British Railways, 1948–73

To S.G.
With Love

Chairmen past and present. Special train organised by Sir Robert McAlpine & Sons Ltd for British Railways Chairmen at St Pancras Station, 1 May 1984 (*back row, left to right*: Lord Marsh; Sir Stanley Raymond; Lord McAlpine of Moffat; Sir Peter Parker; Lord Beeching; Robert Reid; William McAlpine; *front row, left to right*: Sir Henry Johnson; Sir John Elliot) (*McAlpine*).

This image is available in colour for download from www.cambridge.org/9780521188838

British Railways 1948–73

A Business History

oꙨooꙨo

T. R. GOURVISH

Research by N. BLAKE, A. L. FEIST
K. HAMILTON and N. TIRATSOO

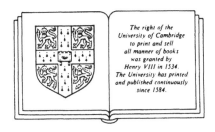

The right of the
University of Cambridge
to print and sell
all manner of books
was granted by
Henry VIII in 1534.
The University has printed
and published continuously
since 1584.

CAMBRIDGE UNIVERSITY PRESS

Cambridge
London   New York   New Rochelle
Melbourne   Sydney

CAMBRIDGE UNIVERSITY PRESS
Cambridge, New York, Melbourne, Madrid, Cape Town,
Singapore, São Paulo, Delhi, Tokyo, Mexico City

Cambridge University Press
The Edinburgh Building, Cambridge CB2 8RU, UK

Published in the United States of America by Cambridge University Press, New York

www.cambridge.org
Information on this title: www.cambridge.org/9780521188838

First published 1986
First paperback edition 2011

A catalogue record for this publication is available from the British Library

Library of Congress Cataloguing in Publication data
Gourvish, T. R. (Terence Richard)
British Railways, 1948–73: a business history.
Bibliography.
Includes index.
1. British Railways – History.   1. Blake, N.
11. Title
HE3020.B76G68 1987   385'.065'41   86–9671

ISBN 978-0-521-26480-8 Hardback
ISBN 978-0-521-18883-8 Paperback

Additional resources for this publication at www.cambridge.org/9780521188838

Contents

Illustrations

Charts, figures and maps

Maps

Tables

Foreword

By Sir Robert Reid C.B.E.
Chairman, British Railways Board

Any professional railwayman of my generation, and many of those who have been our customers over the last 40 years, will turn the pages of this scholarly book with fascination. I joined the old London and North Eastern Railway, after university and War Service, as a Traffic apprentice in September 1947, just four months before the formal start of nationalised railways, in January 1948, when this book begins its historical analysis. The grand events – the relationships between the Board (or rather the Railway Executive as it was then called) and its senior managers, between the former British Transport Commission and the government, between the Board and its financial environment – were distant from the day-to-day railway matters which I saw in my early years. By the time I became Chief Executive in 1980 they began to fill all my vision. But Dr Gourvish's book effectively stops seven years before then; it is a history, an account of the day before yesterday, an account of life as it was not for *my* predecessor Peter Parker, who boldly put this book into commission, but for *his* predecessor and those who came before that.

From gestation to publication this book has taken seven years to appear – hard years of work for the author and his team, hard years of change for the railways. In our business, capital projects take that time and often far more to mature; we are now selecting the locomotives and rolling stock which will run on the railways in the first quarter of the next century. This gives a sense of continuity in physical equipment, a continuity in training and experience, in the self-discipline of those who work in the railways; a sense of continuity which Dr Gourvish rightly emphasises. It is also one of the reasons why, in the past, this great industry displayed a slow rate of change, as is so well documented in this history.

But there have also been, in the more distant past as well as more recently, abrupt discontinuities. The book is rightly and inevitably divided into 'parts', successive slices of time, in each of which there appeared separate issues, problems, styles of management. There is, of course, more than one way of slicing a cake, and I have no wish to substitute my view on that or any other matter of historical judgement for that of the author. Time, and the reviewers, and other historians, will doubtless debate many issues with Dr Gourvish: we on the Railways Board are proud to have commissioned this major project, an independent scholarly history of the first quarter century of the nationalised railways. I am sure it will stand comparison with the other important studies of the business history of different parts of the British economy which have appeared in recent years. It will certainly contribute substantially to one of the great post-war debates – the handling of the nationalised industries in Britain.

I would, however, like to reflect a little on the slices of time that have come since 1973, the terminal date of this book. The last thirteen years have seen three Chairman, eight Ministers of Transport and four Prime Ministers. I certainly do not intend in the ambit of an Introduction to offer a history of those years! Nor do I want to claim that everything in the garden is now lovely, that all the indicators which were negative until a few years ago are now positive, that profitability has at last and irrevocably been achieved. Up-beat Chairman's statements of that sort have their place, but not in the foreword to an academic history.

Some major themes necessarily continue; the competitive struggle for customers, for market shares, already strong in the early 1970s, is now as fierce as in any world market. The technological challenges facing our engineers and their suppliers in British industry are recognisably similar in some respects to those of the early 1970s. The problem of the proper remuneration of our workforce and the best utilisation of their effort and skill is still the daily task of management. We remain a large and widespread organisation, and the managerial challenge which that presents has not disappeared. But there have been changes. In a long process of evolution certain things have *come* together for us, or, more proudly, we can reasonably claim to have *put* certain things together in a constructive way on a number of different fronts. The necessary primary problems remain: some of the secondary, unnecessary complexities have been removed. The result has been that issues which seemed superhuman in their immensity are now rather more man-sized, and we are tackling them with reasonable success.

The change which I would most emphasise is the simplification and unravelling of the strands connecting Minister and Board, and indeed the chain of command between the top managers within the Board and the management team throughout the railway businesses. This has been achieved as a result of the clarification of the short-term objectives of the Board – financial objectives together with a commitment to a quantity and a quality of service – agreed between the railways and the government. Such an agreement has not been easy, and has presented serious challenges to both sides; from the point of view of Board and management, objective tests have been set up by which we must, individually and collectively, stand or fall; from the point of view of the government, once the Board has assumed clearer and more specific financial responsibilities, detailed checking or second guessing of many managerial decisions is clearly no longer necessary.

Equally, there have been major simplifications of the lines of command between myself with the Executive Board members on the one hand, and the railway top management on the other. The key change was the appointment of Sector Directors responsible for each of five businesses that make up the total railway activity. Each Sector Director has clear 'bottom-line' responsibilities delegated to him and he is responsible for specifying to the Regional General Managers the standard of service he requires and the levels of expenditure and investment his business can afford.

This change required the redefinition of the roles and responsibilities throughout the organisation, and today:

the Board remains responsible for long-term policy decisions;
the business Sector Directors have the key bottom-line responsibility which I have just described;
Functional Directors oversee technical and operational performance and standards;
Regional General Managers are responsible for the implementation and co-ordination of production.

Finally, the regional organisation was simplified by removing all 21 Divisional Offices. Local Area Managers now report direct to Regional Headquarters.

I mention this chain of command problem, and what has been done to try to solve it, simply as a specific example of some of the sharp changes which have taken place since 1973. There are others and no doubt there will be more for some future historian to examine. Chairmen come and go; the Muse of History reigns eternal. But I would not wish to give the impression that things are now the same as when Dr Gourvish leaves them, 13 years ago. They are not.

This book will be widely read, both outside and inside the railway community. I know that when my fellow railwaymen go through it, they will be filled not only with a passionate interest in Dr Gourvish's story and analysis, but a readiness to see that things have moved on apace and we are not, in the present, caught in all the traps of the past.

My congratulations to Dr Gourvish and his team, and my thanks to all who have facilitated their work and enabled this valuable enterprise to be brought to completion.

Preface

In 1979 the British Railways Board invited me to write a business history of nationalised railways covering the first 25 years, viz. 1948–73, stipulating that the history should be concerned with 'economic, financial, social and organisational matters, rather than with technical matters'. The work started in March 1980 and the manuscript was completed in November 1985.

I should like to thank all those who in their several ways assisted me in the writing of this book. The project was encouraged by the then Chairman of B.R.B., Sir Peter Parker, and nursed along by a steering committee comprising Michael Posner, a part-time member of the Board (1976–84), Gerry Burt, Chief Secretary, 1976–84, and Professor Donald Coleman, who was Professor of Economic History at the University of Cambridge until his retirement in 1981. The committee met at regular intervals to discuss draft chapters and offer advice on access to records, both internal to the Board and external. The existence of such a committee may seem to imply editorial control. Some comments, it is true, were amended or excised after consultation with the Board's solicitor. But, in general, the committee's criticism was offered in a positive manner, freely, and for the most part, without strings; it was much appreciated by the author. I owe Donald Coleman a particular debt for reading the manuscript over in its several versions, and for repeating the role he performed when I was his postgraduate student 20 years ago. Donald's support has been as ever constructive and reassuring. I imagine that by now he must be getting rather tired of 'Gourvish's puffers'. Michael Posner gave me invaluable help with points of economic interpretation, and Gerry Burt was generous with his wealth of railway experience. All of this should not, of course, be taken to suggest that the steering committee should be held responsible for any surviving errors. These remain the author's sole responsibility.

The Board provided me with generous assistance. A room was set aside for the project at the Board's archives in Porchester Road, W.2. Bert Harrison acted as my liaison officer from 1980 to 1982, and had the task of helping me to set up the history and to locate suitable records in a business where record-keeping had often been sacrificed to the needs of numerous reorganisations and efficiency drives. Robin Linsley, his successor, combined the roles of Liaison Officer and Records Officer, B.R.B., heralding a revived concern for the care of historical records. He also had the job of seeing the manuscript through to completion. Both handled the history beast with patience and good humour. Funds were provided to enable me to appoint four research assistants for two-year terms. Here, the author was extremely fortunate to obtain the services of historians who each showed a dedication, enthusiasm and general support far beyond that which such short-term employment conditions demand. They all contributed both scholarship and comradeship, and quickly mastered the intricacies of railway history. My sincere thanks, then, to Kerry Hamilton and Neil Blake, who introduced me to the ergonomics of Claud Butler; and to Nick Tiratsoo and Andy Feist, who, on the walls of the project room, developed the art of satirical collage to new heights. The writing of the book was also greatly facilitated by the support of the University of East Anglia, which granted me regular periods of study leave.

With the exception of certain highly personal records relating to Board members, I was given totally free access to the records of the Board. The main difficulty was that of locating pertinent material in a very large, dispersed organisation, which had not been operating an archival department since 1973, when the British Transport Historical Records (established by the B.T.C. in 1951) were transferred to the Public Record Office. For some years prior to 1980 parts of the business had followed the practice of many firms in the private sector and destroyed unwanted records after relatively short periods of time. Commissioned histories are sometimes a sequel to the records-gathering process; this one has been both a prelude and an accompaniment. The files of the central secretariat formed the core of the internal evidence used for the business history: in the late 1970s the collection was microfilmed and the originals were then destroyed. The secretariat records were then supplemented by those of other H.Q. departments and the regions, as they became available, and were transferred to the Board's archive over the period 1981–5. Much remains to be done to gather and catalogue this considerable addition to the material already deposited in the Public Record Office at Kew. As the history proceeded, some important classes of record were reported to be missing, presumed destroyed. They included the files of the Railway Executive, 1947–53, the central secretariat's rail closure files and the minutes of informal meetings of the Board, 1963–8. Such lacunae created very real problems when it came to tracking down answers to particular questions. In some cases records reported to be missing or destroyed turned up two or three years after they had been requested; others seem to have disappeared without trace. In relation to government records, the 30-year rule imposed its customary restrictions. A number of Departments kindly allowed me to see files covering the period to 31 December 1955, on the understanding that no published use would be made of them until 1986. The T.U.C. and the rail unions granted access to their own records under similar conditions. I was also able to consult some of the D.O.E. files deposited in the Public Record Office covering the period to the late 1950s.

The writing of 'recent history' under these conditions naturally tempts the historian to try to add the skills of the oral historian to his travelling baggage, and I was no exception. I gained a great deal of useful insights from interviews with some of the principal actors in the story, and in particular the successive Chairmen: Sir John Elliot (Railway Executive), Lord Beeching, Sir Stanley Raymond, Sir Henry Johnson, Lord Marsh and Sir Peter Parker. Many former board members and senior managers offered useful advice and reminiscences: H. P. Barker, Derek Barrie, Miles Beevor, Michael Bonavia, David Bowick, Gerry Fiennes, J. L. Harrington, Fred Margetts, Arthur Pearson, Robin Riddles, Geoffrey Wilson and Sir Reginald Wilson. I spoke to three of the many Ministers of Transport – Lord Boyd, Barbara Castle and Lord Marsh – and to leading civil servants, trade unionists and others – two Permanent-Secretaries, Sir James Dunnett and Sir David Serpell; two General Secretaries, Lord Greene (N.U.R.) and Ray Buckton (A.S.L.E.F.); Sir Alec Cairncross, Lord Kearton and Peter Vinter. All gave freely of their time, and I thank them all. Many people both inside and outside B.R.B. offered me their help with particular problems. I should like to express my thanks to Grant Woodruff, Director of Public Affairs, B.R.B., for granting access to the public relations library; and to M. J. Buscall, George Brown, C. J. R. Clemow, Gordon Hall, C. P. Hopkins, Bernard Kaukas, Frank Paterson, Dave Peters, Tom Twomey, Hugh Wallace, J. A. Walton and Mike Wright, also from B.R.B.; to Colin Smith and Dennis Morris, from the Cabinet Office, Maude Rix (Employment), F. J. McCabe (Environment), R. I. Armitage (C.S.O.), Victor Cox (A.S.L.E.F.), James Dalgleish (B.T.O.G.), Len Dumelow, Secretary of the C.T.C.C., and the Secretaries of the area T.U.C.C.s; to Churchill College, Cambridge, the Centre for the Study of Cartoons and Caricature at the University of Kent, and Philip Bagwell, Eric Cook, Geoffrey Goodman, Tom Hart, Ron Lewis, MP., and Don Murdie. Some of the early drafts and all the interviews were typed in Norwich by Molly Allen, Andrea Francis, Mary Gurteen, Christine Jope, Judy Sparks and Val Striker. The whole of the revised manuscript and subsequent adjustments were placed on word-processor by Kay Alexander at B.R.B. All handled a difficult text most competently. The original graphics were drawn by Steve Mosley and Jacqui White at U.E.A. and modified versions were completed by Kevin Harrison of B.R.B. I should also like to thank William Davies, the editor, Linda Randall, my copy-editor, and all at Cambridge University Press for their help at the publication stage.

In conclusion, it should be emphasised that this is a commissioned but *not* an official history in the sense that it seeks to transmit the views of B.R.B. Over five years of exposure to what some people call 'the culture of the railroad' may have done a little to erode the author's independence, but only a little. Responsibility for most of what follows is mine alone.

Norwich   T.R.G.
November 1985

Abbreviations

A.A.S.	*Annual Abstract of Statistics*
A.C.A.S	Advisory, Conciliatory and Arbitration Service
A.E.I.	Associated Electrical Industries
A.E.U.	Amalgamated Engineering Union
A.P.T.	Advanced Passenger Train
A.S.L.E.F.	Associated Society of Locomotive Engineers and Firemen
A.T.C.	Automatic Train Control
A.U.E.W.	Amalgamated Union of Engineering Workers
A.W.S.	Automatic Warning System
B.R.B.	British Railways Board
B.R.E.L.	British Rail Engineering Ltd
B.S.C.	British Steel Corporation
B.T.C.	British Transport Commission
B.T.H.	British Transport Hotels
B.T.J.C.C.	British Transport Joint Consultative Council
B.T.O.G.	British Transport Officers' Guild
C.B.I.	Confederation of British Industry
C.E.G.B.	Central Electricity Generating Board
C.M. & E.E.	Chief Mechanical and Electrical Engineer
CONGOT	Conciliation grades other than trainmen
C.R.O.	Chief Regional Officer
C.S.O.	Central Statistical Office
C.T.C.C.	Central Transport Consultative Committee
C.W.R.	Continuous Welded Rail
d.c.f.	discounted cash flow
D.M.U.	Diesel Multiple Unit
D.O.E.	Department of the Environment
E.C.	Executive Committee
E.M.U.	Electric Multiple Unit

E.R.	Eastern Region
G.E.	Great Eastern (line or railway)
G.L.C.	Greater London Council
G.N.	Great Northern (line or railway)
G.P.O.	General Post Office
G.W.R.	Great Western Railway
H.S.T.	High Speed Train
I.C.I.	Imperial Chemical Industries
I.P.C.	Investment Programmes Committee
I.R.	Industrial Relations (Dept, B.R.B.)
J.S.G.	Joint Steering Group
L.A.M.A.	Locomotive and Allied Manufacturers' Association
L.C.C.	London County Council
L.M.A.	Locomotive Manufacturers' Association
L.M.R.	London Midland Region
L.M.S.	London Midland & Scottish Railway
L.N.E.R.	London & North Eastern Railway
L.T.	London Transport
L.T.B.	London Transport Board
L.T.E.	London Transport Executive
L.T.S.	London Tilbury & Southend (line or railway)
Memo	Memorandum (official)
memo.	memorandum (internal or private)
M.R.C.	Modern Records Centre, Warwick University
M.S.C.	Management Staff Committee
M.T.	Ministry of Transport
N.C.B.	National Coal Board
N.C.I.T.	National Council on Inland Transport
N.E.D.C.	National Economic Development Council
N.E.D.O.	National Economic Development Office
N.E.R.	North Eastern Region
N.F.C.	National Freight Corporation
N.T.A.C.	Nationalised Transport Advisory Council
N.U.R.	National Union of Railwaymen
Parl. Deb.	*Parliamentary Debates*
PER	Personnel (Dept, B.R.B.)
P.I.B.	National Board for Prices and Incomes
P.R.O.	Public Record Office
P.R. & P.	Public Relations and Publicity (Dept, B.R.B.)
P.S.O.	Public Service Obligation
P.T.A.	Passenger Transport Authority

R. & A.	*Report and Accounts*
R.C.A.	Railway Clerks' Association
R.E.	Railway Executive
R.E.C.	Railway Executive Committee
RENT	Reorganisation of Nationalised Transport
R.Co.A.	Railway Companies' Association
Reshaping	B.R.B., *The Reshaping of British Railways* (1963)
R.M.G.	Railway Management Group
R.P.E.	Road Passenger Executive
R.S.C.	Railway Staff Conference
R.S.J.C.	Railway Staff Joint Council
R.S.N.C.	Railway Staff National Council
R.S.N.T.	Railway Staff National Tribunal
S.A.G.	Stedeford (Special) Advisory Group
S.C. Nat. Ind.:	*Select Committee on Nationalised Industries –*
B.R.	*British Railways* (1960), report, M.O.E., etc.
S.C. Nat Ind.:	*Select Committee on Nationalised Industries –*
Cap. Inv	*Capital Investment Procedures* (1973), report, etc.
S.C. Nat. Ind.:	*Select Committee on Nationalised*
Min. Control	*Industries – Ministerial Control of the Nation-*
	alised Industries (1967–8), report, etc.
S.C. Nat. Ind.:	*Select Committee on Nationalised Industries*
Role of B.R.	*(Sub Committee A) on the Role of British Rail in*
	Public Transport (1976–7), report, etc.
Sc.R.	Scottish Region
S.R.	Southern Region
S.Rly	Southern Railway
T.G.W.U.	Transport and General Workers Union
T.O.P.S.	Total Operations Processing System
T.S.S.A.	Transport and Salaried Staffs' Association
T.T.	Transport Tribunal
T.U.C.	Trades Union Congress
T.U.C.C.	Transport Users' Consultative Committee
W.R.	Western Region

Chronology: railways and government, 1947–74

Year	Events	Chairman	Minister
1947	*Transport Act* B.T.C. and R.E. created	Lord Hurcomb (1947–53)	Alfred Barnes (Labour, 1945–51)
1948 1949 1950 1951	B.T.C., R.E. and C.R.O. organisation; low investment and material shortages Conservatives returned		
1952			John Scott Maclay (Conservative, 1951–2)
1953	*Transport Act* R.E. abolished, B.T.C. reorganised; Area Boards created	General Sir Brian Robertson (1953–61)	Alan Lennox-Boyd (Conservative, 1952–4)
1954 1955 1956	Modernisation Plan developed New B.T.C. organisation Reassessment of Modernisation Plan		John Boyd-Carpenter (Conservative, 1954–5)
1957	Transport (Railway Finances) Act		Harold Watkinson (Conservative, 1955–9)
1958 1959	Reappraisal of Modernisation Plan		
1960	Select Committee, Guillebaud and Stedeford inquiries		
1961	White Paper on Nationalised Industries		
1962	*Transport Act* B.T.C. dissolved, B.R.B. formed; financial reconstruction; railways freed of 'common carrier' obligation; statutory Regional Boards	Dr Richard Beeching (1961–5)	Ernest Marples (Conservative, 1959–64)

Year	Events	Chairman	Minister
1963	'Reshaping': rationalisation drive		
1964	Labour returned		Thomas Fraser (Labour, 1964–5)
1965	P.I.B. inquiry		
1966	J.S.G. inquiry	Sir Stanley Raymond (1965–7)	
1967	White Paper on Nationalised Industries; Raymond sacked		Barbara Castle (Labour, 1965–8)
1968	*Transport Act* Separation of social and commercial roles: transfer of freightliners and sundries to N.F.C.; P.T.A.s established; financial reconstruction; non-statutory Regional Boards	Sir Henry Johnson (1968–71)	Richard Marsh (Labour 1968–9)
1969	McKinsey exercise		Fred Mulley (Labour, 1969–70)
1970	New organisation with emphasis on corporate planning; Conservatives returned		
1971	Economic recession	Richard Marsh (1971–6)	John Peyton (Conservative, 1970–4)
1972	Railway Policy Review		
1973	Field organisation falters		
1974	*Transport Act* Capital reconstruction; P.S.O. support for passenger business		

Introduction: nationalisation

I

The origins of some of the difficulties facing nationalised railways when the newly created British Transport Commission took over in January 1948 lie in the inter-war years and, indeed, in the industry's position before the First World War.[1] As early as 1900, for example, it was clear that the railway companies' freedom to choose and charge the traffic they carried had been severely restricted by legislation designed to encourage a 'public service' obligation in management. Moreover, another important area of managerial concern – labour costs – was for the first time the subject of significant governmental intervention.[2] These were to be some of the industry's most enduring financial and operating problems. A steadily increasing capital burden, already over £1,330 million by the end of 1913, was accompanied by lower and lower operating margins. The 'operating ratio' – working costs expressed as a percentage of revenue – rose from 51 in 1870–4 to 57 in 1895–9 and 62 in 1900–4, where it remained until the war. Such realities were masked by the railways' continuing dominance of inland transport and their ability to provide reasonable returns to investment. In 1910–12, for example, the net rate of return on capital raised (excluding nominal additions to capital) averaged 4.23 per cent, and this was much the same as 40 years earlier when interest rates were higher.[3]

After the First World War, and from the mid–1930s in particular, the transport environment changed radically. Road transport began to challenge rail successfully in a number of markets, but especially in short-distance passenger and short- and medium-distance freight. Although the railways retained their traditional predominance in the long-distance freight business, even here profits were reduced by the instability and shrinking output of Britain's staple industries which came with the slump in world trade. Coal output, for example, which had averaged 270 million tons in 1909–13, was 16 per cent lower in the 'recovery' years, 1934–8, and this was reflected in the coal tonnage carried by rail.[4] But there was no relaxation in the government's control of railway pricing and marketing policies. The Railways Act of 1921 had rejected outright nationalisation in favour of regulated regional monopolies; the four 'main-line' railways, the Great Western, London & North Eastern, London Midland & Scottish and Southern, established in 1923, represented the amalgamation of no less than 123 companies. This search for the efficiency believed to be inherent in regulated, large-scale business units marked the end of the government's faith in inter-railway competition as a protection for consumers.[5] The concept of railways as a monopoly to be regulated became increasingly unrealistic, however, in the new conditions of the 1920s and 1930s. A new structure of freight rates introduced in 1928, which sought, unsuccessfully, to limit the proliferation of 'exceptional' rates, proved to be as inflexible as the old system. Such failures, along with the continued obligation to accept traffic, publish charges, provide a reasonable level of service, avoid 'undue preference' in the treatment of customers and submit to government regulation of wages and conditions, left the railways vulnerable to their more flexible and less constrained competitors.[6]

By 1938 the main-line companies were pressing vigorously for more equitable treatment. In that year net revenue fell by nearly 25 per cent. Although the trade depression was primarily responsible, the railways put some of the blame on the government's one-sided control of freight traffic charges. The 'Square Deal Campaign', initiated by the 'Big Four' railway companies in November, demanded an end to the legal disabilities under which the railways were operating in comparison with the road hauliers – classification, publication of rates, etc. – and the case had been accepted in government circles before the outbreak of war interrupted the legislative programme. The effects of road competition were beginning to show in railway earnings and profitability. The net 'standard revenue' envisaged for the 'Big Four' companies under the 1921 Act – £51,395,095 per annum – was never matched in practice; and in the years 1934–8 the average was some 35 per cent lower at £33,404,092. For Britain's railways as a whole (excluding London Transport) the operating ratio stood at 81 in the same period, 30 per cent higher than before the war. The net rate of return on capital raised (at historic cost, and excluding nominal additions to capital) had fallen to 3.16 per cent, while the return on capital expenditure was a meagre 2.88 per cent.[7] The extent to which the companies were themselves responsible for falling returns is, of course, a controversial matter, and this is not the place to rehearse the debate about performance in the inter-war years.[8] Certainly, the economies of scale envisaged by the 1923 amalgamations were never fully realised, and the new managements may well have remained dangerously complacent for far too long about their position in the transport market. But by 1939 that complacency had certainly disappeared. The decade came to a close in an atmosphere of considerable anxiety for railway management, in which increasing frustration with government control loomed large.

II

The Second World War simply made matters worse. There were many parallels with the situation in the First World War. The railway companies, together with the London Passenger Transport Board, were placed under the control of the Ministry of Transport (from May 1941 the Ministry of War Transport), but operational management was retained by a Railway Executive Committee of railway managers. An agreement with the government established the basis of payment for traffic carried, but charges were frozen and maintenance and renewal were largely sacrificed to the war effort. The final agreement with the government, reached in September 1941 and back-dated to 1 January, gave the railways a guaranteed net revenue of £43.5 million. The government were to take any surplus earned above this figure, but it was agreed that an accumulating trust fund would be established to meet deferred repairs and renewals. Fares and rates were stabilised at the level of April 1941.[9] In retrospect the railway companies were extremely proud of their achievement in carrying greatly expanded traffics under exceptionally difficult operating conditions. To give two examples: in 1944 the net ton-mileage of freight carried was 50 per cent higher than in 1938, and passenger-mileage was up by no less than 67 per cent, and all this without a significant increase in basic equipment.[10] Of course, the rise in traffic volumes owed much to the disruption the war brought to road and coastal transport, and to the need, for strategic reasons, to lengthen average hauls.[11] The comforting statistics obscured the underlying realities of the industry's weakening financial position as wear and tear increased sharply without adequate provision being made for replacement and renewal. When the companies' net earnings fell from £62.5 million in 1945 to only £32.5 million in 1946, there could be no doubt at all as to the potential severity of the post-war situation.

The government's financial arrangements with the railways have been strongly criticised by some historians, not only for the restriction on company profits but also for the freeze on charges. In 1941–5 the railways earned an impressive £412.6 million, equivalent to a decade of pre-war profits, but £195.3 million or 47 per cent was retained by the Treasury. At the same time, costs rose sharply. One company chairman estimated wartime increases to have been 92 per cent for coal, 83 per cent for materials and 75 per cent for labour, while the *Railway Gazette* suggested that the weighted average increase in all railway costs had reached 80 per cent by mid-1947.[12] On the other hand, charges were not adjusted until July 1946, and then by only a modest 7–14 per cent, and by this time earnings had slumped badly. The poor results of 1946, and pessimism about those for 1947, persuaded the government to allow another increase, from October 1947, but with rates at only 55 per cent above their pre-war level the gap between charges and costs remained. Much of the contemporary grumbling about the war-time agreement and its effects came from an industry which had accepted, all too readily, the opportunity to exchange the uncertainty of war-time profits for the security of a guaranteed net revenue and maintenance fund. Whatever the government had decided to do about profits and prices, there would still have remained a serious problem of under-investment as a result of war-time shortages. The companies were probably in a weaker position to initiate early provision for repairs and renewals than they might have been, and there is good reason for criticising the extent to which the railways were allowed to run down during the war, not least because Ministry officials were themselves aware that post-war replacement costs would be both high and incapable of being cleared in the short run. In 1943 Sir Alan Mount, for example, from the Ministry's maintenance division, indicated his anxiety about the railways' arrears; he reckoned that they would take at least ten years to clear after the war.[13] In the following year another official suggested that there was 'great danger in the policy of progressive starvation, which . . . finds this essential service too debilitated to carry the load of which it is capable'.[14] However, the over-riding assumptions were, first, that the government's accumulating trust fund for renewals would be sufficient to meet the bill for replacement at *future* cost, and, second, that there were advantages in deferring expenditure in order that it might be geared more closely to post-war transport needs and motive power policy. As Sir Cyril Hurcomb, the Permanent-Secretary to the Ministry, observed as early as 1942, a major concern was that the money would be 'eaten up by piecemeal expenditure upon purposes which, in certain contingencies, might not be required'.[15]

The results of war-time use and neglect were clear. By 1945, there was a large backlog of repairs and renewals, and this greatly impaired railway operations for the rest of the decade. Despite the considerable increase in traffic, renewal of the permanent way in the years 1940–4 was reduced to under 70 per cent of pre-war levels, and by the end of 1945 the deficiency amounted to nearly 2,500 track miles, or about two years' work under normal (i.e. pre-war) conditions. A similar reduction was evident in the work on structures – tunnels, bridges, buildings, etc.[16] Although motive

Table 1. *Rolling stock under or awaiting repair*

	31 December 1938 (%)	31 December 1946 (%)	Increase (%)
Locomotives	6.04	7.98	32
Coaching stock	6.52	12.52	92
Wagons	2.82	10.79	281

Source: Sir Ian Bolton, memo., 21 November 1947, B.T.C. S17–1–1A, B.R.B.

power was maintained, largely because of the construction of over 1,300 locomotives in 1939–44, a great many engines were close to the end of their useful lives in the immediate post-war period. By December 1946, 7,981 or 39.3 per cent of the total stock, were over 35 years old.[17] The rest of the rolling stock suffered badly from war-time exigencies. The difficulties of maintaining the stock of freight wagons were greatly exacerbated by the requisition and pooling of about 563,000 privately owned vehicles at the beginning of the war. These were markedly inferior to the railway companies' own wagon fleet. At the end of 1946 over 50 per cent of them were more than 35 years old, as compared with less than 10 per cent of the companies' own wagons; so of the total pool of stock nearly 28 per cent were over 35 years old. Many of the requisitioned wagons were, moreover, of inferior technical design, thus worsening the extent of obsolescence.[18] The problem of maintaining the passenger stock was no less acute. Very few vehicles were repaired during the hostilities: the L.M.S., for example, with a total stock of 22,000, renewed only 16 carriages a year during 1940–4. New construction as a whole fell to 16 per cent of pre-war levels in 1940–5, and as a result the total number of vehicles available for traffic was reduced by 13 per cent. At the end of 1946, 12,161 coaching vehicles, 21.6 per cent of the total, were over 35 years old.[19] Everywhere, the queue for essential repairs lengthened and the average age of assets increased. Statistics of rolling stock under or awaiting repair in 1938 and 1946, shown in Table 1, indicate clearly how the position deteriorated.

It may be difficult to accept that a more generous war-time policy towards railway investment would have succeeded in safeguarding assets which were, it is generally agreed, in relatively good shape in 1939. But it remains true that the postponement of essential maintenance and renewals, coupled with the more intensive use of the network and the effects of war damage, proved to be a most unfortunate legacy for post-war managements. The results were felt well into the period of nationalised railways.

III

By disguising the true competitive position of the railways, the war brought welcome relief to the hard-pressed investor. Holders of ordinary stock, with the exception of shareholders in the L.N.E.R., were able to smile for the first time for over a decade, as Table 2 indicates. This comparative bonanza was not only abnormal but was earned on assets which were clearly falling in real value. And the situation did not improve in the immediate post-war period. On the contrary, the years 1946 and 1947 presented difficulties which were certainly as acute, if not more acute, than those experienced in wartime. In the words of Christopher Savage, the official historian of inland transport during the war: 'the problems of restoration and organisation which faced British inland transport when the war ended were scarcely less formidable than the transport problems encountered in the most difficult war years'.[20]

Four months after the Labour Party took office, a clear commitment to nationalisation was made public by Herbert Morrison in a statement on 19 November 1945.[21] This undoubtedly cast a long shadow over managerial decision-making within the main-line companies, diverting attention from the restitution of pre-war standards of service to, first, the pursuance of an anti-nationalisation campaign and then to a struggle to obtain the best terms of compensation for shareholders. Furthermore, the railway companies, together with the L.P.T.B., remained under formal government control until they were vested in the B.T.C. on 1 January 1948. This ensured that the two-and-a-half years of peacetime operation prior to Vesting Day would be regarded by the existing companies as purely transitional in nature, thus putting a firm brake on medium- and long-term strategic planning. It also meant that crucial decisions affecting the railways' financial position – notably those dealing with pricing policy – were left to the newly elected Labour Government to determine. Day-to-day management continued to be a matter for the war-time Railway Executive Committee of general managers, which from 1945 was chaired by Alfred Barnes, the Minister of Transport. This body, under the effective leadership of its Deputy-Chairman, Sir James Milne (G.W.R.), was full of executive competence. Its members included Sir William Wood, President of the L.M.S., Sir Eustace Missenden of the S.Rly, Sir Charles Newton (L.N.E.R.) and Lord Ashfield, the Chairman of the L.P.T.B.: all were distinguished railwaymen, well versed in both operating and commercial practice. However, the Committee was *not* the prototype for a unified executive management of Britain's railways. It was first and foremost a channel of communication by which government instructions were passed down to the constituent companies, and these retained their independent

Table 2. *Main-line railway companies' ordinary dividends, 1929–47 (averages)*

Stock	1929–34 (%)	1935–9 (%)	1940–5 (%)	1946–7 (%)
G.W.R. ord. £42,929,800	4.17	2.80	4.42	6.14
L.M.S. ord. £95,202,450	1.13	0.85	2.67	3.82
S.Rly. deferred ord. £31,490,200	0.63	0.65	1.79	3.54
L.N.E.R. preferred ord. 5% £42,361,000	0.54	0.00	0.00	0.41

Source: Company Reports and Accounts, summarised in *Railway Gazette*, 1930–48.

existence. Unsurprisingly, then, the Committee continued to reflect company divisions after the war and to organise on a relatively loose, federal basis. Very little, if anything, was done to prepare for unification before the second half of 1947, when the first meetings of the B.T.C. (prior to vesting) were held. Direct access to government departments and committees was maintained after 1945, but it is doubtful whether this produced anything more than marginal returns for the industry in its pressing difficulties with material and labour shortages, the maintenance backlog and the search for scarce investment resources. In fact, the practice of dealing directly with government was to have some unfortunate repercussions in that it created an expectation of functional responsibility within the ranks of senior railway management which was to prove difficult to dislodge when the B.T.C. sought to establish its authority over the new organisational system for the railways.

A major cause of anxiety in the period 1945–7 was the patent inability of the companies to restore their physical assets to pre-war standards. Strenuous efforts were made to clear the arrears of maintenance and repair, but post-war shortages, of both raw materials and skilled men, greatly frustrated the work of restitution. Permanent way renewal never went beyond meeting urgent current requirements. For 1947 a target of 1,966 track-miles was set, just above the 1938 level, but it was only possible to deal with 1,434 miles and the 'backlog', based on renewals in 1935–9, remained at about 2,500 miles.[22] Consequently, several sections were in such a dangerously defective state that severe speed restrictions were imposed on most routes. The number of locomotives under or awaiting repair was reduced slightly in the course of 1947 to 1,433 or 7 per cent of the net operating stock; those deemed 'unavailable for traffic purposes' (i.e. undergoing shed repairs, etc.), however, were still numerous at 18 per cent of the total in November 1947.[23] Both passenger and freight vehicles remained in a condition much worse than that of the late 1930s. The shortage of key materials forced the companies to patch up rather than replace rolling stock whose normal life had long expired. Although repair capacity for freight wagons was increased in 1947, and 90 per cent of the target for the heavy repair of rail-owned wagons was completed, the companies continued to complain bitterly of the large blocks of old, unserviceable wagons inherited from private ownership. Operations were greatly hampered by the sharp rise in the total number (rail-owned and requisitioned) under or awaiting repair. This increased from about 140,000 (11 per cent) at the end of 1946 to nearly 203,000 (16.6 per cent) in September 1947.[24] Passenger stock continued to be affected by low government priority. By 31 December 1947 the number under or awaiting repair had risen to 13.6 per cent; construction of new vehicles in 1947 amounted to only 1,199, just over a third of the capacity available in railway and contractors' shops. At the end of the year the total coaching stock was still over 4,000 fewer than in 1939.[25]

Investment in new works was naturally curtailed by government controls. The only major projects to escape the net of Sir Edwin Plowden's Investment Programmes Committee in 1947 were the Liverpool Street–Shenfield electrification (estimated cost: £8 million), and the Manchester–Sheffield–Wath electrification (estimated cost, with the Woodhead Tunnel: £9.1 million), and both were inherited from pre-war programmes. The situation contrasted sharply with the optimism of war-time reconstruction plans which in 1943 had suggested that the 'useful post-war expenditure on railways' should be £500 million at current prices (about £800 million in 1947 prices), including £150 million for a programme of partial electrification and £165 million for the L.P.T.B.[26] The operational consequences of post-war austerity were soon made obvious to all by the glare of peacetime publicity. In early 1946, the railways attracted adverse criticism after a spate of accidents, including a serious collision at Lichfield on New Year's Day, when 20 passengers were killed. Further concern was expressed in October 1947, when two accidents in the space of three days, at South Croydon and Goswick (Northumberland), produced 60 fatalities. Indeed, the number killed in train accidents in 1947 – 121 – was the second highest in railway history.[27] Sir Alan Mount, the Chief Inspecting Officer, in his annual report, was bold enough to suggest that five of the serious accidents (in which 61 died) would probably not have occurred but for the track maintenance arrears and the postponement of work on colour-light signalling.[28] And even where train services were operated without incident, the deterioration in quality of service was a subject of widespread complaint. The shortage of fuel prevented a return to pre-war standards of passenger transport; overcrowding was particularly pronounced in the summer of 1947 after the

February fuel crisis; and the poor quality of locomotive coal was responsible for a series of engine failures and delays. When Hugh Dalton, speaking in the Commons debate on the Transport Bill in December 1946, declared that 'this railway system of ours is a very poor bag of physical assets', he was only echoing a broad sense of dissatisfaction with the postponement of railway recovery.[29]

In theory, of course, the government's financial arrangements for arrears of maintenance and renewal should have proved adequate. The trust funds, established under the Railway Control Agreement, were based on arrears measured against a pre-war expenditure norm for the main-line companies and L.P.T.B. of £56.6 million. By the end of 1945 the account, which had been adjusted for inflation, stood at £148.2 million.[30] The companies also pursued separate claims for abnormal wear and tear and for compensation as a result of war damage. But before 1948 very little was spent under any of these headings. Only £2.5 million was taken out of the trust funds in 1946, leaving a balance of £152.4 million, and £151.4 million was eventually handed over to the B.T.C., on behalf of the controlled undertakings, under Section 27 (3) of the Transport Act of 1947. On Vesting Day, the Commission's abnormal maintenance account showed a credit of £149.7 million, most of which (about £143.5 million) represented the arrears of the main-line companies and the L.P.T.B.[31] The railways' claim for abnormal wear and tear during the war was finally settled by the Ministry of Transport and the Commission at £46 million – certainly no over-estimate – while compensation for war damage was deferred until £24.8 million was paid as a 72.5 per cent grant under the War Damage (Public Utility Undertakings) Act of 1949. On nationalisation, therefore, a conservative estimate of the remaining arrears of maintenance and renewal, including provision for war damage, was as high as £210 million.[32] The problem was not the adequacy of the agreed payments but the urgent need to translate them into tangible assets before they were eroded by inflation. This the railway companies were unable to do. The observation of Reginald Wilson, the B.T.C.'s Financial Comptroller, in 1949 proved to be a prophetic comment on the whole of the decade 1945–54: 'How soon such a sum [for overtaking arrears] could be spent would depend on the materials and labour available, but unless they become available within a reasonable time the existing situation, however abnormal it may seem today, must be regarded as chronic.'[33]

It is difficult to blame the companies and their managers for the arrears problem. Some economic dislocation was expected to occur when Britain's massive war machine was dismantled – especially given the background of substantial borrowing, large-scale disinvestment and the interruption to world trade – but nobody anticipated the exceptional severity of the post-war economic crisis. The railways, like other run-down industries, were victims of the abrupt end to Lend-Lease in September 1945, which put additional pressure on an already serious balance of payments position and forced the government into austerity measures designed to restrict domestic consumption and promote exports. They also suffered in 1947, Dalton's 'annus horrendus'. First there was a fuel crisis in February, following one of the harshest winters on record. Then a run on scarce dollar reserves produced a 'convertibility crisis' in July–August. All this resulted in a further round of rationing and cuts.[34] On the other hand, it is clear that the railway companies, although inhibited by the coming of nationalisation, might have achieved more with a centralised, unified approach to the problems of shortages and restrictions. That there was scope for this, even in the climate of 1945–7, was demonstrated in the latter months of 1947 when, with the new organisational structure for nationalised railways in its embryonic form, successful steps were taken to improve the conduct of freight traffic. Signs of economic recovery, and expectations of a rise in coal output in 1947–8, provided the necessary stimulus. First, a special Wagon Repairs Committee, set up in October under the guidance of R. A. 'Robin' Riddles, one of the newly appointed members of the Railway Executive, was able to create extra repair capacity. As a result, the number of vehicles under or awaiting repair was reduced from 203,000 in September to 159,000 in December 1947 – a reduction of 20 per cent in under three months.[35] Second, an intensive publicity drive was organised by Riddles's colleague David Blee with the aim of cutting wagon turnround time and freeing idle stock. A wagon discharge campaign, which started in November, cut the average daily 'leave-over' of loaded wagons by a third, releasing about 35,000 wagons by the end of the year; and average terminal-user time for all vehicles, loaded and empty, was reduced from 2.13 days at the beginning of the campaign to 1.96 days only four weeks later.[36] These examples, by showing what could be done with more determined management, suggest that the companies had failed to seize earlier opportunities for lessening the effects of austerity restrictions.

Commercially and financially the climate of 1945–7 was equally depressing. The financial results of railway operation in these years are incomplete but the limited data released by the government indicate a marked deterioration after 1945. The estimated net revenue of the controlled undertakings (including the L.P.T.B.) fell from £62.55 million in 1945 to *minus* £16.24 million in 1947, a reduction of 126 per cent.[37] Clearly, some of the decline may be attributed to a return to normal conditions after the exceptional traffic volumes of wartime. The estimated passenger-mileage of the main-line companies fell by 35 per cent from

"Good afternoon. We're from the Ministry of Rail Transport. I suppose you've heard that the country needs all the rolling-stock that is available?"

1 The shortage of rolling stock in 1947: a reaction from Giles, *Sunday Express*, 7 December 1947.

1945 to 1947, while the railways' merchandise net ton-mileage (including free-hauled) fell by 25 per cent over the same period as road haulage firms recovered some of their market-share. Elsewhere, however, the picture was less gloomy. Despite a fall in U.K. coal output of 16 per cent since 1938 the railways' coal/coke ton-mileage for 1945–7 was 11 per cent higher than in 1938, and total freight ton-mileage fell by only 7 per cent from 1945 to 1947.[38] The loss of traffic and revenue was not the major source of concern: gross revenue amounted to £383.9 million in 1945 and £355.6 million in 1947 – a reduction of only 7 per cent – and both figures were well above the equivalent pre-war returns. The railways' difficulties centred on rising costs. Working expenditure increased from £316.9 million in 1945 to £367.2 million in 1947 – a rise of 16 per cent – and the operating ratio jumped from 83 to 103. The government seems to have exaggerated the poor performance of 1947 by debiting the account with £19.99 million under the heading of 'Other special items'. This sum apparently included £16 million as an adjustment relating to the entire period of control. But even if this £16 million is deducted the financial position in 1947 remains grim, with a net revenue of almost zero and an operating ratio of 99.[39] Labour costs were also rising. The average earnings of railwaymen increased by 7.4 per cent, 1945–7, and the Labour Government's commitment to full employment ensured that no shedding of labour could be contemplated. In fact, the companies took on an extra 38,000 employees after 1945.[40]

The major cause of disappearing net revenue in 1947 was undoubtedly the discrepancy between the level of costs and the price of transport. After the freeze on railway charges of April 1941 and the small upward concession of July 1946 the Cabinet still hesitated in 1947 to agree to a further increase, despite clear evidence of continuing inflation and gloomy forecasts about the size of the Exchequer's contribution to the net revenue guaranteed under the Control Agreement. It was only after the railwaymen secured a pay award in July that the Cabinet was jolted into action. A new scale of charges, 55 per cent above pre-war levels, was announced in August and introduced in October, but by this time the cost of most railway inputs was twice as high as in 1939. Labour Party policy had been equivocal, and at ministerial level often contradictory, but it appears that the government was prepared to accept the inflationary implications of paying a large Exchequer subsidy to the controlled undertakings, with all the risks of endangering a 'break-even' position for nationalised railways in 1948, rather than introduce into the economy the 'knock-on' effects of a more realistic increase in transport costs.[41] Admittedly, higher charges might have provoked a serious fall in some traffics (though the elasticity of demand for rail transport under austerity conditions is difficult to predict). On balance, however, it seems likely that the operating account in 1947 would have been in a much healthier state had the government implemented an earlier and more substantial programme to meet the escalation of railway operating costs.

The financial state of the railways on the eve of nationalisation was worse than it had been in the difficult years of the late 1930s. The temporary euphoria caused by war-time dividends had blinded many people – whether directors, managers or shareholders – to the pressing need to respond to developments in road transport by rationalising the rail network, improving productivity and showing a more aggressive attitude in the search for profitable business. However, the immediate prospects of a successful stand against competitors were far from good. Starved of investment and hampered by the enormous backlog of repairs and renewals, the industry could do no more than offer a product much inferior to that of pre-war days. Services were slower and more unreliable; and government restrictions, for example, that on passenger train-mileages in 1947, prevented the companies from responding fully to the market.

The situation was scarcely an ideal one in which to contemplate the difficult transition from regulated regional monopoly to the public owner-ship of an integrated system.[42]

IV

The issue of public ownership versus private enterprise for the railways was as old as the industry itself. In continental Europe the presence of the state had been evident at all stages, in planning, construction and opera-tion, and there were a number of case studies to attract British supporters of nationalisation. And even in Britain, where the development of the railway network had been left largely to the free market, William Glad-stone's Act of 1844 gave the government the option of acquiring the post-1844 companies after 1865 on the basis of 25 years' purchase of the average annual profits for the previous three years. The Act soon lost its raison d'être, however, with the fall in railway earnings which followed the investment 'mania' of the late 1840s. The debate was revived in the late 1860s, and again with more force at the turn of the century, when the formation of the Railway Nationalisation League (1895) and, more particularly, the Railway Nationalisation Society (1908) resulted in renewed lobbying for the implementation of the Act's state-purchase clauses. These societies and their literature were a reflection not only of the increasing influence of corporatist thought in British politics but also of a more widely held view, supported with vigour by hard-pressed industrial-ists and traders, that railways should act more as public corporations than as profit-making businesses.[43] The main thrust, of course, came from the labour movement. In 1894 the Amalgamated Society of Railway Servants demanded railway nationalisation at their A.G.M.; two years later, the T.U.C. declared its support. During the period of the Liberal Governments after 1906 the newly formed Labour Party introduced several bills into the Commons for the nationalisation of railways, together with the canals, tramways and mines.[44]

After the First World War, the precedent of government control led to a spirited discussion of the most appropriate post-war strategy. A recon-stituted Labour Party, with its policy document entitled *Labour and the New Social Order* (1918), pressed for the national ownership of railways and canals and the unified management of the other modes to form a 'combined national service of communication and transport'. In 1919 the pages of the *Railway Gazette* were full of serious schemes for nationalisa-tion. The Railway Nationalisation Society produced a draft bill which provided for the vesting in the government of railways as well as other forms of inland transport under war-time control. The purchase price was to be based on the Stock Exchange valuation of the companies' securities, taken 6–18 months before the bill was introduced in parliament, and payment was to be made in Government Railway Stock. The Railway Clerks' Association offered a similar scheme, but with the purchase price based on pre-war share prices less subsequent depreciation.[45] Enthusiasm was also displayed in more surprising quarters. Within the Coalition Government, Lloyd George had hinted more than once at his support for nationalisation; and Winston Churchill, electioneering in Scotland in December 1918, suggested, somewhat injudiciously, that the government had definitely decided to nationalise the railways. This view was shared by George Barnes, the Minister Without Portfolio.[46] On the other hand, Wilson Fox's Select Committee on Transport, reporting in November 1918, favoured the unification of the railway system but not necessarily its ownership by the state. Opposition to nationalisation intensified with the strengthening of the Conservative element in the Commons after the 'Coupon Election' in December. Although a new Ministry of Transport was created in 1919, the government's more ambitious plans to give it a comprehensive control over all forms of transport, together with powers to nationalise undertakings, were withdrawn following fierce parliamentary opposition from vested interests.[47] Instead, the government went on to deal separately with the various branches of transport. For the railways, the formula adopted was essentially one of compromise. There was to be neither a return to the pre-war system of company organisation nor was there to be nationalisation. The 1921 Act, though grouping the companies into regulated regional units and promising a firmer control of pricing via the Railway Rates Tribunal, maintained the private ownership of capital. The legislators hoped for substantial economies from the enforced mergers but totally failed to consider the place of the railways in a transport world which was being transformed by the internal combustion engine.

If the 1920s were characterised by ad hoc responses to transport problems, the 1930s saw renewed efforts to approach the ideal of integration and co-ordination. The Road Traffic Act of 1930 and the Road and Rail Traffic Act of 1933 responded to the rise of road competition by imposing an element of control on the newcomers. New licensing systems were established to restrict entry into both road passenger transport and road haulage, and these undoubtedly succeeded in checking growth. The L.P.T.B. was established in 1933 as a public authority with a controlled monopoly of passenger transport in the capital. The legislation gave some relief to the railways, but the co-ordination of inland transport as a whole remained a remote concept, particularly since road transport operators were left free to pick and choose traffics and determine charges. The railway companies' 'Square Deal Campaign' (see above, p. 2) had no difficulty in demonstrating that the railways' public service obligations were more onerous than those of their rivals.

The nationalisation not only of the railways but also of other sections of inland transport was never far below the surface of political debate in the inter-war years. The Labour Party led the way, prompted by the railway unions and the T.U.C. The change of emphasis in successive election manifestos is revealing. The statements of 1918 and 1922 had referred to the nationalisation of the railways alone but in 1924 the Party was promising 'a systematic reorganisation, in the national interest and on terms fair to all concerned, of the whole system of Transport', and in 1931 'transport' was included in the list of basic industries to be 'publicly owned and controlled'.[48] By this time Herbert Morrison, Minister of Transport in the 1929–31 Government and chief architect of the L.P.T.B., was a major influence on Labour's internal policy-making, and his position was strengthened after the election defeat of October 1931. He inspired the statement entitled 'The National Planning of Transport', which advocated the extension of the London scheme to most, if not all, of inland transport through the creation of a 'National Transport Board'. This was approved by the Party conference at Leicester in October 1932 and repeated in subsequent publications, including Morrison's *Socialisation and Transport* of 1933 and his *British Transport at Britain's Service* of 1938.[49]

Morrison was certainly not alone in pursuing transport co-ordination by means of state control. As early as 1917, J. H. Thomas, General Secretary of the National Union of Railwaymen, declared that it was necessary to nationalise *transport* and not merely the railways if integration were to be achieved, although his personal commitment to such a policy appears to have wavered with the passage of time. A. G. Walkden, on the other hand, the unusually able Secretary of the Railway Clerks' Association, was more consistent in his approach. Both his 'National Transport Bill' of 1918 and his detailed submission to the Royal Commission on Transport of 1928–30 were in essence blueprints for the Transport Act of 1947. In his memorandum to the Royal Commission he went further than Morrison in spelling out the need to nationalise both road and rail transport and demanding the creation of transport boards on which the unions would enjoy equal representation.[50] The response of the Commission to such lobbying was lukewarm. However, three of its members – Sir Robert Donald, the publishing magnate, Frank Galton, Secretary of the Fabian Society, and former Secretary of the Railway Nationalisation Society, and William Leach, the Labour member for Bradford (Central) – gave their support to the view that compulsion was essential if transport co-ordination were to be secured. For them, a 'real policy of rationalisation' required 'the purchase of the properties of the railway companies, of the motor transport services . . . and the creation of a National Transport Trust'.[51] This suggestion was taken up enthusiastically by the railway unions when, stung by a reduction in wages, they lobbied the Prime Minister, Ramsay MacDonald, in May 1931, and it was subsequently included in a resolution sent to and passed by the T.U.C. at Bristol in October.[52]

As in 1918–19, nationalisation also found sympathisers outside left-wing circles. In May 1931, for example, Charles Williams, the Conservative M.P. for Torquay, asked Ramsay MacDonald in the House when he proposed to introduce legislation to nationalise transport. On being given an inadequate answer he retorted with the complaint: 'How many years have we to wait for this legislation?'[53] Moreover, it was a Conservative Government which demonstrated its enthusiasm for public boards with the creation of the Central Electricity Board and the British Broadcasting Corporation in 1926 (although neither involved a transfer of ownership), and a Conservative-dominated 'National Government' which nationalised coal royalties in 1938 and overseas air services on the eve of the Second World War. The Overseas Airways Act of 1939 merged Imperial Airways and British Airways to form the British Overseas Airways Corporation, a publicly owned body which was very much on the lines of the L.P.T.B. Support for the nationalisation of transport, though strong on the left (but with varying degrees of emphasis), was by no means confined thereto. An increasing body of opinion in all parties certainly favoured a greater measure of governmental control in the interests of both industry and the consumer. This growing consensus makes it difficult to accept the notion of a sharp change of direction, whether during the Second World War or in 1945. Large-scale war, and specifically the need for transport control during hostilities, may well have acted as an important influence in precipitating change. It cannot be simply a coincidence that the Railways Act of 1921 came three years after the end of the First World War and that nationalisation arrived in 1948, three years after the end of the Second World War.

V

During the war civil servants were presented with a number of opportunities to draft plans for the industry's future organisation. The first came in May 1940 when Sir John (later Lord) Reith, the Minister of Transport, having turned his attention to the issue of nationalisation, asked his Deputy-Secretary, Sir Alfred Robinson, to consider a scheme to establish a public utility corporation for all transport. The exercise was given added impetus in August when the government expressed its dissatisfaction with the terms of the Railway Control Agreement of 1939. The commitment to a policy of stabilising railway charges led to a revision, agreed in September 1941, in which a sliding scale of profits was replaced by a guaranteed, fixed payment. This change of strategy raised the more fundamental issue of deciding the best system of war-time management for companies which were to be shorn of the profit incentive. Labour Ministers, led by Attlee and Greenwood, pressed for the immediate unification of railways under public ownership, and Reith responded to the call for a report on the 'transport position generally' by instructing Robinson and Dr W. H. (later Sir William) Coates, a former civil servant who had become a director of I.C.I., to undertake a study of the problem of co-ordinating all forms of inland transport.[54]

The Coates–Robinson report, entitled 'The Transport Problem in Great Britain', was completed in draft form in October 1940, and supported by further papers in November 1940 and January 1941. The proposals were radical. The authors, having examined all available options, came down firmly in favour of a national transport monopoly. Embodying their recommendations in a draft bill, they advocated the formation of a National Transport Corporation which would acquire the undertakings of rail, road, canal and air transport, including the privately owned rail wagons and the docks, and exert a greater measure of control over coastal shipping. Railway shareholders were to be compensated by payment in Government Transport Stock in relation to the average market value of their holdings over three pre-war years.[55] Ministry officials responded with some enthusiasm by investigating the cost implications of sundry schemes of compensation.[56] In the meantime, however, Reith had been replaced by Lt-Col J. Moore-Brabazon (later Lord Brabazon of Tara), whose response to the Coates–Robinson document was more hostile. In December 1940, having asked for a critical brief from his civil servants, he declared that he was frankly 'frightened' by the size of the proposed Corporation and was unable to see how coastal shipping, municipal transport and 'C' licence vehicles* could be included in the scheme. Coates and Robinson made it clear that the scheme had its political pitfalls: 'The Minister to whom it falls to put through Parliament a Bill designed to give effect to these proposals will have no easy task. He will meet a veritable orchestra of opposition all out of tune.'[57] Planning then came to a halt. Robinson retired from the Ministry (he became Regional Transport Commissioner at Bristol) and Coates went to Canada to act as financial

*The 1933 Road Traffic Act established three types of vehicle licence:
  'A' – for those who carried exclusively for hire or reward;
  'B' – for those who carried their own goods and also carried for others;
  'C' – for those who carried only their own goods.

adviser to the High Commissioner. When work was resumed it was undertaken by the new Ministry of War Transport of May 1941, a merger of the Transport and Shipping Ministries, with Lord Leathers as Minister and Sir Cyril Hurcomb as Director-General.

Hurcomb, a career civil servant, had great experience of transport planning. He had been the Permanent-Secretary to the Ministry of Transport from 1927 to 1937, and had established a close rapport with Morrison during his period of office.[58] Leathers, on the other hand, a pragmatic businessman, made it clear that the Ministry's prime objective was to reorganise and improve transport – and particularly rail transport – for the war effort. While his predecessors, Reith and Moore-Brabazon, had been more sympathetic to the view that the problem of railway unification might be tackled along with revision of the Control Agreement, Leathers was strongly opposed to the cluttering up of day-to-day business with wrangles over long-term planning. When, shortly after taking office, he was asked to give the Lord President's Committee his opinion on the basis for a revised agreement, he maintained that 'the war effort would be hindered and not helped by any public declaration at the present time that the railways would be unified after the war, or by any attempt to bring about unification at the present time'. He suggested that 'if rail transport was to be unified it would be necessary to deal also with road transport', but added that 'this was a very difficult matter which should, if possible, be avoided in war time'. The Committee was unable to reach a decision. Its three Labour members – Attlee, Greenwood and Bevin – insisted on the immediate acceptance of 'railway unification under public ownership', but they were opposed by the three Conservatives – Anderson, Kingsley Wood and Duncan – who supported Leathers. The latter view prevailed in the War Cabinet, but it was obviously a close-run affair.[59]

This episode helps to explain Leathers's reluctance to contemplate transport planning during the rest of the war and, in particular, his sluggish response to attempts to engage his Ministry in planning for post-war reconstruction. In July 1941 Arthur Greenwood, Minister Without Portfolio, and responsible for reconstruction, informed him that Churchill had hinted, at a meeting of the War Cabinet, that transport should receive a comprehensive review as part of the reconstruction programme, and he asked for policy drafts to be channelled via his Reconstruction Problems Committee. Leathers did not share Greenwood's sense of urgency. He assured his colleague on 1 October that planning was in progress, but it was not until 18 November that Hurcomb informed his staff that it was proper to proceed. Officials were then instructed to prepare reports on the various transport modes. One of these was to be on 'railway unification', and the Coates–Robinson proposal was brought out of the cupboard to assist those engaged on it.[60] In March 1942 Sir William Jowitt, the Paymaster-General, succeeded Greenwood as Minister in charge of reconstruction. Finding that no progress had been made with transport he pressed Leathers for information, and was told that Coates, having returned from Canada, had been asked to produce a comprehensive review of inland transport 'from a transport and business point of view, and not from any political angle'.[61] In April Coates met Jowitt and his Secretary, Sir Alfred Hurst, and reaffirmed his opinion that a National Transport Corporation should be created. By this time he had come round to the view that short-distance road haulage by 'C' licence holders should be left in the private sector.[62]

Coates produced his second report in July 1942. It was in its essentials a fuller version of the draft bill of 1940, and there were no substantial changes of policy. He did, however, support his position with a lengthy survey of the historical background (which owed much to Gilbert Walker's recently published *Road and Rail* of 1942) and offered a more detailed evaluation of alternative strategies. He maintained that neither free competition nor railway unification was an adequate solution to the problem of transport co-ordination; and he criticised the proposal (put forward by Sir Osborne Mance) for a 'Track Pool' – a public authority to administer the infrastructure of both road and rail – which he considered to be unworkable in practice. Only a single monopoly, he maintained, would be able to secure the efficient and economic deployment of transport resources in the public interest.[63] The report proved to be as unpalatable to Leathers as the 1940 bill had been to Moore-Brabazon. He delayed passing it on to Jowitt until late September, and then made it clear that the Ministry was in no way committed to anything in it. Finally, when pressed by Jowitt at a meeting in March 1943, he admitted that he thought Coates's arguments 'failed to justify the very revolutionary and highly centralised solution proposed'. The report was then shelved pending further investigation, including an inquiry into the views of the main-line railway companies.[64]

Meanwhile, Jowitt, who was becoming increasingly irritated by Leathers's inactivity, turned to other sources. He was particularly impressed by the work of a young economist, Phyllis Deane.[65] In her chapter on 'Rail and Road Transport', in J. R. Bellerby's book, *Economic Reconstruction* (1943), she suggested that no less than three nationalised transport boards or corporations be set up; one for railways, one for London transport, and one for 'A' licence (public carrier) road haulage. 'B' licences would be phased out, but 'C' licences would be allowed to remain outside the public sector. Modal co-ordination in the public interest would be exercised by the Ministry of Transport. Jowitt sent Deane's work in draft form to Leathers in December 1942, hinting that it was a much more useful contribution than the Coates report. He followed this up with an emphatic declaration that something more extensive than railway unification would be required to meet post-war needs.[66] Leathers's continued prevarication was assisted by the cautious attitude of Hurcomb, whose own preference fell far short of a monopoly corporation for inland transport. He argued for an extended pooling arrangement to secure the co-ordination of the railways. After this had been swiftly condemned by one of his colleagues for failing to deal with the major problem of road–rail competition, he went on to review the whole question of inland transport. In memoranda of July and August 1943 he declared the Coates solution to be 'drastic'; suggested a co-ordination scheme for road and rail rates without a radical organisational change; and temporised by stressing the need to wait for a political decision.[67]

The work of reconstruction planning continued throughout the war, of course, and some detailed plans were produced by the Ministry of War Transport. In 1943, for example, Sir Alan Mount prepared a lengthy document on post-war railway investment, with special reference to electrification.[68] However, it was much easier to consider the needs of particular branches of transport in isolation than to examine railway development in the context of a reorganised transport industry, which could be created only by political means. Leathers was able to provide Jowitt with a paper on post-war road construction policy, in July 1943, but apologised for his inactivity on a broader front. In the following year, Jowitt told his successor, Lord Woolton: 'I feel quite sure that the present Minister of War Transport has no intention of making himself responsible for this difficult post-war question if he can possibly avoid it.'[69] There may have been some enthusiasm for a public control board or boards inside the Ministry, but no firm preference for post-war organisation was expressed officially, in spite of the pressure represented by debate in both houses of parliament.[70] Instead, it was stressed that the agreement with the railway companies, which provided for the continuance of control for a full year after the cessation of hostilities, gave ample time for the resolution of issues which, in any case, required Cabinet approval and legislation.[71] Nevertheless, there was common agreement that a return to pre-war railway organisation was undesirable, a view fully supported by Hurcomb and one which even Leathers upheld in his statement to the House of Lords in October 1943.[72]

The railway companies, already in 1941 alerted by rumours that the government was contemplating nationalisation, determined meanwhile to undertake some reconstruction planning of their own. In January 1942 they seized the initiative. On the recommendation of Sir Ronald Matthews, Chairman of the L.N.E.R., the Railway Companies' Association established a planning commission to consider 'how the efficiency of the Railways can be improved in the broadest sense by schemes of post-war reconstruction and reorganisation'.[73] Membership was confined to professional railwaymen. The first Chairman was Sir Ernest Lemon, a Vice-President of the L.M.S., and the other members included Frank Pope, also from the L.M.S., Keith Grand (G.W.R.) and Charles Bird (L.N.E.R.), all experienced senior executives. The move was plainly a pre-emptive one, designed to forestall criticism, particularly from within government circles. In practice it merely served to aggravate existing friction between the railways and the Ministry of War Transport. Not only were the deliberations of this exclusive body to be kept secret, but there had been no prior consultation with the Ministry, a fact which clearly upset its civil servants. From the start the commission proceeded on the assumption that the companies would be restored to private ownership and control after the war, and it was accepted that 'the future structure of the railways' did not lie within its remit.[74] Consequently, its work was confined to a consideration of detailed aspects of operational efficiency. From the spring of 1943 to the end of 1945 it supplied the main-line companies with no less than 19 reports on matters ranging from inter-company wagon control to the centralisation of railway research facilities, from coal distribution methods to station modernisation, not to speak of the extension of continuous brakes to wagons and the optimal lay-out of marshalling yards.[75] But the commission's activities proved to be disappointingly superficial. Members were not relieved of their war-time responsibilities; they experienced great difficulty in extracting information from their overworked colleagues; and there were several changes of personnel. Within a few months Lemon himself was released to advise the Ministry of Production, although he remained Chairman until February 1943, when he was succeeded first by Ashton Davies (to November 1944), and then by Tom Royle (both L.M.S. men). By early 1944 only Bird remained from the original team. The Lemon commission was, in Sir Alan Mount's phrase, 'nearly strangled at birth'. Opposed by a Ministry anxious to ensure that work was not carried out in the government's time, and largely ignored by busy railway managements, its reports could only be rather general and platitudinous in nature. They were certainly not the basis for a unified approach to the rationalisation of the railway system and the improvement of operating efficiency.[76]

Some railway leaders, however, wanted a more positive approach to strategic planning. At a meeting of the Railway Companies' Association in April 1942 it was agreed that the railways should prepare proposals for the industry's future organisation 'which would appeal to the public imagination, overcome the difficulties which had arisen from road transport competition, and meet present criticisms'. To this end a post-war policy committee of railway directors was created. Its task was to report on the post-war development of all forms of transport, with particular reference to the co-ordination of the various modes, and 'to give special regard to private ownership in relation to the public interest'. The Chairman was Colonel Eric Gore-Browne, the banker and Deputy-Chairman of the S.Rly, and the other members were Sir Robert Murrough Wilson (L.N.E.R.), and Sir Edward Cadogan (G.W.R.). Gilbert Szlumper, who had recently retired from the post of General Manager of the S.Rly, was asked to act as the committee's technical adviser.[77] In its circular letter to the company boards in May the committee accepted the premise that both public opinion and political pressure precluded a return to the railways' pre-war organisation, and suggested that some form of amalgamation or pooling of interests should be undertaken. Five policy-options were identified: nationalisation; state purchase of the railways' freehold with the granting of operating leases to the existing companies; amalgamation into one company; regrouping; and unification of operating by means of a central executive body similar to the war-time Railway Executive Committee.[78] The boards then invited their general managers to respond to this remit. Predictably, they produced very different solutions. Sir James Milne (G.W.R.) recommended the incorporation of rail and road interests in boards based on the main-line companies, with a central authority for capital investment. Sir Charles Newton (L.N.E.R.) proposed the state acquisition of railway fixed assets with a lease to a 'British Railways Board' at a low rental (the 'landlord and tenant' scheme). Sir Eustace Missenden (S.Rly) advocated the financial fusion of the railways into one private company, and the eventual reorganisation of the other forms of transport on the same basis. Sir William Wood of the L.M.S. put forward two further proposals. Faced with these conflicting views, the committee found difficulty in formulating a definite scheme. When it finally reported, in October 1942, it outlined three basic principles – private ownership, the necessity of combining road and rail interests and the value of a central board and executive – but suggested that these could be secured by either a pool of the finances and resources of the four railways and the road undertakings, or an outright merger of the two modes of transport.[79]

Whatever its shortcomings as a planning document, the Gore-Browne report represented an exceptionally positive approach by the railways to the problem of post-war organisation. However, like the Coates report, the child was still-born. The companies soon made it clear that they preferred to retain their separate identities after the war. Particular resistance came from the G.W.R. and the L.N.E.R.; only the L.M.S.

directors were prepared to endorse the idea of a road–rail merger.[80] The Gore-Browne proposals were then referred to the general managers for further consideration. In their report in June 1943, Milne, Wood, Missenden and Newton produced conclusions which admirably suited their employers' change of heart. They agreed that the railways should return to their pre-war status at the end of the control period, and suggested that as a first step the companies secure the implementation of the 1938 'Square Deal' proposals on freight transport. The companies' right to their standard revenues was reaffirmed; the cost of uneconomic but socially desirable services should be met elsewhere. Organisational changes were to be limited. The Railway Companies' Association should be reconstituted as a 'Central Railway Board' with wider powers, including responsibility for capital-raising; privately owned wagons should either be taken over by the railways or a separate company formed to operate all wagons; and the railways should seek a controlling interest in Britain's European air services. A proposal that Scotland's railways be worked as one unit was advanced, and the managers were also prepared to support the contention that road and rail 'track' costs should be equalised (though privately their attitude was known to be lukewarm).[81] The general managers' report marked the end of any serious attempt by the railways to anticipate and direct transport policy-making. When Leathers approached the companies for their views on post-war organisation, the chairmen used the report as the basis of their reply in August 1943.[82] They then fell back on an anti-nationalisation campaign which had been set in motion by Milne in the previous year.[83] Leathers's declaration that there could be no return to the status quo, and the subsequent proposals of the Labour Party and Trade Union Congress in 1944 and 1945, which were similar to those in the Coates report, left them unmoved. Only the L.N.E.R., financially the weakest of the four companies, expressed an anxiety about the adequacy of a return to the pre-war position. In an appendix to the general managers' report, Newton had offered the alternative of a net revenue pool with the central direction of railway operating, but this was not taken up by the other companies. No further proposals were published until the spectre of nationalisation became a firm reality with the drafting of the Transport Bill in 1946.[84]

So, by the time the Labour Party was returned to power in 1945, many ideas had long been circulating about the best way to provide a more efficient transport system in the future. Most of them embraced some kind of control board or boards, and while definitions of 'co-ordination' remained vague and often contradictory, it was generally agreed that the relationship between transport modes should be defined more closely. In hindsight, some sort of public control of railways may have seemed inevitable. Nevertheless, the government's proposals for the nationalisation of transport, formulated in the National Executive Committee's report on 'Post War Organisation of British Transport' and clarified by Morrison's statement in the Commons in November 1945, were met by the continuing and generally unconstructive opposition of the railway companies and by a Ministry which, under Leathers's direction, had refrained from detailed planning after the demise of Coates's initiative. There is no doubt that the combination of a hostile private interest and a diffident civil service hindered the process of drafting a complex and wide-ranging bill in a relatively short time.[85]

VI

The story of the drafting of the Transport Bill, its progress through parliament and the provisions of the Transport Act of 1947 have been covered in various books and articles.[86] They do not require elaboration here. However, two factors, decisive in shaping the railways' operating environment in the early years of nationalisation, demand some attention: the choice of organisation and the method of compensating the railway shareholders, which largely determined the capital base of the new concern. In both matters the role of the main-line companies during the drafting stages is of particular interest. It is commonly believed that the railway boards, by rejecting the invitation of Alfred Barnes, the Minister of Transport, in February 1946 to assist in the preparation of the bill, prevented the selection of an optimal form of organisation; and that the simultaneous prosecution of a fierce anti-nationalisation campaign helped their shareholders to win more favourable terms in the compulsory exchange of their securities for British Transport Stock.[87] Is there substance in these allegations?

Before the problem of transport's future organisational structure was taken up in the Ministry in November 1945, Barnes had made it clear that he preferred separate boards for each mode, responsible to a national commission, rather than the concentration of authority in a single giant corporation on the Coates model.[88] This conformed to both stated Labour policy and that of the T.U.C.; Morrison, who as Lord President was given special responsibility for the nationalisation programme, readily agreed to it. The civil servants were then asked to examine ways of introducing such a two-tier system. Three options were examined: 'functional' (delegation by transport mode), 'territorial' (based on the existing main-line railway companies) and 'regional' (non-railway based areas incorporating all transport modes).[89] It was soon decided that the functional form was the most suitable, despite the risk of negating the aim of co-ordinating transport operation. Part I of the Transport Act established a British Transport Commission with the 'general duty ... to provide ... an efficient, adequate, economic and properly integrated system of public inland transport and port facilities', and to cover costs 'taking one year with another'. All assets were to be vested in the Commission, which would determine overall policy, subject to Ministerial supervision, but operation was to be delegated to Executives. Five were named: Railway, Docks and Inland Waterways, Road Transport, London Transport and Hotels (embracing the ex-railway hotels and catering services).[90]

There is no doubt that the railway companies would have preferred a territorial or a regional solution, but it is doubtful whether by participating in the planning discussions they could have achieved either. After all, the major argument in favour of a functional system was its ease of introduction, an important consideration given the intention to act quickly. Moreover, it is clear that both Minister and officials were anxious to avoid an organisational form which would perpetuate 'the railway domination of inland transport'.[91] The railways might have achieved more at a detailed level. They were certainly opposed to the loss of their docks and harbours – the Southern was particularly angry about the fate of Southampton docks – and were also critical of the decision to form a separate body for railway catering and hotels. They might well have secured some changes in the Executive structure.[92] On more general issues there was little room for manoeuvre. In short, a closer involvement by the companies in the drafting procedure would almost certainly have produced nothing more than marginal changes in the basic organisational framework. Certainly, the railway companies would have done little to meet those critics of the bill who, with *The Economist*, contended that the B.T.C. was 'astonishingly small for its task'; and that in all probability it would leave the Executives (who were to be appointed directly by the Minister) free to pursue 'the settled habits of mind of railway men or road operators'.[93] Moreover, some of the harshest criticisms of the initial organisation were levelled at the functional organisation of the Railway Executive itself, and that was determined not by the Act but by the B.T.C. in 1947.[94]

On compensation, the Ministry – impressed by difficulties of implementing a scheme based on net maintainable revenue, which had been advocated by the T.U.C. in 1944 – agreed instead on the more practical use of market values, i.e. London Stock Exchange prices. Discussions then centred on the choice of valuation dates. The Ministry had hoped to apply the mean of the mid-monthly quotations for the pre-election period February–July 1945, but Barnes encountered strong opposition from the company chairmen at his secret meetings with them in June and September

2 'The pertinacious porter', E. M. Shepard, *Punch*, 8 January 1947.
Prime Minister Attlee and the promise of the Transport Act of 1947.
(Reproduced by permission of *Punch*)

1946. His published proposals (18 November 1946) offered the concession of a valuation based on prices in the week 1–8 November 1946, or, where higher, in February–July 1945. Thereby, the railways were to receive about £57 million more than was originally envisaged, in a scheme expected to give the main-line companies £907.8 million in Government Stock with a guaranteed income, assuming a 2.5 per cent interest rate, of £22.7 million.[95] However, by the time of the transfer date, 1 January 1948, a rise in interest rates necessitated the issue of stock at 3 per cent. In this way shareholders reaped the benefit of a stock transfer based on conditions ruling in 1946 and an income based on those of late 1947, while the British Transport Commission's interest burden was increased by about £4.6 million to £27.2 million.[96] Here again, the pressure of railway protest, which was supported by The Economist's influential leader of 23 November 1946 entitled 'Nationalisation on the Cheap', did much to persuade the Ministry that an amelioration in the shareholders' position was appropriate. Indeed, further concessions might have been extracted had the railways abandoned their demand for arbitration earlier and entered into negotiations on a market value basis.[97]

Both episodes illustrate an important – and alarming – element in the framing of the nationalisation proposals. What mattered was political and administrative expediency. Discussion of the implications of the legislation for the economic operation of road and rail transport was conspicuously absent. Economies were expected after the creation of the Commission and the introduction of 'co-ordination' but, as in 1921, these were only vague assumptions. They were not based on detailed investigation. It may indeed be argued that the organisational framework of Commission and Executives was selected in the full knowledge that it was likely to prejudice the co-ordinating aim. The decision to abandon the nationalisation of 'C' licence undertakings carrying for distances of 40 miles and over led in the same direction. The hostility of the railways encouraged the Ministry to conclude that the compensation terms, while fair, were rather mean. Certainly, they were less generous, in relation to shareholders' income, than the schemes drafted in 1940 (when the Coates report was first examined), which had been based on net revenue performance in the mid- to late-1930s.[98] On the other hand, the final valuation was affected by the railways' abnormal profits under war-time control and was undoubtedly generous in relation to future earning-power unless constraints were to be placed on road transport.[99] Because the government had decided that there was no question of buying the railways for less than a Stock Exchange valuation, there was no attempt to examine factors likely to determine future net revenue.[100] The main object of socialising the transport industry, in Barnes's words, 'was to consolidate the various elements of transport . . . into a single whole which would operate as a non-profit making utility service at the least real cost to trade, industry and the travelling public'.[101] But the absence of serious discussions about the future deployment of transport resources after 1947 was one of the most disturbing features of the legislative process attending nationalisation.

PART 1

The British Transport Commission and the Railway Executive, 1948–53

2

Organisation

The Transport Bill of 1946 received the Royal Assent on 6 August 1947, and two days later the Minister of Transport announced the appointment of the B.T.C. Sir Cyril (from 1950 Lord) Hurcomb, Permanent-Secretary of the Ministry, and active in the formulation of the Transport Act, was to be Chairman. Two members were chosen from the ranks of the Railway Executive Committee: Sir William Wood, President of the Executive of the L.M.S., the largest of the main-line companies, and Lord Ashfield, who as Chairman of the L.P.T.B. had unrivalled experience of urban transport. The need to provide an appropriate balance of representation ensured the selection of two trade union officials: John Benstead, the General Secretary of the N.U.R., and Lord Rusholme (Robert Palmer), the General Secretary of the Co-operative Union. However, this did nothing to appease left-wing demands for 'workers' control', i.e. boards elected by workers in the industry.* A part-time member was added with the appointment in September of Captain Sir Ian Bolton, a leading Scottish accountant and partner in the Glasgow firm of McClelland Ker & Co.[1] Periods of office with the Commission were limited to an initial five years for full-time and three years for part-time members. Although these appointments took effect only a few weeks after the Transport Bill became law, they had been the subject of lengthy discussions which had begun in the Ministry as early as April 1946.[2]

How competent was this small team, which had been given the unenviable task of establishing nationalised transport? S. S. Wilson, one of the Ministry officials closely involved in the process, thought them 'hardworking, experienced, elderly, and safe'. He maintained that there was no criticism on the score of 'established reputation and long experience', but more doubt about 'freshness of vision, initiative, and readiness for

---

*Benstead's appointment caused considerable bitterness in the N.U.R. He ceased to be a member of the union's pension fund on taking office.

change'.[3] They were undoubtedly mature, with an average age in 1947 of 61. Hurcomb and Wood were both 64, and Ashfield at 73 was well over retiring age. Benstead, who was 50, must have felt a youngster in such company. Michael Bonavia, who was recruited from the L.N.E.R. to a position in the Commission (he was Assistant Secretary (Works and Development)), has referred to a 'certain drabness' at the top, to a lack of outstanding talent and dynamism.[4] Wood, bereft of his extensive L.M.S. bureaucracy, was uncomfortable in the new role of policy-maker; Ashfield's appetite for such a challenging task appears to have been limited, and in any case, he died in November 1948. Rusholme, amiable rather than forceful, was not very familiar with transport problems, and Benstead, who was clearly able (Hurcomb made him Deputy-Chairman in January 1949), found the transition from trade union leader to management boss a rather difficult one.[5] Hurcomb certainly was no lightweight and he soon came to dominate the team. With a quick, analytical mind, his administrative credentials were first-class, and there is no evidence to suggest that he had lost his enthusiasm for hard work. He was also successful in recruiting experienced officers of high calibre to assist him. Miles Beevor, the Acting General Manager of the L.N.E.R. on nationalisation, became Chief Secretary and Legal Adviser to the Commission, and Reginald H. (later Sir Reginald) Wilson, an accountant with Brown Fleming & Murray who had acquired valuable experience of transport finance while seconded to the Ministry of War Transport, was appointed to the crucial position of Financial Comptroller. Unfortunately, the impact of these appointments was reduced by the keen rivalry between the two men; a rivalry compounded by the fact that Wilson gathered non-railwaymen around him, while Beevor appointed officers from the main-line railway companies. Indeed, the overall impression is of a body inadequately equipped for a formidable task. The usual Ministerial caution had been coupled with government insistence on salaries which were low in comparison with those for senior posts on the main-line railways. For example, Wood's L.M.S. salary of £10,000 was double that fixed by the government for the B.T.C., and the same was true of the other railway chief executives. Furthermore, the Treasury decision to abate Hurcomb's salary by the amount of his civil service pension – he eventually received only £7,000 of his allotted £8,500 – must have caused dismay among highly-paid railway executives lower down.[6] It is perhaps significant that of all those appointed only Benstead had been included in a provisional list of 60 'possibles' drawn up in the Ministry of Transport in May 1946.[7] This niggardliness, part of the Labour Party's anxiety to place the concept of public service before that of adequate remuneration, affected all the nationalised industries.* It encouraged the recruitment of retired businessmen and bureaucrats with fully-paid-up pensions, and tended to exclude dynamic managers in mid-career. The problem worried the government periodically. It was the subject of debate in the Cabinet's Socialised Industries Committee in October 1949, for example.[8] No solutions were offered, however, and the effect of low salaries on the calibre of nationalised industry management has surfaced from time to time ever since.

It had been expected that individual members of the B.T.C. would take up some quasi-functional responsibilities, and in January 1947 Hurcomb had envisaged specialisation in finance, research and development, labour, and Executive co-ordination. At the very first meeting, however, on 13 August, it was agreed that, in accordance with government intentions, the Commission was 'a policy-making and directing body acting collectively and not individually discharging executive functions or charged as individuals with functional responsibilities'.[9] A small functional executive was appointed to assist the Commission in its somewhat cramped offices on the top of 55, Broadway, S.W.1, the headquarters of London Transport. There were three Departments: the Chief Secretary's (Beevor), Finance (Wilson) and Public Relations and Publicity, led by J. H. 'Jock' Brebner, a volatile Scot recruited from the L.P.T.B. The status of these leading officers was reflected in their salaries, which matched those of the Commission itself.[10] In the Secretary's Department executives were made responsible for Staff and Establishment, Works and Development, Traffic, Minutes and Records, law and charges (Parliamentary Assistant Solicitor), and shortly after Vesting Day (1 January 1948) a Secretary for Railway Research, C. E. R. Sherrington, was added with the incorporation of the Main-Line Companies' Railway Research Service. In the Finance Department, five 'Directors' were appointed, for Funds, Accounts, Costs and Statistics, Acquisitions and Audit. A sixth (General Division) had been appointed by the end of 1948, when total staff at H.Q. amounted to 152.[11] The organisation is shown in Chart I.

*Salaries in 1948:

British Overseas Airways Corporation Chairman	£7,500
British European Airways Chairman	£6,500
National Coal Board Chairman	£8,500, members £5,000
British Electricity Authority Chairman	£8,500, members £3,500

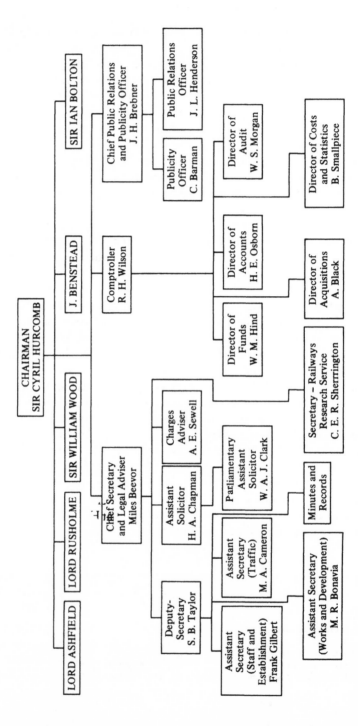

Chart I British Transport Commission organisation, May 1948

II

Much to civil service dismay, and against the advice of his colleagues, Alfred Barnes, the Minister of Transport, had insisted on making the appointments to the transport Executives himself. Apparently, he had accepted the trade unions' belief that if the Commission had been allowed to appoint it would have chosen only technocrats and that workers' representation would have been overlooked.[12] The view that Executives should have a broadly functional organisation was also something established *ex ante* in government circles. Although this anomalous situation was to have an unfortunate effect upon relations between the B.T.C. and the Railway Executive, by far the largest of the five subordinate undertakings, the autonomy it represented was more apparently than real. It is clear that Hurcomb and his colleagues were closely involved from the outset not only in determining the character of Executive organisation but also in the choice of personnel. In August 1947 they decided that each Executive was to have a collective responsibility and would operate 'through a number of highly placed chief officers'; membership would consist mainly of 'persons charged with functional responsibilities'. For the Railway Executive, these functions were to be commercial, operation, engineering, finance and staff. It was also accepted that 'while it was important to choose the best men for each post, some regard must be had at this stage to a reasonable distribution of the appointments among the existing companies'.[13] The selection of Executive members proceeded in tandem with the determination of underlying principles. There was an early setback. Sir James Milne, the General Manager of the Great Western and without doubt the leading railway manager, rejected the invitation to act as Chairman of the Railway Executive. So the Commission decided to recommend Sir Eustace Missenden, the more pedestrian General Manager of the Southern, a nomination which Barnes accepted. At the same time, the name of W. P. Allen, General Secretary of the Associated Society of Locomotive Engineers and Firemen, and a former engine-cleaner with the Great Northern Railway, was forwarded as an ideal candidate for hand-ling labour functions on the Executive. With Missenden in attendance at a further meeting of the B.T.C., a final list of recommendations for the Railway Executive was drawn up for Ministerial approval, and on 12 September the appointments (with the exception of Sir Wilfrid Ayre, a part-time member appointed in October) were announced. The duration of the appointments was the same as that for members of the Commission itself. A profile of the Executive is given in Table 3.

The Railway Executive of 1948 was essentially a body of experienced railwaymen of the old school. Their average age on appointment was 57.

Table 3. *The Railway Executive, 1948*

Name	Age on appointment	Major function	Previous post	Company or equivalent	Appointed	Previous salary in 1947	No. of years in railway industry
Full-time members (salary: Chairman £7,000, Riddles £6,000, others £5,000)							
Sir Eustace Missenden O.B.E.	61	Chairman	General Manager	Southern	1939	£12,000	49
General Sir William Slim G.B.E., K.C.B.	56	Public Relations	Commandant	Imperial Defence College	1946	£ 1,733	Nil
W. P. Allen C.B.E.	58	Staff	General Secretary	A.S.L.E.F.	1940	£ 825	41
V. M. Barrington-Ward C.B.E.	60	Operating; Motive Power[a]	Divisional General Manager	L.N.E.R.	1945	£ 4,500	41
D. Blee	48	Commercial	Chief Goods Manager	G.W.R.	1946	£ 4,000	32
R. A. Riddles	55	Mech. and Elec. Engineering; Motive Power[a]	Vice-President	L.M.S.	1946	£ 6,000	39
J. C. L. Train	58	Civil Engineering	Chief Engineer	L.N.E.R.	1942	£ 4,000	40
Part-time members (salary: £750)							
C. Nevile		Commercial	Chairman Economics Committee	National Farmers' Union		—	Nil
Sir Wilfrid Ayre		Commercial	Chairman and Man. Dir.	Burntisland Shipbuilding Co.		—	Nil

[a] Shared function

General Sir William Slim, who had distinguished himself as Commander-in-Chief of Allied Land Forces in South-East Asia during the war, was the only full-time member with no prior knowledge of railways. The others had all joined the industry before the age of 21 and had accumulated an average of 40 years' service by 1948. With the exception of Michael Barrington-Ward and John Landale Train – who had both attended public schools (Westminster and Dulwich respectively) and had experience of higher education (Edinburgh University, and Hull and Glasgow Technical Colleges) – all of the group had entered the industry straight from school and had thereafter worked for only one company.[14] The composition of the Railway Executive did not engender much enthusiasm in public circles. The absence of Milne was clearly a disappointment and later commentators such as Pearson and Bonavia have emphasised the effect this had in weakening 'the railway team'.[15] Milne was probably the most accomplished general manager of his generation and his position had been strengthened by the retirement in 1941 of Sir Ralph Wedgwood (L.N.E.R.) and the death in an air raid of Lord Stamp of the L.M.S. in the same year.* With the appointment of Wood to the Commission and the retirement from the general managership of the L.N.E.R. of Sir Charles Newton (who was 65), the rather stolid Missenden was the only feasible candidate among the general managers. But Milne at 64 was of retiring age himself, and he had offered to accept the chairmanship on a one-year basis only. This was unrealistic; and his well-publicised antipathy for nationalisation scarcely made him an ideal candidate for the Executive. However, if the effect of losing Milne's personal contribution has been exaggerated, there is no doubt at all that his withdrawal had a most damaging influence upon the attitude of his Great Western colleagues. Both Allan Quartermaine, the company's Civil Engineer, and Keith Grand, the Assistant General Manager, two leading figures, made it clear that they were not interested in joining the new organisation. Quartermaine's rejection of Hurcomb's invitation to join the Executive, coupled with the concern to balance company representation, led to the passing over of Frank Pope of the L.M.S., one of the most experienced commercial managers, and the rather surprising choice of David Blee of the G.W.R. for the important role of commercial specialist. It was expecting a great deal of someone who for much of the war had occupied the modest position of Assistant to the Chief Goods Manager (salary: £1,400–£1,600 per annum) with a company whose freight business was based largely on a single commodity – South Wales coal – to take on the complex commercial

*There have been several explanations for Milne's diffidence. He was a man of substantial means, who probably resented Wood's elevation to the B.T.C. There also appears to have been a clash over outside directorships, which membership of the B.T.C. ruled out.

responsibilities of nationalised railways. He was very much a lightweight.*

Each member of the Executive was given responsibility for specified areas of railway business. No financial appointment was made, but Hurcomb and his colleagues produced a mechanical engineer (Riddles), a civil engineer (Train), and specialists in operation (Barrington-Ward), commerce (Blee) and labour (Allen). Such an organisation carried the risk that it would degenerate into uncoordinated departmentalism. It was to be underpinned by the presence of Missenden as a 'generalist' and by the outsider Slim, who was given a miscellany of interests, the most important of which were public relations and publicity. Little was expected of the two part-timers, Christopher Nevile and Sir Wilfrid Ayre, who were asked merely to take an interest in commercial relations, with particular emphasis on agriculture and Scotland respectively. More important, however, was the small team of senior railway executives appointed to posts which corresponded to those already made at B.T.C. level. Here again, a 'balanced' representation of former company employees was stressed. The L.M.S. supplied a Chief Financial Officer, George Morton, the Southern provided H. L. Smedley, the Legal Adviser and Solicitor, and the Secretary, E. G. Marsden, came from the L.N.E.R. via the Railway Executive Committee. Arthur Pearson and J. L. Harrington, the Chief Officers (Administration), and James Ness, the Chief Officer (New Works), came from the L.M.S., S.Rly, and L.N.E.R. respectively. All were railwaymen with long service records. By June 1948 there was a total staff of 366 (511 by December 1949) at the Executive's headquarters in the Great Central Hotel, 222, Marylebone Road, N.W.1.[16]

The concern to balance company representation certainly resulted in a division of the principal honours among the main-line railways, but lower down, this was less in evidence. Riddles, for example, chose four of his officers from the L.M.S., his old company, while Train appointed two of his staff of four from the L.N.E.R.[17] Given the intensity of the old rivalries, it remained to be seen whether the new organisation could work harmoniously as a team rather than as a collection of individuals pursuing the idiosyncratic procedures of their former employers. The Railway Executive, then, was a body of professional railwaymen, a competent group if not the best that might have been assembled, but with little moderating or stimulating influence from outside the industry. The only major change in personnel in the early years did little to disturb the dominance of the railway specialists: indeed, if anything, it was intensified. In November 1948 Slim resigned to become Chief of the Imperial

---

*One of his colleagues has suggested that he 'couldn't have run a coconut shy'.

General Staff. In his short time with the Executive he had made a good impression, his likeable personality helping to reduce the growing friction between Hurcomb and Missenden. His successor was another army officer, General Sir Daril Watson, formerly the Quartermaster-General, who took office in January 1949. Unfortunately, he was a less charismatic figure, and his quiet demeanour prevented him from restraining his more aggressive colleagues.

Hurcomb explained to Missenden in September 1947, before the Executive had been appointed, that its 'primary task' was to 'unify the four Railways in a real and operating sense, and, at the same time, to do so in such a way as to avoid excessive centralisation and to provide for suitable devolution of authority'.[18] Clearly, if these conditions were to be satisfied, a new regional organisation had to be devised. In practice, not only was policy-making on this crucial issue conducted hurriedly, but discussions took place in an atmosphere of some confusion, with the precise nature of the relationship between the Commission and its Executive uncertain. The B.T.C. began by asking Sherrington, then still with the main-line companies' Railway Research Service, to report on alternative schemes of railway organisation. His memorandum (of 10 September) was then passed on to the Executive, a few days after its appointment, with an instruction to make appropriate recommendations for decentralisation. But the Executive members were at first unsure about the character of their own organisation. Thus, on 30 September, 18 days after appointment, Blee could only write to Missenden that it was understood to be the Minister's intention that the Executives were to assume functional responsibilities, a position encouraged by Barnes who, it appears, had failed to spell things out in the official letters of appointment.[19] The position was not clarified until the joint meeting of Commission and Executive in October.[20]

In these circumstances, the Executive's early thoughts naturally turned to a perpetuation of the status quo. For example, Blee's memorandum of 30 September stated that it would be essential to create regional organisations 'broadly conforming with the existing railway organisations', and that 'regional co-ordination of departmental operations under a regional general manager' would 'prevent separate functional recommendations emerging which are impracticable without inter-functional consideration, adjustment, and balanced judgment regionally'.[21] The Executive endorsed this view, and at a further meeting with the Commission, having presented its scheme allocating functional responsibility for railway departments to its members, suggested that the day-to-day administration of the regions would be in charge of regional general managers, 'to whom all the departmental officers will be responsible'.[22] At this time, the Executive thought that five regions might be introduced on Vesting Day (1 January 1948). A Scottish Region, on which all parties were agreed, required a merger of L.M.S. and L.N.E.R. interests in Scotland, but the others – Western (G.W.R.), Southern (S.Rly), North Eastern (L.N.E.R.) and North Western (L.M.S.) – would be based on the existing main-line companies.[23]

The Commission, under Hurcomb's leadership, had other ideas. It would not accept either the loose form of functional control proposed, with its concentration of authority in the hands of the regional general managers, or the suggested regional structure. It had already determined its role in railway management, having decided in September that it 'would exercise functions similar to those of the Boards of the Main Line Companies, while the Executive exercised the functions of the General Managers'. The implication here was that there was no need for general managers at regional level. The Commission went on to consider the desirability of retaining control of several areas of business, including the negotiation of staff agreements, the settlement of disputes and the approval of senior appointments.[24] The matter was settled in the course of October and November. The 'Scheme of Delegation of Functions by the British Transport Commission to the Railway Executive', which was required under Section 5 of the Transport Act, 1947, was approved at the Commission's meeting of 28 October. Although it granted the Executive the necessary powers to manage, operate and maintain the railways, the B.T.C.'s authority was more than safeguarded by the proviso, in Section 5 (6) of the Act, that Executives were bound 'to give effect to any directions which may from time to time be given them by the Commission'. 'Direction No. 1', signed on 27 November 1947, demonstrated clearly how the Commission intended to operate in the sphere of railway management. The Railway Executive was obliged to obtain the Commission's prior approval for a whole range of activities, including expenditure on renewals over £25,000; new works of £25,000 and above; appointments at salaries of £1,750 p.a. and above: national agreements with trade unions on pay and conditions; land transactions exceeding £5,000; adjustments to the railways' regional structure, including boundary changes; and the closure of any railway line, dock, harbour, hotel, steamer or ferry service.[25] Furthermore, the Commission made it clear, in a separate covering letter, that communications on policy issues should be referred to the Commission. Staff privileges and 'golden handshakes' were also to be the subject of prior consultation. These limitations, along with the Commission's declaration that it was alone responsible for questions of policy, including general financial control, the supervision of research and development and, in accordance with the requirements of the Transport Act, the preparation of a new charges scheme and arrangements for the 'co-ordination of transport', added up to a considerable interference with the 'free hand' in management requested by Missenden on the Executive's behalf.[26]

It is clear, then, that during the period of rushed policy-making in the autumn of 1947 there was a clash between the B.T.C., which was determined to partner its Executive in railway management, and the Railway Executive, which while accepting the functional principle hoped to exercise a general authority over the railways, leaving day-to-day operations in large measure to general managers on the ground. Both bodies were, in effect, trying to reserve to themselves a policy-making and planning role. The B.T.C. prevailed. In the circumstances the Executive had no alternative but to accept, with minor modifications, the commission's organisational scheme, embodied in a draft memorandum on 'Organisation of the Unified Railway System' of 23 October. This gave the Executive the task of imposing a unifying control from the centre, with instructions passed directly by individual members to the relevant departmental officers at regional level. In order to co-ordinate or 'cross-tie' operations locally, Chief Regional Officers were to be introduced, but without the status of 'general manager'.[27]

Hurcomb had less success with the second part of his scheme, namely to introduce a greater measure of decentralisation of railway management. At a joint meeting with the Executive in October Hurcomb suggested seven units for England and Wales: Southern, Welsh, Western, L.M.S.–London (Euston), L.M.S.–Manchester, L.N.E.R.–London (Liverpool St), and L.N.E.R.–York. There was something to be said for breaking up the L.M.S. on the grounds of size, although there would have been considerable operating problems had this been done. However, the only concession made by the Executive, communicated to the B.T.C. two days later, was to divide the L.N.E.R. as proposed, a decision which was facilitated by the existence of such a divisional management structure within the company. So there were to be only six regions including Scotland: London Midland (the L.M.S. in England and Wales), Western, Southern, Eastern (the Southern area of the L.N.E.R.), North Eastern (its North-Eastern area based on York), and Scottish (see Map I).[28]

The B.T.C. had accepted the Executive's view that it was important to avoid a sudden dislocation of existing organisations, but in doing so had helped to create an unbalanced distribution of railway resources. The giant L.M.R., for example, which would have accounted for 29 per cent of the train-miles run in 1946, made a considerable contrast with the tiny N.E.R. whose share would have been only 9 per cent.[29] The choice of

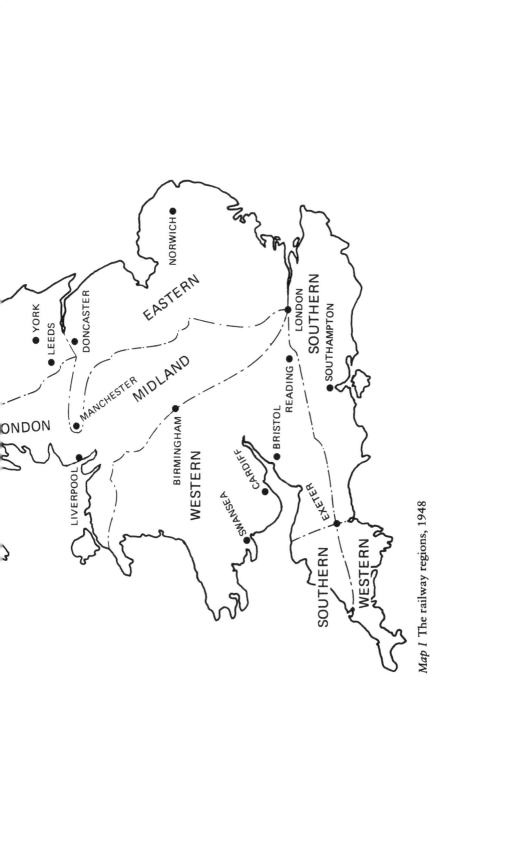

Map I The railway regions, 1948

regions could only be justified by emphasising its purely temporary nature. The Commission stressed that modifications would be made later as experience dictated.[30]

The names of the C.R.O.s were announced at a press conference introducing the new railway organisation in November (see Table 4 and Chart II). They were, like the majority of members of the Executive, senior railway managers of established reputation. With an average age of 52 they were not much younger than the full-timers on the Executive, and their experience of the industry, which amounted to an average of 33 years, was not far behind that of their masters at Marylebone. Indeed, in some ways they could claim superiority. G. L. Darbyshire had been appointed an L.M.S. Vice-President three years before Riddles, while Grand, as Assistant General Manager of the Great Western, and John Elliot, the Deputy General Manager of the Southern, ranked above Blee, Barrington-Ward and Train in the old hierarchy. In terms of formal education, too, the C.R.O.s had every right to be considered equals if not superiors. Charles Bird had obtained a Cambridge First in Mathematics. T. F. Cameron had studied at Edinburgh University, while Elliot (Marlborough and Sandhurst) and Grand (Rugby) had attended major public schools. Starting salaries were a further indication of the C.R.O.s' 'challenge' to the status of the Executive. Darbyshire, who had been earning £7,500 a year with the L.M.S. since July 1946, was allowed to retain that salary as C.R.O. of the London Midland Region, and both Elliot and Grand continued to be paid their former salaries of £6,700 and £5,500 respectively. These officers were thus earning considerably more than their superiors at both Executive and Commission level (cf. above, p. 32, and Tables 3 and 4). Only the more junior C.R.O.s, Hopkins, Bird and Cameron, were appointed at salaries commensurate with the distance the Executive wished to place between itself and its regional officers.[31]

Here, then, were some further seeds of conflict in the new and unfamiliar organisation introduced in 1948. The appointment of leading railwaymen of rather narrow background (like their counterparts on the Executive, they had all worked for only one company) to critical but ambiguous posts of inferior status, when they clearly aspired to general manager positions, only added to the difficulties of administration in the early years of nationalisation.

III

The organisational history of the Executive fits neatly into two distinct periods, the first, under Missenden's chairmanship, from 1948 to 1950, and the second, under John Elliot, from 1951 to 1953. There is no doubt at

Table 4. *The Chief Regional Officers, 1948*

Name	Region	Age on appointment	Previous post	Salary in 1947	No. of years in railway industry
G. L. Darbyshire C.B.E.	London Midland (Euston)	63	Vice-President L.M.S. 1943 (Acting President 1947)	£7,500	50
K. W. C. Grand	Western (Paddington)	47	Assistant General Manager G.W.R. 1941 (Acting General Manager 1947)	£5,500	29
John Elliot	Southern (Waterloo)	49	Deputy General Manager S.Rly 1939 (Acting General Manager 1947)	£6,700[a]	23
C. K. Bird	Eastern (Liverpool St)	50	Goods Manager (Sthn) L.N.E.R. 1943 (Acting Divisional Manager (Sthn) 1947)	£3,500	26
C. P. Hopkins	North Eastern (York)	47	Assistant General Manager (Traffic) L.N.E.R. 1945	£2,250	32
T. F. Cameron	Scottish (Glasgow)	57	Divisional General Manager (Scotland) L.N.E.R. 1943	£3,750	36

[a] Includes £700 in directors' fees.

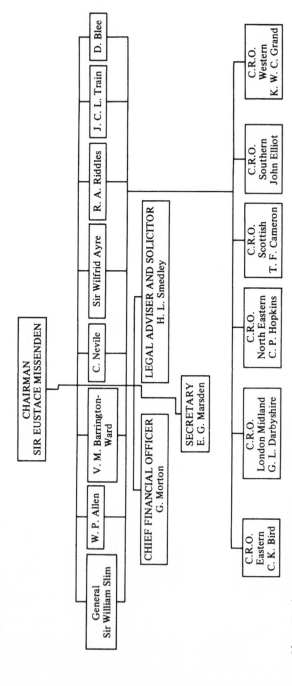

Chart II The Railway Executive and Chief Regional Officers, 1948

all that the earlier period was punctuated by a series of morale-sapping conflicts at all levels of management. As already indicated, tensions between the Commission and the Executive and between the Executive and its regional officers had been unwittingly built into the system from its inception. Furthermore, the climate in which managers were asked to operate was not improved by the open hostility of the press to the new organisation, which only served to reinforce resentment at the imposition of authority from above, whether from 55, Broadway or from 222, Marylebone Road. *The Financial Times*, the *Manchester Guardian*, *The Economist* and the *Railway Gazette* all published critical articles in November and December 1947, in which both the relationship between the Commission and the Executive and the functional organisation of the latter were condemned.[32] Later, Hurcomb was perturbed by an editorial in the *Railway Gazette* on 19 March 1948, which suggested that certain weaknesses in the Executive's organisation were 'not necessarily the fault of the present members of the Executive for, to a considerable extent, at least, the broad outline of the organisation was imposed on them from above'.[33] His anxiety was increased when he discovered that the offending journalist had been briefed by Missenden, Slim and other members of the Executive.[34] By the middle of 1948 the cudgels were being taken up by the popular press. The *Sunday Express*, for example, caused something of a furore with a biting attack upon the C.R.O. organisation. Bernard Harris's article entitled 'Trouble Brewing on the Nationalised Railways' referred to widespread dissatisfaction and frustration among 'key men' with the 'downgrading' of the post of general manager, and provoked immediate concern within the Executive. The C.R.O.s, suspected of leaking information to the press, were then invited to take a more active part in R.E. deliberations.[35]

In this situation Missenden was encouraged to resist the Commission's attempts to encroach upon the Executive's control of operational management. At an early stage he acted to maintain a clear distinction between the two bodies. After discussions in February 1948, the Executive decided to produce, from 1 March, a separate set of minutes known as 'Memorandum of Decisions taken at Meeting . . .'. Typed on green paper and for internal circulation only, the Memoranda were to be additional to the formal minutes which the Executive was obliged to pass on to the Commission for endorsement. The Secretary's explanatory letter to Executive members and chief officers stated that the Memoranda of Decisions would embrace, 'in accordance with standard R.E.C. [war-time Railway Executive Committee] and R.C.H. [Railway Clearing House] practice', departmental committee minutes, items of minor importance and those 'not appropriate or not ready for inclusion in the Official

Minutes'.[36] Further justification of the system of dual minuting was made in later confidential notes in which it was explained that the early, thrice-weekly, meetings of the Executive had been cluttered up with trivial items. The Memoranda were thus an 'administrative convenience', a working guide for functional members and committees as to the state of play on unresolved and minor matters.[37] On the face of it, there was nothing sinister or remiss about such a procedure. But the Commission was not told about the decision to create this Memoranda series. When B.T.C. officers eventually picked up rumours that the Executive was keeping an unofficial set of minutes, they were convinced that this was being done with the intention of withholding information from them. Was there any substance in this allegation?

Unfortunately, both the official and unofficial minutes are cryptic and in the absence of so much supporting material on the Executive's activities, one can only speculate about motives.[38] Certainly, a great many entries in the Memoranda series were concerned with routine items of business. There was no need for the Commission to be informed, of minor operational matters, such as John Train's report of July 1948 on the collapse of a staircase at Alloway Station in Ayrshire, or the decision to ask the Western Region's C.R.O. to report on advertisements on train lavatory mirrors in July 1950.[39] On the other hand, it is clear that much more important matters were discussed, in an atmosphere of secrecy if not conspiracy, and that few of these were passed on to the Commission in the form in which they appeared. For example, in the Memoranda for March 1948, the first month of the new arrangements, there were references to such items as the L.M.S. advisory committee on research, steamship catering, Blee's concern about the availability of covered vans, the loss and pilferage of goods in transit and discussions with the Docks and Inland Waterways Executive on the transfer of railway docks, none of which appeared in the official minutes transmitted to Hurcomb. In addition, there was a fair amount of 'thinking aloud' on the Executive's relations with the Commission, especially on finance.[40] Moreover, while this information was withheld from the Commission, the Executive, in spite of its apparent concern to improve the image of its official minutes by purging them of unimportant matters, continued to feed its masters a diet of trivial operating information. In March 1948, the Commission was told of delays to ferries owing to fog, of cattle straying into tunnels, and that the 'movement of broccoli from Cornwall was again heavy following reduced forwardings due to inclement weather'.[41] Recent recollections support the view that this procedure was part of a deliberate strategy of separation. For example, Robin Riddles has remarked that the Memoranda series was Missenden's way of keeping the Executive's discussions away from

Hurcomb, who for his part had tried to bring the two bodies closer together by means of informal joint meetings.[42]

The cat was finally let out of the bag in the spring of 1950. In March Charles Bird, the Eastern Region's C.R.O., informed his former L.N.E.R. colleague, Beevor, 'off the record', that the Executive was planning to issue revised instructions to its regional officers, and that final approval was to be given at an Executive meeting on 30 March. Nothing was sent to the Commission, however, and it took an 'entirely unofficial' letter from Beevor to Marsden on 20 April to draw forth a copy of the revised instructions. The instructions, which were dated 1 May 1950, were enclosed in a personal note from Missenden to Hurcomb on 27 April, and did indeed refer to a Railway Executive 'resolution' of 30 March. Beevor, in a memorandum to Hurcomb, took the episode to 'confirm the story that I have often heard that the Railway Executive in fact have two sets of minutes, one for the purpose of informing the Commission about matters they consider should be within the Commission's purview and another set of minutes for matters about which they take a contrary view'.[43] The truth of the matter was even more complex. The Executive's resolution was not recorded in the Memoranda series, but came from a 'Special Meeting' held on the same day. Hurcomb, however, chose not to respond. His reply to Missenden's letter merely acknowledged the receipt of the revised instructions.[44]

Motive power policy and regional organisation were two particular areas in which the Executive successfully resisted the Commission's attempts to interfere. The former is analysed in some detail in Chapter 3. Here, it is sufficient to observe that Missenden was deliberately slow in responding to the Commission's call of April 1948 for the creation of a committee to report on the economic advantages of alternative forms of motive power. When a committee was eventually established in December 1948 the Executive ignored the B.T.C.'s request to participate, and did not report until January 1952. Hurcomb's demand that diesel traction be examined more closely met a blank wall. Missenden, replying in December 1950 to the commission's anxiety over the locomotive building programme for 1952, informed them, tongue-in-cheek, that 'Without any knowledge of the conclusions which the Committee . . . may reach and without in any way wishing to anticipate their findings, experience on British Railways points clearly to the fact that . . . the most likely alternative to steam traction, on a long term basis, is electric traction.' Meanwhile, Riddles was given very much a free hand to develop a building programme for standard steam locomotives.[45]

In the railways' regional organisation, Hurcomb clearly wished to see revisions. He wanted smaller units firmly controlled from the centre, for example, the breaking-up of the large London Midland Region into such entities as a Manchester-based 'North Western Region', and a separate region for Wales. The Executive, however, after conferring with the C.R.O.s, decided in June 1948 to retain the existing structure of six regions, and to proceed instead by making adjustments to boundaries and by seeking to eliminate inter-regional routes or 'penetrating lines'. In this way, the London Tilbury & Southend lines were transferred from the L.M.R. to the E.R. and the former L.M.S. lines in central and South Wales were passed to the W.R. The Commission's role in such decisions was largely one of passive endorsement.[46] On the other hand, the dispute over the management of Southampton Docks went against the Executive. Its arguments for retaining Southampton on the grounds that it was a 'packet port' – one whose activities centred on transfers from trains to railway-owned vessels – fell on deaf ears, and after much wrangling it was transferred to the Docks and Inland Waterways Executive on 1 September 1950.[47]

If the Commission was frequently placed in a position of helplessness in its attempts to control the Railway Executive on questions of railway operating, it was determined to impose its authority elsewhere. Consequently, there were several demarcation disputes in the Hurcomb–Missenden period. The B.T.C., in a revised Direction to the Executive of November 1949, made the extent of its control more explicit, maintaining a tight rein on capital expenditure, and emphasising the need for close contact in the conduct of negotiations with the staff on wages and conditions. Although the expenditure levels requiring prior approval were raised – for capital programmes to £50,000 (instead of £25,000), and for land transactions to £10,000 (instead of £5,000) – the Commission insisted that the threshold for salary control remain unchanged at £1,750, and demanded prior notice of all leases where the term exceeded 21 instead of 60 years. The Executive recorded its opposition to both decisions, and complained that it should have been given greater discretionary powers. Control of organisational changes was also amended in the Commission's favour. The Executive had now to obtain prior approval for 'Schemes involving any material alteration in the internal organisation of the Executive and its Regions', though it did succeed in blocking an attempt to add to this the still more restrictive clause 'or in the allocation of duties and responsibilities of its senior officers'.[48] For its part the Executive made it plain that it strongly resented any attempt by the Commission to by-pass it in seeking information, whether by means of contacts between officers of the two bodies, or through direct approaches to railway officers in the regions. As early as October 1947, at a joint meeting, Missenden had secured the B.T.C's agreement that all its contacts with railways and railway officers should go through the Executive, a demand repeated several times by the latter in the period 1948–50. Some of the arguments were very bitter. In May 1950, for example, the Executive reacted angrily to the news that the Commission had made 'direct contact' with a C.R.O.[49]

Some of the fiercest battles were fought over the Commission's plans to introduce 'common services' for its Executives at 55, Broadway, thereby dispensing with separate organisations at Executive level. The Commission's intentions were made clear in March 1948; by the autumn plans for both a centralised legal service and a unified department for commercial advertising were well advanced. From the beginning, Missenden's view, supported by the Executives of both London Transport and Docks and Inland Waterways, was that these services formed part of his Executive's delegated functions. However, he was unable to do more than delay matters by pursuing an obstructionist policy which culminated in the insistence that the Commission proceed formally through specific instructions. The B.T.C. had hoped to establish its new legal organisation on 1 January 1949, but it was not until April that it was able to issue a Direction outlining the first step to this end, namely, the appointment of Michael H. B. Gilmour, the Western Region's Solicitor, as Chief Solicitor to the Commission. Most of the Executives' legal staff were transferred to B.T.C. headquarters in January 1950, and when Smedley retired as Legal Adviser to the Railway Executive at the end of the year, his successor was transferred to Gilmour's department.[50] As early as October 1947 the Commission had decided to undertake an investigation of railway advertising with the aim of securing uniformity of organisation. Shortly after Brebner's appointment as Chief Public Relations and Publicity Officer the Commission accepted the view that commercial advertising should be managed centrally as part of its Public Relations Department (as had been the practice of the L.P.T.B., Brebner's former employer). The idea met with strong resistance from all the Executives, and especially from the Railway Executive, which was naturally anxious to retain control of a useful source of revenue. In 1947, for example, the railways' net revenue from advertising amounted to £654,000, and in 1948 the figure was £686,000.[51] The B.T.C. refused to yield to Executive pressure, but in March 1949 it was forced to issue a formal instrument in order to revoke those parts of the delegation of functions scheme applying to commercial advertising and the production and distribution of films (other than for staff training); and to make the sale and allocation of railway advertising space the responsibility of a Commercial Advertisement Officer in Brebner's department.[52]

Much of the acrimony surrounding areas of authority arose from the clash between Brebner's department and the Executive. Here, the tough exterior and bullying tactics of the B.T.C. officer were an additional irritant. With an extensive experience of public relations at a high level – during the war he had acted as director of the news division of the Ministry of Information and been given several special assignments, including the position of Press Adviser to S.H.A.E.F.* – Brebner was unwilling to deviate from the principle that it was his business to handle the public relations field for the whole of the Commission's undertakings. There was conflict from the beginning. In February 1948 the Executive issued press statements without consulting either Brebner or the B.T.C., and Hurcomb was particularly incensed by Missenden's claim, made at the press conference on improved passenger services of 17 February, that British Railways would be operating at a profit by the end of the year at the current level of charges. The conflict between the two men is amply illustrated in the ensuing exchange of letters. Hurcomb felt that finance was 'a matter affecting major policy . . . If statements of this kind are to be made they should clearly not be made without the full approval of the Commission and, indeed, should be made by the Commission itself.' Missenden responded by emphasising that the Executive should have the freedom 'to take the promptest publicity action on all matters calculated to influence commercial relationships and receipts'.[53]

The Commission's attempt to establish uniformity through a public relations policy committee, consisting of Hurcomb and the chairman of each Executive, supported by a co-ordinating committee of officers, failed to reduce the area of conflict. At the first meeting of the policy committee in April 1948, both Missenden and Slim, the Executive member responsible for public relations, contended that 'public relations was a function of management', a part of the delegated functions. This opinion was repeated in the Executive's Annual Report for 1948.[54] The Executive went on to establish an elaborate public relations and publicity organisation of its own, both at H.Q. and in the regions, while emphasising that such work was seen as an integral part of Blee's commercial functions.[55] Brebner saw nothing in the new arrangements to encourage an 'integrated' approach, and arguments became even more heated after the resignation of Slim. By 1949 it was obvious that the dispute was having a damaging effect on morale at Executive headquarters. Pearson, the Chief Officer (Administration) assigned to public relations work, told Blee: 'I seriously wonder if it is worth while causing this displeasure . . . My conclusion . . . is that I should now go easy with the B.T.C. publicity problem and not bother.'[56] Train reacted to the problem in more humorous vein by sending Blee a proposed

*Supreme Headquarters Allied Expeditionary Force.

entry for *Punch* entitled 'The Fickle Jade Publicity', which carried the strong inference that to operate with the Commission 'through the required channels' was both cumbersome and ineffective. Subsequently, in July 1949, the Executive fed the press the results of the steam locomotive exchange trials of 1948, again without first informing the Commission.[57] Despite some improvement in the atmosphere thereafter, frosty relations with Brebner persisted into the 1950s.[58]

The control of research was yet another area of conflict. Once again, the Commission angered the Executive by reaching towards a 'common service' objective for this activity. In February 1948 it invited a committee, chaired by the distinguished but elderly engineer Sir William Stanier, to report on the organisation of research.[59] The committee's report of the following November recommended the establishment of a consultative council for transport research and the appointment of a chief research officer to co-ordinate operations from the centre. These suggestions were accepted by the Commission, and in May 1949 Dr Henry Merritt, formerly of Vickers, David Brown and the Nuffield Organisation, was appointed Chief Research Officer of the B.T.C., with the task of supervising and co-ordinating both technical and operational research work for the whole of nationalised transport. In July the Commission's Research Advisory Council held its first meeting, with Hurcomb in the chair. The membership was made up of Merritt, five scientists, and the chairman of each of the six Executives. However, the Railway Executive continued to control the major railway research facilities, for example at Derby, and had appointed T. M. Herbert, the former Research Manager of the L.M.S., as its own Director of Research. Merritt's efforts to direct policy from the centre through a research co-ordinating committee made little headway. The Executive offered its customary response that any inquiries received in the regions from Merritt's department should be referred to either Herbert or the Secretary.[60] Its hostility was intensified by the Commission's decision, based again on the Stanier committee's report, to use Sherrington and the Railway Research Service as the nucleus of a transport research library and information centre under Merritt's control.[61] Little progress was made towards the objective of co-ordination. In research as in the other areas of organisational conflict the atmosphere was clouded by distrust and a lack of co-operation. As Hurcomb observed in a letter to Missenden in February 1948, 'I cannot think that organisations like our own can function successfully if there is not some confidence and contact between officers at different levels, particularly in regard to the exchange of information, or if the whole of our communications are to be completely formalised at the top.'[62] Herein lay the fundamental difference in the approach of the chairmen of the two bodies. The antipathy centred on the clash between Missenden's demands for a free hand to manage the railways and Hurcomb's insistence on partnership in decision-making, on the lines of civil service practice. Neither was prepared to give ground.

The Commission, it will be recalled, had instructed the Executive to remodel the railway organisation by introducing standardised practices while at the same time avoiding 'excessive centralisation'. Given the organisation established at the top, however, these aims were almost contradictory. In 1948 the railways had been centrally administered for nearly a decade by the war-time Railway Executive Committee, but this had been a committee of general managers, whereas the nationalised railways were to be controlled by means of a relatively unfamiliar functional organisation, a system of 'line management'. In a document on the 'Organisation of the Unified Railway System' of October 1947, the Commission assumed that while each member of the Executive would accept responsibility for specific railway departments the chairman would be responsible for the general co-ordination of the work of the whole body.[63] Here, Missenden's ability to act as co-ordinator was clearly overestimated. Competent administrator though he was, he was regarded as *primus inter pares* rather than as 'General Manager of British Railways'. His colleagues enjoyed a considerable measure of freedom to determine their role in their respective departments. General management, in short, proved to be somewhat illusory. As Riddles has observed, 'fortunately for me those other boys were so engaged on their own jobs that I could simply say to the Executive, "I'm going to do this" and I did it ... I think we were left a lot to our own devices'.[64] And the chairman himself soon acquired a range of departmental responsibilities: for new works, with a chief officer, James Ness, responsible to him from 1 January 1948; public relations and publicity, on Slim's departure in November 1948; and research, from July 1949.[65]

The Executive sought to establish standardised operating and commercial practices by working through a complex structure of 26 committees (30 by 1948) based on those of the old Railway Clearing House, and by issuing instructions which were sent down the line by the responsible functional member. At the same time, it attempted to rationalise the organisation of regions and, within them, the districts, through the allocation of joint railways, the transfer of lines and the elimination of overlapping local departments. Some progress was evident by the end of 1950. The first standard designs for steam locomotives and carriages were introduced; and the general standardising of equipment was encouraged by the appointment of a materials inspection officer in August 1949 and the creation in 1950 of a small central stores organisation to negotiate the central purchasing of standard equipment. In April 1950 the regional boundaries were redrawn on a geographical basis, and much was done to streamline the local organisations. For example, the number of commercial districts in four regions was reduced by nearly a quarter and a unified service for Greater London quickly established. The number of operating districts in the L.M.R. was halved. The Executive also took steps to break up the empires of the former chief mechanical engineers, by divorcing carriage and wagon engineering from mechanical and electrical engineering, and by standardising motive power control with the appointment of motive power superintendents to all regions and the revision of procedures on the Western and Southern Regions.[66] A standard regional organisation, shown in Chart III, was introduced with 17 chief officers.

However, the disadvantages of pursuing a rationalisation strategy with such a centralised and relatively small management – total staff at 222, Marylebone Road remained under 600, only 200 more than the staffs of the C.R.O.s[67] – soon made themselves evident. In the first place, the Executive was rather slow-moving, since it had to proceed through a cumbersome reporting chain with its proliferation of committees. Second, and more important, its actions only served to erode managerial responsibility at regional level. Here, the B.T.C.'s constant pressure on its subordinate body to share in the policy-making process had the effect of driving the Executive, a team of departmental specialists, into a concern with day-to-day management questions. Some of the difficulty undoubtedly stemmed from the top. Hurcomb, in particular, was unfamiliar with, and underestimated, the strength of the railways' administrative tradition, with its hierarchical structure centring on general management. He considered it vital that the C.R.O.s should play an active part in local management, but as a result of his experience in the Ministry with the former main-line companies, he was hostile to the concept of regional general management and determined to eliminate it from the new organisation.[68] In consequence, the Executive was almost encouraged to strip authority from men who had been accustomed, in their former positions, to a considerable degree of independence. The C.R.O.s were given a very limited freedom to take positive decisions without reference to the Executive. In their initial instructions of 1 January 1948 they were granted the authority to spend on works and equipment up to a limit of £2,000, to make appointments involving salaries of up to £1,000 and to accept tenders and approve contracts of up to £5,000. Otherwise, the position was more uncertain. A C.R.O. was expected to co-ordinate the departments in his region and see that the administration functioned economically and efficiently (for which purposes he was given 'the rights of initiative and oversight'), but at the same time a firm departmental chain of command linked Executive members to regional departmental offices.[69]

How did the two sides react to this difficult and potentially damaging

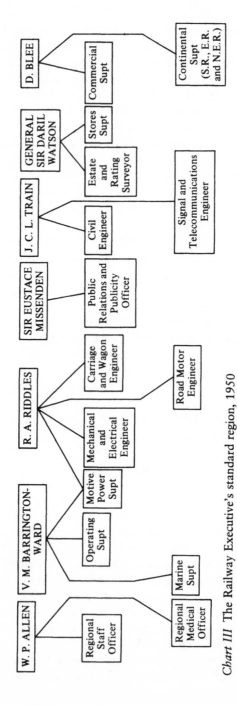

Chart III The Railway Executive's standard region, 1950

Note: in addition, two officers, an Accountant and Treasurer, were linked to the Railway Executive's Chief Financial Officer.

situation? Much depended upon the attitude adopted by the individual members of the Executive. Unfortunately, it became clear all too quickly that the majority paid but scant regard to the C.R.O.s in the decision-making process. Barrington-Ward was a notable offender in this respect. As Train remarked in January 1949, 'he has never been in favour of C.R.O.s and he has been endeavouring to eliminate them so far as his responsibilities are concerned, particularly in regard to Operating'. Elsewhere, they were treated as mere 'postmen', or 'housekeepers'.[70] Not all Executive members were happy with this. Blee, for example, early in 1948, noted that his colleagues had become 'too rapidly immersed in railway management' and that the by-passing of the C.R.O.s 'must . . . create in their minds a sense of frustration and even cynicism'.[71] Early criticisms of the existing organisation made by the C.R.O.s, both confidentially to the Executive and by leaks to the press, led the Executive to attempt to rectify the situation. At first, contact between the two had been established by monthly meetings, the thin agendas of which dealt mostly with problems raised by the C.R.O.s at their fortnightly Conference. But after a heated debate in the summer of 1948, during which the C.R.O.s complained bitterly of 'divided responsibility and divided loyalty' and demanded, unsuccessfully, that the members of the Executive should act through them, they were invited to attend meetings of the Executive itself once a fortnight. The intention, according to Missenden, was to involve them more closely in the Executive's policy-making.[72]

The move had little effect on the C.R.O.'s participation in management and their uneasy relationship with the Executive persisted. They naturally tried to hold on to what they had in the face of the Executive's rationalisation drive. Grand, C.R.O. of the Western Region, was notorious in this respect. He made no secret of his dislike of the new railway organisation and did little to co-operate with the centre. This took the form of attempting to block the transfer of W.R. staff to Executive headquarters. Phillips, his assistant C.R.O., became a pawn in the battle between Blee and Grand before going to headquarters in June 1949 as Acting Chief Commercial Officer.[73] Other squabbles ranged from the serious – the Western's refusal to adopt the standard, upper-quadrant signal – to the petty – its unwillingness to comply with Barrington-Ward's demand that the title of its operating officer be changed from 'Superintendent of the Line' to 'Operating Superintendent'.[74] The Executive responded by trying to break up former company loyalties with its appointments policy. When Darbyshire, the London Midland's C.R.O. and 'elder statesman', retired at the end of 1949, Train and Barrington-Ward suggested that the region might be better run directly by the Executive. Elimination of the C.R.O. structure would have the advantage, it was claimed, of producing substantial economies. No agreement was reached on this draconian solution, however. Instead, careful consideration was given to the alternative of moving officers from one region to another. At first, it was suggested that Grand might be moved from Paddington to Euston, but it was finally agreed to appoint Missenden's Southern Railway protégé, John Elliot, to the vacant post. Elliot, who had no experience of railways north of the Thames, was replaced at Waterloo by C. P. Hopkins from York, whose knowledge of the southern passenger railways was equally limited. The North Eastern position was filled by another ex-Southern man, H. A. Short, the Executive's Acting Chief Officer (Docks). The changes were accompanied by a reduction in salary levels.[75]

This shake-up of senior personnel was matched by further moves lower down. Indeed, the Executive had made it clear to the C.R.O.s in 1948 that the latter's authority to appoint at salaries of up to £1,000 was subject to Executive approval to ensure that there were inter-regional exchanges of staff. It had even attempted to subvert the C.R.O.'s delegated powers by recommending the creation of two appointments committees, each with an Executive member on it, to handle *all* appointments. This plan was abandoned, however, after protests from the C.R.O.s.[76]

The C.R.O.s were anxious to obtain a greater measure of authority to manage their regions, and the issue of decentralisation was not only taken up by the B.T.C. (somewhat ironically in view of its original stance) but was also the subject of political debate. Here, there were two major impulses affecting relations between the B.T.C., the Executive and the C.R.O.s. The first was Prime Minister Attlee's exhortation to restrain administrative costs following the devaluation of sterling in September 1949. The second took the form of a strong attack on these costs by the Conservatives. During the Commons debate on the Commission's First Annual Report in December 1949, it was alleged that nationalisation had created a large number of jobs for the boys. More specifically, Sir David Maxwell-Fyfe claimed – incorrectly – that the establishment of the Executives had produced 1,000 new jobs and added £1 million to administrative costs. This led Dalton and Callaghan on the Labour side to press Hurcomb for a searching examination of management costs, and Hurcomb to ask the Executive to make a careful study of its position since 1947. A greater measure of decentralisation and a pruning of staff at the centre were implied solutions.[77] However, such pressures produced no tangible results in the Missenden period, and the revised instructions to regional officers of May 1950 proved a particular disappointment to the C.R.O.s. The Executive paid lip-service to their anxieties by emphasising that their duties included the requirement to 'contribute to the formation of general policies' and by directing that they were to receive copies of all departmental instructions on matters of principle from Executive members to regional departmental officers. The limits of their financial authority remained unchanged, indeed were defined more tightly than before. And, as Beevor observed, some of the modifications appeared to strengthen the Executive's control of regional management. The deletion of a clause giving the C.R.O.s authority to settle local questions, 'leaving only matters of major principle and general policy to be carried up to the Railway Executive', certainly pointed in this direction, as did the addition of one stating that the 'regional departmental officers will be responsible to and directed by the appropriate Members of the Executive . . . who will give them instructions, guidance and leadership'.[78] The devolution promised by Missenden once unification had been established must have seemed very far away.[79]

The issue of regional boundaries was to prove one of the most intractable organisational problems for the new regime. The decision to introduce geographically-determined boundaries, reached as early as November 1948, was admirably suited to Blee's reorganisation of the commercial departments and promised to strengthen control from the centre. But, as Barrington-Ward made clear from the beginning, the concept was difficult to reconcile with the operating of train services based on the systems of the former companies.[80] The Executive was eventually forced to accept a compromise in which operating and motive power were exempted from a strict geographical division. A number of penetrating lines was thus condoned for operating purposes only (e.g. Birmingham–Bristol, Manchester–Sheffield and Nottingham–Aylesbury), and a 'bizonal' commercial organisation was introduced for the Birmingham-Wolverhampton area. The overall solution, which was introduced in April 1950, pleased no one and only served further to depress morale in the regions. The failure to create self-contained administrative units for all purposes disappointed those who like Blee were in favour of a geographical approach. On the other hand, Barrington-Ward and, to a lesser extent, Train, wanted to return to an organisation based on operating systems. The B.T.C. expressed strong reservations about a scheme which appeared to encourage further centralisation, since routes such as the ex-L.N.E.R.'s Great Central line from Marylebone to Manchester, which now traversed three regional boundaries, clearly cried out for central control, and indeed was managed by one region – the Eastern – for operating purposes only using the 'penetrating line' principle.[81] The C.R.O.s suffered the consequence of these makeshift arrangements. They strongly opposed some of the Executive's moves towards geographical units. The transfer of lines in the West Riding from the L.M.R. to the N.E.R., and adjustments between the Southern and Western, which gave the Western the Southern's lines west of Exeter and the Southern the facilities at Weymouth, caused considerable anger, encouraging a further proliferation of penetrating lines for the operating function. Furthermore, the decision to accept the continuation of these penetrating lines failed to appease local interests, since the provisions for divided responsibility at officer level were regarded as cumbersome. After three years of debate all sides were agreed that no permanent solution had been found.[82]

Issues such as these revealed serious divisions of opinion, both within the Executive itself, and between the Executive and its regions. A draconian approach to unification may have been necessary, but it carried with it the risk of endangering morale and jeopardising administrative efficiency. When, in December 1950, a somewhat weary Missenden announced his intention to retire, he told Hurcomb that 'we have been able to lay down a solid foundation on which those who come after may safely build'. This did not accord with the facts. There was almost universal agreement that fundamental changes in the organisational structure of British Railways were required. Missenden felt that this was a task for a 'fresh mind'.[83]

IV

On 1 February 1951 John Elliot succeeded Missenden as Chairman of the Railway Executive. It was a controversial appointment. Not only did it involve rejecting the claims of existing members of the Executive, but Hurcomb had expressed a preference for Frank Pope, Chairman of the Ulster Transport Authority, who had been passed over in 1947. But there were strong arguments for giving this difficult job to someone who possessed considerable skills in man-management and who had abundant experience of the impact of Executive actions at a regional level.[84] Political misgivings about the level of salary for the post were again present as in 1947, notably in the Cabinet Committee on the Socialisation of Industries, but a figure of £7,000 per annum was eventually agreed.[85] Elliot's was not the only new face at the Executive. In December 1950 Nevile and Ayre, the part-time members, were replaced by Sir Herbert Merrett, Chairman of both Powell Duffryn and Cory Bros. and a director of the National Provincial Bank, and George Nicholson, a director of the Scottish Co-operative Society. Herbert Morrison, Lord President of the Council, expressed some doubts about the choice of Merrett, on accounts of his age and reputation as a tough employer. He eventually relented. However, the posts remained token appointments with little responsibility, a fact which could scarcely have pleased Merrett, who was a man of some stature in the business world. Satisfying political pressure for the inclusion of representatives of the 'celtic fringe' – Merrett was a Welshman, Nicholson a Scot – was a major consideration. The part-timers were given little to do. They had been excluded from the regular Chairman's Conferences attended by functional members, which had been introduced by Missenden in May 1950, and the practice was also applied to Merrett and Nicholson when Elliot began his own 'informal meetings of full-time members' in February 1951.[86] At chief officer level the only major change was the retirement in October 1950 of Morton, the Chief Financial Officer. He was replaced by his assistant and former L.M.S. colleague, V. Radford. In the regions, Elliot's place as C.R.O. (London Midland) was filled by J. W. Watkins, the region's Operating Superintendent, at a salary of £3,750, half that enjoyed by Darbyshire.[87]

There were more significant changes at the top. Hurcomb, having failed to secure Pope's appointment to the Executive, saw him brought on to the Commission as a full-time member from 1 May 1951 (salary: £6,000). With his experience of the L.M.S. and the Ulster Transport Authority Pope was certainly someone capable of arguing with the Executive in its own terms, and he was given the crucial task of developing the Commission's policy on railway reorganisation. He had also acquired experience of the integration of road and rail transport in Northern Ireland. The appointment served to reaffirm Hurcomb's determination to maintain control over railway management.[88] If the Commission required a railway expert it also needed men of more general business experience, and in particular an improvement on the commercial side. Before Pope was appointed Morrison had told Barnes that there was a need to strengthen the Commission with a man of 'wider experience than that of the present members'. Sir Gilmour Jenkins, Permanent-Secretary at Transport, noted that while a first-class businessman was wanted, given the enormous size and complexity of the Commission's business, a salary of £5,000 a year was far too low to attract someone 'unless he feels that his active days are already over'. In the end, the government had to turn to part-time appointees. Several names of prominent industrialists were bandied about, including Ivan Stedeford, Chairman and Managing Director of Tube Investments, who was later to play an important role in determining the organisation of nationalised transport after the B.T.C. (see Chapters 8 and 9). Lt-Col Stephen Hardie from British Oxygen was appointed in July 1950 but resigned shortly afterwards on taking up the post of Chairman of the Iron and Steel Corporation. An attempt to secure the services on a *full-time* basis of A. G. Marsden, Transport Adviser to Lever Bros., also proved abortive.[89] Eventually, two businessmen were found for part-time positions: John Ryan, the Vice-Chairman of Metal Box, in December 1950; and Hugh P. Barker, a director of Parkinson & Cowan, in January 1951.

Finally, there was an important resignation. At the end of June 1951 the Commission lost the services of Beevor, the Chief Secretary and Legal Adviser.* The B.T.C.'s increasing concern with its financial position had encouraged Hurcomb to lean heavily on the Comptroller, Reginald Wilson, who was given a knighthood in the New Year's Honours List of 1951. Wilson's predominance at officer level had greatly disappointed Beevor, whose own more modest functions had been further limited by the appointment of Gilmour as Chief Solicitor. He had also nursed ambitions of becoming Chairman of the Railway Executive when Missenden retired. His successor, S. B. Taylor, was more content to act as a conventional Company Secretary.[90]

Elliot was more relaxed with Hurcomb than Missenden had been, but relations between the two bodies remained chilly. The Commission continued to press its view that services common to the Executive should be centralised. At the end of 1950 it considered the possibility of consolidating the estate and rating organisations, but no positive steps were taken in this direction during the remainder of the Railway Executive's life.[91] The Executive, for its part, persisted in its reluctance to part with information. The B.T.C. frequently complained about the Executive's failure to take it into its confidence, and asserted on more than one occasion that an 'iron curtain' policy was being applied by the railwaymen. One example of this was the belated notice given to the Commission in July 1952 of the degaussing of the Executive's ships in accordance with a Shipping Defence Advisory Committee recommendation of May 1951. When Hurcomb learned about it he commented in exasperation: 'Why do we only hear of this fifteen months after the decision?'[92]

The problem of railway reorganisation cast its shadow over the entire period of Elliot's chairmanship. The Executive spent much of 1951 responding to Hurcomb's request for a review of the organisation. Its report of 8 October suggested that in the light of the provisions of the Transport Act of 1947 the only feasible change would be on the basis of an 'all-in transport management' for the whole of the nationalised undertaking. Drawing upon Barrington-Ward's opinion that the time was ripe for the introduction of integrated 'Transport Regions' for certain functions, the Executive argued that until radical changes of this kind were implemented, it made no sense to alter its existing constitution. Both the functional system, which was 'working well', and the six regions should be retained in their existing form. This decision followed an internal investigation into the pros and cons of merging the E.R. and the N.E.R., the smallest of the six. An ad hoc committee had suggested in April 1951 that

*He became Deputy Managing Director of the Brush Electrical Engineering Co.

the balance of advantage lay with the status quo, and the Railway Executive decided not to proceed.[93] The only immediate alterations required were an extension of the process of decentralisation to the regions, which had 'already gone a long way despite partisan assertions to the contrary'. The Executive now proposed to recognise the C.R.O. as its principal officer in the region rather than as a mere co-ordinator, and to mark the change by altering his title to that of 'Regional Manager'.[94] Hurcomb was not impressed. He told Elliot that he had been looking for a much more detailed examination of the railways' headquarters and regional administrative staff with the aim of securing economies.[95] Pressure for this had built up in 1950, fuelled by parliamentary criticism of the organisation when the Commission's Second Annual Report was debated in October. Here, Hurcomb's concern appeared to be justified. Missenden had not taken the call for a rigorous examination of costs very seriously. Early evidence showed that H.Q. costs had risen in 1948–9, but the matter was left to an ad hoc committee which made little progress. After further B.T.C. pressure in the spring of 1951, Elliot established another committee, staffed this time by retired officers. Their report of June 1951 accepted that the unification drive had produced no real savings, and proposed to make cuts of £40,000 a year, about 10 per cent of headquarters staff costs.[96]

Hurcomb was less convincing in his reaction to the enhanced status of the C.R.O.s. Though favouring greater autonomy in the regions he feared, perhaps irrationally, that the creation of regional 'managers' would encourage a disintegration into six separate organisations. On the broader issue of transport planning Hurcomb warned Elliot that a Conservative victory in the forthcoming election would result in demands for major changes, and suggested that the possibility of eliminating the Road and Rail Executives altogether, and merging them with the Commission or a 'Transport Board', was a very real one.[97] And so it proved. The Conservative Manifesto of July 1949 had promised to sell back road haulage to private enterprise and reorganise the railways into 'an appropriate number of regional railway systems, each with its own pride of identity'. While Labour was still in power, the pressure from the Conservative ranks built up. In November 1950, for example, Lord Teynham introduced a bill into the Lords to extend from 25 to 60 miles the restriction on 'A' and 'B' licensed road hauliers, and to halt the Commission's acquisition of road haulage businesses. This received a second reading in the Commons before being rejected at the committee stage in April 1951. Then, having secured a majority of 16 at the General Election of 25 October 1951, the Conservatives introduced a White Paper on *Transport Policy* in the following May. This, by promising to denationalise the road haulage undertakings and reduce the railways' 'excessive centralisation', rendered both the Commission's and the Executive's existing planning efforts superfluous.[98]

How far did the Executive go in delegating authority to the C.R.O.s? Certainly, Elliot was in favour of involving them more fully in the Executive's deliberations, and on taking office he received strong support from Blee, Train and Pearson, who as early as June 1950 had formed a lobby to press for the narrowing of the gap between H.Q. and the regions.[99] In the course of 1951 the limit of the C.R.O.s' authority to spend on new works and equipment and to settle claims for injury and damages was increased from £2,000 to £5,000. The C.R.O.s were also invited to assume new responsibilities: for example, a closer supervision of regional budgets; recommendations for the closure of unremunerative branch lines and stations; a review of train service punctuality; and the modification of the summer and winter timetables in response to shortages of coal and labour.[100] These changes, which formed the basis of the Executive's claim in its 8 October report that the C.R.O.s should now be regarded as its principal officers in the regions, were extended in February 1952, when the salary limit for the appointment of staff was increased from £1,000 to £1,500.[101] The enhanced status of the C.R.O.s was also reflected in a greater involvement at the centre. In June 1951, for example, Grand was appointed to the Executive's Special Traffic Committee, which was given task of adjusting the winter freight timetable of 1951–2 in response to coal and labour shortages. And Elliot insisted that the C.R.O.s participate in discussions with Commission and Ministry on organisational charges.[102] But it was all very limited. The Executive acceded to Bird's request in April 1951 that the C.R.O.s should receive a full set of Executive Minutes, but did not extend the concession to the Memoranda of Decisions.[103] Indeed, members of the Executive continued to by-pass the C.R.O.s in the ordinary round of decision-making. When the C.R.O.s were invited to participate in the organisational review of 1951 they responded by reiterating their frustration with the system of dual control whereby regional departmental officers were responsible both to the C.R.O. and the functional members of the Executive. Several examples were given of decisions on various operational matters being taken without reference to them, both before and after Elliot's appointment. And they disliked the Executive's policy towards appointments, which often led to officers being switched from one region to another.[104] Obviously little fundamental change had taken place and feelings continued to run high. In February 1953, for example, the Executive voiced particular concern about four cases of serious overspending on new works – three by the L.M.R. and one by the W.R. – and the increased expenditure on minor works under the more liberal spending limits. On the C.R.O.

side, Grand persisted in expressing his opposition to the centre by making unauthorised statements to the press. He occasioned an official rebuke from Elliot by publicly expressing his criticism of the passenger census of October 1952.[105] Such tensions were useful ammunition for Hurcomb, who with Pope had already come to the conclusion that the three-tier organisation of railways should be replaced by a two-tier structure of Commission and regions, a view he put several times to the Conservative Minister, first John Scott Maclay, then Alan Lennox-Boyd, in the course of 1951 and 1952.[106]

In fact, the B.T.C.'s own scheme for the reorganisation of transport, which was presented to the Minister in December 1951, envisaged the fusion of the Railway and Road Haulage Executives in a regional transport organisation.[107] The proposal met with a blank response, and was of course pre-empted by the government's White Paper in May 1952. The demise of the Railway Executive was now almost certain. Some attempts were made to save it. After a scathing attack on the Commission in the *Manchester Guardian*, where it was accused of having 'tried to control everything without accepting direct responsibility for running anything', Viscount Swinton, Chancellor of the Duchy of Lancaster, told Lord Leathers, Secretary of State for the Co-ordination of Transport, Fuel and Power, that he thought there was some merit in retaining the Railway Executive to preside over the railways. However, this was very much a minority view in the Cabinet. The Executive's future was finally resolved when the Transport Bill was first presented on 8 July. Clause 15 required that the scheme for railway reorganisation should provide 'for the abolition (if it has not already been abolished) of the Railway Executive' and for the setting up of area authorities.[108] The Commission, aided by the Executive, reacted swiftly to this challenge by drawing up a plan for reorganisation under existing powers on 1 August. This provided for the immediate absorption of the Executive by the Commission with Elliot becoming one of the full-time members. Responsibility for operating and maintenance was to be delegated to chief regional managers 'to the fullest practicable extent'.[109] Once again, however, the government chose to ignore B.T.C. initiatives. It pressed on instead with a revised Transport Bill which was published in November and became law as the Transport Act of May 1953. This required the Commission to submit a scheme for the reorganisation of railways within 12 months (Section 16). Power to abolish the Executives was also given to the Minister (Section 25).[110]

In the meantime, the members of both the Commission and Executive, whose five-year terms of office had expired in August and September 1952, were re-appointed for a further year. Executive members were asked to assist Pope in drafting plans for the decentralisation of railway management, a procedure in which the C.R.O.s were also invited to participate. Before these were completed, however, the Minister ordered the abolition of all the Executives except London Transport with effect from 1 October 1953.[111] The situation in 1952–3 was scarcely conducive to managerial continuity. While Elliot made strenuous efforts to keep up morale and managed to maintain amicable relations with Pope, the Executive's earlier obsession with planning for institutional survival now gave way to a rather undignified scramble on the part of some members (notably Train) to save their positions in the impending reshuffle.[112] The majority were successful. Barrington-Ward (Sir Michael from 1952) and Riddles, the two most outspoken advocates of centralised control, were asked to retire, but Allen, Blee, Train and Watson survived in the restructured Commission. Hurcomb had hoped that Elliot might become a full-time member of the Commission, but he was moved to the London Transport Executive as Chairman in succession to Lord Latham. A knighthood no doubt provided some compensation for this disappointment. At the Commission, Hurcomb and Wood, who were both 70, retired on 31 August 1953, and Hurcomb's place was taken by General Sir Brian Robertson.[113]

The long interregnum of 1951–3 prevented the Executive from making much progress with its unification strategy. Some steps were taken to develop earlier policies. In the course of 1951 rationalisation at district level proceeded: the number of motive power superintendents was further cut; a new civil engineering district was established at Doncaster, replacing the one at Boston; Western Region carriage and wagon districts were also reduced in number. In July the Executive's central Materials Inspection Unit began to operate, and in January 1952 all Irish shipping services were placed under the control of a single officer. Despite the loss of momentum Elliot was able to claim that the total savings from the unification policy were running at £16 million a year, by the end of 1952. There was also an acceleration in the pruning of the rail network. The route mileage closed to passenger traffic, for example, was considerably increased in Elliot's time, to 1,077 miles (1951–3), compared with only 343 miles in 1948–50.[114]

Elsewhere, the uncertainty surrounding the future organisation, which was exacerbated by the Conservative Government's unwillingness to take the B.T.C. into its confidence, impeded progress. Pricing policy and road–rail integration suffered, in particular, though it has to be said that these areas had been conspicuous for their lack of enterprise before 1951. The B.T.C., which was preoccupied with the purchase of road haulage firms (a process scarcely complete before 1951), was largely to blame for failing to press the Executives to proceed with the integration of road and rail freight services, although there was also indifference from Missenden and stiff resistance from some of the unions. Some tentative first steps were taken in

1951–2: the experimental road–rail commercial service in East Anglia; rail carriage of 'smalls' and parcels for the Road Haulage Executive on certain trunk routes, e.g. London–Manchester and London–Glasgow; and plans to integrate road motor engineering and collection and delivery services on the basis of a scheme already introduced in Scotland. But they were all terminated on the publication of the Conservatives' White Paper.[115]

The Railway Executive had succeeded in making a unified approach to railway working an established fact, but it is quite clear that functional control produced serious resentment from both top (B.T.C.) and bottom (the regions). It also meant that the Executive was, in Elliot's phrase, 'a collection of prima donnas with no conductor'.[116] The Commission was already intent on a restructuring of the organisation of nationalised transport in accordance with the spirit of the Transport Act of 1947, when the Conservatives introduced their own policy. Whatever doctrines and interests may have given impetus to that policy, it seems unlikely that it owed much to any objective critique of the operations of the Railway and Road Haulage Executives. In contrast to the way in which the railways had been run during the war, British Railways appeared to most railwaymen to be an enormous formless body, with the chiefs miles away at 222, Marylebone Road, and the Commission even further away in its ivory tower at 55, Broadway. Thus, the nationalisation period got off on the wrong organisational foot, and the structure erected in 1947 was the first of several defective solutions offered in the quarter century covered by this book. Most of them, it should be noted, were imposed from above, and were not a product of thinking within the railway industry itself. At the Railway Executive, the concern to balance representation from the former main-line companies merely encouraged nostalgic recollections of days past, and to make matters worse the mixture of Missenden, Barrington-Ward, Train and Blee produced all manner of internal tensions. The impact on railway managers' salaries of the modest remuneration fixed by the government for leaders of nationalised industries was another cause of irritation. It may well be true, as was retrospectively observed in 1960, that what destroyed the Executive was a combination of politics, personalities and nostalgia.[117] However, organisational conflict was only one of the problems facing the railways during the lifetime of the Executive. Difficulties were also experienced with capital investment, costs, productivity and the control of pricing. In Chapter 3, attention is given to investment, the first of these issues.

3

Investment

I

The early years of nationalisation were a bleak period in terms of investment, and many writers have traced some of the railways' enduring problems to this situation. Thus, the transport economist Denys Munby, examining the 'Economic Problems of British Railways' in 1962, isolated lack of investment as one of the major factors, pointing out that 'when the Modernisation Plan was produced [in 1954] there had been net disinvestment on the railways for many years on a colossal scale'. Ken Gwilliam, also a transport economist, emphasised the difficulties caused by the accumulated disinvestment of the war and early post-war years, the result, he thought, of both the inadequacy of the war-time financial arrangements and the attitude of the post-war Labour Government. 'Facing inflationary pressure . . . [the government had] deemed that investment in railways was an expendable item in the short run.'[1] Both Munby and Gwilliam, and indeed several other commentators, relied on the estimates of gross and net investment compiled by Philip Redfern of the Central Statistical Office. These indicated that in the period 1938–53 the railways experienced a net disinvestment, at constant 1948 prices, of £440 million (or about £4,730 million at 1983 prices). For 1948–53, on the same basis, gross investment was estimated to be £208 million and net disinvestment amounted to £126 million (in 1983 prices £2,235 and £1,355 million respectively).[2] In the latter period, the explanation for disinvestment, according to Redfern, was the growing average age of the permanent way and buildings ('ways and structures'). His estimates for the other principal category, rolling stock, produced a net *investment* of £16 million at 1948 prices (see Appendix B, Table 6). But in both categories, the investment record compared unfavourably with that indicated by Redfern for the inter-war years. For example, gross railway investment, which averaged £35 million per annum, 1948–53, was significantly lower than the £43 million shown for 1924–38.[3]

Redfern's estimates, as he himself admitted, were defective in many respects. Some defects were of relatively minor consequence, such as those which arose from the absence of satisfactory price data for capital assets and from certain variations in coverage.[4] Thus, a comparison of his data with those for gross investment presented in Munby and Watson's *Inland Transport Statistics,* which are based on the Commission's accounts and relate to 'British Railways' (i.e. the Railway Executive), reveal only very small differences in the figures for 1948–53, if investment in railway ships is included.[5] A far more important defect, however, lies in the definition of capital investment which Redfern used. This differed not only from that accepted in the railway industry by its accountants, but also from that employed by the Treasury and Central Economic Planning Staff when the Labour government first attempted to control capital investment after the war. Redfern included only the expenditure on items which the railway companies (and then the B.T.C.) charged to capital account. This was a more restricted definition than that given in the C.S.O.'s own 'Blue Books', where expenditure on buildings and works charged to revenue account is included.[6] Furthermore, Redfern's method of calculating depreciation represented a considerable departure from conventional railway accounting practice. The railway companies had always assumed that their assets could be maintained indefinitely out of revenue. After nationalisation, the B.T.C. continued to apply this notion to railway buildings and works, although under Reginald Wilson's direction it applied depreciation at historic cost to vehicles and plant. But Redfern depreciated these assets over a period of 100 years. In using this definition of capital investment and this method of depreciation (a simple perpetual inventory formula), Redfern certainly exaggerated the extent of disinvestment as it would have been measured by the railway accountants.[7]

A new method of estimating railway investment has been employed in this book for the period 1948–73. The intention is to capture broad investment trends more satisfactorily than do the data derived from Redfern and the C.S.O. Blue Books. These new estimates are fully described in Appendix B, and do not require a detailed exposition here. The most important point to note is the fact that much, if not all, of Redfern's negative net investment derives from his use of a 100-year life for ways and structures. Since a great deal of Britain's railway route mileage was established in the years immediately following the Victorian 'railway mania' of 1845–7, it biases the calculation if this investment is held to wear out in the late 1940s, irrespective of maintenance work. The new estimates of railway investment, which appear in Table 5, include revised data for ways and structures. While no great claims are made for the results, they show that the railways, far from experiencing disinvest-

Table 5. *Gross and net railway investment, 1948–53 (in current and constant 1948 prices) (£m.)*

Year	Current prices	Gross investment Constant 1948 prices	Net investment Constant 1948 prices
1948	40.3	40.3	14.0
1949	44.1	42.5	14.6
1950	43.4	39.3	10.8
1951	42.3	34.8	7.1
1952	40.0	29.8	−3.0
1953	55.9	39.4	8.8
1948–53	266.0	226.1	52.3
p.a.	44.3	37.7	8.7

Source: see Appendix B.

ment after nationalisation, increased their net capital stock by £52.3 million, or £8.7 million per annum, in the period 1948–53. This should not be taken to imply that all was well, however. The new data, which for gross investment in constant 1948 prices, yield a total of £226 million over the six-year period, £18 million higher than that produced by Redfern, indicate clearly how investment levels deteriorated in the years 1949–52. Moreover, net investment in constant prices fell from £14.6 million in 1949 to *minus* £3.0 million in 1952. The overall picture may look better when the legacy of an arbitrary asset-life for Victorian ways and structures is removed, but it is still bleak enough. And investment levels were grossly inadequate when compared with the amounts needed to compensate the railways for war-time use and the neglect of maintenance.

Nor would the position be altered substantially if a much broader definition of 'investment' were adopted. The revised estimates of investment presented in Table 5 include expenditure on major renewals of ways and structures, which were debited to revenue account. The aim here was to establish a consistent series both before and after 1963, when British Rail's accounting methods were changed (See Appendix B). This expenditure was only a small proportion of the total spent on maintenance and renewals and charged to revenue (including expenditure on rolling stock). How much of this larger sum should properly be regarded as 'investment' and how much as 'operating cost' is difficult, if not impossible, to determine with any precision. Yet there is something to be said for attempting such a distinction. After all, the government itself first adopted a definition of gross investment for planning purposes which embraced not only work normally charged to capital account, but expenditure on maintenance. Although it is true that the planners gradually reduced the area of control until it covered only new additions to capital account, before 1953 they included several revenue-account items, namely replacements of structures, renewals of the permanent way and renewals of rolling stock, plant and machinery.[8] As this Chapter is concerned with the impact of government controls on railway investment as then defined, revenue-account spending on maintenance and renewals is certainly of relevance. This amounted to £670 million at constant 1948 prices (exclusive of ships) over the period 1948–53. A crude, upper-bound estimate of gross investment incorporating revenue-account expenditure yields a total of £870 million at constant prices for 1948–53.[9] Unfortunately, it is not possible to produce an adequate estimate of net investment on the same basis. But since most maintenance work at this time contained a low 'betterment' element,* net investment is unlikely to have amounted to more than a small fraction of the gross figure. However the data are manipulated, there is nothing to indicate that the railways' spending made much of a dent in the backlog of deferred investment, which stretched back to the 1930s.

Low levels of net investment are hardly surprising in an industry losing its market-share, particularly in the circumstances of post-war austerity. The Railway Executive naturally intended to write off life-expired and obsolescent equipment – the accounts reveal that approximately £116 million was written off at gross book value, 1948–53 – but it also needed to undertake a considerable programme of new investment in order to maintain its competitiveness, a need which was jeopardised by the accumulated arrears of maintenance caused by the war and its immediate aftermath. It was the failure of the railways to do much more than patch up the existing system that made the first five years of nationalisation so dismal. From the beginning, the Commission complained bitterly of the effects of government restrictions on capital expenditure and the use of steel. In its Report for 1948, it pointed out that because these controls embraced both new projects and maintenance and renewals, there was little scope for new works other than to complete the electrification of the Manchester–Sheffield–Wath and Liverpool Street–Shenfield lines, to which the railways were already committed under the New Works Programme of 1935–40. Gloomy predictions about the effects of 'serious arrears in investment', and reference to the need 'for a more adequate allocation of the total amount available for national capital investment', were repeated in successive Reports. This was also the approach adopted by the Executive in its more detailed planning exercises, including the five-year development plan of December 1948.[10] Little progress was made. In a

---

* 'Betterment' is that portion of maintenance expenditure which improves the asset and thereby increases its value.

much-quoted passage from the Report for 1953 the Commission declared that while there had been 'a virtually complete post-war re-equipment of the road fleets . . . on the railways, even the arrears of maintenance . . . [had] hardly yet been made good'. It had been 'possible to do little more than continue certain major works started before the war . . .; to deal with cases of war damage and extreme dilapidation; and to make a limited number of improvements on, essentially, a "make-do-and-mend" basis, rather than as stages of a master development plan.' Inflation, shortages of materials, a lack of engineering technicians: all were blamed. But the Commission made particular reference to the 'discouraging and disrupting effects of constantly changing limits upon capital investment'.[11]

When the C.S.O.'s 1954 Blue Book was published the Commission analysed the data in order to show the extent to which the railways had been 'starved' of capital since 1947. During the years 1948–53 gross fixed capital formation in U.K. industry and trade had increased in real terms by 21 per cent but the total for railways had remained relatively static. Consequently, their share fell from 4.4 per cent in 1948 to 3.1 per cent in 1952 (although there was a rise to 3.7 per cent in 1953). This decline was contrasted with the success of the electricity industry in increasing its share (as did the other utilities, gas and water). Moreover, reference to successive *Economic Surveys* produced the disclosure that road transport, unlike the railways, had been able to evade the controls organised by the Cabinet's Investment Programmes Committee. For commercial vehicles, an 'over-shoot' on home sales of no less than 55 per cent was indicated for the period 1948–52. The conclusion, that railways had received 'less than their fair share of investment resources', was included in the report of the B.T.C. Planning Committee which preceded the Modernisation Plan of December 1954.[12] It was subsequently confirmed by Richard Pryke's figures for the 'public enterprise sector'. These show that the railways' share of gross fixed investment (on a C.S.O. basis) fell from 26.4 per cent in 1938 and 19.5 per cent in 1948 to 12.7 per cent in 1952 and 13.9 per cent in 1953.[13]

II

But who, if anyone, was responsible for the inadequacies of railway investment? To what extent did the operation of government controls and investment targets prevent the industry from introducing an expanded and phased programme of capital expenditure? It is difficult to find firm conclusions given the complexity of the several control mechanisms, the use of different definitions of 'capital investment', and the existence of other factors governing the supply of key materials such as steel, cast iron and timber. A detailed history of the effects of the control period remains to be written.[14]

When the Railway Executive took office, decision-making was greatly complicated by the existence of several layers of bureaucratic control. Not only had the B.T.C. reserved to itself responsibility for general financial matters, including the vetting of renewals and new works, but the Transport Act of 1947 had given the Minister of Transport extensive if barely-defined powers in the financial sphere. These included the control of the Commission's borrowing (in partnership with the Treasury), approval of development programmes involving a 'substantial' capital outlay and the ability to give directions on matters which appeared 'to affect the national interest'.[15] Barnes interpreted his position as follows: 'We have powers, partly statutory and partly persuasive to influence the programme of capital investment of the Commission in directions which accord with national policy.' It was his duty to determine whether 'any large project was properly timed having regard to the general economic situation . . . or whether a particular project which would provide useful employment in a particular area could be put higher up in the Commission's order of priorities . . . The Minister could also bring pressure to bear on the Commission to accelerate or slow down their programme.'[16] In addition to this, the Minister and his civil servants were fully involved in the mesh of government controls. The Ministry had acted, since the war began, as the sponsoring body for the transport industry in negotiations for supplies of controlled raw materials, and also exercised a control over building works by organising applications for licences under Defence Regulation 56A.[17] Finally, there were the numerous ramifications of the Labour Government's machinery for economic control, which was strengthened in the wake of the fuel and convertibility crises of 1947: key ministerial committees such as the Economic Policy and Production Committees; inter-departmental committees of civil servants, the most important of which were the Investment Programmes Committee and the Materials Allocation Committee: the Economic Section of the Cabinet Office and the C.S.O.; the Central Economic Planning Staff (C.E.P.S.), responsible to Cripps as Minister for Economic Affairs, and later transferred to the Treasury when Cripps succeeded Dalton as Chancellor in November; and government-sponsored 'quangos' such as the Capital Issues Committee and the Economic Planning Board. In relation to the government's attempts to control investment and ration the consumption of key materials, the hierarchy of decision-making proceeded from Cabinet committee level, where the concern lay with the setting of broad policy objectives, to the I.P.C. This body had been established in August 1947 as a sub-committee of the Official Steering Committee on Economic

Development. Under the chairmanship of Sir Edwin Plowden, Chief Planning Officer of the C.E.P.S., it was given the task of reviewing national investment requirements for 1948 and setting import-saving, export-stimulating priorities. Later in the year it was reconstituted under H. T. Weeks (C.E.P.S.) as a means of exercising a continuous supervision of investment programmes and providing the co-ordinated control lacking in the period 1945–7. The I.P.C. examined departmental spending plans and fixed an annual allocation of investment. After this the Materials Committee, chaired by Douglas Jay, Economic Secretary to the Treasury, determined the detailed allocations to departments of controlled materials such as steel and timber.[18] Given the complexities of the control process, it is scarcely surprising that the newly created Railway Executive should have felt a little remote in its attempts to secure an adequate share of the austerity cake.

The reality of the situation facing the railways in the medium term became only too clear in the late summer and autumn of 1947, before Vesting Day. While Milne and the Railway Executive Committee were busy responding to the call for planning required by the Marshall aid proposals, railway construction was already being restricted by a shortage of steel (despite the industry's priority status) and a lack of labour. This had serious implications for the future due to the lag, of up to 18 months, between the ordering of materials and the completion of the finished product. Milne, in August, presented a programme for rolling stock construction and permanent way renewal sufficient to restore the mainline companies to their pre-war condition over the five-year period 1948–52. This required the annual construction of 740 locomotives, 3,820 carriages and 83,750 wagons, and the relaying of 1,750 miles of track each year. The R.E.C. accepted that existing capacity in both the public and private sectors was insufficient to meet the rolling stock targets in 1948. The maximum output attainable in that year was estimated to be 574 locomotives, 3,070 carriages, and 47,780 wagons, some 20–40 per cent below its recommended annual average for 1948–52.[19] Even these reduced figures were optimistic in relation to actual building in 1947, which was about 50–70 per cent less than this annual average.[20] Moreover, the operation of government controls had ensured that the iron and steel supplied to the railways in 1947 was not only well below their indicated requirements but 10 per cent below the amount which had been allocated to them by the government's Materials Committee.[21] Data for steel alone, supplied to the R.E. (excluding L.T.E.) for the last quarter of the year, shown in Table 6, indicate that the tonnage received amounted to only 74 per cent of estimated requirements and was 10 per cent below the government's allocation.

Table 6. *Railway Executive steel receipts compared with its estimated requirements and government allocations, 1947–50*

Period (Quarter)	Receipts as % of estimated requirements		Receipts as % of government allocations	
	Steel rails	Steel rails/general steel	Steel rails	Steel rails/general steel
1947 IV	83	74	86	90
1948 I	91	82	110	104
1948 II	78	78	95	97
1948 III	74	70	87	94
1948 IV	92	79	103	117
1948 all	84	77	99	102
1949 I	106	73	105	89
1949 II	94	68	100	92
1949 III	91	79	91	88
1949 IV	106	78	107	87
1949 all	99	75	101	89
1950 I	110	91	114	95
Revised %s (adjusting for late deliveries)[a]				
1949 all	80	67	81	80
1950 I	83	80	87	83

[a] Each quarter's receipts include late deliveries of steel estimated for and allocated in an earlier quarter. From 1949 II, these amounts can be separated, yielding a more accurate assessment of how much new steel applied for and allocated actually arrived in the relevant quarter.

Source: derived from Appendix H, Table 1 (q.v. for details).

When the B.T.C. and the Railway Executive took over, investment planning was further affected by the operation of the controls machinery and the planning activity of the I.P.C. The government's attempt to reduce U.K. fixed capital investment in 1948 by £200 (later £180) million provided a clear demonstration of the relatively low priority accorded to transport in Whitehall and of the extent to which the planners were prepared to intervene in the detailed allocation of investment. The I.P.C. not only put a brake on new developments but acted to postpone a number of works already agreed, including the modernisation of Euston Station and the re-signalling of Paddington–Southall. Even those schemes which were allowed to proceed were threatened by its recommendation that the use of contract building labour for transport purposes be cut by no less than 45 per cent.[22] With regard to fixed equipment, the I.P.C. suggested that while the locomotive and wagon programme might proceed at the levels envisaged by the R.E.C. for 1948, carriage building was to be limited to 1,000 vehicles, and permanent way renewal confined to current needs by reducing the R.E.C.'s suggested steel allocation for rails by 20 per cent.[23] Furthermore, the I.P.C. was unable to offer any hope of amelioration in 1949. The results of this planning exercise were incorporated in Cripps's statement to the House of Commons in October and the government's White Paper of December 1947 on *Capital Investment in 1948*.[24] This lack of sympathy for the notion of restoring rail transport, and passenger travel in particular, to its pre-war condition was reinforced by a widespread suspicion among Ministers and senior civil servants, especially in the Treasury, that the industry could absorb cuts without serious repercussions. Although the announcement by Cripps came too late to affect work in hand, it undoubtedly created a climate of uncertainty which influenced the attitude of both Executive and Commission to ordering for 1948 and beyond. The impact on the R.E.'s quarterly supplies of steel in 1948 can readily be ascertained from Table 6. The position in the third quarter of the year was particularly disappointing. Steel receipts (rails and general steel) were only 70 per cent of the R.E.'s estimated requirements, and fell short of the government's allocation by 6 per cent. As Douglas Jay noted, transport was the only important user whose allocation had been cut below that fixed at the beginning of the year.[25] For the year as a whole, receipts fell short of requirements by 16 per cent for rails and 23 per cent for the total.

Investment in 1949 was also blighted by protracted negotiations with the I.P.C. over the steel allocation. Production possibilities had already been limited by the warning in the White Paper that investment would have to be pegged at 1948 levels. But the Railway Executive had to plan in a climate of further restriction. The Ministry of Transport had sought 997,000 tons (later reduced to 900,000) for the railways as a whole, including London Transport and private contractors building for the railways, but the I.P.C., in its report of July 1948, suggested a reduction to 800,000 tons, which was below the current rate of deliveries. It also claimed that there would be no harm in a 9 per cent cut in rail consumption and a 19–25 per cent reduction in the rolling stock programme.[26] Attempts to extract concessions were hindered by planners' suspicions that the railways were overestimating their material requirements and carrying excessively high stocks of steel and timber. This belief had been encouraged at an early stage. A return for December 1947 showing that the railways' stocks of rails and general steel amounted to 21 weeks' supply, with general steel stocks standing at 31 weeks, inspired government allegations of 'hoarding' and made negotiations more difficult. Nor did the position change very much in 1948 and 1949. An internal investigation in March 1950 revealed that the Executive's steel stocks had averaged 18 weeks for all steel and 28 weeks for general steel since nationalisation.[27] Planners' suspicions were also aroused by the candour, not to say naivety, of the Executive in responding all too eagerly to the realities of austerity. In its report on the physical condition of the railways in January 1948, for example, it had produced an estimate for rolling stock and track renewals in 1948 and 1949 which almost halved the steel consumption implied in Milne's earlier R.E.C. forecast.[28]

Delay in determining the likely steel allocation for 1949 undoubtedly prejudiced the Executive's chances of raising production above 1948 levels. The Minister of Transport had argued at the Cabinet Production Committee in July 1948 that the I.P.C.'s proposals for transport were 'ludicrously inadequate; for instance, the allocations proposed by his Department [and rejected] represented replacement rates of 2½ per cent for locomotives, 4 per cent for carriages, and 3 per cent for wagons. The margin of safety for the railways was already dangerously narrow.' However, his submission cut no ice with the Committee, which emphasised that transport services could only be given resources to maintain them at existing levels of efficiency.[29] The allocation was not finalised until September. The I.P.C. having found that another 150,000 tons of steel would be available in 1949, suggested that the railways might be given 40,000 of this, viz. 840,000 tons in all. But Cripps himself produced a distribution formula which gave the railways only 810,000 tons. The combined effect of delay and limitation was to prompt the Executive to reduce its planned production of rolling stock by 50 locomotives and 10,000 wagons, cut track renewal by 88 miles and retain its emphasis on the uneconomic repair, rather than replacement, of life-expired assets.[30] Even then, uncertainty over future steel deliveries persisted, because the quarterly allocations organised through the Materials Committee were not fully co-ordinated with the projections of the I.P.C. There was particular concern over this operation for the first quarter of 1949. The I.P.C./Production Committee's allocation of 810,000 tons for the year included 585,300 tons for the R.E. and L.T.E., net of decontrolled items. But the allocation for the first quarter was only 134,374 tons, or 537,496 tons per annum, a cut of 8 per cent.[31] Investment planning on this basis was in many ways a self-fulfilling prophecy determined by the gloomiest forecast of the previous year. The R.E.'s steel receipts for 1949 were 25 per cent down on estimated requirements, and if late deliveries are excluded the shortfall appears more serious – 20 per cent for rails, 33 per cent for all steel. Moreover, the steel received was lower than the quarterly allocations of the Materials Committee, by 11 per cent, or 20 per cent excluding late deliveries (see Table 6 above, and Appendix H). Consequently, production in 1949 (see below, Table 7) was closer to the I.P.C.'s mid-summer 1948 prescription of 400 locomotives, 1,500 carriages and 30,000 wagons than to the figures which eventually appeared in the *Economic Survey for 1949* (published in March 1949), and implied a consumption of steel for track and rolling stock renewal which was lower than that in 1948.[32]

Conditions did not improve in 1949, in spite of assurances in Whitehall that the next planning round would be expedited. With the emphasis shifting towards control by expenditure limits rather than through the allocation of materials, the Commission had put forward a railway investment programme of £100.2 million (excluding running repairs) for 1950. This figure, which included an allocation of £88 million to the Railway Executive for railway purposes (i.e. excluding ships, etc.), had been scaled down by over 10 per cent to comply with the request that investment plans for 1950 should approximate to 1949 levels. However, the I.P.C. did not consider the proposal until May 1949, when it recommended a reduction to £95 million; the position then remained unclear until the limit was confirmed by the Ministry of Transport in September.[33] Shortly afterwards, uncertainty returned when the devaluation crisis forced the government to seek a further cut of 5 per cent in the investment programmes. For railways, this represented a total reduction in real terms of no less than 18 per cent in the modest proposals advanced by the Commission and Railway Executive at the beginning of the year.[34] In late October, therefore, the Executive was asked to reconsider its investment activity in 1950. It determined to protect both its carriage- and wagon-building programmes, but offered to make cuts in locomotive construction and the renewal of ways and structures. However, the greater part of the savings was to come from a reduction of over 50 per cent in its expenditure on new works.[35] In November, a comprehensive ceiling of £92 million (£82 million for the Railway Executive) was agreed with the I.P.C., the new annual rate to be achieved by the end of 1950.[36] The effect of another lengthy wrangle over investment planning was to curtail spending both in the short and medium term. As Missenden complained to Hurcomb, 'these "investment" variations at short notice throw all our constructive planning thoroughly out of gear . . . it is seldom possible to launch major projects at short notice and it is almost equally difficult to slow down a programme which has once got under way'. Although the I.P.C.'s allocation was topped up belatedly in February 1950 with £2.7 million for a supplementary programme of 7,100 mineral wagons, the Executive experienced particular difficulties with wagon building, where the even-

Table 7. *Railway Executive rolling stock acquisitions (railway workshops and contractors) and track renewals, 1948–53*

Year	Locomotives (all)		Coaching vehicles		Freight and service vehicles		Track renewals (miles)	
	New	Second-hand	New	Second-hand	New	Second-hand	Complete	Total (including partial)
1948	410	563	1,334	—	40,814	61	1,605	2,018
1949	391	39	1,801	3	32,490	339	1,612	1,960
1950	414	—	2,719	—	28,034	5,850	1,485	1,828
1951	340	—	1,923	28	37,796	3,735	1,544	1,844
1952	299	—	1,004	10	28,586	16	1,564	1,825
1953	207	—	1,133	3	41,606	68	1,642	n.a.
1948–53	2,061	602	9,917	41	209,326	10,069	9,452	9,475[a]
p.a.	343.5	100.3	1,652.8	6.8	34,887.7	1,678.2	1,575.3	1,895.0[a]
1947[b]	409		1,198		31,275		1,161	1,434

[a] 1948–52.
[b] 1947 data from *Economic Survey for 1949* (March 1949), P.P. 1948–9, XXIX, Cmd. 7647, p. 51, and R. E., 'Physical Condition of British Railways at January 1948' (n.d., but February 1948), B.R.B.
Source: B.T.C., R. & A. 1948–53; data for locomotives exclude service locomotives (5 (1949), 1 (1951), 1 (1953)).

tual production of 28,034 vehicles (see Table 7) was 2,600 below target. Its final 'capital expenditure' in 1950 (on the government's definition, excluding running repairs and permanent way maintenance) was £67.1 million, about 8 per cent below the permitted level.[37]

The situation was scarcely better in the early fifties. Plans for 1951 and 1952 were initially formulated in the continuing atmosphere of uncertainty following the devaluation of sterling. In November 1949 the Commission and Executive were asked to present two proposals, the first pegging investment at the level fixed for the end of 1950, the second incorporating an additional amount of 'desirable investment'. At this stage, however, it was made clear that the planners considered the lower level to be the more realistic estimate of future possibilities.[38] In January 1950 the Railway Executive supplied estimates for 1951 and 1952 of £63.5/75.5 and £63.5/77.0 million on this basis, and these figures were then increased by £1.8 million in each year for the supplementary wagon programme.[39] The customary delay then ensued. Only at the end of May was the government able to confirm the 1951 target, which on the recommendation of the I.P.C. was close to the upper bound, and a firm figure of £75 million for the Railway Executive was not established by the Commission until 6 June.[40] This more optimistic forecast, stimulated by the government's decision to remove most of the controls on iron and steel in May,[41] was somewhat illusory in view of the difficulties in equating actual production with planning limits at short notice. In July Missenden expressed his Executive's scepticism about the likelihood of spending £75 million in 1951 and asked the B.T.C. to scale down the programme by £2 million.[42]

The outbreak of the Korean War in June 1950 destroyed any hopes of achieving higher levels of investment in 1951 and 1952. Although the I.P.C. confirmed the original plans for 1951 in the following October, the Executive's unduly pessimistic forecast that spending would reach only £61 million in 1950 led it to repeat its demand for a cut in target of £2 million, to £73 million, in March 1951.[43] It then included the figure in its investment submission for 1952–4 and inserted this in its Annual Report for 1950, producing an angry response from both the Minister of Transport and the B.T.C. when it was discovered.[44] By this time the build-up of rearmament orders was having a predictable effect on the railways' steel supplies. In the end, the Executive's 'capital investment' of £70.6 million in 1951 was only £2.4 million (about 3 per cent) short of the revised target. But the Executive could derive no satisfaction from the low level of new works activity and the heavy emphasis on repairs (most of which were no longer subject to planning control) rather than on renewals. The fact remained that the actual construction of rolling stock in 1951, shown in

Table 7, was well below what had been presented to the I.P.C. as 'essential' at the beginning of the year.[45]

In February 1952 steel controls were reimposed and capital investment during the year fell short of the planners' allocation of £76.6 million by £6.8 million or 9 per cent.[46] The main reason was undoubtedly the shortage of steel and other essential materials. But the Executive and its new Chairman John Elliot were also affected by the re-emergence of the planners' insistence on interfering with detailed aspects of the railway programme. In March 1951, for example, the I.P.C. not only cut the Executive's estimated expenditure from £80.5 to £76.0 million, but also suggested where the savings might be found. It recommended that spending on coaching be reduced by £3 million and on building and civil engineering by £1.5 million, including postponement of work on the London Tilbury & Southend electrification scheme first approved by the B.T.C. in November 1950. There was also an instruction that any shortfall in what was clearly regarded as an over-ambitious target of 50,000 wagons should not be used to justify an increase in other parts of the programme.[47] Intervention of this kind was also evident when the programme was renegotiated between November 1951 and January 1952. The I.P.C., in fixing a revised target of £76.6 million which was £8.4 million below the Executive's submission, again suggested that the cuts should fall on coaching and new works.[48]

Whatever the definition employed, 'railway investment' in 1952 was lower in real terms than in any other year before the Modernisation Plan. Both track renewal and the construction of rolling stock were well down on earlier expectations. Production of 300 locomotives, 1,000 coaching vehicles and 28,500 wagons (see Table 7) contrasted sharply with the original plans for 400, 2,500 and 50,000 units respectively, but was also 20–45 per cent below the more realistic estimates of November 1951.[49]

Sympathy for the railways' difficulties had not been encouraged by the industry's tactics in dealing with the planners. The Commission's proposal in November 1951 to submit an unrealistically high figure for 1952 of £90 million is a good illustration of this. The Executive admitted that it was impossible to increase its spending by the £20 million required at such short notice, but was persuaded to increase its submission to £85 million as an expression of 'policy' rather than 'practicality'.[50] Such manoeuvres did little to improve relations with the I.P.C. and the Materials Committee, which were further strained by the actions of the Railway Executive in seeking to increase its allocation of steel in 1952. Its response to the news that its allocation for the first period was to be about 20 per cent below indicated requirements was to propose an unnecessarily draconian reduction in its rolling stock programme, including the total suspension of coach building.[51] However, both the planners and the Ministry of Transport remained unconvinced that the allocation – ultimately 544,000 tons – warranted such an extreme reaction from a concern which had achieved its 1951 output with a tonnage of 516,000.[52]

In 1953 conditions improved, and steel controls were finally abolished in May. Investment planning under the Conservative Government continued to operate much as before, but the B.T.C. attempted to improve its monitoring of investment in 1952 by means of half-yearly progress reports.[53] Nevertheless, the Executive's investment allocation remained a matter for protracted negotiation. In August 1952 government Ministers reduced the railways' submission of £95 million to £80 million (the I.P.C.'s 'lower bound'), although they were prepared to allow the B.T.C. to adjust individual programmes within the global allocation.[54] Thereafter, evidence of more favourable economic conditions, including improved terms of trade, and the willingness of the Conservatives to use bank-rate as an instrument of inflationary control, encouraged a more generous attitude to railway investment on the part of the planners. Early in 1953 the Executive was able to secure a further reduction in the area of control with the elimination from the annual review of expenditure on building repairs and maintenance work.[55] This was followed in April with a relatively generous allocation for 1954 and an upward adjustment of the 1953 target to £71.4 million on a revised basis (about £89 million, including building repairs and maintenance), an increase of about 10 per cent.[56] All this came too late, however, to have more than a marginal impact upon spending during the year, which fell short of the new target by about 7 per cent.[57] There could be only a very modest expenditure on new works, where attention was still focussed on limited schemes already being considered before nationalisation.[58] Arrears in track renewal remained, and although there was an improvement in wagon production in 1953 despite the shortage of sheet steel – 41,600 units were added, 10,000 more than had been considered possible by the Executive at the beginning of the year[59] – carriage construction continued to be limited (see Table 7).

III

It is easy to see why the Commission and its Executive were frequently irritated, and sometimes exasperated, by the uncertainties of the planning and control environment. There was an inherent artificiality, not to say absurdity, about annual programmes for an industry with a lengthy production cycle (especially for new works); and the heterogeneity of railway activities added to the difficulties of forecasting requirements on this basis. It is also clear that the Executive, influenced by the deferential attitude to government of former civil servant Hurcomb and the B.T.C., did respond to the planning restrictions imposed upon it, with the result that capital investment failed to reach the levels feasible under existing conditions.[60] Here, the verdict of an adviser in the economic section of the Cabinet Office is revealing. Reviewing investment control over the nationalised industries in October 1951, he contrasted the disciplined and obedient response of the railways with the more negligent reactions of the coal and electricity industries. The Railway Executive, he observed, had been willing to reduce its requirements in the name of unification but had also asked for an increase in investment in order to restore pre-war efficiency.

The I.P.C.'s aim was rather to keep the railways running with the minimum investment, so as to spare steel and other resources for other investment programmes where a great deal of new capacity was urgently required – e.g. electricity, steel and oil refineries. In following this aim the I.P.C. took risks of dislocating the system either by a shortage of wagons . . . or by widespread speed restrictions.

Within the I.P.C. it was a matter for congratulation that it had resisted the railways' demands for more extensive engineering work and for passenger carriage building 'to bring in revenue'. In this process the railway representatives were observed to have 'acquiesced . . . with understanding and courtesy'. Their investment submissions, in which most of their cards were put on the table, contrasted with the disappointing offerings from electricity and coal.[61]

Both the Executive and the Commission expressed privately their considerable dissatisfaction with the planning mechanisms, which were held to have had a dampening effect on forward investment planning as well as contributing to the failure to achieve expenditure targets. A particular complaint was the lack of liaison between the I.P.C. and the Materials Committee, whose chairman, Douglas Jay, was frequently accused of being 'by no means railway-minded'. Certainly, Jay was no supporter of the railway cause, and he usually got the better of Barnes in arguments over the allocation of materials. Certain in his belief that railways were uneconomic everywhere, he couldn't accept that coal and steel shortages were holding them back. Railway investment was undoubtedly affected when his committee allocated steel at amounts lower than those agreed with the I.P.C.[62] Once decisions had been taken to restrict activities, it was difficult to reverse them quickly, especially if staff had been laid off. Given tight labour markets, it was harder to put on the accelerator than to apply the brake.[63]

On the other hand, the Executive was sometimes at least partly responsible for its own plight. In addition to its general deference, its tendency to resort to guesswork when forecasting annual expenditure (the underestimation of spending in 1950 by £6 million was particularly damaging) and to present its 'ideal' annual requirements as 'essential' scarcely endeared it to the planners. When preparing the case for 1951 James Ness, the Executive's Chief Officer for New Works, warned his colleagues in December 1949 that

there is little prospect of getting anything like as much as we are asking for in our higher programmes . . . only a very strong and well substantiated case will obtain a concession . . . there is nothing to be gained by exaggeration as we may be called upon to substantiate any of the arguments we advance. So far as I can judge hard facts and figures carry much more weight with the planners than hair-raising statements in general terms.

This was undoubtedly true; and the dispute over the steel allocation in 1952, which led the Executive to suspend its carriage-building programme, was a particular example of this truth. The I.P.C., finding the railways able to cope with allocations which were often 20–30 per cent below the level represented as crucial for survival, had little incentive to give more to this non-exporting industry. It was clearly damaging when the Executive issued dire threats that the system would come to a standstill unless a given amount of investment were agreed, if it then avoided catastrophe with less. Sometimes it was the B.T.C. which was responsible for exaggerated claims. When in February 1950 the I.P.C. asked the Commission to produce data showing the economies arising from using new locomotives, Ness estimated the savings from replacing 475 life-expired locomotives with 400 new ones to be £53,000 per annum. But Michael Bonavia, the officer responsible for works and development at the Commission, altered the savings to £267,000 per annum by excluding interest on capital and depreciation.[64]

In general, it seems that the railway managers were only too willing to accept the gloomy allocations they were given. John Ryan, one of the Commission's part-time members, was particularly critical of the Executive's attitude to the steel shortage. An allocation did not guarantee deliveries: it merely provided a licence to order. In a memorandum of January 1953 he contrasted the Executive's complacency with the drive to obtain steel shown by private concerns such as Tube Investments.[65] The disappointingly low investment levels of 1948–53 were primarily a result of shortages in both labour and materials. These were exacerbated by shifts in priorities, induced first by the economic crises of 1947 and 1949 and then by the rearmament implications of the Korean War. The Commission and the Executive may have felt like 'tail-end Charlies', at the end of the queue. But although both the government and the planners gave the railways a fairly low priority, certainly lower than that given to electricity and coal, and the control mechanisms were inhibitive, it is hard to believe that the removal of planning restrictions would have greatly improved the situation. Indeed, the evidence for 1951, when the controls on most iron and steel products had been removed, suggests that the Railway Executive might have found it more difficult to obtain steel supplies in a 'free-for-all'.[66] If low investment was caused by material shortages and planning controls, management attitudes contributed to worsen the difficulties.

IV

From his investigation into the 'Capital-starved Railways' Richard Pryke, in his book *Public Enterprise in Practice*, concluded that British Rail had 'little room for manoeuvre and that the bulk of its investment was well directed'. Limiting his inquiry to expenditure on capital account from 1948 to 1954, he found very few indications of the excessive or ill-advised use of scarce resources. Although investment in wagons took up about half of the total of £284 million, the modernisation of the fleet was a major priority given the large inheritance of obsolescent private owners' wagons. Only in locomotive construction could there be any suggestion that money might have been put to better use. But here Pryke observed that the £28 million spent on steam locomotives before 1955 – some of which was unavoidable given orders placed before 1948 – represented only a fraction of the sums required to undertake a substantial shift to alternative forms of motive power, whether electric or diesel.[67]

What may be said of these conclusions? Pryke did not discuss the railways' spending on maintenance and repairs, but had this been done, it would not have altered the picture of capital starvation. The Executive's expenditure on ways and structures, however calculated, fell far short of what was required to overtake arrears. New estimates of net investment in ways and structures, at constant 1948 prices, indicate only a very small increase in net investment over the period 1948–53 (see Appendix B, Table 2). Travellers and customers could readily see that the routine maintenance of·stations and buildings had been deliberately curtailed. This meant poor working conditions which in turn inhibited the recruitment of staff.[68] Permanent way renewal was naturally accorded a higher priority. Here the level of activity was adequate to preserve safety standards, and some arrears were tackled. But the prevalence of speed restrictions caused by the poor condition of the track was a testimony to the failure to eradicate the legacy of war-time neglect.[69] Train accident figures for 1948–53 remained well above pre-war levels, and although a slight improvement was evident, the increase in passenger fatalities in 1951 and the horrifying accident at Harrow in October 1952, in which 112 people were killed (108 of them passengers), helped to reinforce a growing suspicion that investment was lagging behind the technical possibilities.[70]

This certainly appears to have been true of track circuiting, colour-light signalling and automatic train control (later known as Automatic Warning System or A.W.S.), in which the Executive was unable to make much progress. Bonavia has criticised both the Commission and the Executive for their slowness to act in relation to A.W.S. though the situation was complicated by the existence of alternative systems and doubts about the effect of automatic devices on the vigilance of train crews. Nevertheless, it is likely that a speedier response would have been forthcoming had more investment been available from the late 1940s.[71] Where the resource implications were comparatively modest, the Executive proved itself capable of a more vigorous response. It met the growing staff shortage in track maintenance by importing Italian labour and recruiting women. By February 1952, 721 Italians and 488 women were working on the permanent way. It also made progress with mechanisation by introducing Swiss-made Matisa automatic tamping machines for compacting and consolidating ballast, despite the difficulty in obtaining import licences.[72]

Pryke's analysis of the railways' expenditure on rolling stock also requires further development. The wagon problem inherited on nationalisation remained serious throughout the period, and there were frequent crises in meeting the demands of traffic with existing resources.[73] In the six years to 1953, some 210,000 units (including service vehicles) had been acquired but 338,000 had been scrapped; after various transfers the total stock at the end of 1953 was 117,000 vehicles down on the January 1948 figure. At the same time, about 80,000 life-expired wagons were still in use; and, despite a slaughter of low-capacity private owners' wagons, British Railways were still using about 317,000, of which total 162,000 were of an obsolete (loose-coupled, grease lubrication) type which encouraged operational breakdowns. Parsimony can be a powerful managerial tool to stimulate the efficient deployment of resources. But the Executive had little cause to congratulate itself on resorting to high-cost repairs in order briefly to prolong the life of old vehicles; nor for purchasing 9,000 second-hand 16-ton mineral wagons from French Railways (which had been built in Britain 1944–5) at a time when plans were well advanced for the introduction of wagons with a 24.5-ton capacity. The average size of freight wagons, 12.5 tons at the end of 1948, had risen to only 13.5 tons five years later. The bottleneck of small wagons and restricted freight locations was perpetuated.[74]

The scrapping of coaching vehicles proceeded at a more leisurely pace, with the result that the total stock at the end of 1953 was slightly higher than it had been on nationalisation, and seating capacity had been increased by 2 per cent in the five years to the end of 1953. Despite the difficulties of coping with the seasonal peaks of demand, the number of passenger-kilometres travelled per seat offered in 1954 was lower in Britain than on the continent, where rehabilitation had been proceeding more swiftly.[75] Nevertheless, the low priority accorded to passenger traffic had left a large gap in terms of quality of service. Capital restrictions, exacerbated by internal decisions on the use of steel, meant that it was possible to introduce only 1,800 of the new standard (Mark I) carriages in a total locomotive-hauled fleet of over 37,000.[76]

Any consideration of the Executive's investment in locomotives is necessarily associated with the controversial decision of Riddles and his team to embark on a programme of constructing 12 types of standard steam locomotive. In the period 1948–53, 1,487 new units were built to old company designs. However, the acquisition of alternative forms of traction – electric, diesel and the experimental gas turbine (265 locomotives in all, 1948–53) – was more than offset by the building in 1951–3 of 309 standard steam locomotives, the beginning of a programme which supplied 999 units to British Railways before construction ended in 1960.[77] The arguments for and against the Executive's motive power policy have been rehearsed several times, most recently by Johnson and Long.[78] In such discussions the broader environment in which technical decisions were made has rarely been outlined. Riddles, whose undoubted qualities as a manager have been underestimated as a result of the controversy, claimed that although diesel traction was ideal for shunting purposes, electrification was the natural inheritor of steam for main-line services. Impressed by the French railway's work with a 50-cycle a.c. system, he initiated an experimental conversion of the Lancaster–Morecambe–Heysham line on the same basis in 1953. But as long as this option was blocked by the restrictions on capital investment, he argued, the use of steam locomotives, which were thermally inefficient but had a low first cost, was fully justified.[79]

It should be stressed that in the years immediately preceding nationalisation the general policy of both the Treasury and the relevant ministries (Transport, Fuel and Power) had been similar to that of Riddles. The wartime reports of such transport officials as Hurcomb and Mount did not envisage a large role for diesels, Mount pointing out in 1943 that 'for a country which produces excellent steam coal, but has to import oil, the advantages of imported fuel must be overwhelming before its general use can be justified'.[80] And when Crompton Parkinson raised the possibility of an agreement with General Motors to supply diesel-electric locomotives in 1945, the Treasury made it quite clear 'that they would oppose any proposal for the substantial changeover of main line railways in this country to oil-fired [sic] engines'. The safeguarding of employment in the coal industry was apparently as much a consideration as the saving of imports.[81] After the war, the government exhibited more inconsistency. Coal shortages in 1946 caused the Ministry of Transport to order the railways to convert 1,200 steam locomotives to oil-firing. In fact, only 93 were converted, but the railways were well on their way to spending £3 million of government money on fixed plant before the scheme was suspended following doubts about oil supplies in September 1947. This uneconomic exercise – the R.E. claimed that oil-fired locomotives cost $2\frac{1}{2}$ times more to operate than coal-fired ones – was eventually abandoned in May 1948. Episodes such as this undoubtedly reinforced the general climate of uncertainty which helped Riddles to ignore the Commission and press forward with his steam locomotive policy.[82]

It is quite clear that Riddles carried his enthusiasm for steam much too far. First, his decision not only to persist with this form of traction but to embark on a series of completely new designs made little sense when the locomotive exchanges of 1948 had demonstrated the flexibility of many of the existing company types. Second, it seemed illogical to allow the Western Region to continue its acquisition of steam shunting locomotives when the case for diesels was universally accepted. No less than 293 were added to stock in the years 1948–53, and a further 50 were introduced in 1954–6.[83] Finally, the decision not to proceed with a *full-scale* trial of diesel traction may be questioned. Almost immediately after taking office the Executive abandoned the L.N.E.R.'s plan to introduce 25 1,600 H.P. units for trials on the King's Cross to Edinburgh service, an idea which was taken up subsequently by the Executive's own committee on alternative forms of motive power in 1951, and endorsed by Hurcomb and the Commission.[84] The Executive was quicker to investigate the feasibility of using light-weight diesel units on branch lines and cross-country services. With the encouragement of Pope and Elliot a special committee was appointed in August 1951, but the combination of a lack of enthusiasm in railway circles and a disagreement with the Commission over the selection of test areas delayed the project. Riddles's attitude was demonstrated by his request for a concurrent experiment with steam push–pull units. It was not until the last months of the Executive's life that firm plans were established for the introduction of diesel units in specified areas.[85] Undoubtedly, the effect of the general procrastination was to shift most of the costs of technical transition into the years of the Modernisation Plan (see below, Chapter 8).

Because incentive for prompt decision-making and major forward planning on the part of the Executive was lacking in the depressing environment of the austerity years, the restrictions on investment acted to restrain the introduction of modern technology. It was at best a short-sighted policy to build steam locomotives in the knowledge that alternative forms of power – specifically electrification – had traffic-stimulating properties, and that full employment was making it harder for the railways to attract men into locomotive maintenance work. However, there was a case to be argued for retaining the low first-cost option already in use, and investment restrictions made it easier for Riddles and his team to justify the view that steam should be used until electrification was made available. Certainly, this position was widely accepted in the industry. For example, in the Executive's 'swansong', its hastily prepared Development Programme of April 1953, a third of the proposed expenditure of £500 million was to be for major electrification schemes (see below, p. 259); moreover, enthusiasm for this form of motive power persisted in the regions well after the publication of the Modernisation Plan.[86]

It is debatable whether a higher rate of investment in the period 1948–53 would have led *automatically* to substantial changes of policy, but it seems likely that Riddles would have found it much harder to resist a more enthusiastic experiment with both main-line and branch-line diesels as an alternative to electrification. Certainly, the opportunity to invest more freely in motive power resources might have prevented some of the less desirable aspects of the Executive's steam programme. For example, it is doubtful whether the Executive would have purchased in December 1948 558 second-hand, 'austerities', basic freight locomotives designed by Riddles in 1943 for the Ministry of Supply, given the initial hostility of Barrington-Ward and others to the move on the grounds that they were surplus to estimated requirements. These locomotives, which Riddles had once declared could be 'thrown into the sea' after the war, were expensive to maintain and lacked the operational flexibility of other types. But an undertaking to buy in principle had been made by the Commission as part of its arrangement with the government to effect a quick settlement of the financial legacies of war-time control. In the end, the Executive held out for an advantageous purchase price. The locomotives were bought for £1.5 million, at a unit price which was about half that paid by the L.N.E.R. for 200 of the same locomotives in 1946. This compensated the Executive for rehabilitation and higher maintenance costs, but the episode took the railways further away from their avowed policy of standardisation.[87]

Whatever resources had been available it seems highly probable that the legacy of conservatism in the railways' forward planning and the Executive's natural concern to secure the unification of the four separate companies before taking important decisions about future investment would have left their mark. Nevertheless, it is unquestionable that the restrictive environment in which the railways were forced to work was damaging in several ways. It built up a large backlog of schemes planned as early as the 1930s; helped to strengthen traditional attitudes to motive power; and encouraged resentment at both central and regional level about the difficulty of introducing new ideas, of which there was no shortage. Despite the restrictive environment, Oliver Bulleid, the chief mechanical engineer of the S.R., introduced an ambitious prototype steam locomotive with the double-ended properties of a diesel – the 'Leader' Class – and tried double-deck electric trains in an attempt to relieve rush-hour overcrowding on the S.R. without recourse to longer trains and platforms. He also put into service eight 'tavern cars', restaurant/buffet cars built to resemble mock-Elizabethan inns. All these new developments were controversial. The 'Leader' Class locomotive was a miserable failure. The other two encountered consumer resistance (not to mention in relation to the mock-Tudor taverns the stuffy opposition of the Royal Fine Art Commission) and were eventually abandoned.[88] Nevertheless, these experiments do show that there was a creative response in the industry, one which was inhibited by the lack of investible funds. But most important of all, the failure to spend more money before the mid-fifties had a long-term impact in influencing the attitude of railway managers once the investment brakes were released with the acceptance of the Modernisation Plan in 1955.[89]

4

Revenue, costs and labour relations

I

The Railway Executive must have turned to the task of operating the nationalised railway system with some apprehension. Quite apart from the political distaste most of them felt for the new organisation, there were many practical problems to be resolved. Some have already been mentioned: the need to unify the practices of four stubbornly independent companies; the mounting concern about the level of rates and fares which, having been held down by the government during the war, had patently failed to keep pace with rising costs; the run-down of facilities and equipment; and the threat to recovery presented by the government's restrictive policy towards investment in 1948 and beyond. In addition, informed critics, such as Gilbert Walker, the transport economist, were beginning to express doubts about the Commission's chances of covering its costs, 'taking one year with another', as the Transport Act of 1947 required. The Act's definition of costs embraced not only allocations to general reserve and adequate provision for depreciation or renewal of assets, but also 'proper provision' for the redemption of the Commission's capital within 90 years. If redemption was to be carried out within the present century – as Hugh Dalton, the Chancellor of the Exchequer, had promised – it implied an annual charge of about £20 million on top of the £34 million required to pay British Transport stockholders their 3 per cent. And the burden falling on the railways was very heavy. Of the £1,132 million which had been issued in transport stock by the end of 1948, £927 million or 82 per cent represented the assets of the former main-line companies (including their canals, docks and hotels). At the same time, the Railway Executive's share of the Commission's gross and net book values amounted to 77 and 75 per cent respectively.[1]

The Executive had no immediate worries about its ability to generate a surplus on its operating account. But whether this would be sufficient to meet its contribution to the Commission's central charges, i.e. interest, provision for amortisation and central administrative costs, was entirely another matter. On this issue, as on others, there was a marked contrast between the Executive's private and public prognostications. In its earliest forecast, presented to the Commission in February 1948, it suggested that with existing rates and fares, which had been raised to 55 per cent above their pre-war level on 1 October 1947, net revenue would amount to only about £20 million. Indeed, traffic receipts in the first three weeks of January indicated an annual figure below £20 million. In the Executive's view it was clear that the railways would be unable to meet their interest liability.[2] In contrast, at a press conference on 17 February 1948, called by the Executive without informing the Commission, Missenden infuriated Hurcomb with the promise, devoid of all political sense, that British Railways would be shown to be 'running at a profit' by the end of the year, with the present level of charges.[3]

Although the railways faced considerable operating problems, caused, as The Economist succinctly put it, by 'eight years of over-use and under-maintenance',[4] market prospects were not at first sight unfavourable, in spite of the austerity conditions and the government's gloomy economic predictions for 1948 and 1949. Despite an inevitable fall in the traffic carried after the war, as military movements declined and constraints on road transport and coastal shipping were removed, railway business was still comfortably up on 1938 levels. There was, however, a notable difference between passenger and freight traffic. Although fuel shortage affected all road transport, bus and coach operators recovered relatively quickly after 1945. Indeed, by 1947 their passenger-mileage was approximately 50 per cent greater than in 1938. The successful expansion of public road passenger transport was largely responsible for a fall in the railways' passenger-mileage (including London Transport) of 32 per cent between 1945 and 1947. On the other hand, the railways' hold on the freight market was more secure. The ton-mileage carried fell by only 8 per cent over the same period.[5] A similar picture emerges from estimates of market shares. The railways' share (including London Transport) of the total market for passenger travel amounted to about 28 per cent in 1947, much the same as in 1938. But their share of freight carried was healthier: 49 per cent in 1947, higher than the 41 per cent estimated for 1938 (see Appendix D, Tables 1A and 1B).

Despite this seeming security, the Executive's operating performance was dismal from the very start. As Table 8 column (c) shows, net operating revenue (excluding revenue from ships) in 1948 was only slightly higher than the Executive's gloomy forecast in February of that year, viz. £23.8 million, and this was insufficient to meet its implied share of the Commission's central charges, however these are calculated. And in 1949 a mere

Table 8. *British Railways' operating performance, 1948–53 (including collection and delivery services, but excluding ships) (£m.)*

Year	(a) Gross revenue	(b) Operating costs	(c) Net operating revenue[a]	(d) Contribution to central charges (Commission's basis)[b]	(e) Overall balance	(f) Contribution to central charges (revised basis)[c]	(g) Overall balance (revised)
1948	346.3	322.5	23.8	34.3	−10.5	33.7	−9.9
1949	335.7	325.1	10.6	36.6	−26.0	34.2	−23.6
1950	351.3	326.1	25.2	37.5	−12.3	35.2	−10.0
1951	384.9	351.6	33.3	33.3	0.0	33.0	0.3
1952	416.3	377.7	38.7	34.8	3.9	35.2	3.5
1953	434.7	400.1	34.6	37.3	−2.7	38.3	−3.7
1948–53	2,269.2	2,103.1	166.2	213.8	−47.6	209.6	−43.4
Average p.a.	378.2	350.5	27.7	35.6	−7.9	34.9	−7.2

[a] Includes letting of sites and premises in properties in operational use, and commercial advertising.
[b] Central charges include miscellaneous receipts and interest as a credit. Central administration costs (arguably an operating cost) are also included. The railways' contribution is based upon their share of net book value (excluding ships). The net book value series includes B.T.C. interests in non-controlled undertakings.
[c] Each subdivision of the central charges has been allocated individually to railways and other activities. The main criteria used were:
 i. Interest on the original issues of British Transport Stock: share of net book value at the beginning of 1948.
 ii. Interest on subsequent Stock issues: share of capital expenditure net of depreciation provisions.
 iii. Interest on advances from the Minister (mainly held in suspense account): all to railways.
 iv. Central administration costs: share in B.T.C. annual expenditure.
Source: B.T.C., R. & A. 1948–56.

£10.6 million was earned, producing a deficit, after deduction for central charges, of £26 million. Only in 1951 and 1952 did the Executive appear to 'break even', with net operating revenues of £33.3 and £38.7 million respectively. In fact, this brief period of 'profitability' was probably an accounting fiction, for it may be argued that drawings on the abnormal maintenance fund, which had been set up to enable the Commission to make good war-time arrears, disguised the true operating position. Certainly there is evidence of anxiety about the arrangements for financing maintenance, particularly from 1953, when the fund was running low[6] (this is discussed in more detail below, pp. 173–4, and in Appendix A). In any case, even on the official figures presented, over the period 1948–53 earnings of £166.2 million (£27.7 million a year) left a deficit of £47.6 million (£7.9 million per annum). Put another way, a rate of return on capital averaging only 2.27 per cent was insufficient to meet an interest obligation of 3 per cent on British Transport Stock.[7]

The Executive's shipping services, which were treated separately in the Commission's accounts, enjoyed more success, thanks to a near monopoly of the Irish and cross-channel routes. Even here, however, net earnings of £14.6 million, 1948–53, though more than sufficient to meet shipping's estimated share of central charges (£1.8 million), were clearly too small to alter the Executive's overall position. Moreover, the Commission's heavy reliance upon the railways is clear from its general financial results. Its long-distance road haulage activities were only just being built up when in May 1952 the Conservative Government announced its plans to return these assets to the private sector. With national road haulage barely established, the Commission's accounts revealed an overall loss of nearly £40 million in the years 1948–50, with a deficit of £20.8 million in 1949 alone. Again, ignoring the treatment of maintenance, the improvement shown in 1951–3 – when profits of over £12 million were declared – still left a deficit of about £27 million over the period 1948–53.[8]

II

Why was the railways' performance so disappointing? To what extent were the deficits avoidable?

Some commentators, notably Harold Wilson, strongly criticised the valuation placed on the railways' assets at nationalisation. Wilson also condemned the Commission's obligation to provide for capital redemption as 'illogical and burdensome'. Such criticisms are obviously contentious. But even accepting the argument that British Transport Stock was overvalued – in effect by 20 per cent – and ignoring the Commission's annual provision for the redemption of capital, the Executive would still have exhibited a loss of some £12 million on its railway operations in the years to 1953. And the Commission, by depreciating rolling stock and plant at historic instead of replacement cost, conventional accounting practice at the time, could be accused of having made inadequate provision for depreciation in its accounts.[9]

These observations inevitably raise the question as to whether the Commission's accounts are a true or, at any rate, adequate guide to the 'profitability' of the business, other than within very narrow financial limits. In his book *The Train That Ran Away*, Stewart Joy, who was Chief Economist of the British Railways Board, 1968–72, clearly had his doubts, for he used a cash-flow approach to locate 'The True Losses of BR, 1948–68'. Arguing that in 1948 railway assets were worth no more than their scrap value in relation to aggregate earning power, he ignored the Commission's provision for depreciation and derived net cash flows by deducting annual expenditure on investment from the annual net operating surplus/deficit. A cumulative flow was obtained by compounding annually with a fixed interest rate of 6 per cent. On this basis Joy found that in the period 1948–53 'railway activities', including shipping, hotels and catering, experienced a negative net cash flow only in 1949. By 1953, the cumulative flow amounted to £21.6 million. This, however, was the last year in which the calculation proved positive, and by 1968 the cumulative 'losses' amounted to £2,553 million.[10] But Joy's approach, while undoubtedly useful in indicating the long-run financial problems of British Rail, totally ignores the cost of purchasing the assets in 1948. The assets may have been overvalued, but they were not worthless. His methodology also has the disadvantage of placing the burden of capital expenditure after 1948 unduly heavily upon the years of initial purchases, which makes it difficult to compare single years or groups of years.

I have used an alternative method which gives results on a consistent basis for the whole of the period 1948–73. The data provide a much clearer picture of the performance of British Rail in the quarter century after nationalisation than do either the published accounts or Joy's estimates of 'cash flow'. The new methodology is explained fully in Appendix A, below. In brief, a new series, termed 'gross working surplus', is derived by adding back all capital charges (depreciation and amortisation) to the railways' net receipts. Then, depreciation and amortisation charges are deducted from the gross surpluses on a *current* or *replacement* cost basis. This is an important adjustment, since as early as 1953 Sir Reginald Wilson estimated that the use of *historic* cost depreciation overstated the net results by £13.0 million.[11] Finally, interest charges are deducted, correcting for the overvaluation of assets in 1948 and reducing the railways' subsequent capital burden to square with the use of replace-

Table 9. *The railways' 'true' financial results, 1948–53 (£m.)*

Year	(a) Gross working surplus	(b) Net working surplus	(c) Total balance (after interest)	(d) Total balance at constant 1948 prices	(e) Revised total balance (excluding drawings on abnormal maintenance fund) at constant 1948 prices
1948	43.6	19.4	−1.6	−1.6	−20.1
1949	31.1	5.2	−16.3	−15.8	−29.9
1950	44.7	16.9	−5.2	−5.0	−15.3
1951	49.0	18.1	−4.6	−4.1	−14.6
1952	58.6	24.1	1.0	0.8	−16.6
1953	57.4	21.2	−2.1	−1.7	−18.6
1948–53	284.4	104.9	−28.8	−27.4	−115.1

(a) Net receipts of railways plus capital charges added back.
(b) Gross working surplus less depreciation and amortisation on a current replacement cost basis.
For further details, see Commentary to Appendix A.
Source: Appendix A, Tables 1–3, below.

ment cost accounting. The results for 1948–53 are summarised in Table 9. It is revealed that the railways made 'losses' amounting to £28.8 million, or £27.4 million at constant 1948 prices. Performance improved over the period 1949–52, but only in 1952 is a positive balance or 'profit' suggested. Moreover, the 'true' results were in all probability worse than this. The Commission's drawings on the abnormal maintenance account of £97.5 million were intended to represent abnormal expenditure to make good war-time arrears. If we accept the proposition that they were, at a time of material shortages and controls, in part at least a disguised operating subsidy, the deficit could amount in aggregate to as much as £115 million at constant prices over the six years (column (e) of Table 9). Thus, there was no 'false dawn' of railway profitability in the early 1950s, as the published accounts implied. Nationalised railways experienced difficulties from the start, and however profits are measured, there was no period of comparative prosperity to cushion the industry before the effects of increased road competition from the mid-fifties left their mark.

Many railway managers took their brief from the published information, of course, and it is certainly true that the early results, both operating and overall, were better than those experienced after 1953 (see Chapters 6 and 10). This being so, can it be said that the Commission and the Executive missed an opportunity to restructure the business from a platform of relative security?

In this context, the first thing to observe is that the railways were not placed under immediate pressure in terms of market-share. David Blee, the Executive's commercial member, often expressed anxiety about the competitive challenge from long-distance coaches and 'C' licence lorry operators.[12] But the difficulties the railways experienced in the late 1940s and early 1950s cannot be attributed to any sudden collapse of business. Although coal shortages were frequently blamed for placing constraints on operating, passenger-mileage, for example, while falling slightly after 1948, was only 2 per cent lower in 1953. And the volume of freight carried actually increased in the period. Net ton-mileage (including free-hauled traffic) rose by nearly 6 per cent from 1948 to 1951, and was still 5 per cent above the 1948 level in 1953. Both types of traffic were more abundant than in the immediate pre-war period. It is true that the coal industry, for many years one of the major sources of railway business, had a disappointing record after the war. Annual production remained below the pre-war average and this was reflected in the tonnage carried by the railways, which fell from 191 million tons per annum in 1935–8 to 178 million tons per annum in 1948–53. This 6.8 per cent fall was, however, more than counteracted by a substantial rise in the average length of haul* with the result that coal ton-mileage in 1948–53 was 21 per cent higher than in 1935–8. The *total* volume of both passenger and freight transport in Britain rose in the period 1948–53, by 24 and 16 per cent respectively. The railways did suffer a small contraction of their market-share, from 49 to 44 per cent of freight ton-mileage, and 26 to 21 per cent of passenger-mileage (including private motoring, which expanded rapidly). But there was certainly no downward trend in absolute traffic levels.[13]

In reality the railways' financial performance was strongly affected, if not determined, by the much more deep-seated problems of costs and pricing. 'What is important,' it has been said, 'is the price charged for different traffics and services in relation to costs.'[14] From this viewpoint it is clear that both the Commission and the Executive had a great deal to do if they were to alter the system of pricing and cost-control inherited from the companies on nationalisation. Managerial complacency in an industry long accustomed to the statutory control of rates and fares had encouraged a situation where it was the volume of traffic carried rather than the margin of profit earned which was commonly regarded as an adequate indicator of commercial performance.[15] This attitude was reinforced by the 'in-bred' nature of the railways' executive management at this time. As Arthur Pearson, one of the Executive's chief officers, put it in 1953, 'People come into the railway industry at an early age and stay in it for the rest of

*1935–8: 44.1 miles; 1948–53: 56.6 miles (+ 28%).

their working lives. . . This cloistered system makes for continuity and time for specialising, but it also makes for rigidity.'[16] And nowhere was this rigidity more apparent than in the railways' approach to costing and pricing. Gerard Fiennes, General Manager of the Eastern Region, 1966–7 and author of the uncompromising autobiography which led to his dismissal in 1967, summarised the position as follows: 'It is one of the disasters about British Railways that in the years between 1947 and 1955 no one had done the basic work on what we were there for at all; what traffic should be carried by what methods in what quantities, where from and to, at what rates.'[17] This comment merits close scrutiny. It is clear that an explanation for any implied failing in managerial performance, any implied failure to secure optimal levels of 'profit' in these early years, and indeed later, must centre on a detailed examination of costs and prices.

III

As already mentioned (above, pp. 3–4), the railway companies' concern at the disparity between costs and charges led the government to sanction an increase in October 1947. Both passenger fares and freight rates were raised to a level 55 per cent above the pre-war standard obtaining in October 1937. Railway costs, however, were estimated to have risen by at least 80 per cent over the same period. And inflationary pressures continued to cause anxiety at both Commission and Executive level after Vesting Day. Domestic prices rose by about 5 per cent a year between 1947 and 1953, and there was a sharper increase of 8 per cent, 1950–2, in the wake of the Korean War. Railway costs – and, in particular, labour and fuel which together amounted to about three-quarters of total operating costs in 1948 – more than kept pace with the average trend of inflation.[18] Despite the cushioning effect of rationing, the scarcity of both coal and steel was reflected in price levels. The railways' coal bill was affected not only by general price increases but also by the N.C.B.'s restructuring of its pricing schedules in order to reintroduce differentials for higher quality coal narrowed by flat-rate increases during the war. It is difficult to produce accurate average prices per ton, given the multiplicity of coal grades and the existence of separate purchasing arrangements in each region. But, as an approximation, the cost of railway coal rose from about 44s. 5d. (£2.22) a ton at the end of 1947 to about 64s. 8d. (£3.23) six years later, an annual increase of 6.4 per cent. And the price of steel rails was 83 per cent higher in 1953 than in 1947, representing an average rise of 10.6 per cent per annum.[19]

But the cause of greatest concern was undoubtedly the cost of labour. In its 1948 Report the Commission estimated that no less than 62 per cent of railway operating costs were made up of 'staff costs' – wages, salaries, insurance, pensions, etc. The average weekly earnings of railwaymen had already doubled in the period 1938–48, and a reduction in the working week, from 48 to 44 hours, had been introduced in June 1947.[20] Thereafter, average adult male earnings, while generally tending to fall behind the rise in retail prices, recovered their position in 1953. A 5 per cent increase in earnings, 1948–53, matched the rate of inflation. Average weekly earnings of £6.95 in 1948 had risen to £8.94 by 1953, while retail prices increased by 26 per cent, or 4.7 per cent a year. There was a similar pattern with the 'conciliation grades', the wage-grade traffic staff numbering 393,000 in 1948, some 60 per cent of all railway workers, whose conditions of service had once been determined by the Conciliation Schemes of 1907 and 1911. For this group earnings increased from £6.74 in 1948 to £8.61 in 1953, again a rise of 5 per cent a year. Union leaders such as J. H. B. 'Jim' Figgins of the N.U.R. and James G. Baty of A.S.L.E.F. were nevertheless right to voice their anxiety at the failure of members' earnings to keep up with rising prices. It was only after the pay award of October 1952 that earnings began to out-pace the cost of living (see Table 12, below). Principal pay increases were agreed in February 1948, February 1951, after a strike threat (see below), November 1951 and October 1952. The result was that while numbers employed fell by 7 per cent from 641,000 in January 1948 to 594,000 at the end of 1953, the Railway Executive's wage-bill increased from about £222 million in 1948 to £265 million in 1953, a rise of 19 per cent.[21]

Both the Commission and the Executive, in attempting to explain their financial difficulties, strongly emphasised the lag of fares and rates behind increases in costs. In its 1950 Report, for example, the Commission complained that 'charges can normally be increased only as a result of public enquiries in the nature of litigation which may be prolonged far beyond the date when the need for increased charges becomes clear'. In the following year it pointed out that most of the accumulated deficit in the period 1948–51 was incurred in late 1949 and early 1950, when the Commission was awaiting an approved but delayed increase in freight charges. Later on, the argument was taken further. In an internal memorandum to the Finance Committee drafted by the Commission's Director of Budgets in March 1956, it was suggested that the delay in raising charges to meet increases in wages and other items had cost British Railways £57 million by 1953, £10 million more than the stated deficit. Of this sum, £24 million was attributed directly to the delays imposed by the machinery by which charges were controlled.[22]

How convincing was the Commission's case? There is no doubt at all that the machinery governing charges under the Transport Act of 1947 was just as cumbersome as in the past. All proposals for revision had to be presented to a Transport Tribunal, the successor to the Railway Rates Tribunal set up under the 1921 Act. The Commission was obliged to submit to it new schemes for passenger and freight charges within two years of the passing of the Act, 'or longer as the Minister may allow' (in fact, such schemes were not produced until 1951, for passengers, and 1955, for freight). The Tribunal of three, a president, 'transport member', and 'commercial member', operated as a court and was required to hold a public inquiry whenever an application to alter charges was received. Evidence from both the Commission and complainants, representing transport users, was to be heard before a verdict could be delivered. In addition, a new consultative machinery was created further to safeguard the public interest. A Central Transport Consultative Committee for Great Britain was established which, together with area Transport Users' Consultative Committees, had the task of considering all matters affecting users, including charges. These bodies were appointed by, and had direct access to, the Minister of Transport. Finally, the Minister himself possessed powers to authorise the Commission to make additional charges pending the submission of charges schemes (Section 82 (1)); to order the Commission to implement recommendations from the Central Transport Consultative Committee; and to require the Transport Tribunal to review the operation of any charges scheme, over and above his general powers to issue 'Directions' under Section 4 (1) of the Act.[23]

This relatively complex machinery undoubtedly delayed the implementation of certain fare and rate increases proposed by the Executive and Commission. Two examples stand out. The first involved the Commission's application under Section 82 for an increase of $16\frac{2}{3}$ per cent in freight rates. The application, which was first intimated to the Ministry in a letter from Hurcomb to Barnes on 4 October 1949, had been occasioned by the Commission's financial difficulties in that year. There was also the prospect of a further deterioration arising from the inflationary implications of the devaluation of sterling in September, and the cost of an improvement in railwaymen's pay and conditions – payment in lieu of rest days, and bank and public holidays – agreed in the same month. However, not until 15 May 1950 were freight charges actually raised. Delay had been caused by the need to refer the increase to the permanent members of the Transport Tribunal in accordance with Section 82 of the Act. Further problems arose when Barnes, the Minister of Transport, experienced difficulty in persuading his ministerial colleagues (and Hugh Gaitskell, Minister for Economic Affairs, in particular) to support the increase. These delays were estimated by the Commission to have cost £11 million in lost revenue.[24] The second example is provided by the Commission's passenger charges scheme of 1951–2. The scheme, which embraced charges for both road and rail transport, including London Transport, was presented to the Transport Tribunal in April 1951. There was certainly a case for some adjustment to railway fares in spite of the risk of losing traffic to the roads. While the ordinary third-class single fare had remained constant at its October 1947 level of 2.44d. (1.02p) a mile, the extension of concessionary tickets had had the effect of reducing the average fare paid from 1.40d. (0.58p) a mile in 1948 to 1.25d. (0.52p) in 1951, a fall of 23 per cent in real terms. With Executive support the Commission proposed to retain the ordinary fare but increase a number of the cheaper fares – monthly and day returns, season tickets and workmen's and early morning tickets. The Tribunal began the public inquiry in July by deciding which of the 204 objectors had a statutory right to be heard. The inquiry proper did not open until 8 October – it closed eight weeks later on 3 December – and it was not until 17 January 1952 that the Tribunal announced its interim conclusions.[25] There was some sympathy in both government circles and the press for Hurcomb's view, expressed in a letter to Barnes in May 1951, that the Tribunal machinery was not a suitable instrument of control in a time of sustained inflation. There should be, he argued, 'a rapid and flexible administration'. The argument was received sympathetically by the Cabinet's Committee on Socialised Industries when it considered price policy in July, and Barnes later argued that the Commission ought to be able to adjust its charges 'to meet substantial and unavoidable increases in its costs subject only to *subsequent* ratification by the Tribunal' (my italics). *The Times* endorsed the view that the procedure should be more speedy.[26]

In fact, delays did not result simply from creaking machinery. Public hostility to the fare increases proposed under the passenger scheme – the strength of which was indicated by the large number of objectors and a generally frosty reception in the press – served not only to prolong the inquiry but to stimulate government intervention. The Labour Government had already expressed concern at the implications of higher charges when the Commission presented its interim scheme for London passenger fares to the Minister of Transport in October 1949. This scheme was finally introduced, after a year's delay, on 1 October 1950. There had also been disquiet within the government about the rise in freight rates. Several members of the Cabinet had expressed their opposition to the increase of 1950 and to the first of two increases, each of 10 per cent, applied in April and December 1951 to offset wage awards agreed in February and September.[27] The Conservative Government, which took office at the end of October 1951, while the Tribunal inquiry was proceeding, was prepared to go much further. The result was a Ministerial Direction under Section 4 (1) of the Transport Act.

The circumstances were as follows. The new Minister of Transport, John Scott Maclay, was soon asked to endorse interim increases in charges sought by the Executive and the Commission under Section 82. These were the second of the 10 per cent adjustments to freight rates in 1951 (operational from 31 December), and a 10 per cent increase in monthly return passenger fares, which came into force on 1 January 1952. The latter revision, which raised the fare from 1.59d. to 1.75d. a mile third class, was significant, since about 60 per cent of passenger revenue came from such tickets. It had been insisted upon by the Commission, impatient for the outcome of the Tribunal hearing.[28] Important alterations to both passenger and freight rates had thus been granted before the Tribunal delivered its final judgement on the passenger scheme on 27 February 1952. The Tribunal then gave its blessing to the Executive's plan to increase the level of concessionary fares. The only substantial modification was the requirement that the maximum ordinary fares (single and return) be reduced from 2.44d. a mile to 1.75d. (with powers to raise them to 2.00d. from 1 January 1953). A revised scheme, published at the end of February, was to come into effect on 2 March in the London area and on 1 May in the provinces.[29]

The introduction of the scheme in London caused, in the Commission's words, 'considerable public comment', and it was this which encouraged the government to intervene. Although adjustments made to London bus fares excited the most opposition, there was also much criticism of the higher charges for railway season and early morning tickets and the abolition of 'workmen's fares', both inside and outside London. In March the *Daily Herald* reported that the London County Council had resolved to ask the Minister to set up a Select Committee to inquire into the operation of the Transport Act, and there were predictable howls of protest from aggrieved commuters.[30] The press were not unanimous, however. Both *The Times* and *The Economist* saw the higher fares as justified in relation to rising costs, and they attributed the protest to inept public relations on the part of the Commission and the London Transport Executive. *The Economist* roundly condemned the attitude of the public, suggesting that 'the campaign of protest has demonstrated all the unreason of the small child reviling the bad naughty table on which it has banged its head'.[31]

The government's reactions were mixed. Like the previous administration it ruled out the possibility of offering the Commission a subsidy in order to retain lower charges, but it was also reluctant to court unpopularity by endorsing the higher fares, which had already become a major issue in the L.C.C. election campaign. Prime Minister Churchill took the lead. At a stormy meeting of the Cabinet on 6 March he declared that 'he had been disturbed by the sudden announcement of increased passenger fares... Would it not have been possible to explain that they were made on the authority, not of the Government, but of the Transport Tribunal?' The next day he demanded that a public statement be issued disassociating the government from the passenger charges scheme, and the Minister of Transport was persuaded to refer the whole question of discretionary pricing below the legal maximum rates to the C.T.C.C.[32] To the government's discomfort, this body completely vindicated the railways' position. It reported, on 8 April, that the scheme confirmed by the Tribunal (together with some amendments introduced by the Railway Executive to placate opposition in areas where the proposed increases were high) was 'fair to the travelling public'.[33] The government then reacted with ill-considered haste before the publication of the report, due on 17 April. Not for the first time the relatively weak position of the Minister of Transport was exposed. Maclay was strongly against a policy of direct intervention but he was overruled at another turbulent Cabinet meeting on 10 April, and it is clear that the balance was tilted against him by the personal involvement of Churchill, supported by Leathers and Swinton.[34] Maclay was therefore instructed to exercise his ultimate sanction under an Act which the Conservative Government had already resolved to repeal. By a Direction dated 15 April 1952, the day before the new fares were to be announced by the Commission at a press conference, the Minister ordered the Commission not to raise any of its provincial fares on 1 May. The reduction in the ordinary fares was to proceed. The scheme was once again referred to the C.T.C.C. A Commons debate on the subject on 28 April was led by the Home Secretary, Sir David Maxwell-Fyfe, in Maclay's absence through 'ill-health'. Shortly afterwards, on 7 May, Maclay was replaced by Alan Lennox-Boyd.[35]

The government may have appeased popular opinion, but it won few friends among the more informed. Both *The Times* and the *Daily Herald* were particularly critical of the intervention, which set an important precedent for the rest of the period of Conservative rule and, in *The Times*'s words, opened up the road to 'continuing deficit and subsidy'. Both newspapers correctly exposed the unwisdom of using a general direction 'in the public interest' to support a limited section of the population, or, as Maxwell-Fyfe was forced to concede, merely 'to temper the wind to the flock of more severely shorn lambs'. Finally, the decision to refer the scheme once more to a consultative body which had already pronounced itself in support of the railways on all issues of principle was justifiably criticised as evidence that the government had been stampeded into last minute action.[36]

As far as the Railway Executive was concerned, the Minister's Direction produced considerable administrative problems for its commercial member, David Blee, as well as for the regional passenger superintendents, and promised to cause a further deterioration in its standing with the public. For the Commission it not only threatened to wreck any chance of their reducing the accumulated deficit, but also represented a significant change in their relations with the government. In a formal letter of reply the B.T.C. informed the Ministry that 'the precedent which this Direction has set involves serious consequences for the Commission's finances and may endanger the possibility of their complying with their statutory obligation [to break even, taking one year with another]'. They also deprecated the fact that they were given no prior warning, but 'were merely informed of a decision taken'. Subsequent negotiations produced little but a continuation of the bitter atmosphere.[37]

In June Lennox-Boyd finally announced the basis for a revised passenger scheme, to apply both in London and the provinces. So-called 'substandard' fares were to be treated equally; in other words, all fares were to be raised proportionately, thus removing the relatively high percentage increases sought by the Commission and Executive in order to rid the fare structure of various anomalies. The ruling required the reintroduction of the old bus fare stages in London together with workmen's shift tickets. It also involved the retention of differential fares for a bizarre miscellany of such special groups as patients, escorts and visitors travelling to and from convalescent homes; anglers making day return journeys; members of the Commonwealth Parliamentary Association; shipwrecked mariners; entertainers and music hall artistes; and relatives or guardians visiting children in approved schools.[38] The revised scheme was introduced in London on 31 August and in the rest of the country on the following day. The lag between the first submission and final agreement had thus stretched to 17 months, costing the Commission an estimated £6.5 million in lost revenue. The four-month standstill imposed by the Government cost the B.T.C. an estimated £800,000 alone. In addition, the Minister's modifications were held to represent a loss of a further £1.9 million in a full year, while doing nothing to alter the patchwork of inequalities in passenger pricing which the Executive had sought to rationalise.[39]

There were further delays in 1953. An attempt to bring the fare structures of London and the provinces closer into line, by raising ordinary, early morning and season tickets in London and early morning and season tickets elsewhere, was incorporated into a second passenger charges scheme drafted in the autumn of 1952. This was first intimated to the Minister in November, and lodged with the Transport Tribunal in January 1953. After a 23-day hearing and an unsuccessful reference by the L.C.C. to the Court of Appeal, it was not until 16 August 1953 that the scheme, with some minor modifications, was introduced. The overall impact of the two schemes was, therefore, limited. The average fare paid by passengers rose only slightly, to 1.31d. (0.55p) in 1952 and 1.34d. (0.56p) in 1953, a level which in real terms was 24 per cent below the average paid in 1948.[40]

IV

This clash with the government over passenger fares obviously helped to shape the environment in which railway charges were fixed for the rest of the 1950s, aside from its relevance to B.T.C. finances. But the Commission and the Railway Executive were not merely twin prisoners of a defective Act and a capricious government which together created the mutually inconsistent obligations to break even on the one hand and to make reasonable charges for services provided on the other. What was the attitude of these two bodies to their task of providing, in the Act's phrase (Section 3(1)), 'an efficient, adequate, economic and properly integrated system of public inland transport'?

It is abundantly evident that the members appointed to the B.T.C. in 1947 were ill-equipped to initiate major changes in commercial practice. Although Lord Ashfield and Sir William Wood had a great deal of commercial experience, with the London Passenger Transport Board and the London Midland & Scottish Railway respectively, both failed for different reasons to bring this to bear on the problems of nationalised transport. Ashfield, of course, was well into his seventies and, as already noted, his presence was short-lived. In any case, he was given the comparatively minor job of overseeing the implementation of Section 95 of the Act, which concerned conditions of employment, safety, health and welfare. Wood was younger, but scarcely more dynamic. In February 1948 he was appointed Chairman of the B.T.C.'s Charges Committee, which was given the responsibility of preparing the charges schemes.[41] The Committee's task was a daunting one, particularly in the freight area, and co-operation between the several Executives was at best limited. But there was no effective leadership. Though Wood often had useful advice to offer, he soon made it apparent to colleagues that he was not going to over-extend himself in his new and unfamiliar role as policy-maker. This meant that the initiative was either seized by Reginald Wilson, the Commission's Comptroller, or passed down to the Executives. The only vigorous personalities were Hurcomb and Wilson. It has been said that simply because of his mastery of detail and of the amount of work he did, 'the British Transport Commission *was* Hurcomb', and Wilson was his favoured lieutenant. In 1947, however, both had only a limited knowledge of the commercial problems surrounding the provision of railway services. There were also administrative barriers. Wilson, who was keen that the railways should be more cognisant of costs in relation to pricing, did not control the relevant officers at B.T.C. headquarters. A. E. Sewell, the Charges Adviser, and his successor, H. J. Birkbeck (from January 1950 Principal Charges Officer) were part of the railway-oriented team responsible to Chief Secretary Beevor. The tension between the Comptroller's and the Chief Secretary's department, referred to in Chapter 2, was a further element inhibiting decisive action on costing and pricing.

More important, however, was the interpretation of the Transport Act favoured by Hurcomb and Wilson. Both became fully occupied in chasing two elusive hares. The first was the notion that nationalised inland transport could be 'integrated'; the second was that the Commission could 'break even' while at the same time fulfilling a responsibility to the public to maintain a relatively uniform level of service across the country. Encouraged by Herbert Morrison's pronouncements both in the House of Commons and in the Socialised Industries Committee, the Commission threw its weight behind the contention that some form of cross-subsidisation was inevitable, and even desirable. This was clear in its First Annual Report.

In any nation-wide transport undertaking covering the various forms of transport different services and different methods of transport will show unequal degrees of profitability and will be unable to contribute at a uniform rate to overhead charges. Nor indeed is it possible in such an undertaking to avoid the provision of some services which are unremunerative even perhaps in the sense that they do not support their own direct costs of operation. . . The degree to which one form of transport or one service can and should be called upon to support another will vary from time to time but, within reasonable limits, bold application of the principle may be essential to any adequate system of facilities for the country as a whole.[42]

The difficulties, indeed inconsistencies, in the approach taken by the Commission were evident at an early stage. For example, 'integration' was taken to imply a co-ordination of transport services with policy favouring the mode – whether rail, bus or lorry – where costs were lowest, and, in Wood's words, to avoid 'any duplication of its work by cutting out needless services'. Yet at the same time the Commission interpreted Section 3 (2) of the Transport Act* as precluding it from imposing a

*Section 3 (2) stated: 'Where the Commission are for the time being providing regular goods transport services of different kinds available between the same points, it shall be their duty to allow any person desiring transport for his goods between those points freedom to choose such of the services so provided as he considers most suitable to his needs.'

particular form of transport upon its freight customers against their wishes.[43]

Nor was the B.T.C. free of an initial complacency about the adjustment of charges to meet rising costs. Although there was growing anxiety about the prospect of breaking even from June 1948, the Commission accepted the view expressed by some railway managers (see below, p. 114) that the rates and fares introduced in October 1947 were high enough to have produced a loss of traffic from rail to road transport. In 1948 the steady rise in costs was as unmistakable as was the loss of revenue caused by the reduction in government (H.M. Forces) traffic. But in its First Annual Report, published in July 1949, the Commission conceded that it was reluctant to apply for increased charges, and it was not until the following October that it moved to secure interim increases in freight charges and London passenger fares.[44] In this early period Hurcomb and his colleagues clearly thought it desirable to maximise the volume of railway traffic; and hoped that the Commission's road services, when fully developed, would help to subsidise unremunerative railway operations. Thereby overall finances could be balanced over a number of years. The weakness of this strategy was exposed when the operating results of the road haulage business – British Road Services – were obtained. At the end of 1951, when the bulk of road haulage acquisitions had been completed, the Commission's accumulated deficit stood at £39.5 million. But road haulage operating surpluses (before deductions to meet central charges) of only £1.6 million in 1952 and £8.9 million in 1953 were clearly insufficient to produce much of a dent in the deficit. Indeed, only in 1953 did road haulage profits counter losses on the railways' own road services for collection and delivery. The same may be said of the Commission's bus services. Here the operating surplus derived from provincial English and Scottish buses (there was a small loss on London Transport's road services) amounted to only £3.8 and £4.8 million in the same years.[45] In short, the B.T.C. failed to provide a lead, partly because of its internal organisation, and partly because of its interpretation of the requirements of operating a public service under the Transport Act of 1947. This failure, just as much as government policy, influenced the way railway managers approached the problem of pricing.

Not all of the Commission's work was barren. Under the influence of Hurcomb and Wilson much was done to impress upon the Railway Executive (and others) that a more sophisticated analysis of traffic costs was required. Thus, when the B.T.C. received a memorandum from Blee and Morton in August 1950 which stressed 'the strenuous efforts being made to attract the largest possible volume of passenger travel', Hurcomb was moved to ask: 'Is that not a fallacy? We want to attract traffic in so far as by doing so we can improve our net financial position.' The new mood found particular expression in the Commission's traffic-costing service, which was established in October 1951 under the direction of A. W. Tait.* The aim of the new service, which was directed specifically at the Railway and Road Haulage Executives, was to extend the range of investigative studies already in progress at Executive level, and 'to give advice to the two Executives on the practical relation of the cost findings to the carrying out of the Commission's policies on charges and integration'.[46] Despite some initial qualms on the part of the Railway Executive, Tait was given direct access to railway officers in the regions, and both Executives appear to have co-operated fully with the new unit. Largely as a result of this administrative stimulus, the railways produced statistical material which not only revealed the difficulties in equating prices charged with operating costs for a large number of traffics (given existing maximum charges), but also demonstrated the wide gulf between road and rail costs for given traffic categories. As early as August 1950 Tait informed Blee of his suspicions that the railways' passenger traffic was not making an adequate contribution to net revenue, and later in the same month he produced a draft memorandum for Wilson on passenger transport costs which demonstrated 'that British Railway passenger services as a whole are being run at a substantial loss'. Some of the findings were published in the Commission's Annual Reports. In June 1951 an instructive diagram appeared in the report for 1950 (see Figure 1). This contrasted average road and rail passenger costs for four types of service – long-distance express, stopping, cross-country and branch-line. Road costs were found to be significantly lower (whether calculated per seat-mile or per passenger-mile) in all but the first category. On branch lines rail costs per passenger-mile amounted to over 25d. (10.4p) and for stopping services nearly 14d. (5.8p), compared with under 2d. and 1d. (0.8p, 0.4p) for equivalent bus services.[47] Clearly, with a pricing scheme which comprised a uniform 'standard' fare plus concessions to season-ticket holders, workmen, and so on, the price of railway travel tended to be in inverse ratio to its cost, the express passenger paying more than the workmen on a slow suburban train for a service which was far cheaper to provide.

The costing of freight traffic was a more complex business, but by the end of 1949 principles for a merchandise charges scheme had been produced in which loadability was emphasised, and in December 1950 Tait was able to produce a 'Rail–Road Comparison of Freight Transport Costs' which highlighted the weakness of the railways' merchandise traffic. Merchandise costs per net ton-mile were found to be double that for coal and minerals – 3.221d. compared with 1.549d. (1.34p, 0.65p) –

*Tait had been appointed Principal Costs Officer in January 1950, and Director of Costings in May 1951.

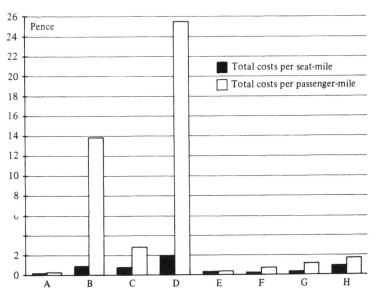

Figure 1 Sample road and rail passenger costs, 1950

RAIL   **ROAD**

A Main-line express service   E Long-distance coach service
B Stopping service on main line   F Inter-City service – mainly double-deck
C Cross-country service   G Country service – mixed fleet
D Branch-line service   H Urban service – single deck

Source: B.T.C., *R. & A. 1950*, I, p. 71.

the discrepancy being largely explained by poor loadings (29 per cent of capacity for merchandise, compared with 81 per cent for coal). In the same study long-distance road costs were put at 1.932d. (0.81p) per net ton-mile. Such problems were also emphasised in the B.T.C.'s Annual Report for 1951, which included an appendix entitled 'Some Notes on Costing'. Here the key elements of loadability and length of haul were isolated, and it was suggested that rail costs were likely to be lower than road costs only where commodities were bulky, the traffic dense, distances long and access direct.[48]

The most telling demonstrations of the unremunerative nature of much of the railways' traffic were not given much publicity. Nor were they the subject of debate at Commission or Executive level before 1954. The first was a confidential estimate of operating margins and total profit or loss for passenger, parcels and freight traffic in 1949, the worst year for the railways before 1955. This produced the depressing conclusion in June 1951 that although all the main categories of traffic covered their direct costs, both passenger and freight failed to cover *total* costs by about £17

Table 10. *Railway operating margins and estimates of profit/loss for specific traffics, 1949 (£m.)*

Traffic	Gross receipts (i)	Direct costs (ii)	Operating margin (i)–(ii)	Joint costs (iii)	Total costs (iv)	Profit/ loss (i)–(iv)
Passenger	115.0	92.6	22.4	40.1	132.7	−17.7
Parcels	29.6	23.4	6.2	4.2	27.6	2.0
Freight	189.5	172.0	17.5	34.9	206.9	−17.4
Total	334.1	288.0	46.1	79.2	367.2	−33.1

Source: B.T.C. traffic-costing calculation, June 1951, referred to in D.M. Dear, memo. to Finance Committee, 20 September 1957, B.R.B. A full discussion of this and subsequent studies is given in Chapter 6 below.

million (Table 10). The exercise shook up management thinking, since it had been often assumed that passenger losses were tolerable while freight charges were high enough to meet all railway joint costs. This situation no longer obtained.

The second study was referred to very briefly in the Commission's Annual Report for 1954. This was the Passenger Train Census of October 1952, which was initiated after an earlier study of loaded passenger-train-mileage in 1951 had produced the hypothesis that all passenger services other than express and suburban trains were failing to cover direct costs. In the week ending 11 October the Railway Executive's regions undertook a survey of train loadings and, with the help of the traffic-costing service estimated revenue and movement costs* for fast, semi-fast, stopping and suburban trains. The results were produced in the course of 1953. Two features clearly emerged. The first was the relatively low loading of the trains. Many services were running with only a handful of passengers per train, and over the system as a whole only a third of the seating capacity was occupied. For some types of train loading fell below 20 per cent.[49] The second was the widespread nature of cross-subsidisation. As shown in Table 11, revenue from fast trains exceeded movement costs by some £448,000 in the Census week, equivalent to £23.3 million a year, but the 'losses' on stopping services amounted to about £341,000, or £17.8 million a year. These services failed by a larger margin to meet their direct costs in all regions except the Southern, where heavy steam-train losses were offset by profitable electric services. Suburban services were also shown to be losing money in three of the five reporting regions. Finally, the

*Here defined as the provision, maintenance and stabling of locomotives and carriages, wages of trainmen and fuel at mid-1952 costs.

Table 11. *Passenger-train operating margins and operating ratios, 1952*

Train type	Region London Midland (£)	Eastern (£)	North Eastern (£)	Scottish (£)	Southern (£)	Western (£)	Total (£)
Fast	188,600 (34)	89,127 (26)	22,690 (28)	26,348 (28)	37,869 (28)	83,204 (20)	447,838 (29)
Semi-fast	64,600 (52)	23,982 (61)	10,967 (73)	14,894 (69)	82,755 (38)	75,298 (37)	272,406 (49)
Stopping	−120,000 (206)	−51,307 (204)	−30,417 (231)	−50,349 (215)	−9,997 (107)[a]	−79,309 (184)	−341,379 (172)
Suburban	−3,200 (129)	25,063 (78)	—	−8,850 (250)	115,138 (48)[b]	−9,218 (146)	118,933 (68)
All	130,000 (75)	86,865 (75)	3,240 (97)[c]	−17,957 (113)	225,765 (60)	69,975 (79)	497,888 (75)

[a] Steam stopping −£52,002 (170), electric stopping + £42,005 (47)
[b] Electric Services only
[c] Weekday results: −£1,003 (101)

Source: Census data by region for week ending 11 October 1952, in B.T.C. Passenger Statistics, AN82/81, P.R.O. The operating ratio, shown in brackets, is here defined as estimated movement costs per train-type divided by estimated revenue × 100. *Note:* some of the figures were amended in Tait's report to the B.T.C. Finance Committee in March 1954, viz:

All:		Total:	
London Midland	£143,190 (76)	Fast	£445,421 (29)
Eastern	£ 84,852 (75)	Semi-fast	£271,730 (52)
North Eastern	£ 3,238 (97)	Stopping	−£331,155 (174)
Southern	£232,808 (58)	Suburban	£130,110 (68)
		All	£516,106 (75)

B.T.C. Finance Committee Minutes, 12 May 1954, B.R.B.

Census revealed that the Scottish Region was failing to cover its overall movement costs by about £18,000 a week (£934,000 a year), while the North Eastern was only just managing to do so – indeed, on weekdays it was showing a small deficit.

The B.T.C.'s concern about the railways' stopping services was evident as soon as the first results were made available. Ironically, it was the Western Region, whose C.R.O., Keith Grand, had made no secret of his opposition to the Census (see above, p. 65), that was first to process its results, in June 1953. Wilson, in an anxious memorandum to the Commission of 8 July, pointed out that the Western's revenue from stopping services not only barely covered half of the movement costs, but when other costs – track and terminals – were taken into account, failed to meet total costs by £11.7 million a year. Even though the estimate was admitted to be speculative, the Western was shown to be making, on this basis, an overall loss of £7.1 million on its passenger services.[50] Here, then, fully ten years before Dr Richard Beeching's report, *The Reshaping of British Railways,* which was to emphasise the unprofitability of such trains, it had been clearly recognised that stopping services were a substantial drain on profitability and that passenger services as a whole were in deficit.[51]

But a big gap lay between recognition of the railways' problems and the introduction of positive steps to remedy them. Two possible solutions – a draconian axeing of unprofitable services, or the adoption of discriminatory pricing on the basis of cost – were discouraged, if not positively ruled out, by the machinery of the Transport Act and the railways' continuing duties as a common (i.e. public) carrier. The latter included the obligation to accept all reasonable traffic offered, to refrain from discrimination between customers under similar circumstances and to publish charges. They were contained in statutes dating back to the mid-nineteenth century which the Transport Act had not repealed. There was also a long tradition of public resistance to the termination of any facility, whether train, station or complete line. In these circumstances, it would have been surprising had the Commission's agent, the Railway Executive, exhibited anything other than conservative attitudes to its obligations as a public carrier, inherited from the days when the railways enjoyed a virtual monopoly of inland transport. In 1948 such attitudes permeated the industry, from Missenden at the top to the passenger and goods superintendents in the regions. It was generally accepted that the aim of pricing was to maximise revenue with the hope of covering (or exceeding) system costs. A retrospective internal study of railway fares policy admitted that the success of pricing strategies was judged by the amount of gross revenue gained, 'without much regard to the costs of the individual services provided'. Freight charges were founded on an antiquated and exceedingly complex classification of commodities by value and on long-cherished notions of 'what the traffic could bear'. In such a strategy retention of the maximum possible traffic level was a major consideration, irrespective of the cost of particular services. Indeed, railway managers customarily asserted that it was difficult, if not impossible, to determine the costs of particular consignments or individual traffics with any accuracy, and that therefore pricing on a cost basis was a futile objective.[52]

Nevertheless, railway managers need not have been so tightly bound by the constraints of their legislative environment. In the 1920s and 1930s, when most senior executives of the post-1947 period began their careers, the railway companies probably interpreted their obligations more widely than was strictly necessary. As Milne and Laing have pointed out, 'the reasonable facilities clause did not command branch lines to be kept open at a dead loss, yet there was no vigorous policy of closure and concentration upon the development of remunerative traffics.'[53] On nationalisation the Railway Executive's commercial responsibilities were exercised by men whose minds were by no means commercially imaginative. Missenden was essentially a 'dyed-in-the-wool' railwayman, risen from the ranks, whose long training in the Southern Railway's traffic department had fully accustomed him to the view that the best way to maximise net revenue was to maximise gross revenue. And although he was in private more flexible in his attitude to pricing than was suggested by his unfortunate public statement on rates and profitability in February 1948, it is evident that he made little attempt to intervene personally in the realm of pricing. This was left to the responsible functional member, David Blee. His role was, therefore, crucial. But, as already indicated (above, pp. 37–8), he was a late and inferior substitute for Frank Pope as the Executive's commercial member. Young and relatively inexperienced at this time, Blee gave everyone the impression of being a fussy and vain lightweight, a view which was strengthened by his disappointing contribution as General Manager of the London Midland Region from 1956 to 1961. His tendency to become bogged down in matters of detail is remarkably demonstrated by his anxiety to record and index his telephone conversations and by his equal concern to see that these records were then preserved for posterity.[54] The changes in personnel in 1951, with Elliot replacing Missenden and the appointment of Frank Pope as a member of the Commission and Vice-Chairman of its Charges Committee, did bring some fresh ideas to the fore. Pope had enjoyed a fair measure of success in dovetailing road and rail services in N. Ireland, where he had been Chairman of the Ulster Transport Authority, and Hurcomb clearly hoped he would apply this experience to the B.T.C.'s problems. But any initiatives were soon dispelled by the announcement of Conservative intentions in relation to road haulage and the plan to wind up the Railway Executive.[55]

Blee's surviving reports and memoranda thus remain the most instructive guide to Executive policy on rates and fares. In general, they demonstrate uncertainty. This is scarcely surprising in view of both Blee's personality and the often contradictory signals he was given by the Commission. For example, in his reports on passenger charges of July 1949 and December 1950 he distinguished between the formulation of an appropriate policy for the railways taken in isolation, and a strategy compatible with the Commission's obligation to integrate inland transport. Unfortunately, as the Annual Report for 1951 illustrates, the B.T.C. was not at all clear about its own objectives. On the one hand it wanted to make the Railway Executive aware of the costs of its services and require it to price accordingly; but on the other hand it continued to stress the railways' public service responsibilities. What was Blee supposed to make of this B.T.C. statement: 'There is no question of withdrawing from customers the services they require and for which they are prepared to pay a reasonable price. . . All the Commission ask is that the customer shall pay the real cost of the service he selects'?[56]

Such doubts and contradictions encouraged conflict between the Executive and the Commission as to the most appropriate pricing strategy. In the passenger business, Blee's emphasis was generally upon the retention of traffic together with a close monitoring of the competition from public road transport. The Executive believed that ordinary fares had reached their competitive ceiling after the increase of October 1947. So its response to falling traffic levels after 1947 was, first, to reintroduce a series of cheap fares in force before the war; and, second, to argue for a substantial reduction in the ordinary fare, from 2.44d. to a minimum of 1.25d. a mile. Wood was prepared to support the Executive; Hurcomb and Rusholme were in favour of raising fares in response to rising costs. Not surprisingly, several clashes ensued before a passenger charges scheme was finally agreed.[57] In all this, the Executive's attitude was influenced by Blee's view that lower rail fares were necessary to promote the aim of integration. Such a policy became harder and harder to justify in the face of rising costs and the deteriorating financial position of the Commission. The Executive's eventual concession that there was a need to raise fares to meet rising costs led to the passenger charges schemes of 1951 and 1953 which attempted to increase the cheaper fares, including the popular monthly return, and remove several low-fare anomalies in national pricing policy. But while the Transport Tribunal, the C.T.C.C., the government and the press debated the issue, railway managers continued to express their concern at the competitive implications of existing fare levels. The railways' share of the market was particularly vulnerable over shorter distances (up to 20 miles), but even over longer distances there was increasing evidence of a loss of business to road transport. For instance, in

October 1950 Phillips, the Executive's Chief Commercial Officer, countered the Commission's allegation that the introduction of cheap tickets had merely diverted business from the monthly returns by producing data showing that the loss of revenue from such tickets had come primarily in the long-distance market (over 50 miles), where few cheap tickets were available.[58] In February 1952, Blee asked a working party of passenger assistants to report to the Executive's Commercial Committee on the impact of long-distance road competition. The report, which was produced in August, revealed not only that bus traffic was growing – Scottish Omnibuses' London–Edinburgh business had doubled, 1947–51 – but that on several routes bus fares were substantially lower. The London–Norwich third-class rail fare, for example, was being undercut by 29 per cent on the ordinary single and 50 per cent on the day return. And when Blee put it to the Commercial Committee in the following November that fares should be raised again to meet rising costs the commercial superintendents expressed grave doubts about prospective yields, the consensus being that 'passenger fares were at present very near the limit which traffic would bear'.[59]

In the freight business, a great deal of the Executive's time was taken up with the framing of principles to be adopted in the freight charges scheme. Much of this work was wasted. Initially, it had been intended that the scheme would embrace road, rail and canal transport, and it was a considerable annoyance to Blee and his officers when early in 1951 the Commission decided that road transport should be excluded.[60] Subsequently, of course, the election of a Conservative Government, the denationalisation of road haulage and the reorganisation of nationalised transport under the Transport Act of 1953 served to delay submission of a more limited scheme until 1955 (see below, p. 184). Meanwhile, however, the very attempt to produce a unified scheme for the three modes had generated much heat among the Executives. In 1949 and 1950 there had been conflict between Blee, A. Henderson (Road Haulage) and Sir Reginald Hill (Docks and Inland Waterways) over a number of issues of principle, not least of which was the suggestion that there should be parity of charging over distances of 40-200 miles. A resolution of such difficulties was far from certain when the idea of a unified scheme was abandoned in 1951.[61]

While work on the freight charges scheme proceeded slowly, the Executive's general response to charges under Section 82 of the 1947 Act was much more enthusiastic than it had been in relation to passenger fares. The upward adjustment of rates in 1950, 1951 (twice) and 1952 together amounted to an increase of 48 per cent, and the average charge per ton-mile rose from 2.00d. (0.8p) in 1948 to 2.77d. (1.15p) in 1953, an increase of 39 per cent. Traffic levels were maintained, so the Executive expressed little anxiety about the higher charges.[62] Not that there were no disputes about freight pricing. Blee was frequently involved in arguments with the Commission about the advisability of introducing differential increases in rates. Hurcomb was firmly of the opinion that the railways' 'exceptional' (i.e. below standard) rates should be raised, and he also encouraged Blee to consider the possibility of raising the charges for the low-rated but profitable heavy freight traffics – coal, other minerals, iron and steel – where demand was relatively inelastic.[63] Blee's dual response was to emphasise both the danger of losing business and the railways' responsibility to the heavy industries. In this context, the report of an ad hoc committee of commercial and accountants' assistants, appointed by Blee in 1949 to examine rate modifications, is very revealing. The committee argued that while it was reasonable to assume that a 50 per cent increase in the rates for coal and heavy minerals would yield £23.5 million in additional revenue, there were 'serious objections to a selective alteration to rail charges of this character'. The 'serious objections' were very much those of managers long accustomed to working under public regulation. They included '*a possible* loss of business' (my italics), an anxiety about the effects on the industries concerned and fears about the likely reception of such rates by the Transport Tribunal.[64]

All too often the Executive's response to its pricing problems was over-cautious. Blee's report on passenger charges of December 1950 is a good example, with its tame comments about costs, loss-making services and discriminatory pricing: 'charges attributable to passenger traffic have not yet been determined. . . It is doubtful whether profitable and unprofitable services can yet be adequately defined. . . the process of curtailing unremunerative services can only be a gradual one. . . [selective fares] would not appear equitable to the public.' To be fair, Blee and the Executive were very much influenced by the requirement to work towards integration. This certainly influenced Blee's view that rail passenger fares should fall in order to achieve parity with bus fares, despite the risks of losing revenue.[65] Yet integration remained an elusive goal. Though some progress was made with the co-ordination of bus and rail services, for example in Devon and North Wales, inter-Executive rivalry persisted and the integration concept was frequently subverted at grass-roots level. George Cardwell and Stanley Kennedy of the Road Passenger Executive were particularly incensed by the railways' introduction of cheap fares which under-cut bus fares in 1949–50.[66]

The integration of the Commission's freight services was also limited. By January 1951 'smalls' traffic (small parcels) collected by the Road Haulage Executive was being conveyed by rail in containers over the London–Manchester and London–Glasgow trunk routes; and in the same month an experimental common commercial service was introduced in

East Anglia, under an Area Freight Superintendent responsible to both the Railway and Road Haulage Executives. The results were disappointing. It was clear that apart from the difficulty of securing co-operation between the Executives the attitude of the trade unions to any rationalisation of service was cool. Attempts to combine the collection and delivery services of the two Executives met with stiff opposition from the unions – and especially Arthur Deakin of the T.G.W.U. and Jim Figgins of the N.U.R. – before the government's White Paper outlined its plans for nationalised road haulage in May 1952. In any case, given the fact that the B.T.C.'s regional organisation did not combine road and rail – surely a *sine qua non* for any real progress in such integration – the efforts of 1949–52 may be seen as a vain pursuit of an impossible task.[67]

The Executive's activities in what may be termed the broad area of 'marketing' were also cautious. There was some investigation of customers' needs, the competitive environment and traffic trends. In 1950, for example, the Executive's commercial investigation bureau produced a report on the impact of 'C' licence vehicle growth on the railways' freight traffic, and by 1953 the commercial superintendents had produced a number of studies of specific initiatives in the passenger field, including tourist and family tickets and 'Starlight Specials', cheap fares from London to Scotland. There is evidence that managers were aware of the strengthening position of road transport, but they produced very few concrete proposals in response. One element of the problem, particularly noticeable in freight, was the separation of the rate-making function from that concerned with 'market analysis'.[68]

Perhaps there should be some retrospective sympathy for the Executive's historical position. It is all too easy to suggest that the railways should have moved quickly to adopt a pricing system based on costs and ruthlessly weeded out their unremunerative traffics.[69] Given its preoccupation with organisational problems and with adjusting to nationalisation, the Executive had little time, let alone inclination, to devote to any dramatic changes in commercial policy. And although early financial results were disturbing, particularly in 1949, and costing studies pointed to the need to improve pricing, traffic levels were considered to be satisfactory. Moreover, diverse directions from the government and the Commission, both formal and informal, were often difficult to reconcile when not contradictory, and there were sound reasons for doubting the legality of certain discriminatory strategies. But even historical sympathy cannot wholly absolve the Executive from the charge of too frequently exhibiting, in pricing policy as in other matters, a complacent attitude to the future. If it was optimistic of the ad hoc committee of assistants to suggest in 1949 that integration 'should result in the long-term in *substan-*

tial economies in costs' (my italics), it was stretching credulity to conclude that 'there was some justification for the assumption that within a period of ten years the present volume of traffics at the existing level of charges would be sufficient to cover expenditure and give an adequate net revenue'.[70]

V

The Executive's response to the question of closing unremunerative services has also been criticised for exhibiting undue complacency. Certainly, the Executive ought quickly to have been aware of large areas of unprofitability. Even before the revelations of the Passenger Train Census of 1952, serious weaknesses were emerging at a regional level. The problems of the Scottish Region were particularly severe: net receipts (i.e. gross revenue less working costs for rail services)* failed to materialise in every year except 1948, and the shortfall in 1953 was £2.4 million. Nor was this all. In 1949, both the London Midland and Western Regions experienced working losses, amounting to £4.0 and £1.6 million respectively.[71] Wilson, as B.T.C. Comptroller, became increasingly concerned about the position, and he wasted no opportunity to present adverse findings to Hurcomb and his colleagues. In March 1953, for example, some months before the Census data had been processed, he circulated the results of a survey of Glasgow's southern suburban passenger services. These indicated a loss of £220,000 a year, and a failure to cover even train-working costs – the shortfall here was £95,000. The situation was explained by light loadings – some trains were being run with only 3 per cent of the seats filled – and the poor utilisation of staff and equipment. Wilson concluded that 'the more we look at these old-fashioned steam-operated suburban services, the more we begin to understand what happens to the profits of those railway services which are really economic'.[72]

On branch-line operations Hurcomb and Wilson pressed the Executive on several occasions to take up the matter of closures with more urgency. The Executive did offer a response. In March 1949 it agreed to establish an ad hoc committee of chief officers, with Arthur Pearson and J. L. Harrington as Joint Chairmen, in order to investigate all branch lines whose earning capacity was in question. Between July 1949 and June 1953 the committee dealt with about 200 cases, recommending the complete closure of over 500 route-miles and the withdrawal of a further 88 passenger services. Estimated net annual savings amounted to about

---

*Including collection and delivery, net receipts from commercial advertising and letting of properties in operational use, but excluding shipping.

£890,000. The Commission's official statistics show that over the whole 1948–53 period 253 miles were closed to passenger and freight traffic, 1,167 miles to passenger traffic only and 359 miles to freight traffic only; passenger and freight facilities were withdrawn from 62 stations, passenger facilities only from 225 and freight facilities only from 84. The total savings were put at £1,159,000 per annum.[73]

These closures were little more than a drop in the ocean. The mileage of track open for traffic was reduced by a mere 1 per cent – from 52,190 miles in 1948 to 51,608 miles in 1953 – and the route-mileage fell from 19,598 to 19,222 miles, a reduction of only 1.9 per cent. Many of the closures put before the ad hoc committee of the Executive were so obviously justified that one can only wonder why action had not been taken before nationalisation. For example, of the 205 proposals for which financial information survives 42 involved no loss of revenue at all, and a further 11 meant a sacrifice of rental income (there was no railway traffic) amounting in total to only £292. Closure schemes included such gems as the London Midland Region's Swannington Incline, which was worked by stationary engine (installed in 1833) until February 1948, and the Western's Corris branch (Aberllefeni–Ratgoed section), worked by horse and gravitation until 1952.[74] The committee adopted an essentially conservative stance, and this was made clear in its terms of reference. Branch-line policy, it declared, 'should not be approached solely from the negative point of view of reducing expenditure. The main object was to increase or maintain net revenue, and this could not be considered without regard to the wider aspects now opened up by transport integration.' In this latter context, the committee gave its full support to the view that the termination of passenger services should be advocated only where the Commission was able to offer alternative bus services through the Road Passenger Executive. It also demonstrated an enthusiasm for other ways of dealing with the branch-line problem, including the substitution of light-weight diesel trains for steam operation, and the introduction of cheap fares, which proved temporarily successful in increasing revenue on the Sunderland–Hetton line.[75] The existence of such alternatives clearly helped to delay any major action to weed out patent loss-making areas.

Of course, public enthusiasm for its railway, however unprofitable, was an important factor to be considered, particularly since consumers were supported by an extensive appeal machinery – the C.T.C.C. and the area T.U.C.C.s. Inhibited by this the Executive maintained a staunch policy of avoiding any sudden contraction in its network, despite the inconsistencies it sometimes produced. Eyebrows must have been raised when, after Missenden had told Hurcomb, at a joint meeting in September 1950, that it would be difficult to find any further lines to close on the Southern and

Western systems, these regions presented over 40 closure proposals in the next three years.[76]

If the Executive's policy in relation to pricing and closures was thus more than a little cautious, it showed more initiative in encouraging improvements in productivity, and particularly in labour productivity. Estimates of output per head indicate an increase of 6.3 per cent from 1948 to 1953. This may seem modest in comparison with the results achieved under Richard Beeching in the first half of the 1960s, but it was obtained in a period when the substitution of capital for labour was effectively blocked by investment restrictions. Regional estimates bear this out. The Eastern Region, which was a major beneficiary of what little investment occurred, produced an improvement of no less than 41 per cent, which contrasts with the 3–7 per cent achieved by the L.M.R., Western and Southern.[77] Reduction in staffing levels accounted for much of the increase in output per head: there was an overall cut of 7 per cent on British Railways from 1948 to 1953. Nevertheless, there is evidence that the Executive might have been more successful in promoting more positive policies had the general economic climate been more favourable. In January 1951, for example, a staff incentive scheme to increase traffic was introduced, only to be abandoned shortly afterwards in the wake of reported coal shortages. Certainly there were broad improvements in operating efficiency. Particular attention was given to the reduction of coal consumption and more efficient freight handling, and the Executive was able to announce record levels in certain operating indices. Net ton-miles of traffic per total freight engine hour, reckoned to be the most comprehensive reflection of efficiency, increased steadily from 547 miles in 1948 to a record 619 miles in 1953, an increase of 13 per cent. Average wagon loads also exhibited a steady rise from 6.54 tons in 1948 to 7.14 tons in 1953, an improvement of 9 per cent. The Executive claimed that by 1952 its programme of unification had produced savings of £16 million a year. Although the scope for further improvement was massive, the Executive did secure some advances in operating efficiency during the period of investment restrictions.[78] An estimate of 'total factor productivity', given in Appendix C below, indicates a very modest improvement of 2.1 per cent between 1948 and 1953, an annual rate of 0.4 per cent.

VI

For a business in which labour costs made up over 60 per cent of total costs, it is obvious that labour relations were a critical area of managerial concern. At first sight the difficulties did not seem to be overwhelming. The railways were traditionally an industry with a disciplined workforce, long accustomed to working to a complex set of rules and regulations. And although militancy sometimes found its expression in sporadic local disputes, the industry's strike record was a comparatively good one. The three national strikes of the first half of the twentieth century – in 1911, 1919 and 1926 – had been a reflection of general economic problems affecting British labour as a whole. After the First World War membership became concentrated in three unions: the N.U.R., founded in 1913, which represented most of the 'conciliation grades' (see above, p. 99) in operating and maintenance; A.S.L.E.F., a craft union founded in 1879 for locomotive men, who were still regarded as something of an elite corps in the railway service; and the Railways Clerks' Association (R.C.A.), a white-collar union founded in 1897 which in 1952 changed its name to the Transport Salaried Staffs' Association.[79] Before nationalisation unilateral action was rare; and a relatively sophisticated negotiating machinery was developed in the inter-war years to cover the three unions as a group. By 1935 this had crystallised into a five-stage system, with local departmental committees; sectional councils, for each main-line railway company; direct negotiations between the companies and the unions on pay and conditions through the Railway Staff Conference; and, failing agreement, reference to first the Railway Staff National Council; and finally, the Railway Staff National Tribunal, an arbitration body comprising one member nominated by the railway companies, one by the three unions and an 'independent' member agreed to by both sides. Negotiations with the railway workshop staff were handled separately through a Railway Shopmen's National Council, established in 1927.[80]

The cohesive qualities of this framework of negotiation were less impressive than the elaborate structure might suggest. And after the Second World War the stability of industrial relations which had characterised the railways was threatened in various ways. The sacrifices made by railwaymen during war-time operations – including the relaxation of restrictive practices, the acceptance of longer hours and the deterioration of working conditions arising from the neglect of maintenance – prompted a ground-swell of demands for an improvement in post-war working conditions. This was particularly evident among the lower-paid grades, who were becoming dissatisfied with the level of remuneration offered for working what were increasingly regarded as 'unsocial' hours. The general mood was demonstrated by the unions' 'National Programme' of March 1945, which brought together a number of demands expressed many times over the previous 30 years. The most important were: a 40-hour week, 12 days paid annual holiday, a pension scheme, the abolition of lodging turns (the rostering of train crews which necessitated lodging overnight in railway hostels) and double-time payment for Sunday working. Such aspirations were given greater impetus by the very process of nationalisation. It is quite clear that the rank and file railwayman, and many of his leaders too, cherished happy expectations of the benefits which would come with the taking of the main-line companies into public ownership. It was believed that not only would pay and conditions improve, but there would be job security together with the satisfaction of the unions' demands for participation in management or even 'workers' control'.[81]

The progress made in collective bargaining with the main-line companies during the period of government control, 1941–7, heightened those expectations. The unions won a number of important concessions; and during the war the wage rates of railwaymen more than kept pace with industrial rates, though the increase in earnings of the 'conciliation grades' did not quite match that enjoyed by industry as a whole. After the war, a series of further advances were obtained. In July 1945 came a 9 per cent increase in wage rates; time and three-quarters for Sunday work (instead of time and a half); and the doubling of paid holidays for 'conciliation grades' from 6 to 12 days (operative from 1 January 1946). In December 1946 there was a consolidation of war wages into peacetime wage rates; improved pay for hybrid grades (e.g. porter-guard); and a reduction in lodging turns. And in July 1947, a further 9 per cent increase in rates was secured, coupled with a reduction in the working week from 48 to 44 hours. The cumulative effect of all these changes was a doubling of average earnings in the period 1938–48, although in common with other industries, differentials for skilled grades were narrowed.[82] At the same time, however, doubts were being expressed about the extent to which such improvements could continue. This was certainly apparent in the response to the unions' claims of January 1947, which were only resolved by referring the matter to a Court of Inquiry established by G. A. Isaacs, the Minister of Labour, and chaired by the Cambridge economist, C. W. Guillebaud. During the negotiations, Barnes, the Minister of Transport, made much of the fact that the railway companies were failing to earn the net revenue guaranteed by the government. Future prospects under the 1947 Act – which the unions held to contain over-generous compensation terms and an unwise concession to 'C' licence lorry operators – were a major source of anxiety on the eve of nationalisation. The B.T.C. and the Railway Executive thus took charge at a time when the chances for the workforce of a gap opening between aspirations and achievement were high; and when the railways, after war-time restrictions and advances in other industries, were losing many of their attractions as a source of employment.[83]

The railways' negotiating machinery was retained by the Executive on nationalisation, and the Commission wisely recognised that no common machinery for railways, railway workshops, buses, road haulage, ships, docks and canals could be established. However, it soon busied itself with the task of creating common procedures for the development of staff welfare, training and education, and by December 1948 had established the British Transport Joint Consultative Council as a means of exchanging information between the Commission, the Executives and the five major transport unions: N.U.R., A.S.L.E.F., R.C.A., T.G.W.U. and the Confederation of Shipbuilding and Engineering Unions. The first meeting was held in January 1949; and both sides certainly believed that this new body represented a step in the right direction.[84] Other attempts to bring management and unions closer together were less successful. Morrison's enthusiasm for the concept of the public board led him on to the conclusion that union representation on the Commission and its Executives would suffice as an answer to the call for 'workers' control'. So John Benstead, the General Secretary of the N.U.R. since 1943, was appointed to the Commission, along with Lord Rusholme, the General Secretary of the Co-op. At Executive level, W. P. 'Bill' Allen, who had served as General Secretary of A.S.L.E.F. since 1938, was appointed to the Railway Executive; Harold Clay, the Assistant General Secretary of the T.G.W.U., joined the Road Transport Executive (from 1949 the Road Haulage Executive); and John Donovan, also from the T.G.W.U., was appointed to the Docks and Inland Waterways Executive. These joined John Cliff, another ex-T.G.W.U. official, who was already serving on the London Passenger Transport Board when it became the London Transport Executive under the terms of the Transport Act.

The attitude of the unions to this limited degree of representation on the new management boards was lukewarm, to say the least. As Sir Reginald Wilson has observed, 'they had expected something rather in the shape of syndicalism, and found themselves fobbed off with the Public Corporation concept'. There was evident hostility towards former general secretaries who obtained highly-paid employment in the new organisation. When, in 1951, the government attempted to persuade the unions to relax their pension rules to permit the freezing of pension rights, Figgins of the N.U.R. explained that although his Executive Committee had agreed to recommend that Benstead should remain a member of the union's pension scheme, the General Conference had refused to confirm the arrangement.[85] Coolness towards the trade unionist turned manager was particularly evident in the relations between Allen, who was given the task of representing the Railway Executive in wage negotiations, and J. G. Baty, his successor, and the other leading A.S.L.E.F. officials. The proceedings of the R.S.N.C. and the R.S.N.T. often proved harrowing for Allen; in the course of difficult negotiations in 1951 Elliot, the Executive's Chairman, was moved to intervene personally in order to relieve his colleague of further strain. The limited realisation of 'workers' control' also disappointed many rank and file unionists. Letters to the N.U.R's *Railway Review* were full of complaints about the failure of the men to be adequately represented on the management bodies of nationalised railways.[86]

Whether the hostility shown to Benstead, Allen and the others was deep-seated or not, another element of the incorporation of trade union leaders into the management was a general stiffening of union attitudes which undoubtedly influenced the course of collective bargaining in the early period of nationalisation. This was certainly true of the N.U.R., where Benstead's departure was followed by the election of Jim Figgins as General Secretary. Figgins, who was elected with the biggest majority since J. H. Thomas's election in 1916, was a Scotsman who had joined the railways as a junior ticket collector in 1907, at the age of 14. A militant left-winger who had supported the Railway Vigilance Movement in the 1930s, he took the union much further to the left. At A.S.L.E.F. Allen was replaced by J. G. Baty, from Newcastle. Baty had joined the industry as a cleaner in 1912, at the age of 16. Although more moderate than Figgins, he was no right-winger and had acquired a considerable reputation as a tough negotiator, especially at the time of a strike in Northern Ireland in 1933.[87]

One way for the Executive, which was regarded in the 1947 Act as the employer of its staff, to tackle the problem of the delays it faced in adjusting transport charges to meet increases in costs was to seek to limit those increases, either by moderating wage demands or by improving productivity. In that way there loomed immense difficulties. At an early stage the Executive resolved to make a concerted effort to raise productivity by improving the utilisation of its labour force. At the same time, however, it had to recognise that serious staff shortages existed in key areas of work, where the pay was low and the conditions sufficiently unattractive to encourage a drift into other jobs. By 1950 there were numerous vacancies in such grades as engine-cleaner, shunter, signalman, goods porter and permanent way labourer.[88] So the principal task for the Executive in its industrial relations strategy was to respond to the challenge of rising costs by restraining wage demands and reducing staffing levels, while attempting to create the conditions which would attract workers into grades where vacancies existed. Unfortunately, it proved impossible to reconcile these objectives.

Although the railway unions expressed full sympathy for the Executive's problems in the raising of charges to meet rising costs,[89] they were naturally less tolerant of the Executive's attempt to play the same game of delaying tactics with wage claims. They were also hostile to suggestions that staffing levels be reduced, a hostility which coloured their attitude to integration. The undercurrent of discontent at grass-roots level, which found expression in sporadic unofficial strikes and 'go-slows', also made such leaders as Figgins less eager to accept the Labour Government's policy of wage restraint. This had followed the publication of the White Paper *Personal Incomes, Costs and Prices* in February 1948, which sought to limit wage increases to cases where either higher productivity had been achieved or there was clear evidence of undermanning. The T.U.C. declared its support for the policy, which was given added impetus by the devaluation crisis of September 1949. The T.U.C. was again prepared to support the government, but this time with the proviso that inflation should be contained.* Trade union support fell away in the course of 1950, but the N.U.R. had been hostile from the start.[90] The situation was exacerbated by the government's continuation until 1951 of compulsory arbitration procedures under a war-time order (No. 1305 of 1940). For the railways this meant an acceptance that disputes would be settled by the R.S.N.T., whose decisions would be final and binding. Growing doubts about the impartiality of this body had induced Benstead of the N.U.R. to appeal directly to the Minister of Labour in 1947, an appeal which led to the establishment of a Court of Inquiry. The combination of an atmosphere of wage restraint, the continuation of a government order which virtually precluded strike action and grass-roots discontent did little to encourage the unions to show moderation in their negotiations with the Executive.

Although, as already indicated, wages kept pace with prices over the period 1948–53, for much of the time earnings tended to lag behind the rate of inflation both for all adult males, and those in the 'conciliation grades' (see Table 12). The difficulties surrounding labour relations in these circumstances were clearly demonstrated by two disputes: the first came with the N.U.R's wage claims of 1948–9, which were accompanied by unofficial strike action over lodging turns in 1949; the second involved the railway unions' claims of 1950 which were finally resolved, after protracted negotiations, by the settlement of February 1951. Both are worthy of further examination.

In 1948 and 1949 the N.U.R. pressed for a substantial wage increase, without having first consulted the other unions and in defiance of the government's policy of wage restraint, confirmed by the T.U.C. The episode did much to set the pattern for future industrial relations. The conflict began in August 1948 when the N.U.R. demanded that the Executive pay the remainder of the £1 increase claimed in 1947, i.e. a flat-

*The T.U.C. had agreed to post-devaluation restraint provided that the interim index of retail prices (1947 = 100) kept within the bounds 106 and 112. The figure for 1950 was 114.

Table 12. *Average weekly earnings of British Railways staff, and index of retail prices, 1948–53*

Year	Average earnings: adult males	Average Earnings: 'conciliation grades'	Index numbers 1948=100		Index of retail prices 1948=100
	(i)	(ii)	(i)	(ii)	
1948[a]	139s.1d. (£6.95)	134s.10d. (£6.74)	100.0	100.0	100.0
1949	140s.0d. (£7.00)	135s. 9d. (£6.79)	100.7	100.7	102.8
1950	141s.9d. (£7.09)	136s. 5d. (£6.82)	101.9	101.2	105.6
1951	158s.6d. (£7.93)	153s. 1d. (£7.65)	114.0	113.5	115.7
1952	168s.2d. (£8.41)	162s. 4d. (£8.12)	120.9	120.4	122.2
1953	178s.9d. (£8.94)	172s. 3d. (£8.61)	128.5	127.8	125.8
Growth rates (p.a.), 1948–53:			5.1%	5.0%	4.7%

[a] The 1948 wage census included data for the main-line companies, London Transport, Manchester Ship Canal, Railway Clearing House and miscellaneous railways not absorbed by the B.T.C. An adjustment was made to the census average of adult males to facilitate a rough comparison with subsequent years. The figure reported here assumes that the difference between 'all grades' and 'conciliation grades' in 1949 also obtained in 1948. 'Conciliation grades' earnings in 1948 were derived by removing the influence of London Transport data using a deflator based on the difference between the wage *rates* of R.E. and L.T. guards.

Source:

(i) Average weekly earnings: British Railways adult males, excluding officers (Census week, March or April), data for 'Principal Grades' in B.T.C., *R. & A. 1949–53*, Table VIII–10. Full census information, not available for all years, produces slightly lower average earnings for the 'conciliation grades', viz. 162s.1d. in 1952, 171s.11d. in 1953: B.T.C., *Transport Statistics* (1952–3).

(ii) Retail prices: interim index, all items, with 17 June 1947 weights, rebased on 1948. B. R. Mitchell and G. Jones, *Second Abstract of British Historical Statistics* (Cambridge: Cambridge University Press, 1971), p.191.

rate increase of 12s. 6d. (62½p) a week, plus additional pay for Saturday working after 12 noon. The claim was discussed by the R.S.C. in September and October, but Allen and the Executive took a firm line, and no agreement was reached. Figgins, like Benstead before him, was reluctant to take the dispute through the rest of the railways' negotiating machinery since Order 1305 was still in force, and just before Christmas he reported the impasse to Isaacs. The Minister, acting on the advice of Sir Robert Gould, his Chief Industrial Commissioner, refused to set up a Court of Inquiry and told the N.U.R. to proceed through the R.S.N.C. and the R.S.N.T. As Gould explained to Figgins on 6 January 1949, 'the root of the difficulty appeared to be that the N.U.R. was acting alone, and out of step with the other unions'.[91] Figgins had no alternative but to present the claim before the R.S.N.T. where, in March 1949, it was roundly rejected. Labour unrest was now evident in several areas. After further discussions with an anxious Ministry the N.U.R. agreed to present a revised claim for an increase of 10s. (50p) a week plus time-and-a-quarter for Saturday work. Following negotiations in May the Executive turned down this claim too, but after another intervention by Isaacs, Allen did offer the N.U.R. an increase of up to 3s. (15p) for the lower-paid grades. This offer, regarded by Figgins as derisory, was rejected by the N.U.R. and another deadlock was reached in June 1949.[92] By this time, the N.U.R.'s relations with the Executive had been soured by the unofficial disputes over new lodging turns (see below, pp. 128–9).

The N.U.R.'s folly in 'going it alone' was readily apparent by the summer of 1949. The other railway unions, anxious to prevent the claim from upsetting existing pay differentials, demanded to be heard and registered their opposition to it. The N.U.R. persisted with a tough stance, refusing to go before the R.S.N.T. and threatening a 'work-to-rule' from 4 July. This persuaded Isaacs to appoint a Board of Conciliation to determine the issue, but Ministry officials were alarmed by the idea, because they felt he was going beyond his brief. An unsigned minute commented that

it has been a cardinal principle of industrial relations over a long number of years, and accepted by all Ministers of Labour, that the Minister takes part in industrial negotiations in the last resort . . . it is particularly necessary that you should not make yourself available to Mr. Figgins whenever he wants to see you. So long as he can run to you whenever he likes there will be no settlement on the railways. Furthermore, the moderate trade unionists are still very angry with Mr. Figgins and are still very critical of the action you took to rescue him from the untenable position in which he had placed himself.[93]

Nothing came of the Board of Conciliation. Despite Figgins's pointed references to the rise in the cost of living since 1947 and the existence of staff shortages, Sir John Forster, the Conciliation Board's Chairman, was greatly influenced by the lack of unity among the unions. In September 1949 the Board, while offering some minor concessions, rejected the claim in all its essentials. The outcome was scarcely surprising, since Forster was also Chairman of the R.S.N.T., which had turned down the N.U.R.'s earlier claim. (Incidentally, he was also Chairman of the Industrial Court of the National Arbitration Tribunal). Thirteen months of negotiations had thus led nowhere.[94]

The absence of inter-union co-operation was a persistent theme. One aspect of it was the dissolution in July 1947 of the railway unions' National Joint Council, following the N.U.R.'s allegation that A.S.L.E.F. was poaching its members among the staff at the Manchester Ship

Canal.[95] When the N.U.R. made a further claim in December 1949, this time for a £5 minimum wage, it did consult with the other unions. Their response was lukewarm as they were supporting the T.U.C.'s policy of wage restraint, but at least the lack of outright opposition from A.S.L.E.F. and the R.C.A. encouraged a more positive outcome. Nevertheless, it was not until 15 August 1950 that the R.S.N.T. finally gave its blessing to the Executive's offer of an additional 3s. 6d. (17½p) on the basic weekly rate.[96] Unilateral union action continued to be common practice. In the autumn of the same year the Executive faced three separate wage claims, for increases of 7½ per cent from the R.C.A., 10 per cent from the N.U.R. and 15 per cent from A.S.L.E.F. And in October A.S.L.E.F., like the N.U.R. before it, tried unsuccessfully to persuade the Minister of Labour to resolve its own claim without reference to the industry's negotiating machinery.[97] The unions' failure to co-operate undoubtedly helped the Executive to avoid making a major pay award between February 1948 and February 1951.

An unofficial dispute over the Executive's introduction of new lodging turns for drivers, firemen and guards in 1949 further illuminated some perennial features of the railways' industrial relations. It provided additional evidence of discontent among the rank and file over both working conditions and the lack of progress in wage negotiations. When the Executive announced its plans to make more train crews lodge away from home in order to increase the productive portion of the eight-hour roster and secure faster train timings, it met with localised resistance, particularly from N.U.R. members working at the locomotive depots of Gateshead, Heaton (Newcastle), York and Grantham. The dispute began with a minor stoppage on Sunday, 15 May, but a week later 3,100 men from nine depots withdrew their labour, seriously disrupting services in the Eastern and North Eastern Regions. The Sunday strikes persisted until 12 June, when despite union exhortations for a return to work, 2,500 men, 86 per cent of those available for work, failed to report to 44 depots in the Eastern, North Eastern and Scottish Regions.[98] In spite of a settlement, which was reached after the Executive had promised to negotiate further, there was renewed action for a short period by Grantham and York crews in August.[99] The attitude of the men was understandable given that the Executive's policy contradicted its earlier actions which in 12 months had resulted in a 57 per cent reduction in enginemen's lodging. The Executive was also in conflict with the policy of the unions, which in their 1945 programme had demanded a total elimination of lodging. Moreover, many railway hostels were in a poor condition. The stoppages were symptomatic of what the R.C.A. called the 'widespread discontent and uneasiness that now exists among all sections of railway staffs', and which was reflected in numerous 'go-slows' between May and September 1949.[100]

The lodging turns dispute also revealed a real fear of redundancy. It was stimulated by the Executive's plans to improve productivity as well as by a general reluctance on the part of the unions to see pay awards linked to specific concessions on working practices. Figgins was incensed when Allen threatened to break off negotiations with the N.U.R. on its wage claim in June 1949, unless the unofficial strikes were ended; and the Executive believed that Figgins was condoning the unofficial action as a bargaining lever. Finally, the dispute provided a further insight into the diverse attitudes of the Minister of Labour and his civil servants. Isaacs often displayed a sympathetic attitude to the plight of the railwaymen but was warned by his officials not to side with the unions. Many civil servants were clearly hostile to Figgins, who was regarded as a dangerous extremist. In June 1949, for example, Gould warned Isaacs not to give in to the N.U.R. leader and, counselling firmness, suggested that 'only by doing this shall we avoid repeated troubles in the railways in future'.[101]

The wage negotiations of 1950–1 involved another bitterly fought contest. The unions, disappointed with the results of previous claims and suspecting that moves to improve productivity would lead to redundancies, faced an Executive which, after the poor results of 1949, was more anxious than ever to hold down labour costs and secure economies in operating. But with inflation persisting, the unions' case for some improvement in wages was justifiable. At the R.S.N.C. in November 1950, Allen, while rejecting the three unions' separate claims (which ranged from 7.5 to 15 per cent), was prepared to make an offer which amounted to about 5 per cent, or £6.75 million on the wage-bill. Whether this alone would have been acceptable to the unions is debatable, but Allen also demanded that the offer be conditional upon the acceptance of measures to reduce costs. These included abolition of the calling-up of trainmen for rostered turns of duty, an increase in the number of lodging turns and an extension of the eight-hour shift to nine hours in order to limit unproductive time. The hostility of Figgins and Baty to this attempt to tie a wage settlement to specific proposals to alter working practices was sufficient to produce a breakdown in the negotiations. A.S.L.E.F. representatives were particularly angry with the position adopted by their ex-colleague Allen, who had not only become less enthusiastic about the retention of A.S.L.E.F. wage differentials in the industry but was also well aware of the scope for improving the productivity of train crews. During the discussions Allen made frequent references to the prevalence of unproductive time in the eight-hour shift, citing a number of examples where the proportion of shift-time spent on the footplate was below 50 per cent. One is worth quoting. Referring to a Willesden–Northampton–Toton freight train, Allen observed:

The first man is on the engine from Willesden and is on responsible duty for 3 hours 6 minutes and travels home passenger. He is booked off duty in 6½ hours. The Northampton man takes over and he is on duty 1 hour 58 minutes and rides home passenger. The Toton man is on duty 1 hour 9 minutes. Three sets of men work the train.[102]

In December a joint union deputation met Isaacs but the Minister was unable to break the deadlock. The N.U.R., like A.S.L.E.F., was angered by the Executive's threat to withdraw its offer entirely unless there were firm guarantees about productivity. Figgins's leader in the *Railway Review* declared 'This is Dictatorship' and claimed that the dispute was a 'challenge to fundamental principles of Trade Unionism' and that the 'whole system of collective bargaining was at stake'. The union demanded that discussions on productivity be separated from the wage claim and dealt with by the existing negotiating machinery.[103] Isaacs, who was clearly worried by the prospect of what he himself called 'strike action by extremists',[104] decided to appoint another Court of Inquiry to resolve the dispute. The Chairman, as in 1947, was C. W. Guillebaud. This time, however, the strategy failed. After a wrangle over the terms of reference the unions were assured that the issue of productivity would be excluded. But when the report of the Court of Inquiry was published in February 1951 it made only marginal adjustments to the Executive's offer of 5 per cent and declared that the award was conditional upon the unions' acceptance of the Executive's productivity package. The court stated that 'after having subjected to a very careful examination the proposals of the R.E. relating to modifications in working arrangements which would make for the more efficient and economic utilisation of railway staff, we have come to the unanimous conclusion that there is an overwhelming case for their adoption'. The unions were left with no alternative but to reject the Court's recommendations, and their action sparked off a number of unofficial local stoppages, notably in Liverpool and Manchester.[105]

Meanwhile, in January 1951, Isaacs had been succeeded as Minister of Labour by Aneurin Bevan. During his brief, three-month stay Bevan proved to be much more willing to play a decisive role in the resolution of labour disputes. When, at a meeting with the railway unions in February, Figgins told him that the existence of unofficial action was serious enough to warrant his personal intervention, he responded by indicating firmly that the government was anxious to avoid a strike. 'Any rash decisions at this stage', he warned, 'would inevitably lead to difficulties which might have a serious effect on the National economy.'[106] Bevan then informed the unions that he had persuaded the Executive and its newly appointed Chairman, John Elliot, to re-open negotiations. Elliot was much more flexible than Missenden had been in the past, and his personal involvement in renewed negotiations in February did much to lower the temperature. But although the Executive raised its offer to about 6 per cent, it could not persuade the unions to settle. It was Bevan's intervention as 'honest broker' on 22 February which ultimately resolved the dispute. After discussions with the unions it was established that a 7.5 per cent offer would be acceptable to them. The linking of pay and productivity remained a sticking point, particularly for Baty and A.S.L.E.F., but Bevan, having told the unions that they must 'be helpful on the question of conditions and [that] there must be a tangible and concrete response from them to help the Railway Executive to remove certain hampering conditions of railway efficiency', urged them to think in terms of a joint declaration. At a Cabinet meeting on the same day it was recognised that 'a general railway strike would dislocate the whole economy of the country'. It was agreed that Barnes should inform the Commission of 'the serious view which the Government took of the likely consequences of a general railway stoppage'.[107] Certainly, the situation had deteriorated. A number of token strikes and 'go-slows' were planned or in progress. Later that day Bevan met Hurcomb, Benstead, Elliot and Allen and urged them to reconsider their offer 'in the national interest'. The following day the unions accepted a revised offer of 7.5 per cent, back-dated to 1 January. The pay package, which was estimated to cost £12 million in a full year, was not made conditional upon the acceptance of productivity arrangements, but in a joint declaration the unions acknowledged 'the imperative need of the fullest co-operation with the Railway Executive in the elimination of waste of man power, in increasing efficiency and improving productivity within the railway industry'. A special joint committee was to be established to examine the Executive's proposals.[108]

Both sides were left with cause for dissatisfaction. Among members of the Commission and Executive there was dismay that they had been required to increase a 'final' pay offer and had failed to persuade the unions to accept specific proposals to raise productivity. Hurcomb, having been told by both Bevan and Barnes that the government did not wish to be faced with a strike and wanted the dispute settled on the best available terms, felt he had no alternative but to instruct John Elliot to settle the claim, even though that meant surrender to the unions. Whether in reality the Commission and the Executive had the appetite for a serious strike remains doubtful. They must have been relieved to see the government, in

Table 13. *Average earnings (adult males), 1948 and 1953*

	1948		1953
Coal	170s. 4d.	Coal	244s. 6d.
Metal manufacture	156s.10d.	Metal manufacture	205s. 4d.
Vehicles	155s. 2d.	Vehicles	204s. 8d.
Engineering, shipbuilding		Engineering, shipbuilding	
and electrical goods	146s. 0d.	and electrical goods	196s. 4d.
Chemicals	137s. 9d.	Chemicals	186s. 1d.
RAILWAYS (conciliation)	134s.10d.	Building and contracting	185s.10d.
Clothing	132s.10d.	Mining and quarrying[a]	179s. 4d.
Transport[b]	131s. 1d.	Textiles	177s. 9d.
Building and contracting	130s. 7d.	Clothing	172s. 6d.
Mining and quarrying[a]	130s. 4d.	RAILWAYS (conciliation)	172s. 3d.
Gas, electricity and water	130s. 3d.	Gas, electricity and water	171s. 9d.
Textiles	129s. 1d.	Transport[b]	170s. 8d.

[a] Excludes coal.
[b] Excludes railways.
Source: A.A.S. (1954), Tables 131, 147, and for railways, B.T.C., *R. & A. 1948, 1949, 1953*.
1948 data: October (for railways an average of April 1948 and April 1949 is taken). 1953
data: March or April.

the shape of the Ministers of Labour and Transport, taking some responsibility for an award which added an extra £5 million to the £7 million award recommended by the Court of Inquiry. By 1951 the Executive was becoming more ambivalent about the desirability of holding down wage levels. Increasingly disturbed by reports of staff shortages and absenteeism among the low-paid grades, Elliot and Blee advocated more positive steps to combat these difficulties. This undoubtedly influenced the Executive's approach to subsequent union claims, which resulted in an 8 per cent increase in September 1951 (agreed in November), and a 7s. a week increase (about 7 per cent) in November 1952.[109] But whatever the attitude of the Executive in 1951, Bevan's intervention undoubtedly set a precedent for the resolution of future disputes.

The unions were also disappointed with the outcome of the 1950–1 negotiations. Although the pay award of February 1951 was an important step towards the recovery of the real value of railway pay, wages were still lagging behind the rate of inflation, and further action was necessary during the remainder of the year and in 1952 before full compensation for the rise in the cost of living was obtained. Furthermore, there remained a widespread belief in the unions that the government by limiting increases in railway charges were forcing railwaymen to subsidise other industries whose wage levels were beginning to outstrip theirs. As is shown in Table

13, average railway earnings of the 'conciliation grades', which in 1948 ranked sixth among the major industries, had fallen to tenth place by 1953.

The seeds of discord which were to influence industrial relations in the late 1950s and beyond had already been sown by 1953. Resentment on the part of the unions at the failure of wages to maintain their real value (until 1953) and keep pace with wages in comparable industries, disappointment within railway management at the failure to tie wage settlements to specific moves to increase productivity and the existence of Ministerial interference: all were clearly established. By the time that the Executive was abolished there was considerable dissatisfaction on both sides of the industry with the progress made on pay and productivity.

PART 2

The British Transport Commission, 1953–62

5

The new railway organisation

With the Transport Act of 1953 the Conservative Government intended to create a new, competitive era in British transport. All ideas of pursuing 'integration' under a public monopoly were now abandoned, and the Commission's duties were re-defined. Long-distance road haulage was to be denationalised and the railways freed from some of their restrictive statutory obligations. Customers would be able thereby to choose the mode which best suited their needs and transport managers would be encouraged to select only those traffics which would secure them a profit. Allocative efficiency was to be secured not by 'socialist' planners, but by the market. The intention, as expressed in the words of a Tory backbencher, was thus to 'hurl against the railways the competition of the road'; or, in the more restrained language of Milne and Laing, to replace regulated monopoly with 'a mixed system of active competition and partial monopoly'.[1] To this end the B.T.C.'s functions in respect of road passenger traffic and ports were to be curtailed and a greater latitude encouraged in the granting of goods vehicle licences, control of which was to be returned to the licensing authorities and traffic commissioners under the legislation of the early 1930s.

In the process of drafting the legislation Ministers had been far from unanimous about the most appropriate way of achieving these objectives. This was reflected in the Act's passage through parliament, where two separate presentations and the use of the guillotine had been required. There was, for example, a great deal of argument about the method of dealing with the enforced sale of the B.T.C.'s road haulage interests. In March 1952 Lord Woolton, Lord President and Chairman of a Cabinet committee on road and rail reorganisation, advocated *inter alia* the payment of compensation to the Commission to meet both the losses involved in selling off its assets and the losses arising from the subsequent transfers of traffic from rail to road. The money was to come either from a levy on road transport or by direct Exchequer subvention. At this stage the Cabinet was prepared to endorse such a strategy, which had the enthusiastic support of Lord Leathers, Secretary of State for the Co-ordination of Transport, Fuel and Power, and senior civil servants in the Ministry of Transport. The idea of compensating the Commission for traffic losses was seen as the core of the plan, a free enterprise solution to the problem of making the whole of transport self-supporting without provoking a sharp rise in rail charges. Churchill summarised the policy as follows:

It does not matter whether the nationalized railways show a deficit, though of course every possible economy should be used in their administration. What is important is that the public should have the best transport service on the roads which can only be furnished by private enterprise. It is necessary that the railways should be properly maintained. For this purpose the Road Transport [sic] should bear a levy and this it can do owing to the greater fertility of private enterprise.[2]

The government's White Paper on *Transport Policy*, published in May, thus included a reference to a goods vehicle levy which would be used to compensate the Commission.[3]

All this was before Maclay's battle with Churchill over the B.T.C.'s plan to raise London fares (see above, pp. 102–4), the replacement of Maclay as Minister of Transport by Lennox-Boyd in May and the mobilisation of road lobby opposition to the levy during the summer recess. Like a good many Ministers of Transport, Lennox-Boyd was a reluctant appointee. He claimed to have told Churchill he thought it 'a job for a rather unprincipled person'. Nevertheless, he quickly threw himself into the task of drafting a bill, and became the focus for opposition to the government's original intentions. By October, the idea of compensating the B.T.C. for the diversion of traffic to private road haulage had attracted considerable opposition, not only inside the Cabinet from Butler and Swinton but on the backbenches and in the press. It may also have been significant that the B.T.C., which was not consulted until Conservative policy had been formulated, indicated its serious misgivings about the introduction of the subsidy principle into railway finance.[4] Lennox-Boyd, taking up a suggestion by Leathers, declared in favour of relying merely upon the abolition of the 25-mile operating limit for private road hauliers (established by the 1947 Act), with no sale of B.T.C. assets and no levy. This plan, intended as a ploy to defeat the levy, was rejected because it did not enable the expropriated road hauliers to return to the industry. The Cabinet was split over the issue, but encouraged by Churchill, who had clearly changed his mind about the levy, it eventually decided to proceed on the basis of a sale of the Commission's assets, the removal of the 25-mile limit and the payment of a sum to cover only the losses arising from the sale of assets.[5]

The Transport Act, which received the Royal Assent on 6 May 1953, omitted all mention of compensating the Commission for any diversion of traffic from the railways which government policy might encourage. Instead, a relaxation of the statutory restrictions on railway pricing was offered up as compensation for the loss of road haulage and the abandonment of the 25-mile limit. This quid pro quo, as many commentators observed, was somewhat illusory. The government retained much of the existing machinery of control, and the remaining charges obligations still represented an 'appreciable burden'. It is difficult to see the change of government direction as more than a capitulation to road interests.[6]

At first sight there was much more agreement among the Conservatives, both inside and outside the Cabinet, about the plan to reorganise the railways. The new government's support for a competitive strategy was linked firmly to a faith in decentralised management. Although the B.T.C. was given 12 months from the passing of the Act, or longer at the Minister's discretion, to submit a new organisational scheme, the basic framework was determined by the politicians. The government was convinced that the Executive structure established by the Act of 1947, and the Railway Executive in particular, had led to an undesirable over-centralisation and should be abandoned. So the Railway Executive, and all the other Executives except London Transport, were abolished by Ministerial Order on 19 August 1953, with effect from 1 October, i.e. before the new scheme had been drawn up. The new solution was to create 'area authorities' (including one for Scotland) to whom operating responsibilities would be delegated. To promote efficiency within the new bodies, a measure of inter-area competitiveness would be encouraged by the publication of regional statistics of operating costs. These elements were mandatory under Clause 16 of the 1953 Act.

However, here too there were elements of doubt, notably about how far the B.T.C. should be placed under government control and how far decentralisation should go. During the drafting stages of the bill there was much argument over the Ministry of Transport's plan to extend Ministerial control, which raised general issues of principle affecting the government's relations with the nationalised industries. In the draft bill of 30 May 1952 the Minister's powers to issue Directions were to be strengthened by providing for intervention in the *public* as well as the national interest (as in the 1947 Act). This clause was dropped in the first bill of July, only to be replaced by one requiring the Chairman of the Commission to 'keep the Minister at all times adequately informed as to all matters connected with the Commission'. There was a lively debate in Whitehall about both clauses. On one side it was argued that without a control mechanism the B.T.C. would become more 'railway minded in its

"HEALTHY COMPETITION"

" THE IDEA IS, YOU FEED THE COW AND HE MILKS IT !"

3 and 4 Comments on the White Paper, 1952 and Transport Act, 1953: Low, *Daily Herald*, 9 May 1952; Vicky, *Daily Mirror*, 30 December 1954.

outlook', with no certainty that it would be 'more amenable or more sensitive to public demand and current Government policy'. Leathers maintained that 'it was not enough to select the best available people for a job of this importance . . . and then leave them alone for five years and hope for the best'.[7] On the other side, there was opposition, particularly from the Department of Economic Affairs and the Ministry of Fuel and Power, to the assertion of Ministerial control in the public interest, which would expose the Minister to pressure from every section of the travelling public. Furthermore, there was the very grave danger of encouraging political intervention. As Sir Donald Fergusson, Permanent-Secretary at Fuel and Power, explained:

with 700,000 miners and hundreds of thousands of railwaymen and electricity and gas employees and with every consumer a voter . . . under a Labour Government the proposed system could be used for promoting general socialism regardless of the efficient running of the particular industries . . . All experience shows that it is not possible to have efficient management of great industries under political democracies if they can be used as instruments for extraneous political purposes.

With Lennox-Boyd more ambivalent than Maclay had been about the idea of new powers, both of the offending clauses were dropped in the revised bill of November 1952 and in the Act itself.[8]

Enthusiasm for the clauses dealing with the composition of the B.T.C. and with railway reorganisation also seemed to wane as the legislation was drawn up. In the draft bill the B.T.C. was to be reconstituted by means of quite specific appointments. The Minister was to be empowered to appoint, *inter alia*, representatives of industry and commerce, agriculture and road haulage, after consultation with outside bodies. An earlier plan had even provided for the appointment of a government nominee, though this was quickly dropped after the practical difficulties had been pointed out. Opposition surfaced here too, and reference to particular types of appointment were watered down in the successive stages of drafting.[9] The provision for consultation was also removed. Furthermore, the government's faith in decentralisation began to waver. Although the government had intended to leave it to the Minister of Transport to decide whether the Commission (with the exception of the Chairman) should now become a part-time body, thereby implying that there might be a substantial devolution to the 'area authorities', they readily accepted, on the second reading, an opposition amendment which maintained the status quo. And some critics had already pointed out that the scope for the area authorities to exercise commercial discretion might well be restricted by the clause reserving to the Commission control over finance and pricing.[10]

Over 18 months were to elapse after the passing of the 1953 Act before the B.T.C.'s new railway organisation was introduced, on 1 January 1955.

This long and uncomfortable interval was very unfortunately timed. The railways had already experienced two years of uncertainty after the election of 1951. Then this interregnum was further extended just when the rigours of post-war austerity were fading away, and the promise of modernisation was in the offing. Railway management was thus left in a hiatus not of its own making, and the new era of direct control of the railways by the Commission began in an atmosphere of pronounced managerial gloom.[11]

During this transitional period there were several changes of personnel at the Commission. The most important was at the top. Lord Hurcomb, who reached the age of 70 in 1953, retired. His place as Chairman was taken by General Sir Brian Robertson, with effect from 15 September 1953. To some of the more jaundiced railway managers, all that had happened was that 'the old civil servant' had been replaced by the 'old soldier'. But it was not quite as simple as that. General Robertson, G.C.B., G.B.E., K.C.M.G., K.C.V.O., D.S.O., M.C., had had a distinguished army career stretching back to the First World War. His father had been a Field Marshal.* Despite this impressive military pedigree he was a comparatively youthful 57 on his appointment to the B.T.C., and his military career had been neither continuous nor conventional. Frustrated by the limited opportunities for promotion in the 1930s, he had resigned his post as major at the end of 1933 and emigrated to South Africa. There he acted as Managing Director of Dunlop's subsidiary company from 1935 until his call-up in 1939. During the war his great success in administration – as Chief Administrative Officer to the Eighth Army in the desert, in the equivalent post for General Alexander in Italy, and as Montgomery's deputy in Germany – led to high office in the early post-war years. After acting as Military Governor and Commander-in-Chief of British Forces in Germany, 1947–9, and subsequently as High Commissioner, he took command of Middle East Land Forces from 1950 to 1953. In these years he added diplomatic skills, particularly in his dealings with the Egyptian government, to his genius for administration. Although he failed to gain the coveted prize of Chief of General Staff, he was about to take up the post of Adjutant-General when Churchill, on Lennox-Boyd's recommendation, invited him to succeed Hurcomb. He thus came to the Commission with a considerable reputation as a military leader. He had specialised in administration and supply, but had taken on a more public role in Germany and Egypt with great success. He also had some experience, if rather fleeting, of business management.[12]

*Field Marshal Sir William Robertson, Bt., G.C.B., G.C.M.G., G.C.V.O. (1860–1933). Quartermaster-General, B.E.F., 1914; Chief of Imperial General Staff, 1915–18; C-in-C, British Army on the Rhine, 1919–20.

What can be said of Robertson's appointment? Early critics referred to his complete lack of knowledge of the railway industry and its problems: operational, technical and, above all, financial. Indeed, the government had taken the view that the chairman 'should not be a person with any previous substantial interest in the management or operation of railways'.[13] On the other hand, a lack of familiarity with the industry was not necessarily a handicap, as Dr Richard Beeching was to demonstrate later. Moreover, the armed services had been a fertile source of railway managers in the mid-nineteenth century, and 100 years later Generals Slim and Daril Watson had performed more than adequately at the Railway Executive. There were obvious parallels between the two activities. Managers had to control large and dispersed staffs, and there was a great emphasis on discipline, obedience and public service.[14] Nevertheless, the arrival of Robertson did little to create a warm relationship between the Chairman and his railway officers. Like Hurcomb before him, Robertson was a shy, austere man of integrity, not without humour, but difficult to know, and above all demanding loyalty and respect. And like Hurcomb he was determined to lead from the top, to command a civilian army providing a service. Indeed command of a labour force of over 850,000 had been one of the main elements attracting him to the post, described by Churchill as 'the most important viceroyalty in the gift of the government'. As he later revealed to Viscount Falmouth, in January 1957, 'when the late Prime Minister asked me to take on my present job, he specifically told me that I should give British Railways leadership'.[15]

Here, then, were the seeds of potential conflict, between the new Chairman and the government, and between the Chairman and his railway managers. Robertson soon made it clear that he had but scant regard for railway officers and claimed that it was his duty to inject 'backbone' into the B.T.C.'s organisation. He did not see his brief as being merely to preside over decentralised management bodies. Instead he was required to manage the railways, to be their 'chief executive', as he told the Select Committee on Nationalised Industries in 1960.[16] But the Transport Act of 1953, vague on details as it was, appeared to stipulate that the Commission should remain a policy unit, with day-to-day management devolved upon area authorities. It was to that end that the Executive structure had been dismantled; and even the surviving London Transport Executive had been re-appointed in October 1953 for a one-year term only (a procedure repeated in 1954), pending the report of a Committee of Inquiry led by Paul Chambers of I.C.I. The issue of centralisation versus decentralisation was far from settled. Not for the first time Churchill's views on transport matters seemed at odds with those of his colleagues. It must therefore have been disconcerting for Robertson to discover that the removal of the Railway Executive had left a large gap to fill at the Commission's headquarters if he was to manage the railway in the way in which both he and Churchill intended.[17]

The other changes at the B.T.C. were less controversial. The new government, while determined to introduce new blood, was also happy to allow a fair amount of continuity. Of the old guard Benstead, Rusholme and Pope remained, together with the part-timers Bolton, Ryan and Barker. At the same time, the Minister made prompt use of the 1953 Act, which had raised the maximum membership from nine to fifteen (of whom two were to have a special responsibility for Scottish affairs). On the demise of the Executives, three new members were appointed to the Commission, with effect from 1 October 1953: Sir Reginald Wilson, the Commission's Comptroller; John Train, the civil engineer and the only member of the Railway Executive to be so elevated; and, on a part-time basis, Sir Harry Methven, former Chairman of the Hotels Executive. These appointments were not unexpected. Wilson had begun to dominate the thinking of the Commission, particularly on the financial side. Train was a technical man who had managed to keep his nose clean during the bitter battles of the previous six years and Methven, an industrialist with considerable experience in the food and catering industries, was an obvious choice to manage the Commission's interests in these fields. In the following year, the Commission was strengthened further with the appointment of Alec Valentine, from the London Transport Executive, and a second Scottish part-timer, Lt-Col Donald Cameron of Lochiel, both from 1 September 1954. Valentine, who had a considerable commercial and operating experience in the capital, had been closely involved in the Commission's passenger charges schemes and was therefore an important addition. The selection of Cameron, however, appears to have been made merely to comply with the terms of the Act as to Scottish representation.[18] With these changes the Commission's membership was increased from 8 to 12, and the average age of the full-time members was reduced from 64 (before the retirement of Hurcomb and Wood) to 58. Of the dozen members, there were only three – Pope, Train and Valentine – who had prior experience of the railway industry (see Table 14).

II

An interim organisation had to be introduced in some haste in the autumn of 1953. As Robertson was unable to free himself of his army duties until early December, it was concocted largely by the Acting Chairman Benstead, assisted by Pope.[19] Some decisions were relatively straightforward. For example, it was a routine procedure to establish 'boards of manage-

Table 14. *The British Transport Commission, September 1954*

Name	Appointed	Age in 1954	Education	Previous post	Experience
Full-time members (salary: Chairman £8,500 (Pope £6,000, others £5,000))					
General Sir Brian Robertson, G.C.B., etc. (Chairman)	1953	58	Charterhouse; Royal Military Academy, Woolwich	C.-in-C. of British Middle East Land Forces	Army; Dunlop (S.A.)
Sir John Benstead, C.B.E. (Deputy-Chairman)	1947	57	King's School, Peterborough	General Secretary, N.U.R.	Trade unions
F. A. Pope, C.I.E.	1951	61	The Leys School, Cambridge	Chairman, Ulster Transport Authority	Railways
Lord Rusholme	1947	64	Local	General Secretary, Co-op. Union	Trade unions
J. C. L. Train, C.B.E., M.C.	1953	65	Dulwich; Hull Technical College; Glasgow Technical College	Member, R.E.	Railways
A. B. B. Valentine	1954	55	Highgate; Worcester College, Oxford	Member, L.T.E.	Transport
Sir Reginald Wilson	1953	49	St. Peter's, Panchgani; St Laurence, Ramsgate; London University	Comptroller, B.T.C.	Accountancy/civil service
Part-time members (salary: Sir Ian Bolton £1,000, others £500 (Methven's salary not drawn))					
H. P. Barker	1951	45	Oundle	—	Engineering
Sir Ian Bolton, D.L., O.B.E.	1947	65	Eton	—	Accountancy/Scotland
Lt-Col Donald Cameron of Lochiel, T.D.	1954	44	Harrow; Balliol College, Oxford	—	Army/Scotland
Sir Harry Methven, K.B.E.	1953	68	'Privately'	—	Hotels/catering
John Ryan, C.B.E., M.C.	1951	60	Wolverhampton Grammar School; Gonville and Caius College, Cambridge	—	Metals

ment' for British Road Services and Docks and Inland Waterways, in place of 'Executives'. But the Commission was required to take on the business of running the railways without a board of management, and here it had to create an effective committee structure and establish adequate links with railway regional officers. Jobs had also to be found for those former Railway Executive members and officers who were to be retained in the new organisation. Although decisions were to be of a temporary nature, action had to be swift. The Commission, having moved from its cramped H.Q. at 55, Broadway to the more spacious premises at 222, Marylebone Road on 1 October, divided railway responsibilities among the five-full time members. Within a fortnight five committees were established: Finance, under Wilson; Works and Equipment, chaired by Pope; Establishment and Staff, under Benstead; and Stores and Property, both chaired by Rusholme. Two more were added in January 1954: Hotels, under Methven, and Research and Development, quickly re-named Technical Development and Research, under Train (see Chart IV for the basic organisation).[20]

The B.T.C.'s declared aim with its interim organisation was to 'control major policy and general direction'. This required a major restructuring of its headquarters staff, and in order to fill obvious gaps on the railway side many former Executive staff were absorbed. As Chart IV shows, three ex-members of the Executive, Daril Watson, David Blee and W. P. Allen became chief officers, for General Services, Commercial Services and Establishment and Staff, respectively. Several former chief officers were appointed to similar posts with the Commission; and four engineers – Roland C. Bond (mechanical), S. B. Warder (electrical), John Ratter (civil) and J. H. Fraser (signal and telecommunications) – were transferred at chief officer level.[21] In the regions, the six former C.R.O.s – Watkins, Bird, Grand, Hopkins, Cameron and Short – looked upon the interim arrangements with some enthusiasm. From 1 October 1953 they were re-named Chief Regional Managers, and given authority over their departmental officers. It was at last agreed that all instructions from the Commission were to pass through their offices.[22]

However much this interim organisation pleased the former C.R.O.s, it was not introduced without friction, nor without some unfortunate repercussions in the longer run. Deposed members of the Railway Executive were naturally distressed by their treatment. Blee, for example, was resentful of Train's elevation and extracted a note of apology from his more successful colleague. He also made it clear to Hurcomb that he would have greatly preferred a regional manager's job to absorption in the Commission's staff. A wider group was critical of the premature retirement of Riddles and the 'demotion' of Elliot, who became Chairman of the

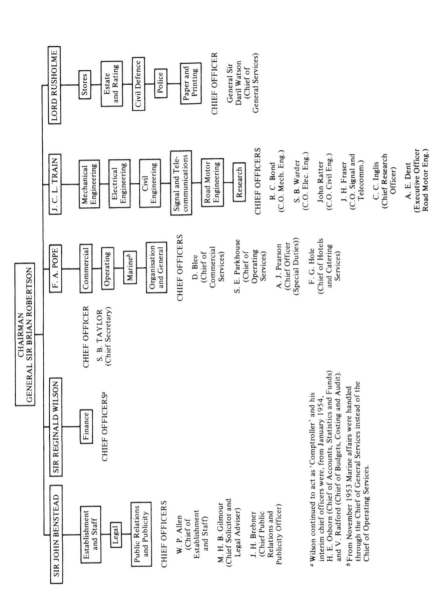

CHAIRMAN
GENERAL SIR BRIAN ROBERTSON

SIR JOHN BENSTEAD

- Establishment and Staff
  - Legal
- Public Relations and Publicity

CHIEF OFFICERS

W. P. Allen
(Chief of Establishment and Staff)

M. H. B. Gilmour
(Chief Solicitor and Legal Adviser)

J. H. Brebner
(Chief Public Relations and Publicity Officer)

SIR REGINALD WILSON

- Finance

CHIEF OFFICERS[a]

CHIEF OFFICER
S. B. TAYLOR
(Chief Secretary)

F. A. POPE

- Commercial
- Operating
- Marine[b]
- Organisation and General

CHIEF OFFICERS

D. Blee
(Chief of Commercial Services)

S. E. Parkhouse
(Chief of Operating Services)

A. J. Pearson
(Chief Officer (Special Duties))

F. G. Hole
(Chief of Hotels and Catering Services)

J. C. L. TRAIN

- Mechanical Engineering
- Electrical Engineering
- Civil Engineering
- Signal and Tele-communications
- Road Motor Engineering
- Research

CHIEF OFFICERS

R. C. Bond
(C.O. Mech. Eng.)

S. B. Warder
(C.O. Elec. Eng.)

John Ratter
(C.O. Civil Eng.)

J. H. Fraser
(C.O. Signal and Telecomm.)

C. C. Inglis
(Chief Research Officer)

A. E. Dent
(Executive Officer Road Motor Eng.)

LORD RUSHOLME

- Stores
- Estate and Rating
- Civil Defence
- Police
- Paper and Printing

CHIEF OFFICER

General Sir Daril Watson
(Chief of General Services)

[a] Wilson continued to act as 'Comptroller' and his interim chief officers were, from January 1954, H. E. Osborn (Chief of Accounts, Statistics and Funds) and V. Radford (Chief of Budgets, Costing and Audit).

[b] From November 1953 Marine affairs were handled through the Chief of General Services instead of the Chief of Operating Services.

Chart IV British Transport Commission 'interim organisation', October 1953

L.T.E. There was also some ill-feeling inside the Commission itself. Several officers who had expected to gain from the upheaval were discomforted by the usurpation of important posts by incoming officers from the Railway Executive. Blee complained to Pope: 'I and my former colleagues are not fully accepted as officers of the Commission, but as quasi-detached railway officers who must not be permitted to see anything that does not relate solely to railways'. The managerial atmosphere was scarcely harmonious.[23]

Far more important was the way in which the B.T.C. chose to take on responsibility for the railways. An astute critic of the interim organisation was Sir Felix Pole, who had been the successful General Manager of the Great Western Railway in the 1920s. In an anonymous leader in the *Reading Standard* on 2 October 1953, which found its way into the files of the Ministry of Transport, he argued that by absorbing Railway Executive personnel the Commission was not decentralising to the regions at all. There was a fair amount of truth in this view. The list of former Executive functions which the B.T.C. decided to reserve to itself was a long one: labour relations 'of a major character'; the general level of charges; broad financial control; commercial policy; the design and manufacture of locomotives and rolling stock; 'the policies and principles to be adopted in railway operation'; 'the inter-regional distribution of wagons'. The regional managers might well have wondered what was left.[24] Moreover, despite all the talk, the autonomy of the Chief Regional Managers was more apparent than real. Their ability to spend on works and equipment without seeking higher authority was restricted to sums below £5,000, just as it had been in the last two years of the Executive. And their freedom to appoint staff was extended only to posts with annual salaries of up to £1,750, little more than the £1,500 limit granted by the Executive in February 1952.[25] In short, the interim period of control, far from helping to introduce decentralisation, established practices which left the initiative firmly at the centre, thus influencing the way in which the new organisation of 1955 was devised. This can be seen in the emergence of Pope and Train as the members responsible for the main areas of railway management. Strengthened by the appointment of officers from the Railway Executive, they fell into the ways of the Executive. They managed the railways, if not functionally, then at least directly through contacts with the Chief Regional Managers. Indeed, the Commission's minutes during the interim period showed all the signs of a body taking a close interest in the details of routine railway administration. On 13 October 1953, for example, the members of the B.T.C. resolved to continue receiving weekly statements of loaded passenger-train-miles; two days later they agreed to continue with 15 separate statistical statements which monitored the production and repair of locomotives, rolling stock and containers. Such concern did not typify devolution from the centre.[26]

The Commission's railway reorganisation proposals were drafted in the early months of 1954, and presented to Lennox-Boyd in April. The scheme was then published as a White Paper in July and, after a change of Minister in the same month – Lennox-Boyd was promoted to the Colonial Office and succeeded by John Boyd-Carpenter – it was debated twice in parliament before it was formally introduced by Ministerial Order on 25 November. The Ministry had taken a keen interest in the Commission's provision for decentralisation to area authorities during the drafting stage. Once Lennox-Boyd learned that the Commission had decided to respond to the Transport Act by establishing Area Boards for the six existing railway regions (the Act had left it open whether the area authorities were to be bodies or merely individuals), he was anxious to ensure that the powers of these new institutions were spelled out, and that decentralisation was real. To that end he requested the B.T.C. not to pack the boards with Commission members as chairmen. On the other hand, Robertson and the Commission had tried to draft as flexible a scheme as possible. There is evidence to suggest that Robertson gave some ground to appease government interests.* Certainly three of the six Area Board Chairmen were recruited from outside the Commission, although they were subsequently appointed as part-time members.

According to the White Paper, the Area Boards were to be policyforming, supervisory bodies. They were not intended to exercise day-today managerial control of regional operations, which was to remain in the hands of the Chief Regional Managers. Nevertheless, they were expected to make 'a very real and big contribution towards increasing the efficiency of the railway industry'. The reorganisation scheme formally delegated to them the following functions:

(a) the management of the railways;
(b) promoting initiative in improving the services and facilities afforded to the public on the railways, and in effecting economies;
(c) ensuring that contact is maintained with transport users so that the requirements of such users in relation to the railways may be met to the fullest possible extent consistent with the general duty of the Commission; and
(d) ensuring that proper measures are taken affecting the safety, health and welfare of persons employed by the Commission on or in connection with the railways.[27]

Appointed by the Commission, in whom ultimate authority resided, the

*He informed the Minister on 15 April 1954 that at the last minute he had persuaded his colleagues 'to swallow an extremely distasteful amendment', but no record of the meeting survives: Robertson–Lennox-Boyd, 15 April 1954, and Lennox-Boyd–Robertson, 6 May 1954, in D.O.E. 52/2/002 Pt 1.

Area Boards were given very limited powers in comparison with the boards of the old railway companies they were thought in some respects to resemble. Delegated management here meant a general supervisory jurisdiction, with the emphasis on commercial, public and industrial relations. This is clear from the details of delegated authority, which were kept out of both the White Paper and the Ministerial Order at Robertson's request. Although the Area Boards were to submit budgets and financial forecasts (for expenditure on both capital and revenue account), their powers to authorise spending on engineering projects and equipment and to appoint staff were strictly limited: for works and equipment, to £25,000, which was half of the limit previously imposed on the Railway Executive; and for appointments, to posts with salaries of up to £2,100 per annum.[28]

Part and parcel of the creation of Area Boards was the restructuring of the headquarters organisation. This was a matter for the Commission alone, since it lay outside the obligations imposed by the 1953 Act, but it naturally had an important bearing on how the statutory scheme of decentralisation would work in practice. Robertson's views on the matter had crystallised by the spring of 1954. At a meeting of the B.T.C. on 8 April he informed his colleagues that something like a 'General Staff' was necessary to co-ordinate the efforts of the several departments, and as a temporary measure Daril Watson was asked to take on the task of chief co-ordinator. There was clearly disquiet about the move, for Robertson was at some pains to point out that he was 'NOT creating a "Director-General" or "Chief Executive", or anything of that nature'.[29] Three months later, he was able to hand Lennox-Boyd a rough sketch of what he proposed to do at H.Q. as a whole (see Figure 2). Robertson's blueprint was endorsed by his colleagues without amendment. Described at length in a staff manual known as the 'Grey Book', it introduced, from 1 January 1955, a complex, multi-tier organisation (see Chart V).

At the top of the new organisation the Commission was assisted by advisory bodies, which were made up of B.T.C. representatives and outside specialists. Two of them, the Research Advisory Council and the British Transport Joint Consultative Council, had been established in 1949. They were joined by others created after the new organisation was introduced: the British Railways Productivity Council, which first met in July 1955, and the Design Panel, which held its first meeting in August

Figure 2 (Opposite) Letter from Sir Brian Robertson to Sir Gilmour Jenkins, Permanent-Secretary, Ministry of Transport, 16 July 1954, enclosing sketch of proposed British Transport Commission organisation

Source: Ministry of Transport file on B.T.C. Railway Reorganisation 52/2/001 Pt. 1, D.O.E.

My dear Jimmom

When I saw the Minister in the House of Commons
on Tuesday I scrawled a sketch of the organisation
which I am developing here.   I took this away with
me, but it occurred to me that it might amuse you to
have it.   I am accordingly making you a present of
..... it herewith.   All writing in ink has been added
since for better explanation.

Yours ever,

Brian.

Sir Gilmour Jenkins, K.C.B., K.B.E., M.C.

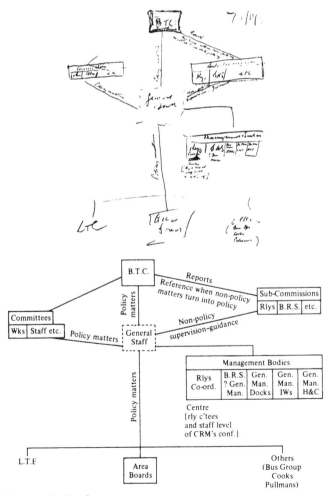

Key to Robertson's sketch

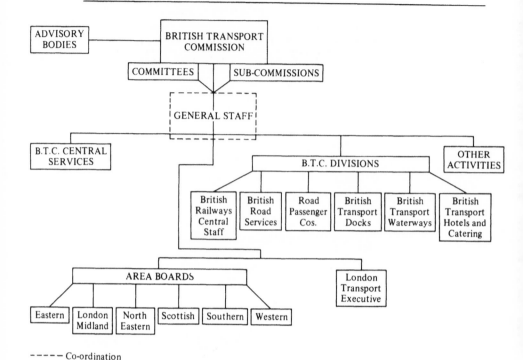

Chart V British Transport Commission organisation, January 1955

----- Co-ordination

1956. Directly responsible to the B.T.C. were two sub-strata, the Committees and the Sub-Commissions, both intended to streamline the work of the Commission proper. The Committees were inherited from the interim organisation and continued with only minor adjustments. Made up of small groups of Commission members and organised on a departmental basis, they were to 'deal with matters relating to the whole of the Commission's activities'.[30] On the other hand, the Sub-Commissions, while having a similar membership, were a new concept. There were nine such bodies, each constituted on a modal or activity basis: Railways, Road Haulage, Road Passenger, London Transport, Shipping, Docks, Inland Waterways, Hotels and Catering and Other Activities (including commercial advertising). The precise role of most of these bodies was left rather vague but the Railways Sub-Commission, made up of Pope, Train, Barker and Cameron, was given a specific brief. It was to 'act as referee on day-to-day matters requiring co-ordination between the Regions when the General Staff [q.v.] are unable to settle them without reference', to 'watch performance and productivity' and to guide the work of the railway committees. These comprised a General Managers' Committee of the six Chief Regional Managers, henceforth to be known simply as 'General

Managers', and thirteen departmental committees, later reduced to ten, with members drawn from the departmental heads in the railway regions and the relevant officers at headquarters. Nevertheless, the Railways Sub-Commission was not to be an executive authority, but an information-gathering entity whose work would assist the Commission in the task of formulating policy. Like the other Sub-Commissions it was to work only through the General Staff, the group of senior officers who were expected to process and filter information as it was passed to and fro.[31]

Further down came the B.T.C. Divisions and Central Services. The Divisions were activity-based, with their chief officers located at the Commission's headquarters to facilitate co-ordination. They included the British Railways Central Staff, officers appointed to deal with those areas of railway business which the Commission had reserved to itself under the scheme of decentralisation (other than those covered by the B.T.C. Central Services). A development of the interim organisation, the Central Staff comprised, initially, ten chief officers, each with specified functions, for operating, commercial policy, staff, the various branches of engineering, finance and research (see Appendix I). This unit possessed some features which were strongly reminiscent of the discredited Railway Executive. Its officers were made responsible, 'in conjunction with the General Managers, for satisfying themselves that the various policies of the Commission are carried out from the point of view of *British Railways as a whole*' (my italics), and to that end provision was made for direct access to the regional departmental officers, a bone of contention with the C.R.O.s in the functional organisation of the past. On the other hand, the Central Staff, like the Railways Sub-Commission, was expected to work through the General Staff, which greatly limited its freedom of action.* The Commission's Central Services were those established as 'Common Services' before 1953 – Research, Commercial Advertising, Film, Archives – together with some new departments taken on during the interim phase, such as Police, Stores and Paper and Printing. They were controlled functionally from headquarters by members of the General Staff.

This whole structure was to be tied together by the controversial General Staff (see Chart VI). Led by the Secretary-General as co-ordinator in chief, this body was to 'ensure the expeditious handling of the Commission's business' by channelling communications from the Area Boards, the L.T.E., Divisions and Central Services to the Commission's Committees and Sub-Commissions. There were seven Advisers, a Chief Secretary and a Chief of General Duties, the last two being directly responsible to the Secretary-General. To this post Daril Watson was appointed, thus ensur-

*The other Divisions functioned through either Boards of Managements (British Road Services (road haulage), Docks, Waterways), Groups (the 'road passenger' businesses of Tillings, and Scottish Omnibuses) or a General Manager (Hotels and Catering).

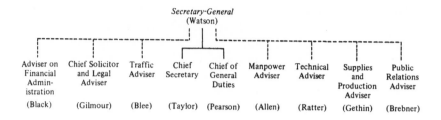

Note: for more details see Appendix I.

Chart VI The British Transport Commission General Staff, 1955

ing that both the Chairman and the head of the General Staff were ex-Generals. The Advisers included two established B.T.C. officers who continued to fulfil their duties in modified form: Gilmour, the Solicitor; and Brebner, the Public Relations chief. Two former members of the Railway Executive, Allen and Blee, had their interim posts renamed Manpower Adviser and Traffic Adviser respectively, with the latter adding operating to his earlier responsibility for Commercial Services.[32] There were three new positions. The post of Comptroller was abolished, and the department was re-titled the Department of Accounts and Finance. Andrew Black, one of Wilson's protégés, was appointed Adviser on Financial Administration.* He was to exercise a general supervision over the department but policy matters were reserved to Wilson and the Finance Committee. John Ratter, Chief Officer (Civil Engineering) in the interim organisation, became Technical Adviser. His job was to guide technical and research development. Finally, the post of Supplies and Production Adviser was established in June 1955 in order to improve the co-ordination of supply and production activities, including the inspection and testing of materials. For this the Commission went outside the existing staff, appointing Ernest L. Gethin, an electrical engineer and Deputy Chief Contracts Officer of the Central Electricity Authority.[33]

The supposed functions of this new General Staff elude precise definition. Apparently without an executive role, the Secretary-General and his team were to advise the Commission on policy and act as a co-ordinating 'filter' of information. Yet they were also expected to wield executive authority over the Central Services; and their position at the centre of the new organisation certainly gave them a clear advantage over the British Railways Central Staff and the General Managers when matters were sent up to the Commission itself. Robertson intended that the General Staff should plug what he saw as a large hole in the organisation at head-

*He had been Director of the Road Haulage Acquisitions Department.

'War Office? Sorry, old boy, can't possibly take any more. There's a drive on against redundancy, y' know'

5 Sir Brian Robertson's 'military style organisation', as seen by McKenna, *News Chronicle*, 19 January 1955.

quarters. But the idea of a co-ordinating policy group was quite unfamiliar in the railway industry, and there was more than a little criticism of the alleged military style of the new regime. Some of it, in appropriately exaggerated form, found its way into the popular press. There was certainly no large-scale exodus from the army into railway management, and Robertson had been at some pains to point out that he was not creating a General Staff in the army sense, but simply a body which could have a general responsibility for all the activities of the Commission.[34] Nevertheless, he had drawn on his army experience in designing the new structure, and was known to have been an admirer of General Eisenhower's organisation at the White House, which included a 'General Staff'. Although the Commission is thought to have consulted large industrial companies such as I.C.I., military precedents were paramount. During the drafting stage, Robertson got at least one member of his team to read a War Office publication entitled *The Conduct of War*.[35] Fuel for the critics was undoubtedly provided when Daril Watson retired as

Secretary-General early in 1955. Robertson promptly replaced one former General by another way by choosing Major-General Llewellyn Wansbrough-Jones, C.B., C.B.E., the Principal Staff Officer to Montgomery at S.H.A.P.E., who joined the Commission at the end of January 1955 and succeeded Watson in May. Aged 55, Wansbrough-Jones had some experience of transport. In the Royal Engineers, he had earlier received some training in the L.M.S. Railway's Derby Works, and during the war had held senior appointments in military transport at the War Office, the Joint Chiefs of Staff H.Q. Washington, and 21 Army Group. But having worked under Robertson in Germany as a staff officer and Chief of Staff, he was first and foremost yet another administrative soldier who had become an administrative railwayman.[36]

III

How well did this new organisation work? How did it influence the way in which British Railways tackled its problems? Such questions are not susceptible to conclusive answers, but certain propositions may be established at the outset. It is clear, for example, that Robertson's organisation, while providing for decentralisation to Area Boards and General Managers, was in practice designed to leave much of the policy initiative at the centre. It is also evident that at 222, Marylebone Road there was a great deal of uncertainty about the exact line of authority, an uncertainty which hit the railway side of the business particularly hard. The B.T.C. had lost its responsibility for co-ordinating inland transport but now had an organisation which perpetuated a false atmosphere of co-ordination. It was much better suited to the other activities than to British Railways. The London Transport Executive, and the various Boards of Management, had genuine foci of managerial authority. But the railways, the Commission's largest element, lacked any such focus and were caught up instead in the administrative tangle at headquarters, with its Committees, Sub-Commissions, General Staff and British Railways Central Staff. This was a basic weakness of the post-1955 organisation. Robertson defended it staunchly in public throughout his period of office, and notably before the 1960 Select Committee on Nationalised Industries, but in private he was more ambivalent. During the investigations of Sir Ivan Stedeford's Special Advisory Group (see below, pp. 300–1) in 1960, for example, he admitted to Stedeford that

The only thing really wrong with our present organisation is that the Commission are trying to fulfil two separate roles. The first is their proper role as headpiece to a great public transport organisation. The second role, which they have been forced to play as a result of the abolition of the Railway Executive, is that of the Headquarters and the Board for British Railways.

Without any doubt the organisation of 1955 was ill-conceived in relation to this second function.[37]

The conflict produced by this unresolved duality was soon apparent in tensions among chief officers – particularly those of the General Staff and the Railways Central Staff. As Bonavia has observed, the Central Staff, specialists in their own right, could expect to be challenged not only by departmental officers in the regions, who could and did appeal to their General Manager or Area Board, but by the General Staff which, by virtue to its special position as an 'inner Cabinet', was able to interpret policy as it was passed up to Robertson and the Commission. Decision-making was sometimes adversely affected by this situation, particularly on technical matters, wherein a kind of decentralisation by default was encouraged. In October 1955, for example, an ad hoc committee of the Central Staff, which had been asked to examine continuous brakes, pronounced itself firmly in favour of making the air brake standard equipment on British Railways. In December this view was enthusiastically taken up by the B.T.C.'s Technical Development and Research Committee and its co-opted expert member, Dr F. Q. den Hollander, President of Netherlands Railways. In the following February, however, the Commission, in deference to regional opinion, decided to retain the vacuum brake, a decision which proved costly before it was finally reversed in 1964.[38] The Central Staff were also unable to prevent the regions from ordering diverse signalling equipment, despite the emphasis on standardisation. Or again, the Western Region, anxious as ever to establish its individuality, was able to persuade the B.T.C. to sanction investment in the ultimately unsatisfactory diesel-hydraulic locomotive, despite obvious qualms at the centre. Such examples will serve to illustrate the absence of a simple, clearly accepted, organisation path from region to Commission. And that absence undoubtedly helped to reinforce regional obstinacy.[39]

Nowhere was the cumbersome and rather remote nature of this complex organisation better demonstrated than at the plenary meetings of the Commission itself. Here members were joined by up to 30 representatives of the constituent elements of nationalised transport, including the Chairmen of the Area Boards and the Divisions, officers of the General Staff and the British Railways Central Staff, and the General Managers of the railways and other activities. The meetings, which began in July 1954, during the period of the interim organisation, were held on the fifth Thursday of the month. They were intended to improve communication and create a unity of purpose within the B.T.C. as a whole. But proceedings were necessarily formal in such large gatherings, and in 1958 the number of meetings was reduced as their usefulness declined. The situation was little better at the Commission's ordinary meetings, which were attended by the General Staff on all occasions, by the heads of the non-railway Divisions on the second Thursday of each month, and by the Area Board Chairmen and railway General Managers on the fourth Thursday. Discussion was inhibited not only by the number of people attending but also by the design of the new board room at Marylebone Road, first used in May 1957. Beeching, who joined the Commission in March 1961 and soon reduced the size of these sessions, observed that

it was more like a lecture hall. The Commission used to sit at a long table all facing the body of the Kirk – they weren't facing each other. They weren't disposed in such a way that they could ever discuss anything among themselves. Brian Robertson was sitting in the middle with the Commission members ranged out on either side, and it was a dialogue between the Commission and the officers, mainly, of course, railway officers.

Robertson's proposal, in April 1956, that the exchange of views within the Commission would be strengthened by the introduction of regular Officers' Conferences was an implicit response to the formality of B.T.C. meetings. The first such conference, on 'The Future Pattern of Freight Traffic', was convened at Balliol College, Oxford, in April 1957. Moreover, the convening of B.T.C. meetings outside London – there were seven of these, 1953–9 – may be seen as a further gesture towards the improvement of relations with more distant outposts of the business.[40]

The imposing personality of Robertson and the industriousness of Wansbrough-Jones prevented any serious breakdown despite these various difficulties of communication. The basic structure of Commission, Committees, Sub-Committees, Area Boards and Divisions remained unchanged. The only modifications of significance were in particular problem areas such as the stores organisation (renamed Supply in 1956) or involved certain central functions such as finance and traffic. These were incorporated in two revisions of the 'Grey Book', which came into operation in January 1957 and January 1960.[41] Some of these organisational problems at H.Q. merit a more detailed examination. The stores or supplies organisation was a particular matter of concern which became more urgent as government money began to flow into the railway industry after the acceptance of the Modernisation Plan of 1955 (see Chapter 8). Here there was a fierce battle between the forces of centralisation and decentralisation. The need for change had been recognised at an earlier stage, in Railway Executive days. An internal report in 1949 had been critical of the existing arrangements, which left much of the responsibility with technical officers at regional headquarters, and recommended a greater measure of central purchasing. This was followed by an Executive Directive of 1950 which provided for the central purchasing of standard materials and advocated a standardisation of the regional apparatus. Action was then interrupted by the uncertainty which followed the change of government in 1951, and the report was shelved.[42]

After the publication of the Modernisation Plan in January 1955, the Commission accepted that a revised organisation was required. E. L. Gethin, who had been appointed to the post of Supplies and Production Adviser in June, was asked to review the position, and the opinions of the General Managers were sought. By the end of the year a working party of the General Staff, chaired by Arthur Pearson, and including Gethin and A. Forbes-Smith, the Chief Stores Officer, was instructed to undertake a broader review, including tendering and contracts procedures, in consultation with the General Managers. In the meantime it was decided, in March 1956, to deal with steel supplies centrally, and in November the Stores Committee was re-named the Supply Committee to herald impending changes. By this time about 40 per cent of total railway materials were being purchased by H.Q.[43] The working party reported in October 1956. Its members were agreed that the existing arrangements for contracts were inadequate; and concern was also expressed about the number of large contracts with firms which were members of price-fixing rings. There were divided views on the solutions to be offered. Gethin, who had been extremely critical of the railways' procedures, was alone in proposing the creation of a separate Progress Section at headquarters under his control. The rest of the working party were in favour of strengthening both Central and Regional Staff. However, the final recommendations leaned heavily in favour of centralised control.[44]

The Commission accepted much of the report. It supported the appointment of a Chief Contracts Officer at H.Q. to handle tenders and conditions of contract and establish regional codes of practice; and endorsed the proposal that responsibility for the commercial and financial aspects of contracting be removed from the technical departments in the regions. However, before the new supplies organisation was approved, on 30 May 1957, certain changes were made. The most important were the abolition of Gethin's post, which followed his enforced resignation in April; and the establishment of two separate central departments for supplies and contracts, each under a chief officer.[45] Personal animosities played a part in all this – Gethin had been very outspoken in his criticisms of the railway's entire purchasing activities – but it is also clear that the Commission acted to appease regional sensibilities, which had been hurt by a move which appeared to cast doubt upon the integrity of regional officers and to contradict the co-existing commitment to decentralisation.[46]

Gethin, who later joined British Oxygen as a Purchasing Manager, refused to lie down. His charges of inefficiency in the B.T.C.'s purchasing of supplies reached the House of Commons, where they were taken up by George Strauss for the Opposition in July 1957. The timing was scarcely propitious. The allegations coincided with an upturn in the inflationary spiral and numerous criticisms of the impact of public sector spending. Fortunately for the Commission its record was upheld by Sir Harold Howitt, senior partner of the accountants, Peat, Marwick, Mitchell & Co., who had been appointed by the Ministry of Transport to examine the case. His generally supportive findings were published as a White Paper in September.[47] Nevertheless, the episode not only publicised obvious organisational difficulties in the railway industry but exposed to full glare a vital area of control which nearly all interested parties from Robertson downwards considered to be in need of tightening up. Certainly, some of the evidence suggests complacency surrounding purchasing arrangements. Forbes Smith, the Chief Stores Officer, who retired in May 1957, was implicated in one of the alleged areas of inefficiency, the purchase of vacuum brakes. He had been happy to buy at Westinghouse prices despite information from the Swindon Works that it was possible to manufacture the equipment much more cheaply. Robertson was moved to comment, to Wansbrough-Jones in July 1957: 'I must say it is not easy to see why Mr. Forbes Smith agreed to pay Westinghouse £31 [per brake cylinder] for the 1957 programme in the face of advice given him in June 1956.' It is also interesting to observe that Robertson went to great lengths to emphasise the need for competitive tendering in the months following the inquiry.[48]

The B.T.C. was also far from satisfied with other elements of its headquarters organisation, and after 1955 adjustments were made in a number of departments. These included the appointment of H. E. Osborn as Chief Accountant and Financial Adviser (a re-titled post), the creation of two new positions – Chief General Accountant, and Chief Railway Accountant – and the amalgamation of the accounts and statistics divisions. It was intended that the Chief Railway Accountant should exercise a firmer control over the regional railway accountants.[49] The traffic organisation was also modified, in order to bring it into line with changes introduced in the regions. After the retirement from the Central Staff of the chief officers for operating and motive-power and for commercial matters, the new post of Chief Traffic Officer was created and Frank Grundy, the Chief Traffic Manager of the North Eastern Region, was appointed to it in December 1957 (see below, Appendix I). The relevant committees were then replaced by a Traffic Conference. There was little improvement in managerial effectiveness, however. The Traffic Advisers, first Blee (1955–6), then T. H. Hollingsworth (1956–61), the 60-year-old Commercial Manager of the Scottish Region who was chosen instead of the younger David McKenna, found it difficult to operate in the surroundings of 222, Marylebone Road, and no effective lead was given.[50] Nor was there much guidance from the Commission itself. In the first Grey Book the members had agreed to establish a 'Joint Traffics Committee' with a broad remit, but this was abandoned after only one meeting as its business was considered to be duplicated by meetings of the full Commission. A Traffic Committee was not set up until January 1960, when Major General G. N. Russell was appointed to chair a body which was given the task of overseeing traffic strategy, including modal co-ordination, pricing policy and modern traffic analysis.[51] Given the B.T.C.'s mounting operating deficits this was a little late in the day, and the role of the Railways Sub-Commission was such that it could not fill the gap in this key area of railway management. Led first by Pope, then Watkins and finally by Grand, the Sub-Commission did not appear to take itself, or to be taken, very seriously. Its minutes, with their frequent reference to operating minutiae – frozen points, the heating of trains, liveries and the paintwork of sleeping cars – read like a truncated version of the expurgated minutes sent by the Railway Executive to the Commission before 1953.[52]

The Commission's efforts to improve its own organisation were not wholly confined to limited and generally ineffective responses to specific problems. The restructuring of its supplies organisation in the mid-1950s was paralleled by a new concern with recruitment and training, work study and 'Organisation and Methods' in general. After Stanley Raymond had produced two influential reports – on 'Work Study Training' and 'Recruitment and Training Arrangements' – in January and March 1956, the Commission adopted a number of measures to improve management development, including the use from 1959 of Woking College as a British Transport Staff College for senior managers.[53] In April 1956 a Director of Work Study, E. J. Larkin, was appointed, and the London Midland's Watford College was used to develop techniques for the improvement of productivity. By July 1959 about 25,000 staff had been 'work studied'. Finally, an Organisation and Methods Officer, H. J. Evans, was appointed, in October 1957, to apply similar principles to administration.[54] The initial impact of such activities, however, was slight. In particular, they did little, at any rate in the short run, to influence the course of regional railway management, where wide disparities in practice remained. The overall impression of the B.T.C. must remain that of a large and cumbersome body which failed to react quickly enough to the competitive challenge of road transport and the difficulties thrown up by the need to modernise the railways. The responses it offered in key areas were all too often ad hoc in character, with only the retirement of senior officers to provide stimulus for action.[55]

In the Commission itself there was a notable continuity of membership, which helped to prop up the creaking dinosaur. There were some new faces, of course. The number of members was soon increased from 12 to 14 with the appointment, from 1 May 1955, of two more industrialists as part-timers: the steel magnate Thomas H. Summerson, who was already Chairman of the Commission's North Eastern Area Board, and Sir Cecil McAlpine Weir, who had, *inter alia*, been head of the United Kingdom Delegation to the European Coal and Steel Community since 1952. They were joined at the beginning of 1957, also on a part-time basis, by Reginald F. Hanks, the Western Area Board's Chairman, who was a leading figure in the British motor industry.[56] Despite these new arrivals, the reality of long service, as Table 15 shows, was unmistakable. The 'inner cabinet' of the B.T.C. – Robertson, Benstead, Wilson, Rusholme and Valentine – together with four of the part-timers – Bolton, Barker, Cameron and Summerson – served for an average period of ten years. Reappointment was usually automatic, and major changes were only forced upon the Commission by ill-health or death. Of the full-time members, only Train, who was 69 in 1958, was not given a further term of office.

Continuity at the Commission also meant that there were only limited opportunities for railwaymen to reach the top. Not that there was much incentive for Robertson to alter his policy: the few railway-trained members proved disappointing as managers. Pope and Train, who had handled railway matters during the interim phase, remained in office until 1958, and in June 1956 they were joined by J. W. Watkins, the General Manager of the London Midland Region, who became a full-time member in a reshuffle which saw David Blee take his place at Euston. Watkins was apparently introduced to relieve Robertson of some of the burden of industrial relations. Despite their experience these three men were very far from being a dynamic trio. Ill-health forced Pope to become a part-timer in May 1955 and he retired three years later; and Watkins, who was 65 on his appointment, died suddenly after a short illness in January 1959. The appointment of his successor, Keith Grand, the General Manager of the Western Region, owed more to internal politics than to anything else. Grand was certainly an able and experienced railway executive, but his promotion was prompted by a determination at headquarters to break up the old regime at Paddington. As a full-time member of the Commission, and Chairman of the Railways Sub-Commission, Grand was better

Table 15. *British Transport Commission members, 1955–62*

Name	Appointed	Departed (if before 31 December 1962)	Period of office (years)
Full-time			
Gen. Sir Brian Robertson (Chairman)	1953	1961	8
Sir John Benstead (Deputy-Chairman)	1947	1961	14
Lord Rusholme	1947	1959	12
F. A. Pope	1951	1958[a]	7[a]
Sir John L. Train	1953	1958	5
Sir Reginald Wilson	1953		9
A. B. B. Valentine	1954		8
J. W. Watkins	1956	1959[b]	3[b]
John Ratter	1958		4
K. W. C. Grand	1959	1962	3
Maj.-Gen. G. N. Russell	1959		3
Dr Richard Beeching (Chairman 1961–2)	1961		2
L. H. Williams	1961		1
P. H. Shirley	1961		1
Sir Steuart Mitchell	1962		1
Part-time			
Sir Ian Bolton	1947	1959	12
John Ryan	1950	1956	6
H. P. Barker	1951		12
Sir Harry Methven	1953	1956	3
Lt-Col Donald Cameron of Lochiel	1954		8
T. H. Summerson	1955		8
Sir Cecil Weir	1955	1960[b]	6[b]
R. F. Hanks	1957		6
Sir Philip Warter (Deputy-Chairman 1961–2)	1958		5
Sir Leonard Sinclair	1958	1961	3
F. Donachy	1959		3

[a] Owing to ill-health Pope became a part-timer from 1 May 1955
[b] Died in office.
Source: B.T.C., *R. & A. 1955–62*, supplemented by B.T.C. Minutes, *passim*, B.R.B.

remembered for his conviviality and love of the turf than for his managerial contribution. He retired early, in July 1962. Of the railwaymen members, only John Ratter's contribution in the technical field after his appointment in October 1958 could be said to have been in any way substantial.[57]

At the same time, businessmen of high calibre continued to be attracted to part-time positions with the B.T.C. In 1958, two years after the departure of Ryan and Methven, Sir Philip Warter and Sir Leonard Sinclair were appointed. Chairman of the Southern Area Board from its inception, Warter was the last of the Area Board Chairmen to be given a seat on the Commission. He was Chairman of the cinema group Associated British Picture Corporation, and held various other directorships. Sinclair was a leading oil man who had become Chairman of the British end of Esso Petroleum in 1951. The only part-time member who was not a businessman was F. Donachy. Appointed in October 1959 to take Bolton's place as a Scottish representative, he was a member of the Executive Committee of the N.U.R. and had joined the Scottish Area Board in January 1958.[58] It is tempting to suppose that the appointment of men such as Summerson, Hanks, Weir, Warter and Sinclair opened up the B.T.C. to a dynamic leadership based on the expert direction of experienced industrialists. In practice nothing of the sort happened. Some of the part-time members made their presence felt in limited areas. For example, H. P. Barker was prominent in discussions of technical and research problems, and Sinclair proved to be both a vocal and a perceptive critic of the Commission's organisation when questioned by the Stedeford Advisory Group in August 1960. On the whole, however, part-time status proved to be an only too effective constraint on dynamic action. The fees paid – a modest £500 a year, increased to £1,000 in 1957 after pressure on the government from Robertson and other chairmen of nationalised industries to raise salaries – were scarcely sufficient to persuade men with wide interests to give disproportionate amounts of their time to the task of running nationalised transport. Indeed, the same might be said of the full-time members. The salary of £5,000 a year, fixed in 1947, remained unchanged until it was increased to £7,500 from July 1957. By this time, salary increases for chief officers, which with the restructuring of the organisation had risen by 25–40 per cent since 1953, had narrowed differentials between the B.T.C. members and their executive managers. The conclusion must be that the combination of a few undynamic railwaymen, under-paid full-timers and poorly-paid part-time business-men was not a very potent managerial cocktail.[59]

IV

The same can be said about the operations of the Area Boards. Here, the cocktail of January 1955 consisted of six members of the Commission (none of whom, incidentally, had been trained in the railway industry) and 29 part-time outsiders.[60] Of the latter, about half came from industry and a quarter from banking and finance. There were three trade unionists, two of them significant figures: Jack Tanner, President of the Amalgamated Engineering Union, 1939–54, and a President of the T.U.C. (Eastern Area Board); and Sir Mark Hodgson, ex-President of the Confederation of Engineering and Shipbuilding Unions (North Eastern). Indeed many of the members were prominent men with national reputations. They included Sir Edmund Bacon and Rt Hon. H. U. (later Sir Henry) Willink (Eastern), Sir Francis Glyn and Sir Basil McFarland (London Midland), Lord Bilsland and Sir Hugh Rose (Scottish) and Sir Herbert Merrett and Sir John Pole (Western).[61] Only two of the Area Board Chairmen were full-time members of the Commission: Rusholme of the London Midland Area (succeeded in April 1960 by Wilson), and Wilson of the Eastern (succeeded in April 1960 by Major-General Russell). And although Wilson was able to address himself to the task of reorganising his area below General Manager level, both he and Rusholme were heavily committed at headquarters. As at the B.T.C. itself, the rewards for those who had agreed to lend their services to the railways were small. Fees were £500 a year, £1,000 for the chairmen. In spite of the impressive qualifications of the members, the part-time character of the Area Boards made it difficult for them to do much more than act as regional public relations agents for the Commission.

After 1955 the B.T.C. extended the powers of the Boards. In the course of the following year the limit upon their authority to agree expenditure on works and equipment was raised from £25,000 to £50,000, and they were empowered to fill all existing posts below that of departmental head. At the same time, responsibility for the buying and selling of property was partially decentralised, the Boards being given the authority to make transactions of up to £10,000. Later, in February and August 1959, the limits on both works and equipment expenditure and property transactions were doubled, reaching £100,000 and £20,000 respectively. Finally, the Commission, in its revised 'Grey Book' of December 1959, made it clear that the Area Board Chairmen were free to attend the meetings of the Railways Sub-Commission.[62] From all this it might be concluded that Robertson and his colleagues were actively carrying out their mandate to proceed with decentralisation as far as was practicable. But how much *real* power was actually devolved upon the Area Boards? An authority to spend £25,000 or £50,000 on new works scarcely meant very much in the context of the railways' modernisation programme. Boards had the freedom to build a new station roof, or re-site a signal box or, with £100,000, to embark on a minor civil engineering scheme, but this hardly amounted to 'devolved authority'. It is difficult to escape the conclusion that such concessions were little more than window dressing, designed to obscure the uncomfortable fact that the Commission had not really followed the spirit of Conservative intentions in 1951–3.

When the B.T.C.'s organisation was placed under the government's microscope in 1960, the Area Boards attracted some support, although most of this came from interested parties. For example, the joint paper of the Area Board Chairmen, presented to the Stedeford Advisory Group, laid great emphasis on the value of the part-time participation of business-men, citing the findings of the Herbert Committee on the Electricity Supply Industry of 1956 in support. Their presence, it was claimed, had helped to counter the conservative, inward-looking approach of the railway managers, and done much to improve the general standing of nationalised transport. 'The advent of so many active practitioners of Private Enter-prise into this nationalised industry', the chairmen declared, 'has already ... eroded away many of the prejudices which had formerly obstructed the Railways' attempts to improve their relations with industry and with much Conservative opinion among the public and in the Right Wing Press.' Support for part-time members also came from Cameron (Scottish Area) and Summerson (North Eastern), who emphasised their contribu-tion in the political, commercial and public relations fields.[63] But in practice, however valuable all this may have been, critical decisions continued to be taken at the centre. For instance, it was the Commission who determined in 1955 to resolve the problem of 'penetrating lines' (see above, pp. 59–60) by insisting on geographical boundaries for the railway regions.[64] And although the Boards and their chief executives, the General Managers, were given a fair amount of commercial freedom, for example, in the fixing of local freight rates, the Commission retained its overall control and arranged rates with major customers on a national basis.[65]

Furthermore, within their limited terms of reference the Boards left much of the initiative to the General Managers. As Hanks told the Stedeford Advisory Group, his Board, the Western, 'acted more as a watchdog than as an initiator of policy'. Henry 'Bill' Johnson, who had succeeded Charles Bird as the General Manager of the Eastern Region in February 1958, was more blunt. His Board, the Chairman apart, was 'little more than a rubber stamp'.[66] When Roberton and Warter tried to convince the Select Committee on Nationalised Industries in 1960 that the relationship between the B.T.C. and its Area Boards resembled that between a holding company and its subsidiaries – Warter referred specifi-cally to the subsidiary companies of I.C.I. – it was scarcely surprising that the Committee should express some scepticism. And while the Committee, in its published report, preferred to make its criticisms *sotto voce*, others were less restrained. Inside the Commission, Sinclair thought there were too many part-time members on the Boards. Outside, Sir Ivan Stedeford quickly came to the conclusion that the Boards, 'with but a part-time interest, with little responsibility, and less authority, have run no risk of having to answer personally for what is done or not done'. His assessment was not far short of the mark.[67]

It might be argued that if the value of decentralisation lay in the opportunity for local responses to local conditions then decentralisation *within* a railway region was more relevant to the improvement of operating and commercial management than delegation of authority from one presiding body (the Commission) to another (the Area Board). Here, some progress was made after 1955, although its extent varied from region to region. The new traffic organisation of the Eastern Region, introduced by Wilson and Johnson from 1956, was particularly successful. Operating, commercial and motive power responsibilities were concentrated in one person's hands at three levels – General Manager, assisted by an Assistant General Manager (Traffic), 'Line Manager' and (District) Traffic Manager. This type of organisation was repeated for the three 'lines', based on the former company systems of Great Northern (London–York–Newcastle), Great Eastern (London–Cambridge/Norwich) and London Tilbury & Southend. Local managers revelled in their new authority, and the chain of command was clear. The Eastern enjoyed the advantage of being able to use existing, system-based units which appealed to railwaymen; and its organisation was staffed by some particularly competent operating managers* who worked to budgetary targets, another Eastern innovation.[68]

In the other regions progress was much slower, and the 'line' concept was not fully applied. Only the Southern Region produced anything resembling the Eastern's organisation. In 1961 it belatedly introduced three system-based Divisions, South-Eastern, Central and South-Western, each with a Line Traffic Manager. Elsewhere, Divisions were established on a geographical basis, and the Divisional Traffic Managers were not given the authority enjoyed by the Eastern's 'Line Managers'. In 1957 the Western Region, which was dominated by Paddington, created a new divisional structure based on Paddington, Bristol, Birmingham and Cardiff, but there was no effective decentralisation of commercial, operating and motive power functions until 1960. Two other regions began the decentralisation of their traffic organisation in 1957. The London Midland introduced a complex structure, devised by David Blee, with a Director of Traffic Services responsible for commercial, operating and motive power duties at regional H.Q. Below him there were six Divisions,

*The three 'Line Managers' were Gerard Fiennes (G.N.), W. G. Thorpe (G.E.), and John Dedman (L.T.S.) H. C. Johnson was Assistant General Manager (Traffic).

each with a Traffic Manager, at Euston, Birmingham, Nottingham, Liverpool, Manchester and Barrow. On the North Eastern, four Areas or Divisions were created, for the West Riding, Teesside, Hull & York and Tyne & Wear, with a Chief Traffic Manager (later an Assistant General Manager) at regional H.Q. Finally, in Scotland, three Divisions were eventually created, in 1960, at Glasgow, Edinburgh and Inverness. The Commission made no attempt either to force the pace of decentralisation or to impose a uniform system on the Area Boards.[69]

Changes of this kind were not welcomed by the majority of officers in the regions. The results of tinkering with the old-established departmental system, with its separation of commercial, operating and motive power functions, were more often than not counter-productive. The chain of authority was too often complicated by a proliferation of Assistant General Managers, who were required to help the General Managers cope with the co-ordination of the new divisions. The London Midland's labyrinthine organisation with its several management layers – General Manager, Assistant General Managers, Director of Traffic Services, Divisional Traffic Managers, Line Traffic Officers (for operating and motive power), and a variety of District Officers – was not found to be working well when Wilson took over from Rusholme as Area Board Chairman in 1960. He tried to inject the 'line' concept into the region by abolishing the post of Director of Traffic Services and appointing three Line Traffic Managers at Derby, Crewe and Manchester. Even so, the region was still in a state of some confusion when Henry Johnson succeeded Blee as General Manager in January 1962.[70]

At the same time the Commission pressed for the reorganisation of the regions' technical departments. The existing structure, laid down by Riddles and the Railway Executive in May 1950, was designed primarily to meet the needs of a steam railway. In each region a motive power department existed to maintain and staff locomotives. There were two separate engineering departments – mechanical and electrical, and carriage and wagon – to handle the construction and repair of rolling stock. However, the introduction of diesel and electric locomotives and multiple-unit stock under the Modernisation Plan blurred the division of responsibility between departments, particularly for maintenance. In February 1957 the B.T.C. outlined a new form of organisation. It proposed a merger of the two engineering departments under one officer, a Chief Mechanical and Electrical Engineer – this had already been done by the Southern in July 1956 – and the progressive elimination of the motive power department. Its functions were to be taken over by operating and engineering. But in order to continue the link between movement (or running) and maintenance, a representative of the operating department (or motive power department while it remained) was to deal with maintenance, although he would be responsible to the C.M. & E.E. and dependent on him for the provision of staff and equipment.[71] The regions were then directed by the Commission to move towards this organisation. The Western acted first, in 1957, and the Eastern, London Midland and North Eastern followed suit in 1959. Running and maintenance officers were appointed at district level as officers of the operating departments responsible for maintenance; the operating departments then took over responsibility for employing the footplate staff; and the motive power departments were disbanded. All six regions had taken some action by 1960, but by no means promptly. Dual responsibility for both running and maintenance added some more confusion over the line of authority and a further dimension to the difficulties associated with attempted decentralisation.[72]

Many of the defects of the decentralisation drive were exposed in detail in the report of management consultants Urwick, Orr & Partners, when they were called in by the North Eastern in 1961 to review the area traffic organisation. Their findings were a scathing indictment of the changes of the mid-1950s, and there was more than the odd side-swipe at the entire organisation of the B.T.C. and its railway regions. The consultants discovered that when the North Eastern's new organisation was introduced in April 1957, firm assurances were given to both district and headquarters officers that the appointment of area traffic managers would in no way diminish their existing authority. The traffic managers, on the other hand, were appointed before the boundaries of their areas had been fixed. 'They had no clear understanding of their role, and inevitably were treated as intruders', the consultants declared.

The first Directive giving their role in even the broadest terms, was not issued for 19 months . . . In essence the old and the new organisations . . . [ran] side by side, with the former dominating . . . The changes were introduced in such a way as to secure the maximum ill-will and frustration with minimum improvement in efficiency.[73]

The consultants went on to make several penetrating comments about the general state of local railway management. The marketing and selling functions were found to be 'totally inadequate', and the provision for management control and accountability received a similar verdict. The Area Traffic Managers had been directed by F. C. Margetts, the Assistant General Manager (Traffic), to secure the 'maximum profit return to the undertaking', but with all the important decisions on fares and rates, staffing levels and quality of service taken elsewhere, either at regional or Commission headquarters, it was impossible for them to respond properly. In any case, as Urwick, Orr observed, this objective was viewed by many of the North Eastern's staff as merely a pious hope when other influences (e.g. political aspects of the closure of unprofitable lines) and such prevalent staff attitudes as 'we have a duty to provide customers with what they want regardless of immediate profit' were still powerful. The consultants recognised that some of the difficulties stemmed from a doctrinaire belief in the merits of decentralisation and from the numbing effects of frequent organisational changes. 'A profound sense of uncertainty, insecurity and cynicism has developed and it is probably stronger today [1961] than ever before. In this sense the organisational arrangements between the national centre and Regional Headquarters have by their uncertainty dissipated concentration and effort on the real job of railway management.'[74] As an instance of the problems created by the Commission they specified the Directive of 1957 on the reorganisation of the technical departments, creating a duality of control. Urwick, Orr were firmly of the opinion that maintenance should be in the hands of the technical departments alone, leaving the running function to the operating department. Likewise, the Commission's insistence on a move towards geographical rather than network-based regional boundaries (i.e. the progressive elimination of penetrating lines) was also seen as causing difficulties, since it made virtually impossible the task of framing regional accounts for management control. So when, in 1962, the then General Manager of the North Eastern Region, F. C. Margetts, was asked by Beeching to present a paper to the Officers' Conference on 'The broad principles of business organisation and their application to the nationalised transport undertakings, with particular reference to the Regional management of British Railways', it was not difficult for a man who had been much influenced by Urwick, Orr's findings to produce a long catalogue of deficiencies.[75]

V

It is, of course, difficult, if not impossible, to measure the precise effects of organisational imperfections on the business performance of any company. There is more to management than charts and flow diagrams; determined personalities may succeed however unpromising the institutional framework. Many large organisations experienced problems after the war, and the failings of the B.T.C. should ultimately be judged in the context of managerial responses in the nationalised industries as a whole. But that context was itself confused. The debate about centralisation versus decentralisation, for example, proved to be a hardy perennial, and the arguments raged in several industries. The Fleck Committee of 1955 criticised the National Coal Board for its excessive decentralisation, but a year later the Herbert Committee found that the Central Electricity

Authority had made insufficient provision for it. For railways that debate also had an international dimension. It is clear that the Commission's moves in the direction of decentralised control were in line with thinking elsewhere, for example in Canada and India.[76] Yet the Commission's record remains unimpressive, and it is difficult to deny that the managerial climate at headquarters encouraged complacency and even cynicism lower down. Although the policy of decentralisation was genuine enough, the balance between the centre and the regions remained tipped in favour of the former. This situation was encouraged not only by the existence of the areas of command which the Commission reserved to itself but also by the Ministry of Transport, whose officials undoubtedly preferred to communicate with a more centralised body, even if they criticised the limited access of the late 1950s, whereby *direct* contact was restricted to Robertson and Wansbrough-Jones.[77]

When decentralising moves were made they were too often doctrinaire responses with little or no thought being given to the action really required to secure effective results. For example, it may have been desirable to establish traffic managers to combine operating, motive power and commercial duties (although strong doubts were expressed about the wisdom of such a policy in the Beeching period), but what was really needed was a new selling and marketing organisation in support. This, however, was left to the regions to develop, and very little of consequence was achieved. 'Uncertainty', 'complexity': these words occur again and again in assessments of the Commission's numerous lines of communication, which were condemned even by those who, like Sir Reginald Wilson, were at the centre. The insistence on a centralised system with elaborate channels of authority, coupled with a failure to establish the balance between central and regional decision-making in key areas of control, allowed a climate to develop which encouraged a lack of urgency, particularly in commercial matters.[78] The organisational steps taken in 1953–5 thus confused many railway managers, leaving them at best uncertain, and at worst cynical and hostile. Of course, an element of uncertainty would have existed whatever organisation had been chosen. Perennial problems in the management of nationalised transport are: the vast size of the undertaking, with 800,000 employees in 1955; and the conflict between the standardisation and financial control needs of the business, which encourages centralisation, and the impact of political influence, which has often promoted decentralisation as intrinsically good. The Conservatives' antipathy for the old monolithic B.T.C. created by Labour merely produced another defective structure, a great semi-military bureaucratic edifice prone to changes of organisational emphasis. Only the determination of Robertson, the administrative competence of Wansbrough-Jones and a fair measure of continuity at the top prevented the organisation from collapsing altogether.

So much for the new railway organisation. What it tried, succeeded or failed to do in running the railways – before it in turn was swept away by yet another reorganisation – is the concern of the remaining chapters of Part 2.

6

Deficits, markets and closures

I

Soon after the new railway organisation had been established, in the mid-1950s, the railways' economic fortunes changed dramatically, and in some areas irrevocably. The contrast with the earlier period under the Railway Executive can be seen clearly if the position in 1951–3 is compared with that in successive triennia. In relation to traffic volumes, the passenger business held up quite well, but it did so at a time when private motoring was expanding rapidly. Consequently, as Table 16 shows, the share of the railways (including London Transport) in total passenger-mileage in Britain fell from over 21 per cent in 1951–3 to about 14 per cent in 1960–2. The decline of the freight business was unmistakable: the ton-mileage carried fell by 23 per cent and the market-share dropped from 45 to 29 per cent.

The railways' operating account plunged into rapid decline and consequently, as Table 17 makes clear, the overall financial position deteriorated to an alarming extent. A positive balance on operating account averaging £35.5 million annually in 1951–3, which was supported by charging maintenance costs of £18 million a year to the abnormal maintenance fund (see Appendix A, Table 3), dwindled away to nothing in the course of the next three years, and the deficits became larger and larger thereafter. The sudden decline in net operating revenue in 1954, £16.4 million compared with £34.6 million in 1953, was in large measure a consequence of the B.T.C.'s application of a revised method of charging maintenance. It was recognised that the sums charged to the abnormal maintenance account, based on a rather arbitrary distinction between 'standard' or normal maintenance, charged to revenue, and abnormal maintenance, were not really a measure of war-time arrears overtaken. From 1954 all maintenance was first charged to revenue; a new maintenance equalisation account was established to finance maintenance regarded as 'special'. There was considerable anxiety inside the Commission about the effect of the change. Wilson even suggested that £5 million

Table 16. *British Railways' traffic volumes and market-share, 1951–62 (triennial averages)*

Period	Passenger traffic Mileage ('000m.)	Market-share (%)	Freight traffic Ton-mileage ('000m.)	Market-share (%)
1951–3	24.2	21.4	22.7	45.3
1954–6	24.2	18.9	21.7	40.5
1957–9	25.3	17.9	19.0	35.1
1960–2	23.5	14.3	17.5	29.2

Source: see Appendix D, Tables 1 and 2. Data include L. T. 1951–3 data not strictly comparable with post 1953 data, which include domestic air travel and pipeline movements.

might be taken out of the fund to reduce the size of the deficit shown for 1954, though this was not in fact done. In the Annual Report, it was admitted that the change involved an additional charge of £19 million to revenue (£18 million for the railways). There was certainly a contrast between the £21.2 million drawn from the fund to benefit railways in 1953, and the £2.5 million transferred *from* revenue in 1954 to build up the new equalisation account. This was more than enough to explain the deterioration in the operating results for 1954. Thenceforth, the railways' operating position was more fully exposed.[1]

Things became steadily worse. In the successive triennia 1957–9 and 1960–2, the average annual working loss amounted to £39.1 and £86.2 million respectively (Table 17). The overall balance, calculated by deducting the railways' share of the Commission's central charges (mainly interest payments), naturally fell in tandem. Whichever of the two methods of allocating these charges is used (see Table 17), the enormity of the railways' financial position remains. On the revised basis (col. (g) in Table 17), the 'break-even' position shown to have been enjoyed by the railways in the years 1951–3 was followed by years of steadily mounting losses, reaching £164 million in 1962. From 1954 the annual losses over successive triennia averaged £41.8, £85.3 and £140.8 million respectively. Furthermore, the position would have been much worse had it not been for the extensive financial concessions provided by the government from 1955 onwards. The Commission's borrowings powers, which had been limited to £275 million by the Transport Act of 1953, were soon in danger of being exceeded, and in 1955 and 1959 these powers were extended to a limit of £600 million and £1,200 million respectively. Then, two further measures gave the B.T.C. considerable financial assistance. The Finance Act of 1956 permitted the Minister of Transport to make advances on loan

Table 17. *British Railways' operating performance, 1951–62 (including collection and delivery services, but excluding ships) (£m.)*

Year	(a) Gross revenue	(b) Operating costs	(c) Net operating revenue[a]	(d) Contribution to central charges (Commission's basis)[b]	(e) Overall balance	(f) Contribution to central charges (revised basis)[c]	(g) Overall balance (revised)
1951–3 (annual average)	412.0	376.5	35.5	35.1	0.4	35.5	0.0
1954	449.3	432.9	16.4	38.0	−21.6	39.4	−23.0
1955	453.9	452.1	1.8	40.0	−38.2	42.2	−40.4
1956	481.0	497.5	−16.5	41.0	−57.5	45.5	−62.0
1957	501.4	528.6	−27.1	41.0	−68.1	45.5	−72.6
1958	471.6	519.7	−48.1	42.0	−90.1	46.4	−94.5
1959	457.4	499.4	−42.0	42.0	−84.0	46.7	−88.7
1960	478.6	546.2	−67.7	45.0	−112.7	50.1	−117.8
1961	474.7	561.6	−86.9	49.0	−135.9	53.7	−140.6
1962	465.1	569.1	−104.0	55.0	−159.0	60.1	−164.1

[a] Includes letting of sites and premises in properties in operational use, and commercial advertising.

[b] These charges include miscellaneous receipts and interest as a credit. Central administration costs (arguably an operating cost) are also included. The B.T.C. claimed that the apportionment could 'not be made by reference to some precise formula', Notes on Accounts (Statement IV-5). However, from 1956 it charged the railways with 70 per cent of the charges, rounded down to the nearest million pounds, and this has been applied to earlier years. In 1961 and 1962 the B.T.C. departed from this formula, allocating 71 and 74 per cent respectively to the railways. A 70 per cent allocation in these years would have been £48.0 and £52.0 million.

[c] Revised calculation as explained in Table 8, above, p. 93.

Source: B.T.C., R. & A. 1951–62.

to the Commission from the Consolidated Fund as an alternative to the issuing of British Transport Stock. In the period 1956–62 £773 million was advanced in this way (£82 million was repaid). The Transport (Railway Finances) Act of 1957 gave to the Commission temporary borrowing powers in order to relieve the burden of interest payments and future railway deficits. First, provision was made for the capitalisation of interest on railway borrowings in the period 1956–65, subject to a time-limit of three years after the year of borrowing. Second, the Minister was empowered to advance sums equivalent to railway deficits in 1956–62, up to a maximum of £250 million (raised to £400 million in 1959), and to cover interest on these advances for a period of five years after the year of borrowing. The deficits and the deferred interest were to be transferred to a Special (Suspense) Account in the B.T.C.'s books. Thus, by deferring interest on capital borrowings for railways purposes, and making advances to cover both the operating deficits incurred from 1956 and the interest thereon, first as loans, then from 1960 as outright grants, the Minister of Transport allowed the Commission to transfer large sums to the Special Account. By the end of 1962 the balance in the account stood at £935 million. But for these provisions, an additional £158 million in interest payments would have been debited to the railways over the period 1956–62, £100 million of which would have been charged to the years 1960–2.[2]

The railways' financial difficulties were so serious that the B.T.C.'s other activities – London Transport, bus services, British Road Services (the rump of the nationalised road haulage interests), ships, property transactions, hotels and catering, inland waterways, docks – were unable to make much of a dent in the deficit. Inland waterways made small but persistent operating losses, while the other businesses produced a modest surplus. If central charges are allocated on the revised basis (as in Table 17), then these activities taken together can be shown to have made an overall profit of £114 million, 1954–62, or £12.7 million a year, enough to wipe off only about 14 per cent of the railways' accumulated losses of nearly £804 million, or £89.3 million a year. Consequently, the B.T.C. as a whole experienced losses amounting to £690 million, 1954–62, a position which was in sharp contrast with the declared profits of £12 million in 1951–3. Of course, thanks to government intervention, the Commission's balance sheets told a rather different story. The overall losses of £11.9 million in 1954 and £30.6 million in 1955 brought the accumulated deficit for 1948–55 to £69.8 million. Thereafter, interest and railway operating losses totalling £707 million were carried to the Special Account, leaving the non-railway activities showing a profit of nearly £60 million in the period 1956–62. If there had been no financial adjustment, the accumulated

Table 18. The railways' 'true' financial results, 1954–62 (£m.)

Year	(a) Gross working surplus	(b) Net working surplus	(c) Total balance (after interest)	(d) Total balance at constant 1948 prices	(e) Revised total balance (excluding drawings on Maintenance Equalisation Account)
1948–53 (ann. aver.)	47.4	17.5	−4.8	−4.6	−19.2
1954	39.0	1.1	−23.0	−18.0	−16.1
1955	22.8	−17.5	−42.7	−32.3	−29.5
1956	12.1	−31.3	−57.7	−41.1	−40.9
1957	4.8	−43.3	−72.0	−49.3	−52.5
1958	−8.6	−61.9	−94.3	−61.7	−67.3
1959	6.8	−52.3	−89.1	−57.4	−64.9
1960	−15.6	−80.6	−122.4	−77.5	−84.5
1961	−27.2	−99.3	−146.1	−89.7	−96.1
1962	−47.8	−125.6	−177.0	−105.1	−105.9

[a] Net receipts of railways plus capital charges added back.
[b] Gross working surplus less depreciation and amortisation on a current replacement cost basis.
For further details, see Commentary to Appendix A.
Source: Appendix A, below.

losses for 1948–62 would have been shown to be about £717 million, and this disregards the treatment of maintenance expenditure.

Table 18 sets out the re-worked data (see above, pp. 95–6 and Appendix A) for 1954–62, together with the annual average for 1948–53. The analysis in no way alters the seriousness of the financial position in these years. The railways, after experiencing modest losses of £4.8 million a year in current prices in 1948–53, are shown to have made losses rising from £23 million in 1954 to £177 million in 1962, a cumulative loss from 1948 of about £850 million. In constant 1948 prices, losses ranged from £18 million in 1954 to £105 million in 1962. Drawings on the newly established maintenance equalisation account made only a marginal difference to the size of the annual deficits. If all maintenance expenditure had been charged to revenue, the losses for 1954–62 in constant prices would have been £558 million instead of £532 million (calculated from Table 18). By 1962 the railways were in a parlous financial state. Indeed, 1961 and 1962 emerge as two of the worst three years in the history of nationalised railways (the other was 1967).

II

Why did the railways' fortunes change so dramatically from the mid-1950s? To produce a list of explanations is easy; to assess their relative importance is much harder. The traffic data reveal that all of the major freight categories were moving into secular decline after 1953. Table 19 shows clearly that although passenger-mileage was maintained almost until 1962, freight ton-mileage began to fall, with minor fluctuations, from 1951 and then markedly after 1957. By 1962 freight traffic was nearly 30 per cent below its level in 1953. The three major categories – coal, merchandise and minerals – exhibited results which did not differ markedly from the general trend, although the fall in minerals did not begin until 1957 and the reduction in merchandise traffic of 23 per cent, 1953–62 was less pronounced than the 32 per cent fall experienced by both types of heavy freight. Railway managers variously accounted for the decline in their freight business. Britain's coal production was well down on the optimistic predictions of the immediate post-war years, and tonnage extracted fell by 12 per cent over the period 1953–62. Changes in the location of heavy industry were, from the mid-1950s, working to reduce the average length of haul of some traffics. The average haul of coal, for example, fell from 56.9 miles in 1953 to 48.3 miles in 1962, a reduction of 15 per cent, while that of minerals fell from 76.9 to 70.1 miles in the same period. Above all, of course, there was the increasingly successful challenge of the road hauliers for both trunk and short-haul transits, a feature encouraged by significant developments in the technical capability

Table 19. *Traffic carried by British Railways, 1948–62 (millions)*

| Year | Passenger-miles[a] | Freight net ton-miles | | | | Freight index 1953 = 100 |
		Coal/coke	Merchandise/ livestock	Minerals	Total	
1948	21,022	9,662[b]	7,041[b]	4,959[b]	21,622[b]	95.2
1951	20,561	10,660	7,078	5,164	22,902	100.6
1953	20,578	10,715	6,790	5,261	22,766	100.0
1954	20,712	10,489	6,542	5,059	22,089	97.0
1955	20,308	10,191	6,087	5,075	21,353	93.8
1956	21,133	10,248	6,008	5,217	21,473	94.3
1957	22,591	9,869	5,944	5,068	20,880	91.7
1958	21,725	8,927	5,231	4,268	18,426	80.9
1959	21,845	8,004	5,376	4,331	17,711	77.8
1960	21,143	8,105	5,706	4,840	18,650	81.9
1961	20,675	7,749	5,553	4,289	17,591	77.3
1962	19,392	7,304	5,200	3,601	16,104	70.7

[a] Post-1958 data adjusted for comparability with 1948–58.
[b] 1948 data adjusted for comparability with 1949–62.
Source: Munby and Watson, *Statistics*, pp. 87, 105.

of the motor lorry. It might be tempting to attribute much of the railways' difficulties to the inexorable march of changes outside the control of the regional freight managers.

Such a temptation should be resisted, however. The railways' financial problems did not follow simply from the decline of the freight business, important though this was. In fact, the *volume* of traffic carried by the nationalised railways in the period 1948–62 remained higher than that carried by the private companies immediately before the war, though by 1962 the freight results were not much different from 1938 levels. As has been stressed earlier, the crucial area of explanation must therefore lie in the relationship between rates and fares on the one hand, and the costs of the traffic carried on the other. This in turn raises questions about managerial strategy and competence, and the perception of the business's role. To what extent did railway managers recognise that there was an imbalance between these crucial elements? What did they do about it and why? To what extent were they confused by external institutional and political constraints?

The following pages will attempt to answer some of these questions. Attention is first given to the general pattern of costs over the period to 1962, in order to provide some background to the following extensive discussion of rates and fares, and commercial policy. Subsequently, the structure of railway costs is examined more closely. The final section of this chapter deals with the B.T.C.'s attempts to curtail operating costs by rationalising unremunerative services. Chapter 7 focusses exclusively on labour, since wages and salaries formed such a high proportion of total costs, and the railways' productivity record in the 1950s is assessed. Finally, Chapter 8 turns to the controversial Modernisation Plan of 1955, which provided for higher levels of railway investment. The question asked here is: how successful was this attempt to break out of the railways' rates/costs vice?

Costs continued to rise steadily from 1953. British Railways' operating costs, which had averaged £377 million a year in 1951–3, and amounted to £400 million in 1953, rose to £529 million in 1957 and then, after some fluctuations, reached £569 million in 1962 (see Table 17). This 42 per cent increase on 1953 compares with an increase in the price level of only 35 per cent over the same period. Moreover, since the industry's 'output', measured in terms of the traffic carried and workshops' production, fell by 13 per cent, 1953–62, it is clear that unit costs rose considerably in real terms.[3] In its Annual Reports, the B.T.C. frequently complained about the rising cost of labour and materials (particularly coal), and its impact upon the railways' operating position, as it had done before 1953. During the years 1956–62, the average cost per ton of coal, the major raw material input, increased by 40 per cent, twice the rate of inflation. Comparison of coal prices with those of other inputs, however, (see Table 20) shows this to be exceptional. Although the price of steel rails, for example, rose by 39 per cent over the longer period 1953–62, most of the rise occurred before 1956 and the 1962 price was held until 1965. And, as the Table also shows, the relative prices of the two substitutes for coal, electricity and diesel oil, moved in the railways' favour, that of diesel oil falling by 38 per cent between 1957 and 1962. The cost of labour, which made up about 60 per cent of total operating expenses, was a very different matter. Over the period 1953–62 average weekly earnings of adult males working for the railways increased by 70 per cent, from 178s. 9d. (£8.94) in 1953 to 304s. (£15.20) in 1962, and those of adult males in the wage-based 'conciliation grades' by 72 per cent, from 172s. 3d. (£8.61) to 297s. (£14.85). Although the rise in earnings was higher than this in many other industries (see below, Chapter 7, pp. 217–18, 244), railwaymen's pay clearly outstripped the 35 per cent increase in retail prices in 1953–62. Five pay increases were granted from January 1954 to January 1956, during a period of disturbed industrial relations which culminated in a strike by A.S.L.E.F. in May–June 1955. There were further significant awards in 1960 and 1962, in the wake of Guillebaud's Railway Pay Committee of Inquiry which reported in March 1960.[4] Thus, while the railway labour force continued to fall, having been cut from 594,000 at the end of 1953 to about 475,000 at the end of 1962, the railways' wage-bill increased from approximately £265 million to £365 million over the same period. Although these figures are

Table 20. *Costs of selected railways inputs, 1953–62*

Year	Coal per ton[a] (£)	Steel rails per ton (£)	Electricity per unit (p.)	Diesel oil per gall. (p.)	G.D.P. Deflator (Feinstein) 1956 = 100
1953	n.a.	30.50 (81)	0.551 (85)	n.a.	89
1954	n.a.	31.50 (84)	0.607 (93)	n.a.	91
1955	n.a.	34.12 (91)	0.629 (96)	n.a.	94
1956	5.06 (100)	37.62 (100)	0.652 (100)	5.84 (100)	100
1957	5.51 (109)	42.25 (112)	0.689 (106)	6.66 (114)	104
1958	5.85 (116)	41.75 (111)	0.682 (105)	5.72 (98)	109
1959	5.87 (116)	41.25 (110)	0.683 (105)	5.64 (97)	110
1960	5.98 (118)	41.25 (110)	0.682 (105)	4.57 (78)	112
1961	6.45 (127)	41.25 (110)	0.697 (107)	4.46 (76)	116
1962	7.06 (140)	42.40 (113)	0.664 (102)	4.14 (71)	120

[a] The data are estimates using the power costs of steam traction divided by the tonnage of locomotive coal used. A series of coal prices per imperial ton at the pithead for *all* coal grades supplied to British Railways by the N.C.B. indicates an increase of 26 per cent, from £4.33 a ton in 1956 to £5.42 in 1962 (although note that the £5.42 price was held from November 1960 to November 1963). Information from N.C.B.
Source: B.T.C., *R. & A. 1953–62*, II, Table VI–1a, X3; steel rails: B.S.C. data on Flat Bottom Sections (109/110A/113A), 1948–82, B.R.B.

only estimates,[*] the suggested rise of nearly 40 per cent certainly exceeded the general advance of prices. Job losses did not lead to any improvement in the railways' labour costs.[5]

Just as in the days of the Railway Executive, the B.T.C. continued to make much of the effect on its financial position of the delays between the increases in its costs, chiefly the resolution of wage claims, and the granting of its applications to raise freight rates and passenger fares in response. For example, its Report for 1955 claimed that the whole of the accumulated deficit of £70 million since 1948 could be accounted for in this way, and a diagram was produced showing the contribution of the several factors to the shortfall (see Figure 3). On seven occasions from the devaluation of sterling in September 1949 to the end of 1955:

the Commission could see, as at each date, that an increase in their Railway and London Transport charges had become inevitable in order to match higher wages and other costs and to preserve the Commission's financial position in real terms, and the Commission took action accordingly to obtain approval. Taking into account the delays involved on each of these occasions before such increases (or modified increases) were sanctioned, the total loss of receipts over this period, it

[*]The first published data on railway 'staff expenses' (including national insurance, retirement benefits, etc.) appear in B.R.B., *R. & A. 1963*, II, p. 44.

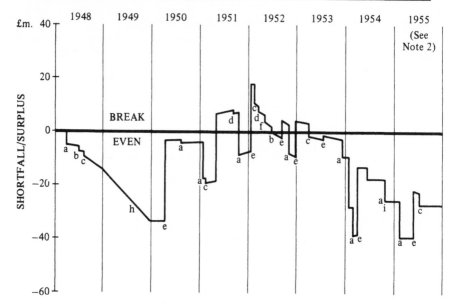

Figure 3 British Railways: approximate trend of net traffic receipts (after eliminating seasonal fluctuations), showing surplus or shortfall compared with minimum contribution required to central charges, 1948–55

Notes:
1. Major changes are shown as follows:
Increases in wage rates and price levels
a Wage rates
b National Insurance contributions
c Coal prices
d Prices of other materials
e Increases in fares and charges
f Decreases in fares
g Charge in treatment of maintenance expenditure
h Devaluation of sterling
i Wages grades pension scheme
2. The estimated effect of the railway strike has been eliminated from the results of the year 1955.

Source: B.T.C., *R. & A. 1955*, I, p. 53.

can be shown, amounted to over £50m. Nor is that the whole story. The Commission have throughout been prevented from keeping any margin in newly adjusted charges to provide against further price movements against them in the period lying ahead. Thus in the various intervals before new applications in turn became inevitable, the Commission were carrying increased and uncovered charges totalling, it can now be estimated, about £50m. Hence it is now apparent that the direct costs of inflation in money terms, as far as British Railways and London Transport are concerned and up to the end of 1955, have been over £100m.

Further complaints about the effect of such lags were made in subsequent Reports.[6]

In 1956 these published incriminations were extended to include the government's direct intervention to restrain increased charges, as part of its price-pause strategy. In February the Commission applied for a 10 per cent increase in railway freight charges to offset the cost of the January wage award, but in the following month the Minister, in the Commission's words, 'decided that it would be expedient to grant only half of this increase'. The B.T.C. was also persuaded to abstain from making any increase in its passenger fares during the year. In return, the government offered the financial concessions which were embodied in the Transport (Railway Finances) Act of 1957. However, they did nothing to help prevent further operating deficits, and there is no doubt at all that the Commission felt that the events of 1956 were damaging in the long term. The Report for 1958 referred in bitter tones to the 'policy of deficit financing which was deliberately introduced in 1956', attributing £55 million of the year's overall deficit of £89 million to this factor.[7] When, in 1969, Sir Reginald Wilson looked back over more than 20 years of nationalised transport, he singled out the circumstances of 1956 for particular attention:

the Commission found itself involved in deliberate deficit-financing when the Minister of the day [Watkinson] not only suggested a general 'restraint' in the interests of stopping the inflationary spiral, but actually over-rode a judgment from the responsible and independent Tribunal in the matter of additional coal freights for railways. The additional annual revenues thus lost by the railways (£17m. on coal freights alone) may not have seemed too formidable – though in all conscience formidable enough – but the principle at stake was vital, and things were never the same again. The Commission's railways were now on the slippery slope of rising cost – of all kinds – but delayed and restricted price adjustments.[8]

There was a good deal of truth in the Commission's complaints as indeed there had been in their complaints of the early fifties. Pricing decisions taken at the centre were in essence ad hoc responses to the cost implications of a wage increase or the budgetary implications of the worsening deficit position. Prompt action was therefore desired. But delays of up to five months in the introduction of revised charges schemes were commonplace, and on some occasions they were much longer. It was nine months, for example, before an increase in London fares, applied for in December 1953, was introduced, in September 1954. By 1958 the Commission was induced to launch bolder pricing initiatives. In September, responding to the Minister's exhortation to stabilise the deficit, it applied to the Transport Tribunal for a 50 per cent increase in the maximum permitted ordinary railway fares – from 2d. to 3d. second-class per mile – in order to give the railways the necessary 'headroom' for pricing in the future. However, this new maximum was not confirmed by the Tribunal until August 1959, and higher charges were not introduced until the following November, 16 months after the Commission had sanctioned the scheme in July 1958.[9]

The Transport Act of 1953 – that symbol of a liberating commercial policy for transport – had done little to simplify the cumbersome machinery surrounding railway charges. Although the Act introduced a special provision (Section 23) enabling the Commission to obtain temporary but limited increases in charges in response to rising costs, and made the first moves towards the granting of full commercial freedom to the railways by allowing them to discriminate between customers, it retained much of the existing framework and added further complications of its own. The Minister's right to intervene 'in the national interest' under Section 4 (1) of the 1947 Act was retained. So too was the Transport Tribunal, although it was now to receive schemes for *maximum* charges instead of standard or fixed ones. These charges were to be published by the B.T.C. For the protection of monopoly traffic customers (where 'merchandise cannot reasonably be carried by any other means of transport') Section 22 enabled them to appeal to the Tribunal if they considered rail charges to be 'unreasonable or unfair'. If the Act freed the railways from the shackles of nineteenth-century restrictions, as has often been claimed, then it also left a fair number of these on the statute book, and the process of altering rail tariffs remained complex.[10] Indeed, the 1953 Act contributed directly to some of the delays experienced by the Commission. Its insistence on the submission of *maximum* charges schemes had the effect of delaying still further the long-awaited introduction of a new merchandise charges scheme to cover all categories of freight, including coal and minerals. As mentioned earlier (see above, p. 115), work on this scheme had started as far back as 1950. A draft scheme, revised to conform with the new legislation, was finally completed in October 1954. It reached the Tribunal in March 1955, after five months of consultation with interested parties. This was not the end of the story. In July 1956 the Tribunal, in an 'interim decision', asked for substantial revisions to the scheme; these, which were eventually confirmed on 31 December, watered down the Commission's plans. Maximum rates were to be replaced by 'reasonable' rates for a substantial tranche of traffic, that carried in owners' wagons or in consignments of 100 tons and over, and reduced maxima were advocated for private siding traffic and goods loaded in bulk. It was not until July 1957 that the modified scheme came into force, seven years after work had first begun on it. Although the difficulties of reshaping the railways' antiquated rate system worked against a speedy resolution of the problem of merchandise charges, changes in the law and the operation of the Tribunal machinery greatly prolonged the delay.

The B.T.C.'s position was also affected by the government's continuing interest in railway charges policy. This interest had been strengthened by the precedent of April 1952 when a Ministerial Direction had been used to block an increase in London fares which had been confirmed by the Transport Tribunal.[11] The gap between the government's expressed faith in competition and commercial freedom for the railways and its attitude to proposed changes in railway tariffs was substantial. This soon became clear during the drafting of the Transport Bill in 1952. On 10 April the Cabinet had approved the draft White Paper on Transport Policy, which contained a paragraph promising to give the Commission freedom to raise railway charges. In a revised draft, considered on 22 April, this was altered to give freedom 'to raise or lower charges'. When it was pointed out that this was hardly consistent with the government's action on London fares seven days earlier, the wording was hastily amended to provide freedom to raise or lower charges 'subject to the over-riding powers of the Minister'![12]

Thereafter, applications to raise passenger fares and freight charges were closely monitored by the Cabinet. In February 1954, after the Commission's application to raise freight rates by 10 per cent had been endorsed by the Tribunal, it was minuted that the 'Government had not resigned themselves to the prospect of periodical increases of railway charges'. However, in the following month, when the Commission's plans to raise London fares were announced, they decided to refrain from direct intervention.[13] Twelve months later the possibility of the Minister, then John Boyd-Carpenter, using his powers to issue a Direction was under active consideration, after the acceptance by the Tribunal of an interim application to increase passenger fares under Section 23 of the 1953 Act. The Cabinet decided against such a move, but instructed Boyd-Carpenter to inform Robertson that no action should be taken by the Commission until evidence could be shown of satisfactory progress to reduce over-manning and restrictive practices in the industry. As the threat of a strike by A.S.L.E.F. emerged in April, the Cabinet resolved to 'let things follow their normal course'.[14]

The 1956 intervention, however, was a significant and direct inter-ference in the pricing of rail transport. The government's price-freeze policy was applied to all the nationalised industries, but the railways suffered more than most from its application. In February the Commis-sion, prompted by the Finance Committee's warnings about the 'extreme seriousness of [its] financial position,' had agreed that freight charges should be raised by 10 per cent. It also decided to make a number of adjustments to passenger fares in both London and the provinces, partly under existing powers, and partly by a further application to the Transport Tribunal under Section 23 of the 1953 Act. After warning noises had been sounded about overheating in the economy by the newly appointed Chancellor, Harold Macmillan, the Minister of Transport, now Harold Watkinson, told Robertson in March that although government policy required the nationalised industries to set prices in such a way as fully to cover their costs, in this instance he felt that it was 'expedient' to raise freight rates by only 5 per cent, half the amount asked for. Pressure was also successfully applied to shelve the increases in passenger fares. Robertson agreed to postpone the application to the Tribunal for six months, and to refrain from using the Commission's existing powers to raise fares for the same period.[15] All this came *before* the government embarked on a more general policy of price restraint for the nationalised industries, in June. Once again Robertson reluctantly complied with the government's wishes. He agreed to make no general increase in passenger fares for the rest of the year, and gave a similar undertaking with regard to freight rates, 'provided that, as a result of the re-assessment of their financial position now being made, a course of action consistent with their statutory obligations and the proper development of their undertaking can be worked out and adopted.'[16]

It is clear that during these exchanges members of the Finance Committee, and Sir Reginald Wilson in particular, were dismayed by the course of events. The railways had good cause to feel indignant. The other nationalised industries had been able to raise their charges before the June freeze was applied – coal and gas prices had been increased on 1 June – while the railways were asked to make a double sacrifice. Moreover, the size of the wage award of January 1956, which was estimated to add some £25 million to annual costs, made a swift pricing response imperative. As *The Economist* pointed out, the prices of coal, gas and to a considerable extent electricity, were 'being solidified at around the temperature of current costs. By comparison the railways present a contrast that is dramatic and frightening.' Robertson, it seems, had given in to the government only after a lengthy meeting with the Prime Minister, Anthony Eden, and his leading Ministers. He had gone, said *The Economist*, 'to the very limit of what the most ardent devotee of the policy of "freezing" could have demanded'.[17] The B.T.C., having seen its cash reserves draining away partly as a result of interference of this kind, was being led down the path of ever-mounting deficits.[18]

The government's interference with the pricing freedom of the Commission elicited the sympathy of many observers. The Select Committee on Nationalised Industries of 1960 was critical of both the Tribunal and the Minister of Transport. It recommended that the services of the former might easily be dispensed with, and suggested that the railways should be fully compensated for the cost of Ministerial interventions in 1952 and 1956. In general in the nationalised industries, and especially on the railways, Whitehall, as Denys Munby observed, had 'exercised power without responsibility, by exerting pressure on the Boards of these "independent" corporations, but in such a way as not to be accountable to the public, and so as to enable blame to be thrown onto the Boards'.[19]

The very process of adjusting railway charges in this manner served to stiffen public resistance to regular price increases. Applications to raise charges, as the B.T.C. frequently lamented, provoked a much fiercer response than did their equivalents in other industries. In its Report for 1960 the Commission complained that the 'long-drawn-out processes of public enquiry and argument about the price of road and rail facilities has [sic] given this a special significance in the mind of the public and has even affected the willingness of the public to pay reasonable fares'. Report after Report pointed out that railway charges, for both passenger and freight services, were lower in real terms than they had been before the war.[20] This was certainly true. Ordinary passenger fares were increased from 1.75d. a mile third-class to 1.88d. in 1955, 2d. second-class* in 1957, and thence by ¼d. steps in 1959, 1960 and 1961 to 3d. in 1962. Some action was also taken to increase special low fares. Season-ticket rates were regularly revised, and early morning fares were abolished over the period 1959–62. However, many low fares persisted, and the debates about passenger pricing in the 1950s, which were sometimes inventive – Robertson suggested a surcharge for travel at peak periods, for example – all too often reflected an anxiety about the market in the face of coach and air competition. The decision to 'taper' long-distance fares when applying an increase in 1959 was indicative of the concern among General Managers and commercial officers about 'strong passenger resistance' to regular fare rises.[21] Consequently, as is evident from Table 21, average receipts per passenger-mile, which had been 1.40d. (0.58p) in 1948 and 1.34d. (0.56p) in 1953, amounted to only 1.54d. (0.64p) in 1959, about 30 per cent below the real value of the charges made by the main-line companies in 1938 and the Railway Executive in 1948. Although fares were hoisted after 1959, by 1962 the average charge per passenger-mile remained below 2d. – 1.99d. (0.83p). In real terms, the 1962 average was 16 per cent lower than in 1948. The real value of freight rates also fell. While the average receipts per net ton-mile for all categories increased steadily in money terms, from 2.00d. (0.83p) in 1948 to 3.32d. (1.38p) in 1957 and 3.37d. (1.40p) in the following year, in real terms railway charges were little above those of 20 years before. The position then deteriorated, and by 1962 the average receipt of 3.34d. (1.39p) was in real terms 10 per cent below the 1938 level, and barely equal to that of 1948. Here, the major weakness was the failure to maintain the real value of merchandise rates.

*Third-class was abolished in 1956 and replaced by second-class.

Table 21. *Average receipts per passenger-mile, and average receipts per net ton-mile, 1938–62 (old pence)*

Year	Current prices				Real relative 1948 prices (1948 weights)			
	Passenger: all categories	Freight: coal/coke	merchandise/ livestock	all categories	Passenger: all categories	Freight: coal/coke	merchandise/ livestock	all categories
1938	0.79	0.93	1.89	1.22	1.43	1.68	3.41	2.20
1948	1.40	1.66	2.90	2.00	1.40	1.66	2.90	2.00
1953	1.34	2.44	3.85	2.77	1.07	1.95	3.08	2.22
1957	1.48	3.11	4.32	3.32	1.01	2.13	2.95	2.27
1958	1.52	3.28	4.22	3.37	0.99	2.15	2.76	2.21
1959	1.54	3.27	3.92	3.27	0.99	2.11	2.53	2.11
1960	1.72	3.22	3.78	3.18	1.09	2.04	2.39	2.01
1962	1.99	3.39	3.89	3.34	1.18	2.01	2.31	1.98

Note: Adjustments were made to the data for 1938 and 1948 to produce a roughly consistent series. The passenger figure for '1938' is for October 1938–September 1939 and those for 1959–62 were adjusted to take account of a change in the calculation of passenger-mileage (see Table 19, above).

Source: B.T.C., R. & A. 1948–62; Munby and Watson, *Statistics*, pp. 93–4, 114; Feinstein, *National Income*, T133.

In current prices, average receipts reached a peak of 4.32d. (1.8p) per ton-mile in 1957, but remained below the 1938 level in real terms. Then the money rates fell back, partly as a result of the Transport Tribunal's decision to cut the maximum rates applied for under the merchandise charges scheme by an average of 14 per cent, and partly as a result of the commercial strategy associated with the new scheme. The 1962 average of 3.89d. (1.62p) per ton-mile represented in real terms a 32 per cent fall on the 1938 rates and a 20 per cent fall on the 1948 rates. Although, as Table 21 also shows, the real value of charges for coal and coke was maintained, even these rates failed to keep pace with inflation after 1958, and by 1962 they had slipped back, in terms of constant prices, to mid-1950s levels.

III

The B.T.C. may readily attract sympathy for having to contend with these externally planted obstacles to change in its pricing policy during the later 1950s. But what of the internal obstacles?

Robertson's own managerial contribution was not left unscathed by his contemporaries inside the Commission. Some thought him much too deferential to the government and therefore at least partly to blame for allowing the gap between costs and charges to develop. As one former colleague put it, 'if you have been a top soldier and a diplomat, as Robertson was, your training is such that in the end you do not disobey your political boss'. Whether Robertson was in fact bullied into accommodating the government in 1956, as the *Manchester Guardian* suggested, or whether he entered into price restraint voluntarily with the hope of gaining assistance with the railways' financial difficulties, he certainly gave his political masters what they required. Yet it is doubtful if a more aggressive personality at the top would have extracted much more from Macmillan and Eden; and highly unlikely that the Commission would have been able to avoid all forms of price control had someone else been at the helm. Robertson's instincts may have been conciliatory, but his statements at several Commission meetings indicate that he fully shared Wilson's concern about the railways' financial plight and the need to bring prices into line with costs.[22]

A more likely internal obstacle to price changes was the fear of traffic losses in the face of competition from road transport. Although the B.T.C. complained about the effects of delays in raising its prices, its Annual Reports also contained strong hints that competitive conditions would prevent the railways from automatically raising charges to match costs. The Report for 1955, for example, said that although freight rates had been raised by 10 per cent in March 1954 and by a further 7.5 per cent in June 1955, on both occasions 'the full amount of the increase has not always been obtainable for competitive reasons'. And in the Report for 1958, a year in which the Tribunal had granted powers to raise maximum rates by 10 per cent, the fall in merchandise rates was attributed largely to the 'selective decreases made ... in order to gain or retain worthwhile traffics'.[23] By 1960 the position had become much clearer. Having been given a greater measure of commercial freedom by the Transport Act of 1953 and the eventual introduction of the merchandise charges scheme in 1957, the Commission was anxious to use it to introduce an element of discriminatory pricing. In its Report for 1959 it expressed satisfaction that in that year general merchandise tonnage had increased for the first time for some years. The improvement, which was a small one (2.3 per cent), was attributed to the 'imaginative commercial action on the part of the railway staff in all Regions'.[24] The internal reality was rather different. Some of the maximum charges fixed by the 1957 scheme were lower than those actually charged, making rate reductions unavoidable. And all too often the new commercial freedom was being applied to cut existing rates in order to retain traffics without considering the costs of handling the business, a policy which ran counter to B.T.C. instructions to the regions to raise charges within the scheme. As early as December 1957 the Finance Committee, monitoring the progress of the charges scheme, observed that rates were being scaled downwards and lamented the fact that 'little progress had been made in applying higher rates to unprofitable traffics which had been and were still being carried at "exceptional" rates'. The Committee emphasised that 'proper progress must be made in the re-negotiation of freight rates to bring them more into line with costs'. But it was not until Beeching succeeded Robertson as Chairman in 1961 that the Commission's Annual Reports began to reflect the determination to price with traffic costs more firmly in mind.[25] There was obviously a gap between the expectation of best pricing practice at the centre, where contracts with the larger customers were specifically costed, and the actions of railway managers in the regions, who acted to reduce many merchandise rates in order to protect the railways' market-share from penetration by road transport.

Stewart Joy, one of the most vocal critics of the railways' pricing operations in the 1950s, has claimed that the B.T.C. in its freight business was 'highly irresponsible in its management and control', providing 'the greatest bargain sale in railway history'. Though conceding that the railways were moving towards a schedule of rates based loosely on costs he castigated the Commission for using the fact that it was difficult, if not impossible, to quote a cost-based rate for *every* consignment to hide fundamental errors in the rate-setting process. The Commission's claim before the Transport Tribunal was that a considerable proportion of its costs was fixed – chiefly track and signalling costs – and could not be varied with changes in traffic levels. This notion, said Joy, which persisted even in the Beeching period, led on to the instruction that managers should price above the floor of direct or variable costs. Any margin above the floor would contribute towards the railways' total fixed or indirect costs, but there was no attempt to allocate such costs to particular traffics. This strategy, which came to be known as 'contribution accounting', might have worked reasonably well, he argued, had it been heeded by the regional managers, but the evidence indicates that it was not, particularly after freight traffic fell off during the recession of 1958. He blamed both central and regional organisation for this failure. In the regions, the separation of the commercial and operating functions meant that the man quoting a rate was not the man responsible for investigating traffic costs. At the top, the Commission did not face up to what it must have known, namely that traffics were being accepted at rates which did not even cover direct, let alone indirect, costs. It 'just sat on its hands and said, in effect, that there was no connection between the prices it could obtain for traffics and the quantity of those traffics it could profitably carry'.[26]

While there is some truth in Joy's allegations, his stance is uncompromising. Joy saw railway management in the 1950s and 1960s simply as a lumbering dinosaur in its death-throes. The ultimate responsibility for weaknesses in the railways' pricing responses must obviously rest with the Commission. Nevertheless, the emphasis needs to be placed more upon the difficulties which it had in controlling its extensive empire than upon the contention that it deliberately flew in the face of unpalatable information about traffic costs. As already noted, there was from the start an anxiety about the way in which regional managers were responding to the pricing of merchandise traffic after the introduction of the new charges scheme in 1957. And after the new organisation of 1955 had been established, the Commission did try hard to encourage the concentration of commercial and operating functions at regional level. If comparatively little success attended their efforts, the obstacle was Robertson's cumbersome organisation. This was the real lumbering dinosaur, for it was unable to accommodate rapid changes in fundamental policy. Moreover, with the exception of the Eastern Region and its 'line management', the regional responses were disappointing.

Despite the efforts of Harold Osborn, the Chief Accountant and Financial Adviser, and the Costings Division, led first by Tait (until 1956), then by D. M. Dear, which produced abundant material for the Finance Committee on traffic costs, hard evidence on the real problems of the freight business emerged only slowly. The long-promised Freight Traffic Survey, analogous to the Passenger Train Census of 1952, was delayed by the preparation of the merchandise charges scheme; it was, in effect, overtaken by other studies. Although reported to be in the course of

Table 22. *Railway operating margins and estimates of profit/loss for specific traffics, 1949–60 (£m.)*

	Gross receipts (i)	Direct costs[a] (ii)	Operating margin (i)−(ii)	Joint costs[b] (iii)	Total costs (iv)	Profit/loss (i)−(iv)
1. Passenger						
1949[c]	115.0	92.6	22.4	40.1	132.7	−17.7
1956	130.6	139.4	−8.8	67.2	206.6	−76.0
1957	142.2	155.2	−13.0	72.9	228.1	−85.9
1958	141.7	156.2	−14.5	75.7	231.9	−90.2
1959	143.9	150.4	−6.5	74.7	225.1	−81.2
1960	155.4	159.2	−3.8	83.9	243.1	−87.7
2. Parcels[d]						
1949[c]	29.6	23.4	6.2	4.2	27.6	2.0
1956	48.5	33.4	15.1	6.6	40.0	8.5
1957	52.3	36.7	15.6	7.5	44.2	8.1
1958	52.8	36.8	16.0	8.0	44.8	8.0
1959	54.1	36.6	17.5	8.4	45.0	9.1
1960	56.3	40.8	15.5	9.5	50.3	6.0
3. Freight						
1949[c]	189.5	172.0	17.5	34.9	206.9	−17.4
1956	301.0	248.8	52.2	56.1	304.9	−3.9
1957	306.9	252.6	54.3	59.2	311.8	−4.9
1958	277.1	243.4	33.7	57.1	300.5	−23.4
1959	259.4	231.3	28.1	54.5	285.8	−26.4
1960	266.9	252.7	14.2	60.8	313.5	−46.6
4. Total						
1949[c]	334.1	288.0	46.1	79.2	367.2	−33.1
1956	480.1	421.6	58.5	129.9	551.5	−71.4
1957	501.4	445.5	56.9	139.6	584.1	−82.7
1958	471.6	436.4	35.2	140.8	577.2	−105.6
1959	457.4	418.3	39.1	137.6	555.9	−98.5
1960	478.6	452.7	25.9	154.2	606.9	−128.3

[a] Direct costs = train-working, marshalling, infrastructure, terminal and documentation costs, loss and damage, commercial costs and road conveyance. Includes interest (at 3%) on value of assets employed. The assumption is made that half of current replacement costs has been accumulated. For buildings, bridges, etc., historic cost is used (1935–7 values).

[b] Joint or indirect costs = track and signalling, general administration and the balance of central charges not absorbed by interest charged directly. These were apportioned on the basis of share of gross ton-miles for track, train-miles for signalling; general admin. costs were spread proportionately to the allocation of direct costs. Some allowance was made for the additional costs incurred by passenger traffic on account of speed, safety and superior facilities.

[c] The 1949 data were calculated on a different basis. Renewal provision was based on gross (not net) replacement cost and revenue from the letting of sites, and commercial advertising was excluded.

completion as late as March 1958, it seems never to have reached the Finance Committee in the form envisaged four years earlier.[27] It might be argued that there was already sufficient information in the Reports of 1950 and 1951 to show that the railways were under-pricing and over-selling much of their merchandise traffic (see above, pp. 108–9), and these studies were supplemented by others in the mid-1950s. For example, a report on freight traffic policy, presented in March 1956 by a traffic survey group established to assist modernisation policy-making, analysed the freight traffic of 1954 and uncovered a number of disturbing features. In the merchandise business, average wagon loadings were only 4.3 tons, which compared unfavourably with 12.0 tons for mineral traffic and 11.6 for coal. Consignments were relatively small: 55 per cent of those weighing over 1 ton, that is, wagon-load traffic, were of 5 tons or less, and 41 per cent were of 3 tons or less. An analysis of traffic location revealed that 69 per cent of the merchandise tonnage originated in private-sidings. Here there was clearly scope for reducing costs by concentrating the business on fewer points of origin and final destination. Finally, a break-down of direct costs for the wagon-load traffic isolated 'wagon provision and maintenance' as the largest single item – 30 per cent of the total – and showed that terminal haulage, terminal shunting and marshalling together accounted for 39 per cent. Both areas were seen as ripe for productivity drives, with the emphasis on concentrated operations.[28] After the merchandise charges scheme had been introduced, more effort was put into analysing the broad areas of profit and loss in railway traffic. In September 1957 the Director of Costings submitted a memorandum to the Finance Committee in which both direct and indirect or joint costs were allocated to specific traffics – passenger, parcels and freight – in 1956. A comparison was also made with results for 1949, which had been produced as part of the costings work of 1950–1. The exercise was repeated in subsequent years and with increasing sophistication. The data for 1961 appeared in the report on *The Reshaping of British Railways*, published by Beeching's British Railways Board in 1963.[29]

So in contrast with a number of published statements on the indivisibility of the joint costs of track and signalling, many of them cited by Joy,[30] the internal evidence shows that the Costings Division was prepared, several years before Beeching's appearance, to make a broad allocation of such costs to the major traffic types for policy-making purposes. The results for 1949 and 1956–60 are summarised in Table 22.

[d] Excludes the costs of parcels carried in passenger train guard's vans.
Source: B.T.C. Costings Division's memos. to the B.T.C. Finance Committee, 20 September 1957, 4 March and 9 October 1961; Finance Committee Minutes, 25 September 1957, 22 March and 11 October 1961, B.R.B.

The initial study, of 1956 traffic, supported the common assumption among senior managers that most, if not all, of the railways' deficit came from the unprofitable passenger sector. As early as November 1954, the Commission had been presented with a reworking of the 1952 Passenger Census data (corrected for seasonal traffics) which suggested that the passenger sector was failing to meet its total costs by about £60 million. Three years later, a more considered estimate appeared. Passenger services were estimated to have lost £76 million in 1956, compared with under £4 million for freight. The parcels traffic was found to be in the black, although this was due to some extent to the difficulty of apportioning costs shared with passenger traffic. Freight services, then, were still regarded as broadly profitable, despite some anxiety at headquarters about losses being incurred in certain areas of the business. There was little change in 1957. As Table 22 shows, the passenger deficit rose to £86 million, and the emphasis remained firmly on 'one of the basic problems of British Railways – the current inability of passenger traffics to make a reasonable contribution to . . . financial stability'.[31]

The recession of 1958 brought radical change. While the passenger deficit, in current prices, remained stable in 1957–60, the freight services slid into substantial deficit. By 1960 the losses on freight amounted to nearly £47 million, and although passenger losses continued to make up the greater part of the overall deficit, most of the latter's growth, from £82.7 million in 1957 to £128.3 million in 1960, could be attributed to poorer freight results as business first fell away and then failed to recover.

The seriousness of the railways' position was clarified when more detailed costings were produced by the Division and presented to the Finance Committee in March 1961. Data for 1959 on passenger and freight traffic were broken down into their principal components as shown in Table 23. In the passenger sector, the exercise confirmed the conclusion of the 1952 Passenger Census that the stopping services were the major area of weakness. Indeed, little progress had been made since 1952. In 1959 these trains failed to cover their direct costs by £39 million, £21 million higher than the imputed deficit of £18 million in 1952, suggesting that there had been little or no short-term gains from the Modernisation Plan of 1955 and the accompanying strategy of service rationalisation. No joint costs were apportioned, but if they had been allocated on the same basis as in the Beeching report, the total loss on stopping services would have been shown to be £62 million, compared with losses of £2 and £17 million on the fast/semi-fast and suburban trains.[32]

The freight results were still more important in illuminating a serious feature of the railways' whole operating problem. The allegation that considerable losses were being carried on the back of the mineral and coal traffics, made by H. P. Barker in November 1954 when the Modernisation

Table 23. *Receipts and costs in passenger and freight traffic,*
1959 (£m.)

Traffic type	Gross receipts (i)	Direct costs (ii)	Operating margin (i) − (ii)	Joint costs (iii)	Profit/ loss (i) − ((ii) + (iii))
1. Passenger					
Fast/semi-fast	89.3	58.0	31.3	—[a]	—
Stopping	23.3	62.3	−39.0	—	—
Suburban	31.3	30.1	1.2	—	—
Total	143.9	150.4	−6.5	74.7	−81.2
2. Freight					
Merchandise/livestock:					
Wagon-load merchandise	61.1	73.7	−12.6	17.9	−30.5
Smalls (under 1 ton)	39.9	50.9	−11.0	7.6	−18.6
Total including livestock[b]	101.1	125.7	−23.6	25.8	−49.4
Minerals	45.8	33.4	12.4	9.8	2.6
Coal and coke	111.5	68.9	42.6	18.9	23.7
Total	259.4	228.0	31.4	54.5	−23.1[c]

[a] No attempt was made to allocate joint costs to passenger categories.
[b] Not shown.
[c] Data exclude £3.3m. for warehousing, which was not apportioned.
Source: D. M. Dear, memo. on 'British Railways Results: 1959', 4 March 1961, B.T.C.
Finance Committee Minutes, 22 March 1961, B.R.B.

Plan was being formulated (see below, pp. 270–1) was now confirmed.
The estimated losses on merchandise, £49 million in 1959, were not
compensated by profits of only £26 million from the heavy freight business
(Table 23). Both the wagon-load and smalls traffics failed to meet even
their direct costs by a substantial margin, with costs exceeding gross
receipts by 21 and 28 per cent respectively. The data for 1960, presented to
the Finance Committee in October 1961, confirmed this situation. By this
time the contrast in earning power between the freight sectors had
widened still further. The merchandise loss was put at nearly £67 million,
while the profits from minerals and coal amounted to only £16 million.
The poor results of the merchandise traffic were attributed in the main to
the implementation of the Guillebaud Report on railwaymen's pay and the
consequent rise in costs. However, such figures suggested not only that the
merchandise losses had to be eradicated, but that the earnings from coal
and minerals needed to be greatly improved.[33] There was thus a fair

amount of costings analysis before Beeching succeeded Robertson in June 1961 and encouraged a series of detailed studies of the railways' trading position. When the B.T.C.'s Report for 1961, published in June 1962, drew the attention of the public to the railways' financial results for 'the various broad classes of traffic', and pointed to the losses on stopping train and suburban traffic, as well as the poor results of the merchandise sector, it was not announcing something discovered as a result of Beeching's initiatives, but something which had been known for some time.[34]

These fundamental weaknesses in railway traffic were also understood at regional level, where similar costing investigations were carried out, especially in the Eastern and Southern Regions. The Eastern carried out Passenger Train Censuses in 1955 and 1957, the Southern followed suit in 1958, and both regions subjected their traffics to detailed analysis in 1960.[35] The passenger surveys were important in that they tempted the Commission to take some comfort in its modernisation strategy. Indeed, it was the prospect of savings from the replacement of steam by diesel or electric traction that stimulated much of the costings work on passenger traffic. The Eastern Census of 1955, for example, was specifically directed at services likely to be affected by the introduction of D.M.U.s. When some of the survey results were passed on to the Stedeford Advisory Group by Wansbrough-Jones in July 1960, he stressed that the operation of multiple-unit trains, whether diesel or electric, was an important factor in improving passenger profitability. The provisional results of the Eastern's census of March 1960 were taken to vindicate the conversion of steam services to D.M.U.s; together with the withdrawal of unremunerative services, this had substantially reduced the gap between movement costs (direct costs excluding terminal costs) and gross receipts.[36] The Southern's Census, taken in March and December 1958, and completed in July 1959, was also passed on to the Stedeford Group. This produced the general conclusion that 'the margin of passenger earnings over direct costs was obtained solely from the multiple unit trains'. These contributed about £13 million to joint costs, while the locomotive-hauled trains, mostly steam-powered, just failed to meet their movement costs and failed to cover direct costs by about £3 million.[37]

These sanguine observations were not shared by all, even internally. The Eastern Region's passenger survey for March 1960, submitted to the Area Board in January 1961, concluded that although total passenger earnings had exceeded direct costs by £10.2 million, the total loss on passenger operations was about £7 million. Furthermore, the stopping services had failed to meet their direct costs by £1.5 million; and although the introduction of D.M.U.s had certainly eliminated the large gap between earnings and *movement* costs, earnings were still insufficient to cover terminal costs. Even the more profitable fast and semi-fast trains were found to have maintained margins at the expense of a substantial loss of traffic, reflected in a lower load factor. A follow-up study for 1961, completed in April 1962, contended that the earlier surveys had been too optimistic. The 1960 study was said to have overstated earnings by £3 million and understated costs by £2.5 million. The results for 1961 revealed that earnings had exceeded direct costs by only £6.5 million, while the stopping services had experienced a shortfall of £2.0 million, with disappointing results evident whatever the motive power used.[38] The results of the London Midland Region's 1960 passenger survey, presented to the Area Board in June 1962, pointed in the same direction. The region's passenger services barely covered their direct costs, earning a surplus of only £134,000 on receipts totalling £41.1 million. The stopping services had failed to cover direct costs by £6.9 million, the suburban services by £1.5 million; losses in Lancashire were particularly high. The introduction of D.M.U.s had reduced but certainly not eliminated the gap between earnings and direct costs. Only one of the 49 diesel-powered stopping services – Birmingham–Leicester–Nottingham – earned a margin over direct costs, and the total shortfall for these services was £1.4 million. Only one of the 15 D.M.U. suburban services – St Pancras–Bedford – made a positive contribution to joint costs. The total shortfall here was £0.3 million.[39] A similarly gloomy picture was evident in the regional freight studies. The information for 1960 was processed too late for submission to the Stedeford Advisory Group, but it was very much part of the post-Stedeford determination to improve regional accounting techniques, construct approximate profit-and-loss accounts for the regions and produce a more accurate picture of the traffic position. The Southern's survey, which was first considered by the Area Board in March 1961, showed how much the region relied on passenger traffic. The originating freight receipts failed to cover direct costs by about £4.5 million a year. The results were disappointing enough to induce the Area Board, at its meeting on 6 April, to resolve that freight operations should be much more heavily concentrated. It decided to reduce the number of marshalling yards, close over half (350) of its freight depots and public sidings by 1964 and cut the number of stations handling the sundries (smalls) business from 130 to 25. A capital investment of £5.25 million associated with the rationalisation was expected to yield savings in annual costs of £1.75 million.[40]

To summarise. Improved information, however carefully prepared, does not necessarily stimulate prompt or pertinent action by management. Some of the more detailed analyses produced under the broad heading of 'costing' were not formally presented to the B.T.C., although they had been read by individual members. But it is wrong to infer, as does Stewart Joy, that the Commission was either ignorant about the nature of the railways' deficit and the costs and earnings of the several traffics or happy to let the deficits mount up in spite of this knowledge. Whatever was formally stated in public, railway managers were prepared to allocate both direct and indirect or joint costs to specific traffics. These broad allocations, it was recognised, were not a blueprint for action in relation to individual services – allocated joint costs would not automatically be saved if a service were abandoned. But they showed at an early stage that passenger losses were responsible for the greater part of the operating deficit, and raised the strong suspicion that much of the wagon-load merchandise business was unprofitable, with charges remaining below costs as regional officers struggled to beat off the challenge of road haulage. By 1961, the position was clear to all. The only traffics which were making a significant contribution to joint costs were the heavy freights – coal and minerals – a potentially vulnerable position which was fully exposed by the recession in the heavy industries in 1958.

IV

Was the B.T.C. slow to act, and was its response inadequate? To what extent should it have anticipated the fall in traffic receipts after 1957? Could costs have been brought more closely and more quickly into line with traffic revenues?

No one should pretend that these vital questions are easy to resolve. Neither the internal documentation, preoccupied as it frequently is with day-to-day concerns, nor the post hoc assessments of retired managers can give the commissioned historian an automatic passport to penetrating insights hidden from others. Nevertheless, the Commission's internal records do indicate that it was in October 1957, not in 1959 or 1960, when the government began to prod the railways more forcefully, that a greater sense of urgency began to be shown. In that month, the Finance Committee, led by Sir Reginald Wilson, took the first steps to impress upon the Commission that it had to respond more vigorously to 'the disquieting financial position' (Wilson's phrase). Unless there was 'a considerable and early improvement in the working results', Wilson argued, 'the running rate of deficit in 1958 would be so great that the Commission's cash resources would be imperilled'. Among the 'urgent and drastic measures' advocated by Wilson were two items normally associated with the Beeching era: a reduction of the labour-intensive small stations and goods depots; and a determined assault on the 'apparent surplus of wagons'. On the first Wilson noted that several locations should have been 'closed many years ago through concentration on railhead working', and on the second he attacked the 'wasteful expenditure' on 'maintaining wagons that were in excess of requirements and in some places . . . were a hindrance to operating'. The capital expenditure budget for 1958 contained expenditure on wagon construction and fitting which, he claimed, 'could not stand up to examination'.[41]

At the same meeting of the Commission John Train argued that the most urgent matter was future freight policy, observing that some members felt that it was here that a 'drastic alteration in methods' was required.* Shortly afterwards, an ad hoc committee, chaired by Train, and including H. P. Barker, Charles Bird and David Blee, was established to examine the problem of freight train working. H. P. Barker produced a far-sighted memorandum on a 'Long Term Freight Policy' in which he deplored the 'wagon fixation' of many railwaymen and suggested that if railway freight were to survive, operating costs had to be cut by shifting the emphasis to train-load and 'freight liner' operations. The committee concluded in February 1958 that a small full-time panel of officers should be appointed to formulate definite recommendations. The Commission agreed, and appointed a small planning team of specially seconded officers, led by A. J. White, the Assistant General Manager of the Eastern Region. The preparation of a report was to be supervised by a full-scale steering committee of the Commission. Action on freight was given added impetus after anxious noises had been made by the Minister of Transport, Watkinson, in January. White's lengthy report on freight traffic policy emerged in August.[42]

The drafting of this report is important in that it illuminates several features of the Commission's response to the emerging traffic crisis. During consideration of the draft chapters by the steering committee it was fully accepted that the passenger business was unprofitable, and that there was no immediate prospect of its becoming profitable. Robertson then made plain his view that 'British railways could not survive without retaining much of the general merchandise traffic, including consignments in less than wagon loads, which they were carrying today. . . The policy should be to retain as much of this traffic as possible by proper charging and good service.' Much of the subsequent discussion in the steering committee, on containerisation, liner train experiments, the need for selective rate reductions and an improved quality and reliability of service, was presented with the aim of winning back the miscellaneous merchandise traffic from road.[43] This strategy was developed at length in White's

---

*The subject for the Officers' Conference at Balliol College in April 1957 had been 'The Pattern of Future Freight Traffic'.

report. He began by isolating four key issues: the contribution to net revenue to be expected from passenger traffic; the future size of the railway network; railway pricing; and the co-operation between the Commission's road and rail undertakings. On the basis of results for 1949–57 freight and parcels were found to have been doing 'quite well financially', but these sectors could no longer be expected to pay for 'the maintenance of an over-large system with very little help from the passenger side'. White emphasised the need for 'a smaller, financially sound railway system' and an accelerated closure programme for branch lines and small stations. A much closer co-operation between the railways and British Road Services, the B.T.C.'s road haulage arm, was also advocated.

On pricing, the report focussed on what was to become a major dilemma for the railways – whether to seek the raising of revenue or the retention of traffic. White condemned the recent emphasis on the former, which he said, had resulted in an increase of 50 per cent in the amount of coal moved by road and a cut of nearly 20 per cent in the volume of rail-carried merchandise since 1952. White concluded:

The question to be faced is whether the railways will ever be able to pay their way if such trends continue. The answer is almost certainly 'no'; if that is agreed, there is really no choice but to stop the erosion now and go all out for much more business, in the knowledge that the margin of profit on many transactions will be rather lower than has hitherto been sought, but also from the firm belief that a vigorous traffic recovery campaign will soon pay off.

Sound business principles were firmly articulated. On commercial strategy, for example, the report recognised that:

The universal availability of road transport has released the Commission from inherited obligations to carry everything for everybody. There is now no general social necessity for the Commission's affairs to be conducted on other than ordinary business principles and it should be made known that the Commission are no longer prepared to perform, except at a profit, any service which is physically capable of performance by someone else. . . The primary objectives of commercial policy should be
a) to get the maximum amount of profitable traffic;
b) to improve the financial results of unremunerative activities which, in modified form, may offer good hope of profitable operation;
c) to discard, by the withdrawal of facilities or by price mechanisms, activities which are unprofitable and likely to remain so.[44]

The policies recommended in the White report were endorsed with minor modifications by the Commission at meetings in October and November 1958. The main thrust of future commercial policy was directed towards the recapture of traffic via a more aggressive pricing strategy. For White, the general aim of pricing was to ensure that direct costs were covered by each traffic and that indirect costs as a whole were recouped 'in accordance with the possibilities in a competitive market', i.e. 'contribution accounting'. It was here that the argument contained elements which were later condemned by Joy when he attacked the Commission for seeking traffic regardless of cost. White argued that the long-run direct cost of carrying a particular traffic was not necessarily the lowest price at which the transaction would be profitable. He contended that

The 'floor' is the out-of-pocket cost – the additional cost of carrying that particular parcel [of traffic] in company with others *for which provision has already been made* [my italics]. A full appreciation of this point is of especial importance to railways, with their so-called variable costs which in fact rise or fall very little in comparison with short-term fluctuations in the volume of traffic.[45]

The correct way of allocating costs to specific parts of the railway business remains a matter of argument. But all the evidence demonstrated that however this was done, the Commission had not made adequate provision for *existing* traffics. There was little point in pricing on a marginal cost basis if average costs exceeded average revenue. But the Commission went on to accept White's view that there should be a two-stage policy for general mechandise, the first designed to recapture traffic in quantity 'without too much immediate regard for profit margins', the second to 'consolidate the gains on fully profitable terms'. In the first stage there was to be 'no hesitation about quoting rates down to, *or even below* the estimated direct costs' (my italics). In this clearly difficult position for the railways, the dilemma lay in deciding whether the Commission should cut rates and gain traffic at unprofitable prices, or raise rates and lose more traffic. White and the Commission believed that if the latter strategy were pursued, the result would be a reduced volume of traffic insufficient to support even a contracted railway network.[46]

Unfortunately, the recommended strategy opened the way to further confusion about pricing at the regional and local levels, and to still larger deficits. Although the White report accepted that railways were 'no longer really in the market for remunerative general merchandise business over short and medium distances', the Commission pressed on with a vigorous effort to double its merchandise tonnage, supported by a selling campaign organised through the publicity consultants C. S. Services Ltd.[47] In so doing, it is clear that the Commission overestimated the size of the market which it could profitably win back to rail. It also overestimated the amount of its business which could be transformed from loss to profit through modernisation or other forms of cost-reduction, and exaggerated its capacity quickly to withdraw services which were recognised to be irredeemable loss-makers. Finally, there were also signs that the Commission had not entirely abandoned notions of its public service obligations, in spite of the fact that the government had made it clear that there were to be no direct subsidies. After White had examined the sundries business and concluded that much of the delivery to rural areas was unprofitable, he nevertheless emphasised that the Commission had to continue to offer a comprehensive service for small consignments, because the public interest demanded a reasonably adequate service and no one else was willing to meet this need.[48] That this kind of approach should have survived after eight years of Conservative rule is a remarkable tribute to the deep impression which the older way of thinking had left in the minds of railwaymen.

For the rest of the Commission's existence, the broad traffic strategy remained one of attempting to win back general merchandise traffic by under-cutting road charges and improving road/rail transfers (collection and delivery services), and of raising passenger fares as much as was practicable in the existing competitive environment. This approach continued into the Beeching period. When Dr Beeching gave his first press conference as Chairman of the Commission, on 12 June 1961, he stated that the anticipated increase in revenue from long-distance passenger services would be insufficient to produce much of a dent in the existing deficit. With the coal trade in decline, and little chance of a dramatic increase in mineral traffic, 'only general merchandise offers prospects of very considerable expansion'. Unless receipts in this sector could be increased considerably, warned Beeching, the main-line railway system would not pay.[49] In reality, the risk in seeking to win this business with the unimpressive organisation and badly co-ordinated commercial structure over which Robertson had presided was that margins of unprofitability would be extended even further. Certainly, there was no improvement in the three years to 1962. The tonnage of merchandise carried, which had amounted to about 42 million tons in 1957 fell to 40 million in 1960, 38 million in 1961, and 36 million in 1962. Estimated losses on merchandise traffic were put at £49 million in 1959, £67 million in 1960 and £75 million in 1961. By this time there was more than a hint of helplessness in regional commercial departments in the face of what were regarded as inexorable market forces.[50]

The B.T.C. evidently did understand the nature of its traffic problems. But it was slow to accept the seriousness of the situation, and it adopted inappropriate commercial strategies. The adverse traffic trends, especially the steady fall in general merchandise tonnage which so disturbed White in 1958, had been identified by 1953, and debated several times thereafter at Commission meetings. The threat to the railway business from new roads and improved lorry designs had been the subject of discussion in the late 1940s and early 1950s.[51] Before 1957–8, however, the Commission had been happy to continue with a considerable element of cross-subsidisation in its activities, throwing the weight of its hopes for the future behind the Modernisation Plan (see Chapter 8) and the merchandise charges scheme. It was only when freight of all kinds started to fall away that the complacency was swept away and the need for an urgent reappraisal of future prospects was accepted. By this time, it could be seen that the Modernisation Plan was neither an immediate nor a medium-term pana-cea for the railways' financial problems, while the new charges scheme had come too late to arrest the considerable loss of merchandise traffic to the road hauliers and 'C' licence operators.

V

If the B.T.C.'s commercial policy is open to criticism, what of its attempts to rationalise its cost structure and improve productivity? From the early 1950s it recognised the need to advance in these areas. Consequently, the Modernisation Plan of 1955 linked the programme of increased invest-ment to the withdrawal of unremunerative services and the promotion of greater efficiency in railway operation. And in the same year the Commis-sion established the British Railways Productivity Council with the aim of encouraging the unions to co-operate with the management in improving productivity outside the existing negotiating machinery. Its specific achievements will be considered in Chapter 7, which deals with the railways' major cost component, wages and salaries.[52] The following paragraphs summarise activity in a second key area of initiative – line and service rationalisation.

As a close reading of the Commission's minutes reveal, there was a continuing recognition of the need to accelerate the pruning of unprofit-able services. In June 1955, for example, the Joint Traffics Committee decided that the Area Boards should be 'brought fully into the matter of dealing with unremunerative passenger services' and asked the General Staff to prepare a policy paper for the T.U.C.C.s, the eleven consumer bodies which considered closure proposals and made recommendations to the C.T.C.C. A policy memorandum, directing attention to the losses on stopping services, was sent to the Area Boards in November, and it was stated that the Commission was looking for 'a substantial transfer of passenger traffic from stopping trains to properly designed road services (or improvised rail services)'. Stopping trains on both branch lines and main lines were to be curtailed. The policy of accelerating closures was explained to the T.U.C.C.s in a document transmitted through the Area Boards in March 1956. The arguments of objectors who claimed that many branch lines could be kept open by alternative operating methods were to be countered; and the Minister of Transport was to be told that it

Table 24. *Withdrawal of unprofitable services and facilities, 1948–59*

Period	Route-miles authorised for closure (miles)			Stations and depots closed (numbers)			Total estimated net annual savings (£)
	Passenger and freight	Passenger only	Freight only	Passenger and freight	Passenger only	Freight only	
1948–53	253	1,167	359	62	225	84	1,159,000
1954–9	568	947	410	70	273	238	2,941,000a
1953	12	162	68	15	29	9	146,000
1954	57	308	44	10	27	17	523,000
1955	118	100	56	13	37	38	276,000
1956	43	97	12	3	58	33	196,000
1957	40	67	2	8	28	23	179,000
1958	199	169	155	18	76	31	1,069,000
1959	111	206	141	18	47	96	701,000a

a Excludes estimated savings from station and depot closures, first shown in 1959 as £121,000 (this sum is included in the data shown in Aldcroft, *British Railways*, p. 147). The data refer to the year of closure authorisation, not the year of withdrawal. A later internal calculation of route-mileage affected by services actually *withdrawn* in 1959, for example, produced figures of 159 (passenger and freight), 228 (passenger only) and 92 (freight only), and net savings of £1,213,000 (including Midland and Great Northern and Hull and Barnsley closures and excluding station/depot savings of £121,000): General Staff memo. 19 January 1961, B.T.C. Minutes, 26 January 1961, B.R.B.

Source: S.C. *Nat. Ind.*: *B.R.*, 1960, Appendix 22 (B.T.C. submission, 16 March 1960).

Table 25. *Closures approved by the Transport Users' Consultative Committees, 1950–62*

Period	Branch lines (no.)	Route-miles to be closed to:			Estimated minimum net annual savings (£)
		Passenger and freight	Passenger only	Freight only	
1950–62	340	811	2,522	796	5,184,952
Annual averages					
1950–62	26	62	194	61	398,842
1950–7	19	29	161	31	209,640
1958–62	37	116	247	109	701,566

Source: Annual Report of the Central Transport Consultative Committee for 1955–62 (1956–63). Figures are rounded to the nearest whole number. The 1962 data end on 31 August 1962. The data for 1961 include the Westerham branch, which was not recommended for closure by the T.U.C.C. but was subsequently closed with Ministerial consent. The data for 1962 exclude proposals relating to the Great Central line (estimated net savings: £232,000), which were only partly accepted (implementation followed in 1963).

was imperative that the T.U.C.C.s should not delay closure decisions by asking for additional information in cases where the financial justification for withdrawal of service was clear.[53]

Nevertheless, most commentators have agreed with Aldcroft's view that 'progress in reshaping the railway system was remarkably slow'; that the advance made in the period 1954–9 was little better than that achieved in the years 1948–53; and that 'only the fringe of the problem had been tackled'.[54] The data he used, which focus on route-mileages affected by authorisations to close services, are summarised in Table 24. The situation was not quite as Aldcroft would have it. The action taken in 1954–9 promised net annual savings of £2.9 million, 150 per cent higher than in 1948–53, and increased attention was directed towards the closure of both passenger and freight services simultaneously (568 miles compared with 253) and the closure of freight depots (238 compared with 84). However, the annual data do indicate that so far from encouraging faster change, the presentation of the Modernisation Plan was followed, in 1956 and 1957, by a period of relative inactivity.[55] It was not until 1958 that the closure programme was really stepped up. This timing is confirmed by the data on closures agreed by the T.U.C.C.s over the period 1950–62, which were published in the annual reports of the C.T.C.C. (see Table 25). The contrast between average annual closures and estimated net savings in 1950–7 and 1958–62 is striking. In the latter period, the T.U.C.C.s approved, annually, the closure of twice as many branch lines and more than double the amount of route-mileage. But conceding that the pace did quicken after 1957, the fact remains that in overall terms the extent of the rationalisation before 1963 was limited. The railways' operating route-mileage, which had stood at 19,222 miles at the end of 1953, was reduced by only 9 per cent, to 17,481, while the track-mileage used fell by only 8 per cent, from 51,608 miles to 47,417.[56] Most of the closures made were so obviously justified in commercial terms that the opposition mounted against them – by local authorities, industry and the public, working through the T.U.C.C.s – was muted. For example, the C.T.C.C. observed, in its annual report for 1960, that 'well over 500' of the 700 proposals relating to station closures were unopposed. Data submitted by the C.T.C.C. to the Stedeford Advisory Group for the period to June 1960 showed that of a total of 919 proposals (lines and stations) submitted since the inception of the T.U.C.C.s, 521 had been unopposed and a further 318 accepted without amendment. Only 55 proposals had been modified and only 25 had been rejected. The withdrawal of the passenger services between Wellingborough and Higham Ferrers in Northamptonshire in June 1959 was a typical example of an unopposed closure. The estimated net annual savings on this $3\frac{1}{4}$ mile stretch of line were given as £8,500, and passengers could be easily accommodated by alternative bus services provided by the United Counties Omnibus Company. C.T.C.C. data compiled in 1960 giving estimated savings from 257 service and line closures since the inception of the T.U.C.C.s revealed a total of £4,117,275 saved, or £16,021 per case; there were 78 unopposed cases with average savings of only £5,754, and 88 opposed cases with average savings of only £5,967.[57]

The timidity of the Commission's response to rationalisation, particularly before 1958, owed something to a dragging of feet in the regions. Some of the senior railway officers were quick to point out that the savings generated by branch-line closures and other rationalisation schemes had been modest, and the case was made for the importance of peripheral services in bringing 'contributory revenue'* to the main lines. The Scottish Region, in its contribution to passenger traffic policy for the Modernisation Plan in 1956, was quite clear that 'it would be unrealistic to contemplate wholesale closure of its [branch] lines . . . for the railways have a social obligation to the communities served'. On the other hand, the Commission itself, in a sudden change of heart, declared itself willing to give a chance to alternative strategies to closures. In June 1956 it agreed that trials should be carried out to test the feasibility of more economic

*The revenue earned on other lines/services as a result of travel on a given service. For example, on a Sheringham–Norwich–London journey, the Sheringham–Norwich service provides contributory revenue to the Norwich–London service. Some of this revenue would be lost if the Sheringham–Norwich line were closed.

operating with, for example, light-weight diesel railbuses. Three weeks later, it accepted a paper from the General Staff which argued that since the regions had made considerable progress in reducing unremunerative stopping-train-mileage (with the possible exception of the Western and London Midland Regions), the scope for further savings was limited. The contributory value of the remaining branch lines, a point stressed by the appended regional reports, was fully accepted by the Commission. Thus, only four months after pressing for a vigorous closure programme, the Commission now decided that the possibility of making large savings had been overemphasised, and minuted that 'serious efforts' should be made to retain branch lines by introducing lower-cost operating methods. The new policy had Sir Reginald Wilson's enthusiastic support, and was incorporated in the B.T.C.'s re-evaluation of its financial position, published as a White Paper in October 1956 (see Chapter 8, below). For some time thereafter the Commission was reluctant, in its own words, 'to take the distasteful step of curtailing facilities'.[58] This dismayed closure enthusiasts among the civil servants in the Ministry of Transport, as well as embarrassing the Minister, Watkinson, who had briefed the T.U.C.C. chairmen to expect a full-scale closure programme. However, it delighted the many political elements who preferred experimentation with services to outright closure. While there was a great deal of justifiable local concern about public transport in rural areas, there was also some sentimentality about the railway branch line. For example, when the B.T.C. met the Conservative Party's transport and agricultural committees in April 1956, one of the M.P.s expressed his concern 'because people would not be able to travel on the line which passed the spot where Tristan and Isolde held hands together'.[59]

Two years later, the arguments for an accelerated closure programme were repeated, following Ministry criticism of the low level of savings in 1957. In May 1958 the Commission asked the Area Boards to make fresh proposals; in June a list of 32 proposed closures with estimated savings of £521,000 was submitted to the Ministry; and in the following September it decided to abandon, wherever possible, its former practice of subsidising the alternative bus services provided when rail closures were introduced. In this the Commission was guided by a General Staff paper which revealed that in 1957–8 subsidies averaging about £2,200 annually had been paid to bus companies in connection with the withdrawal of passenger services on ten branch lines.[60] Efforts were also made to reduce the delays in taking submissions through the formal machinery of T.U.C.C. and C.T.C.C. After lobbying in June 1958, it was found that the average time taken to handle a proposal had been reduced from nine to ten months to eight to ten weeks. In the following February, the Commission agreed to a proposal by the General Managers that the smaller submissions be sent direct to the T.U.C.C.s without obtaining formal B.T.C. approval. These changes were made with the full backing, indeed, active encouragement, of the Ministry of Transport. A much more restricted definition of the railways' 'public service obligation' was now in vogue. Watkinson, having told the chairmen of the T.U.C.C.s at a meeting in June 1958 that 'the Commission could not be regarded as having to provide a social service for all and sundry', soon repeated this view publicly. On 23 July he declared before the Commons that 'the railways are no longer a monopolistic organisation with an obligation to provide all sections of the community with a railway service'.[61]

These new initiatives produced only three major schemes in the period 1958–62. The first was the Eastern Region's closure, in March 1959, of most of the Midland & Great Northern Joint Line, a duplicate route from the East Midlands to Norwich and Yarmouth. Passenger services were withdrawn from 174 route-miles, and 116 miles were closed completely; 43 stations were closed, and a further 18 lost their passenger facilities; estimated job losses were 1,063, and the estimated net annual savings were put at £640,000 (excluding rolling stock renewal), by far the largest of any proposal in the life of the B.T.C. There was only half-hearted opposition to the closure of a line which, as the *Railway Gazette* observed, had lost its raison d'être with the grouping of railway companies in 1923. Passenger loadings outside the summer holiday peak were very light, and the only significant consequence of the closure was the rather bizarre transfer of coal from Norwich (Thorpe) to the coal depot at Norwich (City), barely 2 miles by road, over a rail distance of more than 60 miles.[62] The second major scheme, also in the Eastern Region, was the reduction of passenger services on another duplicate route, the Great Central line from London (Marylebone) to Leicester, Sheffield and Manchester. By taking out a large portion of the train service it was intended to save about £370,000 a year, although only Stage I, the withdrawal of express trains from January 1960 with net annual savings of £140,000, was implemented during the life of the Commission. The third project was the North Eastern Region's closure of most of the 46-mile Hull and Barnsley railway, another redundant monument to the railway competition of the late nineteenth century. Here the total savings associated with the closure of the line in April 1959, including the rationalisation of freight working in the Hull area, amounted to about £200,000 a year.[63]

Elsewhere little progress was made. The failure of the experiment with a single-unit diesel on the Banbury–Buckingham branch line, 1956–9, was accompanied by several statements recognising that the use of diesel traction would not necessarily make stopping services profitable. White's report observed: 'it is already apparent that many stopping services will never pay their way, however cheaply operated'. In May 1960 the Commission examined the results of its decision, four years earlier, to order 22 light-weight diesel railbuses. Estimated losses on the branch lines where these buses had been deployed had been substantially reduced, but none had managed to produce a margin of revenue over movement costs. When terminal, track, signalling and administrative costs were included in the equation the total losses still appeared large. Design failings, teething troubles in operation and Ministry regulations forbidding one-man operation contributed to the disappointing results. But the B.T.C. was forced to conclude that 'there seems no prospect of such services ever becoming remunerative'.[64] Nevertheless, many railway officers remained unconvinced about the efficacy of branch-line closures and the rationalisation of feeder services to main lines. For example, when the London Midland reviewed its progress in closing lines and stations in November 1958, the Area Board was told that 'it was possible to over-emphasise the monetary value obtained from the withdrawal of services and closings in their contribution towards the overall economy requirement'. The Director of Traffic Services 'doubted whether over the whole system there remained many stations where their costs exceeded their earning capacity'.[65]

After 1958 there emerged a curious mixture of managerial stress upon the need to rationalise the network of services, and frequent references to the counter-arguments justifying a 'softly, softly' approach. This indecision undoubtedly served to restrain the move to a smaller railway system promised when the Modernisation Plan was reappraised in 1959 (see below, pp. 297–9). The social service aspect of railway marketing remained firmly in the minds of most senior railway officers, and it was encouraged by the public clamour whenever closure proposals were announced. The insistence of the T.U.C.C.s on the provision of alternative bus services where passenger trains were withdrawn, and the allegations of certain M.P.s that branch lines had been closed by a combination of British Railways' stealth, dishonesty and gross incompetence, played into the hands of those managers who favoured a cautious approach to closures. Thus, despite the Commission's resolution, in September 1958, to end subsidies to bus companies, it was found in June 1960 that subsidies had been promised to the extent of £65,000 (before deduction for bus receipts) for 25 lines, including the Midland & Great Northern; and at the end of 1962 there were still 34 subsidies totalling £86,300. These payments were small in relation to the estimated savings achieved – about 5 per cent of £1.6 million for schemes listed in 1962 – but were indicative of the caution with which the Commission continued to treat the T.U.C.C.s by offering concessions which were not statutory requirements.[66]

Relations between the Commission and the T.U.C.C.s were further strained by two well-publicised cases, where the cries of outrage were out of all proportion to the economic circumstances. The first was the Southern Region's closure in June 1955 of the Lewes–East Grinstead or 'Bluebell' Line. Here, a pertinacious local landowner, Miss R. E. M. Bessemer, great grand-daughter of the inventor of the steel converter, successfully challenged the legality of the move, citing a clause in the original Act of 1878. British Railways were forced to restore a passenger service from August 1956, and there followed a private bill application by the B.T.C., a public inquiry in October 1957 and a Government White Paper in February 1958 before the line was finally closed.[67] What mattered here was not the merit or otherwise of the proposal itself. The timing of Miss Bessemer's challenge was particularly unfortunate, since it coincided with the Ministry's attempts in 1956 to push the B.T.C. and streamline the procedure for dealing with unremunerative services. The B.T.C.'s decision to re-open the line on a skeletal basis only was criticised by both the Southern Region and the Ministry. A civil servant complained angrily in the following terms: 'that they should use scarce footplate staff and coal . . . in the provision of a service that had been proved redundant, indicates the very attitude of mind to the whole question of redundant facilities that we are trying to combat'.[68] The case for closure was a strong one, in fact. In spite of the protestors' claims about the feasibility of more economic operation and their attack upon the grudging restoration of the service – which won British Railways few friends – the C.T.C.C. accepted, after the public inquiry, that closure was fully justified. The line was used by relatively few people, and the substitution of diesels was not expected to transform the financial position. Whether the net annual savings were closer to the £59,700 estimated by the B.T.C. (using 1953 data and including long-run renewals and interest savings) or to the £33,000 considered to be more accurate by the C.T.C.C., they were held to be substantial. However, the protestors' complaints about the inadequacy of the costing formulae used by the Southern Region to estimate savings were taken up. There was an evident gap between the railways' emphasis on long-term costs and the C.T.C.C.'s preference for short-term avoidable costs. In June 1958 the Commission agreed to divulge more detailed financial information to the T.U.C.C.s when putting up proposals, as the C.T.C.C. had suggested in the White Paper, in return for a promise to speed up the machinery. The emphasis in future calculations was to be upon the immediately identifiable net savings, with the calculation of renewal savings on ways and structures limited to a five-year period. The estimated loss of revenue arising from closure was to include an estimate of the contributory revenue lost.[69] The move did nothing to encourage regional enthusiasm for accelerating closures. Opponents of the closure policy could always point to the veiled threat in the C.T.C.C.'s annual report for 1958, in which it was observed that 'there may be a larger proportion of cases in which it will no longer be easy to set the inexorable logic of the Commission's economic situation against the real but imponderable loss of public facility'. By giving more information the Commission was in danger of exposing itself to attack from well-prepared protestors.[70]

This certainly happened in the second controversial case of the period, which concerned the Southern Region's attempt to close the 5-mile branch between Westerham and Dunton Green in Kent. Once again, the justification for closure made by the region in February 1960 seemed to be sound. The line was used by only about 170 London commuters, passenger carryings ranged from 0 to 67 per train, and the net savings, after generous provision for additional bus services, were put at £11,600 per annum. But the objectors, organised by the Westerham Branch Railway Passengers Association, put up a more than reasonable case for the retention of the line using a diesel railbus, presented a number of other suggestions to reduce operating costs and embarrassed the Commission by publicising the fact that the track had only recently been relaid. The London Area T.U.C.C. at first supported the railways' case, but after the C.T.C.C. had intervened on the grounds that full financial information had been denied to the protestors, it changed its mind, and in February 1961 recommended against the closure, a move backed by the C.T.C.C.[71] It was left to the Minister, Ernest Marples, to give consent to the closure of the line, which took place in October 1961.[72] By taking the unprecedented step of reversing a C.T.C.C. recommendation, he showed that he at least was no longer prepared to back dieselisation schemes to reduce but not eradicate losses on marginal routes.*

Many of his fellow M.P.s disagreed. The Westerham decision was followed by a petition to the Commons presented by John Rodgers, the member for Sevenoaks, and an adjournment debate. Indeed, there were a number of such debates, in which several M.P.s lamented the loss of their local train services. In the period 1957–61, for example, the Commons debated not only the rationalisation of the Great Central services, but also such matters as the Foxfield–Coniston line, the North Buckinghamshire, Gravesend–Allhallows, the loss of intermediate stations between Inverness and Wick, Barnard Castle–Penrith and the 'Tutbury Jinnie'. Sometimes the protests became heated. On 1 August 1958, for example, Stephen Davies, M.P. for Merthyr Tydfil, alleged that the B.T.C., in justifying the closure of the line between Merthyr and Abergavenny, had

---

*The M25 was subsequently built over the rail route, but there is no evidence to suggest that Marples was influenced by road planning considerations.

deliberately inflated the deficit shown by spending large sums on station improvements and permanent way renewals when extinction threatened.[73] By 1960, there was no lack of criticism of the existing methods of handling rail closures. While the B.T.C. was accused of deliberately running down services or producing inadequate or misleading data in support of proposals, the consultative procedure itself was condemned for being pro-railway and too remote from the public it was intended to represent.[74] Individual cases provided fuel for the fire. The closure of the Foxfield–Coniston branch in 1958 followed a narrow vote in favour by the North Western T.U.C.C. A two-vote majority included the two votes of the B.T.C. representatives of the Committee, and the C.T.C.C. made critical reference to this example of railway 'influence'. There were also numerous complaints about the way T.U.C.C. hearings were organised, allegedly to the detriment of public protest.[75]

On the Commission's side, the promise of a speeding up of the handling of closure proposals did not materialise. There were several lengthy delays as opposition became more organised, and interested M.P.s pressed the Minister of Transport to intervene. For example, the Barnard Castle–Penrith line, where estimated net annual savings were £89,000, was put up for closure in December 1959. But there was much toing and froing before it was finally closed, in January 1962, after spending over two years in the consultative process. The Southern Region's Gravesend–Allhallows/Grain line was another contentious case. The proposal was rejected by the South Eastern T.U.C.C. in March 1960 when the two B.T.C. representatives were absent. The C.T.C.C. then gave the region another bite at the cherry, and after the case was resubmitted to the T.U.C.C. in December, a recommendation to close was passed by a majority of one. It was another year before the line was closed.[76] The clamour over these cases and the Lewes–East Grinstead and Westerham lines, both inside and outside parliament, certainly gave comfort to those railway officers who claimed that the returns to the considerable effort in preparing and progressing closure proposals were low.

Much more important in the long run was the fact that it was in 1959 that the first tentative steps were taken towards accepting the idea of a separately funded 'social railway'. Significantly, the initiative here came from the Ministry of Transport, not the B.T.C. which had always opposed the notion of government subsidies for specific services. After the reappraisal of the Modernisation Plan, the Ministry informed the Commission that 'considerable interest was being shown by Government Departments in a proposal that financial aid should be provided for certain parts of the railway system which are not economic to operate but which have to be retained for social reasons'. Three 'fringe' areas were selected for examination by the regions: Central Wales (Western); lines west of Exeter (Southern); and ex-Highland lines (Scottish). The concern here was not with branch lines, but with the extremities of main-line routes, although the Commission also observed that the definition of 'social railway' might be extended to stopping services on the trunk lines and to some commuter services. The calculations made indicated that the 1,386 route-miles studied earned £5.2 million gross, while total costs amounted to £8.7 million (excluding a contribution to central charges, and with depreciation based on replacement at historic cost). A General Staff memorandum pointed out that the 'loss' of £3.5 million was small in relation to the railways' total working deficit of £42 million, and since the lines generated about £6.7 million in 'contributory' revenue (gross) – £4.8 million of which was expected to be lost if the lines were closed – a closure policy would probably leave the B.T.C. worse off in the short run and only marginally better off in the long term. When the Commission considered the matter in December 1959, Robertson spoke for many of his colleagues when he expressed his anxiety that the subject of social subsidies might be given an inflated importance in relation to the Commission's overall financial difficulties. Although the document was sent to the Ministry, and later passed on to the Stedeford Advisory Group in May 1960, the initiative was lost in the reorganisation turmoil of 1960–2. The Commission was not prepared to push something it considered of only limited importance, particularly since it feared that to consent to government assistance on such a basis would be to give the Ministry a measure of control over railway operating policy.[77]

The Commission, then, offered an uncertain and vacillating response to service rationalisation and branch-line closures. All too often it was prepared to concede in the face of public opposition, and too much faith was placed in alternative operating methods, such as D.M.U.s and light-weight diesel railbuses, which reduced but did not eliminate operating losses. Most of the facilities closed involved relatively small annual savings. If this policy was a failure, can the same be said of the B.T.C.'s handling of wage costs? This is the subject of the next chapter.

7

Wages, unions and productivity

I

The demise of the Railway Executive in 1953 and the expanded role of the Commission did not lead to any radical alteration in the pattern of labour relations in the railway industry. In the first place, managerial continuity was evident. On the B.T.C., the two trade union representatives, Rusholme and Benstead (the Deputy-Chairman), stayed on until 1959 and 1961 respectively. At senior officer level, W. P. Allen, the ex-A.S.L.E.F. leader, moved in 1953 from the Executive to become Chief of Establishment and Staff in the Commission's interim organisation, and was given the rather grandiose title of Manpower Adviser in Robertson's new organisation of 1955. He continued to act as chief negotiator in pay bargaining talks with the unions, a role he carried out from 1947 until he retired in 1958 and was succeeded by A. R. Dunbar. This continuity on the management side was matched by some changes in union leadership. J. H. B. Figgins, the General Secretary of the N.U.R., reached the compulsory retiring age of 60 in March 1953 and was succeeded by J. S. 'Jim' Campbell, another Scot of left-wing persuasion. In May of the same year and for the same reason the white-collar leader, G. B. Thorneycroft, General Secretary of the T.S.S.A. since 1949, was replaced by W. J. P. 'Bill' Webber, an able moderate from Swansea, who began a ten-year period of office. The other major change came later, in January 1956, when J. G. Baty's retirement as General Secretary of A.S.L.E.F. was followed by the appointment of Albert Hallworth, a long-serving official who had been Baty's assistant since 1948.[1]

The new men were in essence different actors introduced into the same, long-running play. For the Commission, there remained the difficult task of trying to balance the books and restrain the rise in costs and yet at the same time of trying to attract staff into operating jobs with a large number of vacancies, where the pay was low and the working conditions unattractive. For the unions, the anxiety of the leading officials to ensure that wages kept pace with inflation and with advances elsewhere continued to be influenced by the disillusionment of the rank and file membership with the realities of nationalised management, which had not delivered the 'new age' of job security and workers' control. Above all, three features remained as almost constant elements in the conduct of industrial relations: an environment of almost continuous pay bargaining; a lack of co-operation between the three unions; and considerable government interference in the major negotiations. Some new factors did emerge from the mid-1950s, and the emphasis of bargaining shifted in response. The accelerating growth of real wages in the economy as a whole induced railway union negotiators to add the issue of 'pay comparability' to their collective bargaining weaponry, while the Commission's slide into financial deficit stiffened the management's resistance to large claims after 1956. The presentation of the B.T.C.'s Modernisation Plan in 1955, with its associated strategies of rationalisation and productivity achievement (the latter actively encouraged by the government) had the effect of bringing productivity issues to the centre of the stage whenever wage increases were discussed. Nevertheless, the basic framework of the railways' industrial relations remained unchanged.

The available data on earnings and retail prices indicate that railwaymen's pay, having caught up with price rises by 1953, continued to outpace inflation in the period to 1962. Table 26 refers to the two main categories, all adult males, and adult males in the 'conciliation grades', in the period 1953–62. The table reveals that the earnings of both groups increased at about twice the rate of inflation between 1953 and 1962. A similar picture emerges if other categories of railwayman are examined. The average weekly earnings of the 100,000 or so workshop staff increased by just over 5 per cent per annum, 1953–62; the 40,000 clerical workers improved their earnings by about 6 per cent; and the salaried employees in the operating departments experienced an improvement of just under 7 per cent.[2]

The progress made by railwaymen in thus improving their real earnings by roughly 30 per cent in the nine years to 1962 must be assessed in a broader context. In the first place, amelioration was not secured at an even rate. Significant pay advances were concentrated in two periods, the first associated with the troubled industrial relations of 1953–5, which culminated in the A.S.L.E.F. strike of May 1955, the second with the Guillebaud Committee's Inquiry into Railway Pay of 1958, which reported in 1960. Thus, while the earnings of adult males increased at an annual rate of 8.4 per cent over the period 1953–6 and by 7.2 per cent in 1959–62, the growth rate in 1956–9 was much lower, only 2.8 per cent. In the years when earnings were rising faster the issue of pay comparability, the

Table 26. *Average weekly earnings of British Railways staff, and index of retail prices, 1953–62*

Year	Average earnings: adult males (i)		Average earnings: 'conciliation grades' (ii)		Index numbers 1948 = 100 (i)	(ii)	Index of retail prices 1948 = 100
1953	178s.9d.	(£8.94)	171s.11d.	(£8.60)	128.5	127.5[a]	125.8
1954	188s.2d.	(£9.41)	182s.10d.	(£9.14)	135.3	135.6	128.1
1955	207s.6d.	(£10.38)	200s.10d.	(£10.04)	149.2	148.9	133.9
1956	227s.8d.	(£11.38)	218s.10d.	(£10.94)	163.7	162.3	140.4
1957	229s.5d.	(£11.47)	220s. 1d.	(£11.00)	164.9	163.2	145.7
1958	240s.0d.	(£12.00)	232s. 0d.	(£11.60)	172.6	172.1	150.1
1959	247s.0d.	(£12.35)	239s. 0d.	(£11.95)	177.6	177.3	151.0
1960	285s.0d.	(£14.25)	278s. 0d.	(£13.90)[b]	204.9	206.2	152.5
1961	294s.0d.	(£14.70)	283s. 0d.	(£14.15)	211.4	209.9	157.6
1962	304s.0d.	(£15.20)	297s. 0d.	(£14.85)	218.6	220.3	164.3
Growth rates (p.a.), 1953–62:					6.1%	6.3%	3.0%

[a] 1948 'conciliation grade' earnings derived from estimate in Table 12, above.
[b] Census average given as 274s., but inspection of average earnings for each grade indicates that the figure should be 278s.

Source:

(i) Average weekly earnings: adult males, working a full week, from B.T.C., R. & A. 1953–62, Table VIII–10; 'conciliation grades', from Census information in B.T.C., *Annual Census of Staff 1953–62*, supplement to B.T.C., *Transport Statistics* (1953–62). Prior to 1958, calculations were made on the basis of 'equated' staff numbers, 'representing the equivalent number of employees paid salaries or wages in respect of the complete week's work in each grade'. From 1958, actual staff totals were used, but those who failed to work a full week were excluded. The effect in 1958 is to increase average earnings by 0.3 per cent or 8.64d. From 1958 earnings were given to the nearest shilling. Retrospective pay awards are excluded, except in 1960.

(ii) Retail prices: Mitchell and Jones, *Abstract of Statistics*, pp. 191–2.

relationship between railway pay and that of other industrial workers, came to the fore. Comparability was, and of course still is, greatly complicated by the problems surrounding definitions, coverage, the distinction between wage rates and earnings, variations in skill and the statistical methods employed to calculate averages. In bargaining, the ground was constantly shifting, and much of the evidence presented to bodies such as the R.S.N.T. by the Commission and the unions was merely part of what may be termed the 'theatre of conflict'. Nevertheless, as was shown in Table 13, during the period 1948–53 railwaymen had undoubtedly slipped down the pay ladder, and this fact continued to influence the conduct of wage negotiations in the years which followed.

Data on pay comparability need to be treated with reserve, but broad trends may be extracted from Table 27. This compares the weekly earnings of adult males in the 'conciliation' and 'workshop' grades with average manual earnings in building, utilities (gas, water, electricity), manufacturing and all industries, as provided by the Ministry of Labour. The comparisons indicate that the earnings of railwaymen continued to drift down the ladder until 1959. 'Conciliation grade' earnings fell, for example, from 90 per cent of the manufacturing average in 1953 to 88 in 1959; and the equivalent comparison of workshop earnings shows a fall from 99 to 92 per cent over the same years. Similar trends may be observed in the comparisons with the building and utilities industries, where earnings had in 1948 been lower than those of both groups of railway workers. Moreover, the picture appears still gloomier if allowance is made for the downward bias in the Ministry of Labour data, in which no adjustment was made for the effect of including workers who did not work the full week, while the B.T.C. adjusted its staff totals to produce 'equated' figures on a full-time basis. The Commission's Director of Statistics claimed, in a confidential memorandum of March 1955, that the Ministry's data should be increased by at least 5 per cent to produce comparable figures. If this were done, the gap would obviously widen. The situation was well understood inside the Commission. The memorandum, which was circulated to the Manpower Adviser and the Finance Committee, went on to observe that over the period 1948–54 'the conciliation grades would appear to have fallen steadily behind and workshops staff have moved from a relatively favourable position to an unfavourable one. Even if the five per cent corrections applied to the Ministry figures are too great, the deterioration of the railwaymen's relative position still remains clear.'[3]

II

This comment helps to illuminate the background to the unsettled industrial relations of the period 1953–5, which witnessed the first national strike in the industry since the General Strike in 1926. The fuse was lit by the protracted negotiations of 1953. The 7s. per week increase agreed in November 1952 (see above, p. 209) was followed almost immediately by union pressure for further increases. In July 1953 claims of up to 15 per cent were promptly rejected by the Commission. The customary steps in the negotiating procedure were then followed, R.S.C.*, R.S.N.C. and R.S.N.T., but it was not until 3 December that the R.S.N.T., led by Sir John Forster, recommended an increase of only 4s. for male

*Replaced in 1956 as the first rung of the wage negotiating ladder by the R.S.J.C.

Table 27. Earnings of railway staff (adult males) and other groups, 1948–62

| | 'Conciliation grade' earnings as a percentage of: | | | | 'Workshop' earnings as a percentage of: | | | |
Year	Building and contracting	Gas, water and electricity	All manufacturing	All industry	Building and construction	Gas, water and electricity	All manufacturing	All industry
1948[a]	103	104	94	98	112	112	102	106
1953	93	100	90	92	102	110	99	102
1955	94	98	89	92	102	106	97	100
1957	92	96	88	91	101	105	97	100
1959	94	97	88	91	98	102	92	95
1960[b]	104	110	94	99	110	116	99	104
1962	95	100	92	95	95	100	92	95

[a] 1948 data non-railway for October; conciliation = an average of April 1948 and 1949; the workshop average is taken to be 146s.0d. Other years: March or April data.

[b] From 1959 data for non-railway earnings were based on the Standard Industrial Classification of 1958 (earlier data based on S.I.C. of 1948). The change had the effect of raising manufacturing earnings by 3s. in October 1959, but in the other categories cited here the effect was marginal. The 1960 'conciliation grade' earnings = 278s. not 274s. as shown in the B.T.C. Staff Census.

Source: Railway: conciliation and workshop earnings, as for Table 26.
Other earnings: Ministry of Labour Gazette, summarised in D.O.E., British Labour Statistics, Historical Abstract 1886–1968 (1971), pp. 100–3.

adults (with smaller increases for women and juniors). The decision moved the N.U.R. Executive Committee to record its 'profound disgust at the total inadequacy of the amount recommended', while A.S.L.E.F.'s Executive expressed its concern at a decision which, it contended, 'further distorts relativity inside the industry'.[4] On 9 December both unions resolved to take strike action. Not only was the result the most serious conflict since nationalisation, but it also provided yet another illustration of the familiar absence of a united front by the three major railway unions and the familiar presence of intervention by the government. In the negotiations which followed the unions' unprecedented rejection of the Tribunal's award, Robertson offered to undertake a comprehensive review of the railways' entire wage and salary structure. Both A.S.L.E.F. and T.S.S.A. were willing to accept this as the basis for a settlement, but the N.U.R. wanted something more concrete than a promise, and resolved to continue with its plans to take strike action. On 11 December it called a strike to commence on the 21st.

The government was anxious to avoid a national stoppage. At a Cabinet meeting on 14 December Walter Monckton, the Minister of Labour, informed his colleagues that he considered the R.S.N.T. award of 4s. (about 3 per cent) to have been 'unexpectedly low' – it was much lower, for example, than the 6 per cent increase recently obtained by farm workers – and warned that a strike was imminent. The Cabinet agreed that pressure should be exerted on Robertson and the Commission to increase the offer. Two days later, a new offer was produced and this was accepted by the N.U.R., who called off the strike. The 4s. was paid immediately, and the Commission agreed to add to the standard rates on a percentage basis within two months, in addition to the promised wage structure review. In February 1954 an additional 3s. was granted by the Commission, making 6 per cent in all. The total cost of the settlement was about £10 million. A comparable agreement with the workshop staff followed in April.[5]

This capitulation to union demands and government pressure certainly seems a failure on the part of the B.T.C. in the sense that it was scarcely compatible with the railways' declining financial position and did nothing to prevent further union demands in 1954 and 1955. But the situation was, of course, more complex than that. In the first place, both Robertson and Monckton might have been expected to follow a policy of appeasement. Robertson was still very new to the job, and in fact he had only been free of army responsibilities for a few days before the crisis blew up. In these circumstances it would have been very surprising if he had resisted the government's pressure to have the dispute settled. Monckton's position was not dissimilar. He was an inexperienced Minister. Having first become an M.P. in February 1951, he had been appointed by Churchill only eight months later to make Conservative industrial relations more 'harmonious'. Monckton, a lawyer by training, lacked the hard-bitten attitude of the careerist politician and was prone to yield in tense disputes. Indeed, he collapsed with nervous exhaustion shortly after the railway crisis was settled. Although he was much applauded for having personally averted a railway strike, in reality his actions had been entirely consistent with Cabinet policy.[6]

In short, it was the government's attitude, rather than the B.T.C.'s, that was the more important in explaining the N.U.R.'s success in securing a larger wage increase. Robertson had warned Monckton on 15 December that the costs of a more generous settlement would be heavy, but Churchill, ever mindful of press reaction and public opinion, was determined to avoid a Christmas strike, and his colleagues supported him. There was, after all, something in the Prime Minister's reference to the existence of public sympathy for the railwaymen. Certainly, the N.U.R. felt that this had been a factor in its success. Leading articles such as 'Never So Dissatisfied', in the *Manchester Guardian* of 10 November 1953, 'Never So Restive', in *The Daily Telegraph* on the same day, and 'Are Railwaymen Properly Paid?', in *The Times* of 7 January 1954, were indicative of the climate in which the government resolved to press for a settlement. Government intervention was a much more convincing explanation of the capitulation to the N.U.R. than the ex-post justification offered to the Cabinet by Monckton on 29 December 1953. The harassed Minister of Labour, in a volte-face which did him little credit, was now bleating about a 'victory for the Communists' which was 'damaging to the constitutional negotiating machinery and voluntary arbitration'. He blamed the dispute on left-wing elements on the N.U.R. Executive Committee and expressed his bitter regret at the cost of what he deemed 'a surrender to force'.[7]

The unions' claim of 1953 did not end with the settlement of February 1954. There remained the promised review of the wage structure, and this was duly produced by the Commission in the following June. In place of the existing minimum provincial rate for porters of 124s. 6d. per week, a rate of 125s. was offered, with 127s. after 12 months. The footplate staff were offered an additional 4s. 6d. Separate negotiations for the three main groups – salaried, footplate and other 'conciliation' grades – continued throughout the summer, but a full settlement was prevented by the resurgence of inter-union friction over differentials, which had been going on for some time. In September A.S.L.E.F.'s relations with the N.U.R. reached a low point. Its Executive Committee complained that the N.U.R.'s obstructionist tactics, employed to prevent the locomotivemen from putting their case to the R.S.N.C., 'reveals such a distinct absence of identity of interest that no useful purpose could be served by a joint meeting of the unions'. Although by 8 October the three unions, led by the T.S.S.A., were willing to accept an interim offer of an extra £1–£17 a year for the salaried staff, and the N.U.R. had accepted a revised offer for the 'conciliation grades' giving rises ranging from 6d. per week at the bottom to 8s. 6d. at the top, A.S.L.E.F. dug in its toes on behalf of the foot-platemen. Rejecting increases ranging from 6d. for cleaners in the first year to 6s. 6d. for top drivers, it decided to take its claim through the industry's negotiating machinery.[8]

The Commission, neither for the first nor the last time, was subject to a game of leapfrog by A.S.L.E.F. and the N.U.R. The latter, which had exempted its footplate members from the settlement of 8 October in response to the action of its rival, also went before the R.S.N.T. But five days before the arbitration award was announced on 15 November the union's Executive Committee, responding to dissatisfaction at local level with the 8 October offer to the 'conciliation grades', decided to revive the original claim for 15 per cent it had first submitted in July 1953. Thus, by the time the R.S.N.T.'s Decision No. 16 of 15 November had recommended increases for the footplate grades of a further 2s. 6d. 14s. plus accelerated promotion, a decision accepted by the two unions (although A.S.L.E.F.'s vote in favour was a close one), the N.U.R. was trying to reopen the pay issue for the majority of railwaymen.[9] Robertson and Allen, emphasising in talks with the N.U.R. the straitjacket of the B.T.C.'s poor financial position, had little alternative but to resist the union's attempt to renege on the 8 October settlement. Campbell responded by making an appeal, on 13 December, to Boyd-Carpenter, the Minister of Transport. He asked for financial assistance to be given to the Commission to enable higher wages to be paid but, after consulting the Cabinet, Boyd-Carpenter rejected all ideas of a subsidy. Campbell, judging that the mood of the rank and file was still hostile, knew that he would get little joy from the R.S.N.T. Consequently, on 21 December his Executive resolved to strike with effect from 9 January 1955. Only 12 months after successfully rejecting an arbitration award, the N.U.R. was again prepared to test the government's appetite for a strike in the public sector.[10]

The government, in fact, had been closely monitoring the progress of collective bargaining in the railway industry since the beginning of the year. Robertson had kept Monckton and Boyd-Carpenter informed of the various negotiations since A.S.L.E.F. first raised the issue of differentials in April. At this stage Cabinet policy was to encourage Robertson to stand up to the unions in spite of an early strike threat by A.S.L.E.F. The mood changed in the following months. In June Robertson asked the Ministry of Labour to give its approval to a new offer. An internal memorandum records that

Sir Brian Robertson did not wish to make an offer of this sort without prior approval from us, because of the possible repercussions of an increase to railwaymen on other classes of workers. The Secretary discussed this point with the Minister, and I gather that the Secretary will be informing Sir Brian that we would not wish to stand in the way of him making this offer.[11]

The government's attitude in the days leading up to the N.U.R.'s second strike call was more equivocal. The dispute was discussed at considerable length at five Cabinet meetings from 8 to 16 December 1954. At first Ministers, while recognising the 'serious political and economic consequences of a railway strike', were prepared to let Robertson dictate the pace. But the spectre of fuel shortages and transport disruption was still fresh in the mind, and this made the Cabinet more receptive to the view that it should ensure that a strike were avoided. In order to do so it had to convince itself that it was justifiable to make another intervention and cause another addition to the Commission's financial deficit. During the discussions on the 8th, for example, Ministers recognised that railwaymen's wages were comparatively low and expressed the opinion that while a financial subsidy to the Commission was ruled out, higher wages might be bought in return for union agreement to manpower cuts and the economies which a Modernisation Plan might bring. Both sides were playing the same game. During the discussions with Boyd-Carpenter on 13 December Campbell and Robertson tried to use the unpalatable fact of the Commission's deficit, then running at about £39 million per annum, to extract something – whether wages or capital – from the government. Robertson apparently informed the Minister that although prepared to offer a little more to the N.U.R. he would have been willing to concede much more had the Commission's finances been healthier. Asked whether he would budge if the government softened its attitude to the running up of deficits in the short term, he said he was willing to do so if the government made a public statement to that effect. Much of the next two days was taken up with the drafting of a government statement on the dispute. The Cabinet's plan was to make vague promises of financial concessions in return for an N.U.R. promise to proceed via the R.S.N.T. Wishing to avoid a winter strike, which it knew would cost the country more than the N.U.R. claim, the government feared that its political credit would be damaged if it was seen to be pushing the Commission into a more generous settlement.[12]

After the announcement of the strike Monckton had little room for manoeuvre. Since the union had not exhausted the industry's negotiating machinery, and both sides refused to give ground, 'the only practical step', in the Cabinet's words, was to appoint a Court of Inquiry, a strategy which his Labour predecessor, Isaacs, had already been forced to adopt in 1947 and 1950. The Court was appointed on 23 December, with Sir John Cameron, Q.C., as Chairman, and Sir Colin Anderson of Orient Line and Sir Harry Douglass of the Iron and Steel Trades Federation as its other members. With the N.U.R. strike threat very much alive, Monckton, whose health soon gave way again under the strain of office, asked Cameron to produce an early response, and gave him to understand that he would back whatever recommendations were produced. This was certainly a hint that a finding favourable to the N.U.R. would not be automatically ruled out by the government.[13] The Court took up the challenge with enthusiasm. Its interim report of 3 January 1955 began by criticising both sides, the N.U.R. for rejecting an agreement it had ratified and failing to use the existing machinery, the Commission for maintaining that its offers were fair and reasonable but at the same time arguing that its obligation to break even prevented it from paying adequate wages (a position the Court found contradictory and unconvincing). There was no compromise with the recommendations, however. The Court accepted the validity of the N.U.R.'s claim and suggested, in a famous phrase, that 'Having willed the end, the Nation must will the means' if 'fair and adequate' wages were to be paid. The Court thus made a strong hint that the B.T.C. should receive financial assistance from the government to meet the legitimate demands of the men.[14]

Whatever the government's reservations about the Cameron report, it had to back the Court if it wanted industrial peace. The next day Butler, as Chancellor of the Exchequer, suggested to his Cabinet colleagues that the Commission would be justified in running up an increased deficit, which could be made up later through modernisation, pricing flexibility and higher productivity. Monckton then told the N.U.R. that the government supported the interim report and persuaded Robertson to express his willingness to resume negotiations. The union, however, wanted firm assurances that higher wages were in the offing before it would withdraw from strike action, and here, it seems, Campbell was pressed by hardliners on the Executive such as David Bowman and Mark Smith.[15] The deadlock was finally broken on 6 January, when at a meeting between the Commission and N.U.R., presided over by Monckton, now recovered, Robertson gave the necessary promise that wage rates would be improved in accordance with the Court's findings. The N.U.R. called off the strike, and within a fortnight the Commission produced increases for the salaried and conciliation grades which were accepted by the N.U.R. and T.S.S.A. These raised the minimum rate for porters by 6s. to 131s., and there were increases of up to 8s. elsewhere. The offer to footplatemen involved an extra 6s. for cleaners, and 2s. 6d. for drivers, taking the latter's top rate to 195s. (see Table 28, below). The result of the N.U.R.'s action was that rates had been taken close to the 15 per cent demanded by the unions in July 1953.[16]

The press, which had again tended to sympathise with the railwaymen's case, expressed its relief that a strike had been avoided. *The Star* proclaimed that 'Once again the Monckton Magic has worked', and the *Daily Mail* referred to 'Monckton, the Prince of Conciliators'. But any relief on the part of the government must have been tempered by the knowledge that it had orchestrated another surrender to union demands by the Commission, in circumstances which were less defensible than they had been a year earlier. Certain sections of the press were quick to point this out. *The Times* condemned the 'complete divorce from financial responsibility' represented by the Cameron award, while *The Daily Telegraph* complained that since the Commission had been censured by the Court for contending that the railways should pay their way and the government had endorsed this ruling, 'the claim simply had to be conceded'. Monckton's private correspondence reveals the government's doubts. As Iain Macleod told him: 'I hope the sniping you're getting doesn't depress you. God knows the Court of Inquiry has let a litter of cats out of the bag.' Monckton's reply was as follows: 'The choice in this job is never an easy one: it always is of two evils. What we had to do was not good but better than the alternative.' At this point the Cabinet made a move of considerable significance in its approach to nationalised railways. It swung round to the view that a more efficient use of labour should be extracted from the railways with, if necessary, a public inquiry into manpower use. The final report of the Cameron Court of Inquiry echoed this policy on 20 January 1955 when it recommended a 'more searching and detailed inquiry' into efficiency in the industry.[17]

By this time it was A.S.L.E.F.'s turn to take independent action. When the Commission's revised offers were put to the three unions, A.S.L.E.F. expressed considerable anger that the partial restoration of differentials established by R.S.N.T. Decision No. 16 would be eliminated by the proposed increases. On 21 January it decided to take a new claim of 8s. (in place of the 2s. 6d. 6s. offered) to arbitration in order, once again, to restore the position of locomotivemen. But when the claim went to the R.S.N.T. in April, it was turned down (in the R.S.N.T.'s Decision No. 17 of 14 April). A.S.L.E.F.'s immediate response was to call a strike from 1 May.[18]

In the meantime, Churchill had been succeeded by Sir Anthony Eden as Prime Minister on 6 April, and on the 15th, the day of A.S.L.E.F.'s strike call, it had been announced that a general election would be held on 26 May. Whether the Conservatives' attitude to the railway strike threat was affected by their decision to go to the polls is difficult to determine, but it may have encouraged a toughening of their resolve. On 19 April the Cabinet, clearly regretting the N.U.R. settlement, expressed a greater willingness to take on A.S.L.E.F., particularly since the economic implications of a partial stoppage during the summer would not be so serious. It was also confident that the dispute could be presented as an inter-union conflict, which would reduce public sympathy for the railwaymen.[19] The Labour opposition, on the other hand, viewed A.S.L.E.F.'s action with alarm. With a London newspaper strike already in progress – it lasted until 21 April – and trouble brewing in the docks, Labour feared that its election chances might be further jeopardised by a railway strike, and it encouraged the T.U.C., whose Finance and General Purposes Committee had been involved in the dispute from the beginning, to step up its efforts to mediate. The intervention of Sir Vincent Tewson, General Secretary of the T.U.C., was undoubtedly instrumental in producing the decision of A.S.L.E.F. leaders to call off the strike on 30 April, after a promise of resumed negotiations. In fact, Labour fears about the effect of pay disputes on its credibility with the electors were probably exaggerated, since industrial relations were rarely discussed at the hustings.[20] The resumed negotiations proved fruitless. There was a stiffer resolution all round, from the Commission, the Minister of Labour and the Minister of Transport. Inside A.S.L.E.F., Baty, whose health was suffering under the strain, was being pushed by some of the larger branches, for example in the Midlands, which had been angered by the decision to abandon the strike for a promise. As Baty later explained to Monckton, 'The members had severely criticised the Executive for accepting the formula of 30 April . . . The Executive were satisfied that had they not dealt speedily with the situation they would have been faced with widespread unofficial action.'[21]

The Commission did move a little. On 3 May a 'Special Committee on the Remuneration of Footplate Staff' was appointed, under the chairmanship of A. R. Dunbar, then Assistant General Manager of the North Eastern Region. It was asked to

review the rates of pay and earnings of engine drivers and motormen of British Railways and to submit proposals for any practicable adjustments in the existing rates and allowances (such as mileage payments), designed (a) to ensure that the earnings reflect adequate and appropriate recognition of differing degrees of skill and responsibility called for by the work performed and (b) to provide improved incentives to efficiency and/or the acceptance of promotion, where such improved incentives are required.

A report was demanded within a week. The Committee, which was composed of senior officers, clearly felt that there was a case for making differential payments, but was prepared to do so only by re-establishing the principle of 'classification', in which pay was to be related to the type of train worked. In its report of 11 May it concluded that additional payments of 5s. and 10s. for drivers/motormen and 2s. 6d. and 5s. for firemen might be paid on this basis, together with an extension of the system of bonus payments for train-mileage worked. However, at a specially convened meeting of the Commission two days later, members made it clear that they were willing to accept the report only as an indication of the direction in which negotiations might proceed. On 16 May a much more limited offer was put to A.S.L.E.F., with payments of 2s. 6d. and 5s. for drivers, and a more limited extension of the mileage scheme. Since the offer proposed to pay nothing extra to firemen and the 30 per cent of drivers confined to shed and shunting duties, it was immediately rejected by A.S.L.E.F. as 'an insult to locomotivemen'. The union was determined to resist the reintroduction of what it saw as the 'utterly obnoxious principle of classification', and on 20 May it instructed its members to strike from midnight on the 28th. Relations were clearly strained. Baty complained to Victor Feather, Assistant Secretary of the T.U.C., that Benstead had refused to meet the union unless the N.U.R. were also present, and claimed that his Executive 'had no respect for Allen and were angry about Valentine [he had joined the Commission's team of negotiators] who had been insulting to the A.S.L.E.F. in negotiations'.[22]

This time Monckton's 'magic' failed to work. At the prolonged talks of 24–7 May both Monckton and the Commission referred to the N.U.R.'s insistence that negotiations about differentials should not be sectionally based, and Monckton made it clear that he was not prepared to see A.S.L.E.F. 'leap-frogging up an endless staircase'. The union refused to submit to joint talks with the Commission and the N.U.R., and rejected the Minister of Labour's last offer, a Conciliation Board. A modified offer from the Commission, made at the last minute to A.S.L.E.F. members and some N.U.R. grades, received the same treatment. A seventeen-day strike began on 28 May 1955, two days after the Conservatives were returned to office. The N.U.R. and T.S.S.A. decided that they were not parties to the dispute and stood aside, although the salaried workers did offer the strikers 'moral support' and a £1,000 donation to A.S.L.E.F. funds.[23]

The first railway strike for 30 years was not the explosive firework that had been expected. The low-key atmosphere may have been induced, in part at least, by the personal experiences of some of the main protagonists. Baty, the A.S.L.E.F. leader, continued to suffer from ill-health and leaned heavily on his assistant and General Secretary-elect, Albert Hallworth.

Robertson had injured himself playing polo, and Boyd-Carpenter's Permanent-Secretary, Sir Gilmour Jenkins, was in mid-Atlantic on the *Queen Mary*, as if to emphasise his lack of interest in railways. More important, it soon became clear that A.S.L.E.F.'s position was far from strong. The initial sympathy of the press soon evaporated after the second strike call, with the union then being portrayed as an obstinate and anti-social body engaged in a strike aimed more at the N.U.R. than the Commission.[24] Largely isolated from the rest of the trade union movement, A.S.L.E.F. was financially too weak to sustain a long stoppage. Intelligence gathered by the Ministry of Labour included the observation that there was a 'Protection Fund' of £657,000 for a membership of nearly 68,000. This was only enough to pay the minimum strike pay of £2 a week for about five weeks.[25] Furthermore, the strike, though serious, did not cause a total disruption of rail transport. The government announced a state of emergency on 31 May but the railways were able to maintain a skeleton service in most areas. About a quarter of the normal passenger traffic and a third of the freight traffic were carried, and the number of trains run picked up steadily during June. A report from the Federation of British Industries later noted that 'production losses were not nearly as severe as expected'.[26]

Negotiations continued on the first day of the strike. The T.U.C. again involved itself in the horse-trading between the parties, but failed to break the deadlock. Whether its presence served to appease or inflame is a matter of some controversy. Monckton's frequent appeals to the T.U.C. were strongly criticised inside the Ministry by Sir Wilfrid Neden, the recently appointed Chief Industrial Commissioner, who claimed that the strike had been sparked off because the Minister had brought in Tewson over A.S.L.E.F.'s head. Some members of the union's Executive certainly did believe that the T.U.C. had misled them into thinking that there would be more money on the table after the first strike call was abandoned. But there is no evidence to suggest that T.U.C. participation in the resumed talks was responsible for the final breakdown. In the end, it was left to the Commission to resolve the dispute. Robertson, responding to pressure from Eden, took the initiative and saw Baty on 8 June, after the ground had been prepared by Monckton and the T.U.C. By this time Baty was clearly willing to bargain. During talks on 9–13 June he agreed to drop the union's claim for an increase in cleaners' rates, having previously emphasised that the union would only agree to a rise for all of its members. However, an impasse was reached when the Commission offered only to 'examine' drivers' rates and refused even to consider firemen in any settlement. The strike was finally called off on 14 June when Baty accepted Robertson's suggestion that the question of drivers' rates be submitted to the binding decision of an independent referee. It had become clear that A.S.L.E.F.'s action had failed to extract a generous offer from the Commission.[27]

On 20 June the referee, Lord Justice Morris, increased drivers' rates to 176s., 187s. and 198s. (1st, 2nd and 3rd years). The award merely split the difference between A.S.L.E.F.'s claim and the position established by R.S.N.T. Decision No. 17. If the union had gone to war over a decision which, in Hallworth's words, involved 'a serious distortion of the relativity laid down by the Tribunal' in its earlier decision (No. 16), then there was very little to show for the men who had sacrificed about £20–£30 in lost earnings. The drivers got an extra 1s., 2s. or 3s. according to seniority, while the firemen and cleaners received nothing at all.[28] The differentials established by Morris's award were only a little higher than those in existence for some time under nationalisation. As Table 28 shows, the differential rate for both junior and senior drivers, in comparison with porters and guards, was now higher than it had been in 1952–3 but lower than that established by R.S.N.T. Decision No. 16, before the N.U.R.'s counter-claim.

This militancy over the issue of differentials was based upon long-standing complaints by A.S.L.E.F. In its evidence before the R.S.N.T. in November 1954 it emphasised that its real quarrel was with the B.T.C.'s failure to restore the relative position of the grades after the flat-rate increases made during the Second World War. Baty argued that his members' position rested on the National Agreement of 1919, which had created a wages structure in which the relative value of locomotivemen had been fully accepted. This position had been destroyed after 1939. Certainly, as Table 28 indicates, the differentials in existence in 1939 were considerably higher than those of the early 1950s. Concern about this erosion was also shared by the T.S.S.A.[29] Neither the Tribunal's Decision No. 16 nor the Morris award offered much in this context, and the failure continued to rankle with A.S.L.E.F. members. The N.U.R., on the other hand, was unsympathetic to this appeal to the past. The union newspaper pointed out bluntly that 'every modern development is a challenge to the position they [the locomen] have held in the past'; and Campbell, in a 'strike debate' in the *Daily Herald*, suggested that signalmen, yard foremen, carriage and wagon examiners, and running shed foremen also had a good case for higher pay based on their responsibility and skill.[30]

Nobody could take much comfort from the 1955 strike. The government had to all intents and purposes taken on the wrong adversary. Having twice encouraged the Commission to retreat before the N.U.R., it then encouraged resistance over the more limited question of differentials, a situation which many members of the Cabinet found extremely regret-

Table 28. *Differentials between rates of drivers, porters and guards (adult males, provinces), 1939, 1952–5, 1960*

Pay award	Basic rates (s.d.):		Driver (i)'s rate as percentage of:		Driver (ii)'s rate as percentage of:		
	Driver (1st yr) (i)	Driver (max.) (ii)	Porter (1st yr)	Guard (min.)	Porter (1st yr)	Porter (2nd yr)	Guard (max)
September 1939	72/0	90/0	160	144	200	191	138
November 1952 (R.S.N.T. 14)	150/6	168/6	126	121	143	143	121
February 1954 (6%)	159/6	178/6	128	121	143	143	121
October 1954	(164/10)	(185/0)	131	120	148	146	123
November 1954 (R.S.N.T. 16)	172/6	192/6	138	122	154	152	127
January 1955 (Cameron and R.S.N.T. 17)	175/0	195/0	134	122	149	147	122
June 1955 (Morris)	176/0	198/0	134	122	151	149	124
July 1960	220/0	248/0	131	118	148	140	118
(Post-Guillebaud)[a]	234/0	260/0	139	125	155	147	124

[a] 220/0, 248/0 = shunting duties
234/0, 260/0 = train duties

Source: 1939: R.S.C., Statistical Statements for Court of Inquiry, January 1951, I, B.R.B. 1952–5, 1960: R.S.C. circular letters, in R.S.C., 'R.S.N.T. Proceedings Leading . . . to Hearing of Tribunal', October 1952; R.S.C., Wage Negotiations, 1954–5, I, III–VI; B.R.B., Railway Pay Review, 1958–60, I, B.R.B.

table. A.S.L.E.F., while hailing the Morris award as 'a telling victory for our cause', must have privately recognised its Pyrrhic nature. One of the costs of the dispute was the damage done to inter-union relations. The N.U.R. made much of the fact that the co-operation between the three unions which had been so valuable in the wage bargaining of 1951–3 had now collapsed. A.S.L.E.F. criticised the N.U.R.'s attitude during the dispute as 'dictated purely by opportunist considerations' and blamed the larger union for having been responsible for stiffening B.T.C. resistance to its claim. It also inflamed the situation with its promise to 'ensure continued progress by still further upbuilding our craft solidarity'. Conversely, by working normally during the strike, N.U.R. locomen provoked considerable anger among the strikers, and many were induced to change unions in the wake of such hostility. It was scarcely surprising that the three unions should pursue separate wage claims later in the year.[31]

There were other causes for regret. The Tribunal had done little to enhance its reputation by moving towards a restitution of differentials in one decision and then going in the opposite direction in another only five months later. Finally, the Commission itself must bear some responsibility for the troubled industrial relations of 1953–5. Robertson and his colleagues had been only too willing to follow government initiatives in the negotiations with the N.U.R. and took on A.S.L.E.F. only after the government had made it clear that it could not advocate surrender. Yet Robertson's frequent references to the gap between wage and price adjustments and the size of the Commission's deficit (a deficit which appeared larger in 1954 because the Commission was no longer drawing extensively on the abnormal maintenance fund built up during the war) did nothing to draw the unions into a less military posture. As Campbell explained in the *Railway Review*, towards the end of the talks in October 1954 the Commission produced the information that it was losing £500,000 a week, giving notice that it would be more difficult to extract large wage increases in the future without a battle. The Commission also contributed to the escalation of the dispute over differentials. Its promise in December 1953 to examine the wage structure was widely interpreted inside both A.S.L.E.F. and the N.U.R. as a promise to increase differentials for the skilled grades, and the unions' disappointment at what was produced in the summer of 1954 undoubtedly encouraged further industrial action. Allen's argument, before the R.S.N.T. in April 1955, that it was Decision No. 16 that was out of alignment and that the Cameron award had merely corrected it, only fanned the flames.[32] Furthermore, the economic consequences of the events of the period were not something which the Commission could easily slough off. It lost an estimated £12 million in revenue during the A.S.L.E.F. strike, and the pay awards of October 1954–January 1956 added another £45 million to the railways' wage-bill. The settlement with A.S.L.E.F. in June 1955 brought relatively small increases, but here the Commission failed in its attempt to revive the system of classification, where extra payments were related to the effectiveness of the work performed.[33] In short, the Commission's policy was confused. It was torn between resisting union claims, in the face of its financial problems, and yielding to demands which a number of officers inside the organisation felt were fair and reasonable.

III

Before examining the Guillebaud Inquiry of 1958–60, the next major landmark in the history of the railways' labour relations, it is necessary to touch briefly on the events of 1955–8. After the A.S.L.E.F. strike inter-union dealings ceased for a time, and the three bodies chose to conduct their wage bargaining separately, although the N.U.R. made frequent appeals to A.S.L.E.F. about the advantages of co-operation. This lack of unity did not initially appear to damage the unions' position. Claims of 10 per cent by the N.U.R. and 7.5 per cent by A.S.L.E.F. and the T.S.S.A. were met by a Commission offer of 7 per cent at the R.S.N.C. in January 1956. This was accepted eagerly by the unions. The award was criticised by, *inter alia*, the *Manchester Guardian* as proof that the Commission was not being tough enough, while *The Economist* speculated that the Commission's motive in matching the claims so closely was to prevent the possibility of having to concede more at a later stage in the negotiating machinery. The truth of the matter was that while the Commission was extremely anxious to avoid a further increase in costs in 1955, it accepted the force of a case based on the relatively sharp rise in the cost of living. At an informal meeting of the Commission and the three unions in November 1955, Robertson provided confidential information forecasting a deficit of £37 million for 1955, 'a thoroughly dangerous situation for the Commission and for British Railways'. However, he conceded that 'I do understand the onus that falls on you to defend the standard of life of your members. The cost of living is rising. It has risen, I believe, by six points since January of this year when we had our last general settlement. That is a fact which we admit and acknowledge.' This argument was also accepted by the Minister.[34]

The Commission saw things very differently in the next pay round. Once again, there was no concerted union action. When A.S.L.E.F. submitted a demand for 15 per cent on 4 July 1956, only six months after the 7 per cent increase, the T.S.S.A. told the N.U.R. that the time was not ripe for a further claim. Both unions therefore held back for a time. The

Commission was encouraged to adopt a firm stance, particularly as the cost-of-living had changed very little since January. It also enjoyed the backing of the government. A Cabinet reshuffle in December 1955 had taken Macmillan to the Treasury, Iain Macleod to the Ministry of Labour, and Harold Watkinson to the Ministry of Transport. A letter from Watkinson to Macmillan on 12 July 1956 indicated how the government hoped the dispute would turn out:

> As you know, the A.S.L.E.F. have submitted a claim to Robertson. They have obviously done so to try to forestall any action by the N.U.R. whose proposals at their Annual Conference were to try and negotiate with the other railway unions to come forward with some kind of joint proposals. Once again therefore this leaves the railway unions in a confused situation. Robertson's policy will be to play for as much time as possible and of course to oppose any pay claim of any kind.[35]

A.S.L.E.F.'s claim was then rejected by the Commission. It was taken to the R.S.N.T. where in December a 3 per cent increase, justified by the rise in the cost of living, was recommended (Decision No. 19). Although relatively modest, the increase, which was accepted by A.S.L.E.F., was criticised in several quarters for having sparked off a fresh round of inflation.[36]

In October the N.U.R. decided to pursue a claim of its own, this time for 10 per cent. This also went to the R.S.N.T. where in March 1957 a majority of the Tribunal reported that the increased cost of living, 'the only ground upon which an increase in basic rates can be justified', supported only an increase equal to that given to A.S.L.E.F., viz. 3 per cent (Decision No. 20). However, for the first time there was no unanimity. Edwin Hall, the unions' representative, declared in a minority finding that improved productivity justified a much higher increase, encouraging the N.U.R. to resist the majority recommendation. After further talks, the N.U.R. accepted an additional 2 per cent, with effect from 3 March, in return for a commitment to increase productivity. This increment also went to the other unions, although A.S.L.E.F. once again refused to co-operate and made no commitment to raise productivity. Neither side was particularly pleased with the outcome. The N.U.R. had been happy to concede ground on productivity, but its members' earnings had fallen back a little both in real terms and in comparison with workers in other industries, whatever was argued by the Commission and R.S.N.T. (see tables 26 and 27). It was relatively easy for Campbell to produce 'anomalies' at the R.S.N.T. The skilled carriage and wagon examiner, he maintained, was being paid a weekly rate (before the March 1957 settlement) 6d. lower than that paid to Borough Council road sweepers, while senior parcel porters at Euston were paid 47s. less than the postmen they were working alongside, and 57s. less than the higher grade postmen. For the Commission, the persistent pressure of wage demands was a worsening headache. In its Annual Report for 1956, published in June 1957 after having endured the fires of a searching inquiry into both the Modernisation Plan and its overall financial state, it emphasised that the undertaking was 'sorely in need of a truce from recurrent wage problems'. Such a truce was not readily forthcoming, however.[37]

As Philip Bagwell has pointed out in his history of the N.U.R., the Guillebaud Report of March 1960 'was conceived under the threat of one national railway strike and born under the shadow of another'.[38] The reappearance of a militant union attitude owed its origins to the renewed determination of the government to hold down wages, particularly in the public sector, in response to the post-Suez financial crisis. Thus, when the unions presented fresh claims in September and November 1957 for a 'substantial increase' (N.U.R.), 10 per cent (A.S.L.E.F.) and an improvement to 'maintain the purchasing power of salaries' (T.S.S.A.), the government was already preoccupied with a sudden loss of confidence in the economy which had became evident in August. Since it considered that the main cause of the crisis was internal inflation fuelled by the annual wage round, there was little chance of gaining its sympathy. The unions, on the other hand, were still seeking the comparability promised by the Cameron Court of Inquiry, and were encouraged both by Hall's reference to it in his minority finding, and by the T.U.C.'s rejection of wage restraint in September. They were greatly dismayed when the government chose the railways to demonstrate its wages policy. Peter Thorneycroft, Chancellor in Macmillan's new Cabinet of January 1957, told the House in October that he was entirely opposed to 'wage increases unrelated to, and going far beyond, the general growth of real wealth within the country', inducing a hostile response from the N.U.R. and an apt cartoon from Vicky in the *Railway Review*. Further statements in November announced the government's opposition to 'inflationary' wage claims by the railwaymen, moving the *Railway Gazette* to remark:

It is unfortunate that the Government cannot keep its hands off the Commission, for it burns them every time it touches it. If it had been able on more than one occasion to resist the temptation to interfere with matters which should have been left to the Commission as the employer of the labour concerned, much trouble would have been avoided.[39]

The B.T.C. was in no position to give ground without a fight. Dependent on the government for financial support and with its deficit increasing, it could only repeat, in successive stages of the negotiating machinery, that it was unable to pay more. While preparing for a meeting with the N.U.R. at the R.S.N.C. in January 1958, Benstead indicated that the Commission 'must put over to the unions in suitable language that there is no bottomless well from which we can draw the necessary funds to meet these recurring wage claims'. Suitable language was then produced at the meeting.[40] So the claims went once again to the R.S.N.T., where for the second time in succession no unanimous decision emerged. In April 1958 (Decision No. 21) the majority finding stated that although railwaymen's basic rates were low in comparison with those in other nationalised industries and public services, the Commission's desperate financial position precluded any increase in wages at the present time. Another minority report from Hall, on the other hand, recommended an immediate restoration of railwaymen's purchasing power. The unions' reaction to the divided verdict was hostile. The N.U.R.'s Executive Committee recorded its 'deep disgust and concern', condemning the majority report 'as being completely unrepresentative of the facts of the situation'. A.S.L.E.F.'s reaction was similar.[41] But in spite of the rhetoric no one seemed anxious to provoke another major confrontation. The unions were forced to come together in order to obtain further talks with Robertson and the Commission.

The decision of the unions to work together was facilitated by an entirely fortuitous change of leadership at the N.U.R. The old guard at Unity House had been suddenly swept away by a serious road accident. The union had accepted an invitation from the Russian Railway Workers Union to visit the Soviet Union, and a delegation of six was sent at the beginning of November 1957. While the party was in Stalingrad a heavy lorry ploughed into the official car, causing the deaths of Campbell and the union's President, Tom Hollywood. Campbell was replaced by Sidney Greene, who after three months as acting General Secretary was elected unopposed to the post in February 1958. Greene, who had become a Paddington porter in 1924 at the age of fourteen, was a very experienced official of moderate persuasion, a skilful negotiator with a great appetite for the jousts of collective bargaining. He led the N.U.R. until 1975, a seventeen-year spell which was the longest enjoyed by any of the union's general secretaries. It was Greene, then, not Campbell, who took the initiative in bringing the three unions together on 14 April 1958.[42]

The government was also more inclined towards a policy of conciliation by this time. Although in November 1957 both Macmillan and Macleod had warned that there would be no more money on the table for public sector wage increases, the financial crisis had passed by the turn of the year, and the resignations of Thorneycroft and his Treasury team in January paved the way for a mildly expansionist phase under the new Chancellor, Heathcoat Amory. It also appears that the Cabinet had decided to make its stand against the London busmen. Frank Cousins of the T.G.W.U. had presented a large claim of 25s. a week to the London

Transport Executive in October 1957, but this had been rejected. The Cabinet's tough line ultimately forced the union to go to arbitration, where an award in March 1958 of only a third of the sum demanded (and then only to central bus crews) was refused by the T.G.W.U., precipitating a seven-week strike from 4 May. While the government was anxious to make an example of Cousins in the fight against what it saw as wage-push inflation, it had no wish to take on the railwaymen as well.[43] The stage had been set for whisky diplomacy at Number 10. When it was suggested, at a meeting of the Commission and the three rail unions on 16 April, that a direct approach to the government might be made in order to resolve the dispute, the parties readily agreed, and a meeting was held in Downing Street on 22 April. Here Macmillan stressed that any increase in wages would have to be justified by higher productivity, but hinted that the tempo of modernisation might be increased in return for union agreement in abandoning restrictive practices and reducing manpower. However, the negotiations broke down when Robertson contended that even on this basis he could not pay anything more until October. On 7 May the N.U.R. gave notice of its intention to call out its members from the 25th. The issue was finally resolved on 13–15 May, after an intervention by the Minister of Labour. The unions accepted a 3 per cent increase for 'conciliation grades' and salaried staff, payable from 30 June, and the Commission gave an undertaking to establish an independent inquiry to make a full examination of the entire wages structure and the comparability of railway pay with that for similar work in other industries. A programme of service cuts and other economies in railway operating was also drawn up by the Commission and endorsed by the union leaders.[44]

Both the B.T.C. and the unions appear to have been manipulated by certain members of the Cabinet, led by Macmillan who, as a former director of the Great Western Railway, followed Churchill in a sentimental regard for the industry. There was government involvement at all stages of the negotiations, and Robertson was often forced to adjourn the proceedings in order to consult with Macmillan and Macleod. In fact, the unions were negotiating as much with the government as with the Commission. At the critical meeting with the three unions on 13 May, the Commission's strategy, endorsed by the government, was to concede the demand for an earlier increase in return for further savings. Robertson admitted that he had been directed by the government to 'scrape the barrel ... to see whether anything more can be produced' in the way of economies in order to facilitate such an offer.[45] The prospect of additional cuts then made it possible for Macmillan, with the help of Butler and Macleod, to steer the pay increase through a somewhat sceptical Cabinet. Macmillan could content himself that the extra wage costs would be met by an acceleration of the modernisation programme and a determined onslaught on operating costs. Robertson's position was less satisfactory. Both Greene and Hallworth had continually emphasised that a figure of 4 per cent was needed to restore the purchasing power of railway wages, and they had only been able to persuade their Executive Committee to accept 3 per cent after Robertson had promised to investigate the issue of comparability.[46]

The decision to hold an inquiry into railway pay was timely, since there was no sign of any abatement of the unrest among the several groups of railway employee. Shortly after the settlement of May 1958 had been announced, the railway officers and senior administrative staff, represented partly by the T.S.S.A. and partly by the British Transport Officers' Guild,* demanded a matching increase of 3 per cent. They were clearly dismayed when the Commission's offer of only a £30 flat-rate increase was referred to the Chairman of the R.S.N.T. and endorsed by him.[47] This dispute once again brought home to the B.T.C. that it was imperative to seek a pay structure flexible enough to limit the number of 'leapfrog' claims by aggrieved sections of the workforce. More important still was the Commission's growing impatience with the frequent references in pay bargaining to comparability. Prepared to match rises in the cost of living, as it had in January 1956, it was becoming irritated with the uncertainties surrounding arguments over the relative position of railwaymen. Both sides were by 1958 involved in what promised to be an endless and ultimately sterile attempt to link railway pay to that of any other industries wherein the comparisons were found to produce convenient results. Thus, while Campbell drew the attention of the R.S.N.T. in February 1957 to the 'wide disparity' between the lowest railway rate and that in gas, electricity and water supply, building, mining and civil engineering, the B.T.C. argued that much broader aspects should be considered, including promotional opportunities, bonuses, security of employment and the provision of pensions, clothing and free or cheap travel. These elements, it was claimed, helped to tip the scales in favour of the railway as employer. In the next submission to the R.S.N.T. in March 1958 Greene provided tables showing once again how his members' minimum rate compared unfavourably with those of many sections of nationalised industry, including county council roadmen (15s. 5d. above the railway rate), gas, post office and electricity workers (17s. 1d., 22s. 6d. and 22s. 7d.), and surface workers in air transport (35s. 11d.). Conversely, Valentine, for the Commission, argued that railway *earnings*, not rates, should be examined, and these showed that the pay of the 'conciliation grades' was comparable

*Founded in 1945 as the British Railway Officers' Guild, this was an association representing 'out-of-category' officers with annual salaries in the range £1,000–£2,230.

with that in gas and electricity supply, road passenger transport and building, and much higher than that in local authority employment and water supply. Such debates promised to go on forever.[48]

Privately, many inside the B.T.C. were being forced to the conclusion that the unions' case was the stronger. For example, after the R.S.N.T.'s Decision No. 21 had been announced in April 1958, C. H. Brazier, the Commission's Director of Industrial Relations, asked a sub-committee of the R.S.C. to examine the Tribunal's finding that railwaymen's rates were comparatively low. The sub-committee concluded that while the minimum workshop rates were in line with those paid in engineering and shipbuilding, those of the 'conciliation grades' were significantly lower than those in the other nationalised industries and public services. Overtime rates were also more generous elsewhere.[49] The task of preparing briefs for Robertson, Benstead, Valentine and Allen was clearly becoming more difficult by 1958. It was also becoming more complex. The Commission's industrial relations department was stretched even further when asked to respond at short notice to a contention in the *Railway Review* that Britain's railwaymen were the lowest paid in western Europe. Robertson and his colleagues hoped that a full-scale, independent inquiry would establish the ground rules for a more sophisticated comparison of pay and produce firm recommendations acceptable to both sides and to government.[50]

Much to the embarrassment of the union leaders, the Committee of Inquiry was established at a more leisurely pace than had been promised by Robertson during the May negotiations, and once appointed, it took a considerable time to produce its report. It was not until December 1958, seven months after the unions had accepted the 3 per cent increase, that the three members of the Committee were appointed. The Chairman was a familiar figure in railway labour relations, C. W. Guillebaud. Emeritus Reader in Economics in the University of Cambridge, he possessed a vast experience of industrial relations and had headed the Courts of Inquiry into railway pay in 1947 and 1951. He was joined by two other industrial relations specialists: H. A. Clegg, Fellow of Nuffield College, Oxford, and author of a study of labour relations in London Transport; and Edward Bishop, the experienced Secretary of several negotiating bodies in the local government service. Their brief, admittedly, was a challenging one:

To conduct an investigation into the relativity of pay of salaried and conciliation staff in British Railways . . . with the pay of staff in other Nationalised Industries, Public Services, and appropriate Private Undertakings, as agreed between the Parties or on the instigation of the Independent Body, where reasonable and useful comparisons can be made, and in relation to any such comparisons –
  i) to establish the degree of comparability;

ii) to ascertain the rates of pay and such other emoluments of the jobs compared as may be properly taken into account; and

iii) to take account of all such other factors as the Body may consider relevant in assessing the comparability of the jobs.

The Committee was asked to present a report 'with as little delay as possible'. In fact, however, it deliberated for some 15 months before publishing its findings on 2 March 1960.[51]

Meanwhile, as railway basic rates and earnings fell back in comparative terms, rank and file pressure for improvement built up, fuelled by the Commission's efforts to extract more from the staff in its drive for higher productivity and an accelerated programme of rationalisation. 'Waiting for Guillebaud' proved to be extremely trying for the union leadership, and for Greene of the N.U.R. in particular. His position had already been tested during the negotiations of April–May 1958. He had steered the acceptance of the 3 per cent offer through a divided Executive Committee, and glossed over his part in the presentation to the government of the Commission's package of operating economies. By the spring of 1959 he was being pushed hard by a number of Branches and District Councils to submit a fresh claim.[52] In the end the pressure told and on 1 April the N.U.R. broke its undertaking to wait for the Guillebaud report and presented the Commission with a further demand for 'a substantial increase' in wages. This was taken unsuccessfully through the successive stages of the machinery – R.S.J.C. (May–June) and R.S.N.C. (October), and by December the union was proposing to proceed to the R.S.N.T. Its actions had not been supported by the other unions. A.S.L.E.F. turned down the idea of *any* claim as 'inopportune at the present time', while the T.S.S.A. pointed out that the cost-of-living index had risen by only 1.8 per cent since the last settlement. However, the three unions did co-operate in a quite separate demand for a reduction in the working week to 40 hours for 'conciliation grades' and 38 hours for salaried staff, following the rejection of earlier claims in 1957.[53]

By the turn of the year, the patience of some of the more militant N.U.R. areas was exhausted. On 5 January 1960 the London District Council announced that it was calling a one-day strike in the capital on 1 February, and on the 17th Manchester District Council demanded a national strike unless the B.T.C. offered an immediate increase. After initial negotiations with Robertson had proved abortive, Greene gave notice, on 29 January, that his union would strike from 15 February unless an immediate interim increase were granted. Once again, inter-union rivalry contributed to the dispute. Robertson's position was strengthened by the hostility shown by the other unions to the N.U.R.'s claim. At a meeting of the Commission and the three unions on 29 January, the A.S.L.E.F. and T.S.S.A. representatives, W. J. Evans (General Secretary-elect) and W. J. P. Webber, had opposed the idea of an interim increase, fearing that a percentage, 'across-the-board', rise would reduce the amount which would be available after the Guillebaud report to enhance differentials for the locomotive and clerical grades.[54] It required the intervention of both the T.U.C. and the government to settle the dispute. After the N.U.R. had met T.U.C. representatives on 3 and 5 February, the latter offered to inform the 'appropriate authorities' that only an immediate percentage increase would meet the N.U.R.'s claim. Three days later, Guillebaud promised to accelerate the presentation of his report, and Robertson offered the union a back-dated increase (later revealed to be 4 per cent, payable from 11 January) to be paid within a week of the Guillebaud report's publication. This was rejected. At a meeting held at the Ministry of Labour on 12 February, following the intervention of the Minister, Edward Heath, Robertson offered the union an interim payment of 5 per cent, back-dated to 11 January, to be implemented early in March. This offer, drawn up with Macmillan's agreement, was accepted and the strike was called off.[55]

Several factors had combined to break the deadlock. The Cabinet had been influenced by the chaos produced by an unofficial stoppage on the London Underground on 1 February, in which the men had failed to respond to a rather ambiguous instruction by the N.U.R.'s London District Council to abandon the one-day strike. More important, however, was the Cabinet's recognition that Guillebaud would recommend a higher figure than either 4 or 5 per cent. The Commission also had the same information. Pressed by problems of recession, traffic losses and a burgeoning deficit, it was scarcely anxious to pay out in advance of the report, but knew well that the Guillebaud procedure had enabled it to avoid paying anything at all to the railwaymen for 18 months. There remained the obstacle of inter-union conflict. At the difficult talks on 12 February, both A.S.L.E.F. and the T.S.S.A. accepted Robertson's initial offer of 4 per cent, a clarification of his vaguer offer on the 8th. However, the N.U.R. stuck out for 5 per cent, and the opposition of the other unions to the higher figure was only overcome after Heath informed the parties of Guillebaud's assurance that this amount would be containable within the findings of the Committee of Inquiry. Two weeks later, these findings were made known. They had been produced in a climate of considerable unrest, with the largest rail union pressing hard for more money.[56]

IV

The report of the Railway Pay Committee of Inquiry was a complex document of 94 pages and 21 appendices. Basing its calculations on the railways' deviation from the rate of pay in the median industry of those considered,* the Committee found that at the end of 1959 railway rates were approximately 10 per cent below those for comparable occupations (see Table 29). But conditions of employment had also to be taken into account, a point emphasised by the Commission in earlier pay rounds. The Committee, after considering these broader questions, concluded that while a 10 per cent increase for railway salaried staff was still merited, the increase for 'conciliation grades' should be limited to 8 per cent in order to establish a 'fair relativity' with 'outside industries'. The Committee also made a firm statement on the issue of differentials, contending that 'the work of several grades of railwaymen is undervalued in relation to the general level of railway wages'. A number of 'conciliation grades', including permanent way gangers and lengthmen, drivers, shunters, guards, telecommunications staff and signalmen, required an additional 5 per cent to bring them into line with the general run of wages in the industry, while a smaller group, comprising leading signalmen and senior linesmen, merited an extra 10 per cent. Some groups of salaried staff were also singled out for special increases, including manual grade supervisors, traffic controllers and station masters. The Committee went on to recommend a radical simplification of the railways' wages structure. It suggested that the existing system of over 40 wage rates for 153 'conciliation grades' be replaced by only 12 rates for 12 grades. Finally, the Committee advocated the separation of wage and salary negotiations at the R.S.N.C.; criticised the amenities and welfare facilities offered by the railways as 'frequently inferior to the standards prevailing in most other industries'; and condemned many clerical practices as 'unnecessarily elaborate'. There was clearly much to be done if Guillebaud and his team were to be satisfied.[57]

The report was welcomed enthusiastically by the three trade unions. Greene described it as 'a very thorough examination' which confirmed that railwaymen were underpaid. The T.S.S.A. felt that it should be 'accepted as a whole, as vindicating the arguments put forward by the Association for many years' and announced portentously that it would 'borrow the modern idiom to sum up our verdict on the Guillebaud Report ... and pronounce it to be "The Greatest!" '.[58] It was certainly unique. The Committee had been appointed and funded by the B.T.C. and the three trade unions acting together, and it was guided in its work by an advisory committee of Commission and union representatives. It was neither a Court of Inquiry nor an arbitration body working under the aegis of the Minister of Labour, and its findings were intended to form the basis

---

*Not, as the report claimed, the median rate of pay in the industries examined, which would have required a rank-order of workers' rates.

Table 29. Salary and wage comparisons in the Guillebaud report, 1960

(i) Salary Comparisons

Age	Railways clerk class 4 (£)	Median of ten industries (£)	% deviation from railway
18	318	297.5	−6.4
19	336	329.4	−4.9
20	352	365.0	+3.7
21	370	403.0	+9.0
22	387	432.5	+11.8
23	406	461.3	+13.6
24	428	481.6	+12.5
25	451	499.2	+10.7
26	475	521.1	+9.7
27	497	542.7	+11.2
28	521	570.0	+9.4
Max 521		592.5	+13.7

(ii) Wage comparisons

Industry no.	Wages of grades performing comparable work (44-hour week)	% deviation from railway minimum of 156s.
1	189s. 3d.	+21.3
2	188s. 0d.	+20.5
3	185s. 2d.	+18.7
4	185s. 2d.	+18.7
5	182s.11d.	+17.3
6	177s.10d.	+14.0
7	176s.11d.	+13.4
8	176s.11d.	+13.4
9	174s. 2d.	+11.6
10	169s. 7½d.	+8.7
11	167s. 9½d.	+7.6
12	167s. 9d.	+7.5
13	165s. 0d.	+5.8
14	165s. 0d.	+5.8
15	164s. 0d.	+5.1
16	155s. 3d.	−0.5
17	154s. 0d.	−1.3
18	153s. 1½d.	−1.8
Median	171s.10¾d.	+10.2

(iii) Wages of basic manual grades in industries commonly used for comparative purposes (44 hours)

		% deviation from railway minimum of 155s.
Building Labourer A	185s. 2d.	+18.7
Civil Engineering Labourer I	185s. 2d.	+18.7
Electricity Labourer	177s.10d.	+14.0
Gas Labourer	176s.11d.	+13.4
Water Labourer	176s.11d.	+13.4
National Health Service Group I	170s. 4d.	+9.2
L.A. Zone A Labourer (England & Wales)	169s. 6d.	+8.7
Government 'M' Non-skilled	165s. 0d.	+5.8
Municipal Road Transport Depot Worker	164s. 0d.	+5.1
Co. Owned Pass. Transport Depot Worker	162s. 3d.	+4.0
Engineering Labourer	157s. 4d.	+0.9
Road Haulage (Wages Council) Porter	154s. 0d.	−1.3
Median	169s.11d.	+8.9

Source: Report of Railway Pay Committee of Inquiry (1960), Appendices 6 (Salaries), 8 and 9 (Wages).

of subsequent negotiations between the parties. Yet, as Guillebaud later recalled, the Inquiry 'developed an unsuspected and disconcerting dynamic of its own', and its report 'came by force of circumstances to have the effective authority of an arbitration award'.[59] So although the Commission would have preferred to negotiate further, adding to wage comparability such factors as its capacity to pay, external pressures placed it in a position where an offer had to be based closely on the report's findings. Press, radio and television comment exhibited relief that an N.U.R. strike had been avoided, and the government's early endorsement of the findings proved decisive. On 10 March, barely a week after the report appeared, Macmillan told the Commons that 'The Government accept the objective underlying the report of the Guillebaud Committee – that fair and reasonable wages should be paid to those engaged in the industry.' Unions and press alike seized upon this rather than upon his supporting comment that 'others, also, must accept corresponding obligations, including a remodelling of the railway network, higher fares and rates, and a reorganisation of the structure of nationalised transport'.[60]

Correspondence between Robertson and Marples, the Minister of Transport, makes it clear that Marples orchestrated the Commission's negotiations with the unions, which led to a settlement on 24 June. Marples asked Robertson to emphasise that a settlement would be accompanied by a streamlining of the railway system, and his Deputy-Secretary, David Serpell, followed this up with a request that the unions should give a further undertaking on productivity. It was also at Marples's bidding that the Commission prolonged the talks by refusing at first to back-date the award.[61] The eventual settlement followed the Guillebaud formula very closely. Increases of 8 and 10 per cent, back-dated to 4 January and including the interim increase of 5 per cent, were applied to the 'conciliation grades' and salaried staffs respectively, and higher increases were given to the specific grades cited by the Committee in its examination of differentials. A.S.L.E.F. accepted a package which offered additional concessions in return for a form of classification in which shunting drivers were to be paid less than train drivers. The wage structure was reorganised into 14 grades (although no adjustment was made to the salaried grades). The cost to the B.T.C. was £29.8 million, close to the ceiling of £30 million mentioned by Robertson in his talks with the government. But this sum, while large, was not the final bill. Once the Commission had resolved similar demands by those not covered by the report – workshops staff, 'out-of-category' salaried staff and senior officers, as well as workers in other parts of the Commission – the total cost came to £41.5 million.[62]

The implementation of the Guillebaud findings took railway workers' rates close to those of the 'median industry' identified by the Committee. Moreover, as can be seen in Table 27 above, earnings in 1960 approached the average for British industry as a whole. The N.U.R. referred to a 'completely different atmosphere' in wage negotiations which persisted into the mid-sixties, while A.S.L.E.F.'s clamour for higher differentials subsided, if temporarily. This union's stated reaction was that on balance, the Guillebaud report represented 'a tremendous gain and a constructive contribution to the improvement of the general pattern of railway wages'.[63]

The honeymoon, alas, was brief and the industrial peace fragile. By the end of 1962 much of the shine of the Guillebaud settlement had rubbed off. The B.T.C. never shared the unions' enthusiasm for the report, and this undoubtedly influenced its reactions to further wage demands. Although accepting the validity of many of the findings the Commission was particularly concerned lest the report should be used as a concrete statement of norms in future bargaining. An internal analysis, originating in the Finance Department, criticised it on a number of counts. It had been prepared too hastily; had failed to carry out a proper examination of the rates of pay and other emoluments in the non-railway occupations considered; had erred in using basic rates rather than earnings as the basis for comparison; and had neglected both regional wage variations and wide variations in the wage rates of the outside occupations examined. It also revealed statistical imperfections, not the least of which was the failure to use the true median in the comparisons, which almost certainly gave the results an upward bias.[64] Many of these points – and they by no means exhaust the list of objections – were more a reflection of the state of the art in wage investigation and of the lack of data than an attack on the Committee's approach to its task. But the B.T.C.'s disquiet was to resurface later when the railway unions sought to use recalculations of the data presented in appendices 6 and 9 of the report (see Table 29 columns (i) and (iii)) to press for further wage and salary increases. The attitude of the Commission, and later the British Railways Board, to that piece of enterprise was subsequently summarised by Charles S. McLeod, who succeeded C. H. Brazier as Director of Industrial Relations under Dunbar in 1959. He pointed out that the Guillebaud report was regarded by the management as a 'once-only exercise' which could not be adjusted to produce subsequent comparisons. He therefore dismissed the unions' manipulations of appendices 6 and 9: they 'followed after, and were independent of, the Committee's main comparisons'. They were merely useful guides, and certainly did not represent the sole basis of the Guillebaud analysis. Finally, McLeod criticised the use of a small number of industries, some of which were not independent of one another. In the comparison of labourers' rates in appendix 9, for example, two of the twelve industries cited were municipal road transport and company-owned passenger transport, both of which were influenced by wage rates in London Transport, which itself responded to pay changes in British Railways. In these circumstances, 'self-inflation' was 'almost bound to occur'.[65]

If B.T.C. criticism sharpened, so did union enthusiasm wane. The differentials established after Guillebaud, though an improvement in A.S.L.E.F.'s view, really did little more than restore the position established by the Morris award of 1955, particularly for the commonly quoted grades of driver, guard and porter (see Table 28 above). Furthermore, the unions were soon asked to face the reverse side of the Guillebaud coin, with government pressures on the Commission to reduce manpower, accelerate its rationalisation programme and extend its work study schemes. Most galling for the unions, however, was their failure to become linked to what they saw as the 'Guillebaud median'. They were soon falling behind and consequently making fresh claims. Some commentators have contended that Guillebaud opened the floodgates of regular, frequent and high wage increases in the industry, 'a merry-go-round of wage increases trailed by despairing attempts to cover them with increased revenue'.[66] In fact, in the short run at least, railway workers did not enjoy these benefits. They were particular victims of the 'pay pause' strategy introduced by Chancellor Selwyn Lloyd in July 1961 in response to a balance of payments crisis, and the government's attempts to replace it, from March 1962, with a pay limit related to the expected annual growth of productivity, initially 2–2½ per cent, later 3–3½ per cent. Bagwell has summarised the position as the unions saw it: 'railway pay was more effectively restrained than was pay in the twelve industries listed in appendix 9 of the Guillebaud Report. From 31 March 1960 to 1 April 1962, when the next railway pay rise – a modest 3 per cent – was granted, pay in the twelve "outside" occupations had risen by an average of over £1 per week.'[67] By this time, of course, nationalised transport had been thoroughly shaken up by the various committees, inquiries and reports of 1960–1 which presaged the Transport Act of 1962. Both the Treasury and the Ministry of Transport were adopting a much tougher approach to the railways than hitherto, and Marples had secured Beeching's appointment as Chairman of the B.T.C. and Chairman-designate of the British Railways Board.

For the Commission, the post-Guillebaud period was an extremely difficult one. Racked by numerous inquiries and facing an extensive reorganisation, its financial position was worse than ever. With the accounts showing a railway deficit of £84 million in 1959 and £113 million in 1960 (see col. (e) of Table 17 above, p. 175), it was in no state to accommodate large pay claims, however improved the general environment of industrial relations may have been. Consequently, when presented in May and June 1961 with demands for another 'substantial increase' from the N.U.R., a 10 per cent rise from A.S.L.E.F. and 'parity with Guillebaud' from the T.S.S.A., on top of demands for a shorter working week which were proceeding through the negotiating machinery, it had little option but to stall for time. Internal memoranda of May 1961 revealed the stark economic realities only too clearly. Whatever attitude the Commission might have taken to the Guillebaud report, the fact remained that outside wages and salaries had gone up substantially since 31 December 1959, the benchmark date used by the Committee. The parlous financial position of the railways was thus being matched by difficulties in recruiting staff in some areas. Therefore, the memoranda concluded, it was difficult to escape the logic of further pay rises. In order to achieve parity with Guillebaud in March 1961, increases of at least 5 per cent with a two-hour reduction in the working week, or 10 per cent without a reduction in hours, were required. For the minimum-rated staff, increases of 8 per cent (with reduction in hours) or 14 per cent (without) were needed.[68]

Such views could hardly be allowed to surface publicly. Just as the whole Guillebaud process had been 'intended to circumvent political difficulties', so the government took an active part in establishing the post-Guillebaud guidelines for collective bargaining. When Beeching succeeded Robertson in June 1961 and told the unions that he wanted to settle outstanding problems inside the industry, he quickly found that he was constrained by the stance of the government. The 'pay pause' strategy was faithfully pursued by the Commission, so much so that it was not until 23 January 1962 that the unions' claims reached the end of the R.S.N.C. stage of the negotiating machinery. Normally, the Commission would then have replied to the unions' case, but Beeching, acting on instructions from Marples, suggested that instead the demands should be referred to the arbitration of the R.S.N.T. The union expressed considerable anger at this 'interference', clearly designed to be a holding operation. As the T.S.S.A. leaders, Webber and Ray Gunter (President of the T.S.S.A. from 1956 to 1964), were quick to point out at a meeting with Beeching on 31 January, the R.S.N.T. would be asked to take into account not only the Commission's poor financial state but the economic position of the country as well. It was scarcely likely to give a verdict favourable to the unions.[69]

The impatience of the rank and file railwaymen with the long delay since the last increase in January 1960 was demonstrated by an unofficial strike of trainmen on the South Eastern Division of the Southern Region on 29

6 The wage negotiations of early 1962. Beeching fettered by Macmillan:
Vicky, *Evening Standard*, 7 February 1962.

January 1962. When Beeching met representatives of the three unions two days later, he expressed some sympathy for the comparability argument but emphasised that the Guillebaud 'median' was not the only way to assess 'fair and reasonable wages'. The prosperity of the business and the wages necessary to recruit and retain staff were equally valid considerations. He was prepared to offer a modest interim increase of 2½ per cent on the understanding that negotiations could be resumed at the R.S.N.C. later in the year. This was increased to 3 per cent at a meeting of the R.S.N.C. on 5 February. After failing in a direct appeal to Macmillan on 14 February, the unions reluctantly accepted this offer seven days later.[70] The Commission recognised that there was widespread dissatisfaction inside the unions with the progress of the wage claims. Greene admitted to Beeching on 5 February that 'by devious means, we have managed to keep our people, in the main, under control', but his position was more precarious than that. A move by members of his Executive Committee to reject the 'interim' increase and to strike was defeated by only four votes (14–10). Letters of complaint then flooded into the N.U.R.'s headquarters, and the Manchester District Council demanded a more militant response. Lengthy negotiations resumed in the summer, with the Commission's position constrained by an instruction from the Chancellor of the Exchequer, Reginald Maudling, that it should limit any increase in the railways' operating costs to £10 million. Eventually, Beeching offered the unions an additional 6 per cent (after they had rejected 5 per cent) on 7 November. This represented a partial restitution of the 1960 parity, and added over £20 million to labour costs. But by this time the Guillebaud formula was looking distinctly ragged.[71]

The Commission also faced renewed demands for a four-hour reduction in the working week, which were lodged by the unions in January 1960. When the claims reached the R.S.N.C. stage in February 1961, the Commission recognised that a concession was necessary to bring the railways into line with other industries and services. After considerable debate, with Sir Reginald Wilson arguing unsuccessfully for an immediate reference to arbitration, it was decided to offer the unions a two-hour reduction – 40 hours for salaried staff and 42 hours for the 'conciliation grades' – in the hope that the offer might be used as a lever to extract 'valuable changes' in methods of calculating overtime and in the rostering of duties. The offer, made in April, met with a mixed reception. The T.S.S.A. continued to press its claim for a 38-hour week, but this was rejected by the R.S.N.T. in July. Negotiations involving the three unions were then revived, and a settlement seemed likely after the workshops staff had had their 40-hour claim turned down by the Industrial Court and had accepted a 42-hour week with effect from 30 October. But there were two sticking points: the date of implementation; and the rostering of train crews. The latter was the most important, since flexible rostering was one of the main ways in which the Commission hoped to reduce the burden of a concession which, without productivity improvement, would cost it about £13½ million for British Railways staff and £20 million for the total workforce.[72]

The dispute went to the R.S.N.T. The Commission wanted to replace the existing system of 11 × 8-hour turns each fortnight (or 22 each four weeks) with more flexible arrangements, particularly where 'it was impossible to provide productive work for Trainmen for the full 8 hours, typically in suburban passenger services'.[73] It proposed to introduce, in addition to a 21 × 8-hour roster in four weeks, 11 turns of 7 hours 38 minutes each fortnight and, in some cases, 5 turns of 8 hours 24 minutes each week. A.S.L.E.F. was determined to preserve the 8-hour day established by the National Agreement of 1919, and it received a measure of support from the N.U.R., who asked that the 21-roster system be extended to all 'conciliation' staff working an 11-turn fortnight. By a majority decision the R.S.N.T. ruled (Decision No. 25 of 12 December 1961) that A.S.L.E.F.'s position was to be upheld. More flexible arrangements, however, were to apply to 'conciliation' staff other than trainmen. The shorter working week was then introduced, with effect from 1 January 1962. Some productivity measures had been obtained. But the ruling on trainmen's rosters was to prove a significant long-term obstacle to the efforts of successive railway managements to extract operating economies in return for improved wages.[74]

During these years the emphasis in railway labour relations was thus shifting from the cost of living to comparability, with intermittent negotiations over productivity issues. The unions were successful in raising the real value of their wage rates and earnings, but Guillebaud proved to be a brief interlude in a generally unsuccessful attempt to match real wage advances elsewhere, while narrowed skill differentials remained a simmering issue. The Guillebaud report did not settle the problem of determining 'fair and reasonable wages'. But it was an heroic attempt to produce criteria for an industry whose financial position could not justify wage increases without matching productivity gains, but in which the continuance of adequate national services was threatened by a high turnover of labour and the persistence of job vacancies in high-wage areas. The Commission sympathised with many of the unions' claims, but its worsening financial position increasingly placed it in the hands of the government. Here it was encouraged to press the unions to make productivity concessions, although until the negotiations for a shorter working week these were rarely tied specifically to wage increases. As much as anywhere in the public sector, the government set the pace and often determined the detailed content of pay deals. The Conservative administration moved from an obsession with the need to secure industrial peace to an emphasis on pay restraint in the battle against inflation, and finally to support for an incomes policy. This meant more direct involvement in the terms of settlements and a determination (although not usually pressed home) that wage increases were to be bought by fewer jobs. The railways were often at the centre of these changes of policy.

V

References to rank and file discontent, to A.S.L.E.F.'s adherence to the 'principles of 1919', to skill differentials for locomotivemen, and the like, might be taken to imply that the railwaymen offered only a Luddite response to the second main strand of the B.T.C.'s labour policy – the improvement of railway productivity. In fact, existing estimates of productivity growth in the period to 1962 do paint a somewhat cheerless picture. Aldcroft, for example, observed that labour productivity, measured in terms of traffic units per worker, increased by only 2 per cent from 1955 to 1962, compared with a rise of about 13 per cent in the period 1948–55. Criticising the limited progress made in improving the utilisation of equipment, he noted that in the years 1955–62 there was a fall of 9 per cent in loaded wagon-miles per wagon, a fall of 13 per cent in ton-miles run per wagon, and an increase of 20 per cent in wagon turnround time. Although he conceded that the results were affected by the fall off in traffic in the early 1960s, his conclusion was that the progress made was 'by no means spectacular'. Performance after the Modernisation Plan was published in 1955 was apparently no better, and in some cases worse, than before.[75] A more detailed analysis of productivity change in transport, published by B. M. Deakin and T. Seward in 1969, produced even gloomier results. Referring to the period 1952–62, the authors concluded that on the railways (including London Transport) labour productivity declined by 1.6 per cent, while total factor productivity fell by 6.2 per cent. This was attributed to a fall in output of 16 per cent between 1957 and 1962, 'in circumstances where capacity cannot . . . readily be adjusted to match a lower level of demand'.[76]

The methods used by Deakin and Seward impart a downward bias for much of the period in that although their output index is a traffic index, their manpower estimates do not take adequate account of the increasing proportion of railway workshop man-hours devoted to capital construction over the period 1952–9. A revised output index has been calculated which seeks to relate labour inputs to output on a consistent basis. The results, which appear in Table 30, are a little more optimistic. The railways' labour productivity (output per head) is shown to have *risen* by 9.7 per cent, 1952–62, as labour inputs fell, while 'total factor productivity' (output divided by a weighted average of labour and capital inputs) fell by 3.8 per cent, about half the decline suggested by Deakin and Seward. All these calculations are undoubtedly influenced by the drop in railway/workshop output from 1960 to 1962, caused by a combination of falling traffic and the slackening pace of rolling stock construction. Long-run trends can easily be obscured when output fluctuates in this way. However, if we compare periods in which output is at a roughly comparable level, viz. 1948–54 and 1953–60 in Table 30, it can be seen that labour productivity increased at an annual rate of 1.5 per cent, followed by an improvement to 2.0 per cent, while total factor productivity exhibited annual growth rates of 0.7 and 0.6 per cent over the two periods. In the period 1953–60 labour inputs were reduced, but there was an increase in the amount of capital available per head. The resulting modest growth of 'total factor productivity' is also reflected by the available indicators of operating efficiency. For example, net ton-miles of traffic carried per traction-hour, which had stood at 619 miles in 1953, improved to 642

Table 30. *New estimates of British Railways' labour and 'total factor productivity', 1952–62 (1948 = 100)*

Year	Output	Output per head	Capital per head	'Total factor productivity'
1948	100.0	100.0	100.0	100.0
1952	96.7	103.9	110.2	99.9
1953	98.5	106.3	110.5	102.1
1954	99.5	109.5	113.2	104.2
1960	97.9	122.2	140.6	106.7
1962	86.1	114.0	153.4	96.1

Source: see Appendix C, Table 1.

miles in 1960 and fell slightly to 634 miles in 1962. Average wagon-loads, 7.14 tons in 1954, increased to 7.82 tons in 1960 and 8.03 tons in 1962.[77] Our conclusion must be, then, that there was a steady if modest advance in productivity under the B.T.C. Performance was generally below the average suggested for the U.K. as a whole.[78]

How did the Commission orchestrate the modest gains in productivity achieved in the 1950s, and what were the propelling and retarding factors? The B.T.C. pursued its objective to increase productivity through a number of different channels. One of the most obvious was to attach productivity clauses to wage settlements. Most of these, it must be admitted, were cosmetic rather than realistic, designed to appease critics. In December 1953, for example, the agreed statement attached to the 4s. wage increase promised only that the two sides would 'confer in order to evolve ways of increasing the efficiency of the railway organisation'. Attempts were then made to follow this up with local initiatives, including the creation of regional productivity councils, but the results were disappointing, as was revealed in negotiations leading to a similar statement annexed to the settlement with the N.U.R. in October 1954.[79] A further settlement with the N.U.R. in March 1957 was tied to a more specific undertaking. The union agreed to co-operate more fully in productivity initiatives, and, in particular, to discuss jointly the possibility of making progress towards a single-manning agreement for diesel and electric traction. The agreement was then passed to A.S.L.E.F. and the T.S.S.A. with a view to a joint statement, but A.S.L.E.F. declined to co-operate. The unions' commitment to the operating economies introduced in 1958 was also rather vague. The resolution of the impasse over wages (see above, p. 235) included a programme of cuts to which the union leaders were a party, but Greene later denied vigorously that the settlement had carried any strings. Nevertheless, the cumulative effect of such productivity statements did impress upon railwaymen that some progress in operating efficiency had to be made if wage levels were to be improved. This was clearly recognised by 1960–1, during the negotiations for a shorter working week. For the first time, specific productivity improvements were thrashed out before a deal was concluded, which enabled the Commission to reduce the cost of the settlement from £20 million to about £10 million.[80]

In fact, the Commission was able to make more headway outside the wage bargaining arena. Of crucial importance here was the British Railways Productivity Council, a joint forum consisting of a Commission chairman and equal numbers of representatives from the management and the unions (including the Confederation of Shipbuilding & Engineering Unions). This body had a somewhat inauspicious birth, in that it was created in 1955 following the Cameron Inquiry report, largely to forestall government threats of a public inquiry into railway efficiency and the use of manpower. Nevertheless, the council did not become a mere talking-shop. It soon developed into an important channel of communication, through which union co-operation over productivity measures could be sought and won. Initiatives subsequently set in motion by the Council included the development of work study following the opening of the Work Study Training Centre at Watford in March 1957, the reduction of restrictive practices, the single-manning agreement of December 1957 and the first redundancy arrangements.[81]

The Commission's pursuit of a 'slow negotiated path' produced some positive results. It could claim legitimately to be leading the way in the implementation of work study since by 1962 schemes were covering about 57,000 workers, nearly 12 per cent of the railway total, and producing annual savings of about £6 million. Nearly 60 per cent of the men in the civil engineering departments had been covered. The 1957 manning agreement, operative from January 1958, which provided for single-manning of day-time trains over short and medium distances, also decisively punctured traditional practices, although it was always recognised that savings would be prospective rather than immediate.[82] The B.T.C. did in fact persuade its employees to give up some old-established restrictive practices. Reporting to the Joint Advisory Council of the Ministry of Labour in 1956, the Productivity Council identified 14 items impeding 'the full and efficient use of manpower'. This was followed by joint management–union efforts to eliminate the worst examples, such that by April 1959 a follow-up study could report that only five problem areas required further action.[83]

Yet progress was neither as swift nor as straightforward as it might have been. In part this was due to muddled management thinking and the imprecise definition of objectives. For example, the single-manning initiative of 1957 was flawed because an earlier technical decision to persist with steam heating on passenger trains hauled by the new motive power often required the retention of a second man to operate the boiler. The persistence of freight working with loose-coupled wagons also worked against single-manning.[84] Some of the potential gains from the introduction of work study were also lost through a lack of vigour in evaluating the actual work itself. A shortage of trained staff, the temptation to make quick savings and the use of consultants with a vested interest in producing speedy results often meant that there was very little difference between work study operations and existing bonus schemes.[85] Even the somewhat more passive policy of accepting natural wastage in the workforce was not without its problems. As has already been observed (above, pp. 180–1), the total amount of labour employed on the railways fell by 20 per cent between 1953 and 1962, from 594,000 to 475,000. Yet railway managers could do little to modify the market pressures which lay behind much of this shake-out. The result was frequently expressed anxiety about the number of job vacancies in several key operating grades, particularly those associated with freight working and permanent way renewal, and a persistently high rate of staff turnover. Wastage rates in the 'conciliation grades' averaged 57,575 men in 1955–7, about 19 per cent of those employed. Even after the Guillebaud award, it was difficult to recruit men. For example, the General Manager of the Eastern Region complained that in the first eight months of 1961, 55 firemen and 18 passed (i.e. experienced) cleaners had resigned, and only 18 cleaners had been found to take their place. Dissatisfacton with the general conditions of railway working – 'shift work, weekend work, uncongenial hours' – were blamed.[86]

Given these circumstances, it is hardly surprising that union leaders were often far in advance of their members in their preparedness to collaborate with management to effect higher productivity. Grass-roots unease might be lessened by patient joint explanation and exhortation, but all too often the problem lay deeper, in the insecurity and poor rewards which remained the lot of the lower-paid railwaymen. The contentious issue of lodging turns or 'double homers' provides an illustration of the difficulties. The men's resentment at the continuation of these arrangements for rostering train crews persisted after the unofficial strikes in 1949 (see above, pp. 128–9). It had certainly not been assuaged by the establishment in June 1953 of a Joint Lodging Sub-Committee. Made up of representatives from A.S.L.E.F., the N.U.R. and the Railway Executive, it provided some safeguards in return for union agreement to a limited extension of the practice. Unofficial action flared up again in May 1954, with a series of strikes by Western Region locomotive men, who were protesting against the introduction of new lodging turns previously accepted by union leaders through the Sub-Committee. About 2,500 men, three-quarters of the footplate staff at ten depots, failed to report for duty. There was considerable sympathy for their action, so much so that at A.S.L.E.F.'s annual assembly, a resolution calling for the union to seek the total abolition of lodging turns was carried, against the advice of the Executive Committee.[87] The abolition demand was taken to the R.S.N.C., where it was promptly rejected. In any case, the N.U.R. was not so hostile to lodging and, as Greene has pointed out, the turns were welcomed by some men because they enhanced earnings or reduced overtime. The Western Region was also in some ways a special case. Fear of redundancy was very real in a region with few lodging turns and where manning levels were relatively generous, as Raymond and Fiennes, General Managers in the 1960s, were to discover later. Baty and his Executive, feeling that a prolongation of the dispute might prejudice its wage claim, recommended a return to the status quo. The result was a modified form of the 1953 machinery with the resuscitation of the Joint Committee in April 1955. The Commission was able to introduce a number of new turns with considerable savings in staff costs. Despite A.S.L.E.F.'s rhetorical opposition and the discontent of the rank and file, the operation of the Committee after 1954 demonstrated the degree to which the Commission was able to get the unions to co-operate constructively in its efficiency drive. In April 1959, for example, the Productivity Council formally recognised that 'it is worthy of record that on the . . . Committee . . . the co-operation of the . . . Unions has been received provided it could be demonstrated that the turns were . . . necessary and reasonable'.[88]

The gulf between union leaders and their members can also be seen in the results of the Commission's efforts to extend work study. Save in the civil engineering departments, the progress made in the period to 1962 was not impressive. As already indicated, little was achieved in the field of work measurement. Not only did the Commission lack industrial relations experts (men such as Dunbar, Brazier and McLeod had worked their way up through traffic departments), but the build-up of trained work study staff was slow. The unions had, according to Dunbar, displayed a 'passive resistance' to work study, and there had been considerable hostility from local staff, whether belonging to the N.U.R., A.S.L.E.F. or the T.S.S.A. Local opposition was important. James Ness, General Manager of the Scottish Region, gave Dunbar an example of the difficulties he faced in 1958:

For some time we have been endeavouring to negotiate through the L.D.C.* at High Street Goods [Glasgow] an alteration in the hours of duty to deal with the

---

*Local Departmental Committee, the local rung of the negotiating machinery.

Received and Forwarded vulnerable traffic, which would have the dual effect of more efficient working and the elimination of Seven Checkers' posts. The L.D.C. have been most unco-operative in the matter, and in spite of the efforts of the Divisional Organiser of the N.U.R. we have been unable to make any progress . . . the attitude of the Staff Side of the L.D.C. . . . is evidenced by the following extract from the last Minute dealing with the proposed re-organisation: –

After further discussion the Staff Side made it clear that they considered it was their function to resist all economy cuts put forward by the Management and maintained their refusal to submit any proposals affecting the conditions of the staff which would be instrumental in reducing the number of staff employed.

This attitude of mind is clearly not in keeping with the co-operation which has been promised by the Headquarters of the Union.[89]

Union attitudes softened a little in the wake of the Guillebaud report of 1960, and in the two years which followed, the numbers covered by work study doubled. But as Greene pointed out,

We were going round the country trying to get all our people – permanent way staff – to accept work study. They were all resisting it, because they could see that it meant doing away with staff . . . the Unions could only go as far as their members were prepared to agree . . . Nor was it easy to convince all railway workers, to many of whom work study was a novelty, that in present circumstances this was a welcome development.[90]

The Commission certainly accelerated its efforts to tackle problems of manning and overall efficiency, particularly after the re-appraisal of the Modernisation Plan in 1959 and the Select Committee and Stedeford Group inquiries of 1960. But a patient approach to union resistance was counselled by Vice-Chairman Benstead, and action was often tempered by the concern about relatively high vacancy levels and turnover rates. This was evident in the approach to work study. The rather limited single-manning agreement, seen by Robertson as a personal triumph for Allen in his last year in office, may indeed have been proof, as the Commission claimed, 'of the patience and constructive outlook displayed by both sides'. But it was hard to find this outlook below headquarters level, where staff faced the cumulative effect of smaller-scale changes as the Commission pushed the regions to make savings, to adhere to manpower targets and generally tried to encourage an end to restrictive practices. For example, the success of A.S.L.E.F. in resisting the attack on the eight-hour roster in 1961 must be set against the 'widespread extension' of the six-day week to traffic grades in the North East, reported in 1959, which involved the replacement of the 11×8-hour fortnight of duty by 12 turns of 7 hours 20 minutes each. Local staff also faced a more determined assault on the 'unproductive hours of enginemen'.[91]

Throughout this period, the Commission was dogged by a number of serious labour relations problems. Its aim was to drag a leviathan of an industry, with working practices based on Victorian precepts, into the mid-twentieth century. But its chosen methods did not necessarily guarantee success, and sometimes action merely created fresh problems. Work study was by 1962 proving useful in encouraging incentives, but it was also threatening to upset old-established differentials.[92] At the same time railwaymen remained suspicious of many new developments. The industry may have retained its image as a generally peaceful one, but there was an undercurrent of tension, fed by cuts in staffing levels and a decline in the relative position of wage rates and earnings. To the railwayman, as the editor of the *Railway Review* put it, 'justice seems always just out of reach. That feeling is not conducive to an atmosphere in which full co-operation can be expected.'[93] This backcloth ensured that the B.T.C. had little room to manoeuvre, so that a continuing commitment to the patient and constructive negotiation advocated by Allen and Benstead was inevitable.

Beeching's appointment as Chairman of the Commission in 1961 was to transform the position. By 1962, a plan to close 16 of the 32 railway workshops had been announced, and it was accompanied by a new determination to prune the railway network. The unions' immediate response was to call a one-day strike on 3 October, in protest at the rundown of the industry. But in the longer term they were to be faced with a variety of wholly new difficulties, symbolised by the growing problem of redundancy.[94] The new Chairman's appointment was therefore a watershed in labour relations, as it was to prove in so many other facets of the railway business.

8

The Modernisation Plan and investment

I

The B.T.C.'s hopes for future financial viability were pinned on the Modernisation Plan of 1955, one of the most controversial elements in the history of nationalised railways. Published in January 1955, it aimed to establish a 'thoroughly modern system', able fully to 'exploit the great natural advantages of railways as bulk transporters of passengers and goods'. The principal mechanism in this change was to be a long-term investment programme which envisaged an expenditure of £1,240 million over 15 years on the 'Modernisation and Re-equipment of the British Railways'. At its inception it received the warm support of the Conservative Government. R. A. Butler, the Chancellor of the Exchequer, paid tribute to its 'courageous and imaginative conception'. The press was also enthusiastic. The *Manchester Guardian*, for example, announced that 'the new programme stands for a new spirit which the public will welcome', and even *The Economist* initially considered it to be 'carefully thought out' and 'a firm statement of good intentions'. Most observers accepted the Plan as a laudable attempt to rectify a lack of investment in the industry, which stretched back to the inter-war years.[1]

This honeymoon of enthusiasm was relatively short. The Plan soon came to be seen as a flawed response to the problems of railway investment. *The Economist* was one of the most consistent critics. Before the Plan had been published it had struck a cautionary note, warning that 'there will be a tendency to pretend that this will make everything on the railways suddenly all right'. Then, in a leader entitled 'Millions for Cinderella', it observed that 'the mere spending of money does not ensure efficiency; it can be a convenient device for ensuring that inefficiency is chromium-plated. . . Sober analysis suggests that a scheme of this sort is necessary. Grim experience suggests that there are at least three ways in which it could go wrong'. The Plan, it thought, might easily founder on the rocks of unimaginative railway management, competition from road transport and an inadequate response to productivity from railwaymen. The latter was very much a preoccupation. In the wake of the A.S.L.E.F. strike of May 1955, for example, *The Economist* was anxious to emphasise that the Modernisation Plan 'would certainly be a waste of money if it attracted nothing more than Luddite indifference' from the labour force.[2]

Critics became more vocal with the passage of time. In 1956 and again in 1959 the Plan was subjected to critical government review, and in the following year a halt was called. By this time Matthew Stevenson, Under-Secretary at the Treasury, was able to tell the Select Committee on Nationalised Industries that the Plan 'was merely a hotch-potch of the things that the Commission was saying it was desirable to achieve by 1970, ill-qualified and not really readily explainable'.[3] Three years later the economist Christopher Foster, in his influential book *The Transport Problem*, referred to several defects in the Plan, and was particularly severe on the Commission's failure to calculate the rate of return on the investment with sufficient precision. For him the Plan, 'as it was presented originally, should never have been accepted'. Later still, Stewart Joy could dismiss it briefly as 'the greatest shopping spree . . . in railway history', while for supporters of road transport the modernisation of the railways was a waste of resources which would have been better spent on the improvement of Britain's roads.[4] How was it that something which had been welcomed so wholeheartedly could so quickly attract such obloquy? In this chapter, the circumstances surrounding the formulation and acceptance of the Modernisation Plan are examined, and the main features of the Commission's investment under the 1955 programme are analysed. Finally, the government's reactions, and the Commission's response to the railways' failure to halt the trend of increasing deficits are outlined.

II

It is clear that the antecedents of the Modernisation Plan lie in the period of the Railway Executive. Early efforts to lobby the Ministry of Transport and the Treasury began with the change of government in October 1951. Reginald Wilson was firmly of the opinion that the Commission should put something down on paper, and shortly after the dissolution of parliament he encouraged Elliot and the Railway Executive to prepare a report on the railways' long-term capital needs. He claimed that 'his contacts with the Treasury experts were such that he could be quietly creating conditions which would eventually lead to a much higher priority for this type of development'. Pope and Barker were of similar mind. At a meeting with Executive members in January 1953 they suggested that 'a separate and large capital investment authorisation should be sought from the Treasury'. Elliot responded enthusiastically, and a small committee of senior officers was asked to prepare a paper indicating '10 salient directions in which additional capital might be expended, on the assumption that Treasury approval were given to a global additional investment authorisation of perhaps £500m. to be spent over the next 10/20 years'.[5]

The committee reported in April. Its brief confidential memorandum, entitled 'A Development Programme for British Railways', bore all the signs of having been hastily put together. Ten 'salient directions' were produced, each described in only the most general terms, and the estimated expenditure was put at exactly £500 million at current prices (see Table 31). This sum represented the minimum investment level for essential needs and was to be additional to the normal annual programme of maintenance and renewal. It was justified on the grounds that

a modern well-equipped railway system is indispensable for the future of the country as a leading industrial power . . . the volume of heavy freight movement, especially coal and raw materials for the iron and steel and other basic industries, and the density of the relatively short-distance passenger traffic are such that the railways must in the national economic interest remain the backbone of the transport system.[6]

With its generous provision for such things as helicopter terminals, the 1953 'plan' may appear fanciful from a modern standpoint. But coming as it did in the wake of the Executive's report on motive power policy of October 1951, which had fudged the issue of future traction, its support for electrification, which was to consume a third of the total capital, was significant. Only a year or so before the Modernisation Plan itself was concocted, electrification, not dieselisation, was the firm choice of the railway managers. Diesel units were to be given a role on the inter-urban, cross-country and local lines but the main-line strategy was based on electric power. The report recommended the conversion of some 2,900 route-miles, including most of the main lines out of London: both the East and West Coast routes to the north (Euston–Glasgow, King's Cross–Newcastle), Paddington–South Wales, St Pancras–Manchester, Liverpool Street to Cambridge and Ipswich, and the Southern Region's remaining steam lines, to Dover, Bournemouth, and Hastings. This policy, stated the Executive, recommended itself because it made no demands on imported fuel and would free high-grade coal for export. Furthermore, in the longer term, electrification was considered to be 'the most effective means of harnessing atomic power for railway purposes'.[7] In May the Executive's memorandum was passed to the Commission via Frank Pope, but there the initiative was halted. The passing of the Transport Act in the same month, with its promise of a new railway organisation, and the abolition in August

Table 31. *Railway Executive's development programme, 1953*

Proposals	Estimated expenditure (£m.)
Electrification	160
Major improvements to running lines	60
Modernisation of signalling and telecommunications	30
Re-siting and modernisation of marshalling yards	50
Rationalisation and modernisation of freight terminals	50
Fitting of continuous brake to freight rolling stock	40
Introduction of diesel rail-cars	17
Reconstruction of passenger stations	40
Helicopter terminals and services	40
Marine services	13
Total	500

Source: R. E., 'A Development Programme for British Railways', April 1953, p. 3, also reproduced in Johnson and Long, *British Railways Engineering*, p. 96.

of the Executives, provided the Commission with more urgent business.

When the idea of a long-term investment strategy resurfaced, it was taken up by Robertson, who succeeded Hurcomb in September. By the end of the year the B.T.C. had begun to lobby departments and in particular to put some pressure on the Ministry of Transport. Responding to a Ministry request to revise its capital investment forecasts for 1954–6, the Commission agreed in November to inform the Ministry that its new estimates did 'not take into account any broader plans involving a substantial betterment of the undertaking which the Commission are considering for presentation to the Minister in due course'. In April 1954, the climate seemed sufficiently favourable for the Commission to instruct Daril Watson, its Chief of General Services, to

assemble a Planning Committee composed of Chief Officers ... to submit proposals ... for the modernisation and re-equipment of the railways, making the following assumptions:

(a) That the plan shall be spread over a period of years; in principle the plan to be capable of being launched within five years and completed within 15 years.

(b) That H.M. Government will provide a loan of the order of £500m. on special terms.[8]

It seems likely that the Commission took this step in the knowledge that the Conservative Government had come round to the view that some kind of capital support for British Railways might form a legitimate part of its competitive strategy for transport. During the drafting stages of the

Transport Bill in 1952, when the Cabinet examined a number of alternatives to the idea of a compensatory levy on road transport, Churchill raised the possibility of relieving the Commission of some of its fixed interest charges. He took up the idea again in December 1953, after the government had intervened in a pay dispute between the Commission and the N.U.R. (see above, pp. 219–20). Encouraged to offer concessions in order to avert a strike the government was clearly anxious to avoid, Robertson warned Walter Monckton, the Minister of Labour, that the cost of the settlement would be heavy and he 'saw no prospect of recouping this by increased efficiency'. But Churchill's suggestion was condemned by Butler, the Chancellor, who pointed out that to reduce the Commission's interest burden would amount to a transport subsidy. This, he noted, would 'destroy the incentive to secure all possible efficiency of working which is provided by the present requirement to make ends meet'.[9] The Cabinet was thus led, in the wake of its intervention in a railway wages dispute, to the view that a better course would be to offer the railways help to finance modernisation. In February 1954 it was asked to give its blessing to a 10 per cent increase in railway freight charges which, as Lennox-Boyd explained, 'had to some extent been made necessary by the wage increases which the Government had encouraged the . . . Commission to grant'. Concern at the prospect of a never-ending spiral of wage and price increases drew the Cabinet towards Lennox-Boyd's alternative of modernisation with government support, and Butler responded by stating that he was willing to consider any proposals which the Minister of Transport might put forward along these lines.[10]

The change of Chairman at the B.T.C. also helped in inducing the government to support railway modernisation. Lennox-Boyd was very pleased to have got Robertson as a replacement for Hurcomb, whom Churchill had distrusted, and there appears to have been a desire to improve relations with the Commission, which had been soured in 1952 by the clash over fares (see above, pp. 102–4). Confidence in Robertson, whose ability and integrity were widely admired in government circles, certainly influenced Lennox-Boyd's attitude, and during discussions at the beginning of 1954 he offered his nominee some positive encouragement on the modernisation issue.[11] Governmental support for the railways was also influenced by awareness of its earlier and more favourable treatment of other nationalised industries. Investment in electricity supply was considered to be comparatively healthy, despite Lord Citrine's complaints about restrictions, and in 1953 the Conservatives lent their support to a national plan to extend supply to rural areas. The National Coal Board was already working to a 15-year capital development programme devised in 1950. Furthermore, railway supporters were quick to point out that many European countries were pursuing long-term programmes of rail-

1 The war-time Railway Executive Committee in session, April 1940 (*left to right*: Sir Eustace Missenden (S.Rly); Sir James Milne (G.W.R.); Sir William Wood (L.M.S.); W. H. Mills (R.E.C.); E. G. Marsden (R.E.C.); Sir Charles Newton (L.N.E.R.); Frank Pick (L.P.T.B.); Sir Ralph Wedgwood (Chairman); G. C. Deacon (R.E.C.); and Michael Barrington-Ward (Chairman, Operating Committee)) (*Railway Gazette*).

2 First meeting of the British Transport Commission, 13 August 1947 (*left to right*: John Benstead; Lord Ashfield; Sir Cyril Hurcomb (Chairman); Sir William Wood; Lord Rusholme) (*Popperfoto*).

3 British Railways on nationalisation: Sir Cyril Hurcomb (B.T.C.) and General Sir William Slim (R.E.) visit Liverpool Street station, London, on Vesting Day, 1 January 1948 (*B.R.B.*).

4 First meeting of the Railway Executive, 1 January 1948 (*left to right*: E. G. Marsden (Secretary); George Morton (Chief Financial Officer); H. L. Smedley (Legal Adviser and Solicitor); John C. L. Train; R. A. 'Robin' Riddles; Sir Eustace Missenden (Chairman); Michael Barrington-Ward; David Blee; W. P. 'Bill' Allen; Christopher Nevile; W. H. Mills (Assistant Secretary) (*Barratt's*).

5 Miles Beevor, Chief Secretary and Legal Adviser, B.T.C. (*Brush Electrical Machines*).

6 Sir Reginald Wilson, member and former Financial Comptroller, B.T.C., visits new typing pool as Chairman, Eastern Area Board, December 1957 (*B.R.B.*).

7 Freight train operation in the early days of nationalisation: Western Region 2-8-0 locomotive (No. 4809), converted to oil-firing (see Chapter 3 p. 88), near Ilmer Halt, Bucks., September 1948 (*J. S. Russell-Smith Collection*, *National Railway Museum, York*).

8 Western Region's Brown Boverie gas turbine locomotive (No. 18000) on test run, June 1950 (*B.R.B./Railprint*).

9 Ex-L.M.S. diesel-electric locomotive (No. 10000) near Hendon, February 1948 (*B.R.B./Railprint*).

10 'Austerity' (ex-Ministry of Supply) locomotive (No. 90279) with coal train at Peterborough, April 1954 (*B.R.B./Railprint*).

11 'Britannia' Class locomotives, Nos. 70014 and 70004 (the latter showing 'Golden Arrow' train motif), at Stewart's Lane depot, London, 1953 (*M. W. Earley Collection, National Railway Museum, York*).

12 Robin Riddles (third from left) and staff, and 4MT 75000 Class locomotive (No. 75000), Swindon, May 1951 (*B.R.B./Railprint*).

13 Exterior (*B.R.B.*).

14 Interior (*B.R.B.*).

15 Branch-line passenger train in the early 1950s: train at Great Shefford, 1953, on the Lambourn–Newbury branch (closed January 1960) (*M. W. Earley Collection, National Railway Museum, York*).

16 Pay agreement, 23 February 1951 (*left to right*: Jim Figgins (N.U.R.); John Elliot (Chairman, R.E.); James Baty (A.S.L.E.F.) (*Railway Gazette*).

17 Naming of W. R. diesel-hydraulic locomotive No. D800 'Sir Brian Robertson', Paddington, July 1958 (*left to right*: Robertson; Keith Grand (General Manager, W. R.); J. W. Watkins (Member, B.T.C.); Sir John Benstead (Deputy-Chairman, B.T.C.); Reginald F. Hanks (Chairman, Western Area Board) (*B.R.B./Railprint*).

18 With Alan Lennox-Boyd (Minister of Transport, *far left*), at the opening of the new Woodhead Tunnel, June 1954 (*B.R.B./ Railprint*).

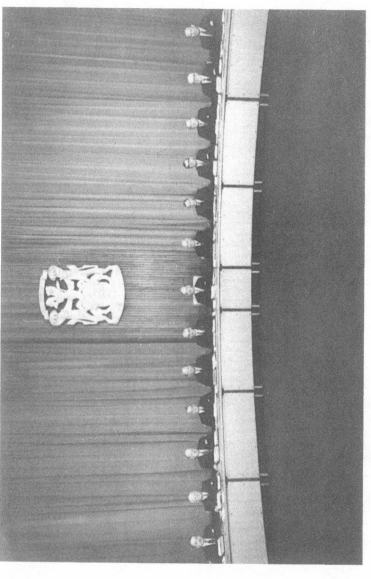

19 A meeting of the British Transport Commission, July 1959, in the Board Room, 222 Marylebone Road (*left to right*: Sir Reginald Wilson; Sir Cecil Weir; Keith Grand; Reginald F. Hanks; Donald Cameron of Lochiel; Sir Ian Bolton; General Sir Brian Robertson (Chairman); Sir John Benstead (Deputy-Chairman); Alec Valentine; John Ratter; H. P. Barker; Sir Leonard Sinclair; Thomas Summerson (not shown: Lord Rusholme; Sir Philip Warter)) (*Bassano*).

20 Pick-up freight train operation, 1960: Glenfield station, on Leicester (West Bridge)–Desford branch line, March 1960 (*author*).

21 Carlisle Kingmoor marshalling yard, 1962 (*B.R.B.*).

22 Experimental single unit railcar, 1956, introduced on the Banbury–Buckingham branch (*B.R.B.*).

23 Railbus: German-built design at White Notley station, on the Witham–Braintree branch line, June 1958 (*B.R.B.*).

24 Guard issuing tickets on Aldeburgh–Saxmundham train, March 1962 (*B.R.B.*).

25 Albert Hallworth (A.S.L.E.F., 1956–60) (*Sunday Citizen*).

26 Sidney Greene (N.U.R., 1958–75), with Harold Wilson (*N.U.R.*).

27 Three of the many classes of diesel-electric locomotive, Ipswich depô November 1959 (*left to right*: all Type 2s: B.R.B. (Derby)-built Class 24 (No. D5022); Brush-buil Class 31 (No. D5544); North British-built Class 29 (No. D6127) (*B.R.B.*)

FAILURE AND SUCCESS IN MAIN-LINE DIESELISATION:

28 Type 4 'Peak' Class 45 diesel-electric locomotive passing freight train at Hassop, Derbyshire, with London–Manchester express, 1963 (*Ransome Wallis Collection, National Railway Museum, York*).

29 Type 5 'Deltic' Class 55 diesel-electric locomotive (No. D9020) at King's Cross with the centenary run of the Flying Scotsman train to Edinburgh, June 1962 (*Photo Source*).

30 Vacuum-braked calcium carbide wagon (*B.R.B.*).

31 Air-braked gypsum wagon (*B.R.B.*).

32 Shunt horse 'Tommy' at Newmarket, with Henry Johnson, General Manager, Eastern Region (*far left*), October 1961 (*B.R.B.*).

33 'Tommy' at work, September 1961 (*B.R.B.*).

ALL RIGHT, NOW LET'S SEE IF WE CAN IMPROVE ON THE ENGINE...

7 The dawn of the Modernisation Plan. Talks between the B.T.C. and Alan Lennox-Boyd, Minister of Transport, in 1954: Vicky, *Daily Mirror*, 31 May 1954.

way modernisation, notably France, Holland and West Germany. Support for railways in the United Kingdom had, without a doubt, been niggardly by comparison.[12]

Daril Watson's Planning Committee took six months to formulate its proposals. These were presented to the Commission in late October 1954, and an amended version was sent to the Minister of Transport, now John Boyd-Carpenter, in December. A document for public consumption was made available in the following month.[13] As Table 32 makes clear, the Plan was in many ways similar to that drawn up by the Railway Executive 18 months earlier. It was now proposed to spend a total of £1,170 million, which was increased to £1,240 million in the published report but, as the Commission explained in its Annual Report for 1954, £600 million

Table 32. *Components of the Modernisation Plan*

Item	(i) Planning Committee report October 1954		(ii) Published report December 1954		(iii) Railway Executive programme 1953
	(£m.)	%	(£m.)	%	%
Track and signalling		207	17	210	17	18
Motive power:						
Electrification	105			185		
Diesel	209	324	27	150	345	28	32
Steam depots	10			10		
Passenger stock and stations (including D.M.U.s)		285	23	285	23	19
Freight services:						
Marshalling yards	80			80		
Terminals	53			60		
Wagons	155	363	30	150	365	29	28
Continuous brakes	75			75		
Miscellaneous		33	3	35	3	3
Total outlay[a]		1,212	100	1,240	100	100
				rounded to		
Net outlay (less displacements)		1,170		1,200		
Funding:						
Internal (provision for depreciation)		300		400		
External (borrowing)		870		800		

[a] Packet ports, welfare, office equipment, research and development.
Source: B.T.C. Planning Committee, 'Report on the Modernisation and Re-equipment of British Railways', October 1954, B.R.B.; B.T.C., *Modernisation and Re-equipment of British Railways* (January 1955); R.E. report percentages from Table 31.

'would in any event have had to be spent over the period of the Plan merely to maintain the existing equipment'.[14] Since normal maintenance had been excluded from the Executive's calculations in 1953, the difference between the two initiatives amounted to only about £100 million. Furthermore, the allocation of total expenditure was similar in many ways. Table 32 shows that the proportionate expenditures to be devoted to track and signalling, freight services and to motive power and passenger services (taken together) were almost identical in the two exercises. The only substantial change of emphasis was the shift from electrification to diesel traction as a replacement for the steam locomotive. No provision had been made for main-line diesels in the Railway Executive's 1953 programme, but in October 1954 the Planning Committee recommended that £183 million of the £209 million to be allocated to diesels should be spent in this way, and this emphasis remained in the published report, although the figures were trimmed to £125 million and £150 million respectively.[15]

The alteration was the result of an order from the Commission which had accepted the argument that, given existing commitments, limits would have to be put on the amount of electrification to be undertaken. It was also influenced by the revised opinion of some of the railway officers on the capability of the diesel locomotive over longer distances. The Planning Committee's sub-committee on motive power had been divided over the future role of diesels, and Riddles's protégé, R. C. Bond, had followed his mentor by arguing strongly for the retention of the standard steam locomotive. However, when in August 1954 it was reported that a 2,000 H.P. diesel-electric locomotive was likely to prove more economical than its Class 7 steam equivalent for annual mileages over 70,000 (and possibly 40,000), without taking into account the diesel's greater availability, the steam lobby's case collapsed. The Planning Committee then approached the Commission for a decision, pointing out that they had been supplied with figures which suggested that the economic range of diesels was wider than had previously been assumed. At the same time, the Chief Regional Managers were pressing for a more vigorous approach to electrification, and had submitted several additional proposals. The Commission responded by declaring that resources would only be sufficient to electrify routes of a given traffic density. It informed the Planning Committee that it was prepared instead 'to look sympathetically at a proposal for a bold programme for the trial of diesel locomotives'. The regional managers had to be satisfied with a strategy which limited main-line electrification to two major trunk routes, from King's Cross to Doncaster and Leeds (and possibly York), and from Euston to Birmingham, Manchester and Liverpool, although the priority accorded to the former in the Planning Committee report was omitted in the published Plan. In addition, the Plan envisaged the electrification of the Southern Region's Kent Coast lines and an extension of the Liverpool Street suburban scheme from Chelmsford to Ipswich, Clacton, Harwich and Felixstowe. Diesel traction, on the other hand, was given a clear green light. The Plan promised 'to build no new express . . . or suburban steam locomotives after the 1956 programme and to terminate the building of all new steam locomotives within a few years'.[16]

Motive power apart, the resemblance of the Modernisation Plan to the Railway Executive's programme was striking. This was scarcely surprising, given the composition of the Planning Committee. Of its 16 members,

13 had been at Executive headquarters prior to 1954, and these included all 5 of the team which had drafted the 1953 programme (see above, p. 258 and n. 5). In any case, there was common agreement among railwaymen about many of the desirable elements in a technically improved railway, and what they wanted in early 1953 they naturally still wanted in late 1954. The importance of improved track, colour-light signalling, automatic train control, larger mineral wagons, continuous brakes and D.M.U.s was universally recognised, and these items would have appeared in a modernisation package whoever had drawn it up.

How much was needed and where it was needed were wholly different questions. Central to the Plan was the stated strategy of establishing a railway system which was 'economically self-supporting'. This would be achieved by a 'purposeful concentration on those functions which the railways can be made to perform more efficiently than other forms of transport'. Not only did this imply a major restructuring, a specialisation on the most cost-effective activities and the shedding of unprofitable elements, but it also implied a winning back of markets, particularly as regards merchandise traffic. Clearly, to put up desirable investments was not enough; these had to be placed within an overall traffic strategy which forecasted how large the efficient railway system of the future should be. The answer depended very largely on estimates of the volume of traffic the railways were likely to retain in the period of the Plan, i.e. to 1974. Forecasting was a tricky business with the tools available in 1954, but some critics have been keen to point out that the composition of the Planning Committee had an important bearing on the Plan's shortcomings in this regard. It has been suggested that the Plan's 'restricted outlook . . . was the inevitable result of the way it was put together. Its compilation was entrusted to a small group of headquarters officers, who appear to have operated in contemplative retreat except for consultation with the chief officers of the six Regions.'[17] In fact, the 'small group of officers' was a 16-strong committee serviced by no less than 9 sub-committees, making a total, with the steering committee of Chief Regional Managers, of 65 men. That the Committee was conservative in character is no doubt true. It was very much a tried and trusted body of railwaymen steeped in the traditions of an industry long accustomed to the notion of operating a relatively fixed network with restricted capital resources. Of the sixteen members, only four were unable to boast of a long career in railways stretching back to their teens or early twenties. Whether or not it lacked imagination, it was certainly staffed by a group more likely to look back to the lost opportunities of the inter-war years than to forecast the railways' requirements in the late 1960s and 1970s.[18] Any attempt to assess the quality of its planning must recognise, first, that the Committee was asked to work in some haste, and, second, that it was encouraged to prepare only a broad outline of optimal requirements for modernisation, built up from regional desiderata and with the detailed justification of major projects left for the future. Treasury pressure on the Commission to produce a plan quickly, which was exerted through the Ministry of Transport, was of key importance. The electricity and gas industries had already published investment plans in anticipation of legislation to extend their borrowing powers; so in June 1954 Treasury anxiety at the delay in obtaining a similar response from the railways was conveyed to the Transport Ministry. Once this had filtered down to the Planning Committee Watson asked the Chief Regional Managers to produce lists of major schemes, without detailed financial justification, in order to speed up the planning process. When the Plan emerged it was fully accepted at B.T.C. headquarters that it was, in Michael Bonavia's words, 'no more than the lumping together of a large number of projects, which on first examination, appear desirable'. 'Plan' was therefore a misnomer: 'Modernisation Policy' would have been a more apt description of what was put together.[19]

These pressing circumstances thus limited the opportunity to pursue sophisticated traffic forecasts and financial calculations. Moreover, as the Commission had only recently begun to encourage the development of this aspect of management there was little that could be pulled out of a drawer in a hurry. The task of preparing 20-year traffic forecasts was given to a sub-committee led by David Blee, which included both the Director of Costings, Tait, and the Director of Statistics, Harris-Burland. Many of their estimates were conservative. The sub-committee assumed that industrial production would grow by at least 2 per cent per annum, 1953–74, and (real) consumers' expenditure by 1 per cent. In fact, both increased at a rate of nearly 3 per cent. Gross revenue from passenger traffic was expected to rise from £115 million in 1953 to £127 million by 1974. The actual 1974 figure, at 1953 fare levels, was £106.3 million, 17 per cent below the predicted level. Given the hazards of long-range forecasting, this turned out to be a reasonable guess.[20] Unfortunately, the forecasts went badly astray in two key areas of the railways' freight business: coal and general merchandise. The sub-committee, making use of the National Coal Board's production plans, estimated that coal carryings by rail would rise from 175 million tons to 190–5 million by 1964 and possibly to 200–10 million tons in 1974. In fact, carryings fell to 147 million tons in 1964 and slumped to only 87 million in 1974. For general merchandise, the sub-committee considered the threat of future losses to road transport and held that it would be 'imprudent . . . to contemplate any increase in the overall tonnage . . . conveyed by rail'. This again proved to be optimistic. Business fell away from the mid-1950s and by 1962 the tonnage carried was about

27 per cent down on the 1953 level. But the sub-committee can hardly be blamed for all its rash judgements. Its coal estimates were based on that industry's own expectations, and the railways did not suggest that their share of the market would increase. Perhaps it should be criticised for failing to predict a fall in merchandise traffic, but while the railways' business was holding up fairly well, as it was in 1954, it was reasonable to assume that increased efficiency via modernisation, together with an improved pricing policy, would help to offset the incursions of the road hauliers.[21]

It is more difficult to excuse the B.T.C.'s inadequate financial justification of the Modernisation Plan. The pressure placed on the Costings Division certainly prevented the Planning Committee from doing much about it. As Tait explained,

it had been hoped to put before each Sub-Committee a rough assessment of the costs and receipts attributable to each part of the railway activities, which ... would have been a valuable guide as to the directions in which modernisation and re-equipment would provide the best financial return. Shortage of time allowed to the Sub-Committee to report did not permit of much more than a cursory study of the economics of the situation, and we were not able to complete our financial and economic assessments before the final reports had to be submitted.[22]

In reality, the responsibility for the plan's financial justification rested firmly upon the Commission itself. After the Planning Committee's report had been submitted, on 18 November 1954, a small ad hoc committee of members, led by Wilson, was asked to assist the staff in licking the report into a shape acceptable for presentation to the Minister of Transport. The chapter dealing with traffic forecasts was to be modified, and a new section inserted on 'the economics of the Plan'.[23] The deliberations of Wilson's committee seem to have been hasty, not to say slap-dash. It removed nearly all the forecasting figures which had appeared in the Planning Committee's report and merely inserted a new estimate that 'gross freight revenue' would rise 'by about one-sixteenth' by the end of the 15–20 year period. This prediction, not apparently based on the Planning Committee's forecasts, proved to be equally wide of the mark. In economic justification of the Plan, Wilson's committee boldly injected a note of optimism and came up with some round figures in support. The introduction to the published Plan declared that the Commission 'should be able to attract and retain sufficient traffic to make it economically self-supporting for many years to come'. The expenditure, it was promised, would 'ultimately attract a return amounting to at least £85 million a year', made up of £35 million from the passenger side of the business and £60 million from freight *less* £10 million for additional joint costs. Since this was apparently a conservative estimate of final benefits the expected yield was 'such as to make it an economic venture of the most promising sort'.[24] But was it?

In the absence of documentary evidence, it is difficult to be certain about the basis of this calculation of £85 million, despite the assurance in the Plan that 'behind this brief presentation . . . there lies a mass of detailed study'. Some assistance was given by the Costings Division. At Wilson's request a further study of revenue and costs was made; this came up with a net revenue improvement of £100 million in 1970, offset by increased charges for interest and replacements. The Commission's files also suggest that equal weight was given to calculations made by Wilson in September 1953 in a report for use in connection with the Railway Executive's earlier initiative. This report began with the statement that 'a bold and imaginative programme could achieve a return of something like 20%'. It is tempting to believe that all the committee did was to dust off the data in Wilson's report, using the information supplied by the Costings Division. Certainly, Wilson's 1953 forecast of an improvement in net revenue of £84 million (with £33 million from passenger services and £58 million from freight) is remarkably similar to that in the published Plan, despite some differences in the composition of the two estimates. Wilson's figures had specifically included savings from the withdrawal of unremunerative passenger services. Although the Plan was rather vague on this point, its estimated improvement of £35 million in passenger services was stated to depend on unprofitable services 'being either turned over to new forms of motive power or transferred to road'. Likewise, the improvement in freight revenue made allowances 'for the transfer to road of certain traffics which cannot be carried economically by rail'. The components of the £85 million are thus of some importance, since savings from a rationalisation of the rail system could have been achieved with little or no additional expenditure and should not properly be included in any calculation of the return to new investment.[25]

This figure of £85 million – not apparently based on the results of a long and searching look at the financial implications of investing £1,240 million in the railway network – attracted considerable attention on its appearance in the published Plan. Initially, observers such as *The Economist* noted that the figure implied a gross return of about 7 per cent on the total expenditure and 10.5 per cent on the £800 million to be raised by new borrowings (i.e. excluding the £400 million which was to be provided internally by depreciation provision – see Table 32).[26] Subsequent commentators have tended to follow *The Economist* in presenting their criticisms in terms of the rate of return on investment, although the Plan itself considered only the extra revenue to be generated in relation to its effect on the Commission's overall financial position, as set out in Table 33. Calculations of the rate of return by other outside critics have tried to

Table 33. *The Modernisation Plan: estimated impact on the B.T.C.'s future financial position (in 1954 prices)*

Financial position in 1954		Forecast financial position after modernisation	
Book deficit (after deducting central charges)	£25m.	Inherited Deficit	−£40m.
		Net Revenue Improvement:	
Additional depreciation	£15m.	Passenger	£35m.
Total deficit	£40m.	Freight	£60m.
		Less additional joint costs	−£10m.
		Less servicing of capital	−£40m.
		Balance	£ 5m.

Source: Modernisation Plan, pp. 31–5.

take cognisance of the Commission's reference to interest charges (it put the cost of servicing the Plan at £40 million or 5 per cent of £800 million), provision for additional depreciation and the railways' 'normal' programme of asset-replacing investment. This was in addition to the problem of separating the savings created by eliminating unremunerative services from the gains arising out of revenue-generating or cost-saving investment.

The economic justification of the Plan was condemned by the economist Christopher Foster as totally inadequate. He argued that provision for depreciation should have been deducted before the rate of return was calculated, criticised the B.T.C. for failing to take due account of the cost of waiting for the Plan to fructify and maintained that it was erroneous for the Commission to assume that interest need not be charged on the £400 million to be raised internally, since it might have been better to reinvest depreciation funds outside the business. He also attacked the Plan's failure to distinguish between investment in the then profitable parts of the railway system and that contemplated in the unprofitable sector.[27] Some of his arguments are convincing, others less so. His criticism that the Commission should have calculated a rate of return net of £15 million in additional depreciation provision is mistaken, despite a long pedigree stretching back to 1955. A careful reading of the Plan reveals that the extra £15 million charge was a quite separate issue. By 1954 the Commission had come round to the view that depreciation provision should in future be based on current replacement cost instead of on historic cost, because of the widening gap between replacement expenditure on capital account and depreciation provision. Additional charges arising from the Plan would have been allowed for in the estimate of net revenue benefits. In any case, Wilson's paper of 1953 argued that modernisation should not result in higher depreciation charges, since the rate of scrapping of the older assets would be accelerated.[28] But the Commission's failure to include a quantified statement of time costs was a real weakness. The Planning Committee had ended their report with these words: 'During the period of fructification of the plan . . . it will be extremely difficult, if not impossible, to meet the additional interest burden.' Yet although Robertson had passed this gloomy message on to the Minister of Transport, it was omitted from the published version of the Plan. Calculations based on the information given by the Commission in 1956, when the problem of time-lag costs was publicly recognised, suggest that about £170 million would have been required to meet interest during the period of 'fructification', an annual charge of about £8 million.[29]

Should the Commission have also included interest charges on the £400 million which it proposed to raise internally? Some commentators argued that the investment which was needed simply in order to maintain the profitable parts of the existing system should not be expected to make any additional return. Accepting their assumption that £450 million would be a reasonable sum to deduct for this purpose, then the rate of return should be calculated not on £1,200 million but on £750 million plus an additional £150 million to cover 'time costs', £900 million in all. On this basis £85 million represents a return of over 9 per cent, comfortably above the assumed test discount rate of 5 per cent.[30] This rate of return must, however, be further modified in order to isolate the benefits deriving from modernisation alone. Wilson's 1953 report suggested that at least £25 million of the anticipated improvement in net revenue of £84 million would come from the pruning of uneconomic services. If the same figure is applied to the Plan then the return falls to £60 million or 6.7 per cent. At this level the economic justification for modernisation would have left little margin for error. And even if the Commission's aggregation of savings from modernisation and rationalisation is accepted, its promise to move into overall surplus appears very fragile. A simple calculation would have shown that *ceteris paribus* the balance of £5 million shown in Table 33 would have been wiped out by the costs incurred in waiting for the investment to bear fruit. Even on the Commission's optimistic assumptions about future prospects more drastic action was clearly required. In the event, traffic did not increase as forecast and the assumption that costs (wages, interest charges, etc.) would move in line with charges was unrealistic, leading to a more serious financial deficit.

III

If the public face of railway management was unduly optimistic about the prospects of a modern railway and the investment plan required to create it, the private face was no less so. Although the Plan promised that there would be a radical reappraisal of the railway services to be provided in the future, there is very little evidence that the B.T.C. and its regional railway managers were prepared in 1955 to make any quick and lively response in this direction. Only H. P. Barker, a part-time member of the Commission, was prepared to challenge some of the Plan's core assumptions from the very outset. In a memorandum to the Commission in November 1954, produced in response to the Planning Committee's report, he launched a strong attack on the obsession with railway *equipment* rather than *operation*:

The report seems to me to accept implicitly a proposal which I deny, namely that the present operational conceptions of British Railways are viable in the long run, given modern equipment. Evidence is now forthcoming and will be forthcoming in increasing quantity in the next two years to show that a solid proportion of our movement operations as carried today are grossly uneconomic, and by inference that no amount of improvement in equipment would make them viable in the conditions of 1970.

In this context he made a pertinent reference to the revised results of the passenger train survey, which the Costings Division had produced while the Plan was being prepared. The survey, which reached the Commission a week before the Planning Committee's report, confirmed the results of the 1952 inquiry (see above, pp. 110–12). Passenger business was not only failing to meet its total costs – the estimated shortfall in 1953 was £60 million at mid-1954 fare levels – but was unable to cover its movement and terminal costs by a margin of £9.25 million.[31] These findings challenged the basic assumption that new forms of motive power would transform the business, particularly in its least profitable sector, the stopping services, which accounted for about 40 per cent of total train-miles run. Here, over half of the trains were so unprofitable that, in Barker's words, there was 'no conceivable equipment which can convert these services into profit-makers'. As for freight, on which less information was then available, Barker expressed his conviction that 'financial enormities' were being supported by the mineral traffic. Here was a problem which improved equipment might ameliorate but would certainly not resolve. An early campaigner for the concept of train-load working (the handling of freight in complete trains), he was clearly disturbed by the report's faith in modern marshalling yards as the saviour of the wagon-load business. Barker's views received short shrift, however. After several decades of capital restrictions, railway managers were in no mood to listen to Cassandras.[32]

If the Modernisation Plan thus contained elements which in both financial and operational terms left important questions unanswered, why was it given the warm support of the government? Why did the Treasury and the Ministry of Transport not demand a more searching evaluation of the railways' investment prospects as some critics have suggested that they should?[33] The tame response from Whitehall was not due to any lack of awareness of the Plan's shortcomings. Letters and notes filed in the early months of 1955 indicate that officials in both the Treasury and Ministry of Transport were concerned about the Plan's defects. In January A. T. K. Grant, Treasury Assistant Secretary, complained to Sir Herbert Brittain, a Second Secretary, about the vague support for the £85 million saving. 'It does not seem possible to show how far it comes directly out of investment, and how far it comes from a more sensible utilisation of labour etc. – i.e. factors which could have [been] brought into play over time without the Investment taking place.' D. M. B. Butt, another junior Treasury official, was even more critical. He wrote:

The few vague figures given do not, it seems to me, establish their case for the financial return . . . much of the £85 million of improved balance is apparently due to things other than the capital expenditure . . . Even if there were nothing else to it, I should have thought a good deal of Treasury investigation would be needed before Ministerial 'approval in principle' could properly be translated into even a vague general blessing to the Plan as an isolated economic project.

The Commission's failure to provide detailed costings of individual projects was also criticised.[34] There was a similar degree of scepticism among Ministers. The Plan was fully discussed at a Cabinet meeting on 20 January 1955. Butler maintained that on the figures presented it was 'possible to take a sanguine and constructive view', but critics suggested that 'the Government should proceed with caution in giving even general approval to this plan. The long-term future of the railways was doubtful: in the years to come roads, and perhaps aircraft, would take over much of the traffic now carried by railways.' Ministers also pressed for more information. If the government were to underwrite the capital borrowed it 'ought to be satisfied that the plan was economically sound'. The argument carried weight because the Commission had already applied for a considerable extension of its borrowing powers. A bill providing for the raising of its borrowing limit from £275 to £600 million was in fact before parliament (it received the Royal Assent on 29 March).[35]

Nevertheless, the government did accept the Plan and indeed defended it in parliament with enthusiasm. It did so partly because investment in transport was an element in its strategy to stimulate economic growth.

Having agreed to invest £400 million in a new roads programme (which included the first motorway projects), Ministers would have found it difficult to refuse support for an industry which all recognised had suffered greatly from financial stringency in the past.[36] But it also accepted the Plan because it was intimately connected with the government's approach to industrial relations. Its intervention in a dispute in December 1953 was repeated a year later when the N.U.R. once more threatened to call a strike (for details see above, pp. 221–3). Both Monckton and Boyd-Carpenter made it clear to Robertson that a strike was to be avoided. At the height of the crisis Boyd-Carpenter asked Robertson whether he would be prepared to raise his pay offer 'if the Government assured him that the Commission need not be unduly concerned about the size of the deficit on the current operations in view of the long term prospects to which they could look forward when their plans for modernising the railways came into effect'. The Cabinet flirted again with the idea of offering the Commission direct financial relief, but once the strike was called off, on 6 January 1955, notions of interest-free loans or the writing-off of accumulated deficits speedily evaporated. This left the government with an obligation to support modernisation as a way of eliminating deficits for which it felt at least a partial responsibility.[37]

Acceptance of the Plan in the form in which it was presented probably owed much to the fact that in 1955 the Treasury was still feeling its way with *all* the nationalised industries. At the time, government control of investment by rationing and programme was only just giving way to the informal vetting of major schemes with the aim of determining their profitability. In the absence of clear guidelines, it is perhaps not surprising that the Treasury should have decided to handle the Commission gently. Discounted cash-flow techniques of investment appraisal had not yet gained wide acceptance, and the investment presentations of the other nationalised industries were scarcely more sophisticated than the railways' Plan, even though some may have been more thorough. Decision-making based on anticipated rates of return was certainly not the norm elsewhere. The British Electricity Authority apparently related its investment decisions to predictions of demand in physical terms, irrespective of any rate of return.[38] And it is doubtful whether either the Treasury or the Ministry of Transport could have produced a clearly reasoned alternative to the B.T.C.'s approach. The academic debate on how exactly railway investment should be determined was still very much alive as late as 1962.[39] The Commission's response in 1954–5 may seem unsophisticated today. But it is well to recognise that the government's control of nationalised industry investment was at this date far more cautious than its handling of both pricing and industrial relations.

IV

The Commission's organisational response to the Plan was made early in 1955. A general instruction issued in April indicated the 'lines of immediate action'. While the B.T.C. reserved to itself the task of determining the broad strategy to be followed, specific investment proposals were to be formulated by the regions, or more exactly, by the newly created Area Boards. Priorities would then 'be fixed by the Commission after taking into account the regional view'.[40] At the centre a modernisation committee was established to co-ordinate activity, supported by a committee of the General Staff and a network of 16 specialist policy-making panels, dealing with such matters as traffic, electrification, main-line diesel locomotives, wagons and marshalling yards. In terms of overall policy, the role of the traffic survey group, one of the panels, was a key one. As the B.T.C. accepted, the Modernisation Plan implied far more than mere physical re-equipment of the existing railway network. The investment programme had to be set in the context of the commercial policy to be followed when the 'charging provisions of the 1953 Transport Act are fully effective'. This required a major reassessment of the commercial strategy of the railway business. The traffic group's terms of reference required it to 'make recommendations in principle on general traffic policy . . . essential if the Plan is to be conceived and executed as a whole and not as a series of separate projects'.[41] The overall monitoring of the work of the panels and regions was organised through regular progress reports passed by the modernisation committee to the Commission. Supervision was further strengthened in July 1956 when Robertson introduced the Chairman's Conference on Modernisation, a series of regular but informal meetings, attended by members of the technical development and research committee and the Railways Sub-Commission. The aim was to discuss problems while they were still in the embryonic stage in order to impose a tighter grip on planning and execution.[42]

Acceptance of the Modernisation Plan in 1955 was certainly followed by a marked upturn in the scale of railway investment. This is clear from the figures of gross investment presented in Table 34. In the period 1954–62 annual expenditure, which had averaged £44.3 million in 1948–53, increased by over 170 per cent, to £120.6 million. And the contrast remains striking even when the data are expressed in real terms. In constant 1948 prices, the annual average investment of £37.7 million in 1948–53 rose to £71.1 million in 1954–62. Over 60 per cent of this higher investment level went into new rolling stock as the switch from steam traction to diesel locomotives and multiple units proceeded rapidly. In the early years under the Plan, 1955–7, this category accounted for three-

Table 34. *Gross investment in railways, 1954–62 (including collection and delivery services, but excluding ships) (£m.)*

Year	Current prices Rolling stock	Total investment	Constant 1948 prices Rolling stock	Total investment
1954	47.4	65.3	31.7	44.5
1955	55.7	71.3	36.3	46.9
1956	66.1	89.0	41.0	55.8
1957	89.9	125.9	52.7	75.8
1958	87.4	141.0	49.5	83.8
1959	97.8	167.8	53.9	98.4
1960	85.9	163.3	46.3	94.2
1961	73.6	146.2	37.9	79.4
1962	62.8	115.3	31.0	60.7
Total	666.6	1,085.1	380.3	639.5
Ann. av. 1954–62	74.1	120.6	42.3	71.1
Ann. av. 1948–53	30.1	44.3	25.4	37.7

Source: see Appendix B, Table 1.

quarters of the total expenditure. Annual investment at current prices grew steadily from £65.3 million in 1954 to a peak of £167.8 million in 1959 – an increase of over 150 per cent – and there were particularly sharp rises in 1956 and 1957. Then investment fell by about a third to £115.3 million in 1962, influenced by the government's tougher policy after January 1960. Nevertheless, it remained comfortably above the pre-Modernisation Plan levels. The picture is very much the same when constant 1948 prices are used (see Table 34). A rise of 121 per cent – from £44.5 to £98.4 million – from 1954 to 1959 was followed by a fall of 38 per cent to £60.7 million in 1962.

The Commission's investment record thus compared very favourably with that of the Railway Executive before 1954. This is further emphasised by estimates of net investment. New calculations indicate that net investment at constant 1948 prices amounted to £242.2 million or £26.9 million per annum over the period 1954–62, with a peak of over £45 million in 1959. This contrasted sharply with the net investment of only £8.7 million a year in 1948–53 and with the negative investment from 1963 (see Appendix B, Table 4). Moreover, the railways increased their share of both national and public sector investment. The proportion of U.K. gross domestic fixed capital formation represented by railway investment rose from 2.4 per cent in 1948–53 to 3.3 per cent in 1954–62, and in the peak years, 1958–60, the percentage was 4.1. Limiting the analysis to nationalised industry, Pryke's estimates show that railways increased their share of the public sector cake from about 15 per cent in 1948–53 to 20 per cent in 1954–62.[43]

How were these more impressive investment figures translated into physical equipment? It has already been observed that a large part of expenditure was devoted to rolling stock. Within this broad category, diesel locomotives, D.M.U.s and E.M.U.s were acquired in comparatively large numbers (see Table 35). In the period 1954–62, the Commission put into service nearly 3,500 diesel locomotives, half of them for main-line working, 4,000 D.M.U.s and 3,800 E.M.U.s. Over half of this new equipment was introduced in the space of only three years, 1959–61 (1958–60 for D.M.U.s). Steam locomotives, which had been expected to continue in operation in the Modernisation Plan, were rapidly phased out. Construction stopped in 1960, and by the end of 1962 the steam fleet had been more than halved, from 18,600 at the end of 1953 to 8,800. The 744 steam locomotives acquired in the period 1954–60, with a 'useful life in service of some forty years', according to the Modernisation Plan, were quickly scrapped. By 1968 all the steam locomotives had gone. This somewhat frantic rush to use diesel locomotion had another important effect: it made the railways more dependent on purchases from outside contractors. In the period 1923–47 the railway companies had built 70 per cent of the locomotives in their own extensive workshops. In 1948–53 the figure was 61 per cent, or 79 per cent if the purchase of second-hand 'austerity' locomotives from the Ministry of Supply is excluded. The specialised steam workshops could not be quickly converted to the more intricate job of constructing diesels and electric locomotives. This limit to productive capacity, together with restrictions imposed by the government and problems associated with obtaining licences, meant that of the acquisitions in 1954–62, some 48 per cent of the diesels – 74 per cent of the main-line units – were bought in, together with nearly half of the D.M.U.s (Table 35). This encouraged two unsatisfactory features of the modernisation of motive power, namely an unnecessary variety of locomotive types, and a commitment to relatively large orders without the testing in service of a prototype (see below, pp. 285–8).[44]

Electrification, with its higher capital costs and longer gestation period, naturally proceeded at a more leisurely pace. Nevertheless, once the Commission had taken the decision to standardise in future on the 25,000-volt a.c. system (except on Southern Region), there was more activity. In the period 1959–62 about 550 route-miles were converted. Although the electrification of the East Coast route from King's Cross was shelved, electric services were introduced in the Eastern Region's commuterland

Table 35. Rolling stock acquisitions, 1954–62

Year	Locomotives					D.M.U.s	E.M.U.s	Passenger carriages (locomotive-hauled)	Total coaching vehicles (including M.U.s)	Freight and service vehicles
	Steam	Diesels: main-line	All[a]	Electric	Total					
1954	208	1	60	6	274	34	294	1,090	2,126	55,325
1955	174	—	136	—	310	111	284	1,321	2,057	59,683
1956	138	—	156	—	294	275	435	1,240	2,112	63,087
1957	144	20	195	—	339	904	222	838	2,560	62,120
1958	62	83	400	1	463	1,070	286	509	2,560	37,006
1959	15	318	601	14	630	832	785	323	2,399	17,326
1960	3	416	751	50	840	575	851	388	2,984	7,660
1961	—	443	631	23	654	183	558	602	1,640	8,898
1962	—	338	506	20	526	93	101	491	757	8,800
1954–62	744	1,669	3,435	114	4,294	4,077	3,816	6,802	19,195	319,905
Per annum	82.7	185.4	381.8	12.7	477.1	453.0	424.0	755.8	2,132.8	35,545.0
1948–53 per annum	399.7	1.0	34.3[b]	9.8	443.8	—	197.2	1,124.1	1,659.7	36,565.8
Percentage built in B.R. workshops	96	26	52	49	60	51	90	71	68	61
Percentage supplied by contractors	4	74	48	51	40	49	10	29	32	39

[a] Includes 1,767 shunting locomotives.
[b] Includes 2 gas turbine locomotives.
Source: B.T.C., R. & A. 1954–62.

(London–Tilbury–Southend, Enfield–Bishop's Stortford, Colchester–Clacton) as well as the Glasgow suburban area, the Kent coast lines (Sevenoaks–Dover/Ramsgate), and the Crewe–Manchester and Crewe–Liverpool sections of the Euston main line.

Progress in other fields was less spectacular, and sometimes flawed. The construction of freight vehicles was stepped up in the years 1954–7, but then fell away to comparatively low levels. As a result the average annual built in 1954–62 was very much the same as in 1948–53 (see Table 35). The percentage of low-capacity wagons (under 14 tons) in use was reduced from 77 per cent in 1953 to 46 per cent in 1962 but average wagon capacity advanced only gradually, from 13.5 to 16.6 tons. Efforts to extend the continuous braking of freight trains were successful in that the number of vehicles so fitted doubled from 166,000 to 320,000 by the end of 1962, in a total stock reduced from 1,107,000 to 849,000. The scope for improvement was, however, limited by handling difficulties, particularly in the antiquated depots of customers; and the choice of the vacuum brake as standard B.R. equipment was short-sighted in view of the superiority of the air brake, proven in 1955 (see below, pp. 290–3). This picture of rather gradual advance was also evident on the permanent way. Track renewals proceeded at much the same rate as in Railway Executive days, about 1,500 miles per annum. Some important steps were taken from the late 1950s, with the installation of 1,000 miles of Continuous Welded Rail, and the application of a newly developed Automatic Warning System to 1,200 route miles of line.[45] The replacement of mechanical semaphore signals by electric colour-light signalling was also accelerated: about 1,300 track-miles were re-signalled in 1959–62, compared with the 600 miles in the previous four years. Nevertheless, these were only modest beginnings in a process which was essential if the benefits of the new motive power units were to be reflected in improved operating performance.

Introduction of the station improvements and new marshalling yards promised in the Plan also proceeded slowly, sometimes delayed by the lengthy planning process, especially where new parliamentary powers were required. When the B.T.C. reported to the Select Committee in 1960 on the progress made by the end of 1959 it could point to only 14 modernised passenger stations and parcels depots, most of these being relatively small projects, as at Banbury, Barrow-in-Furness and Gatwick, though a further 20 new stations were opened before the beginning of 1963. Only three new marshalling yards had been completed before 1960, at Thornton (Fife), Alloa and Temple Mills (London).

V

How effective was the Commission's investment of £1,000 million before 1963? It is obviously very difficult to assess with any real accuracy the results of a programme which was only half-complete before it was subjected to a government-imposed pause in 1960 and then a stringent re-evaluation in the Beeching years. Moreover, many of the major projects completed after 1955 were planned in the Railway Executive period, before the Modernisation Plan had been devised. For example, parliamentary powers for the Thornton marshalling yard, opened in 1956, were acquired in 1948 and the site was cleared in 1953. The Temple Mills yard, opened in 1959, was first passed by the Commission in January 1954.[46] A final obstacle is the lack of sufficiently detailed information on the impact of the individual projects which made up the Plan, particularly before 1959, by which time the closer interest of government was encouraging more activity inside the Commission. Given the shortcomings of the published data, it is scarcely surprising that commentators have tended to fasten on the more glaring mistakes of the period, rather than attempt to isolate projects whose rate of return was either close to the double-figure norm which the government contended was characteristic of private industry or matched the 8 per cent level which it established in 1961 as a target for nationalised industry investment.[47]

Most of the internal data produced to justify major schemes in the 1950s were limited to estimates of the likely improvement in net revenue. Some projects promised to return a reasonable proportion of the capital outlay. This was certainly true of the schemes designed to replace steam with diesel on the main lines. Estimated yields for the three such projects shown in Table 36 ranged from 9 to 12 per cent on the net outlay, and from 13 to 23 per cent on the 'net financial betterment'.* Projects for marshalling yards were more uncertain, but there were hopes of acceptable returns. In the original submission for the Temple Mills scheme, an investment of £2.5 million, of which £1.2 million represented 'betterment', was expected to yield a return of 6.6 per cent on the net outlay, or 13.5 per cent on the betterment portion (Table 36). A final estimate in 1960 raised both capital costs and savings, altering the expected return to 7.9 and 12.8 per cent respectively. The controversial Carlisle Yard was presented to the Commission in 1959 as an even more promising scheme. An estimated expenditure of £4.8 million was expected to yield a return of 11.3 per cent or 13.4 per cent on a betterment basis. The revised estimate of 1962, made as the yard was nearing completion, was more cautious, but it still

*Net outlay less the 'expired life value of assets displaced', i.e. the sum required to maintain the existing assets to present, that is un-modernised, standards.

Table 36. *Examples of British Transport Commission investment submissions, 1954–62*

Date	Estimated net capital outlay (£)	Net additional outlay or 'financial betterment' (£)	Annual net savings/net revenue improvement (£)	Yield on: Net outlay (%)	Net additional outlay (%)
1. DIESEL MAIN-LINE SCHEMES					
A. *Edinburgh–Glasgow* (20 steam locos. replaced by 12 diesels)					
1961	1,284,000	1,218,000	153,947	12.0	12.6
B. *East Coast main line: Deltics* (55 steam locos replaced by 22 diesels)					
1958	3,135,000	1,661,000	375,000[a]	12.0	22.6
			323,000[b]	11.0	21.4
C. *East Coast main line* (345 steam locos replaced by 196 diesels)					
1960	18,235,000	9,929,000	1,683,000	9.2	17.0
2. MARSHALLING YARDS[c]					
A. *Temple Mills, London*					
1954	2,513,553	1,231,332	166,249	6.6	13.5
1960	3,309,758	2,027,000	260,000	7.9	12.8
B. *Ripple Lane, Barking*					
1956	2,289,894	1,852,501	91,859	4.0	5.0
1960	2,910,949	2,467,000	155,000	5.3	6.3
C. *Carlisle (Kingmoor)*					
1959	4,777,000	4,057,000	542,000	11.3	13.4
1962	5,444,000	4,277,000	514,000	9.4	12.0

[a] The Deltic submission assumed a 30-year life (an estimate based on a 10-year life was also given).
[b] Revised calculation assuming a 20-year life for the Deltics.
[c] The Temple Mills and Ripple Lane submissions of 1954 and 1956 included, in the figures for net additional outlay, an allowance for the unexpired life value of assets prematurely destroyed, and for interest on the outlay during construction. These figures were omitted from the final submissions of 1960. The data shown here include an estimate of these two items based on their value in the original submissions and on changing costs and interest rates. No allowance for them was made in the Carlisle data.
Source: submissions to B.T.C. Works and Equipment Committee, Minutes, 6 June 1961, 12 February 1958; submission to Stedeford Advisory Group, 27 April 1960, Beeching Papers, Box 7; B.T.C. Works and Equipment Committee Minutes, 22 January 1954 and 8 November 1960, 25 April 1956 and 12 and 14 January 1960, 8 August 1959, 23 October and 7 November 1962, B.R.B.

promised to return 9.4–12.0 per cent. On the other hand, some projects were passed with estimated returns little higher than the 4 per cent the Commission was using as a yardstick, and below the prevailing borrowing rates of 5–6 per cent. The justification in spending over £2 million on the Ripple Lane Yard in 1956, for example, rested on returns of 4–5 per cent, and the position in 1960 was little brighter (see Table 36, example 2B). Expected returns clearly varied a great deal. When, in November 1959, the Commission's Finance Department was asked to collate data on all schemes in the pipeline costing over £250,000, for the purpose of discussions with the Ministry, the average expected returns were shown as fairly healthy. For example, on the 11 D.M.U. schemes quoted, 11 per cent was expected on the net outlay and 35 per cent on 'betterment'; and on 19 diesel main-line projects (excluding maintenance facilities), 9 and 16 per cent respectively. On the other hand, out of a total of 30 schemes only 14 were estimated to return at least 8 per cent on the net outlay, and some low-return schemes could hope for no more than 4 or 5 per cent on that basis.[48]

Such figures do not mean very much in themselves. The return on the outlay or additional outlay depends on the accuracy of the predicted savings or increase in net revenue. Although information is scanty, there is every reason to believe that the assumptions about freight traffic made in many of the marshalling yard submissions were either out-of-date or too optimistic. In the Carlisle Yard submission of 1959, for example, it was clearly stated that the return depended on the assumption that freight traffic would recover to 1957 levels, and although this was no longer believed in 1962, the revised, more 'realistic', estimate cut the forecast savings by a mere 5 per cent.[49] Equally important, of course, was the profitability of the *existing* assets, a vital matter if the railways' customary practice of considering only the betterment element of capital investment is accepted. The estimates for the electrification of the Kent Coast and Great Northern suburban lines, prepared for the Stedeford Advisory Group, illustrate this point. As Table 37 shows, the Kent Coast scheme involved a net additional outlay of nearly £29 million, which was expected to return £2.5 million in additional net revenue, or 8.7 per cent. However, the existing assets of £33 million were earning only £0.5 million, or 1.5 per cent. Thus, after electrification, the lines were expected to earn less than 5 per cent on a total capital of nearly £62 million. Operational advantages – the removal of a 'steam enclave' in an otherwise electrified system – clearly carried more weight here than purely commercial considerations. The Great Northern scheme, which was halted by the Stedeford Group, offers a similar picture. The return on the net additional outlay was put at an impressive 18.0 per cent on an investment of £12 million, or 8.9 per cent

Table 37. *British Transport Commission investment submissions: electrification schemes, 1959/60*

Year	Net capital outlay (i) £m.	Net additional outlay (ii) £m.	Expected net revenue improvement £m.	Yield on (i) %	(ii) %	Profit/loss Before electrification (actual) Gross revenue £m.	Costs £m.	Net revenue £m.	Capital used £m.	R.R. %	After electrification (est.) Gross revenue £m.	Costs £m.	Net revenue £m.	Capital used £m.	R.R. %
1. Kent Coast lines, Southern Region															
1960	51.0	28.8	2.5	4.9	8.7	8.0	7.5	0.5	33.0	1.52	10.0	7.0	3.0	61.8	4.85
2. Great Northern suburban scheme, Eastern Region															
1960	24.64	12.14	2.185	8.9	18.0	1.65	2.09	−0.44	15.9	—	3.8	2.055	1.745	28.04	6.21
3. Euston main-line scheme, London Midland Region															
1959	159.8	113.2 (129.4)[a]	8.2	5.1	7.2 (6.3)[a]										
1960	153.8	102.9 (122.9)[a]	18.9	12.3	18.4 (15.4)[a]	50.3	36.5	13.8	124.0	11.0	64.6	32.8	31.8	241.0	13.2

[a] These figures take into account interest on outlay during construction. The Euston main-line's profit and loss data do not include diesel traction working from depots on the line to and from points off the line.

Source: L.M.R., 'Electrification of Western Lines' (Blee report), April 1959; data prepared for S.A.G. by B.T.C., July 1960, Wansbrough-Jones Papers, Box 2, B.R.B.

on a total net outlay of £25 million. But the lines were making a loss under steam operation, and after electrification earnings were estimated to be only 6 per cent of the capital employed.

The issue of overall profitability was clearly crucial where money was invested in replacing steam by D.M.U.s on loss-making passenger services. By Beeching's time it must have been obvious that H. P. Barker's gloomy prediction of November 1954 (see above, p. 270) had proved correct. The Commission congratulated itself on the superficially impressive effects of the D.M.U.s in generating revenue, and publicity was given to these in the Select Committee of 1960 and in the B.T.C. Reports for 1959 and 1960. The Leeds–Barnsley service showed the greatest increase. Gross receipts jumped from £8,200 in the last year of steam to £42,100, a rise of 413 per cent. Increases above 200 per cent were also reported on the Birmingham–Lichfield and Leeds–Harrogate routes.[50] But was the investment justified, where the expenditure failed to convert losses into profits? There was little direct information on this until 1961, when the Commission, stung into action by the criticisms of the Select Committee and the Stedeford Group, initiated a pilot scheme to 'back-check' a small number of projects from the regions. One of these was Stage 1 of the London Midland's North Wales dieselisation scheme (Llandudno–Blaenau and Bangor–Amlwch). The results are shown in Table 38. The returns in 1959 were close to the expectations of 1955 and were superficially impressive: 23 per cent on the net outlay, 76 per cent on the 'betterment' portion. But all that had happened was that an annual loss of £109,000 had been reduced to one of £21,000, or £28,000 if additional interest were added. For some of the other schemes tested the 'back-checking' exercise painted a happy picture. Results produced for the Temple Mills Yard in May 1962, for example, showed that effected savings were £233,000, compared with the estimate of £260,000, giving achieved returns on the outlay of 7.0 and 11.5 per cent.[51] Although the yard was operating below capacity, the decision to build it was vindicated on the evidence provided, but no figures were obtained for the *profitability* of the business handled.

It is appropriate to conclude with a comment on the London Midland's Euston main-line electrification scheme (a fuller analysis is provided in Appendix G). It was fortunate that the adverse publicity given to the scheme by the Select Committee of 1960 obscured the facts that the line was profitable, the return to investment promised to be fairly high, and the marginal return over an alternative diesel scheme was also high. Some of the fault lies with the B.T.C. The report produced by Blee and the London Midland Region in April 1959, which was handed over to the Select Committee, did nothing at all to justify the project to critics. Not only were the estimated returns fairly low (see Table 37), but by the report's own

Table 38. 'Back-check' on the North Wales D.M.U. Scheme Stage 1, 1962

Year	Net capital outlay (i)	Net additional outlay (ii)	Improvement in net revenue	Yield on (i)	(ii)	Actual operating profit/loss
Estimate 1955	£202,550	n.a.	£46,416	22.9	n.a.	−£109,200 (steam)
Actual 1959	£387,200	£116,050	£88,000	22.7	75.8	−£ 21,200 (−£ 28,163)[a]

[a] Includes interest on outlay.

Source: submission to B.T.C. Works and Equipment Committee, Minutes, 25 April 1962, B.R.B.

reckoning an alternative diesel scheme would have produced a higher yield, making allowance for interest incurred during construction. The marginal rate of return* comes out at a low 3.4 per cent. The reappraisal of the scheme in July 1960, produced for the Stedeford Group, tackled the problem of justifying electrification more thoroughly. The expected yield on the scheme, shown in Table 37, was not only higher but was claimed to be equal to that expected from a diesel alternative. Furthermore, the marginal rate of return was now a respectable 12 per cent, a figure which re-appeared in an address to the Institute of Transport in 1967 by Henry Johnson, then Vice-Chairman of the British Railways Board. Johnson claimed that the scheme was well on target to achieve by 1970 a 12 per cent marginal rate of return over the diesel alternative. Two years later, however, a private submission to the Ministry revealed that the decline in freight revenue since 1959 had badly dented the original forecast. Indeed, the estimated net revenue of £12.9 million for 1967–8 at 1959 prices was lower than the actual net revenue in 1959 (£13.8 million). A commercial return of the order predicted in 1960 looked a dim prospect.[52]

This brief survey of the limited and speculative data on the Commission's investment appraisals and 'backchecks' suggests an uneven pattern. Some projects promised a healthy rate of return, others patently did not; and in terms of overall profitability many of the schemes were disappointing. Moreover, as any reader of the B.T.C.'s Annual Reports could see, the raised levels of spending under the Plan failed to convert financial deficits into surpluses, or even to halt the slide of ever-increasing deficits. The

*Here defined as the expected improvement in net revenue over and above that expected from dieselisation divided by the excess of net additional outlay for electrification compared with dieselisation.

railways' net operating revenue, a positive £1.8 million in 1955, deteriorated steadily to reach minus £48.1 million in 1958. After a slight
improvement in 1959, the trend was steadily downward, reaching £104
million in 1962 (see Table 17, above, col. (c)). After central charges had
been deducted, the scale of deficit was severe: £38.2 million in 1955,
£159.0 million in 1962 (see Table 17, above, col. (e)). Given the fanfare
announcing the Plan in 1955, this was failure indeed.

VI

Why did the Plan miscarry? To what extent was the Commission responsible, and how much emphasis should be placed on the effects of government intervention? There is no shortage of criticisms in the existing
literature. They range from direct criticisms of the Plan itself, apparently
'doomed to failure', to allegations that the Commission failed to control
investment adequately, from attacks on the government for its complacency to suggestions that the modernisation programme was packed with
technical and financial mistakes. All of these elements require scrutiny.

Government intervention influenced railway investment in three ways:
through the annual round of investment controls and targets, through an
interest in the railways' ordering of new equipment and finally through
direct intervention to review the Plan as the Commission's financial
position deteriorated. Here, the first two of these influences are analysed;
the third is examined in the concluding section of this Chapter. It is
certainly true that the course of railway investment was affected by the
interaction between government and Commission in the setting of annual
investment targets. Although the green light given to the Modernisation
Plan in 1955 had the effect of insulating the railways from some of the
rigours of the Treasury's annual reviews of public sector investment, the
Treasury did impose a reduction of 12 per cent in the 1956 programme at a
late stage, in February 1956; and in September 1957 it insisted upon a 5
per cent cut in the planned investment for 1958 and 1959 (for details see
Appendix F, Table 1). In the latter instance, the railways were given
favourable treatment, since the government did not, as elsewhere, insist
that investment be limited to the actual expenditure in 1957. Nevertheless,
Robertson, reviewing objectives for 1958, complained that the cuts 'had
proved more damaging to the Plan than the Government had expected'
and could discourage managers endeavouring to carry it forward. Some
damage was undoubtedly done. When the government offered substantially higher levels for these years in the following May, the Commission
complained, not for the first time, that it was impossible to turn the

investment tap on quickly.[53] The previously observed tendency (see above, pp. 76–85) for the railways to undershoot their annual investment targets continued in the modernisation period. The regions were prone to over-estimate the activity which was possible; design problems arose; delays were incurred in acquiring parliamentary powers and contractors' deliveries were late. Changes in government investment ceilings also imposed restrictions in 1958 and 1959, and thereafter the closer inspection of railway projects by the Treasury and Ministry of Transport certainly acted as a brake upon future spending. One of the most important decisions came in September 1960, when Marples fixed the railways' investment for 1961 at £125 million plus a reserve of £15 million for electrification. This was 30 per cent below the figure which the Commission had been working to less than 12 months previously.[54] If the fixing of the annual allocation had only a marginal influence on the investment out-turn before 1959, the changed climate thereafter was a major element in the failure of the B.T.C. to achieve its 1962 target by 14 per cent (Appendix F, Table 1) and the overall fall in gross railway investment of 38 per cent in real terms from 1959 to 1962 (see Table 34 above).

The government also took an interest in certain aspects of the Commission's purchasing policy, and at times exerted informal pressure to influence the placing of orders. One of the effects was to encourage the purchase of diesel locomotives from private British contractors. The B.T.C. reaffirmed its broad principles at the end of 1955. It determined to maximise the use of its own workshops wherever equipment could be manufactured on a competitive basis. For locomotives this was soundly based, since studies of comparative cost had shown that units built in the workshops were cheaper than those bought from the contractors, whose existing plant was frequently more antiquated. At the same time, it was conceded that there would be circumstances in which outside orders would be inevitable, and it was agreed that diesel engines and trans-missions would have to be purchased from the private specialist firms.[55] The B.T.C.'s policy had been challenged by the Locomotive Manufac-turers' Association* for some time. It had lobbied the government to persuade the B.T.C. to buy more from the contractors, arguing that a larger and steadier home market would assist the industry's export performance. This view certainly found favour with the government, and it was passed on to the Commission by the Ministry of Transport.[56] When tenders were invited for the initial build of 160 (subsequently 174) locomotives in 1955, the Commission's desire to test a variety of types

*Later the Locomotive and Allied Manufacturers' Association.

prior to standardisation clearly influenced its decision to place most of the orders with private firms. But this was also in accord with the government's anxiety to support the contractors and boost their export performance.[57]

Decisions in detail were also influenced in part by political pressures. One of these was the Commission's rejection of the option of buying diesel locomotives from the United States and specifically from General Motors, the leading manufacturer with the greatest experience in the field. The decision was later condemned by Stewart Joy, who claimed that American firms had been 'expressly excluded by the B.T.C. on chauvinistic grounds'.[58] In fact, the Commission was steered away from buying American by a combination of factors. The need to adapt American diesels to the British loading gauge meant that only a fairly large order would be economic, and it was also suggested that the 2-stroke engines had a high fuel consumption. The initial reluctance of General Motors to consider a licensing arrangement was another obstacle. But it is also apparent that government restrictions on dollar spending through the imposition of import duties influenced the decision. Thus, although the Commission was greatly impressed by the proven reliability of American diesels, particularly after Robertson's visit to the United States in late 1957, it argued that the economic case had to be 'overwhelming' if the political and economic objections were to be surmounted. In the end they were not. By the time Leyland came forward with a proposal to build General Motors locomotives under licence, late in 1958, the policy of purchasing British (with some German and Swiss engines/transmission) was well under way.[59] A great opportunity to obtain a fleet of reliable, standard design had been lost.* Political considerations can also be found in the B.T.C.'s choice of the North British Locomotive Co. of Glasgow as one of the British suppliers. This company was a vocal member of the L.M.A., and political influence was exerted through, inter alia, the Scottish Board for Industry. The Commission's several contracts with North British produced locomotives which were expensive, technically deficient and subject to late delivery. The decision to buy them seems to have owed something, at least, to the fact that it satisfied the government's concern to assist areas of high unemployment.[60]

It is not sufficient to blame the government for the adverse effects of modernisation spending from 1956. The Commission itself must be criticised for failing to control the investment programme properly. Here, the anxiety to secure quick returns was all important. Risks were taken; orders were placed with firms feeling their way in diesel manufacture;

*The same arguments have resurfaced recently. See B.R. Management Brief, 4 March 1985, on 'Main-Line Locomotive Renewal Programme'.

equipment was purchased without adequate testing of prototypes; long-term contracts were entered into without full examination of prices. A prime example is the acceleration of the diesel programme in 1957. The initial build of 174 locomotives involved the placing of orders with seven manufacturers (including B.R. workshops) for frames/chassis, seven for engines and eight for transmissions. This policy could be justified as long as it was accompanied by the promise of a three-year test period prior to standardisation on a limited number of designs. But the plan was abandoned precipitately as the Commission tried to respond to its worsening financial position. The government's first request for a review of the Modernisation Plan produced the White Paper, *Proposals for the Railways*, of October 1956, which promised to give diesels a 'thorough and selective trial'. Purchasing levels of 200 locomotives a year were envisaged only from 1961.[61] A few months later this was set aside. At the Chairman's Conference on Modernisation in February 1957, the arguments for doing so were outlined:

the ultimate object was electrification of all main lines. Diesel locomotives were chiefly needed to replace steam on those parts of the system which could not be electrified under the present plan ... By the end of the century the need for a big fleet of diesel locomotives would have disappeared. The need for diesel locomotives was immediate, in order that the commitments contained in the White Paper of 1956 [*inter alia*, a promise to break even by 1961/2] might be fulfilled. If their purchase were delayed until full experience was available, many of them would be redundant before their life was expired.[62]

The Area Boards were asked to produce revised plans, which were inserted in a report on the passenger services of the future in April. The report emphasised that 'exceptional steps should be taken to secure the authorisation of the diesel locomotives required to be in service by 1962'. A programme of 750–800 locomotives for 1959 was then approved. Standardisation and testing were abandoned in a headlong rush to replace steam. Unfortunately, three years later, the electrification strategy was ruled out by government intervention, and the railways were left with a diesel fleet containing 41 different designs, many of them defective in operation.[63]

It is not difficult to find individual examples of poor investment. Many of the North British locomotives failed to live up to expectations. Their Type 2 diesel-electric locomotives made such an inadequate showing in traffic that the Scottish Region had to reintroduce steam on the Glasgow–Aberdeen services.[64] It was also the North British which satisfied Western Region ambitions for a diesel locomotive fleet with hydraulic transmissions. The move certainly contradicted the standardisation objective, but the region, arguing for cheaper first cost and maintenance, was able to exploit the experimental phase in B.T.C. thinking in 1955–6. More than one railwayman has subsequently referred to the diesel hydraulics as 'an unmitigated disaster'. The locomotives, although working satisfactorily for a time, proved expensive and unreliable and serious operating difficulties became evident after 'some three/four years'.[65] Indeed, the relationship between the B.T.C. and the North British Locomotive Co., which produced 12 contracts worth £15 million to 1961, quickly turned sour. The files are full of internal qualms about inflated prices, late deliveries and technical defects. Shortly before the company went into liquidation, in April 1962, the Commission was contemplating an action to recover £300,000 in compensation for late deliveries. Other locomotives proved less than sound purchases. The Sulzer-engined Type 4s ordered for the London Midland Region were designed with weak crankshafts, and even the Deltics, which performed well on the Eastern, were expensive to operate and required careful maintenance. There is little doubt that had the initial policy of a three-year trial period been followed, many of these expensive mistakes would have been avoided.[66]

The opening of the floodgates of railway investment in the mid-1950s put pressure on existing suppliers of equipment to increase their productive capacity, and they often exploited this problem in the bargaining over contracts. The evidence suggests that the Commission surrendered the advantage too readily, allowing manufacturers to pass on additional production costs and to insist upon long-term contracts with heavy penalty clauses. For example, when the North British Locomotive Co. increased the price of 52 diesel hydraulics in June 1957 by about 20 per cent, from £2.8 to £3.3 million, the Works and Equipment Committee recommended acceptance without further investigation. This surprised the Commission, and the Chief Accountant thought it 'a most unsatisfactory way to deal with these orders involving very large amounts'. Nevertheless, the new price was finally accepted. Later on, in 1961, the Chief Railway Accountant complained about the failure to compare costs when placing orders with Brush and English Electric, suggesting that the orders were 'being influenced by the *need* to ease the contractors' difficulties in production'.[67]

Many of the Commission's difficulties could be attributed to organisational factors. The panel system was soon found to contain inherent weaknesses. The inclusion of regional representatives often produced a loss of impetus, such that 'the inevitable compromise resulted in the lowest common denominator having to be accepted'. At the same time, the panels often defined their brief much too narrowly. Thus, when the marshalling yards panel recorded its progress in January 1958, the B.T.C. was moved to minute its dissatisfaction. It asked for a comprehensive yard plan 'so as to assure the Commission that the problem was not being dealt with exclusively on a Regional and individual yard basis'. This came after nearly two years of deliberation by the panel.[68] Such defects would not have been quite so damaging had the pivotal Traffic Survey Group performed well. By March 1956 the Group had produced a document on passenger policy, but it proved to be a rather pallid piece of work. Its progress with freight was even more disappointing. A preliminary report was circulated to the Commission in July 1956 but was not discussed, and although some revealing statistics were produced on the weakness of wagon-load traffic (see above, p. 192), the promised detailed examination did not materialise. Wansbrough-Jones summarised the position a year later:

> I am afraid the preparation of the Freight Traffic Survey is at present at a virtual standstill. The immediate reason for this is the illness of Mr. Hollingsworth but a more serious reason is the apparent cleavage of opinion within British Railways as to the future pattern of freight traffic. There are those who feel that we should do the best we can with the present conventional type of equipment and those who feel that something more revolutionary is required.[69]

The lack of firmly established guiding principles was extremely damaging, given the inter-relatedness of investment in freight facilities. Eventually, the Commission was moved to create an ad hoc committee, and the White Report, described in Chapter 6, was the outcome. In the meantime, large sums of money were committed to freight modernisation without a clear and unanimous statement of future policy. The Commission's wagon-building programme, the design of freight terminals and depots and the entire strategy to recover lost business was jeopardised.[70]

The failure of the marshalling yard programme may be interpreted in this light. In view of the challenge to the railways' wagon-load traffic promised by faster, larger lorries in conjunction with the new motorways, it was just as well that only three new yards were completed before 1960. Unfortunately for the Commission, and whatever it may have felt about its future freight prospects after the poor results of 1958 and the reappraisal of 1959, the policy drift of the mid-1950s meant that it was too late to halt the completion of several more yards. By the end of 1962 another six had been brought into total or partial operation, at Perth, Millerhill (Edinburgh), Newport (Teesside), Margam (Port Talbot), Ripple Lane (Barking) and Ashford, and others were well advanced, including Carlisle (Kingmoor), Healey Mills (Wakefield), Lamesley (Tyneside) and Tinsley (Sheffield). The rationale for many of these schemes, the legacy of an earlier faith in the viability of a refurbished wagon-load business, disappeared long before they were opened.[71] It is possible to sympathise with the B.T.C. for planning facilities for freight traffic which was promised by customers but which did not materialise. The provision made for the Fife coalfield at Thornton is a case in point. Planned in the late 1940s on the basis of Coal Board promises, the viability of this marshalling yard was threatened soon after its opening in 1956 by the run-down of the Rothes Pit. On the other hand, there were some obvious planning disasters. The decision to site marshalling yards at former company exchange points far from the main centres of production and consumption was a fundamental flaw in the investments at Carlisle, Perth and Millerhill.[72] Another monument to the Commission's dilatoriness in accepting that freight operations should be rationalised around the train-load concept was its support for the London outer ring freight route. Improvements along this route – from Cambridge to Ashford via Oxford, Reading and Tonbridge – had been advocated by a Railway Executive working party in 1949. The intention was to relieve congestion at London junctions by keeping north–south freight traffic out of central London. The cost (including that of associated projects) was put at £15 million in 1958, altered to £11.7 million in the following year, an expenditure which the Commission recognised was 'never expected to show a direct financial return'. This was an under-statement. At least one expensive white elephant was proceeded with in the shape of the Bletchley Flyover (cost: £1.6 million) and land acquired for another, a marshalling yard at Swanbourne (Bucks), before the scheme was abandoned after 1960.[73]

Only one or two gleams of light shone in this gloomy picture of freight investment before 1963. A solution to the inefficiency of the wagon-load traffic was offered by the first steps taken in the development of container or liner trains. In 1959 the 'Condor' train from London to Glasgow was introduced. Offering a fast, door-to-door service for container traffic, it was followed by others, including one from Sheffield to Glasgow, and the 'Tees–Tyne' and 'King's Cross Freighter'.[74] Defending its slow progress in freight improvements, the B.T.C. claimed that it had been difficult to respond quickly without falling back on schemes which the regions had kept in their store cupboards, and that several technological choices had had to be made before concerted action could be taken. The sudden encouragement given to the railways in 1954–5 also left them with the task of mobilising resources in an industry which had been marking time for decades, as well as of tackling several bottlenecks, particularly on the engineering side, when it attempted to accelerate the programme after 1956.[75]

The decision in February 1956 to fit the freight rolling stock with vacuum brakes was followed by a series of technical and commercial difficulties. The policy, which had been one of the frustrated ambitions of the Railway Executive, was an integral part of the Modernisation Plan and

£75 million had been allocated for it in the published report (see Table 32, above). Some aspects of this unfortunate story have been recounted in Chapter 5, namely the B.T.C.'s decision in 1955 to continue with the vacuum brake in preference to the technically superior air brake, and the criticisms of its handling of the contracts to supply brake cylinders, particularly from Westinghouse Brake & Signal Co., which led to the official inquiry into purchasing by Sir Harold Howitt in 1957. A more detailed analysis of the problem reveals the risks taken by the Commission when it embarked on a spending programme before the technical and commercial implications had been fully investigated.

The choice of the vacuum brake in preference to the air brake was largely the result of resistance by the regional General Managers, who put current operating considerations above the planning of freight services in the future. This was undoubtedly a costly mistake which gave road haulage an unnecessary advantage.[76] The same regional myopia lay behind the greatest weakness in the programme – the insistence that *all* railway wagons should be fitted with vacuum brakes, in accordance with the objective of a fully compatible fleet. Not only did this serve to delay the returns to early investment, but it revealed a failure to grasp the realities of freight movement in the 1950s. Services were still predominantly of wagon-load or pick-up freight type, which did not allow vacuum-braked wagons to be usefully employed in conjunction with non-fitted wagons during the long period of transition. The idea that partly fitted freight trains could usefully be run was more theoretical than practical; in reality most of these trains were likely to be operated with the vacuum brakes disconnected. Braked wagons only made sense when fully employed in trains which avoided intermediate marshalling, but the concept of the train load was only tentatively being explored by the B.T.C. Not for the first time, it was left to the part-time member, H. P. Barker, to expose the frailties of the initial policy. In a critical paper in March 1960 he argued that it had rested on two unsound foundations, 'namely that it was practicable to modernise the present fleet and implicitly that if this were done the economic ends would justify the means'.[77] Unfortunately, freight policy remained confused in the second half of the 1950s, and the anxiety to fit large numbers of wagons as quickly as possible not only failed to overcome operational discontinuities but brought with it technical and contractual difficulties. The cost of the brakes programme also escalated. By mid-1957 the total cost was put at £175 million, an increase of £100 million.[78]

The introduction of vacuum brakes created problems in a related piece of technology, wagon couplings. The old-fashioned railway couplings had to be replaced by either 'instanter' link couplings or the British or continental type of screw coupling. But many argued that this was merely an intermediate step, to be adopted until a suitable automatic coupler could be developed, which would accelerate speed through the marshalling yards and cut labour costs. The raison d'être for automatic couplings was rightly challenged from the start. In November 1956 the General Managers found that the savings would be small compared with the large capital outlay required, and argued that marshalling yard movements would diminish with modernisation. The problem was expected to be resolved by the Freight Policy Group, but no firm proposal emerged. Tests with prototype automatic couplers in 1956 and 1958–9 eventually produced a workable design, but by this time the whole strategy had been questioned. In 1960 Barker dismissed the notion of a fully fitted wagon fleet with automatic couplings as a 'pipe dream'. He reached the conclusion that 'the only feasible application . . . is in the case where it is unnecessary, namely the circuit worked train with vacuum brakes. We have been chasing an illusion.'[79]

More problems came with the attempt to fit brakes to the mineral wagon stock. The operation of heavy mineral and steel carrying trains required the heavier continental screw coupling, but the Commission was rightly apprehensive about the reactions of guards and shunters to handling this more cumbersome equipment. More important still was the adverse reaction of British Railways' leading customers. Both the British Iron and Steel Federation and the National Coal Board refused to accept the new fitted mineral wagons in their terminal and sidings. The fitting of brakes and screw couplings had to be suspended.[80] A more embarrassing difficulty came with the fitting of clasp brakes to mineral wagons in order to counter the adverse effects of braking at high speeds. It was found that all of the 550 privately owned end-tipplers* were unable to take the wagons without fouling the brake gear. About a quarter of the other types of tippler also required modification. The cost of modifying the plant was estimated to be £1.25 million. Angry at this fiasco, which had led to 'considerable loss of money and prejudice to the Commission's business', the Commission went to some lengths to reprimand the culprits. The policy of fitting brakes to mineral wagons was then suspended, and in May 1960 the policy of fitting the entire fleet was formally abandoned.[81]

On top of this dismal story of planning and technical deficiencies, the anxiety to fit brakes quickly also led the Commission to tie itself to long-term contracts with outside manufacturers, often at high prices. One of the largest contracts involved an undertaking by Westinghouse to supply 295,000 brake cylinders at £23 each over a five-year period. The suspen-

---

*Tipplers are devices to unload railway wagons by tipping them, either on their ends, or sides.

sion of the mineral programme and government investment cuts caused the Commission to reduce its purchasing. The company submitted a hefty claim for damages in 1961, and this was eventually settled at £1.6 million. Sums totalling £0.5 million were also paid to other manufacturers for cancelled contracts. Nor was this all. The Westinghouse claim produced the revelation that its £23 price had been too high, with both labour and material production costs overestimated.[82]

There is much for which the Commission must be directly criticised in its approach to the challenge of modernisation. The anxiety to speed up the programme in order to gain quick results, the need to respond to government requirements, the need to negotiate properly with private industry and, above all, the need to work to a defined commercial strategy placed a great strain on the B.T.C.'s organisation and planning mechanisms. The evidence suggests that all too often these were unequal to the task. Some technical decisions were taken too quickly, while important decisions relating to traffic were taken too late. The strength of regional operating opinion was frequently apparent. No firm grip was imposed.

VII

How did the government respond to the progressing of the Plan, as the Commission's financial position deteriorated, and what was the outcome of the review and reappraisal activity of 1956 and 1959–60? How adequate was the Commission's defence of its spending programme? These questions are answered in this final section.

The defects inherent in the hurried B.T.C. submission of 1954 are perhaps excusable; much less so is the Commission's defence of its position during the process of revision and reappraisal in 1956 and 1959. Likewise, Whitehall's response to the Commission's growing financial difficulties, despite the obvious unease shown by some senior officials, was notably feeble. In December 1955 Harold Watkinson succeeded Boyd-Carpenter as Minister of Transport, thus becoming the fourth Conservative Minister in four years of government. In March 1956 he informed the Commons that the Commission had made a further application to raise railway freight charges, and stated that an essential element in the government's response was to insist upon a reassessment of the Commission's entire 'economic and financial future'. The latter's finances, meanwhile, were showing signs of progressive deterioration. The accounts for 1955, published in June 1956, indicated that the railways' annual deficit, after meeting central charges, was now running at about £40 million. The B.T.C.'s consolidated revenue account for all activities revealed a net loss for the year of £31 million, making the accumulated deficit since 1948 almost £70 million.[83] The financial climate in which the government was now asking for a revised strategy was thus much harsher than it had been two years earlier.

The Commission's reply, for which Wilson and Harold Osborn, the Chief Accountant, were largely responsible, was incorporated in a White Paper, *Proposals for the Railways*, published in October. It covered all aspects of the Commission's strategy, including pricing, productivity and the elimination of unprofitable services; and a key section was devoted to modernisation. In the latter the Commission provided a more detailed account of its investment plans in physical terms; offered some rough estimates of annual investment expenditure for 1956–62; and made a clearer, although still rather sketchy, statement of the expected impact on its financial position in 1961/2 and in 1970. This time, the benefits arising from modernisation were distinguished in part from those arising out of other activities, such as the pruning of unremunerative services, and the application of greater flexibility to railway pricing. As Table 39 shows, the B.T.C. now estimated that modernisation would improve the net revenue contribution of the railways by £35 million in 1961 or 1962. This was just over half of the total improvement which, it was claimed, would not only meet the interest on modernisation borrowings but would also eliminate the annual deficit, put at £40 million in 1956. A state of current balance would thus be achieved within five to six years, although, as was clearly pointed out, this did not take account of the interest burden on the accumulated deficits. By 1970, however, even this problem would be resolved. Modernisation would indeed produce the £85 million claimed in the original Plan. With the other contributions, a healthy surplus of £48 million would be earned, more than sufficient to meet interest on the accumulated deficits.[84] The government's official response was once again supportive. Watkinson followed his three predecessors in as many years in making optimistic noises. The Commission, he declared in his introduction to the White Paper, had 'prepared a comprehensive statement . . . including a re-examination of the whole scope of the reorganisation, modernisation and re-equipment of the railways . . . with [a] *full financial and statistical background*' (my italics). While accepting that annual deficits would continue 'for some years', he believed that the Commission had 'presented a convincing case' and 'had spared no effort to lay before the nation *as full and detailed an examination . . . as is possible*' (my italics).[85]

Watkinson's remarks did not, of course, fool any of the more knowledgeable critics. This revised justification of the Modernisation Plan was little more than a dressing-up of the hurried calculation made earlier. Much of the B.T.C.'s effort, such as it was, had been put into the provision

Table 39. *British Transport Commission: revised financial estimate,*
1956

Item	Position in: December 1956 (£m.)	1961 or 1962 (£m.)	1970 (£m.)
Annual rate of deficit[a]	−40	−40	−40
Improvement in non-railway activities	—	+5	+5
Improvement in railways' contribution:			
(a) Modernisation	—	+35	+85
(b) Pruning services	—	+3	+3
(c) Productivity	—	+5	+10
(d) Pricing freedom	—	+20	+25
		+63	+123
Less: interest on modernisation borrowings	−2	−25	−40
	−2	+38	+83
Balance	−42	+3	+48
Balance after deducting interest on accumulated deficits (B.T.C. estimate)	−48	−17	+38

[a] Excludes interest on accumulated deficits (assuming a 5 per cent rate, £6m. in 1956, £20m. in 1961/2 and £10m. in 1970) and financing of the Modernisation Plan.
Source: Proposals for the Railways, October 1956, p. 29, P.P. 1955–6, XXXVI, Cmd. 9880.

of details of *physical* planning only. The estimated gain in net revenue of
£85 million remained unaltered, although it now applied to 1970 instead
of 1974. And its appearance without further analysis did nothing to
inspire confidence in its accuracy. It was particularly unfortunate that no
attempt was made to show what proportion of the £85 million would
come from the ending of unremunerative services, since the Commission
admitted that this was a 'considerable' element. The £3 million for
'pruning of services' in Table 39 was merely an incremental addition to an
unspecified sum. Another disquieting feature was the omission of any
reference to the £15 million charge for replacement cost depreciation.
Although the Commission showed an access of realism in formally
accepting that interest on deficits would need to be met, some of the
assumptions on which its calculation were said to rest were clearly
unrealistic. For example, it is difficult to see how the figures in Table 39
could have been taken seriously when they were based *inter alia* on the

premise that 'the Commission will not be prevented from adjusting their charges without delay to cover increases in costs'. Not only did this fly in the face of the government's record, but it also conflicted with Watkinson's remarks, in the same White Paper, that general increases in charges were to be avoided and that to increase substantially the rates on the heavy bulk traffics would be 'against the broad national interest'.[86] Even more vulnerable was the assumption that charges would move in line with costs. Labour costs had outstripped inflation in the past and would obviously be likely to do so in the future. After all, the Commission, in its Report for 1955, had admitted that there existed serious labour shortages. They were particularly evident in the low-paid grades in which the level of wages had fallen behind that in comparable occupations. And the mood of the railway unions during the disputes of 1953–5 should have told the Commission that it was highly unlikely that, having slipped down the pay ladder, they would be satisfied with stationary real wages over the next 15 years. The failure to heed this factor was a very serious weakness.[87]

In short, this 1956 review, which was used to justify an acceleration of the Plan and financial support from the government, should not have convinced anyone that the Commission would achieve a net revenue surplus in 1970 let alone in 1961 or 1962.

Nevertheless, the Commission received a considerable measure of financial assistance from the government. In the period 1956–8, £221 million was advanced under the Finance Act of 1956, which gave the Minister of Transport powers to lend money to the B.T.C. as an alternative to the issuing of British Transport Stock.[88] In addition, temporary borrowing powers, promised in the White Paper, were given to the B.T.C. by the Transport (Railway Finances) Act of 1957, in order to relieve the burden of interest payments and future railway deficits (see above, p. 176). Deficits and the deferred interest were then transferred to a Special Account in the B.T.C. books in order to meet Robertson's somewhat pious hope that the Commission should be seen to be 'turning over a fresh financial page'.[89]

Soon after this, the Commission revalued the cost of the Modernisation Plan at £1,500 million, and added a further £160 million for new projects. But the railways' financial position continued to deteriorate, in spite of attempts to accelerate the programme. In 1956 and 1957 deficits of £57.5 and £68.1 million were announced, and in 1958, when the recession hit the freight business particularly hard, the deficit amounted to £90.1 million, making a total of nearly £216 million for the three years. By the end of the year the Minister had advanced a total of £191 million under the 1957 Act, and the Special Account stood at £308.2 million. The critics were more than vindicated.[90] By the beginning of 1958 Watkinson had grown more than a little anxious. In a letter to Robertson in January he pointed out that the increased cost of the Plan, coupled with the downward trend in the freight business, meant that 'a lot more questions are going to be asked about the worthwhileness of all you are planning on the freight side and about the likelihood of your being equipped in time to stop the rot that at least some people think has set in'. He asked for detailed answers to several questions about the freight strategy and the benefits expected by the 'break-even date' of 1961/2. In the course of the year the position deteriorated still further. By September Robertson was forced to inform his Minister that the annual deficit would be a great deal larger than had previously been anticipated. Watkinson responded by agreeing to extend the limit on deficit advances (under the 1957 Act) from £250 to £400 million, and to increase the Commission's general borrowing powers from £600 to £1,200 million. The quid pro quo was another reassessment. Presenting the proposals to the Commons on 11 December, Watkinson announced that at his request the B.T.C. had begun a 'full, detailed, and urgent review of the whole modernisation plan' and a 'complete revision and re-shaping of the 1956 prospectus'.[91]

This second review was carried out during the first half of 1959 and published in July as a White Paper, *Re-appraisal of the Plan for the Modernisation and Re-equipment of British Railways*. As requested by the Minister, the Commission reviewed the progress made with modernisation over the first four years (to the end of 1958). It then offered a forecast of its traffic and a recalculation of its financial prospects over the following five years, to the end of 1963. As in 1956, it dealt competently with the physical aspects of its modernisation activity. Detailed information was given about the various investment categories, and an estimate of rolling stock requirements for 1963 proved to be very close to that which actually obtained. However, the traffic forecasts again proved to be too optimistic. It was expected that in 1963 freight revenue would be at about the same level as in 1957. A fall in coal receipts would be matched, it was thought, by increases in the revenue from minerals and general merchandise. It was also estimated that passenger traffic would increase by about 15 per cent over the same period. In fact, not only did the coal business decline but so too did the other items. Consequently freight revenue fell by about 20 per cent (at 1957 rates). The passenger business also fell away. There was a decrease of 13 per cent in both volume and revenue terms (at 1957 fares).[92]

Although the B.T.C. was once again proved wrong, its forecasts, despite the views of some critics, were not wholly 'unrealistic'.[93] In the economic climate of the time it could not readily have foreseen in 1959 that its railway traffics were in secular decline. The Commission's officers had been advised by government departments to work to annual growth rates of 2.5 per cent for G.N.P. and 3.5 per cent for industrial production, and they were scarcely at fault in failing to anticipate the recession of 1963. The hopes for the mineral traffic rested on the optimistic figures supplied by the iron and steel industry. Furthermore, the assumptions about coal traffic were not only sound but, unlike the 1954 estimates, they had been drafted without the advantage of any co-operation from the National Coal Board. At a time when the railways were facing one of the biggest crises in their history, it must have galled Robertson to be told by Sir James Bowman, the N.C.B. Chairman, that since the coal industry was also in the middle of an investment planning exercise, it could not supply the Commission with a revised forecast of coal production for the years to 1963. The Commission's independent prediction of 200–210 million tons for 1963 was remarkably close to the actual production of 202 million and therefore very creditable.[94] Where the traffic forecasts were noticeably defective, as with the general merchandise and passenger businesses, it seems likely that they were manipulated to square with the desired financial forecast. In the light of the Commission's cautious comments about merchandise traffic in 1954 (see above, p. 265), its expressions of hope for an increase in 1957–63 can hardly be taken seriously. Likewise, the predicted growth in passenger traffic is simply incompatible with its claim to have taken full account of the growth of private motoring and the impact of motorway-building.[95]

The financial calculations in the 1959 *Re-appraisal* were extremely vague. This time the Commission confined the argument to the operating account. In contrast with the 1955 Plan, the lion's share of the expected improvement in net revenue was to come from passenger traffic. The £60 million freight/£35 million passenger breakdown of 1955 (see Table 33) was replaced by £5–35 million freight/£50–70 million passenger. After deducting extra costs, the Commission hoped to achieve an improvement of £45–95 million, converting the working deficit of £27 million in 1957 to a surplus of £18–68 million in 1963. For the Commission's activities as a whole, a working loss of £4 million in 1957 would become a surplus of some £50–100 million. Further improvements were expected after 1963. In fact, the railways' operating account revealed a deficit of nearly £82 million in that year. The 1959 calculation was an improvement on the earlier review, to the extent that the Commission had made it clear that in estimating future working costs it had allowed for rising wage levels and included a sum of £14 million for additional depreciation. But it still did not produce a more realistic result; the misplaced optimism remained. The net revenue estimates of £45–95 million for 1963 were consistent with the 1956 estimate of £63 million for 1961/2 (see Table 39 above).[96]

Whatever the validity of the forecasted operating surplus, the 1959

White Paper was certainly not a proof of future solvency. A separate section on the B.T.C.'s central charges made it clear that by 1963 the interest burden would be almost as large as the upper-bound of the predicted gain in net revenue, and much higher than this in later years. The Commission therefore made a strong plea for a fresh consideration of its capital structure. Nor was the White Paper strictly a 'reappraisal' of the economics of the Modernisation Plan. For all its detail, there was no attempt to disentangle the returns to investment from the wreckage of deficit-trading and mounting debt. The government was merely left with Robertson's assurance that the exercise had proved that the plan was 'soundly based'. Although the Commission stepped up its emphasis on the need to create a more 'compact' railway, its overall view was that no fundamental changes to its modernisation strategy were required. Indeed, it argued that investment should be accelerated so that the bulk of the Plan could be completed within five years.[97]

VIII

There were few signs of a railway recovery in the months after the White Paper was published. The operating deficit in 1959 amounted to £42 million and the total deficit was £84 million. Ministerial advances to the Commission totalled £238 million during the year.[98] By this time the mood in Whitehall was visibly changing. At the Ministry of Transport, officials who favoured a tougher response to the railway problem came to the fore. In 1958 James Dunnett moved from the Ministry of Supply to take up one of the posts of Deputy-Secretary, and in April 1959 he succeeded Sir Gilmour Jenkins as Permanent-Secretary. Jenkins, who had been Permanent-Secretary since 1947, had not taken a very close interest in inland transport, and had left much to his Deputy-Secretaries. He was generally sympathetic to the railways and had established a good relationship with Robertson. All this changed with Dunnett's appointment. He soon made it clear that he was keen on the idea of moving towards a much smaller but more cost-effective railway system. The new attitude was strengthened when he obtained David Serpell's transfer from the Treasury to Transport at Deputy-Secretary level. These moves were matched by political changes after the General Election of October 1959. Watkinson was moved to Defence. His successor as Minister of Transport (now shorn of Civil Aviation) was Ernest Marples, a lively and energetic politician who had impressed Macmillan both when acting as his Parliamentary Secretary at the Ministry of Housing (1951–4) and in his work as Postmaster-General (1957–9). Marples, a qualified accountant and founder of the road construction business of Marples, Ridgeway &

Partners, was known to prefer motorway-building to railway modernisation as the solution to Britain's transport problems. The prospects for the B.T.C. soon became much bleaker.[99]

The new mood of criticism quickly produced results. By the end of 1959 a Select Committee on Nationalised Industries had been established to examine the Commission's railway activities. The Committee of 13 members, which included Sir Toby Low (Chairman), Austen Albu, John Peyton (later Secretary of State for Transport, 1970–4), Enoch Powell, Jeremy Thorpe and Dame Irene Ward, took evidence between January and May 1960 and reported in July.[100] Before this process was completed, however, Marples decided to take independent action. In January 1960 he, along with other Cabinet Ministers, received a joint memorandum from the Treasury and the Ministry of Transport on the *Re-appraisal*, which was produced after a series of meetings with B.T.C. officers. This poured a large dose of cold water on the B.T.C.'s sums. It argued that over-optimistic traffic forecasts and an underestimate of future wage costs had greatly exaggerated the estimate of net revenue improvement in 1963. The promised £50–100 million should thus be reduced to a sum nearer £35–50 million. Although the predictive powers of the civil servants proved to be little better than the Commission's, their argument about wages was certainly convincing, not least because an extensive inquiry into railway pay comparability, established in late 1958 under C. W. Guillebaud (see above, pp. 237–9), promised to lead to higher wage levels. The memorandum also criticised the Commission for failing to provide precise estimates of the expected rate of return to individual projects; condemned the practice of considering only the 'betterment' element of capital expenditure when estimating returns; and concluded that the return to investment was likely to be small in 1963 and much smaller thereafter, when interest liabilities would swallow up 'the very speculative increases in working surpluses'. There was no prospect of the Commission's meeting its full interest burden without continued capitalisation of interest, and even with this assistance its chances of doing so were very slim. The possibility that it would be able to pay off the accumulated deficits was regarded as even more remote.[101] This gloomy report was given greater impact when the Guillebaud pay inquiry reported, in March 1960, that an 8 per cent increase in railway wages was merited. A Special Advisory Group was then appointed to assist Marples in examining the 'structure, finance and working' of the Commission's activities. The Group was essentially a committee of businessmen. More will be said in Chapter 9 of their qualifications, activities and views (see below, pp. 308ff.). Suffice it here to note that the Chairman was Sir Ivan Stedeford, head of Tube Investments, and that the other members were Dr Richard Beeching of

I.C.I., Henry Benson, an accountant from Cooper Brothers, and Frank Kearton from Courtaulds. They were joined by two civil servants, Matthew Stevenson (Treasury), and David Serpell (Transport).[102]

The full story of the redrafting of the Conservatives' transport strategy, from the Select Committee and the Stedeford Advisory Group to the Transport Act of 1962 and the abolition of the British Transport Commission, is told in Chapter 9. At this stage it is necessary to observe only that in the process of this considerable upheaval the Modernisation Plan was in effect halted, five years after its launch, while a detailed inquiry into the viability of outstanding projects was undertaken. The climate of criticism was advanced by the published statements of the Select Committee. In its report in July 1960, it made good use of the evidence provided by the interested civil servants and, in particular, Dunnett and Stevenson. Although the Committee accepted that it was difficult to measure the effects of modernisation as it proceeded, and that many schemes had produced good results in terms of revenue generated, it censured the Commission for failing to apply adequate financial tests to the return on individual projects. It suggested that 'large expenditures have been undertaken on modernising parts of the undertaking without any precise calculation of what the profitability of those parts will be on completion'. The Commission was also criticised for its failure to carry through some of the priorities in the Plan and, in particular, the rationalisation of the network and the improvement of freight operation. The Select Committee was equally critical of the past record of the government departments. The Ministry of Transport and the Treasury should have demanded a detailed justification of the projects undertaken with the government's financial assistance before the Commission had slid into a financial mess. Yet it was not until the beginning of 1960 that the Minister had asked to examine all schemes costing over £250,000. The Committee concluded that 'there was no question that the agreement to the Modernisation Plan meant the handing over of a blank cheque to the Commission'. The departments had obviously been slow to respond to the recommendations of the Committee's predecessor which, in looking at the Coal Board's affairs more than two years earlier, had suggested that there should be a much closer supervision of investment in nationalised industries.[103]

When the Committee examined one of the major schemes in detail, the Euston–Birmingham–Liverpool/Manchester electrification, it uncovered an extremely confused situation. The scheme had been costed in the original Plan at £75 million. By 1959 this figure had reached £161 million; and the expected yield, a mere £8 million net, represented a return below the current interest rate. The Commission argued that the rate of return should be measured on a 'betterment' basis by deducting £48 million for 'the expired life value of assets displaced'.[104] Both Ministry and Treasury witnesses expressed their surprise and dismay at this procedure, and a lengthy debate then ensued. The Select Committee did not adjudicate, but merely observed that millions must already have been spent on schemes which had been allowed to go forward 'on the basis of figures which apparently meant completely different things to the two sides'. Noting that the Commission had decided to electrify the line largely on the basis of traffic density, it expressed astonishment that no one had asked for a consideration of diesels as an alternative. It did not, however, recommend that the project should be abandoned, despite its apparently low return.[105]

Stedeford's Advisory Group, in its private deliberations of April–October 1960, covered much of the same ground. Encouraged by a Minister who made it clear that his Department was planning an extensive road-building programme which would limit the railways' future prospects,[106] its members soon reached the conclusion that the Modernisation Plan was unsound and should be 'stalled'. After taking evidence from members of the B.T.C.'s finance and works and equipment committees, the Group agreed that the Plan had been determined on its technical merits without proper regard to capital cost or commercial justification. Its recommendation to Marples in June was that those parts of the Plan which had been started but had not reached 'the point of no return' should be held up pending a further examination.[107] The Group was far from unanimous, however, about its role in the review process. Beeching and Benson wanted to undertake a thorough investigation of the railways' position, including detailed aspects of the Modernisation Plan. On the other hand, Stedeford, supported by Kearton, preferred to seek the co-operation of the Commission, and had obtained Robertson's agreement to a joint review. Not for the last time, the four businessmen were divided 2–2. After much argument, Marples decided that the study of the railways' future and the details of modernisation investment were best left to an entirely separate body, and that Stedeford's Group should concentrate on organisation and finance. In August 1960, therefore, Marples set up a Ministerial Group on Modernisation, consisting of representatives of the Ministry, the Commission and the Board of Trade. So there were now two Groups and a Select Committee officially examining the railways in one way or another.[108]

The Stedeford Group continued to take an interest in the modernisation issue. In July, it fulfilled its prior commitment to examine schemes in progress. The Commission submitted 120 projects, costing £227 million, listed under four heads: (a) too far advanced to be sensibly stopped; (b) self-evidently justified; (c) unavoidable replacement; and (d) started but had not passed the point of no return (£4 million of a total of £73 million had been spent). The Group recommended that while most of the schemes in Schedules (a)-(c) should be allowed to proceed, all those in (d) should be halted, and the Crewe–Liverpool electrification should be transferred from (a) to (d). Indeed, the Euston electrification scheme caused further argument within the Group. Beeching was convinced that diesels would be more cost-effective, and he pressed his colleagues to recommend it to Marples and the Ministerial Group. But Stedeford was much more sympathetic to the Commission's position, and after a further review he used his influence to secure a more guarded recommendation.[109] In spite of Beeching's clear opposition to the scheme, it survived its examination by the Ministerial Group and was duly endorsed by Marples in January 1961. If, as the Select Committee had observed, the glitter had gone out of the Plan, then it is also fair to point out that Stedeford's attitude, together with the creation of the Ministerial body, deflected some of the more hawkish tendencies which had emerged within the Advisory Group.[110]

Having saved the Euston electrification scheme, the Commission submitted a four-year modernisation programme for the period 1961–4. This was still under consideration by the Ministry when Beeching was appointed to the Commission in March 1961. The task facing the critic-turned-railway manager was an immense one. The published accounts for 1960, which were made available in June 1961, the month in which Beeching succeeded Robertson as Commission Chairman, revealed that the railways' position was worse than ever. The year's operating loss was £67.7 million, and the total deficit, after allowing for central charges, was put at £112.7 million.[111]

This account of the Plan's 'reappraisal' in the years 1956–61 indicates that if there were villains, then they were to be found as much in the corridors of Whitehall as in 222, Marylebone Road. Certainly the B.T.C.'s handling of its investment programme had been amateurish and periodically complacent. Initially unprepared for the progressing of expenditure on the scale proposed in 1954, it had contented itself with working to Wilson's broad strategy, 'a policy not a blueprint', as he described it to the Stedeford Group. The regions submitted schemes on their supposed technical or operating merits without regard to the precise financial consequences which in any event would have been difficult to unravel. They were then processed by the Works and Equipment Committee led by Ratter, a technical expert, with no financial specialist in attendance. The Finance Committee was not involved at all. If Wilson, its Chairman, had considerable talents as a financial theorist he had no appetite for investment control. In short, he was no finance manager. Given this lack of attention to financial detail, it was unfortunate that the Commission was noticeably cool to the initial probings of the Ministry and Treasury.[112] Yet the continuing debate about the correct method of assessing the returns to investment projects obscured some of the more important questions, namely, what size of railway system was to be supported, and how much investment was it to receive? In this context the attitude of shocked surprise adopted by the civil servants in 1960 was merely a diversion. The Commission's calculations may indeed have been capable of refinement, but investment appraisal elsewhere, whether in nationalised or private industry, was not always in accordance with either theory or best practice, as the evidence to the Radcliffe Committee on the Working of the Monetary System in 1958 demonstrated. Statements by representatives of such companies as Ford, Shell and Vickers indicated that investment decisions were often little more than guesses.[113] Furthermore, the Commission may have been rash to embark on an ambitious programme to modernise much of the 1950s' network without adequate financial testing, but successive Ministers made no attempt to search for answers to the central issues of size and profitability before the recession of 1958. It was maintained that the railway was to be an economically viable one but, as Robertson explained to Stedeford in 1960, the Plan had been presented 'at a time when the idea of contracting the system was entirely strange to thinking in the country generally'.[114] This problem was recognised by the Departments but they remained complacent about it until the Commission's finances deteriorated. Many of the schemes implemented during the modernisation period were worthwhile and would have satisfied more stringent tests, had they been applied. Even those schemes which were not really justified in purely commercial terms reduced operating costs and cut the railways' deficit. It is not difficult with hindsight to proclaim that the B.T.C. should have concentrated its investment in the more profitable areas of the business and pursued rationalisation more ruthlessly. To do that, however, it would have had to convince a public which expected to see improved rail services over a network barely reduced in size. And until 1960, there was little pressure from the Ministry of Transport to pursue such goals. The B.T.C. had wanted to modernise the railways after years of neglect. The public wanted a modern railway network of roughly the same size as in 1955. The government wanted the Commission to fulfil its obligation to break even. Much of the review activity, like much of the investment activity, was not about justifying the Plan financially but about the attempt, made under government pressure, to reconcile these objectives. Not surprisingly, it proved impossible to do so.

PART 3

The British Railways Board, 1963–73

9

The 'Beeching Revolution': organisation and reorganisation

I

As will have been evident from the preceding chapters, the late 1950s saw the B.T.C. faced with a set of problems of growing seriousness for nationalised railways. The sharp decline in freight traffic from 1958, a worsening financial deficit, the government's increasing doubts about the Modernisation Plan, unhappy industrial relations culminating in the Guillebaud Inquiry: all placed Robertson and his colleagues in a vulnerable position. The outcome – in the shape of the various inquiries which finally led to the Transport Act of 1962 and the replacement of the Commission by the British Railways Board in January 1963 – was strongly influenced by a marked shift in attitudes within government circles towards the performance of the nationalised industries in general and the railways in particular. Both the Treasury and the Ministry of Transport experienced a shake-up. Changes in personnel, such as the consolidation by the Treasury in 1958 of all its nationalised industries work into one division under Matthew Stevenson and the appointment of James Dunnett as Permanent-Secretary at the Ministry of Transport in 1959, were symptomatic of the new approach. So too was the appointment of a group of officials under Sir Thomas Padmore, a Treasury Second Secretary, to examine organisational changes in public sector energy and transport and their relations with government. Their judgement was that organisational issues were secondary to the need to establish clear economic and financial objectives, a contention which led on to the Government's White Paper on *The Financial and Economic Obligations of the Nationalised Industries* in April 1961. A similar view can be found in the report of the Select Committee appointed in November 1959 (see above, pp. 300–2). It saw the key to profitable railway operation as being a concentration on commercial objectives combined with improved accounting and investment appraisal.[1] There were, however, some quite penetrating criticisms of Robertson's cumbersome dinosaur of an organisation in the pages of its report. The weak position of the Area Boards attracted its attention, for example, although here one of the proposed remedies – separate accounts for each railway region – led the railways down a false and time-consuming trail until the idea was quietly dropped.[2] More important was the Committee's observations about work at the centre. The Commission had been handicapped by the distractions offered by its non-railway businesses:

> it cannot have helped to achieve efficiency in the higher direction of British Railways that there should have been no one authority whose only duty in the field of transport was to ensure an efficient system of railways . . . Your Committee say this in the conviction that the British Railways are, to an important degree, a single integrated system.

In the main, though some inherent defects were exposed, organisational problems were kept in the background of the Select Committee's report and it concluded that 'the general lines on which the Commission are now working – both in central co-ordination and in decentralisation of managerial responsibility – are right'.[3] The defects were to be examined in full in the parallel proceedings of Stedeford's Special Advisory Group.

As outlined in Chapter 8, the setting-up of this Group in March 1960 was the work of Ernest Marples, Macmillan's appointee as Minister of Transport in October 1959. The organisational changes imposed on the railways owed much to him and to the Stedeford Group. Its task was to guide the Minister after the publication of the Guillebaud report had carried with it the strong suggestion that the railways' wage-bill, and hence the financial deficit, would increase still further unless drastic surgery were applied. On 10 March Macmillan's statement to the Commons on the Guillebaud report included the announcement that 'the Commission must accept a radical alteration of its structure, so as to secure a more effective distribution of functions and a better use of all its assets'. Macmillan envisaged further measures to decentralise the business, with the railway regions made 'fully self-accounting and responsible for the management of their own affairs'. The 'detailed application of these principles' was to be worked out by a special planning board.[4]

The 'special planning board' turned out instead to be a Special Advisory Group, as Marples told the House on 6 April. The quality of its membership – four businessmen and two civil servants – was impressive; Sir Ivan Stedeford, Chairman and Managing Director of Tube Investments, and Chairman of the Group; Frank Kearton, Joint Managing Director of Courtaulds; Henry Benson, partner in Cooper Brothers, a leading firm of accountants; Dr Richard Beeching, Technical Director of I.C.I.; Matthew Stevenson, Under-Secretary at the Treasury; and David Serpell, Deputy-Secretary, Ministry of Transport. The Group had been assembled by

Marples and Lord Mills, the Paymaster-General, with the aim of creating a small and cohesive body of businessmen who had been successful in the private sector and were experienced in organisation matters, but who had some knowledge of nationalised industry. Stedeford had been a member of the Committee of Enquiry into the B.B.C. in 1949–50, and had completed a five-year appointment to the U.K. Atomic Energy Authority in 1959. Here he had met Frank Kearton, who joined the Authority in 1955. Benson had been Deputy-chairman of the Fleck Committee of 1953–5, which had reported on the organisation of the coal industry, and made a notable contribution to its work. The choice of a technical member proved to be more difficult, but Beeching had impressed Mills with his reorganisation of I.C.I. Metals (he had become Chairman of the Metals Division in 1955). The intention was that the Group should formulate the general organisational strategy for the B.T.C. As Marples explained,

The task of the advisory body will be to examine the structure, finance and working of the organisations at present controlled by the Commission and to advise the Minister of Transport and the British Transport Commission, as a matter of urgency, how effect can best be given to the Government's intentions as indicated in the Prime Minister's statement.

John Hay, one of Marples's Parliamentary Secretaries, pointed out that the Group's members all had 'extensive and detailed knowledge of the problems of organisation and management of large-scale business in modern, twentieth-century conditions . . . The problem with which the group has to deal is a problem of organisation.'[5]

The appointment of the Group riled the Labour Opposition. In a Commons debate in April 1960 Alfred Robens and Wedgwood Benn found it easy enough to expose some of the inconsistencies in the government's prescription for transport. Effective points were scored with the observations that the Group was narrowly-based, lacking both Commission and union representatives; that it was needlessly duplicating the existing representation of businessmen on the Commission and its Area Boards; that although the Group's remit was intended to be broad and flexible, it was effectively limited by Macmillan's precise statement of 10 March; that its deliberations were to be kept secret; and that the government, having previously supported the Commission's existing decentralisation scheme, now proposed to replace it with something else. A great many M.P.s agreed with Robens when he remarked: 'I wonder whether these four businessmen realise that they may well have been brought in to be the handmaidens of Government policy.'[6] Penetrating though these comments may have been, they failed to note the fundamental difference in approach between those who, like Macmillan and Marples (and presumably the Cabinet), believed that the pressing need was to get the organisation right and those who considered that the real priority was to establish adequate management targets for nationalised industry. The Stedeford Advisory Group was born out of the former initiative as the government began to take a new, hard look at performance in the public sector. But the difficulties in accommodating two distinct strategies were soon revealed when, only four months after Macmillan's Commons statement had isolated organisational change as a major issue, the Select Committee concluded its deliberations with a quite different emphasis.

The Stedeford Group soon found itself split by this issue of priorities. When it first assembled, on 12 April, Stedeford reminded the members that decentralisation 'was an essential point in the Terms of Reference' and he placed it at the top of his list of subject headings. As a consequence, the early interviews with members of the Commission, senior railway managers and representatives from the railway trade unions tended to focus on the existing organisation and its defects. After only a few meetings, however, it became clear that an alternative approach was feasible, and the Group quickly divided itself into two rival factions, with Stedeford and Kearton on one side, and Beeching and Benson on the other. Here, disagreement was heightened by the clash between Stedeford's intuitive approach to problem-solving and Beeching's firm emphasis on the value of detailed analysis. Thus, Stedeford had sketched out his ideas for a new organisation as early as 20 April, and encouraged Benson to produce a paper on 'Basic Organisation'. Beeching, on the other hand, at a meeting on 29 April, argued that recommendations on organisation could only be made after the Group had acquired 'a close understanding of the basic economics of railway operation in order to assess the future place of the railways in the country's transport system' and had interviewed railwaymen at comparatively low levels in the hierarchy. Although Stedeford argued strongly against Beeching's view, pointing out that the Group was neither competent nor had the time to produce what was envisaged, even he had to accept the force of his opponent's logic, a logic which gathered strength as the financial plight of the Commission was revealed to the Group. On 11 May Beeching presented a paper on the 'Interpretation of the Terms of Reference', which placed organisational changes fourth in a list of priorities, behind: (1) the size and pattern of the railway system; (2) the general soundness of the modernisation proposals; and (3) the changes necessary in the Commission's financial structure.[7]

Stedeford, who had been briefed by the Ministry on the government's thinking in relation to the reorganisation of the B.T.C., was anxious to resolve the issue, and he persisted in his opposition to Beeching's more ambitious plans. He asked the Treasury's representative, Matthew Stevenson, to prepare a short note on the basic elements of organisational change, and this was also considered by the Group on 11 May. Stevenson, who with David Serpell, had been given a watching brief on the Group's deliberations, pointed out that any solution would have to accommodate two potentially conflicting requirements from the Ministry of Transport and the Treasury. Marples, in a document sent to members with the terms of reference, had declared in favour of reconstituting the Commission as a holding company, to be renamed the British Transport Council, and reorganising the separate activities of the Commission as fully self-acounting units 'on a *Limited Company* pattern'. On the other hand, Heathcoat Amory, the Chancellor, told Marples, in a letter passed on to the Group, that any new organisational and accounting arrangements should continue to allow the government to offer financial assistance to nationalised transport in aggregate rather than to its individual parts. There was a danger, said Stevenson, that the creation of a superior body to meet the Chancellor's wishes could thwart the Minister of Transport's intention to increase the degree of decentralisation in railway management. A week later, Stedeford produced an outline scheme which he hoped would eventually lead to a solution to the problem. He visualised a three-tier organisation comprising: six Regional Railway Boards with managerial functions; a Central Railway Board with 'overall executive responsibility'; and a superior body, the British Transport Council, with presiding powers, at the top. As the minutes record, 'some doubts were expressed about the need for the Transport Council', but further discussion was halted while the Group concentrated its attention upon the control and curtailment of the Modernisation Plan (see above, pp. 302–3). It was this subject which consumed most of the Group's time over the next three months.[8]

When the Advisory Group returned to the subject of organisation in August, the Beeching/Benson v. Stedeford/Kearton alignment was a firm fixture. The later proceedings, as one participant has recalled, became 'really a tussle of wills between Beeching and Stedeford . . . and without any doubt Beeching won the argument'. In fact, both sides stuck rigidly to the broad positions they had reached in the early stages of debate. There was a consensus of opinion that both the Commission and the Area Boards should be abolished, and that the Commission should be replaced by a 'superior body' to 'exercise a general surveillance' over nationalised transport. But when the Group examined two weighty memoranda on organisation from Stedeford and Beeching, two fundamental areas of disagreement were revealed. The first concerned the powers of the 'superior body', the second the extent of the decentralisation to the railway regions. Stedeford retained his preference for a superior body with important direct powers, particularly in relation to investment and finance, and wanted the maximum amount of decentralisation of authority to Regional Railway Boards. He therefore suggested that the Regional Board chairmen and the managing directors (initially the former General Managers) should also sit on a Central Railway Board, assisted by a few functional directors. Beeching and Benson, on the other hand, wanted a stronger Central Railway Board with functional responsibilities. Its membership, they contended, should be limited to professional railwaymen serving full time, reinforced by a part-time element. The regional chairmen and managing directors would be excluded: they could not do two jobs. Beeching claimed that 'in a very real sense the proposed British Railways Board may be regarded as a successor to the Transport Commission'. Since there was agreement that most of the non-railway activities of the Commission should be separately constituted, the only practical role for the 'superior body' was a purely advisory one. These conflicting prescriptions were merely extensions of the options which had been outlined by Stedeford in April and then by Benson and Stevenson and had resurfaced intermittently thereafter.[9]

The next six weeks were spent in trying to find a way out of this impasse. Although Beeching and Benson raised considerable doubts about the effectiveness of the Stedeford scheme of holding company and powerful regional boards in relation to the management of the railways as a whole, the Group's Chairman could not be argued out of his view. He also continued to enjoy the support of Kearton, in spite of the fact that the latter, having found the Group's preoccupation with detail frustrating, had largely lost interest in its deliberations. Beeching was clearly disconcerted by Stedeford's stubbornness. 'You could argue him to a standstill now,' he recalled, 'and the next time you met he would start precisely where he started before, totally ignoring any argument, any yielding that had occurred under pressure of argument on previous occasions. So we all came back to square nought every time we met, and this made it very, very tedious.'[10] In fact, Stedeford's refusal to budge may have arisen not only from an anxiety to implement Marples's ideas about decentralisation, but also from a loyalty to Robertson, with whom he had built up a considerable rapport. As early as 14 April Robertson had told the Group that the Commission was 'broadly in harmony with the Government's intentions', and his private note to Stedeford of 10 June indicates that the two men had come to an informal understanding that the conversion of the Commission into a loose holding company, along the lines established by the Electricity Council in 1958, might serve the Minister's purpose.[11] A final attempt to break the deadlock was made in September when, at Serpell's suggestion, it was agreed that the two civil servants should try to produce a single paper encompassing the two positions. Their efforts to synthesise the arguments resulted in a document which leaned very much Beeching's way, and Stedeford refused to let it be used as the basis of a recommendation to the Minister. It was eventually decided, at the Group's last meeting on 3 October, that Marples should be given the advantage of receiving a 'unanimous' recommendation. The Group's advice for the Minister was contained in a series of Recommendations, numbered 1–8. So the final one, No. 8, included two policy options for the railways, 'Scheme A' from Stedeford and Kearton, and 'Scheme B' from Beeching and Benson. This was sent to the Minister with supporting papers on 7 October.[12] The two options are outlined in Charts VII and VIII.

Despite the ambivalence of Recommendation No. 8, the Group was unanimous in holding that the Commission should be fundamentally reorganised. Earlier Recommendations had suggested: that a financial reconstruction was imperative, including the writing-off of the railways' accumulated deficits and capital losses (No. 4); that manpower should be substantially reduced, charges raised, capital investment subjected to closer scrutiny and a vigorous attack made on unremunerative lines and services (No. 5); and that the remaining statutory obligations and restrictions on railway operating be removed, including the restrictions on the Commission's powers to develop land and property (No. 6). But the organisational proposals, along with the disagreement over the handling of the Modernisation Plan and, in particular, the Euston Electrification Scheme revealed sharp differences within the Advisory Group which scarcely helped the Minister to proceed to a straightforward solution to the Commission's difficulties. Stedeford's holding company, the 'British Transport Corporation', contrasted with Beeching's advisory 'British Transport Council'. Stedeford saw the new British Railways Board as an 'intermediate' body dominated by regional representatives (although he dropped his earlier idea of full membership for Regional Board chairmen), while Beeching regarded it as very much the dominant element in railway management, and to that end recommended that Regional Board members be specifically excluded from it. For Stedeford, the Regional Railway Boards were to be incorporated by statute and to have 'the maximum degree of autonomy'; for Beeching, they were merely the executive arm of the Central Board. The two schemes also differed in their prescriptions for London Transport, the docks, inland waterways, the railway workshops and the management of the Commission's property interests.[13]

SCHEME 'A'
(Stedeford/Kearton)

1. 'Superior Body'

> BRITISH TRANSPORT CORPORATION
> 6–12 Governors, part-time with a full-time
> Chairman and Financial Governor. Apptd
> by Minister. A holding co. but without
> over-riding authority. Advisory to both
> Minister and 'Constituent Bodies', esp.
> re. appointments, investment, organisation.
> Served by a Central Staff of functional
> officers.

2. 'Intermediate Bodies'

> BRITISH RAILWAYS BOARD
> Preferably 11 full-time members, apptd
> by the Minister, including the Managing
> Directors of each region and some
> functional directors (Regional Board
> Chairman free to attend). A full-time
> Chairman independent of regions.
> To ensure railways are run as an
> effective entity, to co-ordinate
> regions; responsibility for overall
> financial performance and for matters
> best dealt with centrally, e.g. wages,
> rolling stock, safety.

> CO-ORDINATION COUNCIL
> To resolve disputes between
> 'Constituent Bodies'

3. 'Constituent Bodies'

1	Southern Region
2	Western Region
3	London Midland Region
4	North Eastern Region
5	Eastern Region
6	Scottish Region

Railway regions grouped under British Railways Board

Each incorporated and given maximum degree of autonomy. Each with Executive Board of part-time Chairman, apptd by the Minister, and full-time Executive Directors (including a Managing Director) apptd by the Constituent.

7	London Transport
8	British Road Services
9	Tilling Buses
10	Scottish Buses
11	Hotels (excluding Rly Catering)
12	Docks
13	Thomas Cook
14	Property Co.

Each incorporated. Board with Chairman and part-time Directors apptd by the Minister and full-time Executive Directors apptd by the Constituent.

Source: S.A.G. Recommendation No. 8, 11 October 1960, Beeching Papers, Box 8, B.R.B.

Chart VII Stedeford Advisory Group: alternative recommendations on organisation, October 1960

SCHEME 'B'
(Beeching/Benson)

TRANSPORT COUNCIL
8–12 members, mainly part-time.
Apptd by the Minister. Advisory
– no executive or administrative
authority.

BRITISH RAILWAYS[a]

LONDON TRANSPORT
BRITISH ROAD SERVICES
ROAD PASSENGER TRANSPORT
DOCKS
INLAND WATERWAYS
ROAD FREIGHT SHIPPING
THOMAS COOK

Each unit incorporated, financially
autonomous and directly responsible to
the Minister.

[a] Railways to be one business with assests
vested in a *British Railways Board* of
10 full-time and 4 part-time members
apptd by the Minister. All except Chairman
and Deputy-Chairman to have functional
responsibilities.

To determine general policy, administer
central functions, supervise Regional Boards
and retain control over matters of concern
to railways as a whole, e.g. investment,
budgets, labour relations, rates and fares.

Managerial responsibility for most functions
delegated to Regional Boards, each with a
part-time Charman and 6–8 full-time
executive members. None would sit on the
British Railways Board.

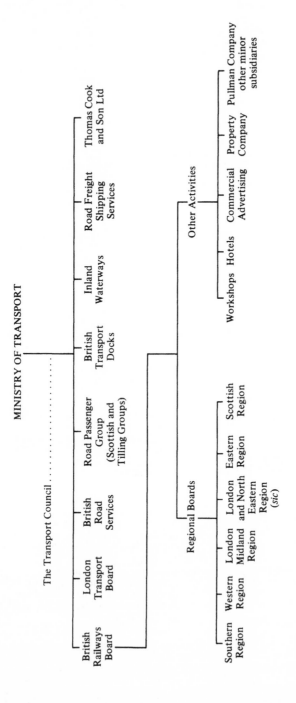

MINISTRY OF TRANSPORT

The Transport Council ....

British Railways Board

London Transport Board

British Road Services

Road Passenger Group (Scottish and Tilling Groups)

British Transport Docks

Inland Waterways

Road Freight Shipping Services

Thomas Cook and Son Ltd

Regional Boards

Southern Region

Western Region

London Midland Region

London and North Eastern Region (sic)

Eastern Region

Scottish Region

Other Activities

Workshops

Hotels

Commercial Advertising

Property Company

Pullman Company other minor subsidiaries

Functions under the Regional Boards:

(a) Ships
(b) Packet Ports
(c) Restaurant Cars and Catering Services

Chart VIII The Scheme B organisation

II

The indecisiveness of the Group's Recommendation No. 8 did nothing to relieve the uncertainty as to the future amongst the ranks of the B.T.C. As in 1951–4, this made it difficult for members and senior railway managers to concentrate properly on day-to-day administration. Indeed, the Commission had been distracted by the Advisory Group from the start. In March 1960, while it still remained a possibility that Marples would include a Commission representative as a Group member, Robertson and his colleagues had put a considerable effort into planning their own solution to the organisation problem. Robertson, who was prepared to accept the Commission's relegation to holding-company status, had by early April developed a response based largely on the Electricity Act of 1957, and this strategy, as already noted, was offered to Stedeford in more complete form in June. The arrival of Recommendation No. 8 brought dismay at the sight of the Advisory Group pointing in two quite different directions, with Beeching's formula threatening to spell the end of the existing Commission in any meaningful sense.[14]

Robertson, having sought the views of his colleagues before discussing the recommendation with the Minister, found a majority totally hostile to the Advisory Group's findings. The Chairmen of the Area Boards, in particular, resented the proposals in both Schemes to replace their part-time Boards with Boards dominated by full-time executive directors. The reaction of T. H. Summerson, Chairman of the North Eastern Board was particularly pungent and is worth quoting in extenso:

I am strongly of the opinion that we should not 'accept' Recommendation No. 8. It is based on faulty premises; much of the argument is superficial and gives the impression that it has not really been thought out; and several of the most important recommendations themselves run directly counter to the teachings of experience, if not almost to commonsense.

Contrary to what we were given to understand, the membership of the Advisory Group, with the sole exception of their Chairman, did not match up to the importance and scope of their subject. How he, the Chairman, came to sign this Recommendation, I am at a loss to understand. . .

I am convinced that if the greater part of Recommendation No. 8, involving either of the two alternative Schemes, were put into effect, it would very seriously prejudice the future of the railway industry. For that reason, I think that it is the Commission's duty to try to do their best to discredit it by informed argument. . . I therefore counsel that we content ourselves, in the first place, with preparing a documented criticism of Recommendation No. 8, while adding an undertaking to submit our considered views as to the reorganisation which the Government might adopt . . .

As to Schemes A and B, the functional Regional Board that is proposed would not be a Board at all, merely a Management Committee; they would not get 'eminent men' to serve on the purely advisory type of Transport Council which is proposed under Scheme B; they would not get Regional Chairmen worthy of appointment to accept office under either set of rules; the proposed reduction in the number of part-time members on the Regional Boards would gratuitously jettison half the advantages, political, commercial and public relations, of these appointments. Either Scheme would fall short of the present arrangements, which work quite well and have recently been approved by an intelligent and probing Select Committee.[15]

There were a few dissentients from this hostility, including Sir Leonard Sinclair, who had attacked the Area Boards in his evidence before the Group, and John Ratter, who was quite happy with the proposal to introduce a professional executive core at regional level. In addition, H. P. Barker was characteristically maverick in expressing enthusiasm for the idea of a strong central railway board which, he felt, would bring with it all the strengths of the pre-1953 Railway Executive.[16] But on the whole, the Commission shared Summerson's position, and when Robertson saw Marples on 11 November 1960, he informed the Minister that the Commission was opposed to both Scheme A and Scheme B.

In the horse-trading which followed, Robertson told Marples that the Commission completely rejected Beeching's Scheme B, since it not only threatened to remove all traces of co-ordination between the constituents of nationalised transport but was also at odds with the decentralisation aims of the Transport Act of 1953 and Macmillan's statement of March 1960. On the other hand, Robertson suggested that the Commission might be able to live with Stedeford's Scheme A, provided that a number of alterations were introduced. He accepted that the idea of a British Transport Corporation was workable, as it was 'not suitable for a Ministry to exercise direct control of commercial organisations, especially when they are in constant and direct competition with private enterprise'. But the Commission felt it unwise to make a statutory stipulation that there should be a full-time financial member of a mainly part-time body, and suggested that co-ordination was best left to the proposed Corporation rather than to a separate Co-ordination Council. While happy with the 'general concept of a British Railways Board', Robertson emphasised that the Regional Board chairmen, *not* the managing directors, should be formal members of it, and he dismissed the notion of incorporating the railway regions as creating a fiction. It was also considered a mistake to rule out the appointment of part-time directors, both for the Central Board and the Regional Boards.[17] Marples seems not to have been anxious to co-operate with Robertson in framing alternative proposals which would leave open the possibility of reconstituting the existing Commission in another guise. Whether his prime objective was to press ahead with the government's organisational solution for the railways' financial difficulties, or whether he had decided that the important thing was to get rid of Robertson, as has been alleged, is not clear. But it is evident that the Ministry and the Cabinet, in preparing the White Paper, *Reorganisation of the Nationalised Transport Undertakings* which appeared in December 1960, took no more account of railway opinion than it had in 1952, when preparing the ground for the Transport Act of 1953.

The preamble to this White Paper stated that the government had taken into full account the views of the B.T.C. and the trade unions. But by accepting in large measure the Scheme B devised by Beeching and Benson, it ran into direct conflict with the views expressed by Robertson and his colleagues in the November discussions. Chart IX outlines the government's organisational proposals, which were very similar to those in Scheme B (Chart VIII). The only fundamental change was the grouping of the smaller constituent activities, such as British Road Services and the bus companies, under a Holding Company, which was also given the task of running the railway hotels (a responsibility taken from the British Railways Board as in Scheme B). In matters of detail the government did demonstrate that they had accepted the force of some of Robertson's arguments. In order to make the concept of a Nationalised Transport Advisory Council work, its membership was to consist of the chairmen of the new Boards – British Railways, London Transport, Docks, Inland Waterways and the Holding Company – and the Council was given the specific duty of co-ordinating transport services.* The White Paper also refrained from specifying in detail the particular duties of members of the British Railways Board and retained the idea of part-time members for both the Board and its Regional Boards. These points had been raised by the Commission in its objections to Recommendation No. 8. However, the government did nothing to ease one of the Commission's more important fears, that of Ministerial interference in the working of the new organisation. Its qualms were not really answered by a document which proposed to give both the Minister and the British Railways Board control over finance and investment.[18]

The government's proposals ran into a barrage of criticism. All sections of the press condemned its lack of clarity in relation to the future size of the railways system and the position of uneconomic services, the modernisation programme and the functions of the new Boards. It was pointed out that the organisational package ran counter to the government's promise to introduce a substantial measure of decentralisation. The unions deplored the removal of the last vestiges of the concept of transport

---

* The N.T.A.C. proved to be a very limited body. It met only five times between 27 May 1963 and 16 March 1965, and did little to further the cause of co-ordination. See M.T. files, RA 12/91/01 and 02, D.O.E.

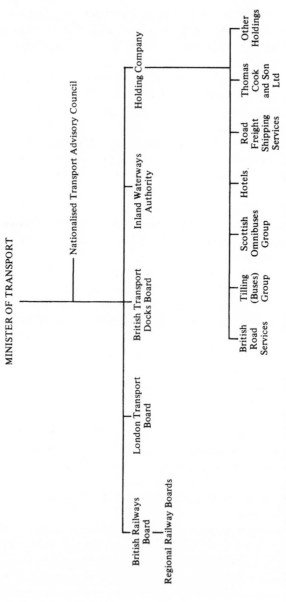

Chart IX Reorganisation of nationalised transport: White Paper, December 1960

integration established by the Transport Act of 1947, and the 'hiving off' of the profitable sectors of nationalised transport, albeit under a publicly owned holding company. The *Manchester Guardian* spoke for frustrated railway managers when it pointed out that the new organisation looked 'suspiciously like the structure before the 1953 Act'. Its labour correspondent, John Cole, explained that 'what railway officials fear above all else is that the White Paper will usher in another long "interim" period. They complain that the politicians have made their lives one long "interim", and that they must, some day, be left alone to run their railways under a clearly defined set of rules.'[19]

There was no prospect of relief on that score. Indeed, the White Paper heralded another vexatious, even comical interlude in the history of nationalised railways. The discredited B.T.C., condemned to death, was required to work closely with its political masters in helping to frame the details of legislation designed to effect its demise. Robertson had given an undertaking that the Commission would assist the government in implementing the necessary changes, and at the request of the Ministry of Transport two joint informal bodies began to operate from February 1961. The first was a working party of officials led by an Under-Secretary, on which the Commission was represented by the Assistant Secretary-General, an Assistant Chief Solicitor and the Director of Budgets. The second operated at a higher level as a Steering Committee. David Serpell, Deputy-Secretary at Transport, was the Chairman, and the Commission was represented by the Secretary-General, Wansbrough-Jones, the Chief Solicitor and Legal Adviser, Gilmour, and the Financial Adviser, Osborn. Working under the acronym RENT (Re-organisation of Nationalised Transport) the two groups put in a considerable effort in preparing the ground for the Transport Act of 1962. The exercise was a wide-ranging one, taking in all aspects of nationalised transport, including the Minister's powers, the removal of statutory controls on the railways, finance and the composition of the new Boards. It is quite clear from the Commission's internal records that this co-operation with the Ministry placed the railway officers concerned in a somewhat ambiguous position *vis-à-vis* their masters, the members of the Commission, who were not informed about the deliberations.[20]

Robertson had also promised Marples, as he revealed in a press statement in December 1960, that the Commission would co-operate with the Minister in order that 'the men who are to occupy the key positions in the new organisation are given the status, authority and machinery necessary to enable them to exercise the responsibilities of those positions as soon as possible'.[21] This introduced the rather bizarre prospect of the B.T.C.'s being required not only to preside over nationalised transport until the new Act came into force (in fact, for another two years to 1 January 1963), but also to bring in and control a 'shadow' railway management team designed to ease the problems of transfer. Under the existing legislation the new team would of course be subject to the over-riding authority of the institution it would ultimately replace. The idea appeared particularly ludicrous to such specialist commentators as the editor of the *Railway Gazette*. Having read in the White Paper that the government thought it important that 'the nationalised transport under-takings should produce their own leaders', he envisaged the Minister reaching down into the ranks of the existing senior railway managers to make up the new Board. The names of Ratter and Grand were mentioned as likely candidates for the post of Chairman, and since they were both full-time members of the Commission and members of the Railways Sub-Commission the probability of a confusion of roles was great.[22] In fact, the situation was eased when Marples dashed any hopes the Commission may have nursed of managerial continuity and, having chosen Beeching's 'Scheme B', asked its principal architect to implement it. On 15 March 1961 it was announced that Beeching would replace Robertson as Chair-man of the Commission on 1 June (he would serve in the meantime as a part-time member), and would lead the British Railways Board when it was established. It was Beeching rather than Robertson who worked with Marples in selecting a 'shadow' railway administration, and, as described below, they were very much concerned with bringing *new* managerial talent into the industry.

III

The appointment of Dr Richard Beeching came as something of a surprise. He had had little or no experience of transport, whether road or rail, before joining the Stedeford Advisory Group, and it took a fair amount of persuasion on Marples's part to arrange his secondment from I.C.I. In the end, Beeching agreed to a five-year period of office to 31 May 1966, although the formal documents provided for the termination of the appointment at any time. Marples also agreed to match Beeching's existing I.C.I. salary of £24,000 a year.[23] When the appointment was announced, both the Commons and the press focussed on this figure of £24,000. It was wholly exceptional for a leader of a nationalised industry, dwarfing the £10,000 paid to Robertson and the Chairmen of the Coal and Electricity Boards, and indeed public sector salaries as a whole (Marples, for example, was paid only £5,000 and his Permanent-Secretary Dunnett £7,000). The press also seized on the significance of that salary. It demonstrated clearly that private sector pay had outstripped that in the

Is there any secret understanding between Mr. Marples and Dr. Beeching about the railway policy Dr Beeching is to pursue?
—Mr. George Strauss (Lab. Vauxha'l)

8 The appointment of Dr Beeching as Chairman, B.R.B.: the reactions of Emmwood to Beeching's salary, *Daily Mail*, 22 March 1961.

public sector. *The Economist* produced data showing that 35 directors of I.C.I. and Shell shared £729,000 (exclusive of pension contributions), an average of £20,829 each. If non-geriatric managers were to be attracted into the railway industry, or other nationalised enterprises, then salaries and pensions required drastic revision. Furthermore, as *The Times* observed, Beeching's exceptional salary presaged an exceptional role. There is no doubt at all that Beeching was to be paid a great deal. Eleven years later, after a period of considerable inflation, Peter Parker was paid

" I MAY HAVE NO EXPERT KNOWLEDGE OF THE RAILWAYS, BUT I AM A
VERY PRACTICAL MAN — DR. BEECHING, MARCH 16. 1961.

9 The appointment of Dr Beeching as Chairman, B.R.B.: the promise of
rationalisation as seen by Vicky, *Evening Standard*, 23 June 1962.

only £23,538 as Chairman of the B.R.B., the equivalent of £6,573 in 1961
prices. The salary paid to Beeching was commensurate with the Minister's
expectation that he would shake up the railways. Robertson was retired
early in order to give way to someone who, unlike his predecessors, would
apply private sector strictures to public sector operations. The ink was still
wet on the government's White Paper on *The Financial and Economic
Obligations of the Nationalised Industries* which declared that managements should achieve a break-even position over a five-year period and
attain defined rates of return to investment. Beeching was appointed to
give effect to government intentions for its largest loss-maker by a Minister
bent on redirecting resources into road transport.[24]

Beeching, aged 47 in 1961, proved more than able to lead a managerial
revolution at 222, Marylebone Road. Born in 1913, the son of a journalist,
he was educated at Maidstone Grammar School, where a former school-
friend remembered him as a prefect and 'constructor of a telescope
contraption in wood and ply'.[25] A successful career as a scientist followed.
At Imperial College, London, Beeching took a First in physics and then a
doctorate for research into electrons. During the war he had been

seconded from Mond Nickel to work in armaments design for the Ministry of Supply, and he continued in peacetime as Deputy Chief Engineer of Armaments Design until he joined I.C.I. in 1948. A large, portly man with a small moustache, he presented an image of avuncular geniality. According to Anthony Sampson, with his 'slow gravelly voice' Beeching 'might be mistaken at first for one of those large phlegmatic men who tell long stories over a pint of beer in a country pub'.[26] But colleagues soon found that this persona belied the man. Beneath the lazy, reserved manner there was a quick, incisive mind and a positive enthusiasm for the exhaustive analysis of business problems. There was also a strong determination to cut through some of the bureaucratic formalities which railway management had gathered to itself from the nineteenth century, and which had been reinforced after nationalisation by the choice first of a former Permanent-Secretary and then of an army General as successive Chairmen.

Like Robertson before him Beeching came to the job with a reorganising mission, but there the resemblance ended. Beeching was no cool, austere presence with a faith in complex organisational chains. His attitude to the existing structure was quickly revealed when he showed his contempt for the co-ordinating bodies in Robertson's 1955 scheme – the General Staff and the eight Sub-Commissions – and set about streamlining work at headquarters. In his 18 months as Chairman of the Commission he did much to prepare the ground for the post-1962 organisation. The Sub-Commissions, which continued to meet, were largely disregarded until they were placed in 'abeyance' or formally dissolved.[27] Most of the major departments at H.Q. were reorganised, and in April 1962 a British Railways Committee was established as a shadow Railways Board. The new Chairman also made it clear from the start that he favoured the introduction of a comprehensive system of management development, i.e. the selection and training of staff for higher management, and in September 1961 new appraisals were made of the 400 senior officers with maximum salaries of £3,000 and above.[28] Nothing demonstrates Beeching's managerial style better than his dislike of Wansbrough-Jones's 'Grey Book', the organisational manual setting out structure and responsibilities. He showed such continuing dislike for it that at a B.T.C. meeting in the summer of 1962 he finally exclaimed 'Throw the damn thing out of the window! Chaps know what they are supposed to be doing – we don't need to have it all written down in a "Grey Book".'[29]

Beeching's appointment also had repercussions on the preparation of the Transport Bill by the RENT joint working parties. There were two important departures from the White Paper. First, Beeching intervened personally to keep the railway hotels within his sphere of influence. In June 1961 he told Marples that the shares in the proposed hotels company should be held by the Railways Board and not by the Holding Company, and this suggestion was accepted by the Ministry. Second, Beeching's aim of establishing a strong Board with functional duties led the bill's draftsmen to drop the White Paper's emphasis on decentralisation and regional autonomy.[30] This intention became clear when Marples, acting on Beeching's recommendations, appointed three new full-time members of the Commission, in place of Benstead, Sinclair and Grand.

The new men were all non-railwaymen, and they were required to undertake functional responsibilities both on the Commission and on the Railways Board when it was established. In September 1961 Leslie Harry Williams* joined the Commission as a commercial specialist, after a 30-year career with Shell, spent mainly in Africa and the Middle East. He had been Managing Director of Shell Chemicals from 1955 to 1960, and had had a brief spell with Shell International before retiring in June 1961 at the early age of 52. He was joined in October 1961 by Philip H. Shirley, an Australian accountant who was seconded from Unilever to act as finance member. Aged 49, he had worked for Peat Marwick Mitchell and for Rank before joining Unilever, where he had been quickly promoted, in 1952, to the post of Chief Accountant. From 1958 he had been Chairman of the Unilever subsidiary, Batchelor Foods. Shirley had been recommended to Beeching by his Stedeford Group associate, Henry Benson of Cooper Brothers. Benson considered him 'a good technician and full of thrust and drive' who 'might be useful to you bearing in mind the appalling weakness on the financial side'.[31] The third new face was that of Sir Steuart Mitchell, a war-time colleague of Beeching's at the Ministry of Supply. Born in 1902, Mitchell joined the Navy at the age of 14, and first went to Naval Ordnance in 1931 as Assistant Superintendent of Design. He met Beeching when he became Chief Engineer and Superintendent of the Armament Design Establishment in 1945. Subsequently Controller of the Royal Ordnance Factories (1956–9) and of Guided Weapons and Electronics, Ministry of Aviation (1959–62), Mitchell seemed to Beeching to be an ideal choice to direct the reorganisation of the railway workshops under centralised control. He joined the Commission on 1 February 1962. Beeching's enthusiasm for outsiders in railway administration was further demonstrated when he selected Sir Philip Warter, a part-time member, to succeed Benstead as his Deputy-Chairman on 1 October 1961. He also chose a number of non-railwaymen to run Railway Sites Ltd, a subsidiary set up in September 1961 to develop the Commission's property interests.[32] Once again, salary levels were comparatively high for the Commission newcomers. Shirley was to be paid £12,000 in order to match his pay and conditions at Unilever, and although the salaries of Williams (£7,500),

* Not to be confused with Leslie *Henry* Williams, Deputy-Chairman of I.C.I., 1960–7.

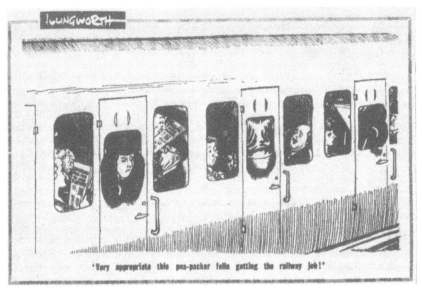

'Very appropriate this pea-packer fella getting the railway job!'

10 The appointment of Philip Shirley, Chairman of Batchelor Foods, frozen pea manufacturers, to B.R.B. in October 1961: Illingworth, *Daily Mail*, 18 August 1961.

Mitchell (£8,000) and Warter (£6,000) were lower, they retained external benefits either in the form of pensions or, in Warter's case, as Chairman of the cinema chain, A.B.C. Beeching and the government were stressing again that this was the way to obtain men of calibre, or, as *The Financial Times* expressed it, 'The Men To Put the Railways Right'.[33]

The new members were soon required to make a positive contribution. The B.T.C.'s records reveal that they were given the task of pursuing economies and improving the running of departments. There was no set formula: some departments were divided into more effective units, others were amalgamated. Sometimes, it was merely a question of putting new men into redesignated posts. Shirley, for example, took the lead in remodelling both the Finance Department and that of Supplies and Contracts. For finance, this involved the creation in April 1962 of a financial management services section, led by a chief officer, P. G. James, formerly the Chief Accountant, and the establishment in June of the posts of Management Accountant and Administration Accountant. Shirley firmly believed that the pursuit of regional accounting was futile: his aim was to strengthen the central direction of O. & M., management accounting and cost-consciousness throughout British Railways. Supplies and contracts were tackled in a similar manner. Having secured the merger of the two departments, Shirley commissioned a study of the railways' purchasing and stores control methods by an outside expert, from Woolworths, whose report was used to justify the complete centralisation of purchasing, leaving the regions to concentrate on the monitoring of stock levels.[34]

The Commission also took steps to consolidate its work on investment programmes and project development; in the commercial sphere, S. C. Robbins, the Chief Contracts Officer, was transferred to the commercial department as Chief Development Officer: and a number of senior marketing directorships were established. Operational research was also given further encouragement. The atmosphere at Marylebone Road was intense. Shirley and Williams were instructed, in October 1961, to investigate the broad problem of clerical costs. The existing administrative, clerical and technical staff numbered nearly 75,000, and it was felt that there was a 'high potential for economy'. Their report of May 1962 must have sent a shudder down more than a few spines. A strong case was made for cuts in staffing levels, to be achieved partly by centralising routine work, and partly by eliminating 'cumbersome relics' of clerical procedure. The report also contained the ominous comment that 'management may not be giving the same amount of thought to the higher levels in their organisation. Parkinson's Law works at all levels and not only in the clerical grades.' Reviews of both regional and headquarters staffing followed.[35] Everywhere, the complexity of the organisation was challenged. As in the private sector, so in railways numerous administrative bodies were proving ripe for removal. In December 1961 Shirley turned his attention to the need to reduce the multiplicity of committees, advisory panels, councils and conferences with which the Commission and the regions were beset. He uncovered an astonishing number of such bodies – a 'review' in 1958 had still left over 200 on the books – and emphasised the consequent drain on regional staff time. Ness, the General Manager of the Scottish Region, had told him that 'no less than ninety first class sleeper berths are occupied each week in each direction for Scottish representatives attending meetings in London'. Wansbrough-Jones set about pruning the number of committees in January 1962, and further action was taken by the Commission in the summer. But the problem was clearly a deep-seated one.[36]

Few activities were left unscathed. Preparations were made to split up the common legal service, and to create a road motor division to control the railways' collection and delivery vehicles. Commercial advertising was passed to a limited company, British Transport Advertising, which was incorporated in November 1961. One of the more significant changes involved the Manpower Department. In July 1962 it was divided into two main sections: Industrial Relations, under C. S. McLeod who became

Chief Industrial Relations Officer; and Management Staff, where J. E. M. Roberts was appointed to the new post of Chief Management Staff Officer. The improvement of managerial performance by education and training and better selection methods, and a more effective labour relations organisation, were key elements in Beeching's strategy for reshaping the railways.[37]

Further action was encouraged by the establishment, on functional lines, of the shadow Board, the British Railways Committee, in April 1962. Marples had been rather slow to commit himself on this matter, since he was worried that Beeching's appointments might compromise his own promise to the Commons Standing Committee that trade unionists would be kept in mind when selecting Board members and that nationalised transport undertakings would select their own leaders. Discussions stretched from November 1961 to February 1962, before Beeching was able to convince the Minister that it was important to remove the anxiety of Commission members as to their future. A 16-strong committee was then assembled. It included: Beeching and his appointees, Warter (Deputy-Chairman), Williams (Commercial Activities), Shirley (Finance) and Mitchell (Workshops); the six Area Board Chairmen, Wilson (London Midland), Russell (Eastern), MacNaughton Sidey (Southern), Hanks (Western), Summerson (North Eastern) and Cameron of Lochiel (Scottish); and two part-time members, Barker and Donachy. There were places for only three railwaymen, Ratter (Technical), who was already a member of the Commission, Dunbar, the Manpower Adviser (Manpower), and Margetts (Operating and Planning). Margetts was the only new face at headquarters. Appointed General Manager of the North Eastern Region in September 1961, he had impressed Beeching at the Officers' Conference at Balliol in 1961 and on the Chairman's subsequent visits to the North-East.[38]

In the six months of its life, May–November 1962, the British Railways Committee was concerned mainly with the nuts and bolts of railway administration. Some hardy perennials were subjected to firmer policy initiatives, including line closures, station amenities, single-manning, the poor utilisation of diesel locomotives and the excessive size of the wagon fleet. But the Committee also handled some organisational issues, as the functional members flexed their muscles. In July it processed Mitchell's plan for the railway workshops and Ratter's accompanying revision of the duties of the regional engineering departments. A Main Workshops Committee and an H.Q. Division were established to give effect to Mitchell's programme of rationalisation, and the regional Chief Mechanical and Electrical Engineers were given full responsibility for the running and maintenance functions. The Committee also gave further impetus to the traffic studies which Beeching had encouraged to provide the data base for his 1963 report, *The Reshaping of British Railways.*[39]

IV

The Transport Act of 1962, which was given the Royal Assent on 1 August, swept away the remaining traces of the integration or co-ordination strategy of 1947. The B.T.C. was broken up into five separate bodies. The railways' debt burden was eased, and commercial freedom was emphasised with the removal of most of the constraints relating to pricing, facilities and the exploitation of assets (property, pipelines, and the like). Organisations were encouraged which, it was hoped, would be appropriate to the self-contained search by each undertaking for a break-even position within five years. Macmillan's commitment to decentralisation found expression in the establishment of Railway Regional Boards but, as already observed, railways emerged as a separately defined business with a strong central direction, in very much the way Beeching and Benson had envisaged in 1960.

The reorganisation of 1962–3 did, however, necessitate some changes of personnel as the British Railways Committee became the British Railways Board. In September 1962 two members, Warter and Wilson, were appointed to the Transport Holding Company as its Chairman and Deputy-Chairman and Managing Director respectively. Then two of the old Area Board chairmen decided to retire – Hanks (Western), at the end of 1962, and Summerson (North Eastern), ten months later. Both had expressed some disquiet at the course of events following the Stedeford Group recommendations. Summerson, in particular, was disappointed that Beeching and Shirley had flatly rejected his Board's policy initiative of July 1961, in which it was argued that the break-even objective for the railways was unrealistic, and that the government should be asked instead to provide financial help to subsidise railway services. Shirley's response was crisp and clear:

I do not believe frankly that the Railways are yet in a position at which they can fairly ask for legislation in their aid for, to my mind, they have not yet done nearly enough of the things which are in their own power to do . . . The Railways have continued, long beyond the point of proved social or economic need, to operate a great many services which are no longer required . . . I would be more sympathetic to the thoughts your Board express if I started from the point of believing that we have done everything we could have been reasonably expected to do on our own behalf.

Summerson clearly found the new approach uncongenial.[40] As for the rest of the Commission there was room for everyone except Valentine, who had not been a member of the shadow Committee. He remained at the head of London Transport, with the Executive's conversion to a Board.

Although there was no need to replace the men who had departed, since the 1962 Act allowed for a membership of 12–19, three further appointments were made. The first, in December 1962, brought a second trade unionist onto the Board as a part-time member. Frederick Hayday, of the National Union of General and Municipal Workers, was a life-long trade union official with a considerable experience of national negotiating. A member of the T.U.C. General Council since 1950 – he acted as Chairman in 1962–3 – Hayday's appointment served both to strengthen the Board's industrial relations expertise and to satisfy those critics who had asked Marples to increase trade union representation. Hayday was followed by two railway officers, Raymond and Ness, who took up full-time appointment on 1 October 1963. Stanley Raymond had been recommended to Beeching by Robertson as a coming man. A former Dr Barnardo's boy, he had joined the railways via London Transport and road haulage, and was not tarred with the operating brush of the archetypal railway manager. After a spell in the Scottish Region he came to headquarters in July 1961 as Traffic Adviser, and quickly gave impetus to the traffic studies which were to be central to Beeching's *Reshaping* strategy. Then in January 1962 he was sent to Paddington as General Manager with an instruction to flush out the old guard, and there he enjoyed a considerable measure of success. Ambitious, energetic, blunt and even aggressive he seemed the ideal personality to break down the old attitudes to the running of the railways. He was appointed to take on the passenger and organisational aspects of the commercial function, leaving Williams free to concentrate on freight. The choice of James Ness was more puzzling. Nearing the end of his career – he was 60 – he had been General Manager of the Scottish Region since 1955, and there is no evidence to suggest that he had been involved in any radical initiatives during the Robertson regime. He was also a rather paranoid character who frequently clashed with colleagues. But he was obviously a Beeching man, another railwayman who could be trusted to carry out the 'new policy'. He was brought on to the Board to assume responsibility for the planning function, hitherto part of Margetts's brief, and was to give much of his time to the preparation of plans for the future rail network and the improvement of 'Freightliner' design.[41] With Mitchell taking Warter's place as Vice-Chairman, Beeching's 15-strong Board assumed its final shape in October 1963, ten months after the first meeting on 6 December 1962 (see Table 40 and Chart X).

It has been generally agreed by informed commentators that the arrival of Beeching helped to shake up the railway industry, but many doubts have been expressed about the competence of his Board. There is a consensus of opinion among those associated with the Beeching period that he was a

Table 40. *The British Railways Board, 1 November 1963*

Name	Date of appointment	Age on 1 November 1963	Education	Previous post	Experience	Left B.R.B.
Full-time members (salary: Chairman £24,000, Vice-Chairman £8,000, Shirley £12,000, others £7,500)						
Dr Richard Beeching (Chairman)	1962 (1961)[a]	50	Maidstone Grammar School; Imperial College, London	Technical Director, I.C.I.	Ministry of Supply; Chemicals	May 1965
Sir Steuart Mitchell, K.B.E., C.B. (Vice-Chairman)	1962	61	Edinburgh Academy; R.N. Colleges, Osborne and Dartmouth	Controller of Guided Weapons and Electronics, Ministry of Aviation	Royal Navy; Ministry of Supply; Royal Ordnance Factories	July 1964
Maj. Gen. G. N. Russell, C.B. C.B.E.	1962 (1959)[a]	64	Rugby; Royal Military Academy, Woolwich	General Manager, British Road Services, and member, Eastern Area Board, B.T.C.	Army; B.T.C.	Sept. 1968
Philip Shirley	1962 (1961)[a]	51	Sydney C. of E. Grammar School	Chairman, Batchelor Foods	Accountancy (Peat Marwick, Rank, Unilever)	Dec. 1968
L. H. Williams	1962 (1961)[a]	54	Portsmouth Grammar School; Jesus College, Cambridge	Director, Shell International	Oil (Shell)	Aug. 1966
A. R. Dunbar, O.B.E.	1962	59	Whitehill School, Glasgow	Manpower Adviser, B.T.C.	Railways	Jan. 1968

Name	Year	Age	Education	Position	Field	Date
John Ratter, C.B.E.	1962 (1958)[a]	55	St Peter's York; Durham University	Technical Adviser, B.T.C.	Railways	March 1970
F. C. Margetts, M.B.E.	1962	57	Driffield Grammar School, St Martin's, Scarborough Grammar School	General Manager, N.E.R.	Railways	Jan. 1968
S. E. Raymond	1963	50	'Grammar School in Middlesex'	General Manager, W.R.	Civil Service; L.T.; B.T.C.; Railways	Dec. 1967
J. Ness	1963	60	No information	General Manager, Sc.R.	Railways	Jan. 1966
Part-time members (salary: £1,000):						
H. P. Barker	1962 (1951)[a]	54	Oundle	—	Engineering	Dec. 1967
Lt-Col Donald Cameron of Lochiel	1962 (1954)[a]	53	Harrow; Balliol College, Oxford	—	Army/Scotland	Sept. 1964
F. Donachy, C.B.E.	1962 (1959)[a]	64	Elementary Schools (Glasgow, Edinburgh)	—	Trade unions (N.U.R.)	Dec. 1967
F. Hayday, C.B.E.	1962	51	No information	—	Trade unions (General and Municipal Workers' Union)	Dec. 1975
J. MacNaughton Sidey, D.S.O.	1962	49	Exeter School	—	Shipping (P. & O.)	Dec. 1968

[a] Date of first appointment to B.T.C.

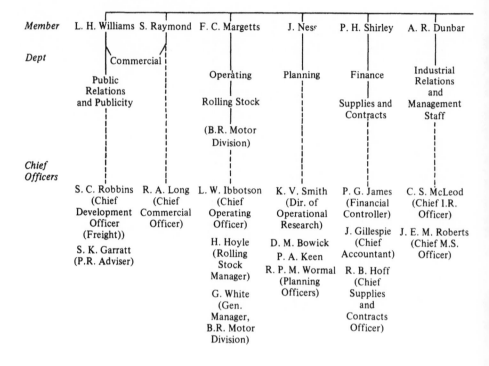

Member	L. H. Williams	S. Raymond	F. C. Margetts	J. Ness[a]	P. H. Shirley	A. R. Dunbar
Dept	Public Relations and Publicity	Commercial	Operating Rolling Stock (B.R. Motor Division)	Planning	Finance Supplies and Contracts	Industrial Relations and Management Staff
Chief Officers	S. C. Robbins (Chief Development Officer (Freight)) S. K. Garratt (P.R. Adviser)	R. A. Long (Chief Commercial Officer)	L. W. Ibbotson (Chief Operating Officer) H. Hoyle (Rolling Stock Manager) G. White (Gen. Manager, B.R. Motor Division)	K. V. Smith (Dir. of Operational Research) D. M. Bowick P. A. Keen R. P. M. Wormal (Planning Officers)	P. G. James (Financial Controller) J. Gillespie (Chief Accountant) R. B. Hoff (Chief Supplies and Contracts Officer)	C. S. McLeod (Chief I.R. Officer) J. E. M. Roberts (Chief M.S. Officer)

[a]Chairman of

Chart X Beeching's Functional Board, November 1963

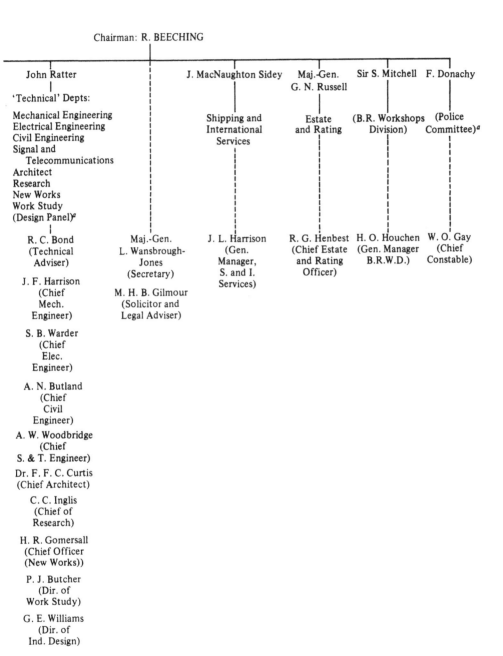

Chairman: R. BEECHING

John Ratter	J. MacNaughton Sidey	Maj.-Gen. G. N. Russell	Sir S. Mitchell	F. Donachy

'Technical' Depts:

Mechanical Engineering
Electrical Engineering
Civil Engineering
Signal and
    Telecommunications
Architect
Research
New Works
Work Study
(Design Panel)[a]

		Shipping and International Services	Estate and Rating	(B.R. Workshops Division)	(Police Committee)[a]

R. C. Bond (Technical Adviser)	Maj.-Gen. L. Wansbrough-Jones (Secretary)	J. L. Harrison (Gen. Manager, S. and I. Services)	R. G. Henbest (Chief Estate and Rating Officer)	H. O. Houchen (Gen. Manager B.R.W.D.)	W. O. Gay (Chief Constable)

J. F. Harrison
(Chief
Mech.
Engineer)

M. H. B. Gilmour
(Solicitor and
Legal Adviser)

S. B. Warder
(Chief
Elec.
Engineer)

A. N. Butland
(Chief
Civil
Engineer)

A. W. Woodbridge
(Chief
S. & T. Engineer)

Dr. F. F. C. Curtis
(Chief Architect)

C. C. Inglis
(Chief of
Research)

H. R. Gomersall
(Chief Officer
(New Works))

P. J. Butcher
(Dir. of
Work Study)

G. E. Williams
(Dir. of
Ind. Design)

bad picker of men. The B.R.B. Headquarters Library copy of Bonavia's *Organisation of British Railways* contains this anonymous and intriguing pencilled annotation: 'It has been a criticism of Dr Beeching that, despite his great abilities, his selection of top level "new blood" was poor, and that indeed this "blank area" in an otherwise great man was a serious handicap to him and to B.R.' This view was also offered to the author in interviews with several surviving members or officers of the B.T.C. and/or B.R.B.; and it has found its way into the popular literature.[42]

There was more to Beeching and his Board than such criticisms imply. It is important to understand the Beeching style of management, which inevitably placed a greater strain on those appointed to assist him. He spent much of his four-year period as Chairman in preparing and publicising his report, *The Reshaping of British Railways* of March 1963, with its recipe for a smaller rail network and emphasis on profitable traffic flows. Ironically for a man who was at first unnerved by the glare of publicity surrounding his job, Beeching quickly came to appreciate the value of good public relations and improved industrial relations. Indeed, the railways' publicity machine was revolutionised during his period of office, and here he was well served by a new appointee, S. K. Garratt, who came from Shell International Chemicals to take up Brebner's post as Public Relations Adviser in October 1961. Garratt, together with Eric Merrill, Chief Public Relations Officer since 1959, worked closely with Beeching in mounting an effective campaign in connection with the *Reshaping* report. For the first time, the railways made a concerted and sophisticated effort to create a favourable climate of opinion. Their success scotches any idea that Garratt's appointment was a poor one.[43]

In other areas, Beeching was usually content to set the agenda for change, leaving others to implement specific policy initiatives. He slimmed down the organisational machinery, reduced the number of meetings – his Board met fortnightly instead of three times a month – brought in outsiders and gave impetus to functional control from the centre. If the Beeching period was really one in which bad appointments were made, then we should look not only at Board members, but at senior officers and General Managers as well.

Regional autonomy was challenged in a number of ways after 1961, not least by shuffling round the General Managers. Some decisive moves were made in January 1962. At Euston Blee was asked to retire, being replaced by Henry Johnson of the Eastern Region. The undynamic Roy Hammond was moved from the Western to the Eastern Region, and his post at Paddington was taken by Raymond. David McKenna, Chief Commercial Officer at headquarters, succeeded Hopkins as General Manager of the Southern Region a year later. The places vacated by Margetts (from the

North Eastern), Raymond (Western) and Ness (Scottish) on their elevation
to Board status in 1962–3 were filled by Arthur Dean (Eastern), Gerard
Fiennes (also Eastern) and W. G. Thorpe (London Midland). In no case,
then, was an internal succession permitted, and it would be very difficult
to sustain the view that these men were in any way inferior to their
predecessors. As far as the General Managers were concerned, Beeching
chose wisely from the resources available.[44]

A key feature of the 'Beeching Revolution' was the readiness to
introduce managerial talent from outside the railway industry. In addition
to Board members, a large number of officers were recruited, mainly to
headquarters, but also to posts in the regions. Nearly 40 officers were
imported between October 1961 and April 1963 from *inter alia* Shell,
I.C.I., General Electric, English Electric, Lever Brothers, Beaverbrook
Newspapers and Jaguar Cars. Their quality naturally varied; some made
little or no impact. Others, in contrast, achieved much in bringing new
arguments and ideas to bear on a situation dominated by managers of the
old school. According to Gerard Fiennes, 'Railwaymen were an enclosed
order, far worse than the Benedictines, or whoever is an enclosed order.
They're inbred, inward-looking, they've got plenty to do looking after
railways. The people who came in for the first years did an absolutely
fantastic job with the arguments.' In addition to Garratt, already mentioned, there was H. O. Houchen, formerly of British Overseas Airways
Corporation and the Metal Industries Group, who was appointed General
Manager of the B.R. Workshops in December 1962 and who in August
1964 took Mitchell's place on the Board. From the same pool of recruits
came three more future Board members: Dr Sydney Jones, radar research
scientist, former Director of Applications Research, C.E.G.B. and Technical Director of R. B. Pullen, who became Director of Research in March
1962 and joined the Board in 1965; A. V. Barker, Joint General Manager
of N.A.A.F.I., who was appointed Assistant General Manager of Southern
Region in October 1962 and a Board member in 1968; and Geoffrey
Wilson, Senior Consultant with Production-Engineering Ltd, who joined
headquarters staff as Cost (later Management) Accountant in March 1963
and joined the Board in 1968.[45] Another important acquisition by British
Railways was Terry House, Marketing Equipment Co-ordinator with
Shell-Mex and B.P. Ltd, who was appointed Commercial Development
Officer in April 1962, on the introduction of Williams, and later became a
Director of Marketing Development. He proved to be the driving force
behind Williams's enterprise in capturing oil traffic for the railways in
1963–4. The sort of initiatives which House and Williams took were very
unlikely to have been taken by the old brigade. It seems quite clear
therefore that the introduction of new faces in the strategic areas of

accounting, marketing and public relations, as well as in general management, helped to transform the railways' approach to its business operations.[46]

This leaves the Board members, where once again opinion is firm among those who recall their activities. Beeching's selection of the volatile Shirley and the more affable Williams is the most commonly cited criticism, but there are also many who feel that the limited representation of railwaymen was a mistake. Certainly, the strengths and weaknesses of individuals were fully exposed by the functional organisation of the Board, which encouraged departmentalism. Williams was a useful acquisition if only for his oil industry contacts, and he did make a valuable contribution here, although his success was in large measure due to the support of his subordinates. Outside this area his impact was minimal and he was frequently by-passed. By 1965 many of his former responsibilities had been taken up by others – commercial affairs by Raymond, then by Shirley, and publicity by the Chief Commercial Manager, R. A. Long.[47]

Shirley was a key figure in Beeching's organisation. At one and the same time he was Chairman of four major committees – Finance, Supply, Works and Equipment and Property – and Chairman of the subsidiary companies, Railway Sites and British Transport Hotels. He was also a controversial character whose overall impact is difficult to gauge. He was like an emetic: the first dose works wonders, but problems arise when the medicine is taken repeatedly. Anecdotes about him abound. One former colleague saw him as 'a bloody good finance manager' whose troubleshooting role in the fields of stores, purchasing and finance often brought dividends. But he also had a highly abrasive manner which progressively antagonised railway managers the longer he remained. His weaknesses were more visible after his appointment as a Vice-Chairman (together with Raymond), following Mitchell's resignation in July 1964. He then became, as another colleague put it, 'an absolute menace. He would have an idea about every three months and the previous idea he'd had wouldn't be anywhere near completed by then, but he'd take everybody off that previous idea, and put them onto the new one, so nothing got done at all.' He was thus a force for both change and frustration: 'a great catalyst . . . a swash-buckling, cost-cutting, knocker-down of sacred cows . . . [but] . . . naive to the complexities of the business'. On the credit side, he is remembered for his prompt action in pressing for the removal of the Commission's costly system of multiple bank accounts. It was discovered that 60 per cent of banking costs came from interest on maintained balances, resulting in an annual loss of £150,000. His initial drive on railway stock levels also produced savings. With all sorts of personal initiatives he succeeded in cutting paper and printing stocks from £1.1

million to £457,000 in the three years to the end of 1963, and in selling surplus material as scrap to the value of £20 million in 1963 alone.[48] On the debit side, the irritant manner of Shirley's probings often riled regional managers with the result that suggestions were rarely pushed through. For example, his warnings in 1962 about high administrative costs may have caused a flutter, but Raymond was able to complain in 1967 that H.Q. staff numbers had increased from 1,723 in December 1962 to 4,052 three years later, a far higher increase than was justified by the shift in authority from the regions to the centre.[49] Amongst many Shirley stories familiar in British Railways history and legend, one must suffice to convey the nature of the man, in his regional manifestations, and of the reactions he provoked. On one of his visits to the Scottish Region, he had occasion to complain about the unnecessary cost of railway fencing. The official party was travelling on the West Highland Line, accompanied by the General Manager, Gordon Stewart. As the train ran along the side of a loch Shirley noticed that the fencing had become partly submerged in the water. This incensed him, and after a tirade lasting about five minutes he said, 'Now then, Stewart, what earthly use is that fencing over there?' Stewart's immediate response was: 'It's to prevent the salmon from coming up and nibbling the fishplates.'[50]

Of the others, Mitchell performed competently in rationalising the workshops, and there were valuable, if restricted, contributions from some of the part-timers, notably H. P. Barker and Hayday. The four career railwaymen (that is, excluding Raymond) may have had rather narrow backgrounds. They had all been employed by the L.N.E.R. as young men, and two of them, Dunbar and Margetts, had begun as traffic apprentices with the company. They were really 'rough and tumble railwaymen' rather than ideal candidates for Board status, but given the dearth of managerial talent at the time – a factor to which much attention was paid in the Beeching years – it is difficult to criticise their appointments. Critics of Beeching's choice of colleagues seem to have forgotten that the earlier Chairmen, Hurcomb and Robertson, were no more successful therein. Blee, Riddles, Train, Pope and Reginald Wilson were in their own way just as controversial as Williams, Shirley and Raymond.

In trying to assess the organisational achievements under Beeching, it must be recognised that he did not give himself much time to cement the changes he had encouraged. While Robertson presided over the railways for eight years, Beeching did so for only four. He was Chairman of the B.R.B. for only two-and-a-half years, from December 1962 to May 1965, and since, as already observed, the full Board was not assembled until November 1963, the period of 'consolidation' amounted to only 18 months. The approach remained strictly functional. The Board operated through eleven main committees, six of them of long standing, namely, Finance, Technical, Works and Equipment, Supply, Property and Management Staff (formerly Establishment and Staff). The others were of newer vintage. The Commission's Traffic Committee was wound up after only two years in February 1962. Its policy-making role later passed to a Planning Committee established in August 1963. New committees for the Main Workshops and for Shipping Services were introduced in January and February of the same year. Then, in November 1964 a Commercial Committee, led first by Raymond, then by Shirley, formed part of a further reorganisation of commercial affairs at H.Q. Another important innovation was the Chairman's Monday Conference, informal meetings of the Board's full-time members which were introduced in December 1962 to prepare the ground for Board meetings. Beeching also established informal meetings with the General Managers. These were later formalised with the creation of a British Railways Management Committee, attended by full-time Board members and the General Managers, which first met in September 1963. The intention was to involve the regions in policy-making at the centre. With the continuance of the three special committees, for the Police, Staff College and Design, the total of 14 committees represented a considerable organisation. Beeching's structure was a simplified and slimmed-down version of Robertson's dinosaur, but it did not eliminate the possibility of fragmented decision-making.[51]

Relatively few adjustments were made to the departmental organisations at H.Q. in the period 1963–5. The only changes of significance concerned operating, research, engineering and commercial matters, and all followed from the emphasis on centralised control and the clarification of lines of command. In operating, three new managerial posts were created in November 1963, for Movements, Terminals and Liner Trains, and they were followed by the abolition of the Road Motor Division in January 1964. In April of the same year the redundant Research Advisory Council was abolished. In October 1962 the design and development departments of Mechanical Engineering had been centralised, and the four regional design offices were taken under direct control. This was followed, in January 1965, by the fusion of the Mechanical and Electrical Engineering departments. Finally, the changes in commercial organisation in October 1964 involved the separation of passenger and freight responsibilities and the creation of redesignated posts of Chief Commercial Manager, Chief Passenger Manager and Chief Marketing Manager.[52]

As time went on, some Board members began to voice their concern that managerial effort was becoming increasingly compartmentalised. Although both the Chairman's informal conference and the Management Committee offered a forum for inter-functional debate, it was felt that

Beeching's 'Revolution' had proceeded too far in the direction of the old Railway Executive. This opinion surfaced immediately after Beeching was succeeded by Stanley Raymond. Thus, in a memorandum to full-time members on 28 June 1965, Raymond pointed to the 'apparent lack of co-ordination on some major issues at headquarters'. He cited a specific instance: 'the General Managers mentioned to me last week at dinner that they were receiving communications from eight different Members and Chief Officers at Headquarters on various aspects of the procurement of rolling stock'. Ratter responded with the observation that 'we have overdone the functional division of duties and this has brought back departmentalism'.[53] Signs of the tensions which this encouraged may be seen in the relationship between the Board and the new Regional Railway Boards. Although the latter were strengthened by the introduction of railway executives, their authority was not increased in spite of the promises which had appeared in the White Paper of 1960. Indeed, many of the initiatives undertaken at H.Q. served to weaken regional autonomy. The six Regional Boards were in essence Boards of General Managers and their Assistants. From the start three of the Boards were chaired by the General Manager – London Midland (Johnson), Southern (McKenna) and Western (Fiennes) – and by October 1964 the number became five after Dean had succeeded Summerson at York and W. G. Thorpe took Cameron's place at Glasgow. Of the remaining members, nearly half were Assistant General Managers. This had followed the restructuring of the regional organisation in 1963. Beeching and his colleagues took up the recommendations in Urwick Orr's report on the North Eastern in 1961 (see above, pp. 169–70) and insisted that the regions removed the 'line' tier of management and operated with only two tiers – 'region' and 'division'. The functional Board at H.Q. was to be reflected at regional level by the appointment of at least four Assistant General Managers, with specific responsibility for finance, commercial affairs, movements (i.e. operating) and technical matters. In each region, between two and four of these men were given Board status. Five of the new posts went to Beeching 'out-siders', but the changes also involved the promotion of a considerable number of younger internal candidates.[54]

Although the Regional Boards possessed a greater degree of railway expertise than had their predecessors, the Area Boards, they also faced a much tighter control from the centre. Beeching's preference for strong central direction, evident during the Stedeford Group's deliberations, soon found expression when he joined the railways. Although initially sympathetic to a proposal to re-title the regions as 'Railways', he eventually decided against the idea. The formal delegation of authority to the Boards under Section 2 (4) of the 1962 Act then reserved a long list of functions to the B.R.B. itself. They included: national negotiations on pay and conditions; overall control of finance and investment; determination of the size of the railway network; major questions of commercial policy; purchase of certain stores and equipment; senior staff appointments; the design, procurement and allocation of rolling stock and track; control of the main workshops; research and development; shipping; and property development policy. Much of this was familiar territory but some elements, such as central purchasing and workshop control, were new. Further modifications to regional powers in the course of 1963 included the raising of the limit on property transactions from £20,000 to £25,000, a move which corrected the position for the inflation which had occurred since 1959. The Regional Boards' authority in relation to works and equipment expenditure and to staff appointments was diminished rather than enhanced: the salary limit placed on appointments by Regional Boards, for example, was reduced from £3,600 per annum to £3,000.[55] Finally, the regions experienced a further diminution of their powers with the creation in March 1963 of a Central Wagon Authority for wagon distribution, which was organised through the Rolling Stock Department at H.Q.[56]

There was undoubtedly some regional opposition to these moves, but examples of outright rebellion were rare. Railwaymen are a disciplined breed of men and in any case Beeching's shake-up of regional appointments destroyed the continuity of top management, particularly in the Eastern and Western Regions, which served to discourage dissent. Nevertheless, in the early part of 1963 Summerson (North Eastern) and Johnson (London Midland) voiced complaints about central purchasing and the new salary limit for appointments, and Johnson and McKenna (Southern) were critical of the plan to standardise the regional organisations. While Hammond at Liverpool Street accepted the abolition of the Eastern's line management without demur, an exception was made of the London Midland on grounds of size. McKenna only reluctantly accepted that he needed separate Assistant General Managers for the movements and commercial functions, and took a year to appoint them.[57] Attempts by the Board to bring in further measures of centralisation, with economy in mind, were similarly frustrated as the regions dragged their feet. The General Managers, led by Johnson, expressed disquiet over any move to dilute their authority, and this occasioned lengthy discussions over regional boundaries, surveying, medical services and commercial advertising. The process of management development, which was intensified after November 1963, also caused offence in the regions where it involved managers being transferred against the wishes of their region.[58]

More important than the mere fact of this squabbling between H.Q. and the regions is the light it throws upon the working of Beeching's functional management system. The minutes of both the Management Staff Committee and the British Railways Management Committee, through which these issues were focussed, reveal that the centre often failed to press home its advantage. Johnson, as the senior General Manager, was certainly handled very carefully by Shirley, Margetts, Dunbar and the rest. The Management Staff Committee quickly came round to the view that 'there were too many Regions and that boundaries and administrative headquarters were in the wrong place'; that the London Midland's line management should, after all, be scrapped; and that there were very real savings to be gained from further measures of centralisation. But it took a considerable time to effect the necessary changes in the face of regional prevarication.[59] Johnson was consistent in demanding that line management should be retained. He had found the Euston organisation in some disarray (see above, pp. 167–8) when he took over in January 1962 and there was force in his argument that it was undesirable to introduce further drastic changes so soon after the districts had been reorganised into divisions. However, both the Management Staff Committee and the Board, which had been happy to retain line management in May 1963, took the entirely opposite view less than a year later, and in May 1964 Johnson was asked to submit a suitable scheme within six months. It was only after David Bowick was moved from the Central Planning Unit to Euston as Assistant General Manager (Planning) in January 1965 that the necessary plans were drawn up, and the line structure was not abandoned until June 1966.[60] There was a similar time-lag, although with less justification, in the transfer of responsibility for the fixing and maintenance of commercial advertising sites from the regions to the subsidiary, British Transport Advertising Ltd. Johnson cast doubt upon the predicted staff savings (£63,000) and additional revenue (£647,000), but although the new subsidiary complained energetically about the deficiencies of dual control, it was not until September 1966 that the firm plans of January 1964 were implemented.[61] Such delays were symptomatic of the too frequent lack of vigorous and unified decision-making. This was perhaps the major weakness of the Beeching period. Cost-consciousness, management development, the new name style 'British Rail' (adopted in 1964) and the impetus from the centre: all were undoubtedly beneficial in many ways, but functional control was taken too far, and the Board rarely acted as a unified team. Planning was certainly encouraged by Beeching, but it was in no sense corporate. The absence of a co-ordinated planning mechanism made it difficult for Board members to take on the General Managers with confidence.

V

Beeching was always firmly identified with the Conservatives' transport policy, and his unpopularity in union circles made his position insecure when a Labour Government, headed by Harold Wilson, was elected in October 1964. Within seven months, Lord Beeching (he was ennobled in the New Year's Honours List of 1965) was back at I.C.I. Labour, however, came to office with no firm plans for transport. The Party's manifesto had promised to draw up a national plan to co-ordinate services, halt 'major rail closures', extend the operation of British Road Services and examine transport in rural areas in order to ensure a reasonable level of service. But nobody seemed to know what 'co-ordination' meant. Marples was succeeded as Minister by Tom Fraser. Described by *The Economist* as 'a very nice man . . . courteous, sympathetic and gentle', he was a Scottish miner with limited experience of government. His appointment served to demonstrate that Wilson did not rank transport very highly in his list of priorities for the new government, despite his close involvement with its problems in the late 1940s and early 1950s.[62] During Fraser's period of office little seemed to change. The new Minister attracted odium in union circles by continuing the policy of rail closures, and made no fuss when the second part of Beeching's *Reshaping* report appeared in February 1965. This comprised Ness's report on trunk routes, which recommended that the Board should concentrate on the development of only 3,000 of its 7,500 miles of through routes.[63] Fraser was also criticised for the government's failure to make progress with its promised investigation of transport co-ordination. His problems as a Minister were to have considerable long-term repercussions for they led to his replacement by Barbara Castle in December 1965 and to a much more aggressive transport policy from Labour.

The sorry tale of the Ministry of Transport's attempts to produce a transport plan in 1965 is of some interest here, since it was bound up with Beeching's resignation. In November 1964 Fraser, with Wilson's encouragement, invited Beeching to undertake, in effect, another Stedeford-type exercise, this time covering the whole of inland transport. Unfortunately, the plan blew up in his face when Cabinet opposition to Beeching surfaced, and strings were attached to the job, requiring the latter to work alongside an advisory committee of 'independent assessors' representing sectional interests. Beeching then withdrew, having decided to return to I.C.I. on 1 June 1965, exactly four years after his initial secondment. Fraser turned instead to Lord Hinton, the former Chairman of the C.E.G.B., who was appointed Special Adviser on Transport Planning in February 1965. The episode was mildly embarrassing to the government, as the approach to Beeching had been extensively leaked. But it also raised more fundamental issues concerning the political environment in which transport reorganisation could be contemplated. The Cabinet's opposition to Beeching, which was apparently led by Cousins and Crossman, could be interpreted simply as Labour's distaste for the Conservatives' anti-rail axeman.[64] But there was probably more to it than that. The publication in 1964 of a study by B.R.B. of the comparative true costs of freight by rail and road transport, part of its evidence to the Geddes Committee on Carriers' Licensing, had made it plain that Beeching believed that the same rigorous, cost-based analysis which had been applied to the railways should be extended to road haulage and inter-city air services. So far from being anti-rail, Beeching was seen in some quarters as anti-road. The blunt anti-Beeching sentiments of some Cabinet members – not for nothing did Cousins proudly claim to have 'sacked' Beeching – may well have got mixed up with the pro-road leanings of others.[65]

No attempt was made to cast the net widely in the search for Beeching's successor. For the first time in the 19-year history of nationalised railways an internal candidate was selected, a man who had experience of running the railways at both H.Q. and regional level. Stanley Raymond, then aged 51, was known to have Labour sympathies, a feature in marked contrast to the views of his fellow Vice-Chairman and chief rival, Philip Shirley. He was reported to be a member of the Fabian Society and a close friend of Callaghan, then Chancellor of the Exchequer. But this implied patronage did not bring with it a salary to equal Beeching's. Hailed in the press as the 'Half-Pay Rail Chief', Raymond was to be paid £12,500 p.a., the same salary paid to Lord Robens at N.C.B.[66]

The choice of Raymond probably owed much, in Cabinet circles, to the conviction that his experience in the industrial relations field would prove useful as the railways faced up to the implications of *Reshaping* – staffing cuts, single-manning and liner trains. *The Financial Times* referred to the breadth of his experience:

with experience in both the Western Region and the Scottish, the staff side and traffic control, quite apart from his recent spell in the thick of planning, the new chairman can claim to have gone right through the mill . . . the accent has swung to implementation and the man at the top will need diplomacy, experience and drive to take the Beeching reforms through to all levels. Mr. Raymond has yet to make this imprint, but his background suggests these qualities are there.[67]

Raymond certainly had experience and drive but little diplomacy. There were few signs that his blunt and aggressive manner had been tempered during his short spell as a Board member. It was his personality, as much as anything else, that was later to cost him his position. He occupied the post for only two-and-a-half years, precipitating a period of instability at the top.

There were no dramatic changes in the Board's organisation in the wake of Raymond's appointment. The new Chairman talked much about the need to improve internal communications, canvassing the full-time members for their views as to how they might be improved and encouraging the production of a document setting out more clearly the precise duties of Board members and chief officers. But he rejected the idea of re-establishing something like Robertson's General Staff and made no attempt to abandon the functional organisation of the Board, despite the many internal criticisms of it which landed on his desk.[68] The few practical improvements which he did introduce were in the financial, technical and planning fields and resulted from his determination to improve the calibre of the Board.

With Fraser's consent, he appointed P. G. James, the Financial Controller, to the Board in June 1965. The aim was to free Shirley of responsibility for direct financial work, allowing him to concentrate on commercial affairs. James took Shirley's place as Chairman of the Finance Committee and Shirley became Chairman of the Commercial Committee in lieu of Raymond. The post of Financial Controller was then abolished.[69] In October Fraser invited Raymond to put forward further proposals to strengthen the Board, Raymond having declared his intention to cut out dead wood. Ness was at the top of his list (his antipathy for the Scotsman stretched back to his days as Chief Commercial Manager in Glasgow), and Williams was a close second. Ness was asked to retire early, with effect from January 1966 (although his formal contract did not expire until June 1968), and Williams's appointment was not renewed when it ended in August of the same year. Good replacements were not easy to find. Raymond ruled out the existing General Manager for various reasons. The most likely candidates, Johnson and McKenna, were needed in their regions for the time being, and, in any case, Raymond thought Johnson would not willingly serve under Shirley. Admitting a weakness on the technical side, where Ratter was, apparently, finding it difficult to 'carry the full range', the Chairman proposed to promote the 54-year-old Sydney Jones, the Chief of Research, to Board status, giving him functional responsibility for research, design and development. Further changes were contingent upon this step. Houchen would then combine the functions of workshops and mechanical engineering, while Ratter would take over the planning work relinquished by Ness. Once Jones was appointed, on 15 November 1965, a Technical Group, consisting of Ratter, Houchen, Jones and H. P. Barker, was established to improve the co-ordination between the technical departments and research and to keep a tighter rein on mechanical engineering. Planning was then re-defined as an 'all-department activity'; and Ratter was given the job of supervising central planning (including operational research) as Chairman of a reconstituted Planning Committee. Margetts took over responsibility for the trunk routes.[70]

Fraser was not happy with the new arrangements. He expressed doubts about the quality of James; 'mentioned the opinions held within the Trade Union movement about the unsuitability of Mr Dunbar [Industrial Relations] for his present post' and suggested that there was a need to improve public relations. In an exchange of letters in November, Fraser asked Raymond to consider new appointments in planning and in capital investment and budgeting:

From my own point of view, I shall find it difficult to pursue policies designed to influence traffic from road to rail unless I can be confident that the railways will be able not merely to cope with the additional traffic but to provide a progessively better and more attractive service. This will not be achieved unless there is active management bringing energy and enthusiasm to the day-to-day tasks and producing a constant stream of new ideas. What I have seen of the Board's work in the last year leads me to think that too much of the burden is shouldered by too few members.[71]

Fraser was particularly critical of the assignment of planning to the overloaded Ratter. He was right, for the planning function was badly in need of regeneration. The creation of the Planning Committee and the Central Planning Unit under Margetts in July 1963 had been closely bound up with the *execution* of Beeching's *Reshaping* strategy, with operating matters such as route closures and motive power. The Committee's role was 'not to form policy but to carry out the policies which the Board had formulated'. Unfortunately, the notion of creating a pool of 'bright young men' failed to live up to expectations. The Committee and the Unit were hampered from the start by an ill-defined chain of command. Planning continued elsewhere at H.Q. and in the regions, creating severe problems of co-ordination. This is demonstrated by the Planning Committee's memorandum on diesel locomotives in November 1963, where it was admitted that 'too many uncertainties exist about future planning and the outcome of present planning to allow a reliable forecast to be made'. The arrival of Ness, whose appointment as Board member for planning owed more to his antagonistic behaviour as General Manager, Scottish Region, made little difference. He later admitted that when he was appointed, the Board 'took no decisions on the scope and functions of the post'. After an informal conference in January 1964 he was told to 'stimulate planning and act as a medium for getting work done', but there was no intention to supplant the work of the several departments or to inhibit regional initiatives. Ness concentrated on the preparation of a trunk route report and took a keen interest in the details of freightliner design. Beeching's planning legacy was therefore unsatisfactory, despite his own personal reputation for study and analysis. The danger inherent in the Board organisation operated by Beeching and Raymond, where executive and planning functions were combined in a small group of nine full-timers (eight after the departure of Williams) and four part-timers was that 'planning' in the broader sense of long-term policy-making would suffer. This indeed is just what seems to have happened. There was insufficient co-ordination and planning tended to proceed haphazardly without reference to precise financial goals. A further attempt to improve matters came in March 1966 – by which time Fraser had been replaced by Castle – when the Commercial Committee was re-titled the Commercial and Operating Committee and asked to act as a central policy-making body for both functions.[72] It required the growing problems of the railways' freight business to force the elevation of 'planning' to a more central position in the Board's priorities (see Chapter 11).

Finally, and before Barbara Castle's appointment sparked off yet another major reorganisation of the industry, Raymond made some progress in such other matters as the long-discussed merger of the Eastern and North Eastern Regions; the transfer of control of advertising from Public Relations to the Chief Commercial Manager; and, on the retirement of Wansbrough-Jones, the Board Secretary, the merging of the posts of Legal Adviser and Secretary, under M. H. B. Gilmour, a return to the practice of the Commission before Beevor's resignation in 1951.[73] These steps were in the right direction, but they did nothing to appease critics within the Ministry.

VI

Barbara Castle's appointment as Minister of Transport in December 1965 came about partly because Fraser failed to produce his promised plan for the co-ordination of transport. The appointment of Hinton as Special Adviser, hailed as a sound move by the serious press, proved to be a mistake. Aged 64, Hinton was abrasive and uncompromising. If he was, as Hannah contends, 'deeply imbued with the public service ethos', then he was certainly not a political animal and to his colleagues he often appeared bloody-minded. His experience of transport was limited, although he had served a six-year apprenticeship at Swindon in 1917–23 before going on to Trinity College Cambridge, I.C.I., the Ministry of Supply, the Atomic Energy Authority and the C.E.G.B.[74] Hinton, unlike Beeching, accepted the fetters of a Transport Advisory Council, but appears to have disregarded it. His reports to the Minister, which were produced in the spring, were not published, and *The Economist* speculated that either Hinton submitted plans unacceptable to the government or he found that there was no sound case for the co-ordination of road and rail transport. In fact, the Hinton papers confirm that the latter interpretation was correct. Hinton had to write his reports without staff support from the Ministry: 'I set about the job alone and I do not think that I have felt so isolated . . . without help and with limited time it had only been possible to "broad brush" the problems.' In his two-part report on inter-urban traffic and urban transport, he contended that co-ordination could best be secured by 'natural competition and evolution', while his response to the problem of urban transport was that 'there is little advice that I can usefully give'. The only thing to emerge was a second report, on smalls (sundries) traffic, where Hinton argued for an entirely new nationalised organisation for collection and delivery, embracing B.R.B. and British Road Services – anticipating the National Freight Corporation set up under the 1968 Act. Otherwise, Fraser was unable to produce anything from Hinton's work. As the latter noted, 'the Minister and the Government had hoped for a report that would whitewash them in restructuring the growth of road transport and bolstering up the railways but that was what they did not get'. In December 1965 the Minister turned instead to the heads of various public transport organisations for a report on operational co-ordination.[75]

Fraser may also have leaned too far in the direction of his predecessor's policies. As Garratt noted, in a memorandum to Margetts in March 1965, 'the Minister is anxiously seeking all possible support so that he can implement those of our proposals which he knows to be right but which nevertheless are a liability to the party platform'. Garratt thought that the main task was to counteract 'the more emotional and political pressures' to which Fraser was subjected by his colleagues. The N.U.R. also lobbied Wilson for his removal. In December he became a casualty of a Cabinet reshuffle. Castle was moved from Overseas Development, Wilson pointing out to her that transport policy had been one of the government's great failures. 'He went on, "I *must* have a Minister of Transport who can act".'[76]

Like many a Minister of Transport, Barbara Castle had no experience of the industry, and had been extremely reluctant to leave her previous post. Nevertheless, she quickly brought her characteristic bustle and enthusiasm to the new job. Six months later, a White Paper on *Transport Policy* was produced, outlining Labour's intentions to modernise the industry, subsidise 'socially necessary' rail passenger services and integrate publicly owned road and rail services. The White Paper also announced that a Joint Steering Group had been established to review aspects of the railway industry, including costing, pricing, investment and management structure. From September to December of the following year, four more Papers appeared, on *British Waterways, Railway Policy, The Transport of Freight* and *Public Transport and Traffic,* which prepared the ground for the Transport Act of 1968. Another lengthy period of major reorganisation was under way, embracing two General Elections, in 1966 and 1970, a change of Minister and a change of British Rail Chairman.[77]

The Ministry, like the railways themselves, required improved planning mechanisms and a better co-ordination of departments. Castle was apparently shocked to find that she had been posted to 'a huge, sprawling jungle' of 7,000 civil servants, patently in need of major departmental reform. While Dunnett had brought a new vigour to Transport in the period 1959–62, his successor as Permanent-Secretary, Sir Thomas Padmore, presided over few comparable organisational changes. With 12 Under-Secretaries and 14 main departments, there was little co-ordination, even with the major sections dealing with roads, nationalised transport and planning. As the *Guardian* observed, 'like Gaul, it is divided into three parts, but its administrative performance in recent years has compared unfavourably with the Romans' '. The impetus for change was lacking with a Permanent-Secretary who was known to favour 'separate development' for the various transport modes.[78] Fraser, in fact, made the first reforming moves when he appointed Michael Beesley, an L.S.E. economist, as a part-time Economic Adviser in February 1965, following this up with a measure of reorganisation in October, which gave more emphasis to policy-making and research and included the establishment of a separate policy division for London. Castle took this a stage further and brought in some new blood. In January 1966 she announced the setting-up of a new Economic Planning section to assist her in the formulation of a White Paper. Its Director-General was Christopher Foster, a young economics don of 35, who was Senior Economic Adviser in the regional section of George Brown's Department of Economic Affairs. Foster had impressed with the cost-benefit study of the Victoria Line project in 1963, undertaken jointly with Beesley. At the same time, Castle strengthened her team in the Commons by the appointment, as Joint Parliamentary Secretary with Stephen Swingler, of the relatively young John Morris, barrister and M.P. for Aberavon. The Ministry then organised a comprehensive programme of consultations with transport interests.[79]

Raymond and his Board were concerned that the new Minister would not only serve to check the *Reshaping* strategy and its rail closure proposals but would herald another major shake-up of the industry's organisation. *The Times* added fuel to the fire when it reported that the Ministry was thinking of bringing in consultants to investigate British Rail's planning and managerial efficiency, since she had been struck both 'by the generally poor quality of management and decision-making in the railways' and by the Board's 'extraordinarily negative relationship' with the Ministry. Raymond was determined, in his own words, 'to retain the initiative' he felt had existed in Fraser's time.[80] Shortly after taking office he had invited Board members to suggest items which might be included with advantage in any future Transport Bill. One of these, the notion of a National Highway Authority to administer both road and rail, was advanced by Raymond in a kite-flying exercise in early January 1966, and behind the scenes the Board drew up proposals for a Freight Sundries Division, a joint parcels organisation with the Transport Holding Company, and separate authorities for transport in the major conurbations. By the end of the month, the Chairman had been provided with a well-argued paper by three of his leading managers, R. A. Long (Chief Commercial Manager), K. V. Smith (Commercial Research Manager) and F. T. Gray (Director of Costings), which rejected the Highway Authority approach for one based on Public Service Obligation, where the government would be invited to support non-commercial parts of the railway for 'social' reasons.[81]

So when Raymond met Castle on 2 February for what was described as 'a long, personal conversation', he was supported by a considerable amount of internally-generated proposals. Castle, on the other hand, was equally determined to keep the initiative for change inside the Ministry. Consequently, both this meeting and a more formal one which followed it a fortnight later were tense affairs. Raymond and Castle together produced a volatile and potentially explosive cocktail, the ingredients of which were obstinacy and a coercive instinct. Both were in their early fifties (Raymond was 52, Castle 54), but their backgrounds and political affiliations were very different. Castle was a tax inspector's daughter with a conventional education behind her – Bradford Grammar School and St Hugh's, Oxford. She was part of the intellectual left-wing of the Labour Party, eager to fuse the reforming zeal of the 1940s with the central planning obsession of the 1960s. Raymond's politics were moderate and he was proud of having pulled himself up by his bootstraps. Their confrontation ushered in a long and bitter struggle over the future organisation and financing of nationalised transport, which culminated in Raymond's 'enforced resignation' in November 1967. The February 1966 talks were dominated by Labour's anxiety to slow down the rate of rail closures and encourage the retention of a larger network than had been envisaged under Beeching. There was also considerable discussion about investment, the implications of an integration strategy and the handling of the rail deficit. The full story will be told in subsequent chapters. For present purposes, the important thing to emerge was the establishment of a Joint Steering Group to examine the railways' financial problems and prepare amendments to the 1962 Act. Part of the Group's remit was still another investigation of the railways' management structure.

It came about as a result of Castle having taken up Raymond's suggestion that a working party might look at the financial problem. She supported an independent assessment by consultants. Raymond complained that 'the railways had probably had enough independent inquiries recently', and suggested that the investigation be conducted jointly by the Board and the Ministry.[82] Castle then moved towards the idea of a Joint Steering Group, but emphasised that it should include some independent members in order that it be 'accepted politically as a genuine exercise' (her position in the Cabinet was not unassailable and in Labour's *National Plan* British Rail had been given the target of breaking even by 1970). The Group would control the work of an expert working party staffed by accountants, management consultants and the Ministry's new team of economists. The agenda would include costing, the identification of loss-making elements with a view to grant-aid, investment, pricing and organisation. Raymond saw much similarity between this and previous investigations, but agreement was reached when Castle accepted the inclusion in the terms of reference of a commitment to what was called a 'substantial railway network for the foreseeable future', and a study of the 'standby' element in railway infrastructure costs.* The proposal was then consolidated over the next three months and summarised in the White Paper in July. By this time, Labour had increased its overall majority from 4 to 98 following the General Election in March.[83]

The Joint Steering Group, like the Stedeford Inquiry, was another painful turn of the screw of detailed Ministerial involvement in railway management. Raymond, having welcomed it initially on the grounds that its joint nature would help to sustain the morale of railway managers, later had cause to regret his decision. Johnson, his senior General Manager, saw through the exercise from the start. Writing to Raymond in March 1966, he remarked: 'I had always thought that some consultants might be forced upon us . . . We all know what can happen when such an enquiry is started by such a mixed group with such a very broad remit.' He urged Raymond to act as its Chairman, but in April Castle decided that Morris should do so.[84]

The J.S.G. began its work in June 1966. The Board was represented by

---

*Standby capacity, it was argued, was needed for unpredictable traffic surges, transfers from other transport modes in bad weather and defence.

Shirley, Margetts and James, who with Raymond formed a small policy-making team. There were four civil servants of Under-Secretary rank, two from the Ministry of Transport and one each from the Treasury and the Department of Economic Affairs.[85] Three 'independents' were chosen: J. P. Berkin, former Managing Director of Shell; J. G. Cuckney, Managing Director of the Standard Industrial Group; and A. J. Merrett, Professor of Finance at the London Business School. The Group was completed by J. W. Wardle, Running Movements Supervisor at British Rail's Tyseley Depot, Birmingham. His name emerged after Castle had insisted, to Raymond's consternation, on including 'a representative of the workers'. She had rejected the idea of appointing trade union officials 'because they would, in her view, take too partisan a line'. Wardle was, in fact, recommended to the Minister by the General Secretary of A.S.L.E.F., Albert Griffiths.[86] The Group was assisted by two Joint Executive Directors, Roy Hammond, Chief Officer (Special Duties), for the Board, and P. E. Lazarus, for the Ministry. No 'expert working party' was created. Instead, the Group worked through teams of expert advisers. Two firms of consultants were appointed, Cooper Brothers and Production-Engineering, although the latter was subsequently dropped.[87]

The Board's policy team accepted that organisation would have to be included in the J.S.G.'s terms of reference, given the government's plans for a national freight authority and for regional transport bodies. The precise wording was agreed as follows: 'to consider the suitability of the Board's management structure and procedures for the future operation of the system in the light of the contents of the White Paper and the changes which may stem therefrom'. Shirley was certainly prepared for the organisation issue to surface at an early stage and believed that something fundamentally different was required. But his colleagues were not keen to commit themselves, and the majority view inside the J.S.G. was that the subject would have to wait until the consultants had dealt with the other five of their six remits. Consequently, no organisational proposals were presented in the Group's interim report of January 1967.[88] Then, in February, after concern had been expressed at the tightness of the timetable if a bill were to be prepared by the end of the year, the Group agreed to accelerate discussion on the Board's management structure.[89] The organisation issue exposed a fundamental difference of opinion both within the J.S.G. and between Raymond and Castle. The Board had argued that it could not present sensible proposals on its own internal structure until the Minister decided upon the shape of the national freight organisation and 'the extent of the further sub-division of the railway structure'. It therefore limited its initial response to the formulation of broad principles for the industry as a whole. In October 1966 Raymond gave Castle a rough outline which envisaged a top or parent Board to control the assets of both B.R.B. and the Transport Holding Company and a series of Management Boards to deal with specific functions (railway management, freight traffic, passenger traffic and transport services). This ambitious scheme for integration, which enjoyed Raymond's full support, became redundant when Castle moved towards the concept of a 'free-standing' National Freight Corporation outside British Rail, taking over the sundries and the freightliner businesses. The N.F.C. fell far short of her original intentions for transport integration.[90]

Raymond and his colleagues clearly accepted that much was wrong with the internal organisation. But their response was disappointing, partly because there was no consensus about how to effect improvement. When Raymond (by this time Sir Stanley) canvassed the full-time members for their views in February 1967, he reflected a general concern that the existing organisation was cracking under the strain of fulfilling three roles – running the business, planning the business and conducting the external planning required by the J.S.G. The answers he received seemed to 'cancel each other out'. Some favoured a strengthening of the functional approach, others a delegation to the regions.[91] The most cogent contributions came from James and from Leonard Neal, who had been brought onto the Board in January from Esso to strengthen the industrial relations side. James reiterated the views he had put forward in September 1966. He was highly critical of the existing functional approach. The resultant confusion of responsibilities and loyalties encouraged a lack of clarity at the centre and a suspicion between H.Q. and the regions; and the co-ordination offered by the British Railways Management Committee was not working. The General Managers wanted to be informed, 'but they wish to be left alone to run their own business, happy in the thought that Headquarters will deal with the really difficult problems such as getting cover for their deficits and coping with Ministers and Ministries'. He advocated a downgrading of the regions, and a smaller, non-functional Board with a Vice-Chairman as Chief Executive (i.e. a Managing Director). Three or four members would have defined areas of interest, but functional duties would be left to senior managers. Neal was struck by what he called a 'quasi-military structure'. He also felt that 'to combine the functions of over-all policy-making with that of general management in a small Board' was 'likely to get the worst of both worlds'.[92]

Raymond warned: 'I have jealously guarded our right to participate in the formulation of national policy and having won that right we must ensure that our contribution is of the highest quality.'[93] Unfortunately, his Board was reluctant to put forward radical solutions, and slow to present proposals of any kind to the J.S.G. This served to encourage the Ministry to play an active part in the creation of a new Board structure. The independents, Cuckney and Berkin, found it hard to understand why the Board's representatives had not been more assertive in putting forward their view. Stewart Joy, who was one of the Ministry's economists on the J.S.G. assignment, has since explained it as 'the expected reaction of a group of tired managers, feeling misunderstood, groggy with inquiry, and beyond embarrassment about the mounting and apparently uncontrollable deficit'. This was true enough in the sense that both Margetts and James were ill during the Group's deliberations, but the Board's team also felt strongly that internal organisation was a matter for the Board itself to determine, and that to proceed otherwise would be to put one's head on the block.[94]

The Board's paper on management structure was finally produced in April 1967 and considered by the J.S.G. on 2 May. In it British Rail advocated a strengthening of functional control within the existing mix of functional and general (or 'line and staff') management. This process, it explained, had been encouraged by changes developed in 1966 – the creation of a B.R. Sundries Division, and the merger of the Eastern and North Eastern Regions. The Regional Boards, which were condemned as serving no essential purpose, were to be wound up. A new emphasis on the division, rather than the region, was proposed as the legitimate focus of 'territorial management'. On Board composition, it was suggested that there be two Vice-Chairmen, one 'inward-looking', to deal with operating and technical aspects, the other 'outward-looking', responsible for planning, commercial policy and finance. The remaining ten to fourteen members would include at least seven with functional duties. Co-ordination of the functional and the general elements of management would be secured by an Executive Policy Group consisting of the Chairman and two (or possibly three) Vice-Chairmen. Considerable emphasis was placed on the need for flexibility in approaching these goals. The Board wanted the freedom to introduce progressive and gradual changes. For this reason it suggested that the forthcoming Act should not prescribe rigidly and in detail. The railways should be allowed to submit a scheme for Ministerial approval, as they had done under the 1953 Act.[95]

It soon emerged that some very different ideas were circulating inside the J.S.G. In June the results of a straw poll of members, conducted by John Pears, senior partner in Cooper Brothers, at the Group's request, revealed a majority in favour of a *non*-functional Board and a Chief Executive. This approach was also favoured by Cooper Brothers' own report as well as by Pears himself.[96] The J.S.G. were in agreement with much that the Board proposed. Members were unanimous in recommending that the Regional Boards should go; that the General Managers be retained for the foreseeable future; and that it was desirable to retain flexibility in the legislative reference to organisation through provision for a scheme (as in the Iron and Steel Act of 1967). But the Board representatives found themselves in a minority when it came to a suitable constitution for the Board itself. Most of the J.S.G. wanted to follow the fashion for 'corporate planning'. This meant a small, non-functional planning Board led by a non-executive Chairman, plus a Chief Executive as Deputy-Chairman (in effect, a Chief General Manager to co-ordinate the running of the railways). The Chief Executive would be supported by specialists to handle corporate planning, finance and industrial relations (see Chart XI). The new organisation would satisfy the need for a more effective planning mechanism, to formulate and execute on a co-ordinated basis comprehensive 'profit' plans for each sector of the business. Despite Shirley's hostility to the notion of a Chief Executive and non-functional full-time Board members, and despite the embarrassing revelation that Coopers had not formally consulted the Board members before submitting their report, the 'Coopers' view' was duly incorporated into the J.S.G.'s final report of July 1967 and reproduced in the White Paper, *Railway Policy*, in November.[97]

By this time, the estrangement of Board and Ministry had become acute. Raymond worked doggedly towards his own conception of organisational improvement and pressed for the maximum flexibility for the future. For example, only two days after the Board had completed its submission on organisation and before it had been considered by the J.S.G., he pressed Castle to appoint Henry Johnson as a second, 'inward-looking' Vice-Chairman, as well as making other proposals for appointments to the finance and commercial functions. There was some logic in strengthening the Board, given the ill-health of Margetts and James and the strain being put on Raymond himself, but Castle found it hard to interpret this move as anything other than a plan to cement the existing functional framework. Nevertheless, she did consent to the appointment of Johnson, then 60, for a three-year period (salary: £10,000), and this was welcomed inside the business.[98]

Raymond also encouraged other changes during this interim period. On Johnson's appointment in June 1967 he created an informal Executive Group of Chairman and Vice-Chairmen. Further moves were designed to enhance the responsibility of chief officers. In August there was a belated attempt to improve planning at H.Q. by reorganising the planning staff and appointing R. A. Long as Chief Planning Manager, responsible to the Executive Group. The main impetus for this was the growing concern over railway freight and the wagon-load traffic in particular.[99] In October, the Board agreed to a major restructuring of its committee system. The British Railways Management, Management Staff, Planning and Workshops

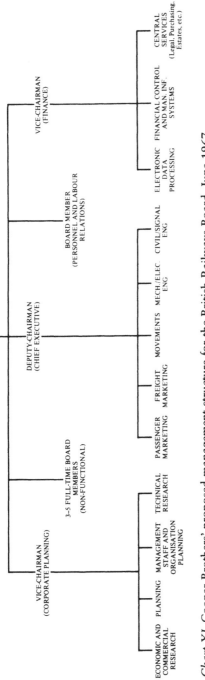

Chart XI Cooper Brothers' proposed management structure for the British Railways Board, June 1967

CHAIRMAN

VICE-CHAIRMAN (CORPORATE PLANNING)

DEPUTY-CHAIRMAN (CHIEF EXECUTIVE)

VICE-CHAIRMAN (FINANCE)

3–5 FULL-TIME BOARD MEMBERS (NON-FUNCTIONAL)

BOARD MEMBER (PERSONNEL AND LABOUR RELATIONS)

ECONOMIC AND COMMERCIAL RESEARCH

PLANNING

MANAGEMENT STAFF AND ORGANISATION PLANNING

TECHNICAL RESEARCH

PASSENGER MARKETING

FREIGHT MARKETING

MOVEMENTS

MECH./ELEC ENG

CIVIL/SIGNAL ENG

ELECTRONIC DATA PROCESSING

FINANCIAL CONTROL AND MAN. INF. SYSTEMS

CENTRAL SERVICES (Legal, Purchasing, Estates, etc.)

Committees were to be wound up (although, in fact, the latter continued to meet until the establishment of British Rail Engineering Ltd in 1970). A Production Committee of officers was set up under Johnson to run the railway; a Commercial Committee of officers, with Shirley as Chairman, was to co-ordinate the sales effort; and Neal was given the task of handling all staff matters except management development (which was to be the Chairman's responsibility). Contacts with the regions were to be co-ordinated by Johnson, and the Informal Conference of General Managers was transformed into an official Committee of the Board.[100]

One of the most pressing matters was the appointment of new Board members. Five men – Dunbar, Margetts, Ratter, H. P. Barker and Donachy – were due to retire at the end of 1967 and James was to follow in June 1968. Castle made it clear that she would take a close personal interest in filling these places and, much to Raymond's annoyance, insisted on specifying the duties of new appointees. In July, Raymond offered no objections to the departure of four of the five members (Ratter, he thought, might be retained for a short time). He also offered Shirley as a sacrificial lamb, barely a year after he and Castle had agreed to give him a second five-year term.[101] Tyzacks, the management consultants, were then asked to find suitable candidates for planning and finance. Unfortunately, no names were produced quickly, and the situation deteriorated further in October when Shirley, having asked to be released as a full-time member at the end of the year, cabled Raymond from Barbados to say that he was moving to Cunard as Deputy-Chairman.[102]

In addition to these tensions about appointments Raymond and Castle were also sharply divided over the organisation issue. In September Castle indicated that the Cabinet wanted to make the measures for financial reconstruction in the forthcoming bill conditional upon the Board's simultaneous implementation of the proposed changes in management structure. She also indicated that the J.S.G.'s report would be published in the White Paper on *Railway Policy*. In short, the Minister determined that there should be no transitional period, no flexibility in moving to a non-functional Board. Feelings ran high when she claimed, in a letter of 4 October, that the reference to flexibility in the J.S.G. report had only been inserted to spare the feelings of the Board representatives, an allegation which Raymond strenuously denied.[103] At the end of October the Board's disarray was complete when Raymond himself joined the list of casualties. The handling of his resignation reflected little credit on Castle. As Raymond later explained, in *The Sunday Times*:

It was a rather devastating experience to be pulled out of an important trade union meeting, summoned to see the Minister of Transport, informed that a report was appearing in the *Daily Mail* next day saying that I had been 'sacked', and told that if I resigned immediately and accepted a non-existent part-time job the story could be denied.

The job was the post of Chairman of the Freight Integration Council, a new body which Castle hoped would provide a measure of integration of road and rail transport. It was turning the knife in the wound to ask Raymond to lead this totem to a failed policy.[104]

There have been several attempts to explain Raymond's departure, not least by the two protagonists. Raymond saw himself as faced with a Minister who wanted to run the railways her way, which was something he could not agree to. Castle has contended that it was the Ministry who disliked him, believing him to be both inadequate and difficult, and arguing that he would not meet financial targets. She saw herself as getting on with him well enough while the civil servants were demanding a man with more management expertise. She has also explained that the three independent members of the J.S.G. did not believe that their recommendations would be implemented by B.R.B. as long as Raymond was Chairman, and pressed her to remove him. There is substance in both views, though Castle's disinterested stance is hardly convincing. Raymond was genuinely surprised by her decision, but it was the culmination of months of disagreement on a broad front. Raymond had strongly opposed the proposal to give British Rail's freightliner business to the National Freight Corporation. There had been problems with industrial relations and with pricing, where the Minister had asked for the deferral of a fare increase. She had also gone slow on rail closures. But it was Raymond's opposition to the organisation formula of the J.S.G. that tipped the balance, and his harsh dismissal of Gerard Fiennes, General Manager of the Eastern Region, in September 1967 for publishing an autobiographical critique of railway management, gave a further justification for his own enforced resignation.[105] As Castle pointed out, in an exchange of letters on 16 November, 'The Government's new policies will give the railways fresh terms of reference involving a different outlook in matters of finance and long-range planning. That is why I have concluded that there should be a change of leadership.'[106]

Raymond was a difficult man, but he was probably more sinned against than sinning. He was asked to put the Beeching steamroller into reverse, and had to submit to one of the most searching inquiries into a nationalised industry's affairs. He, more than anyone, had cause to resent the disturbance of government intervention. 'In my twenty-one years in public transport', he recalled, 'I calculate that at least half my time has been devoted to organisation, reorganisation, acquisition, denationalisation, centralisation, decentralisation, according to the requirements of the now regular political quinquennial revaluation of national transport policy.'[107]

On the debit side, Raymond was naive to suppose that a full integration of road and rail was a political possibility, given the record of the B.T.C. and the dismal performance of British Rail's sundries business; and he failed to produce any truly imaginative proposals to improve an internal management structure which he knew well was not functioning properly.

VII

Raymond formally resigned with effect from 31 December 1967, and for the last two months of the year British Rail was a rudderless ship with a dispirited crew. One can only sympathise with Raymond's predicament when he complained to Castle, on 29 November: 'In extremely difficult circumstances I am endeavouring to keep this business running.'[108] In fact, it proved extremely difficult for Castle to find a replacement for Raymond and to fill the other vacancies on the Board. The explanation is partly political and partly financial. Castle was determined to resist the attempt to replace Raymond with a right-wing financier, but competent businessmen with left-wing leanings were far from abundant. The name of Peter Parker, 43-year-old director of Booker McConnell, surfaced at an early stage, but doubts were expressed about his toughness, and Castle procrastinated. For the first time an attempt was made to trawl for a railway Chairman. John Tyzack produced a list of names, and informal soundings were taken. Morris made an approach to N. J. MacMillan, Chairman and President of Canadian National Railways, who had given advice to both Board and Ministry in the wake of the J.S.G. inquiry. Lord Robens offered the name of Matthew Stevenson, ex-member of the Stedeford Group and Permanent-Secretary at the Ministry of Power. Duncan Dewdney, Managing Director of Esso was a serious candidate, and so was Arthur Knight, Finance Director of Courtaulds. Johnson was the only railwayman to be considered. The press speculated about others, including Lord Campbell of Eskan, former Chairman of Booker McConnell, Frank Cousins and Arnold Weinstock of G.E.C.[109]

After much agonising Castle finally settled on Peter Parker, who had been recommended to her by Campbell. Parker was keen to take the post, but equally keen to see that the salary matched 'the competitive realities of management'. As he told the Minister, 'the effect of slipping in a new Chairman at the repressive level of the existing appointment would . . . be damaging to internal morale . . . Furthermore, a number of new key appointments will have to be made from outside; no Chairman could promise you success in recruitment at the top under the present conditions.' Parker asked for £17,500 a year, wanted Johnson as his Chief Executive at £15,000 and asked for authority to appoint from outside at

£13,500–17,500.[110] This problem could hardly have been unexpected. There was much contemporary debate about salary drift in the nationalised industries, encouraged by the recent appointment, in April 1967, of Lord Melchett as Chairman of the British Steel Corporation at £16,000, and his Deputy-Chairmen at £20,000–24,000, with which Parker had been associated as a member of the steel organising committee. The low level of remuneration in British Rail, both for Board members and senior managers, had been singled out for criticism by the J.S.G.[111] A stalemate was reached when Castle failed to get Parker's package through the Cabinet – her application coincided with Labour's decision to devalue the pound – and Parker refused to accept an abated rate of £12,500. As he explained to Castle on 24 November:

The authority of the top management will come under the sort of stress and strain you will know better than anybody. Therefore, the inner confidence and clarity of the command group in its relations with one another are the essentials of success . . . The sort of compromise which looks as if I will do anything to get the job puts me on a banana skin from the start. My recommendation is, once again, that you must build around Bill Johnson. He would be able to hold the situation for at least two years, and by that time new solutions may be possible.[112]

Castle then accepted Parker's advice, and on 13 December, Henry Johnson was duly installed as Chairman for the period from 1 January 1968 to 11 September 1971, which would be his 65th birthday. His salary was fixed at the 'normal' level of £12,500. The appointment was made with time running out, and there were some doubts as to whether the most appropriate man had been chosen. Castle, wanting someone to bring in fresh ideas, had been forced to turn instead to an out and out operating railwayman in his 62nd year. Champion of the General Managers, and with under six months' experience at the Board, he had been thrust suddenly into the arena. It was difficult to accept him as the ideal man to introduce a new organisation with a non-functional emphasis and to preside over the dismantling of regional authority.[113]

Johnson's preference for railway managers was soon evident when he turned to his first task – choosing his colleagues. After meetings with Castle and Tyzack in January, it became clear that financial constraints on salaries would make it difficult to attract able external candidates for the planning and finance roles, and this helped Johnson to press the case for internal appointments. He was also encouraged by the fact that corporate planning was such a new concept in Britain that external candidates could offer very little advantage over a good railway manager prepared to pick up the jargon from business school seminars. Cooper Brothers's report on 'Corporate Planning in British Railways' of November 1967 strengthened Johnson's position. This jargon-laden and somewhat imprecise document may have given the Board, as has recently been claimed, 'a useful outline of the procedures which should be followed to prepare a corporate plan'. But having maintained that such planning could not be satisfactorily introduced under the existing functional system, it encouraged a move back in this direction by suggesting that there should now be Board members with specific responsibilities for passenger traffic, freight and technical matters (see Chart XII, and cf. Chart XI).[114] Railwaymen were thus put up for promotion. It had already been decided to retain Ratter for another year. Then Johnson pressed Castle to accept three nominations for full-time posts: W. G. Thorpe, General Manager, London Midland Region, as Vice-Chairman and Chief Executive; David McKenna, General Manager of the Southern Region, as Planning Member; and A. V. Barker, Assistant General Manager, London Midland Region, with commercial functions in mind (including shipping and hotels). Castle agreed to appoint Thorpe and Barker with effect from 11 and 12 January respectively.[115] Difficulties arose over the planning and finance posts, however. Castle blocked the appointment of McKenna, who was supported by Tyzack as the best available candidate, because she believed it to be politically inexpedient to promote the manager of a region suffering adverse publicity after problems with its 1967 timetable and a serious accident at Hither Green (5 November 1967). He should, she said, 'sweat out the problems of the Southern'. Some potential outsiders were found for finance but nothing came of them. No progress was made before April 1968, when Castle was moved to the Department of Employment and Productivity, and succeeded by Richard Marsh, the 40-year-old Minister of Power.[116]

Marsh was the third Labour Minister of Transport in four years, a depressing record of impermanence paralleled only by the Conservatives' Ministerial changes in 1952–4. Like Castle before him, he 'could not see the slightest reason why I should be shifted into a Ministry about which I knew nothing and cared less'.[117] Indeed, it made no administrative sense to move Ministers while they were in the process of making major initiatives in the running of two key nationalised industries, steel and transport. Marsh had to familiarise himself quickly with the Transport Bill of December 1967, which fell to him to steer through parliament, and at the same time solve the appointments conundrum. The latter brought him into conflict with Johnson. By this time, Michael Bosworth had emerged as a serious candidate. Born in 1921, he had been a partner in the leading accountancy firm of Peat, Marwick, Mitchell & Co. since 1960, and had undertaken several major assignments, involving Bowaters, Rank Xerox and the Egg Marketing Board. Marsh wanted to appoint him as Vice-Chairman and member for 'finance planning', but Johnson persisted with McKenna's name, and thought it inadvisable to bring in a newcomer at

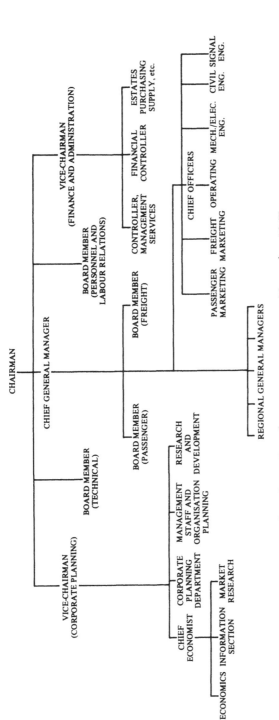

Chart XII Revised proposal for British Railways Board management structure, November 1967

such an exalted level. The Minister had his way. Bosworth was seconded for a three-year term in June 1968, at the specially arranged salary of £13,000 a year (on top of which the Board paid his annual pension contribution of £2,000). Marsh did agree to McKenna's appointment as a member without portfolio. He also joined the Board in June, and was asked to give his attention to the passenger side of the business, conurbation transport development, publicity and advertising.[118] The appointment of a Board member for finance was eventually resolved in the autumn. Three more outsiders were given serious consideration, but the best of these was said to require £16,000 a year. In the end, Marsh agreed that an internal candidate should be appointed. He was Geoffrey Wilson, the recently appointed Chief Officer (Financial Services) and protégé of Johnson and Thorpe. The rising star of British Rail's management development scheme, he was at 39 by far the youngest member of the Board, which he joined in October at a salary of £8,000 a year, half the reputed 'going rate'.[119]

Despite Ministerial preference for non-railwaymen, then, three of the four new full-time members came from inside the business. And the change of leadership left the initiative with career railwaymen. Johnson and Thorpe were close associates. Both had been traffic apprentices on the L.N.E.R. before the war. Both were past members of what Fiennes has called 'the gang from Whitemoor Yard', by which was meant managers who had reached the top via a Fenland outpost of freight operations, near March in Cambridgeshire. Thorpe had been a railwayman since 1927. He had worked under Johnson at Liverpool Street and Euston, and had been General Manager of the Scottish Region for four years before taking Johnson's place on the London Midland in 1967. He was very much Johnson's man. The same could be said of Barker and Wilson. Although they were technically outsiders, having come from the N.A.A.F.I. and Production-Engineering Ltd respectively, they both had experience of two regions at Assistant General Manager level, and both had served under Johnson and Thorpe at Euston. This is not to deny the variety of backgrounds and experience in Johnson's Board (see Table 41), a variety which was further enhanced by the acquisition of two new part-time members, Lord Taylor of Gryfe, from the Scottish Co-op, and Sir John Hunter, Chairman of Swan Hunter, the shipbuilders. But railway managers wanted a breathing-space after Raymond, Castle and the J.S.G., and this attitude was taken up by the Chairman and by Thorpe in particular. They accepted that further change was inevitable, but wanted to introduce this 'in a calm and reflective atmosphere'.[120]

"He's still breathing – what he really needs now is someone to put new heart into him!"

11 Reviving the railways with the Transport Act of 1968. Harold Wilson, Ray Gunter, Minister of Labour, and Barbara Castle, Minister of Transport, at the bedside: Emmwood, *Daily Mail*, 7 December 1967.

VIII

The Transport Act of 1968, which received the Royal Assent on 25 October, was the longest and the most important piece of legislation affecting nationalised transport. The emphasis was redirected from 'efficiency' and 'competition' towards 'service' and 'modal integration' in public transport. Several new bodies were established on and from Vesting Day, 1 January 1969, to give effect to this: the National Freight Corporation, Passenger Transport Authorities and their Executives, the Freight Integration Council (which took the place of the defunct Nationalised Transport Advisory Council set up in 1962), the National Bus Company and the Scottish Transport Group. The Transport Holding Company was to be dissolved. References to the railways were comparatively succinct. British Rail's recently established Sundries and Freightliner Divisions were passed to National Carriers Ltd and Freightliners Ltd, subsidiaries of the N.F.C. (with the Board retaining a 49 per cent stake in Freightliners Ltd). The Act provided for a major reconstruction of the Board's finances, and a distinction was made between 'commercial' and 'social' passenger rail services, the latter being eligible for grant-aid. In terms of organisation, the

Table 41. *The British Railways Board, 1 November 1968*

Full-time members (Salary: Chairman £12,500, Bosworth £13,000, Thorpe £10,000, Ratter £9,000, Houchen, James and McKenna £8,500, Jones £7,000, others £8,000)

Name	Date of appointment	Age on 1 November 1968	Education	Previous post	Experience	Left B.R.B.
Sir Henry Johnson, C.B.E. (Chairman)	1968 (1967)[a]	62	Bedford Modern	Vice-Chairman B.R.B.; General Manager, L.M.R.	Railways	Sept. 1971
W. G. Thorpe (Vice-Chairman)	1968	59	Nunthorpe Grammar School	General Manager, L.M.R.	Railways	Oct. 1974
J. M. W. Bosworth (Vice-Chairman)	1968	47	Bishop's Stortford College	Partner, Peat, Marwick, Mitchell & Co.	Accountancy	June 1983
A. V. Barker, O.B.E.	1968	58	Whitley and Monkseaton High School; L.S.E.	Assistant General Manager, L.M.R.	Accountancy; NAAFI; railways	Nov. 1974
H. O. Houchen	1964	61	Canterbury College, University of New Zealand	General Manager, B.R. Workshop	Air transport; electrical industry	July 1969
P. G. James	1965	64	Amersham Grammar School; L.S.E.	Financial Controller, B.R.B.	Accountancy (London Transport)	June 1969
Dr Sydney Jones	1965	57	Cyfarthfa Castle Grammar School; Cardiff Technical College; Birmingham University	Chief of Research, B.R.B.	Scientific research (Radar, C.E.G.B. etc.)	June 1976

Name		Age	School/University	Previous position	Background	Date
David McKenna, C.B.E.	1968	57	Eton; Trinity College, Cambridge	General Manager, S.R.	Railways; London Transport	Aug. 1978
L. F. Neal	1967	55	L.S.E.; Trinity College, Cambridge	Labour Relations Adviser (Esso)	Trade unions (T.G.W.U.); oil industry	Oct. 1971
John Ratter, C.B.E.	1962	60	St Peter's York; Durham University	Technical Adviser, B.T.C.	Railways	March 1970
Geoffrey Wilson	1968	39	Bolton Grammar School; Birmingham University	Chief Officer (Financial Services), B.R.B.	Management accountancy; railways	Jan. 1971
Part-time members (Salary: £1, 000):						
F. Hayday, C.B.E.	1962	56	No information	—	Trade unions (General and Municipal Workers' Union)	Dec. 1975
Sir John Hunter, C.B.E.	1968	55	Oundle; Cambridge and Durham Universities	—	Shipbuilding (Swan Hunter)	June 1971
Philip H. Shirley	1968 (1961)[a]	56	Sydney C. of E. Grammar School	Vice-Chairman, B.R.B.	Accountancy (Peat Marwick, Rank, Unilever)	Dec. 1968
J. MacNaughton Sidey, D.S.O.	1962	54	Exeter School	—	Shipping (P. & O.)	Dec. 1968
Lord Taylor of Gryfe	1968	56	Bellahouston Academy, Glasgow	—	Co-op	June 1980

[a] Date of first appointment to B.T.C./B.R.B.

Board's composition of Chairman, one or two Vice-Chairmen and 10-16 members under the 1962 Act, became a Chairman and 9-15 members. The Board was, like the N.F.C., to undertake a review of its activities 'so far as regards the direction thereof', and to report to the Minister within 12 months of the passing of the Act. Provision was also made for the submission of further reviews, on the initiative of either party. A new departure was the clause prohibiting the Board from making any substantial change in its organisation without Ministerial consent. Finally, the statutory requirement for Regional Railway Boards was removed.[121]

In January 1968, the Board encouraged preparatory work on a new organisation by creating a Headquarters Committee consisting of Hammond, now the Chief Secretary, and Arnold Kentridge, Chief Management Staff Officer. It produced draft schemes on the basis of the J.S.G. recommendations. However, some opposition to the idea of moving towards a non-functional organisation surfaced at Board level, and it also became clear that a great deal of further work would be needed to convert draft outlines into a scheme for submission to the Minister. So in April the Board decided to bring in another firm of management consultants to assist it in this task. The employment of consultants, it was argued, would help to validate the recommended changes both internally and in the eyes of Government. McKinsey & Co. was the firm selected. It was already examining the provision of a suitable organisation for British Rail's Shipping and International Services Division, which had been established on a more centralised basis in January.[122] The McKinsey exercise set in motion yet another long and often agonising process of organisational change. The consultants reported in three stages – August 1968, March 1969 and August 1969 – and a scheme was put up to the Ministry at the end of November 1969. The new Board organisation was finally introduced on 1 January 1970, nearly five years after Raymond had declared that something was wrong. Even then, Stage II of the operation, a revised structure for the regions, whose Boards were allowed to continue in non-statutory form after 1968, remained to be tackled.

Parallel with the Board/McKinsey deliberations, the business still had to be run, and several 'interim' adjustments to the organisation were necessary in 1968 and 1969. Some of these were the direct result of the 1968 Act. The Sundries Division, for example, which had been created in December 1966, had to be passed to the N.F.C. at the beginning of 1969. The same was true of the Freightliner business, which had also been set up as a separate Division. Other moves followed on from the J.S.G.'s recommendations while the Transport Bill was proceeding through parliament. In February 1968 the Board delegated certain functions to a Headquarters Executive Committee, established under W. G. Thorpe as Chief Executive to deal with the executive administration of the railways. The new

Committee, which was renamed Executive Committee (Railways) in January 1969, replaced the existing Production, Commercial, and Commercial and Operating Committees. It brought together chief officers from finance, engineering, operating, industrial relations and public relations, and the Chief Secretary, Hammond, whose department had been separated, once again, from the legal department. The intention was to enable the Board to concentrate upon its proper task, 'to overlook and direct the business as a whole', and to improve inter-departmental co-ordination at the centre. The Board also moved from fortnightly to monthly meetings in June 1968.[123]

Could it be said that a non-functional Board was now operating? Only in part, since the original idea of creating a *small*, planning Board had dissolved during the deliberations of the J.S.G. in favour of a half-way house between a functional and planning body, with a Chief Executive and a planning member grafted on to what already existed, and statutory provision for a fairly large Board of 10-16 members. This conception of the new organisation, which enjoyed Johnson's support, was given further impetus when Bosworth and McKenna joined the Board in June 1968. Bosworth was made responsible for corporate planning, while McKenna was asked to assume responsibility for the passenger side of the business, leaving A. V. Barker to concentrate on freight selling. In addition, Barker and James were to handle the transfer of the Sundries and Freightliners Divisions, and James was to deal with grant-aided services and the surplus capacity issue. How far these responsibilities were truly 'functional' in the sense that they carried authority 'down the line' is difficult to determine. Certainly McKenna and Barker were directed to work 'in collaboration with the Chief Executive', and the arrangements were regarded as temporary pending the outcome of McKinsey's report. Nevertheless, there were Board members who continued to support a functional emphasis, and the continuation of the Board's committee structure – Finance, Supply, Works and Equipment (re-named Investment in October 1968), Workshops, Property, and so on – served to perpetuate the status quo. Clearly, the success or failure of a non-functional reorientation depended upon a precise definition of the role and authority of the Chief Executive in relation to his colleagues with 'special areas of interest'. This was one of the most important elements of the McKinsey exercise.[124]

The circumstances in which McKinsey & Co. were invited to assist the Board reveal basic divisions inside 222, Marylebone Road. By April 1968 the Hammond/Kentridge Committee's work had shown that the Board was split into two camps. One favoured a clear non-functional, that is non-executive, Board, with day-to-day management left to a Chief Executive supported by senior officers as executive directors. The other supported the retention of functional management for the non-railway activities (shipping, hotels etc.), and a measure of functional responsibility in railway finance, manpower, selling, and engineering. Some Board members were not keen to give up their authority, and the latter view was given a nudge by allowing two former Board members, Margetts and Dunbar, who had been retained on a part-time basis, to have their say.[125] There was also a disagreement over the choice of consultants. Hammond wanted to appoint Cooper Brothers who, like McKinsey, were already advising the Board, in this instance on its freight marketing organisation. Kentridge, on the other hand, supported McKinsey. This alignment was rather puzzling, since McKinsey was known to favour a pure non-executive Board and a Chief Executive, on which Kentridge had expressed doubts. Hammond was clearly worried about the impact McKinsey would make. He claimed to have evidence 'which indicates that their approach has in many instances been radical and has caused difficulty', and examples of dissatisfied customers were offered as evidence, including I.C.I., Shell and the Dutch airline K.L.M. Nevertheless, at an informal meeting of full-time members on 8 April, McKinsey got the vote. They were certainly the pre-eminent specialists in the organisation field and in 1968 were also employed by the B.B.C. and the Bank of England.[126]

It was agreed that McKinsey would report in two stages, the first a general assessment of the Board's role, the second a more detailed analysis of the whole management structure. The McKinsey team, led by Hugh Parker, made its initial views known in a paper entitled 'Organizing the Board for the 1970s' in August 1968. This went further than the J.S.G. formula and recommended that the Board be converted from its present semi-functional structure into a fully non-executive form, with the Chief Executive enjoying full 'line' authority for the railway business. Full-time members would be given a number of specified non-executive interests. The change, said the consultants, would require a drastically remodelled railway organisation below the Chief Executive, with improved management information, planning and control systems.[127]

McKinsey's views could hardly have been unexpected, since Hugh Parker had written much the same thing in The Director in May. But they encountered further opposition inside the Board, notably from Neal, Ratter and James. The latter, who had argued against the functional form in 1966 and 1967 (see above, p. 354), now made it clear that to him 'non-functional' (or non-executive) did not preclude a Board with members who would have 'overall supervisory power over a range of functions . . . with a Managing Director pulling all together'. He was hostile to the idea of a Board 'thinking in a vacuum', becoming a group of 'uncommitted thinkers'.[128] Self-interest (and possibly self-preservation) was a motivating force. As Hammond wryly observed, 'most Members have been closely and directly involved in management, and it will be rather like transplant-

ing them from the nettlebed of management to the cold frame of thinking!'. Although, therefore, the Board agreed to accept the report as the
basis for further work, some members continued to express reservations
about moving to a fully non-executive system.[129]

The next six months saw some give and take between the consultants
and the Board. McKinsey, like Cooper Brothers before them, found
themselves being pulled back from the concept of a simple, non-executive
Board. Parker was put under some pressure to modify his scheme. He was
reported as saying that he had never been faced with a more difficult
assignment. McKinsey's second report, on 'Proposed Board and Management Structure' of March 1969, provided a more detailed analysis of the
Board's future headquarters organisation. It also attempted to ease the
anxiety over the terms 'non-functional' and 'non-executive', making an
important distinction between the 'corporate' functions of the Board and
the 'management' functions of executives. The Board would be non-
executive, but individual members were to be assigned 'specific corporate
"functional" and other non-executive responsibilities'. In other words,
some members would retain their existing interests, but would not exercise
authority down the line. The distinction was intended to pacify the
doubters on the Board. The Chief Executive was to be given 'full profit
accountability and executive authority (a) for the current management of
British Rail, and (b) for developing future railway plans for Board review
and approval'. In order to ensure his successful functioning, it was
suggested that his 'span of command' be reduced by combining 20 or so
headquarters departments into five major units, each led by a 'General
Manager' (subsequently, the agreed title was 'Executive Director'). The
five posts were in Systems and Operations, Freight Services Planning/
Marketing, Passenger Services Planning/Marketing, Finance (excluding
Corporate Finance) and Personnel (industrial relations, education and
establishment control). In addition, the five Regional General Managers
were to report directly to the Chief Executive in a 'line' relationship
pending a reassessment of the regional structure. The Chief Executive was
thus to have a management team, in essence an 'Executive Board', of ten
managers. Finally, Thorpe's dual role as Chief Executive and Deputy-
Chairman was criticised, McKinsey recommending instead that the posts
of Chairman, Deputy-Chairman and Chief Executive should be
separate.[130]

On 10 April 1969 the Board accepted the report, with minor modifications, as a discussion document to be used to obtain the Minister's general
approval of the new organisation. The passages referring to Thorpe's dual
position were excised, but the issue was put to the Minister in a letter from
Johnson. It was then decided that McKinsey should proceed to the next
stage, to work with the new management team in defining the new

organisation in detail and its working relationship with the regions. The consultants' promised work on a new regional structure and revised planning and control procedures was deferred.[131] The Board, pressed by Thorpe in particular, had anticipated events by taking further steps to create an effective executive machinery. In December 1968, some months before endorsing McKinsey's second report, it created a Research and Development Committee and decided to establish a new post of Executive Director (Passenger Services), appointing R. A. Long with effect from May 1969. In January 1969 Arnold Kentridge was appointed in Long's place to the retitled post of Controller of Corporate Planning. In March the industrial relations and management staff departments were merged under David Bowick as Executive Director (Personnel). S. C. Robbins was earmarked for the post of Executive Director (Freight). All these moves were made before the organisation draft was sent to the Ministry.[132]

Marsh, and his Permanent-Secretary, Sir David Serpell, who had succeeded Padmore in November 1968, were prepared to support the move to a non-executive Board. But by the beginning of June Marsh had made it plain that he thought the 'pure McKinsey doctrine', in proposing a Chief Executive with overall responsibility for the railway business, went much further than the J.S.G. formula. He was in favour of the Chief Executive working with the 'corporate functional' members for planning and finance as a 'team'. As Hugh Parker noted, 'there seems to be a belief in the Ministry that important Board functions will not be properly discharged unless they are assigned to specially appointed Members'. At the same time, Marsh insisted that the Chief Executive be a member of the Board, a view he later opposed when Chairman. This was entirely a question of controlling appointments. Marsh could not appoint the Chief Executive unless he were on the Board, and he could not discharge his statutory duty to ensure that the railways were properly organised unless he made the appointment.[133]

The argument between the Minister and the Board on these essentials was matched by a division within the Board on the choice of a Chief Executive. When Thorpe asked his colleagues for names in April 1969, there was no consensus of opinion. Robert Lawrence (London Midland) and Lance Ibbotson (Southern) emerged as contenders among the General Managers, but there was also a strong lobby in favour of Thorpe's remaining in his dual position. The response of Geoffrey Wilson, the youngest and least experienced member, was revealing. Maintaining that the job was too big for a General Manager, he asked if the field were open to Board members, and offered his own name together with that of McKenna.[134] Thorpe at first felt that Lawrence might understudy the post, but by May had moved in favour of appointing Wilson at the end of the year. Johnson appeared to agree with him. But his draft letter to the Minister of 2 July, 'strongly recommending' Wilson, was not sent, and in discussions with Marsh the Chairman played for time.[135] Another attempt to resolve the dispute was made on 13 August. Once again, the Board was divided, and the Wilson supporters, Johnson, Thorpe and Bosworth, found themselves in a clear minority. A fortnight later a compromise was reached. Thorpe was to remain as Chief Executive until at least mid-1970, and Wilson was to give up his corporate responsibilities for finance to Bosworth and act as Thorpe's assistant. This arrangement was put to Marsh in September. The idea of including a young, non-railwayman in the top three posts was pressed despite the concern of some Board members that none of the General Managers (three of whom were over 60) had been offered an Executive Directorship.[136]

It was not an easy time at the Board. The finishing touches to the new organisation were made in an atmosphere of acrimony, which was not eased by the consultants' preference for theoretical concepts rather than practical suggestions. The failure to secure a clear choice of Chief Executive – a crucial matter since the Board was delegating a considerable part of its business to this man – and Bosworth's new role combining planning *and* finance scarcely impressed a Minister who favoured something closer to the original J.S.G. proposals. Barker and Neal continued to express disappointment with their reduced role, and three disgruntled full-time members – Houchen, James and Ratter – retired or resigned in the course of the year.[137] Marsh's appointment of two part-timers as replacements – Alan Walker, Chairman of Bass Charrington, and Derek Palmar, Director of the merchant bankers Hill Samuel – also produced an element of discord. Johnson had recommended Walker, a part-time member of the London Midland Regional Board, but was opposed to Palmar who, like Bosworth, had formerly been with Peat Marwick, on the grounds that he had enough financial expertise already. Furthermore, the appointments were made just when the part-time member Lord Taylor of Gryfe had reported to the Minister that the new organisation threatened to make it even harder for part-timers to play an effective role.[138]

The final ironies in the McKinsey exercise were a reversion to 'J.S.G. principles' by the consultants and yet one more shake-up of Transport in Whitehall. McKinsey's 'Proposed Charter for the British Railways Board' was submitted in August 1969, discussed with the trade unions in September, and a further paper, 'Organizing for the 1970s', was then discussed in detail with the Ministry. Serpell drew particular attention to the change of emphasis, in the Chief Executive's terms of reference, from running the railway to planning. McKinsey were now prepared, moreover, to see corporate planning, finance and industrial relations as 'exceptions to

the non-executive rule'. A fee in excess of £150,000 was a great deal to pay
for consultancy which had boldly departed from the J.S.G. recommendations only to be pulled back towards them.[139] And, then, in the middle of
the consultations, Marsh was sacked by Harold Wilson, on 5 October.
Another Minister appeared in the shape of Fred Mulley. As though to
underline the low priority and status accorded to Transport in the pecking-
order of political office, Mulley was appointed without Cabinet rank and
Transport, it was announced, would be merged in a new Department of
Environment. It was Mulley who gave his consent to the final B.R.B./
McKinsey report on organisation on 1 December. His stay was also short.
On 18 June 1970 the Conservatives were returned with an overall majority
of 30 and John Peyton became the Minister in a Department led by Peter
Walker.[140]

IX

The new organisation, which came into effect on 1 January 1970, was
outlined in a White Paper printed on 11 December 1969. The B.R.B. was
henceforth 'mainly non-executive'. There was a chief executive for each
business – railways, hotels, property, B.R.E.L. (now with wider powers to
sell equipment), shipping, hovercraft and advertising (a joint interest with
the National Bus Company) – and each of the non-railway activities was
controlled through a subsidiary Board led by a main Board member (see
Chart XIII). The aim of the organisation was to establish a clearly defined
structure, with every manager 'fully accountable for the results he
achieves', and a 'systematic planning and control process', based on the
setting of objectives and the development of long- and short-term plans.
The Board would concentrate on 'corporate planning, policy making and
longer term direction'.[141] The Chief Executive (Railways) was supported
by a Railway Management Group, which had been first established in
August 1969 by fusing the Executive Committee (Railways) with the
General Managers' Committee. Its membership in 1970 is set out in Table
42.
    Much depended on how successfully the Board could distinguish clearly
between its corporate (i.e. all activity) departments such as planning, its
railway departments centred on the Chief Executive and its subsidiary
businesses such as hotels and shipping. The new Board retained distinct
executive (or functional) features, and the relationship between the Chief
Executive and his Board colleagues remained to be worked out in detail.
Bosworth as Vice-Chairman was responsible for both corporate planning
and corporate finance, and Neal was responsible for the corporate personnel function. Both men exercised 'line authority' over the relevant H.Q.

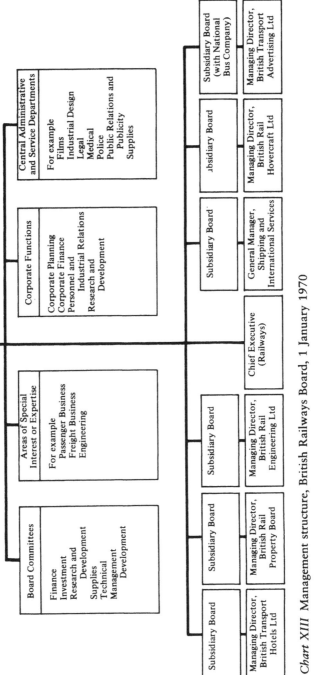

Chart XIII Management structure, British Railways Board, 1 January 1970

Table 42. *The Railway Management Group, 1970*

W. G. Thorpe (Chairman)	Chief Executive
Geoffrey Wilson (Deputy-Chairman)	Board member
D. M. Bowick	Executive Director (Personnel)
A. G. Kentridge	Executive Director (Planning)
R. A. Long	Executive Director (Passenger)
W. O. Reynolds	Executive Director (Systems and Operations)
S. C. Robbins	Executive Director (Freight)
A. W. Tait	Executive Director (Finance)
J. Bonham-Carter	General Manager (Western)[a]
I. M. Campbell[b]	General Manager (Eastern)
L. W. Ibbotson	General Manager (Southern)[a]
R. L. E. Lawrence	General Manager (London Midland)[a]
G. W. Stewart	General Manager (Scottish)[a]
A. E. Robson	Managing Director (B.R.E.L.)
Eric Merrill	Controller, Public Relations and Publicity (Associate member)

[a] Also Chairman of non-statutory Regional Board.
[b] D.S.M. Barrie to May 1970.

departments, and Neal was expected to work closely with the Executive Director (Personnel), David Bowick. But Bowick was also in a direct 'line' relationship with the Chief Executive, whose remit included the taking of action 'to meet ad hoc developments (e.g. industrial strikes . . .)'. There was also a potential clash with Bosworth, in that the Chief Executive had a duty to contribute to 'top-level policy making and decision taking for the railway *and the Board as a whole*' (my italics), and to develop both one- and five-year plans. Planning and finance had both a 'corporate' and a 'railway' existence. On the technical side, where the Board had lost the services of Ratter and Houchen, the engineering departments reported through Reynolds, the Executive Director (Systems and Operations), to the Chief Executive. But Thorpe did not control Research and Development, which remained the responsibility of Sydney Jones as a non-executive Board member and Chairman of the Board's R. & D. and Technical Committees.[142] The remaining Board members retained 'areas of special interest or expertise' – McKenna, for example, looked after publicity and London and South East passenger transport – and the central service departments such as Legal, Public Relations and Publicity, and Supplies (see Chart XIII) were allocated to individuals. There was a range of main Board Committees, for Finance, Investment, Management Development, and so on. The introduction of a Chief Executive represented an organisational improvement, but the Board remained a multifaceted entity, a mix of the executive and non-executive, with the Chief Executive combining 'line' and 'staff' functions. Given the element of overlapping responsibilities in this shift to a more modern managerial style, the way in which individuals interacted was critical – as soon became evident during 1971.

The administration of the railways under the Thorpe/Wilson regime in 1969–71 revealed the many difficulties in bedding down the new organisation. The minutes of the Board, Chairman's Conference, and Railway Management Group suggest a new dynamism, led by the enthusiastic Wilson, and a considerable effort to pursue the long list of Board and railway objectives. These included the production of a corporate plan and its major constituent, the Rail Plan, and the development, in conjunction with McKinsey, of a management information and control system (MIPAC)* and a new 'field' organisation for the railway regions. But there were problems in relating the Chief Executive's initiatives to those generated by the Board itself as well as in determining the relationships between his team of Executive Directors and, on the one hand, the functionally responsible Board members and, on the other, the General Managers. No sooner had the Railway Management Group been established in August 1969 than there were hints of a lack of clarity in determining the dividing line between the 'railway' and the 'corporate' roles for finance and personnel. Thorpe and Wilson also introduced private informal meetings with the Executive Directors. These meetings, known from November as the Executive Directors' Conference, were no doubt vital for the smooth working of the management team, but the exclusion of the General Managers ran counter to the idea of integrating the latter in centralised decision-making.[143]

Thorpe's view of his joint role was that it was both burdensome and contradictory. When at last the Board agreed that Wilson should take on the post of Chief Executive, with effect from 1 February 1971, Johnson obtained the consent of the new Minister, John Peyton, to Wilson's resignation from the Board. In this way it was hoped that the line of authority from Board to Chief Executive would be made clear.[144] Wilson's place on the Board was filled by Robert Lawrence, General Manager of the London Midland Region since 1968, who was also appointed on 1 February. A career railwayman with both engineering and operating experience, he had, like Johnson and Thorpe, the characteristic background of numerous changes of job and location since first appointed as a traffic apprentice in 1934.[145]

Wilson's appointment as Chief Executive was uncomfortably brief for in May 1971 he suddenly resigned, the resignation taking effect as from 11

*Management Information Systems for Planning and Controlling Railway Activities.

July. This young, thrusting newcomer had caught the eye several times, notably as Shirley's protégé in a cost-cutting exercise for the Central Division of the Southern Region in 1964, and later in Scotland, where he participated in the region's moves towards a two-tier organisation in 1966.[146] But, committed though he was, his abrasive, and dogmatic manner had ruffled many feathers during his swift rise up the promotional ladder, and opposition to his appointment within the Board persisted. This was evident when the matter of his salary was debated. Since five members of the Railway Management Group were being paid £10,200-10,700, Johnson argued that Wilson should receive an advance on his Board salary of £11,000 and had obtained Peyton's agreement to a salary range of £10,000–15,000 for the post. Wilson's Board colleagues agreed to a rise of only 5 per cent to £11,550, and insisted that Thorpe continue as Chairman of the Railway Management Group.[147] But the precise reasons for what the Board minutes of 12 and 13 May record as Wilson's resignation in 'special circumstances' remain obscure. There is a suggestion that the continuing uncertainty as to the precise authority and functions of the post contributed to his decision to leave British Rail after eight years' service. This emerges from a letter he wrote to Richard Marsh who took over from Johnson as Chairman of B.R.B. shortly after Wilson's departure. 'My concern', he explained, 'stems primarily from the principle that in my opinion the Board should not delegate authority to the Chief Executive to such an extent that it becomes almost an abdication of the Board's responsibility which in the last resort it cannot escape.' In certain key areas, such as passenger and freight pricing, delegation to the Chief Executive had become almost absolute. He deplored the lack of clarity in the responsibility for generating long-term strategic planning for the railway business. There may of course have been other reasons for his going when he did. There are hints of some sort of personal crisis. There may, or may not, be truth in The Economist's suggestion that he looked with concern at the appointment of Marsh who, while Minister, had been critical of some of the railways' investment proposals with which Wilson had been much associated. The second stage of the McKinsey exercise, a new 'field' organisation, on which Wilson had worked, was drawing to a close and promised a long and bitter struggle to implement it. Finally, there is a suggestion that he felt that some of the wage settlements concluded by Neal would prejudice the short-run performance of the railways, for which he was responsible.[148]

Whatever the reasons, his sudden departure did not resolve the problem of establishing a Chief Executive in a mixed Board. At a private session of the Board on 22 June 1971, the members agonised again over the post. By this time Marsh had become the Chairman-designate. He felt that 'the job was one of the top ten in the country and . . . found difficulty in seeing how any one man . . . could possibly completely fulfil requirements'. Derek Palmar maintained that the job specification was wrong. He wanted to appoint a Chief General Manager (Railways), and to reconstitute the Railway Management Group as an executive committee of the Board consisting of Board members. There was clearly no consensus. Eventually, the Board agreed to appoint David Bowick in Wilson's place. Bowick, the former Executive Director (Personnel), had succeeded Lawrence as General Manager of the London Midland Region. His appointment as Chief Executive in July 1971 came after only five months at Euston.[149] Even then, the problem of determining the Chief Executive's role surfaced from time to time. In May 1975, for example, Marsh and Mulley, Minister of Transport for a second time when Labour was returned to office in 1974, clashed over the latter's proposal to link Lawrence's appointment as Vice-Chairman with the announcement that he would relieve Bowick of some of his duties. Marsh made it clear that it would undermine Bowick's position to 'share out the executive authority of a Chief Executive'.[150] In the following year Bowick was appointed to the Board and in 1977 he combined the roles of Vice-Chairman and Chief Executive. The posts were separated again in 1978 when I. M. Campbell became Chief Executive (and also functional member for engineering), but his successor, R. B. Reid, later acted in both capacities (but with no additional functional responsibilities). The precise role of a Chief Executive within the Board's structure does not appear to have been conclusively resolved.*

What, then, was the organisational legacy of the Johnson/Thorpe/ Wilson period? The new organisation of 1970 was an advance on past practice in its enthusiasm for corporate planning, management by objectives and the setting and monitoring of detailed business plans. The new executive management structure promised a more effective control of the business from the centre, though it did not begin to work properly until the mid-1970s. Furthermore, the second stage of the reorganisation, a slimmed-down and more cost-effective regional organisation in which the five regions were to be replaced by eight territories, was only accepted in principle after Johnson's retirement.

The Johnson period will always be associated with the railways' pursuance of the corporate planning objective. Aided by Cooper Brothers

---

*Since September 1982 a triumvirate has been responsible for the railway business. It first consisted of Reid as Chief Executive and two Deputy Chief Executives, one responsible for Sectors, the other for Resources. The organisation survived Reid's appointment as Vice-Chairman, in January 1983, and Chairman, in September 1983. A further adjustment was made with effect from February 1984. Reid continued to act as head of the railway business, but without the title of Chief Executive, and his deputies were re-designated Deputy Managing Directors (Railways).

and McKinsey, the Board made considerable progress in this key area of systematised financial and managerial control, gaining the reputation of being relatively advanced in comparison with the other nationalised industries and many large firms in the private sector.[151] In reality, however, both the Board and its planning managers were feeling their way very tentatively in the initial work on a corporate plan, to which the frequent changes in organisation testify. A major source of difficulty, as already indicated, was the relationship between 'railway planning' and 'corporate planning' for the Board as a whole. When Kentridge took up the post of Controller of Corporate Planning in March 1969, his aim was to codify and rationalise the several business plans to be generated by each of the eight businesses, including the railways. M. H. Harbinson was appointed as Planning Manager (Rail), reporting via K. V. Smith, the Corporate Planning Manager, to Kentridge. But the organisation chart also showed a 'dotted line' link to the Chief Executive (Railways). In the reshuffling of staff, some planners were transferred to passenger and freight marketing while the new works section was absorbed, which also contributed to the state of flux. There were differences of opinion over the placing of financial specialists – Wilson and Tait wanted to retain them as a corporate planning team within the Finance Department, while Bosworth wanted to position one in each business sector – and over the provision for engineering planning. A further complication was the remit of Stewart Joy, who had been appointed Chief Economist within the Corporate Planning Department in November 1968, but who was intended to be used as a resource by Board members and others. As Bowick admitted at the time, nobody had a clear enough idea of what was required of the Planning Department to be dogmatic about its organisation.[152]

It was soon realised that the pressures on Harbinson, who had the task of assisting the Chief Executive in preparing five-year and one-year rail plans without adequate staff, were too great. In February 1970 Bowick recommended the establishment of a separate railway planning department under Kentridge, who would report to the Chief Executive as Executive Director (Planning). He was to be supported by Harbinson as Railway Planning Officer and C. J. R. Clemow as Planning Officer (Development). The new department was set up in March. In consequence, K. V. Smith was appointed to the regraded post of Controller of Corporate Planning. Joy was to report directly to Bosworth. At the same time, the Corporate Planning Department's market research section was transferred to an independent subsidiary company called Transmark (Transportation Systems & Market Research Ltd) run initially by Margetts as Chairman and Acting Managing Director.[153] In effect, the balance of power shifted from the 'corporate' to the 'railway'.

The March 1970 organisation also proved to be short-lived. Only five months later, the need to embrace satisfactorily long-term planning led to a further internal reorganisation. The Corporate Planning Department was divided into two main sections, the first under a Corporate Planning Officer, the second under a Planning Manager (Development). Subsequent experience with the First Corporate Plan, which was presented to the Minister in December 1970, raised serious doubts as to the need for two separate planning departments. There was a particular difficulty with the 'corporate' and 'railway' elements in long-term strategic planning.[154] In February 1971 Kentridge asked Ian Todd, the Organisation Planning Officer, to undertake a review of the Railway Planning Department, paying particular attention to the apparent duplication of strategic planning work by the Planning Officer (Development) and the Planning Manager (Development). Todd discovered that the problem of duplication ran much deeper:

It seems we really have a problem of planning hierarchy on our hands. The present arrangement where the Corporate Planning Department has a total responsibility for presentation of the Board's 5 year Corporate Plan which includes the 5-year rail plan is open to question. The rail plan itself constitutes by far the greatest factor in the total corporate group and whilst the other businesses are not insignificant by any means, it is extremely doubtful if they have any effect on the rail plan at all.[155]

Kentridge then presented proposals to amalgamate the two departments once more. The aim, as he explained in April 1971, was to avoid 'problems related to the interface between Rail and Corporate Planning', and, equally important, to achieve staff savings in an area of rapidly escalating cost. Bosworth supported the change, and Kentridge was duly installed as Controller of Corporate Planning again in September. His new organisation of three principal officers, for Corporate Planning (G. R. Burt), Rail Planning (Harbinson), and Strategic Planning (P. Corbishley), was in place by November.[156] The frequent changes in the handling of the planning function indicate the experimental nature of much of the work. There was a shared dissatisfaction with the early corporate planning effort and at times a confusion of roles. The Board itself tended to rubber-stamp the various business plans as they emerged. It was not really acting in a truly corporate fashion, and in consequence some of the full-time members took refuge in their executive responsibilities for the subsidiary businesses. It was not until the mid-1970s that corporate planning was satisfactorily established in British Rail.

X

Johnson's term of office was to expire in September 1971. His successor, Richard Marsh, was found by Peter Walker, the Secretary of State for the Environment in Edward Heath's Conservative Government. Walker and Marsh were old friends, despite their apparent political differences. In fact, Marsh, though still a member of both the Labour Party and the National Union of Public Employees, had become somewhat disillusioned with politics since his dismissal by Harold Wilson. He had since then collected a string of minor directorships, and, having turned to 'managerialism rather than socialism', relished the prospect of putting his ideas about nationalised industry into practice. He came to the Board in May as Joint Deputy-Chairman and Chairman-designate, and in September succeeded Johnson at the existing salary level of £20,000.[157]

Marsh inherited Johnson's organisation and Johnson's Board (see Table 43). Very few changes were made in the early part of his five-year term of office. Neal departed in October 1971 to become Chairman of the Commission for Industrial Relations. He was not immediately replaced. Marsh turned to the firm of management consultants, Michael Saunders Management Services, of which he had been Chairman, to find a successor, and in January 1972 H. L. Farrimond, Director of Personnel, Dunlop, joined the Board as member for Corporate Personnel. In the following October Thorpe stepped down as Deputy-Chairman in favour of Bosworth, and was appointed for a further two years on a part-time basis. Of the part-time members, Palmar left in September 1972, and was eventually replaced, in July 1973, by Sir Alastair Pilkington, Deputy-Chairman (later Chairman) of the glass firm. Marsh found it difficult to attract part-timers given the basic salary of only £1,000, which he criticised as 'derisory' and which remained unchanged from 1958 to 1978.[158]

Most of the organisational initiatives undertaken during Marsh's period of office followed on from the progress made by his predecessor. At Board level, Taylor had been asked, in January 1971, to review the Board's procedures, with the aim of involving members more fully in policy-making and long-term planning, particularly for the railway business. A small ad hoc committee, consisting of Taylor, Bosworth and Hammond and advised by Parker of McKinsey, reported in April. While the report concluded that the new organisation was working 'reasonably well', it pointed out that the Board was not fulfilling its planning and policy roles effectively enough and criticised the lack of involvement in railways by the full-time non-executive members. The committee's detailed proposals were examined by the Board in October, once Marsh was installed. Some

Table 43. *The British Railways Board, 1 November 1971*

Name	Date of appointment	Age on 1 November 1971	Education	Previous post	Experience	Left B.R.B.
Full-time members (Salary: Chairman £20,000, Thorpe £16,000, Bosworth £15,000, others £11,000)						
The Rt. Hon. Richard Marsh (Chairman)	1971	43	Jennings School, Swindon; Woolwich Poly; Ruskin College, Oxford	Minister of Transport; Deputy-Chairman, B.R.B.	Trade unions (N.U.P.E.); politics (Labour)	Sept. 1976
W. G. Thorpe (Deputy-Chairman)	1968	62	Nunthorpe Grammar School	General Manager, L.M.R.	Railways	Oct. 1974
J. M. W. Bosworth (Vice-Chairman)	1968	50	Bishop's Stortford College	Partner, Peat, Marwick, Mitchell & Co.	Accountancy	June 1983
A. V. Barker, O.B.E.	1968	61	Whitley and Monkseaton High School; L.S.E.	Assistant General Manager, L.M.R.	Accountancy; NAAFI; railways	Nov. 1974
Dr Sydney Jones, C.B.E.	1965	60	Cyfarthfa Castle Grammar School; Cardiff Technical College; Birmingham University	Chief of Research, B.R.B.	Scientific research (radar, C.E.G.B. etc.)	June 1976
R. L. E. Lawrence, O.B.E., E.R.D.	1971	56	Dulwich College	General Manager, L.M.R.	Railways	Sept. 1983
David McKenna, C.B.E.	1968	60	Eton; Trinity College, Cambridge	General Manager, S.R.	Railways; L.T.	Aug. 1978
Part-time members (salary: £1,000)						
Sir Frederick Hayday, C.B.E.	1962	59	No information	—	Trade unions (General and Municipal Workers' Union)	Dec. 1975
Derek J. Palmar	1969	52	Dover College	—	Accountancy (Peat, Marwick); Banking (Hill Samuel)	Sept. 1972
Lord Taylor of Gryfe	1968	59	Bellahouston Academy, Glasgow	—	Co-op	June 1980
H. Alan Walker	1969	60	No information	—	Brewing (Bass Charrington)	Jan. 1978 (died)

of these had already been agreed or implemented, such as the amalgamation of the Corporate Planning and Railway Planning Departments, while others were accepted in principle, for example, the need to improve the flow of railway information. Some proposals were flatly rejected, however. The Board disagreed that the appointment of Board members as chairmen of subsidiary businesses was in any way distracting; refused to increase the frequency of Chairman's Conference Meetings; and defended its earlier decision to separate responsibility for Corporate Planning and Corporate Finance.[159] In December Thorpe asked the Chief Legal Adviser, Evan Harding, to conduct a further assessment of the position. Reporting in March 1972 Harding proposed that some of the part-timers' anxieties would be relieved if the Chairman's Conference were made a formal part of the organisation and suggested that the terms of reference of the Board's main committees required revision. Proposals were also advanced in relation to research and development, technical affairs and supplies. The main thrust of Harding's report was endorsed by the Chairman's Conference.[160]

The most pressing problem was undoubtedly that of the 'field' organisation. Once again, much had been done before Marsh's arrival. The joint Railway/McKinsey team, reporting in January 1971, had proposed to replace the five regions by eight territories, each with a manager combining passenger, freight and systems and operations functions. Their report was accepted in principle by the Board in February 1971 and an implementation team was established in May.[161] The Scottish Region had showed what could be achieved by eliminating its traffic divisions and operating a two-tier organisation of 'region' and 'area' from 1969, and plans to follow suit were being considered by the Southern Region.[162] The proposal was then firmed up in the course of 1971, was presented to the Minister in April 1972, and received his consent in July.[163]

At first, neither the trade union officials nor the General Managers were outwardly hostile to the idea of major change. The latter had at times advanced some fairly radical plans themselves, as for example in 1965 when they put forward a proposal to break up the Eastern Region and transfer parts of it to a new South Eastern Region. Administrative staffing in the regions had already been reduced by 22,000 from 1963 to 1970 with estimated savings of £42 million at 1970 pay-roll costs. Nor was the Board's plan as radical as might appear at first sight. Three of the eight territories, with headquarters at Glasgow, Cardiff and London (South), were based on the existing Scottish, Western and Southern Regions. Only the Eastern and London Midland were to be broken up, into three and two parts respectively, with H.Q.s at Newcastle, York and London (East), and at Manchester and Birmingham (see Map II). In fact, the scheme was in line with the preliminary thoughts of the General Managers, expressed as early as September 1968.[164] Nevertheless, a proposal of this magnitude, which not only aimed to save 4,500–6,500 jobs and some £8–12 million a year but also involved a considerable upheaval for the retained staff, was bound to attract fierce opposition in a conservative industry. Some progress was made towards the objective in 1972–3, led by Bowick and orchestrated by a steering group (set up in August 1971) and an implementation team under Dear. A formal agreement was reached with the T.S.S.A. in January 1973, and the operating and engineering organisations were slimmed down at area level. Office blocks were built in Cardiff and Birmingham. But opposition from the T.S.S.A., British Transport Officers' Guild and A.S.L.E.F. intensified, particularly at the local level, and in January 1975 the Board decided to abandon the territory scheme. So a key element in the organisational strategy of 1967–70, if not indeed of 1963–70, namely a streamlined regional framework to match a smaller rail network and a substantial reduction in regional responsibilities, was only partially achieved. Much remained to be done.[165]

In the ten years to 1973 the Board had given a great deal of its attention to organisational matters. It had moved first under Beeching to a heavily centralised functional regime in which co-ordination had been weak, then progressed slowly and at times painfully to a primarily (but by no means exclusively) non-executive or non-functional form. In common with some of the other ailing industries of nineteenth-century origin, it had introduced new managerial blood, new techniques and a greater cost-consciousness.[166] The day-to-day management of the railways had undoubtedly been improved with the introduction of a Chief Executive, the Railway Management Group, the one-year and five-year planning round and a stronger management services department with the use of computing services. Nevertheless, the transition to 'modern management' had not proved easy. None of the organisational changes was given much time to take root, and the prevailing atmosphere of inquisition, created by the Stedeford Advisory Group, The Joint Steering Group, Cooper Brothers and McKinsey, not to mention the inquiry of the National Board for Prices and Incomes in 1965 (see below, pp. 534–7), only served to distract railway managers from the central task of improving financial performance. As the Board itself observed, 'with each successive change the attention of management had to be diverted from running the business to reshaping the organisation'.[167] The government intervention which produced such inquiries was motivated principally by concern over the railways' continuing deficits, but all too often the means to create improvement, whether in relation to network size, investment or labour relations, were seen purely in terms of organisation. Indeed, the Ministry's interest in

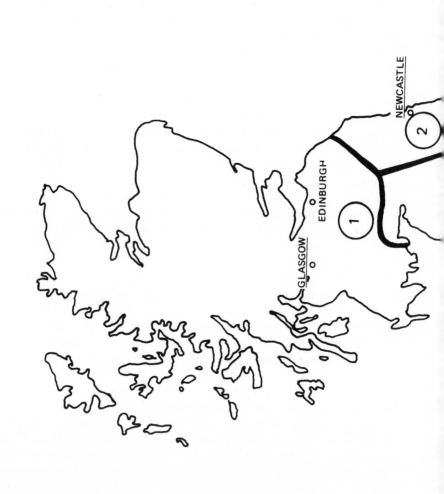

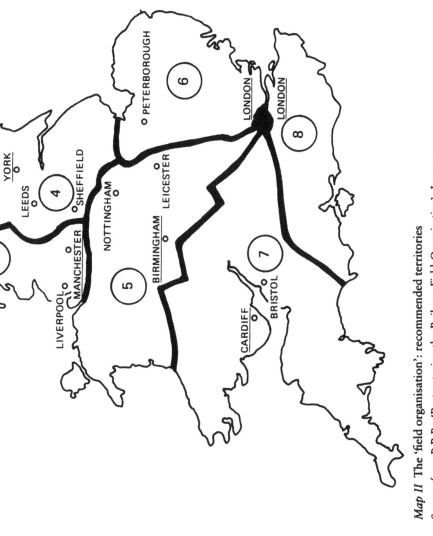

Map II The 'field organisation': recommended territories

Source: from B.R.B., 'Restructuring the Railway Field Organisation', January 1971, B.R.B.

organisational solutions, which had been established with the changes of 1955 and 1963, became a permanent and statutory feature with the Act of 1968. Unfortunately, the J.S.G. and McKinsey exercises demonstrated how difficult it was to apply a straightforward organisation manual for a manufacturing business – planning board, chief executive, etc. – to a complex, highly specialised business like the railways. The sheer size and dispersed nature of B.R.B.'s activities made it extremely difficult to implant the glib simplifications of management consultants. Regional resistance to change, the attempt to protect regional 'empires', continued to dog the administration, as the collapse of the field scheme demonstrates, again distracting it from more important issues. It was the 'culture of the railroad' that required change, rather than the organisation. The series of organisational tinkerings made it more difficult for Beeching and his successors to attack the commercial and operating attitudes associated with the culture. One thing was quite clear. It was difficult, if not impossible, to justify the organisational changes in terms of 'profitability' or 'viability'. Surpluses on current account in 1969 and 1970 appeared to support the new direction under Johnson, but they were soon eclipsed by the losses in 1971–3 (see below, pp. 396–8). The idea, fashionable in government circles in the 1960s, that organisational change coupled with financial reconstruction would place the railways on a firm foundation proved mistaken.

10

Financial performance and rationalisation

I

In the Board's first decade, the prime objective was to hold on to a profitable traffic while at the same time removing unprofitable operations. As Table 44 shows, the railways' overall traffic volumes, both profitable and unprofitable, stabilised at a level just below those of 1963–5, though these in turn were lower than hitherto (see above, pp. 173–4). But as there had been a marked expansion in inland transport generally over the period 1963–73 – in terms of passenger-miles an increase of 56 per cent and in freight ton-miles an increase of 31 per cent – this amounted to a decline in the railways' market-share. The share of the passenger market, which had been about 14 per cent in 1960–2, fell to under 10 per cent in 1966–8 and to 8 per cent in 1971–3. The share of freight, 29 per cent in 1960–2, fell to 19 per cent in 1966–8 and to under 18 per cent in 1971–3 (making allowance for the National Freight Corporation's freightliner and sundries businesses carried by rail). The market-shares fell still further after 1973, particularly that of freight. By 1982 the railways' share of passenger-mileage had dropped to under 6 per cent, and the freight share to only 10 per cent.[1]

In the *public* transport of passengers (i.e. excluding private motoring), however, the railways' share actually increased, especially in the Inter-City business: British Rail's share of public passenger-mileage rose from about 35 per cent in 1963 to 38 per cent in 1973; by 1982 it had reached 42 per cent. In the freight market, the railways not only failed to prosper from the expansion in general merchandise traffic but saw their traditional mainstays – coal, and iron and steel – experience considerable problems from the late 1960s onwards, and this constrained demand for rail transport. The possibilities of participating vigorously in the movement of oil and fuel were also limited by the increasing use of pipelines. Only 500 million ton-miles of traffic had been transported in this way in 1963, but by 1973 the figure was 2,100 million.[2]

Table 44. *British Rail's traffic volumes and market-share, 1963–73 (triennial averages)*

Period	Passenger traffic		Freight traffic	
	Mileage ('000m.)	Market-share (%)	Net ton-mileage('000m.)	Market-share (%)
(1960–2)	(23.5)	(14.4)	(17.5)	(29.3)
1963–5	22.4	11.5	15.6	22.1
1966–8	21.2	9.4	14.4	18.7
1969–70[a]	21.9	9.0	15.9[b]	18.8
1971–3	21.8	8.1	14.9[b]	17.7

[a] Two years' average.
[b] Includes estimates for freightliner and sundries traffic controlled by N.F.C. Averages for B.R.B. only: 14.2 (1969–70), 13.5 (1971–3).
Source: see Appendix D, Table 2. Data include L.T.

The period 1960–75 was very much the new age of road transport. It witnessed the 'largest road building programme ever started in Britain', which by 1975 had produced 11,500 miles of new road, including 1,100 miles of motorway. The number of road vehicles in use increased by 149 per cent. The rise in car ownership was marked: in 1958 77 per cent of households were without a car; by 1975 the figure had fallen to 43 per cent. The freight market came to be dominated by road haulage, which was transformed by the introduction of faster and heavier lorries. The freight ton-mileage carried by road increased by over 70 per cent, 1962–75, and the average length of haul rose by a third. The most important element here was undoubtedly the shift to higher capacity lorries, which reduced transit costs. For example, the limit on articulated lorry length was raised by 40 per cent over the period 1955–68, while the weight of 4-axle lorries was increased by 25 per cent between 1955 and 1972. This transformation was underlined by the increased amount of traffic carried by the heaviest lorries, those over 8 tons in unladen weight. This group carried only 11 per cent of total ton-mileage in 1962, but 62 per cent in 1976. Engine capacity and performance matched the increase in size and weight. These developments represented a considerable competitive challenge to the railways, particularly in terms of quality and reliability of service.[3]

To understand the problems confronting railway management in the period, it is necessary to break down both gross traffic receipts and costs into their several components. The crude allocation of total costs to specific traffics, developed by the B.T.C. Costings Division in the late 1950s and published for 1961 in the *Reshaping* report, was repeated in submissions to the Finance Committee until 1968, and the results for 1965–7 also appeared in the Board's Annual Reports. It must be emphasised that these calculations are *not* consistent with those presented later in the chapter. They relate to railway operations only, and all ancillary income and costs, redundancy payments and workshop closure costs are excluded. Depreciation is provided for at replacement cost. The allocation of costs is very approximate; the profitability of parcels and mails traffic in particular is almost certainly exaggerated by the methods used. But the results offer an interesting guide to traffic-sector profitability both during and after the 'Beeching Revolution'. Table 45 indicates how little the profile of revenue and costs changed from 1961 to 1967. The passenger business, which had failed to cover its direct costs in 1961–3, was shown to be covering them in the years 1964–7, by a margin of £7, £11, £17 and £11 million respectively, but the gap between revenue and total costs settled down around £80–85 million in current prices. Parcels and mails traffic, barely profitable in 1961–5, was apparently losing money in 1966 and 1967. The freight sector also deteriorated, as revenue fell and its failure to cover even direct costs persisted. British Rail's operating results, following Beeching's drive towards a slimmed-down railway and the change of emphasis by Raymond and Castle in 1966, were disappointing. Expressed in terms of an 'operating ratio', that is, operating costs expressed as a percentage of gross revenue, an improvement in the passenger sector, 1961–7, was more than offset by a decline elsewhere, and the aggregate result for 1967 was slightly worse than in 1961 (see Table 46). As the Director of Costings observed in May 1968, when he presented the 1967 data to the Board's Finance Committee, for the first time in five years, total railway revenue had been insufficient to cover allocated direct costs.[4]

Turning to the individual components of passenger and freight traffic, it can be seen that none of the passenger sub-sectors managed to make an adequate contribution to allocated total costs, though, as is evident from Table 46, there was a marginal improvement in the operating ratio of all three. Coal traffic, on the other hand, which had earned a small surplus over total costs in 1961, slid into deficit, and the sundries traffic also exhibited a marked deterioration, despite efforts to rationalise activities. The decline in freight business also had the effect of worsening the passenger results, since that traffic had had to carry a greater share of indirect costs. The Director of Costings also observed in May 1968 that a 'disturbing feature' of the cost-allocation exercise for 1967 was the continuation of a rising trend in total indirect costs since 1963. The assault on railway costs had reduced direct movement costs, leaving indirect costs, i.e. track and signalling and general administration costs, to rise. Thus,

Table 45. *Allocation of gross receipts and total costs to categories of passenger and freight traffic, 1961–7 (£m.)*

Traffic type	1961 GR	1961 OM	1961 P/L	1962 GR	1962 OM	1962 P/L	1963 GR	1963 OM	1963 P/L	1964 GR	1964 OM	1964 P/L	1965 GR	1965 OM	1965 P/L	1966 GR	1966 OM	1966 P/L	1967 GR	1967 OM	1967 P/L
Passenger	162	−8	−103	166	−6	−107	164	−1	−93	170	7	−83	176	11	−82	182	17	−76	183	11	−85
Parcels/mails	57	17	7	57	15	4	58	16	5	58	17	5	58	14	1	58	12	−1	55	7	−6
Freight	256	−13	−76	242	−26	−91	241	−8	−73	240	−4	−71	232	−5	−78	224	−13	−85	201	−20	−92
Total	475	−4	−172	465	−17	−194	463	7	−161	468	20	−149	466	20	−159	464	16	−162	439	−2	−183
Passenger components:																					
Fast/semi-fast	91	18	−22	94	21	−23	90	21	−20	93	26	−14	95	22	−21	101	27	−16	102	26	−19
Stopping	31	−26	−56	29	−27	−56	28	−25	−54	27	−24	−52	29	−16	−42	28	−14	−39	28	−17	−42
Suburban	40	−	−25	43	−	−28	46	3	−19	50	5	−17	52	5	−19	53	4	−21	53	2	−24
Freight components																					
Coal	109	25	3	106	22	−	111	26	−	105	21	−4	102	19	−8	103	18	−10	91	15	−11
Minerals[a]	44	7	−4	39	7	−3	35	6	−3	38	7	−4	37	6	−6	35	−2	−14	32	−3	−15
General merchandise[b]	65	−32	−54	61	−39	−63	64	−22	−44	67	−17	−41	66	−14	−40	61	−12	−36	56	−14	−40
Sundries	38	−13	−21	36	−16	−25	31	−18	−26	30	−15	−22	27	−16	−24	25	−17	−25	22	−18	−26

Key: GR Gross Receipts
OM Operating Margin (GR−Direct Costs)
P/L Profit/Loss (OM−Indirect Costs)
[a] From 1966 'iron and steel'.
[b] From 1966 'other'.

Source: B.R.B., R. & A. 1965, I, p. 70, 1967, I, p. 51. Results for 1962–4 from R. G. Smith, memo. to Finance Committee on 'British Railways Results: 1966', 25 April 1967, B.R.B.

Table 46. *Operating ratios, 1961/7*

Sector/sub-Sector	1961 (%)	1967 (%)
Passenger	164	146
Parcels/mails	88	111
Freight	130	146
Total	136	142
Fast/semi-fast	124	119
Stopping	281	250
Suburban	163	145
Coal	97	112
Minerals/iron and steel	109	147
General merchandise/other	183	171
Sundries	155	218

Note: the 'minerals/iron and steel' and 'general merchandise/other' categories are not of course strictly comparable. A comparison of the two groupings in 1963 indicates that 'minerals' were more profitable than 'iron and steel' and 'general merchandise' was more unprofitable than 'other'.
Source: taken from Table 45 (costs = GR plus *loss* or minus *profit*).

while direct costs fell from £466 million in 1963 to £441 million in 1967, indirect costs rose from £168 to £181 million.[5]

By this time B.R.B. had made a number of attempts to pass on some of the burden of indirect costs. In 1964 the Board published a *Study of the Relative True Cost of Rail and Road Freight Transport over Trunk Routes*, in which it argued that heavy lorries were paying far less than their true road costs, and put the case for an equalisation of road and rail 'track costs'. However, when the Geddes Committee on Carriers' Licensing reported in 1965, it declared itself unconvinced by British Rail's arguments, maintaining instead that the scope for a transfer of traffic from road to rail was limited without draconian restrictions on road haulage. This was followed in 1968 by a report from the Ministry of Transport on *Road Track Costs*. Though accepting that heavy goods vehicles did not contribute as much as other road users in relation to attributable costs, it found that these vehicles paid more in taxes than the road costs they incurred. Although the 'track costs' issue was not resolved beyond all doubt – the Ministry's position was influenced for example by the low value placed upon environmental cost – the findings inhibited the efforts of both B.R.B. and the Labour Government to encourage a transfer of freight to rail. The final blow came with the abandonment of Labour's plans, included in the 1968 Act, to introduce a quantity licensing system for long-distance road haulage.[6]

The Board's strategy moved from an emphasis on cost equalisation to a plea for government subsidy. In 1966 Raymond had opened his debate with Castle by reviving the idea of a National Highway Authority to administer both road and rail 'tracks' and charge operators for their use. This was quickly abandoned in favour of an attempt to get the government to foot the bill for British Rail's 'standby' capacity, that part of track-mileage which the Board was required to maintain above that which was commercially justified.[7] In the end, the government, following criticisms of the 'standby' notion by Ministry of Transport economists such as Stewart Joy, rejected it but agreed instead to support unremunerative passenger services by paying for both their direct and joint costs, and to provide temporary grants, up to a maximum of £50 million, to support surplus capacity in track and signalling, pending its eventual elimination. But not even these initiatives, together with financial reorganisation, managed to establish long-term financial viability for British Rail.[8]

In July 1968 the Board's Finance Committee resolved that in future, statements of revenue and costs on a total cost-allocation basis should not be published in the Annual Report. By this time it was known that the impending reorganisation would make comparisons with earlier years virtually meaningless. Not only was a large slab of the passenger business about to receive direct subsidy, but British Rail was also going to lose direct control of its freightliners and sundries traffics to the National Freight Corporation. All these areas had been making losses, including freightliners which, though dubbed by Raymond 'the brightest jewel in British Rail's crown', had by 1968 failed to produce more than £6.4 million in gross revenue, with a net loss of at least £3.0 million.[9]

No one should pretend that there is a uniquely correct formula for allocating railway costs. Methods changed with the broad policies adopted for the railways, and all carried an element of controversy. Many economists would argue that, necessarily and correctly, overheads must be recovered mostly from those customers who are most prepared to pay, and least from those customers who have alternative modes of transport readily available. As there emerged the post-Castle strategy of identifying a 'social' railway to be subsidised, so the Board began to move away from the idea of policy-making based on total cost-allocation exercises in favour of other formulae, thus starting a long process of adjustment in the treatment of costs, both direct and indirect, both specific (to a particular traffic or service) and shared. British Rail analysts have since pointed out the weakness of total cost allocation, which could give misleading indications to managers about the profitability of traffics through arbitrary identification of costs with parts of the business as well as false impressions of the potential for cost reduction by withdrawing or pruning services (see below, pp. 432–4). But new methods of cost allocation became more a matter of extracting the maximum advantage out of the grants system and of presenting a good face to government than of searching for the soundest approach in theoretical terms. This can be seen in the fact that while from 1969 grants for unremunerative passenger services were calculated on a total cost-allocation basis (the 'Cooper Brothers formula'), the 'commercial railway' was expected to generate only a 'contribution' to indirect or infrastructure costs (track and signalling, etc.), since these costs were regarded as an indivisible entity (the 'contribution accounting method'). Furthermore, where the continuation of a 'social' passenger service provided the sole justification for the retention of a route, the government agreed that the grant should cover *all* track and signalling costs, leaving freight traffic to cover only its direct costs.[10]

The application of new formulae to suit changing conditions can also be seen in the adoption of an 'avoidable costs' approach in 1975, which isolated those infrastructure costs which would be associated with an activity and calculated the total costs which would be saved if the activity ceased to exist. The method was used to determine the level of support following the Railways Act of 1974, when government grants to individual passenger services were replaced by a Public Service Obligation to the passenger business as a whole. In practice, freight and parcels traffic were charged with their avoidable costs, leaving the rest to be attributed to the passenger business. More recently, two more conventions have been devised, as the emphasis has shifted towards the search for performance indicators to guide the main sectors of the railway business. The 'Prime User' approach attributes all costs which cannot be identified as the avoidable costs of a particular activity to the principal user. Here, the rump of infrastructure costs is charged to the most appropriate passenger user, whether Inter-City, London and South East Suburban or Provincial, the aim being to give a firmer financial responsibility to the Sector Managements operated from 1982. Still more recently (1984) this approach has been replaced by the 'Sole User' convention, which charges sectors with the cost of facilities which would be required if that sector were the only user of the line. The requirements of secondary and tertiary users are then added and charged. The principal objective here is to secure the viability of the Inter-City business, which could not be shown to be profitable under the 'Prime User' approach. It also has the advantage of identifying surplus capacity. Each method used may have been, in the words of a recent British Rail paper, 'a direct response to managerial pressure for knowledge about the business', but it was also a reaction to the political environment in which railway management has been working to reduce the gap between costs and revenue.[11]

For present purposes, the important thing to observe is that these more sophisticated developments spelled an end, after 1967, to the broad apportionment of *total* costs to individual categories of traffic, since this was no longer deemed to be relevant either to strategic planning or to sector control. Furthermore, the frequent changes in accounting convention make long-term assessments very difficult indeed. However, the data on sector revenue and working expenses (not costs) prepared for the Board's Railway Policy Review of December 1972 and the findings of the 1971 studies of wagon-load traffic in greenfield areas suggest that continuing problems beset most if not all of the Board's commercial sectors, despite the financial reorganisation, the loss of sundries and freightliners and the provision of passenger grants. All sectors covered their working expenses in the early 1970s, but were unable to generate adequate contributions to track and signalling costs, administration or interest charges. Economic recession, pricing restraint and the declining fortunes of coal and iron and steel contributed to the poor showing of freight, which from a revenue of £202 million in 1971, generated only £38 million towards such costs, in that year. In fact, there was a major shift in the composition of the railways' revenue. In 1963 rail freight (excluding parcels and mails) was clearly the major business, earning £235 million gross, compared with £162 million from passenger traffic. In 1973 the positions were reversed. Passenger revenue amounted to £297 million, while freight earned only £199 million (all in *current* prices). Another decade later, in 1983, passenger revenue was more than double that of freight.[12]

II

The appointment of Beeching, the publication of the *Reshaping* report in 1963 and a new emphasis on cost-consciousness and profitability failed to reverse the railways' persistent weakness on operating account. Table 47 shows clearly that net operating revenue, which had been in deficit since 1956, continued to be negative until the introduction of substantial grants to unremunerative passenger services in 1969. Running at £104 million in current prices in 1962, the deficit had come down to £82 million in 1963 and £68 million in 1964 but by 1967 the net operating deficit had topped the £90 million mark again. Nor was the payment of grants more than a temporary palliative. Payments of £61 million in 1969, rising to £91 million in 1973 (see Table 48), maintained a railway net profit for only four years. By 1973 the railways were in deficit again.

The contribution of the subsidiary businesses – ships, hotels, harbours, hovercraft, non-operational property and the workshops (the latter shown separately from 1969) – was in general positive.[13] But, as in the late 1950s, their net profits were too small to make much of a dent in the railway

Table 47. *British Railways Board profit and loss account, 1963–73*
(£m., current prices)

Year	(a) Gross revenue[a]	(b) Operating costs	(c) Net operating revenue[a]	(d) Net operating revenue (all businesses)[b]	(e) Interest charges[c]	(f) Profit/loss
1963	468.6	550.2	−81.6	−75.8	58.1	−133.9
1964	474.1	541.6	−67.5	−62.5	58.4	−120.9
1965	472.6	545.7	−73.1	−71.5	60.9	−132.4
1966	470.5	542.1	−71.6	−70.5	64.2	−134.7
1967	445.7	536.1	−90.4	−86.5	66.5	−153.0
1968	463.6	547.1	−83.5	−80.1	67.3	−147.4
1968[d]	463.6	551.5	−87.9	−80.1	67.3	−147.4

Year	Gross income[e]	Expenditure	Operating profit[e]	Profit before interest (all businesses)[f]	Interest charges	Profit/loss
1969	540.2	491.6	48.6	56.2	41.5	14.7
1970	579.4	532.0	47.4	51.7	42.2	9.5
1971	604.2	578.0	26.2	30.2	45.6	−15.4
1972	642.9	625.1	17.8	24.9	51.1	−26.2
1973	683.5	688.6	−5.1	5.7	57.3	−51.6

[a] Includes net revenue from rail catering, commercial advertising and leasing of sites in operational use.
[b] Ships, harbours, hovercraft (from 1966), hotels, letting of sites not in operational use, plus other income/costs (includes redundancy payments amounting to £23.9m., 1963–8).
[c] Net of interest charged to capital – £7.4m., 1963–6.
[d] Revised allocation of costs using 1969 headings.
[e] Includes net income from grants, catering, commercial advertising and operational property letting.
[f] Ships, hovercraft, harbours, hotels, non-operational property lettings, workshops, freightliners (49 per cent share), and from 1970 'corporate expenses'.
Source: B.R.B., R. & A. 1963–73.

deficit. In 1963–8 railway operating losses amounted to £472 million; they were reduced by only £25 million or 5 per cent if the subsidiary activities are taken into account.* As is evident from Table 47, they appear more significant after the financial reconstruction of 1968. In 1969–73 total railway operating surpluses of £135 million were increased by 25 per cent to £169 million when all the businesses were included. Even so, the Board's financial plight could not possibly be alleviated by the limited

*Calculations involve use of second (revised) costs figure for 1968 in Table 47.

amount of diversification allowed under the Acts of 1953, 1962 and 1968.

All this of course takes no account of the Board's interest burden inherited with nationalisation. Though eased by the financial adjustments of 1962 and 1968, it was certainly not removed. In 1963–8 the Board's liability, net of capitalised interest of £7 million, amounted to £375 million, an annual burden of nearly £63 million. Consequently, the Board's overall loss averaged £137 million per annum. The £134 million deficit in 1963 was cut only in 1964, and by 1967 the position was as bad as ever, both in current and constant prices (the 1967 deficit of £153.0 million was equivalent to £135.6 million at 1963 prices). After 1968, the continuing interest burden averaged £47.5 million a year. Consequently, the final balance was positive only in 1969 and 1970. In 1973 the Board declared a loss of over £50 million, about £30 million in 1963 prices.

The comparative improvement after 1968 was the result not only of a capital write-down and lower interest payments, but of direct government grants. In addition to the substantial payments for unremunerative passenger services, which may legitimately be regarded as compensatory income, there were payments under Section 40 of the 1968 Act for the temporary maintenance of surplus track and signalling. Without these grants, £15 million in 1969, £12 million in 1970 and £45 million in all to 1973, there would have been no positive balance shown in 1969 and 1970. Furthermore, the 1972 loss – £26.2 million – was substantially reduced by a grant of £27 million paid under the Transport (Grants) Act to compensate the Board for the effects of government pricing controls. Notwithstanding all these manipulations, the viability of British Rail remained as elusive as ever. Additional 'Special Grants', of £32 and £72 million, were paid by the government in 1972 and 1973 to meet the Board's cash-flow shortfall.[14]

The Board's continuing difficulties can also be clearly seen in the estimates of the 'true financial results of British Rail' for 1948–73 (see Appendix A). Presented in summary form for 1963–73 in Table 48, the data show how little the railways' position really changed after the 'crisis' years of 1961 and 1962. The overall deficit, measured on a consistent basis over the 25-year period, was, at constant 1948 prices, much the same in 1968 as in 1963, and the results for 1967 rank with those for 1962 as the worst since nationalisation. After 1968, the deficit was reduced with the payment of grants for unremunerative passenger services, but it still remained sizeable, and at constant 1948 prices was higher in 1972–3 than in 1956–7. The accumulated losses for 1963–73, £775 million (constant prices), were much higher than those made under the Commission in 1948–62 – £560 million (ignoring maintenance equalisation adjustments) or £673 million (charging all maintenance to revenue account).

The data which lie behind Table 48 can be re-arranged to show gross revenue and total costs (including capital charges) on a consistent basis.

Table 48. *The 'true' financial results of British Rail, 1963–73 (£m.)*

Year	(a) Gross working surplus[a]	(b) Net working surplus	(c) Total balance (after interest)	(d) Total balance at constant 1948 prices
B.T.C.				
1961	−27.2	−99.3	−146.1	−89.7
1962	−47.8	−125.6	−177.0	−105.1
B.R.B.				
1963	−24.8	−105.5	−159.2	−92.7
1964	−8.7	−94.2	−148.4	−84.7
1965	−12.9	−103.9	−159.0	−87.6
1966	−9.3	−103.6	−160.2	−84.9
1967	−26.1	−129.4	−186.6	−96.2
1968	−18.5	−128.4	−184.6	−92.0

	Gross working surplus[b]	Passenger grants	Net working surplus	Total balance (after interest)	Total balance at constant 1984 prices
1968	−2.4	—	−110.4	−166.6	−83.1
1969	13.5	61.2	−40.6	−94.5	−45.4
1970	17.2	61.7	−43.5	−92.7	−41.3
1971	2.3	63.1	−64.8	−109.9	−44.4
1972	−36.2	68.2	−108.6	−147.8	−54.2
1973	−47.0	91.4	−118.6	−153.1	−51.5

[a] Net receipts of British Rail plus capital charges, net results of rail catering and, from 1969, B.R.B.'s share (49 per cent) of freightliner profits/losses.
[b] Excludes £18m. loss on freightliner/sundries divisions transferred to N.F.C. Ignores grants. Includes profits from external sales from B.R.B. workshops/B.R.E.L.
Source: see Appendix A, Table 2.

The results for 1960–73 are shown in the form of a graph in Figure 4. Here, it can be seen that the assault on railway costs inspired by Beeching, Shirley *et al.* did produce a real reduction in their level. However, since it was accompanied by a decline in traffic revenue, which was itself partly a product of the rationalisation drive, the overall effect was to leave the size of the deficit more or less unchanged. The transfer of the loss-making sundries and freightliner divisions to the National Freight Corporation, and the payments of grants from 1969, naturally brought revenue and costs closer together. Unfortunately, from 1970 the pattern observable in the Beeching period seemed to be repeating itself, namely falling revenue and falling costs, with the former falling more sharply than the latter. Net margins, i.e. gross revenue minus total costs (including capital charges)

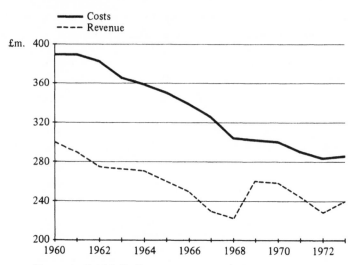

Figure 4 British Railways revenue and costs in constant 1948 prices, 1960–73

Source: data from Appendix A, Table 4, cols. 1 and 2. For 1960–2 costs are shown before the B.T.C. drew on the maintenance equalisation account (see Appendix A, Table 3).

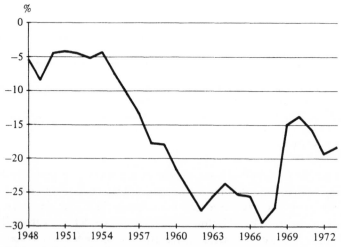

Figure 5 British Railways 'net margins', 1948–73

Source: Appendix A, Table 4.

expressed as a percentage of total costs, deteriorated steadily from 1954 to 1962, then, as Figure 5 shows, improved briefly during the Beeching and Johnson years, both periods coinciding with financial reconstructions. However, the pressures on the Board encouraged further deterioration.

III

There were several ways in which B.R.B. responded to the financial problems it faced in the decade after 1963, embracing cost-control, commercial strategies and planning, investment and productivity. The first major managerial initiative, and perhaps the most important, was the Beeching Plan of 1963, with its considerable emphasis on rationalisation. The remainder of this Chapter is concerned with the Plan and its attempts to restructure the railway business, and with the general attack on costs.

The Beeching Plan or, more exactly, the Board's report on *The Reshaping of British Railways* of March 1963, was one of the most important single publications on transport in the post-war period. Marking the culmination of Beeching's investigation of the 'railway problem', encouraged by Marples and the Conservative Government, it put forward a reasoned and detailed case for the rationalisation of railway services. In future, the Board would seek to concentrate on the traffic which the railways handled best, namely the inter-city passenger and long-distance train-load freight, where traffic flows were large enough to justify the cost of operation. While considerations of social benefit and quality of service were not ruled out, *Reshaping* stressed the need to relate the costs of transport provision to the revenue generated for the various categories of traffic, and to eliminate those elements of the railways' business found to be so unprofitable as to be irredeemable. In short, Beeching and his Board proposed to 'shape the railways to meet present day requirements'. This meant creating the conditions whereby they could 'provide as much of the total transport of the country as they could provide well'. It also meant facing up to the realities of making the railways pay in a transport system dominated by roads.[15]

The report, based on a series of traffic studies commissioned by Beeching in 1961, came up with a 16-point programme for improvement. Its proposals were presented as 'conservative' in relation to closures, and 'restrainedly speculative with regard to new developments'. Even so, a contraction of some 5,000 miles, about 40 per cent of the route-mileage open for passenger traffic, was promised, together with a substantial reduction in the number of stations handling this traffic (2,100 of the existing 4,300 were listed for closure).[16] The planned rationalisation of the railways' freight services was also radical. The report recommended concentration on a much smaller number of stations and depots, and there was to be a drastic pruning of the wagon fleet from the 848,591 vehicles at the end of 1962 to 500,000, in the space of three years. The sundries business, which was using 950 depots, was to be concentrated on about 100 main locations, and cartage provision was to be reorganised in a similar fashion. On the positive side, 'liner trains', carrying containerised consignments in bulk, the block working of coal trains, diesel traction and selected inter-city services were all to receive active encouragement. In this way, a financial improvement in the region of c.£115–147 million was predicted if the plan was *implemented with vigour*. This would have the effect of eliminating *much (though not necessarily all)* of the Railways' deficit . . . by 1970' (my italics).[17]

The *Reshaping* Plan was very much identified with Beeching personally, and it is clear that he himself drafted the report.[18] But an examination of the making of the document and the studies supporting it reveals how much of it rested on initiatives and studies rooted in the 1950s. In the first place, as critics such as Munby were quick to point out, the idea of a severe pruning of services was not new, having been part of the Modernisation Plan of 1955. The reappraisal of the Plan in 1959 promised a reduction of about 10 per cent of the network, about 1,800 route-miles. In the same year the London Midland Region had produced a passenger services plan outlining its long-term rationalisation strategy, and in December 1960 the Commission, responding to pressure from the Ministerial Group on Modernisation (set up during the Stedeford Inquiry), produced a four-year modernisation programme which included detailed listings of passenger service and line closure proposals for 1961–4.[19] Second, a great deal of the miscellaneous statistical material offered in the 148-page report was based on work undertaken by the Commission's Costings Division and by the regions in the 1950s. This can be demonstrated if the traffic studies and supporting data are dissected in a little more detail.

Two important sections of the *Reshaping* report, the table of 'Revenue and Assessed Costs by Main Traffics' for 1961, and the results of a detailed survey of wagon-load traffic, produced by an all-region census for the week ending 24 April 1961, were pre-Beeching initiatives. The revenue and costs results for 1961 were merely a continuation of the costings data prepared for the years from 1956, based on 'full cost allocation' (in which joint indirect costs were allocated to specific traffics in relation to estimated use of facilities). The wagon-load survey had been a response to the Commission's earlier concern about the poor loading and loss-making character of much of this traffic, as seen in the White report of 1958. The proposal emerged in October 1960 as part of the Traffic Committee's investigation of the Commission's future traffic pattern.[20]

What, then, did Beeching inspire on his arrival at the B.T.C. in 1961, and what was novel about his *Reshaping* report? When the subject of costing was considered at the Commission's meeting in May, Beeching maintained that in the past there had been 'too much emphasis on seeing whether the total "costs" for various classes of traffic balanced with actual expenditure'. He wanted the costings effort directed towards an examination of traffic types, the method of conveyance used (with the aim of introducing improvements) and the characteristics of traffic being moved by other modes of transport. Shortly after this he asked, more specifically, for new traffic studies to be carried out. These were announced at a press conference in June and were subsequently listed in the Commission's Annual Report for 1961. They were designed to determine:

1. the cost of handling existing rail traffic by existing methods;
2. the types of traffic which railways did handle and could handle more satisfactorily and more cheaply than other modes;
3. the traffic volumes flowing through the rail network, with the aim of establishing levels of utilisation, revenue-generating ability and profitability for particular parts of the system or for individual services;
4. the pattern of U.K. traffic flows both by rail and by other modes, to establish 'the volume of traffic favourable to rail'; and
5. the ways in which railway freight operations might be modified in order 'to attract the maximum amount of remunerative traffic'.[21]

To expedite the studies Beeching appointed Stanley Raymond as Traffic Adviser, in succession to Hollingsworth, in July. Work on four separate inquiries was then instituted, dealing with:

1. non-railborne wagon-load traffic (except coal) favourable to rail;
2. a national plan for sundries traffic (less than wagon-load);
3. non-railborne coal traffic favourable to rail; and
4. traffic flows and densities and utilisation of the system.

The studies, which were each organised through a working party and involved a close collaboration of regions and H.Q., took on board existing initiatives. These included a road traffic and costs exercise started in March 1961, and a study of the 'smalls' or sundries traffic, encouraged by the Commission in February. The latter was given impetus by the Traffic Committee's concern over the poor results for 1959, where sundries failed to cover their direct costs by £11 million, or 44s. (£2.20) per ton. Some of the regions had also made progress in formulating plans to concentrate both their wagon-load and their sundries operations, and had begun to collect information on merchandise traffic which was not going by rail.[22]

What Raymond's studies added to the railways' existing effort was a new emphasis on traffic flows and an attempt to ascertain the size of the market which the railways might win back. Both required the application of more sophisticated data-gathering techniques, including the use of computers. For the wagon-load survey, district traffic intelligence cards were distributed to the regions, to record how each major trader sent out his products.[23] The study of network utilisation involved the use of 'Station Basic Record Cards' by district traffic managers. The cards were intended to isolate those stations and depots where originating revenue failed to cover local costs. Beeching himself contributed to this emphasis on analysing traffic flows by giving the General Managers copies of density flow maps prepared by three divisions of I.C.I.[24]

Much of the basic information was collected in the course of 1961, before Raymond was appointed General Manager of the Western Region.[25] His successor at H.Q., Margetts, who joined the interim British Railways Committee in April 1962 as Operating and Planning member, was given the job of collating the material, ironing out the inconsistencies in the way data was being assembled at regional level, and assisting Beeching in the preparation of the text of the report. There was also a major contribution from Garratt and Merrill, of the Public Relations and Publicity Department, since Beeching had emphasised from the start that the way in which the *Reshaping* strategy was presented to both the public and railwaymen was vitally important. There was much patient explanation of the policy to the unions by Beeching at the British Transport Joint Consultative Council. The media were also fully briefed well in advance of the report's publication in March 1963. Some of the findings appeared earlier. The financial results for the main classes of traffic in 1961 were given in rough outline in the Commission's Annual Report for 1961, published in June 1962, and in the same month passenger and freight traffic density maps were released which revealed the low utilisation of much of the network.[26] The data in the *Reshaping* report were thus based in large measure on existing work and on conditions ruling in 1960 or 1961, but the attention given to network utilisation, traffic flows, the winning of markets and the public relations effort on rationalisation were very much Beeching innovations.

Old or new, the findings published in the report put forcefully to all the financial implications of maintaining railway services at their existing level. As Table 49 shows, the traffic category figures for 1961, based on full-cost allocation, were far worse than anything privately considered inside the Commission for earlier years. For the first time total railway traffic failed to cover its directly attributable costs, the shortfall amounting to nearly £4 million. Stopping passenger trains (−£56 million) and general merchandise wagon-load traffic (−£54 million) were the heaviest loss-makers. With an operating ratio (operating costs expressed as a percentage of revenue) of 281 and 183 respectively, they accounted for nearly two-thirds of the total deficit. Only fast and semi-fast passenger traffic, parcels and mails, and heavy freight earned a margin over direct costs, and when indirect costs were added, only coal and parcels and mails showed a surplus.[27]

The results of the wagon-load survey and the four new traffic studies

Table 49. *Receipts and costs in passenger and freight traffic, 1961 (£m.)*

Traffic type	Gross receipts (i)	Direct costs (ii)	Operating margin (i) − (ii)	Joint costs (allocated indirect cost) (iii)	Profit/Loss (net revenue/deficit) (i) − ((ii) + (iii))
1. Passenger					
Fast/semi-fast	91.2	72.7	18.5	40.3	−21.8
Stopping	30.8	56.9	−26.1	29.8	−55.9
Suburban	39.8	40.3	−0.5	24.5	−25.0
Total	161.8	169.9	−8.1	94.6	−102.7
2. Freight by coaching train (Parcels, mails, etc.)	57.3	40.2	17.1	10.3	6.8
3. Freight					
Coal	108.3	83.5	24.8	22.0	2.8
Minerals	44.5	36.9	7.6	11.3	−3.7
General merchandise:					
Wagon-load	64.8	96.6	−31.8	22.0	−53.8
Sundries ('smalls')	38.0	51.5	−13.5	7.8	−21.3
Total freight	255.6	268.5	−12.9	63.1	−76.0
4. Grand total	474.7	478.6	−3.9	168.0	−171.9

Note: estimated costs include interest and provision for depreciation in 'present money values'.
Source: 'Table No. 1. Revenue and Assessed Costs by Main Traffics for British Railways, 1961', *Reshaping*, I, p. 8.

introduced a new dimension into the debate about the railways – the low utilisation of much of the existing network and equipment. Pruned as it had been by some 2,000 miles since the end of 1950, the retained system of 17,481 route-miles (at the end of 1962) was shown to be poorly used. This applied in particular to all the 5,900 route-miles of single-track branch line. On half of the existing network the revenue earned was insufficient to cover route-maintenance costs (track and signalling). Likewise, half the network carried only about 4 per cent of the passenger-miles travelled and about 5 per cent of the freight ton-miles run. In 1961 there were about 7,000 stations, one for every 2½ miles of route. Many of these were relics of the horse-drawn society of the nineteenth century. A third of the 4,300 stations open to passenger traffic handled, in 1960, less than 1 per cent of the total revenue from passengers. In contrast, the largest 34 stations, under 1 per cent of the total number, produced 26 per cent of the passenger revenue.[28]

On the freight side, half of the 5,000 stations and depots produced less than 3 per cent of the revenue in 1960, while 57 of them accounted for 35 per cent. The wagon-load survey of April 1961 revealed a similar picture in terms of freight tonnages. Of the 4,371 stations (excluding private sidings) examined, 2,633 or 60 per cent each handled less than 100 tons in the survey week and accounted for only 9 per cent of total railway tonnage. Much of the freight business was shown to be characterised by light loadings – the average was only 9.3 tons – and short lengths of haul. Half of the tonnage surveyed was carried a distance of only 1–50 miles. Traffic using the higher-cost terminal facilities, for example that containing a road–rail transfer element, exhibited particularly low loadings and was generally unprofitable. Indeed, all traffic requiring shunting/marshalling was found to be of dubious worth. Only the siding-to-siding traffic, in which wagon-loads were comparatively high (12.7 tons) and a great deal of the traffic was moved in complete train loads, earned a surplus over direct costs. Even here, a third of the traffic was carried over short distances (1–25 miles) and failed to cover such costs. Furthermore, the analysis of flows revealed that 78 per cent of the siding-to-siding traffic was being moved through only 15 per cent of the total number of sidings.[29] Thus the strong implication of the *Reshaping* report, with its mass of data and supporting maps (see Maps III and IV), was that the existing network should be reduced by half, to about 8,500 miles.

In presenting the case for rationalisation of the passenger business *Reshaping* went into considerable detail. An appendix listed the 266 passenger services to be withdrawn and a further 71 to be modified. Similar lists were provided for stations and halts, showing that 2,363 would lose their passenger facilities (this total included 435 stations under consideration for closure before the report appeared, of which 234* had already closed). Action on this front was expected to produce a net saving of £18 million per annum (after allowing for loss of contributory revenue from retained parts of the network), and a further £11–13 million as a result of line closures and the reduction of track and signalling maintenance to freight standards. The passenger closures policy was supported by some telling statistics relating to ten selected services. For the first time, British Railways shared with the public the discovery that a change of motive power to diesel multiple-unit or diesel railbus was no panacea for the problem. For two of the services quoted, Gleneagles–Comrie in Perthshire and Thetford–Swaffham in Norfolk, the traffic was ludicrously small – only five and nine passengers per train respectively. Yet both had benefited from the new motive power.[30] The report also provided an example of the economics of operating low density services, contending that 'even with relatively low cost diesel multiple unit trains there will be losses up to quite high levels of traffic'. However, as Denys Munby was quick to point out, the figures provided to demonstrate the unprofitability of services patronised by fewer than 10,000 passengers a week (17,000 if there was no freight traffic) exaggerated the case for closure. The example assumed a comparatively high level of service, used upper-bound train-mile costs and a fixed fare of 2d. per passenger-mile, and gave very short shrift to cost-saving alternatives.[31]

What then, should be made of the report? Academic critics pronounced themselves dissatisfied with the inadequacy of the data-base provided, and drew attention to the fact that the Board's references to 'direct' and 'indirect' costs were both inconsistent and misleading, since neither could be equated with 'fixed' and 'variable' costs as an economist would define them. Joy, writing in 1964, was particularly critical of Beeching's dependence for his diagnosis on the proposition that the railways' track and signalling costs were both high and fixed in the long run. He argued strongly that some attempt could be made to scale down capacity to meet the levels of traffic offering. Later on, he went further and condemned the report as 'lacking in arithmetic, logic and a sense of priorities'.[32] Criticism was also directed at the quality of the estimates of financial benefit to be derived from the *Reshaping* strategy, shown in Table 50. With the aid of a little hindsight, some have labelled them superficial and over-optimistic. Despite the clamour about route and station closures, and the rationalisation of passenger services in particular, savings under these heads were expected, as Table 50 indicates, to produce only about 28 per cent of total

*235 given in the text, but only 234 listed in *Reshaping*, appendix 2.

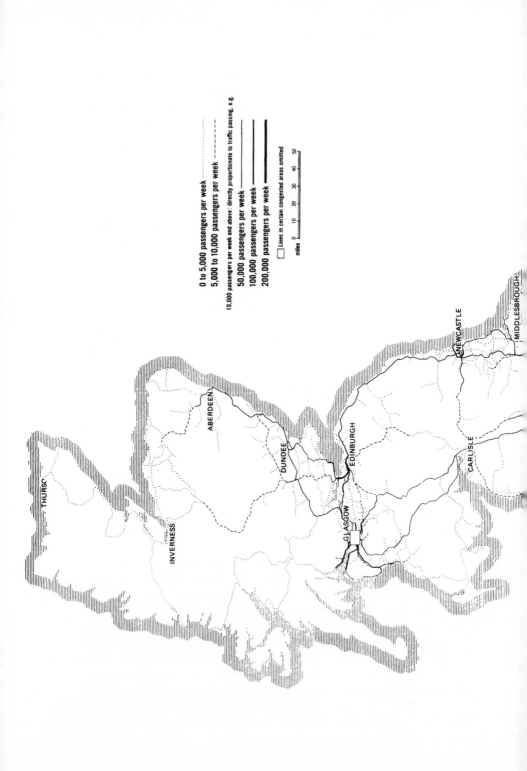

0 to 5,000 passengers per week ⋯⋯⋯⋯⋯

5,000 to 10,000 passengers per week ⎯ ⎯ ⎯

10,000 passengers per week and above : directly proportionate to traffic passing, e.g.

50,000 passengers per week ⎯⎯⎯⎯

100,000 passengers per week ⎯⎯⎯⎯

200,000 passengers per week ⎯⎯⎯⎯

☐ Lines in certain congested areas omitted

miles   0 10 20 30 40 50

THURSO

INVERNESS

ABERDEEN

DUNDEE

EDINBURGH

GLASGOW

CARLISLE

NEWCASTLE

MIDDLESBROUGH

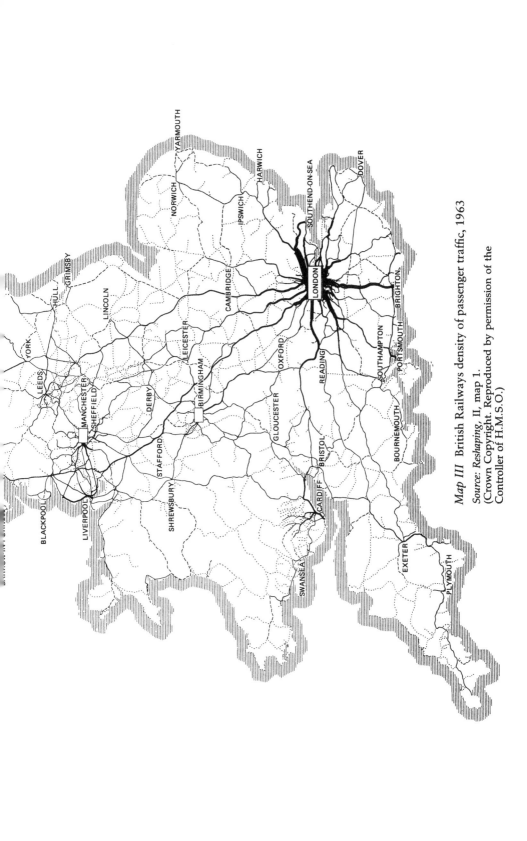

Map III British Railways density of passenger traffic, 1963

Source: Reshaping, II, map 1.
(Crown Copyright. Reproduced by permission of the
Controller of H.M.S.O.)

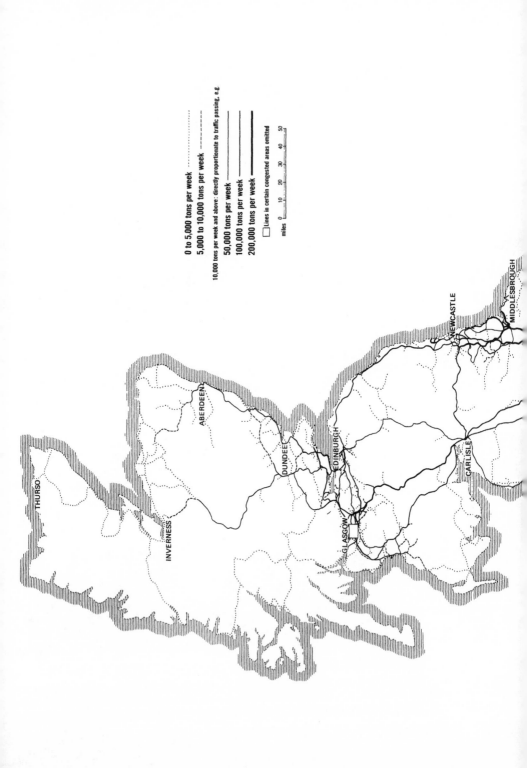

0 to 5,000 tons per week ················

5,000 to 10,000 tons per week ----------

10,000 tons per week and above: directly proportionate to traffic passing, e.g.

50,000 tons per week ────────

100,000 tons per week ━━━━━━

200,000 tons per week ━━━━━━

☐ Lines in certain congested areas omitted

miles 0 10 20 30 40 50

THURSO

INVERNESS

ABERDEEN

DUNDEE

GLASGOW

EDINBURGH

CARLISLE

NEWCASTLE

MIDDLESBROUGH

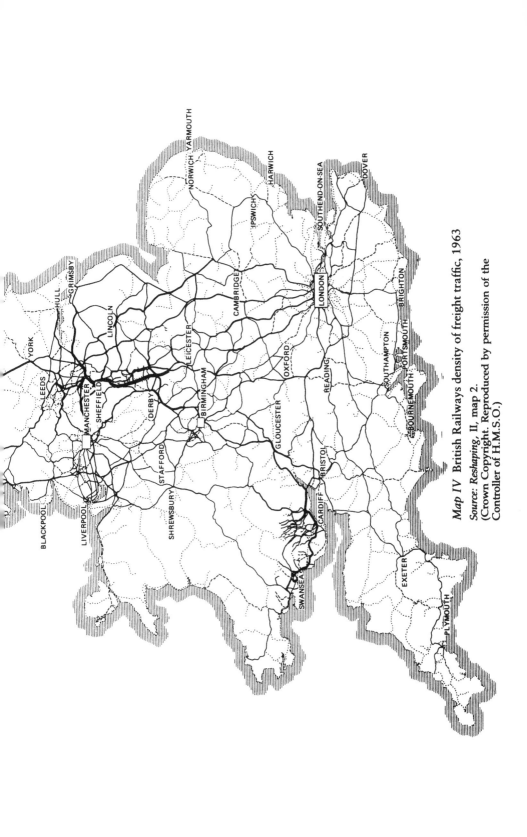

Map IV British Railways density of freight traffic, 1963

Source: Reshaping, II, map 2.
(Crown Copyright. Reproduced by permission of the
Controller of H.M.S.O.)

Table 50. *The Reshaping Plan: estimated 'financial consequences'*

Item	Estimated benefit £m. p.a.	Percentage of total savings (using upper-bound estimates)
Passenger service closures/service cuts	18	12 ⎤
Line closures and reduced track maintenance following passenger closures	11–13	9 ⎬ 28
Freight closures	5–10	7 ⎦
Reduction in passenger coach fleet	2–3	2
Reduction in wagon fleet	10–12	8
Workshop rationalisation: cut in standing charges	4	3
Further replacement of steam by diesel traction	15–20	14
Reduction in coal traffic operating costs	7–10	7
Concentration of sundries traffic	15–20	14
Net earnings from liner trains (1968)	10–12	8
Commercial measures to reduce losses on unprofitable traffics	5–6	4
Acquisition of traffic not on rail	10–15	10
Reduction in general administration costs	3–4	3
Total	115–47	101

Note: estimates were held to be 'not fully additive'. It was also admitted that interest charges would be incurred on the £250m. required for diesels, liner trains, and the reorganisation of sundries.
Source: Reshaping, I, pp. 54–5.

savings (21 per cent from passenger services). The bulk of the financial benefit rested on such imponderables as the prospects of future investment in diesel motive power, the likelihood of liner trains winning back a substantial amount of traffic from the roads within five years and the chances of securing considerable reductions in operational costs. Here, neither the counteracting effects of escalating wage costs nor the burden of new interest payments was built into the calculation (although the latter was mentioned in the supporting text). Indeed, the forecast of a break-even position by 1970 ran counter to the reality of a still heavy capital burden as established by the Transport Act of 1962.[33]

The assumption that £10–15 million might be gained from traffic won back to rail, together with another £10–12 million from the new liner trains, was rightly judged to be particularly fragile. The traffic study had isolated some 93 million tons of freight 'potentially favourable to rail', but the report conceded that by no means all of this would be profitable to carry. In fact, with 38 million tons in the hands of 'C' licence operators and 26 million tons of a short-haul character (under 51 miles), this was an understatement. Only 13.4 million tons of traffic could be won back to siding-to-siding operation, where the prospect of profit was highest. Later experience, moreover, was to confirm the suspicion that the rationalisation of freight facilities might result in traffic losses.[34] Many other criticisms could be offered. The presentation of the liner train investment proposal was insubstantial, no attempt being made to justify the expenditure in terms of rate of return or discounted values. It certainly gave the impression of having been put together rather hastily. The estimate of *'net earnings'* of £10–12 million by 1968, which appeared in the text, conflicted with the expectation of £12.5 million as *'a contribution over direct costs* by 1970' in the appendix (my italics).[35] The same was true of the section on manpower savings, which was amended at the last minute, where the imprecise nature of the estimates added to the anxiety of the unions. The N.U.R. and the Confederation of Engineering and Shipbuilding Unions had already shown their reactions to the planned rationalisation of the workshops with a one-day strike in October 1962.[36]

Finally, the presentation of the passenger closure policy has attracted considerable criticism. It has been suggested that the long lists of service reductions and station closures not only served to stiffen public resistance to rationalisation – stimulating such pro-rail bodies as the National Council on Inland Transport and the Scottish Railway Development Association (later the Scottish Association for Public Transport), both established in 1962 – but also encouraged a closure mentality in regional railway staff to the exclusion of all other considerations. Both propositions are difficult to substantiate, but it does seem that in this area the *Reshaping* report contained too much precision, rather than too little. Certainly, the passenger listings contained several entries about which it was difficult to argue. From Glemsford to Glenwhilly, from Edward Thomas's Adlestrop to Amlwch, and from Cullompton to Culloden Moor, there were dozens of relics of the Victorian railway. However, as Freeman Allen noted, the report did not merely threaten to remove Britain's branch lines but promised to deprive some major centres such as Nottingham and Grimsby of their direct connections with London. Nottingham, in fact, was asked to contemplate a substantial reduction in its services to neighbouring cities, such as Leicester, Birmingham, Lincoln and Sheffield. Here, Beeching undoubtedly raised the temperature of concern. Most important of all, the *Reshaping* exercise, which focussed attention unduly on the pruning of residual passenger services, implied that a network of a given size, shorn of its unprofitable tentacles, could break even under the terms of the Transport Act of 1962. Subsequent experience was to suggest that this was a false premise. As Joy put it, the report 'lulled the Government, community and railway management into a false sense of security'. In the Board's Annual Reports for 1965 and 1966 further analyses of revenue and assessed costs (see Table 45, above) indicated continuing losses in *all* traffic categories, and showed that the report, by giving fast passenger and suburban services a comparatively clean bill of health, had been too optimistic. Furthermore, in 1972, a decade after the report, Richard Marsh argued, in a confidential report to the Minister, that it was impossible to find any network size that could be viable, even under the more favourable conditions established by the Transport Act of 1968.[37]

Whatever its shortcomings, Beeching's report did represent the clearest statement to date of the dilemma facing this nationalised industry. For all the quibbles of the professional transport pundits, what Beeching managed to achieve was, in Freeman Allen's words, 'to make the public face up to the question of striking a balance between the social necessity of public transport in areas where it cannot pay its way, and the financial burden on the rest of the community of providing such transport'. The public relations campaign surrounding *Reshaping* was a notable success for the Board. Despite the criticisms of economists, press coverage was both lengthy and generally favourable, and the same was true of the reactions of radio and television. B.B.C.'s *Panorama* programme, for example, used as the core of its coverage a British Railways-produced film on the report. The response of *The Observer* and *Guardian* was typical of the general mood. For the former, the 'metaphysics of the railways has been replaced by the mathematics of the railways; ideology has given way to accountancy'; for the latter the economic argument could now be regarded as 'conclusive'.[38] Beeching's Minister, Marples, was delighted with the outcome. Writing to the Chairman in April 1963, he remarked: 'I feel that the presentation of the plan ... was a superb effort. We had almost unanimous praise from all sections of the Press, and we hogged the television programmes.' Former Chairman Robertson was also greatly impressed with the *Reshaping* document. 'If I had put in such a report five years ago,' he told Beeching, 'I should have had my head knocked off. But the climate is quite different now. I expect the balance of re-action, especially from the more serious-minded, to be strongly in your favour.'[39]

The *Reshaping* report, then, was not really intended to be a precise account of railway operating economics designed to impress the specialist transport economists. The aim was to polarise the economic and social arguments about running the railways in a roads-dominated transport system. The Board hoped to use the new emphasis on traffic flows and densities to present a reasoned case to the intelligent layman, if not the man on the Clapham omnibus, then at least the man on the 8.00 a.m. from Brighton. In this Beeching and his colleagues succeeded, at least in the short run. For the first time, the management of nationalised railways attempted to lead rather than merely respond to public political debate about the industry's future. The extent to which the planned programme of route, freight and passenger rationalisation was implemented is, of course, another matter and it is to this that we now turn.

IV

The rationalisation of railway facilities and routes proceeded in tandem with the second stage of the *Reshaping* strategy. This involved the identification of a basic network consisting of the major trunk routes, which would be developed intensively over the next two decades. The work, which, as outlined in the previous chapter, was led by James Ness, the Board member responsible for planning, was very much associated with the concentration of freight facilities. As the Board's memorandum to the J.S.G. of April 1967 recalled, 'freight traffic being demonstrably the more important aspect of our business, the density of freight movement over the network . . . formed the starting point of investigations designed to produce a first outline of the trunk route requirements of the future'. Planning for the concentration of freight movement in terminal-to-terminal block trains, and tests of route capacity to meet future demand were the central elements in this work.[40]

In fact, the investigations were some time in the making. A preliminary examination of routes had been part of Margetts's reshaping strategy in 1962–3, and some progress was made in identifying surplus duplicate routes, particularly in Scotland; likewise a joint Western/Southern team examined the two routes to Exeter and found in favour of the Western line via Westbury. But, as Margetts recognised, there was 'much to be done'. Route rationalisation was only one of a large number of objectives being pursued simultaneously under the *Reshaping* banner.[41] It was not until January 1964 that Ness was asked to prepare a draft plan on the trunk network, and the final result, the Board's *The Development of the Major Trunk Routes*, was not published until February 1965.[42] At first sight, the continuing delay is difficult to explain. The main conclusion of this report, that 3,000 miles of the existing 7,500 miles of trunk route should be earmarked for intensive development to 1984, followed on naturally from the *Reshaping* maps of 1963 (see 1964 maps, Maps V–VIII). But the

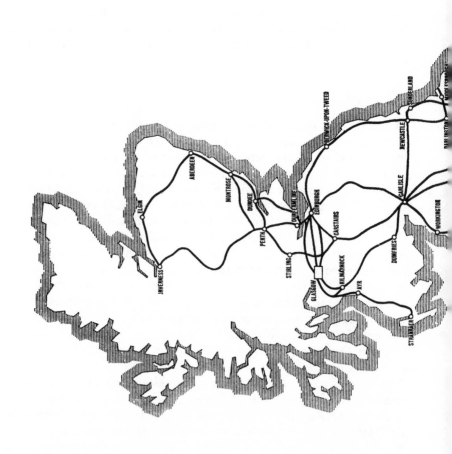

Map V British Railways 1964: through routes (approximately 7,500 route-miles)

Source: B.R.B., *The Development of the Major Railway Trunk Routes* (1965), Map 1.

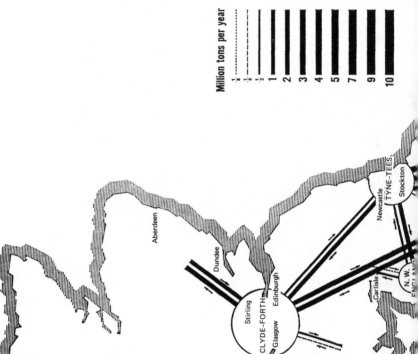

Million tons per year

Stirling
CLYDE-FORTH
Glasgow   Edinburgh

Dundee

Aberdeen

Carlisle

N. W.
ENGLAND

Newcastle
TYNE-TEES
Stockton

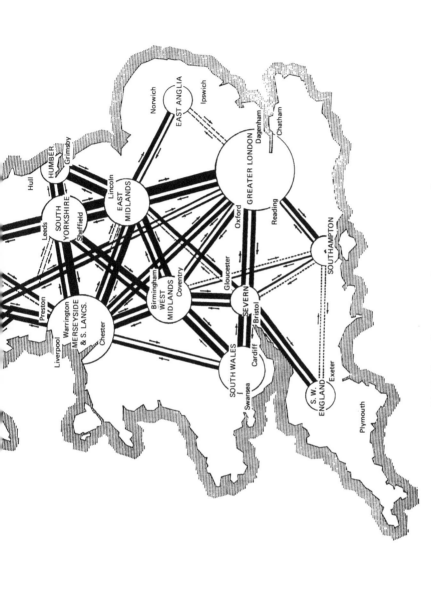

Map VI British Railways 1964: flows between main centres – total freight

Source: B.R.B., *The Development of the Major Railway Trunk Routes* (1965), Map 8.

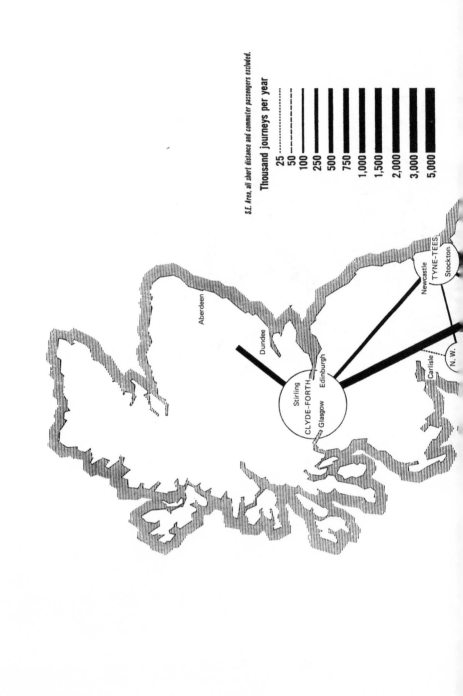

S.E. Area, all short distance and commuter passengers excluded.

Thousand journeys per year

25
50
100
250
500
750
1,000
1,500
2,000
3,000
5,000

Aberdeen

Dundee

Stirling
CLYDE-FORTH
Glasgow   Edinburgh

Newcastle
TYNE-TEES
Stockton.

Carlisle
N. W.

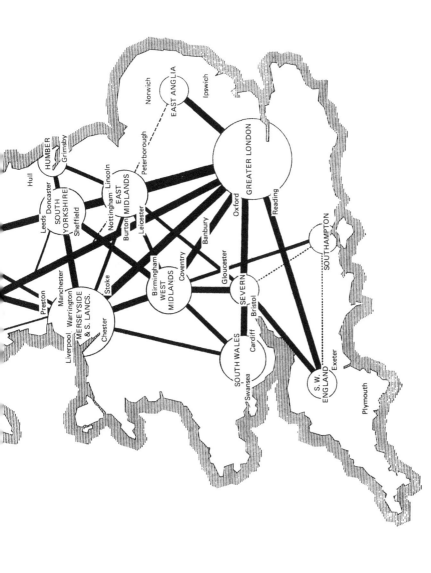

Map VII British Railways 1964: flows between main centres – passenger

Source: B.R.B., *The Development of the Major Railway Trunk Routes* (1965), Map 10.

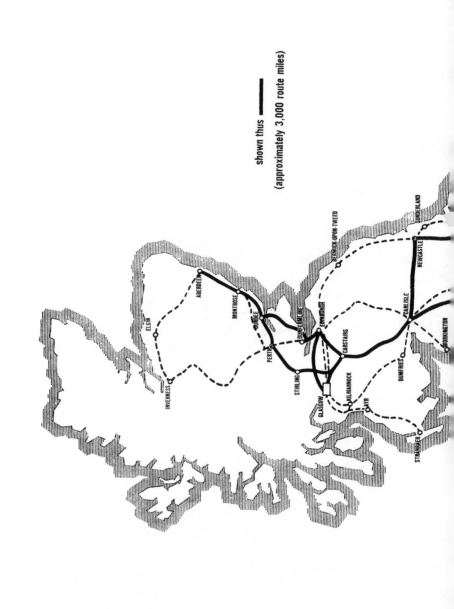

shown thus ▬▬

(approximately 3,000 route miles)

Map VIII British Railways 1984: routes selected for development

Source: B.R.B., *The Development of the Major Railway Trunk Routes* (1965), Map 21.

nature of the inquiry stretched the available resources at H.Q., and those of Ness and his small planning team in particular, in three ways. First, projections of such variables as economic growth, population, industrial location, energy use and motorway-building were required. Second, regional information on the long-term maintenance and operating costs for the various routes had to be collated, and the regions' existing initiatives for the concentration of freight traffic flows (encouraged by Margetts as part of the overall *Reshaping* strategy) needed to be carefully co-ordinated. And third, there was the problem of appeasing internal critics. A first draft of the report was subjected to detailed scrutiny from October 1964. The General Managers naturally expressed some concern over the details of route selection. This was scarcely surprising, since the preferred network included, for example, only one Anglo-Scottish route, the West Coast line from Euston to Glasgow, and went against regional opinion by identifying the line from Paddington to Plymouth via Bristol (not Westbury) as the only route to the West Country. Henry Johnson also made it clear that the managers felt the trunk passenger traffic forecast was 'unduly pessimistic'. Some of the Board members, and Williams in particular, were far from convinced that publication of the report was desirable after the change of government.[43]

Given the information available in 1964, the *Trunk Routes* report was a fairly sober assessment of likely economic trends, although some of the projections now appear fanciful. The Board elected to use the N.E.D.C.'s upper-bound prediction of a 4 per cent growth rate to 1984, in order to ensure that it had sufficient trunk route capacity in the future. It was also assumed that industrial growth would occur evenly in existing centres, and that population would grow by 15 per cent. The report then forecast a fall in passenger traffic, wagon-load freight and trunk coal traffic (the latter by 25 per cent), but held that these losses would be more than offset by substantial increases in the railways' other freight businesses, viz. oil (up 200 per cent), iron and steel (60 per cent) and other freight, mostly freightliner (200 per cent). Consequently, total freight ton-mileage in 1984 was expected to be 60–70 per cent higher than in 1964. With modern technology and sophisticated train diagramming, a network of only 3,000 miles would be able to handle these expanded freight flows.

More important than its predictions, which time has eroded, the 1965 report hinted at an important change in emphasis in the *Reshaping* strategy. The Board was now arguing more firmly than before that route costs could be scaled down to meet the traffic offering. Note, for example, the following comment: 'a prime requirement is that the costs of providing the railway track and signalling per unit of traffic passing over it should be reduced to a level which enables services to be provided on a competitive basis'. Regret was now expressed that the public should have focussed on the negative aspects of pruning the network instead of the positive proposals for developing its core.[44] But the Board itself was largely to blame for encouraging this public reaction. In 1962 and 1963 Beeching, Margetts, Shirley and others had encouraged railway managers to think chiefly in terms of cutting out traffics, sometimes with scarcely any examination of costs. By the end of 1963 there was evidence of a change of heart, in some quarters at least. This can be seen in the discussions about the future of wagon-load traffic. In January 1964 Raymond was arguing in the Planning Committee that the existing preoccupation with shedding traffics should give way to a policy of handling general merchandise more cheaply in order to bring unprofitable traffics into profit. There is also evidence to suggest that this kind of thinking was surfacing at regional level.[45] At the Board, some members began to share Raymond's view that the Beeching emphasis on track costs should be questioned. James's reaction to the draft report on *Trunk Routes* was that route costs had been 'given too dominating a status'.[46] By the time the report was published, internal opinion had thus begun to move away from a strategy which had concentrated upon the reduction of track costs by closure to one which embraced movement costs and the possible retention of some traffics via an assault on *total* operating costs. All this meant that much of the early rationalisation activity was undertaken without a clear and consistent idea of the final end to which the Board was working.

The Board declared that the 1965 report was not 'a prelude to closures on a grand scale: it is, rather, a basis for more definitive, stepwise planning of route rationalisation.'[47] In fact, it was scarcely even this. Ness and his team deliberately omitted any consideration of the feeder and suburban routes to be retained, which were to be the subject of a second report. Without an evaluation of the supplementary network no report on the shape of the future system could be regarded as final. By August 1965 separate studies of passenger and freight requirements had 'reached a stage where it was apparent that ultimately some 4,000–5,000 route miles might be necessary to supplement the 3,000 mile Trunk Route System, although not all of this could be considered as profitable'. These findings, which pointed to the conclusion that a network of 7,000–8,000 miles could fully meet all British Railways' requirements over the next 20 years, remained confidential.[48]

By this time, of course, much water had flowed under the political bridge. A Labour Government was in power, and there was much talk of a return to 'transport co-ordination'. Indeed, Lord Hinton was appointed to advise the Minister on the subject in the same month that the *Trunk Routes* report appeared. The Board may have wanted to use it as the basis for future planning, but as Beeching told the Management Committee, the government was hardly likely to express a view until Hinton had reported to Fraser.[49] Another indication that the climate was changing was to be found in a letter from George Woodcock, General Secretary of the T.U.C., to Fraser which gave the reactions of the General Council to the *Trunk Routes* report. The Council made the point that the B.R.B. approach did not appear to give the non-selected routes a fair chance of future viability.[50] Before the feeder information was produced, Beeching was succeeded by the new government's nominee, Raymond, and both government and Board were on the brink of a major change of policy, culminating in the establishment of the J.S.G., the 'Network for Development' of March 1967 and a new Transport Act. The implementation of the second stage of *Reshaping* was in effect still-born.

The striking thing about the railways' rationalisation of its freight services, however, was the speed of response, particularly in the closing of stations and depots, as is evident from Table 51. On 1 June 1963, when the closure programme began in earnest, there were still about 5,070 freight stations open. The Western Region offered the keenest response, closing 10 per cent of its stations in the first three months, and a further 10 per cent by March 1964.[51] But with the exception of the Southern, which had rationalised many of its freight facilities before 1963, all regions quickened the pace. In the first year a quarter of the total number of stations was closed, and by the end of 1965, over 3,100 had been dealt with, 62 per cent in the space of only two and a half years. By the end of 1968, only 912 stations were left, 18 per cent of the total open six years earlier. The number fell to 542, about 10 per cent of the 1962 figure, at the end of 1973.

The railways' response was facilitated by earlier planning. The basic groundwork had been carried out in the autumn of 1962 as part of the *Reshaping* exercise, when Margetts obtained outline closure plans from the regions. These were then up-dated in April 1963. The only hiccup was the delay caused by the Minister in determining the notice of closures to be given the public under Section 54 of the 1962 Act. A direction on this subject was not sent to the Board until the end of July 1963.[52] The initiative for producing and implementing closure proposals remained with the regions. As Hammond later recalled, 'Mr. Margetts kept a fairly loose hand on it, giving the Regions an occasional prod.'[53] Nevertheless, the policy orientation was made quite clear by headquarters. At the outset Margetts reminded the General Managers that 'the majority of small stations handle very little freight traffic indeed, and what they do handle is predominantly of the worst kind', and he frequently wrote to them urging more acceleration in the course of 1963. Although no precise target was

Table 51. *Rationalisation of freight facilities and equipment, 1962–73*

Date: end of	Freight Stations and Depots Freight only (i)	All (ii)	Marshalling yards (iii)	Route-mileage open to freight (iv)	Freight vehicles Merchandise (v)	All (vi)	Index numbers (1962=100) (i)	(ii)	(iii)	(iv)	(v)	(vi)
1962	2,479	5,175	602	17,481	325,407	862,640	100	100	100	100	100	100
1965	1,109	1,934	378	14,920	204,344	610,998	45	37	63	85	63	71
1968	598	912	184	12,447	135,632	437,412	24	18	31	71	42	51
1970	422	646	146	11,799	111,355	370,917	17	12	24	67	34	43
1973	364	542	124ᵃ	10,801	62,229	248,682	15	10	21ᵃ	62	19	29

[a] End of 1972 figure. Yards were re-defined in 1973 to exclude local yards.
Note: in 1969/70 13 miles of route were transferred to L.T. An unexplained alteration of the marshalling yards data was made in 1963. The B.T.C.'s Accounts for 1962 give the total as 815.
Source: B.R.B., R. & A. 1963–73.

given in the *Reshaping* report itself, it was clearly understood by Margetts's team that the 60 per cent of stations, which handled only 3 per cent of the traffic volume and each handled under 200 tons of business in the survey week in 1961, should go.[54] This freight station closure policy was judged by the Board to have been highly successful over its first three years. The notional target of 60 per cent was reached by the end of 1965, and this with no significant contraction in the volume of freight carried by rail. Indeed, the tonnage carried in 1965 was a little higher than that carried in 1962. Furthermore, there were few protests from industry and traders. Margetts was able to inform his colleagues in December 1964 that 'the policy of proceeding to close stations individually has undoubtedly paid off as the volume of objections and complaints would appear to have been negligible'. In the following July, the newly appointed chairman, Raymond, made a point of congratulating the General Managers and Margetts on the satisfactory progress made.[55]

Though successful in these terms, the policy also had its limitations. The speedy response to freight rationalisation was largely confined to the closure of small stations, where most customers could transfer to alternative locations. The railways' overall freight facility *was* scaled down, but not quite so quickly, as Table 51 demonstrates. By the end of 1965, the Board had closed 37 per cent of the marshalling yards open at the end of 1962, and dispensed with 29 per cent of its vehicle stock. But Beeching's promise, in the *Reshaping* report, to scrap at least 348,000 wagons by the end of 1965 was not fulfilled until 1967.[56] Furthermore, the route-mileage open to freight contracted by only 15 per cent over the same period, from 17,500 to just under 15,000 miles. The Board was also rather slow to introduce concentration schemes for domestic coal traffic and to rationalise its loss-making sundries depots. Beeching's freight programme certainly represented a much more intensive strategy of rationalisation than the railways had ever experienced. At the same time, the freight business held up remarkably well until 1966. Economic conditions were of course comparatively favourable in these years, but it was the slower rate of route-mileage reduction and problems in dealing swiftly with the coal and sundries traffics that help to explain why the Board was able to maintain its traffic volumes.

The slower reduction in the route-mileage of the railways' freight network is easily explained. While the Board could move quickly to close individual freight stations, where no formal procedure for evaluating hardship applied, it was a very different matter where freight and passenger facilities co-existed. Here, there came into operation the complex and time-consuming process of public inquiry by the T.U.C.C.s and reference of closure proposals to the Minister of Transport for a final decision. Where a line was seen to be surplus to requirements, action to remove both freight and passenger services was necessary. There is evidence to suggest that regional managers had to be prodded to act in this way, and to remove freight facilities in anticipation of a passenger closure on the same line.[57] This had the effect of limiting progress, as will be evident when passenger rationalisation is examined (see below, pp. 436–60).

Plans for the concentration of coal traffic were neither drawn up nor implemented as speedily as B.R.B. planners had hoped. This was not entirely disadvantageous, since it allowed the Board to scale down the ambitious scheme of 1963, whereby customers were to be encouraged to build 250–300 fully mechanised depots, to a more modest 80–90 depots two years later. By this time it had been realised that a large consuming area was too close to the coalfields to provide the operational economies to justify investment.[58] Nevertheless, slow progress during the first phase of the post-*Reshaping* activity meant that about 800–900 station closure proposals were frozen pending the development of the new coal facilities, and the problem persisted into the late 1960s.[59] The N.C.B. was reluctant to commit investment to railhead operations at a time of falling demand for household coal, and at many pits it had little incentive to invest in the loading and storage facilities needed for block train working as long as railway wagons could be used for storage. It also felt that it was important to give the trade the widest choice of fuels available, which meant that it was not keen to disturb the existing fragmented pattern of distribution. Coal merchants showed a similar disinclination to invest. The anxiety of some local authorities when considering planning applications for urban depots was an additional complication. The regions, moreover, were not keen to dump their long-established customers, the local coal merchants, despite the fact that many of them were operating through depots of very low volume indeed: the *Reshaping* report had revealed some 1,790 stations which were each handling a *maximum* of only 50 tons or one to five wagons a week.[60] All these factors combined to retard coal concentration. The much-publicised depot at West Drayton in London, which opened in December 1963 with an estimated annual throughput of 200,000 tons, was an exceptional example of sponsorship by the N.C.B. At the end of 1965 only 14 fully mechanised depots were open, and a year later the number had increased to only 22, well short of the 56 planned for completion by that date. Only five of these were designed for traffics in excess of the 80,000 tons a year identified as the minimum to make a mechanised depot viable. British Railways' effort in relation to coal concentration, which had been advocated as early as the Modernisation

Plan of 1955, was too little too late. By 1966, the eventual loss of the domestic coal traffic to road was being gloomily forecast at headquarters.[61]

In July 1962 a National Sundries Plan had been drawn up by a joint headquarters/regions working party. It contended that a capital investment of £11 million would make this loss-making traffic viable, the definition of viability being that revenue would cover direct costs and make a contribution of £3 million to joint costs. The strategy involved a reduction in the number of depots from about 950 (550 main and 400 secondary) to 152 (97 and 55). But implementation of the Plan was hindered by growing doubts inside H.Q., led by Margetts, as to whether it could satisfy the *Reshaping* report's intention that the traffic 'must be made to pay'. The working party was instructed to take a second look at the Plan and this produced revised figures in July 1963: capital investment of £8.5 million, a £4 million contribution to joint costs and 141 depots (91 main and 50 secondary).[62] Although the General Managers declared themselves in favour of the Plan, Margetts continued to press the view that as long as the sundries traffic was handled in the old way concentration would not produce the planned viability. He was firmly of the belief that sundries operations could be linked with the development of the freightliner, something which the working party had challenged. The continuing uncertainty over the future of sundries undoubtedly acted as a brake on wholehearted rationalisation. In September 1963 the Management Committee instructed the regions to press on with depot closures but at the same time discouraged them from spending money on concentration schemes.[63] Regular reports of poor service, traffic losses to road and teething troubles at depots where concentration had been applied made for depressing reading. Another plan, formulated at the beginning of 1965, recommended concentration on only 61 main depots, and it was suggested that about half of the existing traffic could be associated with the planned freightliner network. However, the first experimental freightliner service, from London to Glasgow, did not materialise until November 1965. Depot closures *were* introduced, but not as quickly as desired at H.Q. At the end of 1964, British Rail sundries were still being handled at 497 locations, and a year later, there were still 360.[64]

In 1966, a new policy emerged which profoundly influenced the progress of both freight and passenger rationalisation. Raymond and Castle together discussed the latter's wish to reverse Beeching's *Reshaping* thrust, with the intention that in future British Railways management would concentrate on the 'improvement rather than the reduction of the system'. The Board, taking the initiative, suggested that a network of about 11,000 of the existing 15,000 route-miles might be retained. In the government's White Paper on *Transport Policy* of July 1966, which announced the setting-up of the J.S.G., it was declared that 'the country's transport system must include a substantial railway network', and a map outlining revised proposals for the 11,000 miles as a 'Network for Development' was published jointly by the Ministry and the Board in March 1967 (see Map IX, below).[65]

The new direction, endorsed by Raymond, Castle and the Labour Government, set more restricted limits to the planned extent of rationalisation schemes. It helped to appease internal disquiet in the ranks of senior and middle management both about the extent to which freight traffic, and particularly wagon-load traffic, should be jettisoned, and about the ability of a 3,000-mile trunk network to handle the traffic volumes forecast in Ness's report of 1965 (Map VIII). Nevertheless, given the relatively limited response to rationalisation before 1966 (except for freight station closures), there remained much to be done, even with a target network of 11,000 miles. After all, the Board's National Freight Train Plan of July 1965 had argued for the concentration of wagon-load traffic flows, and the Standby Committee of the J.S.G. gave further impetus to decisions on route closures by identifying, in 1967, a 'national freight grid' of freightliner services of only 3,600 miles and a 'core network' of 6,000 miles.[66]

Between the end of 1965 and the end of 1973, 4,000 route-miles of line were closed to freight traffic. And with the emphasis of rationalisation firmly on lines rather than stations, the contraction achieved in 1965–8 was just as vigorous as in 1962–5 (see Table 51). Concentration on routes also meant concentration on a limited number of marshalling yards. In accordance with the National Freight Train Plan of 1965, these were pruned considerably to allow the concentration of wagon-load traffic on a smaller number of modern facilities. By 1967, 55 yards had been closed and about 5 million train-miles per annum had been saved.[67] The number of yards was halved between 1965 and 1968, and there were further reductions thereafter. By the end of 1972, there were only 124 in use, compared with 602 at the end of 1962. There was also a further reduction in the wagon fleet. By the end of 1973 British Rail was operating with 249,000 vehicles, only 29 per cent of the 1962 number, for a traffic volume which, in terms of net ton-miles, was still 87 per cent of the 1962 level.

After Beeching's departure, the rationalisation of freight was accompanied by considerable debate at H.Q. about the optimum scale of such a strategy. On one side, the Treasury exerted pressure on the Board via the Ministry to continue the reduction of loss-making elements, following further heavy deficits on revenue account of £132, £135 and £153 million in the years 1965–7. Thereafter, a clear by-product of the

Transport Act of 1968 and its grant-aid for loss-making passenger services was the assumption that the freight business would have to pay its way. In these circumstances, both Raymond and Johnson were moved to encourage the closure of more unprofitable stations and freight-only lines in 1967–8.[68] There was support for such a policy at headquarters. Shirley and Margetts, in particular, were concerned about the limited impact rationalisation had made on the losses incurred by the wagon-load traffic. The results for 1965 confirmed this, with merchandise traffic failing to cover its total costs by £40 million, compared with a deficit of £54 million in 1961. No improvement over the position in 1963 was evident. Even in the transformed political atmosphere of 1968, Margetts, in reviewing the achievements of *Reshaping*, stated quite simply that although 'quite a lot of progress [had] been made . . . it just has not been enough . . . there is still too much railway'.[69] Others, however, felt that a simple policy of rationalising the freight network in a draconian way would not solve any of the railways' fundamental problems. They continued to press for the retention and development of the wagon-load business. As early as 1964, Raymond referred to regional doubts about the prospect of recovering costs, and by 1966 these views had gained considerable momentum. Long, the Chief Commercial Manager, expressed grave concern over the realisation that 'with the worst loss makers out of the way, it is now more difficult to show early savings from eliminating the unremunerative business. The next stage could involve severe net revenue losses in the short term as the receipts drop faster than the costs.'[70] The crude allocation of total costs to specific traffics, developed in the 1950s and employed in the *Reshaping* report, was increasingly being questioned in relation to commercial strategies at a detailed level. It was recognised that the contribution of wagon-load traffic to the railways' joint or indirect costs was considerable; in short, it was 'too uneconomic to be tolerated but too valuable to be jettisoned'.[71]

This realisation did something to halt the Board's policy of drift in relation to wagon-load freight. Moreover, a clear by-product of Labour's promised transport legislation was that freight services would have to break even. The result was that considerable managerial resources were devoted to deciding how best to deal with the freight sector, something which Beeching and his managers had essentially failed to do. The formulation of an 'interim freight policy' in May 1968 led on to the production of the substantive Freight Plan of October, which came down firmly in favour of the development of wagon-load services.[72] Evidence of this new approach can be found in a study of freight services in 'greenfield' areas by Robbins, the Executive Director (Freight), presented to the Railway Management Group in May 1971. His conclusion was that given the existing mix of traffics, including grant-aided passenger services, most of the 12 areas and 16 freight-only lines studied could be expected to yield in 1976 'a worthwhile contribution to overall system costs – mainly from wagonload services'.[73] This emphasis on retention and development was then repeated in the B.R.B.'s Second Corporate Plan of February 1972, and in the Railway Policy Review in December. The Board's position was that as long as the existing rolling stock could be employed, a general contraction in freight facilities would only result in a fall in the contribution made to system costs. Terminals with low throughputs would be closed, but only where the revenue lost could be matched by cost savings.[74]

If the changing attitudes of B.R.B. managers were an important determinant of the pace of freight rationalisation, there is little evidence of any direct Ministerial involvement in the process of freight closures, although disquiet about the overall prospects of railway freight surfaced from time to time, and was certainly evident in the deliberations of the J.S.G. in 1966–7. The Ministry of Transport was also reluctant to sanction investment in wagon-load.[75] The only examples of direct pressure for specific closures occurred when the Minister and his officials were pressed by their Highways Department to use railway track-beds to cut the constructional costs of road improvement schemes. Thus, in February 1969, P. E. Lazarus, an Under-Secretary at the Ministry, wrote to Hammond in an attempt to prod the Board into closing the Welwyn–Blackbridge (Dunstable) line, which was being used in connection with a London rubbish disposal contract, in order to avoid bridging costs for an improvement to the A1 road. Similar informal pressure was exerted in an attempt to reduce by £300,000 the costs of a by-pass on the A35 near Poole in Dorset. In these cases, both the Board and the region concerned were willing to accommodate the Ministry provided that there were no long-term prospects of freight revenue.[76] In general, freight rationalisation remained a matter for railway managers, not the government.

What then, did the Board's freight rationalisation programmes achieve in the period 1963–73? It is difficult to find a simple answer to match that given in the *Reshaping* report, where savings of £5–10 million were forecast for 'freight closures', and an upper-bound of some £63 million was expected to be saved from closures, wagon fleet reductions and the concentration of coal and sundries traffics.[77] No global estimate appears to have been attempted at H.Q., but if Long and James were correct in assuming, in October 1964, that about £8 million per annum could be saved for every 100,000 wagons eliminated and £6 million saved for every 1,000 miles of double track line closed, then there is every reason to believe that savings of the order forecast in 1963 were ultimately achieved.[78] Another clue may be found in regional information on the expected savings (both in the short and long term) from station and depot closures. By summing the London Midland's data for 800 depot closures from 1963 to 1969, a saving of £1.3 million is produced, which suggests that total savings for British Railways from the elimination of some 4,500 stations and depots, 1963–73, amounted to about £7 million.[79]

Of course, estimates like these are defective on a number of counts. The data available are invariably in current prices, and it would be an extremely laborious task to make adjustments for inflation, particularly since total savings accrue over extended periods of time after closure. In any case, there is every reason to be sceptical, as indeed the Board was, about the quality of the information produced by the regions. In the first stage of *Reshaping*, the formulation of closure proposals, it was clear that there was no consistency in the methods used. For freight, two regions, the London Midland and Eastern, used the old T.U.C.C. formula, which compared immediately identifiable savings in local movement and terminal costs with an estimate of 'throughout' revenue lost, that is both local and contributory revenue. The others adopted the more sophisticated approach of comparing the estimated reduction in costs with estimated loss of gross revenue. Some regions included contributory revenue in their calculations, others did not. Not surprisingly, the clear message from Margetts and his team was that the low-volume depots were such obvious loss-makers that there was no need for regions to calculate precise figures to support closure. Margetts also saw no value in drawing up aggregates of estimated financial savings.[80] Some concern at regional level about the method of formulating closure proposals led the H.Q. *Reshaping* team to make a distinction between small and other stations, and to circulate a screening procedure in October 1963, which supplied the regions with yardstick costs and invited them to consider proposals on the basis of a failure to cover 'throughout' direct costs. But regional inconsistencies persisted, and this was evident when savings figures were given to the unions as part of the staff consultation process. When the emphasis shifted in 1964 from the closure of stations to that of lines and branches, the General Managers were asked merely to provide information on local costs, where 'a degree of estimation' was stated to be 'acceptable'. Headquarters staff clearly did not think very much of regional freight data, and this makes it very difficult to find a serious estimate of financial effect.[81] Certainly, there is evidence to suggest that paper savings were not always achieved. This point was put most forcefully by James. In a memorandum on costs and freight traffic in February 1966 he emphasised that the recovery of costs was not automatic: it required determined management action and a full consideration of the time-scale involved.[82]

Did rationalisation drive away profitable or potentially profitable traffic? It is difficult to come to a firm conclusion here since the rationalisation of freight facilities was only one of a number of factors which may have influenced a trader's decision to switch from the railways to road haulage. This was particularly true in the first five years after *Reshaping*, when there was no firm policy of development for wagon-load traffic, and reliability was at a particularly low level. Nevertheless, it seems likely that during the period 1962–5, when the emphasis was overwhelmingly on the need to effect station closures quickly, some traffics were shed which might have been financially beneficial in the long run. Regional uncertainty as to which stations to close and the lack of co-ordination between the closing of small freight stations and the opening of new concentration depots undoubtedly played into the hands of the road hauliers. Indeed, in May 1966, Griffiths, the Commercial Planning Officer, when reviewing the effects of the station closure programme, admitted that 'we have lost more traffic than was expected'.[83] In the second part of the decade the pendulum began to swing the other way, especially when the 1965 directive to the regions, that all traffic should cover its direct costs plus 20 per cent of indirect costs, was superseded in 1967 by the instruction that henceforth traffic should be retained as long as it covered direct costs.[84] The subsequent adoption of the Freight Plan of 1968 further lessened the chances of potentially profitable traffic being deliberately discarded. By the early 1970s it was quite apparent that the railways were continuing to handle unprofitable traffics, for the sake of a contribution to system costs.[85]

The rationalisation of freight facilities was an obvious response to the poor prospects of much of the existing business in the early 1960s but, as we have seen, it was neither a continuous nor a wholehearted policy. More was done to eliminate small stations and life-expired wagons than to prune network size, although the latter was determined in large measure by the change of political direction in 1966. The bald facts are that much antiquated equipment was still being used ten years after *Reshaping*, and the profile of rail freight did not change a great deal. This emerges from the analysis of freight business activity in 1974, which was drawn up by British Rail's Operations Planning team in August 1975. At the end of 1974, 53 per cent of the 240,000-strong wagon fleet had no power braking system at all, and only 5 per cent had the preferred air brakes. One of the conclusions of the analysis was that 'the overall picture' was that of a 'highly variable, geographically fragmented, and low volume workload, with marked differences in traffic density'. Freight operations remained 'manpower intensive [and] lacking in robustness'.[86]

V

The rationalisation of passenger services put British Rail firmly under the microscope of government scrutiny, at both a central and a local level. The process also induced at best anxiety and at worst outright hostility from consumers. But in spite of this clamour comprehensive data on the closure programme has proved elusive for the historian. A broad indication of post-*Reshaping* activity can be obtained from the Reports and Accounts (Table 52). Here, it can be seen that the closure of passenger stations was neither as quick nor as extensive as was that of freight stations (cf. Table 51 above). Although 27 per cent of the stations open at the end of 1962 had been closed by the end of 1965, Beeching's promise to shut over 2,000 stations was not quite fulfilled in our period. Closure of route-mileage, on the other hand, was on much the same scale as that of freight, 4,000 route-miles having been closed to passenger traffic in the years 1963–73, about a third of the network open at the end of 1962.

To penetrate further than these bare facts detailed information is needed on such matters as British Rail's proposals for line, service and station closures; successful closures and estimates of their financial effect; and a detailed evaluation of the working of the machinery for monitoring closure proposals established by the Transport Acts of 1947, 1962 and 1968. Unfortunately, it is not at all easy to obtain this information. The formulation and justification of passenger closures was, like the freight closures, left to regional initiative, subject to the broad guidelines established by the *Reshaping* report. In 1962 Margetts had encouraged the use of passenger train surveys to ascertain earnings and direct expenses and to provide a common basis for the quantification of aggregate long-term savings. But not all regions followed this practice, the Western, for example, continuing to use the old, pre-1963 T.U.C.C. formula of immediately identifiable savings; and there was a distinct lack of homogeneity in approach, particularly in relation to contributory revenue. The situation made it difficult to monitor progress at the centre.[87]

There was little incentive for the regions to provide carefully formulated data. The new procedure established by the Transport Act of 1962, which effectively transferred responsibility for public decisions on opposed closures from the T.U.C.C.s and the C.T.C.C. to the Ministry, placed no obligation on British Rail to publish any financial information in support of its proposals. The role of the T.U.C.C.s was limited to an evaluation of the 'hardship' suffered by users. Nevertheless, after negotiations with the Ministry and C.T.C.C., the Commission agreed to supply the T.U.C.C.s with rudimentary data, for line closures, on revenue and direct movement

Table 52. *Rationalisation of passenger facilities, 1962–73*

Date: end of	Passenger stations open (i)	Route-mileage open to passengers (ii)	Index (1962 = 100) (i)	(ii)
1962	4,306	12,915	100	100
1965	3,161	10,884	73	84
1968	2,616	9,471	61	73
1970	2,423	9,095	56	70
1973	2,355	8,932	55	69

Source: B.R.B., *R. & A. 1963–73.* Passenger station data exclude stations open for parcels traffic.

and terminal costs, on an 'expense' basis,* together with the track and signalling costs attributable to passenger train working. Estimated renewal and maintenance costs over a five-year period were also to be given. For station closures, originating receipts and direct costs were to be supplied. These figures were endorsed in October 1963 by Sir William Carrington, past-President of the Institute of Chartered Accountants in England and Wales, in a report commissioned by Marples following criticism of the new procedure, particularly in the House of Lords. However, the information supplied was very bare indeed, far less detailed in fact than that given under the arrangements agreed in 1958 (see above, p. 210). In these circumstances, figures were often produced hastily from out-of-date surveys. Where closure proposals were opposed, the Ministry of Transport was also given financial information. In the case of line and service closures, this was more substantial including estimates of contributory gross revenue, the expected loss in total revenue and the 'estimated net financial effect' of closure (as was supplied for specific examples in 'Table No. 1' on pages 100–1 of the *Reshaping* report). But there is no reason to suppose that the figures supplied to the Ministry were superior in quality to the outline data given to the T.U.C.C.s.[88] Indeed, the regions frequently confused the two sets of data, and there were numerous errors and omissions. Track and signalling costs were not always included, particularly in the early proposals. Contributory gross revenue, information reserved for the Minister, was erroneously included in revenue figures supplied to the East Midlands T.U.C.C. by the London Midland Region in its submission for the Rugby–Peterborough (East)

---

* 'Expense' basis calculations exclude interest and provide for renewal at historic instead of replacement cost.

service in 1965. Attempts by the region to rectify its mistake after a question in the Commons merely led to more confusion.[89] Concern was expressed at headquarters when the same region admitted, later in the year, that it had made the same error in its submission for the Hope Valley line from Manchester (Central) to Sheffield (Midland), and had produced an inflated figure for movement costs by incorrectly calculating on a cost rather than an expense basis.[90]

As the closure process accelerated, it became more difficult for B.R.B. to put an exact figure on the financial effect of the closure programme. This was certainly evident in December 1966, when British Rail was asked to give detailed information about aggregate passenger savings in response to a parliamentary question from the Earl of Kinnoull. The Board admitted that it could not provide the details concerned, the Director of Budgets conceding privately that 'to analyse the information in the manner requested would entail research into records widely dispersed in the Regions in respect of some 250 services'.[91]

Now, more than 20 years after the *Reshaping* report, the data are even harder to find. Complete regional information has not survived, and the headquarters closure files, based on submissions to the T.U.C.C.s and the Minister (which were never a complete record of all cases) were destroyed some years ago. The C.T.C.C. has not retained information on all individual cases, and the Ministry's files, to which access was not granted, are, it appears, no longer complete. Nevertheless, an analysis has been built up by drawing on a wide variety of sources. It provides a fairly comprehensive indication of British Rail's closure proposals, closures and part-closures effected, route-mileage reductions and the maximum financial effect based on the figures supplied to the T.U.C.C.s.[92]

A summary of the results is given in Table 53. Data are available for 482 of the 488 closure proposals submitted under the Transport Acts of 1962 and 1968 from 4 June 1963 to the end of 1973. In addition, there is more limited information on the line and service closures undertaken during Beeching's period as Chairman from 1 June 1961, under the old pro-cedure, including cases in the pipeline, which were dealt with between 1 October 1962 and 4 June 1963. Although the results must be treated with some caution, it can be seen that the bulk of the Board's effort in relation to closure proposals fell in the 18-month period from June 1963 to December 1965, when 330 or 68 per cent of the 482 cases examined were presented. Most of these (286) came during Beeching's Chairmanship. The most important period for closures effected – the timing of which was influenced by such external factors as the extent of public opposition, the efficiency of the T.U.C.C. hearing procedure and the attitude of the Minister – was clearly 1964–6. In these three years 258 closures were made, involving about 2,350 route-miles and with total estimated maxi-

Table 53. *Rationalisation of passenger services, 1961–73, by calendar year and by Chairman's period of office*

Year	Proposals (no.)	Full and part closures (no.)	Route-mileage	Estimated savings (maximum) (£)
1961[a]	n.a.	11	283	314,308
1962	n.a.	39	702	1,272,999
1963	173[b]	26	177	648,375
1964	100	112	902	3,517,286
1965	57	78	859	3,142,506
1966	48	68	583	3,917,347
1967	41	51	307	976,786
1968	35	44	332	1,373,737
1969	6	27	270	1,597,926
1970	11	22	251	1,545,139
1971	4	5	23	80,636
1972	6	10	68	638,500
1973	1	5	41	78,900
1 June 1961– 3 June 1963	n.a.	74	1,153	2,232,341
4 June 1963– 31 December 1973	482	424	3,644	16,872,104
Chairmen				
Beeching (1 June 1961– 3 June 1963)	n.a.	74	1,153	2,232,341
Beeching (4 June 1963– 31 May 1965)	286	145	1,326	4,874,329
Beeching (all)	n.a.	219	2,479	7,106,670
Raymond (1 June 1965– 31 December 1967)	129	166	1,333	6,682,937
Johnson (1 January 1968– 11 September 1971)	48	96	877	4,596,238
Marsh (12 September 1971– 31 December 1973)	5	17	109	718,600

[a] June–December.
[b] Proposals from 4 June 1963 only.
Note: data relate to proposals published, full and part closures effected, with route-mileages (rounded to nearest mile) closed. The savings data are maxima since they relate to savings estimated for full proposals. Where a part closure was made, no attempt was made to scale down the savings figure. See Appendix J.
Source: see Appendix J.

mum savings (on the T.U.C.C. basis) of £10.5 million. These figures represent about two-thirds of the totals for 1963–73.

The trend of actual closures, unlike that of closure proposals, cannot be attributed primarily to Beeching's post-*Reshaping* strategy, important though this was. The incomplete information available for the first two years of Beeching's period of office, from June 1961 to June 1963, reveals nonetheless that the rationalisation he pursued under the old machinery compared favourably with that of the next two years. The closure of at least 1,153 route-miles was broadly comparable with the 1,326 miles which followed, and estimated savings in 1961–3 of £2.2 million were nearly half of the aggregate for 1963–5. These findings contradict the impression given by some writers that there was a long moratorium while the *Reshaping* strategy was being formulated. To say, as has Aldcroft, that 'from the end of 1960 investment and closures were being held up, and between September 1962 and June 1963 closures were suspended altogether' is simply not true. Several 'pipeline' cases were dealt with in this period, including the Brecon lines rationalisation, introduced on 31 December 1962, for which the estimated savings (T.U.C.C. figures) were given as £287,463.[93] If there was a moratorium, it surely came in 1963 as a result of the T.U.C.C./Ministerial procedure. Of the 173 closure proposals published by British Rail from 4 June to 31 December, only two came to fruition by the end of the year.[94]

In fact, while the *Reshaping* report produced a marked acceleration in the presentation of closure proposals, actual closures were as much a feature of the Raymond and Johnson periods. Raymond, in spite of his association with Barbara Castle's new policy towards network size and passenger services from 1966, presided over more closures, in terms of numbers, route-miles and estimated savings, in his two-and-a-half year term than Beeching did in the two years to June 1965. Johnson's period of office, from January 1968 to September 1971, when grant-aid for unremunerative passenger services was firmly established under the Transport Act of 1968, witnessed the closure of a fairly sizeable mileage, 877, with estimated savings of £4.6 million (see Table 53). Finally, the rationalisation programme must not be seen merely as a matter of working through the list of planned closures given in Appendix 2 of the *Reshaping* report. Nearly a quarter (104) of the 424 closures introduced from June 1963 had not appeared in the report but were the result of subsequent planning.[95]

Table 53 does show clearly that the railways' efforts to close passenger facilities, as measured by the number of proposals, fell off steadily after 1963, with a marked decline after 1968. From the data, it is tempting to attribute the rationalisation initiative to Beeching and Marples, his Minister for much of the period, and the subsequent 'flight from Beeching' to a change of government, Castle's policy initiative, the work of the J.S.G. and the Transport Act of 1968. While there is much truth in this generalisation, it masks the complexities of the situation facing the Board as it struggled to reduce the deficit on passenger services. Both the presentation of closure proposals and the final implementation of closures were subject to a variety of internal and external influences, which determined the tempo of change. It is to these that we now turn.

Although the Commission's attitude to rationalisation had been rather equivocal in the 1950s, there were signs of a stiffer resolve before Beeching's arrival. Prodding from the Treasury and the Ministry of Transport was clearly evident. As already observed (above, p. 402), concrete proposals based on regional lists were included in the four-year modernisation programme produced in December 1960. These ultimately envisaged the withdrawal of passenger services from 1,176 route-miles by 1964.[96] Throughout 1961 and 1962, Chairman and Minister were at one in their anxiety to accelerate passenger closures in response to Treasury concern about the Commission's considerable financial deficit. This anxiety was further demonstrated by the curtailment of the public's right to challenge closure proposals via the machinery of the T.U.C.C. and C.T.C.C. The Commission had always complained about the time taken to prepare presentations and the delays while cases were being examined. Marples, after dealing with one or two contentious cases, notably the Westerham line (above, p. 211), was willing to assume a more positive role in the process. The Ministry, and no doubt the Commission also, were keen to revise a system in which persistent objectors had used data 'to comment on the alleged shortcomings of the railway management'.[97] Under the 1962 Act, the C.T.C.C. became a purely supervisory body, and the work of the T.U.C.C.s was confined to reporting to the Minister on the extent of hardship and how to alleviate it. The Commission, later the Board, was no longer to be represented on the C.T.C.C. and the T.U.C.C.s. It was the Minister's sole responsibility to balance hardship against cost.[98]

If the legislators believed that this would streamline the process of public consultation then they were mistaken. Disquiet about the new rules persisted throughout the 1960s, but was particularly marked in 1962–3. After discussion between the interested parties, the Commission agreed to supply the T.U.C.C.s with the outline data described above (pp. 436–7). But the figures were intended only for guidance, to help the T.U.C.C.s determine the comparative costs of bus services as an alternative to rail. They were no longer to be the subject of discussion by objectors or indeed by the Committees themselves. The Carrington report of October 1963 was an attempt to legitimise the data. Rejecting the idea of 'profit and loss statements' as unduly complex and likely to confuse, Carrington declared British Rail's T.U.C.C. data to be 'well founded, and sound in principle'. The only note of criticism was his plea for more consistency at regional level. This was just what the Board and the Ministry wanted to hear. Unfortunately, it did little to reassure protestors. They continued to express the belief that the figures were defective, that the costs of cheaper rail operations were not being properly examined and that the 'savings' figures suggested by the T.U.C.C. data were exaggerated.[99]

By the end of 1963, with the Conservatives' long period of office coming to an end, Marples was put under pressure from colleagues who were doubtful about the electoral appeal of rail closures in rural and suburban areas. There was also more interest in regional economic policy following Edward Heath's appointment as Secretary of State for Industry, Trade and Regional Development. In December Marples voiced his concern to Beeching, who offered to produce financial information on selected cases for a private meeting with interested M.P.s. The B.R.B.'s response to the Minister's request for information on 66 specific proposals was to say that these proposals involved about 20 per cent of the £29–31 million saving expected from passenger closures (including track and signalling savings) in the *Reshaping* report (cf. Table 50).[100] Beeching declined to give the Ministry full details for all these cases but, as agreed with Marples, produced ten examples favourable to the Board's point of view. With the exception of the Inverness–Wick–Thurso line, they promised average savings of £120,000. Beeching also fully grasped the point that by including only track and signalling costs attributable to passenger operation the data understated the scope for savings where freight traffic could not support the remaining costs. In the case of the Inverness–Wick–Thurso line, the expected loss of revenue was £202,500 (including contributory revenue lost), while the direct costs amounted to £209,000, producing a 'saving' of £6,500, which Marples described as 'very small'. Beeching then pointed out that the balance of track and signalling costs was £235,300, which would also be saved, since the Board intended to withdraw freight facilities if consent were given to the passenger proposal. He was plainly irritated to be asked to justify his position. As he told Marples in January 1964, 'it is very frustrating to all of us who are putting so much effort into this task to experience growing resistance from those who profess to support the plan and to find that the number of closures actually achieved is disproportionately small'.[101]

By this time the honeymoon period with the government was over. Long delays, refusals and part-refusals now appeared at the Ministerial stage. After turning down two 'pipeline' cases, Haltwhistle–Alston and Woodside–Selsdon, in 1963,[102] Marples rejected seven cases in full and seventeen cases in part in the first nine months of 1964. The most important were the Central Wales line (Llanelly–Shrewsbury), a 'pipeline' proposal of June 1962, which was rejected in February 1964, and the Inverness–Wick–Thurso and Inverness–Kyle lines, both refused in large measure in

April. They were followed by a cluster of rejections in the run up to the General Election of October.[103] Of equal concern to the Board was the time taken by the Minister to come to a decision. Although some proposals were dealt with promptly, others remained on Marples's desk for a long time. No obvious pattern was discernible, but it is clearly true that 'in the Marples reign selection out of sequence was made on more than one occasion . . . conceivably for political expediency'.[104] In July 1964 the Board's Public Relations and Publicity Department produced a list of 30 outstanding cases which had been reported to the Minister from September 1963 to February 1964. Of these 17 had been awaiting a decision for six months or more, including Bath–Bournemouth (Somerset and Dorset line), Bletchley–Buckingham and Carlisle–Settle–Hellifield. The list was sent by Eric Merrill, Chief Public Relations Officer, to his opposite number in the Ministry, in the hope that it might provoke some action. In the same month, Margetts informed the Board that the cost of delays was running at about £4 million a year.[105] Marples, it is true, handled an exceptionally large number of proposals – 148 – and the average time taken to process those settled during his period of office was under four months. He also pointed out that he was not responsible for delays caused when he asked either the Board or the T.U.C.C.s for additional information. Nevertheless, the Board's evident frustration found its way into its Annual Reports.[106]

The change of government did nothing to improve the position from the Board's point of view. The immediate response of the newly appointed Minister of Transport, Tom Fraser, was to introduce an adjustment to the procedure known as the 'early sift'. Operative from October 1964, it required the Board to submit proposals for Ministerial vetting *before* they were published. The intention was to prevent lengthy T.U.C.C. hearings of cases which were likely to be, in Fraser's words, '"non-starters" from the outset'. He had been influenced by Marples's rejection of the Manchester (Piccadilly)–Buxton proposal in July 1964, where the North Western T.U.C.C. had found hardship to be so extensive that it had not considered it necessary to document it in detail in its report.[107] Fraser also obtained the Board's undertaking that it would not in future lift the track after a closure was authorised, in case restoration were to be recommended in forthcoming regional transport plans. From April 1965 both the 'early sift' proposals and all outstanding cases were referred to the newly appointed Regional Economic Planning Boards and Councils for their consideration. The climate was clearly more restrictive. Fraser was under pressure from the strong anti-Beeching elements in his Party and in the trade union movement. As he admitted to Beeching, 'I am being pressed on all sides to bring the whole programme to a stop.'[108]

Under Fraser the delays certainly lengthened. The 'early sift' mechanism usually added about two to three months to the decision-making process. Secondly, the new Minister took longer to decide about a T.U.C.C. report: the average for proposals finalised during his period of office, 5.3 months, contrasts with the figure of 3.8 months established by his predecessor. These factors contributed to a lengthening of the average time taken to deal with a proposal from start to finish. The figure for cases published in 1964 was 21.7 months, which contrasts markedly with the 14.9 months for cases published in 1963 (Appendix J, Tables 3 and 4). Fraser also sat upon a number of more difficult cases inherited from Marples, notably the Penrith–Workington proposal, which was reported on in October 1963 and left for Barbara Castle to decide in January 1966. In April 1965 Margetts reported to the Management Committee on the state of play. He found that two years after the *Reshaping* report, over half of the cases were still awaiting decisions for one reason or another. Ministerial delay was singled out for criticism. Margetts produced half a dozen cases which had been with the Ministry for a year and more, including two, Penrith–Workington and Bath–Bournemouth, reported on in 1963.[109] The number of rejections by the Minister also increased relative to proposals. Fraser turned down twenty proposals, eleven of them in part, and rejected three at the 'sift' stage. Most of these were not entirely unexpected in that they were either suburban services or 'trunk' routes in sparsely populated areas, such as Carlisle–Hellifield and Fort William–Mallaig.[110] The Board continued to complain about the cost of delays and refusals. Its Report for 1964, published in May 1965, claimed that refusals to the end of 1964 had prevented the railways from eliminating losses of £1.5 million a year. Privately, Fraser was subjected to considerable pressure from Beeching. In December 1964 he received the Board's calculation that Ministerial delays and refusals had added £2 million to the 1964 deficit. It was followed by five months of argument in which Beeching tried to convince the Minister that further delay would jeopardise the Board's planned improvement in the 1964 budget. The Board also threatened to take steps to run down services or increase fares on lines where decisions were outstanding.[111]

Fraser's stance was not a doctrinaire one. Like Marples he blamed both the Board and the T.U.C.C.s for contributing to delays, and pointed out with justification that these were likely to increase since the Board had already dealt with the more obvious candidates for closure (about half of the *Reshaping* proposals had been processed by the end of 1964). While he had told the C.T.C.C. that the T.U.C.C.s should expect continuity in government policy towards closures, he told Beeching that the problem would be 'the increasing difficulty and complexity of the cases now coming forward'. Fraser showed an increasing reluctance to withdraw services in the main conurbations, in isolated rural areas with a poor road system, in areas where bus operators could not provide adequate alternative services and in holiday areas. He also requested that in some cases the Board should cost an alternative to closure in the form of a cheaper or modernised service. This strategy had been rejected by the Board in the past on the grounds that though losses might be reduced, they would not be eradicated.[112] Another irritant was the attitude adopted by some of the Regional Planning Councils and Boards. For example, the rather negative approach of the North West Council, led by Charles Carter, Vice-Chancellor of Lancaster University, caused the Minister particular concern when it brought a halt to decisions affecting the Liverpool and Manchester conurbations in 1965.[113]

The debate continued on Raymond's appointment as Chairman in June 1965. At this stage Fraser showed himself to be more amenable to the Board's pleas for assistance. The climate improved partly because Raymond, unlike Beeching, did not try to convince the Minister that the difficulties with passenger closures were an important factor in the Board's failure to deliver the promised reduction in its deficit.[114] In the summer of 1965 the Ministry made a determined effort to dispose of the outstanding cases, and Fraser lent his support to the Board's plans to deal more quickly with the redundant urban termini such as Glasgow's St Enoch and Buchanan Street stations.[115] He accepted a number of closure proposals in the six months to December 1965, including the Somerset and Dorset line, Salisbury–Exeter, and Leeds/Lancaster–Morecambe–Heysham, where in each case the gap between revenue and direct costs was stated to be £200,000–300,000. The Board's deteriorating financial position was an important motivating force for all concerned (the deficit in 1965 was £132 million, £11 million higher than in 1964). The moves caused considerable disquiet in Labour circles. Philip Noel-Baker, for example, a member of the Party's transport group, told the technical adviser to the National Council on Inland Transport, Prof. E. R. Hondelink, that Fraser had 'fallen into the hands of the civil servants who had four years of Marpleization'. However, there still remained a backlog of contentious cases. Over 30 (where the T.U.C.C. report had been completed before November 1965) were handed to Fraser's successor, Barbara Castle, when she replaced him on 23 December 1965, and seven of these were of old vintage, having been passed on to Fraser by Marples.[116]

When Castle took office, the Board was about to embark on the second stage of its passenger rationalisation programme, a systematic evaluation of all its passenger services in order to weed out those which, in Margetts's words, were 'suspect in the sense that earnings (ignoring contributory revenue) do not cover direct costs'.[117] But this initiative was put to one side with the change of direction in 1966, which involved the identification of a larger, 11,000-mile network for development and a group of passenger services which would qualify for government subsidy. Castle was certainly expected to be more hostile to closures, particularly by those on the Labour backbenches and in the rail unions who had attacked Fraser for perpetuating the Beeching–Marples approach. One of the myths of railway history is that the new Minister, by championing the cause of the commuter and rural rail user, finally nailed the lid on the *Reshaping* coffin.[118]

Once again, the truth is not quite so straightforward. During the two years and three months of Castle's term, Chairman and Minister developed an alternative strategy of direct governmental subsidy for loss-making services which were considered necessary on wider, socio-economic grounds. It might be expected that there would be, from 1966, a long moratorium on outstanding cases and a large number of Ministerial refusals. Evidence can be found to support these suppositions. Castle took longer than her predecessors to process new proposals put to her, 7.2 months on average compared with 3.8 months by Marples. She also turned down four proposals at the 'early sift' stage and withheld her consent on 38 occasions, 18 involving complete refusals. Over a third of these cases were in the North-West. They included the substantial proposals for Manchester–Glossop, Liverpool–St Helens–Wigan, Liverpool–Fazackerly–Wigan and Liverpool–Chester (General), where the T.U.C.C. 'savings' figures amounted in total to £336,000 per annum. As for length of time between the receipt of a T.U.C.C. report by a Minister and a subsequent decision (by the same Minister), 9 of the 15 longest lags involved Castle. The Wrexham–Chester–New Brighton proposal, for example, took her two years to deal with. And like Fraser, she handed on over 30 cases to her successor, Richard Marsh. These included Manchester (Exchange)–Huddersfield, which had been sent to the Ministry in May 1965, and six others received in 1966.[119]

However, there was another side to Castle's activities. While she admitted that she was very nervous about proceeding with closures before her transport policy had been fully worked out, an attitude strengthened by the 'feedback' she received during the 1966 election campaign, she agreed to no less than 71 proposals.[120] Among them was the largest one of all, the closure of the Great Central (73½ miles) with estimated T.U.C.C. savings of £539,000. Castle also agreed to the closure of Manchester (Central) station, where annual costs were put at £235,000, and two sizeable proposals in Scotland, Aberdeen–Keith–Elgin and Stanley Jnc.–Forfar–Kinnaber Jnc. In all, she gave her consent to the withdrawal of passenger services from 606 route-miles, compared with 819 miles agreed by Fraser.

Whatever the final outcome, it is quite clear that relations between the

Board and the Ministry were strained during Castle's period of office, and that the passenger services issue took up an inordinate amount of management time, both at the centre and in the regions. The drafting of the map giving the jointly agreed 'network for development' of 11,000 miles was a very lengthy process, and the negotiations provide a fascinating insight into the horse-trading that surrounded decisions on outstanding closure proposals in 1966–7. When Castle was first shown British Rail's 'watershed' map in February 1966, which divided lines into those marked black (main – for retention), red (others – for retention) and green (for immediate closure), she remarked that there were 'at least a few [lines] which we would regard at first glance as very doubtful starters'.[121] This was an understatement. The Ministry, it seems, was prepared to downgrade two Scottish routes – Dingwall–Kyle and Fort William–Mallaig – from 'red' to 'green', in return for movement in the other direction affecting nearly 500 miles, mostly in Wales and the West of England, where the Ministry felt that closure was 'politically impossible'. Castle was particularly keen to preserve rail links with holiday resorts such as Skegness. Her officials gave a clue as to the political tactics involved when they admitted that two proposals in East Anglia – Saxmundham–Aldeburgh and the East Suffolk line – would make useful refusals to balance 'awkward consents' such as the Great Central.[122] Discussions continued for over a year, and were complicated by the reference of a first draft to the Regional Planning Councils in July 1966. Their deliberations resulted in a number of alterations to the lines earmarked for closure, now coloured 'grey'. Castle caused another complication herself by announcing, at a full-scale press conference in September 1966, that she had decided to reprieve a number of lines, some of which had been agreed with the Board for closure. The final Map was not published until March 1967 (Map IX).[123]

At the same time, the J.S.G. established by Raymond and Castle was busy examining, with the help of consultants, such matters as British Rail's costing methods; ways of reducing the operating costs of unremunerative services; and the methods by which subsidies might be calculated. The atmosphere created by both the J.S.G. inquiry and the network exercise gave some impetus to a retentionist lobby within the regions. This had never been entirely eradicated by Beeching, and after the introduction of the 'early sift' most regions expressed disquiet at having to prepare detailed submissions and consult affected staff for cases which might never materialise. On a number of occasions the cost-cutting alternative to closure was followed. Two London Midland cases may serve as illustrations. In 1963 closure of the Richmond–Broad Street service promised a net saving of £70,000, but since much of the allocated direct expenses (station costs in particular) were shared with other services they could not be escaped, and the 'real' saving was put at no more than £2,800. The service was retained, and the deficit on direct expenses was reduced from £90,000 in 1962 to £61,000 in 1964. When the future of the service was examined again in 1965, several options were considered, but closure was rejected. The General Manager pointed out that

the present attitude of the Minister makes it almost certain that the closure submission would not go beyond the 'sifting' stage. To produce the information required for submission would absorb a great deal of clerical and managerial time and it would seem pointless to proceed if it is accepted that there is little or no chance of closure.

The second case involved the Chester–Holyhead local trains, which were found to be losing £302,000, in 1964. However, contributory revenue amounted to £935,000 and the region contended that all but £80,000 of this would be lost on closure, leaving it worse off by £553,000. It decided to seek the replacement of the existing steam services by semi-fast trains operated by D.M.U.s.[124]

Two General Managers were strong advocates of retention in circumstances where savings appeared to be small. One of them, Gerard Fiennes, General Manager of the Western, 1963–6, argued in 1964 that lines such as Yatton–Clevedon, Taunton–Minehead and Bodmin–Padstow were worth keeping, since direct costs did not greatly exceed direct revenue, and contributory revenue was comparatively large. This argument cut no ice with Margetts and his colleagues at H.Q. They condemned Yatton–Clevedon as a 'bus service on rails', and stressed that 'arguments based on loss of contributory revenue should not prevail'.[125] Fiennes continued to press his views after a transfer to the Eastern in January 1966. He made strenuous efforts to save the East Suffolk line (Ipswich–Lowestoft), a proposal then with the Ministry, by advocating conversion to 'basic railway operation' (single-track, automatic crossings, etc.). The Board was sceptical about the viability of this low-cost proposal, but had no alternative but to support the region in principle when the Minister reprieved the line in June 1966. However, the investment for conversion was not made available until the 1980s. In his autobiography Fiennes contrasted his approach with that of his pro-Beeching predecessor, Roy Hammond. In fact, Hammond, who was moved to H.Q. to assist Margetts, had suggested a similar policy for the East Suffolk in March 1964, and had also proposed the retention, with cheaper operation, of the Romford–Upminster line. The Board had overruled him on both occasions.[126] Fiennes packed a bigger punch than Hammond. When asked by Margetts in July 1966 to accelerate the submission of 'sift' cases he prevaricated, and in December he put up 12 cases for retention, most of which had earlier been agreed for closure and coloured 'grey' on the draft network map. Low direct savings and a large contributory revenue were characteristic features of these lines, which included Witham–Braintree and the seaside services of King's Lynn–Hunstanton and Norwich–Sheringham. Although the application caused considerable annoyance to Margetts, James and Hammond at H.Q., Fiennes was able to extract some concessions.[127]

At Waterloo David McKenna pursued a similar policy in relation to the Southern Region's Ashford–Ore–Hastings and Alton–Winchester lines. In February 1964 regional data were produced which appeared to cast doubt on the wisdom of closing the first of these. Although, on the basis of T.U.C.C. data, direct costs exceeded direct revenue by £20,500 per annum, the expected loss of revenue, including loss of contributory revenue, was £34,500 *more* than expected savings, assuming the continuation of existing freight working. The argument rested on the belief that about 80 per cent (£116,000) of the direct revenue of £61,000 and contributory revenue of £79,000 would be lost on closure. After freight had been withdrawn (with the exception of the nuclear flask traffic serving Dungeness Power Station), the passenger service had to meet higher track and signalling costs. But in May 1965 McKenna pressed for the line's retention. The revised financial data showed only a meagre financial benefit, he argued, and this became negative when the cost of a bus subsidy was added. The case was apparently stronger still when conversion to single-line working was included. Margetts's response was to cast doubt on the estimated loss of contributory revenue, while the Costings Division argued that the capital expenditure of £95,000 required to convert the line would not be justified. The line was eventually put up for closure in April 1967, but was retained after examination by the Minister.[128]

In June 1967 McKenna told H.Q. that he was unable to 'make an economic case for the closure of the Alton–Winchester line'. Although on the basis of a Ministerial submission (using data based on Table 1 of the *Reshaping* report) a net saving of £20,900 was indicated, McKenna considered the figures 'a very misleading basis for action'. Citing the Cooper Brothers report of November 1966 to the J.S.G. on British Rail's costing, he argued that £30,000 of the line's expenses of £70,900 were 'truly joint' in the sense that they could not be escaped and would have to be carried by the remaining services. This attitude was not dissimilar to that emerging in relation to wagon-load freight, discussed earlier. The new tactic caused more alarm at H.Q. James wrote to Margetts: 'I think the Alton–Winchester case is a good example of the sort of things being done in two Regions (the Southern and the Eastern) to protect their existing level of operations. While I understand their approach to life I do not think we can permit them to continue this kind of obstruction.' The line was put up for closure in December 1967, and eventually closed in February 1973, though not before the circulation of widespread allegations that British Rail had deliberately allowed the service to deteriorate.[129]

It is possible to sympathise with both the regional and the headquarters positions. In the regions, much of the difficulty stemmed from the data they were asked to produce to justify a closure. These did not express the full reality of earnings and costs, nor that of contributory revenue, where contributory service costs had also to be taken into account. More sophisticated methods were understood by the Costings Division, including the difference between the estimated savings accruing from closure and the costs of continuing to provide a service, but these were rarely emphasised in dealings with the regions.

The resurgence of a retentionist spirit, together with the reappearance of the idea that some loss-making services might be cross-subsidised by grouping them with profitable ones, clearly dismayed James, Margetts and others concerned with costing and implementing *Reshaping* at headquarters.[130] Not only were they reluctant to redraw the network map after the long grind of negotiations with the Ministry, but they had come to appreciate the full extent of passenger service losses and hence the size of the potential area for subsidy. A costings evaluation of all services outside London for October 1966, commissioned by Margetts, provided some uncomfortable moments for the Board when it received the results in December 1966. The data revealed an unsurprising shortfall (direct costs minus direct revenue) of £13.9 million on stopping and suburban trains. But, on top of this, 8 main-line services were failing to cover their direct costs, by a total of £900,000, including Manchester–Sheffield, Glasgow–Dundee and St Pancras–Manchester, and 13 services were barely covering costs, including St Pancras–Glasgow, Euston–Inverness and Liverpool/Manchester–Bournemouth.[131] The problem of passenger losses ran much deeper than the 'grey' lines on the network map. Thus, when Cooper Brothers and the Costings Division were asked to provide the J.S.G. with an 'order of magnitude' estimate for likely subsidy, they produced a figure of £83 million. A précis of the situation was available for readers of the Board's Annual Report for 1967. Here it was shown that the cost to B.R.B. of closure refusals amounted to £4 million, while proposals losing another £4 million were caught up in the closure machinery. In 1967 passenger services exceeded direct costs by only £11 million and failed to cover total costs by £85 million.[132]

Margetts, in particular, showed considerable frustration with the difficulty in processing closure proposals in 1966–7. Not only had the regions become more critical in relation to outstanding cases, but the Minister added many more complications to the procedures. These included negotiations with the unions, the prospect of local authority support for certain services and plans to establish conurbation transport authorities, which blocked many decisions. There remained several proposals which the Minister contended were of a political character. They included several lines where either the bus operators were unwilling to operate replacement services or bus operating costs were higher than the expected rail savings. In the summer of 1967, for example, the Minister gave a decision on five 'grey' lines in the West of England which had been caught up in the 'sift' process. Data provided by the Western Region's Divisional Manager at Bristol showed that in three cases bus costs were much greater than estimated savings, and Castle recommended against publication for closure. She also asked that a fourth, Taunton–Minehead, should be examined on a cost-benefit basis.[133] Negotiations such as these disheartened Margetts. He had never accepted the flight from *Reshaping* either for passenger or freight traffic. His reaction to the 11,000-mile network was that the extra 3,000 miles 'contained no railway with a financial case behind it and we know that even with [retained] lines only we are not going to break even – yet – if ever'. Throughout 1967 he complained about the cost of delays and refusals.[134]

Richard Marsh's appointment as Minister of Transport in April 1968, in succession to Castle, made little difference to the Labour strategy for transport. The Transport Act of 1968 gave legislative effect to Castle's grant-aid proposals, despite the strong reservations of the Chancellor of the Exchequer, Roy Jenkins. The Act also provided for the active participation of the new conurbation authorities, the P.T.A.s, via their Passenger Transport Executives, in the planning and provision of rail services in their areas. Most of the 369 cases submitted by British Rail in 1967 for possible subsidy found their way into the first list of subsidised lines of services. In 1969, 302 lines and services received grants totalling £61 million, including temporary payments for 56 proposals still in the closure machinery.[135]

The new apparatus promised to be one of the most significant changes in railway–government relations since 1947. At long last British Rail's management was apparently relieved of one of the great charades of the post-nationalisation period, that of seeking to remove loss-making services in order to satisfy the statutory requirement to 'break even' only to find the way blocked by Ministerial intervention. In the Report for 1969 Johnson's Board expressed some satisfaction at having been relieved of the 'odium of seeking to withdraw a passenger service in circumstances where the loss of social benefit to the community clearly exceeds the savings to the railway'.[136] It was also clear from the list of subsidised services that grant-aid was not merely a matter of dealing with the residue of Beeching's *Reshaping* proposals. By including loss-making main-lines and commuter routes not previously listed for closure, the British Rail subsidy reflected more of the realities of railway passenger operations.

Unfortunately, however, the system of grant-aid did not put an end to the formulation of closure proposals and the periodic publication of Ministerial consents and refusals. For British Rail, the 'odium' of having to run the gauntlet of hostile public opinion was not ended. By giving grants on a one to three year basis the government were not providing the means to retain services in the long term. Indeed, the Board, in its 1968 Report, pointed out that the number of subsidised services must in time 'be expected to diminish'.[137] The logic of Labour policy was that non-subsidised lines should be closed. This affected not only those cases in the pipeline, but additional proposals published by British Rail following the Ministry's refusal of a subsidy. In his 18-month term to October 1969 Marsh gave his consent to closure in 37 instances, including the Waverley Line (Carlisle–Hawick–Edinburgh), where estimated savings on the T.U.C.C. basis were given as £256,000, and Manchester (Exchange) station, with costs of £142,000. Fred Mulley, Marsh's successor, gave 13 consents in his eight-month period of office to June 1970, including Colne–Skipton and Skipton–Carlisle, and the much disputed cases of Barnstaple–Ilfracombe and Taunton–Minehead. After the change of government in June 1970, John Peyton, the Conservative Minister, gave 14 consents to the end of 1973, including the much deferred case of Alton–Winchester, and Birmingham–Wolverhampton–Langley Green, with declared savings of £227,000. Rationalisation may have proceeded at a diminished rate, but it did not disappear.

Nor too did political intervention. With an election looming, the Labour administration was not unmindful of the consequences of consenting to the closure of lines in 'politically sensitive' areas, including marginal constituencies. Under Marsh and Mulley the Ministry, while leaving Minehead and Ilfracombe without a railway, much to the consternation of the area T.U.C.C.,[138] refused its consent on no less than eleven occasions affecting lines marked 'grey' on the 1967 Map. They included Manchester–Wigan–Southport, where savings were put at £229,300, the Central Wales line, a resubmission with estimated savings of £122,450, Norwich–Sheringham and Edinburgh–North Berwick. The two Ministers also refused their consent in part to 12 proposals.[139] At the same time, some contentious cases were left on the shelf for the incoming government. Five of those passed on to Peyton took three years to leave the Ministry. Among them was the Alton–Winchester proposal. The subject of much argument between McKenna and Margetts in 1967, it was eventually published in December 1967 and reported on by the South Eastern T.U.C.C. in July 1968 and again in July 1970. It was not until August 1971 that Peyton gave a positive decision, and the line was not shut until February 1973, five years and two months after it had been put up.[140] The treatment of this and similar pipeline cases ruptured relations between the Board and the Ministry (which from 1970 became the Department of the Environment). Two bones of contention were the Department's early introduction, in 1970, of the 'pooling' of South-Eastern commuter services for grant-aid purposes, reducing the overall grant by about £2 million, and the expiry of the temporary one-year grants for pipeline cases at the end of 1969, which meant that operating losses then had again to be carried by British Rail. Of the 56 cases, 12 were refused consent, 11 did not close until 1970, 4 encountered problems with bus services and 6 were still awaiting decision late in 1971. The same thing happened at the end of the year, when Peyton apologised to Marsh, now Chairman of B.R.B., for failing to clear all the cases for which grant-aid was due to expire.[141] One of these was the Machynlleth–Pwllheli (Cambrian Coast) line. Marked 'grey' on the network map, it was put up for closure by the London Midland Region in 1967 following a closer look at the data and a decision to withdraw freight. Publication was delayed by the Minister's suggestion that the line be used as a model for cost-benefit analysis. The Ministry's study of 1969 found that the costs outweighed the benefits, but this inspired considerable argument in academic circles. The line was grant-aided in 1969–71 then put up for closure. However, British Rail had to carry its losses until July 1974, when Mulley, Minister for the newly elected Labour Government, refused his consent.[142] In the meantime, the Conservatives had made a number of refusals, including Inverness–Kyle, Marks Tey–Sudbury, Romford–Upminster and Marylebone–High Wycombe.

Certainly, the involvement of government in its many forms continued to complicate the situation facing railway managers. A good example is the closure of the Edinburgh–Cowdenbeath–Kinross–Perth route in January 1970. This had been coloured 'thick black' (for retention and development) on the 1967 Map, but when an application for grant-aid was made by British Rail in 1968, the Minister contended that re-routing of the Edinburgh–Perth–Inverness trains via Stirling would offer 'better value for money'. The closure procedure was set in motion, and in April 1969 the Scottish T.U.C.C. found little evidence of hardship on the line, while the Scottish Region's figures showed that direct expenses exceeded receipts by £83,190. Consent to closure was given in October 1969. In fact, the idea of re-routing the services had been first suggested at a joint meeting of the Ministry, the Scottish Development Department, B.R.B. and the Scottish Region in April 1968. After a feasibility study carried out by the region, the plan was endorsed by both the Scottish Economic Planning Board and the Scottish Economic Planning Council. A major consideration in the decision was the prospect of using the track-bed at Glenfarg to save the Scottish Roads Division £250–500,000 in constructing the M90 Motorway. Although British Rail was consulted at all stages, it is difficult to escape the conclusion that the Ministry acted both as judge and jury in the case. The Scottish Region was left with the task of accelerating journey times and pricing competitively on a much longer route. It is not clear from the grant-aid figures that the government secured significant savings.[143]

The 'rail lobby' also made more work for railway managers. The inexorable growth of private motoring did nothing to dampen its enthusiasm. Any expectations that there would be an improvement in relations with the public after the Transport Act of 1968 proved unfounded. This was due in no small measure to the fact that the new legislation failed to improve the public consultation procedure. The T.U.C.C.s remained confined to a consideration of user 'hardship' defined in a rather narrow sense. From January 1969 no financial information on the 'expense' basis endorsed in 1963 by Sir William Carrington (see above, pp. 436–7) was to be supplied to T.U.C.C.s. It was agreed, however, that when the Ministry refused grant-aid, press notices should contain both this information, essentially the short-term financial savings, and details of the grant-aid applied for. The latter was calculated on the Cooper Brothers/B.R. costings formula of attributable long-term annual costs, including interest plus renewals at replacement cost.[144] The alleviation of the Board's obligation to provide bus subsidies – which reached a peak of £1.0 million in 1968 – was no doubt welcome relief,[145] but it did nothing to alter the damaging effects on public opinion of lines agreed for closure continuing to operate because adequate alternative services could not be provided.

Early opposition from protestors ranged from the informed and aggressive to the marginal, ineffectual and mildly absurd. An important factor in the opposition to the Inverness–Wick–Thurso proposal in 1963–4, for example, was the work of a north of Scotland conference of local authorities and other bodies. Many closure proposals spawned action committees which rallied support. The Oxford–Cambridge case in 1964 produced nearly 1,300 written objections, over 700 of them on printed postcards provided by the N.U.R. The second submission of the Central Wales line in 1968 was met by 1,900 objections, including 1,600 using a duplicated letter organised by a joint campaign committee of railwaymen.[146] On the other hand, individual objectors often made noises out of all proportion to the hardship involved, while objections by local authorities appeared cheek-by-jowl with those from organisations with a more limited function. Amid the concern about the economic implications for the Border Counties of the Waverley line proposal in 1966 was a protest from a body with the resplendent title of the South of Scotland Budgerigar and Foreign Bird Society, to the effect that closure would 'spell the death warrant of all bird societies in this area'.[147]

Many protests included the allegation that British Rail had neglected a service or deliberately allowed it to run down. It is difficult to come to a satisfactory generalisation here. The closure of the Great Central line involved a phased programme of withdrawal, for example, but in the majority of cases both the Board and the regions were reluctant to upset T.U.C.C.s by varying services while proposals were being considered. In any case, protestors often argued both ways at once when they complained on the one hand that a service was being run down and on the other hand that British Rail was not taking steps to operate it more efficiently.[148] Financial information proved to be the greatest area of difficulty. It was never intended that the Carrington figures should be used by protestors to challenge the validity of a proposal, but this did not prevent several attempts to do so, or to argue on broader, socio-economic grounds. On many occasions the T.U.C.C.s themselves had doubts about the accuracy of what they were given. When in December 1964 the Secretary of the Welsh T.U.C.C. received from the London Midland Region figures relating to a proposal to modify the Chester–Holyhead services, he spotted that the movement costs, given as £687,400, were based on steam working instead of diesel, which was about to be introduced. The region hastily amended the movement costs to £505,400.[149]

Data relating to station closures sometimes caused problems out of all proportion to the savings involved. This was because the information given was usually confined to a statement of direct costs and revenue originating at the station. In 1966 the East Midlands T.U.C.C. Secretary queried British Rail data for the closure of South Aylesbury Halt, which gave station receipts of £130 per annum and direct costs of only £26 (excluding renewals). This produced a reprimand from the Acting Secretary of the C.T.C.C. in the following terms:

The general question of financial information has, I am sorry to say, been the cause of more confusion than any other single aspect of the closure procedure. A great deal of this has been brought about by muddled thinking on the part of the objectors, and even some T.U.C.C. members (who shall be nameless) have unfortunately allowed themselves to probe into figures unnecessarily.

The T.U.C.C. subsequently found 'no actual hardship if the Halt were closed'. The railways' case had been supported by anticipated renewal costs of £2,500. Similar problems arose with Folkestone (East) station in 1964, where originating receipts were £14,600 and costs £4,900. Most of the receipts were expected to transfer to another station. Difficulties were also encountered with service modification cases. Of the 18 stations put up for closure in 1965 as part of the Chester–Holyhead scheme 10 showed an apparent surplus over direct costs, occasioning T.U.C.C. concern. Such information ignored the wider revenue/cost position.[150]

The rail lobby became more authoritative as it became more informed, recruiting ex-railwaymen, professional economists, engineers, planners and environmentalists. The National Council on Inland Transport, led in the Lords first by Lord Stonham, then by the Earl of Kinnoull, was a relatively sophisticated pressure group from its formation in October 1962. For example, at the Manchester–Buxton hearing in May 1964 it was represented by Samuel Silkin Q.C., in an unsuccessful attempt to widen the definition of 'hardship' to permit consideration of alternative operating methods.[151] The Council's technical adviser, Professor Hondelink, caused the Board some headaches when he condemned the proposed closure of the 'profitable' Great Central, and many bodies, including local authorities, turned to academics to supply social or cost-benefit studies of threatened services.[152] By the early 1970s the lobby had become more formidable. Academics and transport specialists were recruited. Changes of name denoted broader ambitions: a body called the Branch-Line Re-invigoration Society had grown into the Railway Invigoration Society; the Scottish Railway Development Association had become the Scottish Association for Public Transport; and in December 1972 the N.U.R. helped to establish Transport 2000, a more vigorous pressure group representing a broad spectrum of interests. Such bodies were rarely content to limit the argument to the hardship of individual users. Speculation about the extent and significance of contributory revenue, excluded from T.U.C.C. figures, was made on a number of occasions. Regional economic strategies, road congestion costs and other issues were raised by the Scottish Railway Development Association when objecting to the Kinross and North Berwick proposals in 1968–9, much to the annoyance of the Scottish T.U.C.C.[153] All this must have made regional railway managers ask themselves whether the savings really justified the managerial time and effort put in to secure them.

How much, then, did the passenger rationalisation programme achieve? What was the aggregate net financial effect of closures and service modifications? Given the figures used by British Rail and the Ministry, this is difficult to quantify. None of the available series, even were they complete, could provide a satisfactory answer. Some of the problems have been discussed earlier. Data given to the T.U.C.C.s showing estimated earnings and direct expenses provide a clue to expected short-term savings, although there is no guarantee that these were actually achieved following closure. The more detailed data supplied to the Minister based on Table 1 of the *Reshaping* report provide an estimate of the 'net financial effect' expected by British Rail, equal to direct expenses (assumed to be saved) *minus* the expected loss of both direct and contributory revenue. The balance of track and signalling costs is also given where relevant to the case, for example if freight was also to be withdrawn (see examples in Table 54). But the validity of such statements is totally dependent upon the judgement of regional officers about travel patterns in the event of closure.[154] It is therefore difficult to contend that one set of data is superior to the other. We should also scotch the suggestion that British Rail submissions to the T.U.C.C.s persistently overstated losses in comparison with submissions to the Ministry. Certainly, in those cases where the region found a large contributory revenue and felt that much of it would be lost, the 'net financial effect' given to the Minister would be lower than the 'savings' figure inferred by protestors using T.U.C.C. data. On the other hand, where freight was to be withdrawn with the passenger traffic, large track and signalling savings would be declared to the Minister but hidden from the T.U.C.C. The Inverness–Wick–Thurso proposal of 1963 (see Table 54) illustrates both effects. A simple opportunity to test the proposition on a broader basis is given by the financial information for 20 cases published in response to a parliamentary question from Lord Stonham in March 1964. The total financial saving on a 'Table 1' basis is £738,000, while the figures presented to the T.U.C.C.s yield 'savings' which sum to £684,000, certainly not markedly higher![155]

From 1968 data were prepared in support of grant-aid applications. Based on British Rail's established costing procedures recently endorsed by the consultants to the J.S.G., Cooper Brothers, the submissions excluded contributory revenue, but produced an estimate of long-term direct costs, including renewals at replacement cost. Joint costs, including for the first time administration, were allocated as before on the basis of use (for example, track costs were allocated on the basis of gross ton-miles, signalling on train-miles). This Cooper Brothers formula was, however, soon rejected by British Rail in favour of cost allocations which recognised the problem of cost-escapability and the relationship between passenger and freight traffic. The grant-aid data, of which an example is given in Table 54, were never regarded as more than a rough guide to service costs. And they are of little help in computing the financial effects of Beeching's passenger rationalisation programme.

Although many private and public references were made to the cost implications of delays and Ministerial rejections, the only published figure of aggregate savings was that given to Tom Bradley, M.P. for Leicester (North-East), in the form of a written answer on 25 November 1966. In response to his request for the estimated annual financial saving of all

Table 54. 'Savings' and grant-aid data for selected closure proposals

	Inverness–Wick–Thurso 1963	Manchester–Buxton 1963/4	Great Central 1965	Taunton–Minehead 1968
1. T.U.C.C. basis				
Estimated direct earnings	88,340	140,000	438,000	48,700
Estimated direct expenses				
Movement	86,030	142,600	347,000	46,800
Terminal	15,180	70,600	91,000	18,700
Track/Signalling[a]	107,820	51,350	539,000	62,550
Total	209,030	264,550	977,000	128,050
'Saving'	120,690	124,550	539,000	79,350
2. Ministry (Table 1) basis				
Estimated earnings	88,340	140,000	438,000	48,700
Contributory gross revenue	196,800	22,700	22,000	140,000
Expected loss in total revenue	202,440	145,300	101,000	62,700
Estimated direct expenses (as T.U.C.C.)	209,030	264,550	977,000	128,050
Estimated net financial effect	6,590	119,250	876,000	65,350
Balance of track/ signalling costs	235,250	44,350	—[b]	—[b]
3. Grant-aid basis				
Earnings	—	—	—	42,000
Costs				
Movement	—	—	—	63,000
Terminal	—	—	—	20,000
Track/Signalling	—	—	—	82,000
Administration	—	—	—	11,000
Interest	—	—	—	7,000
Total	—	—	—	183,000
Grant	—	—	—	141,000

[a] Where freight services were run, costs = additional expenses incurred in maintaining and renewing track and signalling to passenger-train standards.
[b] Freight already withdrawn.
Source: B.R.B. Sc.R. RT/TS2/24/79/ Pt 1; B.R.B. L.M.R. 7–19–46; East Midlands T.U.C.C. report, 30 November 1965, EM494; J. E. Dewdney–J. H. H. Baxter (M. T.), 22 January 1965, D.O.E.; B.R.B. W.R. KU 6207 Pts. 4, 5; B. A. Payne (M.T.)–E. G. Gomm (South Western Area T.U.C.C.), 28 August 1970, South Western Area T.U.C.C. 95.

branch-line and station closures completed since the publication of the *Reshaping* report, it was stated that the 'present financial improvement is about £17 million per annum'.[156]

The answer was not without controversy. Not only was the Earl of Kinnoull's request for further details (see above, p. 438) turned down in the following month, but it became evident that some politicians were misled into the belief that the figure of £17 million referred to an annual average saving over the period 1963–6, instead of the *accumulated* annual average reached only in 1966. Even the Ministry was in the dark about the precise coverage of this savings figure, which is hardly surprising given the fact that during the frequent exchanges between the Board and the Ministry over British Rail's failure to achieve its savings targets, calculations had been offered on quite different bases. The internal correspondence makes it clear that the figure of £17 million was an aggregation of the 'net financial effect' of each proposal (as supplied to the Ministry), plus the balance of track and signalling costs saved when freight traffic was withdrawn at the same time as passenger traffic. It also included £5.5 million for 'pipeline' cases dealt with in 1962–3. A revised figure for the end of 1967 was £18.75 million per annum, gross of bus subsidies paid by British Rail, then running at £0.69 million per annum.[157]

The savings data shown in Table 53 were taken from British Rail submissions to the T.U.C.C.s. They exclude both the contributory revenue factor and the balance of track and signalling costs. The accumulated annual saving from 1962 to 1967 appears as £13.5 million, while the total 'savings' from June 1963 to the end of 1973 is shown to be £16.9 million. There are many reservations about the calculation (see notes to Appendix J for details). It should be considered an 'upper-bound estimate' since no attempt has been made to scale down the data for those proposals for which part-consent only was granted.[158] It contains no adjustment for bus subsidy costs. On the other hand, it excludes the capital expenditure British Rail was able to avoid. Proposals to close stations and lines were supposed to contain an indication of anticipated expenditure on major renewals and maintenance over a five-year period. The data are far from complete, but an examination of 75 cases considered by the North Western and South Western area T.U.C.C.s indicates that the additional savings from this source amounted to about two-thirds of the direct savings. This would make the total 'saving', from June 1963 to the end of 1973, £28.2 million.

The true value of savings is anybody's guess. A clue is contained in a note on passenger closures sent to the Executive Director (Finance) in September 1972. This observed that 'files prior to 1964 budget have been destroyed' and that 'detailed regional submissions are available from 1966 budget only'. These showed actual net savings (reduced expenses less reduced receipts) of only £2.8 million for 1966–9, compared with the estimated maximum 'saving' of £7.7 million shown in Table 53. In these years, at least, there was clearly quite a gap between expectation and achievement.[159] In any case, whether the savings forecast in the *Reshaping* report – £18 million directly, plus £11-13 million from subsequent track cost savings – were achieved or not, they were no answer to the overall problems of passenger profitability.

VI

The savings derived from passenger closures were probably not a major component of the post-Beeching rationalisation drive, in spite of the considerable managerial time devoted to them. More significant for long-run costs were other resource savings. Indeed, general cost-control became a preoccupation of H.Q. management after Beeching's arrival. There was a greater degree of central purchasing of materials, and the Board, like the B.T.C. before it, continued to take prime responsibility for the negotiation of wage and productivity agreements. As already noted, the rising trend of overall operating costs was halted after 1962, and this for the first time since nationalisation. Operating expenditure, which had risen to £561.6 million in 1961 and £569.1 million in 1962, fell to £536.1 million in 1967. Even the increase of £11 million in 1968 was lower than the prevailing rate of inflation. Although this success has to be set against the countervailing trend of falling gross real income, as shown in Figure 4 above, the 19 per cent reduction in real costs over the period 1962–8 remains an impressive achievement. After the reorganisation of nationalised transport in 1969, real costs continued to fall, although the pace was more gentle.

Where were the economies made? Three areas of managerial initiative demand particular attention: the complete elimination of steam locomotives by 1968, far earlier than had been anticipated; the closure of 19 of British Rail's 32 main workshops; and the general reduction in manpower, coupled with a determination to improve the productivity of the railway workforce. These activities were not new. They all owed their origins to the pre-Beeching period and, in particular, to the Modernisation Plan of 1955 and its subsequent reviews in 1956 and 1959–60. But it was Beeching and his team that gave them added impetus, and the achievements under these heads, summarised in Table 55, went beyond the expectations of the *Reshaping* report. Some of the savings were swallowed up by the extra costs associated with the diesel locomotives which replaced steam (see above, pp. 285–8), and by wage increases and relatively generous redundancy and resettlement payments. Nevertheless, overall

Table 55. *Rationalisation, 1962–73: steam locomotives, main workshops and manpower (numbers)*

Date: end of	Steam locomotives	Main workshops	Manpower			
			Workshops wages staff	Salaried staff (railway/ workshop)	Total railway staff[a]	Total B.R.B. staff[b]
1962	8,767[c]	32[d]	56,326[e]	99,009	476,545[f]	502,703
1965	2,987	20	39,079	84,935	365,043	387,663
1968	3	15	33,032	79,163	296,274	317,478
1970	—	14	31,485	64,752	250,777	273,063
1973	—	13	26,863	61,872	228,590	250,083

[a] Include those employed in common services and operational/non-operational property.
[b] Include those employed in ships, hovercraft, harbours, hotels and rail catering.
[c] Given as 8,796 in *Reshaping*, I, p. 139.
[d] Official figures vary from 28 to 32. Here, 32 workshops cover 24 locations, with two main workshops at Ashford, Eastleigh, Swindon, Doncaster, Derby and York. Darlington (Faverdale) and Temple Mills counted separately from Darlington (North Road) and Stratford respectively.
[e] Mid-year estimate.
[f] Given as 474,538 in *Reshaping*, I. p. 50.
Source: B.R.B., R. & A. 1963–73; Sir Steuart Mitchell, confidential report on 'Main Workshops. Future Plan', 31 July 1962; 'Memo. of Information Passed at a Meeting on 22 August 1962 by Sir Steuart Mitchell to Representatives of the N.U.R. and Confed. of Shipbuilding and Engineering Unions', 20 August 1962, B.R.B.

savings were considerable, and because these activities attracted far less publicity and far less political interest than the passenger closure programme, the returns to managerial effort were much higher.

The *Reshaping* report made no firm promise about a date for the total elimination of steam traction, but private expectations were that there would still be about 4,000 locomotives in use in 1967, and that steam would not disappear completely until 1972. This prediction was soon found to be unduly pessimistic, following a determined assault on the surviving steam fleet by Beeching's managers. Action to raise the tempo began in the summer of 1962, with the acceptance by the British Railways Committee of the arguments of Margetts and Shirley for an accelerated rate of scrapping. The policy of withdrawing whole types of locomotive in order to save maintenance costs and reduce stores was also accepted. In that year alone the number of steam locomotives was reduced by a quarter, from 11,700 to under 8,800. The strategy was taken a stage further at the end of 1963, after it had been realised that the utilisation rate of diesel locomotives had been underestimated. Margetts's forecast of December was that steam would be withdrawn from the Eastern and Western Regions by 1965, and from the remaining regions by the end of 1967. This plan was then executed. No steam services were run on British Rail after August 1968.[160]

Beeching's strategy for the workshops was established by Sir Steuart Mitchell's plans of April and July 1962. Those advocated the transfer to central control of the regions' main workshops, which was implemented in January 1963, and the closure of 16 of the 32 existing works, with a reduction in the wage-paid labour force from 56,000 to 37,000. It is important to observe that this initiative, widely regarded as a draconian when made public in September 1962, merely followed an earlier plan of February 1959 to scale down capacity more gradually to meet the change from steam to diesel and electric traction. By 1960 this had already resulted in the closure of eight redundant locomotive works, including Brighton, Gateshead and Inverness.[161] The case for accelerating the programme then became stronger. The low utilisation of labour in the existing works – 0.77 of a fully manned single shift on average – was accompanied by the scaling down of the railways' investment plans after the 1960 government review. The scrapping of steam locomotives was stepped up. In addition, the Conservatives, in their Transport Act of 1962, extended the prohibition on the railway workshops from competing with the private railway construction industry for outside orders (this was rescinded six years later by the Labour Government's Act). All these developments helped to make a substantial measure of rationalisation more or less inevitable.[162]

The workshops plan was implemented successfully. Both the closure programme and the reduction in manpower were completed on schedule. The only minor hiccups were the delays in closing Cowlairs works in Glasgow and the old carriage and wagon works at Swindon, and the fact that manpower losses proved too great in 1963–4. Generous redundancy payments and the ease with which many displaced workers found new jobs undoubtedly helped to smooth the path to a lower level of capacity. The estimated savings – £4 million from the reduction in fixed overheads and £5 million from sales of surplus buildings and sites – also materialised.[163] Further difficulties with the Board's investment plans from the late 1960s and the decline in its freight business made it necessary to take more action. Much to the dismay of the unions, the Board went beyond the original plan in transferring Town Hill (Fife) Wagon Works to the Scottish Region in 1968, and closing the Inverurie and Barassie works in 1969 and 1972 respectively.

Finally, there was the more general feature of staff cuts. This phenomenon was in part a reflection of the initiatives described earlier –

the rationalisation of routes, the removal of steam locomotives and the pruning of workshop capacity – but it was also the result of economies introduced in all areas of the business. The manpower section of the *Reshaping* report charted the progress of manpower reduction since 1948 and forecast that there would be additional job-losses of only 32,000 as a result of the *Reshaping* programme. This rather reassuring statement, for the unions at least, indicated that the railway labour force (excluding those employed in ancillary activities) would fall from about 476,000 in 1962 to 370,000 by 1970.[164] In fact, the actual reduction was much greater. There were only 250,000 railwaymen by the end of 1970 and under 229,000 by the end of 1973 (Table 55). The workforce had thus been reduced by more than half, much of the reduction coming in 1962–8. The fall in salaried staff numbers, however, was not so pronounced, a reduction of 38 per cent being achieved by 1973. Clearly, the rationalisation objective carried an administrative price.

There were other difficulties confronting these management initiatives. The removal of steam locomotives promised cheaper operating and maintenance costs, but these were partially offset by abnormal expenditure on diesel locomotives, particularly in the 1960s. The savings obtained from the switch to diesel traction were reduced by higher running and maintenance costs caused by the poor performance of several loco-motive types, including the Western Region's Maybach-engined 'Warship' and 'Western' classes and the Beyer Peacock 'Hymek', all diesel-hydraulics, and the Sulzer-engined Type 4s. The non-availability of the latter reached crisis proportions in 1965, costing the Board an estimated £2 million a year in 1965 and 1966 and necessitating a costly £10 million programme of rehabilitation.[165] An examination of workshop main-tenance expenditures over the period 1962–6 indicates that although expenditure on steam locomotives fell sharply from £16.3 million to £1.2 million in current prices, the cost of diesel and electric maintenance, including the servicing of multiple units, rose from £9.0 million to £22.3 million, producing an overall saving of only 7 per cent. However, if constant prices are used, the improvement amounts to 23 per cent.[166] The reduction in the labour force brought with it the familiar problems of turnover costs and unplanned staff shortages encountered in the 1950s. The turnover of railway staff was a costly business. An estimate of 1969, for example, showed that costs were running at £8.5 million a year, of which £5 million was considered to be avoidable. The experience of the railways was also found to compare unfavourably with that in other industries of comparable size. Cuts in staffing, in which control of recruitment was an important element, also brought with them the risk of clusters of vacancies in key operating grades, particularly where the pay was low. There are numerous reports of the deleterious effect which shortages had on the quality of service provided, particularly in the handling of wagon-load freight.[167]

At a more general level, the pace of rationalisation and cost control depended on the way in which the regions responded to central directives and annual budget targets. Here, the response seems to have been patchy, although it is difficult to attribute this to variations in managerial performance. One factor was the final abandonment of any serious attempt to construct separate regional profit and loss accounts as instruments of management control. Progress towards this objective, which had been encouraged by the 1953 Act and the creation of the Regional Area Boards in 1955, had been slow. Macmillan's statement in the Commons in March 1960 (above, p. 308) roused the B.T.C. to make a more serious attempt to establish regional profit and loss accounting, and the firm of Deloitte, Plender, Griffiths & Co. was engaged as consultants. The policy was also supported by both the Select Committee of 1960 and the Stedeford Advisory Group.[168] No immediate results followed, however, and with the arrival of Beeching and Shirley in 1961 and the new emphasis on traffic *flows*, the concept of regional accounting was quietly laid to rest. The view that the difficulties and cost of constructing meaningful accounts outweighed the advantages for management control had been a widely held one, not only at H.Q. and in the regions, but in the Ministry of Transport as well.[169] Shirley gave these doubts added impetus. Under his encouragement the Commission, and later the Board, moved towards an emphasis on accounting by activity not region, on improving the general level of costing and management accounting and on the package of centralised financial reforms, designed to eliminate waste, outlined in Chapter 9. The control of the regions was to be maintained by monitoring their annual budgets and reducing their level of autonomy.[170]

The regions continued to produce the more limited breakdowns of revenue and working expenditure and these are useful in indicating something at least of the response to cost control (see Appendix E). With all their limitations they usefully show that, whatever the global financial results for British Rail may have been, the Beeching–Shirley emphasis on cost-control was translated into positive action in some regions by aggressive general management. The impact of Raymond and of Fiennes, successive General Managers at Paddington, from January 1962 to August 1963 and from September 1963 to December 1965, was apparently formidable enough to justify some florid accounts which talked of 'cataclysm' and the 'hoisting of storm cones'.[171] There may have been fat to be trimmed here, but it was certainly trimmed. In the space of three years, 1962–5, the Western Region's working expenses were reduced by

Table 56. *Western Region receipts and working expenses, 1961–8, in current prices (£m.)*

Year	Gross receipts	Working expenses	Net receipts
1961	78.6	108.1	−29.5
1962	77.3	105.0	−27.7
1962[a]	70.0	90.3	−20.4
1963	71.6	85.9	−14.3
1964	71.4	83.3	−11.9
1965	66.8	73.6	−6.9
1966	67.0	76.9[b]	−10.0
1967	60.6	75.1	−14.6
1968	59.7	69.0	−9.3

[a] Second 1962 data on 1963 basis, including rail catering, with administration allocated to H.Q., and adusting for regional boundary charges.
[b] From 1966 wagon hire charged to region.
Source: B.T.C. and B.R.B. Accounts, Appendix E.

18 per cent, and the gap between those expenses and gross receipts fell dramatically from £20.4 to £6.9 million, an improvement of 66 per cent (Table 56). The position was then held by the next General Manager, Lance Ibbotson, in the more difficult trading circumstances of 1966–8. Cost-cutting, though on a less impressive scale, was also evident in the accounts of the Eastern, North Eastern and Scottish Regions (see Appendix E). Nevertheless, the reluctance of the regions to tackle the problem of profit and loss accounting and the variable response to cost-control were indicative of some of the difficulties facing H.Q. planners. The files contain a number of indications that regional managers did not always pursue rationalisation directives with the same enthusiasm. There were complaints, for example, that unremunerative wagon-load traffic was being retained in the mid-1960s in spite of a clear understanding that it was unprofitable.[172]

What, then, was the overall impact of these cost-reducing activities on the profile of British Rail costs? A rudimentary breakdown of operating expenses, isolating labour and fuel and power costs, is given in Table 57. The major change in the years after 1962 was the decline in importance of fuel and power costs, associated with the rapid removal of the coal-powered steam locomotive. In 1948 locomotive coal cost the B.T.C. £36.4 million (11 per cent of total operating expenses) and in 1962 £44.3 million (8 per cent). Coal costs then fell rapidly to £31.5 million in 1963 and £0.8 million in 1968, and disappeared completely from the 1971 accounts. The transfer to diesel and electric power was not only advantageous in terms of

Table 57. *British Railways' operating expenses by input 1963–73, in current and constant 1948 prices (£m.)*

Year	Current prices					Constant prices		
	Staff	(%)	Fuel and power	(%)	Total	Staff	Fuel and power	Total
1948	(326.4)		(39.8)		322.5	(326.4)	(39.8)	322.5
1962	(364.6)		(61.3)		569.1	(216.4)	(36.4)	337.7
1963	344.4	63	47.6	9	550.2	200.5	27.7	320.3
1964	345.4	64	44.2	8	541.6	197.1	25.2	309.1
1965	348.6	64	34.3	6	545.7	192.0	18.9	300.5
1966	351.4	65	29.8	5	542.1	186.2	15.8	287.3
1967	341.9	64	25.8	5	536.1	176.3	13.3	276.5
1968	340.2	62	25.4	5	547.1	169.6	12.7	272.7
1969	307.9	63	24.0	5	491.6	148.0	11.5	236.3
1970	338.5	64	25.1	5	532.0	150.8	11.2	237.1
1971	359.2	62	25.6	4	578.0	145.1	10.3	233.5
1972	416.7	67	28.1	4	625.1	152.8	10.3	229.2
1973	455.9	66	29.6	4	688.6	153.3	10.0	231.6
1982	1,593.3	59	185.6	7	2,681.1	157.5	18.3	265.0

Source: B.R.B., *R. & A. 1963–73, 1982.* 'Staff costs' include salaries and wages, national insurance payments, clothing and retirement benefits; fuel and power include coal (to 1968), oil and electricity. Not shown: 'materials, supplies and services' and 'depreciation and amortisation'.

Data for 1948, 1962 and 1982 are not comparable with those for 1963–73. 'Staff costs' for 1948/62 are estimated wages and salaries, and 'fuel and power' are taken from 'train and vehicle operating expenses' and do not appear to square with later data. Data for 1982 are for all 'rail businesses'. 1963–73 data exclude catering, and letting of operational and non-operational property.

From 1970 'corporate expenses' are shown separately (£2.8m. in 1970).

work done per unit of energy consumed, but fuel prices also moved in the Board's favour, as Table 58 illustrates. In most years the price of oil and electricity rose less steeply than the general price level. Consequently, fuel and power costs fell from 9 per cent of total costs in 1963 to 5 per cent in 1966–70 and 4 per cent in 1971–3.[173] After that the oil crisis put an end to the period of cheap diesel oil. This fall in fuel costs was indeed one of the main causes of the fall, to 1968, in operating expenses. In constant prices, the cost of this input fell to a third of its 1962 level.

In contrast to the success with fuel costs, the action taken to restrain labour costs had very modest results. In the period 1963–6 staff costs *rose* in current prices, and although there was a fall of 7 per cent in real terms

Table 58. *Diesel oil and electricity prices, 1962–73*

Year	Diesel oil price per gallon (1962 = 100 = 4.14p)	Electricity price per unit (1962 = 100 = 0.664p)	G.D.P. deflator
1962	100.0	100.0	100.0
1964	113.5	105.0	104.0
1967	103.6	111.0	115.1
1970	106.5	112.4	133.2
1973	161.6	134.6	176.4

Source: information from B.R.B. Electricity prices quoted are for traction purposes only.

this was very disappointing given the fact that staff numbers fell by 17 per cent over the same period. It should also be added that the staff costs shown in the revenue accounts excluded redundancy and resettlement payments, which increased as a result of new agreements signed in 1962–3. Substantial sums were paid out – £15.8 million in all over the period 1963–6. And despite a reduction in the workforce of 48 per cent from the end of 1963 to the end of 1973, the reduction in real staff costs over the same period was limited, as is evident from Table 57, to a more modest 24 per cent.

One of the factors here was a failure to restrain white-collar employment. The number of salaried staff fell from 94,600 at the end of 1963 to 61,900 by the end of 1973, but this 35 per cent drop includes the loss of some 7,000 staff on the transfer of the Freightliners and Sundries Division to the N.F.C. in 1969. Administration and general expenses amounted to 10.5 per cent of total railway working expenses in 1963. A decade later, they had risen to 17.6 per cent of the total.[174] But the principal cause of the more limited success with staff costs was undoubtedly the fact that higher productivity was rewarded by the Board in the form of higher real wages, a point emphasised in the Annual Reports. The Board, like the Commission before it, had always to balance restraint on pay levels with a due regard for wastage and recruitment rates as well as the general competitiveness of railway wages and conditions. In the pay negotiations of November 1964, for example, Beeching openly conceded that there was a gap between 'our wages and what could be regarded as the middle of the wages spread for comparable occupations'. In April 1967, Raymond, in a confidential note to the Board, claimed that 'All the savings from large investments on modernisation have gone to the staff . . . the 1966 results will show that the Railways are now a more labour intensive industry than they were when we started in 1962 . . . Despite a reduction of some 150,000 in staff [1961–6] our wage bill is the same.' Nevertheless, he defended the policy of increasing wages as 'necessary in large measure because railwaymen were underpaid'.[175] The subject of labour relations, wage levels and productivity will be examined in Chapter 12. Here, it is important to observe that the returns from staff cuts were reduced by the conscious decision to raise wage levels and seek productivity improvements in return. Sometimes, this strategy appeared to misfire. The pay award of June 1972, for example, helped to lift staff costs from 62 per cent of total operating costs in 1971 to 67 per cent in the following year, shown in Table 57. But on the whole the increase in real earnings of British Rail staff (adult males), which amounted to an annual average of 4.5 per cent over the period 1962–73, does not appear to have been exorbitant, particularly in the light of the considerable gains in productivity achieved at the time (see below, pp. 562–5).

11

Markets, pricing and commercial strategy

I

If one critical area of managerial responsibility in the post-Beeching years was costs, then the other was revenue. Increasingly, the major problems for British Rail concerned the price charged for the railways' 'output', the relationship between railway fares and rates and rail costs, the quality and reliability of rail services, particularly in the freight sector, and the declining competitiveness of the industry compared with private motoring and road haulage. The *Reshaping* plan was not merely a matter of rationalisation and cost-cutting; considerable emphasis was also placed on the need to maintain and improve services for those traffics which were 'best suited to rail'. This meant the development of appropriate marketing strategies, including a close attention to pricing, and associated projects of new investment. In this chapter attention is given to the revenue side of the equation, and in particular to the commercial strategy followed in the wake of the 1962 Transport Act. The first section deals with pricing, since price variation in the passenger sector continued to promise a path to increased net revenue. This fact led, as will be seen, to considerable government interest and intervention. In the freight sector, by contrast, price was not the key variable, since the railways' competitive position was much weaker. Here, the crucial task for railway managers was to develop commercial and planning policies designed to improve profitability and maintain market-share. An evaluation of the railways' response forms the concluding section.

The general pattern of British Rail's pricing after 1962 may be stated quite simply. The trends which had been established over the period 1948–62 were reversed. In the days of the Commission, passenger fares fell in real terms by about 16 per cent, while real freight rates held up quite well (see Table 21, above, p. 188). In 1962–73 the Board succeeded in raising the real value of average passenger fares, though there was a slight deterioration in 1971–3, and, as Table 59 shows, fares still remained

Table 59. *Average fares per passenger-mile and average receipt per net ton-mile, 1962–73, in current and estimated real relative prices (1948 weights) (new pence)*

Year	Current prices					Real relative prices				
	Passenger: All categories	Freight: coal/coke	Iron/steel	Other	All categories	Passenger: All categories	Freight: coal/coke	Iron/steel	Other	All categories
1948	0.58	0.69	n.a.	n.a.	0.83	0.58	0.69	n.a.	n.a.	0.83
1962	0.83	1.41	n.a.	n.a.	1.39	0.49	0.84	n.a.	n.a.	0.82
1963	0.83	1.38	1.31	1.87	1.53	0.48	0.80	0.76	1.09	0.89
1965	0.92	1.41	1.25	1.67	1.46	0.51	0.78	0.69	0.92	0.80
1967	0.98	1.46	1.28	1.47	1.43	0.51	0.75	0.66	0.76	0.74
1969	1.10	1.47	1.27	1.07	1.29	0.53	0.71	0.61	0.51	0.62
1970	1.19	1.54	1.36	1.00	1.29	0.53	0.69	0.61	0.45	0.57
1971	1.38	1.69	1.44	1.00	1.34	0.56	0.68	0.58	0.40	0.54
1972	1.50	1.55	1.57	1.03	1.33	0.55	0.57	0.58	0.38	0.49
1973	1.59	1.55	1.62	1.00	1.32	0.53	0.52	0.54	0.34	0.44
1982	5.40				4.93	0.53				0.49

Source: 1948, 1962: Table 21 (passenger = average *receipt* per passenger-mile); 1963–73: B.R.B., *R. & A.* 1963–73, Tables 5A, 5B; 1982: B.R.B., *R. & A.* 1982, Tables 6A, 6B. Price deflator: Feinstein, *National Income*, 1948–65, then G.D.P. information in *A.A.S.*, 1976, Tables 344, 354, and 1984, Table 14.1, 14.8–9.

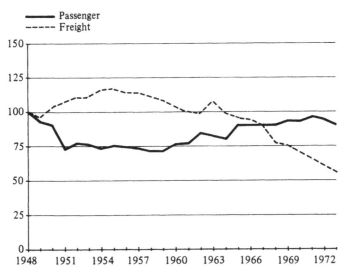

——— Passenger
----- Freight

Figure 6 Average real fares per passenger-mile and average real receipts per net ton-mile, 1948–73

Source: B.R.B. data base.

below their real value in 1948. On the other hand, real freight rates fell sharply, as road transport took an increasing share of the market, and by 1973 they were little more than half of their 1948 level. Figure 6 exhibits in graphical form the striking divergence between passenger and freight rates.

The maintenance of the real level of passenger fares was undoubtedly aided by the declining importance of concessionary fares in total journeys and receipts to 1971. There was little change in the relative prices of season tickets, reduced fares and full ordinary fares.[1] But the main element was the application of regular, across-the-board increases in fares, notably in 1965, 1968, 1970 and 1972, and the introduction in 1968 of selective pricing, which meant an end to the practice of basing fares rigidly on the distance travelled. In the freight business, the dramatic fall in real rates cannot be attributed to a major change in the composition of the traffic. The only development of significance was the declining importance of coal and coke traffic, whose share of the railways' net ton-mileage fell from 51 per cent in 1963 to 40 per cent in 1973.[2] Here, what mattered, in general, was an overall decline in the demand for railway freight services; and, in particular, the reduction of short-haul rail transits and a shift in relative rates. Charges in the 'other traffic' category, which included agricultural goods, building materials, petroleum, chemicals and general merchandise, exhibited the sharpest decline of all, 69 per cent in real terms over the period 1962–73. By 1970 the Board's freight rate structure had been turned on its head. The rates for heavy freight traffic, far from being lower than average, were now *higher* (see Table 59). The change certainly reflected the relative competitiveness of rail and road in this sector. But it remains a fact that, in the railways' strongest markets, the Board did not increase coal/coke and iron and steel rates to a level which would have maintained their real value of 1963, let alone that of 1948.

The trends in real railway charges should be examined in conjunction with those of other variables analysed in this book. Over the 25-year period to 1973 railway productivity improved considerably, matching national performance, and railway wages too responded to the rise in real earnings elsewhere in the economy (see Chapter 12, Table 63, Figure 9 and Appendix C). In these circumstances it is not a surprise to find that the real prices charged to passenger customers stabilised at a level just below that of 1948 (Table 59). This was accompanied by a relatively stable passenger-mileage but a falling share of a rapidly expanding market (see Chapter 10, Table 44). In the freight market, however, real rail charges fell after 1962, a response to the inexorable squeeze of declining competitiveness, which made both road haulage and the 'own account' lorry business attractive to customers irrespective of relative transport charges. The railways attacked their costs, but these remained exposed against both their prices and the costs of their competitors. The fundamental difficulty lay in the rapid reduction in real costs and rapid increase in performance of road haulage, bus and air transport and private motoring. While railway productivity improved in pace with the average performance of the economy as a whole, other modes of transport improved much faster. Technological change and heavy national infrastructure investment in roads and airports produced quality and cost changes to which railway managers had to respond.

Can it be said that British Rail's pricing policies were a failure? How much was inevitable and how much avoidable? How far did government intervention in rail pricing, which was much in evidence before 1963, damage the Board financially? In many ways, the story was the same. The B.R.B. followed its predecessor, the B.T.C., in complaining about the effects of government interference and specifically about the effects of price 'restraint' and 'freeze'. There was also no shortage of external critics of the railway industry in the 1960s and 1970s. Whether consultants to the J.S.G., witnesses before the several meetings of the Select Committee on Nationalised Industries or the National Board for Prices and Incomes, established in 1965, they all echoed past commentators in condemning what they saw as unimaginative commercial policies, inadequately supported by market research.[3]

One thing did change. The Transport Act of 1962 removed passenger fares (except in London) from the jurisdiction of the Transport Tribunal which, as described in earlier chapters, had exercised a general control of rail pricing since its inception in 1921. The railways were now largely free to charge whatever they liked, to discriminate between users and to price differently in different markets and regions, subject to the over-riding consideration that pricing should reflect the commercial objectives for the Board laid down in the Act.

The reality was rather different, however. Under Sections 45–6 of the 1962 Act, fares charged for travel within the London Passenger Transport area could not exceed those authorised by the Transport Tribunal, following a public inquiry. Provision was also made for the Minister to order the Tribunal to review London fares at any time. Furthermore, although freight pricing was in general free of control, the Minister was empowered under Section 53 of the Act, to consider and issue directions in relation to complaints about rail charges from the coastal shipping industry (both for competitive rates and for rates to and from ports). More informal mechanisms for pricing supervision were also perpetuated. The railways' long-standing obligation to break even was supplemented by the White Papers of 1961 and 1967 on the economic and financial objectives of the nationalised industries, the latter recommending that pricing should be based on long-run marginal cost.[4] Finally, though free to price in the provincial passenger market, the Board agreed to 'test the temperature' in regular, informal discussions with the Ministry of Transport about prospective fare increases.[5]

The impact of these miscellaneous constraints is difficult to measure precisely. Certainly, as will be made clear later, London fares were subject to persistent interference, notably during 1965–7. The effects of the coastal shipping clauses are less clear. The Board, in its submission to the Select Committee on Nationalised Industries in April 1967, expressed the view that they imposed 'considerable commercial inhibitions'. There was only one Ministerial Direction, however, in October 1964 when Marples ordered an increase in the rates for china clay carried from Cornwall to Kent.[6] The episode certainly annoyed Raymond and Beeching. The bone of contention was the interpretation of the Act, which provided for Ministerial intervention if charges were 'inadequate having regard to the full cost of affording the service'. Beeching complained with some force to Marples that 'we have followed normal commercial practice . . . in that we have quoted a rate which improved our financial position, although the margin over the direct costs associated with the traffic does not cover what might be deemed to be the full allocation of system cost'. Although there was only one more reference under the Act, an unsuccessful complaint about a coal rate for Yorkshire–Plymouth traffic, it seems that the clauses acted as a psychological barrier to a rail challenge for traffic carried by coastal shipping.[7] Contacts with the Ministry in relation to passenger pricing acted as a barometer of government thinking in relation to price increases, and had the same effect as the coastal shipping clauses, even before prices and incomes policy became a matter of legislative fact.

II

The most important single feature of pricing control was the impact of the prices and incomes policies pursued determinedly by the Wilson governments from 1964, and more reluctantly by the Heath administration from 1971. Shortly after Labour took office in October 1964, a new Department of Economic Affairs was created with George Brown as its Minister. He in turn established the National Board for Prices and Incomes in March 1965, with the aim of monitoring pay and price increases, and of encouraging the linking of pay increases to productivity growth in accordance with the 'Declaration of Intent' signed by the government, employers and the unions in December 1964. In the initial, voluntary phase, an 'early warning system' for pay and price increases was introduced in November 1965. It applied to a wide variety of goods and services but it seems that the nationalised industries were more effectively restrained than the private sector; and of the nationalised industries the railways were subject to closer monitoring than the others.[8]

At this time, the prime example of government intervention in railway pricing affected London fares. Two increases, each of 10 per cent, had been made in June 1962 and June 1963. Twelve months later, the Board used the temporary authorisation procedure under Section 48 of the 1962 Act to raise short-distance fares and season-ticket rates, in response to earlier action by the London Transport Board. An application was then made to the Transport Tribunal both for confirmation of the increases and to seek a further 5 per cent increase in season-ticket rates and the withdrawal of day-return fares. But in January 1965 the Tribunal turned down the application in respect of season tickets and made it clear that it was opposed to any departure by the Board from the established practice of 'assimilation', whereby since 1950 British Railways and London Transport had agreed to adopt as far as possible a common fare structure.[9]

Raymond, then the Board's commercial member, had advanced sound arguments for differential pricing in the London area, emphasising that the markets of the two bodies were different. While the L.T.B. derived most of its revenue from short-distance traffic, British Railways were more dependent on travel over longer distances, from 10 to 30 miles, and on season tickets, which made up 50 per cent of its London revenue, compared with only 7 per cent for the L.T.B. However, the 'assimilation' principle had to be kept in mind when the Board, responding to the L.T.B.'s plans, made known in March 1965, to use Section 48 to raise fares from 2 May, prepared an application to the Tribunal to match the increase.[10] At this stage the Board was caught up in the government's intervention in the affairs of London Transport. In response to the L.T.B.'s disappointingly low surplus of £1.3 million in 1964, the government decided to undertake a thorough investigation of the position. In the meantime, it requested the L.T.B. first to postpone the fare increases for two months, then in June 1965 to do so for the rest of the year. Fraser, the Minister of Transport, now invoked the principle of equal treatment, if not that of 'assimilation', when he told Raymond, now Chairman of the Board, that the standstill should also apply to British Railways. This request was reluctantly conceded, although the pill was sweetened by the government's promise that any consequential increase in the railways' financial deficit would rank for a grant under Section 22 of the 1962 Act. Fraser later warned Raymond that any use of Section 48 (the 'quick' procedure) in the meantime would not be consistent with the government's prices and incomes policy, since George Brown had insisted that all prospective price increases should be examined in detail via the P.I.B.[11]

The position deteriorated further over the next two years, when pricing restraint became one of the many sources of conflict between Raymond and the new Minister, Castle. In January 1966 the Board followed the L.T.B. in implementing the postponed fare increases, using Section 48. It then applied to the Tribunal for additional increases, including the raising of the fare for longer journeys (11 miles and over) from 3d. to 3¼d. a mile. However, the procedural delay was such that the Tribunal did not reach a decision, which was in the Board's favour, until 18 July. Two days later Harold Wilson made his statement establishing a statutory prices and incomes freeze, in response to a deteriorating balance of payments which culminated in the devaluation of sterling in November 1967.[12]

Efforts to have the Tribunal award of 18 July implemented and to make further adjustments to cover rising costs after the freeze ended, on 31 January 1967, fell on deaf ears. The 'freeze' was followed by a six-month period of 'severe restraint', but the change brought no prospect of amelioration. In February 1967, Castle asked the Board once again to fall in line with a further deferment of London fare increases, both past and prospective, which had been pressed on the L.T.B. The reason given was political rather than economic, namely the prospect of the G.L.C. taking a leading role in a new transport authority for London. (The L.T.B. was in fact replaced by a G.L.C.-controlled London Transport Executive, with effect from 1 January 1970.)[13] Five months later, in July 1967, when the period of 'severe restraint' was due to expire (it formally ended on 12 August), the Board approved another attempt to secure higher charges from the Tribunal. Shirley, in his presentation, pointed out that the longer-distance fares (13 miles and over) had not been altered since June 1962. But Castle, having given clearance for the implementation of the Tribunal award of 1966, changed her mind in August. She told Raymond: 'The London problems are still not resolved. Moreover, my colleagues and I are still very much concerned about the whole question of price increases . . . I am afraid that I must ask you to continue to defer introducing the increases.'[14] Despite the Board's deteriorating financial position, the government asked it not only to postpone a further application to the Tribunal, but also to 'refrain from increasing any other prices to which you are not already committed' and, in addition, to stop its planned workshop rationalisation measures. The Minister's promise to accelerate decisions on closures (see above, p. 446) was scant compensation. It is little wonder that the Board, at its meeting on 10 August 1967, formally minuted that 'they were being discriminated against in comparison with other nationalised industries, e.g. Electricity and the Air Corporations'.[15]

The proposals for London fares, together with those for provincial fares and freight rates, were referred to the P.I.B. in accordance with the Prime Minister's statement of 7 September that all future price increases by nationalised industries should be so treated. The period of delay was lengthened still further. The P.I.B. took until May 1968 to report favourably in relation to the London proposals, which matched those already put up successfully by the L.T.B.[16] Subsequent applications by the L.T.B. and the Board to the Tribunal for what proved to be the last time (the London fares division was abolished by the Transport (London) Act, 1969) were only partially successful. The proposals for short-distance ordinary fares were moderated considerably. It was not until September 1968 that British Rail's London fares were altered, the first increases since January 1966.[17] The financial implications of these successive postponements and modifications may not have been large in relation to the Board's published rail deficits of some £72 million in 1966 and £90 million in 1967 (see above, Table 47 col.(c)) but nor were they trifling. The deferments of 1965–6 cost the Board approximately £1.4 million in net revenue foregone, while those of 1966–8 cost about £4.5 million.[18] At a time when inflation was gathering pace, the London fares issue represented an inhibitive factor, both irksome and time-consuming, for a business which had been encouraged to believe it had gained commercial freedom and had been exhorted to behave accordingly.

The effects of government prices and incomes policies were, of course, much more extensive, both provincial fares and freight rates being caught up in sundry interventions from 1966 onwards. Ordinary passenger fares and season-ticket prices had been raised in February 1965, by about 8 per cent (to 3.25d. a mile) and 5 per cent respectively, and in the following January the 'taper' rates for long journeys had been raised to 2.75d. a mile (201–300 miles) and 2.25d. (301 miles and over). Freight rates had been increased by 4 per cent in February 1965, the first general adjustment since 1957, and in January 1966 there had been increases of 5 per cent for wagon-load traffic and 10 per cent for sundries and general merchandise. Further proposals to respond to inflation were then affected by the Wilson government's 'freeze' and 'restraint'. Although the Board was certainly not the only victim, it again had good reason to believe that it suffered more than most.

Discussions with Castle on these issues began in October 1966, and in the following month specific proposals were presented to the Ministry with the aim of introducing selective increases in passenger and freight charges during the period of 'severe restraint'. The Board hoped thereby to avoid a reference to the P.I.B., which would have resulted from a proposal to raise charges on a broader front.[19] After some delay, the Ministry's response, in March 1967, was that the Board could renegotiate freight contracts on a selective basis. Castle told Raymond, however, that she had 'important reservations' about the passenger proposals.[20] Some idea of the detailed nature of government interference during this period may be gleaned from the episode. The Board had planned to remove the price 'taper' for journeys of 200 miles and over and to withdraw the summer mid-week concession fares. After examining the proposals, and passing them to the Department of Economic Affairs, the Ministry not only declared that they should be scaled down but handed Raymond specific instructions on how much to charge. Castle wrote to Raymond:

In view of the considerations of Prices and Incomes Policy which obtain during the period of severe restraint, it has been decided by the Government that the mileage taper in ordinary fares should be modified (to 3d. and 2½d. per mile respectively for journeys of 200–300 miles and over 300 miles) rather than being completely removed. Similarly it was thought right that the mid-week Summer concessionary fares should be reduced from 20% to 15% rather than being withdrawn altogether.

These more limited adjustments were introduced in April 1967. In these conditions, the commercial freedom of the railways was clearly a nonsense.[21]

As the budget position deteriorated in the course of 1967, it became obvious to B.R.B. that it could no longer postpone a general application to raise its charges. In May the Ministry was informed that the Board intended to raise passenger fares outside London by 5–8 per cent, coal rates by 6–10 per cent and parcels and sundries rates by 6 and 7.5 per cent. Government prevarication culminated in Castle's instruction in August to desist from making the increases. Raymond's response was one of exasperation:

The Board find it difficult to understand why the Railways should be singled out for action of this kind particularly in relation to increases which had already been agreed in principle but which, for reasons known to you, have not been applied. This decision seems to be wholly inconsistent with what is happening elsewhere in the Nationalised Industry field.

Eventually, in accordance with a statement by the Prime Minister on 7 September, the proposals were referred to the P.I.B., in October. In December the Board asked the P.I.B. to examine additional proposals to raise the rates for iron and steel, bulk traffic and general merchandise, by 7.5 per cent, and in February 1968 it asked for 'headroom' to make further increases in 1969.[22]

The conditions of the P.I.B. inquiry were to be more intrusive than hitherto. Following public concern over an increase in electricity prices announced in April 1967 (to apply when the period of 'severe restraint' ended), the government considered the idea of subjecting the public sector to an 'efficiency audit', a proposal which drew loud howls of protest from the chairmen of the nationalised industries. Harold Wilson's statement in September included the announcement that the P.I.B. should carry out such an audit in the course of its price investigations.[23] The news was scarcely welcome at 222, Marylebone Road. Detailed investigations into the railway business were already running at a high level. There was the J.S.G. (see above, pp. 352–6) which, with the help of consultants, had examined most, if not all, aspects of the industry between July 1966 and September 1967; then there was a joint inquiry with the unions into pay and productivity, sponsored by the Minister of Labour, Ray Gunter, which ran from May 1966 to September 1967 (see below, pp. 547–8). The Transport Tribunal had also conducted two full inquiries into London fares. Now the P.I.B., which had already pronounced on railway wages in January 1966, had been given an 'efficiency' remit which led it to appoint the accountants Price Waterhouse as its consultants. Still more hands were going to reach into British Rail's filing cabinets. The Board was naturally anxious to retain as much control as possible and to limit contacts to H.Q. level. As Raymond explained to his Vice-Chairmen, Shirley and Johnson, in September 1967, 'we should try and ensure that the Prices and Incomes Board has regard for what has already been done by the Ministry, [the] Steering Group, the Consultants, and the London Tribunal . . . [and] that the enquiries and the consultants are not allowed to roam unsupervised over the business'.[24] Early indications were that the P.I.B. inquiry would not produce a major upheaval. Although Price Waterhouse were asked to study a wide range of issues, including cost increases, financial results, the allocation of costs between passenger and freight traffic, the investment programmes and investment criteria, they were anxious to make use of the work of others. As James noted on 13 November, 'Six young men have arrived today . . . Winchester [Chief Officer (Financial Research)] has made it clear that he does not see a great amount of original work for Price Waterhouse Staff to do . . . I think we can contain this enquiry within the bounds of reason . . . So far the young men appear anxious to be led by us.'[25]

Confidence turned to disappointment when the results of the inquiry were published in May 1968. Not only did the P.I.B. reject the Board's proposals for general percentage increases, but it also impugned the railways' entire pricing strategy. The main complaint was that British Rail had failed to base its case

on any refined assessments of different demand elasticities for various services; by and large it had adopted the traditional approach of broad general percentage increases, the market response to which might vary according to different traffics. The policy of relying on general increases and adopting standard fares as maxima with discounts at the discretion of the Regions had inhibited the development of a marketing strategy based on individual market sectors.[26]

Criticisms of railway marketing were not new, of course. Innumerable consultants had referred to weakness in this area, including Urwick, Orr (in 1961), Production-Engineering, and Cooper Brothers (in the course of the J.S.G. inquiry of 1966–7). The significant development in 1968 was that the P.I.B. was recommending *publicly* that in future railway pricing, both for passenger and freight traffic, should be based on flexibility and selectivity, part of the government's general encouragement of price discrimination in the public sector. For example, in the passenger market there should be differential pricing by route and type of service, e.g. for first-class Inter-City travel. The P.I.B. recognised that cost allocation was a major management challenge in the industry, and that it would be difficult for the Board to relate rail prices to long-run marginal costs, as the White Paper, *Economic and Financial Objectives of the Nationalised Industries,* had just advocated. In these circumstances, it recommended that British Rail should set its flexible prices above avoidable costs but not higher than the market would bear.[27]

Whatever the merits of the P.I.B. recommendations – the Board apparently took the view that the report was generally 'fair and reasonable' – railway managers had cause for concern and irritation at the impact of this exercise on the 1967 and 1968 budgets. The proposed increases had been under consideration for over a year, eight months of which had been taken up by the P.I.B. The end result was that only minor immediate increases had been granted, while the exhortation to move to selective pricing could not be implemented overnight. The entire process probably cost the railways about £14 million in revenue: Johnson, the new Chairman, told Marsh, the new Minister of Transport, that each month's delay meant more than £1 million lost. It was, as James noted, echoing Reginald Wilson's complaints in the 1950s, 'another case of the Board's finances being adversely affected through the protracted delay in increasing fares and charges to meet rising costs'. Moreover, revenue maximisation had become a more urgent task for management as the weapon of cost-reduction ran out of easy targets and the aim shifted to the much more difficult challenge of getting the unions to deliver real productivity in return for higher pay.[28]

A further irritant to the Board was the implication in the P.I.B. report that the railways had not considered alternatives to the use of standard mileage fares, charges and discounts. This was not true. As early as 1964, in response to an acceptance that 'far too little was known about the passenger business', Raymond had raised the possibility of introducing a new national fare structure based on selective pricing by route and the relative popularity of trains at different times of the day. The plan involved a three-tier system of business, off-peak and cheap tickets. Unfortunately, the response of the Management Committee, in February 1964, was that the simplicity of the existing structure was an advantage, and the plan was subsequently dropped in May 1965, after regional trials.[29] Further criticisms of the passenger marketing effort were made by the Board in the following August. Three years before the P.I.B. report, it was formally minuted that 'decision-making was perhaps taken on too low a level and the effort dissipated by too many "bargain offers"'.[30] The concept of market pricing was then seriously evaluated. Proposals were put to the Minister in May 1967, and the overall strategy was endorsed by the consultants to the J.S.G., Cooper Brothers, in July. It was then 'fed' to the P.I.B. by the Board, both in its submission in October 1967, when it proposed to 'exercise local market flexibility', and in February 1968, when it made a request for 'headroom'.[31]

The central problem was a big gap between the best intentions of policy-makers at H.Q. and the attitudes of middle managers and commercial officers in the regions. The Board had left far too much to regional initiative, and this shortcoming had been exacerbated by a lack of specialist staff at the centre.[32] Before 1968 only the Eastern Region had been prepared to use the opportunity offered by the 1962 Act to price high, action which attracted the favourable attention of Cooper Brothers. Elsewhere, it seems that railway managers were, in James's words, 'unduly timid' in their response.[33] The effects of prices and incomes restraint and the P.I.B. exercise were thus positive as well as negative. While the way to simple, standard increases was blocked, the rail business was given impetus to move to more sophisticated, selective pricing, which meant that many of its subsequent decisions were taken out of the P.I.B. arena. After May 1968 the Board took up the challenge of differential pricing with vigour. At the same time, Johnson was keen to avoid the detailed interference which had characterised the Raymond–Castle period. He instructed the Chief Passenger Manager to keep the Ministry at bay when planning selective changes. For a while, a less intrusive atmosphere prevailed. Nevertheless, Marsh as Minister was bound to take a continuing interest in rail prices in the name of industrial cost-control. 'You will realise', he told Johnson, 'that, despite the freedom which the N.B.P.I. Report had now given to the Railways Board, there will inevitably be a lot of political interest in the way your pricing develops and we must be realistic and recognise that pressures may build up for further Governmental interference.' One area where the Ministry considered it had a right to intervene was the pricing of grant-aided services, and it was here that some of the inducement to raise prices was removed, since there was no monetary incentive to do so.[34]

Although inhibiting at all levels, the effects of the government's prices and incomes policy are not easily determined with real precision. There was pay restraint as well as price restraint, and both operated against a backcloth of recession and industrial dispute affecting British Rail's customers. Thus in 1966 the estimated loss of revenue attributable to the price freeze, £3.9 million, was offset in large measure by the expected savings of £3.5 million from the postponement of wages increases. The cost to the Board of the seamen's strike, put at £2 million, was probably more important in net terms. This said, there was some substance in the Board's complaint that in 1967–8 it had been held back more than other nationalised industries. The Electricity Council, and the airlines, for example, were able to make more progress in 1967; and others, such as Gas, had their applications to the P.I.B. resolved before the railways. It was not until September 1968 that the first batch of selective passenger fare increases was introduced. As Johnson reminded Marsh, although the P.I.B. report offered 'opportunities for increasing our revenue, it certainly will not enable us to achieve the targets we expect – either this year or next ... We have had to wait whilst other nationalised industries received preference.'[35] It seems likely that the positive results of the Board's pricing policy only became evident in the period 1968–70. In the passenger business, price changes were estimated to have increased income by £3.4 million in 1968 (1.9 per cent), £8.7 million in 1979 (4.6 per cent) and £8.9

million in 1970 (4.3 per cent). Selective pricing was applied with increasing sophistication, and it is unfortunate that it was not introduced earlier.[36]

III

The Heath government, elected in June 1970, eschewed the whole idea of a prices and incomes policy, and the P.I.B. was wound up in March 1971. Nevertheless, it retained in truncated form an early warning system for major price rises, and the pressure to exercise some control over price and wage increases soon built up as the inflation rate accelerated. In June 1971 the Cabinet was happy to pin its faith on a voluntary initiative sponsored by the C.B.I., which proposed that its leading 200 members should limit unavoidable price increases to 5 per cent, and refrain from raising prices more than once in a 12-month period. In return, the Chancellor offered a measure of economic reflation. The strategy, which was remarkably similar to Labour's voluntary phase of 1964–5, was accepted in principle by the chairmen of the nationalised industries in July.

After some prevarication, B.R.B. agreed, in August, to back the C.B.I. initiative provided that it was adequately compensated for loss of income, something to which the government had not given much thought. The Board had been planning to raise its prices by about 10–11 per cent. The effect on its cash flow of adopting the C.B.I. proposals was estimated to be a loss of £1.3 million in 1971 and £35.7 million in 1972. Additional losses of £0.6 and £2.4 million were expected from an extension of the 5 per cent ceiling to the price variation clauses of freight contracts.[37] As already shown, the Board's finances deteriorated badly in the course of 1972. Notwithstanding a grant of £27 million, intended to cover the pricing 'gap', an additional 'special' grant of £32 million had to be paid to the Board to cover its cash-flow shortfall. The Annual Report for 1971, published in May 1972, was predictably gloomy:

The Board's obligation to act commercially implied increases in fares and charges considerably in excess of 5 per cent . . . the effect of price restraint will continue to affect corporate profit adversely even after restraint is lifted. When prices have been artificially held down it is seldom feasible to raise them to their proper level immediately.[38]

The pricing problem was not the simple, black-and-white issue that such statements implied. Since 1970 doubts had been voiced in the Finance Committee about the effect on railway revenue of regular price increases, particularly in the passenger business. These doubts resurfaced in June 1972 after a wage settlement, and on the eve of the expiry of voluntary restraint. The Board had raised fares selectively by about 5 per cent in

April 1972. In June, Bowick, the Chief Executive, argued that it would be more profitable to introduce one increase at the beginning of 1973 instead of two, in September 1972 and April 1973, since 'the commercial interests of the Railway business would not be served by the raising of charges in 1972 on a stagnant market'. The government, on the other hand, was keen to see a price increase linked with the recent pay award. Whether through government pressure – Marsh had promised Peyton, the Minister for Transport Industries, that there would be such a link – or political prescience – some Board members feared that there would be a price freeze later in the year – the Board decided to raise charges in September 1972, and passenger fares by about 7.5 per cent. Two months later, a statutory price and pay freeze was imposed.[39] This episode may serve to indicate the complexities of pricing strategies. In the absence of pricing restraint in 1971–2, the Board might well have moderated its planned increases in response to the level of economic activity. The sacrifice involved in voluntary restraint, while real enough, was not as severe as was sometimes claimed. Furthermore, it applied to all of the nationalised industries. More important in some ways, and certainly specific to British Rail, was the insistence of the Heath government in October 1970 that the London and South East network should cease to be a grant-aided 'lame-duck' by 1973. In pursuance of this vain objective, the level of grant-aid was reduced, forcing the Board to increase its fares in March 1971 to bridge the gap. Here was a case of government policy bringing about an *increase* in prices.[40]

The difficulties created by the prices and incomes interventions of 1972–4 were considerable, and since they resulted from economic conditions which were more volatile than those of 1964–70 their impact was more damaging. On 6 November 1972 the government announced a statutory freeze for 90 days, with an option to extend it for a further 60 days, after the failure of prolonged discussions with the C.B.I. and T.U.C. It was followed in April 1973 by 'Stage II', a period of managed restraint based on the formulation of a Price and Pay Code, and the establishment later in the year of new monitoring bodies, the Pay Board and Price Commission. 'Stage III', operative from November 1973, was planned to last for a year, but it was destroyed by the sharp rise in oil prices, and the coalminers' challenge to the government's pay policy. In February 1974 a Labour Government was returned, committed, like Heath had been, to a non-statutory policy. However, it retained the existing statutory price machinery, and in August 1975 was forced into another round of controls.[41]

The railways' experience during the Heath regime was, once again, not unique, but the Conservative brand of prices and incomes policy generated plenty of resentment on the part of Richard Marsh as Chairman of B.R.B. He was particularly critical of the emphasis on using the nationalised industries as an instrument of control. This had first become evident in the non-statutory period, 1970–2, when an attempt had been made to confine wage increases in the public sector to $n-1$ (i.e. pay settlements should not exceed last year's settlement minus 1 per cent). Marsh saw Heath as having used the nationalised industries quite openly and consciously as instruments of economic planning, to a much greater extent than any Labour Government did. He believed Heath's contempt for industrialists to have been equalled only by Harold Wilson's contempt for trade unionists. On one occasion he told Heath in no uncertain terms that freezing prices at a time of double-figure inflation was likely to have more than a marginal effect on the public sector borrowing requirement. A further bone of contention was the government's failure to repeat the compensatory grant of 1972.[42]

The manner in which the nationalised industries would be treated was made clear from the start when John Davies, Chancellor of the Duchy of Lancaster, explained the position to the Chairman on 6 November 1972. 'Ministers', he said, 'would not use their discretion so as to drive a private sector firm into bankruptcy. It could not be assumed that nationalised industries would similarly be allowed to avoid deficit.'[43] Thus, in 'Stage II', the Price Code laid down that an application for price increases should be related to 'allowable' cost increases incurred after 30 September 1972, but in the case of a nationalised industry in deficit, to containment of its deficit in 1973 to the actual level in 1972. As a result of the new government guidelines, the Board's plans to raise freight charges by 4 per cent from January 1973 and passenger fares by 5 per cent from January 1973 had to be abandoned. Instead, an application under the Price Code was required.[44]

In 1973, as on previous occasions, B.R.B. had good cause to complain that the delay in obtaining authorisation for price increases prejudiced its budget position. This was made worse by the leisurely way in which the Price Commission was set up, and by the more rapid escalation of costs. In February 1973, the Board planned modest increases of 5–6 per cent, pitched low in the hope of getting early approval. An additional increase was planned for the autumn. The combined effect of procedural delay and a Price Commission ruling, influenced by the Minister, which rejected important elements of the application was to limit 'allowable' pricing to 2.5 per cent. The cost to the Board was £9 million in 1973. Fares and charges were raised on this basis in June. However, correspondence with the Chairman of the Price Commission, seeking further adjustments to

34 Dr Richard Beeching and his Board, 14 February 1963 (*left to right*: A. R. Dunbar; Philip Shirley; Dr Richard Beeching (Chairman); Sir Steuart Mitchell (Vice-Chairman); Leslie H. Williams (others not shown)) (*Observer*).

35 Philip Shirley, management catalyst. As Vice-Chairman, B.R.B., making a presentation to A. Ballantyne of United Biscuits, a major freightliner customer, September 1966 (*Harrison & Laking*).

36 Sir Stanley Raymond (Chairman, B.R.B., 1965–7) and Barbara Castle (Minister of Transport, 1965–8), at the opening of the new administrative wing of the British Transport Staff College, Woking, 10 November 1967. The visit took place shortly after Raymond had been asked for his resignation (see Castle, *Diaries*, p. 321) (*P.A. Studios*).

37 Sir Henry Johnson (Chairman, B.R.B., 1968–71), at the Railway Technical Centre, Derby, February 1969 (*third from left*). *Also shown*: P. E. Lazarus (Ministry of Transport), *far left*; Richard Marsh, Minister of Transport, *second from right*; Dr Sydney Jones (Board Member, B.R.B.), *far right* (*B.R.B.*).

38 Richard Marsh (Chairman, B.R.B., 1971–6), talking to M.P.s visiting mock-up of the Advanced Passenger Train, November 1971 (*B.R.B.*).

39 Hayling Island station, after closure, 1966 (*John Goss*).

40 Gloucester–Hereford line: track recovery, 1965 (*John Goss*).

41 Liverpool Central (High Level) station, after closure, 1967 (*John Goss*).

42 Last train on the Cromford & High Peak line, 1967 (*John Goss*).

43 Gerard Fiennes, General Manager, Eastern Region (1966–7), at Peterborough (North) station, March 1966 (*B.R.B.*).

44 Wagon-load freight train in the mid-1960s: leaving Tinsley Yard (Sheffield) for Port Talbot, August 1965 (*B.R.B.*).

45 Bescot steam depot, January 1950 (*B.R.B.*).

46 Finsbury Park diesel depot, April 1960 (*B.R.B.*).

47 Poster advertising last steam train, 11 August 1968 (*John Goss*).

48 The last steam train at Carlisle hauled by 'Britannia' Class locomotive (No. 70013) (*B.R.B.*).

49 Matisa ballast-tamping machine, 1957 (*B.R.B.*).

50 Rail-lifting by hand, Broxbourne, 1958 (*B.R.B.*).

51 Plasser tamping machine, 1967 (*B.R.B.*).

52 Laying pre-fabricated track panels, 1969 (*B.R.B.*).

53 'Merry Go Round' coal trains, at Aberthaw Power Station, 1982 (*B.R.B.*).

54 'Merry Go Round' train unloading at Ferrybridge Power Station, 1966 (*B.R.B.*).

55 London–Glasgow freightliner service, June 1966 (*B.R.B.*).

56 Drott 'Travelift' crane for loading/unloading containers, at York Way terminal, London, 1966 (*B.R.B.*).

57 Euston main-line: Euston station (*B.R.B.*).

58 Bournemouth: Waterloo train passing Pokesdown, 1968 (*John Scrace*).

59 Prototype High Speed Train, Derby, 1972 (*B.R.B.*).

60 Prototype Advanced Passenger Train, St Pancras, 1975 (*B.R.B.*).

61 Oil train at Milford Haven, 1963 (*Studio Jon*).

62 B.R.B. and trade union negotiators at New Lodge, Windsor, September 1968
(*Railway Gazette*).

63 The railway visit. Sir Cyril Hurcomb, on a visit to Sheffield (Darnall) motive power depot, July 1948 (*B.R.B.*).

64 The Hancock report. Illustration from *The Truth About the Railways. The Hancock Report*, a public relations brochure prepared in the wake of Beeching's *Reshaping* report of 1963 (*B.R.B.*).

65 The General Manager's lunch. Lunch for Lance Ibbotson, General Manager, Southern Region (1968–72), at Charing Cross Hotel, November 1971, with table-top transport provided by model railway (*Pic Photos*).

66 Celebrating 25 years of nationalisation: party, 31 January 1973 (*left to right*: Sir Stanley Raymond; Lord Beeching; John Peyton (Minister of Transport, 1970–4); Lord Hurcomb; Richard Marsh; Ernest Marples (Minister of Transport, 1959–64)) (*B.R.B.*).

meet rising costs, proved abortive. So B.R.B.'s terse public observation ran: 'costs rose by 6 per cent: we were allowed to increase prices by 3 per cent'.[45]

The events of 1973 had a knock-on effect in 1974, made worse by Labour's attitude to a similar pricing strategy on the part of the Board, namely two modest increases planned for the spring and autumn. A draft application to the Price Commission under 'Stage III' early in 1974 had to be revised after Ministerial scrutiny. The main change was an enforced reduction in the increase in season-ticket rates from 13½ to 12½ per cent. In June passenger fares were raised by 12½ per cent and freight rates by 18 per cent.[46] More damaging was the government's rejection of the Board's immediate, follow-up application to raise charges by about 5–8 per cent in the autumn. The request was considered modest by Bosworth, the Deputy-Chairman, when he informed the Minister, Mulley, that costs had risen by 12–19 per cent since the last application. Mulley's response was that the government was unhappy with the proposal in relation to passenger traffic. He told Marsh on 5 August: 'We consider that it would not be in the public interest for there to be a further increase in passenger fares as soon as the Board had in mind.' Requesting British Rail not to approach the Price Commission, he added that 'the Government would not in any event be prepared to approve such an increase'.[47]

The decision infuriated Marsh and his colleagues. The cost was estimated to be £39 million, without considering the damage that would be done to the pricing plans for 1975. The Board formally minuted that the government had 'completely negated the Board's pricing policy'.[48] The situation was made worse by the government's complete turnround three months later, when Chancellor Healey announced that the nationalised industries were now free to price up to commercially justified limits. This was not the last time that government policy changed suddenly. The Report for 1974 noted that by the time the go-ahead was given to raise prices, 'the price base was so low that the market could not take the increase needed. The result: costs rose by 33 per cent and we were enabled to increase prices by 16 per cent.'[49] The last word should be Marsh's. Replying to the Minister in August 1974 he warned of the

rapidly growing gap between pricing and costs . . . In the year 1974 inflation will have increased our costs by at least £165m. and all our forward plans have been directed towards achieving some relationship between costs and revenue. This objective was overwhelmingly dependent upon our assumption in two key areas, the elasticity of the market and our view of Government intentions in relation to the control of inflation . . . The decision conveyed in your letter of 5th August means that against a background of a rapidly escalating call on public funds, one of the two basic influences upon our pricing policy is indeterminate. There is clearly no need to emphasize the dangers of such a situation in present circumstances for an industry which has been in such a parlous financial situation for as long as the Railways.[50]

The situation in 1973–4 was not unlike that of 1967–8 in that the government was prepared to fund the mounting rail deficit while bringing in another new legislative deal, this time the Transport Act of 1974. For the Board, there was nothing but frustration at the way in which the exigencies of government wrecked a delicately balanced pricing policy based on the knowledge that there was considerable customer resistance to large and sudden price increases in the highly competitive transport market in which the railways operated. 'Hard pricing', in railway terms, could only be sustained over short periods, and the timing was crucial. Vulnerability to government 'directions' was undoubtedly a destabilising factor.[51]

IV

Government intervention in pricing may have been extremely irritating for the Board, but it did not lessen the need for an accurate perception of the market for rail transport. The problems facing commercial managers handling the railways' freight business, where government involvement was less pronounced than it was with passenger, demanded internally generated solutions, and, above all, a radical approach. Indeed, British Rail's attempts to improve the marketing of its freight services after 1962 merit a detailed examination.

The *Reshaping* report gave the distinct impression that B.R.B. would respond positively to the new commercial freedom provided by the 1962 Transport Act, and launch a major drive to win new and profitable traffic. The 'Survey of Traffic Not on Rail', summarised in the report, had suggested that a far greater effort would be made to attract new freight business. In organisational terms, changes were made to strengthen the commercial function at H.Q. In October 1964 commercial responsibilities were separated from the operating side, with which they had hitherto been merged. Passenger and freight functions were divided, and the new posts of Chief Commercial Manager, Chief Passenger Manager and Chief Marketing Manager were created. Parallel changes were introduced at regional level. Beeching's appointment of a large number of managers from private industry was also part of the response, being intended to improve market awareness and hence lead to the securing of additional traffics.[52] Several positive steps were then taken to improve the profitability of the railways' freight business: the development of train-load operations, with a drive to win new bulk traffics, particularly oil; measures to transform the movement of the railways' traditional traffic, coal, which included the establishment of 'Merry-Go-Round' trains* incorporating automatic loading and unloading; and the introduction of the freightliner concept, the trunk-haul transit of containers in the merchandise market. These initiatives were exciting and promised to enhance the quality and reliability of service. However, as will be evident from the following narrative, they were certainly not an unqualified success.

The B.R.B. oil traffic contracts represent the major marketing success of the early 1960s. Beeching brought Leslie Williams on to the Board from Shell to undertake commercial responsibilities, and he obtained the services of Terry House, former Marketing Manager with Shell-Mex and British Petroleum. House's five-year term in freight marketing from April 1962 had most positive effects in securing significant quantities of oil traffic to B.R.B. on a long-term basis. Here, of course, there existed an identifiable market which was confidently expected to grow rapidly during the 1960s. But when House joined the Commission, the railways' share of the market had fallen sharply from 28.7 per cent in 1954 to 12.5 per cent in 1962, and the expansion of inland pipelines promised to make the situation much worse. Under the guidance of this newly appointed manager, B.R.B. persuaded the oil industry to commit much of its distribution to rail on a long-term basis. By 1965, 10-year contracts (and one for 15 years) had been successfully negotiated with all the major oil companies selling in the U.K. The 17 contracts were designed to provide maximum benefits for the railways, and in this they contrasted with many of the contracts for equipment signed in the name of modernisation in the 1950s. The oil companies undertook to offer minimum guaranteed tonnages which were linked to an escalator clause reflecting increased deliveries of petroleum for inland consumption. In other words, the contracts were designed to encourage an increase in rail carryings as the market expanded, and in this they were successful. The railways carried 86.8 million tons in the period 1964–70 instead of the minimum contracted volume of 54.5 million, and their share of the oil market was increased to 14 per cent.[53] Other features of the oil contracts were also advantageous to the Board. The use of price escalator clauses, for example, which provided for the automatic adjustment of the negotiated rate for cost inflation, prevented revenue from being eroded. More important still, the provision of oil tank wagons by the oil companies, rather than by B.R.B., released the latter from investment responsibilities at a time when resources were becoming particularly scarce (see below, pp. 508–9).

*The near continuous use of fixed train-sets between the collieries and points of consumption, viz. electricity power stations. Some trains carried gypsum to cement works, and the concept was also applied to iron ore for B.S.C.

Unfortunately, the intervention of the Minister of Transport prevented the Board from making the most of the situation. Beeching had been anxious to have the new wagons built in the B.R. workshops, where in spite of the rationalisation programme there was much spare capacity as steam was phased out and large cuts were made in wagon and coach building. Underemployment and overheads at the works at Shildon and Darlington, for example, were said to be costing £0.5–1.0 million per annum. But Marples refused to sanction Beeching's request, on the grounds that it conflicted with the prohibition on manufacture for sale in the 1962 Transport Act. Nonetheless, the private investment produced new air-braked wagons of high capacity (up to 100 tons) which committed the oil companies to rail for a longer period than the formal contracts implied.[54]

Given these advantages, it was a great disappointment when the anticipated profitability of this traffic did not materialise. In 1963, on the signing of the first contracts, it had been estimated that under future conditions, i.e. diesel traction and increased traffic volumes, the average contribution to indirect costs from oil conveyed in full train loads would be 100 per cent over direct costs. In fact, in spite of a 7 per cent increase in the length of haul, and tonnages well above the contracted minima, the margin above direct costs was found in 1966 to be a mere 12 per cent. Had B.R.B.'s own guidelines for shedding unprofitable traffics been followed, the contracts would have been terminated.[55] The main reasons for this unsatisfactory state of affairs were an irregular pattern of train-load consignments and a tendency for the oil companies to cancel scheduled services at short notice. Although the schedule of rates was intended to encourage train-load working, it was based on a charge per ton, not a charge per train. This allowed the oil companies to offer relatively small quantities at frequent intervals, producing low pay loads for B.R.B. By 1970 the operation of the contracts had been tightened up and returns improved. The results for May 1970 showed that the margin above direct costs had risen to about 54 per cent. At the same time, the Board was negotiating for the right to reject loads under 300 tons.[56] In the 1970s B.R.B. may have looked back on the oil contracts as 'a superb success story', but it should be noted that they were very much an exception to the rule, and not a particularly profitable exception at that.[57] Other train-load initiatives in the 1960s, where traffic growth was not so spectacular, involved the carriage of cement, motor cars, limestone and steel. Here too returns appear to have been on the low side. A report on B.R.B. freight marketing by Cooper Brothers in 1968 concluded that much of the cost-reduction derived from more economic train-load operating had had to be handed back to the customer to compensate him for investing in additional facilities and for having to carry higher stocks.[58]

The railways' coal traffic was also tackled as part of the train-load strategy. Two elements sprang from *Reshaping*, with mixed results: the establishment of coal concentration depots for the more efficient distribution of domestic coal; and the expansion of the 'Merry-Go-Round' train concept through the provision of bunkering facilities at N.C.B. collieries and unloading facilities at the electricity power stations. The first has already been examined briefly in the discussion of freight rationalisation (see above, pp. 429–30). The idea was not new. In July 1958, for example, Charringtons had opened a fully mechanised depot in north-east London, and it was followed by a railway-sponsored depot at Enfield Chase in 1962. The Beeching management tried to accelerate the process, and enjoyed a measure of success in bringing together the three sides – B.R.B., N.C.B. and the coal merchants. But once again, the financial results were disappointing. The Chessington depot in Surrey certainly achieved the planned volume of 50,000 tons per annum in 1963–4, but estimated losses were put at £12,000. By this time, 80,000 tons were regarded as the minimum for viable operations. The explanation for the Board's difficulties lay in the failure to attract adequate tonnages in train-load quantities. The trade was such that coal flows were often insufficient to generate regular train loads of economic size.[59] The concentration concept was sound in theory, but success depended upon a sophisticated control of the commercial and operating environment. This was lacking. One of the most important inhibiting factors was the lukewarm response of the N.C.B. to the declining domestic coal market. It did co-operate with B.R.B. in financing a new large depot at West Drayton, opened in December 1963, but in general was reluctant to invest in new facilities for rail operations. The N.C.B. also influenced the profitability of rail traffic through its unwillingness to rationalise coal supplies and its attempt to use pricing to shift more of the small domestic consignments from road to rail. An investigation into the state of the London Midland's coal traffic in May 1969 revealed that deliveries to station yards and concentration depots were failing to cover total costs by about £5 million per annum. Serious thought was then given to the possibility, eventually rejected, of withdrawing from the household coal market altogether. B.R.B.'s train-load strategy for domestic coal was therefore disappointing, and it is interesting to note that today's rail traffic is carried not in train loads but via 'Speedlink', the air-braked wagon-load service.[60]

In contrast, the expansion of the Merry-Go-Round system was one of the most important sources of net revenue improvement, even though its potential was limited by the N.C.B.'s unwillingness to commit investment to it. Beeching's management strategy again owed something to the past, and specifically, to an agreement signed by the B.T.C. and the Central

Electricity Generating Board in September 1958, which provided for the conveyance of coal in high capacity wagons in train-load formation.[61] But a supplementary agreement of December 1963, operative until the end of 1972, promised to be a significant advance. The Board introduced a new pricing schedule designed to encourage longer coal transits, made possible by technical improvements in handling coal at the power stations and by the development of large, 32-ton hopper wagons. The C.E.G.B. was asked not only to invest in coal-fired power stations with automatic unloading equipment but to site them away from the coalfields in areas of consumption. The results were certainly revenue-enhancing, though they fell short of the optimal. The C.E.G.B., in anticipation of the new agreement, applied for planning consent to build a 2,000 megawatt station at Didcot. When operational in 1970, this gave B.R.B. coal transits of over 120 miles. But the other new power stations – at West Burton,* Ferrybridge and Ratcliffe, for example – were located close to coal sources, and the length of haul was rarely above 20 miles.[62]

   Merry-Go-Round trains could be profitable even when run over short distances, particularly where large tonnages were moved between pit and power station in a continuous chain. There was a clear cost-reducing advantage over conventional wagon-load operations, but the pay-off was greatest when 'full Merry-Go-Round' was introduced, that is, when automatic rapid loading and unloading facilities were provided at both ends. Here, full exploitation was hindered by the negative attitude of the N.C.B. to the financing of the new rapid-loading bunkers required. In 1964, for example, there was considerable argument over the proposal to equip Monktonhall Colliery, near Edinburgh, for Merry-Go-Round services to the South of Scotland Electricity Board's Cockenzie power station six miles away. The Coal Board demanded a tonnage levy on all coal loaded into railway wagons to finance its investment, a proposal which the General Manager of the North Eastern Region contended would threaten the entire advantage of Merry-Go-Round over conventional wagon-load operation. Eventually, after nine months of negotiation, Beeching and Robens, the N.C.B. Chairman, were drawn into the argument, which was finally resolved when B.R.B. reluctantly agreed to a 7d. per ton payment. The first services ran in March 1967.[63] Investment for the pits to serve the new power stations in Yorkshire and the East Midlands was handled differently. B.R.B. and N.C.B. agreed in 1966 to make a joint investment, with the former reimbursing the latter over a 20-year period. This arrangement was applied to bunkering in ten pits before it was decided to revert to a levy system in 1971.[64] The reluctance of N.C.B. to invest in

*The first Merry-Go-Round trains ran from Manton Colliery to West Burton in November 1965.

rapid loading facilities certainly jeopardised the utilisation of the new 32-ton wagons developed after the agreement of all three parties. Difficulties also arose from the uncertainty displayed in the N.C.B. and C.E.G.B. negotiations to identify the pits capable of supplying the power stations for a guaranteed long-term period. All this put a brake on the implementation of Merry-Go-Round. In 1967, only 35 daily trains were running, though the number had increased to 148 by 1972. The C.E.G.B. contract, worth about £30 million a year in the late 1960s, was the largest single sector of rail freight, and was a profitable business. But it was some time before the full benefits of the investment in new wagons and loading bunkers were realised. Because the Board had to price keenly in order to encourage the C.E.G.B. to retain coal-firing at a time of great uncertainty about future fuel policy, a transfer from conventional wagon-load working to Merry-Go-Round often depressed gross revenue levels in the short run. The agreed tariffs promised very large margins over direct costs – 100–300 per cent for distances of 5–20 miles according to 1966 estimates[65] – but full exploitation of the new technique was prejudiced by technical problems in the new power stations, production problems at several pits, uncertainty about C.E.G.B. intentions and the difficulties rail managers had in encouraging a high and stable volume of traffic.[66]

The freightliner was another admirable attempt to improve the quality of railway freight services. Based on the ideas of H. P. Barker and others, and developed from the London Midland Region's 'Condor' service of 1959, it was intended not only to attract new general merchandise traffic to a fast, reliable scheduled service for containers, but was also *Reshaping*'s response to the unprofitability of the large sector of existing general merchandise traffic carried in wagon-loads. The freightliner would take over a portion of this traffic, converting loss into profit. Beeching and his team focussed on inland traffic flows, identified 93 million tons of traffic 'potentially suitable for rail haulage' and hoped to attract 30 million tons to freightliners, rising to 40 million in ten years.[67] The fragility of this initial optimistic forecast has already been dealt with (see above, p. 413). In this Chapter our main concern is to contrast expectations with the actual financial results, particularly before the transfer of the freightliner business to the N.F.C. in 1969, under the terms of the 1968 Transport Act. The *Reshaping* plan had envisaged a network of services operating from about 55 terminals. The first stage, operational in 1965–6, connected London, Liverpool, Manchester and Glasgow. Then, following optimistic noises by the Board with its proposals for a National Freight Grid, London was connected with Aberdeen, Cardiff, Heysham (for Belfast), Sheffield, Newcastle, Leeds and Stockton, and eight provincial services serving Birmingham, Cardiff and Glasgow were introduced by the end of 1967, making 21 services in all. By May 1968 another 12 services were added, connecting London with Hull, Edinburgh, Southampton and Paris, and there were extensions of the Maritime Freightliner network embracing Harwich and Felixstowe.

Here too the operating reality failed to square with forecasted returns. The figures which appeared in *Reshaping* estimated that the full freightliner network would make a contribution to indirect or system costs of 21 per cent above direct costs, in 1968, rising to 37 per cent by 1973. A subsequent examination of the most promising 15 routes produced the more optimistic figure of 56 per cent. When the first stage went to the Board for approval it was supported by figures promising a contribution of £1.125 million or 37.5 per cent to system costs, and the extension of routes which followed the Freight Train Grid concept aimed at £2.2 million or 35 per cent. None of these forecasts turned out to be remotely accurate.[68] Indeed, as early as October 1963 doubts were being raised at H.Q. about the viability of the long-term network, which contained a large volume of short-distance traffic. The Chief Officer (New Works) argued that although there was 'a prima facie case for liner trains over a limited number of routes . . ., there [was] equally a prima facie case for not extending liner train services to the full network suggested in the Re-Shaping Report'.[69] By 1968 serious difficulties had been encountered with the operation of the limited freightliner network. Some of these concerned industrial relations – the attitudes of both rail and road unions to the use of the terminals – and are examined in the following chapter (pp. 544–7). But there were also numerous technical problems, including the faulty design of the early container-carrying vehicles and the difficulties with the Drott 'Travelift' cranes used to transfer containers from rail to road. Quality of service was found to have declined substantially at some terminals, particularly, as at Gushetfaulds, in Glasgow, where the volume of traffic built up quickly and outstripped physical capacity. All this meant lost business, and led the General Managers' Committee to ask 'whether the freightliner system could be built up to break even with the equipment provided'.[70] Later in the year, Margetts, writing as Chairman of B.R.B.'s short-lived Freightliner Division (created in March), admitted that the financial results had been disappointing. He estimated the loss for 1968 as £4.6 million, a figure amended to £3.0 million in the published Annual Report. Margetts conceded that rates had been pitched too low in order to attract business to freightliners, but he put much of the blame on the fact that development had 'lagged seriously behind the original intentions'. This was not true. Losses were made because prices did not match costs, and the latter had risen substantially above original expectations. As the Chief Marketing Manager explained in December 1968, 'the main reason for the worsening of profitability since the submission to the Ministry [in 1966] is an estimated increase in costs of £4m.'. The principal factors were wage increases, a failure to achieve planned levels of efficiency, a substantial rise in terminal costs caused by the need to take on additional staff to maintain quality of service and a reduction in the estimated number of train services which could be handled in Glasgow.[71] Only belatedly were attempts made to recover some of these costs from the customers. The situation improved in the 1970s, as the amount of maritime container traffic grew, and a break-even point was reported in 1971. But if this was Raymond's 'brightest jewel in British Rail's crown', it was a tarnished one.[72]

The Beeching initiatives were bold in concept and sound in theory, but the medium-term returns were very disappointing indeed. Some of the explanation lies in factors beyond the Board's control, but the principal weakness had been managerial. This was spelled out by the Director of Costings in 1968.

Planning in the abstract, for optimum traffic/lowest cost solutions is relatively simple; what has not proved possible so far is our ability to control the commercial and operating situations to ensure that in practice planned performance can be achieved. We have had unhappy experiences in respect of coal concentration, train load movement of oil and the initial Freightliner services. In every case the pattern of operations assumed was advised by the officers responsible but because of the absence of any simple system of back checking of performance things have not worked out as planned.[73]

V

The train-load, 'Merry-Go-Round' and freightliner initiatives also had a detrimental effect on the substantial wagon-load services operated by British Rail. The bulk of this traffic had been identified as unprofitable: the Board's dominating policies of cost-reduction and increased resource utilisation demanded that it be abandoned where it could not make an adequate contribution to system costs. All this was quite logical, and taken independently the individual components of B.R.B.'s freight strategy promised an improved financial performance, even if the initial results from freightliner et al. were poor. But the assumption that costs attributed by an abstract formula could necessarily be saved in practice proved incorrect. And the most damning indictment of Board policy in 1963–8 was the failure to assess the freight position as a whole and develop a positive policy for wagon-load, a traffic which as late as 1967 contributed two-thirds of total freight revenue.[74] Its relative neglect helped to erode still further the declining confidence of customers in its future.

One of the more far-sighted members of the Board realised the serious implications for wagon-load and for freight prospects as a whole at an early date. In December 1963 Raymond asked the pertinent question 'what is our policy for wagon load traffic?'. Not only did he argue that the uncertainty surrounding the traffic should be ended, but he also maintained that it was quite 'impracticable to build up an aggressive and keen commercial sales staff on the basis of train load working only – we must offer a wagon load service'.[75] His plea fell on deaf ears. With the unprofitability of so much wagon-load traffic proven in the *Reshaping* report, and managerial attention clearly focussed on the new initiatives in freight, most of the Board were in no mood to listen sympathetically to such arguments. Only the National Freight Train Plan of July 1965, which aimed to improve operational reliability and optimise the use of marshalling yards and wagons, could be regarded as anything like a positive approach. Criticisms of the absence of an overall freight plan incorporating the wagon-load business were made in the reports on B.R.B. marketing undertaken by the consultants, Production-Engineering, in February 1967, part of the J.S.G. exercise, and by Cooper Brothers in August 1968. Although the former report was dismissed as shoddy and superficial by the Board, the consultants' criticisms were clearly acknowledged by some Board members.[76]

The problems of the wagon-load business were also exacerbated considerably by the encouragement given to many customers to abandon it in favour of the faster and more reliable freightliner or train-load services. This left the sector with a residual of poor traffics which were difficult, if not impossible, to organise into regular and reliable transits. McKenna, the General Manager of the Southern Region, who in 1968 blamed the deterioration in freight operating margins on misguided management policies, had come to the conclusion that 'transfer of traffic to freightliners without regard to . . . the adverse effect on profit and performance of the residual services' had been partly responsible for the decline.[77] The situation facing the Southern Region was a peculiar one, of course – it was dominated by passenger traffic – but there was a real point here. Board members such as Shirley had regarded containerisation as a panacea for B.R.B.'s freight problems, and had argued for the swift abandonment of wagon-load – 'that expensive and now obsolescent process of handling wagons one at a time'. This kind of thinking was fed into the Board's submission of the Freight Grid to the Ministry in 1966, and probably influenced the latter's subsequent reluctance to authorise investment in a revitalised wagon-load system in 1969.[78]

Furthermore, the assault on operating costs personified by Shirley went beyond the closure of routes and the rationalisation of terminals described in Chapter 10 (pp. 415–31). Economies made without adequate attention to the operational implications damaged the reliability of the remaining services, and of wagon-load in particular, and thus had depressing effects on revenue which went beyond the savings made. In some ways this was a self-fulfilling prophecy. Another detailed study of wagon-load services in March 1966 produced the gloomy conclusion that in spite of some improvements in loading and consignment size and the shedding of unremunerative traffics the cost position was very much the same as in 1961. Not only were the poor financial results in part a consequence of cost-cutting, but the findings provided a brief for more cuts.[79] The lack of co-ordination between the railways' operating and commercial functions and between division and regional headquarters, and the inadequate attempts to quantify market reactions, meant that policies undertaken in the name of economy often damaged relations with the customer. The drive to reduce the wagon fleet was a sound strategy in view of the conclusion that the number of wagons was greatly in excess of requirements. But the way in which it was tackled frequently led to a deterioration in the quality of service provided, and, in particular, to longer transit times. The consultants Production-Engineering reported that reductions in the wagon fleet had suffered from a 'lack of detailed commercial justification', and this was privately conceded by Margetts. He observed: 'If one looks back over the years one cannot deny – or at least I can't – that much of what P-E Consulting Group say is correct. We have cut the [coaching stock] and wagon fleets without a clear commercial policy.'[80] All too often the blame for poor quality of freight service was attributed to staffing difficulties instead of accepting that it was also a product of the unforeseen consequences of management initiatives.[81]

Nor did the National Freight Train Plan produce a rapid improvement. On the contrary, with its emphasis on low-cost operating and the reduction of train-mileage, its implementation from 1966 did very little to improve punctuality and transit times. There was a conflict between greater resource utilisation and a higher quality of wagon-load service, and this was picked up by the consultants investigating B.R.B.'s marketing. Cooper Brothers observed that the reduction of services between marshalling yards had made the overall service less flexible and therefore less attractive to the customer. Another criticism was that by giving priority of movement to traffics considered 'commercially important' B.R.B. was encouraging an overall decline in the quality of service. The plan had been formulated by operating managers working largely in isolation; this had prevented commercial managers from specifying the level of service required by customers.[82]

The seriousness of the situation can only be appreciated if we accept the crucial point that competitiveness in the freight transport market was increasingly determined not by price, but by reliability of service and speed of delivery. It was here that road haulage scored well in the 1960s, while the railways performed badly. By 1970 it had been conceded by railway managers that cost-cutting had damaged reliability. Geoffrey Wilson, the Chief Executive, put the matter bluntly. 'During the 1960s, the "minimum cost" approach towards the provision of freight services sought to achieve viability through cost reduction – notwithstanding the consequential impact upon quality. The resultant worsening of transit times and reliability inevitably widened the competitive gap in favour of the road haulier.' By this time, the emphasis had shifted within B.R.B. from cost-reduction to revenue-maximisation as a means to improve net revenue.[83] Studies commissioned by the Ministry of Transport in 1970 pointed in the same direction. A study of the allocation of freight traffic found B.R.B. wanting in terms of both speed of delivery and loss and damage levels. The persistence of intermediate marshalling was identified as the principal factor responsible for adverse criticisms.[84] The consequent loss of traffic from rail to road was charted in a study of the industrial demand for transport, by the government economists, Bayliss and Edwards. A survey of 720 companies undertaken in 1966–7 produced the conclusion that about 10 per cent had changed their mode of transport in the two years before the survey period. Moves from rail transport represented 60 per cent of the total number of changes. The main movement came in industries which provided an insignificant amount of rail traffic, but there was an ominous loss of business in chemicals and iron and steel, two of B.R.B.'s major customers. The reasons for this desertion of rail are illuminating. The most important was 'slowness and delays', followed by loss and damage, making up 63 per cent of the explanations offered. Increased charges were cited in only 21 per cent of cases.[85] Some losses of traffic to road transport, whether road haulage or own-account lorries, were inevitable in the 1960s and early 1970s. But the inadequacies of B.R.B.'s policy for wagon-load traffic resulted in losses of traffic which could have been made to cover direct costs and yield a contribution to system costs. Poor quality of service was largely responsible for this weakness.

The problem of quality undoubtedly lay at the root of B.R.B.'s inability to raise its freight charges during the early 1960s. The study of productivity in transport by Deakin and Seward included a comparison of charges by road and rail in 1966 for a wide variety of commodities. This showed that in nearly all cases railway rates were cheaper than those quoted by road hauliers.[86] In spite of the fact that there was no general freight rate increase between 1957 and 1965, losses of traffic and revenue were considerable.[87] A good example of poor quality of service inhibiting revenue levels can be found in the Board's relations with the Post Office. In June 1963 the G.P.O. diverted a considerable proportion of its East Anglian parcels to road vehicles, following a report critical of the standards of the rail service. The success of the move led to a threat to withdraw large amounts of business from rail. B.R.B. averted this by successfully negotiating a new ten-year contract operated from April 1964, which re-secured the East Anglian traffic and promised the railways a 90 per cent share of the parcels market. However, there was a price to pay for the G.P.O.'s custom. The railways' share of parcels revenue was cut from 40 to 32.5 per cent over a three-year period, and a change in the method of calculating the volume of rail traffic was adjusted in the G.P.O.'s favour. The net effect of the modifications was a reduction in revenue of about £2 million per annum. On top of this, retention of the parcels business was made conditional on the maintenance of a satisfactory service, and to ensure this strict obligations were laid down, including station scheduling. Inside B.R.B. the new arrangement was described as a 'pistol-point contract'. Poor quality of service had weakened the Board's position in negotiating with a major customer. It produced the pithy remark from the Public Relations and Publicity Department that 'if regional managers were *made* to run their trains efficiently most of our customer relations problems would disappear'.[88]

Because unreliability reduced many of the operational advantages the railways had once enjoyed over longer distances, the approach to pricing was usually cautious, influenced by the fear of wholesale desertions of traffic. As long as management action was focussed upon cost-reduction and the application of costing formulae to traffics, the equally important objective of revenue-maximisation was neglected. Even the cost-conscious Margetts was moved to admit in 1966 that insufficient attention had been given to the raising of revenue.[89] This was not always so in the regions, which retained a wide responsibility for pricing, particularly in relation to small or irregular consignments. As early as 1964 Raymond had reported that the inability to save in the short run at least the equivalent of the gross revenue obtained from wagon-load traffic had caused some regions to challenge the wisdom of commercial rationalisation.[90] Two years later, when there was much heart-searching at H.Q. about the way in which freight traffic was being accepted, James produced a long and complex paper on costs and freight traffic. This indicated how much was still to be done to encourage regional officers to depart from pricing decisions based only on the covering of direct costs. But the reaction of regional managers was that 'they were not in favour of losing the revenue from business for which there was existing capacity unless savings at least equivalent to the revenue could be realised'. The overall unprofitability of much of the wagon-load business in the 1960s was accepted in the regions but, as James remarked to Raymond in January 1967, 'some of them don't wish to believe the figures and have done little about this loss-making traffic; some have even increased it by taking traffic at marginal prices'.[91] This regional intransigence would have been praiseworthy had it been accompanied by a concerted effort to improve the quality of service. Unfortunately, it was not.

Of course, the increasing significance of centrally negotiated long-term contracts with major customers reduced the impact of regional attitudes, and the pricing of these contracts demands close attention. The bulk of freight traffic – about two-thirds by tonnage and a half by revenue in the early 1970s – was priced in this way. The arrangements involved traffics such as coal, iron ore, steel, oil, chemicals, cement, parcels and motor vehicles; and such major British concerns as the National Coal Board, the C.E.G.B. and the Post Office, already mentioned, as well as the British Steel Corporation, British Petroleum, I.C.I., Ford and Portland Cement. Although it is not easy to generalise about the prices charged, because of the wide variation in the conditions under which the traffic was handled, it is clear that by the mid-1960s most long-term contracts contained 'escalator' or 'price variation' clauses. These to some extent insulated British Rail freight prices from the government's prices and incomes interventions, particularly during periods of 'restraint'. Such clauses were not always a blessing. Customers sometimes complained about having to pay higher prices during periods of freeze. There was also a danger that train-load rates covered by contract would get out of line with individually quoted rates for more casual customers (which were not covered by escalator clauses), a problem which Raymond put to Castle during the 1966–7 restraint.[92] Furthermore, much depended on the base rate and the size of the escalation provided for. In June 1970, for example, it was noted in the Railway Management Group that rate increases to the full extent merited by rising costs 'were frustrated by the nature of price variation clauses in contracts, and by undertakings which had been given not to seek further increases before the expiration of certain periods of time'.[93] Nevertheless, a survey of some of the most important contract rates, involving the C.E.G.B., the oil companies, the Post Office and the British Steel Corporation, showed that rates had kept pace with wholesale prices over the period 1968–72 (see Table 60).

The most important point is whether the contract base rates were, in the first place, 'commercial', that is, made a real contribution to profits. Did British Rail exploit fully the few remaining areas of quasi-monopoly left to it, namely the bulk traffics? The average rates per net ton-mile, as shown in Table 59 above, although at best a very rough indication of pricing trends, suggest that it did not. Coal rates fell by 38 per cent in real terms, 1962–73;

Table 60. *'National escalation and B.R. pricing', 1968–72*

	1968 (%)	1969 (%)	1970 (%)	1971 (%)	1972 (%)	1968–72 (%)	Approx. revenue (£m.)
Price series							
Retail	+4.6	+5.4	+6.4	+9.4	+6.4	+36.9	
Wholesale	+3.9	+3.1	+7.5	+8.8	+5.7	+32.4	
British Rail pricing							
Price variation clauses							
C.E.G.B.	+5.3	+2.8	+8.0	+9.5	+6.2	+35.9	31
Oil	+4.3	+5.0	+5.9	+8.7	+6.1	+33.8	11
Post Office	+4.8	+3.8	+7.8	+9.9	+6.0	+36.6	25
Negotiated				+8.5			
B.S.C.	+5.5	+5.5	—	+5.0	+5.0ᵃ	+35.4	35
				+2.75			
			+6.5	+10.0			
Domestic coal	+6.0	—	+8.5	+5.0	+5.0ᵃ	+46.4	20
Govt Depts	+5.0	+5.0	+10.0	+12.5	+5.0ᵃ	+41.5	3

ᵃ 5 per cent increases applied under C.B.I. restraint rules.
Source: Bowick–Marsh on 'Pricing', 9 June 1972, Marsh Papers on Pricing, 1970–5, B.R.B. Figures as given (1968–72 for Govt Depts should be +43.3%?).

iron and steel rates by 29 per cent, 1963–73. By the later 1960s these rates were admittedly higher than those charged for other products. But even so British Rail could have done more to extract what the market would bear. The earlier references to the oil contracts and to 'Merry-Go-Round' indicate that there was little point in setting prices at a competitive level in anticipation of economic traffic volumes if these did not materialise.

Discussions about the budget for 1968 reveal some understanding of this at H.Q. In August 1967, Johnson, then joint Vice-Chairman, argued that for coal traffic British Rail should 'demand a price which covers our full costs of doing the job'. The matter was becoming more urgent with the C.E.G.B.'s move to fuels other than coal. As Johnson observed,

the run down in coal output may result in some mines being retained with more regard to their social utility than to their economic value ... the Electricity Generating Board will turn more and more to the policy of using coal fired power stations to meet seasonal peaks in demand ... If we are not careful some of the costs of these policies will fall on the railways ... It is no longer possible to continue to provide concealed subsidies for other activities or industries.

It is not clear how far Johnson's views were taken up.[94]

No one would pretend that rail pricing was easy, in a declining competitive position: simple marginal cost formulae could not be operated. Moreover, it would be expecting a great deal of managers steeped in the 'culture of the railroad' to preside enthusiastically over the rapid run-down of uneconomic rail traffic by encouraging high prices. There were other complications too. Traffic concentration often led to rate cuts to compensate customers who incurred additional terminal costs, and lower rates were also used to encourage companies into the private ownership of wagons, something which gathered pace in the 1970s. Managers had been caught up in the uncertainty of deciding between relating prices to costs – whether direct or indirect or both, long-term or short-term – and of charging what they perceived the market would bear, a rough and ready practice more suited to the railways' monopoly position in the nineteenth century, but which in late twentieth-century conditions meant setting prices to reflect the price and quality of service of competitors. Although, as will be evident from the discussion which follows, British Rail woke up to the need to conduct sophisticated market research and pursue disaggregated market pricing – and there was no shortage of consultants, government bodies and quangos to point them in the right direction – by the time the railways were ready to adopt market pricing they were caught up, like the other nationalised industries, in the trammels of prices and incomes policy. The defensive and not particularly impressive response of British Rail to Pryke and Dodgson's allegations of underpricing, made before the Select Committee on Nationalised Industries of 1976–7, suggests that all had not been well.[95]

VI

The change in B.R.B.'s approach towards freight pricing and marketing followed the recognition that the deterioration of this sector was the major element in the failure to restrain deficits in the 1960s. When Raymond succeeded Beeching in June 1965, one of his first actions was to warn the Minister of Transport, Fraser, that the financial results for the year would be some £15–20 million worse than had been forecasted. Fraser's response was to call for a joint examination of the Board's finances, and in September a confidential report found that a fall in freight revenue of £15 million had been largely responsible for the estimated deterioration of £21.5 million. The prospect of achieving viability by 1970, promised by *Reshaping*, was now formally recognised to be 'extremely doubtful'.[96] The joint inquiry stimulated an undertaking by Raymond to give attention to ways of increasing revenue by improving quality of service, in addition to the continuation of a cost-cutting strategy, but, as has already been outlined, there was no immediate change of attitudes, especially in relation to wagon-load, and much of the search for quality was based on the National Freight Train Plan of 1965, which was not very successful. It was left to Castle to ram home the message that the freight sector problem had to be tackled in a more determined and systematic way. The deliberations of the J.S.G. established by Castle and Raymond helped to bring to a head the growing disquiet about the future of railway freight services. The Group was able to compute a reasonable estimate of the future financial position of the passenger business, but found it difficult to do so with freight, since the 'management options were wide enough [e.g. what to do with wagon-load] to cause uncertainty about the future stability of the industry'.[97] On top of this, in May 1967 Castle was forced to press Raymond about the Board's failure to limit the rail deficit to the budget figure of £128 million agreed with the Ministry (the eventual deficit was £153 million). Once again, freight problems were blamed. Observing that things were going 'seriously wrong' due to a fall in the traditional traffics such as coal, she suggested that the Board proceed quickly to develop long-range planning and 'a clear picture of the future for wagon-load traffic'. Some kind of response to this challenge was inevitable.[98]

Ministerial probings coincided with internal disquiet within B.R.B. to produce change. By 1966 the dilemma facing railway management over freight – whether to emphasise cost-reduction or revenue-maximisation, whether to encourage pricing on the basis of fixed contribution formulae or allow a more flexible approach to system costs – had begun to surface. For example, the Chief Commercial Manager, Long, noted in August that further rationalisation of services could produce 'severe net revenue losses . . . as the receipts drop faster than the costs'.[99] At the end of the same year action to develop a comprehensive freight plan was encouraged by the news that Castle was determined to establish a free-standing National Freight Organisation (later, the N.F.C.). Arthur Dean, General Manager of the North Eastern Region, which was on the point of being merged with the Eastern Region, was invited to H.Q. to assist Ratter, Margetts and Shirley in a preliminary planning exercise. Dean's reports of January and March 1967 made use of the wagon-load traffic test of 1966 to identify several weaknesses in the freight business. But his principal recommendation was that a forward planning unit be set up at headquarters. He pointed out:

Whilst the way to achieve substantial economies in working will emerge, without an Overall Forward Plan, vital knowledge as to the longer term integrated freight service products and their net earnings potential will not be realised . . . The biggest single clarification required . . . is to determine what is to be the whole range of the freight train products which we can evaluate.[100]

At the same time, an 'Integral Freight Plan', produced by the central

planning unit, used the computer program FRATE* to develop positive
proposals for the improvement of wagon-load services on trunk routes,
which included higher speeds and the introduction of new wagons.[101]

The reports were used as the basis for a major change in the planning
function at H.Q. Long was appointed to the post of Chief Planning
Manager and was put in charge of a central freight 'steering' committee.
The role of planning was accorded a high priority, and the moves
coincided with criticisms made to the J.S.G. by Cooper Brothers that
B.R.B.'s planning organisation needed recasting in a 'corporate' mould
(see above, pp. 355–7).[102] As the freight business slid into decline in 1967,
the Board referring to a 'depressing state of affairs', the new planning
organisation was instructed to concentrate upon the production of a
freight plan.[103] Several indications of a fundamental reappraisal of the
freight sector emerged in 1968, before the production of 'The Freight Plan
1968' in October. A Planning Department memorandum in February
acknowledged the fact that neither the train-load nor the freightliner
services could entirely replace the wagon-load business. Confidence was
lacking 'both inside and outside the industry', and there was an urgent
need for its restoration to prevent the wagon-load system from falling
apart in an uncontrolled manner.[104] The Board responded by announcing
an 'interim freight policy' in May, designed to restore confidence by
encouraging a more positive approach by managers, an improved reliability and better marketing. Cooper Brothers were employed as consultants to make recommendations about the latter. However, by this time
it was proving difficult to convince major customers that the railways
would not soon be withdrawing from the business. Robbins, for example,
pointed to the concerns of the British Steel Corporation on this score.[105]

The new approach to wagon-load was set out at length in the 1968
Freight Plan. It was a landmark in two ways. First, it established a
commitment to a wagon-load system of some kind in the future. This was
not of course incompatible with further steps to prune the number of
terminals and routes; in 1971, for example, consideration was given to the
feasibility of withdrawing from certain 'greenfield areas', and from East
Anglia in particular, though both tests proved negative.[106] But the Plan
highlighted the significant level of resource interdependence affecting
train-load and wagon-load traffic, and stressed the need to establish for
both a core of high quality services which would not be jettisoned in a
haphazard fashion. It thus provided the base from which a competitive
successor to the old wagon-load services emerged. In October 1972 British
Rail introduced its first high-speed scheduled service using air-braked

*Formulation of Routes and Technical Equipment.

wagons, which laid the foundations for the subsequent development of the 'Speedlink' network.[107] Second, the Freight Plan was a tangible demonstration of the value of sophisticated planning mechanisms applied to key management decisions. The urgency of the freight problem had encouraged a quick response in organisational and planning terms. Many of the techniques employed were subsequently used in the production of B.R.B.'s first five-year Corporate Plan in 1970. Indeed, the work in 1968 was advanced in comparison with that undertaken by much of private industry in Britain; the Board had been forced to look to the U.S.A. and Canada, where corporate planning was more developed. The Ministry's reaction to the contents of the Plan may have been a little lukewarm, but officials were 'enormously impressed' by the planning approach – Lazarus referred to 'a real breakthrough in planning methods'.[108] The Freight Plan was not a magic wand, nor were its forecasts perfect. Some Board members followed the civil servants in expressing reservations about the accuracy of the forecasting. But it was a bold attempt to estimate B.R.B.'s competitive position in the freight transport market at a time when the 1968 Transport Act required the Board to make its freight services break even.[109]

The essential aim of the Plan was to assess the effect on the Board's revenue position of two strategic options: (i) selectively to develop freightliner, train-load, and wagon-load services; and (ii) to develop freightliner and train-load, but abandon the wagon-load business. Both options were examined with the help of sophisticated computer programs, such as EMEWS, PUFF and ROUTESTRAT,* and such crucial variables as the effect of quality of service on revenue and costs were carefully assessed. The conclusion was that option (i) offered the best financial results. Although many of the figures were tentative, a snapshot evaluation for 1974 on a cost-attribution basis found that retention of wagon-load would produce an additional £115 million in gross revenue, £21 million over direct costs, and a margin over total costs of £5 million, compared with a loss of £20 million in option (ii). Calculations of discounted cash flows for 1969–90 yielded a balance in favour of wagon-load of £130–225 million, though it was conceded that most if not all of this might be matched by savings accruing from withdrawal. In all, wagon-load was 'likely to be only a modest financial success'. Most of the arguments in support of retention involved rejecting the notion of a railway with no wagon-load traffic. It would mean lower investment needs and lower financial risks, but would produce a rapid reduction in the size of the

*Economic Model for the Evaluation of Wagonload Systems; Programme for the Utilisation of Fractional Freightliners; and Route Strategy for working any trunk route system of 100 marshalling yards for a pre-determined quality of service to give minimum cost.

network and the loss of 50,000 jobs. Since other traffics shared resources with wagon-load, the loss of the latter would raise the unit costs of train-load and expose more of the passenger traffic to grant-aid status. The Plan concluded that there was 'a real risk that a spiral of decline would be started which would undermine the prospect of maintaining a national rail system'.[110] It was therefore recommended that marketing be improved, along the lines suggested by Cooper Brothers in their report of August 1968; that there should be more co-ordination between marketing and operating, and between the train-load and wagon-load sectors; and that there should be a drive to improve the speed and reliability of wagon-load by, *inter alia*, investing in new wagons and introducing a computerised system of wagon-control and traffic regulation.[111]

The Board continued to express some doubts about the wisdom of supporting one of its least profitable sectors, but agreed to make a move in this direction, and in particular to make an initial investment in new wagons. At this stage its scepticism was reinforced by that of the Ministry. After a joint conference at Watford, the Ministry indicated, early in 1969, that while it agreed that the implications of a railway without wagon-load were 'extremely serious' it was far from convinced by the traffic forecasts supporting the viability of the wagon-load option. This attitude was also evident when the Board submitted its proposal to spend £12.7 million on 3,200 new wagons. In August 1969, the Ministry expressed its reservations about a submission which did not include a quantified financial justification, and Marsh's consent to it included the rider that investment should not be undertaken until a thorough test of alternative suspension systems had been carried out. Nor was the authorisation to be interpreted as indicating any government support for wagon-load in the future.[112] In fact, only 600 wagons were built prior to the development of the first 'Speedlink' service, from Bristol to Glasgow, in 1972, by which time the Board itself had reassessed its requirements in the light of further freight studies.[113]

Although the uncertainties about the future viability of wagon-load services persisted, influenced by the bleaker economic climate of the 1970s and the abolition of road carriers' licensing (in December 1970), the Board's policy of retention with limited development was maintained. As long as the existing rolling stock could be employed, a general contraction in freight facilities would only produce a worsening of financial performance, since the contribution to system costs would be lost. The Board's insistence that rationalisation proposals be supported by direct evidence of cost escapement, and that traffics making a contribution, however small, to system costs should be retained, supported the argument for a core of wagon-load services. This policy was fed into the Board's second Corporate Plan of February 1972 and repeated in the more confidential Railway Policy Review in December.[114] It did not pre-empt the key objective of improving the quality of service. Here, several important initiatives were planned and developed after 1969, although their full potential was not realised until the mid–late 1970s.

One of the most important of these was the successful introduction of a comprehensive system of information and transit control. Measures to improve operating control can be found as early as 1965, when a manually-operated Advance Traffic Information system – A.T.I. – was first applied to limited parts of the trunk network. Doubts about the results of the scheme – the General Managers of the London Midland and Western Regions expressed some reservations in 1968 – were swept away by the Freight Plan and its emphasis on reliability. The scheme was then extended to the national trunk network in 1969–70.[115] The next stage was to computerise the monitoring of wagons and extend the area of control to feeder and local lines. The T.O.P.S.* system, developed in the U.S.A. by the Southern Pacific Railroad, was selected, and a £10 million investment sanctioned by the Board in 1971. This had been applied to about half the network by the end of 1974 and was fully operational a year later. Although once again the government, in the shape of the D.O.E., raised doubts about the returns, T.O.P.S. promised to give the railways a substantial boost in the area of wagon-load reliability. It was vigorously defended by David Bowick, one of its main advocates, in evidence to the Select Committee of 1976–7.[116] The 'Speedlink' services were another important development. Following the introduction of a pilot service in 1972, three more scheduled air-braked services were added in 1973–4, supported by an investment proposal for 650 wagons. But as with many new developments, hopes of early financial improvement were frustrated by operating difficulties, and there was plenty of late running.[117] Efforts were also made to improve revenue gained from private-sidings, where sloppy wagon control was evident.[118]

The final area of improvement was in B.R.B. marketing and market research. There is a great deal of evidence to show that this activity was transformed in the 1970s. An improved organisation, the formulation of commodity marketing plans and the integration of marketing and movements planning were the main elements. At both H.Q. and regional level five-year rolling marketing plans were developed for each commodity and major customer, and market information and forecasting were improved, with the application of new computerised systems such as FORWARD† (1973). By identifying growing markets where increased rail business

---

*Total Operations Processing System.
†FORecasting With Accurate Regular Data.

could be obtained, the first step was taken to increase revenue to compensate for the decline of traditional traffics such as wagon-load coal. The railways' earth and stone traffic increased by a third between 1967 and 1971, and there were also gains in car traffic and waste disposal.[119] Pricing also became a much more sophisticated activity in the 1970s. If the Beeching period and indeed the costings work of the 1950s had been useful in diagnosing broad areas of weakness in profitability, the lessons for freight in the 1960s were that simple cost-attribution provided no guide to rate-making at a detailed level. By 1973 pricing involved the strategy of seeking the highest rate compatible with market conditions and of maximising the contribution to system costs. This was a far cry from the use of yardstick costings formulae to determine whether to accept or reject a traffic and then pricing high to drive the 'unprofitable' traffic away, which was the message in the early 1960s. That approach was now condemned because the use of such yardsticks 'would be influenced by many factors extraneous and completely inappropriate to the specific circumstances of the flow under review. Such lack of discrimination would almost certainly distort the traffic mix required to maximise net revenue for British Rail.' Effective pricing by the alternative route meant acquiring a lot of good market intelligence and an ability to look at groups of traffics. By 1973 this involved a more sophisticated budget system and the use of 700 sub-sectors of activity called 'profit centres'.[120]

All this sophistication, the new jargon-packed environment with its welter of acronyms, did not guarantee financial success. The problem of unprofitability remained: in 1976, for example, it was reported that the much reduced wagon-load services were running at a loss of £30 million a year.[121] Other factors influencing the financial out-turn included road investment, the further incursions of road transport, a depressed economy and high inflation. Many of the initiatives described above failed to achieve a reasonable return in the medium term not only because of managerial difficulties but because there were teething troubles associated with constraints on investment and industrial relations problems. These areas are examined in the next chapter.

12

Investment, labour relations and productivity

I

Capital investment and labour, the two major factor inputs, continued to present railway managers with considerable problems as they sought to improve railway productivity and financial performance in the 1960s and beyond. These problems cut across the shifts in overall strategy determined by changes of chairman, changes of government, the appearance of new legislation and fluctuations in economic growth. Both were essential elements, for example, in a cost-cutting and a revenue-maximising objective, and both invited a substantial amount of government intervention, as they had done in the past. There is no doubt at all that the government was responsible for constraining the level of investment resources available to the railways after 1960; it also intervened in detail on a number of occasions and took a greater interest in investment appraisal techniques. In the labour relations field the government maintained its role as a watchdog on public sector wage claims. Furthermore, the obverse side of the prices and incomes coin which had affected pricing (see above, pp. 474–86) was a control of wage increases, and this is examined here. The government also continued to encourage the industry to improve its productivity. In this chapter an attempt is made to determine the effectiveness of both internal and external influences. An assessment of B.R.B.'s productivity record to 1973 then forms the conclusion.

Rationalisation and investment were clearly intended to go hand in hand. The rationalisation of the workshops, for example, was accompanied by a £16.8 million investment programme to modernise the retained works, of which £16.2 million was actually invested.[1] Elsewhere, investment in new equipment was expected to accompany closures and the concentration of existing facilities, whether in traction, rolling stock, trunk routes, freightliners or stations and depots. Unfortunately, while the story of the 1950s was one of investment with minimal rationalisation, it

Table 61. *Gross investment in railways, 1963–73 (£m.)*

Year	Current prices		Constant 1948 prices	
	Rolling stock	Total investment	Rolling stock	Total investment
1954–62				
(ann. ave.)	74.1	120.6	42.3	71.1
1963	47.2	90.6	22.7	46.8
1964	47.0	100.7	21.4	50.3
1965	54.5	113.7	23.5	54.0
1966	39.3	102.8	17.2	49.4
1967	31.3	86.0	12.6	38.4
1968	26.7	79.0	10.3	33.2
1969	15.3	62.0	5.5	25.1
1970	20.2	77.9	6.8	29.1
1971	21.2	91.2	6.8	31.5
1972	19.1	102.8	6.0	30.5
1973	24.9	109.4	7.1	26.6
1963–73	346.7	1,016.1	139.9	414.9
1963–73				
(ann. ave.)	31.5	92.4	12.7	37.7

Source: see Appendix B, Table 1. Investment includes collection and delivery, but excludes ships and ancillaries.

changed thereafter to one of rationalisation with precious little investment. The Board's investment programmes were, like the passenger rationalisation initiative, hampered by a long-running and time-consuming dialogue with the government, making for considerable uncertainty about both long-term and medium-term forecasts. The losses made by the Board under Beeching and his successors to 1968 and, after the financial reorganisation, the deterioration in the Board's overall profitability from 1971, made it extremely difficult to convince governments that they should release resources.

Gross investment, whether measured in current or constant 1948 prices, proved to be disappointing in comparison with the heady days of 1959 and 1960. As is evident from Table 61, there was a persistent downward trend in constant terms from the peak in 1959, and a deterioration was particularly noticeable after 1965. In 1969, annual investment at £62.0 million, or £25.1 million in 1948 prices, was little more than a quarter of the figure for 1959 of £98.4 million. The average level of investment for 1963–73, at constant prices, was little more than half of that achieved in 1954–62. Consequently, net investment (see Figure 7), which had been positive from 1948 to 1962, except in 1952, became negative again in 1963 and remained so throughout our period. The series indicates a

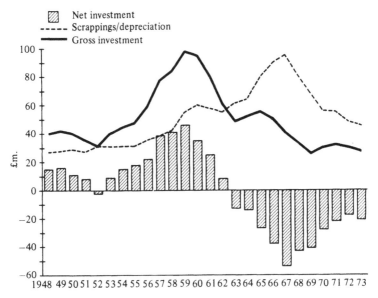

Figure 7 British Railways investment, 1948–73 (constant 1948 prices)
Source: Appendix B.

trough in 1967 of −£54.8 million in 1948 prices as scrappings and depreciation intensified (for steam locomotives and wagons in particular). Aggregate disinvestment in 1963–73 totalled £317.3 million at constant prices, which more than cancelled the positive net investment of £294.5 million in 1948–62. Railways also consumed a reduced share of U.K. investment resources. The proportion of gross domestic fixed capital formation represented by railway investment fell from about 3.3 per cent in 1954–62 (4.1 per cent in 1959–60) to 1.1 per cent in 1963–73. Pryke's estimates of public sector investment for 1948–68 indicate that the railways' share of the nationalised industry cake fell sharply from 20 per cent in 1954–62 to only 10 per cent in 1963–8. And there was a further deterioration thereafter.[2]

Dissatisfaction with the scale of railway investment was a perennial theme for the Board. One of the major difficulties with its corporate planning from the late 1960s was the vulnerability of its forecasts of future investment to changes in government policy. Richard Marsh, who as Minister had been severely critical of some of B.R.B.'s investment plans, made the Board's position clear in the Annual Reports for 1972 and 1973. In the first, he complained that 'in terms of capital investment for renewal, research development and improvement the railways' share has not been comparable with the millions poured into other forms of transport'. A year later, he drew attention to the fact that 'within three weeks of the announcement that investment in British Rail for five years would total £891 million [November 1973], a 20 per cent reduction in the investment for the first year was imposed as part of a general cutback in the public sector'.[3] By this time, as can be seen from Table 62, the Board had begun to hire or lease equipment as an alternative to outright purchase, but even here government intervention was evident.

The picture was not, however, quite as gloomy as the industry frequently made out. In view of the ending of the expenditure programme under the Modernisation Plan in the mid-1960s and the rationalisation of railway facilities under Beeching and his successors, it was only to be expected that requirements for some items would diminish in the short run. This was certainly true of rolling stock which had consumed 62 per cent of total investment resources in 1954–62 but only 34 per cent of the total in 1963–73 (see Table 61). No D.M.U.s were acquired after the 40 obtained in 1963, and acquisitions of diesel locomotives virtually ceased after the 1967 purchases and the leasing of 50 locomotives from English Electric in 1967–8 (see Table 62). The modest pace of electrification meant that the only new electric locomotives required were for the west coast route from Euston, where new services were introduced to Liverpool/ Manchester in April 1966 and to Birmingham in March 1967. The Board's attention was firmly fixed on the development of a new generation of trains for the 1970s – the Advanced Passenger Train and the High Speed Train. However, turning off the tap was to prove easier than turning it on again. By the late 1960s it was realised that some of the lumpy investment of the previous decade would need to be replaced sooner than anticipated because of increased utilisation and higher train speeds. There was some concern about the life-span of the D.M.U.s, although it was accepted that the case for replacement could not be justified commercially. In the confidential Railway Policy Review of December 1972 specific reference was made to the age and condition of the D.M.U., E.M.U. and wagon fleets.[4]

Investment in ways and structures, which made up only 32 per cent of total investment in 1954–62, took 59 per cent of the total in 1963–73 (see Appendix B for details). More attention was paid to the laying of Continuous Welded Rail (C.W.R.) and improved ballasting, to the extension of modern colour-light signalling, and to Automatic Warning Systems (A.W.S.). There was steady if not spectacular progress in these areas. Although British Rail lagged behind the railways of continental Europe in the standard of its infrastructure, B.R.B. was unable to convince the Ministry of Transport of the need to accelerate existing investment

Table 62. Components of railway investment, 1963–73

Year	Locomotives Diesel	Locomotives Electric	Locomotives Total	DMUs	EMUs	Passenger carriages	Total coaching vehicles	Freight vehicles	Continuous welded rail (single track-miles)	Route-miles fitted with Automatic Warning System[a]	Net additions — Locomotives Diesel	Net additions — Locomotives Electric	Net additions — EMUs	Net additions — Passenger carriages	Net additions — Wagons
1963	382	16	398	40	113	377	543	3,001	367	253	—	—	—	—	—
1964	408	6	414	—	36	98	134	769	399	44	—	—	—	—	—
1965	354	79	433	—	238	50	288	1,815	552	95	—	—	—	—	—
1966	168	63	231	—	194	185	399	1,500	518	129	—	—	—	—	—
1967	59	1	60	—	360	110	482	1,590	456	38	4	—	—	—	—
1968	4	—	4	—	91	227	354	2,120	466	106	46	—	—	—	—
1969	1	—	1	—	184	175	373	1,228	561	271	—	—	—	—	—
1970	—	—	—	—	210	186	387	1,180	662	88	—	—	—	—	—
1971	—	—	—	—	8	—	12	41	627	169	—	—	228	230	1,226
1972	2	—	2	—	74	8	107	2	608	477	—	—	96	244	656
1973	—	16	16	40	157	218	398	383	574	165	—	12	324	186	295
1963–73	1,378	181	1,559	40	1,665	1,634	3,487	13,629	5,790	1,835	50	12	324	660	2,177
p.a.	125.3	16.4	141.7	3.6	151.4	148.5	317.0	1,239.0	526.4	166.8	4.5	1.1	29.5	60.0	197.9
(1954–62 p.a.)	381.8	12.7	477.1	453.0	424.0	755.8	2,132.8	35,545.0	113.9	136.9	—	—	—	—	—

[a] B.R. standard Automatic Warning System. In addition, there were 1,390 miles of non-standard equipment on W.R., which had been reduced to 681 miles by the end of 1973.

Source: B.R.B., R. & A. 1963–73; Continuous Welded Rail data from B.R.B. 1984, and Automatic Warning System data from B.R.B. New Works 145–1–2 Pt. 7. The 50 leased diesel locomotives (Type 4, Class 50) were purchased in 1974.

programmes. About 5,800 single-track-miles of C.W.R. were laid in the period 1963–73, an annual rate of 526 miles, which was a marked advance on the 1,000 miles laid (under 115 miles a year) in 1954–62. But in spite of a total expenditure at current prices of £254 million in 1963–73, overall investment in track (C.W.R. and jointed-rail) declined. By the end of 1973, the 6,800 miles of track laid with C.W.R. producing annual savings of £6.6 million, still amounted to less than a third of British Rail's total track-mileage, and under a half of the principal routes scheduled for the new technology. Dissatisfaction with the progress made was expressed in the policy review of 1972.[5]

There were similar difficulties with the extension of multi-aspect colour-light signalling. This system, which embraced about 3,000 single-track-miles at the end of 1962, was applied to a further 2,500 miles in 1963–6 with an annual investment of about £13 million. An attempt to accelerate the tempo was made through a National Signalling Plan in 1966, which envisaged an expenditure of £197 million over ten years, with an increased level of £24 million per annum in 1968–70. Unfortunately, the initiative foundered at Ministry level after the Board failed to provide an estimate of the financial effect.[6] Spending thereafter was at much the same rate as before – £168 million at current prices on signalling and telecommunications in 1963–73, or £15 million per annum. After 1966 another 3,500 single-track-miles were resignalled, making 9,453 in all by the end of 1973, three times the amount installed before 1963. The number of signal boxes also fell sharply over the eleven-year period, from 8,700 to 3,300. Nevertheless, the mileage modernised was still only 40 per cent of the total track-mileage (22,561), and there was a striking contrast between the 30 new signal boxes each controlling an average of 110 miles and the remaining 3,282, controlling only 5.9 miles.[7] The introduction of A.W.S. also proceeded at a rather leisurely pace, influenced not only by the scarcity of investment resources but also by problems on two regions. The Western had inherited 1,400 route-miles with non-standard equipment, and on the Southern A.W.S. had to be integrated with third-rail electrification and high-density operation. At the end of 1962, there were 2,600 route-miles of A.W.S., including the Western Region mileage. Eleven years later, the figure was 3,795, which included the conversion of 700 miles on the Western. This amounted to little more than half of the mileage earmarked for A.W.S., and in the early 1970s there was some concern about the slow pace of change in view of the prospect of higher train speeds in the future.[8]

Electrification schemes were few and far between. The largest project, the 25 kV a.c. electrification of the Euston–Birmingham/Liverpool/Manchester lines, comprising a total of 495 route-miles at a cost of £160 million, had been inherited from Commission days. The Board completed only one more main-line scheme before the end of 1973, the 90-mile Bournemouth line from Brookwood to Branksome, which was opened on the 750-volt d.c. third-rail system in July 1967. In addition, about 70 miles of suburban electrification were completed – in and around Glasgow (Gourock, Wemyss Bay, Lanark and Hamilton Circle) in 1967, the Lea Valley line near London (Clapton–Cheshunt) in 1969 and the conversion to 25 kV a.c. of the Manchester–Altrincham line in 1971.[9] The route-mileage electrified increased from 1,560 (9 per cent of the total) at the end of 1962 to 2,151 (19 per cent) by the end of 1973. Two major projects were under construction. The 235-mile extension of the Euston scheme from Weaver Junction, north of Crewe, to Glasgow at an estimated cost of £55 million received Ministerial authorisation in February 1970, was opened to Preston in the summer of 1973 and completed in May 1974. The £35 million project to electrify the Great Northern suburban lines out of King's Cross was given government approval in August 1971. Work began in 1973, and the two stages were completed in February 1978. Preparatory work also began on the conversion of the Liverpool Street lines from 6.25 kV to 25 kV. These schemes were undoubtedly important, but the progress made to 1973 was limited in comparison with the aspirations of the Modernisation Plan. Several routes remained to be electrified, including the East Coast main line from King's Cross, and the extension of the Eastern Region schemes to Norwich and Cambridge – only now being tackled in the mid-1980s.

Despite the shortage of funds, the decade to 1973 saw several features of what might be called 'the modern railway'. In terms of train technology, there was the introduction in 1963 of the Mark II series coaches, which from 1970 were air-conditioned and electrically heated, and the prototype Mark III coaches, put into service in 1973; the freightliners from 1966; the permanently-coupled 'Merry-Go-Round' trains for coal and gypsum, with automatic loading and unloading; the new privately owned 100-ton wagons for petroleum, iron ore and liquid gas. Prototypes of both the A.P.T. and the 'intermediate technology' H.S.T. were being tested in 1972. While the A.P.T. was dogged by technical problems, the H.S.T. was put into service in 1976. British Rail's shipping services were transformed by the new hovercraft of Seaspeed (B.R. Hovercraft Ltd) and the drive-on drive-off ferries marketed by the subsidiary, Sealink. Further develop-ments included the gradual replacement of manned level crossings by automatic half-barriers. Over 200 were installed before the momentum was halted by a serious accident at Hixon, Staffordshire, in January 1968. A national telecommunications plan in 1969 produced British Rail's own extension trunk dialling system. The computerised system for controlling freight traffic operations, T.O.P.S., was authorised in 1971 and intro-duced in stages in 1973–5. In 1973 test boring for the Channel Tunnel was started near Dover, following a lengthy planning process. This ambitious and ill-fated project was eventually scuppered by the government in January 1975, but a decade later it has been taken up again with more determination on all sides. Developments in train technology, telecommunications, the use of computers: all suggest that the expenditure from the mid-1960s was put to more imaginative use than the investment under the Modernisation Plan a decade earlier.

The Board also paid attention to the modernisation of its station sites, linking this with property development and an awareness of the importance of road–rail connections. The most extensive project was the building of the new Euston station at a cost of about £16 million, which was opened in 1968. Here, the estimated net financial effect, calculated in 1965, was a disappointing loss of £152,000. Attempts to exploit the opportunities for property development had only a limited success, after the L.C.C.'s refusal, in March 1963, of planning permission for a large office development which had promised to yield an annual income of £400,000–500,000.[10] Other projects showed a better return, although they were often disappointing in comparison with crude rates of return or, after the introduction of discounted cash-flow techniques, test discount rates, in the private sector. The re-building of Birmingham (New Street) in 1964–6 was followed by the construction of a shopping mall on a raft over the station, completed in 1972. There were numerous office and shop developments accompanying station schemes, for example at Cannon Street, Waterloo and Wembley (Central) in the London area, and at Sheffield, Manchester, Cardiff and Southport in the provinces. Expected returns for Cannon Street were put at about 3 per cent before interest charges, while at Birmingham an expenditure of £8.3 million was expected to yield 7 per cent.[11] The first of the 'Park and Ride' stations was more successful. Bristol Parkway, close to the M4, soon repaid the investment of £230,000 after its opening in April 1972, although the second station, Alfreton and Mansfield Parkway, near the M1, which opened in 1973, was less profitable. All in all, the railways' exploitation of their station properties via the subsidiary company Railway Sites Ltd was far from dynamic, particularly when compared with the activities of the private property developers.[12]

II

After the problems the Commission had experienced in 1960 in trying to convince several sceptical bodies – a Select Committee, an Advisory Group, the Ministry of Transport and the Treasury – about the soundness of its investment plans and appraisal techniques, both the Commission and, from 1963, B.R.B. were put under a stronger microscope during the customary annual round of investment review and the setting of a Treasury ceiling. The Minister's powers to oversee major investment proposals* were extended in the 1962 Transport Act, and the Treasury remained the sole source of long-term loan capital. Under Beeching, the railways were expected to provide a firmer long-term indication of investment intentions, usually over five years, following the presentation of a plan for 1961–4 by Robertson in December 1960. In addition, the railways, in common with the other nationalised industries, were expected to seek a minimum rate of return of 8 per cent, as prescribed in the 1961 White Paper on *The Financial and Economic Obligations of the Nationalised Industries*. The workings of this procedure for investment monitoring and control, which applied in one way or another to all nationalised industries, were, as observed in earlier chapters, both complex and time-consuming. A summary of what was involved in the 1960s can be found in the evidence of both sides to Sub-Committee A of the Select Committee on Nationalised Industries which inquired into Ministerial Control in 1967.[13] However, a more immediate visual demonstration may be obtained from a chart showing the annual timetable, which was drawn up when the Board adjusted its internal procedures in 1968 (see Chart XIV). It is clear that a considerable burden was placed on railway management: on regional officers, charged with initiating proposals; on headquarters officers and the members of the Works and Equipment Committee (from 1968 the Investment Committee), who had to sift and 'salt' proposals, that is, relate regional submissions to what could be achieved in a given period; and Board members engaged in the several negotiations with relevant government departments. Further complications came with more sophisticated techniques in investment appraisal. Social cost-benefit studies were applied to certain projects which were unlikely to pass conventional commercial tests. From 1965, the Board agreed to adopt d.c.f. methods for its major projects, following a recommendation from the Treasury.

The development of an agreed appraisal procedure with the Ministry took three long years of debate. After the recommendations of the Stedeford Advisory Group had been received in October 1960, the Ministry asked the Commission to agree revised criteria for railway investment. There were fundamental areas of disagreement. The Ministry insisted that the railways had concentrated too much on necessary replacement and technical improvement and not enough on expected returns. The Commission, and later the Board, resented Ministerial

*Projects over £100,000 to be reported, those over £250,000 to receive specific approval.

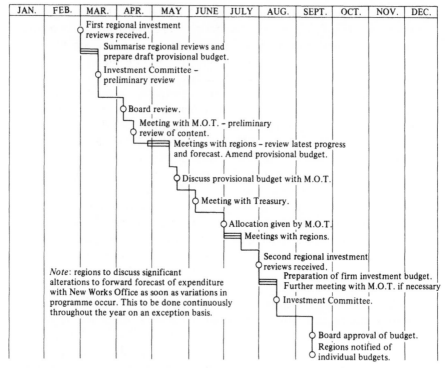

| JAN. | FEB. | MAR. | APR. | MAY | JUNE | JULY | AUG. | SEPT. | OCT. | NOV. | DEC. |

First regional investment reviews received.

Summarise regional reviews and prepare draft provisional budget.

Investment Committee – preliminary review

Board review.

Meeting with M.O.T. – preliminary review of content.

Meetings with regions – review latest progress and forecast. Amend provisional budget.

Discuss provisional budget with M.O.T.

Meeting with Treasury.

Allocation given by M.O.T.

Meetings with regions.

Second regional investment reviews received.

Note: regions to discuss significant alterations to forward forecast of expenditure with New Works Office as soon as variations in programme occur. This to be done continuously throughout the year on an exception basis.

Preparation of firm investment budget.
Further meeting with M.O.T. if necessary

Investment Committee.

Board approval of budget.
Regions notified of individual budgets.

Source: John Ratter–General Managers, 22 October 1968, B.R.B. New Works 23-4-2.

Chart XIV British Railways Board investment budget procedure – annual timetable, 1968

pressure to distinguish between 'unproductive' (i.e. straight replacement) expenditure and 'productive' expenditure and felt that there was inadequate appreciation of the railways' need to replace life-expired assets in order to keep trading. There was also disagreement about suitable tests of project worth. For example, the railways wanted to retain, in some circumstances at least, the existing approach of considering only the 'betterment' portion of an investment (net additional outlay), i.e. excluding expenditure to maintain existing assets.* It was also argued that project worth should be determined on a broader basis than mere rate of return.[14] Eventually, the Ministry, after taking advice from Binder, Hamlyn & Co., produced a draft procedure in August 1962. This was eventually accepted in September 1963, six months after the *Reshaping* report had been published, and was given its final form in January 1964.

*By 1961, however, they were prepared to substitute expenditure on the simplest possible renewal for renewal 'like for like'.

The Ministry requested both a one-year and a five-year 'rolling' programme of investment, with statements of purpose, spread and return. It also made a strong plea for back-checks on earlier projects. The new rules accepted that a crude rate of return (before interest charges) should be used as a convenient measure of worth, but emphasised that other considerations were important, including revenue flows, the pay-off period and alternative scheme-sizes and time-scales. The Board was also asked to divide its projects into those which were viable, i.e. profitable; those which were unprofitable but were necessary for safety or welfare reasons; and those intended for unprofitable facilities which had to be retained owing to the Minister's refusal of consent to closure. The emphasis throughout was on viability under the terms of the 1962 Act and on a more critical appraisal of no-return schemes of replacement, but no target return was specified.[15] The new rules were not entirely unwelcome at H.Q., although there were some doubts raised about the obligation to provide accurate five-year forecasts. Internal evidence reveals that in 1960–1 there had been an element of disagreement between the Commission's Finance and Works and Equipment Committees as to the most appropriate way of justifying projects financially. Furthermore, Beeching's arrival produced moves to tighten central control of both project presentation and spending, with the accent on the need to secure a 'proper return'. These intentions were codified in new instructions to the regions in February 1962, which included a request for the financial appraisal of minor works.[16]

In 1965 d.c.f. was taken on board. The technique had been under discussion in the Treasury as early as 1962, with a view to its application to nationalised industry investment. At this time it was still relatively new to British industry. The method proceeded from the assumption that all investment had a terminable life and that investment would only be justified financially if discounted net income was at least sufficient to repay capital cost. It permitted a fairer financial evaluation of projects where the pattern of spending and income over asset life was irregular. The Treasury eventually produced a discussion paper in January 1965 which gave a detailed account of investment appraisal and advocated the application of d.c.f. with a minimum test discount rate of 8 per cent.[17] The Board's response was enthusiastic. Both Shirley and James welcomed the move, and James produced a draft document in May 1965 which represented a considerable advance on earlier railway attitudes. Intended as a set of operative instructions, it advocated the use of d.c.f. for all but the simplest investment proposals, and specified a test rate of at least 8 per cent, with 12–15 per cent a 'reasonable target'. James also emphasised the need for frequent back-checks (not less than a year after completion for major projects), suggested that assumptions about future increases in real wages should be built into calculations and criticised the 'betterment' approach for having led railway managers to take for granted the need to maintain existing facilities and capacity. A Finance Department manual incorporating these revisions was issued in September 1965.[18]

In August 1965, negotiations began with the Ministry over a revised document on investment control and appraisal. Although no formal agreement was reached, a draft statement was accepted by P. G. James as a 'reasonable interpretation' of relationships with the Ministry. This codified both the Board's acceptance of d.c.f. and existing procedures developed in the course of 1965. These included an agreed annual timetable for the processing of one-year and five-year programmes; and the categorisation of investment schemes into those requiring Ministry approval, those allowed to proceed and those requiring further examination (usually large projects or those where no marked financial improvement was indicated).[19] The publication in November 1967 of the White Paper, *Nationalised Industries. A Review of Economic and Financial Objectives*, produced a new set of guidelines for both investment and marginal cost pricing. It shifted the emphasis from the setting of broad financial objectives (in the case of British Rail to break even as required by the 1962 Act) to the use of techniques such as d.c.f. to secure the optimal allocation of resources. Previously, it had been argued, in the 1961 White Paper, that the nationalised industries should make a return sufficient to cover replacement cost depreciation and to make an adequate contribution towards capital development. Now industries were expected to make 'a satisfactory return in commercial terms'. Thus, the use of d.c.f. with a common test rate of 8 per cent was recommended because it represented the rate consistent with the real return expected of marginal low-risk projects in the private sector. At the same time, the 1967 White Paper expressed some of the non-commercial realities facing those concerned with railway investment, and indeed with investment in nationalised industry as a whole. First, it contended that a project which 'passed the test' would not automatically be undertaken, given government policy on the scale and priorities in public sector borrowing. Second, it suggested that it might be appropriate to use social cost-benefit analysis in certain cases where the commercial test would be failed.[20] The technique had been used to evaluate London Transport's Victoria Line project in 1963, and was currently being applied by the Ministry of Transport to the Cambrian Coast line. It was clearly of relevance to a number of potential railway projects, particularly for unremunerative lines and services which were being earmarked for grant-aid. However, the Board's first attempt to make use of cost-benefit analysis for investment purposes was not a success. In

1963, acting on a suggestion from the Ministry, it commissioned Christopher Foster to examine a proposal of long standing, the electrification of the Great Northern suburban services based on King's Cross. The project had an unhappy history. There were several disagreements about cost and traffic assumptions, and problems with the data. When Foster reported in 1965 that he was unable to find a positive case for any of the 13 proposals he had examined, he received a frosty reception at headquarters.[21]

The procedure for investment control of 1966 and the White Paper of 1967 continued to serve as the basis for Board–Ministry contacts, and were endorsed by the report of the Select Committee on Nationalised Industries of July 1968.[22] The only substantive change was the raising of the test discount rate from 8 to 10 per cent in 1969. However, Ministry vetting procedures were modified in response to the new conditions created by the Transport Act of 1968 and the promise of corporate planning. A new document drawn up in February 1970 prepared the way for control via a 'continuously up-dated Corporate Plan' in place of control over individual projects, which was welcomed by the Board as an important step in reducing the 'previously excessive detailed control of investment by the Ministry'. The document also made provision for co-operation with the National Freight Corporation in relation to joint investment, and made reference to investment in grant-aided services, investment grants and leasing as an alternative to investment. The new procedure began after the presentation of the Board's First Corporate Plan in December 1970. A comprehensive corporate manual, which included a revised document entitled 'Relationships with the Department of the Environment', was agreed in May 1972 and presented to the Select Committee on Nationalised Industries dealing with investment procedures in February 1973.[23] In October 1968 the Board issued a revised manual on investment appraisal to its regions, following recommendations made by Cooper Brothers in December 1967, at the end of the J.S.G. exercise.[24] This was a much more sophisticated document than that of 1965. Use of d.c.f. was to include not only the net present value of cash flows but the internal rate of return,* and the year in which discounted receipts would 'break even' with discounted expenditures. The new instructions also took note of the changed conditions of grant-aid, asked regions to place an added emphasis in their submissions on the alternative to investment of doing nothing and provided improved guidelines for the examination of profitability, risk and alternative timings.[25]

Further modifications were suggested in the course of 1970–1 as corporate planning developed, and in April 1972 another appraisal

*The rate which discounts the cash flows of expenditure and of receipts so that the discounted values equate over the life of the project.

document was produced, which with new investment regulations was included in the corporate manual. There were no major developments of principle. Improvements to the presentation of submissions were included. The use of d.c.f. continued to be supported, but was placed in context: 'The Board, like any business, is judged on the revenue account performance and it is very necessary to consider alongside d.c.f. evaluations the shorter term effects on revenue account.' More emphasis was therefore put on profit contribution, and on the use of a crude rate of return on net outlay for smaller projects with a quick pay-off. For larger projects, risk was to be evaluated in more depth, using the computer program PRAM.* It is scarcely surprising that when the Select Committee on Nationalised Industries reported in December 1973 it noted that the Department of Environment considered British Rail's methods to be 'highly developed'.[26]

By this time, of course, some of the rules of the game had changed. The more difficult economic conditions facing the U.K. had caused government policy to shift from encouraging pricing at marginal cost to using price controls in the public sector as a means to damp inflationary pressure. This, together with a decline in economic performance in the nationalised industries generally, had led the Select Committee to reconvene, although its immediate concern was Post Office investment in telephone equipment. But it was another five years and another White Paper, that on *The Nationalised Industries* of 1978, before the government moved away from reliance upon the test discount rate as the sole basis for investment evaluation and control. After the Treasury had admitted that it had 'not fully lived up to expectations', it was supplemented by a 'required rate of return' of 5 per cent in real terms, a return thought to be comparable with that which the resources might earn elsewhere in the economy and therefore intended to represent the opportunity cost of capital.[27]

III

The effects of the government's closer involvement in railway investment planning are extremely difficult to measure with any precision. Even broad influences were a matter of argument. Howls of public protest must be set against smirks of internal satisfaction. On the railway side, there were long-running complaints about the shortage of investment resources and periodic cash crises, and their prejudicial effect upon the attempt to establish a modern railway. As in the past, it was also alleged that the investment actually achieved – the 'out-turn' – was adversely affected both

*Project Risk Analysis Method.

by the delay in firming up annual figures for the investment 'ceiling', a decision not usually made until July or August in the preceding year, and by subsequent adjustments to investment allocations. One railway manager spoke for many when he observed in 1972 that 'the level of investment in railways has been constantly manipulated, mostly downwards but sometimes upwards at short notice, as part of government's strategic planning for the economy'.[28] On the government side, the suspicion that investment projects were being put up by B.R.B. with at best a thin justification was slow to die, despite the obvious progress made in the area of investment appraisal. There were regular requests for 'back-checks' on earlier projects, to see whether reality squared with forecasted benefits. The Ministry also contended that the responsibility for 'under-shooting' the investment targets set rested firmly on the shoulders of railway management. It was regarded as a persistent feature which owed more to problems of construction, raw materials and manpower than to the vicissitudes of macro-economic management.[29]

Close government monitoring was certainly a fact of life for all the nationalised industries after 1960, and there was little to be gained from complaining stridently about it. Raymond, in fact, in his evidence to the Select Committee in April 1967, admitted that 'we have one of the best machines for dealing with investment as between a nationalised industry and a sponsoring department that exists', and considered that good relations had existed for the past three years. In February 1973, Michael Bosworth, the Deputy-Chairman, and J. E. H. Skerrett, Chief Officer (New Works), told the Committee much the same thing. Referring specifically to a Department undertaking to process major projects within 28 days, Bosworth said that 'normally the situation has worked quite well over the last three or four years'. Skerrett's view of the vetting procedure was that the questions asked by the Department were 'sensible and sound . . . we have never yet not come to an agreement'.[30]

These comments, which suggested that all was sweetness and light, did not prevent the railway witnesses complaining about the effects of inter-ference at a detailed level. Raymond made much of the disagreement with the Ministry over a major scheme of 1966 to provide 2,500 air-conditioned coaches over ten years, and the episode was documented at length in the Select Committee's proceedings. The Ministry, in response to a first proposal of July 1964, had deferred a decision in October until it received evidence that the Board could compete effectively with other forms of transport. It then took the Board 18 months to produce a revised submission based on a survey of the major Inter-City services. By this time, the Ministry had been reinforced by Barbara Castle, and Christopher Foster and his team of economists, who challenged the market assumptions underlying this major project, estimated to cost £12–14 million for a three-year build. After much argument about 'market research' and 'optimum coach life', the Ministry approved a truncated programme of 400 coaches for 1967–8, stating that they were 'somewhat in the dark about the real financial effect of the proposed investment', and insisting that the Board carried out market research to support the 1969 programme. The episode produced another Raymond–Castle row. At a stormy meeting in August 1966, Castle and C. P. Scott-Malden, an Under-Secretary at the Ministry, accused the Board of failing to provide information requested a year earlier and of not being 'organised to provide the answers required'. Raymond noted that the point at issue was that the Board's answers were not acceptable.[31] There were similar difficulties with the proposal to build 600 coaches, most with air-conditioning, in 1969. As Scott-Malden reminded Bosworth in March 1969, when Marsh's approval was confirmed, 'the most troublesome question was the assessment of the earning power of the new stock, particularly as compared with the refurbished stock . . . We should have been happier if the validity of the conclusions drawn from the market research, and the factors fed into your quantified financial assessments, could have been more convincingly demonstrated.'[32] The nub of the matter was financial justification. As James expressed it, 'if passenger services are to be kept in being as a matter of policy, rolling stock replacement obligations must be accepted even if they cannot individually be justified in normal financial terms'. There was, for instance, a clash between Raymond and Foster over the possible consequence for Southern Region passengers of the railways not being able to provide specific financial justification for the renewal of coaching stock which was 25, 30 or even 35 years old, life-expired and becoming dangerous.[33]

Such cases were undoubtedly exceptions to the rule. In general, projects got through the vetting process without difficulty, as they did in other nationalised industries. Gomersall, Chief Officer (New Works), explained the position in a note of March 1969. He looked back on the previous five years with satisfaction. The relationship with the Ministry might appear to be unduly submissive, he remarked, but it was

based on the philosophy that one accepts the rules of the game as laid down but plays the game better than the Ministry. It is not a popular philosophy, but it has the merit of working very well in our interests. In the last five years over 300 projects have been put to the Ministry and all have been approved. Despite the frustration and irritation that occasionally occurs, most projects are cleared reasonably quickly and in a trouble-free way. The only real difficulty we have is when the projects are of indifferent quality, such as the loco-hauled coaching stock project, or where they are in some way caught up with national politics. The method also has the advantage that it is not necessary for us to give to the Ministry any information other than that strictly necessary to prove the project . . . The Ministry have never been happy with this arrangement as, to quote their own words, they regard the investment provisions in the Act as 'the only door' through which they can see the Board at work and influence its policies and decisions. Evidence given in the recent Select Committee by Ministry officials and economists shows a much greater frustration in St. Christopher House than at '222'.[34]

Gomersall went on to argue that the government's enthusiasm for corporate planning was far from being a disinterested concern with improving management techniques in nationalised industry but was seen as a means of obtaining more information on the Board's operations. There was something in this view. The changes of 1970 meant that the Board was exchanging the risk of interference in individual projects, which had hitherto been limited, for the prospect of more informed interference by the Department in the broader, strategic objectives of the business. If the microscope was being lifted, then a searchlight was being put in its place.

Two elements support Gomersall's contention that the Board did not go out of its way to supply the Ministry with all the information it might have done. The first was the Board's reluctance to include d.c.f. calculations as specified in the internal investment manuals from 1965. At the Select Committee of 1967–8 the Ministry officials complained about the lack of financial information in many cases. Of the 57 proposals submitted in 1966, for example, only ten came with d.c.f., and another three were only added after pressure from the Ministry. This was not simply a case of bloody-mindedness, but an argument about the applicability of the technique. There was strong support within railway management, particularly at regional level, for the view that since essential renewals had no logical alternative, a d.c.f. exercise was rather futile. Occasionally, the absence of such calculations caused the Board problems. The lack of detailed support for its National Signalling Plan undoubtedly contributed to its poor reception at the Ministry. On the whole, most of the large projects were supported by d.c.f. A parliamentary answer by Marsh in November 1968 revealed that of 29 major projects submitted in January 1967–September 1968, with an estimated cost of £138 million, d.c.f. information was given for 13, costing £104 million. Nevertheless, the Ministry remained unhappy with the Board's undertaking that it was providing d.c.f. in all cases considered to be 'appropriate', since the two parties disagreed about the appropriate circumstances. The problem persisted in the 1970s.[35] The second cause of tension was the Board's failure to supply the Ministry with regular back-checks on the results of earlier investments. At the regular joint meetings, Ministry officials made repeated requests for such information, but these fell on deaf ears. There was a quite natural reluctance on the part of British Rail representatives to give information which might jeopardise existing submissions. However, the problem ran deeper than this. The regions were not keen to carry out the work, even for internal purposes. Back-checking was a time-consuming and complex task which was made even more difficult by the frequent changes in investment appraisal and the 'indivisibility of railway operations'. It appears that specialist teams were created in the regions, but they achieved very little, and were soon diverted to new project work. Checking required the participation of those people who had been involved in the original appraisals, but they gave it a low priority. There was a strong feeling in British Rail that 'practical difficulties ruled it out in most cases'.[36]

Were there skeletons in the cupboard? There may have been some. It is quite clear that some projects were very sloppily presented, particularly before the late 1960s, and failed to achieve forecasted returns. A back-check carried out by the H.Q. Audit Department in 1968 on the Derby Technical Centre Project (cost: £1.1 million) of 1965 revealed an 'inadequacy of basic information', and an 'almost complete lack of proper working papers'. Mistakes were due in large measure to the haste with which the proposal was advanced. Running costs were underestimated, staff savings were over-estimated and rents from released buildings failed to materialise. The estimated annual savings were given in 1965 as £128,500 (this failed to allow for depreciation, and should have been £111,500). In fact, the savings given in the 1968 budget were only £19,500. The construction of a new hotel at St Andrews, opened in June 1968, was equally disappointing. The authorised outlay of £700,000 was exceeded by 20 per cent, and the results for the third year of operation, 1970, revealed a loss of £60,000 instead of the forecasted profit of £123,500 submitted to the Ministry.[37]

Following the Select Committee's report and the circulation of a Treasury paper on 'Post-Audit of Investment Decisions' of December 1968, the Ministry of Transport, along with other Departments, made a concerted effort to get more information. In February 1969 the Board took part in discussions with government officials, although it was formally minuted that 'care would be taken ... to discourage any excessive investigation from outside on the subject'.[38] By this time the Board was 'seriously in arrears' in responding to a request for information on specific cases, made in March 1966. Only four back-checks, from a list of over 30, had been supplied by August 1969, when the Board was asked to report on another 12 cases, making 41 in all. In January 1970, an attempt was made to reduce the number of outstanding cases, and to give only outline information.[39] In September 1970 the Investment Committee agreed to institute a new form of project control based on the concept of a project manager who would incorporate checking into the overall process of project management, using completion certificates. This, it was considered, pre-empted the need for back-checks on the old basis, and in October the Department was asked to 'wipe the slate clean'. It agreed to this request, provided that the Board completed checks on three of the outstanding cases. Only one of these was a railway project, the Glasgow–Gourock/Wemyss Bay electrification. A report was sent to the Department in November 1971.[40] Very little had been allowed to percolate through to the Department, and the new control system produced no tangible results before 1974. The Serpell report of 1983 suggests that the same elements – lack of back-checks, concern over project appraisal – persisted.[41]

The Board may have experienced comparatively little difficulty in advancing and justifying its investment projects, but it certainly felt the pinch of government policy in relation to its overall investment ceilings. A summary of a very complex situation is given for 1963–73 in Appendix F.* British Rail was entirely dependent on the Exchequer for direct borrowings and for the financing of deficits when they arose. Most, if not all, of its investment was directly or indirectly funded by the government. The industry was thus vulnerable both to the government's 'fine-tuning' measures in the economy, and to responses to economic crises such as the devaluation crisis of 1967. The tendency of British Rail to undershoot its investment targets continued. The frequent adjustments to government ceilings, while not the whole story, did affect the out-turn. In most years there was some kind of intervention. In June 1964, for example, Beeching was asked to reduce calls on the building industry, and he promised to cut his 1965 budget by about £3–4 million.[42] Any hopes that the change of government and Labour's preparation of a National Plan would encourage Departments to 'stand by forward investment estimates to a greater extent than had been necessary in the past' were soon dashed. The Plan, published in September 1965, referred to railway investment levels of £135 million per annum for 1966–8. However, in the previous month, Callaghan, the Chancellor, asked Raymond to respond to the worsening balance of payments position by postponing building starts and running down stocks. Raymond's riposte was that the railways had been pared to the bone by dependence in large measure on their own resources, direct borrowing from the government having been limited in 1963–5. Nevertheless, he offered to defer renewals, station improvements and other works amounting to £1.5 million in the short term and, if considered necessary, expenditure amounting to £8 million in the following year,

*The position was complicated by new capital accounting rules in 1970, the appearance of investment grants of various kinds and the separation of investment in London and the South-east.

1966. A £6-million reduction in the ceiling was agreed. The Board's submissions for 1966–8 were well down on the forecasts in the National Plan.[43]

In July 1966 the government imposed a £10-million cut for 1967 which had a considerable effect in postponing investment in stations, hotels and ships. Projects were chosen which interfered 'least with the development of the basic continuing railway', according to a parliamentary written answer, but it is clear that the timing of freightliner investment was disrupted.[44] The devaluation of sterling in the following year was accompanied by cuts of £5 million in 1968 and £18.5 million in 1969. One of the most tangible results was the postponement of the extension of the West Coast electrification from Weaver Junction to Glasgow.[45] The British Rail submission was also considerably reduced in 1970, from £90 to £75.5 million. Projects affected included the extension of C.W.R., wagon construction and spending in the Southern Region. For the first time, however, attempts were made to compensate for under-shooting. The Investment Committee agreed to add £5 million to the 1969 budget, and £7 (later £10) million to the 1970 budget. In the latter year, the out-turn exceeded the ceiling for the first time in the Board's experience.[46] From 1969 more fundamental cash-flow problems were beginning to constrain investment possibilities in the new climate established by the Transport Act of 1968. The Board had found very little of its investment in 1963–8 from direct borrowings, £65 million out of a total of about £575 million in current prices. The rest had come from depreciation provisions paid for by government support of the deficit, and by sales of property and displaced assets. The writing-down of the Board's capital debt was no panacea. As the Report for 1968 warned, B.R.B. was left with 'a physical system requiring further substantial investment and possessing no financial reserves available for this purpose'.[47] In 1968 James and Gomersall stressed that the Board could generate only about £50 million a year from its own resources, and suggested that investment should in future be nearer £70 million than £100 million. If money was to be borrowed, it should be spent only on schemes which would be profitable. The cash available from asset disposal was expected to decline with the stabilisation of railway operations. The new concern led to the new investment regulations and criteria of October 1968 mentioned above.[48]

Management faced a very real dilemma in trying to determine how much the railways could afford to invest. When the Railway Management Group met in August 1969 to discuss 'The Task Ahead', it observed that

one of the difficulties would be to decide between the two conflicting pressures – to limit capital expenditure in order to protect the short-term revenue situation, or, alternatively, to adopt a higher rate of investment, so putting the short-term revenue situation at risk, in order to ensure the modernisation of the system, and, as a result, the provision of an improved and more attractive standard of service in the future.

There was certainly no shortage of projects. In planning for 1970, for example, the Investment Committee reduced bids from the regions totalling £116 million to £90 million. The eventual ceiling of £75.5 million was thus only about two-thirds of desired investment.[49] The early 1970s saw many changes to the rules. Infrastructure grants, grants for the elimination of surplus track and signalling equipment, employment grants and leasing – all complicated the picture. In addition, the publication of the Board's first corporate plans was followed by a separation in the government's allocations of investment in London and the South East and investment in the commercial railway outside London (plus ancillary businesses), which applied from the year 1972. One thing is clear. The Board continued to express its frustration with investment cuts, and pressed for upward adjustments. It also continued to add to budgets to compensate for undershooting.[50] However, the Board's attempt to introduce a particularly advantageous method of leasing assets was frustrated by government intervention. Based on advice given by the bankers Morgan Grenfell, it involved the establishment in 1971 of Railway Finance Ltd, a consortium of profitable private companies such as Barclays, A.E.I. and Williams & Glyn's. A eurodollar loan was raised by B.R.E.L., and used to enable the new company to purchase rolling stock required by B.R.B. This was then leased to the Board on favourable terms. The consortium were able to use investment allowances to offset their tax liabilities, and 90 per cent of the sums saved were passed to B.R.B. Not only was this a way of circumventing investment 'ceilings', it was also an important addition to cash flow. Naturally, the Inland Revenue and the Treasury were concerned about this 'commercial' activity by a nationalised industry, and fearing an escalation they asked the Board to terminate its arrangements with Railway Finance Ltd in 1973. The loophole was then closed.[51]

One of the main difficulties was the gulf between realistic expectation and optimistic forecasting. This came out clearly from the preparation of the First Corporate Plan and its main constituent, the Rail Plan, in 1970. In September the Railway Management Group reached the gloomy conclusion that there would be a rail deficit of £8 million in 1975 and felt that investment would have to be limited to the cash flow that could be generated. However, the Corporate Plan persisted with projections which erred on the optimistic side. The correspondence shows that the Department of the Environment were sceptical about the figures, and this influenced their approach to railway submissions. It should not be supposed, however, that railway management erred badly in this respect. As has been observed by one of the participants, the annual round of submission and the setting of a ceiling, now linked to corporate planning, was something of a game in which the bidding party always over-estimated its needs in the knowledge that some cuts would come. And no one, not least the Treasury, would have accepted gloomy prognostications based on high real wage gains, industrial recession or the collapse of British Rail's main freight base – coal, iron and steel. As James noted in 1972:

> there were periodic complaints from Ministry and Treasury officials that Railway forecasts were always too optimistic. This is probably true, but here the fault does not lie wholly on our side. Advance estimates for Treasury budgeting purposes that forecast out-of-line wage increases or traffic recessions would not have had much chance of being accepted. Nor was much enthusiasm shown for forecasts of 'between £Xm. and £Ym.' ... [Estimates in the J.S.G. exercise and the First Corporate Plan] could not, politically, allow for wage increases of the order experienced in recent years, nor could they assume a deep and long-lasting industrial depression.[52]

How successful, then, was railway investment to 1973? The answer depends as much on a socio-economic judgement as on a business assessment, on how large 'The Necessary Railway' was to be. Investment levels were too low to renew the run-down parts of the system, to replace worn-out D.M.U.s and wagons. Increasingly, the concentration was on the more profitable elements of the business, although renewals merely to 'keep trading' continued to consume large portions of the annual budget. The experience of railway investment managers was demonstrated in microcosm in 1973. The year began full of optimism, following an instruction to *accelerate* investment in order to reduce unemployment. It ended in gloom, with the swingeing cut in future investment complained of by Richard Marsh. The licence given to the industry in 1955–60 was not to be repeated. British Rail had to live with the realities of government inspection, and the scepticism of officials who suspected that much railway investment would not realise commercial returns.

The meagre information we have on the actual returns to investment bear this out. In 1969, the Board justified the extension of the West Coast electrification to Glasgow on the basis of a discounted rate of return of 15 per cent and a net present value, discounted at 10 per cent, of £11.9 million. Asked by Marsh to include a back-check on the first stage, electrification from Euston to Birmingham/Liverpool/Manchester, John-son provided what he called a 'provisional report'. This made gloomy reading. While passenger revenue had increased more rapidly than fore-cast in 1959, freight traffic, and particularly coal traffic, had proved disappointing. The results for 1967/8 showed net revenue of £17.1

million, or £12.9 million at 1959 prices. Not only was this lower than the forecast for 1970 of £31.8 million, but it was lower than the actual net revenue in 1959 of £13.8 million. There was a long way to go before this premier investment could claim to have produced a commercial return.[53] Back-checks for other projects provide similar results.[54] The government, working through the 1962 and 1968 Acts, wanted a commercial railway. It also wanted a railway of a given size. Much of the investment put up by British Rail to maintain this was unlikely to pass commercial criteria. For the Board this meant a long struggle with the government for investment resources and a series of disputes about the best way to measure the effectiveness of railway investment. The situation has continued into the 1980s.

IV

Wages costs, that most important element of railway costs, were caught up in the aftermath of the Guillebaud 'comparability' award of 1960, discussed in Chapter 7, then influenced by the attempt to relate pay increases to productivity growth, a policy which emerged in earnest in Wilson's Labour Governments of 1964–70. Whether the issue was 'comparability' or 'productivity', railway pay and associated problems in industrial relations were inevitably enmeshed, like railway pricing, in the prices and incomes policies which operated with varying degrees of rigour throughout the period.

The progress of railwaymen's pay, expressed in terms of average weekly earnings, is difficult to assess from the published data. The annual accounts, for example, give staff census figures only for 1966–70. And their presentation makes them difficult to use: the staff numbers, for example, refer to the total employed in each grade but the average earnings quoted for each grade relate only to those railwaymen who worked a full week or more. The average earnings data quoted in Tables 63 and 64 were derived from unpublished census books. Table 63 indicates that the average weekly earnings of railwaymen outpaced inflation throughout the period, real earnings increasing by 4.5 per cent per annum, 1962–73. The Beeching years, 1962–6, saw a higher than average advance, 5.4 per cent. It came in the wake of the Guillebaud award and was influenced by the Board's acceptance that railway pay was, in relation to recruitment, uncomfortably low. The census data also show that the main grades of staff shared more or less equally in the general advance (Table 64). Precise comparisons are hindered by frequent changes in the grade structure and by the application of successive stages of pay and productivity agreements. With this reservation, however, it is evident that much the same rate of

Table 63. *Average weekly earnings of British Railways staff (adult males) and index of retail prices, 1962–73*

Year	Average earnings (£)	Index (1962 = 100)	Retail price index (1962 = 100)	Index of average real earnings
(1953)	8.94	58.8	76.6	76.8
1962	15.20	100.0	100.0	100.0
1963	—	—	102.0	—
1964	—	—	105.3	—
1965	(19.45)[a]	(128.0)[a]	110.3	(116.0)[a]
1966	21.50	141.4	114.7	123.3
1967	22.48	147.9	117.5	125.9
1968	22.92	150.8	123.0	122.6
1969	25.74	169.3	129.7	130.5
1970	29.79	196.0	138.0	142.0
1971	33.46	220.1	151.0	145.8
1972	38.04	250.3	161.7	154.8
1973	43.38	285.4	176.6	161.6
Annual growth rates				
1953–62	6.1%		3.0%	3.0%
1962–6	9.0%		3.5%	5.4%
1966–70	8.5%		4.7%	3.6%
1970–3	13.4%		8.6%	4.5%
1962–73	10.0%		5.3%	4.5%

[a] Estimate.

Note: figures refer to adult males working a *full week*. There was no full census in 1963–5. Source: B.R.B., Annual Staff Census, B.R.B. I.R. Cassette 5001 Pts. 1 and 2. Retail price index from A.A.S., 1975.

growth in earnings was enjoyed by all the main groups. Salaried staff fared a little worse than average in the 1960s, trainmen and workshop staff a little worse overall, but there is nothing here to indicate that existing differentials were significantly disturbed.

It is perhaps ironic that railwaymen should have made their greatest real gains in the Beeching years, when cost-consciousness was high. In practice, as already noted, the cost-cutting policy of the 1960s was aimed at what were later admitted to be easy targets – excising the worst traffics, slimming down the workshops and changing over to non-steam motive power – and therefore the pressure to effect productivity increases by actions other than simply allowing the staff to run down was limited. Furthermore, Beeching and his colleagues had considerable sympathy for the relatively low pay of railwaymen in general. For some years after Guillebaud, then, both sides were prepared to play the 'comparability'

Table 64. *Average weekly earnings of conciliation, CONGOT, trainmen, workshop and salaried staff (adult males), 1962–73*

Year	Conciliation (£)	CONGOT[a] (£)	Trainmen (£)	Workshop (£)	Salaried (£)	All (£)
1962	14.85	14.44	16.20	14.90	16.85	15.20
1966	21.20	20.45	23.60	21.00	22.85	21.50
1968	22.45	21.91	24.30	22.40	24.60	22.92
1970	29.32	28.58	31.31	28.59	32.22	29.74
1973	42.45	41.83	44.29	41.27	48.27	43.38
Annual growth rates						
1962–6	9.3%	9.1%	9.9%	9.0%	7.9%	9.0%
1962–73	10.0%	10.1%	9.6%	9.7%	10.0%	10.0%

[a] CONGOT: conciliation grades other than trainmen.
Source: as in Table 63.

game. The 1960s also saw a continuation of the traditional, railway approach to industrial relations. Though Beeching's arrival and the introduction of 'new blood' into the management team did much to transform attitudes, industrial relations remained largely unreformed. Negotiations were organised through a rather old-fashioned, non-specialist team, led by A. R. Dunbar as the functionally responsible Board member, and C. S. McLeod, the Chief Industrial Relations Officer. Both men were former traffic apprentices who had worked their way up through the operating departments.[55] The complex, multi-layered negotiating machinery of R.S.J.C., R.S.N.C. and R.S.N.T., with its formal, legalistic atmosphere (see Chapter 7) continued to dominate contacts between management and the unions. The British Transport Joint Consultative Committee, a joint body through which informal contacts had been established, was regarded by both sides as a fairly harmless 'talking shop'.

Nor was there much change in the unions. Sidney Greene continued to lead the N.U.R., acting as General Secretary until succeeded by Sidney Weighell in 1975. W. J. Evans, General Secretary of A.S.L.E.F. from 1960, retired in 1963. He was followed by Albert Griffiths, who served until his death in February 1970. At the T.S.S.A., William Webber (General Secretary, 1953–63) was replaced by J. G. Bothwell (1963–8). The leadership remained predominantly right-wing in character. There was more variety at Executive Committee level, and it was not always easy for the leaders to control the left-wing. Within A.S.L.E.F., the Executive Committee, dubbed by Bowick 'the Arkwright Road Apaches', contained a strong Communist support, and there were tied votes on several key issues, which were resolved only by the casting vote of the President.[56] Nevertheless, the more conservative influences within the railway unions generally held sway. These influences supported the contention that the Guillebaud award of 1960 had been a real victory and that 'comparability' had to be kept in the forefront of pay bargaining until the maximum advantage had been extracted.

The pay awards of 1963 and 1964 were quite generous. The unions had submitted their claims, in October 1963: for 10 per cent (A.S.L.E.F.); for 'Guillebaud comparability' (T.S.S.A.); and for a 'substantial increase' (N.U.R.). The Guillebaud argument was emphasised in the negotiations. As Greene explained to the R.S.J.C., 'I want to say again that this claim is being based on the principle laid down by the Guillebaud inquiry and we are prepared to stand by that evidence.' The Board accepted the comparability framework but used different arithmetic to arrive at an offer of 6 per cent for 'conciliation grades' and 3 per cent for salaried staff. This was accepted by N.U.R. and A.S.L.E.F., but the T.S.S.A. took its claim, now defined as 4.6 per cent, to the R.S.N.T., which eventually awarded it 3.75 per cent, an extra 0.75 per cent.[57] Everything was settled by 14 February 1964. This remarkable speed was due to the fact that the Board agreed to take the short cut of replying at a higher level to a claim put before the R.S.J.C. According to McLeod, who provides an outline of railway industrial relations in his book, *All Change*, 'the Board felt that an increase was justified because the railwaymen had fallen behind in the general industrial rise in wages, and appreciated the fact that the unions had exercised patience by waiting nearly a year since the previous settlement.' Even so, the 6 per cent settlement failed to eliminate the gap between railway pay and the median pay of the 12 industries listed in Appendix 9 of the Guillebaud report, which had been 13.5 per cent according to N.U.R. calculations.[58]

After only four months, in April 1964, the unions presented a further set of claims. When these were heard before the R.S.N.C. in November, Beeching accepted that there was a gap between railway wages and pay for comparable occupations. In offering increases of 4, 5 and 6 per cent for clerical, supervisory and 'conciliation' staff respectively, from December 1964, he expressed the hope that the offer would convince the unions that the Board intended to 'narrow the gap as soon as we can'. The unions rejected the offer, however, and at the R.S.N.T. hearing the issue of 'Guillebaud comparability' dominated their case. It was argued, for example, that the deviation from the Appendix 9 median had again reached 13 per cent for 'conciliation grades'. The Board responded in familiar vein by emphasising its inability to pay given its financial deficit and declaring in favour of productivity-related agreements. But although it rejected median calculations as a meaningful basis for fixing wage rates, it allowed itself to be drawn into an argument over the figures when it suggested that the real deviation from the Appendix 9 median was not 13 per cent but 9.4 per cent.[59] The R.S.N.T., in its award of 21 December 1964, endorsed the Board's offers to the clerical and supervisory staffs but recommended a much higher increase of 9 per cent for the 'conciliation grades', adding another £6 million to the £15.5 million increase in costs represented by the Board's original offers. The award was accompanied by a rather empty appeal to both sides for improved productivity in the railway industry. The two main unions reluctantly accepted the award, while the T.S.S.A. pressed for a further review of salaries, but without success.[60]

Almost immediately, the climate changed. Five days before the R.S.N.T.'s award, the Labour Government had signed the joint 'Declaration of Intent' on prices and incomes with the employers and the T.U.C., which thrust productivity into the forefront of future pay bargaining. The Board, which had relied hitherto on cost-cutting and workshops rationalisation instead of a serious assault on existing working practices, and had made only a modest start with work study, was now forced to consider the pay-productivity issue more seriously. Two separate initiatives proceeded in tandem. First, the need for improved productivity was introduced more directly in the pay talks of 1965–6, with the active encouragement of the government. Second, an attempt was made in 1965 to extract higher productivity from the A.S.L.E.F.-dominated trainmen. Both moves were significant in terms of the long-run implications for the agenda of railway pay bargaining, but the tangible results were very disappointing indeed.

In May 1965, both the N.U.R. and A.S.L.E.F. submitted claims for another 'substantial' pay increase, and repeated earlier demands for a two-hour reduction in the working week, together with the promise of improvements in holiday pay and pensions. The response of the Board, now led by Raymond, was not only conditioned by the government's overall strategy on pay, which involved a recommended 'norm' of 3–3½ per cent, but was also affected in detail by the active participation of interested Ministers. So when Raymond met George Brown and Tom Fraser in June, it was agreed that the unions should be offered a package deal: '3½ per cent this autumn, with a further increase at about the same level in the autumn of 1966, and the introduction of a 40-hour week which would be deferred as late as possible – perhaps until March 1966.' Raymond also convinced the Ministers that, in the event of a breakdown, the dispute would be steered towards the P.I.B. rather than the railway arbitration machinery, since the unions had achieved too much at the recent Tribunals. The parties agreed that the negotiations would require delicate handling, and it was decided that they would keep 'in the closest touch throughout'.[61]

In August 1965 the Board offered the unions a staged programme of improvement – a 40-hour week for 'conciliation grades' and a 38-hour week for salaried staffs, both operative from April 1966, a 3 per cent increase in October 1965 and a further 3 per cent increase in October 1966, plus improvements in holidays and pensions. The offer was met by considerable union resistance, particularly from the N.U.R., who told the Board on 7 October that it would remit its claims to the R.S.N.T. Raymond then discussed the problem with Fraser. He emphasised that arbitration would produce an unsatisfactory result from B.R.B.'s point of view, since

> arbitrators did not have to take prices and productivity into account; they were only bound to ensure that claims before them were just on the basis of comparability. If the claim went to arbitration, therefore, it was likely to give an increase greater than the amount which the government thought suitable without compensating benefits in e.g. productivity.

The government would therefore need to act quickly and propose a reference to the P.I.B. with a wide remit.[62] Brown and Fraser responded on 15 October by persuading the unions to accept a reference to the P.I.B. in return for an immediate 3½ per cent increase. The unions appear to have reacted favourably to the suggestion, with only token resistance being shown by A.S.L.E.F. In fact, Brown oiled the wheels by emphasising that a P.I.B. reference was in the unions' best interest. He is reported as saying:

> If you go to the Tribunal it will be a shooting match for everyone . . . I would like you . . . to submit this case to the Prices and Incomes Board . . . If you are prepared to do that, I am prepared to implement the present package deal which Management have offered as soon as possible. I am also prepared to say that if you are not satisfied you can still go to the Tribunal.

The unions took this to mean that their claims would be justified by productivity already delivered.[63]

The Board was pleased with the outcome, since it promised to shift the argument from comparability to the more promising area of productivity. As Bagwell has observed, the very nature of the P.I.B. remit – 'to examine the issues in dispute in the light of the considerations set out in the White Paper on Prices and Incomes Policy (Cmnd. 2639), in particular paragraph 15' – was crucial, since paragraph 15 emphasised that the most important precondition of granting improvements in pay was to make a 'direct contribution towards increasing productivity'.[64] More specifically, it soon emerged that Aubrey Jones, the Chairman of the P.I.B., was not unsympathetic to the Board's position. At a preliminary informal meeting with Raymond he showed himself opposed in principle to the continued use of comparability and was willing to make himself available to Raymond at regular intervals in order to exchange views. Unfortunately, it proved far easier to make noises about productivity increase than to formulate specific proposals. The Board's case to the P.I.B., which was contained in 28 formal papers on all aspects of the rail business, was primarily directed towards a justification of the offer that had been made, and there was correspondingly little on how the railways could escape from the 'Guillebaud trap'. As Raymond admitted when pressed by Aubrey Jones for a solution, 'it was easier to reject suggestions than to make them'.[65]

The overall strategy which the Board wished to pursue was, in fact, outlined clearly during the P.I.B. investigation. The railways' financial position made it imperative that in future emphasis should be placed on productivity-generated increments to pay. Here, the Board drew an important distinction between 'soft' productivity based on staff economies and 'hard' productivity created by changes in working practices. The Board's view was that in the past too much attention had been given to the former. In paper 27, a summary of its case, it contended that in the railway industry, where the labour content of working costs was high, economies from improved productivity came largely from staff reductions, 'but the capacity of the remaining staff to contribute to savings by increased effort' was relatively small. In future, attention would be given to the development and exploitation of new equipment and techniques, and to the rewarding of workers according to their participation in these processes. More rapid progress was needed in exploiting the freightliner and container technology, implementing single-manning for night-time operation, removing the guard from freight trains, introducing greater versatility of employment in grades where work was seasonal and extending work study in the workshops. As Raymond confessed to Aubrey Jones, 'the time had come for some shock treatment which would force the Railway Unions to realise that unless there was more rapid acceptance of change and the consequence of change the industry would go on declining at an accelerating rate'.[66]

What lay behind these fine words was less certain. Dunbar, the Board's member for industrial relations, gave an impression of complacency to the P.I.B. investigating committee when he informed it that 'there is no great group of restrictive practices which mean anything. They are not very numerous' and conceded that 'we have not been prevented on any large scale from doing what we wanted to do on our investment programme except on Liner trains. The three unions have co-operated well'.[67] Raymond was embarrassed by the fact that the railways had been slow to bring forth positive ideas. As he told the General Managers in February 1966,

one of my difficulties had been that although I am enjoined all round to ensure that we get a productivity or efficiency quid pro quo, when we come to list and quantify what we want to do – other than Liner Trains and single manning, which we have known of for a long time – the catalogue is not very impressive. Indeed, this is the criticism that I am now encountering in government circles.[68]

A further source of embarrassment was the Board's failure to discredit the unions' case. The most persuasive document was the N.U.R.'s evidence to the P.I.B., which was published as *National Union of Railwaymen and the P.I.B.* in January 1966. Here, the call for a return to Guillebaud comparability was given added strength by its revelation that British Rail had flirted with Guillebaud in every settlement since 1960. The union was also able to show that whatever the Board was now arguing about the need for real productivity, it had in the past frequently congratulated the unions on their co-operative attitude to the intensification of work.[69]

What, then, emerged from the P.I.B. inquiry? Its report was published as a White Paper, *Pay and Conditions of Service of British Railways Staff*, in January 1966. It attacked the emphasis on comparability and it went on to conclude that it was 'desirable for the railways and their workers to move away from a system of wage determination that relies exclusively on bringing up to date selected parts of the detailed comparisons with outside industries in the Pay Inquiry Report [Guillebaud]'. The P.I.B.'s own comparative studies of earnings led to the conclusion that 'conciliation' and workshops grades had kept pace with industrial earnings generally between 1960 and 1965 and therefore no further adjustment was necessary. On the other hand, it found that the earnings of clerical staff had fallen behind those of their counterparts elsewhere – this had been a factor in the degree of militancy shown by T.S.S.A. in 1963–5 – and suggested that an award of 5 per cent from 1 January 1966 was merited, instead of the 3½ per cent offered by the Board.[70] The main thrust of the report was that a 'New Approach to Earnings on the Railways' was required. To enable the industry to exhibit a 'more effective financial discipline', both management and unions should strive to transform working practices, particularly by ensuring 'a more flexible, and thus more economic, use of manpower and a reduction in overtime'. Rewards to groups of workers contributing to this process would be directed by new joint Pay and Productivity Councils, one for workshops staff and one for other railwaymen, which would combine the responsibilities of the existing R.S.N.C. and Railway Shopmen's National Council and the British Railways Joint Productivity Council. A first programme was to be tabled by October 1966.[71]

The response of both sides to these recommendations was predictable. While Raymond welcomed 'an important Report by a responsible and independent body', Greene, for the N.U.R., rejected it and called for a strike to begin on 14 February 1966. The union was furious about the rejection of Guillebaud and felt that its claims were more than justified by productivity improvements already delivered.[72] The move set off a hectic round of tripartite meetings, involving B.R.B., the rail unions and Ministers, with the latter calling most of the shots. The participation, not to say interference, of government in the industrial relations of the railway industry reached another high point, as it usually did when a strike was in the offing. Thus, after discussions between the Board and the Minister of Transport (now Barbara Castle) on 19 January, and between the Board and Castle, Ray Gunter (the Minister of Labour and former T.S.S.A. President) and George Brown, on 24 January, Raymond was simply handed a set of instructions which had been drawn up by Brown, Callaghan (Chancellor of the Exchequer), Gunter and Castle at a meeting of Ministers on 31 January. These authorised Raymond to reopen negotiations provided the strike threat were removed. In that event,

he would have Ministerial authority:
  (i) to offer a 40 hour week one month sooner, i.e. from 1st March 1966;
  (ii) to offer one additional day's holiday for men with more than 10 years' service;
  (iii) in the *last* resort, and only if Mr Raymond judged that this additional offer would turn the scales, he could offer to bring forward by one month, but by no more, the operative date of the 3½ per cent pay increase.

Raymond was also informed that a settlement on these terms 'must be accompanied by the unions' agreement to hold early talks on the productivity and pay proposals in the [P.I.B.] Report, including the specific suggestions made in the Report'.[73]

The events culminating in Harold Wilson's meeting with union leaders at No. 10, Downing Street on 11 February are well known. The N.U.R. refused to withdraw its strike threat, and on 4 February rejected Raymond's improved offer which deployed (i) and (ii) of the government's instructions. George Brown had no more success when he brought (iii) into play, and offered to pay the 3½ per cent increase from 1 September. Finally, the unions gave way after a long meeting with the Prime Minister and his colleagues. The N.U.R. accepted the existing offer by the narrow majority of 13–10 and on Harold Wilson's promise personally to inaugurate an investigation into the pay structure. An underlying loyalty to the Labour Party appears to have swung the vote in favour of acceptance but it is clear that Wilson and Castle were forced to employ all their political skills. According to Castle, the 'Commies' on the N.U.R. Executive Committee were only countered after she had promised a new deal for the railway industry.[74] No immediate changes in working practices were agreed with the settlement. Instead, there began an exhaustive series of further investigations which eventually culminated in the Penzance and Windsor Pay and Productivity Agreements of 1968 (see below, pp. 552–5). Specific moves to improve productivity in pay rounds were thus delayed for another two years.

At the same time, the issue of train manning and footplate bonuses also ran its course, again with rather disappointing results. The background to the problem lay, first, in the limited nature of the 1957 Manning Agreement, which had sought to reduce the manning of locomotives as the shift from steam to diesel and electric motive power made the fireman redundant (see Chapter 7); and, second, in attempts by British Rail to introduce a national freight train incentive scheme for footplate staff and guards.

In the early 1960s, when British Rail made determined efforts to extend the scope of work study and other bonus schemes, it was agreed with A.S.L.E.F. that local experimental bonus schemes for footplate staff would be introduced in certain problem areas, such as Birmingham, where staff shortages had inhibited freight movements. From 1961 an incentive scheme based on punctuality was successfully applied in the Birmingham area, but attempts by the London Midland and Western Regions to extend it met with resistance from the unions, who feared redundancy. A.S.L.E.F. had insisted from the start that productivity payments should be made to all footplate staff on a national basis, and a claim to this effect was presented to the R.S.J.C., with N.U.R. support, in August 1964. When the Board rejected this demand, a lengthy bargaining period ensued. Unofficial action by drivers from the South Eastern Division of the Southern Region on 10–20 November helped to take the claim to the next stage, the R.S.N.C., where it was agreed, in December, that a joint sub-committee should examine both bonus payments and associated productivity measures.[75]

The existing additional payments to footplate staff were many and varied, thus hindering moves to introduce productivity-related changes. In December 1964, for example, about half of the 54,000 footplate staff were receiving some form of bonus payment. There were 25,000 men in receipt of mileage bonuses for 'short' (65–139 miles) and 'long' (140 miles and over) distances. A further 1,300 men were being paid bonuses generated either by work study (300) or by the experimental Birmingham freight scheme (1,000). About 2,300 men were paid in accordance with pre-war incentive schemes for short-distance freight operation in the north-east of England and eastern Scotland.[76] After an examination of the position by a British Rail working party, it was concluded that it would take too long to extend work study, while the incentive schemes of the Birmingham type would yield insufficient savings. The answer was to press for a relaxation of the 1957 Manning Agreement, which permitted single-manning in only a limited set of circumstances. Four specific modifications were required: to the limitation on the aggregate mileage of scheduled train running; manning during night hours (12 midnight to 6 a.m.); the duration of rostered turns; and the duration of physical needs breaks. In return the working party recommended the introduction of special improved redundancy arrangements and either enhanced mileage payments or a specific single-manning allowance. Savings of at least £6 million were envisaged.[77]

During the course of the Board's negotiations with the two unions, it became clear that although Griffiths and his fellow A.S.L.E.F. negotiators may have been amenable to the idea of relaxing the 1957 Agreement, theirs were not the only voices in A.S.L.E.F. A considerable body of grass-roots opinion was antithetical to the Board's proposals. A particular bone of contention among Southern Region men was that they had done more than most to concede single-manning but the prevalence of short hauls effectively excluded them from mileage payments. More generally, there was resentment at the way differentials were being upset by work study schemes being applied elsewhere in the industry. So while informal discussions between British Rail and A.S.L.E.F. in December 1964 suggested that the union would be fairly co-operative over the proposed relaxation of the 1957 Agreement, the theatre of negotiations in the R.S.N.C. joint sub-committee involved a union demand for payments without negotiations on manning.[78] In May 1965 the Board offered the two unions an improved package in which enhanced mileage payments and a protective redundancy clause ('The Board are prepared to introduce arrangements which will provide for Footplate staff surplus to requirements at a depot as a result of the introduction of the [new] arrangements ... remaining at their depot until absorbed into permanent posts ...') were offered in return for the abandonment of double-manning at night and an increase in the length of the rostered turn from eight to eight and a half hours. The proposed new mileage payments included payments to drivers travelling less than 65 miles.[79]

The position in A.S.L.E.F. was very delicate indeed. With the Executive Committee equally divided over the Board's offer, Les Kirk, the President, used his casting vote in favour, but when the offer was put to the Annual Assembly of Delegates in June 1965, it was rejected. Led by the left-wingers Ronksley and Milligan, the delegates pressed for incentive payments without the strings of manning changes. Griffiths then enlisted British Rail's aid in an attempt to reverse the resolution, urging the Board to drop its plan for longer rosters and improve the financial quid pro quo. However, he lost control again when drivers from the South Eastern Division of Southern Region began a 'go-slow' on 7 July in protest at the lack of progress.[80] This unofficial action lasted for three weeks, causing considerable disruption in the London commuter area. After the intervention of Gunter, A.S.L.E.F. agreed to recall its Assembly of Delegates, and on 11 August this body reversed its earlier decision and backed the Executive Committee's proposal to resume negotiations, albeit on rather restrictive conditions.[81] After further talks in the R.S.N.C. sub-committee, the negotiations foundered on the issue of night manning. The unions were prepared to concede a one-hour relaxation for D.M.U. and E.M.U. operations, but the Board rejected this as insufficient. It had calculated that single-manning at night would contribute £1.8 million or 17 per cent of total expected savings, and therefore informed A.S.L.E.F. that a reduced scale of mileage payments would operate if single-manning at night were not agreed.[82] This impasse, which was accompanied by the threat of further unofficial action on the Southern Region, led Gunter first to threaten and then to impose a Court of Inquiry. On 9 September 1965 the Court was duly appointed, under the Chairmanship of A. J. 'Jack' Scamp, a director of G.E.C. Scamp was a personnel manager with an impressive record at Plessey and Massey-Ferguson behind him. In 1964 he had been appointed to the Industrial Arbitration Board, and in February 1965 had been seconded to George Brown's Department of Economic Affairs as Industrial Adviser.[83]

Raymond was aware of the potential difficulties posed by a Court of Inquiry which was to investigate productivity-related payments for only one section of railway staff. Publicity might be useful in demonstrating the crucial importance of improving productivity in the industry but the issue had to be handled very carefully, since 'so many other sections of staff not yet in receipt of bonus or other additional payments will be watching the results'.[84] In the end, Raymond's worst fears were realised in a disappointing settlement which not only produced very little in the way of footplate savings but spilled over into the question of bonuses for guards.

The Court of Inquiry was certainly not slanted in the unions' favour. For example, the terms of reference, agreed with Raymond – 'to inquire into the issues arising in the negotiations for increasing the productivity of footplate staff and for the payment of a related bonus' – effectively ignored A.S.L.E.F.'s argument that its members had already done enough to merit extra payments. But the Scamp report, completed on 22 September, was scarcely a victory for the Board. Recognising that the issue of night manning was the main stumbling block, the Court offered a sensible compromise. While it supported the Board, it recognised that there were

Table 65. *Estimate of net annual savings attributable to single manning, 1965–9 (£m.)*

Year	Annual saving	Cumulative saving
1965	−2.4	−2.4
1966	−0.9	−3.3
1967	+0.3	−3.0
1968	+1.1	−1.9
1969	+1.5	−0.4

Source: B.R.B., Memo. on 'Manning Agreement 1965', 6 March 1967, L. F. Neal Papers, R.S.C./I.R. Box 281, Folder marked 'Scamp 13/4/1967', B.R.B.

strong union objections, and recommended that while the existing restrictions should remain in force, single-manning should be phased in over 'the next year or two at most'. On the question of rewards, the Court found against the Board. Referring to the Board's rather candid assessment of its final, reduced offer as 'a compromise, a poor one, a bit illogical and a bit unjustified by any standards', it argued that British Rail had underestimated the likely savings from relaxation of the 1957 Agreement. It concluded that the Board should have settled for something nearer their original, more generous offer, even though restrictions on single-manning at night were to remain.[85] The two sides accepted the findings of the Scamp report as the basis of a new Manning Agreement signed on 28 October 1965. This extended single-manning by lifting mileage limitations and other restrictions, but single-manning at night did not come until Stage I of the Pay and Efficiency Agreements in 1968.[86]

Almost immediately, the Board realised that the new Agreement would not produce the intended savings. Indeed, the break-even point, when cost savings exceeded the extra bonus payments, was probably not reached until 1969, as Table 65 shows. The Board erred in believing that the displaced firemen, protected by the no-redundancy guarantee, would soon be absorbed. In fact, increasing redundancies among drivers caused by factors other than single-manning ensured a large surplus of second-men, 1,630 in May 1967.[87] To try to solve this problem British Rail offered, first, special severance payments in September 1967, and then a package of measures, including lump sum inducements, from the end of 1968. The visible proof of this failure of the 1965 Agreement caused considerable disquiet inside the organisation in the course of 1967–8. It prompted Margetts to put the blame on Beeching, who had apparently sanctioned the offending redundancy clause himself, one of his last actions as Chairman.[88]

The 1965 Agreement also left unanswered the question of a national bonus scheme for freight train crews. Scamp had recommended that the parties should press ahead with negotiations for a scheme, but internally the Board struggled to finalise a satisfactory set of proposals. An outline offer was put to the unions in May 1966, but was first caught up in the prices and incomes freeze, then blocked after criticism from the Management Committee in August. A.S.L.E.F. became increasingly impatient with the delay and, after putting their case directly to Harold Wilson, threatened a work-to-rule and overtime ban from mid-January 1967. Dunbar's view was that A.S.L.E.F.'s militancy stemmed from rivalry with the N.U.R., which made it necessary for them to secure an industrial relations victory, but it is also clear that there was genuine impatience with the lack of progress and a determination to secure a wider protection against redundancy. Eventually, the issue of redundancy was referred to Scamp who, in a judgement of 12 January 1967, supported the unions in declaring that the protection against redundancy offered to footplate staff in the 1965 Agreement should henceforth apply to any staff covered by an incentive scheme.[89] The Board argued that not only would the cost of the freight incentive scheme outweigh the savings, but that it would also trigger off claims elsewhere. It did not help its case, however, by using some inept and muddled arguments during the subsequent negotiations.[90] With the government, in the shape of Wilson and Gunter, eager for a settlement, the Board agreed to introduce six pilot schemes from mid-1967. Further extensions were arranged on a depot-by-depot basis until the scheme was included in the Pay and Efficiency settlements from 1968. There was little here on which the Board could congratulate itself.[91]

The issue of mileage payments to guards was another problem to arise from the 1965 Manning Agreement. The guards had won the right to such payments after the R.S.N.T. Decision of May 1964, and by Decision No. 38 in June 1965 had obtained payments on terms marginally better than those currently paid to firemen (second-men). The Manning Agreement then restored the differentials in favour of the firemen, but this merely prompted the N.U.R. to press, from December 1965, for a restoration of the guards' position, where it was argued that the new manning arrangements had given this group additional responsibilities. Another delicate situation was thereby created. The Board was anxious to avoid the failures of the 1965 Agreement and reach a settlement which would secure an unambiguous return in terms of higher productivity. The N.U.R., on the other hand, claimed that this had already been delivered. Negotiations dragged on throughout 1966 and 1967, punctuated by threats of industrial action. A ban on second-man duties in April 1967 led to the establishment of a joint working party, but no agreement was reached.

The atmosphere became tense, and rank and file pressure induced the N.U.R. to break off negotiations. On 11 September a further ban on second-man duties began, accompanied over the next fortnight by instances of unofficial action by N.U.R. members. Gunter then intervened and established another Court of Inquiry, under Prof. Donald Robertson, an economist from Glasgow University. Robertson criticised the Board for having 'gravely miscalculated' in its over-generous treatment of the drivers in 1965. But did the guards merit the same treatment? Robertson thought not. His findings were not accepted by the N.U.R. and for a time labour relations were very strained indeed, with the Board threatening to suspend the guaranteed week. Eventually, serious talks were resumed which culminated in an agreement granting more generous mileage payments to guards in return for productivity concessions, including the abolition of brake-vans on fully-fitted freight trains. Even so, the Board estimated that it was 'giving away' about 90 per cent of the overall savings in the form of higher bonuses.[92]

The matter did not end there, however. In the familiar leap-frogging pattern of union activity observed in several disputes since nationalisation, A.S.L.E.F., which had not been brought into the negotiations with the N.U.R., now declared that its members would not work trains in which the guard was to travel in the rear cab of the locomotive. Scamp was called in for a third time to adjudicate, and this time he ruled in favour of the Board, in November 1967.[93] The union was not deterred, however, and a ban on rest-day working and a work-to-rule began on 4 December. Gunter, who had called the dispute 'the silliest of the decade', threw his weight behind the Board, and the influence of the T.U.C. was also brought into play. Eventually, after another long session at No. 10 on 5–6 December – though without beer and sandwiches, according to Wilson – the drivers agreed to return to normal working.[94] The 1965 Manning Agreement may have achieved some savings eventually but the costs, both direct and indirect, were far from small. Furthermore, double-manning did not disappear. In 1971, for example, 70 per cent of programmed rosters for passenger trains hauled by locomotive were double-manned; and for all trains, including D.M.U. and E.M.U. operations, the figure was 28 per cent. In 1984 the percentage was about 17.[95] The slow removal of a practice which clearly added to operating costs cannot be attributed merely to union intransigence and inter-union rivalry, real though these elements were. Some significant barriers to single-manning had been the result of poor management decisions, including the persistence with steam heating which necessitated the presence of a second-man, and a number of operating practices, such as the use of pilot engines, which were within the control of management to reduce or eliminate. A report on train-crew productivity in 1971 concluded that a great many of the opportunities for cost-reductions *within the terms of the existing agreements* had not been realised.[96]

V

Another industrial relations/productivity problem surrounded the Board's introduction of the new freightliner technology from the mid-1960s. Here again, the early results were disappointing, but the reasons were more complex than those surrounding train-manning, going beyond mere managerial shortcomings or resistance from the rail unions. There were more ingredients in the pot, and volatile ones at that – the reactions of the road haulage industry and the road transport workers' unions to the use of freightliner terminals, and the attitude of the Minister of Transport and the Labour Government to the question of rail-road freight transfers. A brief summary of events must suffice.

When the 'Liner Train' concept was being developed during the Beeching years, the Board's policy from the start was that the terminals should be open to *all* road transport operators, whether British Rail, British Road Services, road haulage firms or 'C' licence operators. Beeching emphasised this in a letter to Sidney Greene of the N.U.R. in February 1964, indicating that union assurances on this point were a condition of further capital investment in the project. The union's reply in May was that it was not prepared to concede access to the private road hauliers, which would threaten railway staff with possible redundancies, an attitude which 'gravely disappointed' Beeching.[97]

Unfortunately, the issue was allowed to drift on unresolved. As McLeod has observed, 'discussions . . . over the next four years resembled a long series of rugby scrums at Murrayfield on a wet November afternoon'.[98] Early in 1965 the Minister of Transport, Fraser, declared his firm support for the Board's case that to restrict access to the terminals would jeopardise freightliner viability and spark off a rate war with the road haulage industry. This had no impact on the N.U.R., however, which not only reiterated its opposition to the private hauliers but insisted that the new freightliner trains be worked with brake-van and guard.[99] The government continued to take much of the initiative in the negotiations, with Fraser making a statement in the Commons on 28 April 1965 that capital expenditure for the new services had been authorised on the basis of open terminals. But the issue was not resolved and the emphasis in Board–union talks shifted to the question of redundancies. Once again, the Board offered very generous safeguards in an attempt to win union support. In August 1965 Raymond promised that guards would travel in accommodation separate from the locomotive, and pledged that any staff made redundant by freightliner services would be able to stay at their home depot without loss of earnings as long as that depot remained open. Unfortunately, no agreement was reached, and the Board was forced to proceed on the basis of using freightliners for rail-only traffic, hoping to extend the facilities to 'C' licensees and the private road hauliers in stages.[100]

The first freightliner service, from London to Glasgow, began on this limited basis in November 1965, and in the following year Manchester and Liverpool were included in the network. The slow growth of freightliner traffic was not merely a question of restricted access to the terminals. The first series of flat wagons required a number of modifications, and traffic growth was also hindered by a shortage of containers. As late as February 1967 the supply of containers represented only two-thirds of requirements.[101] At the same time, the new technology attracted a good commercial response, and the Board was heartened when the road haulage unions, led by the T.G.W.U., agreed to allow British Road Services access to the London–Glasgow service on an experimental basis. Against this optimistic background, the Board made a further submission to the Ministry for capital investment of £12 million in October 1966, hoping to resolve the open-terminals question by further negotiations with the unions.[102] The Minister, now Barbara Castle, was not impressed by the Board's submission, which lacked a d.c.f. assessment, but she agreed to authorise it. Her decision was not given publicity because she accepted the Board's view that the N.U.R. were more likely to accept open-terminals if the issue were 'played down'. While further negotiations with the unions proceeded, the government began a concerted campaign designed to win the co-operation of the N.U.R. Castle met the union's Executive Committee in May 1966, and in July addressed its Annual Conference. She had been encouraged by Greene to believe that persuasion would succeed. In her recently published diaries she reports Greene as having said 'he would consider how I could best help him to persuade his Executive. Personally, if he were Raymond he would go ahead and risk a strike: he didn't think much would come of it.'[103] In fact, the union proved much more difficult to shift, and Castle, like Fraser, was forced to resort to threats. Wilson joined in when he reiterated the government's determination that the new services should go ahead on the basis of open terminals.[104]

By early 1967 the freightliner problem was becoming acute. On the railway side, there was an urgent need to counter aggrieved road operators who, having been excluded from the freightliner grid, were threatening to contest the railways' right to a cartage fleet sufficient to satisfy their own services. At the same time, Castle was complaining of pressure from the road transport lobby, both inside and outside the House of Commons.[105] On the other side, genuine opposition to open-terminals inside the N.U.R. must not be underestimated. When Castle tried to force the issue by appealing directly to union members in their newspaper, the *Railway Review*, it aroused a spirited response from rank and file activists. One of them wrote:

I ... welcome the freightliner service ... but in existing circumstances its full technical and financial benefits are not going to accrue to the public sector. The provision of the low-cost long-haul element to the private road haulier will give him a larger marginal profit with which to undercut existing public road service rates, and free access to our terminals gives him the right-of-way for consolidating the private road sector with a view to further inroads should a Tory government be returned.[106]

The issue finally came to a head over the activities of Tartan Arrow, a small long-distance haulage firm specialising in London–Glasgow traffic. The firm had entered into an agreement with B.R.B. in 1965 to construct its own private terminals on railway land, with the idea of using rail for trunk haulage. Before anything was done, however, the Transport Holding Co. acquired a substantial stake in the business, with 50 per cent control. The move gave Tartan Arrow automatic access to British Rail's freightliner services, and the N.U.R., smelling a rat, expressed immediate opposition to its plans to operate company trains as from February 1967. A period of hard bargaining then followed, involving the Board, the Ministry, the N.U.R. and the Transport Holding Co. In the process, Sir Reginald Wilson, Chairman of the latter, decided to buy up Tartan Arrow completely, and this was widely regarded as a move to outmanoeuvre the union.[107] The N.U.R. Executive Committee was far from unanimous in its opposition to open-terminals, but the talks were nearly wrecked when someone leaked the news that British Rail had also been negotiating a private liner-train deal with the Transport Development Group, one of the largest private haulage companies.[108] Union opposition only disappeared after Castle had offered to give railwaymen equal job opportunities in Tartan Arrow, and arranged for British Rail to take a 50 per cent stake in the firm. But the main concession was another generous employment guarantee from the Board. The final agreement with the N.U.R., signed on 7 June 1967, not only gave a guarantee against dismissal for terminals and cartage staff displaced by the transfer of traffic to liner trains, but promised that men held surplus to requirements would have their earnings maintained on the basis of an eight-week representative period.[109] The agreement, together with the T.G.W.U.'s decision to allow British Road Services full access to freightliners, seemed to have resolved the problem, but trouble flared up again briefly over the new international freight terminal at Stratford, in east London. The terminal, designed to replace three existing sites, was planned around 'self-contained enclaves' to be leased to the major forwarding agents. Railway staff would handle only a small proportion of the traffic, that consigned and received direct by the customer. The fate of the 35 men to be displaced by the new arrangements was taken up by fellow workers in London when the terminal was opened on 19 June. Sympathetic strike action spread to 26 terminals employing 5,000 men, and the action was declared official on 22 June. For Greene, the dispute was a simple one: 'You don't open a new coal mine and then ask the distributors to go down and hack out the coal.' The Board had to resort to concessions to win the support of the N.U.R. The 35 jobs were guaranteed, and the matter was resolved after a positive vote at the union's A.G.M. in July.[110]

McLeod's bland conclusion on the open-terminals dispute – 'Thus the long drawn-out affair came to an end to the advantage of all concerned: management, staff and customers' – makes light of the costs of concessions. Even the General Managers expressed their concern at the guarantees given in the Agreement of June 1967, with Ibbotson complaining to McLeod that the safeguards would prejudice the strategy of cutting staff costs.[111] Of course, a more uncompromising stand by the Board from the start might have back-fired, thus delaying the introduction of the new services. But once again, it seems that the anxiety of the Board to reach a settlement, produced an agreement on redundancies which ate into the economic returns generated.

VI

There is a fair measure of agreement among British Rail managers that the appointment in January 1967 of Leonard Neal, to replace Dunbar as the Board member responsible for industrial relations, heralded a new era in the railways' labour relations, marking the beginning of major initiatives to link pay advances to improvements in productivity. What is less certain, however, is the extent of the savings which accrued from the Agreements inspired by Neal, and in particular the Pay and Efficiency Agreements, Stage I, of August 1968, and Stage II, of August and September 1969.

In order to assess the position we need to go back to the Board's bargaining with the unions on pay from 1966. It will be recalled that on 11 February 1966 a strike threatened by the N.U.R. had been averted after a promise by the government that there would be another inquiry into the railways' pay structure. A month later Harold Wilson, with Brown, Gunter and Castle in attendance, suggested the future agenda: 'a fresh look at the basis on which the pay of railwaymen was settled'; an examination of 'how far it was possible to link pay and efficiency together to a greater extent than in the past'; and 'a new look at the present negotiating and consultative machinery'. This was followed by a meeting on 10 May, chaired by Gunter, which established a wide-ranging joint inquiry into railway pay. Some 50 meetings were held under the auspices of the Ministry of Labour between May 1966 and September 1967, supported by the detailed investigations of joint working parties.[112]

The new inquiry gave additional impetus to a drive for more productivity which had begun in earnest with the P.I.B. inquiry. It was recognised by most Board members and senior managers that recent progress in this area had been unsatisfactory. Productivity had grown largely through injections of capital, it was argued, and although staff numbers had fallen sharply, by 28 per cent, 1962–6, total labour costs had changed very little.[113] Raymond was determined to avoid the piecemeal approach of his predecessors, in which 'crisis management' had characterised much of the discussions with the unions, but the disappointing initial response of the General Managers in February 1966 to his plea for suggestions did little to inspire confidence. Furthermore, it was clear that the existing wage structure would not provide sufficient leverage to shift staff productivity. The Board had developed incentive schemes for skilled grades, though with mixed results, but 80 per cent of the 'conciliation grades' were still outside the scope of work measurement.[114]

The debate within British Rail then began to change. There was a much greater acceptance of the need for a major overhaul of the existing pay and grade structure. The Industrial Relations Department began a detailed investigation under McLeod. The message was clearly getting through. The General Managers' Conference, now anxious to make a positive response, gave the process of policy-formulation a jolt, when in March 1966 they established their own committee of inquiry on the pay structure under the chairmanship of David Bowick, Assistant General Manager of the London Midland Region. Johnson and Dean were particularly keen on the idea of formulating general principles quickly. The Managers' response to the Industrial Relations Department in setting up their own inquiry was a rare example of scant regard for the bureaucratic hierarchy of decision-making in British Rail.[115] Bowick's committee produced an interim report in June 1966, and this was influential in establishing an agenda for change. The report recognised that the nature of railway work was changing. It was increasingly being organised in larger, concentrated sites, akin to factories, which were connected by the major routes. In these locations, the committee contended, there was considerable scope for a more intensive use of labour. A new pay structure should take account of this reality and extract the maximum amount of versatility from the staff while at the same time maximising the utilisation of equipment. The committee recommended a skill-based pay structure with six groupings, with rewards allocated after job evaluation. The strategy bore some resemblance to the work study initiatives of the early 1960s, but there was now a clearer recognition of the need to increase real productivity throughout British Rail.[116] The Industrial Relations Department fully shared these sentiments. A balance-sheet terminology began to dominate the policy documents. There were frequent references to the key issue of balancing the expense of assimilating the existing grades by cost savings from greater efficiency. It was also recognised that it would be necessary to establish new or modified institutions to give expression to the new policy. Borrowing from the P.I.B.'s findings, the Board moved towards the concept of a 'parliament' to deal with pay and productivity. One idea current in 1966 was to convert the R.S.N.T. into a Railway Council which would, *inter alia*, organise a staged programme of pay and productivity measures.[117]

Of course, it was one thing to formulate policy and quite another to implement it successfully. The lesson of the 1950s and 1960s was that railway management had to work with, not against, the unions. The need for a new approach emerged during the somewhat ponderous joint talks presided over by the Ministry of Labour in 1966–7. Both the Industrial Relations Department and the Bowick committee had warned that the trade unions would simply view a new pay structure as an assimilation exercise bringing free gifts for a number of existing grades. Greene certainly appeared to see it this way, when he emphasised that the problem was one of low pay, which could be resolved by merging the three lowest-paid grades into one. A.S.L.E.F., on the other hand, posed a different problem. Griffiths maintained throughout the joint talks that the attendance of his union should not be taken to imply that it wanted any change at all in the existing structure as it affected footplate staff.[118] To get through this thicket of difficulties would clearly require from British Rail management a far higher degree of competence in industrial relations than had been displayed in the past.

The necessary competence was supplied in large measure by Leonard Neal. He had the support of an enthusiastic disciple in David Bowick, who was seconded to the Industrial Relations Department and then succeeded McLeod as Chief Industrial Relations Officer in March 1968. Neal quite simply breathed fresh air into the staleness of railway bargaining. He was first and foremost a brilliant negotiator, with experience of both sides of industry. Leaving school at the age of 14, he became a meat porter at Smithfield, where he soon became actively involved in the process of unionisation. He was elected Secretary of a new Smithfield branch of the

T.G.W.U., and later rose to the position of National Officer with the union. After studying industrial relations as a mature student at the London School of Economics he won an adult scholarship to Trinity College, Cambridge, where in 1955, at the age of 42, he graduated with an upper-second-class degree in economics. Disappointed with the response of his union to his belated educational achievements, Neal joined Esso Petroleum. Here, as Employee Relations Manager at the Fawley Refinery he was closely involved in the productivity agreements signed by Esso and the T.G.W.U. in 1960–2, which broke new ground in British industrial relations.[119] He had just been appointed to a labour relations post with Esso (Europe) when he attracted the attention of the headhunters for nationalised industry. Neal was not the first or even the second choice for a post which both Raymond and Castle accepted was vital to the new strategy for the railways. As Raymond put it in July 1966, 'he has no experience at senior management level in a large organisation. He also lacks Boardroom experience and all that goes with it.' But they agreed that Neal had proved himself both as a trade union official and as a modern industrial relations manager. He was also content to specialise in this facet of management, leaving others to handle staff matters such as management development, education and welfare. So when Neal was appointed in January 1967, Dunbar continued to act as chairman of the Management Staff Committee until his retirement at the end of the year.[120]

Neal arrived at a time when the joint talks were in danger of breaking up with little achieved, and when the atmosphere of pay freeze and restraint was beginning to erode trade union support for the Labour Government's strategy. Furthermore, the various specific issues already mentioned – surplus firemen, freight train crew bonuses, payments to guards – had still to be settled. Neal's response was immediate. As at Fawley he favoured a rolling programme of pay and productivity change, which was the direction in which British Rail managers were already moving (Bowick's committee, for example, had examined the Fawley precedent). He gave the policy impetus by emphasising the need for collaboration, an approach which had proved so successful with the T.G.W.U. In stressing the need to work with the rail unions he helped to blow away some of the cobwebs of old-style railway negotiating, which was rooted in the master-and-servant, courtroom environment of the nineteenth century, characterised by the proceedings of the R.S.N.C. and R.S.N.T. Neal preferred to invite the union leaders into his confidence and to thrash out problems without reference to the existing arbitration machinery. During his five years with British Rail only one dispute was taken to the R.S.N.T.; and the R.S.N.C., the top in-house body, was convened only rarely to rubber stamp things which had been agreed informally. As one of his colleagues has recollected, we used to live with the trade unions . . . we'd have an inspection saloon out for a couple of days and we'd have members of the executive committee of that union and that union on it and we'd push off and we'd have a great piss up . . . a lot of understanding was created . . . at one o'clock in the morning you'd be saying to Bill Ronksley of A.S.L.E.F., 'Well, you understand why I want to bloody well do this, don't you Bill?' . . . it was very, very informal, but it paid off.[121]

Neal inherited and helped to develop a considerable measure of agreement on both sides about how to simplify the grade structure, but found it difficult to make progress on the issues of pay and the negotiating machinery. By the summer of 1967 it was agreed in the joint talks that workers in the lower groups should be merged into two grades – 'railman' and 'leading railman', an impressive piece of rationalisation which compressed 50 grades into two, and covered 77,000 staff, 60 per cent of the 'conciliation grades other than trainmen' (CONGOT).[122] Unfortunately, pay discussions made little headway and attempts to overhaul the existing negotiating machinery were resisted by the unions. The problem of pay threatened to jeopardise the progress of productivity talks masterminded by Neal. Within the unions, rank and file impatience at the lack of progress since February 1966 was building up, fuelled by the fact that the joint talks had been kept confidential and that the $3\frac{1}{2}$ per cent increase in pay agreed for September 1966 had been caught up in the pay freeze and was not paid until March 1967. In June and July the N.U.R. and A.S.L.E.F. decided to take straight pay claims (divorced from the productivity issue) through the existing machinery. Gunter told Neal that it was essential to achieve something within six months, the length of time he could hold the N.U.R. and retain the support of the T.U.C. This timetable proved to be too tight. Having failed to make progress at the R.S.J.C. and R.S.N.C. in August– November, the two unions informed the Board that they would proceed to arbitration at the R.S.N.T. stage. The Board maintained the stance that pay should be linked to the existing productivity talks, and after the manner of Esso's *Fawley Blue Book*, produced a booklet, *Pay and Efficiency* in November, which set out the broad objectives of the joint management–union discussions.[123] The threat of a reference of union claims to the R.S.N.T. induced the Board to act quickly. A set of comprehensive proposals was formulated in January 1968 and distributed in a booklet entitled *The Board's Offer* in February. The Board proposed to simplify the grade structure for CONGOT staff by establishing four 'versatility' grades – railman, leading railman, senior railman and chargeman (yard foreman) – and seven 'specialist' grades. Here the aim was to give staff a wide variety of duties, breaking down the barriers of demarcation in labour-intensive activities. Parallel changes were proposed for supervisory, clerical and workshop staff, and although trainmen were excluded, as a result of resistance from A.S.L.E.F. during the joint talks, provisional plans for footplate staff were outlined in the document, including the integration of duties of second-men and freight train guards. In return, higher rewards were offered, including a basic pay of £12.50 for railmen and £13.75 for leading railmen, in place of existing scales of £11.30–13.40. When the proposals were put to the unions on 23 February, their reactions were not enthusiastic. Johnson, the Chairman, was thus faced with the situation he had hoped to avoid: 'a conventional reference to the Tribunal with a significant risk of industrial trouble'.[124]

At the R.S.N.T. in May 1968, the unions once again stressed comparability and productivity gains already achieved, while the Board argued that pay and productivity talks were about to produce a constructive solution to the industry's problems. The Tribunal, in Decision No. 41 of 6 June, sat on the fence. Much of the report was an exhortation to both sides to conclude their long-standing deliberations, refrain from 'skirmishing for position' and 'adopt a more flexible attitude'. Clearly in two minds over the question of making an interim award, the Tribunal was persuaded to recommend a temporary supplement to low-paid railway workers (50p. a week to those paid £12.70 or less, 25p. to those paid £13.15–13.40), with the increase to be absorbed in any final award from the pay and productivity negotiations. In the R.S.N.T.'s view, an agreed timetable was essential, and in order to prod the two sides it warned that it would return to the claims before it in the latter part of 1968. The Board welcomed the report, seeing it as encouraging negotiations on its offer of February 1968, but the unions' response was negative. Both N.U.R. and A.S.L.E.F. began an official work-to-rule, as well as a ban on overtime and rest-day working, as from 24 and 25 June respectively. The action cost the Board £3 million, and disrupted commuter services on the Southern Region.[125]

The Board made several attempts to resolve the dispute. On 22 June Neal suggested that the timeworker's allowance of 3 per cent, to be paid to certain workers in the specialist grades under the February proposals, would be paid instead to all CONGOT grades not receiving bonus payments. After the unions rejected the idea, the Board offered to pay 3 per cent plus the interim payments to the low-paid recommended by the R.S.N.T. The offer was communicated to the N.U.R. on 1 July, the first day of its Annual Conference at Penzance. The following day, the conference rejected the proposals, but resolved to elect a negotiating body to meet the Board. Contrary to expectation, the Annual Conference proved to be no more moderate than the Executive Committee.[126] At this stage, the government intervened. Castle, now Secretary of State for Employment and Productivity, met Marsh, the Minister of Transport, and Johnson and Neal of British Rail on 3 July. It is clear that the group was divided into two hawks, Johnson and Marsh, and two doves, Castle and Neal. Johnson, backed by the General Managers, was prepared to suspend the guaranteed working week to force a showdown. Neal argued for moderation, and it was eventually agreed that he and his team should fly down to Penzance to meet the N.U.R. negotiators. Agreement was finally reached on 5 July in relation to CONGOT staff, and on the following day, a parallel agreement was signed with A.S.L.E.F. officials for the trainmen. It was a considerable triumph for Neal to pull agreements with both unions out of the bag.[127]

The price was not small, however, £5.6 million in a full year, and most of the newspapers regarded the Penzance agreements as a 'sell-out'. Criticism was also levelled at the government for allowing a settlement which breached the terms of its prices and incomes policy.[128] In fact, what had happened was that the negotiating strategy had been pushed from a concentration on rewards to the lower-paid railwaymen and those excluded from bonus schemes to higher pay for all. Thus, from 8 July 1968, the lower-paid received an additional 50p. a week, as recommended by the R.S.N.T., and all other staff received a flat 3 per cent increase, whether they were enjoying bonus schemes or not. The deal helped Greene to appease colleagues who did not share his emphasis on the plight of the lower-paid. The British Rail team, led by Neal and Bowick, derived considerable satisfaction from the outcome, despite its cost. The agreements exposed the fact that N.U.R. had agreed to redistribute the monies available for the interim settlement from the low-paid to all grades, and the team hoped that the low-paid would respond by pressing the union for an early introduction of the Pay and Efficiency proposals, which promised to raise their basic rates (the target date agreed at Penzance was 2 September 1968). Moreover, the unions had agreed to the freezing of bonus rates, which in the past had normally moved up with changes in basic rates. The stipulation that bonuses were to remain at existing levels was regarded as an important change of principle. Finally, the Penzance Agreements were a clear departure from the conventional wage bargains of the past, opening the door to the linking of pay and productivity.[129]

The first Pay and Efficiency Agreements were signed on 14 August 1968 for CONGOT staff, and on 29 August for trainmen. Here, there was a novel departure from the way in which industrial relations were normally conducted. Representatives of both the Board and the unions closeted themselves away in the Board's training college, New Lodge, Windsor, for two-and-a-half weeks of intensive discussions in order to thrash out the details of the first productivity deal. A typical feature of Neal's approach, it created anxiety in both the Board and the non-participating members of the unions' executive committees that they were no longer in control of events. The 'incarceration at Windsor' produced a committed group pledged to make headway. As one of the railway participants has recalled,

there was resistance from the Board. Johnson would ring up from time to time to talk to Neal and say, 'The Board wants to know what's bloody well going on down there. What are you committing us to, Len?' Fortunately the management side and the trade union side ignored their bosses and just got on with it . . . I felt my role in labour relations in the railways was something in between the trade union and the management and I didn't feel totally committed to the management.[130]

The CONGOT agreement eliminated many of the traditional lines of demarcation. No less than 170 job titles were concentrated in a simplified structure of 35 jobs with 10 rates of pay. The 'versatility' grades outlined in the proposals of February 1968 were introduced, and one grade of guard was to replace the passenger guard, goods guard and train ticket collector, and a new post of conductor guard was created for Inter-City services. The agreement also provided for flexible rostering, with the 40-hour week divided into four consecutive turns of 10 hours each. Three days' extra holiday for the long-service staff was to be accompanied by economies achieved through the grouping of rest days in a roster cycle. In return, the Board introduced a new pay structure which subsumed the Penzance Agreements. The four 'versatility' grades received new basic rates of £13, £14, £14.65 and £16. The increases ranged from 3-15 per cent, but the greatest gains were made at the bottom. Those on £11.30 and £11.70 received £13, increases of 15 and 11 per cent respectively. At the same time, the widening of the gap between bonus and non-bonus staff was halted. Bonus payments were frozen at the July 1968 levels. The agreement with the trainmen was not so radical, but it did resolve some of the long-standing problems. Single-manning at night was at last conceded by A.S.L.E.F., and moves to encourage the more effective employment of second-men protected against redundancy were made with a promotion scheme and transfer allowance. Bonus payments and mileage payments were frozen, but basic rates were increased by 4.9–8.0 per cent.[131]

The Penzance and Windsor Agreements were a watershed in railway industrial relations. In return for a pay award which increased earnings by an average of 4.6 per cent, the unions agreed to major concessions in productivity, and the comparability arguments fashionable since the Cameron (1955) and Guillebaud (1960) inquiries were silenced. Furthermore, the agreements provided for both a rolling programme of change in the future and for close monitoring of the financial results with the unions, so that savings would not evaporate. The monitoring machinery was established by Bowick and Geoffrey Wilson in September 1968, and inserted into the Board's budgetary reporting system. Bowick was asked to provide the Board with quarterly reports.[132] These permit an assessment of the first stage of the Pay and Efficiency programme. They show that savings did not accrue at the rate expected by the Board. The target figures, staff cuts of 13,930 with savings of £20.9 million, were circulated to the General Managers in early October 1968. In many areas, regional managements acted with commendable speed in implementing changes. However, the outcome appears to have been as follows. The total gross cost of the 1968 Agreements was £19.0 million. The net value of the targets agreed with the regions was finally set at £16.6 million, £4.3 million lower than the original target. The savings agreed up to 1 November 1969 amounted to only £9.9 million, and the expected savings by the spring of 1970 were put at £12.0 million, £4.6 million less than the target, and £7.0 million short of the break-even point. These figures, taken from Bowick's progress reports, conflict with Neal's recollection of events. He told Bagwell, for example, that 'we had spent £19 million in extra remuneration to employees and saved, in the same twelve months, £18 million'.[133] But if the savings were not as large as the Board sometimes liked to make out, they were nevertheless sizeable. The alternative to Pay and Efficiency Stage I, as Neal and Bowick were quick to emphasise, was a 5 per cent settlement with no strings, which would not have produced anything to offset the higher cost.

Stage II was concluded in August and September, 1969. Here, the results were rather disappointing. A major factor was the loss of enthusiasm on the part of the trade unions. The N.U.R., for example, was divided in its response. The signalmen, in particular, complained strongly that they had gained very little from Stage I, while the lower-paid grades were so surprised at the speed with which regional managements acted to implement it that the union was forced to withdraw its co-operation for a short time in September 1968.[134] But above all, the rail unions could see that the government's prices and incomes policy was failing. As Castle busied herself with the ultimately disastrous *In Place of Strife*, the White Paper of January 1969 which proposed strike-curbing legislation, the statutory ceiling of 3½ per cent for pay increases introduced in March 1968 for the period to the end of 1969 was being widely disregarded. Pay settlements, particularly in the private sector, were producing higher percentage gains with fewer strings. For example, Ford workers gained an 8–10 per cent increase in March 1969, and the British Overseas Airways Corporation pilots obtained 15 per cent in April. Even in the public sector, manual workers gained rises of 6–7 per cent from mid-1968 to the end of 1969. All this did nothing to encourage N.U.R. and A.S.L.E.F. to co-operate in Stage II as they had done in Stage I.[135] At the same time, the Board had two objectives to consider. It was important to retain the initiative of Stage I and prevent the unions making a general application for a percentage increase, but there were also advantages in spinning out the negotiations, and Bowick indicated that the Board's aim should be to establish an interval of at least 12 months between Stage I and Stage II. Serious talks began in December 1968, with the appointment of seven working parties. By July 1969, Bowick, now Executive Director (Personnel), was able to tell the Board that 40 specific areas for action had been isolated, including the introduction of 'spreadover turns' (i.e. rosters extending beyond eight hours). On the union side, the importance of improving pay for the staff who had received only 3 per cent in August 1968 was a priority. However, when the package of measures was passed to the General Managers for comment, their response was hostile. Considerable doubt was cast upon the real savings which would accrue.[136]

The scepticism of the General Managers was borne out by the settlement for CONGOT, footplate, clerical and workshops staff, which followed on from an eleven-day joint session at the British Rail training centre at Watford. The CONGOT agreement introduced further measures of versatility, including Do-It-Yourself procedures for basic maintenance work, and improved rostering by creating weekday 'spreadover turns'. The footplate agreement made further attempts to improve the utilisation of second-men. Both agreements gave a specific commitment to joint studies of subjects such as worker participation and the bonus system. By comparison, the new pay scales, applied from 4 August 1969, were much more concrete. CONGOT staff received increases of 5.0–5.4 per cent, with 7.5 per cent for senior railmen and 8.1–8.4 per cent for senior signalmen. There were rises of 4.9–5.3 per cent for the trainmen. In addition, several improvements in conditions were granted from 1 January 1970, relating to holidays, sick pay, the closed shop and 'established' or salaried status for the upper echelons of the wages staff.[137] The estimated annual gross cost of Stage II was put at £15 million, while the identified savings amounted to only £1.25–2.25 million. It is scarcely surprising that Bowick should concede that Stage II was merely a 'shadow' of Stage I.[138] The failure of Stage II was not merely a function of union resistance. By 1969 there was evidence of tension within British Rail, between those who like Neal and Bowick were busy developing a long-term strategy for labour costs, and managers such as Geoffrey Wilson and Thorpe, who were responsible for the railways' annual financial results. This can be seen in the discussions within the Railway Management Group in September 1969, after Stage II had been completed. On one side, Bowick argued that there was a case for giving labour more of the benefits flowing from capital investment and new technology. He wanted future projects to contain built-in estimates of staff savings to be set aside for this purpose. From the other side came the argument that the staff had already received far too much from earlier capital investment, and that the Stage II agreements would prejudice the short-run railway performance. The strength of the latter faction was important in inhibiting further developments on the Board's part.[139]

What, then, did Pay and Efficiency achieve? The results for 1967–9 showed that the strategy may have failed to pay for itself, but it demonstrated what management–union co-operation could achieve in eliminating job demarcation. The strategy was also successful if viewed in a broader context. Neal's submission to Johnson in November 1969 showed that retail prices had increased by 11.5 per cent in the period March 1967 to September 1969. Over the same period British Rail wages had increased by 12.0 per cent, but the national rate of increase had been 14.4 per cent. Moreover, the Stage II increases of about 5 per cent compared well with settlements for several groups in August–October 1969, to which no productivity conditions had been attached. They included the milkmen (8.3 per cent), busmen (5.6), government industrial workers (8.5), firemen (17.0) and electricity workers (10.0).[140]

VII

The productivity strategy developed by Neal and his team in 1967–9 was finally blown off course by events beyond B.R.B.'s control, specifically the reaction of the rail unions to the 'wages explosion' in the British economy in 1969–70. Rank and file railwaymen responded by initiating a series of unofficial actions, putting union leaders under pressure to deliver some kind of cash package. The clock was put back to the early 1960s when, in February 1970, the three rail unions demanded 'substantial' pay increases, with A.S.L.E.F. lodging a specific claim for 10 per cent. At the R.S.J.C. Ray Buckton, increasingly the voice of A.S.L.E.F. (he became General Secretary in June 1970), underlined the unions' predicament when he emphasised the difficulty his Executive Committee were having in 'holding the men'.[141] With the threat of widespread action imminent, the Board agreed to meet the unions at Watford on 17–18 March, and a settlement was concluded a week later. This granted an 8 per cent rise from 4 May and a further 3 per cent from 3 August. Neal defended the deal at the Railway Management Group with the argument that urgent and exceptional action had been needed to arrest a deteriorating situation created by external influences. He hoped to resume the rolling programme of productivity bargaining. This proved to be an unrealistic aim. Some advances were made, including the introduction of a minimum wage of £16, a rationalisation of drivers' mileage payments and an interim incentive scheme for signalmen. But negotiations with the unions to 1974 were dominated by the response to inflation and the pay settlements secured by other groups of workers.[142]

The 1970–1 pay round was accompanied by a greater volatility of prices and wages, mounting left-wing influence in the unions and a hardening of the attitudes of Heath's Conservative Government to industrial relations. Not surprisingly, the rail unions began to disengage themselves from the close contact with management which had characterised the Penzance and Windsor Agreements. By early 1971 they saw the 'rolling programme' as a way of securing the icing on the cake of unrelated pay increases. At grass-roots level, railwaymen were critical of the imbalance of the pay structure, which continued to favour bonus staff, and there were justifiable complaints that since 1967 a larger amount of overtime was required to maintain earnings. Above all, the 11 per cent increase of 1970 was widely regarded as meagre when set against much higher awards secured by other workers later in the year. Comparability returned to the centre of the stage.[143] Claims for further substantial increases – the N.U.R. asked for 25 per cent – were lodged in July–September 1970. After a leisurely process of negotiation, matters came to a head in March and April 1971, amidst considerable unrest in both the N.U.R. and A.S.L.E.F. (the latter worked to rule for a period in April). The eventual settlement was based on earnings rather than rates. It represented an increase of about 9 per cent, plus some consolidation of bonuses in the basic rates. The minimum earnings level was also raised by 14 per cent, from £16 to £18.25. Neal was able to derive some satisfaction from the settlement, which bore some of the marks of the former consensus. Both Greene and Buckton had been nervous of the government's reaction to high claims; there had even been an attempt to outflank the left-wing faction on A.S.L.E.F.'s Executive Committee.[144] Given the size of pay awards in 1971, the British Rail increases were reasonable. In addition, the first real steps had been taken to consolidate bonuses in the basic pay structure.[145]

The 1972 pay talks were conducted in a different and in many ways more hostile environment. First, Neal had gone. He resigned with effect from 31 October 1971 to take up the post of Chairman of the Commission on Industrial Relations, which was established in 1969 to encourage the improvement of collective bargaining following the recommendations of the Donovan Commission. It became a precursor of the present A.C.A.S. under the Conservatives' Industrial Relations Act of 1971. Neal's departure was perhaps unfortunate, but he had been bitterly opposed to the dilution of his functional command under the Board's new organisation of 1970 (see above, pp. 373–6), and in any case the industrial relations function was at the same time brought more firmly under the control of the corporate planners and their budgets. Neal was followed by H. L.

Farrimond, the Personnel Director of Dunlop, who proved rather less successful than his predecessor in handling the unions.[146] There were other changes, too. Johnson was succeeded as Chairman by Marsh, at a time when the government, armed by its Industrial Relations Act, began to take a more interventionist line with major industrial disputes. The contrast with the period 1967–70 was marked. At the time of the Penzance talks, Bowick phoned up his opposite number in the Ministry of Transport, to be told, 'do appreciate that you're steering between Scylla and Charybdis'. In 1972 instructions became much more precise, much to the annoyance of a Chairman who had played the same game for the other side.

Tension between the Board and the government was created immediately when the latter's strategy for 1971–2 was defined as a limit to pay rises of 7 per cent, moving down by steps to 5 per cent, with the promise of 'a continuous conversation throughout negotiations'.[147] This dismayed the Industrial Relations Department, which had found that the unions had a good case, both in terms of minimum wage rates and the movement of retail prices. In addition, the Board's efforts to curtail overtime in 1971 had left it vulnerable to comparability arguments when earnings were chosen as the basis for comparison. All this made a double-figure settlement seem inevitable. External events also fanned the flames in the early months of 1972. The miners' strike was followed by a major defeat for the government's policy of limiting public sector pay increases by the $n-1$ formula (see above, p. 484). The award by Lord Wilberforce of about 20 per cent was not only high. It encouraged A.S.L.E.F. drivers to believe that, like the miners, they were a 'special case' owing to responsibility, danger and skill, and the N.U.R. to believe that low-pay arguments applied equally to them.[148]

The Board's negotiations with the unions were conducted against a background of militancy and unofficial action, particularly in the London area. British Rail's starting offer of 8 per cent was raised to 11 per cent in March 1972, but this produced no response from the unions. Farrimond's early relations with Greene and Buckton were far from cordial.[149] When the unions called a work-to-rule from 15 April, the Secretary of State for Employment, Maurice Macmillan, was moved to intervene. His offer of arbitration was rejected on 13–14 April, but with industrial action imminent, Marsh persuaded the unions to accept an unofficial reference to an independent chairman. That chairman, Alex Jarratt, Managing Director of the International Publishing Corporation, suggested a 'compromise' award of 12 per cent, payable from 1 May 1972, and a minimum wage rate of £20, in place of the existing £17.20, payable from 1 January 1973. This was rejected by the unions, who wanted a settlement in the region of 14–16 per cent, with an immediate payment of the £20 minimum.[150]

Tempers became frayed when the union leaders were summoned to a meeting with Macmillan in the early hours of 17 April. The Minister's uncompromising response did much to undo the earlier progress made in railway industrial relations. After two days of industrial action, with widespread disruption to rail services, the government decided to make use of the legal sanctions contained in its Industrial Relations Act of August 1971. On 18 April Macmillan applied to the National Industrial Relations Court established by the Act for a three-week 'cooling-off' period. On the following day a 14-day period was ordered by the Court. The outcome merely demonstrated that the Act, like Labour's *In Place of Strife*, was ill-conceived. The cooling-off period did nothing to lower the temperature, and the resumed talks from 1 May 1972 soon broke down over the question of the starting-date for implementation of a settlement. By this time, the Board was coming round to the opinion that appeasement was the most appropriate strategy. Bowick, now the Chief Executive, pointed out that the cost of the outstanding difference – whether the award should be paid on 1 May or on 5 June – was lower than that of a prolonged 'Go-Slow'.[151] The government, however, stung by its defeat at the hands of the miners, demanded a hawkish response. Against the advice of Marsh and Farrimond, Macmillan applied to the Industrial Relations Court for a compulsory strike ballot. This turned out to be nothing short of a disaster for the government. The ballot, held on 29 May, following union protests about its legality (rejected by the Court of Appeal) and five more days of industrial action, produced an overwhelming vote in favour of the continuation of this action. The current Conservative myth that the rank and file were more moderate than their leaders was firmly nailed. Marsh continued to stand firm as directed when the unions used the ballot result to press for an improved offer. Eventually, after the unions had called for further industrial action from 13 June, the government decided to cave in, and Marsh was instructed to put more on the table. The Board agreed to the N.U.R.'s suggestion that lump sums be paid in lieu of back-dating the award to 1 May. A £20 minimum rate with minimum earnings of £20.50 was introduced. Pay-bill costs were increased by 13½ per cent.[152]

All this swept away much of the Neal consensus. British Rail had returned to the familiar world of industrial conflict, comparability and union rivalry. The government had oscillated wildly between stubborn resistance and instantaneous surrender, and Macmillan had brought to the dispute 'all the patience and persuasion of a Glasgow Rangers supporter meeting a Spanish policeman'.[153] Marsh became profoundly disillusioned with his job. In his autobiography he comments:

Ministers gave constant advice along the lines of, 'when you meet the unions, we suggest you say this, that and the other, and when they reply this way, you then say the following'. It was a Walter Mitty world and total nonsense because only people who have never been involved in complex union negotiations think you can write the script in advance . . . Over and over again we could have settled much more cheaply by settling more quickly but, at each stage, we were told that we must not settle quickly because the Government really were going to fight this one to the bitter end . . . The end result was an undignified collapse in the last few days.[154]

By 1973 railway industrial relations had deteriorated again. Government intervention continued with a statutory freeze in November 1972, followed by their own 'Stage II' which, in April 1973, limited pay rises to £1 a week plus 4 per cent of the previous year's pay-bill costs. The railwaymen's pay award in April 1973 was in line with this diktat, adding 8 per cent to British Rail's staff costs. The basic rate for railmen was raised to £21.80, the minimum earnings level to £22.50.[155] Of more importance, however, was the uncertainty inherited from the 1972 pay settlement, in which the two sides had agreed to establish joint working parties to make a further examination of the pay structure. Another long and painful period of negotiation began in September 1972. A.S.L.E.F., whose members' position within the pay ladder had deteriorated with the freezing of bonus payments in 1968–73, pushed strongly for the re-establishment of their differential status, a claim backed up by considerable militancy. The N.U.R., on the other hand, continued to press for higher rewards for the low-paid. A.S.L.E.F.'s relations both with the Board and the N.U.R. deteriorated, spilling over into parallel negotiations over the manning of the new A.P.T./H.S.T. trains. The whole issue of the pay structure review had to be taken to the R.S.N.T. in April 1974. After the Tribunal's award in July, the Board made further concessions, including a 10 per cent increase in trainmen's basic rates, in return for progress with the consolidation of bonuses.[156]

In the period 1968–73 some real advances were made by the Board to reform railway working practices, and these were secured with the active co-operation of the rail unions. Versatility was perhaps the most important principle to emerge at the Penzance and Windsor talks in 1968. There were a great many examples of management–union agreement in introducing new technology. A little publicised example was the B.R.U.T.E. trolley,* successfully introduced from the mid-1960s to cut handling costs at stations and depots.[157] But union co-operation was paid for in improved pay and conditions; and the progress made in 1968–9 came too close to the 'pay explosion' of the early 1970s to allow the Board to consolidate and extend the gains which had been made. Train-manning and trainmen's rostering were two particular examples of problems which lingered on into the 1980s. The early productivity agreements also failed

*British Railways Universal Trolley Equipment.

to eliminate two major elements in the pay structure which conditioned the response of rank and file railwaymen. The first was the effect of bonus payments on pay inequalities within the grade structure, a problem reduced but not removed by the settlement in 1974. The second was the persistence of a fairly large group of poorly-paid staff. Figures produced confidentially by British Rail for the Department of the Environment in February 1972, for example, showed that whatever the average earnings may have been, rewards were modest for those at the bottom, and long hours had to be worked to obtain a reasonable standard of living. 'Railmen' earned on average £28–50 for a 52-hour week, but nobody earned more than £30 in a standard week; and for all hours worked, including overtime, more than a quarter earned less than £25.[158] The problems of differentials and of low-pay were persistent in railway industrial relations.

VIII

How far did B.R.B. succeed in its objective to improve productivity? All the indicators show that after a very modest increase in productivity in the Commission's period (see above, pp. 249–50), the Board presided over a marked improvement. One indication of this is the fact that real costs fell

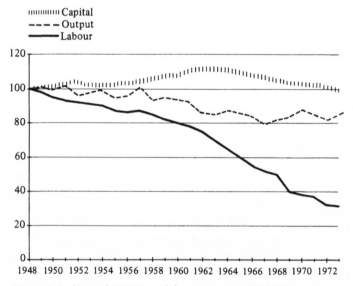

Figure 8 Indices of output and factor inputs, 1948–73

Source: Appendix C, Table 1.

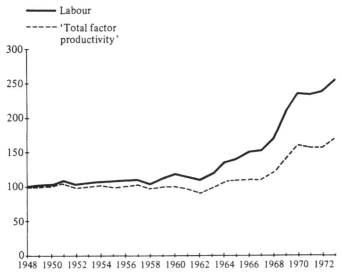

Figure 9 Railway productivity, 1948–73

Growth rates per annum (%)

	Labour (output per head)	'Total factor productivity'
1948–60	1.68	0.54
1960–70	6.68	3.99
1970–3	2.89	1.89
1948–73	3.80	2.07

Source: Appendix C, Table 1.

by 28 per cent from 1962 to 1973, with output exhibiting a tendency to fall only slowly.[159] This impression is reinforced by the new estimates of labour and 'total factor productivity', given in detail in Appendix C and shown graphically in Figures 8 and 9 for the entire period 1948–73. Output showed a downward tendency throughout though the reduction observable in 1960–7 was counterbalanced by a recovery to 1970. Labour inputs fell steadily from 1948, accelerating after 1961, and boosted by the loss of staff associated with the reorganisation of 1969. Capital inputs increased with the higher investment levels associated with the Modernisation Plan of 1955, reaching a peak in 1963. They then fell back, and by 1973 had reached 1948 levels. The result was that labour productivity, after a modest growth of 1.7 per cent per annum in 1948–60 (measuring from output peak to peak), exhibited a growth rate of 6.7 per cent in 1960–70, and the measure of 'total factor productivity' for railways, after growing by only 0.5 per cent per annum in 1948–60, increased by 4.0 per cent per annum over the next decade (Figure 9). In contrast, the progress made in the early 1970s was more modest, despite the greater emphasis

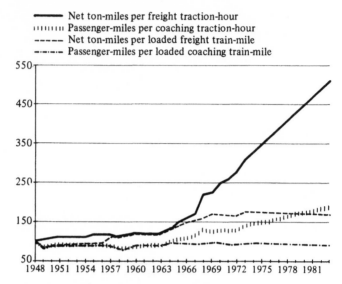

Figure 10 Productivity measures, 1948–83 (1)
Source: B.R.B. data base.

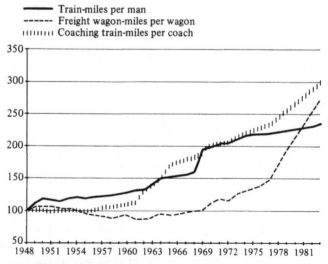

Figure 11 Productivity measures, 1948–83 (2)
Source: B.R.B. data base.

being placed by the Board and the rail unions on the linking of pay awards to productivity agreements.[160] The growth of productivity was obviously rather low in the 1950s, and even in the mid-1970s much still remained to be done, for example in train-manning, signalling and administration. Nonetheless, the 1960s were clearly a period of spectacular improvement, and this may be attributed to the pruning of the least productive elements of the railway system, the transfer from steam to diesel traction and the first steps to create staff 'versatility'. The importance of this decade has also been stressed by *inter alia*, C. D. Jones, and Richard Pryke, the latter contrasting the productivity achieved to 1973 with the more disappointing results over the next five years as output fell.[161] The Board's productivity record also compared favourably with the average achievement in the economy, not only in 1960–70, but over the entire period from 1948 to 1973. Estimates of U.K. 'total factor productivity', drawn up to provide a comparison with the railway estimates, indicate annual growth rates of only 1.8 and 1.7 per cent respectively, compared with 4.0 and 2.1 per cent for British Rail.[162]

Substantial productivity gains in the 1960s are also evident in various measurements of work done in railway operation. For example, the average wagon-load at the starting point, under 8 tons in 1948 and only 10.6 tons in 1962, nearly doubled to 20.5 tons in 1973. Net ton-miles of traffic per freight traction-hour, 547 miles in 1948, and 634 miles in 1962, jumped to 1,678 miles in 1973. Figures 10 and 11 display these and other measures of railway operation, both freight and passenger, in graphical form. They extend the time-scale for purposes of comparison to 1983 and show clearly how the 1960s saw the beginnings of real improvement though some operations, notably certain measures of rolling stock utilisation (see Figure 11), did not show marked advance until after 1973.[163]

Not all problems were solved and there was disappointment that some of the potential gains from new technology were lost. But in overall terms, the productivity gains of the period were striking. Output held up quite well, and operating costs were brought under a measure of control. Some of the progress made was not sustained after 1973, and there were difficulties when output fell and fuel costs (particularly oil) rose. Nevertheless, the pattern was set for a more efficiently operated railway. Anxiety about profitability may have been a perennial theme, but Britain's railway system of the 1970s was very different from that which existed when the industry was nationalised on 1 January 1948.

13

Conclusion

This *business* history of the nationalised railways should not be regarded merely as one more book to be added to the list of serious accounts of modern businesses. Naturally, there are some similarities with the experiences of both private and other public enterprise over the quarter-century to 1973, and these have emerged in earlier chapters. For example, the lack of sophistication in investment appraisal, characteristic of the railways in the 1950s, can be found throughout British industry, and the zeal for reforming unwieldy business organisations in the early 1960s, which culminated in the introduction of American-based corporate planning techniques, was certainly not something confined to the railways. But British Rail is not another I.C.I., Unilever or Courtaulds; nor should it be assumed to resemble closely such nationalised industries as electricity and coal. As a business, the railways present special features which greatly complicate the task of evaluating managerial performance in conventional terms. Three long-standing elements stand out: size; dispersed operations; and the existence of government control. Company concentration was an established fact in the industry as early as the 1850s, and the size of the leading railway companies has always dwarfed most, if not all, of Britain's businesses. In 1938, for example, the four main-line railways had issued capitals ranging from £150 to £414 million and annual turnovers of £26 to £73 million, which put them in the top rank along with the companies such as I.C.I., Lever Brothers & Unilever and Imperial Tobacco.[1] Furthermore, despite post-war growth and merger and the expansion of the multi-national enterprise, the amalgamated railway business established by the 1947 Transport Act was by any standards large. First of all, there was the umbrella organisation of the British Transport Corporation, with its staff of 873,000, an issued capital stock of £1,132 million (at the end of 1948) and an annual turnover in 1948 of £462 million, or £4,790 million in 1983 prices. Then the British Railways Board, a more modest enterprise established after the break-up of the B.T.C., began life in 1963 with a staff

Table 66. *Company size, 1948 and c. 1963*

Company	Date	Sales/ turnover[a]	Capital employed[b]	Employees
B.T.C.	1948	£461.6m.	£1,132.0m.	873,257
I.C.I.	1948	£163.9m.	£143.1m.	120,000 (U.K. only, 1949)
B.R.B.	1963	£523.2m.	£1,562.1m.	502,703
Unilever	1963	—	£722.1m.	294,000 (worldwide, 1965)
Courtaulds	1963–4	£227.7m.	£262.4m.	72,000 (worldwide, 1965)
Bowater	1963	£138.8m.	£197.7m.	29,000 (worldwide, 1964)
Pilkington	1965–6	£84.9m.	£92.8m.	29,670 (worldwide, 1966)

[a] B.T.C. and B.R.B. = gross receipts, *all* activities, for others 'sales' with Pilkington = 'sales to outside customers'.
[b] B.T.C. = issued capital stock, B.R.B. = capital liabilities, including suspended debt. For I.C.I., Unilever, Bowater and Pilkington = 'capital employed', for Courtaulds = total net assets.
Source: B.T.C., *R. & A. 1948*; B.R.B., *R. & A. 1963*; W. J. Reader, *Imperial Chemical Industries. A History*, II (London: Oxford University Press, 1975), p.497; Charles Wilson, *Unilever 1945–1965* (London: Cassell, 1968), pp. 46, 130; D. C. Coleman, *Courtaulds. An Economic and Social History*, III (Oxford: Clarendon Press, 1980), pp. 257–8, 290; W. J. Reader, *Bowater. A History* (Cambridge: Cambridge University Press, 1981), pp. 363, 367; T. C. Barker, *The Glassmakers. Pilkington: The Rise of an International Company 1826–1976* (London: Weidenfeld & Nicolson, 1977), pp. 408–9.

of 503,000, capital liabilities, including suspended debt, of £1,562 million and a turnover in 1963 of £523 million (£3,275 million in 1983 prices). All this added up to a complex giant of a business in comparison with leading firms in the private sector, as Table 66 demonstrates. In 1948, for example, I.C.I.'s turnover was only about a third of the B.T.C.'s, and both capital and labour inputs were much lower. By the 1960s the position of the railways was less dominant, with the spectacular growth of large multi-nationals such as Shell and British Petroleum. But as late as 1963, B.R.B. was nearly twice the size of the Anglo-Dutch conglomerate, Unilever, in terms of capital and labour employed, and was much bigger than companies such as Courtaulds, Bowater and Pilkington, which have been the subject of recent business histories (see Table 66).

The second distinguishing feature of the railways is the long-standing influence of government in key areas of decision-making. Britain's railways may have been a prime example of free enterprise capitalism, but government control was in evidence from the industry's birth, when parliament supervised company formation, thereby influencing network development, and set maximum charges to protect the public from 'monopoly'. By the end of the nineteenth century, control had become more specific, affecting merger activity, pricing, the provision of services, labour conditions and safety standards.[2] Nationalisation in 1947 was the end-product of this long process of state intervention, with its emphasis on public service. Consequently, scholars concerned with the business history of the railways have always been faced with the task of determining the extent to which responsibility for performance rested with the market and the competitive environment; with the independent actions of railway managements; or with the restrictive conditions imposed by government. After nationalisation the government dimension expanded and the rules of the game became more complex. But the essential intellectual problem remains unaltered.

Recent work on railways in the later nineteenth century has done much to exonerate railway managers from the criticisms they previously attracted, and has emphasised the strength of the constraints on business freedom imposed by statute and case-law.[3] Should managers be given similarly favourable treatment in the period 1948–73? Certainly, the sheer size of the nationalised railway business and the ramifications of government intervention invite a number of general questions, not only on the difficulties of measuring 'performance' in a nationalised industry but also on the hypothesis that public ownership brings with it barriers to effective management. Was size a constraining factor on management? Were the railways too large and too dispersed a business to be managed effectively? It may not be entirely coincidental that they appear to have been better run after the break-up of the cumbersome B.T.C. in 1962 and the beginning of a serious rationalisation drive, although firmer management also owed much to Beeching's managerial team and a renewed emphasis on centralised control. The search for effective units of management in the industry continued throughout the period 1948–73 and indeed beyond, with first centralising then decentralising initiatives. The current enthusiasm for management by 'sector' – the creation in 1982 of five managerial units for freight, parcels, Inter-City, provincial passenger and London and the South East passenger services – represents only one of a number of options which have been tried, including the Railway Executive, the idea of fully accountable regions and the attempt to establish a 'field' organisation of 'territories'.

What lessons can the railways provide in the perennial debate about the merits of private v. public enterprise? Did government intervention produce a damaging instability in the environment, which served to inhibit managerial initiative? Did nationalisation confuse managers about the purpose of the railways? Is there a correlation between public ownership and a slow rate of change? What part did tradition play in the actions of railway management? These questions are naturally easier to pose than to resolve. Although much has been written about the nationalised industries and the nationalised railways at a general level, comparatively little has been offered *in detail* about the precise influence of government on the activities of state industries. A recurrent theme of this book has been the complex interplay of government and internal management in the decision-making process.

Scratch a railway manager, it is said, and he will complain that post-war governments have greatly harmed the railways by continually organising or reorganising nationalised transport, thereby creating a perpetual climate of uncertainty. Government intervention has been intermittent, as in 1947–51, or more comprehensive and regular, as in Castle's period of office as Minister, 1966–8. Sir Reginald Wilson echoed the opinions of many managers when he referred to the disenchantment of the B.T.C. 'with attitudes on the part of Westminster and Whitehall towards an organisation that was, to its great disadvantage, both servant and non-voter'.[4] His remark may also be applied to the British Railways Board when it was subjected to detailed scrutiny, as, for example, by the Prices and Incomes Board in 1965, or by the Joint Steering Group and its consultants in 1966–7, or more recently by the Serpell Committee in 1982–3. Stanley Raymond complained about the constantly changing environment shortly after his dismissal in 1967, and so did Peter Parker, Chairman from 1976 to 1983, when in the Dimbleby Lecture of 1983 he referred to 'the intrusion of adversarial politics far beyond the capacity of ideologies to resolve'. Parker even suggested that an independent Council of Industry should be set up to interpose itself between government and industrial management.[5] The establishment of the Select Committee system for the nationalised industries in the 1950s was a necessary step in the attempt to reassert parliamentary responsibility, as opposed to that of Cabinet, Treasury and Department. But it also increased the amount of investigation. For the railways, the important inquiries took place in 1960, 1967–8, 1973 and again in 1976–7. There is much in the argument that the government's uncertainty about the role and prospects of the railways in the post-war mixed economy, with the shift of emphasis from 'co-ordination', 'integration' and 'public service' to 'competition', 'commercial freedom' and 'viability', has distracted railway managers from the essential tasks of marketing, planning and cost-control. Since the late 1950s each government has felt impelled to instigate its own investigation of the 'railway problem'. A plethora of select committees, advisory groups, committees of inquiry and consultants has probed the dark corners of the business, from Stedeford in 1960 to Serpell in 1982, producing an environment which was more often in a state of flux than in a state of equilibrium. Not only was the B.T.C. and B.R.B. subject to numerous changes of government and Minister – no less than 11 Ministers in the 25 years covered by this book – but they were often left in a state of suspended animation. Over the quarter-century, 13 years were spent preparing for major Transport Acts and reorganising after them – in 1948–9, 1951–4, 1959–62 and 1966–9 (see Chronology, above). The situation did not improve in the later 1970s and early 1980s. Parker called it a state of 'perpetual audit'.[6]

Many areas of responsibility which might properly be regarded as the province of managers have been influenced to a greater or lesser extent by government. Although there has been broad support for the Morrisonian public corporation, legally and financially independent of departments of state, Ministerial intervention has gradually increased since 1945. Nowhere has this been more apparent than in the sphere of organisation, one of government's great obsessions. Both Parties have clearly felt that the key to efficient operation lies in establishing a suitable form of organisation, though the rationale for this is less certain, and there have been several changes of position. Of course, an organisational change, accompanied by suitable publicity, is tangible if ephemeral proof that a government is 'doing something about the railways'. A series of specific directions has been issued, pointing the way either to decentralisation, as in 1953–5, or to centralisation, as in 1960–2, or to a confused mixture of the two, as in 1947. The environment has never remained unaltered for very long. The Labour Party's emphasis on the integration of diverse transport undertakings, including road and rail, under the 1947 Transport Act, soon gave way to the Conservatives' denationalisation of the B.T.C.'s road haulage acquisitions from 1953, with all its damaging implications for the Commission's long-term financial prospects. In 1968 the government moved in the opposite direction. For the first time, British Rail's workshops were permitted to manufacture for sale, having been expressly forbidden to do so by earlier legislation. More recently, there has been another turn of the wheel with the Conservative Government's privatisation drive, which has seen the sale of B.R.B.'s hotels, hovercraft and the shipping arm, Sealink.

One of the great organisational challenges for nationalised railways was to determine the right balance between centralised control and decentralisation, a problem to be faced, indeed, by all business enterprises, public and private. In this context, we should note that there has been considerable academic interest in the relationship between organisational structure and the strategy, including growth, of the firm, stimulated by the work of Edith Penrose and Alfred Chandler.[7] Whether the choice of organisation is determined by market conditions and business strategy or vice versa is a fascinating intellectual puzzle for which there is no space here. But it is certainly true that post-war economic conditions have been accompanied by a distinct preference among the larger companies for the multi-divisional form of organisation, with a considerable measure of decentralisation to production units, and broad strategy determined by a planning board at the centre. For the railways, however, there have been periods of movement in the opposite direction, seen in the centralising activity of the Railway Executive, 1947–53, and under Beeching and his successors in the 1960s. The disappointing results of the McKinsey exercise in 1968–9 (see Chapter 9) demonstrated how difficult it was to apply a simple manufacturing model to a business as complex as the railways. Furthermore, both 'strategy and structure', to borrow Chandler's phrase, have been complicated and confused by government involvement in both. The organisation has generally been established before the strategy, and in any case, for most of our period the strategy of the railway business was left rather vague. There was always the precedent of the four private companies which operated in the inter-war years. Indeed, the government's preference for decentralisation in the 1950s owed a great deal to the nostalgia for railways past. The idea that a return to something resembling the Great Western Railway or the L.M.S. would improve managerial performance surfaced when the 1953 Act was being drawn up, and was still evident when the future of the B.T.C. was determined in 1960–2. Harold Macmillan, a former director of the G.W.R., was notable in this regard. For example, one of his interventions came when the Transport Bill was being formulated in 1952. Writing to Lord Leathers, his contribution to the debate about the future of the B.T.C. and the Railway Executive was as follows:

Why not restore the old names and titles? For instance, Western Region should be called the Great Western Railway. The head of it should be called the General Manager, as he always was. It would also give great pleasure if the old colours were restored. Our men used to be proud of their chocolate brown suits and all the rest; the Great Western institutions such as the Operatic Troupes, Concerts, Boy-Scouts and all the rest should go back to the old names and become distinctive. The regimental system is a great one with the British and it is always a mistake to destroy tradition. I am quite sure from my own talks with old friends in the G.W.R. that they would welcome recovering their identity. They don't care about who owns the shares, what they care about is their own individuality.[8]

Behind this kind of thinking, more often attributed to diehard regional managers than to politicians, lies a crucial question: what is the optimal organisational form for the railways? The first point to make here is that no one has been able to produce a simple formula for the business. Indeed, many of the solutions offered since 1947 have suffered from being far too complex and unwieldy. As will have become evident from the preceding chapters, the history of nationalised railways has been marked by much tension between those at the centre, whether B.T.C., R.E. or B.R.B., and the chief managers in the regions. Whatever the arguments for a centralised or for a decentralised emphasis, it seems clear that moves in the latter direction have frequently been exploited by regional managers bent on resisting change, while periods of faster change have coincided with a preference at Board level for stronger centralised command. The intervention of government has prevented internal evolution, and the way in which this intervention has been introduced has often made for unexpected results. For example, the encouragement given to decentralisation by the Conservatives in the 1950s was hampered by the considerable time-lag between the announcement of their intentions in 1951, the passing of the Transport Act in 1953 and the introduction of Robertson's new organisation in January 1955. The long 'interregnum' put considerable power into the hands of those who remained at B.T.C. headquarters. They operated an 'interim' organisation which put a firm brake on the decentralising initiative (see Chapter 5). It remains to be seen whether managerial efficiency and the speed of response would improve if a considerable measure of autonomy were passed down the line. The record of the regions in relation to investment appraisal during the Modernisation Plan period and to rationalisation in the 1950s and 1960s certainly provides little comfort for the decentralisers.

Because the government has always determined appointments to the boards of nationalised industries, it has been able to exercise an indirect influence over the broad managerial strategies pursued by each industry, transcending the general requirements inserted in the Acts to 'break even' or provide 'adequate' levels of service. A key factor in the way in which the railways have been managed at the top since 1947 has been the government's insistence that the Chairman should not normally be a professional railwayman. This was demonstrated by the choice of B.T.C. Chairmen: Cyril Hurcomb in 1947, Brian Robertson in 1953 and Richard Beeching in 1961, a senior civil servant followed by a soldier, and then by a technocrat-businessman. Although Raymond broke the mould in 1965 when he succeeded Beeching as Chairman of B.R.B., his was not the conventional background of the railway manager, that is, a traffic apprenticeship with one of the main-line railway companies. Nor is it known whether he was the first choice for the post. Johnson, his successor, certainly was not. Barbara Castle's diaries reveal unmistakably her preference here: 'I told him [Johnson] frankly that, as he knew, I would have preferred Peter Parker but that I had always had him in mind as a second choice and some people had always thought he ought to be my first choice.'[9] The next Chairman was Marsh, in 1971, and he was followed in 1976 by Parker, a career politician followed by a businessman. The current Chairman, Sir

Robert Reid, is thus only the second railway-trained manager to come through the business to the top.[10] This preference for leadership by outsiders is further emphasised by the fact that career railwaymen were often in the minority as full-time members of the B.T.C. and B.R.B., a phenomenon particularly striking in Robertson's and Beeching's time. All this has given the railway business a clear message that the government has some doubts about the quality or the intentions of its internally-trained managers.

More important still, the government-imposed limits on top salaries in the nationalised industries has had a damaging effect, not only by narrowing the field available for appointment to the board, but also because low board salaries have a knock-on impact on executive salaries, reducing recruitment potential and lowering the morale of able middle-managers. The standard salary for B.T.C. members was fixed at £5,000 in 1947, and it remained unchanged until it was increased to £7,500 in the middle of 1957. Consequently, pay was much lower than that enjoyed by directors and senior executives in privately owned companies of comparable size, such as I.C.I., Shell and Unilever, a fact which was underlined when Beeching was recruited from I.C.I. His salary of £24,000 a year dwarfed the £10,000 paid to his predecessor, Robertson. Beeching, of course, was very much an exception to the rule. In the late 1960s most members of the British Railways Board were being paid only £8,000–8,500, within the government's fixed range of £7,000–9,500, established in 1964. Such rewards were well down on those available in the private sector, a point often stressed by those who were offered the chance of high office. A report by the P.I.B. in 1969 revealed that companies with net assets of £250 million or more were paying their board members an average of £18,760, while fringe benefits and pensions were much higher than those available in nationalised industry.[11] The government took some steps to narrow the gap between private and public in 1969–71, and the problem was accorded official recognition with the establishment of a top salaries review body under Lord Boyle. However, its several recommendations were not acted upon. By 1977, recently retired chiefs of nationalised industry, such as Sir Richard Marsh, Sir Montague Finniston (British Steel) and Alfred Singer (Post Office GIRO), were recording their frustration with a four-year pay freeze during a period of severe inflation. Marsh was quoted as saying that British Rail had recently been without a finance director for seven months 'because the rate being offered would not buy the fifth man in an average London firm of accountants'.[12] The report of the top salaries review body in June 1978 admitted that 'current salaries in the nationalised industry Boards remain even more seriously out of date', producing a harmful compression of the salary structure lower down. Not for the first time, the review body emphasised that there was a need to pay 'realistic salaries . . . if the right calibre of top management is to be recruited and retained'.[13] All this had a rather hollow ring. The appointments files of British Rail indicate that attempts to attract leading managers have often foundered on the rock of inadequate salaries and pension rights. Further difficulties have been produced by the compression of executive pay-scales. For example, when Beeching tried to improve managerial performance by importing a large number of outsiders in the early 1960s, he found that many of them had to be paid 'special' salaries which were considerably higher than those of their railway colleagues. The impact on morale was predictable.

Government intervention was not confined to questions of organisation and personnel. 'The early history of the nationalised industries' may have been 'mainly concerned with the evolution of norms of conduct in a previously unexplored territory',[14] but the railway industry found that much of this territory was mapped out fairly quickly, even if the degree of control fluctuated. Finance was naturally a major area of concern. Not only did the government call the financial tune, but it also rewrote the score on a number of occasions. Significant interventions with regard to the B.T.C.'s borrowing powers and interest and debt liabilities from the mid-1950s were followed by the major capital reconstructions of 1962, 1968 and 1974, as the business continued to incur large annual deficits. Political anxiety about what would now be termed 'bottom-line' perform-ance surfaced at an early stage, and by 1958 the Minister of Transport was endeavouring to get the B.T.C. to work towards a precise figure for the next year's deficit.[15] More recently, the Public Service Obligation subsidy for the passenger business, introduced after the 1974 Act, marked an important step forward in the financial relationship between government and B.R.B., replacing the rather cumbersome funding of specified services under the 1968 Act. But thereafter managers have had to cope with the very close monitoring demanded by the setting of detailed financial targets and 'cash limits'. Ever since the early 1950s the government's interest in the size of the railways' operating deficit and the final balance (after meeting interest and central charges) has coloured its attitude to other matters in which it has taken a close interest, including industrial relations, pricing, investment and the provision of services. All are key areas of managerial decision-making; all have been plagued by political inter-ference, often of a rather general nature, but sometimes quite specific in character. For example, Ministerial attitudes to the prospect of a railway strike certainly served to determine the pace and content of collective bargaining, particularly in the 1950s and 1960s. The debate about the size of the railway network and the level of services to be provided was very much one for government, which not only orchestrated the acceleration of rail closures in the early 1960s but also encouraged the switch to a 'social railway' concept later in the same decade. Pricing and investment suffered from similar interventions. Government anxiety about committing funds to an industry in decline has encouraged a close scrutiny of individual schemes. The Modernisation Plan of 1955 was quickly made the subject of government-inspired reviews in 1956 and 1959, and the periods 1960–2 and 1966–8 saw a very detailed examination of specific components of the railways' investment programme. The situation was repeated in the tighter economic conditions of the 1970s. Government-imposed investment ceilings, which were often altered at short notice, created uncertainty in an industry where the gestation period of new projects was long. Consequently, long-term planning and spending have been inhibited. In the 1960s the government's advice to nationalised industries, contained in the White Papers of 1961 and 1967, included a direction to work to specific rates of return and include d.c.f. techniques in project appraisal. These clear, if not entirely consistent, instructions contrasted with the vaguer approach of the late 1940s and 1950s, but were set aside in the early 1970s, when the government used the railways, along with other public enterprises, as instruments of macro-economic control in an attempt to curb inflation.[16] In short, the influence of government has been considerable.[17]

So 'public' an industry as the railways must expect a close contact with government. An essential part of British Rail's managerial task has therefore been, and presumably still is, to secure the right balance between a relationship – whether with the Minister, Permanent-Secretary or whomever – which is uncomfortably intrusive and a contact which is too much at arms-length to inspire confidence in Whitehall. In the late 1950s the railways' relationship appears to have been too remote; in the mid-1960s too close. It is a continuing management problem for all the nationalised industries. From the late 1950s the widespread enthusiasm in political circles for greater industrial efficiency produced a move towards closer contact. The enthusiasm was directed at both the public and the private sector, and it is clear that the larger private companies also experienced problems caused by government interference.[18] Nevertheless, the nationalised industries generally bore the brunt of this penchant for interventionism, and among them the railways often suffered more than most. Railway planning in relation to output, prices, wages and investment was on several occasions disturbed or even negated by the need to respond to pressures which either originated in party political conflict or were the product of measures taken ad hoc to meet a major economic crisis. The dangers of this kind of action were recognised at an early stage. In 1952, for example, a senior civil servant argued that:

all experience shows that it is not possible to have efficient management of great industries under political democracies if they can be used as instruments for extraneous political purposes, or subjected to ephemeral pressures from party political struggles. And this country cannot afford not to have efficient management of its Coal, Railways, Electricity, and Gas.[19]

Since then the goal of efficient management, inadequately defined and accompanied by platitudes about 'breaking even', has often been challenged by the government's demand that the nationalised industries should contribute to crisis management and at the same time set a good example to private industry. In the early 1970s this meant bearing the brunt of the assault on inflation. Moreover, the railways, with a long tradition of state control and a management accustomed to discipline and obedience, have been particularly susceptible to this kind of appeal. At the same time, their comparatively weak market position has caused governments to raise doubts about the industry's long-term future. Managers have been able to complain not only that the government has given considerable encouragement to road transport and to road building since 1951, and particularly during Ernest Marples's period of office as Minister of Transport (1959–64), but that its general financial support for the United Kingdom's railway network has been more niggardly than that of most countries in western Europe.[20]

That the political and economic environment in which the railways, like the other nationalised industries, were required to operate was complex and frustrating is not in doubt. Interventions were often costly, and both the B.T.C. and the B.R.B. lost no opportunity to compute the financial effect of a blocked or delayed price increase or of a wage settlement urged upon them 'in the national interest'. But it would be facile to suppose that the industry's disappointing financial record and managerial shortcomings can be attributed only to government intervention and the uncertainties of the political environment. The transport co-ordination policy of the 1947 Transport Act, its ending and the subsequent support for road building were all political decisions. But the increasing importance of road transport in the economy was to a considerable extent inevitable given the flexibility and higher quality of service it was able to provide. Moreover, though government interventions in railway affairs were numerous, they were not always pressed home in a determined fashion. Intervention certainly fell far short of a full efficiency audit and the kind of surveillance experienced by, say, the French and Swedish state industries.[21] Assuming that the prime function of a business is to optimise its financial performance *within* its environment, there is a great deal to criticise in the response of railway management to its admittedly difficult task. Many of the errors of judgement made in relation to marketing, investment and the choice of technology can be traced directly to decisions taken inside the B.T.C. and B.R.B. with little or no government participation. Political change has created uncertainty, but it cannot be blamed for such matters as the railways' persistence with vacuum brakes and steam heating. At one time, and particularly in the 1950s, railway managers were unduly cautious and conservative. In the next decade, they can be found displaying quite contrary tendencies, for example as they rushed headlong into dieselisation. Serious mistakes have littered the 25-year path of nationalised railways, as they have done in other enterprises, both public and private.

Where, then, has railway management proved to be deficient? The first point to stress concerns the nature of the bureaucracy within which the railways have been managed. The observation that the railways are a monastic order of disciplined, committed enthusiasts is as much a cliché as the observation that the industry has suffered from political intervention. But it remains true that the 'culture of the railroad', rooted in its nineteenth-century domination of the transport system, has survived all attempts to tinker with the organisational structure, from the dismantling of the main-line companies in 1947 to the establishment of an organisation dominated on paper by corporate planning and the use of executive directors in 1970. Some would argue that it will survive the introduction of 'sector management' and the privatisation drive of the 1980s. The 'enclosed order of railwaymen' exhibits strengths in its loyalty and discipline, necessary qualities in an industry where operational safety is rightly emphasised. But it also encourages a close-knit group antagonistic to outsiders and hostile to new ideas. Some of the costs of this kind of management may be seen in the heavy reliance on commercial and marketing practices developed in the late nineteenth and early twentieth centuries, which became increasingly inappropriate in the post-war world, and in the courtroom atmosphere of much collective bargaining before the late 1960s. All this was cemented by the 'traffic apprentice' system of management development, which gave an advantage to managers trained in the operating departments. The disciplined functioning of an industry brought up on rule books and elaborate procedures also encouraged the first Chairmen, Hurcomb and Robertson, who were both from disciplined backgrounds themselves, to err on the side of being too deferential to their political masters. At times they appeared only too willing to place their heads under the cosh. Whatever the reasons for the improvement in railway management in the 1960s, it is clear that the new ideas and the new

faces introduced by Beeching, Shirley *et al.* had a great impact, with all
their imperfections. It was Shirley who set out to puncture the railways'
overblown bureaucracy, with its numerous committees and its mass of
paper work, much of which was produced by administrators isolated from
the selling function and therefore insensitive to the changing needs of
customers.

That large businesses such as the B.T.C. and B.R.B. should have
developed complex organisational structures is in itself scarcely surprising. Operations were widely dispersed. Both concerns operated a number
of subsidiaries, and manufactured a range of products as well as providing
a variety of transport services. It is only to be expected that they would
need considerable time to recover from the kind of disruptive effects
produced by the Transport Acts of 1947, 1953, 1962 and 1968. The loss
of road haulage after 1953, the break-up of the B.T.C. in 1962, the loss of
sundries and freightliners in 1968 – all produced upheaval, and the effects
were probably more damaging because the business was so large.[22] But by
no means all of the railways' organisational deficiencies were imposed
upon them from outside. In the period 1947–53, for example, the tensions
between the Railway Executive and the Commission, while partly a
reaction to an unfamiliar type of organisation, also owed something to
nostalgia for the old main-line companies. The numerous squabbles
between Hurcomb and Missenden, for example, reflected little credit on
those involved. Robertson's 'dinosaur' – the cumbersome, multi-tier
structure of 1955 – was very much a personal choice. Nor was Beeching's
period of office without its organisational problems. The drive to central
control and the use of Board members with functional (i.e. executive)
responsibilities were probably taken too far, with the result that decision-
making became excessively compartmentalised. Planning was a notable
area of weakness. In Raymond's time, there were several discussions with
the Minister about the need to improve the calibre of the Board, and the
finance and planning functions were identified as ripe for improvement.
The Board's organisational response to the J.S.G. exercise was not very
impressive, revealing a fundamental split among the members over the
issue of a policy versus a functional structure. In Johnson's period, this
disagreement influenced the outcome of the McKinsey exercise. The early
1970s saw considerable difficulty in bedding down the new organisation
based on a Chief Executive (Railways), and a failure to introduce the
promised 'field' organisation for the regions. Throughout the period, the
clash between centre and regions complicated the decision-making process. The government sometimes gave this additional impetus, for example
when it declared in favour of decentralised management, as in 1953, or
regional accounting, as in 1960, but the problem of delegated authority

persisted at other times too, and often slowed down centrally inspired initiatives. In the 1960s, for example, the Board's progress with pricing, traffic costing and passenger service rationalisation was constrained by the more conservative views held at regional level.

The improvement in the railways' business approach after Beeching, while real, was far from complete. Many of the old attitudes, based on notions of quasi-monopoly, public service and the maximisation of traffic volume irrespective of cost, were challenged, and the *Reshaping* report brought a new emphasis on cost-control and rationalisation. But, as shown in Chapter 11, most of the more positive aspects of the *Reshaping* strategy proved to be rather disappointing in net revenue terms, in both the short and medium run. This was true, for example, of the development of special train-load traffics such as oil, the Merry-Go-Round trains and the freightliner services for general merchandise container traffic. Equally, the wagon-load freight traffic, unprofitable but a major contributor of gross revenue, was allowed to drift without a clearly defined policy for far too long. All this meant that although railway costs were successfully tackled from 1961, the improvement was more than offset by an accompanying fall in gross revenue. Behind this lay several factors, not least of which was the increased competitive strength of the railways' main rivals in transport. The government must also accept its due share of the blame for a continuing uncertainty about the ultimate size of the railway network and about where the dividing line between the 'commercial' and the 'social' railway should be drawn. Whatever may have been put on paper in the *Reshaping* and *Trunk Routes* reports of 1963 and 1965, the long-term strategy of British Rail remained a matter for argument, political and managerial. In the circumstances, the managers' failure to give sufficient attention to the quality of service in bread-and-butter freight operations was a notable area of weakness, if perhaps an understandable one, as was the post-Beeching precept that the attribution of both direct and indirect costs to particular traffics might be used to facilitate decisions about individual traffic flows. The railways' record in relation to investment and labour relations was not without blemishes. The Modernisation Plan was a hastily conceived and, in several particulars, flawed response to the need to make up lost ground. Technical errors, together with inadequate investment appraisal and the suspicion of low rates of return, did much to persuade the government to establish more restrictive investment conditions after 1960. In the crucial area of labour relations, managers faced the very real difficulty that railwaymen were falling behind other occupations in terms of both pay and conditions, a situation underlined by the findings of the Cameron and Guillebaud inquiries. Most of the early gains from labour shedding in the 1960s were returned to the men in the form of higher wages, and although Neal and Bowick inspired a more positive approach to productivity with the Pay and Efficiency Agreements of 1968–9, here too the productivity had to be paid for and the net gains were small. The attempts to bring an end to the formal atmosphere of collective bargaining were shattered by the wages explosion of 1969–70 and the bitterness which followed. Finally, there was much to be done to persuade employees to accept more flexible and less labour-intensive operating conditions.

Thus, whatever the scale and frequency of government intervention over the 25 years since 1948, railway management itself has in several respects been found wanting. Nor is this something which has occurred only to outsiders. When the Board's Railway Policy Review was being formulated in 1972, for example, Tait, the Executive Director (Finance), recognised that managerial shortcomings were as much a part of the story of nationalised railways as government interference, although he could naturally see little point in highlighting this observation in a submission to government. As he explained privately:

I am a little doubtful whether my purpose would be served by dwelling on the deficiencies of management in the past.

These would be more fittingly the theme of a comic opera than a White Paper and I am sure if I were commissioned to write the libretto I could make it quite lively. The title might be 'Shipwreck' or 'The Voyage of the Railway Queen' and the theme chorus might go something like this:

'So, if Cyril and Brian, Dick, Stan and Bill,
couldn't manage to sink her, then nobody will'.[23]

In more sober, and more public, vein, the current Chairman has also acknowledged many of the past deficiencies. In a lecture to the Institute of Administrative Management in April 1985 he argued that the Engineering and Operating Departments had set service patterns and quality standards without an adequate knowledge of the market's requirements, that investment projects had been 'sponsored by operators and engineers, and were not market-led' and that the geographically-based regional organisations had produced long and weak lines of communication.[24]

Such comments should not be taken to imply that the calibre of railway managers was any worse than elsewhere, or that no progress was made by the railways before the 'business-led management revolution' of the 1980s.[25] The industry changed considerably in the quarter-century after 1947. Much of the Victorian atmosphere was swept away. Productivity gains were considerable, matching those achieved in the national economy as a whole, and at times clearly outstripping them. In the period 1960–70, for example, the railways' output per head increased by 6.7 per cent per annum, compared with an increase of 2.7 per cent for the U.K. (Appendix C, Tables 1 and 2). British Rail improved its track and signalling, replaced steam locomotives with diesel motive power and additional electrification and began to make good use of telecommunications and computers for train control and administration. By the early 1970s much had been done to gear investment and service provision to areas where rail retained a strong advantage, for example in bulk freight and long-distance Inter-City passenger services, and to transform operating practices. The corporate management structure after 1970 bore little resemblance to the way in which Hurcomb and Missenden operated in the B.T.C. and Railway Executive of the late 1940s. Furthermore, by European standards British Rail's performance in the 1970s has been creditable, in spite of the comparatively mean financial support from the government. A joint report from B.R.B. and the University of Leeds in December 1979 was able to show that of the ten leading rail systems, British Rail was second only to Sweden in its self-financing ratio (the extent to which revenue covers costs), and surpassed only by Sweden and Holland in labour productivity (train kilometres/staff numbers, excluding B.R.E.L.).[26]

If success is measured purely in terms of financial results, then of course there was none. Deficits have remained a persistent theme, in spite of the financial reconstructions of successive Transport Acts. But it would be foolish to write off British Rail as a 'lame duck', part of the 'soft, sodden morass of subsidised incompetence' complained of by the Conservative Government in the early 1970s.[27] The railways managed to raise their productivity in line with the national average, though labour market pressures ensured that railway pay also responded to the rise of real wages in the economy as a whole. Passenger fares, too, maintained their real value, but freight rates did not. Developments elsewhere in the transport industry left railway costs 'high and dry' against its prices. Had the railways' competitors not showed above average productivity and a higher quality of service, all would have been well. But a combination of cost-reductions, technological change and heavy national investment in roads and airports gave an advantage to road haulage, bus and air transport and transformed the economics of private motoring. British Rail may be held to have performed fairly well in isolation, but not well enough to bring costs down to the point where they could support the stable or reduced real pricing which was a reaction to the price and quality changes of competitors' products (see Table 59, above, p. 470). To have prospered British Rail would have had to perform as well as its rivals, which was a tall order.

In many ways, then, this is a business history where some of the conventional yardsticks of performance and managerial behaviour are difficult to apply. It is difficult to look for entrepreneurship in the Board when the government hires and fires, controls investment levels and intervenes in pricing, wage levels and 'production' levels. As indicated above, even if the railways had been an exemplar of best management practices, they would have found it difficult to prosper under nationalisation in a mixed economy. The market for rail transport would have been equally depressing for a private railway system, although private owners might have benefited from more autonomous control, might have exhibited a swifter response in commercial terms and would surely have been allowed to diversify into road and air transport, as the main-line companies did in the inter-war years. 'Profitability' under public ownership could only have come from a coherent policy of integration in which either the revenue from rail and road transport was pooled, or road transport was subjected to economic and environmental constraints. Since neither was politically feasible, the only course open was to try to optimise results within a framework of subsidy, an experience common to the railways of the developed world. Indeed, one of today's ironies is that Japan, currently a model of business success and managerial competence, has recently embarked upon a Beeching-type rationalisation (and privatisation) exercise in an attempt to restore the flagging fortunes of its state railway system.[28] Many of the problems facing the railways since nationalisation have persisted, not only over 25 but also over 40 years. The relationship with government, changes in organisation, investment shortages and industrial relations difficulties, for example, remain live issues. Above all, the basic precepts surrounding the purpose and role of the industry are still fluid, as the Serpell report recently demonstrated. What is the optimal size of the railway network? How is viability to be measured? What is the right balance between private and public enterprise? Can a line be drawn between the 'commercial' and the 'social'? How is the profitability of a sector, line, traffic or service to be determined? A greater sophistication and creativity has been brought to bear on these crucial issues since 1973, but it might be argued that we are just as far from their resolution as we were in 1947.[29] If this is so, then railway managers in the future are likely to encounter as many problems as their predecessors did.

Statistical Appendices

Neil Blake, Andrew Feist and Nick Tiratsoo

The 'true' financial results of British Railways, 1948–73

Table 1. *In current prices (£m.)*

Year	Gross working surplus	Depreciation and amortisation		Net working surplus	Interest	Total deficit/surplus
1948	43.6	24.2		19.4	21.0	−1.6
1949	31.1	25.9		5.2	21.5	−16.3
1950	44.7	27.8		16.9	22.1	−5.2
1951	49.0	30.9		18.1	22.7	−4.6
1952	58.6	34.5		24.1	23.1	1.0
1953	57.4	36.2		21.2	23.3	−2.1
1954	39.0	37.9		1.1	24.1	−23.0
1955	22.8	40.3		−17.5	25.2	−42.7
1956	12.1	43.4		−31.3	26.4	−57.7
1957	4.8	48.1		−43.3	28.7	−72.0
1958	−8.6	53.3		−61.9	32.4	−94.3
1959	6.8	59.1		−52.3	36.8	−89.1
1960	−15.6	65.0		−80.6	41.8	−122.4
1961	−27.2	72.1		−99.3	46.8	−146.1
1962	−47.8	77.5		−125.6	51.4	−177.0
1963	−24.8	80.7		−105.5	53.7	−159.2
1964	−8.7	85.5		−94.2	54.2	−148.4
1965	−12.9	91.0		−103.9	55.1	−159.0
1966	−9.3	94.3		−103.6	56.6	−160.2
1967	−26.1	103.3		−129.4	57.2	−186.6
1968	−18.5	109.9		−128.4	56.2	−184.6

Year	Gross working surplus	Depreciation and amortisation	Passenger grants	Net working surplus	Interest	Total deficit/surplus
1968	−2.4	108.0	—	−110.4	56.2	−166.6
1969	13.5	115.3	61.2	−40.6	53.9	−94.5
1970	17.2	122.4	61.7	−43.5	49.2	−92.7
1971	2.3	130.2	63.1	−64.8	45.1	−109.9
1972	−36.2	140.6	68.2	−108.6	39.2	−147.8
1973	−47.0	163.0	91.4	−118.6	34.5	−153.1

Table 2. *In constant 1948 prices (£m.)*

Year	Gross working surplus	Depreciation and amortisation	Net working surplus	Interest	Total deficit/surplus
1948	43.6	24.2	19.4	21.0	−1.6
1949	30.2	25.2	5.1	20.9	−15.8
1950	43.2	26.8	16.3	21.3	−5.0
1951	44.0	27.8	16.3	20.4	−4.1
1952	48.3	28.4	19.9	19.0	0.8
1953	45.9	29.0	17.0	18.6	−1.7
1954	30.6	29.7	0.9	18.9	−18.0
1955	17.3	30.5	−13.2	19.1	−32.3
1956	8.6	30.9	−22.3	18.8	−41.1
1957	3.3	32.9	−29.6	19.6	−49.3
1958	−5.6	34.9	−40.5	21.2	−61.7
1959	4.4	38.1	−24.6	23.7	−57.4
1960	−9.9	41.2	−51.0	26.5	−77.5
1961	−16.7	44.3	−61.0	28.7	−89.7
1962	−28.4	46.0	−74.5	30.5	−105.1
1963	−14.4	47.0	−61.4	31.3	−92.7
1964	−5.0	48.8	−53.8	30.9	−84.7
1965	−7.1	50.1	−57.2	30.3	−87.6
1966	−4.9	50.0	−54.9	30.0	−84.9
1967	−13.5	53.3	−66.7	29.5	−96.2
1968	−9.2	54.8	−64.0	28.0	−92.0

Year	Gross working surplus	Depreciation and amortisation	Interest	Total excluding grants	Passenger grants	Total including grants
1968	−1.2	53.8	28.0	−83.1	—	−83.1
1969	6.5	55.4	25.9	−74.9	29.4	−45.4
1970	7.7	55.6	21.9	−68.8	27.5	−41.3
1971	0.9	52.6	18.2	−69.9	25.5	−44.4
1972	−13.3	51.6	14.4	−79.2	25.0	−54.2
1973	−15.8	54.8	11.6	−82.2	30.7	−51.5

Note: columns have been rounded to one place of decimals

Table 3. *Revised results for 1948–62 (excluding drawings on abnormal maintenance fund, 1948–53, and maintenance equalisation account, 1954–62) (£m.)*

Year	Net charges to equalisation accounts (current prices)	Revised deficit/surplus (current prices)	Revised deficit/surplus (constant 1948 prices)
1948	18.5	−20.1	−20.1
1949	14.5	−30.8	−29.9
1950	10.6	−15.8	−15.3
1951	11.6	−16.2	−14.6
1952	21.1	−20.1	−16.6
1953	21.2	−23.3	−18.6
1954	−2.5	−20.5	−16.1
1955	−3.7	−39.0	−29.5
1956	−0.2	−57.5	−40.9
1957	4.8	−76.8	−52.5
1958	8.5	−102.8	−67.3
1959	11.6	−100.7	−64.9
1960	11.0	−133.4	−84.5
1961	10.4	−156.5	−96.1
1962	0.9	−177.9	−105.6

Table 4. *Gross revenue, total costs, and 'net margins', 1948–73, in constant 1948 prices (£m.)*

Year	Gross revenue	Total costs	Balance	'Net margin' (%)
1948	346.7	366.8	−20.1	−5.5
1949	325.7	355.6	−29.9	−8.4
1950	338.7	354.0	−15.3	−4.3
1951	345.6	360.2	−14.6	−4.1
1952	343.0	359.6	−16.6	−4.6
1953	347.3	365.9	−18.6	−5.1
1954	352.0	368.1	−16.1	−4.4
1955	343.0	372.5	−29.5	−7.9
1956	342.2	383.1	−40.9	−10.7
1957	343.0	395.5	−52.5	−13.3
1958	308.4	375.7	−67.3	−17.9
1959	294.7	359.6	−64.9	−18.0
1960	303.1	387.6	−84.5	−21.8
1961	291.5	387.6	−96.1	−24.8
1962	276.2	381.8	−105.6	−27.7
1963	272.8	365.5	−92.7	−25.4
1964	270.6	355.3	−84.7	−23.8
1965	260.2	347.8	−87.6	−25.2
1966	249.3	334.2	−84.9	−25.4
1967	229.9	326.1	−96.2	−29.5
1968	223.1	306.2	−83.1	−27.1
1969	259.3	304.7	−45.4	−14.9
1970	258.1	299.4	−41.3	−13.8
1971	244.2	288.6	−44.4	−15.4
1972	226.0	280.2	−54.2	−19.3
1973	239.2	281.7	−51.5	−18.3

Note:

Balance: from Tables 2 and 3 above.

Cost: include capital charges in Table 2, and also abnormal maintenance/maintenance equalisation adjustments, which are considered to be costs.

Gross revenue: includes passenger grants for 1969–73.

'Net margin': gross revenue minus costs divided by costs, expressed as a percentage.

1968 figures are up-dated ones (see Table 2).

Sources: except where specially stated, all data in the tables and text to Appendix A have been taken from B.T.C., *R. & A. 1948–62*, and B.R.B., *R. & A. 1963–73*. Constant prices derived from Feinstein's G.D.P. deflator, in *National Income*, supplemented by C.S.O., *National Income and Expenditure 1965–75*.

NOTES TO TABLES 1 AND 2

The published accounts of the B.T.C. and B.R.B. fail to give a clear impression of the financial situation of the railways for several reasons. The problem lies in the ways of charging for the capital assets used. There are problems of under and overcharging and of discontinuities all of which serve to cloud the picture. The areas of concern may be briefly listed as follows.

(i) Depreciation provisions

In accordance with contemporary accounting practice the B.T.C., then B.R.B., provided for depreciation on a historic cost basis. In 1953 Sir Reginald Wilson estimated that the depreciation of rolling stock on a replacement cost basis would add £13m. to the charge calculated on book values. This excluded interest on the increased cost of replacement if financed externally, estimated as £12.5m. by the end of the replacement cycle (see Wilson, draft memo. on 'Economics of Reconstruction and Re-equipment', 9 September 1953, B.R.B. 23-10-1 Pt 1C). By 1983 the gap between historic and current depreciation provision had risen to £184m. (including £24m. for the difference between historic and current cost amortisation provision) although £93m. of this was met by the Special Replacement Allowance received under the Public Service Obligation (B.R.B., R. & A. 1983, pp.28, 30–2). The cause of the shortfall was that provisions based on the purchase cost of assets were inadequate to cover the replacement cost due to inflation. A more accurate picture of railway finances would have been had by making provisions based on replacement cost.

(ii) Amortisation provisions

The B.T.C. continued the traditional practice of charging the renewal of ways and structures assets to revenue account. The B.R.B. accounts from 1963 introduced a new system by which assets were first charged to capital account and then amortised over a number of years related to the expected length of life of the assets. This system, which was similar to the depreciation provisions made for other assets, also used a historic rather than a replacement cost formula (B.R.B., R. & A. 1963, notes to accounts, p.14). The change in accounting practice in 1963 represented a major break in the series of financial results. As a consequence the charge on revenue for ways and structures assets fell heavily from £21.9m. in 1962 (this figure is derived from the estimated total investment in ways and structures of £47.7m., Appendix B, Table 1, minus the investment on capital account of £25.8m., B.T.C., R. & A. 1962, II, Table V-10) to £13.2m. in 1963. Any consistent series outlining the financial results of British Rail must seek to eradicate this discrepancy.

(iii) Interest payments

Interest charges made against British Railways came from a variety of sources. In the beginning the B.T.C. had to carry a fixed interest debt on the compensation paid to shareholders on nationalisation. Originally this was not allocated between the different constituent parts of the B.T.C., although later it was decided that 70 per cent could be attributed to railways. In 1956 interest charges and central administration charges attributed to the railways were £41m. Of this £22.4m. represented interest on the original British Transport Stock. The level of compensation was determined by the stock market value of transport company shares prior to nationalisation. This in itself tended to overvalue the capital value as the stock market prices were largely determined by buoyant traffic levels and the knowledge of impending nationalisation. This had little relation to the actual earning power of the assets. Furthermore the stock market valuation was made when the long-term rate of interest was 2½ per cent, while British Transport Stock carried a rate of 3 per cent, the actual rate on nationalisation. This automatically overvalued the stock by 20%.

(iv) Capital write-downs
The reorganisation and capital reconstruction of the railways in 1962 and 1968 seriously affect any attempts to compare financial statistics across these years. Both the book values of assets and interest bearing debt were revalued. In consequence interest charges attributable to railways fell from £77.4m. in 1962 (£38.9m. of which was placed in a suspense account) to £59.9m. in 1963. The 1968 Transport Act reduced the interest burden of the B.R.B. from £67.3m. to £41.5m. In addition the gross book value of the assets was written down by £535m. with consequent reduction in the level of depreciation and amortisation provisions. These alterations were carried out either in order to place a more realistic capital burden on the railways or to help remove from the railways the stigma of constant deficits. For our purpose they mask the true picture of railway finances.

(v) Grants and subsidies
In several years grants of various kinds were received. Between 1960 and 1962 grants totalling £392m. were made by the Minister in respect of railway deficits. From 1969 to 1973 £45.3m. was received under the heading of 'Surplus Track Grant'. Their inclusion in certain years clouds comparison of those years with others. Similarly a payment of £27.0m. was made to the B.R.B. in 1972 to cover 'frustrated pricing'. While it is true that the government's prices and incomes policy adversely affected railway finances in 1972 it was no less so than in 1973 or in the famous case of 1952. The grants for unremunerative passenger services are of a different nature. The payments were intended to be a realistic charge for railway services provided at the government's behest, and we have chosen to credit them to the operating account.

Creation of a consistent set of accounts, 1948–73

Two sets of statistics have been generated. One is termed the 'gross working surplus'. This represents gross receipts net of all expenses except capital costs. The second gives capital costs on a current replacement cost basis with no write-downs, and these are then deducted from the 'gross working surplus' to give the overall surplus or, in the vast majority of cases, deficit. Grants are *ignored*, except those for unremunerative passenger services from 1969.

(a) Gross working surplus
All capital charges on operating account (i.e. depreciation and amortisation provisions) are added back to the figures for net receipts. Before 1963 this includes the investment expenditure which was charged to revenue. Other adjustments, i.e. the inclusion of the net results of rail catering and a contribution to the central administration charges of the B.T.C., are also made. From 1969 the B.R.B.'s share of freightliner profits is included in net receipts. Two figures are given for net

receipts and depreciation and amortisation provisions in 1968. The first is comparable with pre-1969 data. The second excludes the £18m. loss on the freightliners and sundries divisions which were transferred to the N.F.C. at the end of 1968 and is comparable with post-1968 data.

(b) Capital costs

Total capital costs consist of three categories: depreciation provisions, amortisation provisions and interest charges. The depreciation provisions were calculated from the new investment data with minor amendments. Steam locomotives constructed after nationalisation were depreciated over a full 25 years despite the fact that the last one was withdrawn in 1968. The rationale for this is that premature displacement should be treated as a capital cost since the retirement of unprofitable assets will not only benefit finances in a single year. No depreciation charges were made for road freight vehicles after 1968 (after 1967 for the second calculation for 1968) to allow for their transfer, and their loss was not made an additional depreciation charge as in the calculations of the capital stock. Assets leased in the 1971–3 period are not included since the leasing charges were made directly into the operating account. Finally, the estimated depreciation charges at 1948 price levels were multiplied by the relevant price indices to give current-cost depreciation provisions. Amortisation provisions were dealt with in two ways. Expenditure after nationalisation was charged for over a period of 40 years. This was also multiplied by the ways and structures price index to convert it into current cost terms. This leaves charges for the amortisation of pre-1948 construction. An estimate of this was gleaned from B.R.B., R. & A. 1963. Total historic costs were put at £56.7m. for railways for both depreciation and amortisation. In the notes on accounts it was stated that,

If the book values of all operational fixed assets represented in the capital account other than land had been calculated at mid-1963 levels of prices and had the depreciation and amortisation provisions for the year 1963 been calculated on these notional book values they would have been greater by some £25m. Of this amount about £1m. related to ships. (II, p.15).

Assuming the extra provisions due to harbours and hotels to be negligible (they formed less than 1 per cent of the historic cost provisions), this indicates current cost provisions totalling £80.7m. in 1963 (£56.7m. plus £24m.). Deducting the estimated £63.0m. depreciation provisions leaves £17.7m. as the current cost amortisation provisions. Of this £12.3m. can be attributed to post-nationalisation assets leaving £5.4m. to pre-nationalisation assets. This is equal to £3m. in 1948 prices. Assuming that the provision for 1948 represented a fortieth of accumulated investment over the previous 40 years and that this investment was evenly spread then the provision for 1948 would have been £4.8m. (If x = 1948 provision, the 1963 provision would be

$$\frac{40x - 15x}{40} = 3.0, \therefore x = 4.8,$$

as the 'gross stock' of assets to be amortised, constructed before 1948, would decline by £xm. per annum in constant prices, i.e. £0.12m. (4.8/40) in each subsequent year). Provisions so calculated were converted to current cost levels and added to the provisions for post-nationalisation assets. Interest charges also fall into two sections: interest on investment since nationalisation, over and above depreciation and amortisation provisions; and interest on the initial purchase of railway assets. The first charge was made as described with the rate of interest being taken as equal to the average yield on consols for each year. Whenever depreciation and amortisation charges exceeded actual investment this was treated as a negative charge or credit.

The charge for interest on the value of assets on nationalisation was based on the value of British Transport Stock issued in compensation. This amounted to £1,066.8m. Allocating this to railways on the basis of their share in total net-book values gives a figure of £838.5m. This was then adjusted to take into account the change in interest rates between the valuation and issue of the stock to give a value of £699m. It should be noted that the interest subsequently charged is much less than that actually charged to the Commission and the Board. This is partly because of the lower cost of acquisition charged in 1948. However, it is mainly due to the application of assumed current cost depreciation and amortisation charges. Consequently less had to be borrowed to finance investment and so interest charges are lower. After 1967 the provisions exceeded investment. This was taken as a paying back of the capital debt, reducing interest charges yet further. These figures do not include interest on previous deficits, a fact which also tends to make them smaller.

NOTES TO TABLE 3

Maintenance accounting and the railways' financial results

The abnormal maintenance account (see B.T.C., *R. & A. 1948–53*, Table V13) was designed to compensate the B.T.C. for the fact that maintenance had fallen heavily into arrears during the war, which necessitated abnormal expenditure in the immediate post-war years. It was estimated that the total cost of war-time arrears was between £100 and £150m. Because it was difficult to distinguish between normal and abnormal expenditure, the B.T.C. applied as a proxy a 'standard charge', based on the average maintenance expenditure of the main-line companies in 1935–7 and adjusted for changes in price and asset levels. Expenditure in excess of the standard was charged to the abnormal maintenance fund (see R. H. Wilson, memo. on 'Standard Charge for Maintenance', 23 May 1949, B.T.C. S21-1-1, B.R.B.). The net charges to the fund made for the railways (including collection and delivery) for 1948–53 are shown in Table 3. Although annual drawings on the account fell up to 1950, as had been expected, they then increased as a result of inflation; by 1952 it was apparent that a new procedure was urgently required, and it was agreed that the 'standard charge' would be abandoned in 1954. As a step in this direction it was discontinued for locomotives and coaching vehicles in 1953. The abnormal maintenance fund, which had stood at £149.7 million in January 1948, had fallen to £45.6m. by December 1953. All but £1m. of this residue, together with £14.2m. provided for the restoration of war damage, was then transferred to a new maintenance equalisation account. After 1 January 1954, maintenance expenditure was first charged to revenue; exceptional or 'special' maintenance was charged to the new account, in order to equalise year-to-year expenditure. As Table 3 shows, the railways' operating account continued to benefit from drawings on the new account. However, in 1954–6, sums were debited to revenue to build up the account (for details see B.T.C. Finance Committee Minutes, 24 February 1954 and 10 February 1955, B.R.B. and B.T.C., *R. & A. 1954*, notes to accounts).

The B.T.C. was clearly anxious about the implications of abandoning the 'standard charge' procedure (see R. H. Wilson, memo. on 'Commission's Financial Outlook: June 1953', 30 June 1953, B.T.C. Minutes, 9 July 1953, and H. E. Osborn, memo. on 'Commission's Financial Outlook', 10 November 1953, B.T.C. Finance Committee Minutes, 12 November 1953, B.R.B.). The accounts for 1954 revealed that the change had added about £19 million to the B.T.C.'s costs charged to revenue, about £18 million of this attributable to the railways' operating account (B.T.C., *R. & A. 1954*, I, p.68, and notes to accounts). Had the revised procedure been in operation in 1953, it would have added an extra £14m. to costs shown on revenue account for ways and structures alone (H. E. Osborn, memo. on 'Maintenance Equalisation – British Railways', 3 February 1955, Finance Committee Minutes, 10 February 1955, B.R.B.). The situation was serious enough for Wilson, the B.T.C. Comptroller, to suggest that 'a rather better view of the results of British Railways' might be obtained for 1954 if the Commission agreed to withdraw about £5m. from the remaining abnormal maintenance reserve (Wilson, memo. on 'Closing the Budget Gap', 18 December 1953, repeated in memo. on 'Financial Outlook of British Railways', 5 April 1954, B.T.C. S21-4-1, B.R.B.). However, concern was expressed about the attitude of the auditors to such a move, and it was abandoned. The drawings on the abnormal maintenance fund amounted to £104.1m. over the period 1948–53. The railways consumed £97.5m. This sum would represent a subsidy to operating if the maintenance expenditure taken to be normal or the 'standard' was an underestimate of maintenance in normal circumstances. Clearly, it was quite proper that the railways should be compensated for war-time neglect; equally clearly, there was internal acceptance in the B.T.C. that the 'standard charge' used was an arbitrary way of determining how that compensation should be charged. Given the circumstances of post-war shortages and controls – the steel allocations, building licences and shortages of labour – it is highly likely that the railways were failing to spend at abnormal levels. There is certainly empirical evidence to suggest that the level of physical maintenance in 1948–53 remained below pre-war standards and that the maintenance of structures in particular had been curtailed (see Chapter 3, p. 85). Although controls and shortages played their part here, there were those at the Commission who were keen to keep maintenance expenditure at a minimum in spite of the existence of the abnormal maintenance fund. In 1949, for example, Wilson had stated that 'the fact that these arrears . . . had occurred does not mean, of course, that all of it [*sic*] will have to be made good'. He was referring to circumstances where constantly deferred annual maintenance did not lead to cumulative arrears, or where neglected maintenance might ultimately be compensated for by the purchase of a replacement asset. Wilson also recommended periodic reviews of the physical standards of maintenance, and argued that the 'standard charge' and actual expenditure should be reduced wherever possible. The aim was to ensure that 'the excess off-charged to the reserve will be reduced more rapidly than our Opening Reserve allows for in which case we shall be left with a free balance . . . which must then be dealt with as the Commission may determine' (Wilson, memo. on 'Standard Charge for Maintenance', 23 May 1949, B.T.C. S21-1-1, B.R.B.). In contrast, Hurcomb was critical of the idea of using any residue from the abnormal maintenance account for other purposes, for fear of adverse criticism (Hurcomb, memo. to B.T.C. 26 May 1949, S21-1-1, B.R.B.).

The data in Table 3 provide an upper-bound estimate of this 'subsidy', since it is assumed that *all* drawings on the account represented 'normal' maintenance and should have been charged to revenue. Certainly, the sharp change in the railways' fortunes in 1954 owed a great deal to the change of accounting method. In 1954 £2.5m. was transferred from the railways' revenue account to the new maintenance equalisation account; in the previous year, revenue had benefited to the tune of £21.2m. from a transfer in the opposite direction. The 'profits' and 'healthy' operating performance in 1951–3 would seem to be little more than an accounting illusion.

In 1954–6 £6.4m. was paid into the maintenance equalisation account from railway revenue; in 1957–62 £47.2m. was transferred to the railways' operating account. The net benefit to railways was thus £40.8m. The account, designed to 'equalise' year-to-year expenditure levels, appears to have done little more than distribute, mainly in 1958–60, the residue of the original fund. Again, Table 3 provides an upper-bound estimate of the 'subsidy' which may have been incorporated in such a procedure. The severity of the overall deficits in 1954–62 is not affected.

Gross and net investment and the capital stock, 1948–73

Table 1. *Gross investment in British Railways (including collection and delivery), 1948–73, in current and constant prices (£m.)*

Year	Current prices: Rolling stock	Ways and structures	Total[a]	Constant 1948 prices: Rolling stock	Ways and structures	Total[a]
1948	27.6	10.0	40.3	27.6	10.0	40.3
1949	29.2	11.7	44.1	27.7	11.7	42.5
1950	29.4	10.5	43.4	26.2	10.0	39.3
1951	33.0	6.5	42.3	27.8	5.0	34.8
1952	25.0	11.6	40.0	18.4	9.1	29.8
1953	36.1	14.4	55.9	24.7	11.0	39.4
1954	47.4	11.6	65.3	31.7	8.5	44.5
1955	55.7	10.3	71.3	36.3	7.2	46.9
1956	66.1	17.0	89.0	41.0	11.3	55.8
1957	89.9	29.5	125.9	52.7	19.2	75.8
1958	87.4	46.2	141.0	49.5	30.2	83.8
1959	97.8	61.7	167.8	53.9	39.9	98.4
1960	85.9	70.2	163.3	46.3	44.0	94.2
1961	73.6	66.4	146.2	37.9	38.3	79.4
1962	62.8	47.7	115.3	31.0	27.1	60.7
1963	47.2	40.5	90.6	22.7	22.7	46.8
1964	47.0	49.1	100.7	21.4	26.2	50.3
1965	54.5	53.1	113.7	23.5	27.5	54.0
1966	39.3	52.1	102.8	17.2	25.9	49.4
1967	31.3	45.9	86.0	12.6	21.4	38.4
1968	26.7	44.1	79.0	10.3	19.5	33.2
1969	15.3	42.5	62.0	5.5	17.9	25.1
1970	20.2	53.2	77.9	6.8	20.6	29.1
1971	21.2	65.4	91.2	6.8	23.0	31.5
1972	19.1	78.6	102.8	6.0	22.7	30.5
1973	24.9	78.8	109.4	7.1	17.7	26.6

[a] Categories not listed separately include plant and equipment, electric plant and road freight vehicles. In 1948, investment in these categories was £1.1m., £0.1m. and £1.5m. respectively.

NOTES TO TABLE 1

Gross investment at current prices 1948–73

(i) Ways and structures 1948–62
Most of the data in this table are taken from the expenditure on capital account shown in the Annual Reports and Accounts of the B.T.C. (V–8, V–10) and B.R.B. (3–A, 3–B). The principal exception to this is the ways and structures series between 1948–62. During this period, the B.T.C. charged a substantial amount of expenditure on ways and structures to the revenue account. Consequently data from the Reports and Accounts had to be supplemented with additional material. The other sources used were as follows:
(a) B.R.B., Rail Policy Review, 1972: data prepared for the review and supplied by B.R.B. (cf. B.R.B. Finance 23-1-14).
(b) Investment Programmes Committee Minutes, CAB134/440-2, 938, P.R.O., and B.T.C. S21-1-2 A-H, K, B.R.B.
(c) Investment Reviews, B.R.B. 23-4-2 Pts. 1-3.
(d) B.R.B. New Works 23-4-5.

(ii) Rolling stock 1971–3
A further complication arises from the introduction in 1971 of the practice of leasing assets. Here again, the figures for capital investment given in the Reports and Accounts are inadequate for our purposes, because they take no account of leased assets. Adjustments to compensate for the effect of leasing have been made to the figures 1971–3, using information supplied by B.R.B.

Gross investment at constant prices 1948–73

This series was obtained by dividing the current price series by the appropriate price indices given in Table 1a. The ways and structures index was taken from the 'Cost of Building and Civil Engineering Structures Related to Cost in 1830' used by B.R.B. The road freight vehicles index was taken from the C.S.O. The remaining indices were constructed from series used to calculate current replacement cost by B.R.B. (see B.R.B. Finance 252-5-8). The rolling stock index is a current weighted average price index of locomotives, coaches and freight vehicles.

Table 1a. *Price indices for capital goods: summary 1948–73*

Year	Rolling stock	Ways and structures	Plant and equipment	Electric plant	Road freight vehicles
1948	100.0	100.0	100.0	100.0	100.0
1949	105.3	100.3	107.8	105.4	101.7
1950	112.2	105.3	115.2	112.6	108.8
1951	118.6	129.7	133.0	137.4	131.5
1952	136.0	128.0	149.7	148.9	147.0
1953	145.9	131.1	148.8	148.9	139.1
1954	149.6	136.4	152.4	149.7	135.6
1955	153.6	143.2	168.9	169.8	135.6
1956	161.4	150.5	182.5	178.6	145.1
1957	170.5	153.6	190.8	170.0	149.5
1958	176.6	152.8	193.8	168.5	152.0
1959	181.3	154.7	195.3	174.3	147.0
1960	185.6	159.6	206.6	178.2	142.4
1961	194.2	173.2	217.4	182.0	144.7
1962	202.8	175.7	219.3	183.1	147.2
1963	208.1	178.7	220.8	183.8	140.8
1964	219.2	187.1	222.2	193.0	141.3
1965	231.8	193.2	238.2	201.2	143.4
1966	228.4	201.2	243.4	208.7	144.9
1967	249.0	214.7	246.9	207.6	147.5
1968	260.4	226.3	258.3	220.5	152.9
1969	279.5	238.0	264.5	233.5	160.6
1970	296.9	258.2	268.9	248.5	170.1
1971	311.5	284.0	305.9	253.0	188.4
1972	320.2	345.8	317.6	267.3	200.1
1973	350.6	444.9	333.3	299.4	215.2

Table 2. *Ways and structures: changes in the capital stock 1948–73 at constant (1948) prices (£m.)*

Year	Gross investment	Scrappings	Net investment	Capital stock[a]
1948	10.0	6.9	3.1	1,603
1949	11.7	8.1	3.6	1,607
1950	10.0	8.6	1.4	1,608
1951	5.0	7.6	−2.6	1,606
1952	9.1	12.6	−3.5	1,602
1953	11.0	10.6	0.4	1,602
1954	8.5	10.2	−1.7	1,601
1955	7.2	9.7	−2.5	1,598
1956	11.3	12.1	−0.8	1,597
1957	19.2	14.3	4.9	1,602
1958	30.2	17.7	12.5	1,615
1959	39.9	26.1	13.8	1,629
1960	44.0	31.1	12.9	1,642
1961	38.3	25.9	12.4	1,654
1962	27.1	23.6	3.5	1,657
1963	22.7	29.5	−6.8	1,651
1964	26.2	33.6	−7.4	1,643
1965	27.5	49.5	−22.0	1,621
1966	25.9	53.2	−27.3	1,594
1967	21.4	55.8	−34.4	1,560
1968	19.5	35.4	−15.9	1,544
1969	17.9	36.6	−18.7	1,525
1970	20.6	26.6	−6.0	1,519
1971	23.0	25.0	−2.0	1,517
1972	22.7	20.5	2.2	1,519
1973	17.7	19.5	−1.8	1,517

[a] At end of year.

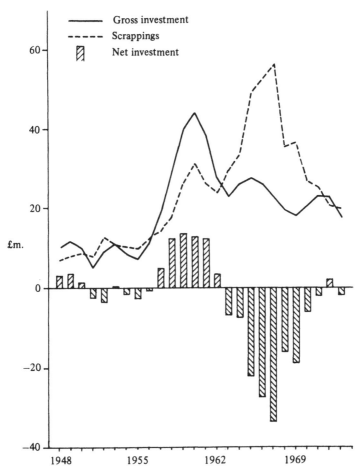

Investment in ways and structures, 1948–73 (constant 1948 prices)
Source: Appendix B, Table 2.

Table 3. *Rolling stock, etc.:*[a] *changes in the capital stock 1948–73 at constant (1948) prices (£m.)*

Year	Gross investment	Depreciation	Net investment	Net capital stock[b]
1948	30.3	19.4	10.9	233
1949	30.8	19.8	11.0	244
1950	29.3	19.9	9.4	254
1951	29.8	20.1	9.7	263
1952	20.7	20.2	0.5	264
1953	28.4	20.0	8.4	272
1954	36.0	20.4	15.6	288
1955	39.7	21.0	18.7	306
1956	44.5	21.7	22.8	329
1957	56.6	23.0	33.6	363
1958	53.6	25.0	28.6	391
1959	58.5	26.9	31.6	423
1960	50.2	28.6	21.6	445
1961	41.1	29.7	11.4	456
1962	33.6	30.3	3.3	459
1963	24.2	30.6	−6.4	453
1964	24.0	30.6	−6.6	446
1965	26.5	30.6	−4.1	442
1966	23.5	34.3[c]	−10.8	431
1967	17.0	36.9	−19.9	412
1968	13.7	41.3[d]	−27.6	384
1969	7.2	29.5	−22.3	362
1970	8.5	28.9	−20.4	341
1971	8.5	28.5	−20.0	321
1972	7.8	28.1	−20.3	301
1973	8.9	27.7	−18.8	282

[a] Includes plant and machinery and road vehicles.
[b] At end of year.
[c] Jump in series due to final phasing out of steam power.
[d] Jump in series due to loss of collection and delivery service; capital value of road freight vehicles (£11.7m. gross, £7.5m. net) written out of series.

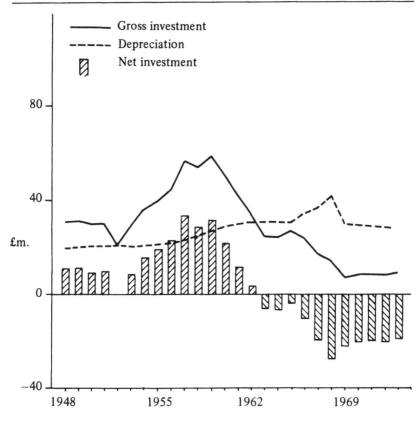

Rolling stock investment, 1948–73 (constant 1948 prices)
Source: Appendix B, Table 3.

Table 4. *Depreciation and net investment, 1948–73 at constant 1948 prices (£m.)*

Year	Depreciation	Net investment
1948	26.3	14.0
1949	27.9	14.6
1950	28.5	10.8
1951	27.7	7.1
1952	32.8	−3.0
1953	30.6	8.8
1954	30.6	13.9
1955	30.7	16.2
1956	33.8	22.0
1957	37.3	38.5
1958	42.7	41.1
1959	53.0	45.4
1960	59.7	34.5
1961	55.6	23.8
1962	53.9	6.8
1963	60.1	−13.2
1964	64.2	−14.0
1965	80.1	−26.1
1966	87.5	−38.1
1967	92.7	−54.3
1968	76.7	−43.5
1969	66.1	−41.0
1970	55.5	−26.4
1971	53.5	−22.0
1972	48.6	−18.1
1973	47.2	−20.6

Table 5. *Value of the gross and net capital stock employed in British Railways, 1947–73 in constant 1948 prices (£m.)*

Year (end of)	Gross capital stock	Net capital stock
1947	2,065	1,822
1948	2,076	1,836
1949	2,082	1,851
1950	2,083	1,862
1951	2,085	1,869
1952	2,074	1,866
1953	2,082	1,875
1954	2,094	1,888
1955	2,112	1,905
1956	2,142	1,927
1957	2,195	1,965
1958	2,250	2,006
1959	2,308	2,052
1960	2,349	2,086
1961	2,376	2,110
1962	2,386	2,117
1963	2,379	2,104
1964	2,372	2,090
1965	2,361	2,063
1966	2,337	2,025
1967	2,294	1,971
1968	2,255	1,928
1969	2,224	1,887
1970	2,208	1,860
1971	2,199	1,838
1972	2,189	1,820
1973	2,173	1,799

Note: data rounded to nearest £m.

Table 6. *Railway investment, 1948–53: Redfern's estimates (£m.)*

| Year | At current prices: | | | | At constant 1948 prices: | | | |
| | Rolling stock | | All | | Rolling stock | | All | |
	Gross	Net	Gross	Net	Gross	Net	Gross	Net
1948	28	5	36	−21	28	5	36	−21
1949	29	5	38	−20	28	5	37	−20
1950	31	4	40	−19	28	4	38	−18
1951	33	4	42	−26	27	3	34	−21
1952	27	−5	36	−37	20	−4	27	−28
1953	37	4	49	−24	27	3	36	−18
1948–53	185	17	241	−141	158	16	208	−126
p.a.	30.8	2.8	40.2	−24.5	26.3	2.7	34.7	−21.0

Source: P. Redfern, 'Net Investment in Fixed Assets in the United Kingdom, 1938–53', *Journal of the Royal Statistical Society*, Series A, CXVIII (1955), 153–60. The figure of £37m. for gross investment in rolling stock in 1953, derived from the C.S.O. Blue Book of 1954, is given as £36m. in later editions.

NOTES TO TABLES 2–6

Investment and the capital stock

Introduction

Discussion of investment and the capital stock falls naturally into two parts. One, the level of gross investment, is relatively uncontroversial. The other concerns the size of the capital stock and the net additions or deductions from it. This part depends heavily on chosen definitions and methods, the results of which can never be certain.

The usual method of estimating the capital stock is to add up gross investment over a given number of years taken to represent the average length of life of the assets in question. Changes in the gross capital stock are then equal to gross investment less gross investment at some time in the past. Similarly net investment, or changes in the net capital stock, is equal to gross investment less a moving average of past levels of gross investment. This method, known as the perpetual inventory method, of estimating the value of the capital stock can have serious shortcomings. The estimate of removals from the capital stock depends totally on past levels of investment and pays little attention to current policy decisions. This can lead to a serious bias being present in the estimates and to very misleading derived estimates of capital productivity. In some cases estimated trends in capital productivity move in the opposite direction to the true movements. For example when there is technological change (which is the normal case), capital investment will be attractive in order to embody the new technology. With perpetual inventory estimation this is likely to increase the capital stock as the level of scrappings or depreciation depends totally on past levels of investment and is independent of current policy. Consequently, unless output expands more than the estimated increase in the capital stock the estimation will point to a fall in capital productivity. The actual picture of events is likely to be very different from this.

The introduction of more productive capital is likely to displace a greater amount of the existing capital stock, leading to a higher level of capital productivity. Examples of where this could happen are numerous in the railway industry. Capital employed in diesel locomotives, for example, will have a smaller observed effect on productivity if the steam locomotives they replace are still counted as being included in the capital stock. More importantly, much of the modernisation and rationalisation of the network which took place in the years 1948–73 will fail to be adequately captured by perpetual inventory methods of estimation. The accelerating cuts in the system of the first half of the sixties obviously increased capital productivity. However, if estimated scrappings take no account of current policy (i.e. cuts) there is no reason why the estimate of the capital stock, whether gross or net, should indicate an increase in the level of capital productivity.

The attraction of the perpetual inventory method is that it requires relatively little data. All that is needed (although this in many cases may be difficult or impossible to obtain) are constant price estimates of past levels of investment and information on the average length of life of assets. An alternative method requiring information on actual assets in use at any particular time would need information which in all probability would be impossible to obtain, as information on gross investment (or more likely capital expenditure) is more commonly collected than data on capital stocks in any real sense. Due to these problems the perpetual inventory method has been used for a large part of the estimation of the capital stock of British Railways. There are, however, two important exceptions to this. One is the case of capital invested in locomotives. As mentioned above this is a clear example of created bias. The introduction of diesel locomotives represented substantial embodied technical change. This has been taken care of explicitly within the perpetual inventory framework since estimates are made of the value of steam locomotives retired prematurely because of the new technology. The other exception is the case of ways and structures, which is treated quite differently. This is a major adjustment since the category is estimated to have formed 88 per cent of the total value of the net capital stock at the beginning of 1948. In this case an attempt is made to estimate actual retirements from the stock on a basis other than previous investment levels. The accuracy of the results is uncertain but it is thought that the method is justified due to the complete inappropriateness of the perpetual inventory method for ways and structures.

The actual estimates (Table 1) show gross investment in constant prices falling in the immediate post-war years owing to rationing and investment controls. From 1953 investment picked up and reached a peak of £98.4m. in 1948 prices in 1959. After 1959 investment fell off in real terms following renewed government constraints and the worsening financial situation of British Rail. Investment reached a low point in 1969 and then recovered a little thereafter. The value of the net capital stock reached a peak in 1962 (Table 5) having grown by an estimated 1 per cent per annum from the beginning of 1948 to the end of 1962. From 1963 onwards the net capital stock fell continuously under the impact of falling investment and cuts in the network.

Ways and structures
The perpetual inventory method of estimating the value of the gross or net capital stock can lead to serious errors in the case of railways' ways and structures. The reason for this lies partly in the nature of the assets and partly in the system of capital accounting used by the railways. Major works could be maintained and

renewed almost indefinitely and the cost charged to revenue in the pre-1963 accounting system. Even after 1962 heavy maintenance expenditure meant that the age of an asset was no pointer to its value. The idea of depreciation is not therefore relevant to ways and structures. Furthermore the idea of a gross capital stock based on perpetual inventory estimation has little relevance when the length of life of assets could be almost indefinite depending on the level of maintenance expenditure. The major factor affecting the scrapping of an asset was managerial decision based largely on fixed capital requirements rather than on the age of the asset.

The pure perpetual inventory method of estimating the gross capital stock, as used by Redfern, assumes a fixed length of life for the assets. This overlooks the fact that current policy considerations are at least as important as the age of assets in scrapping decisions. Redfern took the length of life for railways' ways and structures to be an, admittedly, arbitrary one – viz. 100 years. Though this figure is meant to represent an average, it does imply that by 1948 the railway system contained no pre-1849 assets. This is clearly an absurdity. About 30 per cent of the existing route-mileage in 1948 had been laid down before 1850 and today this proportion is probably higher (owing to the closure of more recent parts of the system). A 1953 survey of the age of bridges in the North Eastern Region of British Rail showed that 13.5 per cent had been built before 1849 and that 20.3 per cent were over 100 years old (B.R.B. Eastern Region Civil Engineer's Records, AN28/6, P.R.O.). A fixed 100-year figure is not realistic. Furthermore, as assets are removed from the gross capital stock calculation after 100 years there is a problem that the estimated changes in the capital stock tend to mirror, often exceptional, levels of gross investment 100 years earlier. The method now employed by the C.S.O. attempts to counter this problem by smoothing the series. A fixed length of life is not assumed. Instead the scrapping of assets is assumed to be evenly distributed between 120 and 80 years after construction. The effect of this is to smooth out the fluctuations by a moving average process. While this provides more plausible results the problem of a fixed average length of life still remains.

An example of the various estimates can be had by taking 1948, the first year of nationalised railways. The simple perpetual inventory method, as used by Redfern, indicates a level of scrapping of £19.32m. at 1848 prices, equal to the level of gross investment in 1848. This amounts to £92m. at 1948 prices. Given a level of gross investment in 1948 of £10m. this clearly indicates heavy disinvestment. The chosen level of scrapping is largely a statistical freak. 1848 was one of the peak years of the 'Railway Mania'. The assumption that all the assets built in that year were scrapped in 1948 indicates the problem of using a fixed length of life. The C.S.O. method indicates a level of scrapping of £27.9m. This still indicates disinvestment, though the level of £18m. is much less than that suggested by Redfern. As the C.S.O. figure in effect averages out past levels of investment the figures are likely to be more plausible. However, the assumption of a constant average length of life is more relevant to a growing or stable industry where assets are unlikely to be prematurely scrapped. The assumption is on very uncertain ground when applied to an industry facing a shrinking market, as with the railways.

For a further indication of the level of scrapping we can turn to the annual accounts of the B.T.C. Figures are given for assets displaced and not replaced, but at historic cost levels. In 1948 this figure was £76,739. To bring this up to 1948 prices it is strictly speaking necessary to deflate each proportion of this sum represented by a given year's vintage by a price index relevant to that year. Clearly we lack the detailed information to do this. An approximation can be had, however, by applying an average price index if this is appropriate. Most of the assets displaced and not replaced in the post-war years would have been constructed in the later years of the nineteenth and early years of the twentieth centuries. These were the marginal parts of the system, the many branch lines and a few main lines which duplicated others. Between 1870 and 1913 the 'Cost of Building and Civil Engineering' index gives an average price level of 25 (1948 = 100) when weighted by the volume of investment. This can be taken as a representative price index to see how the series compares. Applying this to the historic cost displacement level indicates a value of assets displaced and not replaced of £0.3m. in 1948 prices. For comparability with the C.S.O. data the value of assets displaced and replaced must be added. This will be equal to the level of investment (new series) less expenditure on capital account. This is £10m. less £3.4m., or £6.6m., giving a total for scrapping of £6.9m. for 1948. This figure is considerably less than the C.S.O. figure of £27.9m. and far removed from Redfern's figure of £92m. In terms of changes in the gross capital stock the difference is even more marked. While the C.S.O. data show a fall of £17.9m. the new figure actually points to a small increase of £3.1m. Such a wide variation in the estimates must make us wary of using any of them. Table A below illustrates the difference between the two estimates for the entire 1948–62 period.

Although the trend in both scrapping series is upwards there are substantial year-to-year differences in the variations exhibited about this trend. The C.S.O. series moves continuously upwards. This is a feature of the moving average

Table A. *Changes in the gross capital stock: ways and structures, alternative estimates*

Year	Scrapping 'C.S.O.'[a]	New estimate	Total change (Net investment) 'C.S.O.'[a]	New estimate
1948	27.9	6.8	−17.9	3.1
1949	28.6	8.1	−16.9	3.6
1950	29.4	8.6	−19.4	1.4
1951	30.4	7.6	−25.4	−2.6
1952	31.4	12.6	−22.3	−3.5
1953	32.5	10.6	−21.5	0.4
1954	33.8	10.2	−25.0	−1.7
1955	35.1	9.7	−29.0	−2.5
1956	36.4	12.1	−24.0	−0.8
1957	37.6	14.3	−19.9	4.9
1958	38.6	17.7	−8.6	12.5
1959	39.4	26.1	−2.2	13.8
1960	40.1	31.1	0.0	12.9
1961	41.0	25.9	−2.7	12.4
1962	42.0	23.6	−14.9	3.5

[a] The C.S.O. data here = our gross investment series minus C.S.O. figures for scrappings = 'C.S.O. "net" investment'.

procedure by which it is generated. The scrappings figure for 1948 is essentially gross investment up to 1868 averaged out. The figure for 1962 is the average level of gross investment 1842 to 1882, obviously a higher figure. The new estimate, on the other hand, fluctuates considerably, with the increase slackening off in 1954–5 and 1960–2. The new series is more likely to reflect actual policy in the period in question rather than the distribution of nineteenth-century investment. The low scrapping levels indicated in the early post-nationalisation period were due to the need to retain older assets when faced with an investment shortage. As the 1950s passed the investment situation became much easier, especially with the onset of the Modernisation Plan. Contrast for example the £10.0m. investment in 1948 (or only £5.0m. in 1951), with £44.0m. in 1960 (all at 1948 prices). With the greater availability of new assets more ageing assets could be scrapped. The branch-line closure programme also points to higher scrapping levels.

As scrapping should relate to actual physical changes in the capital stock an indicator of the reliability of the three series can be had by relating them to the physical evidence. The Annual Reports and Accounts give data on the closure of track and stations in the period. Table B shows simple correlation coefficients for these two items and the alternative Redfern, C.S.O. and new estimates of 'assets displaced and not replaced'. 'Assets displaced and not replaced' are defined as the total scrapping estimates less replacement investment (the 'new' investment series less investment charged to capital account). Replacement investment is excluded on the grounds that it would not show up in physical changes. Route-mileage and station closures are lagged by one year to allow time for the changes to appear in the books. The conclusions of Table B are quite clear. The new estimate corresponds fairly well with the physical indicators while the C.S.O. data show no significant level of correlation and Redfern's series actually shows negative correlation.

To be fair to Redfern his series was not meant to be a particularly accurate measure. It was intended for estimating the gross capital stock with the intention of arriving at depreciation estimates and measures of net investment, and this for the economy as a whole rather than a single industry. The argument followed in this note has been that depreciation is not a relevant concept when assets can be maintained in good working condition almost indefinitely out of revenue. Redfern's figures are quoted for comparison only. It is not claimed that he intended them to have any real relevance to actual changes in the gross capital stock.

It appears that scrappings did not depend entirely on the age of the assets. Decisions as to the desired size of the system were all important, and these were taken with reference to available replacement investment as well as to the age of assets. The estimation of scrapping levels by adding together displacements, calculated from the historic cost levels in the Reports and Accounts, and replacement investment appears to be a far more accurate way of capturing the actual fluctuations in the 1948–62 period. The actual magnitude must remain in some doubt. The levels of replacement investment are fairly reliable (and this accounts for over half the total), but the rest depends on the multiplier chosen to convert the historic cost figures into 1948 prices. This cannot be determined with any great certainty. A figure of 4 was chosen as being representative of prevalent prices in the period in which most of the assets likely to be scrapped were built. For the new estimates to average out at the same level as the C.S.O. figure the multiplier would have to be of the order of about 15. This is obviously unrealistic. On the basis of the 'Cost of Building and Related Structures' index, in only eleven years since 1830

Table B. *Physical indicators and alternative estimates of displacements, etc. (correlation coefficients)*

| | Closures | |
	Route-mileage	Stations
New estimate	0.86	0.81
C.S.O.	0.02	0.08
Redfern	−0.47	−0.55

were prices less than a sixth, let alone a fifteenth, of the 1948 level, and these were all before 1861. This is further evidence that the new estimate's order of magnitude is more likely than that of the C.S.O. This in combination with its more accurate short-term movements appears to make it the superior series.

Changes in the capital stock after 1962

The capital accounting procedure of the B.R.B. differed substantially from that of the B.T.C. From 1963 major replacements were incorporated into the capital account and no longer charged to revenue. Capitalised investment was then amortised over a given number of years. Estimates for the displacements of assets that actually took place were no longer given. If the method of estimating scrappings on an alternative basis is to be continued some other way must be found of estimating the actual level of displacements without replacements and major renewals.

A pointer to a possible way of doing this can be found in Table B. Displacements (without replacements) show a high degree of correlation with both changes in route-mileage and stations (lagged by one year). If the relationship between displacements and scrappings can be found for the 1948–62 period it can be used to extrapolate data forward in the post 1962 years. To begin with we know that the level of assets displaced (and not replaced) was related to closures:

$$\text{Dis.}_t = f_1 \text{ (closures }_{t-1}, \text{ age of assets)}$$

The age of assets is also likely to have been of some influence. In addition replacement investment must be considered. This will be related to the total level of investment, replacements tending to increase with the resources available for new investment. (The correlation coefficient between replacements and gross investment 1948–62 is 0.96):

$$\text{Rep.}_t = f_2 \text{ (Investment}_t)$$

Adding these together gives:

$$\text{Dis.}_t + \text{Rep.}_t = f \text{ (Closures}_{t-1}, \text{ Investment}_t, \text{ age)}$$

Using regression analysis experiments were made with various variables based on this postulated relationship. The best version uses the C.S.O. scrappings estimate as a proxy for age of assets and changes in route-mileage as an indicator of closures. This was:

$$Sc_t = \ -2.91 + 0.12 \ Sc_{t-1} + 0.03 \ R.M._{t-1}$$
$$(-1.60) \quad (2.75) \quad\quad (7.92)$$
$$+ \ 0.35 Inv_t + 0.20 \ C.S.O._t - 0.74 r_{t-1} + r_t$$
$$(16.3) \quad\quad (3.24) \quad\quad (3.85)$$
$$r^2 \ = 0.998 \quad h = -1.79 \quad n = 14$$

Table C. *Changes in the gross capital stock: alternative estimates*
1963–73

Year	Scrappings C.S.O.	New estimate	Net investment C.S.O.	New estimate
1963	42.7	29.5	−20.1	−6.8
1964	43.4	33.6	−17.1	−7.4
1965	43.7	49.5	−16.2	−22.0
1966	43.3	53.2	−17.4	−27.3
1967	42.3	55.8	−19.6	−34.4
1968	40.9	35.4	−21.4	−15.9
1969	39.4	36.6	−21.5	−18.7
1970	38.5	26.6	−17.9	−6.0
1971	38.3	25.0	−15.3	−2.0
1972	38.4	20.5	−15.7	2.2
1973	38.7	19.5	−21.0	−1.8

Estimation was by autoregressive least squares. The 'h' statistic is Durbin's test for
first order autoregressive errors when a lagged dependent variable is present. It has
a standard normal distribution. The variables are:

Sc	= Total Scrappings
Inv	= Gross Investment
C.S.O.	= C.S.O. estimate of scrappings
R.M.	= Changes in Route-Mileage
r	= residual term

The estimated equation has a high explanatory power. Over 99 per cent of the
variation in estimated scrappings in 1948–62 is explained. Although there is no
firm reason for assuming that the parameters would remain stable into the post-
1962 period, it does form some basis for extrapolating the data, which should be
superior to the C.S.O. estimate, given the shortfalls of that series in the pre-1963
years.

The alternative estimates, 1963–73, are given in Table C. Once again there are
substantial differences between the estimates. This time the new estimate for
scrappings actually exceeds the C.S.O. estimate from 1965 to 1967 as it captures
the effects of the Beeching cuts which escape the perpetual inventory estimate.

Value of the gross capital stock (ways and structures)
The procedure outlined above derives estimates for net additions (or deductions) to
the gross capital stock 1948–73. In order to find the total value of the capital stock
we need to have an estimate of its value for one of these years. Redfern derived an
estimate for 1948 of approximately three billion pounds. Having rejected the
perpetual inventory method of estimating net changes it would be inconsistent to
use it to estimate the gross value. In any case there are reasons for believing that this
may be too high. This is partly due to the problems of estimating past levels of
investment and partly because of the inability to take into account war-time
damage and the loss of value due to deficient maintenance in wartime. An
alternative estimate can be had from Sir Reginald Wilson's paper of September
1953 on 'Economics of Reconstruction and Re-equipment' (B.R.B. 23-10-1 Pt 1C).

In this the following estimates of the replacement cost, at 1953 prices, of railways' ways and structures are given:

Permanent way, etc., requiring renewal	£678m.
Buildings	more than £300m.
Rest of infrastructure (bridges, tunnels, embankments, culverts, etc.)	more than £1,000m.
Total	more than £1,978m.

The figure gives a lower limit for the value of the gross capital stock in 1953. Converting this figure to the value at the beginning of 1948 gives a value of £1,516m. (by deflating by the price index and removing any net investment). This is our lower limit for the base year. The actual total may be much higher, but there is no way of saying by how much. We have taken this figure rounded up to the nearest £100m. (the degree of accuracy suggested by the Wilson figures) as the base figure.

Conclusions
Our estimates for the gross value of ways and structures are admittedly uncertain. The scrappings data are based on a mixture of historical cost figures and extrapolation and the base estimate for 1948 of the stocks value is only an 'informed guess'. What is claimed, however, is that these estimates are a substantial improvement on other figures. The scrappings estimates actually mirror the historical changes in the railway industry in a way in which other estimates completely fail to do.

Estimates of productivity, 1948–73

Table 1. *British Railways: factor inputs and productivity (1948=100)*

Year	Output	Labour	Capital	Output per head	Capital per head	'Total factor productivity'
1948	100.0	100.0	100.0	100.0	100.0	100.0
1949	101.0	98.7	100.8	102.3	102.1	101.5
1950	99.4	95.4	101.6	104.2	106.5	101.6
1951	101.2	93.5	102.2	108.2	109.3	104.5
1952	96.7	93.1	102.6	103.9	110.2	99.9
1953	98.5	92.7	102.4	106.3	110.5	102.1
1954	99.5	90.9	102.9	109.5	113.2	104.2
1955	97.0	88.4	103.6	109.7	117.2	103.0
1956	98.8	87.9	104.5	112.4	118.9	104.9
1957	102.3	88.7	105.7	115.3	119.2	107.5
1958	94.5	87.1	107.8	108.5	123.8	99.6
1959	97.1	82.9	110.1	117.1	132.8	104.6
1960	97.9	80.1	112.6	122.2	140.6	106.7
1961	93.4	78.7	114.5	118.7	145.5	102.2
1962	86.1	75.5	115.8	114.0	153.4	96.1
1963	86.1	70.6	116.2	122.0	164.6	99.9
1964	90.0	64.6	115.4	139.3	178.6	110.5
1965	86.6	58.9	114.7	147.0	194.7	112.6
1966	84.1	54.3	113.2	154.9	208.5	115.5
1967	80.0	50.6	111.1	158.1	219.6	115.4
1968	83.2	47.3	108.2	175.9	228.8	126.3
1969	84.8	40.2[a]	105.8	210.9[a]	263.2[a]	143.2
1970	90.8	38.9	103.6	233.4	266.1	157.8
1971	86.0	37.2	102.1	231.2	274.5	154.4
1972	84.2	35.9	100.9	234.5	281.1	155.1
1973	88.7	34.9	99.9	254.2	286.2	166.9
Growth rates: % p.a.						
1948–54	−0.08	−1.58	0.48	1.52	2.09	0.69
1953–60	−0.09	−2.07	1.37	2.01	3.50	0.63
1948–60	−0.18	−1.83	0.99	1.68	2.88	0.54
1960–70	−0.75	−6.97	−0.83	6.68	6.59	3.99
1970–3	−0.78	−3.55	−1.20	2.89	2.46	1.89
1948–73	−0.48	−4.12	0.00	3.80	4.30	2.07

[a] Includes loss of 27,000 staff with transfer of freightliners and sundries to N.F.C.

NOTES TO TABLE 1

(i) Output
This is a weighted index of passenger and freight traffic, mail and parcels traffic, collection and delivery services, and workshops capital goods output. Weights, based on costs, are for 1948–62 the geometric mean of 1948 and 1961 weights. Weights for 1963–73 are based on the geometric mean of 1963 and 1973 cost-based weights.

(ii) Labour
This index represents numbers employed by British Railways (average of beginning and end of year), including workshops staff. It has not been found possible to separate man-hours applied to maintenance work from that applied to capital construction. The reduction in 1968–9 is explained partly by loss of staff to N.F.C. (Freightliners and Sundries).

(iii) Capital
This is an index of the value of 'net capital stock' (gross for ways and structures, net for other items) at beginning of each year, in constant 1948 prices. For derivation see Appendix B.

(iv) 'Total factor productivity'
This is derived from a simple Cobb-Douglas function:
$$Y \text{ (output)} = A\,K^{\alpha}\,L^{1-\alpha}e^{r},$$
where K is Capital inputs and L is labour inputs. α is estimated to be 0.4, based primarily on an estimate of factor shares in total costs (railways became less labour intensive over the period). Thus,

$$\text{T.F.P.} = \frac{Y}{K^{0.4}L^{0.6}}$$

The calculation should be regarded as a rough approximation of total factor productivity in the railway industry, since it rests, like all productivity measures, on a number of assumptions which are difficult to justify, e.g. elasticity of substitution assumed to be constant and equal to 1.

Table 2. *Estimate of U.K. productivity (1948=100)*

Year	G.D.P.	Capital stock	Labour force	Output per head	'Total factor productivity'
1948	100.0	100.0	100.0	100.0	100.0
1949	103.7	102.0	100.8	102.9	102.6
1950	107.4	104.5	102.1	105.2	104.6
1951	109.4	106.6	102.8	106.4	105.4
1952	110.0	108.6	102.5	107.3	105.8
1953	114.4	112.0	103.2	110.9	108.6
1954	119.0	114.2	104.9	113.4	111.0
1955	123.3	117.1	106.4	115.9	113.1
1956	124.8	120.2	107.3	116.3	113.1
1957	127.0	123.7	107.5	118.1	114.1
1958	126.6	127.1	106.7	118.7	113.6
1959	131.6	130.7	105.5	124.7	118.2
1960	139.0	134.9	109.9	126.5	120.2
1961	142.5	139.5	111.2	128.1	121.1
1962	144.4	144.0	111.8	129.2	121.3
1963	150.3	148.8	112.0	134.2	125.0
1964	158.6	154.7	113.5	139.7	129.3
1965	163.2	160.7	114.5	142.5	130.9
1966	166.0	166.4	113.6	146.1	132.8
1967	169.7	174.4	112.7	150.6	135.0
1968	177.1	182.0	112.5	157.4	139.6
1969	181.3	188.2	112.2	161.6	141.9
1970	184.7	198.2	111.6	165.5	143.4
1971	187.6	205.3	109.5	171.3	146.4
1972	192.4	213.1	111.6	172.4	146.6
1973	206.5	223.4	113.3	182.3	153.8
Growth rates: % p.a.					
1948–54	2.94	2.24	0.80	2.18	1.75
1953–60	2.82	2.69	0.90	1.90	1.46
1948–60	2.78	2.53	0.79	1.98	1.55
1960–70	2.88	3.92	0.15	2.72	1.78
1970–3	3.79	4.07	0.51	3.28	2.36
1948–73	2.94	3.27	0.50	2.43	1.74

Note: the method used reflected that used for the railway calculations, e.g. in the use of gross capital stock changes for buildings, etc. (cf. ways and structures in railways), and use of labour numbers not man-hours. For 'T.F.P.' the weights used were: labour 0.75, capital 0.25.

Source: capital stock (gross for buildings/construction, net for rest), from Feinstein, *National Income,* supplemented by C.S.O. Macroeconomic and Financial Statistics Databank. Labour force (civilian) and G.D.P. from C.S.O. Databank (G.D.P. is average estimate at factor cost).

APPENDIX D

British Railways market share, passenger and freight, 1935–73

Table 1. *Railway share of passenger and freight traffic in Great Britain, 1935–8 and 1946–53*

A. Passenger Miles ('000 million)

Year	Road transport		Rail transport				Rail transport as % of total
	Private	Public (buses, coaches, etc.)	Main-line cos./ Railway Executive	London Transport	Total		
1935	25.0	22.9	18.9	2.6	69.4		31.0
1936	27.0	23.9	19.5	2.7	73.1		30.4
1937	28.7	24.7	20.2	3.1	76.7		30.4
1938	30.2	27.2	19.0	2.7	79.1		27.4
1946	22.8	39.6	28.1	3.6	94.1		31.9
1947	25.5	41.5	22.1	3.5	92.6		27.6
1948	26.3	44.5	21.0	4.0	95.8		26.1
1949	29.4	49.9	20.9	4.0	104.2		23.9
1950	32.2	50.2	20.0	3.9	106.3		22.5
1951	34.9	50.9	20.6	3.7	110.1		22.1
1952	37.8	50.1	20.5	3.6	112.0		21.5
1953	42.1	50.7	20.6	3.6	117.0		20.7

Source: private road transport (including taxis and hire-cars): data based on vehicles with a current licence, and the number of passenger miles travelled per vehicle extrapolated from post 1953 information. See *A.A.S.*

Public road transport: 1950–3 data from Ministry of Transport, *The Transport Needs of Great Britain in the Next Twenty Years* (1963), p. 25. 1946–9 data obtained by extrapolation, using data on passenger journeys and the average length of journey in Munby and Watson, *Statistics*, Tables B6.1, B6.3, C7. 1935–8 data from R. Stone and D. A. Rowe, *The Measurement of Consumers' Expenditure and Behaviour in the United Kingdom, 1920–1938*, II (Cambridge, 1966), p. 71. Data include trolleybuses and trams, but exclude taxis and hire-cars throughout. Note: Aldcroft, in *British Railways*, p. 125, excluded trolleybuses and trams in 1938, but included them in 1950 *et seq.*

Rail transport: 1948–53 data from B.T.C., *R. & A. 1956*, Table XI. 1935–8, 1946–7 data from Munby and Watson, *Statistics*, Table A18, C6.5, C7, adjusted to be comparable with 1948–53.

B. Freight ton-miles ('000 million)

Year	Road	Coastal shipping	Rail	Total	Rail as % of total
1935	14.7	6.8	16.7	38.2	43.7
1936	15.9	7.0	17.7	40.6	43.6
1937	16.7	7.2	18.6	42.5	43.8
1938	17.0	7.1	16.9	41.0	41.2
1946	14.3	6.0	21.6	41.9	51.6
1947	15.2	6.6	21.0	42.8	49.1
1948	15.9	7.1	21.7	44.7	48.5
1949	16.8	7.7	22.0	46.5	47.3
1950	18.0	7.7	22.1	47.8	46.2
1951	18.3	8.4	22.9	49.6	46.2
1952	17.8	8.9	22.4	49.1	45.6
1953	19.7	9.0	22.8	51.5	44.3

Source: road transport: *A.A.S.* The data were derived from the observed relationship between ton-miles by road, the number of licensed haulage vehicles, ton-miles by rail and industrial production 1953–62. The relationship was:

$$\ln TM - \ln VR = -1.69 \quad -1.24 \ln VRt \quad - \quad 0.73 \ln RMt \quad + 1.59 \ln Yt$$
$$(-0.92)\ (-3.44) \qquad\qquad (-3.30) \qquad\qquad (3.67)$$
$$r^2 = \quad 0.87 \quad \text{Durbin-Watson stat.} = 1.87$$

Where TM is ton-miles by road, VR vehicles registered, RM ton-miles by rail and Y industrial production.

Coastal shipping: *A.A.S.* The data are based on the tonnage of ships arriving with cargo only. Before 1953 the number of ton-miles per ton of shipping was assumed to be constant at the 1953 level. Rail transport: Munby and Watson, *Statistics*, Table A12. Pre-1948 data were adjusted for comparability with 1948–53.

Table 2. *Railways' market share, 1954–73*

Year	Passenger-miles ('000m.)			Freight ton-miles ('000m.)		
	Rail (incl. L.T.)[a]	Total[b]	Rail as % of total	Rail[c]	Total[d]	Rail as % of total
1954	24.2	121.6	19.9	22.1	52.3	42.3
1955	23.8	128.1	18.6	21.4	53.5	40.0
1956	24.5	132.9	18.4	21.5	54.7	39.3
1957	25.9	132.0	19.6	20.9	53.7	38.9
1958	25.0	141.6	17.7	18.4	53.4	34.5
1959	25.0	151.6	16.4	17.7	55.4	31.9
1960	24.3	157.6	15.4	18.7	58.5	32.0
1961	23.8	165.2	14.4	17.6	60.3	29.2
1962	22.5	169.3	13.3	16.1	60.9	26.4
1963	22.4	180.2	12.4	15.4	66.0	23.3
1964	23.0	196.3	11.7	16.1	72.2	22.3
1965	21.8	206.5	10.6	15.4	73.7	20.9
1966	21.5	215.7	10.0	14.8	76.1	19.4
1967	21.2	225.8	9.4	13.6	75.5	18.0
1968	20.8	233.1	8.9	14.7	79.5	18.5
1969	21.6	238.3	9.1	15.3[e]	82.8	18.5
1970	22.2	248.1	8.9	16.4	86.2	19.0
1971	22.0	261.1	8.4	14.8	83.1	17.8
1972	21.6	270.4	8.0	14.3	83.5	17.1
1973	21.9	280.7	7.8	15.6	86.4	18.1

[a] 1948–62 series includes adjustments for 1958–62 to A.A.S. data to provide a consistent series.

[b] Includes domestic air travel (including N.I. and Channel Is.).

[c] From 1965 excludes all free-hauled traffic.

[d] Includes pipeline movements (except gases). Prior to 1965 data for pipelines of less than 10 miles were excluded. The method of calculating coastal shipping-mileage was altered in 1967 (no adjustment made here for pre-1962 period).

[e] From 1969 includes estimated freightliner and sundries traffic by rail.

Source: A.A.S., 1965 and 1974.

British Railways regional accounts (including collection and delivery and net receipts from commercial advertising, and letting of property in operational use), 1948–73

Table 1. *Gross receipts, working expenses and net receipts (£m.)*

| | Region | | | | | | | | | | | |
| | L.M.R. | | | E.R. | | | N.E.R.[a] | | | W.R. | | |
Year	GR	W/E	NR	GR	W/E	NR	GR	W/E	NR	GR	W/E	NR
1948	111.8	109.5	2.3	58.1	57.3	0.8	33.4	25.4	7.9	56.9	56.3	0.5
1949	97.5	101.5	−4.0	56.1	55.7	0.4	43.4	34.5	8.9	57.7	59.4	−1.6
1950	105.2	101.7	3.4	58.7	55.7	3.0	45.4	34.4	11.1	60.3	59.7	0.6
1951	116.0	110.0	6.0	64.8	59.7	5.1	50.1	36.9	13.2	67.2	64.8	2.4
1952	126.2	117.9	8.3	71.4	63.6	7.8	54.0	39.9	14.1	72.3	70.1	2.2
1953	134.2	123.3	10.9	73.4	65.7	7.7	55.0	43.5	11.5	75.6	75.0	0.6
1954	139.0	130.8	8.2	76.1	71.0	5.0	57.8	46.5	11.3	76.7	85.8	−9.1
1955	140.0	132.9	7.1	77.9	72.5	5.4	59.4	49.9	9.5	79.6	91.4	−11.8
1956	148.9	145.9	3.0	81.4	80.0	1.3	63.4	55.7	7.7	83.6	101.4	−17.8
1957	153.1	153.6	−0.6	84.5	85.4	−0.9	66.2	59.1	7.1	86.6	106.6	−20.1
1958	141.5	155.6	−14.1	82.1	82.7	−0.7	66.1	57.5	3.7	79.5	101.9	−22.4
1959	134.9	150.1	−15.2	80.7	81.0	−0.3	58.2	54.1	4.1	77.2	96.4	−19.1
1960	136.6	162.6	−26.0	85.6	89.0	−3.3	61.6	60.1	1.4	80.8	105.1	−24.3
1961	133.5	168.2	−34.7	86.1	90.9	−4.8	59.6	61.7	−2.1	78.6	108.2	−29.5
1962	129.9	170.5	−40.7	86.7	91.1	−4.4	54.3	60.3	−6.1	77.3	105.0	−27.7
1962	140.5	185.0	−44.5	87.5	89.5	−1.9	54.4	57.9	−3.4	70.0	90.3	−20.4
1963	137.4	184.2	−46.8	90.4	87.2	3.1	53.8	55.7	−1.8	71.6	85.9	−14.3
1964	137.7	178.2	−42.4	92.2	87.8	4.5	56.4	54.9	−1.5	71.4	83.3	−11.9
1965	124.1	162.4	−38.3	87.8	81.7	6.2	53.9	50.5	−3.4	66.8	73.6	−6.9
1966	124.3	171.4	−47.0	88.3	85.1	3.2	51.8	54.6	−2.8	67.0	76.9	−10.0
1967	118.0	164.1	−46.2	84.4	84.2	0.2	47.5	53.9	−6.4	60.6	75.1	−14.6
1968	112.0	148.7	−36.7	133.9	133.4	0.5				59.7	69.0	−9.3
1969	118.9	143.5	−24.6	141.5	127.4	14.1				65.8	68.5	−2.6
1970	128.2	147.5	−19.3	151.0	129.6	21.5				72.6	71.9	0.6
1971	131.5	157.7	−26.2	151.1	139.9	11.1				75.6	80.5	−4.9
1972	128.4	166.8	−38.4	151.0	147.5	3.5				74.5	82.8	−8.3
1973	139.5	179.5	−40.1	162.8	159.6	3.2				81.0	89.7	−8.6

[a] From 1968 merged with E.R.

Key:
L.M.R.	London Midland Region	W.R.	Western Region	GR	Gross Receipts
E.R.	Eastern Region	S.R.	Southern Region	W/E	Working Expenses
N.E.R.	North Eastern Region	Sc.R.	Scottish Region	NR	Net Receipts

S.R.			Sc.R.			H.Q.			B.R. Workshops			National Carriers		
GR	W/E	NR	GR	W/E	NR	GR	W/E	NR	GR	W/E	NR	GR	W/E	NR
50.1	38.0	12.1	36.1	35.9	0.2	—	—	—	—	—	—	—	—	—
46.7	38.2	8.5	34.4	35.9	−1.5	—	—	—	—	—	—	—	—	—
46.5	39.0	7.5	35.2	35.6	−0.4	—	—	—	—	—	—	—	—	—
48.7	42.0	6.7	38.2	38.2	0.0	—	—	—	—	—	—	—	—	—
52.1	45.2	6.9	40.3	40.9	−0.7	—	—	—	—	—	—	—	—	—
54.7	48.5	6.2	41.7	44.1	−2.4	—	—	—	—	—	—	—	—	—
57.1	52.0	5.1	42.6	46.8	−4.2	—	—	—	—	—	—	—	—	—
51.9	54.8	−2.9	45.1	50.6	−5.5	—	—	—	—	—	—	—	—	—
56.1	59.6	−3.5	47.6	54.8	−7.2	—	—	—	—	—	—	—	—	—
60.1	64.8	−4.7	51.0	59.2	−8.2	—	—	—	—	—	—	—	—	—
60.8	65.8	−5.0	46.6	56.2	−9.6	—	—	—	—	—	—	—	—	—
62.0	65.2	−3.2	44.3	52.6	−8.3	—	—	—	—	—	—	—	—	—
67.7	71.5	−3.8	46.3	57.9	−11.6	—	—	—	—	—	—	—	—	—
70.7	73.6	−2.9	46.1	59.1	−12.9	—	—	—	—	—	—	—	—	—
72.5	76.5	−4.0	44.5	58.9	−14.4	0.0	6.7	−6.7	—	—	—	—	—	—
70.9	69.6	1.3	44.6	58.1	−13.4	0.0	21.0	−21.1	—	—	—	—	—	—
71.2	69.7	1.4	43.9	56.7	−12.8	0.4	10.8	−10.4	—	—	—	—	—	—
74.6	69.8	4.9	43.8	54.6	−10.9	−0.1	13.0	−13.2	—	—	—	—	—	—
72.9	70.9	2.1	40.6	49.4	−8.7	26.3	57.3	−30.9	—	—	—	—	—	—
74.3	74.2	0.2	38.5	51.0	−12.5	26.2	28.8	−2.6	—	—	—	—	—	—
73.5	76.4	−2.9	36.0	51.2	−15.1	25.6	31.1	−5.5	—	—	—	—	—	—
71.5	77.5	−6.0	36.0	48.4	−12.4	27.2	31.3	−4.1	—	—	—	23.4	38.8	−15.4
78.4	79.4	−1.0	37.7	45.1	−7.3	97.8	27.9	70.0	94.8	94.3	0.5	—	—	—
86.2	87.3	−1.0	39.5	46.7	−7.1	101.8	48.9	52.9	101.4	101.3	0.1	—	—	—
100.8	98.6	2.2	42.0	51.3	−9.2	103.2	50.1	53.2	114.5	114.3	0.2	—	—	—
106.1	104.7	1.4	42.0	55.3	−13.3	140.9	68.0	73.0	114.7	114.3	0.4	—	—	—
115.2	114.0	1.1	45.7	62.0	−16.2	139.2	83.7	55.5	122.9	122.6	0.4	—	—	—

Notes: The limitations of the regional data should be acknowledged. First of all, until 1957 several 'sponsorship' arrangements existed. For example, all parcel post receipts were allocated to S.R.; ticket agency receipts were kept by the sponsor region; Woolworth's traffic receipts were allocated to L.M.R. (freight) and S.R. (coaching); mail receipts were allocated according to the old company contracts (none therefore went to N.E.R. and Sc.R.); administration costs of Railway Clearing House and B.R. Central Staff were charged to E.R.; depreciation of rolling stock was debited to the region where the assets were listed in the capital account, irrespective of use or location (thus all ex-private wagons were included in L.M.R. accounts). See B.T.C., *The Scope and Content of Accounts* (March 1956), p. 23. More importantly, inter-regional traffic receipts were kept by the region in which the traffic originated, with working expenses being charged to the region in which the motive power depot was situated. This procedure created 'imbalance' which made the 'net receipts' data impossible to use as a guide to inter-regional performance. From 1957 adjustments were made to the accounts to remove most of the biases created by the 'sponsorship' arrangements. At the same time, Osborn attempted a re-working of the data for 1955 to examine the effects of ironing out inter-regional traffic imbalances and of debiting the regions with central charges (see Table 2).

Regional data for 1948–57 are given in AN12/26, P.R.O., but they differ from the data used here in that collection and delivery, and the net receipts from commercial advertising, and letting of property in operational use, are included only for 1956 and 1957.

1962–73 data include rail catering in regions' accounts.

From 1962 an H.Q. Division was created. The second of the data sets for 1962 allocates administration expenses to H.Q. and takes into account regional boundary changes effective from 1 January 1963.

The H.Q. series changes several times. From 1965 the cost of wagon repairs and receipts from the Post Office were allocated to H.Q. In the following year, H.Q. charged wagon and container hire to the regions, to meet maintenance and depreciation charges (working expenses fell by *c.* £30m.)

After 1968, payments from Freightliners Ltd for train-hire were allocated to H.Q.; grants for unremunerative passenger services and the special grants paid in 1972 and 1973 were also credited to H.Q.

Source: 1948–62: B.T.C. Regional Account Books, B.R.B.; 1962–73: Supplementary Schedules to Annual B.R.B. Accounts, B.R.B.

Table 2. *Conversion of regional accounts to full profit and loss status – Osborn's calculation for 1955 (£m.)*

Region	Net receipts (from regional books (Table 1))	Net receipts adjusted for sponsorship arrangements	Net receipts adjusted for inter-regional working, etc.	Net receipts after allocation of central charges
L.M.R.	7.1	6.9	9.1	−3.4
E.R.	5.4	5.7	0.3	−6.2
N.E.R.	9.5	9.4	2.6	−1.9
W.R.	−11.8	−12.0	−0.5	−8.0
S.R.	−2.9	−2.5	−1.2	−5.7
Sc.R.	−5.5	−5.5	−6.1	−10.6

Note: The results of adjusting for sponsorship and inter-regional working indicate that the regional accounts cited in Table 1 tend to exaggerate the net receipts of the E.R. and N.E.R. and understate those of the W.R. and S.R. The W.R. in particular was disadvantaged by the 'originating receipts' method of allocation. The L.M.R. was the healthiest region in 1955, and the Sc.R. the weakest. After debiting central charges, all regions were shown to be in deficit.

Source: H. E. Osborn, confidential memo. on 'British Railways: Financial Results by Region', 19 February 1957, Finance Committee Minutes, 27 February 1957, B.R.B.

APPENDIX F

Investment submissions, government ceilings and actual investment, 1955–73

Table 1. *British Transport Commission: British Railways (excluding collection and delivery), 1955–62 (£m.)*

Year	B.T.C. submission	Government allocation	Actual investment
1955	78 (1954)	78 (1954)	70
1956	103 (1955)	103 (1955) 91 (1956)	87
1957	123 (1956)	120 (1956)	124
1958	151 (1956)	143 (1957)	140
1959	148 (1956)	143 (1958)	167
	163 (1958)	169/178 (1958)	
1960	190 (1958)	175 (1959)	162
	177 (1959)	155 (1960)	
1961	200 (1959)	140^a (1960)	145
	160 (1960)		
1962	145 (1961)	133 (1961)	114

^{a} Includes reserve of £15m. for L.M.R. main-line electrification.

Notes:

(i) Figures for 'actual investment' differ from those given in Appendix B, because of the exclusion of investment in collection and delivery. For submission purposes, collection and delivery investment was considered part of the Commission's 'other activities' and not part of British Railways. Although this practice was changed for the 1962 investment submission, the figures have been adjusted for consistency.

(ii) The figures quoted above attempt to portray the most representative picture of what were extremely complex negotiations between the B.T.C. and the Ministry of Transport. For one year, 1960, the Ministry merely allocated an overall 'planning' ceiling for the B.T.C.; this has necessitated the estimation of the allocation for British Railways.

Source: 1955–6: B.T.C. Finance Committee Minutes and background papers, 1954, 1955, B.R.B. 1956–62: B.R.B. 23–4–2 Pts. 1–4.

Table 2. *British Railways Board: Railways (including collection and delivery and ancillary businesses), 1963–73 (£m.)*

Year	B.R.B. submission	Government ceiling	Actual investment
1963	120 (1962)	115 (1962)	96
1964	105/110 (1963)	110 (1963)	108
1965	140 (1964)	122 (1964)	121
1966	126 (1965)	126 (1965)/120 (1966)[a]	107
1967	110 (1966)	112 (1966)/102 (1966)[a]	97
1968	105/110 (1967)	110 (1967)	87
1969[b]	97 (1968)	76 (1968)[c]	74
1970	90 (1969)	76/78 (1969)[d]	83 (5)[e]
1971	95 (1970)[f]	84/91[f] (1970) 90 (1970)	99[f] (1)[e]
1972	123 (1971)	113/120 (1971)[g]	116 (4)[e]
1973	121 (1972)	130/143 (1972)[g]	131 (6)[e]

[a] Reduction following Treasury imposed cut.

[b] Investment in N.F.C. and Scottish Transport Group excluded from 1969.

[c] Excludes £2.7m. agreed separately for the provision of Merry-Go-Round wagons.

[d] New accounting rules applied from 1970; £76m. is the ceiling under the old rules, £78m. that under the new. These totals include a separate allocation of £5.4m. for Freight Plan wagons.

[e] The bracketed figures refer to infrastructure grant expenditure and are not included within the out-turn totals quoted. Infrastructure grants had been made available to B.R.B. since the 1968 Transport Act, although it was only in the latter part of 1969 that the Ministry of Transport proposed that they should in future be considered separately from B.R.B.'s overall investment ceiling. The situation was complicated during 1971 by the Ministry's decision to allocate separate 'resource ceilings' for the constituent parts of B.R.B. – London and South East, Other than London and South East and Non-railway businesses. Within the London and South East ceiling, no distinction was made between 'infra-grant' and 'non-infra-grant' expenditure. Consequently, the out-turn totals for 1971–3 and the submission and ceiling totals for 1972–3 include that element of infrastructure expenditure covering London and South East. Conversely, the bracketed infrastructure figures for 1971–3 cover only those of the Passenger Transport Executives.

[f] B.R.B.'s original (1969) 'bid' for 1971 was reduced by the Ministry from £90m. to £80m. (both these figures exlude any allocation for the Weaver Junction–Glasgow electrification). B.R.B. felt this was unacceptably low and unsuccessfully attempted to raise the ceiling in 1970 to £95m. (including £3m.–5m. for essential renewal projects on the Southern Region). However, early in 1970, the Minister finally approved the Weaver Junction scheme; the final ceiling of £91m. includes an allocation of £7.2m. for this purpose. Unfortunately, the comparison between government ceiling and actual investment in 1971 is virtually meaningless. The out-turn figure of £99m. is inflated by the inclusion of infrastructure grant spending, in London and the South East, and should not be compared with the ceiling figure of £90m. (see n.[e]). A revised ceiling figure comparable with the out-turn of £99m. would be £103m., indicating an underspending of £4m.

[g] Ceilings increased by £7m. and £13m. after government request to accelerate investment in areas of high unemployment e.g. by laying Continuous Welded Rail.

Note: the discrepancy between the out-turn figures above and those figures for gross investment at current prices 1948–73, given in Appendix B, is due to the inclusion within the figures given above, of B.R.B. ancillaries (hotels, ships, harbours and subsequently hovercraft). In addition, the capital manufacturing cost of items subject to leasing arrangements (after 1971) is included in the out-turn figures given above.

Source: B.R.B. 23–4–2 Pts. 4–9; New Works 23–4–200 Pts. 1–8, 23–4–208, Pts. 1–3, 23–4–2, Pts. 1–10.

The Euston main-line electrification scheme

A major component of the 1955 Modernisation Plan was the electrification of the main line of the London Midland Region from Euston to Birmingham, Crewe, Liverpool and Manchester.[1] No financial justification was given of individual schemes in the Plan, and such a justification was not forthcoming for some years. The line was chosen on the basis of its traffic density, which for some time had been the criterion used in assessing electrification schemes. The Weir report of 1930 set the trend in expressing the justification for electrification in terms of traffic density. It arrived at a break-even point of 2.3m. trailing ton-miles (m.t.t.m.) per mile of single track per year.[2] The first post-war justification put the break-even point at 3.0–3.6 m.t.t.m. and was published in 1950.[3] In the same year a Dutch report had recommended a traffic density of 38 trains per day, or approximately 6 m.t.t.m.[4] Significantly, only the Dutch paper compared electrification with diesel traction, which by the 1950s was the real alternative (and not steam). The Weir report included a map illustrating the traffic densities of the main British lines: 34 per cent of the system then had a traffic density of over 4 m.t.t.m. per annum, including the L.M.S. Euston main line.

Soon after the publication of the Modernisation Plan a major step in the electrification programme was taken with the decision to standardise on the 25 kV a.c. system successfully tested in France, rather than the 1,500V d.c. system under construction on parts of the British network. At the same time a separate report showed expected savings for the Euston scheme of £6m. in capital costs and £1m. in annual running costs under the 25 kV system.[5] In October 1955 the

---

[1] B.T.C., *Modernisation and Re-equipment of British Railways* (London: B.T.C., 1955), p.15.

[2] M.T., report of the Committee on Main Line Electrification (Weir report), 1930.

[3] R.E./L.T.E., report of the Railway Electrification Committee (1948) (Cock report), 1950, p. 16.

[4] H. J. Van Lessen, 'Electric and Diesel Traction on the Netherlands Railways', *Proceedings of the Institution of Electrical Engineers*, XCVII (1950), 75; A. H. Emerson, 'Electrification of the London Midland Main Line from Euston', *Proceedings of the Institute of Mechanical Engineers*, CLXXXI (1966–7), published as *Euston Main Line Electrification* (1967), p. 19.

[5] B.T.C. Minutes, 17 November 1955, B.R.B., and *System of Electrification for British Railways* (London: B.T.C., 1956); S. B. Warder and J. W. Watkins, 'Electrification of L.M.R. Main Lines: Report on Comparisons of 50 Cycle A.C. and 1500 D.C.', September 1955, B.T.C. Minutes, 19 October 1955, B.R.B.

Commission agreed to use the Crewe–Manchester section of the scheme (Styal line) as a proving ground for the new system, and in the following month decided to standardise on 25 kV for the whole of British Railways (except the Southern Region).[6] Preparatory work was started, and an expenditure of nearly £3.4m. had been authorised by the end of 1956. In April, 1957 the Commission authorised an expenditure of £14.3m. for the Crewe–Manchester section and for preparatory work for the Crewe–Liverpool line. At the same time it asked for a broad assessment of the scheme's financial effects. This did not materialise, however, until April 1959.[7]

As financial pressures mounted the Commission pressed for an acceleration of the electrification project. The minutes of 23 October 1958 record the opinion that the scheme was proceeding too slowly and should be speeded up, possibly at the expense of the East Coast route. The scheme was given further priority at a meeting of the Chairman's Conference on Modernisation and at a further Commission meeting in December.[8] The London Midland Region initiated a study by way of response, and produced a report, entitled 'Electrification of Western Lines', in April 1959, which was passed to the Commission on 21 May. The original scheme had envisaged completion of six stages by 1968 and of the North Staffs. line by 1970. The report proposed a schedule for the completion of the bulk of the scheme within five years. The project was supported by fairly detailed costings and financial forecasts, the first that had been prepared for the electrification. The gross cost was estimated at £161.0m. (£159.8m. net). Deducting the expenditure that would have been necessary to maintain the line in any case left a net additional expenditure or 'betterment' of £113.2m. It was predicted that this expenditure would lead to an improvement in net revenue of £8.2m. a year, equal to a return of 5.1 per cent on the net outlay, or 7.2 per cent on the net additional outlay. These estimates covered electrification as far as Liverpool and Manchester. Further estimates showed that the extension of the scheme to Gretna Junction (the limit of the London Midland Region) would push the anticipated return on the additional outlay up to 9 per cent. Of course, the only logical extension of the scheme was to Glasgow in the Scottish region.

Costings and forecasts were also given for an alternative diesel scheme. Surprisingly, these showed a considerable margin in favour of diesels: an expected return of 10 per cent, compared with 7 per cent for electrification. In terms of the marginal rate of return, the diesel scheme was expected to increase net revenue by £1.3 million per annum less than under electrification, but at a cost of £43.5 million less in additional outlay. This was equivalent to a marginal rate of return in favour of electrification of only 2.99 per cent (£1.3/43.5m.). This was not thought to be sufficient to justify abandoning electrification, however. £11m. had already been spent and a better performance was expected from the use of electric power. In any case, this was not a direct comparison between electrification and a comparable diesel alternative. The electrification scheme included 3,300 H.P. locomotives, whereas the diesel alternative had included locomotives with a maximum power of 2,500 H.P. Supplementary notes by David Blee, General Manager of the London Midland, attached to the report when it came before the Commission in July,

---

[6] B.T.C. Minutes, 19 October and 17 November 1955, B.R.B.

[7] L.M.R., 'Modernisation of Euston Main Line', July 1960, Appendix A; B.T.C. Minutes, 24 April 1957, B.R.B.

[8] B.T.C. Minutes, 23 October and 18 December 1958; Chairman's Conference on Modernisation Minutes, 2 December 1958, B.R.B.

quantified this discrepancy. They showed that the substitution of 2,000 H.P. electric locomotives would reduce the cost of the scheme by £2.2m., or alternatively, that the use of 3,300 H.P. 'Deltic' locomotives where necessary in the diesel scheme would increase its cost by £16.5m. This would reduce the return on the diesel scheme to 8 per cent (£6.8/86.2m.) on the net additional outlay, and increase the marginal rate of return in favour of electrification to 4.8 per cent (£1.3/27.0m.).[9]

While the report put forward some justification for electrification as opposed to steam traction, it did not recommend it over and above diesels, on a purely financial basis, even taking into account the £11m. already spent. It is quite likely, as was claimed, that the electrifisation would lead to better results than actually shown in 1959. If this were true then it was a great pity that such expectations were not quantified and included in the financial justification. The April 1959 report provided the first financial estimates for the scheme. It was important that they demonstrated a clear case for electrification over the alternatives. That this was not the case owed more to the inadequacy of the calculations than to the inferiority of the choice of power. The figures produced provoked harsh criticism when they were given to the Select Committee on Nationalised Industries. This reported that 'if the calculation . . . shows that a loss is unavoidable, it seems to be going a little far if you then justify the scheme on the ground that your calculation was bound to be wrong, any way'.[10] There were similar difficulties with the early justification of the Kent Coast scheme, which Benson criticised strongly in a paper for the Stedeford Advisory Group in July 1960.[11] The costs given in the April 1959 report failed to include the cost of capitalising interest on the outlay during construction. Given the size of the project this was a serious omission. Using the planned time profile of investment shown in the report and an interest rate of 4 per cent (also used in the report), this may be estimated at an additional £16m. on the net additional outlay. A parallel calculation for the diesel scheme is difficult to make due to the lack of a similar time profile. However, assuming that it would have taken two years to implement, interest would have added £5m. to costs. The marginal rate of return in favour of electrification would then be 3.4 per cent (£1.3/38.0m.). If we include all our adjustments to the original figures in the report – for interest, high-powered diesels, writing off the £11m. spent – the marginal rate of return becomes 5.5 per cent. This seems rather low to justify such a major capital project.

As he was unable to attend the Commission meeting, H. P. Barker penned a memorandum on the report. He thought that it tended to overstate equipment requirements, particularly for supplementary diesel traction in the electrification scheme, although Blee denied this in his supplementary notes. Barker also noted a tendency to understate the case, since most real economies would come from new operating patterns, 'and not simply by substitution of new gadgets for old'. He also considered it wrong to consider electrification which stopped short of Glasgow, noting the illogicality of terminating at Gretna, and claimed that the costs 'grossly understated' the problems of the construction and changeover period. The Commission approved the report with a few reservations. It was suggested, however, that 'the financial results ought to be better'.[12] In March 1960 the scheme came

[9] B.T.C. Minutes, 9 July 1959, B.R.B.
[10] Report of S.C. Nat. Ind.: B.R., July 1960, p. li.
[11] Henry Benson, memo. July 1960, p. 10, Beeching Papers, Box 2, B.R.B.
[12] H. P. Barker, memo. to Robertson, 30 June 1959, B.T.C. Minutes, 9 July 1959, B.R.B.

under severe criticism from the Select Committee. The Commission responded with a paper setting out their arguments in favour of electrification. This stated that 'Decisions reached primarily by way of calculation were often proved pessimistically wrong or incomplete. Experience in electrification all over the world has given conclusive evidence that electrified railways are the best railways, when the density of traffic justifies that system of traffic.'[13] The logic of this statement is unclear. It appears that calculations are not to be relied on unless they concern density, presuming of course that the relationship between economy and density has manifested itself in some form of calculation. The Commission's density criterion rested on outdated calculations comparing electrification with steam traction. By 1960 steam was no longer a realistic option. Little wonder that the Select Committee should question the Commission's approach.

Since June 1959 the Commission had had in its possession a new study of the density criterion, comparing diesel and electric traction. This had been produced by independent consultants, Merz and McLellan.[14] For some reason the Commission chose not to make use of this in the controversy surrounding the Euston scheme. The report concluded that 'If the traffic density is equivalent to about 15,000 [electric loco. miles p.a.] per track or more, electrification always pays: while if the traffic density is equivalent to 10,000 or less, diesel working always pays.' The average number of tracks on the London Midland scheme was about 3.7, giving a required traffic density of 55,500 electric-locomotive-miles per route-mile per annum. The planned traffic density for electric locomotives was 51,500, which falls within the 'uncertain' range of the report's findings. A planned density for E.M.U.s of 180,000 set miles per annum per route-mile, however, pushes the aggregate density above the break-even point. The consultants' report was a thorough investigation, and given its favourable findings it is difficult to see why more use was not made of it.

Further pressure on the electrification scheme came from the Stedeford Advisory Group. The Commission this time responded by making a complete reassessment, which was completed by the London Midland Region in July 1960 and presented to the Commission and the Group in August. This document revised the original figures in several ways. The estimated net outlay was reduced to £153.8m., and the additional outlay became £102.9m. The cuts were largely the result of removing the carriage heating programme from the scheme. The scheme was now expected to be completed by 1964: £25.1m. had been spent, and a further £12.5m. committed by contracts placed. New estimates of future net revenue forecasted an improvement by 1970 of £18.9m. The increase over the 1959 estimate came from the inclusion of all traffic using the line rather than only the originating traffic, and by forecasting a growth in the demand for travel. These figures gave an average expected rate of return of 18 per cent. Revised figures were also included for an alternative diesel scheme. These put the additional cost at £82.8m. and the expected net revenue improvement at £14.8m. – also a return of 18 per cent. The marginal rate of return in favour of electrification from these figures is 20.4 per cent. On this basis electrification was clearly an attractive proposition.[15]

[13] L.M.R., memo. on 'The Electrification of the West Coast Main Line', 11 May 1960; B.T.C. Minutes, 12 May 1960, B.R.B.

[14] Merz and McLellan, Report on the Relative Economics of Electric and Diesel Traction, June 1959, B.R.B.

[15] L.M.R., memo. on 'Modernisation of Euston Main Line', July 1960; B.T.C. Minutes, 18 August 1960, B.R.B.

If the 1959 report had badly understated the case for electrification, the 1960 report tended to do the opposite. In doing so it attracted the criticism of Dr Richard Beeching of the Stedeford Group, in a memorandum circulated in August 1960. While many of his criticisms were equally attributable to the costings for the diesel alternative – for example, the exclusion of carriage heating costs and major station modernisation, and the over-optimism of the freight traffic projections – others merit closer attention. The new figures assumed that diesel traction would attract £2.3m. less than electrification in increased passenger business. This was said to be because 'Diesel traction has not proved its reliability to the degree experienced with electric traction and, in addition, electric operation is cleaner. It is assumed, therefore, that electric passenger services will be more popular than diesel.' Beeching, on the other hand, thought that it was 'difficult to take [this] seriously except as an indication of bias'. There was some justification for the Commission's position. Electric traction was (and is) more reliable and previous experience had shown that it was more popular with passengers. In any case, the estimated increase in receipts with electrification of 39 per cent was not outrageously higher than the 30 per cent increase expected from diesels. Beeching also questioned the increased cost of diesel locomotives used in the 1960 Reassessment. The average cost of a diesel locomotive had risen from £100,000 in the 1959 report to £138,000, due to the inclusion of Deltic locomotives where necessary at a cost of £150,000 each (incorporating the suggestion in Blee's supplementary notes). Beeching doubted whether 'any diesels of more than 2,500 H.P. are really necessary'. However, experience on the East Coast main line has shown the need for high-powered diesels when electrification is not undertaken. The number of Deltics thought to be needed does appear to be rather high, nonetheless. Of the 538 diesels contemplated in the alternative scheme, 207 were to be of the Deltic type. The East Coast route made do with 22 Deltics in a total fleet of 218. If the requirements of the West Coast route had been similar, a figure of 50 Deltics is suggested. This would reduce the capital cost of the diesel scheme by £7.9m., and increase the expected net revenue improvement by £0.3m. A more important criticism concerned the effects on traffic during the period of construction. That disruption was a serious factor was undeniable, although in the case involved there were alternative routes from London to Birmingham and from Manchester to Birmingham. All in all, while some of Beeching's comments were pertinent, they did not prove that the balance in favour of electrification had been unfairly tilted.[16]

Once again the financial justification in the 1960 Reassessment failed to take into account the cost of capitalising interest on the outlay during the period of construction. Given the rise in interest rates and the alteration to the expected completion date this would have been more substantial in 1960. Based on an interest rate of 5 per cent a rough calculation indicates that these capitalisation costs would have amounted to about £20m. for electrification and £6m. for diesels in 1960. The amendments to the figures given in the 1960 Reassessment appear in the table.

Although this shows an average rate of return on diesels that is higher than that for electrification, the marginal rate of return in favour of electric traction of 12 per cent on the extra expenditure, or 9 per cent when the allowance for lower-powered diesels is made, is still quite high. For the purposes of investment appraisal it is this

[16] Dr Richard Beeching, 'Comments upon the London Midland Region Report, August 1960, on the Modernisation of the Euston Main Line', 21 September 1960, Beeching Papers, Box 8, B.R.B.

	(i) Electrification	(ii) Diesels	Excess of (i) over (ii)
Additional outlay (1960 report)	£102.9m.	£82.8m.	£20.1m.
Capitalisation of interest	£20.0m.	£6.0m.	£14.0m.
Allowance for lower-powered diesels	—	−£7.9m.	£7.9m.
Total:	£122.9m.	£80.9m.	£42.0m.
Increase in net revenue (1960 report)	£18.9m.	£14.8m.	£4.1m.
Allowance for lower-powered diesels	—	£0.3m.	−£0.3m.
Total:	£18.9m.	£15.1m.	£3.8m.
Rate of return	15.4%	16.7%	12.0%
Rate of return (allowing for lower-powered diesels)	15.4%	18.7%	9.0%

marginal rate which should attract attention. The figure of 9 per cent was higher than the cost of borrowing to the Commission, and above the 8 per cent norm established by the government in 1961. The figures suggest that the project was financially justifiable. When account is taken of the money already spent on the project, the marginal rate of return jumps to 22.4 per cent, well above any test discount rate that may have been considered. The 1960 report formed the basis of a letter from Robertson to Stedeford, on 30 August 1960. Robertson pointed out that the line was already profitable, that the estimated cost of the scheme had been revised downwards, and emphasised the size of the expected improvement in net revenue and the capital already spent. Robertson contended:

If the Commission had their original decision to make again, they would decide again in favour of electrification of this line. While the estimates show that in the short term . . . the comparative economics of the two systems are not wildly different, they have more confidence in the ability of an electrified service (where the density of traffic justifies its introduction) to stand up to the growing competition of air and road transport.[17]

The Commission was unrepentant, in spite of the dubious nature of some of its calculations. The scheme was finally given permission to proceed by Ernest Marples, in a letter of 30 January 1961.[18] The total expenditure approved was £175m., which included the carriage heating programme and major station reconstruction. A reappraisal of the cost made in 1964 reduced this figure to £159.8m., primarily because of revised requirements on the lines to be electrified (savings of £13.4m.), and elimination of some of the more lightly loaded lines from the scheme (£10m.). This turned out to be the final gross cost of the scheme. Figures relating to the actual financial outcome of the scheme are difficult to find. In an address to the Institute of Transport in November 1967, Henry Johnson, then

[17] B.R.B. 23–4–2.
[18] B.T.C. Minutes, 9 February 1961, B.R.B.

Vice-Chairman of the Board, claimed that the scheme was well on target to achieve a 12 per cent marginal return over the diesel alternative by 1970.[19] A 'provisional' back-check produced for the Ministry in 1969 was less sanguine, however. The expectation in 1959 was an increased net revenue of £18m. by 1970. In 1967/8 earnings were £0.9m. down on 1959 levels at constant 1959 prices.[20]

[19] *Journal of the Institute of Transport*, XXXII (January 1968), 295–302.
[20] Johnson–Marsh, 30 September 1969, B.R.B. New Works 182–6–22 Pt.9.

APPENDIX H

British Railways steel requirements, allocations and receipts, 1947–50 (tons)

Period	Steel rails only			General steel and steel rails		
	R	A	Rec	R	A	Rec
1947 IV	63,780	61,700	52,942	202,363	166,755	150,390
1948 I	74,680	61,490	67,592	194,650	154,941	160,416
1948 II	75,020	61,100	58,338	195,037	156,942	152,204
1948 III	74,920	63,550	55,554	202,812	149,970	141,544
1948 IV	70,480	63,080	65,188	189,408	127,410	148,891
1948 all	295,120	249,220	246,672	781,907	589,263	603,055
1949 I	66,250	67,170	70,365	178,460	146,885	130,411
1949 II	66,800	62,490	62,522[a]	182,590	135,377	124,557[a]
1949 III	63,620	63,620	57,655[a]	148,700	134,527	118,213[a]
1949 IV	62,873	62,370	66,580[a]	170,469	152,738	133,618[a]
1949 all	259,543	255,650	257,122	680,219	569,527	506,799
1950 I	62,270	59,950	68,437[a]	147,380	141,655	134,624[a]

Key: R Estimated Requirements
A Government Allocations
Rec Actual Receipts

[a] From 1949 II, figures include amounts received against previous periods. Excluding these late deliveries, receipts are as follows:

> 1949 II rails 46,979 all 109,014
> 1949 III rails 41,151 all 101,709
> 1949 IV rails 48,833 all 115,871
> 1950 I rails 51,965 all 118,152

Note: figures relate to priority and non-priority steel, and exclude L.T.E. submissions, small supplementary re-allocations, etc.

Source: R.E. Stores Committee Minutes, 26 January 1948–25 April 1950, AN97/192, P.R.O.

British Transport Commission and British Railways Board staff, 1955–73

1. *The General Staff*

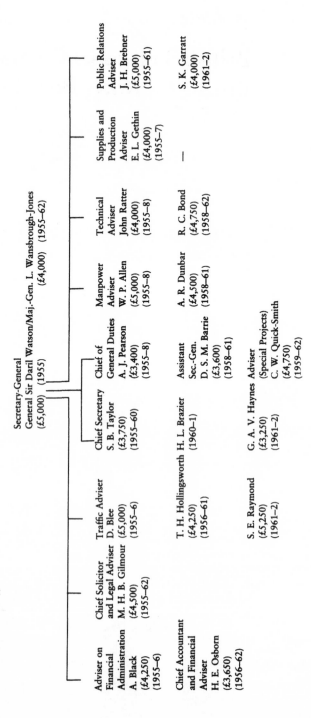

2. General Managers

Eastern Region	London Midland Region	North Eastern Region	Scottish Region	Southern Region	Western Region
C. K. Bird (£4,750) (1955–7)	J. W. Watkins C.V.O., D.S.O. M.C. (£4,750) (1955–6)	R. A. Short C.B.E., M.C. (£4,750) (1955–61)	T. F. Cameron (£4,750) (1955)	C. P. Hopkins (£4,750) (1955–62)	K. W. C. Grand (£5,000) (1955–9)
H. C. Johnson (£5,000) (1958–61)	D. Blee (£5,000) (1956–61)	F. C. Margetts (£5,500) (1961–2)	A. E. H. Brown (£4,000) (1955)		J. R. Hammond (£5,000) (1959–61)
J. R. Hammond (£5,580) (1962)	H. C. Johnson (£6,850) (1962)	A. Dean (£5,500) (1962)	J. Ness (£4,000) (1955–62)		S. E. Raymond (£5,700) (1962)

[a] Managing Director, British Transport Advertising Ltd.
[b] Managing Director, Railway Sites Ltd.

Chart II British Transport Commission central services and General Managers, 1955–62

Eastern Region	North Eastern Region	London Midland Region	Scottish Region	Southern Region	Western Region	B. T. Hotels	B. R. Workshops
J. R. Hammond (£5,580) (1962–5)	A. Dean (£5,500) (1962–6)	H. C. Johnson (£6,850) (1962–7)	J. Ness (£4,000) (1955–63)	D. McKenna (£6,000) (1963–8)	S. E. Raymond (£5,700) (1962–3)	F. G. Hole (£4,000) (1955–69)	H. O. Houchen (£6,000) (1962–5)
G. F. Fiennes (£8,000) (1966–7)	then merged with Eastern Region	W. G. Thorpe (£8,000) (1967–8)	W. G. Thorpe (£5,500) (1963–7)	L. W. Ibbotson (£8,000) (1968–72)	G. F. Fiennes (£5,750) (1963–5)	G. R. Hill (£8,500) (1970–6)	R. C. Bond (£6,750) (1965–8)
D. S. M. Barrie (£7,000) (1967–70)		R. L. E. Lawrence (£7,500) (1968–71)	G. W. Stewart (£6,250) (1967–71)	D. S. Binnie (£8,665) (1972–4)	L. W. Ibbotson (£6,350) (1966–8)		A. E. Robson[a] (£7,350) (1968–73)
I. M. Campbell (£7,700) (1970–73)		D. M. Bowick (£9,800) (1971)	A. Phillip (£8,550) (1971–4)		J. Bonham-Carter (£7,500) (1968–71)		
W. O. Reynolds (£11,800) (1973–6)		J. Bonham-Carter (£10,600) (1971–5)			D. Mathewson-Dick (Acting) (£8,310) (1971)		
					F. M. Wright (£8,610) (1972–6)		

[a] From 1970 Managing Director, B.R.E.L.

Chart III B.T.C. and B.R.B. General Managers, 1962–73

1. *Central Services*

Chief Stores
Officer
A. Forbes
(£3,000)
(1955–7)

Chief Police
Officer
W. B. Richards
M.V.O.
(£2,800)
(1955–6)

Chief Paper and
Printing Officer
J. O'Neill
(£2,750)
(1955–61)

Chief Research
Officer
C. C. Inglis
(£3,500)
(1955–62)

Chief Officer
(Films)
E. Anstey
(£2,300)
(1955–62)

Chief Commercial
Advertising
Officer[a]
G. Dobson-Wells
(£3,450)
(1955–62)

Chief Estate
and Rating
Surveyor[b]
W. S. Barnes
(£3,500)
(1955–62)

Chief Supplies
Officer
R. B. Hoff
(£3,750)
(1957–62)

Chief Constable
N. McK. Jesper
(£2,500)
(1956–8)

A. C. West
(£3,000)
(1958–62)

Chief Contracts
Officer
S. C. Robbins
(£4,400)
(1957–62)

Chief Supplies and
Contracts Officer
R. B. Hoff
(£4,750)
(1962)

2. British Railways Central Staff

Chief Commercial Officer	Chief Operating and Motive Power Officer	Chief Establishment and Staff Officer	Chief Mechanical Engineer	Chief Carriage and Wagon Engineering Officer	Chief Electrical Engineer	Chief Civil Engineer	Chief Signal Engineering Officer	Chief Financial Officer	Director of Research
J. R. Pike (£3,600) (1955–7)	R. F. Harvey (£3,750) (1955–8)	F. Gilbert (£3,600) (1955–6)	R. C. Bond (£4,000) (1955–8)	A. E. Robson (£3,200) (1955–8)	S. B. Warder (£3,750) (1955–62)	C. W. King (£3,000) (1955–61)	J. H. Frazer (£3,000) (1955–9)	V. Radford (£4,000) (1955–6)	H. M. Herbert (£2,550) (1955–61)
			J. F. Harrison (£4,750) (1958–62)			A. N. Butland (£4,850) (1962)	A. W. Woodbridge (£4,250) (1959–62)	—	Dr S. Jones (£4,500) (1962)

Chief Traffic Officer
F. Grundy (£4,000) (1957–9)

E. W. Arkle (£4,750) (1960–1)

Chief Commercial Officer
D. McKenna (£5,500) (1961–2)

Chief Operating Officer
G. F. Fiennes (£4,750) (1961–2)

Chief Development Officer
S. C. Robbins (£5,100) (1962)

Chart 1 British Transport Commission headquarters staff, 1955–62

Passenger service rationalisation, 1961–73

The data collected on closures relate to those cases (stations, services or lines) which were eligible for T.U.C.C. investigation. It should be noted that this definition is not necessarily coterminous with those adopted by either B.R.B. or *Hansard*.

Information on each case was collected from a number of sources:

(i) Dates – five relevant dates (of publication, T.U.C.C. hearing, T.U.C.C. report, Ministerial decision and closure) are recorded in various Parliamentary Written Answers, and, in particular *Parl. Deb. (Commons)*, vol. 725 (Session 1965–6), 28 February 1966, *202–18*, and vol. 800 (Session 1969–70), 27 April 1970, *237–46*. This source was cross-checked against the partial lists kept by B.R.B.

(ii) Mileages – see *Parl. Deb. (Commons)*, vol. 851 (Session 1972–3), 1 March 1973, *437–46*. Supplementary information came from a range of B.R.B. sources.

(iii) Financial Data – taken from T.U.C.C. reports, located in local offices, supplemented by additional material from regional closure files, B.R.B.

It should be noted that this data base suffers from a number of defects:

(a) All official lists were found to contain sufficient errors to require cross-checking against alternative sources.

(b) T.U.C.C. and *Hansard* sources do not detail closure proposals which had been processed before the 1962 Act came into force (the first proposals published under the Act were those of 4 June 1963, while the first closure took place on 9 September 1963). Data on pre-1962 Act proposals were derived from a wide range of sources, including B.T.C. Minutes, 25 January 1962, B.R.B.; B.R.B. 33-1-14; G. Daniels and L. Dench, *Passengers No More* (London: Ian Allan, 3rd edn., 1980).

(c) The 1968 Transport Act altered the rules governing the provision of financial information in closure cases. The pre- and post-1 January 1969 summations are therefore not strictly comparable.

In addition to these defects, there are a number of straight lacunae, affecting later proposals in particular. Consequently the summations which draw attention to various characteristics of the cases examined do not necessarily refer to similar base totals. For example, route-mileage figures were available in only 292 of 296 relevant cases; savings data could not be found in 20 of the 424 relevant cases.

Reference must be made, finally, to the fact that the individual savings figures used in the compilation of this data base refer to the maximum impact of any given proposal. No allowance can be made, then, for part closures; and some summations therefore inflate the overall financial saving involved in a given time period because part-closures are assessed for this purpose as if they had been full closures. Mileage figures, it should be noted, always refer to actual lengths closed.

With the various qualifications in mind, it is now possible to turn to the actual presentation of the data. Table 53 (p. 439) and Appendix J, Table 1, measure activity in several given time periods: how many proposals and how many closures there were in 1963, for example. Table 2, by contrast, looks at Ministerial action, by isolating decisions made by each successive Minister. Finally, Tables 3 and 4 examine various kinds of lag. Table 3 takes proposals presented each year and measures how long those that were agreed for closure actually took to be implemented (date i = date of proposal; date v = date of closure). Table 4 focusses on Ministerial action: what was the average time in which Ministers dealt with T.U.C.C. reports presented to them (date iii = T.U.C.C. report; date iv = Ministerial decision)? The compilation of the lag data also allowed an insight into cases which were handed on from Minister to Minister and some illustrations on this theme are offered in Chapter 10.

Table 1. *Full and part closures, June 1963–December 1973*

Time period	Part closures				Full closures				Full and part closures			
	No.	No. in reshaping report	Mileage actually closed	Financial saving	No.	No. in reshaping report	Mileage actually closed	Financial saving (£)	No.	No. in reshaping report	Mileage actually closed	Financial saving (£)
1963	—	—	—	—	2	2	8	3,341	2	2	8	3,341
1964	11	11	55	488,664	101	97	847	3,028,622	112	108	902	3,517,286
1965	10	10	57	984,415	68	59	802	2,158,091	78	69	859	3,142,506
1966	13	12	49	1,091,650	55	39	534	2,825,697	68	51	583	3,917,347
1967	7	6	56	463,500	44	24	251	513,286	51	30	307	976,786
1968	8	7	85	791,676	36	16	247	582,061	44	23	332	1,373,737
1969	6	6	28	356,900	21	10	242	1,241,026	27	16	270	1,597,926
1970	5	3	113	578,700	17	9	138	966,439	22	12	251	1,545,139
1971	—	—	—	—	5	2	23	80,636	5	2	23	80,636
1972	—	—	—	—	8	4	68	638,500	10	4	68	638,500
1973	—	—	—	—	5	3	41	78,900	5	3	41	78,900
1963–73	60	55	443	4,755,505	364	265	3,201	12,116,599	424	320	3,644	16,872,104
Beeching 3 June 1963–31 May 1965	14	14	79	642,709	131	127	1,247	4,231,620	145	141	1,326	4,874,329
Raymond 1 June 1965–31 December 1967	27	25	139	2,385,520	139	94	1,194	4,597,391	166	119	1,333	6,682,937
Johnson 1 January 1968–11 September 1971	19	16	326	1,727,276	77	37	651	2,868,962	96	53	877	4,596,238
Marsh 12 September 1971–31 December 1973	—	—	—	—	17	7	109	718,600	17	7	109	718,600

Table 2. *Ministerial action, 1963–73*

| Minister | Decisions taken | | | Mileage closed | Savings (£) |
	Accepted	Part-accepted	Rejected		
Marples (4 June 1963– 17 October 1964)	124	17	7	1,436	5,265,294
Fraser (18 October 1964– 22 December 1965)	77	11	9	819	4,254,619
Castle (23 December 1965– 5 April 1968)	71	20	18	606	3,405,515
Marsh (6 April 1968– 5 October 1969)	37	10	8	419	2,197,419
Mulley (6 October 1969– 22 June 1970)	13	2	3	227	1,085,679
Peyton (23 June 1970– 22 December 1973)	14	—	6	90	619,586

Table 3. *'Total' lag (date i–v) by year of proposals, 1963–73*

Year	No. of cases	Total lag (months)
1963	162	14.9
1964	86	21.7
1965	48	15.6
1966	43	17.6
1967	35	16.6
1968	29	18.7
1969	5	7.0
1970	6	15.3
1971	3	12.3
1972	5	14.2
1973	1	9.1

Table 4. *'Ministerial' lag (date iii–iv) by Minister*

Minister	No. of cases	Ministerial lag (months)
Marples	148	3.8
Fraser	76	5.3
Castle	70	7.2
Marsh	23	6.4
Mulley	3	3.3
Peyton	16	9.2

Notes

Explanatory Note

The records of the British Transport Historical Records archive at 66, Porchester Road, London, W.2, were transferred to the Public Record Office, Kew, and are filed under two main class references: RAIL (mostly pre-nationalisation, but also contains some records for the B.T.C. and R.E. period) and AN (after nationalisation). Duplicate copies of some of these records were retained by the Board, and are sometimes to be preferred to the P.R.O. series. For example, the retained Minutes of the B.T.C. for 1947–62 contain detailed indexes. These and other retained records are now housed at 66, Porchester Road.

The B.T.C. Secretariat 'S' file series, which covers the period 1947–54 (some files were maintained until 1962), was retained by the Board, but will be transferred to the P.R.O. in the near future. References to this series are made as follows: 'B.T.C. file number, B.R.B. (location)'. The remainder of the Secretariat file series, continued by the B.R.B. from 1963, was microfilmed in the late 1970s. Reference to this series is 'B.R.B. file number'. Both the B.T.C. and the B.R.B. Minutes are accompanied by Guard Books which contain the main papers discussed by the Commission or Board. Reference here is, for B.T.C. material, 'B.T.C. Minutes, date, B.R.B. (location)', and for B.R.B. material, 'B.R.B. Minutes, date'.

File numbers used by the B.T.C. and B.R.B. Secretariat are not discrete, but may also be used by other departments. Thus, 'B.R.B. 99–1–1' refers to a Secretariat file, while 'B.R.B. Finance 99–1–1' refers to a Finance Department file with the same number.

A distinction is made between 'Memo.', an official memorandum passed from one institution to another, e.g. from the B.T.C. to the M.T., and 'memo.', an internal communication passed from one official or committee to another, or from either to the Board.

1. Introduction: nationalisation

1 As the B.T.C. itself understood. See, for example, B.T.C., *Reorganisation of Railways* (Submission to the Minister of Transport) (April 1954), pp. 3–4.
2 See T. R. Gourvish, *Railways in the British Economy 1830–1914* (London: Macmillan, 1980), pp. 52ff.
3 Ibid., p. 42. Data are for the U.K.
4 Unfortunately, there are no comparable railway statistics for the pre- and

post-1912 period, and both coverage and method change several times thereafter. However, U.K. coal tonnage carried (excluding free-hauled) was 225,601,000 tons in 1912, and the average for *Great Britain* (*excluding London*) was 177,448,000 tons per annum, 1934–8, which suggests a fall of about 20 per cent. See D. L. Munby and A. H. Watson (eds.), *Inland Transport Statistics: Great Britain 1900–1970*, I (Oxford: Oxford University Press, 1978), pp. 83, 188–9.

5 Scepticism about the extent of inter-railway competition can be seen before the war in the *Report of the Departmental Committee on Railway Agreements and Amalgamations* of 1911.

6 For a general summary of the railways' problems in the 1930s see, *inter alia*, D. H. Aldcroft, *British Railways in Transition: The Economic Problems of Britain's Railways since 1914* (London: Macmillan, 1968), pp. 47–88, and T. C. Barker and C. I. Savage, *An Economic History of Transport in Britain* (London: Hutchinson, 1974), pp. 153–9.

7 *Railway Returns.*

8 For contrasting views see Aldcroft, *British Railways*, and M. R. Bonavia, *British Railway Policy between the Wars* (Manchester: Manchester University Press, 1981).

9 I.e. 16.66 per cent above most pre-war charges, and 10 per cent above pre-war season and workmen's tickets and London Transport fares. Sir Norman Chester, *The Nationalisation of British Industry 1945–51* (London: H.M.S.O., 1975), p. 701.

10 Munby and Watson, *Statistics*, pp. 86, 104–5. Data are for main-line companies (for passenger-mileage in 1938 the authors' estimate of 19,800 million less 3 per cent is used).

11 C. I. Savage, *Inland Transport* (London: H.M.S.O., 1957), p. 634n.

12 Col Eric Gore-Browne, address to Southern Railway shareholders, 7 March 1946, in file on 'Nationalisation of Railways, British Railways Stockholders' Union, 1945–7', RAIL258/205, P.R.O.; *Railway Gazette*, 15 August 1947.

13 Mount, memo. 14 August 1943, Ministry of War Transport Correspondence and Papers: Post-War Planning and Reconstruction: Finance, Railways and Transport Generally, MT47/275, P.R.O.

14 Quoted in Savage, *Inland Transport*, p. 638.

15 Memo. 21 December 1942, MT47/275, P.R.O.

16 *Railway Gazette*, 1 August 1947, 19 March 1948, B.T.C., *R. & A. 1948*, p. 123

17 R. Bell, *History of the British Railways during the War, 1939–45* (London: Railway Gazette, 1946), pp. 109–10; R.E.C., 'Five-Year Plan for Construction and Repair of Railway Rolling Stock for Main-Line Companies' (Memo. to the Minister of Transport, 26 August 1947), Ministry of Transport Correspondence and Papers: R. E. C. Minutes of Meetings, MT6/2805 Part II, P.R.O.

18 Over two-thirds of the requisitioned stock were still fitted with grease axle-boxes at the time of nationalisation, whereas 99 per cent of the rail-owned wagons were using the superior oil-boxes. R.E.C., 'Five-Year Plan', P.R.O.; R.E., confidential report on 'Physical Condition of British Railways at January 1948' (n.d., but February 1948), pp. 10–11, B.R.B.

19 Michael Bonavia, memo. on 'White Paper, *Capital Investment in 1948* (1947, Cmd.7268)', 3 December 1947, B.T.C. S17–1–1A; construction and stock

availability data for main-line railways 31 December 1939 and 1946, in B.T.C., Memo. on 'Construction of Railway Coaching Stock', 31 December 1947, S17–3–1A, B.R.B.; R.E.C., 'Five-Year Plan', P.R.O.

20 Savage, *Inland Transport*, p. 639.

21 *Parl. Deb. (Commons)*, vol. 416 (Session 1945–6), 35.

22 R.E., 'Physical Condition of British Railways', p. 16, B.R.B.

23 R.E., 'Mechanical & Electrical Engineering on British Railways' (July 1952), Appendix VIII; Wood, memo. on 'Locomotive Position', 5 February 1948, B.T.C. Minutes, 15 February 1948, B.R.B.

24 R.E., 'Physical Condition of British Railways', p. 10, B.R.B.; Captain Sir Ian Bolton, memo. on 'Rolling Stock', 21 November 1947, B.T.C. S17–1–1A, B.R.B.; B.T.C., *R. & A. 1948*, p. 111.

25 R.E., 'Mechanical & Electrical Engineering' (July 1952), Appendix VIII; R.E., 'Physical Condition of British Railways', pp. 8–9, B.R.B.; B.T.C., *R. & A. 1948*, p. 110.

26 Mount, memo. on 'Planning for Post-War Reconstruction: Main-Line Railways and London Transport Facilities', 15 January 1943, MT47/275, P.R.O. Mount later raised his figure by £200m.: Mount, memo. 10 July 1943, Ministry of War Transport Correspondence and Papers: Railways: Post-War Reconstruction, MT6/2634, P.R.O. The Investment Programmes Committee was a sub-committee of the Official Steering Committee on Economic Development, part of the Labour Government's complex machinery for economic control during the post-war austerity period. Its specific aim was to draw up priorities for investment. See below, pp. 73–4.

27 Mount, *Report to the Minister of Transport upon the Accidents which Occurred on the Railways of Great Britain during . . . 1946* (1947), and *1947* (1948); *Daily Mail*, 28 October 1947.

28 Cit. in *Railway Gazette*, 30 July 1948.

29 *Parl. Deb. (Commons)*, vol. 431 (Session 1946–7), 17 December 1946, 1809.

30 The pre-war norm was based on 1935–7 for the main-line railways and the year 1938–9 for the L.P.T.B. Reginald H. Wilson, memo. on 'Standard Charge for Maintenance', 23 May 1949, B.T.C. S21–1–1, B.R.B.; *Government Control of the Railways. Estimates of the Pooled Revenue . . . for the Year Ended 31 December 1945* (April 1946), P.P.1945–6, XX, Cmd.6797.

31 Barnes, Written Answer, 27 January 1947, *Parl. Deb. (Commons)*, vol. 432 (Session 1946–7), *128*; *Government Control . . . 31 December 1946* (April 1947), P.P.1946–7, XVIII, Cmd.7106, p. 3, and *Government Control . . . 31 December 1947* (May 1948), P.P.1947–8, XX, Cmd.7399, p. 4; B.T.C., *R. & A. 1948*, Table V-13, p. 258; Wilson, memo. 23 May 1949, B.T.C. S21–1–1, B.R.B.

32 Wilson, memo. 23 May 1949 B.T.C. S21–1–1, B.R.B.; C. Coates–W. M. Hind, 14 June 1949, Ministry of War Transport Correspondence and Papers: Finance: War Damage, MT47/263, P.R.O.

33 Wilson, memo. 23 May 1949, B.T.C. S21–1–1, B.R.B.

34 See, *inter alia*, G. D. N. Worswick and P. H. Ady (eds.), *The British Economy 1945–1950* (Oxford: Clarendon Press, 1952), *passim*, M. Sissons and P. French (eds.), *Age of Austerity* (London: Hodder, 1963), pp. 169ff., and J. C. R. Dow, *The Management of the British Economy 1945–60* (Cambridge: Cambridge University Press, 1965), pp. 13–28.

35 Hurcomb–Missenden correspondence, 14–15 October 1947, and Riddles,

memo. on 'Wagon Position', 5 November 1947, B.T.C. S17–1–1A, S59–3–
1A, B.R.B.

36 R.E.C. Minutes, 4–18 November 1947, MT6/2805 Part II, P.R.O., and R.E.,
Wagon Discharge Campaign, file, 18 November–17 December 1947, B.R.B.

37 *Government Control* . . ., P.P.1945–6, XX, Cmd.6797, and 1947–8, XX,
Cmd.7399.

38 Coal output was 190.1m. tons per annum, 1945–7. See *A.A.S. 1938–49*
(1951), pp. 131, 220 (comparisons are approximate due to changes in
methods of compilation, Munby and Watson, *Statistics*, pp. 190, 200–2).
The fall in merchandise traffic was also influenced by the priority for coal
traffic established by the Ministry of Transport's orders under the Control
Agreement. See B.T.C. S110–2–1, B.R.B.

39 *Government Control* . . ., P.P.1947–8, XX, Cmd.7399, and *Railway
Gazette*, 7 and 28 May 1948. Data for gross revenue and working
expenditure exclude collection and delivery services and other subsidiary
activities.

40 Munby and Watson, *Statistics*, pp. 61, 73. The figures are for British
Railways, including the L.P.T.B. and the Railway Clearing House. For
problems of comparison, see ibid., pp. 174–82.

41 Chester, *Nationalisation*, pp. 701–7.

42 This résumé of the position in 1948 is the railways' own. See B.R.B., Railway
Policy Review, report to the Minister for Transport Industries, December
1972, p. 2, B.R.B.

43 G. Alderman, *The Railway Interest* (Leicester: Leicester University Press,
1973), pp. 224–8, and E. E. Barry, *Nationalisation in British Politics*
(London: Cape, 1965), pp. 87–104.

44 Barry, *Nationalisation*, pp. 96–102.

45 *Railway Gazette*, 31 January 1919.

46 P. S. Bagwell, *The Railwaymen. The History of the National Union of
Railwaymen*, I (London: George Allen & Unwin, 1963), p. 405.

47 See, for example, P. S. Bagwell, *The Transport Revolution from 1770*
(London: Batsford, 1974), pp. 240–6.

48 F. W. S. Craig (ed.), *British General Election Manifestos 1900–74* (London:
Macmillan, 1975), pp. 32, 40, 63, 96.

49 B. Donoughue and G. W. Jones, *Herbert Morrison. Portrait of a Politician*
(London: Weidenfeld & Nicolson, 1973), pp. 182–6.

50 Bagwell, *The Railwaymen*, I, pp. 370, 404–5, 529; Barry, *Nationalisation*,
pp. 238–9. However, Morrison did include long-distance road transport in
his scheme of 1933: see *Socialisation and Transport* (London: Constable,
1933), p. 100.

51 *Royal Commission on Transport Final Report: The Co-ordination and
Development of Transport* (December 1930), 'Additional Recommendations', P.P.1930–1, XVII, Cmd.3751, p. 230. Donald, Galton and Leach had
all been appointed by the Labour Home Secretary, J. R. Clynes, to replace
retiring members in 1929.

52 Letter from T.U.C. General Council, January 1932, in *Communications
Received from Certain Organisations in Response to the Ministry of Transport's Request for Their Observations on the Conclusions and Recommendations of the Final Report of the Royal Commission on Transport*,
P.P.1931–2, XX, Cmd.4048, pp. 76–7.

53 *Parl. Deb. (Commons)*, vol. 252 (Session 1930–1), 14 May 1931, 1346.
54 Robinson, memo. 29 May 1940, Ministry of War Transport Correspondence and Papers: Co-ordination of Transport (Proposed National Transport Corporation), 1940–1, MT64/10; memo. (unsigned), 22 August 1940, and notes of a meeting of Jowitt, Coates and Hurst, 27 April 1942, in Cabinet Committee on Reconstruction Problems: Transport Policy File, CAB117/226, P.R.O. See also J. C. W. Reith, *Into the Wind* (London: Hodder, 1949), pp. 390–1. For details of the renegotiation of the Control Agreement see Savage, *Inland Transport*, pp. 283ff., and on Coates see W. J. Reader, *Imperial Chemical Industries. A History* (2 vols., London: Oxford University Press, 1970, 1975), I, pp. 420–1, II, pp. 137, 310.
55 Memo. on 'The Transport Problem in Great Britain', 15 October 1940, signed 'W.H.C.' and 'A.T.V.R.', in Ministry of War Transport Correspondence and Papers: Co-ordination of Transport, MT64/11, with supporting memos. in ibid.: Sir Alfred Robinson's Supplementary Memoranda, MT64/16, P.R.O.
56 See calculations and discussion in Ministry of War Transport Correspondence and Papers: Co-ordination of Transport, MT64/15, and MT47/275, P.R.O.
57 Anon., 'Conversations with the Minister', 3 December 1940, and Coates, report, p. 18, MT47/275, P.R.O.
58 Donoughue and Jones, *Herbert Morrison*, pp. 131–3, 153–4.
59 Sir John Anderson, draft memo. on 'The Future of the Railways', n.d. (probably July 1941), pp. 4–5, Rail Priorities Committee (Lord President's Committee), CAB 123/69, subsequently printed as War Cabinet Paper (41) No.158, 11 July 1941, CAB66/17; War Cabinet Minutes, 15 and 24 July 1941, CAB65/19, P.R.O.
60 Greenwood–Leathers, 31 July 1941, and Leathers–Greenwood, 1 August and 1 October 1941, CAB117/266; Hurcomb, address to internal meeting, 18 November 1941, MT47/275, P.R.O.
61 Jowitt–Leathers, 16 March 1942, Leathers–Jowitt, 3 April 1942, CAB117/266, P.R.O.
62 Short-distance = up to 30 miles (later altered to 15 miles). Notes of meeting, 27 April 1942, CAB117/266, P.R.O.
63 Coates, (Secret) Report on the Transport Problem in Great Britain, July 1942, copies in MT64/9, MT74/7, MT47/275 and CAB117/266, P.R.O. Chester, *Nationalisation*, pp. 392–3, and J. B. Cullingworth, *Environmental Planning 1939–1969*, I, *Reconstruction and Land Use Planning 1939–47* (London: H.M.S.O., 1975), p. 36, summarise the report though without reference to its antecedent of 1940. Sir John F. Heaton, Chairman and Managing Director of Thomas Tilling and a member of the Inland Transport War Council came independently to the same conclusion as Coates: Heaton, memo. to Minister, April 1942, in Hurcomb, memo. on 'Co-ordination of Inland Transport', July 1943, Ministry of War Transport Correspondence and Papers: Nationalisation of Transport: Policy, MT74/1, P.R.O.
64 Leathers–Jowitt, 24 September 1942, and notes of a meeting of Jowitt, Leathers, Hurcomb, Hurst and Philip Noel-Baker, 29 March 1943, CAB117/266, P.R.O.
65 Later (1981) Professor of Economic History at Cambridge.
66 Draft of P. Deane, 'Rail and Road Transport', later published in J. R. Bellerby

(ed.), *Economic Reconstruction. A Study of Post-War Problems* (London: Macmillan, 1943), in Jowitt–Leathers, 3 December 1942, and meeting notes, 29 March 1943, CAB117/266, P.R.O.

67 Hurcomb, memo. on 'Unification of Railways', 2 July 1943, and reply by W. M. Hind, 9 July 1943, MT47/275; memos. on 'Co-ordination of Inland Transport', July and August 1943, MT74/1, P.R.O.

68 Mount, memo. 15 January 1943, MT47/275, P.R.O.

69 Leathers–Jowitt, 17 July 1943, CAB117/266; Jowitt–Woolton, 5 April 1944, Cabinet Papers: Minute on Post-War Organisation of Transport, CAB127/189, P.R.O.

70 See the Lords debates on 'British Railways', 14 October 1941, 'Public Services', 17 June 1942, and 'Inland Transport', 27 October 1943: *Parl. Deb. (Lords)*, vol.120 (Session 1940–1), 215–31, vol. 123 (Session 1941–2), 415–30, and vol. 129 (Session 1942–3), 353–90; and the Commons debates on 'Transport', 13 February 1940, and 'Ministry of War Transport', 5 May 1944, *Parl. Deb. (Commons)*, vol. 357 (Session 1939–40), vol. 399 (Session 1943–4), 1581–682.

71 Memos. of Mount, 10 July 1943, and P. Faulkner, 23 July 1943, MT6/2634, P.R.O. Mount was worried about the Ministry's complacency in its approach to railway planning.

72 Hurcomb, memo. July 1943, MT74/1, P.R.O.; *Parl. Deb. (Lords)*, vol. 129 (Session 1942–3), 384.

73 R.Co.A. Minutes, 14 April 1942, RAIL1098/9, P.R.O.

74 P. Wilson–R. H. (Sir Reginald) Hill, 20 January 1942, and Hill–Hurcomb, 24 January 1942, MT6/2634; R.Co.A. Minutes, 14 April and 6 August 1942, RAIL1098/9, P.R.O.

75 The reports can be found in RAIL1098/29–47, P.R.O.

76 Mount–Hill, 9 March 1942, Ministry of War Transport Correspondence and Papers: Post-War Transport Reorganisation, MT6/2770; Chairman's Report to the L.M.S. Board, April 1944, RAIL418/116, P.R.O.

77 R.Co.A. Minutes, 14 April, 5 May and 17 November 1942, RAIL1098/9, P.R.O. Szlumper had left the S.Rly on 'leave of absence' in 1939 to work for the War Office as Director-General of Transportation and Movements. Missenden, who had taken his place, made it clear that he was not prepared to work merely as an 'acting' General Manager. When Szlumper's work for the government ended in 1942 he was retired by the railway company. See Sir John Elliot, *On and Off the Rails* (London: George Allen & Unwin, 1982), pp. 49–52.

78 Gore-Browne Committee, Report on Post-War Policy, 16 October 1942, RAIL1098/48, P.R.O.

79 Ibid., pp. 5–7, 15 and Appendix I.

80 Great Western Chairman's File on Post-War Policy, RAIL258/552, L.N.E.R. Post-War Policy Committee Minutes, 8 July and 16 December 1942, RAIL390/14, and L.M.S. Board Minutes, 27 and 28 January 1943, RAIL418/11, P.R.O.

81 Report by the General Managers of the Main-Line Companies on Post-War Policy, July 1943, RAIL1098/49, and Missenden, private report to Southern directors on 'Post-War Policy', June 1943, RAIL1100/3, P.R.O.

82 Memo. to the Minister of War Transport on Post-War Transport Proposals, August 1943, RAIL1098/50, P.R.O.

83 A Railway Public Service Committee was established to prepare propaganda. Its Chairman, Sir William Wood, and Arthur Pearson, both of the L.M.S., produced initial drafts in April 1943. R.Co.A. Minutes, 17 November 1942, RAIL1098/9; 'The Case against the Nationalisation of the Railways', April 1943, L.M.S. Chairman's correspondence and papers, 1943–4, RAIL424/29, P.R.O.

84 General Managers' Report, Appendix B, p. 20, RAIL1098/49, P.R.O., R.Co.A., *British Railways and the Future* (London: R.Co.A., 1946), and L.N.E.R., *The State and the Railways: An Alternative to Nationalisation* (London: L.N.E.R., 1946). See also L.M.S./L.N.E.R. Joint Committee Minutes, 28 February–25 September 1946, RAIL390/14, P.R.O.

85 Serious planning did not begin until October/November 1945. See MT74/1 *et seq.*, and Ministry of Transport Correspondence and Papers: Finance: Nationalisation of Inland Transport, Preliminary Discussions on General Policy, MT47/202, P.R.O.

86 See, for example, Chester, *Nationalisation*, pp. 106–39, 261–77, 319–31, 351–8, 391–405, 665–77, 1019–21; G. Walker, 'The Transport Act, 1947', *Economic Journal*, LVIII (March 1948), 11–30, and 'Transport Policy Before and After 1953', *Oxford Economic Papers*, V (1953), 90–116; B. Williams, 'Transport Act, 1947: Some Benefits and Dangers', *Journal of the Institute of Transport*, XXIV (May 1951), 153–8. An important primary source is Ministry of Transport, 'Transport Act 1947. Guide to Official Papers', September 1947, B.T.C. S214–2–1, B.R.B.

87 Lord Portal–Barnes, 6 February 1946, and Barnes–Portal, 14 February 1946, Ministry of War Transport Correspondence and Papers: Nationalisation of Transport: Policy 1946, MT74/2, P.R.O.; A. J. Pearson, *Man of the Rail* (London: George Allen & Unwin, 1967), p. 97; M. R. Bonavia, *The Birth of British Rail* (London: George Allen & Unwin, 1979), pp. 21–2.

88 Meeting of Barnes, Morrison and others, 8 October 1945, in MT74/1, P.R.O.

89 S. S. Wilson–Hurcomb, 27 and 28 November 1945, MT74/1, P.R.O. Wilson was one of the major architects of the Transport Bill.

90 Transport Act, 1947, S.3 (1), 4 and 5 (1).

91 Wilson–Hurcomb, 27 and 28 November 1945, MT74/1, P.R.O. The Parliamentary Secretary, Noel-Baker, and Wilson's colleague, W. M. Hind, were less critical of the territorial option. See meeting, 8 October 1945, and Hind, memo. 30 November 1945, MT74/1, P.R.O.

92 A. J. Pearson, 'Developments and Prospects in British Transport', *Journal of the Institute of Transport*, XXV (May 1953), 2–3. Southampton Docks were not handed over to the B.T.C. until September 1950.

93 *Economist*, 7 December 1946.

94 See Chapter 2, pp. 47ff.

95 Ministry of Transport Correspondence and Papers: Finance: Negotiations with Main-line Companies' Chairmen, MT47/222, P.R.O.; H. Wilson, 'The Financial Problem of British Transport', report in typescript to T.S.S.A., N.U.R. and A.S.L.E.F., 20 December 1951, pp. 7, 11, T.U.C. Library.

96 Based on compensation of £907.8m. The final sum was £927.3m. (interest £27.8m.) and with L.P.T.B. £1,055.4m. (£31.7m.).

97 *Economist*, 23 November and 14 December 1946, and *Railway Gazette*, 8 and 18 November and 13 December 1946. The railway chairmen continued negotiations with the Ministry until July 1947: MT47/222, P.R.O.

98 MT47/275 and MT64/15, P.R.O.
99 For a critical Stock Exchange view of the process, see N. Davenport, *Memoirs of a City Radical* (London: Weidenfeld & Nicolson, 1974), p. 181.
100 Final terms amounted to over 24 years' purchase of the Control Agreement's guaranteed net revenue of £43.5m. The railways' net operating surplus was £26.3m. per annum, 1948–52.
101 Barnes, memo. to Cabinet Socialisation of Industries Committee, 23 May 1949, in Treasury Correspondence and Papers: Socialised Industries (Control of Investment), T229/339, P.R.O.

2. Organisation

1 Bolton had also been a director of the L.M.S.
2 See, *inter alia*, Ministry of Transport: Transport Act, 1947, Bill Files and Papers, MT74/141, P.R.O. Note that Ashfield's term of office was limited to three years: B.T.C. Minutes, 15 September 1947, B.R.B.
3 Wilson, memo. 22 October 1947 and Wilson–Dickinson, 23 October 1947, MT74/141, P.R.O. Wilson directed his remarks not only at the B.T.C. but also at three of its Executives: Railway, London Transport and Docks and Inland Waterways. His opinions were shared by *The Economist*, 16 August 1947.
4 M. R. Bonavia, *The Birth of British Rail* (London: George Allen & Unwin, 1979), p. 23. See also his *British Rail. The First 25 Years* (Newton Abbot: David & Charles, 1981), pp. 30–1.
5 These impressions have been taken from a variety of sources, and in particular, David Blee's pen-pictures of the B.T.C., memo. 16 February 1949, Blee Papers, AN6/27, P.R.O.
6 The original intention was to reduce Hurcomb's salary to £6,500. For the circumstances surrounding the abatement of his salary see Dalton–Barnes, 29 May 1947, S. A. Bailey (M.T.)–L. L. H. Thompson (Treasury), 14 August 1947, and reply, 16 August 1947, and Thompson, memo. 29 August 1947, Ministry of Transport Correspondence and Papers: Establishment and Organisation, B.T.C. Appointments, Salaries of Members, MT45/500, P.R.O. Wood's salary is given in L.M.S. Board Special Minutes, 29 May 1941, RAIL418/13, P.R.O. Both Wood and Missenden were offered their posts *without* deduction for their railway pensions.
7 S. S. Wilson's list, 15 May 1946, MT74/141, P.R.O. The list, which contained six sub-divisions – 'politicians with administrative experience', 'other administrators', 'trade unionists', 'some transport experience', 'independent' and 'women' – included two men later appointed to Executives: Lord Latham (London Transport) and Henry Clay (Road Haulage).
8 Cabinet Socialised Industries Committee Minutes, 20 October 1949, CAB134/690, P.R.O.
9 Hurcomb, memo. on 'B.T.C.', 10 January 1947, MT74/141, P.R.O.; B.T.C. Minutes, 13 August 1947 (appendix), B.R.B. Cf. S. S. Wilson, 'Notes on Points to be Brought to the Notice of the B.T.C., 8 August 1947', Ministry of Transport: Transport Act 1947, Bill Files and Papers, B.T.C.: Policy and Practice, 1946–7, MT74/97, P.R.O.
10 Salaries were: Beevor, £6,500; Wilson, £5,000; and Brebner, £5,000. B.T.C.

Minutes, 21 August, 15 September and 11 November 1947, and Beevor's memo. 10 November 1947, B.R.B.

11 B.T.C. Minutes, 20 January, 17 February and 28 September 1948, and memos. of Beevor, 16 January and 10 February 1948 and Reginald Wilson, 27 September 1948, B.R.B.

12 See, *inter alia*, S. S. Wilson, brief for Barnes, 24 April 1946, and Viscount Addison–Barnes correspondence, 21 and 23 May and 2 June 1947, MT74/141; G. R. Strauss–Barnes, 31 January 1947, and Wilson, note, 15 July 1947, Ministry of Transport: Transport Act 1947, Bill Files and Papers, B.T.C.: Appointment of Executives, 1947, MT74/99, P.R.O. Hurcomb was also openly critical of Ministerial appointment of Executive members: cf. Hurcomb–Alan Lennox-Boyd, 14 November 1952, B.T.C. S201–4–2C, B.R.B.

13 B.T.C. Minutes, 13 August 1947, B.R.B.

14 Excluding the changes which came with the amalgamations of 1923. *Railway Gazette,* 19 September 1947.

15 A. J. Pearson, *Man of the Rail* (London: George Allen & Unwin, 1967), pp. 97–8, and Bonavia, *British Rail. The First 25 Years,* pp. 23–4. For details of the appointments process see Ministry of Transport Correspondence and Papers: B.T.C., Railway Executive Appointments, MT96/41, P.R.O.

16 R.E., Review of Railway Executive and Regional Headquarters Staff, October 1951, Elliot Papers, AN6/5, P.R.O.

17 There was also no G.W.R. man in Barrington-Ward's staff of five. R.E., List of Executive Officers, 1948, Blee Papers, AN6/8, P.R.O.

18 Hurcomb–Missenden, 3 September 1947, reproduced in B.T.C. Minutes, 16–17 September 1947, B.R.B.

19 B.T.C. Minutes, 25 August and 16–17 September 1947, B.R.B.; Blee, memo. to Missenden on 'Transport Act, 1947: The Railway Executive', 30 September 1947, p. 1, Blee Papers, AN6/7, P.R.O. In reply to a questionnaire on organisation of July 1952, all R.E. members said 'No' to the question 'Were you advised of your functions in writing on appointment by the Minister?'. Barrington-Ward claimed that his functional capacity was explained verbally: R.E. memo. 25 July 1952 and supporting appendices, Blee Papers, AN6/41, P.R.O.

20 'Note of Meeting between the B.T.C. and R.E.', 2 October 1947, and Confidential Memo. (unsigned) on 'Origin of the Functional Method of Organisation of the Railways as Shown in the Official Records', 6 January 1948, both in Elliot Papers, AN6/58, P.R.O. The creation of the B.T.C. and R.E. organisation is outlined in M. R. Bonavia, *The Organisation of British Railways* (London: Ian Allan, 1971), pp. 44–52.

21 Blee, memo. 30 September 1947, AN6/7, P.R.O.

22 R.E., draft memo. on 'Organisation of British Railways', 8 October 1947, summarised in Confidential Memo. 6 January 1948, and 'Note of Meeting between the B.T.C. and R.E.', 10 October 1947, AN6/58, P.R.O.

23 'Note of Meeting . . .', 2 October 1947, AN6/58, P.R.O. The proposal was repeated in the R.E.'s draft memo. of 8 October: see memo. on 'Inception of the Regions', 8 February 1951, AN6/58, P.R.O.

24 B.T.C. Minutes, 16–17 September 1947, B.R.B.

25 B.T.C. Minutes, 28 October 1947; B.T.C., Direction No. 1, 27 November 1947, B.R.B.

26 Beevor–Marsden, 11 November 1947, AN6/7, P.R.O.; B.T.C., Memo. on 'Organisation of the Unified Railway System', 28 October 1947, B.T.C. Minutes, 23 October and 4 November 1947, B.R.B. Missenden's plea for a 'free hand' is in 'Note of Meeting . . .', 2 October 1947, AN6/58, P.R.O.

27 B.T.C., draft memos. on 'Organisation of the Unified Railway System', B.T.C. Minutes, 23 October and 4 November 1947, B.R.B.

28 B.T.C. and R.E. Joint Meeting Minutes, 27 October 1947, summarised in memo. on 'Inception of the Regions', February 1951, AN6/58, P.R.O.; Missenden–Hurcomb, 29 October 1947, B.T.C. S92–1–1, B.R.B.

29 Data from B.T.C. press release, 26 November 1947, B.R.B.

30 This view was incorporated in the B.T.C.'s Memo. for the 'Information and Guidance of All Officers and Staff of the Main Line Railways as to Procedure during the Period Beginning 1st January 1948', November 1947, B.T.C. Minutes, 6 November 1947, B.R.B. See also the correspondence in B.T.C. S92–1–1, B.R.B.

31 Beevor, memo. on 'Railway Executive: Appointment of Officers', 20 January 1948, B.R.B., and private communications from Sir John Elliot, 18 May 1981, and C. P. Hopkins, 16 June 1981. Only Hopkins received an increase in salary (his former salary with the L.N.E.R. was £2,250), although Bird was earning £2,500 a year until his appointment as acting Divisional General Manager (Southern) L.N.E.R. at £3,500 from 1 October 1947.

32 *Railway Gazette*, 28 November and 4 December 1947 (the latter contains references to articles in *The Financial Times* and *Manchester Guardian*), and *The Economist*, 29 November and 6 December 1947.

33 *Railway Gazette*, 19 March 1948.

34 Hurcomb, memo. on 'Railway Executive Organisation', 20 March 1948, B.T.C. S4–9–1A, B.R.B.

35 *Sunday Express*, 23 May 1948: R.E., Memoranda of Decisions Taken at Meeting (hereafter 'Memoranda'), 24 May, 5 and 19 July 1948, AN4/9; R.E. Minutes, 29 July 1948, AN4/1, P.R.O.

36 Marsden, Confidential Memo. on 'R.E. Meetings and Procedure', 28 February 1948, in R.E., 'Terms of Appointment of and Reference to R.E. Committees and Instructions in Regard to R.E. Meetings and Procedure', B.R.B. Hurcomb's request for copies of all R.E. Minutes was made in Hurcomb–Missenden, 19 September 1947, B.T.C. S26–2–1, B.R.B.

37 Memo. (unsigned) on 'R.E. Meetings and Procedure', 25 February 1948, B.T.C. S26–2–1, B.R.B., and Marsden, confidential note on 'The Railway Executive Minutes and Memoranda of Decisions', 5 November 1948, AN6/58, P.R.O. The existence of two sets of minutes was first revealed in Bonavia, *Organisation*, pp. 53–4.

38 Very little has survived apart from the formal minutes and memoranda.

39 R.E. Memoranda, 5 July 1948 and 27 July 1950, AN4/9 and 10, P.R.O.

40 Ibid., 1, 8, 11, 15 and 18 March 1948, AN4/9, P.R.O.

41 R.E. Minutes, 1, 4, 8, 11 and 24 March 1948, AN4/1, P.R.O. Note especially: 'The 6.30pm sailing from Waterford to Fishguard on Saturday did not leave until 2.45pm yesterday owing to fog' (Min.408, 1 March) and 'Working was dislocated in the Stafford area this morning from 4.58am until 6.25am on account of cattle straying in Shugborough Tunnel' (Min.524, 24 March).

42 Conversation with Riddles, 30 September 1980. The first informal joint meeting was held on 20 January 1948. See B.T.C. Minutes, 6 January 1948;

Beevor, memo. 7 January 1948, Beevor–Marsden, 13 January 1948, and
B.T.C./R.E. Minutes, 20 January 1948, in B.T.C. S26–2–2A, B.R.B.
43 Beevor, note on 'R.E. Administrative Instructions', 29 March 1950,
Bonavia–Beevor, 19 April 1950, Missenden–Hurcomb, 27 April 1950,
Beevor–Hurcomb, 1 May 1950, B.T.C. S92–1–1; and R.E., Instruction to
Officers in the Regions, printed handbook, 1 May 1950, B.R.B.
44 R.E. Special Meeting Minutes, 30 March 1950, bound with ordinary
minutes, AN4/3 (prior decisions appear in R.E. Memoranda, 1 September
1949, 30 January and 6 March 1950, AN4/9, 10, P.R.O.); Hurcomb–
Missenden, 15 May 1950, B.T.C. S92–1–1, B.R.B.
45 Hurcomb–Missenden, 13 April 1948, and reply on 'Future of Diesel Traction', 22 April 1948; Missenden–Hurcomb on 'Future Forms of Motive
Power', 20 December 1948, B.T.C. S44–1–1A; B.T.C./R.E. Minutes, 14 May
and 15 December 1948, S26–2–2A, B.R.B.; Missenden–B.T.C., 7 December
1950, S17–2–1A, B.R.B.; R.E. Memoranda, 17 February 1949, AN4/9,
P.R.O. On Riddles's policy see below, pp. 87–9.
46 See, *inter alia*, B.T.C. Minutes, 8 January and 1 July 1948, B.R.B.; R.E./
C.R.O.s Joint Meeting Minutes, 27 May and 21 June 1948, AN99/1, P.R.O.;
Missenden–Hurcomb on 'The Railway Regions', 17 June 1948, AN6/58,
P.R.O.
47 Beevor, memo. 10 November 1949, B.T.C. Minutes, 29 November 1949 and
12 January 1950, B.R.B.; B.T.C., *R. & A. 1949*, pp. 1–2.
48 B.T.C., Direction No. 2 to the Railway Executive, 10 November 1949, AN6/
58, P.R.O. For B.T.C.–R.E. discussions on this issue, see B.T.C./R.E.
Minutes, 22 September 1949, B.T.C. S26–2–2B; Beevor, memo. on 'Revision
of Direction No. 1 to the Railway Executive', 8 November 1949, B.T.C.
Minutes, 10 November 1949, B.R.B.
49 B.T.C./R.E. Joint Meeting Minutes, 2 October 1947, AN6/58; R.E.
Memoranda, 8 and 18 May 1950, AN4/10, P.R.O. See also Beevor's
comments at informal meeting, 15 September 1949, recorded by Blee, Blee
Papers, AN6/10, P.R.O.
50 Beevor, memo. on 'Common Services', 25 February 1948, Hurcomb, memo.
on 'Common Services', 20 August 1948, B.T.C. Minutes, 2 March and 24
August 1948; Missenden–Hurcomb, 30 September 1948, Beevor–Hurcomb,
11 October 1948, B.T.C. S195–1–1; Beevor, memo. on 'Common Services –
Legal Organisation', 9 March 1949, B.T.C. Minutes, 10 March 1949, B.R.B.;
B.T.C., *R. & A. 1950*, pp. 4–5. On Missenden's obstructiveness see Beevor–
Smedley, 15 February 1949, B.T.C. S195–1–1, and correspondence re
B.T.C./R.E. Joint Meeting Minutes, 16 November 1948, S26–2–2A, B.R.B.
51 Data from Brebner, memo. on 'Commercial Advertising', 20 May 1949,
B.T.C. Minutes, 24 May 1949, B.R.B. (the figure for 1948 is given as
£667,000 in B.T.C., *R. & A. 1948*, p. 300). For the background to the
advertising service see B.T.C. Minutes, 23 October 1947, 8 and 20 April, 11
May 1948; report by Chairman of the Co-ordinating Committee (Brebner)
on 'Commercial Advertising', 18 August 1948, B.T.C. S32–1–1; Minutes of
meeting between B.T.C. and Chairmen of the Executives, 31 August 1948,
S195–1–1, and correspondence in S55–1–1, B.R.B.
52 B.T.C. Minutes, 30 November 1948, and B.T.C. confidential memo. 7
December 1948; Beevor, memo. on 'Common Services – Commercial
Advertising', 8 March 1949, B.T.C. Minutes, 8 March 1949, and *Instrument*

No. R/EX/9 *Issued Pursuant to a Scheme of Delegation of Functions by the British Transport Commission to the Railway Executive*, 10 March 1949, in B.T.C. S195–3–1, B.R.B. Similar instruments were issued to the other Executives. The dispute over films and the continuation of the squabble over commercial advertising after March 1949 are outlined in the same file.

53 Hurcomb–Missenden, 18 February 1948, Missenden–Hurcomb, 23 February 1948, B.T.C. S32–5–1, B.R.B.

54 B.T.C. Public Relations Policy Committee Minutes, 26 April 1948, B.T.C. S32–1–2, and R.E., confidential report to the B.T.C. on 'British Railways. First Annual Report for Year Ended December 31, 1948' (n.d.), p. 35, B.R.B. See also Slim, memo. on 'Demarcation of Publicity Responsibility', 9 January 1948, B.T.C. S26–2–2A, B.R.B.

55 R.E., memo. on 'Public Relations and Advertising [subsequently changed to 'Publicity'] Organisation, British Railways', December 1948, in Beevor, memo. 1 January 1949, B.T.C. Minutes, 4 January 1949; notes of a meeting of B.T.C. and R.E., 17 January 1949, in Beevor, memo. on 'Railway Executive: Public Relations and Publicity Organisation', 19 January 1949, B.T.C. Minutes, 20 January 1949, B.R.B.

56 Brebner, memo. on 'Railway Executive Public Relations and Publicity Organisation', 13 December 1948, in Beevor, memo. 1 January 1949, B.T.C. Minutes, 4 January 1949, B.R.B.; Pearson, 'very private' letter to Blee, AN6/8, P.R.O. The letter is undated, but the author suggests it was written in 1949: private communication from Pearson, 11 April 1981.

57 Train, memo. on 'The Fickle Jade Publicity', 28 January 1949, AN6/27, P.R.O.; Beevor–Hurcomb, 4 July 1949, B.T.C. S17–2–39, B.R.B. Train was commenting on the Executive's press notice on locomotive standardisation, issued without reference to the Commission, which was followed up by an agreed statement on flat bottom rails. See B.T.C./R.E. Joint Meeting Minutes, 20 January 1949, B.T.C. S26–2–2A, B.R.B.

58 E.g. Blee memos. 7 July 1949, 28, 29 and 30 October 1953, AN6/10, P.R.O. Brebner's approach was also well known in the Ministry of Transport. When, shortly after his appointment to the B.T.C., he wrote a hasty letter to *The Daily Telegraph* (2 December 1947) criticising an article by J. C. Johnstone on the new railway organisation, a civil servant commented: 'I am afraid Breb's habit of popping in letters is going to be awkward for the B.T.C.!': Ministry of Transport: Transport Act, 1947: Administrative Action, MT6/3031, Part II, P.R.O.

59 Stanier (1876–1965) had been Chief Mechanical Engineer of the L.M.S.

60 B.T.C. Minutes, 14 July 1949, B.R.B.; R.E. Memoranda, 15 August 1949, AN4/9, P.R.O.; B.T.C., *R. & A. 1948*, p. 34, *1949*, pp. 2–3; Bonavia, *Organisation*, pp. 52–5.

61 Beevor, memo. on 'Future of the Railway Research Service', 16 January 1948, B.T.C. Minutes, 20 January 1948, B.R.B.; R.E. Memoranda, 27 June 1949, AN4/9, P.R.O.; Missenden–Hurcomb, 29 August 1949, and reply, 9 September 1949, B.T.C. S34–1–9, B.R.B.

62 Hurcomb–Missenden, 24 February 1948, B.T.C. S55–1–1, B.R.B.

63 B.T.C., Memo. on 'Organisation of the Unified Railway System', 28 October 1947, B.T.C. Minutes, 4 November 1947, B.R.B.

64 Conversation with Riddles, 30 September 1980; Sir John Elliot, *On and Off the Rails* (London: George Allen & Unwin, 1982), p. 68.

65 B.T.C., *R. & A. 1949*, p. 59; R.E., Examination of Organisational Functions: Chairman's Department, July 1952, AN6/41, P.R.O.

66 B.T.C., *R. & A. 1949*, pp. 58–9, 63, 77, 83; *1950*, pp. 91–3, 109, 113. The R.E. also appointed an Architect, Chief Medical Officer, Fire Officer, Welfare Officer and Chief Officer (Police). The Railway Police were not organised as a B.T.C. 'common service', but instead the R.E. acted as agents for the Docks and Inland Waterways and Hotels Executives in controlling a united British Transport Police force.

67 R.E. staff totalled 577 on 31 December 1950, cf. 367 C.R.O. staff, R.E., Memo. on 'Review of Railway Executive and Regional Headquarters Staff', 26 October 1951, AN6/5, P.R.O.

68 Notes of a meeting between B.T.C. and R.E., 10 October 1947, AN6/58, P.R.O.

69 R.E., Confidential Instruction No. 6 (Western Region) (1 January 1948), B.R.B. Instructions to the L.M.R. (No. 2) are reproduced in Bonavia, *Organisation*, pp. 48–50.

70 Train, confidential memo. to Missenden on 'Regional Boundaries', 4 January 1949, AN6/27, and see also Blee, memo. 10 November 1950, AN6/10, P.R.O. It is significant that in the review of organisational functions in July 1952 only Barrington-Ward stated that his function was 'to *provide general managership* for the operating, motive power . . . branches of railway service' (my italics), 'Appendix A', circulated with memo. on 'Organisation', 27 July 1952, AN6/41, P.R.O.

71 Blee, memos. 27 April and 13 May 1948, AN6/10, P.R.O. According to Beevor, only Missenden, Slim, Watson and Allen sent their instructions for the regions direct to the C.R.O.s: memo. on 'Railway Executive: Regional Boundaries and Organisation', 16 February 1949, B.T.C. Minutes, 17 February 1949, B.R.B.

72 R.E. Minutes, 29 July 1948, AN4/1, P.R.O. The C.R.O.s Conference began on 7 January 1948, and the first of the regular R.E./C.R.Os meetings was held on 28 January 1948. For the details of the organisational conflict see R.E./C.R.O.s Informal Meeting Minutes, 1 and 10 December 1947; C.R.O.s' Conference Minutes, 23 March 1948; R.E./C.R.O.s Joint Meeting Minutes, 27 May, 21 June and 12 July 1948, B.R.B.; C.R.O.s' memo. 16 June 1948, notes of R.E./C.R.O.s' meeting of 12 July 1948, in Elliot Papers, AN6/1, P.R.O.

73 Unsigned R.E. letter to Grand, 2 December 1947, Blee–Allen, 2 January 1948, and Grand–Blee, 5 November 1948, AN6/8, P.R.O.; B.T.C. confidential memo. 8 December 1949, B.R.B.

74 Elliot, *On and Off the Rails*, pp. 69–70. The W.R. was not alone in its resistance to HQ: the S.R. continued to call its staff officer 'Chief Officer for Labour and Establishment' instead of 'Regional Staff Officer'.

75 Hopkins and Short were appointed at £3,750 and £3,500 respectively, and the annual cost of the three posts was trimmed from £16,750 to £13,250. Elliot retained his salary of £6,700 and the appointments took effect from 1 January 1950. B.T.C., confidential memo. 8 November 1949, B.R.B.; Train, memo. on 'Regional Organisation', 2 November 1949, Blee Papers, AN6/23, P.R.O.

76 R.E./C.R.O.s Joint Meeting Minutes, 1 and 29 April 1948, AN99/1; R.E. memo. on 'Staff Arrangements', 8 June 1948, and C.R.O.s' reply (n.d.), Blee,

notes, 15 July 1948, AN6/8; R.E. Memoranda, 8 June 1948, AN4/9, P.R.O.
77 Barnes–Hurcomb, 28 November 1949, Dalton (Chancellor of the Duchy of Lancaster)–L. J. Callaghan (Parliamentary Secretary to M.T.), 8 December 1949, Callaghan–Hurcomb, 10 December 1949, Beevor, memo. on 'Staff and Staff Costs', 16 December 1949, and on 'Economies in Headquarters Administration and Overhead Costs', 28 February 1950, B.T.C. S19–26–1, and see also S324–1–1, B.R.B.; *Parl. Deb. (Commons)*, vol. 470 (Session 1949–50), 1 December 1949, 1358–9 (Maxwell-Fyfe).
78 R.E. Confidential Instruction No.6 (Western Region) (1 January 1948), p. 1, and R.E Private Instructions to Officers in the Regions (1 May 1950), pp. 4–13; Beevor, memo. on 'Railway Executive Instructions to Officers in the Regions', 5 May 1950, B.T.C. S92–1–1, B.R.B.
79 Sir Eustace Missenden, 'The First Two Years of British Railways – I', *Railway Gazette*, 21 April 1950.
80 Barrington-Ward, memos. 4 June and 15 December 1948, cit. in R.E. Memoranda, 18 November and 16 December 1948, AN4/9, and Pearson, paper on 'Summary of the Present Position Regarding Penetrating Lines', 13 November 1953, Blee Papers, AN6/17, P.R.O.
81 Beevor, memos. 26 January, 10 and 16 February 1949, B.T.C. Minutes, 17 February 1949, B.R.B.; Blee, memo. 7 February 1949, AN6/10, and see also material in AN6/12, AN6/17 and AN6/27, P.R.O.
82 Blee, notes, 15 and 16 July 1948, memo. 18 October 1948, in Pearson, paper on 'Penetrating Lines', and R.E. printed pamphlet on 'Regional Boundaries', January 1950, AN6/8, AN6/17, AN6/22, P.R.O. For later developments see Chapter 5, pp. 166ff.
83 Missenden–Hurcomb, 6 December 1950, MT96/41, P.R.O. This was subsequently published in *Railway Gazette*, 5 January 1951.
84 Elliot, notes, 18–21 January 1951, Elliot Papers, AN6/6, P.R.O.; Elliot, *On and Off the Rails*, pp. 80–2.
85 D. Stephen (Treasury)–P. J. E. Dalmahoy (M.T.), 6 February 1951, and Dalmahoy–B. D. Fraser (Treasury), 19 September 1953, MT45/500; Cabinet Socialisation of Industries Committee Minutes, 30 January 1951, CAB 134/692, P.R.O.
86 Morrison–Barnes, 20 and 28 November 1950, Ministry of Transport Correspondence and Papers: B.T.C. Appointments, 1950–6, MT96/36, J. A. Payne (Ministry of Agriculture), note, 2 November 1950, MT96/41, P.R.O.; *Railway Gazette*, 12 January and 2 March 1951; R.E., Minutes of the Chairman's Conference of Functional Members, 1 May 1950–29 January 1951, B.R.B., and R.E., Minutes of Informal Meetings of Full-Time Members, 12 February 1951–28 September 1953, AN4/8, P.R.O.
87 *Railway Gazette*, 6 and 13 October 1950; R.E. Memoranda, 12 February 1951, AN4/10, and R.E. Minutes, 1 March 1951, AN4/4, P.R.O.; B.T.C. confidential memo. 24 June 1952, B.R.B. There was some dispute over the choice of Watkins. Cf. Blee, memo. 5 February 1951, AN6/8, P.R.O.
88 Barnes–Morrison, 29 January 1951, MT96/36; Stephen–Dalmahoy, 6 February 1951, MT45/500, P.R.O.
89 Morrison–Barnes, 9 March 1950, Jenkins–Sir John H. Woods (Board of Trade), 24 March 1950, Morrison–Barnes, 16 and 21 June, 20 November 1950, Barnes–Morrison, 23 June and 25 October 1950, MT96/36, P.R.O.
90 Taylor was appointed on 1 July 1951 at a salary of £3,750: B.T.C. confiden-

tial memo. 26 June 1951, B.R.B. See also B.T.C., *R. & A. 1950*, p. 1; Barnes–Hurcomb, 7 December 1950, MT96/36, P.R.O.

91 Beevor, memo. on 'Estate Management', 14 November 1950, B.T.C. S195–4–1, and B.T.C. Minutes, 4 November 1954, B.R.B.

92 Hurcomb, annotation on S. B. Taylor's confidential B.T.C. memo. 24 July 1952, B.R.B. See also the complaints of Reginald Wilson, in Blee, memo. 11 October 1951, AN6/10, P.R.O.

93 Report of ad hoc committee on 'Eastern and North Eastern Regions', 30 April 1951, R.E. Informal Meeting of Full-Time Members Minutes, 26 February and 4 June 1951, AN4/8, P.R.O. For the opposition of Train and Blee to the merger plan see correspondence in Blee Papers, AN6/35, P.R.O.

94 R.E., confidential 'Review of Present Organisation', 8 October 1951; Barrington-Ward–Elliot, 14 February and 11 July 1951, AN6/6, P.R.O.

95 Hurcomb–Elliot, 10 October 1951, and Elliot, memo. on 'Railway Executive Organisation', 12 October 1951, AN6/6, P.R.O.

96 *Parl. Deb. (Commons)*, vol. 478 (Session 1950–1), 18 October 1950, 2078, 2087 (Thorneycroft), 2112–13 (A. E. Davies), 2157 (Maxwell-Fyfe), 2166–8 (Callaghan); R. E. Memoranda, 12 June 1950, 12 April 1951, AN4/10; Report of Committee Appointed to Investigate the Staffing and Organisation of the Railway Executive Headquarters (Chairman O. W. Cromwell), June 1951, and Marsden, memo. 1 September 1951, Blee Papers, AN6/31; R.E., memo. on 'Review of Railway Executive and Regional Headquarters Staff', 26 October 1951, AN6/5, P.R.O. H.Q. and regional staff numbered 24,203 on 31 December 1947, and 24,600 on 16 June 1951.

97 Elliot, memo. 12 October 1951, AN6/6, P.R.O.

98 Conservative Party, *The Right Road for Britain* (1949), pp. 27, 29, and see also *Britain Strong and Free* (1951), p. 21; *Transport Policy*, P.P.1951–2, XXV, Cmd.8538, May 1952. For Teynham's bill see *Parl. Deb. (Lords)*, vol. 169 (Session 1950–1), 2 and 21 November and 12 December 1950, 145, 396–450, 865–91, vol. 170 (Session 1950–1), 13 February 1951, 274–98; *Parl. Deb. (Commons)*, vol. 484 (Session 1950–1), 23 February 1951, 1615ff.; and B.T.C. S241–15–4, B.R.B.

99 Pearson, draft memo. (undated) on 'The Railway Executive and its Critics'; Train, memo. 5 June 1950 and letter to Blee, 8 June 1950, AN6/27, P.R.O.

100 R.E., Memo. (anon.) on 'Review of Organisation', 12 October 1951, AN6/6, and R.E. Minutes, 1 January, 5 April, 26 April (includes Elliot's letter to C.R.O.s on 'Supervision and Administration of the Regions', 27 April), 31 May, 14 and 28 June, 19 July, 16 August and 20 September 1951, AN4/4, P.R.O.

101 Elliot, note on 'Authority of the C.R.O.s', 20 May 1952, AN6/6, P.R.O. 'Revised Instructions to Officers in the Regions' were ordered to be prepared in October 1951: R.E. Memoranda, 11 October 1951, AN4/10, P.R.O.

102 R.E., Memo. (anon.), 12 October 1951, AN6/6; R.E. Minutes, 7 June 1951, AN4/4, P.R.O.

103 R.E., Informal Meeting of Full-Time Members Minutes, 2 April 1951, AN4/8, P.R.O.

104 C.R.O.s' memo. on 'Review of Organisation', 1 September 1951, AN6/6, P.R.O.

105 See below, p. 112. For the leak see *Railway Gazette*, 30 October 1952, article entitled 'Statistics Run Wild'; Reginald Wilson, memo. 3 October 1952, B.T.C. Minutes, 7 October 1952, B.R.B.; R.E. Memoranda, 19 February

1953, AN4/11; Elliot–Grand, 16 October 1952, and Blee, memo. 24 October 1952, AN6/5, AN6/10, P.R.O.

106 Pope, draft memo. on 'Organisation of British Transport', 17 September 1951, AN6/5, P.R.O.; *Parl. Deb. (Commons)*, vol. 509 (Session 1952–3), 15 December 1952, 1034 (Lennox-Boyd).

107 This is summarised in an aide-mémoire on 'Organisation', 22 December 1952, Blee Papers, AN6/39, P.R.O.

108 *Manchester Guardian*, 9 May 1952; Swinton–Leathers, 9 May 1952, in Ministry of Transport Correspondence and Papers: Lord Leathers's Papers: Transport Policy, MT62/144, P.R.O.; Transport Bill, 8 July 1952.

109 Secret 'Draft Plan of Railway Reorganisation Practicable Under Existing Powers', 1 August 1952, AN6/41, and aide-mémoire, December 1952, AN6/39, P.R.O.

110 1 & 2 Eliz. II, c.13.

111 B.T.C. (Executives) Order, 19 August 1953, Order No. 1291, in *Statutory Instruments 1953*, Pt. II (1954), p. 1457. For background papers see AN6/5, 6, 39 and 41, and MT96/36, P.R.O.

112 Pope–Elliot, 24 March 1953, AN6/6, and Train–Elliot, 8 May 1952, enclosing self-justifying memo. 'To Whom It May Concern', 6 May 1952, AN6/5, P.R.O.

113 Lennox-Boyd–Jenkins, 2 April 1953, MT96/36, Elliot's notes of a conversation with Hurcomb, 7 July 1953, AN6/6, P.R.O.; B.T.C., *R. & A. 1953*, I, pp. 1, 83–4.

114 Elliot's comment in R.E., '[Confidential] British Railways' Report for 1952' (March 1953), p. 76, B.R.B.; B.T.C., *R. & A. 1951*, pp. 9, 91, 119, *1953*, I, p. 27.

115 R.E., '[Confidential] British Railways' Report for 1951' (March 1952), p. 84, and 'British Railways Report for 1952' (March 1953), pp. 69–71, B.R.B.; B.T.C., *R. & A. 1951*, pp. 4–5, *1952*, pp. 7–8.

116 Elliot, *On and Off the Rails*, p. 84.

117 H. P. Barker, paper on 'Management Structure of British Railways', 27 October 1960, Beeching Papers, Box 8, B.R.B.

3. Investment

1 D. L. Munby, 'Economic Problems of British Railways', *Bulletin of the Oxford Institute of Statistics*, XXIV (February 1962), 24; K. M. Gwilliam, *Transport and Public Policy* (London: George Allen & Unwin, 1964), p. 170.

2 P. Redfern, 'Net Investment in Fixed Assets in the United Kingdom, 1938–53', *Journal of the Royal Statistical Society*, Series A, CXVIII (1955), 141–76, cit. in Munby, 'Economic Problems', 24–5; Gwilliam, *Transport and Public Policy*, p. 170; D. H. Aldcroft, *British Railways in Transition: The Economic Problems of Britain's Railways since 1914* (London: Macmillan, 1968) p. 151; H. Pollins, *Britain's Railways* (Newton Abbot: David & Charles, 1971), pp. 184–5; A. W. J. Thomson and L. C. Hunter, *The Nationalized Transport Industries* (London: Heinemann, 1973), p. 133

3 Redfern, 'Net Investment', 160.

4 The C.S.O. data used by Redfern not only included information on railways in London (London Transport Executive) and Northern Ireland (Ulster

Transport Authority), but were also drawn up on a different basis from the figures published in the B.T.C.'s Annual Report and Accounts. Ibid., 144–6, 150–1, 175, and cf. W. Harris-Burland (Director of Statistics, B.T.C), memo. on 'The Railways' Share of Gross Fixed Investment', 29 October 1954, B.T.C. S21–1–2K, B.R.B.

5 I.e. £241.3m.; cf. Redfern's £241m. D. L. Munby and A. H. Watson (eds.), *Inland Transport Statistics: Great Britain 1900–1970*, I (Oxford: Oxford University Press, 1978), pp. 40–3, and B.T.C., *R. & A. 1948–53*, Tables V–8, V–10. Gross investment in ships totalled £7.9m., 1948–53.

6 The 'Blue Book' of 1954, Redfern's principal source, gives the railways' gross investment as £273m. at current prices, which is £32m. higher than Redfern's figure. The figure was amended to £264m. in later editions. C.S.O., *National Income and Expenditure 1946–53* (August 1954), Table 46; C. H. Feinstein, *National Income, Expenditure and Output of the United Kingdom, 1855–1965* (Cambridge: Cambridge University Press, 1972), T92–3.

7 B.T.C., *R. & A. 1948*, pp. 44–5, 196–7, and cf. C. H. Newton, *Railway Accounts* (London: Pitman & Sons, 1930), pp. 164–83. The B.T.C., having applied depreciation at *historic* cost to vehicles and plant, from 1949 quoted the additional sums which would be needed to provide for depreciation at *replacement* cost. The accounting changes, together with the requirement in the 1947 Act that the B.T.C. should amortise its capital over 90 years, were intended to impress upon railway accountants that the capital assets should no longer be regarded as something to be maintained in perpetuity. See Reginald H. Wilson, memo. on 'Accounting for Capital Assets', 27 April 1949, B.T.C. Minutes, 5 May 1949, B.R.B., and Wilson, 'The Accounting and Financial Structure of British Transport', *British Transport Review*, I (April 1950), 30–3.

8 At first, the B.T.C./R.E. submissions to government on 'capital investment' included all expenditure on maintenance (renewals and repairs). The I.P.C. then asked in April 1948 for a distinction to be made between renewals and repairs, and in May 1949 attempted to exclude 'running repairs' (but not permanent way repairs) from the estimates. From February 1950 permanent way repairs were also removed. Further adjustments came in 1953, by which time the definition was limited to expenditure on capital account. See White Paper on *Capital Investment in 1948* (December 1947), P.P.1947–8, XXII, Cmd. 7268; I.P.C. Minutes, 1 April 1948, 14 February 1949, 13 February 1950, and 17 December 1952; the draft reports on 'Capital Investment in 1949' (July 1948), p. 30, 'Capital Investment in 1950–2' (May 1949), p. 43; and 'Report on Capital Investment in 1951 and 1952' (24 April 1950), p. 34, 'Investment in 1953 and 1954' (January 1953) pp. 3–19, I.P.C. Minutes and Memoranda, CAB134/438–41, 982, P.R.O.; and supplementary papers in B.T.C. S21–1–2A–H, B.R.B.

9 I.e. £670m. plus £226m. from Table 5 above less double-counting of revenue-account spending on ways and structures. B.T.C., *R. & A. 1948–53*.

10 B.T.C., *R. & A. 1948*, pp. 29–30, *1950*, pp. 20, 56; R.E., 'Major Development Schemes: Five Years 1948 to 1952' (December 1948), and 'Standard Stocks and Types of Locomotives, Carriages and Wagons' (April 1949), produced for I.P.C., B.T.C. S21–1–2D, B.R.B.

11 B.T.C., *R. & A. 1953*, I. p. 23 (a fuller quotation appears in Aldcroft, *British Railways*, p. 151.)

12 Harris-Burland, memo. on 'The Railways' Share of . . . . Investment', pp. 1–3; B.T.C. Planning Committee, 'Report on the Modernisation and Re-equipment of British Railways' (October 1954), p. 39, B.R.B. It should be noted that road *building* was also constrained in the period.

13 Richard Pryke, *Public Enterprise in Practice. The British Experience of Nationalization over Two Decades* (London: MacGibbon and Kee, 1971), p. 289.

14 War-time controls are analysed in detail in J. Hurstfield, *The Control of Raw Materials* (London: H.M.S.O., 1953), and there are general surveys of post-war controls in G. Walker, *Economic Planning by Programme and Control in Great Britain* (London: Heinemann, 1957), Jacques Leruez, *Economic Planning & Politics in Britain* (London: Martin Robertson, 1975), pp. 37–77, and the recently published A. Cairncross, *Years of Recovery. British Economic Policy 1945–51* (London: Methuen, 1985), pp. 299–353. See also A. A. Rogow, *The Labour Government and British Industry 1945–1951* (Oxford: Blackwell, 1955), *passim*, J. C. R. Dow, *The Management of the British Economy 1945–60* (Cambridge: Cambridge University Press, 1965), pp. 144–77.

15 10 & 11 Geo. VI. c.49, s.4(1), 4(2), 88(1) and 88(2). For early concern inside the Ministry about the interpretation of the Minister's powers, see 'Report of the Working Party on the Relations between the Minister and the British Transport Commission', and S. S. Wilson's Note of Reservation, both 23 December 1947, MT45/343, P.R.O.

16 Barnes, memo. to Cabinet Socialisation of Industries Committee, 23 May 1949, T229/339, P.R.O.

17 When the B.T.C. and R.E. took office, building licences were required for all work costing over £10. This sum was subsequently raised to £100, £500 and £1,000 before controls were finally removed in November 1954. See Beevor, memo. on 'Relation between Government Departments, the Commission, and the Executives', 23 January 1948, B.T.C. S65–1–6, B.R.B., and *Statutory Instruments, 1947–54.*

18 P. Vinter (Treasury, Joint Secretary to I.P.C.), 'Note on the Development of Work on Investment Programmes', 29 November 1949, Treasury Correspondence and Papers: I.P.C. Composition, Terms of Reference and Procedure, T229/332, P.R.O., and conversations with Lord Plowden, 12 November 1981, Sir Alec Cairncross (Board of Trade representative, I.P.C.), 2 December 1981, and Peter Vinter, 2 January 1982. The I.P.C. included representatives of the C.E.P.S., Economic Section of the Cabinet Office, Ministry of Works, Ministry of Supply, Board of Trade and Treasury.

19 Wagon-building forecasts assumed an increase in capacity to 16 tons and a coal output in 1952 of 245m. tons (10 per cent higher than was mined). R.E.C., Memos. to the Minister of Transport on 'Five-Year Plan for Construction and Repair of Railway Rolling Stock for Main-Line Railway Companies' and 'Five-Year Plan for Restoration of the Railways' Permanent Way, Signal, Telegraph and Telephone Equipment to Pre-War Standard', both 26 August 1947, in B.T.C. S17–2–1A, B.R.B.

20 I.e. 409 locomotives, 1,198 carriages and 31,275 wagons (see Table 7).

21 Data for 'Railways', *including* London Transport (except trams), but *excluding* private builders and repairers: steel, cast steel and iron (excluding cast iron):

estimated needs: 803,186 tons
allocated: 619,517 tons
delivered: 555,928 tons
See B.T.C. ref. S65–2–3A (n.d.), included in Beevor–Missenden, 1 July 1948, S21–1–2C, B.R.B.

22 See I.P.C. Minutes, 15 August, 24 September and 8 October 1947, CAB134/437; Plowden–Hurcomb, 15 August 1947, Sir Reginald Hill–Missenden, 6 September 1947, Ministry of Transport: Investment Programmes Committee Correspondence and Papers, MT6/2831, P.R.O.; C. A. Birtchnell (M.T.)–Beevor, 10 March 1948, and reply, 19 April 1948, B.T.C. S110–2–1 and S19–1–14, B.R.B. The suggested reduction in the railways' use of contract labour was not achieved. See monthly returns and correspondence in B.T.C. S19–1–14, B.R.B.

23 I.e. from 314,000 to 250,000 tons. See I.P.C. draft report, 8 October 1947, in MT6/2831, P.R.O. The target for carriage building was subsequently increased to 1,200 (i.e. actual production in 1947) after lobbying from the R.E., B.T.C. and M.T. See I.P.C. Minutes, 10 and 17 February 1948, CAB134/438, P.R.O., and Hurcomb–Barnes, 1 March 1948, and other correspondence in B.T.C. S21–1–2A, B.R.B.

24 Parl. Deb. (Commons), vol. 443 (Session 1947–8), 23 October 1947, 280–1 (Sir Stafford Cripps); Capital Investment in 1948, Cmd. 7268, pp. 20, 24–5.

25 Jay, draft memo. to Production Committee on 'Steel Allocation Period IV, 1948' (n.d., but April 1948), Treasury Correspondence and Papers: Steel Supplies and Allocation 1948, Periods III and IV, T229/78, P.R.O. Jay's remarks referred to Period III.

26 I.e. from 265,000 to 240,000 tons for rails, 516 to 400 locomotives, 2,012 to 1,500 carriages and 37,000 to 30,000 wagons. I.P.C., 'Report on Capital Investment in 1949' (July 1949), pp. 13, 33, CAB134/439, P.R.O. At this time there was some confusion about the figures for the railways' steel requirements. The reference to 900,000 tons apparently excluded 35,000 tons for civil engineering and building. See Bonavia, memo. on 'Steel Requirements', 25 June 1948, Beevor–Ministry of Transport 29 June 1948, Beevor–Missenden, 1 July 1948, and Minutes of B.T.C./R.E. Steel Allocation Committee, 2 September 1948, B.T.C. S21–1–2B and C, B.R.B. Annual deliveries were estimated to be running at 876,000 tons: B.T.C., draft notes for Minister, 27 July 1948, B.T.C. S21–1–2C, B.R.B.

27 Beevor–Marsden, 23 April 1948, R.E. Memo. on 'Railway Stocks of Steel', 3 May 1948, B.T.C. S65–2–3A; Return of 'Steel Stocks' for 31 December 1947–31 December 1949, March 1950, S65–2–3B, B.R.B.

28 R.E., confidential report on 'Physical Condition of British Railways at January 1948' (n.d. but February 1948), B.R.B., and remarks by Pearson, I.P.C. Minutes, 14 February 1949, CAB143/440, P.R.O. The implied reduction in steel was in fact about 40 per cent. R.E. representatives also informed civil servants that, despite getting far less than they had asked for, their new building and repair programmes for 1948 were being 'substantially achieved': Bonavia, notes for a meeting with Slim on 20 August 1948, B.T.C. S21–1–2C, B.R.B.

29 Production Committee Minutes, 23 July 1948, CAB134/636, P.R.O.

30 I.P.C. Minutes, 5, 9 and 11 August 1948, and supplementary report, 1 September 1948, CAB134/438–9; Production Committee Minutes, 6 September 1948, CAB134/636, P.R.O.; Bonavia–Hurcomb, 3 September

1948, B.T.C. S21–1–2C, B.R.B.; R.E., Memo. on 'Effect of Allocation to British Railways and London Transport of 810,000 Tons of Steel for 1949', 8 September, and memo. by Barrington-Ward, Riddles, Train and Slim on 'Steel Allocation for 1949', 30 September 1948, R.E. Minutes, 9 and 30 September 1948, AN4/1, P.R.O.

31 Bonavia–E. S. Foster (M.T.), 30 June 1949, B.T.C. S65–2–3B, and see also Pearson's comments at an informal meeting with P. Vinter and W. Strath of I.P.C., reported in Bonavia, memo. on 'Investment Programmes Committee', 18 November 1948, S21–1–2C, B.R.B., and I.P.C. Minutes, 17 February 1949, CAB134/440, P.R.O. The allocation referred to here differs from that given in Appendix H, Table, because it excludes items decontrolled during the planning round.

32

Item	B.T.C./R.E. submission for 1949	I.P.C. forecast mid-1948	Economic survey 1949	Actual construction 1949
Locos.	516	400	500	396
Carriages	2,012	1,500	2,100	1,801
Wagons	37,000	30,000	27,000	32,490

While there is a difference between steel receipts and steel consumption, the annual figures for rails and general steel receipts are 603,055 for 1948 and only 506,799 for 1949 (Appendix H, Table). A rough estimate of consumption in 1948 and 1949 may be derived from data on track renewals (2,108 and 1,960 miles) and rolling stock production (Table 7), using the following tonnages per vehicle: locos., 78.8; carriages, 21.0; wagons, 7.2 (B.T.C. S21–1–2C, B.R.B.).

33 The figures £100.2m. and £95m. included provision for London Transport's railways and buses. I.P.C., 'Report on Capital Investment in 1950–1952' (May 1949), pp. 43–6, CAB134/440, P.R.O.; B.T.C., submission 4 February 1949, and Beevor, memo. to B.T.C., 18 May 1949, B.T.C. Minutes, 19 May 1949, B.R.B.; Birtchnell–Beevor, 2 September 1949, and Beevor–R.E. and L.T.E., 7 September 1949, B.T.C. S21–1–2D, B.R.B.

34 A reduction to £90m. involved a cut to £80m. for the R.E., whose original submission of £88m. was equal to £98m. at current (October 1949) prices. See Missenden–Hurcomb, 24 October 1949, B.T.C. S21–1–2D, B.T.C. Minutes, 27 October 1949, B.R.B., and I.P.C. Minutes, 28 October 1949, CAB134/440, P.R.O.

35 Savings of £18m. were to be found by reducing the programme by £1.5m. (locomotives), £6.6m. (ways and structures) and £9.6m. (new works). The cut in new works was contingent upon the successful cancellation of some existing contracts, and involved postponement of the Potters Bar widening scheme (part 1), York colour-light signalling, Willesden carriage shed, etc. Missenden–Hurcomb, 24 October 1949, B.T.C. S21–1–2D, B.R.B.

36 The extra £2m. was allocated to ways and structures, but Missenden was critical of the inadequate notice given to the R.E. I.P.C. Minutes, 14 November 1949, CAB134/440, P.R.O.; I. Wild (Director of Finance, M.T.)–Bonavia, 15 November 1949, Missenden–Hurcomb, 16 November 1949, Missenden–Beevor, 12 December 1949, B.T.C. S21–1–2E, B.R.B.

37 Missenden–Hurcomb, 23 January 1950, B.T.C. Minutes, 31 January 1950,

B.R.B.; I.P.C. Working Paper, 9 February 1950, and Minutes, 13 February 1950, CAB134/441, P.R.O.; Wild–Hurcomb, 21 February 1950, B.T.C. S21–1–2E, B.T.C., 'Summary of Correspondence, etc. with the R.E. on Wagon Building', 16 January 1950, S89–1–2B, B.R.B.; B.T.C., *R. & A. 1950*, p. 334. The figure of £67.1m. was first revealed in Bonavia–Ness, 16 July 1951, and Ness–Taylor, 9 August 1951, B.T.C. S21–1–14 and S21–1–2G, B.R.B.

38 Wild–Beevor, 30 November 1949, and Bonavia, note of a discussion with Vinter on 13 December 1949, B.T.C. S21–1–2E, B.R.B. Hurcomb shared the planners' pessimism: Hurcomb–Missenden, 21 November 1949, ibid.

39 R.E., 'Investment Programme Committee: Investment Review 1951–1952', January 1950, in B.T.C. Minutes, 31 January 1950, B.R.B.; I.P.C. Minutes, 13 February 1950, and 'Report on Capital Investment in 1951 and 1952' (24 April 1950), p. 34, CAB134/441, P.R.O.

40 The government's allocation of £73.9m. plus £1.5m. for the purchase of wagons from the S.N.C.F. (France) was reduced by the B.T.C. to £73.5m. plus £1.5m. Wild–Hurcomb, 31 May 1950, B.T.C. S21–1–2F and B.T.C. Minutes, 6 June 1950, B.R.B.

41 Except for sheet steel under 3mm. thick, and tinplate. See Control of Iron and Steel (No. 79) Order, 1950 (operative 27 May 1950), *Statutory Instruments 1950*, Vol. III (1952), p. 771.

42 Missenden–Hurcomb, 25 July 1950, B.T.C. S21–1–2F, B.R.B., and cf. also Missenden–Hurcomb, 23 January 1950, B.T.C. Minutes, 31 January and 1 August 1950, B.R.B.

43 Plowden, letter to departments, 4 October 1950, I.P.C. Minutes, 31 January 1951, and 'Report on Capital Investment in 1951, 1952, and 1953' (March 1951), pp. 41–2, CAB134/441–2, P.R.O.; Wild–Hurcomb, 10 October 1950, Beevor–Missenden, 16 November 1950, and Wild–Bonavia, 20 March 1951, B.T.C. S21–1–2F, B.R.B.

44 R.E., 'Investment Programmes Committee: Investment Review 1952–1954' (December 1950), B.T.C. S21–1–2F, B.R.B.; I.P.C. Minutes, 31 January 1951, CAB134/442, P.R.O.; B.T.C., *R. & A. 1950*, p. 19; Ness–Taylor, 9 August 1951, Barnes–Hurcomb, 7 September 1951 (and reply, 27 September 1951), and Missenden–Taylor, 25 September 1951, B.T.C. S21–1–2G, B.R.B.

45 Taylor, memo. on 'Capital Investment 1953', 29 September 1952, B.T.C. Minutes, 30 September 1952, B.R.B. Rolling stock:

	R.E. submission January 1950 'minimum essential'	R.E. submission December 1950	Actual construction 1951 (Table 7)
Locos.	350/400	380	340
Carriages	2,695	2,440	1,923
Wagons	39,975	47,000	37,796

Source: Ness, memo. to R.C. Bond, Arthur Dean, S.E. Parkhouse *et al.*, 28 December 1949, Bonavia–Wild, 5 February 1951, B.T.C. S21–1–2E and F, B.R.B.

46 Iron and Steel Distribution (No. 2006) Order, 1951, and Iron and Steel Distribution (Amendment No. 1) (No. 172) Order, 1952 (operative 4

February 1952), *Statutory Instruments 1951*, Vol. III (1952), pp. 459–73, *1952*, Pt III (1953), p. 3291; I.P.C., 'Report on Capital Investment in 1952' (February 1952), p. 3, CAB134/982, P.R.O., and Wild–L. B. Marson, 1 January 1952, and Taylor–Hurcomb, 3 January 1952, B.T.C. S21–1–2H, B.R.B.; B.T.C., *R. & A. 1952*, p. 3.

47 This programme was approved in July 1951. I.P.C., 'Report on Capital Investment in 1951, 1952, and 1953' (March 1951), pp. 41–2, CAB134/442, P.R.O., and Wild–Taylor, 2 July 1951, B.T.C. S21–1–2G, B.R.B. For complaints about I.P.C. interference, see Elliot–Beevor, 3 April 1951, and Beevor–M.T., 4 April 1951, B.T.C. S21–1–2F., B.R.B. The electrification of the London Tilbury & Southend line, approved in principle by the B.T.C. on 16 November 1950, was later delayed by opposition in the Eastern Region.

48 I.P.C., 'Report on Capital Investment in 1952' (February 1952), p. 3, CAB134/982, P.R.O.

49 Viz. 380 locomotives, 1,800 carriages and 46,000 wagons: R.E., 'Investment Programmes: Annual Investment Review' (revision), in Elliot–Hurcomb, 30 November 1951, B.T.C. Minutes, 4 December 1951, B.R.B.

50 B.T.C. Minutes, 22 and 27 November 1951; Taylor, memo. on 'Capital Investment Programme; Railway Executive', 3 December 1951, and Elliot–Hurcomb, 30 November 1951, in B.T.C. Minutes, 4 December 1951, in B.T.C. S21–1–2G, B.R.B.

51 The plan included a reduction in track renewals of 150 miles, and a reduction in railway workshop construction from 300 to 150 (locomotives) and from 19,000 to 11,900 (wagons). Taylor–Hurcomb, 19 December 1951, Marsden–Taylor on 'Steel Supplies', 14 January 1952, B.T.C. S65–2–3D, B.R.B. For B.T.C. objections, see Hurcomb–Maclay, 21 January 1952, ibid., and B.T.C./R.E. Informal Meeting Minutes, 17 January 1952, B.T.C. S26–2–2D, B.R.B.

52 Bonavia, note on 'Steel Allocations and Capital Investment', 12 August 1952, Taylor–Elliot, 22 August 1952, and Jenkins (M.T.)–Hurcomb, 2 September 1952, B.T.C. S21–1–2H, B.R.B. There was some confusion owing to the use of different methods of calculation. The data quoted here are from Bonavia–Ryan, 19 March 1953, B.T.C. S65–2–3E, B.R.B. Note that steel deliveries in 1952 amounted to 506,000 tons, i.e. 7 per cent below the allocation: ibid.

53 The intention was to ensure that a higher proportion of the allocation was actually spent. See Taylor, memo. 4 February 1952, Taylor–Elliot, 23 July 1952, and R.E., Memo. 15 August 1952, B.T.C. S21–1–2G, B.R.B. The removal of controls on steel (except tinplate) was operative from 6 May 1953: Iron and Steel Distribution (Amendment No. 4) (No. 775) Order, 1953, *Statutory Instruments 1953*, Pt II (1954), p. 2220.

54 I.P.C., 'Report on Investment in 1953' (June 1952), p. 6, Joint Secretaries' note, 15 August 1952, CAB134/982, P.R.O., and Wild–Bonavia, 17 September 1952, B.T.C. S21–1–2H, B.R.B. See also B.T.C. Minutes, 30 September and 13 November 1952, B.R.B.

55 I.P.C. Minutes, 17 December 1952, and 'Report on Investment in 1953 and 1954' (January 1953), pp. 3, 19, CAB134/982, P.R.O.

56 I.P.C., Joint Secretaries' note, 9 April 1953 (Annex), CAB134/982, P.R.O.; Wild–Bonavia, 16 April 1953, Bonavia–Elliot, 22 April 1953, and Elliot–Taylor, 14 May 1953, B.T.C. S21–1–2H, and Taylor, memo. 18 May, in B.T.C. Minutes, 19 May 1953, B.R.B.

57 This calculation is complicated by yet another change in the definition of 'capital investment' under government review. In 1953 capital investment in 'fixed assets' ('new building' and 'plant') amounted to £50.1m. and the target expenditure was £53.6m. See I.P.C. Joint Secretaries' note, 9 April 1953 (Annex), CAB134/982, P.R.O., and Form I.S./7.R (Railways) 8 June 1953, B.T.C. S21–1–2H, B.R.B.

58 R.E., 'Investment Programmes: Annual Investment Review, November 1952', B.T.C. S21–1–2H, B.R.B., and B.T.C., R. & A. 1953, I, pp. 23–6. Such schemes as Potters Bar station and route widening, Battersea Park/Bricklayers Arms–Coulsdon North colour-light signalling and the change of electric current frequency on the Southern Region were referred to in negotiations between the Ministry of Transport and the I.P.C. in August 1947: see correspondence in MT6/2831, P.R.O.

59 I.P.C. Minutes, 17 December 1952, CAB134/982, P.R.O.

60 Bonavia, memos. on 'The Commission and the Planners', 18 February 1948, 'Planning and the Commission', 3 March 1948, draft letter to Lord Plowden, December 1949, 'A Note on Capital Investment in Railways', 17 October 1950, and 'Capital Expenditure Restrictions', 13 July 1951, B.T.C. S21–1–2A, E and F, B.R.B.; conversation with Bonavia, 19 November 1981.

61 F. J. Atkinson, memo. on 'Investment Control over the Nationalised Industries', 8 October 1951, T229/339, P.R.O.

62 E.g. for the first quarter of 1949, see above, n. 31 and see the data in Appendix H. On Jay, see Bonavia–Beevor, 21 October 1948, reporting remark by F. W. Smith (C.E.P.S.), B.T.C. S65–2–3A, B.R.B., and Jay, note to Cripps, 6 November 1948, commenting on a memo. by Barnes on the B.T.C.'s finances, Treasury Correspondence and Papers: I.P.C. Ministry of Transport, T229/523, P.R.O.

63 See, inter alia, W. R. Maunder, memo. 5 February 1948, Ministry of Transport Correspondence and Papers: Railways, MT6/2833, P.R.O.; Missenden–Beevor, 12 December 1949, Missenden–Hurcomb, 23 January 1950, Wild, extract from I.P.C. Minutes, 13 February 1950, Elliot–Beevor, 3 April 1951, Bonavia–Ness, 16 July 1951, in B.T.C. S21–1–2E–H, S21–1–14, B.R.B.

64 Ness, memo. to Bond, Dean, Parkhouse et al., 28 December 1949, B.T.C. S21–1–2E; Ness–Beevor, 31 March 1950, with enclosures, including 'Financial Effect of Replacing 475 Life Expired Locomotives with 400 Locomotives of Modern Design', and Bonavia–Ness, 4 April 1950, enclosing revised calculation, B.T.C. S21–1–2F, B.R.B.; and I.P.C. Minutes, 13 February 1950, CAB134/441, P.R.O.

65 Ryan, memo. on 'Steel Supplies for the Railways', January 1953, B.T.C. Minutes, 15 January 1953, B.R.B.

66 R.E. Minutes, 11, 18 and 25 October 1951, AN4/4, P.R.O.; A. Forbes-Smith (R.E.)–M. Churchard (M.T.), 3 December 1952, B.T.C. S65–2–3E, B.R.B.; and Ryan, memo. on 'Steel Supplies . . .', B.T.C. Minutes, 15 January 1953, B.R.B. See also Parl. Deb. (Commons), vol. 497 (Session 1951–2), 3 March 1952, 158 (John Scott Maclay, Minister of Transport).

67 Pryke, Public Enterprise, pp. 43–4. Pryke's findings contrast with the curious and unsubstantiated remark in Hannah's recent book on electricity that the 'nationalised railway industry . . . incurred mounting annual losses, yet persisted in uneconomic investment programmes': L. Hannah, Engineers,

Managers and Politicians. The First Fifteen Years of Nationalised Electricity Supply in Britain (London: Macmillan, 1982), p. 58.
68 For comments from a variety of sources, see 'Rover', 'What's Wrong on British Railways?', *Railway Review*, 28 October and 4 November 1949; Marsden–Beevor on 'Staff Shortages', 22 May 1951, B.T.C. S71–1–35; Bonavia, memo. 17 October 1950, S21–1–2F; Ministry of Transport Note to B.T.C. on 'Inland Transport Problems', 21 September 1951, S131–16–1, B.R.B.; *Economic Survey for 1952* (April 1952), P.P.1951–2, XXV, Cmd.8509, p. 30; F. McKenna, *The Railway Workers 1840–1970* (London: Faber and Faber, 1980), pp. 143, 226.
69 The total number of speed restrictions, about 120 per annum before the war, averaged 236, 1948–51, and 170, 1952–3 (January–June only for 1953). Restrictions caused by the 'condition of the track' averaged 42.5, 1948–51, and 19.5, 1952–3. R.E., Monthly Reports to B.T.C., 1948–53, B.R.B. Staff shortages were isolated as an important area of concern, e.g. Monthly Report for May 1950.
70 Train accidents averaged 1,212 per annum, 1948–53, 53 per cent higher than the 794 per annum, 1935–8, and with a reduction of over 9 per cent in train-miles run. See *Reports of the Inspecting Officer (Ministry of Transport)*, Lt-Col G. R. S. Wilson, and particularly *1950* (20 July 1951), pp. 6, 32–3, *1951* (25 July 1952), pp. 4, 32, *1952* (15 October 1953), pp. 9, 32–3 (Wilson claimed that 28 per cent of fatalities in accidents (inquiry cases), 1912–52, might have been prevented by an Automatic Warning System), *1953* (26 July 1954), p. 31; Munby and Watson, *Statistics*, pp. 130, 133.
71 B.T.C./R.E. Minutes, 14 July and 16 December 1948, B.T.C. S26–2–2A, and R.E., Confidential Memo. 'Outlining Consideration given to Automatic Train Control . . .' (n.d. but *c.* 1953), B.R.B.; M. R. Bonavia, *The Birth of British Rail* (London: George Allen & Unwin, 1979) pp. 84–5. For more information on A.T.C./A.W.S., including discussions in the inter-war period, see J. Johnson and R. A. Long, *British Railways Engineering 1948–80* (London: Mechanical Engineering Publications, 1981), pp. 471–80.
72 R.E., Monthly Report to the B.T.C., February 1952, B.R.B. After successful trials with a Matisa tamping machine purchased in 1947, 12 more were ordered from Materiel Industriel S.A. of Lausanne in 1948, but only 4 were delivered before the devaluation of sterling led to increased costs: B.T.C. Minutes, 9 March 1948 and 29 November 1949, B.R.B. Subsequent orders were for British-built machines, and a further 45 had been ordered by July 1953: R.E., Monthly Report to the B.T.C., July 1953, B.R.B.
73 A situation also exacerbated by staff shortages. See B.T.C., *R. & A. 1950*, pp. 115–16, and *1951*, pp. 94–5; R.E., Special Traffic Committee correspondence, esp. Elliot–Hurcomb, 5 October 1951, and Elliot–Pope, 17 July 1953, B.T.C. S131–16–1, B.R.B.
74 Data from B.T.C., *R. & A. 1948–53*. For the purchase of 9,200 French wagons see *1950*, p. 114, and for 24.5 ton wagons see *1951*, p. 117, and *1953*, I, p. 29.
75 B.T.C. *R. & A. 1948, 1949, 1953*. In 1954 the number of passenger-kilometres travelled per seat offered was:

British Railways (all):	13,400
British Railways (Southern Region):	22,500
French Railways	20,100

German Railways (West Germany)   25,900
Dutch Railways   73,000
Harris-Burland, 'Statistical Comparisons between British, French, and Netherlands Railways', 20 September 1956, B.R.B. 250–1–1.

76 The actual figure was 1,774: B.T.C., *R. & A. 1953*, I, p. 28.

77 B.T.C., *R. & A. 1948–53*. Note: the steam locomotives data include five service locomotives.

78 Johnson and Long, *British Railways Engineering*, pp. 40–3, 49–56, 120–45. See also E. S. Cox, *Locomotive Panorama*, II (London: Ian Allan, 1966) pp. 7–8 (beware of errors); A. J. Pearson, *Man of the Rail* (London: George Allen & Unwin, 1967), pp. 110–12; S. Joy, *The Train That Ran Away. A Business History of British Railways 1948–1968* (London: Ian Allan, 1973), pp. 36–40; D. H. Aldcroft, 'Innovation on the Railways: The Lag in Diesel and Electric Traction', in *Studies in British Transport History 1870–1970* (Newton Abbot: David & Charles, 1974), pp. 243–62; Bonavia, *Birth of British Rail*, pp. 52–69.

79 Correspondence in B.T.C. S34–1–8, B.R.B., and conversation with Riddles, 30 September 1980. See also H. C. B. Rogers, *The Last Steam Locomotive Engineer: R. A. Riddles, C.B.E.* (London: George Allen & Unwin, 1970), pp. 133–92.

80 Mount, memo. on 'Post-War Railway Electrification', 23 April 1943, and Hurcomb, memo. on 'Railway Electrification', 5 June 1943, in Ministry of War Transport Correspondence and Papers: Co-ordination of Transport, MT64/5, P.R.O.

81 Mount, memo. 9 March 1945, W. Graham (M.T. (Commercial Services)) – Mount, 1 May 1945, F. L. Tribe (Ministry of Fuel and Power)–Hurcomb, 22 May 1944, in Ministry of War Transport Correspondence and Papers: Post-War Reconstruction: Diesel–Electric Traction, MT6/2776, P.R.O.

82 See the correspondence in B.T.C. S47–1–1, B.R.B., R.E., Report on 'The Coal–Oil Conversion Scheme on British Railways 1945–48', 1949, AN88/84, P.R.O., and Johnson and Long, *British Railways Engineering*, pp. 41–2.

83 C. J. Allen, *The Locomotive Exchanges, 1870–1948* (London: Ian Allan, 1949), and *New Light on the Locomotive Exchanges* (London: Ian Allan, 1950). Cox, *Locomotive Panorama,* II, p. 8.

84 R.E., Report on the Committee on Types of Motive Power (Chairman: J. L. Harrington), October 1951, pp. 179–80 and paras. 454–63; B.T.C. Minutes, 12 February and 8 May 1952; B.T.C., Pope Committee Report on Motive Power Policy, April 1952, B.R.B.

85 R.E. memoranda, 7 June and 9 August 1951, 26 February 1953, AN4/10 and 11, and R.E. Minutes, 14 May 1953, AN4/6, P.R.O.; R.E., Report of the Light Weight Trains Committee (Chairman: H. G. Bowles), March 1952, and Second Supplementary Report, July 1953; B.T.C. Minutes, 28 August and 11 September 1952, 17 February and 6 August 1953; Blee–Taylor, 26 August 1952, B.T.C. S44–1–1A; and Hurcomb–Elliot correspondence, 8–17 August 1953, in B.T.C. Minutes, 20 August 1953, B.R.B. The Lincolnshire scheme was not approved until November: B.T.C. Minutes, 12 November 1953, B.R.B.

86 R.E., A Development Programme for British Railways, April 1953, B.R.B. £160m. was earmarked for electrification. See also *Railway Gazette*, 23 November 1956. On enthusiasm in the regions for electrification see Pearson, *Man of the Rail*, pp. 128–31.

87 Bonavia–Beevor, 31 May 1948, B.T.C. memo. on 'Purchase of Austerity Locomotives', 1 June 1948, Morton, Riddles and Barrington-Ward, memo. to R.E., 21 October 1948, Elliot, memos. May, 29 August and September 1953, B.T.C. S17–2–25, B.R.B.; conversation with Riddles, 30 September 1980.

88 See B.T.C. S17–3–26, S320–1–1 and S17–5–5; R.E., memo. on 'Mixed Traffic 0–6–6–0 "Leader" Class', February 1951, B.T.C. Minutes, 6 March 1951, B.R.B.; and Johnson and Long, *British Railways Engineering*, pp. 43–4, 133–4.

89 See Chapter 8, below.

4. Revenue, costs and labour relations

1 Gilbert Walker, 'The Transport Act, 1947', *Economic Journal*, LVIII (March 1948 (the article was written in November 1947)), 17; and see also *The Economist*, 17 April and 6 December 1947; B.T.C., *R. & A. 1948*, Tables V–7, V–8, V–14. R.E. gross and net book values exclude ships, but include interests in non-controlled undertakings.

2 R.E., confidential report on 'Physical Condition of British Railways at January 1948' (n.d., but February 1948), pp. 34–5, B.R.B.

3 See above, Chapter 2, p. 52. For newspaper comments see *Daily Telegraph*, *Manchester Guardian* and *Daily Express*, all 18 February 1948, and *Sunday People*, 22 February 1948.

4 *The Economist*, 29 November 1947.

5 Railways' passenger-mileage (including L.T.) estimated at 37.9m. (1945), 25.9m. (1947) (originating journeys), and freight ton-mileage at 22.0m. (1945), 20.2m. (1947) (net, including free-hauled traffic): D. L. Munby and A. H. Watson (eds.), *Inland Transport Statistics: Great Britain 1900–1970*, I. (Oxford: Oxford University Press, 1978), pp. 86, 105, 543. These estimates differ from those shown in Appendix D, Table 1, which aim at consistency pre- and post-1948. The passenger-mileage of buses, coaches, trams and trolley-buses is estimated at 27.2m. (1938), 41.5m. (1947), Appendix D, Table 1A (note: D. H. Aldcroft's figure of 19.4m. for 1938, in *British Railways in Transition: The Economic Problems of Britain's Railways since 1914* (London: Macmillan, 1968), p. 125, appears to be for buses and coaches only, though his post-war data include trams and trolley-buses).

6 For details of the abnormal maintenance fund see Reginald Wilson, memo. on 'Standard Charge for Maintenance', 23 May 1949, Hurcomb, memo. on same, 26 May 1949, B.T.C. S21–1–1; Osborn, memo. to Finance Committee, 10 November 1953, B.T.C. Finance Committee Minutes, 12 November 1953, B.R.B.; and B.T.C., *R. & A. 1954*, I, p. 68.

7 The estimated rate of return is derived from the railways' net operating revenue minus their contribution to central charges (Commission's basis, excluding ships). This figure is then expressed as a percentage of the railways' share of the capital value of interest-bearing British Transport Stock, shown in B.T.C., *R. & A. 1948–53*, Table IV–8. The railways' share, estimated at £1,062.2m. in 1948 rising to £1,173.0m. in 1953, is based on their share of B.T.C. net book values.

8 The financial position of the B.T.C. for 1948–53 (and 1954–8) is conveniently summarised in N.U.R., *Planning Transport For You* (London: N.U.R, 1959), p. 38.

9 The railways' share of central charges would have been reduced from £213.8m. (Table 8, column (d)) to £178.4m. The overvaluation of 20 per cent is based on the observation that B.T. Stock was valued in relation to Stock Exchange prices ruling when interest rates stood at 2½ per cent not 3 per cent. See H. Wilson, 'The Financial Problem of British Transport', report in typescript to T.S.S.A., N.U.R. and A.S.L.E.F., 20 December 1951, p. 42, T.U.C. Library, and G. Walker and R. H. B. Condie, 'Compensation in Nationalised Industries', in W. A. Robson (ed.), *Problems of Nationalised Industries* (London: George Allen & Unwin, 1952), pp. 64–5, 70–2.

10 S. Joy, *The Train That Ran Away. A Business History of British Railways 1948–1968* (London: Ian Allan, 1973), pp. 13–15.

11 Wilson, memo. on 'Economics of Reconstruction and Re-equipment', second draft, 9 September 1953, B.R.B. 23–10–1 1C.

12 E.g. Blee, report on 'Charges Schemes – Passenger Fares', 14 July 1949, and report on 'National Passenger Charges Scheme', 12 December 1950, and R. E. Commercial Investigation Bureau, report on '"C" Licensed Road Vehicles', May 1950, Blee Papers, AN6/24, 25 and 28, P.R.O.

13 See Appendix D, Tables 1A and 1B. For coal traffic see Munby and Watson, *Statistics*, pp. 85–7, 98–9.

14 Aldcroft, *British Railways*, p. 123. He is not the only commentator to make such an observation.

15 This problem has a long pedigree. See T. R. Gourvish, *Railways in the British Economy 1830–1914* (London: Macmillan, 1980, pp. 46–9, 54.

16 A. J. Pearson, 'Developments and Prospects in British Transport', *Journal of the Institute of Transport*, XXV (May 1953), 6.

17 G. F. Fiennes, *I Tried to Run a Railway* (London: Ian Allan, 1967), pp. 76–7.

18 B.T.C., *R. & A. 1948*, p. 54, and for the increase in war-time railway costs see *Report of a Court of Inquiry into Applications by the Trade Unions Representing the Employees of the Railway Companies for Improvements in Wages and Reductions in Weekly Hours of Work*, 24 June 1947, P.P.1946–7, XIV, Cmd. 7161, p. 26. Prices are taken from C. H. Feinstein, *National Income, Expenditure and Output of the United Kingdom, 1855–1965* (Cambridge: Cambridge University Press, 1972), T133 (G.D.P. deflator).

19 Coal data: Slim–Beevor, 3 August 1948, and Schedule of 'Increases in Coal Prices since July 1947', 17 August 1948, B.T.C. S89–4–1; General Sir Daril Watson, memo. on 'Coal Prices', 3 May 1954, B.T.C. Stores Committee Minutes, 5 May 1954, B.R.B. Steel data: B.T.C. data on Flat Bottom Sections (109/110A/113), 1948–82, B.R.B. The figure for 1947 was derived by interpolation using information supplied by the R.E. to the Court of Inquiry investigating the unions' pay claims of 1950, R.S.C., Financial Statements, January 1951, B.R.B.

20 B.T.C., *R. & A. 1948*, pp. 54–5; *Report of Court of Inquiry . . .*, Cmd. 7161, p. 30. Labour costs were put at 60 per cent of total costs in 1949: B.T.C., *R. & A. 1949*, p. 44.

21 Wage-bill estimates derived from B.T.C., *R. & A. 1948–53*. Average weekly earnings are multiplied by 52 and then by the average of the number of employees at the beginning and end of each year. The figure for 1948 is derived by assuming that the same differential between all employees and male adult 'conciliation grades' obtaining in 1949 existed in 1948.

22 B.T.C., *R. & A. 1950*, p. 39, *1951*, p. 17; W. I. Winchester, memo. to Finance Committee on 'Accumulated Deficit', 1 March 1956, B.T.C. Finance Com-

mittee Minutes, 7 March 1956, B.R.B. For 1948–56 £90m. of the total of £140m. was attributed to delays.

23 10 & 11 Geo. VI, c. 69, s. 4 (1), 75–8, 80, 82; see also A. M. Milne and A. Laing, *The Obligation to Carry* (London: Institute of Transport, 1956), pp. 34–7. (Directions under Section 82 were issued as Statutory Instruments.) Applications to the Minister under Section 82, 1948–51, and to the Transport Tribunal, 1950–8, are summarised in E. W. Godfrey (Assistant Secretary, M.T.)–R. R. Goodison (Under-Secretary, M.T.), 3 December 1958, with enclosed statements, Ministry of Transport Correspondence and Papers: B.T.C. (Borrowing Powers) Bill, MT56/358, P.R.O.

24 Hurcomb–Barnes, 4 October 1949, B.T.C. S21–4–1, B.R.B.; Cabinet Conclusions, 12 and 23 March, 24–5 April 1950, CAB128/17, P.R.O.; B.T.C., R. & A. 1950, pp. 38, 41–2.

25 Final conclusions appeared on 27 February. B.T.C., R. & A. 1951, pp. 76–7; Transport Tribunal, report on *B.T.C. (Passenger) Charges Scheme, 1951* (17 January 1952), and material in B.T.C. S60–6–11A, B.R.B. For fares see Munby and Watson, *Statistics,* p. 114.

26 Hurcomb–Barnes, 31 May 1951, B.T.C. S21–4–1, B.R.B.; Cabinet Committee on Socialised Industries Minutes, 12 July 1951, CAB134/692, P.R.O.; Barnes, memo. to Cabinet on 'Long Term Financial Prospects of the British Transport Commission', 10 September 1951, CP (51) 245, CAB129/47, P.R.O.; *Times,* 21 September 1950, 18 March 1952.

27 *Times,* 18 March 1952, *Daily Herald,* 19 March 1952, and *Daily Express,* 17 April 1952; Cabinet Conclusions, 12, 15 and 19 March 1951, CAB128/19, P.R.O. See also Godfrey–Goodison, MT56/358, P.R.O.

28 B.T.C., R. & A. 1951, p. 78. The fares quoted here are the actual rates charged and not the 'theoretical' fares of 1.63d. and 1.79d. a mile. See Blee, 'Report on the National Passenger Charges Scheme', 12 December 1950, Blee Papers, AN6/25, P.R.O. The monthly returns made up 59 per cent of total passenger revenue in 1948: Blee, report on 'Charges Schemes – Passenger Fares', 14 July 1949, Blee Papers, AN6/24, P.R.O.

29 Gilmour, note on 'B.T.C. (Passenger) Charges Scheme 1952', 4 March 1952, B.T.C. Minutes, 6 March 1952, B.R.B.; B.T.C. R. & A. 1952, p. 54. Blee estimated the lost revenue from the lower ordinary fares, which effectively ended the sale of monthly return tickets, priced at the same level, at £1.7m. per annum: Blee–Hurcomb, 12 February 1952, B.T.C. S60–6–11A, B.R.B.

30 B.T.C., R. & A. 1952, p. 54; *Daily Herald,* 19 March 1952; *Sussex Daily News,* 11 March 1952, and *Star,* 27 March 1952, cuttings in B.T.C. S60–6–11A and B, B.R.B.

31 *The Economist,* 15 March 1952, *Times,* 19 March 1952.

32 Cabinet Conclusions, 12 and 19 March, and 4 December 1951, and 6, 7 and 18 March 1952, CAB128/19–24, P.R.O.; *Railway Gazette,* 14 March 1952.

33 C.T.C.C., Report on British Transport Commission (Passenger) Charges Scheme 1952, 8 April 1952, draft copy in B.T.C. S60–6–11B, B.R.B. The report was subsequently published on 17 April as Cmd.8513, P.P.1951–2, XVIII. The principal concessions were the retention for at least a year of the 8.30 a.m. time limit for early morning tickets in North-West England (instead of 8 a.m.), and the replacement of sub-standard ordinary fares in the Central Belt of Scotland with cheap-day tickets: Hurcomb–Maclay, 29 March 1952, S60–6–11B, B.R.B.

34 Cabinet Conclusions, 10 and 16 April 1952, CAB128/24, P.R.O. Lord Leathers was Minister for Co-ordination of Transport Fuel and Power, and Lord Swinton was Chancellor of the Duchy of Lancaster and Minister of Materials. On Churchill's role see, *inter alia*, Lord Moran, *Winston Churchill: The Struggle For Survival, 1940–1965* (London: Constable, 1966), p. 385.

35 The Direction and other correspondence are in B.T.C. S60–6–11B, B.R.B.

36 The government's poor showing in the L.C.C. elections in early April was also a contributory factor. *Times*, 17 and 18 April 1952, *Daily Herald*, 17 April 1952, and *The Economist*, 19 April 1952; *Parl. Deb. (Commons)*, vol. 499 (Session 1951–2), 28 April 1952, 1031 (Maxwell-Fyfe).

37 Secretary, B.T.C.–Secretary, M.T., 18 April 1952; notes of a meeting of B.T.C., R.E. and L.T.E., 30 April 1952; B.T.C., Report to M.T. on 'Sub-Standard Fares and Charges', 13 May 1952; Lennox-Boyd–Hurcomb, 24 May 1952; and W. V. Wood, notes of a meeting with Lennox-Boyd, 10 June 1952, all in B.T.C. S60–6–11B; and B.T.C. Minutes, 13 and 29 May, 10 and 12 June 1952, B.R.B.

38 *Parl. Deb. (Commons)*, vol. 502 (Session 1951–2), 16 June 1952, 780–1 (Lennox-Boyd). The special groups were mentioned by Churchill in vol. 499 (Session 1951–2), 21 April 1952, 37ff. A full list is given in memo. by H. J. Birkbeck, Principal Charges Officer, B.T.C., 26 March 1952, B.T.C. S60–6–11B, B.R.B.

39 B.T.C., *R. & A. 1952*, p. 55; Cabinet Conclusions, 10 June 1952, CAB128/25, P.R.O.

40 Munby and Watson, *Statistics*, p. 114. A request for a 5 per cent increase in freight rates was handled more promptly. The application was made in October 1952, and the rates raised on 1 December. See B.T.C. explanatory memo. 22 October 1952, B.T.C. S60–14–2, B.R.B.; B.T.C. *R. & A. 1952*, pp. 56–7, *1953*, I, pp. 1–2.

41 The other members were David Blee (R.E.), A. Henderson (Road Transport Executive), Sir Reginald Hill (Docks and Inland Waterways Executive), Alec Valentine (L.T.E.) and A. E. Sewell (the B.T.C.'s Charges Adviser). B.T.C. Minutes, 17 February 1948, B.R.B. Sewell was appointed to the Transport Tribunal in October 1949.

42 B.T.C., *R. & A. 1948*, pp. 40–1. On Morrison, see *Parl. Deb. (Commons)*, vol. 431 (Session 1946–7), 2080, quoted in Walker, 'The Transport Act, 1947', 18; Cabinet Committee on Socialised Industries (M) Minutes, 15 November 1949, discussion of Morrison's memo. 26 April 1949, CAB134/690, P.R.O.

43 W. V. Wood, memo. on 'Charges Policy', 27 November 1947, B.T.C. Minutes, 2 December 1947, B.R.B.; B.T.C., *R. & A. 1948*, pp. 25–6. However, as a following sub-section made clear, Section 3(2) did not impose an obligation on the B.T.C. to continue services, or prevent it from quoting different charges.

44 B.T.C., *R. & A. 1948*, p. 17. In 1948, coal costs rose by £3.8m., wages by £6m., and national insurance added £3.5m. See B.T.C., *R. & A. 1950*, pp. 37–8.

45 B.T.C., *R. & A. 1951*, p. 11, *1952–3*, Table IV–1.

46 Blee and Morton, memo. on '1950 Passenger Receipts', 2 August 1950, Hurcomb, note, 25 August 1950, B.T.C. S107–1–12; B.T.C. Minutes, 3 May

1951; Wilson, memo. on 'Traffic Costing Service', 23 October 1951, B.T.C. Minutes, 1 November 1951, B.R.B.

47 Blee, memo. 3 August 1950, AN6/10, P.R.O.; Tait–Wilson on 'Passenger Transport Costs. I – Rail', 25 August 1950, B.R.B.; B.T.C., R. & A. 1950, p. 71.

48 B.T.C., *Draft Outline of Principles Proposed to be Embodied in a Charges Scheme for Merchandise* (December 1949); Tait, memo. December 1950, Table B, Blee Papers, AN6/29, P.R.O.; B.T.C., R. & A. 1950, p. 21, 1951, pp. 73–4. Tait appears to have stretched the point that rail costs for merchandise traffic were higher than by road. The road cost of 1.932d. per capacity ton-mile quoted was taken from A. H. Barlow's Manchester–London traffic, but other examples of long-distance traffic revealed costs of 2.716d. and 2.842d.

49 Average loads (passenger-miles as a percentage of seat-miles provided) were: London Midland, 31 per cent; Eastern, 27 per cent; North Eastern, 29 per cent; Scottish, 33 per cent; Southern, 27 per cent; and Western, 33 per cent. The all-regions average was 30 per cent. Loads were particularly low on the following trains: London Midland stopping and Scottish suburban, 18 per cent; Southern suburban, 19 per cent; Eastern stopping, 21 per cent (42 passengers per train). B.T.C., Passenger Statistics, AN82/81, P.R.O., and Tait, Monthly Report, March 1954 (incorporates some revisions to data), B.T.C. Finance Committee Minutes, 12 May 1954, and B.T.C. Minutes, 11 November 1954, B.R.B. For the background to the census see B.T.C. S107–1–12, B.R.B.

50 Wilson, memo. on 'Traffic Costing: Western Passenger', 8 July 1953, B.T.C. S21–8–1, B.R.B. Movement costs were put at £16.9m. per annum, track costs at £6.0m. and terminal costs at £4.6m. Grand had suggested that the burden of work involved in collecting data for the Census would encourage the cutting of corners, thereby impairing accuracy. See 'Statistics Run Wild', in *Railway Gazette*, 3 October 1952, and Tait, memo. to Wilson, 3 October 1952, B.T.C. Minutes, 7 October 1952, B.R.B.

51 Tait, in his monthly report of March 1954, defended the accuracy of the Census and suggested that an operating ratio of 60 per cent (movement costs/revenue) was required if all costs were to be covered. The Census produced an overall operating ratio of 75 per cent: B.T.C. Finance Committee Minutes, 12 May 1954, B.R.B. The unprofitability of passenger services was also mentioned in W. I. Winchester and J. M. Roberts, 'Survey of Railway Fares Policy' (n.d., probably late 1954), Blee Papers, AN6/26, P.R.O. Cf. *Reshaping'*, I, pp. 15–19.

52 Winchester and Roberts, 'Survey of Railway Fares Policy', AN6/26, P.R.O. Railway attitudes owed much to Sir William Acworth. See his *The Elements of Railway Economics* (Oxford: Oxford University Press, 1924 edn), pp. 57ff., and also P. Burtt, *Railway Rates. Principles and Problems* (London: Pitman & Sons, 1926), and Milne and Laing, *Obligation to Carry*, pp. 20–7, 35, 110–13. For the views of railwaymen, see M. R. Bonavia, *British Railway Policy between the Wars* (Manchester: Manchester University Press, 1981), ch. 4, and esp. p. 67 (comment by A. A. Harrison).

53 Milne and Laing, *Obligation to Carry*, p. 33.

54 Blee, telephone conversations, 1956–8 (indexed), in Blee Papers, AN6/57, P.R.O.

55 B.T.C. Minutes, 3 May 1951, B.R.B.

56 B.T.C., *R. & A. 1951*, p. 16, and see also p. 29; Blee, report on 'Charges Schemes – Passenger Fares', 14 July 1949, and 'National Passenger Charges Schemes', 12 December 1950, AN6/24–5, P.R.O.

57 B.T.C./R.E. Joint Meeting Minutes, 17 March 1949, 9 August 1951, B.T.C. S26–2–2A and C; Wood, note on 'Passenger Fares', 25 March 1949, S60–1–1A; notes of a meeting of B.T.C., Blee, Cardwell (R.P.E.) and Vane Morland, 12 May 1950, S60–1–1B, B.R.B.; Blee, notes of a meeting with Hurcomb, 7 September 1950, and memo. 9 January 1951, AN6/10, P.R.O.

58 H. H. Phillips, memo. to Blee on 'Receipts from Passenger Traffic. Effect of Cheap Fares Policy', 19 October 1950, AN6/20, P.R.O.

59 R.E. Commercial Committee Minutes, 6 February and 11 November 1952, RAIL1080/728, and R.E., Report of Working Party of Passenger Assistants on the Competition of Long Distance Passenger Road Services, 7 August 1952, in B.T.C. Passenger Statistics, AN82/81, P.R.O. Blee continued to voice his anxiety about plans to raise fares and, in particular, the ordinary fare from 1.75d. to 2.00d. See his memo. on 'Possible Increase in Passenger Charges', 17 November 1952, B.T.C. S60–1–21, B.R.B.

60 R.E. Informal Meeting of Full-Time Members Minutes, 19 March, 2 April and 19 December 1951, B.R.B.

61 Blee, notes of a meeting with Hurcomb, 7 September 1950, AN6/10, P.R.O.

62 See, for example, R.E. Commercial Committee Minutes, 6 February 1952, RAIL1080/728, P.R.O.; B.T.C. Transport Statistics, 15 March 1960, B.R.B.

63 Hurcomb–Missenden, 30 August 1949, B.T.C. S21–4–1; B.T.C./R.E. Joint Meeting Minutes, 16 November 1948, 18 January 1951, S26–2–2A and C; Blee–Hurcomb, 19 November 1951, S60–14–1B, B.R.B.

64 R.E. Commercial Committee Minutes, 23 February and 29 June 1949, RAIL1080/727, P.R.O.

65 Blee, report on 'National Passenger Charges Scheme', 12 December 1950, AN6/25, P.R.O.

66 B.T.C. Standing Conference on the Co-ordination of Inland Transport Minutes, 28 January 1949, and *Modern Transport*, 26 March 1969, extracts in B.T.C. S50–8–1A, B.R.B. On undercutting see Beevor–Wood, 22 July 1949, Beevor–Marsden, 12 January 1950, and other correspondence in S50–8–1A; B.T.C./R.E. Joint Meeting Minutes, 19 January and 16 February 1950, S26–2–2B; Cardwell–Beevor, 12 March 1951, Blee–Beevor, 15 March 1951, and Beevor, memo. to B.T.C., 17 April 1951, in B.T.C. Minutes, 3 and 17 April 1951, B.R.B.

67 R.E. Commercial Committee Minutes, 31 May 1950, RAIL1080/727, P.R.O.; B.T.C. Standing Conference on Integration of Inland Transport Minutes, 14 December 1951, and Taylor, memo. 21 May 1952, in B.T.C. S50–7–1, B.R.B.; notes of a meeting of B.T.C., R.E. and Road Haulage Executive, 16 January 1952; Deakin, in *Transport & General Workers Record*, May 1952; Marsden–Taylor, 20 May 1952, B.T.C. S50–6–2C, and see also S50–16–1, B.R.B.

68 R.E. Commercial Investigation Bureau, report on 'C Licence Growth', May 1950, Blee Papers, AN6/28; R.E. Commercial Superintendents, report on 'The Development of Passenger Traffic – Creation of Additional Traffic', 17 March 1953, and on 'Starlight Specials', 12 August 1953, B.T.C. Commercial Committee Reports and Memos., AN97/32, P.R.O.; J. C. Stewart, 'The

Marketing and Pricing of Railway Freight Transport', *Journal of the Institute of Transport*, XXXI (May 1966), 376–82.

69 Aldcroft, *British Railways*, pp. 134–49; Joy, *Train That Ran Away*, pp. 60ff.

70 R.E. Commercial Committee Minutes, 29 June 1949, RAIL1080/727, P.R.O.

71 See Appendix E, Table 1. The data cited here are unadjusted for 'sponsorship' arrangements and inter-regional working but have been adjusted to produce a consistent series for 1948–62 (see Notes to Table 1). Figures available to the B.T.C. at the time showed a small net revenue in Scotland of £0.1m. in 1951, a shortfall of £2.6m. in 1953 and 1949 'losses' of £2.3m. (L.M.R.) and £1.9m. (W.R.): B.T.C. Statistics, AN12/26, P.R.O.

72 Wilson, memo. on 'Railway Passenger Suburban Services', 24 March 1953, in B.T.C Minutes, 26 March 1953, B.R.B. The Glasgow services were: East Kilbride, Cathcart Circle, Kirkhill and Uplawmoor.

73 B.T.C./R.E. Joint Meeting Minutes, 17 March and 22 September 1949, and 21 September 1950, B.T.C. S26–2–2A–C, B.R.B.; Blee, memo. 7 July 1949, AN6/10; R.E. Minutes, 31 March 1949, AN4/2; R.E. Branch Line Committee Minutes, 1949–53, AN97/19–22, P.R.O.; B.T.C., *R. & A. 1953*, I, p. 27; Aldcroft, *British Railways*, p. 147.

74 R.E. Branch Line Committee Minutes, 1949–53, AN97/19–22, and particularly 22 February 1951, 7 March and 24 April 1952, AN97/20–1, P.R.O. Munby and Watson, *Statistics*, p. 118.

75 R.E. Branch Line Committee Minutes, 7 July 1949, 4 December 1952, AN97/19, 21, P.R.O. Cheap fares matching those charged by bus and an hourly service were introduced on the Sunderland–Hetton branch in January 1950, but the increase in revenue was matched by an increase in costs, and the line was finally closed in January 1953. See B.T.C. S99–1–54, B.R.B., and E. W. Arkle, 'The Branch Line Problem', *Journal of the Institute of Transport*, XXIV (March 1951), 124–8.

76 B.T.C./R.E. Joint Meeting Minutes, 21 September 1950, B.T.C. S26–2–2C, B.R.B., and R.E. Branch Line Committee Minutes, 1950–3, AN97/20–2, P.R.O.

77 Labour productivity (output per head) from Appendix C, Table 1. Regional estimates, constructed on a different basis, show the following results for 1953 (1948 = 100): L.M.R. 106.0; W.R. 102.7; S.R. 107.2; E.R. 141.1; and Sc.R. 112.6.

78 R.E., Memo. on 'Economy', 15 March 1950, B.T.C. S324–2–2; R.E., 'British Railways Report for 1952', March 1953, pp. 75–6, B.R.B., *R. & A. 1953*, I, p. 52, *1956*, II, pp. 262–3. For other measures of improvement – engine availability, engine-mileage per mechanical failure, repair costs per engine-mile, coal consumption per engine-mile – see Pearson, 'Development and Prospects', 6. For the 1951 incentive scheme see B.T.C. S324–9–1, B.R.B.

79 For an authoritative account of general developments and a detailed history of the N.U.R. see P. S. Bagwell, *The Railwaymen. The History of the National Union of Railwaymen*, I (London: George Allen & Unwin, 1963), which covers the period to *c*.1960. On A.S.L.E.F. see the much slighter Norman McKillop, *The Lighted Flame. A History of the Associated Society of Locomotive Engineers and Firemen* (London: Thomas Nelson, 1950), and B. Murphy, *ASLEF 1880–1980. A Hundred Years of the Locoman's Trade Union* (London: A.S.L.E.F., 1980).

80 Bagwell, *The Railwaymen*, I, pp. 435, 541–4, 566, II, *The Beeching Era and*

After (London: George Allen & Unwin, 1982), pp. 233–4. A rare example of unilateral action was A.S.L.E.F.'s ten-day strike in January 1924.

81 Cf. *Railway Review*, 1944–6, *passim*; Bagwell, *The Railwaymen*, I, pp. 605–6; McKillop, *Lighted Flame*, pp. 278, 289, 300–4.

82 Bagwell, *The Railwaymen*, I, pp. 589, 605–8; McKillop, *Lighted Flame*, pp. 305–7, 313, 318–19; B.T.C., *R. & A. 1948*, pp. 54–5.

83 Bagwell, *The Railwaymen*, I, p. 607; F. McKenna, *The Railway Workers 1840–1970* (London: Faber and Faber, 1980), p. 63–4, 143. On conditions and, in particular, complaints about locomotives see S. Cannon (Swindon Branch Secretary, A.S.L.E.F.)–T. Reed, M.P., 22 November 1947, 5 January 1948, in B.T.C. S17–8–2, and Baty–Barnes, 21 November 1947, S17–6–2, B.R.B.

84 B.T.J.C.C. Minutes, 25 January 1949 *et seq.*, B.R.B.; B.T.C., *R. & A. 1948*, pp. 34–40.

85 Wilson, letter to author, 31 March 1983; Note of a discussion between Ministers and representatives of the General Council of the Trades Union Congress on 'Trade Union Members of Public Boards', 31 July 1951, 3 August 1951, Socialised Industries (M) Committee Memorandum SI (M) (51) 40, CAB134/692, P.R.O. Allen's A.S.L.E.F. pension was frozen: B.T.C. confidential memo. 24 April 1958, B.R.B.

86 R.S.C. Salaried and Conciliation Staff: Court of Inquiry proc., January 1951, notes of meeting between . . . R.E., N.U.R., A.S.L.E.F. and the R.C.A., 19 and 20 February 1951, B.R.B.; R. Burton, 'The Mysticism of Workers' Control', *Railway Review*, 4 November 1949. See also J. Street, 'The Origins and Development of Trade Union Involvement in the Management and Control of British Industry, Especially Nationalized Industry, 1930–1951', unpublished University of Oxford D.Phil. thesis, 1981, pp. 356ff.

87 Bagwell, *The Railwaymen*, I, pp. 626–7, McKillop, *Lighted Flame*, pp. 338–45. On the Railway Vigilance Movement, a left-wing faction which opposed the official union policy in the 1930s, see McKenna, *The Railway Workers*, pp. 129–35.

88 See, *inter alia*, notes of meetings with locomotive running and motorman inspectors and firing instructors, November–December 1949, in R.E. Motive Power Committee Minutes, 30 December 1949, AN97/138; ibid., 28 April 1950, and 27 September 1951; Blee, notes on staff shortages, 14 June 1951, AN6/35, P.R.O.; Bonavia, memo. 17 October 1950, B.T.C. S21–1–2F; Marsden–Beevor on 'Staff Shortages', 22 May 1951, S71–1–35, B.R.B., R.E. Commercial Committee Minutes, 4 April 1951, RAIL1080/728, P.R.O.

89 As is clear from the comments of Deakin, Franklin and others at the meetings of the B.T.J.C.C.: Minutes, 31 March 1950, 26 January 1951 and 4 April 1952, B.R.B. See also *Railway Review*, 12 May 1950.

90 For further information on N.U.R. policy see Bagwell, *The Railwaymen*, I, pp. 608–9, 613; *Railway Review*, 13 February and 11 June 1948 and 9 December 1949; P.P.1947–8, XXII, Cmd.7321.

91 Notes of a meeting between Gould and representatives of the N.U.R., 6 January 1949, in Ministry of Labour and National Service: Industrial Relations Department: Passenger Transport, R.E. and N.U.R. 12/6 claim, LAB10/800, P.R.O. The Ministry's decision was supported by a ruling from the National Arbitration Tribunal. See B.T.C., *R. & A. 1948*, p. 96, *1949*, pp. 66–7, and 'Memo. on Differences between the Railway Management and

Railway Trade Unions 1947 to Date', 18 October 1950, in Ministry of Labour and National Service: Industrial Relations Department: Passenger Transport (Railways), R.E. and A.S.L.E.F., LAB10/996, and see also ibid., N.U.R. and R.E. Question of Wage Increase, LAB3/631, P.R.O.

92 R.S.N.T. Decision No.11, 18 March 1949, B.R.B.; Minutes of meeting of Isaacs and N.U.R. representatives, 26 April 1949, Figgins–Isaacs and Allen–Gould, 20 May 1949, in Ministry of Labour: Industrial Relations Department: Passenger Transport. British Railway Executive and N.U.R. claim for 10s. per week, LAB10/840, P.R.O.

93 Figgins–Isaacs, 28 June 1949; unsigned minute to Minister, 16 July 1949, LAB10/840, P.R.O.

94 The concessions offered by the Executive and the Conciliation Board are listed in B.T.C., R. & A. 1949, pp. 66–7. See also B.T.C. S71–1–22, B.R.B.

95 Bagwell, The Railwaymen, I, p. 610.

96 The increase was introduced on 4 September. R.S.N.T. Decision No. 12, 15 August, B.R.B.

97 B.T.C., R. & A. 1950, p. 166; Baty–Isaacs, 12 October 1950, and Gould–Isaacs, 23 October 1950, LAB10/996, P.R.O.

98 R.E., Memos. on 'Enginemen's "Lodging Turns" Dispute', 24 May 1949, and 'Enginemen's Lodging Turns Dispute. The Facts', (n.d.), B.T.C. S19–1–72, B.R.B.; correspondence in Sir Robert Gould's file on 'Lodging Turns', and, in particular, Missenden–Gould, 13 June 1949, in LAB10/840, P.R.O.; and S. Weighell, 'The Story of Lodging Turns', Railway Review, 4 October 1953. The loss of revenue from the Sunday stoppages was put at £85,000: Marsden–Beevor, 12 July 1949, B.T.C. S104–2–1, B.R.B.

99 Hurcomb, draft letter to Barnes and Gould, 11 August 1949, B.T.C., memo. on 'Lodging of Trainmen', 15 August 1949, and on 'Lodging Turns Dispute', 24 August 1949, in B.T.C. S19–1–72, B.R.B. On the impact of the strike on train services, see R.E. Minutes, 23 May, 2, 8 and 13 June 1949, AN4/2, P.R.O., and Marsden–Beevor, 12 July 1949, B.T.C. S19–1–72, B.R.B.

100 R.C.A. Statement, 30 June 1949, in LAB10/840, P.R.O. On lodging hostels see McKenna, The Railway Workers, pp. 197–229, and on 'go-slows' see Missenden–Gould, 2–3 June and 22–3 September 1949, LAB10/840, and R.E. Memoranda, 4 July 1949, AN4/9, P.R.O.

101 Gould–Isaacs, 13 June 1949, Figgins–Isaacs, 13 June 1949, LAB10/840; R.E. Minutes, 13 June 1949, AN4/2, P.R.O.

102 R.S.C. Court of Inquiry Proceedings, January 1951, I, notes of meeting of R.S.N.C., 7 November 1950, B.R.B.; unsigned note on 'Railways', and Allen–Gould, 7 December 1950, Ministry of Labour and National Service: Private Office Case (J. G. Baty (A.S.L.E.F.), J. B. Figgins (N.U.R.); G. B. Thorneycroft (R.C.A.): asking Minister to receive Deputation...), LAB43/32, P.R.O.

103 Railway Review, 15 December 1950.

104 Isaacs–Lord Porter, 20 December 1950, Ministry of Labour and National Service: Industrial Relations Department: Court of Inquiry into Claims made by Railway Trade Unions, LAB10/1008, P.R.O. The letter thanked Porter for accepting the invitation to act as Chairman of the Court of Inquiry. In fact, ill-health forced him to stand down, and he was replaced by Guillebaud.

105 Report of Court of Inquiry ... , 13 February 1951, P.P.1950–1, XVI, Cmd.8154, Figgins–Isaacs, 14 February 1951, and Baty–Isaacs, 15 February

1951, in Ministry of Labour and National Service: Industrial Relations Department: British Railways and N.U.R. and A.S.L.E.F. Apprehended dispute in connection with the findings of the Court of Inquiry, 1951, LAB10/1021, P.R.O. For local stoppages see Bagwell, *The Railwaymen*, I, p. 614.

106 Notes of a meeting of Bevan and the railway unions, 16 February 1951, LAB10/1021, P.R.O.

107 Notes of meetings of R.E. and the railway unions, 19–21 February 1951, R.S.N.T. Papers, B.R.B.; note of meeting, 22 February 1951, LAB10/1021; Cabinet Conclusions, 22 February 1951, CAB128/19, P.R.O. On Bevan's general approach see M. Foot, *Aneurin Bevan. A Biography*, II, *1945–60* (London: Davis-Poynter, 1973), pp. 317–18.

108 *Joint Statement to the Staff of British Railways...*, March 1951, B.R.B.; *Railway Gazette*, 2 March 1951; Sir Norman Chester, *The Nationalisation of British Industry 1945–51* (London: H.M.S.O., 1975), pp. 824–5.

109 B.T.C., *R. & A. 1951*, pp. 80–2, *1952* pp. 81–2. For R.E. concern re staff shortages see Blee, memo. 23 August 1951, Blee Papers, AN6/33, and Motive Power Committee statistics, in AN6/34, P.R.O.; R.E. Full-Time Members Minutes, 7 August 1951, B.T.C./R.E. Joint Meeting Minutes, 4 October 1951, and note of a B.T.C./R.E. meeting, 15 November 1951, B.T.C. S26–2–2D, S19–6–1, B.R.B.

5. The new railway organisation

1 Tory backbencher cit. in Lord Hurcomb, 'The Obligation to Carry', *Journal of The Institute of Transport*, XXVII (January 1957), 57; A. M. Milne and A. Laing, *The Obligation to Carry* (London: Institute of Transport, 1956), p. 37; Conservative Party, *Britain Strong and Free* (1951), p. 21.

2 Lord Woolton, memo. on 'Reorganisation of Road and Rail Transport', 20 March 1952, and memo. 8 April 1952, Cabinet Memoranda, CAB129/50; Cabinet Conclusions, 25 and 27 March and 10 April 1952; CAB128/24; Churchill–Leathers, 7 April 1952, Leathers–Churchill, 6 July 1952, MT62/144, P.R.O.; Reginald Wilson, note on 'Draft Transport Bill', 23 June 1952, B.T.C. S201–4–2A, B.R.B.

3 An annual sum of £4m. was mentioned: *Transport Policy*, May 1952, P.P.1951–2, XXV, Cmd.8538.

4 Conversation with Lord Boyd of Merton, 9 December 1982; Butler, note to Churchill, 21 May 1952, MT62/144; R. Assheton–Chief Whip, 15 May 1952, enclosed in Churchill–Leathers, 23 May 1952, M.T., 'A Review of Press Comment on the Transport Bill, 1952', 14 July 1952, Ministry of Transport Correspondence and Papers: Lord Leathers's Papers (1952 Transport (Amendment) Bill), MT62/138, P.R.O.; Hurcomb–Lennox-Boyd, 8 July 1952, and Reginald Wilson, note, 23 June 1952, B.T.C. S201–4–2A, B.R.B.

5 Churchill–Leathers, 28 September and 16 October 1952, Leathers–Churchill, 17 October 1952, Ministry of Transport Correspondence and Papers: Lord Leathers's Papers (1952–3 Transport (Amendment) Bill), MT62/145; Swinton, memo. on 'Transport Bill', 2 October 1952, Leathers, memos. 2, 20 and 21 October 1952, Lennox-Boyd, memo. 21 October 1952, CAB129/50; Cabinet Conclusions, 7, 22 and 29 October 1952, CAB128/25, P.R.O.

6 2 Eliz. II c.13, s.12–15. The B.T.C. was allowed to retain *c*.3,500 road

vehicles owned by the companies prior to nationalisation. The number was increased to c.15,000 by the Transport (Disposal of Road Haulage Property) Act, 1956, 4 & 5 Eliz. II c.56. For criticisms of Conservative policy see *Times*, 6 November 1952 and 6 May 1953, *Manchester Guardian*, 7 November .1952, *The Economist*, 21 March 1953, and for the roads lobby see *Commercial Motor*, 13 and 27 February and 15 May 1953.

7 Draft Bill, 30 May 1952, Transport Bill (No.128), 8 July 1952; H. E. Robson–Sir Cyril Birtchnell (M.T.), 7 May 1952, enclosing memo. on 'Draft Transport Bill – Points for Submission to the Road and Rail Committee' (n.d.), and Leathers–Lennox-Boyd, 25 June 1952, MT62/138, P.R.O.

8 Fergusson–G. W. Lloyd (Minister of Fuel and Power), 16 June 1952, and note, 18 June 1952; Sir Arthur Salter (Minister of Economic Affairs)– Leathers, 21 May 1952, MT62/138, P.R.O.; Transport Bill (No.1), 5 November 1952.

9 Robson–Birtchnell, 7 May 1952, Salter–Leathers, 21 May 1952, Fergusson– Lloyd, 11 June 1952, MT62/138, P.R.O., and Transport Bill (No.128), 8 July 1952, Transport Bill (No.1), 5 November 1952.

10 *Railway Gazette*, 27 March and 3 April 1953; G. Walker, 'Transport Policy Before and After 1953', *Oxford Economic Papers*, V (1953), 108; *Times*, 7 May 1953.

11 'Wondering', 'To Be or Not To Be', *Railway Gazette*, 14 August 1953; A. J. Pearson, *Man of the Rail* (London: George Allen & Unwin, 1967), p. 105; *Railway Gazette*, 17 July 1953; conversations with Arthur Pearson, J. L. Harrington, and Michael Bonavia.

12 *Times*, 30 April 1971.

13 Robson–Birtchnell, 7 May 1952, MT62/138, P.R.O.

14 For a nineteenth-century example, see T. R. Gourvish, *Mark Huish and the London and North Western Railway* (Leicester: Leicester University Press, 1972), pp. 27–8.

15 Conversation with Lord Boyd; Robertson–Falmouth, 14 January 1957, B.R.B. 21-8-1. Falmouth had questioned the structure of executive control on the railways in a debate on the 1956 White Paper on Railways.

16 Evidence of Robertson, *S.C. Nat. Ind.: B.R.*, 10 February 1960, QQ.242-3, P.P.1959–60, VII (254-1), cit. in M. R. Bonavia, *The Organisation of British Railways* (London: Ian Allan, 1971), p. 77.

17 B.T.C. Minutes, 24 September 1953, 16 and 30 September 1954, B.R.B., *Railway Gazette*, 6 and 13 August 1954; Sir John Elliot, *On and Off the Rails* (London: George Allen & Unwin, 1982), pp. 87, 89. The Chambers Committee reported in January 1955, and the L.T.E. members were re-appointed for five-year terms on 1 October 1955. See correspondence in Ministry of Transport Correspondence and Papers: L.T.E. Appointments, MT96/37, P.R.O.

18 B.T.C. Minutes, 24 September 1953, 2 September 1954, B.R.B.; *Railway Gazette*, 25 September 1953, 3 September and 10 December 1954.

19 Robertson did make his initial views on organisation known to the Commission in September 1953. See his confidential memo. 17 September, and B.T.C. Minutes, 17 September 1953, B.R.B. On the role of Benstead and Pope see Benstead's confidential memos. 3 September and 6 November 1953, and B.T.C. Minutes, 3 September–7 December 1953, B.R.B.

20 B.T.C. Minutes, 29 September, 6 and 15 October, and 10 November 1953, 28 January and 25 March 1954, B.R.B. The interim organisation is also outlined in Bonavia, *Organisation*, pp. 65–8.
21 B.T.C. Minutes, 24 September 1953, B.R.B.; B.T.C., 'Interim Railway Reorganisation. Instructions to Officers as to Procedure during the Period Beginning 1 October 1953', draft copy, in B.R.B. 30-2-4.
22 B.T.C., 'Interim . . . Instructions', B.R.B. 30-2-4; Robertson's comments, B.T.C. Minutes, 26 November 1953, B.R.B.
23 Train–Blee, 14 August 1953, Taylor–Blee, 11 September 1953, and Blee–Taylor, 17 September 1953, and Blee's private notes, 1956, AN6/9, P.R.O.; Bonavia, *Organisation*, pp. 67–8; Pearson, *Man of the Rail*, p. 121; Blee–Pope, 6 January 1954, AN6/10, P.R.O.
24 Newspaper cutting in D.O.E., retained file on 'B.T.C. Railway Reorganisation', 52/2/001 Pt. 1; description of the interim organisation in the White Paper *Railways Reorganisation Scheme* (July 1954), p. 9, P.P.1953–4, XXVI, Cmd.9191.
25 B.T.C., 'Interim Railway Organisation. Instructions to Officers' (confidential booklet), (n.d., September 1953?), pp. 6–11, B.R.B.
26 B.T.C. Minutes, 13 and 15 October 1953, B.R.B.
27 Cmd.9191, pp. 2–3, 17.
28 Robertson–Jenkins, 14 June 1954, D.O.E. 52/2/001; B.T.C. Minutes, 23 December 1954, B.R.B.
29 Robertson's remarks at meeting of the Commission, B.T.C. Minutes, 8 April 1954 (Appendix), B.R.B.
30 B.T.C., 'The Organisation of the British Transport Commission' (confidential 'Grey Book'), December 1954 (operative from 1 January 1955), pp. 3–6, AN84/116, P.R.O. The Productivity Council and Design Panel were listed in the revised Grey Book of November 1956, operative from 1 January 1957, pp. 6–8 (although the Design Panel was considered to be a special committee of the Commission in the revision operative from 1 January 1960): AN84/117, 118, P.R.O.
31 Grey Book, December 1954, pp. 7–8, 15–16.
32 Blee's functions were expanded on the retirement of S. E. Parkhouse on 1 January 1955. Grey Book, December 1954, pp. 9–13; B.T.C., confidential memos. 2 and 9 December 1954, B.R.B.
33 B.T.C., confidential memo. on 'Supplies and Production Adviser', 28 April 1955, B.T.C. Minutes, 12 May 1955, B.R.B.
34 'Notes of Chairman's Statement to the Commission', 2 December 1954, B.R.B. 30-2-4. The only ex-army officers in the organisation, other than Robertson and Wansbrough-Jones, were: Maj.-Gen. G. N. Russell, former Chairman of the Road Haulage Executive, General Manager of British Road Services from 1955, subsequently (1957), a member of the Eastern Area Board (Chairman in 1960), and a member of the Commission (from 1959); and Maj.-Gen. H. Reginald Kerr, General Manager of British Waterways from 1955.
35 Pearson, *Man of the Rail*, pp. 125–6. The Commission apparently consulted with both I.C.I. and Unilever: *Modern Transport*, 11 December 1954.
36 Wansbrough-Jones was paid £4,000 a year (£6,000 from July 1959). Benstead, confidential memo. on 'Appointment of Secretary-General', 14 December 1954, and B.T.C., confidential memo. 16 June 1959, B.R.B.

37 Robertson's evidence, *S.C. Nat. Ind.: B.R.*, 10 February 1960, Q.237; Robertson, personal note to Stedeford, 10 June 1960, Wansbrough-Jones S.A.G. Papers, Box 2, B.R.B.

38 B.T.C., 'Report on Continuous Brakes on Freight Trains', October 1955; B.T.C. Technical Development and Research Committee Minutes, 8 December 1955, 8 March 1956; Grand–Wansbrough-Jones, 13 February 1956, B.R.B. 170–4–10 Pt.1; B.T.C. Minutes, 16 February 1956; B.R.B. Technical Committee Minutes, 26 June 1963; Planning Committee memo. on 'Proposal to adopt the Air Brake as Standard on British Railways', 2 October 1964, and B.R.B. Minutes, 8 October 1964, B.R.B. See also M. R. Bonavia, *Organisation*, p. 75, and *British Rail. The First 25 Years* (Newton Abbot: David & Charles, 1981), p. 215; J. Johnson and R. A. Long, *British Railways Engineering, 1948–80* (London: Mechanical Engineering Publications, 1981), pp. 111–13, 297.

39 On signalling see B.R.B. 206–66–2 Pt. 1; B.T.C. Minutes, 28 February 1957, B.R.B. Diesel hydraulics are examined in more detail in Chapter 8, pp. 287–8.

40 Conversation with Lord Beeching, 8 July 1980; B.T.C. Minutes, 19 April, 31 May, 21 June and 11 October 1956, 9 August 1961, B.R.B. B.T.C. meetings were held at Edinburgh, York and Birmingham (1955); Cardiff (1956); Manchester and Sheffield (1958); and aboard the S.S. *Falaise*, Southampton Docks (1959).

41 Grey Book, November 1956, and December 1959. Other post-1955 changes included the reorganisation of shipping under J. L. Harrington in 1956 and the creation of a Shipping Advisory Council in 1960 (which replaced the Sub-Commission); the appointment of D. S. M. Barrie as Assistant Secretary-General on the disbanding of Arthur Pearson's General Duties Department in 1958; and the replacement of the General Manager's Committee by an informal Conference in 1956.

42 P. R. Hickman (Stores Superintendent, L.M.R.), report on 'Present and Proposed Organisation of Stores Department', June 1949, pp. 124–33, B.R.B.; R.E. Memoranda, 17 February 1949, AN4/9; Pearson Committee, report on 'Supplies Organisation of the British Transport Commission', October 1956, pp. 7-10, AN8/6, P.R.O.

43 Ibid., p. 11; B.T.C. Minutes, 8 March and 22 November 1956, B.R.B.; Ministry of Transport and Civil Aviation, *Report on the Purchasing Procedure of the British Transport Commission*, September 1957, P.P.1956–7, XIX, Cmd.262, p. 11 (the Howitt report).

44 Pearson Committee Report, pp. 65–75, and see also Robertson's comments at a meeting of B.T.C. members and Howitt on 25 July 1957, B.R.B. 232–1–8.

45 B.T.C. Minutes, 28 February, 28 April and 30 May 1957; General Staff memos., 26 February and 23 May 1957; Benstead–Gethin, 29 March 1957, and Gethin–Benstead, 10 April 1957, confidential memo. No. 130, B.R.B.; Robertson's Report to the Minister of Transport, 23 July 1957, printed in the Howitt report, pp. 53–61; B.T.C., *R. & A. 1957*, I, pp. 18–19. Gethin was paid £5,500 in compensation. The new officers were R. B. Hoff (who had succeeded Forbes Smith), Chief Supplies Officer, and S. C. Robbins, Chief Contracts Officer.

46 Robertson's comments are in B.T.C. Minutes, 30 May and 19 September

1957, B.R.B., and for Pearson's views see A. J. Pearson, *Railways and the Nation* (London: George Allen & Unwin, 1964), pp. 88–90, and *Man of the Rail*, pp. 126, 162–4.

47 Howitt report, pp. 49–50; *Parl. Deb. (Commons)*, vol. 573 (Session 1956–7), 10 July 1957, 484–94 (G. R. Strauss). Gethin joined British Oxygen in 1958; he died in 1965 (information from British Oxygen).

48 Robertson–Wansbrough-Jones, 27 July 1957, and see also Osborn–Valentine, 23 July 1957, in B.T.C./B.R.B. 232–1–8; B.T.C. Minutes, 19 September 1957, B.R.B.

49 Osborn, memo. on 'Finance Department: Organisation', 21 August 1956, and B.T.C. Minutes, 31 May, 20 September and 8 November 1956, B.R.B.

50 McKenna had been first choice for the post: Benstead, confidential memos., 22 June 1956 and 25 November 1957; Valentine, memo. 14 June 1956, B.T.C. Minutes, 28 June 1956, 28 November and 19 December 1957, B.R.B.

51 Grey Book, December 1954, p. 6; 'Explanatory Notes to Amendments to the Grey Book', (n.d., but 1956), B.R.B. 30–2–4; B.T.C. Minutes, 29 October and 12 November 1959, B.R.B.; Grey Book, December 1959, Section III, Annexe A (vi), and amendment, 14 January 1960; B.T.C., *R. & A. 1959*, I, p. 19.

52 B.T.C. Railways Sub-Commission Minutes, e.g. 24 March and 28 April 1955, 22 March 1962, B.R.B.

53 The idea of a Staff College had been raised in an earlier report by the Gilbert Committee in 1952. A College was also opened at Windsor for middle management. S. E. Raymond, 'Interim Report on Work Study Training', 17 January 1956, and confidential report on 'Recruitment and Training Arrangements', March 1956, B.T.C. Minutes, 26 January and 12 July 1956, B.R.B.

54 For work study see B.T.C. Establishment and Staff Committee Minutes, 23 February 1955; B.T.C. Minutes, 23 February, 15 March and 25 October 1956, 7 November 1957 and 30 July 1959, B.R.B. For 'O. & M.' see Marsden, report for the General Staff on 'Organisation and Methods', 15 May 1956; General Staff memo. on 'Organisation and Methods', 23 May 1957; B.T.C. Minutes, 30 May 1957, 30 July 1959, B.R.B. London Transport had had an 'O. & M.' Department for some years.

55 The Commission decided to respond to the early challenge of modernisation by co-opting experts such as Allan Quartermaine, the retired Chief Engineer of the Great Western Railway, and E. J. Larkin, Assistant Mechanical and Electrical Engineer of the London Midland Region. See B.T.C. Minutes, 24 March 1955, B.R.B.

56 Summerson, Chairman of Summerson Holdings Ltd of Darlington, was also Chairman of British Steel Founders Association and Copelaw Engineering. Weir, partner in Schrader Mitchell & Weir (Leather Merchants) and Chairman of the British Tabulating Machine Co., was also a director of British Enka and Pyrene. Hanks, who had succeeded Sir Herbert Merrett at Paddington in July 1955, was a director of the British Motor Corporation and Vice-Chairman of Morris Motors, one of its main subsidiaries. *Directory of Directors*, 1955, and *Railway Gazette*, 11 March, 24 June and 8 July 1955.

57 On Watkins's appointment see Watkinson–Robertson, 8 February 1956, Ministry of Transport Correspondence and Papers: Labour and Staff Relations, MT115/10; Watkinson–Eden, 1 March 1956, MT96/36, P.R.O.

58 Rusholme also retired in 1959, his place being taken by Maj.-Gen. G. N. Russell. Warter was Chairman of Enfield Cables, and Managing Director of the British & Foreign Wharf Co.; Sinclair's past directorships included Cleveland Petroleum, Redline–Glico, and Eagle Star Insurance. *Railway Gazette*, 8 April 1955 and 28 February 1958, and *Directory of Directors*, 1958.

59 The fees received by Summerson, Hanks and Warter included an additional £1,000 a year each for acting as Chairman of an Area Board. On the pressure for increased salaries see Robertson–Boyd-Carpenter, 17 November 1954, Sir Miles Thomas (B.O.A.C.)–Boyd-Carpenter, 22 November 1954, and undated memo. by the Minister, in Ministry of Transport Correspondence and Papers: Remuneration of Board Members and Senior Executives, Policy 1954–9, MT96/46, P.R.O., and *Parl. Deb. (Commons)*, vol.572 (Session 1956–7), 1310 (Macmillan).

60 Members were listed in the *Railway Gazette*, 31 December 1954. By April 1960 the Boards were manned by 9 members or ex-members of the Commission and 30 outsiders: B.T.C., 'Transport Directory', XII (January 1960), with pencilled amendments, B.R.B.

61 The third trade unionist was J. E. Binks (Southern Area), former President of the N.U.R. Bacon was a director of Lloyd's Bank, Lord Lieutenant of Norfolk and later Chairman of the British Sugar Corporation; Willink, Master of Magdalene College Cambridge, had been Minister of Health in Churchill's war-time government; McFarland was a director of the Belfast Banking Co.; Glyn was Chairman and Managing Director of Glyn Mills & Co.; Bilsland was a director of the Bank of Scotland, John Brown and Burmah Oil; Rose was Chairman of the Scottish Provident Institution and a director of the Union Bank of Scotland; Merrett was Chairman of Cory Bros. and Powell Duffryn; Pole was Chairman of Cornwall County Council. There was a broadly similar composition in April 1960. Of the 30 'outsiders' half came from industry, 6 from finance and there were 5 trade unionists, including James Haworth, President of the T.S.S.A. 1953–6 (London Midland), Percy Morris, also of T.S.S.A. (Western), and John Bowman of the A.E.U. (North Eastern).

62 Grey Book, December 1959, Section IV, p. 3. Only Russell, who attended the Sub-Commission twice in the period 1959–62, availed himself of this opportunity. On Area Board powers, see B.T.C. Minutes, with supporting papers, 24 February, 22 September and 27 October 1955, 15 and 22 March, 21 June and 19 July 1956, 26 February and 27 August 1959, B.R.B.

63 Area Board Chairmen's memo. on 'Functions and Membership of Area Boards', 30 May 1960, Beeching Papers, Box 4, and Cameron–Robertson, 1 November 1960, Summerson–Robertson, 4 November 1960, Box 8, B.R.B.

64 The General Managers, while accepting that penetrating lines were a nuisance, favoured a system or network division. See General Managers' confidential report on 'Proposals for the Elimination of Penetrating Lines', August 1955; B.T.C. General Staff memo. on 'British Railways: Penetrating Lines', 26 October 1955, and report on 'Lines of Demarcation between Regions', 1956; B.T.C. Minutes, 24 November and 15 December 1955, 24 May and 27 September 1956, 25 April and 28 November 1957, B.R.B.; B.T.C., *R. & A. 1955*, I, p. 2, *1957*, I, pp. 19–20; Bonavia, *Organisation*, pp. 80–7.

65 Sir Reginald Wilson's evidence, *S.C. Nat. Ind.: B.R.*, 31 March 1960, QQ.1184–5, 1217–18.
66 S.A.G. Minutes, 4 May 1960, Beeching Papers, Box 1, B.R.B.
67 Report of *S.C. Nat. Ind.: B.R.*, July 1960, p.xiii, evidence of Robertson and Warter, 10 February 1960, and Warter's exchange with the Chairman, Sir Toby Low, QQ.247–9; Sinclair, statement to S.A.G., Minutes, 4 August 1960, Beeching Papers, Box 1, and Stedeford, note on 'Draft Proposals on Organisation', 17 August 1960, box 7, B.R.B.
68 B.T.C. Minutes, 24 May 1956 and 21 February 1957, B.R.B.
69 Cf. Robertson, statement at B.T.C. Plenary Meeting, Minutes, 31 January 1957, B.R.B. On regional developments see B.T.C., *R. & A. 1957–61, passim*, and Bonavia, *Organisation*, pp. 87–93.
70 London Midland Area Board Minutes, 6 April and 6 October 1960; B.T.C. Minutes, 10 March, 18 and 25 August 1960, B.R.B.
71 B.T.C. Minutes, 19 July 1956; General Staff paper, 20 June 1956; General Staff memo. on 'Organisation of Technical Departments of British Railways', 9 January 1957, and revised version, 23 February 1957, and B.T.C. Minutes, 17 January and 28 February 1957, B.R.B.
72 See Western Area Board Minutes, 15 May 1957; B.T.C. Minutes, 22 January and 21 May 1959; North Eastern Area Board Minutes, 17 July 1959; B.T.C. Minutes, 14 January and 12 May 1960, B.R.B. For a later critique see H. P. Barker–Raymond, 15 October 1965, B.R.B. 171–7–1.
73 North Eastern Area Board Minutes, 20 January and 20 October 1961; Urwick, Orr & Partners Ltd, confidential report on 'British Railways: North Eastern Region Area Traffic Organisation', 25 July 1961, B.R.B.
74 Ibid., pp. 7–9, 13–15.
75 Margetts, 'Organising a Railway as a Business', private paper, presented to B.T.C. Officers' Conference, York, April 1962 (copy kindly supplied by the author).
76 See, *inter alia*, W. A. Robson (ed.), *Problems of Nationalized Industries* (London: George Allen & Unwin, 1952), pp. 78–118; Sir Norman Chester, *The Nationalisation of British Industry 1945–51* (London: H.M.S.O., 1975), pp. 1027–34; L. Hannah, *Engineers, Managers and Politicians. The First Fifteen Years of Nationalised Electricity Supply in Britain* (London: Macmillan, 1982), pp. 163–7; *Railway Gazette*, 9 September 1960.
77 Chester, *Nationalisation*, pp. 1030, 1034. Sir James Dunnett, the Permanent-Secretary, told the Stedeford Group that 'the most important defect in the Ministry was that there were only two points of contact – one between the Minister and Sir Brian Robertson, and the other between the Ministry and the Secretary-General': S.A.G. Minutes, 9 May 1960, Beeching Papers, Box 1, B.R.B.
78 Conversation with Wilson, 18 July 1980; Stedeford, 'Note', 17 August 1960, and memo. 16 September 1960, Beeching Papers, Box 7, B.R.B.

6. Deficits, markets and closures

1 Reginald Wilson, memo. 30 June 1953, B.T.C. Minutes, 9 July 1953, and memo. 18 December 1953 and 5 April 1954, B.T.C. S21–4–1, B.R.B.; B.T.C., *R. & A. 1954*, I, p. 68, and note to accounts, p. 10. For more details see Appendix A, notes to Table 3.

2 B.T.C., *R. & A. 1957–62*, II, Tables V–16, V–17, V–19. These sums are net of £12.5m. of suspended interest repaid by the B.T.C. in 1958–62 (most of it in 1960–2). It is assumed here that in the absence of financial concessions the B.T.C. would have raised the same amount of capital for railway purposes; Finance Act 1956, 4 & 5 Eliz. II c.54, extended by the Finance Act 1958, 6 & 7 Eliz. II c.56; Transport (Railway Finances) Act 1957, 5 & 6 Eliz. II c.9.

3 Output is a weighted average of the several categories of passenger and freight traffic mileage, mail, parcels, the carryings of the collection and delivery service and workshops' capital goods. See Appendix C for details.

4 For details, see below, pp. 215ff.

5 Published estimates suggest a rise of 45 per cent, from £254m. to £369m., D. L. Munby and A. H. Watson (eds.), *Inland Transport Statistics: Great Britain 1900–1970*, I (Oxford: Oxford University Press, 1978), p. 75. The revision employed here is based on four-weekly staff data in B.T.C., *Transport Statistics*, with average annual earnings adjusted to take account of wage increases during the year:

Year	Workforce (adjusted)	Average earnings (adjusted)	Estimated wage bill
1953	600,619	£441.48	£265.2m.
1962	486,467	£749.75	£364.7m.

6 B.T.C., *R. & A. 1955*, I, p. 11 (based on Winchester's memo. on 'Accumulated Deficit', of 1 March 1956, B.R.B.). See also *R. & A. 1956*, I, pp. 12, 61, *1957*, I, p. 48, *1960*, I, p. 1.

7 Ibid., *1956*, I, p. 11, *1958*, I, p. 2.

8 Transport Holding Co., *Report and Accounts, 1968* (1969), p. 32. My thanks to Sir Reginald Wilson for this reference.

9 Winchester, memo. 1 March 1956, B.R.B.; 'List of Applications to the Transport Tribunal', 1947–58, in Godfrey–Goodison, 3 December 1958, MT56/358, P.R.O.; B.T.C. Minutes, 10 and 24 July, 20 and 27 November 1958, 15 and 22 January, and 27 August 1959, B.R.B.

10 1 & 2 Eliz. II c.13, s.20–4.

11 See above, pp. 102–4.

12 The full text ran: 'Within presented limits they will be free to raise or lower their charges with subsequent approval by the Transport Tribunal and subject to the over-riding powers of the Minister.' Cabinet Conclusions, 10 and 22 April 1952, CAB128/24, P.R.O.; P.P.1951–2, XXV, Cmd. 8538, May 1952, p. 3.

13 Cabinet Conclusions, 10 February and 31 March 1954, CAB128/27, P.R.O.

14 Ibid., 23 March and 22 April 1955, CAB128/28–9; Boyd-Carpenter, memo. on 'British Transport Commission: Revenue and Charges', 9 March 1955, and further memo. 21 March 1955, CAB129/74, P.R.O.

15 B.T.C. Minutes, 9 and 16 February, 15 March and 11 April 1956, B.R.B. and correspondence in B.R.B. 99–1–1 Pt.1; Watkinson, in *Parl. Deb. (Commons)*, vol. 550 (Session 1955–6), 19 March 1956, 827–8. See also H. Macmillan, *Riding the Storm 1956–1959* (London: Macmillan, 1971), p. 8; Sir Anthony Eden, *Full Circle* (London: Cassell, 1960), pp. 324–6; Nigel Fisher, *Iain Macleod* (London: Deutsch, 1973), p. 109.

16 B.T.C. press statement, 27 June 1956, B.T.C. Minutes, 28 June 1956, B.R.B.
17 'Unfreezing the Railways', *The Economist*, 30 June 1956.
18 Soon after this, Wilson gave serious thought to the possibility of returning to private practice as an accountant: communication with author, 28 March 1983.
19 Report of *S.C. Nat. Ind.: B.R.*, July 1960, pp. xci–ii; D. L. Munby, 'The Nationalised Industries', in G. D. N. Worswick and P. H. Ady (eds.), *The British Economy in the Nineteen-Fifties* (Oxford: Clarendon Press, 1962), p. 384.
20 B.T.C., *R. & A. 1960*, I, p. 63, and see also *1956*, I, pp. 61–2.
21 General Staff memos. 14 November 1956, 26 June and 3 July 1958, H. C. Johnson–T. H. Hollingsworth, 9 March 1960, Traffic Conference Report, 18 April 1961, Traffic Conference Minutes, 12 December 1961, B.R.B. 99–2–1, Pt. 2; Blee, memo. 31 March 1960, London Midland Area Board Minutes, 6 April 1960; B.T.C. Minutes, 5 January and 14 May 1959, B.R.B.
22 *Manchester Guardian*, 29 June 1956; B.T.C. Minutes, 23 January 1958, B.R.B.
23 B.T.C., *R. & A. 1955*, I, p. 6, *1958*, I. p. 65.
24 Ibid., *1959*, I, pp. 70, 84.
25 Cf. B.T.C. Minutes, 1 April 1954; General Managers' comments, 14 October 1954, in B.R.B. 96–6–14 Pt. 2; B.T.C. Finance Committee Minutes, 11 December 1957, and see also 25 September 1957, 12 March 1958, B.R.B.; B.T.C., *R. & A. 1961*, I, pp. 2–5.
26 S. Joy, *The Train That Ran Away. A Business History of British Railways 1948–1968* (London: Ian Allan, 1973), pp. 43, 58–67. Not surprisingly, internal reactions were hostile. Tait described the book as 'readable . . . but marred by backstairs gossip, and on past and present personalities, often ill-informed and sometimes malicious'. Tait, notes, 11 April 1973, B.R.B. 21–12–92 Pt. 2.
27 See B.T.C. Finance Committee Minutes, 22 January and 12 March 1958, B.R.B.
28 B.T.C., 'First Report of Traffic Survey Group, Part I – Freight Traffic Policy', March 1956. The study was the work of J. R. Pike, R. F. Harvey and A. W. Tait. See Wansbrough-Jones Papers, Box 12, B.R.B. The emphasis on the need to concentrate both station and private-sidings operations contrasts with the more impressionistic analysis offered by Richard Pryke, *Public Enterprise in Practice. The British Experience of Nationalization over Two Decades* (London: MacGibbon and Kee, 1971), p. 235.
29 Dear, memo. 20 September 1957, B.T.C. Finance Committee Minutes, 25 September 1957, B.R.B.; *Reshaping* I, pp. 7–8.
30 Joy, *Train That Ran Away*, pp. 62–3, citing Osborn, and B.T.C. statements to the *S.C. Nat. Ind.: B.R.*, 1960, Appendices 9 and 39.
31 Tait, memo. on 'Survey of British Railways Passenger Train Services', October 1954, B.T.C. Minutes, 11 November 1954; Osborn, memo. on 'British Railways: Financial Results', 6 November 1958, B.T.C. Finance Committee Minutes, 12 November 1958, B.R.B.
32 The ratios between indirect costs and train-miles run for the three passenger sectors in 1961, shown in *Reshaping*, I, p. 8, were applied to the 1959 data. This method produces cost figures for the individual sectors at 1961 costs. The costs were then scaled down to 1959 cost levels.
33 Barker, memo. on 'Re-equipment of British Railways', 16 November 1954,

filed with B.T.C. Minutes, 18 November 1954; Dear, memo. on 'British Railways Results: 1960', 9 October 1961, B.T.C. Finance Committee Minutes, 11 October 1961, B.R.B. The 1960 data were drawn up on a new basis, with interest calculated at 4 per cent instead of 3 per cent as before. In Table 22 alternative data for 1960 are quoted to provide comparability with earlier years.

34　B.T.C. *R. & A. 1961*, I, pp. 4–5.

35　Eastern Region, 'Census of Passenger Trains March and September 1955', 1956, AN82/16–17, P.R.O.; 'Passenger Census September 1957', May 1958, Eastern Area Board Minutes, 10 June 1958, B.R.B.; 'Survey of Passenger Train Services 1960', October 1960, AN82/11, P.R.O.; 'Freight Survey', referred to in Eastern Area Board Minutes, 14 February 1961, B.R.B. The Eastern also conducted a survey of coal traffic in October 1956, see interim report 1957, AN82/18, P.R.O. Southern Region, 'Passenger Census 1958', July 1959, in Wansbrough-Jones–Gingell, 8 July 1960, Beeching Papers, Box 4, B.R.B.; report on 'Freight Traffic on the Southern Region', February 1961, AN103/15, P.R.O., and Southern Area Board Minutes, 2 March 1961, B.R.B.

36　From £25,400 a week to £9,500: Wansbrough-Jones–Gingell, 8 July 1960, Beeching Papers, Box 4, B.R.B.

37　Southern Passenger Census 1958. 'Ocean Liner' boat trains were excluded from the survey.

38　Steam: −£1.0m., D.M.U.s: −£0.8m. and E.M.U.s: −£0.2m. Eastern Region, 'Survey 1960', and 'Survey of Passenger Train Services August 1961', April 1962, AN82/98, P.R.O. A more detailed evaluation of the 1960 results, uplifted to 1961 levels, is in AN82/97, P.R.O.

39　London Midland Region, 'Passenger Train Survey 1960', London Midland Area Board Minutes, 6 and 7 June 1962, B.R.B. The L.M.R. also carried out tests of wagon-load traffic (including coal) from 1959. For the test of April 1962 see Area Board Minutes, 6 September 1962, B.R.B.

40　Hopkins, memo. on 'Freight Traffic Policy S.R.', 27 February 1961, AN103/15, P.R.O., and Southern Area Board Minutes, 2 March and 6 April 1961, B.R.B.

41　B.T.C. Minutes, 24 October 1957, B.R.B.

42　Wansbrough-Jones–Robertson, 3 January 1958, in Wansbrough-Jones, memo. on 'Long-term Traffic Policy', 9 January 1958, Wansbrough-Jones Papers, Box 13; B.T.C. Minutes, 30 January 1958, Barker, memo. on 'Some Aspects of a Long Term Freight Policy', 11 February 1958; General Staff memo. on 'Freight Traffic Policy', 11 February 1958, with recommendations of the ad hoc committee, Wansbrough-Jones Papers, Box 15; B.T.C. Committee on Freight Traffic Policy Minutes, 13 February 1958; B.T.C., Confidential Report on Freight Traffic Policy, August 1958 (the White report), B.R.B.

43　B.T.C. Committee on Freight Traffic Policy Minutes, 10 and 24 April, and 22 May 1958, and see also B.T.C. Minutes, 16 and 23 October 1958, B.R.B.

44　White report, pp. iv–v, 121–2.

45　Ibid., pp. 68–9.

46　Ibid., pp. 66, 69–70, 122.

47　Ibid., p. 32; B.T.C. Minutes, 30 October 1958; B.T.C., confidential memos. on 'Campaign for Rail Freight Traffic', 7 July 1959, 20 July 1960, 21 December 1961, B.T.C. Minutes, 9 July 1959, 21 December 1961, B.R.B.

48　White report, p. 49.

49 'Can British Railways Pay?', summary of remarks by Dr Richard Beeching, 12 June 1961, B.R.B.
50 Munby and Watson, *Statistics*, p. 84; 1959 and 1960 data from Table 23 above, and p. 195; 1961 data from *Reshaping*, I, p. 8.
51 See the remarks of Wilson, Grand and Watkins at an informal conference on 'Finance and Freight Budgets', 4 December 1953, B.R.B. 99–6–12; B.T.C. Minutes, 25 August 1955 and 26 April 1956, B.R.B.
52 See below, pp. 251–2.
53 General Staff memos. on 'Passenger Services', 10 January 1956, 'Unremunerative Railway Passenger Services', 20 March 1956, and 'Economic Operation of Passenger Services in Rural Areas', 15 June 1956, B.T.C. Minutes, 12 and 26 January, 22 March, 12 April and 28 June 1956, B.R.B.
54 D. H. Aldcroft, *British Railways in Transition: The Economic Problems of Britain's Railways since 1914* (London: Macmillan, 1968), pp. 146–8.
55 This feature was observed by Pryke: *Public Enterprise*, p. 238.
56 B.T.C., *R. & A. 1953*, II, p. 149; B.R.B., *R. & A. 1963*, II, p. 53. The post-1953 data are affected by changes in coverage, e.g. the removal of dock route-mileage from British Railways' route-mileage.
57 C.T.C.C., *Report, 1960*, p. 4; C.T.C.C.–S.A.G., 9 August 1960, Appendix A, Beeching Papers, Box 7; London Midland Area Board Minutes, 3 July 1958, with General Manager's submission of 24 June 1958, B.R.B.; C.T.C.C. closure data, 23 November 1960, C.T.C.C. File 1010 Pt. 2.
58 General Staff memos. on 'Proposed Passenger Traffic Policy of British Railways', 20 July 1956, 'Unremunerative Passenger Services', 9 July 1956, B.T.C. Minutes, 28 June, 19 and 26 July 1956, B.R.B.; *The British Transport Commission. Proposals for the Railways*, October 1956, p. 20, P.P.1955–6, XXXVI, Cmd.9880; Wilson-Hugh Molson (Joint Private Secretary, M.T.), 18 July 1956; B.T.C., memo. for C.T.C.C., 27 September 1957, in Ministry of Transport Correspondence and Papers: Withdrawal of Unremunerative Services: Policy 1950–8, MT115/3, P.R.O.
59 Presumably the Lostwithiel–Fowey line, put up for closure in October 1963 and closed in January 1965. Copy of Whip's note on joint meeting, 11 April 1956, and for Ministry attitudes see J. R. Willis–Molson, 28 January 1956, and Alison Munro–Willis, 14 April 1956, MT115/3, P.R.O.
60 Robertson–Watkinson, 2 June 1958, ibid.; General Staff memo. on 'Unremunerative Rail Passenger Services. Bus Services in Rural Areas', September 1958; B.T.C. Minutes, 1 May, 12 June and 11 September 1958, B.R.B.
61 General Staff memo. on 'Withdrawal of Unremunerative Services: Acceleration of Consultative Committee Procedures', 18 February 1959, B.T.C. Minutes, 18 December 1958, 26 February 1959, B.R.B.; *Parl. Deb. (Commons)*, vol. 592 (Session 1957–8), 23 July 1958, 421 (Watkinson).
62 *Railway Gazette*, 20 June 1958; Eastern Region, confidential report on 'Proposed Withdrawal of Train Services from Part of Former Midland & Great Northern Joint Line', September 1958, B.R.B.; Johnson's comments at joint meetings of East Midlands and East Anglia Area T.U.C.C.s, 30 September 1958, and note for file, 16 April 1959, T.U.C.C. (East Anglia) records, Norwich.
63 B.T.C. Minutes, 22 December 1960, London Midland Area Board Minutes, 2 November 1960, Eastern Area Board Minutes, 8 November 1960; H. A.

Short, memo. 6 November 1958, B.T.C. Minutes, 20 November 1958, B.R.B.; *Railway Gazette*, 8 January 1960, 15 February 1963.
64 C.T.C.C., *Report, 1959*, pp. 13–14, *1960*, p. 10; White report, p. 7; General Staff memo. on 'Diesel Rail Buses', 19 May 1960, B.T.C. Minutes, 26 May 1960, B.R.B. The five buses used on the E.R. had turned a shortfall of 99.41d. a train-mile into one of 6.08d., while six used in Scotland had reduced the shortfall from 102.97d. to 7.71d. Regional estimates of the financial effect of railbuses were complicated, however, by differences of calculation. The E.R. included a portion of through bookings in revenue, the Sc.R. confined revenue to local stations only, and the situation was further confused by an inability to separate revenue earned from railbuses and revenue from supplementary steam and D.M.U. services operated over the same lines.
65 E. W. Arkle, reported in London Midland Area Board Minutes, 6 November 1958, B.R.B. This view was repeated by the General Manager, Blee, ibid., 5 February 1959.
66 General Staff memo. on 'Withdrawal of Unremunerative Railway Services: Subsidies to Bus Companies', 9 June 1960, B.T.C. Minutes, 23 June 1960, B.R.B.; B.T.C., *R. & A. 1962*, I, p. 6.
67 Southern Area Board Minutes, 3 May and 2 August 1956, B.R.B.; 'Low Comedy in Sussex', *Trains Illustrated*, September 1956; *Railway Gazette*, 12 July 1957, 21 February 1958; M.T., *Proposed Withdrawal of Train Services from the Lewes–East Grinstead Railway*, February 1958, P.P.1957–8, XVIII, Cmd.360; C.T.C.C., *Report, 1958*, pp. 3, 6. There are two large M.T. files on the line: Correspondence and Papers: Withdrawal of Unremunerative Services: Southern Region: East Grinstead–Lewes line, 1954–6, MT115/8, 1956–7, MT115/9, P.R.O.
68 Alison Munro, Minute, 21 June 1956, MT115/9, P.R.O.
69 C.T.C.C., *Report, 1958*, pp. 16–18.
70 Ibid., p. 4.
71 General Manager's memo. 25 February 1960, Southern Area Board Minutes, 3 March 1960, B.R.B.; T.U.C.C. (London) Minutes and papers, 21 July, 4 October and 8 December 1960 and 8 February 1961, and *Report, 1961* (1962), p. 5, T.U.C.C. (London) records, London.
72 L. J. Dunnett (Permanent-Secretary, M.T.)–E. G. Whitaker (C.T.C.C.), 7 September 1961, Ministry of Transport File on Withdrawal of Unremunerative Services. Southern Region, Westerham branch line, M.T. RB3/5/011 Pt. 2, D.O.E.; Marples, written answer, 2 August 1961, *Parl. Deb. (Commons)*, vol. 645 (Session 1960–1), *180*; B.T.C. Minutes, 26 October 1961, B.R.B. A back-check in March 1963 indicated that £10,000 had been saved in the first year: Wansbrough-Jones–C. P. Scott-Malden (M.T.), 11 March 1963, M.T. RB3/5/011 Pt. 2, D.O.E.
73 *Parl. Deb. (Commons)*, vol. 646 (Session 1960–1), 17 and 19 October 1961, 2, 517–30 (Westerham), vol. 592 (Session 1957–8), 1 August 1958, 1875–6 (Merthyr–Abergavenny).
74 Cf. M. Howe and G. Mills, 'The Withdrawal of Railway Services', *Economic Journal*, LXX (June 1960), 348–56, and 'Consumer Representation and the Withdrawal of Railway Services', *Public Administration*, XXXVIII (Autumn 1960), 253–62; D. St J. Thomas, *The Rural Transport Problem* (London: Routledge, 1963), pp. 36ff.

75 Thomas, *Rural Transport Problem*, pp. 143–9; C.T.C.C. Minutes, 7–8 July 1958, Wansbrough-Jones–General Managers, 14 July 1958, and correspondence in B.R.B. 31–14–4. The Foxfield–Coniston case was followed by an instruction to B.T.C. representatives to abstain from voting at T.U.C.C. meetings.
76 B.T.C. Minutes, 23 June and 27 October 1960, 26 January, 23 March, 22 June and 26 October 1961, 25 January 1962, B.R.B., and B.R.B. 33–1–14.
77 General Staff memo. on 'Fringe Areas', 14 December 1959, with draft letter to M.T., B.T.C. Minutes, 17 December 1959, B.R.B.; Wansbrough-Jones–Ministry, 23 December 1959, and other information in B.R.B. 242–8–16. Some of the papers were passed on to S.A.G. members on 5 May 1960, Beeching Papers, Box 4, B.R.B.

7. Wages, unions and productivity

1 *Locomotive Journal*, LXIX (February 1956), 48–9; *Railway Service Journal*, XLVI (September 1949), 399; *Transport Salaried Staffs Journal*, L (June 1953), 263; P. S. Bagwell, *The Railwaymen. The History of the National Union of Railwaymen*, I (London: George Allen & Unwin, 1963), pp. 662–3.
2 Earnings (male adults):

	1953	1962
Workshop staff	189s. 4d.	£14 18s.
Clerical staff	177s. 9d.	£15 2s.
Salaried staff (operating)	211s. 3d.	£19 5s.

B.T.C., *R. & A. 1953, 1962*, II, Table VIII–10, and *Annual Census of Staff 1953, 1962*.

3 W. Harris-Burland, confidential memo. on 'Wages, Earnings and Hours of work', 17 March 1955, B.T.C. Finance Committee Minutes, 24 March 1955, B.R.B. The deterioration was less pronounced with wage rates. Cf. S. G. Peitchinis, 'The Determination of the Wages of Railwaymen: A Study of British Experience, with a Comparative Study of Canadian, since 1914', unpublished University of London Ph.D. thesis, 1960, pp. 245ff.
4 A.S.L.E.F. E.C. Minutes, 9 December 1953, A.S.L.E.F.
5 Cabinet Conclusions, 14 and 15 December 1953, CAB128/26, P.R.O.; B.T.C. Minutes, 14 December 1953, B.R.B.; B.T.C., *R. & A. 1953*, I, p. 21, *1954*, I, pp. 26–7.
6 Lord Birkenhead, *Walter Monckton* (London: Weidenfeld & Nicolson, 1969), pp. 274–6, 291–3. See also Lord Butler, *The Art of Memory: Friends in Perspective* (London: Hodder & Stoughton, 1982), pp. 135–7.
7 Newspaper cuttings from Ministry of Labour and National Service: Industrial Relations Department file on 'British Railways and N.U.R. . . . Wage Claim', LAB10/823; Monckton, memo. on 'Industrial Disputes', 29 December 1953, and Cabinet Conclusions, same date, CAB129/64, CAB128/26, P.R.O.
8 A.S.L.E.F. E.C. Minutes, 21 September 1954, A.S.L.E.F.; Allen, memo. on 'Revised Salaries and Wage Structure – Railway Salaried and Conciliation Staff other than Footplate Staff', 13 October 1954, B.T.C. Minutes, 14

October 1954, B.R.B.; B.T.C., *R. & A. 1954*, I, p. 26; *Railway Gazette*, 15 October 1954.
9 A.S.L.E.F. E.C. Minutes, 18 November 1954, A.S.L.E.F.; N.U.R. E.C. Special Meeting, 10 November 1954, N.U.R. Proc., 1954, I, N.U.R.
10 Campbell, in *Railway Review*, 19 November 1954; Cabinet Conclusions, 13 December 1954, CAB128/27; note of a meeting between N.U.R. representatives and the Minister of Labour, 23 December 1954, in Ministry of Labour and National Service: Industrial Relations Department file on 'Difficulties Arising from Proposals for a New Wage Structure 1954–5', LAB10/1319, P.R.O.
11 Note of a meeting of Lennox-Boyd, Jenkins, Benstead and Monckton, 6 April 1954, and C. F. Heron (Monckton's Principal Private Secretary)–C. J. Maston (Assistant Secretary), 10 June 1954, LAB10/1319; Cabinet Conclusions, 7 April 1954, and see also 27 August, 8 and 21 September and 6 December 1954, CAB128/27, and correspondence in Ministry of Transport Correspondence and Papers: Labour and Staff Relations, MT115/14, P.R.O.
12 Cabinet Conclusions, 8 and 13–16 December 1954, CAB128/27, P.R.O.
13 Ibid., 22 December 1954; Birkenhead, *Monckton*, pp. 293–4.
14 *Interim Report of a Court of Inquiry into a Dispute between the British Transport Commission and the National Union of Railwaymen*, January 1955, pp. 4–7, P.P.1954–5, V, Cmd.9352; P. S. Bagwell, *The Railwaymen*, II, *The Beeching Era and After* (London: George Allen & Unwin, 1982), pp. 160–1.
15 Cabinet Conclusions, 4 and 6 January 1955, CAB128/28, P.R.O.; report of N.U.R. Negotiating Committee, 6 January 1955, and N.U.R. E.C. Special Meeting, 6 January 1955, N.U.R. Proc., 1955, I, N.U.R.; *Railway Review*, 14 January 1955.
16 Notes of a meeting between representatives of the B.T.C., N.U.R. and Monckton, 6 January 1955, Ministry of Labour and National Service: Industrial Relations Department file on 'Court of Inquiry. Dispute between N.U.R. and B.T.C. 1954', LAB10/1352, P.R.O.
17 I. Macleod–Monckton, 16 January 1955, Monckton–Macleod, 20 January 1955, Monckton Papers, Bodleian Library Oxford. *Star*, 7 January 1955 (cit. in Birkenhead, *Monckton*, p. 294); *Daily Mail*, 6 January 1955; *Times*, 6 January 1955; *Daily Telegraph*, 8 January 1955; and see also 'Lessons from the Railways', *The Economist*, 15 January 1955; Cabinet Conclusions, 3 and 24 January 1955, CAB128/28, P.R.O.; *Final Report of a Court of Inquiry . . .* January 1955, p. 25, P.P.1954–5, V, Cmd.9372.
18 A.S.L.E.F. E.C. Minutes 14 and 21 January, 15 April 1955, A.S.L.E.F.; Bagwell, *The Railwaymen*, I, p. 650.
19 Cabinet Conclusions, 19 April 1955, and see also 26 April 1955, CAB128/29, P.R.O.; notes of a meeting between representatives of A.S.L.E.F. and Monckton, 21 April 1955, Ministry of Labour and National Service: Industrial Relations Department file on 'A.S.L.E.F. Claim 1955–6', LAB10/1390, P.R.O. On the government's presentation of the dispute note Eden's radio broadcast of 29 May 1955, extract in Sir Anthony Eden, *Full Circle* (London: Cassell, 1960), pp. 284–5.
20 Cabinet Conclusions, 27 and 29 April, 3 May 1955, CAB128/29, P.R.O.; *Manchester Guardian*, 2 and 3 May 1955; T.U.C. *Congress Report 1955*, pp. 137–8, D. E. Butler, *The British General Election of 1955* (London:

Macmillan, 1955), pp. 88–9. For evidence of Labour Party pressure on A.S.L.E.F., exerted through the T.U.C., see note of A.S.L.E.F. meeting with T.U.C. 21 April 1955, A.S.L.E.F. file 51U, A.S.L.E.F., and Vic Feather's note, 29 April 1955, T.U.C. file on 'Industrial Dispute 1955. Locomotive Engineers and Firemen', T.U.C. 253–43, T.U.C. According to Birkenhead, *Monckton*, p. 300, Gaitskell thought that strikes were one of the main factors in Labour's defeat, but there is no reference to this in P. M. Williams, *Hugh Gaitskell: A Political Biography* (London: Jonathan Cape, 1979), and the issue remains clouded. Cf. *The Economist*, 23 and 30 April 1955, *New Statesman*, 21 May 1955.

21 Baty, in notes of a meeting between reps. of A.S.L.E.F. and Monckton, 24 May 1955, LAB10/1390, P.R.O.; B.T.C. Minutes, 21 April 1955, B.R.B.; J. Boyd-Carpenter, *Way of Life* (London: Sidgwick & Jackson, 1980), p. 114; *Manchester Guardian*, 25 April, 3 May 1955; *Locomotive Journal*, LXVIII (April 1955), 110.

22 Feather, confidential memo. on 'Railway Dispute: A.S.L.E.F.', 20 May 1955, T.U.C. 253–43; confidential report of B.T.C. Special Committee on Remuneration of Footplate Staff, 11 May, and additional note, 12 May 1955, in B.T.C. Special Meeting Minutes, 13 May 1955, B.R.B.; notes of a meeting between B.T.C. and A.S.L.E.F., 19 May 1955, and memo. on 'Railway Disputes', 26 May 1955, LAB10/1390, P.R.O.; B.T.C. 'Proposals in Regard to Drivers, Motormen, Firemen and Asst. Motormen', 16 May 1955, in R.S.C., Wage Negotiations, 1954–5, VI, B.R.B.

23 Cabinet Conclusions, 27 May and 2 June 1955, CAB128/29; 'Points for Minister's Opening Statement to A.S.L.E.F.', 26 May 1955, and notes of meetings, 24–8 May 1955, LAB10/1390, P.R.O.; N.U.R. E.C. Special Meeting Minutes, 25 April 1955, N.U.R. Proc., 1955, I, N.U.R., and Campbell–Allen, 13 May 1955; R.S.C., Wage Negotiations, 1954–5, VI B.R.B.; T.S.S.A. E.C. Minutes, 9 and 10 July 1955, M.R.C.

24 Boyd-Carpenter, *Way of Life*, pp. 108, 113; *Times*, 23 April, 10 and 21 May, 1 June 1955; *Manchester Guardian*, 19 April 1955; *Daily Mail*, 30 May 1955; *Daily Express*, 23 April, 30 May 1955; *Daily Herald*, 30 April, 1 June 1955; *New Statesman*, 23 April, 4 June 1955.

25 C. J. Maston, note, 19 April 1955, LAB10/1390, P.R.O. In fact, £340,000 was spent on the strike: A.S.L.E.F., *Annual Report for 1955*, p. 3.

26 Report by F.B.I. to the National Production Advisory Council on Industry on the 'Long Term Effects of Rail and Dock Strikes', circulated 29 June 1955, T.U.C. 253–43; *The Economist*, 18 June, *Railway Gazette*, 17 June 1955. The needs of industry were reduced during the strike by extending the Whitsun holiday: *New Statesman*, 4 June 1955.

27 Feather, memo. 20 May 1955, T.U.C. 253–43; Birkenhead, *Monckton*, p.296; Robertson–Baty, 6 June 1955, Robertson–Monckton, 8 June 1955, notes of meeting at Ministry of Labour, 11 and 13 June 1955, in R.S.C., Wage Negotiations, 1954–5, VI, B.R.B.; notes of Neden's discussion with Robertson, 10 June 1955, LAB10/1390; Cabinet Conclusions, 13 and 14 June 1955, CAB128/29, P.R.O.; B.T.C. Minutes, 16 June 1955, B.R.B.

28 Hallworth–Allen, 15 April 1955, in R.S.C., Wage Negotiations, 1954–5, V, B.R.B., and see also Hallworth–Neden, 25 April 1955, LAB10/1390, P.R.O.; *Railway Gazette*, 22 April and 24 June 1955.

29 Baty, in Minutes of Proceedings before the R.S.N.T., 4 November 1954, in

R.S.C., Wage Negotiations, 1954–5, III, B.R.B.; T.S.S.A. Special E.C. Minutes, 21 August 1954, M.R.C.

30 *Railway Review*, 27 May 1955; *Daily Herald*, 6 June 1955.

31 Cabinet Conclusions, 26 April 1955, CAB128/29, P.R.O.; *Locomotive Journal*, LXVIII (special strike issue, July–August 1955), 221–6; *Railway Review*, 27 May 1955; B.T.C., *R. & A. 1955*, I, p. 24; B. Murphy, *ASLEF 1880–1980. A Hundred Years of the Locoman's Trade Union* (London: A.S.L.E.F., 1980), p. 53.

32 *Railway Review*, 15 October, 19 November 1954; Allen, in Minutes of Proceedings before the R.S.N.T., 4 April 1955, in R.S.C., Wage Negotiations 1954–5, VI, B.R.B.

33 B.T.C., *R. & A. 1955*, I, p. 3; *The Economist*, 28 May 1955.

34 *Manchester Guardian*, 21 January, *The Economist*, 28 January 1956; Robertson, in notes of a discussion at an informal meeting between reps. of B.T.C. and of the N.U.R., T.S.S.A. and A.S.L.E.F., 24 November 1955, in R.S.C., Wage Negotiations, 1955–6, III, B.R.B.; Watkinson–Eden, 20 January 1956, Ministry of Transport Correspondence and Papers: Labour and Staff Relations, MT115/10, P.R.O.

35 Watkinson–Macmillan, 12 July 1956, LAB10/823, P.R.O.; T.S.S.A. E.C. Minutes, 13 October 1956, M.R.C.; N.U.R. E.C. Minutes, 10 September, 17 October 1956, N.U.R. Proc., 1956, I, N.U.R.

36 Robertson–Watkinson, 12 April 1957, and anon. memo., 18 June 1957, in B.R.B. I.R. 82–2–2.

37 R.S.N.T., Decision No.20, 19 March 1957, pp. 5–8, 10–11, B.R.B.; B.T.C., *R. & A. 1957*, I, p. 5.

38 Bagwell, *The Railwaymen*, I, p. 654.

39 *Railway Review*, 8 November 1957, *Railway Gazette*, 22 November 1957. The Commons debate was on 29 October.

40 L. J. Hamblin (Industrial Relations and Welfare Officer, B.T.C.), notes of a meeting in Sir John Benstead's Room, 10 January 1958, B.R.B. I.R. 82–2–14 Pt.2.

41 R.S.N.T., Decision No.21, 10 April 1958, pp. 6–10, B.R.B.; N.U.R. Special E.C. Minutes, 10 April 1958, N.U.R. Proc., 1958, I, N.U.R., A.S.L.E.F. E.C. Minutes, 11 April 1958, A.S.L.E.F.

42 Bagwell, *The Railwaymen*, I, pp. 663–4, II, p. 90.

43 H. Macmillan, *Riding the Storm 1956–1959* (London: Macmillan, 1971), pp. 711–14; M. Stewart, *Frank Cousins: A Study* (London: Hutchinson, 1968), pp. 53–7; G. Goodman, *The Awkward Warrior. Frank Cousins, His Life and Times* (London: Davis-Poynter, 1979), pp. 164–76.

44 B.T.C. Minutes, 24 April, 1 and 22 May 1958, B.R.B.; notes of meetings between reps. of the B.T.C. and of the N.U.R., A.S.L.E.F. and T.S.S.A., 16 April, 6, 7, 13 and 15 May 1958, and correspondence between Robertson and Watkinson, esp. private note from Robertson, 2 May 1958, B.R.B. I.R. 82–2–14 Pt. 4.

45 Notes of meeting . . . , 13 May 1958, B.R.B. I.R. 82–2–14 Pt. 4; T.S.S.A. Special E.C. Minutes, 14 May 1958, M.R.C. The Commission offered savings in the form of cuts in passenger services, while the government agreed to give the railways £25m. per annum more in investment in 1958 and 1959, and to relieve the Commission of certain obligations to maintain bridges and level crossings.

46 Notes of meetings . . . , 16 April, 13 May 1958, B.R.B. I.R. 82–2–14 Pt. 4. The extent to which the unions had committed themselves to operating cuts was a matter for argument. A.S.L.E.F. felt it had given no such commitment. See Minutes of meetings of the three rail unions, 17 and 28 April, A.S.L.E.F. File 51Y, A.S.L.E.F.

47 British Transport Officers' Guild (B.T.O.G.) Minutes, 4 December 1957, 12 June and 11 September 1958; Stanley Howes, 'The Foundation of the British Transport Officers' Guild', typescript, 1974, p. 9, B.T.O.G.

48 R.S.N.T., Decision No.20, 19 March 1957, pp. 10, 17, Decision No.21, 10 April 1958, pp. 11, 35, B.R.B. See also evidence of Greene and Valentine, 17–18 March 1958, in R.S.C., Wage Negotiations, 1957/8, B.R.B.

49 R.S.C. Sub-Committee Minutes, 22 April 1958, B.R.B. I.R. 82–2–14 Pt. 4. Brazier was Allen's assistant. The sub-committee was chaired by A. H. Nicholson who later became a Director of Industrial Relations at B.R.B. H.Q.

50 Notes of a meeting in Sir John Benstead's Room, 10 January 1958, B.R.B. I.R. 82–2–14 Pt. 2; Robertson, at meeting with the unions, 13 May 1958, B.R.B. I.R. 82–2–14 Pt. 4. The example of the Civil Service Pay Research Unit represented a precedent. Cf. *Times*, 18 August 1958.

51 *Report of Railway Pay Committee of Inquiry*, 2 March 1960, p. 8.

52 *Railway Review*, 18 July 1958, 27 February and 20 March 1959.

53 N.U.R. E.C. Minutes, March 1959, and Special Meeting Minutes, 31 March 1959, N.U.R. Proc., 1959, I, N.U.R.; A.S.L.E.F. E.C. Minutes, 23 March 1959, A.S.L.E.F.; Hallworth, press statement, 26 March 1959, and transcript of Greene, interviewed by Kenneth Harris for B.B.C. Home Service, 7 April 1959, in B.R.B. I.R. 82–2–20 Pt. 1; T.S.S.A. E.C. Minutes, 12 April 1959, M.R.C.

54 Notes of meeting between reps. of B.T.C. and of N.U.R., A.S.L.E.F. and T.S.S.A., 29 January 1960, in R.S.C., Railway Pay Review, 1958–60, I, B.R.B.; T.S.S.A. Special E.C. Minutes (at Ministry of Labour), 12 February 1960, M.R.C.; Bagwell, *The Railwaymen*, I, p. 656. Evans succeeded Hallworth in October 1960.

55 T.U.C., *Congress Report 1960*, p. 131; Guillebaud–Robertson, 8 February 1960, B.R.B. I.R. 82–2–16 Pt. 2; notes of meeting between reps. of B.T.C. and of N.U.R., A.S.L.E.F. and T.S.S.A., 12 February 1960, in R.S.C., Railway Pay Review, 1958–60, I, B.R.B.; T.S.S.A. E.C. Minutes, 12 February 1960, M.R.C.

56 Notes of meeting . . . , 12 February 1960, in R.S.C., Railway Pay Review, 1958–60, I, B.R.B. For pre-Guillebaud reactions see H. Macmillan, *Pointing the Way 1959–1960* (London: Macmillan, 1972), p. 219; J. Gillespie–H. E. Osborn, 2 June 1959, B.R.B. I.R. 82–2–20 Pt. 1; R.S.C., 'Application from the N.U.R. for a substantial Increase in Rates of Pay . . .', October 1959, B.R.B. I.R. 82–2–20 Pt. 2. The B.T.C. did extend holiday and overtime payments from 1 January 1959: B.T.C., *R. & A. 1959*, I, p. 15.

57 *Report of Railway Pay Committee of Inquiry*, pp. 22–3, 30–7, 39–42.

58 Greene, in *Railway Review*, 11 March 1960; T.S.S.A. E.C. Minutes, 6 March 1960, M.R.C., and *Transport Salaried Staff Journal*, LVII (April 1960), 114.

59 C. W. Guillebaud, *The Role of the Arbitrator in Industrial Wages Disputes* (Welwyn: Nisbet, 1970), pp. 7–8.

60 Macmillan, *Parl. Deb. (Commons)*, vol. 619 (Session 1959–60), 10 March 1960, 642–4.

61 Marples–Robertson and reply, 22 March 1960, Robertson–Marples, 6 May 1960, and reply, 9 May 1960, Robertson–Marples, 11 May 1960, Dunbar Papers on Railway Pay Review, 1960, B.R.B. I.R. 82–2–16 (Dunbar's File).

62 A. R. Dunbar, memo. to B.T.C. Establishment and Staff Committee on 'Cost of Wage and Salary Settlement', 19 December 1960, in B.T.C. Minutes, 22 December 1960, B.R.B.

63 *Locomotive Journal*, LXXIII (July 1960), 198; N.U.R., *National Union of Railwaymen and the PIB* (London: N.U.R., 1966), p. 10.

64 The analysis was drafted by D. W. Glassborrow, Economics Officer, B.T.C. Finance Department: confidential memo. on 'Report of the Railway Pay Committee of Inquiry', March 1960, B.R.B. I.R. 82–2–16 Pt. 2.

65 Charles McLeod, *All Change. Railway Industrial Relations in the Sixties* (London: Gower Press, 1970), pp. 108–9. McLeod became Chief Industrial Relations Officer in 1962.

66 Geoffrey Freeman Allen, *British Rail After Beeching* (London: Ian Allan, 1966), p. 12. See also R. Kelf-Cohen, *Twenty Years of Nationalisation. The British Experience* (London: Macmillan, 1969), p. 162.

67 Bagwell, *The Railwaymen*, II, p. 163, quoting from N.U.R, *National Union of Railwaymen and the P.I.B.*, pp. 11–12.

68 Glassborrow, memos. to Dunbar on 'The Guillebaud Report and Current Railway Wage Claim', 11 May 1961, and 'British Railways Wages and Salaries', 31 May 1961, B.R.B. I.R. 82–2–16 Pt. 2. For a similar view at regional level see H. C. Johnson (General Manager, E.R.)–Dunbar, 11 September 1961, B.R.B. I.R. 82–2–30 Pt. 1.

69 Dunbar–Sir Philip Warter (Deputy-Chairman), 24 January 1962, B.R.B. I.R. 82–2–30 Pt. 2; Memo. of meeting between the Chairman of the B.T.C. and reps. of N.U.R., A.S.L.E.F. and T.S.S.A., 31 January 1962, in R.S.C., Wage Negotiations, 1961–2, B.R.B.; Bagwell, *The Railwaymen*, II, pp. 163–4.

70 B.T.C., *R. & A. 1962*, I, p. 20; Memo. of meeting . . . , 31 January 1962, R.S.N.C. Minutes, 5 and 21 February 1962 (with note of discussion at the meeting on 5 February), in R.S.C., Wage Negotiations, 1961–2, B.R.B.; Webber–Macmillan and Greene–Macmillan, 7 February 1962, and press communiqué, 14 February 1962, B.R.B. I.R. 82–2–30 Pt. 2.

71 Note of discussion, 5 February 1962, and R.S.N.C. Minutes, 7 November 1962, in R.S.C., Wage Negotiations, 1961–2, B.R.B. Dunbar had estimated the cost of the 3 per cent award at £11.3m. for British Railways staff and £15.2m. for all staff: memo. 7 June 1962, B.T.C. Minutes, 14 June 1962, B.R.B. The 6 per cent award would be approximately twice these amounts.

72 Dunbar, memo. on 'Shorter Working Week', 22 February 1961, B.T.C. Minutes, 23 February 1961; B.T.C., confidential memo. on 'Shorter Working Week', 23 March 1961, attached to Minute 14/124; R.S.N.T., Decision No. 24, 20 July 1961, B.R.B.; B.T.C., *R. & A., 1961*, I, pp. 13–15.

73 R.S.N.T., Decision No. 25, 12 December 1961, p. 7, B.R.B.

74 At the R.S.N.T. Sir Roy Wilson, the Chairman, and Robert Willis were in favour, and the Commission's nominee, Sir Richard Sneddon was against: ibid., pp. 8–10. Wilson, Sneddon and Willis had replaced Forster, Aspley and Hall. The clerical section of the salaried staff obtained a 38-hour week from 24 December 1962. See R.S.N.T., Decision No. 26, 24 October 1962, and McLeod, memo. on 'Weekly rostered hours for clerks', 3 December 1962, R.S.C., Wage Negotiations, 1961–2, B.R.B.

75 D. H. Aldcroft, *British Railways in Transition: The Economic Problems of Britain's Railways since 1914* (London: Macmillan, 1968), pp. 168–72.

76 B. M. Deakin and T. Seward, *Productivity in Transport. A Study of Employment, Capital, Output, Productivity and Technical Change* (Cambridge: Cambridge University Press, 1969), pp. 190, 197, 205.

77 Note that the wagon-load statistics are affected by changes in freight traffic composition. For 1953–62, for example, coal wagon-loads increased from 11.16 to 13.32 tons, while merchandise loads increased from 3.85 to 4.27 tons. B.T.C., *R. & A. 1953–62*, II, Table XI.

78 Estimates of U.K. productivity for 1948–54 and 1953–60 indicate annual growth rates of 2.1 per cent and 1.9 per cent (G.D.P./labour force), and 1.8 per cent and 1.5 per cent ('total factor productivity', applying the method used for railways to the U.K.). See C. H. Feinstein, *National Income, Expenditure and Output of the United Kingdom, 1855–1965* (Cambridge: Cambridge University Press, 1972), T52–3, 97–8, 126–7, C.S.O., *National Income and Expenditure 1965–75* (1976), and Appendix C, Table 2.

79 *Railway Gazette*, 25 December 1953; Statement, October 1954, in B.T.C. Minutes, 14 October 1954, B.R.B.; T.S.S.A. Executive Sub-Committee Minutes, 13 February and 12 June 1954, and Special E.C. Minutes, 21 August 1954, M.R.C.

80 *Railway Gazette*, 29 March and 5 April 1957; McLeod, *All Change*, pp. 116–17. McLeod gives figures of £18m. and £10m., but the true position is unclear. The Finance Department included a figure of £15m. for the shorter working week in the estimated costs for 1962, but the regions put the extra cost at only £9m., and data provided for the first six months of 1962 indicate that the annual cost for regional salaried, conciliation and workshop staff was under £7m. These figures exclude H.Q. and non-railway staff. See B.R.B. I.R. 72–7–7 Pts. 5 and 7.

81 Cabinet Conclusions, 24 January 1955, CAB128/28; memo. of discussion held on 27 January 1955, n.d., in LAB10/1319, P.R.O.; Watkinson, *Parl. Deb. (Commons)*, vol. 536 (Session 1954–5), 3 February 1955, 1288–9; correspondence in B.R.B. I.R. 81–2–3 Pt. 1.

82 *The Economist*, 26 April 1958; A. R. Dunbar, 'Progress Report on Work Study', 22 February 1963, with report from E. J. Larkin on 'Work Study. Progress and Development 1956–1962', B.R.B. Minutes, 14 March 1963, B.R.B.; W. P. Allen, quoted in *Railway Review*, 3 January 1958. The single-manning agreement provided for single-manning of non-steam passenger trains (except where steam-heated) for scheduled non-stop runs of 200 miles or two hours (with diagrams limited to 200 miles or six hours) and of non-steam freight trains working with vacuum brakes up to 75 miles or two hours non-stop. Night working (12 midnight–6 a.m. with concessions to 1 a.m. and from 5 a.m.) was excluded.

83 British Railways Productivity Council Minutes, 30 November 1956, 24 April 1959; B.T.C. Minutes, 28 February, 21 November and 19 December 1957, B.R.B.

84 Dunbar and Margetts, memo. on 'Manning . . .', 17 July 1962, B.R.B. I.R. 171–14–1 Pt. 8. It should also be pointed out that the failure to build new locomotives with an automatic on/off boiler switch close to the driver, or to site controls for the water pick-up gear on Type 4 locomotives near the driver, helped to perpetuate double-manning.

85 G. H. K. Lund, 'The Study of Work', *British Transport Review*, VII (December 1962), 8.
86 Wastage rates from notes of meeting of R.S.N.C., 14 January 1958, supplementary statement No. 14, B.R.B. I.R. 82–2–15 Pt. 1. E.R. info. from H. C. Johnson–Dunbar, 11 September 1961, B.R.B. 82–2–30 Pt. 1.
87 A.S.L.E.F. Annual Assembly of Delegates, Report 1954, 27 May 1954, A.S.L.E.F.; Allen, memos. to B.T.C. Establishment and Staff Committee, 24 December 1954 and 21 November 1955, B.R.B.; Frank Gilbert (Chief Establishment and Staff Officer), memo. on 'Lodging Turns of Duty for Trainmen', 6 January 1956, in B.R.B. I.R. 72–9–1; memo. on 'British Railways – Western Region. Strike Against . . . Extra Lodging Turns' (n.d.), Ministry of Labour and National Service: Industrial Relations Department file on 'British Railways . . . Difficulties arising from the introduction of Lodging Turns 1954', LAB10/1298, P.R.O.
88 A.S.L.E.F. E.C. Minutes, 11 June, 18 August and 21 October 1954; Special Assembly of Delegates, 3 November 1954 and File 51/O, A.S.L.E.F.; memo. of meeting between reps. of B.T.C. and of N.U.R. and A.S.L.E.F., 16 November 1954; Sub-Committee Minutes, 6 October 1955; Allen, memos. to the B.T.C. Establishment and Staff Committee, 20 June 1956, and 10 April 1957, B.R.B. I.R. 72–9–1; British Railways Productivity Council Minutes, 24 April 1959, B.R.B. A.S.L.E.F. represented its demand for a total abolition of lodging at the R.S.N.C. in 1958, again without success.
89 Dunbar, evidence to Stedeford Advisory Group, S.A.G. Minutes, 23 May 1960, Beeching Papers, Box 1, B.R.B.; Ness–Dunbar, 20 June 1958, B.R.B. I.R. 80–10–3.
90 Greene, evidence to S.A.G., S.A.G. Minutes, 5 August 1960, B.R.B.; conversation with Lord Greene, 24 May 1982.
91 B.T.C. Minutes, 30 July 1959, 19 December 1957; B.T.C. Railways Sub-Commission Minutes, 22 December 1955, 20 December 1956, B.R.B.; *Railway Review*, 13 March 1959.
92 McLeod, *All Change*, pp. 53–5.
93 *Railway Review*, 1 July 1955. On the railways' image see H. A. Clegg, *The Changing System of Industrial Relations in Great Britain* (Oxford: Blackwell, 1979), p. 287.
94 Redundancy was a relatively minor phenomenon in the late 1950s. See *S.C. Nat. Ind.: B.R.*, 1960, Appendix 36, Annex 2. Of 20,825 salaried and 'conciliation' staff declared redundant in 1957–9, only 1,267 had been dismissed, most of them casualties of the closure of the Midland and Great Northern line.

8. The Modernisation Plan and investment

1 B.T.C., *Modernisation and Re-equipment of British Railways* (December 1954) (London: B.T.C., 1955) (hereafter '*Modernisation Plan*'); *Parl. Deb. (Commons)*, vol. 536 (Session 1954–5), 3 February 1955, 1307 (Butler); *Manchester Guardian*, 28 January 1955; *The Economist*, 29 January 1955. See also *Railway Gazette*, 28 January 1955.
2 *The Economist*, 15 and 29 January and 2 July 1955.
3 Evidence of Stevenson, *S.C. Nat. Ind.: B.R.*, 4 February 1960, Q. 152, cit. in A. J. Pearson, *Railways and the Nation* (London: George Allen & Unwin,

1964), pp. 82–3. Stevenson later denied that the expression 'hotch-potch' implied that the Plan was an ill-considered document: Q. 179.

4 C. D. Foster, *The Transport Problem* (1st. edn, London: Blackie, 1963), pp. 93–116, repeated with amendments in the second edition, 1975, pp. 97–119; S. Joy, *The Train That Ran Away. A Business History of British Railways 1948–1968* (London: Ian Allan, 1973), p. 43; *Commercial Motor*, 28 January 1955.

5 Wilson, remarks at a dinner, 10 October 1951, in Blee's notes, 11 October 1951, AN6/10, P.R.O.; meeting of R.E. Members with Pope and Barker, 23 January 1953, reported in R.E. Informal Meeting of Full-Time Members Minutes, 2 February 1953, B.R.B. Elliot later told Robertson that the Plan 'started with a talk between Wilson, Pope and myself' and claimed that there was an earlier R.E. plan to spend £100m.: Elliot–Robertson, 25 January 1955, Elliot Papers, AN6/2, P.R.O., and *Railway Gazette*, 23 November 1956. The members of the special committee were J. L. Harrington, John Ratter, S. B. Warder, A. C. B. Pickford and S. E. Parkhouse.

6 R.E., 'A Development Programme for British Railways', April 1953, Elliot Papers, AN6/3, P.R.O.

7 Ibid., and cf. R.E., Report of the Committee on Types of Motive Power, October 1951, B.R.B.

8 R.E. Informal Meeting of Full-Time Members Minutes, 11 May 1953; B.T.C. Minutes, 26 November 1953, 14 April 1954, B.R.B.

9 Churchill–Leathers, 30 May 1952, MT62/144; Leathers–Churchill, 3 October 1952, MT62/145; Leathers, memo. on 'Transport Bill: The Transport Levy', 2 October 1952, CAB129/50; Cabinet Conclusions, 15 December 1953, CAB128/26; Butler, memo. 30 December 1953, CAB129/50; Cabinet Conclusions, 10 February 1954, CAB128/27, P.R.O. See also note of a meeting of Ministry of Transport officials, 1 December 1954, in Ministry of Transport Correspondence and Papers: Finance Division: Modernisation and Re-equipment: Plan for British Railways, MT47/405, P.R.O.

10 Cabinet Conclusions, 10 February 1954, CAB128/27; Lennox-Boyd, memos. on 'B.T.C. Increase in Charges', 1 January and 6 February 1954, CAB129/65, P.R.O.

11 Conversation with Lord Boyd, 9 December 1982. On Robertson's lobbying, which was connected with a request for increased borrowing powers, see Robertson–Boyd-Carpenter, 18 October 1954, Ministry of Transport Correspondence and Papers: Parliamentary Bills and Orders (Transport (Borrowing Powers)), MT47/401, P.R.O.

12 L. Hannah, *Engineers, Managers and Politicians. The First Fifteen Years of Nationalised Electricity Supply in Britain* (London: Macmillan, 1982), pp. 49–51, 57–8, 74, 294; R. Kelf-Cohen, *Twenty Years of Nationalisation. The British Experience* (London: Macmillan, 1969), pp. 48, 199–200.

13 B.T.C. Minutes, 18 November 1954; B.T.C., Report on The Modernisation and Re-equipment of British Railways, October 1954 (hereafter 'Planning Committee report'), B.R.B.; B.T.C., *Modernisation Plan*.

14 B.T.C., *R. & A. 1954*, I, p. 32.

15 Planning Committee report, p. 40; *Modernisation Plan*, p. 18.

16 B.T.C., 'Confidential Reports of the Sub-Committees of the Planning Committee', October 1954 (contains second report of sub-committee No. II on 'Forms of Motive Power', 11 August 1954), pp. 39–42; B.T.C. Minutes, 19

August 1954, B.R.B.; Planning Committee report, pp. 17–18; *Modernisation Plan*, pp. 11, 14–15; M. R. Bonavia, *British Rail. The First 25 Years* (Newton Abbot: David & Charles, 1981), pp. 94–6 (Bonavia was one of the members of the sub-committee and later drafted the published version of the Plan).

17 *Modernisation Plan*, pp. 5–7; Geoffrey Freeman Allen, *British Rail After Beeching* (London: Ian Allan, 1966), p. 6.

18 Of the four 'outsiders', General Sir Daril Watson, Michael Bonavia, C. C. Inglis and S. B. Warder, only Watson was really new to railways. Inglis had served an apprenticeship with the London and South Western Railway, although he did not rejoin the industry until the age of 52 (in 1952), while Warder and Bonavia joined pre-nationalised companies when in their mid-thirties (in 1936 and 1945 respectively).

19 A. T. K. Grant (Assistant Secretary, Treasury)–I. Wild (Under-Secretary, M.T., and Director of Finance), 14 June 1954, MT47/405, P.R.O.; Watson, comments reported in notes of meeting, 24 June 1954, and Bonavia, memo. 21 October 1954, in B.R.B. 23–10–1 Pt. 1C.

20 B.T.C., confidential reports . . . , October 1954 (sub-committee No. I on 'Forecast and Brief Analysis of Traffic'), B.R.B.; Planning Committee report, p. 6; B.R.B., *R. & A. 1974*, p. 43 (1974 revenue derived from 1974 passenger-miles and average fares per mile in each category in 1953).

21 B.T.C., confidential reports . . . , October 1954 (sub-committee No., I), B.R.B.; Planning Committee report, pp. 7–10; B.T.C., *R. & A. 1962*, II, p. 154; B.R.B., *R. & A. 1964*, II, p. 37, *1974*, p. 44. For further details see Richard Pryke, *Public Enterprise in Practice. The British Experience of Nationalization over Two Decades* (London: MacGibbon and Kee, 1971), pp. 294–6, who also considers the railways' steel and raw material forecasts to have been reasonable in the circumstances.

22 Tait, 'Progress Report for July–September 1954', 7 October 1954, B.T.C. Finance Committee Minutes, 13 October 1954, B.R.B.

23 The other members were Pope, Ryan and Valentine. B.T.C. Minutes, 18 November 1954, B.R.B.

24 *Modernisation Plan*, pp. 5, 7–8, 34. The forecast of a 6 per cent increase in freight revenue by about 1974 may be contrasted with the (approximately) 30 per cent fall which occurred (1974 revenue derived from 1974 net ton-miles and average rates per ton-mile in each of the major categories in 1953).

25 Ibid., pp. 5, 33–4; Wilson, memo on 'Economics of Reconstruction and Re-equipment', 9 September 1953, B.R.B. 23–10–1 Pt. 1C; Tait, 'Progress Report for October–December 1954', 21 January 1955, B.T.C. Finance Committee Minutes, 10 February 1955, B.R.B. Wilson's memo., which was never formally considered by the Commission, estimated passenger benefits at £33m., freight benefits at £58m. and track savings at £7m. £14m. was then deducted as the cost of providing substitute road services.

26 'On the Right Track', *The Economist*, 29 January 1955.

27 Foster, *Transport Problem*, pp. 96–8.

28 *Modernisation Plan*, p. 31; Wilson, memo. 9 September 1953, B.R.B. 23–10–1 Pt. 1C. The difference between existing provision and the amount necessary to provide for depreciation at replacement cost was about £18m. for railway rolling stock in 1953, using Redfern's estimates, and £13m. as estimated by Wilson in 1953: B.T.C., *R. & A. 1953*, II, p. 46; P. Redfern, 'Net Investment

in Fixed Assets in the United Kingdom, 1938–53', *Journal of the Royal Statistical Society*, Series A, CXVIII (1955), 157, 171. The confusion over the purpose of the £15m. charge can be found in *The Economist*, 29 January 1955, Butler's statement to the Commons, 3 February 1955, *Parl. Deb. (Commons)*, vol. 536 (Session 1954–5), 1309, and (in ref. to the rate of return) M. Beesley and A. A. Walters, 'Investment in British Railways', *Westminster Bank Review* (May 1955), 5–6.

29 Robertson–Boyd-Carpenter, 7 January and 1 April 1955, MT47/405, P.R.O.; Planning Committee report, p. 43; *The British Transport Commission. Proposals for the Railways*, October 1956, pp. 29, 40, P.P. 1955–6, XXXVI, Cmd. 9880 (forecasts of net revenue improvements were extrapolated between the points in the table on p. 29, and the investment profile was assumed to follow the shape indicated by the annual totals given in Appendix B, p. 40).

30 Beesley and Walters, 'Investment', 6–7. Estimates of 'time costs' naturally vary with the capital sum to be spent. Here, costs are £150m. with an expenditure of £750m. (cf. the earlier estimate of £170m. with an expenditure of £800m.).

31 Barker, memo. on 'Re-equipment of British Railways', 16 November 1954, B.T.C. Minutes, 18 November 1954; Tait, 'Survey of British Railways Passenger Train Services', October 1954, B.T.C. Minutes, 11 November 1954, B.R.B.

32 Barker, memo. 16 November 1954, B.R.B.

33 Foster, *Transport Problem*, p. 96; D. H. Aldcroft, *British Railways in Transition: The Economic Problems of Britain's Railways since 1914* (London: Macmillan, 1968), p. 155.

34 Grant–Brittain, 8 January 1955, and Butt–Grant, 19 January 1955, Treasury file on British Transport Commission: Modernisation Plans, HOP89/01A, Treasury. See also Grant–Wild, 6 April 1955, and note of a meeting of Treasury, Ministry of Transport and B.T.C. representatives, 19 April 1955, MT47/405, P.R.O.

35 Butler, memo. on 'The Finances of the Railway Modernisation Plan', 19 January 1955, CAB129/73; Cabinet Conclusions, 20 January 1955, CAB128/28, P.R.O. (see also Lord Cherwell–Churchill, 14 January 1955, HOP89/01A, Treasury); British Transport Commission (Borrowing Powers) Act, 1955, 3 & 4 Eliz. II c.10.

36 Cabinet Conclusions, 13 and 20 January 1955, CAB128/28, P.R.O.

37 Ibid., 13 and 16 December 1954, 4 and 13 January 1955, CAB128/27–8, and cf. Wild–Stedman, 7 December 1954, referring to earlier discussions with the Treasury, MT47/405, P.R.O.

38 Grant–Wild, 6 April 1955, MT47/405, P.R.O. For information on other nationalised industries see Pryke, *Public Enterprise*, Part III, *passim*; M. V. Posner, 'Pricing and Investment in Nationalised Industries', in Alec Cairncross (ed.), *The Managed Economy* (Oxford: Blackwell, 1970), p. 95, and Hannah, *Engineers*, p. 52.

39 D. L. Munby, 'Economic Problems of British Railways', M. E. Beesley, 'Financial Criteria for Investment in Railways', and G. Mills and M. Howe, 'On Planning Railway Investment', in *Bulletin of the Oxford Institute of Statistics*, XXIV (February 1962), 1–59. See also C. D. Foster, 'Surplus Criteria for Investment', ibid., XXII (November 1960), 337ff.

40 General Staff memo. 21 March 1955, B.T.C. Minutes, 24 March 1955; B.T.C., Modernisation and Re-equipment of British Railways, General Instruction No. 1, 12 April 1955, Wansbrough-Jones Papers, Box 10, B.R.B.

41 Wansbrough-Jones–C. Barman, 13 April 1955, Wansbrough-Jones Papers, Box 12, B.R.B. The panels were operational by June 1955, and the Modernisation Committee's first meeting was on 6 July. The full list of panels is as follows: Coaching Stock, Communications, Continuous Brakes, Diesel de Luxe Multiple Units, Diesel Main Line Locomotives, Diesel Multiple Units, Electrification, Freight and Parcels Terminals, Marshalling Yards, Motive Power Depots, Packet Ports, Passenger Stations, Permanent Way and Bridges, Signalling, Traffic Survey and Wagons.

42 B.T.C. Minutes, 26 July 1956; Chairman's Conference on Modernisation Minutes, 21 September 1956, B.R.B. 22–40–15.

43 C. H. Feinstein, *National Income, Expenditure and Output of the United Kingdom, 1855–1965* (Cambridge: Cambridge University Press, 1972), T92–3; Pryke, *Public Enterprise*, p. 289.

44 Cf. B.T.C. General Staff memo. on 'Locomotive Construction', 10 May 1954, B.T.C.Minutes, 11 May 1954, B.R.B., and see also R. M. Tufnell, *The Diesel Impact on British Rail* (London: Mechanical Engineering Publications, 1979), pp. 11ff.

45 Track renewals, 1954–62: 14,101 miles or 1,556.8 miles per annum (cf. 1,575.3, 1948–53); C.W.R., 1954–62: 1,026 miles; A.W.S. 1,232 miles. B.T.C., *R. & A. 1954–62*, supplemented by information from B.R.B.

46 *Railway Gazette*, 27 December 1957; B.T.C. Minutes, 28 January 1954, B.R.B.

47 White Paper on *The Financial and Economic Obligations of the Nationalised Industries*, April 1961, p. 5, P.P. 1960–1, XXVII, Cmnd. 1337. The target return of 8 per cent 'after allowing for depreciation at historic cost', was omitted from the White Paper, but had been included in earlier drafts (see para. 23, draft White Paper and Marples–Robertson, 2 March 1961), B.T.C. Confidential Memo. for Minute 14/99, 1961, B.R.B.

48 E.g. D.M.U.s for Marylebone–Aylesbury–Princes Risborough (4 per cent return estimated on net outlay of £2.4m., 8 per cent on 'betterment' of £1.3m.) and diesels for Longsight Depot, Manchester (4 per cent on £2.6m., 5 per cent on £2.0m.). B.T.C. Finance Department Schedules of 'Investment 1960/61/62. Financial Effect of Schemes Included in Works and Equipment Budgets', November 1959, B.R.B. New Works 23–4–2.

49 Submissions to the B.R.B. Works and Equipment Committee, Minutes, 8 August 1959, 23 October 1962, B.R.B.

50 *S.C. Nat. Ind.: B.R.*, 1960, Appendices 9 and 10 (shows Leeds–Barnsley increase as 416 per cent); B.T.C., *R. & A. 1959*, I, pp. 81–2, *1960*, I. pp. 81–2.

51 B.T.C. Minutes, 26 January 1961; report on Temple Mills by Eastern Region Traffic Survey and Costing Office, 24 May 1962, Works and Equipment Committee Minutes, 7 November 1962, B.R.B. Net additional outlay was given as only £437,000 in the 'back-check', producing a 'return' of 53.3 per cent. Cf. note to Table 37.

52 H. C. Johnson, 'Main Line Electrification – A First Appraisal', *Journal of the Institute of Transport*, XXXII (January 1968), 295–302, and see Johnson–Marsh, 30 September 1969, B.R.B. New Works 182–6–22 Pt. 9.

53 B.T.C. Minutes, 9 and 16 February, 22 November 1956, 28 November 1957, 30 January 1958, B.R.B.; Watkinson–Robertson, 19 September 1957, B.T.C. General Staff memo. on 'Review of Investment, 1958 and 1959', 16 October 1957, B.T.C. Minutes, 17 October 1957, and Wansbrough-Jones–General Managers on 'Capital Investment Programmes 1958/1959', 3 June 1958, B.R.B. 23–4–2 Pt. 3.

54 Marples–Robertson, 26 February and 15 September 1960, B.R.B. 23–4–2 Pt. 3 and 4. Cf. R. W. R. Price, 'Public Expenditure', in F. T. Blackaby (ed.), *British Economic Policy 1960–74* (Cambridge: Cambridge University Press, 1978), p. 93.

55 General Staff memo. 8 December 1955, B.T.C. Minutes, 15 December 1955, B.R.B.; R. C. Bond–J. C. L. Train, 10 March 1954, J. H. Conway and J. Crowther, interim report of B.T.C. and L.M.A. Joint Cost Investigation, 18 July 1955, B.R.B. 171–6–1 Pt. 1.

56 M. Churchard (M.T.)–S. B. Taylor, 3 February 1954, ibid., and Watkinson–Robertson, 10 May 1956, B.R.B. 81–1–1 Pt. 1.

57 S. B. Warder, R. C. Bond, V. Radford and R. F. Harvey, memo. to Works and Equipment Committee, 29 September 1955, B.R.B. 171–6–5. See also Tufnell, *Diesel Impact*, pp. 11–12.

58 Joy, *Train That Ran Away*, p. 50.

59 Warder *et al.*, memo. 29 September 1955, B.R.B. 171–6–5; B.T.C. Minutes, 28 November 1957, 13 and 20 November 1958; Chairman's Conference on Modernisation Minutes, 10 January 1958, B.R.B. 22–40–15, and see also B.R.B. 171–3–1 Pt. 1.

60 Cf. T. A. Crowe (Chief Managing Director, North British Locomotive Co.)–Robertson, 26 January 1954, and Scottish Board for Industry Minutes, 15 October and 19 November 1954, B.R.B. 171–6–1 Pt. 1; Train, memo. 14 October 1954, B.T.C. Minutes, 26 October 1954; S. C. Robbins (Chief Contracts Officer), confidential memo. on 'North British Locomotive Co. Ltd.', 24 February 1961, Supply Committee Minutes, 3 March 1961, B.R.B. 232–88–3. See also Tufnell, *Diesel Impact*, pp. 16, 35, 40, 50, 139–51.

61 B.T.C. Works and Equipment Committee Minutes, 17 November 1954; B.T.C. Minutes, 26 July 1956; General Staff memo. on 'Standardisation of Main Line Diesel Locomotives', February 1959, B.R.B. 171–3–2 Pt. 1; *Proposals for the Railways*, Cmd.9880, p. 33. See also J. Johnson and R. A. Long, *British Railways Engineering* (London: Mechanical Engineering Publications, 1981), pp. 168–9, Tufnell, *Diesel Impact*, pp. 23–9.

62 B.T.C. Minutes, 31 January 1957, Chairman's Conference on Modernisation Minutes, 15 February 1957, B.R.B.

63 B.T.C., confidential report on 'Diesel and Electric Traction and the Passenger Services of the Future', April 1957, B.R.B.; General Staff memo. on 'Diesel Main Line Locomotives', 11 September 1957, B.T.C. Minutes, 19 September 1957, B.R.B.

64 R. A. Long–G. A. Culverwell, 7 March 1962, B.R.B. New Works 10–11–110 Pt. 13.

65 J. F. Harrison, 'Proposals for Further Investment in Diesel Locomotives', 3 January 1964, B.R.B. New Works 10–11–101. See also B.T.C. Technical Committee Minutes, 29 September 1961; Robbins, memo. on 'Locomotive Building Programme: Diesel Hydraulic Locomotives', 30 November 1961,

B.R.B. 171–748–2; B.R.B. Department of Chief Engineer (Traction and Rolling Stock), report on 'Diesel Electric and Diesel Hydraulic Locomotives on British Railways', August 1965, AN7/128, P.R.O. The locomotives are also discussed in E. S. Cox, Locomotive Panorama, II (London: Ian Allan, 1966), pp. 121–7, and Allen, British Rail After Beeching, pp. 109–14.

66 B.T.C. Minutes, 27 June and 19 September 1957, 26 June 1958, 14 September 1961; H. E. Osborn–Wansbrough-Jones, 4 July 1957, Ratter–Wansbrough-Jones, 9 August 1957, Robbins, memo. 3 March 1961, Ratter–Beeching, 21 September 1961, B.R.B. 232–88–3. For data on reliability and maintenance costs in 1971 see Railway Gazette International (December 1972).

67 Osborn–Wansbrough-Jones, 4 July 1957, note of meeting held in Secretary-General's Room, 29 July 1957, B.R.B. 232–88–3; J. Gillespie–J. F. Harrison, 6 April 1961, B.R.B. New Works 10–11–209 Pt. 2.

68 A. J. Pearson–Wansbrough-Jones and Ratter, 25 July 1956, Wansbrough-Jones Papers, Box 10; B.T.C. Minutes, 23 January 1958, B.R.B.

69 B.T.C. Traffic Policy Group, 'First Report. Part II – Passenger Traffic Policy', March 1956, 'Part I – Freight Traffic Policy', July 1956, Wansbrough-Jones Papers, Box 12; B.T.C. Minutes, 11 July 1956; Pearson, draft memo. on 'Future Freight Traffic Policy of British Railways', 20 November 1956; Wansbrough-Jones–Train and Watkins, 5 September 1957, Wansbrough-Jones Papers, Box 15, B.R.B.

70 Wansbrough-Jones–Train et al., 6 December 1957, Wansbrough-Jones Papers, Box 15, B.R.B.

71 S.C. Nat. Ind.: B.R., 1960, Appendix 17 (B.T.C. Memo. 4 February 1960); B.T.C., R. & A. 1960–2.

72 G. F. Fiennes, I Tried to Run a Railway (London: Ian Allan, 1967), pp. 77–8. Some schemes were stopped, notably Swanbourne (Bucks), Brookthorpe (Gloucester) and Walcot (Shrewsbury).

73 The London Midland Area Board was still acquiring the land for the project in 1961, and was unsure of B.T.C. intentions as late as September 1962: London Midland Area Board Minutes, 2 February 1961, 5 and 6 September 1962, B.R.B. For details of the ring route see, inter alia, B.T.C. Minutes, 26 February 1959, General Staff memo. 22 February 1960, B.T.C. Minutes, 25 February 1960, B.R.B.

74 B.T.C. Minutes, 23 April 1959, 26 May 1960, B.R.B.; Modern Railways, January 1960. Technical details are given in Allen, British Rail After Beeching, pp. 240ff, and Johnson and Long, British Railways Engineering, pp. 298ff.

75 Some of the problems were described in report of S.C. Nat. Ind.: B.R., July 1960, pp. lxvi–lxxii.

76 B.T.C. Minutes, 16 February 1956, B.R.B.; B.R.B. Technical Committee Special Meeting Minutes, 26 June 1963, B.R.B. For M.T. doubts about the decision see Stedman, note for Minister, 18 April 1956, MT115/3, P.R.O.

77 Barker, memo. on 'The Problems of the Wagon Fleet', 18 March 1960, B.R.B. 170–4–10 Pt. 6. Barker had warned of the dangers two years earlier in Barker–Robertson, confidential notes on 'Some Aspects of a Long Term Freight Policy', 11 February 1958, Wansbrough-Jones Papers, Box 15, B.R.B.

78 General Staff memo. on 'Fitting of Continuous Brakes to All Freight

Wagons', 15 April 1958, B.T.C. Minutes, 24 April 1958, B.R.B. The main reason for the cost escalation was the failure to include the costs of modifying couplings, buffers and axle boxes.
79 Barker, memo. 18 March 1960, B.R.B. 170–4–10 Pt. 6; General Staff memo. on 'The Economic Case for Automatic Couplers', 5 November 1956, B.R.B. 170–6–4 Pt. 1.
80 General Staff memo. 15 April 1958, B.R.B. The N.C.B. agreed to accept the wagons if the couplings were unscrewed and the vacuum pipes disconnected.
81 General Staff memo. 15 April 1958, B.R.B.; B.T.C. Minutes, 17 July 1958; Robertson, confidential memo. on '16 Ton Mineral Wagons with Fitted Brakes and Continental Screw Couplings', 24 July 1958, B.R.B.; Ratter, memo. 8 February 1960, and Minutes of a joint meeting of the Technical and Traffic Committees with the General Managers, 25 March 1960, B.R.B. 170–4–10, Pt. 6; B.T.C. Minutes, 26 May 1960, B.R.B.
82 Alec Valentine, confidential memo. to B.T.C., 8 September 1961; 'Claim for Damages Concerning the Agreement for the Manufacture and Supply of Vacuum Brake Cylinders to the British Transport Commission', 27 October 1961, B.R.B. 170–4–10 Pt. 7; B.T.C. Minutes, 14 September 1961, B.R.B.; R. B. Hoff, memo. to Supply Committee, 11 December 1963, B.R.B. 170–4–10 Pt. 8; confidential note to Beeching, 29 January 1964, and press release, 14 February 1964, B.R.B. 232–97–7.
83 *Proposals for the Railways*, Cmd.9880, p. 3; B.T.C., *R. & A. 1955*, II, pp. 3, 16A.
84 *Proposals for the Railways*, Cmd. 9880, pp. 28–9. It was realised that the government's concurrent plans to advance capital to cover interest and future railway deficits would alter the forecast shown in Table 34. The deficit in 1956 was estimated to be £45m., not £48m., and the surplus in 1970 was put at £35m. instead of £38m., ibid., p. 7.
85 Ibid., p. 3.
86 Ibid., pp. 5–6, 11, 20–3; J. E. Hartshorn, 'Doublethink about Transport Deficits', *The Banker*, CVI (December 1956), 765–71.
87 B.T.C., *R. & A. 1955*, I, pp. 3–4. Joy, *Train That Ran Away*, p. 48, also makes this point, although his arithmetic is confusing. Of course, higher wage costs might have made some of the returns to modernisation higher, where there was a significant labour-saving element.
88 4 & 5 Eliz. II c.54, extended by the Finance Act, 1958, 6 & 7 Eliz. II c.56; B.T.C., *R. & A. 1957–8*, I, Table V–16. The £221m. was borrowed at 5¼–6 per cent repayable over 25 years. By the end of 1958 £8.3m. had been repaid.
89 5 & 6 Eliz. II c.9; Robertson–Watkinson, 31 August 1956, B.R.B. 21–12–1 Pt. 1.
90 Robertson–Watkinson, 19 September 1957 and Benstead–Watkinson, 29 October 1957, B.R.B. 23–10–1 Pt. 2; Hartshorn, 'Doublethink', 771.
91 Watkinson–Robertson, 3 January 1958, MT47/405, P.R.O.; Watkinson–Robertson, 18 November 1958, B.T.C. Minutes, 20 November 1958, B.R.B. *Parl. Deb. (Commons)*, vol. 597 (Session 1958–9), 11 December 1958, 522–3 (Watkinson). Some of the correspondence was published as *British Transport Commission (Exchange of Correspondence): An Exchange of Correspondence between the Minister of Transport and Civil Aviation and the Chairman of the British Transport Commission*, September–October 1958,

P.P.1958–9, XXV, Cmnd.585. Borrowing Powers were extended by the Transport (Borrowing Powers) Act, 1959, 7 & 8, Eliz. II, c.16.

92 *The British Transport Commission. Re-appraisal of the Plan for the Modernisation and Re-equipment of British Railways,* July 1959, pp. 4–17, 19–24, 32–40, P.P.1958–9, XIX, Cmd.813; B.R.B., R. & A. 1963, II, *passim,* and see also B.R.B. 23–10–1 Pts. 2–4.

93 Cf. Pryke, *Public Enterprise,* pp. 296–8.

94 T. H. Hollingsworth, memo. to General Managers, 3 March 1959; Bowman–Robertson, 10 March 1959; Robertson–Watkinson, 12 March 1959, B.R.B. 23–10–1 Pt. 2. Additional information supplied to the government by the Commission put the railways' coal traffic in 1963 at 155–65m. tons and revenue at £166–24m. In fact, 1963 traffic amounted to 151.4m. tons and revenue to £107.9m. or £101.1m. at 1957 rates. See Treasury/Ministry of Transport Joint Memo. on 'Reappraisal of the Plan for the Modernisation and Re-equipment of British Railways', December 1959, Beeching Papers, Box 4, B.R.B.; B.R.B., R. & A. 1963, II, p. 49.

95 *Re-appraisal,* Cmd.813, pp. 22–4.

96 Ibid., pp. 27, 29. In 1959 prices the 1956 estimate would be *c.*£70m.

97 Ibid., pp. 13, 16, 28–31.

98 B.T.C., R. & A. 1959, I, p. 55, II, p. 64.

99 *Railway Gazette,* 17 April and 23 October 1959. Marples retained shares in Marples Ridgeway until 1960, when they were transferred to Nutraco Nominees Ltd.

100 *S.C. Nat. Ind.: B.R.,* 1960.

101 Treasury/Ministry of Transport Joint Memo. December 1959. The Memo. thought the Commission's predictions about coal too optimistic, and its forecasts about mineral traffic to be too pessimistic. Both suppositions proved incorrect. See also G. C. Wardale and R. Le Goy (M.T.), 'Departmental Examination with the Commission's Officers of the British Transport Commission's Reappraisal Report', 5 October 1959, Dunnett, memo. on 'The Railway Problem', 4 January 1960, Ministry of Transport Correspondence and Papers: Capital Investment: Reappraisal of Railway Modernisation Plan, MT115/77, P.R.O.

102 S.A.G. Minutes, 12 April 1960, Beeching Papers, Box 1, B.R.B.

103 Report of *S.C. Nat. Ind.: B.R.,* July 1960, pp. xlii–liii, lxxxvii–iii; Marples–Robertson, 26 February 1960, B.R.B. 23–4–2 Pt. 3.

104 Report of *S.C. Nat. Ind.: B.R.,* July 1960, pp. l–li. The earlier estimate of £75m. excluded signalling and the partial use of diesel locomotives. 'Expired life value' was defined as the theoretical accrued liability for renewal of the assets on a sinking fund basis: ibid., Appendix 25.

105 Ibid., pp. liii, lxxxix. To justify electrification, the Commission used a density yardstick of 4m. trailing ton-miles per mile of track per annum. Wilson defended the 'betterment' procedure in his memo. 'Modernisation v. Simple Replacement v. Scrapping', 9 June 1960, Wansbrough-Jones S.A.G. Papers, Box 2, B.R.B. (There is nothing wrong with the procedure *providing*: (i) the assets retained can be used elsewhere; (ii) allowance is made where assets are scrapped prematurely; (iii) the assets in question are already producing a return. For further criticisms of B.T.C. investment appraisal, see Beesley, 'Financial Criteria', 1962, 32–8.)

106 See reports of the Minister's views in S.A.G. Minutes, 11 and 20 May 1960, and confidential notes of a meeting between Marples and Stedeford, 26 May 1960, Beeching Papers, Box 7, B.R.B.

107 S.A.G. Minutes, 12 April, 13, 16 and 18 May, 3 June 1960; S.A.G. Recommendation No. 1, 22 June 1960, Beeching Papers, Box 8, B.R.B.

108 S.A.G. Minutes, 29 April, 20 and 27 May, 3, 8, 13 and 17 June (the meetings on 8 and 17 June were with Marples, the Paymaster-General, Lord Mills and Dunnett); Marples–Stedeford correspondence, 20–2 June 1960; S.A.G. Recommendation No. 2, June 1960, Beeching Papers, Boxes 7 and 8, B.R.B.

109 S.A.G. Minutes, 1 and 20 June, 6, 11 and 14 July, 14, 28 and 29 September 1960; Robertson–Stedeford correspondence, 24 and 30 June, 12 July, 30 August 1960; Marples–Stedeford, 7 July 1960; S.A.G. Recommendation Nos. 3 and 7, 27 July and 30 September 1960, Beeching Papers, Boxes 2, 7 and 8, B.R.B. The Group also moved the Newport (Teesside) marshalling yard scheme from category (a) to (d).

110 Beeching, 'Comments upon the London Midland Region Report, August 1960, on the Modernisation of the Euston Main Line', 21 September 1960, Beeching Papers, Box 8; Marples–Robertson, 30 January 1961, B.T.C. Minutes, 9 February 1961, B.R.B.; report of S.C. Nat. Ind.: B.R., July 1960, p. liii.

111 Four-Year Review, enclosed in Robertson–Marples, 19 December 1960, Beeching Papers, Box 4, B.R.B.; B.T.C., R. & A. 1961, I, p. 55.

112 S.A.G. Minutes, 13 and 16 May 1960; note of a meeting between Marples and Stedeford, 26 May 1960 (included caustic evaluation of Wilson by Stedeford), Beeching Papers, Box 7, B.R.B. On the Commission's coolness, see I. Wild–J. R. Willis, 13 April 1955, MT47/405, P.R.O., and V. Radford's memo. to the B.T.C. Finance Committee, 1 September 1955, commenting on the investment allocation fixed by the Treasury for 1955, Finance Committee Minutes, 7 September 1955, B.R.B.

113 Evidence Submitted to the Committee on the Working of the Monetary System (1960), II, pp. 773–98 (evidence of Lord Knollys (Vickers), Sir Patrick Hennessy (Ford), Viscount Chandos (A.E.I.), Lord Heyworth (Unilever), Lord Godber (Shell) and Stedeford (Tube Investments), 4–20 November 1958). The relevant extracts were noted inside the Commission. See Osborn–Wansbrough-Jones, 23 August 1960, Wansbrough-Jones S.A.G. Papers, Box 1, B.R.B.

114 Robertson–Stedeford, 3 June 1960, Wansbrough-Jones S.A.G. Papers, Box 2, B.R.B.

9. The 'Beeching Revolution': organisation and reorganisation

1 P.P.1960–1, XXVII, Cmnd.1337; Sir Richard Clarke, Public Expenditure, Management and Control (London: Macmillan, 1978), pp. 13–14; report of S.C. Nat. Ind.: B.R., July 1960, pp. lxxxiii, xcii–iii.

2 See below, p. 464.

3 Report of S.C. Nat. Ind.: B.R., July 1960, pp. lxxxiii–iv.

4 Macmillan, Parl. Deb. (Commons), vol. 619 (Session 1959–60), 10 March 1960, 644.

5 S.A.G. Minutes, 12 April 1960, Beeching Papers, Box 1, B.R.B.; Marples, Parl. Deb. (Commons), vol. 621 (Session 1959–60), 6 April 1960, 394; Hay,

ibid., 13 April 1960, 1395. Stedeford had once been suggested for member-ship of the B.T.C. See above, p. 61.

6 Robens and Wedgwood Benn, *Parl. Deb. (Commons)*, vol. 621 (Session 1959–60), 13 April 1960, 1343–9 (quotation, 1347), 1381–91.

7 S.A.G. Minutes, 12, 20 and 29 April 1960, 11 May 1960; Benson, paper on 'Basic Organisation', 21 April 1960; Beeching, 'Interpretation of the Terms of Reference of the Special Advisory Group', 3 May 1960, Beeching Papers, Box 7, B.R.B.

8 'Reorganisation of the British Transport Commission' (n.d.), and 'Extract of Letter from the Chancellor of the Exchequer to the Minister of Transport Dated 24th March 1960', documents circulated by Marples with the terms of reference, Beeching Papers, Box 8; Stevenson, 'Structure of Transport Industry in National Ownership', 6 May 1960, Box 6; S.A.G. Minutes, 11 and 18 May 1960, B.R.B.

9 Stedeford, 'Draft Proposals on Organisation', 17 August 1960, and Beeching, 'Reorganisation of Activities Controlled by the British Transport Commission', 19 August 1960, S.A.G. Minutes, 22 August 1960, B.R.B. Cf. earlier memoranda, and S.A.G. Minutes, 8 and 13 June 1960.

10 Conversation with Lord Beeching, 8 July 1980; S.A.G. Minutes, 2, 9, 14 and 21 September 1960, B.R.B.

11 S.A.G. Minutes, 14 April 1960; Robertson–Stedeford, 10 June 1960, in Wansbrough-Jones S.A.G. Papers, Box 2, B.R.B. On the Electricity Council and the organisation of 1958, see L. Hannah, *Engineers, Managers and Politicians. The First Fifteen Years of Nationalised Electricity Supply in Britain* (London: Macmillan, 1982), pp. 193ff.

12 S.A.G. Minutes, 21, 28, 29, 30 September and 3 October 1960; Serpell and Stevenson, memo. on 'Recommendations on the Structure and Organisation of the British Transport Commission', 28 September (revision, 29 September) 1960; S.A.G. Recommendation 8, 7 October 1960, Beeching Papers, Boxes 7 and 8, B.R.B.

13 S.A.G. Recommendation 8, and note also 'Comparison of S.A.G. Papers on Organisation', n.d. (a comparison of the September proposals of Stedeford and Beeching), Beeching Papers, Box 8, B.R.B. Stedeford envisaged the workshops under regional control, and property as a constituent body separate from B.R.B. Beeching wanted central B.R.B. control of the work-shops, and property as a B.R.B. subsidiary.

14 Notes of meetings of members of the Commission, 24 and 31 March, 6 April (the latter at Balliol College, Oxford) 1960, and Robertson, personal and confidential memo. on 'Organisation of the British Transport Commission to conform with the Policy of H.M.G. "The Broad Lines"', draft 30 March 1960 and revision, n.d., in Wansbrough-Jones S.A.G. Papers, Box 2, B.R.B.; Robertson–Stedeford on 'Reorganisation of the British Transport Commission', 10 June 1960; Stedeford–Robertson, 7 October 1960, enclosing Recommendation 8, Beeching Papers, Box 8, B.R.B. This Box contains the comments of most of the B.T.C. members in letters sent to Robertson, 1–9 November 1960.

15 Summerson–Robertson, 4 November 1960, Beeching Papers, Box 8, B.R.B.

16 Sinclair's 'minority view' is referred to in Hanks–Robertson, 10 November 1960; Ratter–Robertson, 9 November 1960; Barker, 'Management Struc-ture of British Railways', 27 October 1960, ibid. Sinclair and Hanks also

pressed Robertson to demand the integration of B.R.B. and British Road Services, but he refused to put this to the Minister: Hanks–Robertson, 10 November 1960, and reply, 14 November 1960, ibid.

17 Based on 'Aide-Mémoire Approved by the Commission for Use by the Chairman in Discussing with the Minister Recommendation No. 8 (Organisation) of the S.A.G.' n.d., ibid.; B.T.C. Minutes, 16 November 1960, B.R.B.

18 M.T., *Reorganisation of the Nationalised Transport Undertakings*, December 1960, P.P.1960–1, XXVII, Cmnd.1248, pp. 4–8, 14. The issue of the Minister's role was raised by *The Economist*, 24 December 1960.

19 *Manchester Guardian*, 21 December 1960 (this view was also expressed by G. R. Strauss in a Commons exchange on the White Paper: *Parl. Deb. (Commons)*, vol. 632 (Session 1960–1), 21 December 1960, 1302); *Railway Gazette*, 23 and 30 December 1960, 6 January 1961; *Times, Financial Times* and *Daily Worker*, all 21 December 1960; *Railway Review*, 30 December 1960; *Locomotive Journal*, February 1961.

20 Wansbrough-Jones–Beeching, 11 October 1961, Wansbrough-Jones–Serpell, 31 October 1961, Wansbrough-Jones's RENT Papers, Boxes 5, 6, B.R.B. On RENT see D. S. M. Barrie, memo. on 'Organisation', 7 February 1961, and M.T., Memo. on 'Reorganisation of the Nationalised Transport Undertakings. List of Main Topics to be Covered by Legislation Arising from the White Paper Proposals (Revise)', R.E.N.T.1, February 1961, RENT Box 7, B.R.B. The Treasury also had a representative.

21 B.T.C. press statement, 20 December 1960, RENT Box 7; B.T.C. Minutes, 22 December 1960, B.R.B.

22 *Railway Gazette*, 27 January (and see also 6 and 13 January) 1961; *Reorganisation*, Cmnd.1248, p. 8. Ratter and Grand had both been members of the Ministerial Group on Modernisation, set up in August 1960 to examine railway investment and the future size of the railway network.

23 Marples–Beeching, 30 March 1961, B.T.C. S1–1–22E, B.R.B.; Formal Documents of Appointment, December 1962, B.R.B. In conversation with the author (8 July 1980) Beeching said that his private understanding with Marples was that he would serve for three years.

24 *The Economist*, 25 March 1961, *Times*, 16 March 1961; *The Financial and Economic Obligations of the Nationalised Industries*, April 1961, Cmnd.1337, pp. 7–9.

25 Peter Brome (Marks and Spencer)–Beeching, 7 April 1960, Beeching Papers, Box 6, B.R.B.

26 A. Sampson, *Anatomy of Britain Today* (London: Hodder & Stoughton, 1965), p. 582.

27 B.T.C. Minutes, 13 September 1961, 11 July 1962, B.R.B. The Waterways Sub-Commission was resuscitated in August 1962 prior to the establishment of an Inland Waterways Board: B.T.C. Minutes, 23 August 1962, B.R.B.

28 Appraisals were extended to 8,000 staff in 1962. See Wansbrough-Jones, note to W. J. Sharp (M.T.) on 'Preparation for Higher Management: Staff Appraisals', 23 January 1962, RENT Box 6; B.T.C. Minutes, 8 June 1961; Dunbar, memo. on 'Preparation for Higher Management', 19 February 1962, B.T.C. Minutes, 22 February 1962, B.R.B. On the earlier origins of management development, see B.T.C. Minutes, 20 February 1958, 19 November 1959, 16 March 1961, B.R.B.

29 Conversation with Beeching, 8 July 1980. The incident occurred at the B.T.C. meeting of 18 June or 11 July 1962.

30 Beeching–Marples, 9 June 1961, Marples–Beeching, 22 June 1961, and supporting papers in RENT Box 3; Wansbrough-Jones–Beeching, 11 October 1961, RENT Box 5, B.R.B.

31 *Financial Times* and *Times*, 18 August 1961; *Who's Who*, 1983; *Who Was Who 1971–80*; Benson–Beeching, 21 March 1961, B.R.B. 48–2–13.

32 Maj.-Gen. G. N. Russell (Chairman); H. L. 'Roy' Matthews, Chairman of Crosse and Blackwell and a Southern Area Board member (Deputy-Chairman); Sir Reginald Wilson (Managing Director); and the property developers, F. J. Howe and Harold Samuel. *Financial Times*, 19 and 25 August 1961; B.T.C. Minutes, 27 July and 12 October 1961, 13 June 1962, B.R.B. Howe was ex-Chairman of Liverpool Victoria Friendly Society, while Samuel was Director of Land Securities Investment Trust Ltd.

33 *Financial Times*, 18 August 1961; B.R.B. 48–2–5, 10 and 13.

34 See, *inter alia*, Shirley, memo. 15 March 1962, memo. on 'Stores Organisation', 24 August 1962, memo. on 'Finance Group', 30 March 1962; B.T.C. Minutes, 7 and 15 March, 14 June and 12 September 1962, B.T.C. Supply Committee Minutes, 23 August 1962, B.R.B.; B.R.B. 30–10–2 Pt. 6.

35 Dunbar, memo. to B.T.C. Establishment and Staff Committee, 28 February 1962; Warter, confidential memo. 26 February 1962; B.T.C. Minutes, 8 February, 8 March, 14 June and 11 July 1962; Shirley and Williams, memo. on 'Administrative and Clerical Staff', 3 May 1962, B.T.C. Minutes, 9 May 1962, B.R.B.

36 Shirley–Wansbrough-Jones, 29 December 1961; Wansbrough-Jones, memo. 29 January 1962, and other material in B.R.B. 30–19–2; B.T.C. Minutes, 13 June and 11 July 1962, B.R.B. Cf. the way in which Kearton set about sweeping away the too numerous committees in Courtaulds's organisation in the early 1960s: D. C. Coleman, *Courtaulds. An Economic and Social History*, III, *Crisis and Change 1940–1965* (Oxford: Clarendon Press, 1980), p. 246.

37 B.T.C., *R. & A. 1962*, I, p. 24; Dunbar, memo. on 'Manpower Organisation, British Railways', 8 June 1962, B.T.C. Minutes, 14 June 1962; memo. on 'Manpower Organisation: British Railways', 23 July 1962, B.R.B. 30–2–5 Pt. 2.

38 Marples–Beeching, 20 November 1961, 12 January and 27 February 1962, Beeching–Marples, 25 January 1962, B.R.B. 30–2–4 Pt. 2; B.T.C. Minutes, 7 March and 11 April 1962, B.R.B. There were functional roles for Russell (Estate and Rating, Railway Sites) and Summerson (Design Panel), and Williams also had responsibility for Public Relations and Publicity.

39 British Railways Committee Minutes, 24 May, 26 July, 27 September and 25 October 1962; Ratter, memos. of 24 and 31 July 1962, B.R. Committee Minutes, 23 August 1962; B.T.C. Minutes, 11 April, 14 June and 8 August 1962, B.R.B.

40 He was also an opponent of the diminution of regional authority (see below). Shirley–Summerson, 21 December 1961, commenting on North Eastern Area Board memo. on 'Government Policy for Inland Surface Transport', 18 July 1961, in B.R.B. 21–12–1 Pt. 2 and see also B.R.B. 48–2–4.

41 B.R.B. 48–2–6, 48–2–14, 48–2–16; memo. on 'Commercial Organisation. British Railways Board Headquarters', 7 October 1963, B.R.B. Minutes, 10

October 1963, B.R.B.; Ness, memo. on 'Planning', n.d. (mid-1965), B.R.B. 30–2–10 Pt. 1.

42 See e.g. Graham Turner, *Business in Britain* (London: Eyre & Spottiswoode, 1969), p. 185; J. Johnson and R. A. Long, *British Railways Engineering, 1948–80* (London: Mechanical Engineering Publications, 1981), p. 74.

43 Garratt, aged 45, was appointed at a salary of £4,000: Dunbar, confidential memo. 27 September 1961, B.T.C. Minutes, 28 September 1961, B.R.B. On Publicity and Public Relations see: B.T.C. Minutes, 12 December 1962; Beeching's address to the Public Relations and Publicity Committee, Minutes, 10 January 1962, and Garratt, memo. on 'Organisation: Publicity Division of the Public Relations and Publicity Department', 9 July 1965, in B.R.B. P.R. & P. 301–1–1 Pt. 1; Marples–Beeching, 25 April 1963, Garratt–Ness, 24 February 1964, and Garratt, memo. on 'The Presentation of "The Reshaping of British Railways"', 6 August 1964, in B.R.B. P.R. & P. 21–12–12 Pt. 2.

44 B.T.C. Minutes, 13 December 1961, 7 November 1962, B.R.B., and see Appendix I, Chart III. McKenna had been Assistant General Manager of the Southern Region before moving to H.Q. in 1962.

45 Conversation with Fiennes, 8 September 1983; B.R.B. 48–2–22, 23, 31.

46 B.T.C. Minutes, 22 March 1962, B.R.B. Oil traffic amounted to 5.1m. tons in 1962. Williams's forecast for 1972 was 20m. tons – actual traffic was 21.3m., B.R.B., *R. & A. 1973*, p. 5. Other newcomers in 1962–3 included: R. B. W. Bolland (Head Wrightson), Assistant General Manager, Scottish Region; T. G. P. Bond (Lever Bros.), Director of Marketing Development; P. J. Butcher (I.C.I.), Director of Work Study; F. H. Culpin (Asiatic Petroleum), Executive Member, London Midland Board; J. R. G. Flynn (Shell), Assistant General Manager, Western Region; J. W. Fraser (Great Universal Stores), Assistant General Manager (Finance), North Eastern Region; J. H. Nunnelly (Beaverbrook Newspapers), Chief Publicity Officer, later Chief Development Officer (Passenger); B. J. Rusbridge (I.C.I.), Industrial Relations Officer; and G. White (G.P.O.), General Manager, Road Motor Division.

47 Cf. Williams–Raymond, 24 August 1965, in B.R.B. 30–2–10 Pt. 1.

48 J. S. Birch (Director of Funds), memo. to Finance Committee on 'Future Banking Arrangements for British Railways', 11 December 1962, B.R.B. Finance Committee Minutes, 12 December 1962, and *British Railways Management Quarterly*, No. 3 (November 1964), 33–6; Shirley, memos. on '"The Paper Chase"', 26 June 1963, 'Supplies Department', 1 August 1963, 'Supplies and Contracts Department', 6 February and 7 August 1964, B.R.B. Minutes, 8 August 1963, 13 February and 13 August 1964. Sales of scrap also realised £20m. in 1965: Shirley, memo. on 'Supplies Department', 28 January 1966, B.R.B. Minutes, 10 February 1966.

49 Raymond, private and personal memo. on 'H.Q. Organisation', 3 February 1967, B.R.B. 30–2–10 Pt. 1.

50 This is based on two separate accounts of the same incident. Both contend that Stewart was General Manager (he succeeded Thorpe on 1 July 1967), but the only record of a visit to Scotland by Shirley is in May 1966, when Stewart was an Assistant General Manager: Scottish Regional Board Minutes, 3 and 4 May 1966, B.R.B.

51 B.T.C. Minutes, 7 March and 13 December 1962, B.R.B.; B.R.B. Minutes, 14

February, 11 July 1963, 22 August and 22 October 1964; British Railways Management Committee Minutes, 25 September 1963, B.R.B.

52 The officers were R. A. Long, J. H. Nunneley and S. C. Robbins. On these organisational changes, see B.R.B. Minutes, 28 November 1963, 23 January and 27 February 1964; J. F. Harrison (Chief Engineer, Traction and Rolling Stock), confidential report on 'The Working of the C.M.E. Department', 1 November 1963, B.R.B. Minutes, 14 November 1963, 10 December 1964; B.R.B., 'Commercial Organisation at H.Q. Arrangements to be Introduced on Monday 26 October 1964', B.R.B. I.R. 48–30–1 Pt. 2; *British Railways Management Quarterly*, No. 3 (November 1964), 9–10, B.R.B.

53 Raymond, private memo. 28 June 1965, and Ratter–Raymond, 30 July 1965, B.R.B. 30–2–10 Pt. 1.

54 The outsiders were A. V. Barker (Southern), R. B. W. Bolland (Scottish), J. R. G. Flynn (Western), J. W. Fraser (North Eastern) and F. H. Culpin (London Midland) (the latter was not formally an Assistant General Manager, but was considered to be of that rank – he was an Executive Member of the Regional Board). Later on, in January 1965, J. E. Brenan (Canadian National) became Assistant General Manager (Finance), Eastern Region. On regional organisation see J. E. M. Roberts (Chief Management Staff Officer), memos. to M.S.C. on 'North Eastern Region: Developments in Management Structure and in Functional Organisation', 1 January and 7 February 1963, M.S.C. Minutes, 16 January, 6 February, 15 May 1963, Mitchell, memo. on 'Management Structure', 16 May 1963, B.R.B. Minutes, 23 May 1963.

55 Garratt–Williams, 27 April 1962, B.R.B. P.R. & P. 301–1–1 Pt. 1; British Railways Committee Minutes, 22 November 1962; Wansbrough-Jones–Regional Railways Boards on 'Delegation of Functions and Authority to Regional Railways Boards', 31 December 1962, and 15 August 1963, B.R.B. 30–21–1, Pt. 3; Russell, memo. on 'Committees. Terms of Reference: Property Committee', 17 May 1963, B.R.B. Minutes, 23 May 1963; B.R.B. Minutes, 13 and 20 December 1963; B.R.B. Works and Equipment Regulations, January 1963, B.R.B. Minutes, 10 January 1963. The salary limit became £3,300 in 1964; Dunbar–Boards, 18 August 1964, B.R.B. 30–21–1 Pt. 4.

56 Margetts, memo. on 'Development and Control. Wagon and Container Fleets', 8 October 1962, British Railways Committee Minutes, 25 October 1962, B.R.B., and memo. 4 July 1963, B.R.B. Minutes, 11 July 1963; B.R.B. 172–1–7.

57 The delay was in part explained by the decision not to appoint an external candidate, J. H. Halsall, ex-Managing Director of Tube Investments (Export): see Dunbar, memo. to M.S.C., 16 September 1963, M.S.C. Minutes, 2 October and 4 December 1963, B.R.B. For regional dissent see, *inter alia*, North Eastern Area Board Minutes, 14 September 1962; Johnson–Wansbrough-Jones, 1 January 1963, B.R.B. 30–21–1 Pt. 3; London Midland Board Minutes, 9 and 10 January 1963, B.R.B.

58 Roberts–Dunbar on 'Next Steps in Management Development', September 1964, in Dunbar, memo. 30 September 1964, M.S.C. Minutes, 7 October 1964, B.R.B. 'Poaching' by the centre led the General Managers to demand representation on the M.S.C.: British Railways Management Committee Minutes, 23 September, 21 October 1964, B.R.B.

59 Memo. (by Dunbar?), 24 March 1964, in B.R.B. 30–3–50 Pt. 1. On the treatment of Johnson see B.R.B. 30–3–65.

60 The full introduction of a two-tier movements organisation in the region was planned to come into effect in 1969. Roberts, memos. to M.S.C., 3 April and 12 May 1964, M.S.C. Minutes, 17 March, 15 April, 20 May 1964; London Midland Board Minutes, 31 March and 1 April 1965, 6 July 1966; L.M.R., private and confidential report on 'Organisation Changes in the London Midland Region', March 1965, M.S.C. Minutes, 11 and 17 March 1965, B.R.B.

61 W. J. Oliver (British Tourist Authority)–R. W. Crawshaw (Public Relations and Publicity Officer, L.M.R.), 21 December 1964, M.S.C. Minutes, 27 January 1965; Johnson–Williams, 11 January 1966, Williams, memo. on 'Fixing and Maintenance . . .', 3 May 1966; British Railways Management Committee Minutes, 22 and 29 January 1964, 27 January 1965, 25 May 1966, B.R.B.; B.R.B. Minutes, 11 June 1964, 28 January 1965, 26 May 1966.

62 Labour Party, *Let's Go With Labour for the New Britain* (1964), pp. 11–12; *The Economist*, 1 January 1966. Fraser, born in 1911, had been M.P. for Hamilton since 1943. He was Parliamentary Private Secretary to the President of the Board of Trade, 1944–5, and Joint Parliamentary Under-Secretary of State for Scotland, 1945–51. On Labour's unpreparedness see D. Coates, *The Labour Party and the Struggle for Socialism* (Cambridge: Cambridge University Press, 1975), p. 101, and on Wilson see above, pp. 94–5.

63 B.R.B., *The Development of the Major Railway Trunk Routes* (London: B.R.B., 1965); British Railways Management Committee Minutes, 24 February 1965, B.R.B.

64 Cabinet Conclusions, 15 December 1964; the memoirs of Christopher Hinton, pp. 486–7, HINT4/8, Hinton Papers, Churchill College, Cambridge; *Times*, 23 and 25 November, 17, 21 and 24 December 1964; *Observer*, 14 February 1965, *The Economist*, 2 January 1965, *Financial Times*, 9 February 1965; G. Goodman, *The Awkward Warrior. Frank Cousins, His Life and Times* (London: Davis-Poynter, 1979), pp. 426–7; R. Crossman, *The Diaries of a Cabinet Minister*, I (London: Hamish Hamilton and Jonathan Cape, 1975), pp. 100–3.

65 B.R.B., *A Study of the Relative True Costs of Rail and Road Freight Transport over Trunk Routes* (London: B.R.B., 1964); Cousins, *Parl. Deb. (Commons)*, vol. 720 (Session 1965–6), 16 November 1965, 1058, and cf. Fraser's denial, vol. 721, 1 December 1965, Written Answer, 60. See also *Times*, 24 December 1964; *The Economist*, 2 January 1965; Arnold Strang in *New Statesman*, 29 July 1966; Beeching's conversations with Kenneth Harris, printed as 'Beeching: What I Would Do', *Observer*, 17 and 24 January 1965; H. Wilson, *The Labour Government, 1964–70. A Personal Record* (London: Weidenfeld & Nicolson, 1971), p. 184.

66 Fraser–Raymond, 10 May 1965, B.R.B. 48–2–14; *Daily Mail, Daily Telegraph, Guardian* and *Daily Worker*, all 22 April 1965.

67 *Financial Times*, 22 April 1965.

68 See correspondence in B.R.B. 30–2–10 Pt. 1.

69 James, aged 60, the former Chief Financial Officer of the London Transport Executive, had joined the Commission in 1960 as Chief Accountant at H.Q.,

and succeeded Osborn as head of the Finance Department in January 1963. He was duly appointed for a three-year term (salary: £8,000). Raymond–Fraser, 21 May 1965, B.R.B. 48–2–2; Raymond, memo. 18 June 1965, B.R.B. 48–2–20; B.R.B. Minutes, 12 August 1965. Dunbar took Raymond's place as Chairman of the M.S.C.

70 'Appointments to the British Railways Board. Notes of a Meeting in Room 8/57 St. Christopher House on 22nd October 1965'; Raymond, note, 28 October 1965, B.R.B. 48–2–1 Pt. 1. Jones had succeeded Inglis as Chief of Research in August 1964: B.R.B. 48–2–23.

71 Meeting, 22 October 1965, and Fraser–Raymond, 12 November 1965, B.R.B. 48–2–2.

72 Fraser–Raymond, 12 and 23 November 1965, B.R.B. 48–2–2; Planning Committee memo. on 'Planning Policy: Diesel Main-Line Locomotives', 13 November 1963; B.R.B. Minutes, 11 July and 14 November 1963; Planning Committee Minutes, 18 September 1963; Ness, memo. on 'Planning', 1965, B.R.B. 30–2–10 Pt. 1; B.R.B. Minutes, 10 March 1966; Cooper Bros., report to J.S.G. on 'B.R. Management Structure', 5 June 1967, B.R.B.

73 The E.R./N.E.R. merger was discussed at the meeting on 22 October 1965, B.R.B. 48–2–1 Pt. 1. See also M. R. Bonavia, *The Organisation of British Railways* (London: Ian Allan, 1971), pp. 106–7. On advertising and the Secretary's Department see B.R.B. Minutes, 12 August 1965, and B.R.B., *R. & A. 1965*, I, p. 11.

74 'Mr. Fraser's Trump', *The Economist*, 13 February 1965; 'The Human Steamroller', *Observer*, 14 February 1965; Hannah, *Engineers*, pp. 186, 264. *The Financial Times*, 9 February 1965, noted that Hinton and Beeching were both 'men who have acquired very tough reputations because, with unshakeable confidence in their lucid minds, they move like bulldozers once they have come to a conclusion'.

75 Hinton memoirs, pp. 488–90, HINT4/8; Hinton, reports on 'Inter-Urban Traffic. Stage I', 'Urban Transport. Part Two' and 'The Carriage of Parcels and Smalls', M.T. retyped versions, dated January 1968, HINT1/3–5, Hinton Papers, Churchill College, Cambridge; Cabinet Conclusions, 15 June 1965, Cabinet Office; *The Economist*, 20 November 1965; Report to the Minister of Transport on Operational Co-ordination of Public Passenger Transport (January 1966), presented by the Chairmen of B.R.B., L.T., Transport Holding Co. and British Electric Traction Omnibus Services Ltd., B.R.B. Hinton's work on sundries was facilitated by contacts with B.R.B. See Hinton–Raymond, 30 July 1965, etc., B.R.B. 30–3–44 Pt. 1.

76 Garratt–Margetts, 11 March 1965, B.R.B. P.R. & P. 21–12–12 Pt. 2; P. S. Bagwell, *The Railwaymen*, II, *The Beeching Era and After* (London: George Allen & Unwin, 1982), p. 151, B. Castle, *The Castle Diaries 1964–70* (London: Weidenfeld & Nicolson, 1984), p. 79.

77 M.T., *Transport Policy*, July 1966, *British Waterways*, September 1967, P.P.1966–7, LIX, Cmnd.3057, 3401; *Railway Policy*, November 1967, *The Transport of Freight*, November 1967, and (with Scottish Development Department and the Welsh Office), *Public Transport and Traffic*, December 1967, P.P.1967–8, XXXIX, Cmnd.3439, 3470, 3481. These were followed by *Transport in London*, July 1968, Cmnd.3686.

78 *Guardian*, 6 January 1966, *Sunday Times*, 9 January 1966, *The Economist*,

15 January 1966. For Padmore's views see *Sunday Times*, 9 January 1966, and Castle, *Diaries*, pp.79–80, 83, 89. *The Economist* had earlier called the Ministry 'a bumbling ant-heap', 4 September 1965.

79 *Financial Times*, 30 September 1965; *Times*, 7 and 12 January 1966; *Motor Transport*, 14 January 1966; Castle, *Diaries*, pp. 89–92.

80 British Railways Management Committee Minutes, 22 December 1965, B.R.B.; *Times*, 17 January 1966. Raymond was here referring to the initiative re rail closures. He later suggested that Castle herself had been responsible for the 'leaks' to the press.

81 Margetts–Raymond, 12 August 1965; R. A. Long–Raymond, 26 January 1966, enclosing memo. on 'Railway Deficit', same date, B.R.B. 21–12–17 Pt. 1; Raymond, 'My Dispute with Barbara Castle', *Sunday Times*, 7 January 1968.

82 W. W. Scott (Principal Private Secretary to Castle), note, 4 February 1966; Raymond–Castle, 4 February 1966, with enclosures on 'The Future of the Railways', 'Railway Policy', etc.; 'Note of a Meeting Held at 222 Marylebone Road . . . on 16th February, 1966', and '. . . in Room 8/27 St Christopher House on 16 February, 1966' (Ministry's account), and 'Notes of Meeting between the Minister and the Chairman 16th February 1966' (B.R.B. account), in B.R.B. 21–2–11. Cf. Castle, *Diaries*, pp. 97, 99.

83 Notes, B.R.B. 21–2–11; *The National Plan*, September 1965, P.P. 1964–5, XXX, Cmnd.2764, p. 129; *Transport Policy*, Cmnd.3057, pp. 35–6 (Annex); Raymond–Castle, 17 March and 2 June 1966, Castle–Raymond, 31 May 1966, B.R.B. 21–12–17 Pts. 1 and 2.

84 Raymond–Castle, 25 May 1966, Johnson–Raymond, 10 March 1966, Raymond, confidential notes, 6 April 1966, B.R.B. 21–12–17 Pt. 1.

85 They were: C. P. Scott-Malden and G. C. Wardale, M.T.; J. J. B. Hunt, Treasury; and D. O. Henley, Department of Economic Affairs (Henley was an Assistant Under-Secretary of State). For B.R.B., Margetts was taken ill in 1967 and was replaced by Johnson in June.

86 Raymond's confidential notes, 6 April 1966, and Castle–Raymond, 21 July 1966, enclosing draft letter to the trade unions, B.R.B. 21–12–17 Pts. 1 and 2; Castle, *Diaries*, p. 113.

87 Hammond had moved from Eastern Region to H.Q. on 1 January 1966, when Fiennes was moved from Paddington to preside over the eventual merger of the Eastern and North Eastern Regions. His initial task was to assist Margetts. On the J.S.G. consultants, see J.S.G. Minutes, 5 July, 13 December 1966, 3 January 1967, B.R.B., and Scott-Malden, note, 15 December 1966, B.R.B. 21–2–28 Pt. 3.

88 *Transport Policy*, Cmnd.3057, p. 36; Shirley, memo. to Margetts and James on 'Steering Group', 14 June 1966, B.R.B. 21–2–11; J.S.G. Minutes, 11 July 1966; J.S.G., 'Railway Police Review. J.S.G. Interim Report', 10 January 1967, B.R.B. The six remits are in *Railway Policy*, Cmnd.3439, Appendix J, pp. 66–7.

89 J.S.G. Minutes, 17 February 1967, and note by Joint Executive Directors on Group's Work, February 1967, B.R.B.

90 Raymond–Shirley, Margetts and James, 5 October 1966, and B.R.B., Confidential Memo. on 'A Future Organisation for Nationalised Transport', 21 November 1966, B.R.B. 30–2–10 Pt. 1; *Sunday Times*, 7 January 1968.

91 Raymond, private and personal note to full-time members, 3 February 1967, and note, 2 March 1967, with replies, in B.R.B. 30–2–10 Pt. 1.

92 James, confidential memo. on 'Organisation of the Railway', 2 September 1966, sent to Raymond on 14 September, and private and personal note to Raymond on 'Headquarters Organisation', 10 February 1967, B.R.B. 30–2–10 Pt. 1, 21–2–47 Pt. 1; L. F. Neal, private and personal note to Raymond on 'H.Q. Organisation', 28 February 1967, B.R.B. 21–2–47 Pt. 1. On Neal's appointment see B.R.B. 48–2–21, and in particular Raymond–Castle, 18 July 1966.

93 Raymond, note, 3 February 1967, B.R.B. 30–2–10 Pt. 1.

94 J.S.G. Minutes, 7 March 1967, and Cuckney–Morris, 15 March 1967, B.R.B.; S. Joy, *The Train That Ran Away. A Business History of British Railways 1948–1968* (London: Ian Allan, 1973), p. 92. Joy joined the Directorate-General on a short secondment from Monash University in November 1966, M.T. Memo. to J.S.G., 24 October 1966, B.R.B.

95 B.R.B., 'Report on Management Structure', 26 April 1967, B.R.B., and for Sundries and Eastern/North Eastern merger see B.R.B. Minutes, 8 and 22 December 1966. Bonavia, who acted as Secretary to the team drafting the report, has suggested that it was a cautious, watered-down version of an earlier draft of 6 April: *Organisation*, pp. 118–22. In fact, the draft, in B.R.B. 21–2–47 Pt. 1, which was more aggressively functional in its recommendations, was written, ironically, by James, and was altered under Raymond's direction to give him more flexibility in his discussions with Castle.

96 'Letter from Mr. Pears on B.R.B. Proposals for Management Structure', 2 June 1967, 'Proposals for Management Structure. Report by S. J. Pears with "Consensus of Views Expressed by the Members . . ." ', 2 June 1967, and Cooper Bros. & Co., report on 'British Railways Management Structure', 5 June 1967, B.R.B. There is also a summary in Bonavia, *Organisation*, pp. 122–4.

97 J.S.G. Minutes, 6, 19/20 June, 18 July 1967; Bonavia–Raymond on 'Cooper Bros. Report', 8 June 1967, and Bonavia–Hammond, 14 June 1967, B.R.B. 30–2–10 Pt. 1; Cooper Bros., report, 5 June 1967, p. 12; J.S.G., 'Railway Policy Review. Report to the Minister of Transport and the Chairman, British Railways Board' (July 1967), pp. 31–52, B.R.B.; *Railway Policy*, Cmnd.3439, pp. 28–34.

98 Raymond–Castle, 28 April 1967; Castle–Raymond, 22 June 1967, and letters to Raymond from Fiennes, McKenna and Ibbotson, 19 May 1967, B.R.B. 48–2–1, Pt. 1, 48–2–24. Raymond suggested that the Finance post be offered to J. J. B. Hunt, Treasury representative on the J.S.G., and the commercial post to S. C. Robbins, Chief Marketing Manager of B.R.B.

99 E. Harding, private and confidential memo. on 'Organisation of the Board', 19 June 1967, B.R.B. Minutes, 22 June 1967; Dunbar, memo. on 'Organisation of the Planning Function at Board Headquarters', 1 August 1967, B.R.B. 48–8–1 Pt. 1. Three Directors of Planning were then appointed – K. V. Smith, A. E. T. Griffiths and Michael Bonavia – together with a Planning Services Manager (P. Corbishley): B.R.B. Minutes, 28 September 1967.

100 Neal, memo. 17 July 1967; memo. on 'Organisation of the Board', 2 October 1967, considered at Informal Meeting of Full-Time Members, 2 October 1967; Production Committee Minutes, 1 November 1967, General

Managers' Committee Minutes, 22 November 1967, B.R.B. 30–2–10 Pt. 1, 30–21–1 Pt. 4; B.R.B. Minutes, 12 October 1967.

101 Castle–Raymond, 22 June, 3 July 1967, Raymond–Castle, 23 June 1967, Gilmour–Raymond, 5 July 1967, 'B.R.B. Appointments. Note of the Minister's Meeting with Sir Stanley Raymond on 13 July 1967', B.R.B. 48–2–1 Pt. 1. Castle had needed some persuading before she agreed to renew Shirley's appointment. Raymond–Castle, 18 April, 9 June 1966, Castle–Raymond, 3 June, 8 July 1966, ibid.

102 Padmore–Raymond, 16 October 1967, Shirley–Raymond, same date, Raymond's notes, 30 October 1967, Shirley, cable to Raymond, n.d. (28 October?), Castle–Shirley, 19 December 1967, B.R.B. 48–1–13.

103 Raymond–Castle correspondence, esp. Castle–Raymond, 8 and 21 September, 4 and 11 October 1967, and Raymond–Castle, 19 and 28 September, 5 and 12 October 1967, B.R.B. 21–12–17 Pt. 3. When Raymond, after his resignation, tried to press the point that the J.S.G. had genuinely wanted to build in flexibility in its organisational proposals, Castle decided to wind the Group up. See Castle–Raymond, 5 and 8 December 1967, Raymond–Castle, 5 and 11 December 1967, note of meeting, 13 December 1967, and Raymond, note on 'Joint Steering Group', 13 December 1967, in P. H. Shirley's file on 'B.R.B. and MoT. J.S.G.', B.R.B. 21–2–10.

104 *Sunday Times*, 7 January 1968; Castle, *Diaries*, pp. 292, 295–6, 298, 314–15. The meeting took place on the 26th of October, and the news broke on the 27th. Raymond was 'completely devastated', Raymond–Bond, 27 October 1967, B.R.B. 48–2–14. The trade union meeting concerned the dispute over guards' bonuses. Castle had blamed the *Daily Mail* 'leak' on Ray Gunter.

105 B.R.B. Minutes, 23 February and 25 September 1967. The offending article was G. F. Fiennes, 'Running a Region: WR and ER', *Modern Railways*, XXIII (October 1967), 532–6, which contained extracts from his autobiography, *I Tried to Run a Railway* (published on 21 October 1967). Fiennes was not the innocent party that some commentators have suggested. He had had frequent disagreements with H.Q. over policy, particularly in relation to unremunerative passenger services (see below, pp. 448–9). He had refused to submit the manuscript for permission to publish, and was due to retire in February 1968 in any case.

106 Castle–Raymond, 16 November 1967, B.R.B. 48–2–14, and see also Castle, *Diaries*, pp. 297–8, 304.

107 *Sunday Times*, 7 January 1968.

108 Raymond–Castle, 29 November 1967, B.R.B. 48–2–1 Pt. 1.

109 MacMillan–C. D. Foster, 11 September 1967, and Raymond–MacMillan, 1 December 1967, and Commons Written Answer, 23 November 1967, in B.R.B. 30–2–10 Pt. 2; Castle, *Diaries*, pp. 294–5, 311–12, 316. Lord Robens, *Ten Year Stint* (London: Cassell, 1972), p. 149; *Times*, 14 October 1967.

110 Parker, draft confidential memo. to the Minister of Transport (n.d.), B.R.B., and Parker, 'Minding Our Own Businesses', *New Statesman*, 15 December 1967; Castle, *Diaries*, pp. 320–2.

111 J.S.G. Minutes, 20 June 1967; Hay–MSL Ltd, report to J.S.G. on 'Analysis of Senior Positions and Salary Practices . . .', September 1967; J.S.G., report, July 1967, pp. 42, 51, B.R.B.; Sir Richard Marsh, *On and Off the Rails. An*

Autobiography (London: Weidenfeld & Nicolson, 1978), pp. 75–84. The steel salaries were subject to an abatement of up to 12½ per cent until April 1969: Marsh, *Parl. Deb. (Commons)*, vol. 743 (Session 1966–7), 15 March 1967, 420.

112 Parker, confidential memo. to Castle, 24 November 1967, B.R.B.; Castle, *Diaries*, pp. 322–7, 330, 333–4. It was ironical that Castle had apparently opposed the steel salaries put up by Marsh and Parker: Marsh, *On and Off the Rails*, pp. 78, 82 (Castle denies this in *Diaries*, p. 322, however). Parker accepted the post of B.R.B. Chairman in 1976.

113 Castle–Johnson, 13 December 1967, in B.R.B. 48–2–24; *The Economist*, 16 December 1967.

114 Cooper Bros., report, 17 November 1967, B.R.B.; J. Harris and G. Williams, *Corporate Management and Financial Planning. The British Rail Experience* (St Albans: Elek., 1980), p. 92.

115 Castle–Ratter, 2 August 1967, B.R.B. 48–2–18; 'Note of the Minister's Meeting with Mr. H. C. Johnson on 2nd January, 1968', B.R.B. 48–2–1 Pt. 1; B.R.B. Minutes, 25 January 1968. See also B.R.B. 48–2–25, 26.

116 Notes of meetings, 2, 11 and 25 January 1968; Castle, confidential letter to Campbell, Berkin and others, 13 February 1968, Johnson–Castle, 27 March 1968, and Tyzack–Padmore, 20 March 1968, B.R.B. 48–2–1 Pt. 1 and 48–2–28. On the problems of Southern Region see *Railway Gazette*, 21 July and 6 October 1967, 5 January and 4 October 1968.

117 Marsh, *On and Off the Rails*, p. 123.

118 Marsh–Johnson, 29 April 1968, and reply, 30 April 1968; Marsh–Johnson, 8 and 10 May 1968; Johnson, memo. 8 May 1968, B.R.B. 48–2–1 Pt. 1; Bosworth's C.V. and memo. on 'Informal – 13 May 1968', 14 May 1968, B.R.B. 48–2–27 Pt. 1 (Peat, Marwick, Mitchell & Co. had been the Board's auditors since 1963); memo. 13 June 1968, B.R.B. 48–2–28. At the same time the appointments of James and Ratter were extended for one and two years respectively.

119 Johnson, memo. 29 August 1968, and M.T. press release, 14 October 1968, B.R.B. 48–2–1 Pt. 1.

120 B.R.B. 48–2–25, 26, 29–31; B.R.B., *R. & A. 1969*, I, p. 4.

121 16 & 17 Eliz. II c.73.

122 Chairman's note, 29 January 1968, and 'Remit for Committee'; Hammond, note to Johnson and Thorpe, 2 April 1968, B.R.B. 30–2–10 Pt. 2; B.R.B. Minutes, 11 January 1968.

123 Hammond, memo. on 'Board Committees', 7 February 1968, B.R.B. Minutes, 11 January, 8 February and 14 March 1968; B.R.B. Headquarters Executive Committee Minutes, 26 February 1968, B.R.B.

124 Hammond, memo. on 'A. Responsibilities and Interests of Individual Board Members. B. Memberships of Committees, etc.', 6 June 1968, B.R.B. Minutes, 13 June 1968, B.R.B. Barker also retained responsibility for hotels, catering and shipping.

125 'The Organisation and Structure of the British Railways Board', March 1968, B.R.B.Org. 1 and revised version, April 1968, B.R.B.Org. 1/A, circulated by Hammond, and ibid., 'Part 1. The Functions and Composition of the Board', April 1968, B.R.B.Org. 2, circulated by Kentridge, B.R.B. 30–2–10 Pts. 2, 3. There was some confusion as to the intentions of these documents. Ham-

mond later claimed they were 'virtually identical in intention', memo. on 'B.R.B. Organisation', 18 April 1968, ibid. Pt. 2. On the retention of Margetts and Dunbar and their views, see B.R.B. 48–2–11, 12, Margetts, note to Johnson and Thorpe, 23 April 1968, and Hammond, memo. 24 April 1968, B.R.B. 30–2–10 Pt. 3.

126 Hammond–Johnson and Thorpe, 2 April 1968, Kentridge–Johnson and Thorpe, 8 April 1968, P. A. Satchwell–Hammond, 18 April 1968; Informal Meeting of Full-Time Members ref. to in Hammond, memo. on 'McKinsey & Company Inc.' 18 April 1968, B.R.B. 30–2–10. Pt. 2. On McKinsey see *Times*, 18 November 1968, *The Economist*, 8 June 1968.

127 Summary in McKinsey & Co., 'Proposed Charter for the British Railways Board', 6 August 1969, B.R.B.

128 H. Parker, 'Managing the Managers. The Role of the Board', *The Director*, XX (May 1968), 272–6; James–Johnson, 28 August 1968, memo. on 'B.R.B. Organisation – McKinsey "Discussion Draft" August 1968', 30 August 1968, and James, private note to Johnson with paper on 'Organisation', 19 February 1969, B.R.B. 30–2–10 Pts. 3, 4.

129 Hammond, memo. 27 August 1968, memo. on 'Meeting at McKinsey's HQ', 14 October 1968, and 'McKinsey's: Organizing the Board for the 1970s', 28 October 1968, B.R.B. 30–2–10 Pt. 3.

130 Hammond–Johnson on 'B.R.B. Organisation. McKinsey's "Discussion Draft", August 1968', 28 August 1968; Hammond–Johnson, 3 February 1969, and Hammond's notes on 'McKinsey's', 4 February 1969, B.R.B. 30–2–10 Pts. 3, 4; McKinsey & Co., 'Proposed Board and Management Structure' (Discussion Draft), March 1969 (contains Parker–Johnson, 27 March 1969), B.R.B. The Chief Executive's team of ten was later increased to eleven with the addition of a Planning Manager.

131 B.R.B. Chairman's Conference Minutes, 1 and 21 April 1969, and B.R.B. Minutes, 10 April 1969; B.R.B. 'Proposed Board and Top Management Structure', April 1969; McKinsey & Co., Memorandum of Proposal, 17 April 1969, B.R.B. 30–2–10 Pt. 4.

132 B.R.B. Minutes, 12 December 1968, 9 January and 13 March 1969; Hammond, memo. 18 February 1969, and Hammond–Johnson, note for meeting with Minister, 17 March 1969, Thorpe–Johnson, 22 April 1969, B.R.B. 30–2–10 Pt. 4; C. J. Doyle–Hammond, 2 April 1969, B.R.B. 48–8–1 Pt. 2.

133 Marsh–Johnson, 4 June 1969, Parker–Johnson, 12 May 1969, Marsh–Johnson, 7 May and 4 June 1969, Hammond–Johnson, 8 May 1969, B.R.B. 30–2–10 Pt. 4; for earlier correspondence and meetings, see Marsh–Johnson, 25 February 1969, Johnson–Marsh, 15 May and 2 July 1969, B.R.B. 48–2–1 Pt. 2, 48–2–2. Note that Serpell, while admitting to a 'favourable first impression' of the scheme, insisted on seeing McKinsey's original draft: Johnson–Marsh, 22 April 1969, and note for papers, 23 April 1969, B.R.B. 30–2–10 Pt. 4. On Marsh's later views see his notes of meeting with Sir Idwal Pugh, 30 January 1974, B.R.B. 48–2–1 Pt. 2.

134 Thorpe, memo. on 'Board Organisation', 10 April 1969, and replies of Ratter, McKenna, James, Houchen, Jones, Neal, Bosworth and Wilson, in B.R.B. 48–1–10. On members' preferences see Hammond, memo. on 'Board Organisation', 7 July 1969, ibid.

135 Thorpe–Johnson, 22 April 1969, and memo. to Chairman's Conference, 25

April 1969 (not considered at the Conference on 7 July: Hammond, memo. 7 July 1969, B.R.B. 48–1–10); Thorpe–Johnson, 22 May 1969; Johnson–Marsh, 2 July 1969 (marked 'Not Sent'), Marsh–Johnson, 15 July 1969, B.R.B. 48–1–10, 30–2–10 Pt. 5.

136 Hammond, 'British Railways Board Meeting, 13 August 1969. Unofficial Note of Private Discussion on the Election of Chief Executive', B.R.B. 48–1–10; confidential memo. 14 August 1969, B.R.B. Minutes, 13/14 August 1969; Hammond, confidential memo. on 'Chief Executive (Railways)', 25 August 1969, and on 'Chairman/Minister Meetings, 15/9/69', 16 September 1969, B.R.B. 48–2–25, 30–2–10 Pt. 5.

137 Ratter left on 31 March 1970; he had been appointed for a further two years to 1 January 1971 in 1968, B.R.B. Minutes, 23 May 1968, 12 March 1970. See Barker–Johnson, 27 October 1969, Ratter–Serpell, 14 October 1969, Ratter–Mulley, 31 December 1969, etc., in B.R.B. 48–2–18, 48–2–26.

138 Johnson–Serpell, 24 January 1969, Marsh–Johnson, 25 February and 8 May 1969, Johnson–Marsh, 15 May 1969; 'Note of Private Meeting Minister/Chairman', 8 July 1969, note for Johnson, 5 August 1969, Marsh–Johnson, 4 September 1969; Taylor of Gryfe–Marsh, 23 June 1969, B.R.B. 48–2–1 Pt. 1, 48–2–2. Two part-timers, MacNaughton Sidey and Shirley, had left the Board in December 1968.

139 McKinsey & Co., 'Proposed Charter for the British Railways Board', 6 August 1969, and 'Organizing for the 1970s', September 1969; B.R.B. Minutes, 13/14 August 1969; Chairman's Conference Minutes, 8 September 1969, B.R.B.; 'Preliminary Ministry of Transport Comments on BRB Paper of 11 September 1969', 26 September 1969, B.R.B. 30–2–10 Pt. 5. The payment to McKinsey of £155,123 included £17,623 in expenses.

140 Marsh, On and Off the Rails, pp. 142–3; B.R.B. Minutes, 12/13 November 1969; Mulley–Johnson, 1 December 1969, B.R.B. 30–2–10 Pt. 5.

141 B.R.B., Report on Organisation, 11 December 1969, P.P.1969–70, XXVIII, HC.50. The Chairmen of the Subsidiary Boards were: Bosworth (B.R.E.L.); McKenna (Shipping and International Services Division and British Transport Advertising); Barker (Hotels and Hovercraft); Johnson (Property); and Margetts (Transmark).

142 Ibid., pp. 12–15; Hammond, memo. on 'A. Responsibilities of Board Members B. Memberships of Boards, Companies and Committees', 5 November 1969, Chairman's Conference Minutes, 3 November, and B.R.B. Minutes, 12–13 November 1969.

143 Informal Meeting of Executive Directors Minutes, 29 August and 27 October 1969, B.R.B. Minutes, 8 January and 24 August 1970; Railway Management Group Minutes, 26/27 August 1969, Executive Directors' Conference Minutes, 17 November 1969, B.R.B.

144 Johnson–Peyton, 14 January 1971 (two letters), Peyton–Johnson, 19 January 1971, B.R.B. 48–2–31. Wilson has said that it was his idea to resign from the Board.

145 Lawrence experienced 36 changes of job and 21 changes of location, 1934–71, B.R.B. 48–2–34. Cf. the 45 jobs and 38 locations of Thorpe, 1927–68, B.R.B. 48–2–25. He was appointed to act as Chairman of B.R.E.L., relieving Bosworth. He was also Chairman of BRE-Metro, and Transmark was part of his 'area of special influence'.

146 See Wilson, report, November 1964, and other material in B.R.B. 30–3–68, and B.R.B. Minutes, 10 December 1964. On Wilson and the Scottish two-tier organisation see below, p. 384.

147 B.R.B. Minutes, 28 January 1971; Johnson–Peyton, 26 January 1971, and reply 2 February 1971, Hammond, 'Confidential Note for Private Session of the Board 10/11 February', 4 February 1971, and confidential memo. 11 February 1971, B.R.B. 48–2–31.

148 Wilson–Marsh, 28 June 1971, B.R.B. 48–1–10; *The Economist*, 10 April and 22 May 1971; *Sunday Times*, 23 May 1971; Railway Management Group Minutes, 23/24 September 1969, B.R.B.

149 B.R.B. Special Board Minutes (Private Session), 22 June 1971, and B.R.B. 48–2–41.

150 Mulley–Marsh, 14 May 1975, and reply, 19 May 1975, B.R.B. 48–2–1 Pt. 2, 48–2–41. Lawrence was appointed Vice-Chairman in November 1975.

151 P. H. Grinyer and J. Wooller, *Corporate Models Today: A New Tool for Financial Management* (London: Institute of Chartered Accountants in England and Wales, 1975), cit. in Harris and Williams, *Corporate Management*, p. 90; Geoffrey Freeman Allen, 'Corporate Planning', *Modern Railways* (September 1968), 478–83; British Institute of Management, *Is Corporate Planning Necessary?* (London: B.I.M., 1968); *Railway Gazette International*, August 1971.

152 Unsigned memo. on 'Corporate Planning Department Organisation', 17 January 1969, Kentridge, memo. on 'Organisation for Corporate Planning', 5 March 1969, and Bowick, note on 'Corporate Planning Organisation', 3 April 1969, B.R.B. 48–8–1 Pt. 2; B.R.B. Minutes, 13 March 1969; E.C. (Railways) Minutes, 17 February 1969, B.R.B. On Joy see B.R.B. Minutes, 14 November 1968, and Long, 'Job Specification', 8 January 1969, in B.R.B. PER 48–8–3.

153 Bowick, memo. on 'Corporate and Railway Planning Organisations', 3 February 1970, and memo. 13 February 1970, B.R.B. 48–8–1 Pt. 3; Chairman's Conference Minutes, 9 February 1970, B.R.B. Minutes, 13/14 August 1969, 12 February 1970.

154 The officers were G. R. Burt (appointed August 1970) and P. D. Ings (February 1971). K. V. Smith and Bowick, memos. on 'Corporate Planning Organisation', July 1970, Chairman's Conference Minutes, 20 July 1970; Railway Management Group Minutes, 17 December 1969 and 21 January 1970, B.R.B.

155 J. E. Todd–Kentridge, 18 December 1970; Todd–D. Cook, 15 February 1971 (with note of discussion with Clemow, 8 February), B.R.B. 48–8–1 Pt. 3.

156 Kentridge, memo. to Cook, 7 April 1971, ibid. (a similar memo. by Bosworth, 16 July, was endorsed by the Chairman's Conference on 19 July 1971, and by the Board on 12 August); T.R. Barron (Chief Management Staff Officer)–Bosworth on 'Planning Organisation', 19 October 1971, and confidential memo. on 'Planning Organisation', Chairman's Conference Minutes, 8 November 1971, B.R.B. Joy remained in the department but his job was not to be renewed when his contract ended. Barron succeeded Kentridge in June 1972, B.R.B. Minutes, 8 June 1972.

157 Marsh, *On and Off the Rails*, pp. 85–6, 155ff. Marsh was Chairman of Michael Saunders Management Services and Midland Plant Transport, a director of Concord Rotaflex and a member of the Council for the Founda-

tion of Management Education. B.R.B. 48–2–35; *Times*, 6 April, and *Financial Times*, 7 April 1971; C. King, *The Cecil King Diary 1965–1970* (London: Jonathan Cape, 1972), pp. 290, 323.

158 B.R.B. 48–2–5, 21, 31, 36 Pt. 1, 37. On salaries see Marsh, memo. 17 November 1972, and Marsh–T. L. Beagley, 15 October 1973, B.R.B. 48–2–2. (Part-timers were paid additional sums for extra duties, e.g. Chairman of a committee, subsidiary, or regional Board.)

159 Chairman's Conference Minutes, 25 January 1971, B.R.B. Minutes, 28 January 1971, B.R.B.; confidential report of the enquiry on 'Conduct of the Board's Business', April 1971, B.R.B. 30–2–20 Pt. 1; Hammond, memo. 8 October, Chairman's Conference, 11 October 1971, and B.R.B. Minutes, 12–13 May and 14 October 1971; B.R.B. Minutes, 12 August 1971.

160 Thorpe, memo. 16 March 1972, containing E. Harding, report on 'British Railways Board: Duties and Powers: Delegation: Organisation', March 1972, B.R.B. 30–2–20 Pt. 2; Chairman's Conference Minutes, 20 March 1972, B.R.B. The Research and Development Committee, established in December 1968, was subsequently transformed into an unincorporated subsidiary Board, B.R.B. Minutes, 13 July 1972, and see B.R.B. 30–16–25.

161 The team, established in May 1970, was led by D. M. Dear, Chief Officer, Special Duties, B.R.B., and Earl le Grande of McKinsey. B.R.B., 'Restructuring the Railway Field Organisation', January 1971; Railway Management Group Minutes, 16 December 1970, 27 January 1971, Executive Directors' Conference Minutes, 1 February 1971, B.R.B. Minutes, 10–11 February and 13 May 1971, Chairman's Conference Minutes, 10 May 1971, B.R.B. There is a summary of the report in Bonavia, *Organisation*, pp. 140–50.

162 B.R.B. Minutes, 8 August 1968, 8 October 1970 (the Scottish initiative had its origins in actions taken in 1964: A. Philip (Chief Establishment and Staff Officer), report, 7 January 1965, Scottish Regional Board Minutes, 12–13 January 1965); B.R.B., report, January 1975, and 'Retrospective Study on the Introduction of a Two-Tier Management Structure on the Scottish Region', December 1970; Railway Management Group Minutes, 16 December 1970, B.R.B.

163 B.R.B., *Second Report of the Board on Organisation*, 21 April 1972, P.P.1971–2, XXXIX, HC.223; Bowick, Progress Reports, August and November 1971, etc., in B.R.B. 30–1–118 Pts. 1, 2.

164 General Managers' report, 10 March 1965, B.R.B. Minutes, 25 March 1965; B.R.B., report, January 1971; Kentridge, memo. to Chairman's Conference, 30 September 1968, B.R.B. 30–2–10 Pt. 3.

165 Bowick, confidential memo. on 'Railway Field Organisation', 7 February 1975, B.R.B. 30–1–118 Pt. 5; B.R.B. Minutes, 9 January and 13 February 1975. On trade union opposition see, *inter alia*, Railway Management Group Minutes, 23 February 1972, 18 April 1973, B.R.B., and *Sunday Times*, 26 January 1975.

166 E.g. shipbuilding in the 1960s and 1970s.

167 B.R.B., 'A Future Organisation for Nationalised Transport', 21 November 1966, B.R.B. 30–2–10 Pt. 1. Under Parker from 1976 the Board reverted to a more executive form and made greater use of its part-time members: the main reorganisation took effect on 10 January 1977. See G. R. Burt, memo. on 'Board Organisation and Procedures', 5 December 1976, B.R.B. Minutes, 9 December 1976.

10. Financial performance and rationalisation

1 C.S.O., *A.A.S.* (1984), p. 195. Passenger data used here exclude pedal cycles.
2 *A.A.S.* (1974), p. 226. The data exclude movement of gases, and (before 1965) pipelines of less than 10 miles.
3 British Road Federation, *Basic Road Statistics 1979* (1979); Stephen Plowden, *Taming Traffic* (London: Deutsch, 1980), pp. 43, 54–5; David Starkie, *The Motorway Age* (Oxford: Pergamon, 1982), pp. 108–10; George Charlesworth, *A History of British Motorways* (London: Telford, 1984), pp. 50, 71.
4 R. G. Smith, memo. on 'British Railways Results: 1967', May 1968, Finance Committee Minutes, 24 July 1968, B.R.B.
5 Ibid.
6 B.R.B., *A Study of the Relative True Costs of Rail and Road Freight Transport over Trunk Routes* (London: B.R.B., 1964), pp. 24–5; M.T., *Report of Committee on Carriers' Licensing* (Chairman: Lord Geddes) (1965), pp. 5–7, 66–76, 88–94; M.T., *Road Track Costs* (1968). For a summary see J. J. Hillman, *The Parliamentary Structuring of British Road–Rail Freight Coordination* (Evanston, Illinois: Northwestern University Transportation Center, 1973), pp. 141–2, 167–87.
7 B.R.B., Memo. to J.S.G. on "'Standby Capacity'", September 1966, B.R.B.
8 On the rejection of the 'standby' argument and the provision of temporary grants see M.T., note to J.S.G., 23 September 1966; report by the J.S.G. Committee on Standby Capacity, 31 March 1967, confidential report by the J.S.G. Committee on Surplus Track Capacity, 16 June 1967, B.R.B.; S. Joy, *The Train That Ran Away. A Business History of British Railways 1948–1968* (London: Ian Allan, 1973), pp. 106–13.
9 Data from B.R.B., *R. & A. 1968*, I, pp. 13, 32. No profit/loss calculations were made for freightliners before 1969, but internal evidence suggests that the reported loss of £3.0m. in 1968 was an underestimate. See Margetts (Chairman, Freightliner Division), memo. on 'British Railways Freightliner Division', 30 November 1968 (with data in Appendix 7), B.R.B. Minutes, 12 December 1968. Raymond's comment was a response to the transfer of freightliners to the N.F.C.: *Sunday Times*, 7 January 1968.
10 This approach, known as 'Method 2', also applied to the Southern Region network (Method 1 is total cost allocation/Cooper Bros. formula). The practice was criticised by the Exchequer and Audit Department in 1969, and from 1970 a revised formula was used. This charged freight a 'wear and tear' toll (as originally recommended by Cooper Bros.), and excluded short lines (0–5 miles), and lines where the only other user was a commercial passenger service or viable freight service. See Bosworth, memo. on 'Grant Aided Passenger Services: Method of Calculation of Track and Signalling Costs for Inclusion in Grant Claims', 25 September 1970 (enclosing report of M.T./B.R.B. Working Party on 'Review of Method 2 Basis . . .'), B.R.B. Minutes, 5 October 1970, and Joy, *Train That Ran Away*, pp. 110, 125.
11 D. Allen (Director, Sector Evaluation), memo. to Strategy Committee on 'The Development of Infrastructure Attribution and Sole User', May 1983, Strategy Committee Minutes, 17 May 1983, B.R.B. and memo. to Board on 'Infrastructure Costing and Sector Management: The Sole User Regime', 23

July 1984, B.R.B. Minutes, 2 August 1984. See also B.R.B., *Measuring Cost and Profitability in British Rail* (London: B.R.B., 1978), pp. 1–30.

12 B.R.B., Confidential Railway Policy Review, December 1972, 'Support Paper A – The Freight Business', Appendix AI, B.R.B. (data are given for passenger (1971), and parcels and freight (1969–71), in the Review); B.R.B., *R. & A.* 1963, II, p. 60, *1973*, p. 52, *1983*, p. 56. 1983 figures: passenger £1,149.5m.; freight £528.6m.

13 Losses were made by hovercraft, 1966–72; harbours, 1966, 1970–1; rail catering, 1968, 1970, 1973; and freightliners, in which B.R.B. had a 40% stake, 1969, 1970, 1972 (earlier losses included in the rail accounts).

14 B.R.B., *R. & A. 1972*, pp. 26–7, *1973*, p. 12.

15 *Reshaping*, I, pp. 1–2.

16 At the end of 1962, 12,915 route-miles were open for passenger traffic, and there were 6,801 stations, of which 4,306 were open for passengers. The report listed 2,363 closures, but they included 234 stations which had already closed. *Reshaping*, I, pp. 19, 96–136, and B.R.B., *R. & A. 1963*, II, p. 53.

17 *Reshaping*, I, pp. 2, 39, 48, 54–5, 59–60. See also D. L. Munby, 'The Reshaping of British Railways', *Journal of Industrial Economics,* XI (July 1963), 161–82; Geoffrey Freeman Allen, *British Rail After Beeching* (London: Ian Allan, 1966), ch. 1; D. H. Aldcroft, *British Railways in Transition: The Economic Problems of Britain's Railways since 1914* (London: Macmillan, 1968), pp. 185ff.; Richard Pryke, *Public Enterprise in Practice. The British Experience of Nationalisation over Two Decades* (London: MacGibbon and Kee, 1971), pp. 249ff.; and Joy, *Train That Ran Away*, pp. 54–71.

18 Beeching's Private Secretary to E. Atkinson, Archivist, British Transport Historical Records, 5 July 1963, B.R.B. 21–12–12 Pt. 1.

19 Blee, memo. on 'London Midland Region Passenger Services', 4 March 1959; London Midland Area Board Minutes, 5 March 1959; B.T.C., confidential 'Programme of Modernisation 1961–1964', 19 December 1960, B.R.B.; *The British Transport Commission, Re-appraisal of the Plan for the Modernisation of British Railways*, July 1959, p. 8, P.P.1958–9, XIX, Cmd.813; Munby, 'Reshaping', 161. Regions' listings of planned closures are in B.R.B. 33–1–14.

20 B.T.C. Traffic Committee Minutes, 17 May, 7 and 21 June, 23 August and 25 October 1960, B.R.B. The officers concerned were T. H. Hollingsworth, the Traffic Adviser, G. W. Quick-Smith, Adviser (Special Projects), and H. E. Osborn, Financial Adviser.

21 B.T.C. Minutes, 11 May 1961, B.R.B.; B.T.C., *R. & A. 1961*, I, pp. 2–3.

22 B.T.C. Minutes, 23 February and 13 July 1961; Hollingsworth, memo. to Traffic Committee on 'Handling of Less than Wagonload Traffic', 16 June, Traffic Committee Minutes, 25 April and 20 June 1961, B.R.B.; Memo. of meeting held at B.T.C. headquarters, Friday 21 July 1961, B.R.B. Finance File on 'Traffic Studies 1961/62', F6/314, and 'Notes for Meeting . . .', F6/314/ 1(a); Wansbrough-Jones, memo. on 'Concentration of Freight Traffic', 22 November 1960, B.R.B. 95–1–1 Pt. 4.

23 Raymond–General Managers, 25 July 1961, enclosing 'Study to Help Determine the Pattern and Characteristics of Traffic not at Present Carried by Rail' (T.S.1/1), and Raymond–General Managers, 27 July 1961, enclosing

'Study to Help Determine the Pattern and Characteristics of Coal, Coke and Patent Fuels not at Present Carried by Rail' (T.S.1/3), B.R.B. Finance F6/314/1(a) and (b).

24 Raymond–General Managers, 3 August 1961, enclosing 'Study of Present Traffic Flows and Densities, and Utilisation of the System' (T.S.2/1), B.R.B. Finance F6/314/3(a); 'Study . . .' (T.S.1/1); Memo. of meeting held at B.T.C. H.Q. Tuesday 16 January 1962 on 'Traffic Studies: Cartographical Representation', B.R.B. Finance F6/314.

25 E.g. Raymond and Osborn–General Managers, 27 December 1961, enclosing first results of wagon-load traffic survey; Traffic Conference Minutes, 2 March and 17 April 1962, B.R.B.; memo. on 'British Railways: Freight Traffic Survey', 27 April 1962, B.R.B. 95–1–1 Pt. 4. A study of winter traffic congestion was also conducted: Raymond–General Managers, 26 July 1961, ibid.

26 Margetts–Hammond et al., 30 November 1962, B.R.B. 21–12–12 Pt. 1; B.T.C. Minutes, 11 October 1962; British Railways Committee Minutes, 22 November 1962; British Transport Joint Consultative Council Minutes, 16 April 1962, B.R.B.; Public Relations memo. on 'Public and Internal Relations Case Study. Presentation of "The Reshaping of British Railways"', n.d. (prob. 6 August 1964), B.R.B. P.R. & P. 21–12–12 Pt. 2.

27 The Costings Division recognised that the somewhat arbitrary allocation of costs influenced the results for parcels and mails in particular. Later, 'full cost allocation' was abandoned for methods which took account of cost escapability. See above, pp. 394–5.

28 Reshaping, I, pp. 10–11, 65. Some of the statistics quoted here were selected in a report to the J.S.G.: B.R.B., Memo. on 'Sequence of Events between 1963 and 1967 Culminating in the Publication of the British Railways Network for Development', 28 April 1967, B.R.B.

29 Reshaping, I, pp. 11, 34–7, 69, 71, 73, 77, 84–5. Data for stations and private sidings: 2,356 of the 4,995 locations (47 per cent) each handled under 100 tons, 2 per cent of total tonnage, ibid. p. 75. Both data sets refer to merchandise and mineral traffic forwarded/received, and to coal class traffic received. Maps supporting the data were published in Part II. Note that not all road–rail traffic was poor – e.g. small amounts of road/dock traffic in loads over 12 tons, and road/siding traffic over 16 tons: Munby, 'Reshaping', 169–72.

30 Reshaping, I, pp. 54, 97–136.

31 Ibid. pp. 16–18; Munby, 'Reshaping', 172–81. Munby, who was critical of the report for its errors and misprints, erred himself in giving receipts per passenger-mile as 1s. 1d.–1s. 5d. instead of 1.15d.–1.46d., 'Reshaping', 177. Freeman Allen found Munby's argument somewhat exaggerated, British Rail After Beeching, pp. 30–1.

32 S. Joy, 'British Railways' Track Costs', Journal of Industrial Economics, XIII (November 1964), 74–87; Joy, Train That Ran Away, pp. 70, 74–5. See also C. D. Foster, The Transport Problem (1st edn., London: Blackie, 1963), pp. 81–8. Later, British Rail found that 80–90 per cent of track and signalling costs did not vary in response to changes in traffic volume: see B.R.B., Measuring Cost, p. 5.

33 Aldcroft, British Railways, pp. 193–4; Pryke, Public Enterprise, pp. 249–50; Joy, Train That Ran Away, pp. 73, 78.

34 *Reshaping*, I, pp. 41, 90–2; Pryke, *Public Enterprise*, pp. 219–22, 232; Allen, *British Rail After Beeching*, pp. 24–5, 27–8.

35 *Reshaping*, I, pp. 55, 148; Foster, *Transport Problem* (1963 edn), p. 113n.

36 *Reshaping*, I, pp. 50–3; Margetts, memos. 15 and 18 March 1963, B.R.B. 21–12–12 Pt. 2. Changes in type-setting in the manpower section were noticed by Munby, 'Reshaping', p. 166n. The section forecast 16,200 job-losses from passenger services, 10,900 from line closures, 8,600 from sundries concentration and 4,900 in train working/maintenance savings.

37 Allen, *British Rail After Beeching*, pp. 28–30; Joy, *Train That Ran Away*, pp. 16, 71, 79; B.R.B., Confidential Report to the Minister for Transport Industries. Railway Policy Review, December 1972, pp. 12–19, B.R.B.

38 Allen, *British Rail After Beeching*, p. 33; B.B.C. *Panorama* Programme, 27 March 1963, *Observer*, 31 March 1963, *Guardian*, 28 March 1962, and see 'Presentation of "The Reshaping of British Railways"', B.R.B. P.R. & P. 21–12–12 Pt. 2. Only the *Daily Worker*, 28 March 1963, was critical of the Plan.

39 Marples–Beeching, 25 April 1963, Robertson–Beeching, 27 March 1963, B.R.B. 21–12–12 Pt. 2.

40 B.R.B., Memo. to J.S.G., 28 April 1967, B.R.B.

41 Margetts, 'Railway Planning Report, July 1963', 18 July 1963, B.R.B. Minutes, 25 July 1963; Planning Committee Minutes, 18 January 1964, Fiennes–Ness, 10 January 1964, Long–Raymond, 13 February 1964, etc., B.R.B.

42 British Railways Management Committee Minutes, 22 January 1964, 11 February 1965, B.R.B.

43 H. C. Johnson–Ness, 31 March 1965, B.R.B. 33–1–30; B.R.B. Minutes, 22 October and 12 November 1964, B.R.B.; Williams–Beeching, 9 November 1964, B.R.B. 33–1–30.

44 B.R.B., *The Development of the Major Railway Trunk Routes* (London: B.R.B., 1965), pp. 16–21, 33–6, 48–51. None of the Board's predictions has materialised. G.D.P. growth to 1983 was at a rate of 1.5 per cent per annum (not 4 per cent), population growth was 4 per cent not 15 per cent, and total freight ton-mileage *fell* by a third to 1983. Oil ton-mileage increased by 100 per cent (not 200 per cent), iron and steel *fell* by 60 per cent.

45 Raymond–Margetts and Ness on 'What is Our Policy for Wagon Load Traffic?', 30 December 1963, Planning Committee Minutes, 15 January 1964, B.R.B. Allen, writing in 1965, quoted a 'high Regional officer' as saying: 'There's far less money to be got from pulling up the track after we've shut down a service than from pruning the movement costs of a service while it's still running': *British Rail After Beeching*, p. 70.

46 James–Shirley, 2 November 1964, B.R.B. 33–1–30.

47 B.R.B., *Trunk Routes*, p. 46.

48 B.R.B., Memo. to J.S.G., 28 April 1967; B.R.B., draft report on 'The Selection of the Railway Feeder Line System', May 1965; Planning Committee Minutes, 19 May 1965, B.R.B.

49 British Railways Management Committee Minutes, 24 February 1965, B.R.B.

50 Woodcock–Beeching, 4 March 1965, enclosing Woodcock–Fraser, 25 February 1965, B.R.B. 33–1–30.

51 Margetts, 'Railway Planning Report', 19 September, B.R.B. Minutes, 26 September 1963; 'Railway Operations Report', March 1964, B.R.B.

Minutes, 12 March 1964. No one at B.R.B. H.Q. seems to have been quite sure how many freight stations were open on 1 June 1963. Internal reports in 1963–7 gave six different figures (5,070 is mean; range is 5,047–5,103).

52 David R. Serpell–Wansbrough-Jones, 29 July 1963, enclosing 'Directions and Determinations by the Minister of Transport under Section 54 . . .', B.R.B. Minutes, 8 August 1963. On delays see notes of a meeting of the General Managers' Informal Conference, 20–1 April 1963, in General Managers' Conference Minutes, 1963, B.R.B. and Margetts–General Managers, 14 June 1963, B.R.B. 33–1–1.

53 Hammond–Thorpe, 26 February 1968, B.R.B. 33–1–1.

54 Margetts–General Managers, 4 April and, subsequently, 14 May, 14 June and 9 August 1963, ibid., and 'Railway Operations Report', November 1963, B.R.B. Minutes, 14 November 1963, B.R.B. Data for stations *and* private-sidings, *Reshaping*, I, p. 75, cit. in A. E. T. Griffiths (Commercial Planning Officer), summary report on 'Closure of Freight Stations', 5 May 1966, B.R.B. 33–1–1.

55 Margetts, memo. to British Railways Management Committee on 'Freight Station Closures', 18 December 1964, B.R.B. 33–1–1; British Railways Management Committee Minutes, 21 July 1965, B.R.B. Freight tonnage was 228.1m. in 1962 and 228.5m. in 1965.

56 *Reshaping*, I, p. 48; B.R.B., *R. & A. 1963–7*, II. 306,494 vehicles were scrapped, 1963–6 (including 7,737 brake vans, etc.) and 392,056, 1963–7 (9,926 vans, etc.).

57 Cf. Hammond–General Managers, 1 February 1966, B.R.B. 21–12–17 Pt. 1.

58 Shirley, memo. on 'Progress Report on Coal Concentration', 20 October 1965, B.R.B. Minutes, 28 October 1965; *Reshaping*, I, p. 32; B.R.B., *R. & A. 1965*, I, p. 13.

59 Margetts, 'Railway Progress Report', 19 September 1963, B.R.B. Minutes, 26 September 1963, and memo. to British Railways Management Committee, 17 April 1964, Minutes, 22 April 1964, B.R.B. For later problems, see General Managers' Commitee Minutes, 27 March 1968, B.R.B.

60 *Reshaping*, I, p. 68; Margetts–General Managers, 8 August 1963, B.R.B. 102–14–4 Pt. 1.

61 Note of a meeting of B.R.B. and N.C.B., 21 February 1963, Memo. on 'Coal Concentration', n.d. (prob. August 1965), B.R.B. 102–14–4 Pt. 1; Shirley, memo. 20 October 1965, B.R.B.

62 See Margetts, memo. on 'Freight Sundries Traffic', 19 September 1963, and other material in B.R.B. 95–1–6 Pt. 1.

63 Margetts–General Managers, 2 August 1963, and 'Summary of Main Points in Replies . . .', 16 September 1963, British Railways Management Committee Minutes, 25 September 1963; Margetts, memo. to British Railways Management Committee, 9 October 1963, enclosing 'Review of the National Sundries Plan', B.R.B.

64 B.R.B. Minutes, 10 September 1964; L. W. Ibbotson (Chief Operating Manager)–General Managers, 2 February 1965, B.R.B. 95–1–6 Pt. 2; Planning Committee Minutes, 17 February 1965, B.R.B.; B.R.B., *R. & A. 1964*, I, p. 18, *1965*, I, p. 26.

65 M.T., *Transport Policy*, July 1966, p. 4, P.P.1966–7, LIX, Cmnd.3057; M.T. and B.R.B., *British Railways Network for Development* (London: H.M.S.O., 1967).

66 B.R.B., confidential report of Working Party (Chairman: J. R. Legg) on 'National Freight Plan', July 1965, B.R.B. 95–1–16; B.R.B., Memo. to J.S.G., 28 April 1967, B.R.B.

67 B.R.B., report of Working Party on 'National Freight Train Plan', July 1965; Operating Committee Minutes, 14 February 1967, Movement Conference Minutes, 12 July 1968, B.R.B.

68 British Railways Management Committee Minutes, 25 October 1967, H.Q. Executive Committee Minutes, 4 March 1968, B.R.B.

69 Shirley, memo. on 'Traffic Profitability', 19 March 1965, B.R.B. Minutes, 25 March and 22 July 1965; B.R.B., R. & A. 1965, I, p. 70; Margetts, memo. 28 August 1968, B.R.B. 21–12–12 Pt. 2.

70 Raymond, memo. 16 October 1964, British Railways Management Committee Minutes, 25 November 1964; Long, memo. on 'Costs and Freight Charges for Wagonload Traffic', 25 August 1966; Commercial and Operating Committee Minutes, 1 September 1966, B.R.B.

71 James, memo. on 'Costs and Freight Traffic', 23 February 1966, British Railways Management Committee Minutes, 27 April 1966, B.R.B.; J. Johnson and R. A. Long, British Railways Engineering (London: Mechanical Engineering Publications, 1981), p. 299.

72 B.R.B. Minutes, 9 May and 11 December 1968; Chairman's Conference Minutes, 21 October and 28 November 1968; B.R.B., Freight Plan 1968, October 1968, pp. 53–6, B.R.B.

73 Robbins, confidential report on 'Studies into the Possible Withdrawal of Freight Services from Selected Areas and Lines', May 1971, and A. W. Tait, memo. 25 May 1971, R.M.G. Minutes, 25 and 26 May 1971, B.R.B. The estimated short-term cut in net revenue from withdrawing all the services examined was 'as high as £8.6m.', ibid.

74 R.M.G. Minutes, 28 October 1970, 25 and 26 May and 27 October 1971; B.R.B., Second Corporate Plan, February 1972, B9, C3–4; B.R.B., Railway Policy Review, December 1972, 'Support Paper A – The Freight Business', B.R.B.

75 J.S.G. Minutes, 11 July and 24 November 1966, 7 March and 6 June 1967, B.R.B.; P. E. Lazarus (Under-Secretary, M.T.)–Long, 24 February 1969, B.R.B. New Works 95–1–100 Pt. 2.

76 Lazarus–Hammond, 14 February, 5 and 17 March 1966, Hammond–Lazarus, 18 March 1966, B.R.B. 33–1–1. The Welwyn–Blackbridge line closed in October 1970. The Upton–Lytchett Minster by-pass on the A35 crossed the Hamworthy–Broadstone line. Here, the track was retained pending local authority plans for the region.

77 See Table 50 above (the figure of £63m. includes the upperbound total for line closures, £13m., less the £2m. included in it for the effects of reducing passenger-standard lines to freight-only standards). See Costings Division paper on 'Savings on Passenger Service Closures', 6 April 1964, B.R.B. FC351/10.

78 Long (Chief Commercial Officer) and James (Financial Controller), memo. on 'Traffic Costs and Freight Charges Policy', 16 October 1964, British Railways Management Committee Minutes, 25 November 1964, B.R.B. To 1973 about 600,000 wagons and 7,000 route-miles were dispensed with. Joy, Train That Ran Away, p. 76, was critical of B.R.B. assumptions about savings from wagon-fleet reduction.

79 L.M.R., Register of Line, Service and Depot Closures, c.1963–9, B.R.B. The register is incomplete and contains several inconsistencies.

80 Margetts–General Managers on 'Re-shaping of the Railways', 30 November and 20 December 1962, Margetts–General Managers, 4 April 1963, B.R.B. 21–12–12 Pt. 2; M. A. Cameron (Principal Officer (Administration))–F. T. Gray (Director of Costings), 17 May 1963, B.R.B. FC351/9.

81 Margetts and Williams–General Managers, 9 August 1963, and Margetts–General Managers, 19 September 1963; Long–General Managers, 10 October 1963, enclosing Costings Division memo. on 'Criteria for Screening of Traffics at Small Stations', October 1963; B. A. Coulson (Traffic Costing Officer, York)–Gray, 8 January 1964, R. A. Taylor (Director of Traffic Survey)–Long, 3 April 1964, D. S. M. Barrie (Assistant General Manager (Commercial), N.E.R.)–A. H. Hencriffe (Sectional Council), 13 July 1964, B.R.B. FC351/9; letters to General Managers from Margetts and C. A. Haygreen (Planning Officer, Reshaping), 4 May 1964, B.R.B. 33–1–1. On costing variations see Gray, memo. 11 October 1964, Commercial Committee Minutes, 19 October 1964, B.R.B.

82 James, memo. 23 February 1966, B.R.B.

83 Long–Margetts, 13 June 1963, B.R.B. FC351/9; Griffiths, memo. 5 May 1966, B.R.B. 33–1–1. A study of the reasons for rail customers switching to road found that closures were not as important as 'slowness and delays', 'increased charges' and 'losses and damage': B. T. Bayliss and S. L. Edwards, *Industrial Demand for Transport* (London: H.M.S.O., 1970), p. 68.

84 British Railways Management Committee Minutes, 24 November 1964, Commercial Conference Minutes, 12 March 1964, Commercial Committee Minutes, 16 August 1967, B.R.B.; memo. on 'The Wagon Load.System', 22 April 1968, B.R.B. 95–1–30.

85 This was admitted in Support Paper A of the Railway Policy Review, December 1972.

86 B.R. Operations Planning, confidential report on 'Analysis of the 1974 Freight Business Activity', August 1975, B3, and 'significant features and areas for study', p. 10, B.R.B.

87 Margetts–General Managers, 30 November 1962, B.R.B. 21–12–12 Pt. 2; W.R., notes of a meeting held on 4 April 1963 on 'Re-shaping of British Railways – Submissions to the T.U.C.C.s', W.R. divisional closure files, General Policy File, 1/KU7 Pt. 2, B.R.B. The view of G. Dickinson, Principal Traffic Costing Officer (Paddington), was that broad estimates based on unit costs for *Reshaping* 'would not stand the test of close examination', ibid. See also Raymond–Margetts, 23 September 1963, B.R.B. FC351/103 pt. 1.

88 See Margetts–General Managers, 2 December 1963, B.R.B. FC351/101 Pt. 1; J. E. Dewdney (Planning Officer, Reshaping)–Margetts, 22 June 1965, B.R.B. FC351/10; Memo. of discussion held at B.R.B. 9 June 1966, B.R.B. FC351/101 Pt. 2. For more detail on the administrative procedure see, *inter alia*, M. Howe, 'The Transport Act, 1962, and the Consumers' Consultative Committees', *Public Administration*, XLII (Spring 1964), 45–56.

89 R. D. Gardiner (Divisional Manager, Leicester)–S. W. Walton (Secretary, East Midlands, T.U.C.C.), 28 May and 4 June 1965; L. A. Metcalf (Line Manager's Office, Derby)–Walton, 12 August 1965, East Midlands T.U.C.C. Files, EM456; *Parl. Deb. (Commons)*, vol. 714 (Session 1964–5), 16 June 1965, Written Answer by T. Fraser to J. Farr, 75–6.

90 Johnson–Dewdney, 10 August 1965, L.M.R. Closure Files, 7–19–51, B.R.B.

91 W. I. Winchester–M. H. B. Gilmour (Legal Adviser and Secretary), 8 December 1966, B.R.B. FC351/103 Pt. 2. Kinnoull's question followed an earlier one from Tom Bradley asking for the total financial saving since *Reshaping*. See *Parl. Deb. (Commons)*, vol. 736 (Session 1966–7), 25 November 1966, S. Swingler–Bradley, *371, (Lords)*, vol. 278 (Session 1966–7), 15 December 1966, Lord Champion–Earl of Kinnoull, 1825–6.

92 For details see Appendix J.

93 Aldcroft, *British Railways*, p. 200; B.R.B. W.R., Brecon Lines Rationalisation, Briefs submitted to T.U.C.C.s, II, B.R.B.

94 The two cases (both unopposed) were: Newcastle–Washington and Flax Bourton station (near Bristol).

95 See Appendix J, Table 1.

96 B.T.C., 'Programme of Modernisation 1961–1964', 19 December 1960, B.R.B., modified in General Staff paper on 'Rationalisation of Railway Facilities in 1961', 17 April 1961, B.T.C. Minutes, 27 April 1961, B.R.B. Lists of lines and services are in B.R.B. 33–1–14.

97 E. C. V. Goad (M.T.), speaking at meeting of T.U.C.C. Secretaries, 2 October 1962, Yorkshire T.U.C.C. Files, YC249(2). On the Ministry's anxiety about the system, see Serpell, note of 23 May 1961, and correspondence in Ministry of Transport Correspondence and Papers: Transport Users Consultative Committees Policy, MT96/22, P.R.O.

98 Serpell–E. G. Whitaker (member, C.T.C.C.), 13 August 1962, and notes of a meeting of T.U.C.C. Chairmen, 11 September 1962, Yorkshire T.U.C.C. YC249(2); C.T.C.C. Minutes, 11 July 1961, 13 March 1962, C.T.C.C.; Serpell–Wansbrough-Jones, 22 October 1962, B.R.B. FC351/1.

99 Shirley–Beeching, 8 October 1963, B.R.B. FC351/12; *Parl. Deb. (Commons)*, vol. 682 (Session 1962–3), 24 October 1963, Written Answer, Marples–G. Wilson, *253–4*. On protestors see the activities of N.C.I.T., Railway Development Association, etc.

100 Marples–Beeching, 19 December 1963; B.R.B., 'Financial Information Given to the Minister of Transport about Passenger Withdrawal and Modification Proposals', n.d., B.R.B. FC351/10.

101 Beeching–Marples, 10 January 1964, enclosing 'Selected Cases', B.R.B. FC351/10. In this exercise, the data supporting closure were rounded.

102 A third, the Central Wales line, was refused in February 1964.

103 E.g. Manchester–Buxton, Newcastle–Tynemouth, Middlesbrough–Whitby. It is sometimes difficult to distinguish 'full' and 'partial' closures, and official statistics (*Hansard*, B.R.B. reports, and B.R.B.'s internal 'Refusals and Part Refusals to Closure Applications since 1962 Act') vary. Related proposals are often considered as one. Cf. A. W. Allen–R. G. Smith, note for papers on 'Parliamentary Question', 8 March 1967, B.R.B. FC351/103 Pt. 2.

104 C. T. Rogers (Special Duties Officer, P.R. & P.)–Eric Merrill, 28 May 1965, B.R.B. P.R.& P. 33–2–2 Pt. 4.

105 Rogers–Merrill, 9 July 1964, Merrill–F. D. Bickerton (Chief Information Officer, M.T.), 10 July 1964, ibid. No response is recorded in the file. Margetts, memo. on 'Service, Line and Station Closures – Passenger and Freight', 1 July 1964, B.R.B. Minutes, 9 July 1964, B.R.B. 'Cost' here was merely direct revenue *minus* direct costs for proposals as reported to T.U.C.C.s and Ministry, from the expiry date for objections to the Minister's decision or the end of June 1964.

106 Marples–Beeching, 27 April 1964, B.R.B. 33–1–5 Pt. 4; B.R.B., *R. & A.*

1963–8, section on 'unremunerative passenger services'. For information on Ministerial action see Appendix J, Tables 2 and 4.

107 Fraser–Beeching, 2 and 10 November 1964, Beeching–Fraser, 16 November 1964, B.R.B. 33–1–5 Pt. 5; North Western T.U.C.C., 'Report to Minister . . .', 15 June 1964, North Western T.U.C.C. Files, NW No. 36. The 'sift' process was applied to all cases published after the Labour Government took office on 16 October.

108 Fraser–Beeching, 2 and 10 November 1964, B.R.B. 33–1–5 Pt. 5, and cf. B. Castle, *The Castle Diaries 1964–70* (London: Weidenfeld & Nicolson, 1984), p. 19. The undertaking not to lift the track until Ministerial assent was obtained was altered in June 1966 to an undertaking not to dispose of the formation, i.e. the track *bed*. Rails could now be sold.

109 Margetts, memo. 7 April 1965, British Railways Management Committee Minutes, 21 April 1965, B.R.B. The other four cases were: Lincoln–Firsby, Leeds–Knottingley, Wakefield–Goole and Brighton–Shoreham (Christ's Hospital). Three of the six cases were handed on to Barbara Castle.

110 Other cases included Glasgow–Shotts–Edinburgh, Glasgow–East Kilbride, Crewe–Shrewsbury, Romford–Upminster and Manchester (Victoria)–Bury–Bolton. The three 'sift' refusals were Cramlington station, Exeter–Barnstaple and Exeter–Okehampton.

111 Beeching–Fraser, 7 December 1964, 13 January and 14 May 1965, Fraser–Beeching, 23 December 1964, 21 January 1965, B.R.B. 33–1–5 Pt. 5. See also B.R.B. FC351/10.

112 Minister's address to C.T.C.C., 1 December 1964, C.T.C.C. Files, CC1010/7; Fraser–Beeching, 21 January 1965, Margetts–General Managers, 15 February 1965, B.R.B. 33–1–5 Pt. 5. Of course, refusals and substantial part-refusals forced such a policy on the Board.

113 The Council refused to endorse individual closure proposals until regional plans were finalised. C. P. Scott-Malden (Under-Secretary, M.T.)–Margetts, 13 August 1965, Fraser–Raymond, 20 August 1965, B.R.B. 33–1–5 Pt. 5.

114 Beeching–Fraser, 13 May 1965, Fraser–Raymond, 3 June 1965 and reply 21 June 1965, ibid., and see also correspondence in B.R.B. 240–1–5 Pt. 2.

115 Fraser–Raymond, 13 July 1965, Margetts–General Managers, 23 September 1965, B.R.B. 33–1–5 Pt. 5; British Railways Management Committee Minutes, 21 July 1965, B.R.B. The Minister was concerned that the consents should be reflected in an improvement in the 1966 budget: see 'Discussion between B.R.B. and M.T., 7th July 1965'; Costings Division, 'Note for Papers', 31 August 1965; R. G. Smith–Winchester, 6 August 1965, B.R.B. FC351/113.

116 Noel-Baker–Hondelink, 22 July 1965, Noel-Baker Papers, Churchill College, Cambridge, NBKR 3x/9. The seven cases were: Penrith–Workington, Leeds–Knottingley, Watford–Croxley, Liverpool–Gateacre, Wakefield–Goole, Cambridge–St Ives–March and Felixstowe Beach Station.

117 Margetts, memos. 23 September 1965, 2 February 1966, B.R.B. 33–1–5 Pt. 5.

118 Cf. P. S. Bagwell, *The Railwaymen,* II, *The Beeching Era and After* (London: George Allen & Unwin, 1982), p. 151.

119 Three of the four 'sift' cases were also in the North-West: Manchester (Piccadilly)–Hayfield–Macclesfield (part) and Liverpool–Ormskirk–Preston (part), April 1966, and Liverpool–Tydesley–Manchester, March 1967. The other was Bridgend–Treherbert, February 1967.

120 Raymond, confidential note, 6 April 1966, B.R.B. 21–12–17 Pt. 1.
121 Notes of meeting between the Minister and the Chairman, 16 February 1966, B.R.B. 21–2–11, and Castle–Raymond, 4 March 1966, B.R.B. 21–12–17 Pt. 1.
122 Margetts–Raymond, 18 April 1966, Hammond, note on 'Watershed Map', 31 March 1966, and 'Watershed Map. Changes suggested by the Ministry' (n.d.), B.R.B. 21–12–17 Pt. 1. Only Saxmundham–Aldeburgh was in fact closed, the East Suffolk line being retained. Castle–Raymond, 16 June 1966, ibid.
123 Lines reprieved included Cardiff–Coryton, Bolton–Blackburn–Burnley–Skipton, Penrith–Keswick and Castle Cary–Dorchester. Castle–Raymond, 16 June 1966 and reply 21 July 1966, B.R.B. 21–12–17 Pt. 2; Hammond–Raymond, 22 September 1966, Raymond, note, 5 October 1966, B.R.B. 33–1–5 Pt. 6.
124 Griffiths (Traffic Survey Officer (Euston))–Haygreen, 18 November 1963, B.R.B. FC351/107 Pt. 1; Johnson, memo. 1 June 1965, L.M.R. Closure Files, 7–19–33, Johnson–Haygreen, 6 August 1964, 7–19–97, B.R.B. On the general position see Margetts, memo. 15 April 1966, B.R.B. 33–1–5 Pt. 6.
125 Note on 'Yatton–Clevedon', 17 December 1964, note to Margetts on 'Proposal to Modify instead of Withdrawing the Bodmin Road/Bodmin North to Padstow Passenger Service', 6 February 1964, and other material in B.R.B. FC351/107 Pt. 1.
126 Fiennes–Hammond, 27 May 1966, Hammond–Scott-Malden, 7 June 1966, Hammond, draft memo. March 1964, ibid.; Eastern Railway Board Minutes, 8 July 1964, and see also 14 April 1964, B.R.B.; G. F. Fiennes, *I Tried to Run a Railway* (London: Ian Allan, 1967), pp. 112–20; B.R.B. and Association of County Councils, *Review of Rural Railways* (London: 1984), p. 15.
127 Fiennes–Hammond, 15 December 1966, Hammond–Margetts, 21 December 1966, Margetts–Dewdney, 4 August 1967, B.R.B. FC351/107 Pt. 2; Hammond–Margetts and James, 2 February 1967, Margetts–James and Hammond, 6 February 1967 ('this blatant use of "seaside" contributory revenue just isn't on'), Margetts–Fiennes, 15 February 1967, in B.R.B. Reshaping File (unreferenced).
128 Data in Costings Service (Waterloo)–Gray, 14 February 1964, B.R.B. FC351/107 Pt. 1. The inadequacy of proposed alternative bus services kept the line open. McKenna–Margetts, 13 May 1965, Margetts–McKenna, 4 October 1965, R. G. Smith–Dewdney, 26 May 1965, Dewdney–Margetts, 28 September 1965, Smith–Hammond, 16 March 1966, ibid. McKenna's data showed a net financial effect of £5,500–10,500 after payment of bus subsidy, and with single-line operation, −£5,700 and −£21,700.
129 James–Margetts, 1 August 1967, a response to McKenna–Margetts, 7 June 1967, and R. G. Smith–Dewdney, 20 June 1967, B.R.B. FC351/107 Pt. 2; South East T.U.C.C., 'Further Report to the Minister of Transport on the Proposed Withdrawal of Passenger Train Services between Alton and Winchester', 31 July 1970, S.E. T.U.C.C.; John Arlott, 'Transport through the Looking Glass', *Guardian*, 28 November 1967.
130 James–Raymond, 12 July 1967, B.R.B. 33–1–14; James–Margetts, 1 August 1967, B.R.B. FC351/107 Pt. 2.
131 Only 19 of 51 principal services, and 15 out of 62 secondary services were making a satisfactory contribution to indirect costs. Margetts, memo. 7 December 1966, James and Margetts, memo. 9 December 1966, B.R.B.

Minutes, 9 December 1966, British Railways Management Committee Minutes, 22 December 1966, B.R.B.

132 Cooper Bros., report to the J.S.G. on 'Subsidies for Loss-Making Passenger Services: Order of Magnitude Estimate', 17 May 1967, B.R.B.; B.R.B., R. & A. 1967, I, pp. 2, 51. The £83m. was made up as follows: £14m. 'grey' lines; £14m. London suburban; £10m. other suburban; £26m. stopping; £19m. principal and secondary services.

133 B.R. Divisional Manager (Bristol)–Ibbotson (General Manager), on 'Branch Lines in Devon and Cornwall', W.R. File, 117/X8/43, B.R.B., and see also Hammond–Ibbotson, 2 November 1967, ibid., and Castle–Raymond, 27 July and 31 October 1967, B.R.B. 33–1–5 Pt. 7.

134 Margetts–Raymond, 16 May 1966, B.R.B. 21–12–17 Pt. 1, and see Margetts–Raymond, 19 and 27 July 1967, B.R.B. 33–1–5 Pt. 7.

135 R. Crossman, The Diaries of a Cabinet Minister, III (London: Hamish Hamilton and Jonathan Cape, 1977), p. 124, cit. in Bagwell, The Railwaymen, II, p. 30; B.R.B., R. & A. 1969, I, pp. 64–71.

136 B.R.B., R. & A. 1969, I, pp. 19–20. A recent study of the social effects of branch-line closures, commissioned by B.R.B., found considerable hardship after closure and noted also a loss of contributory revenue: M. Hillman and A. Whalley, The Social Consequences of Rail Closures (London: Policy Studies Institute, 1980), pp. 61–2, 110–18.

137 B.R.B., R. & A. 1968, I, p. 8.

138 See South Western T.U.C.C., 'Report on . . . Ilfracombe and Barnstaple Jnc.', 4 November 1968, S.W. T.U.C.C.94; 'Report on . . . Taunton and Minehead', 30 December 1968; protests of M.P.s Tom King and Edward du Cann; Lt-Col J. K. MacFarlan (Chairman, S.W. T.U.C.C.)–Mulley, 3 April 1970, and reply, 13 April 1970, and Lazarus–McFarlan, 2 June 1970, S.W. T.U.C.C.95.

139 Including Manchester (Exchange)–Huddersfield, and Manchester–Woodhead–Sheffield.

140 Note that Romford–Upminster, Bradford–Ilkley, Marks Tey–Sudbury and Paignton–Kingswear were all with the Ministry for three years.

141 See correspondence in B.R.B. 33–60–1 Pts. 2 and 3, and, in particular, Johnson–Mulley, 10 February and 22 April 1970, Mulley–Johnson, 25 March 1970; Marsh–Peyton, 18 August and 21 September 1971, Peyton–Marsh, 10 September, 7 October and 30 December 1971.

142 See L.M.R. Closure File, 7–19–86 Pts. 1 and 2, B.R.B., including David Bowick–Dewdney/Satchwell, 2 November 1964, Bowick–Hammond, 19 April 1967, and John Morris–Hammond, 1 August 1967; Hammond–Raymond, 1 and 2 June 1967, in B.R.B. 33–1–10; M.T., The Cambrian Coast Line (London: H.M.S.O., 1969), and criticisms, e.g. by K. Richards, 'The Economics of the Cambrian Coast Line', Journal of Transport Economics and Policy, VI (September 1972), 308–20.

143 Brief for Liaison Officer, B.R. and other material, including R. J. E. Dawson (Assistant Secretary, M.T.)–Hammond, 10 October 1969, Sc.R. Closure File, RP/TS24/96 Pts. 1–3, B.R.B. The 1969 grant to the Kinross route was £219,000, to Edinburgh–Stirling £121,000. The 1970 grant to Edinburgh–Stirling–Perth was £444,000. B.R.B., R. & A. 1969–70.

144 Notes of meeting between Morris, Castle and Chairmen of the T.U.C.C.s, 5 June 1967, C.T.C.C. File CC1000/30; notes of a meeting of South East

T.U.C.C., 11 December 1968, and M.T., Memo. to C.T.C.C., November 1968, in B.R.B. 33–1–5 Pt. 8.

145 Bus subsidies paid by B.R., £1.012m. in 1968, fell to £0.31m. in 1969, largely as a result of a transfer of responsibility to the National Bus Company and Scottish Transport Group. See B.R.B., *R. & A. 1968*, I, p. 31.

146 Objection No. 15 (Inverness–Wick–Thurso), 13 December 1963, Sc.R. RT/TS2/24/79 Pt. 3, B.R.B.; East Midlands and East Anglia T.U.C.C., draft reports (Oxford–Cambridge), October 1964, East Anglia T.U.C.C. Box 6A; Welsh T.U.C.C., report, 25 June 1968, Welsh T.U.C.C. file no. 576.

147 G. Jamieson (Secretary, Bird Society)–J. Bonar (Secretary, Scottish T.U.C.C.), 4 October 1966, Scottish T.U.C.C. File R738/1.

148 Cf. brief for Liaison Officer, B.R., for Edinburgh–Hawick–Carlisle (Waverley Line), Sc.R. RT/TS24/41 Pt. 3, B.R.B.

149 J. Royston (Line Manager, Crewe)–Johnson, 29 December 1964, Johnson–Dewdney, 5 February and 28 May 1965, L.M.R. 7–19–97, B.R.B.

150 L. E. Plenty–C. E. Cresswell, 1 February 1966, East Midlands T.U.C.C. report, 19 July 1966, E.M. T.U.C.C. File EM506; Dewdney–Margetts, memo. on 'Financial Information to M.O.T. and T.U.C.C.s', June 1965 (cites Folkestone and Chester–Holyhead cases), B.R.B. FC351/10.

151 G. Lambert (Line Traffic Manager, Manchester)–Johnson, 28 May 1964, J. C. Chambers (Secretary, C.T.C.C.)–Sir Patrick Hamilton (Chairman, North Western T.U.C.C.), 7 July 1964, L.M.R. 7–19–46, B.R.B. On Stonham's challenge re B.R.B. data, and the definition of 'hardship', see *Parl. Deb. (Lords)*, vol. 250 (Session 1962–3), 19 and 20 June 1963, 1347–55, 1368, 1466–74, and correspondence with Raymond and Margetts, 22–9 July 1963, in B.R.B. 21–12–12 Pt. 2. Silkin later became Attorney-General in the Labour Government of 1974–9.

152 E. R. Hondelink, *Stopping Trains* (1963), and cf. *Nottingham Evening Post*, 8 August 1966. East Lothian County Council commissioned a study of the North Berwick line by R. White (University of Newcastle) and K. Alexander (Strathclyde): East Lothian County Council–W. Ross (Secretary of State for Scotland), 15 November 1968, Scottish T.U.C.C. File R787.

153 T. R. Gourvish (Secretary, Scottish Railway Development Association)–L. A. Dumelow (Secretary, Scottish T.U.C.C.), 20 November and 18 December 1968, 13 January 1969, Scottish T.U.C.C. File R787; Objection No. 26, Sc.R. RP/TS24/96, B.R.B.

154 For internal criticisms of regional inconsistency see Memo. of discussion held at B.R.B. 9 June 1966, Arthur Dean–Margetts, 3 June 1966 ('one asks what would a reasonable man do'), Gray, draft memo. on 'Passenger Services: Financial Estimates, Earnings and Contributory Revenue', June 1966, B.R.B. FC351/101 Pt. 2.

155 In fact, data for 21 cases with savings of £838,000 were given: *Parl. Deb. (Lords)*, vol. 256 (Session 1963–4), 14 March 1964, Chesham–Stonham, 714–15. But the Swansea–Pontardulais proposal (savings: £100,000) cannot be readily compared with T.U.C.C. data, since it was part of a 'pipeline' case (Central Wales line) reported on before 1963.

156 *Parl. Deb. (Commons)*, vol. 736 (Session 1966–7), 25 November 1966, Swingler–Bradley, 371.

157 Beeching–Fraser, 14 May 1965, B.R.B. FC351/10; D. G. Fagan (M.T.)–Dewdney, 23 January 1968, and reply, 5 February 1968, and see Winchester–

Gilmour, 8 December 1966, B.R.B. FC351/103 Pt. 2. For a parliamentary reaction see *Parl. Deb. (Commons)*, vol. 757 (Session 1967–8), 22 January 1968, N. Carmichael, G. Wilson and T. G. D. Galbraith, 107–8.

158 60 of the 424 consents/part-consents, 1963–73.

159 Winchester–Tait, 13 September 1972, B.R.B. Finance 27–1–14. It is quite possible, of course, that regions failed to take note of *all* savings elements.

160 Margetts, memos. 22 October and 17 December 1962, B.R.B. 171–2–4 Pt. 1; British Railways Committee Minutes, 26 July and 26 October 1962, B.R.B.; Margetts, memo. on 'Steam Locomotive Stock', 11 December 1963, B.R.B. Minutes, 26 September and 19 December 1963, 8 August 1968, B.R.B.

161 Report of Working Party on 'Repair and Production Policy for Locomotives and Rolling Stock', February 1959, B.T.C. Minutes, 19 and 26 March 1959; General Staff memo. on 'Report on Progress in Reduction of Workshop Facilities and Staff', 24 October 1960, B.T.C. Minutes, 27 October 1960, B.R.B.

162 General Staff memo. on 'Workshop Policy', 14 December 1961, B.T.C. Minutes, 21 December 1961, and see also 10 and 24 August 1961; Sir Steuart Mitchell, memo. 17 September 1963; B.R.B. Minutes, 10 October 1963, B.R.B. A summary of the workshops story is given in Johnson and Long, *British Railways Engineering*, pp. 502–45.

163 Cf. A. E. Robson (General Manager, B.R. Workshops), report to B.R.B., August 1968, B.R.B. Two favourable academic responses to B.R. policy were P. L. Cook, *Railway Workshops: The Problem of Contraction* (Cambridge: Cambridge University Press, 1964), and D. Wedderburn, *Redundancy and the Railwaymen* (Cambridge: Cambridge University Press, 1965).

164 Mitchell, confidential report on 'Main Workshops. Future Plan', 31 July 1962, B.T.C. Minutes, 23 August 1962, and memo. on 'Information Passed to Representatives of N.U.R. and Confederation of Shipbuilding and Engineering Unions', 20 August 1962, London Midland Area Board Minutes, 6 September 1962, B.R.B.; *Reshaping*, I, pp. 50–2.

165 H. O. Houchen, memo. 8 September 1967, British Railways Management Committee Minutes, 27 September 1967, B.R.B., and info. in B.R.B. 171–201–2 Pt. 1.

166 R. C. Bond (General Manager, Workshops), memo. 14 December 1966, B.R.B. Minutes, 22 December 1966. In current prices, overall maintenance expenditure fell from £25.3m. to £23.5m.; in constant 1962 prices, it fell from £25.3m. to £19.6m.

167 B.R.B. Minutes, 12 November 1964, General Managers' Committee Minutes, 23 July 1969, B.R.B.

168 Report of *S.C. Nat. Ind.: B.R.*, July 1960, pp. lxxv–vi; S.A.G., Recommendation No. 5, September 1960, Beeching Papers, Box 8, and Deloitte, Plender, Griffiths & Co., report, 24 October 1960, in Osborn, memo. on 'Regional Accounts', 1 December 1960, and confidential memo. on 'Sectional Accounts', same date, Finance Committee Minutes, 7 December 1960, and B.T.C. Minutes, 22 December 1960, B.R.B.

169 Cf. First Progress Report of Conference on Regional Accounts and Traffic Trading Accounts, 1 November 1961, Finance Committee Minutes, 22 November 1961, B.R.B., and E. W. Godfrey–R. R. Goodison, 21 January 1959, Ministry of Transport Correspondence and Papers: British Transport

Commission: Finances: Regional Accounting for British Railways, 1959–1960, MT56/450, P.R.O.
170 Shirley, memo. 20 February 1962, B.T.C. Minutes, 7 March 1962, B.R.B.
171 See 'The Western's £30 Million Saving' and 'The Western Will Be in the Black This Year' (interview with Fiennes), *Modern Railways* (January 1965), and Fiennes, *I Tried to Run a Railway*, pp. 94–111.
172 James, memo. on 'Costs and Freight Traffic', 24 February 1966, British Railways Management Committee Minutes, 27 April 1966; Commercial Conference Minutes, 13 May 1966, B.R.B.
173 Oil prices rose more steeply than the G.D.P. deflator in 1963 and 1964, and prices were exceptionally high – 5.02p a gallon – in 1968. Electricity prices increased more than average in 1963–6.
174 B.R.B., *R. & A. 1963*, II, p. 20, *1973*, p. 29. This point is also made by Richard Pryke, *The Nationalised Industries. Policies and Performance since 1968* (Oxford: Martin Robertson, 1981), p. 84.
175 Beeching, verbatim notes of R.S.N.T. proceedings, 6 November 1964; Raymond, confidential note, 10 April 1967, Raymond Papers, B.R.B.

11. Markets, pricing and commercial strategy

1 Real price changes, 1963–73: all categories, 1.0 per cent; season tickets, 1.8 per cent; reduced tickets, 1.25 per cent; ordinary full fares, 0.7 per cent. Reduced fares made up 40 per cent of journeys and 34 per cent of receipts in 1963. In 1973 the percentages were 23 and 27.
2 At the same time the share of the 'other' category, i.e. all traffic other than coal, coke, iron and steel, went up from 32 per cent to 43 per cent.
3 E.g. Production-Engineering Ltd, report to J.S.G. on 'Commercial Activities, and Particularly the Marketing of Passenger and Freight Services', February 1967, B.R.B.; report of *S.C. Nat. Ind.: Min. Control*, July 1968, P.P.1967–8, XIII; *S.C. Nat. Ind.: Role of B.R.*, 1976–7, M.O.E., and report, April 1977, P.P.1976–7, XXXIV; P.I.B., Report No. 72 on *Proposed Increases by British Railways Board In Certain Country-Wide Fares and Charges*, May 1968, P.P.1967–8, XXVIII, Cmnd.3656.
4 10 & 11 Eliz. II, c.46; *The Financial and Economic Obligations of the Nationalised Industries*, April 1961, P.P.1960–1, XXVII, Cmnd.1337, and *Nationalised Industries. A Review of Economic and Financial Objectives*, November 1967, P.P. 1967–8, XXXIX, Cmnd.3437.
5 Beeching–Marples, 3 and 15 July 1964, Marples–Beeching, 14 July 1964, B.R.B. 99–2–1 Pt. 4; report of *S.C. Nat. Ind.: Min. Control*, July 1968, p. 87, and M.O.E., QQ.1449–54, 1918.
6 B.R.B., Memo. 1 March 1967, *S.C. Nat. Ind.: Min. Control*, 1967–8, M.O.E., 27 April 1967; Ministerial Directions (2), 5 October 1964, repro-duced in B.R.B., *R. & A. 1964*, I, pp. 75–6.
7 Beeching–Marples, 16 July 1964, B.R.B. 95–44–4; British Railways Management Committee Minutes, 24 May 1967, B.R.B.; note of a meeting between the Minister and Beeching, 19 November 1964, and information relating to 1967 complaint about rates from Yorkshire Collieries to Plymouth Gasworks, B.R.B. 102–15–18.
8 *Prices and Incomes Policy: An 'Early Warning System'*, November 1965,

P.P.1965–6, XIII, Cmnd.2808; report of *S.C. Nat. Ind.: Min. Control*, July 1968, pp. 88–9. There is an abundant literature on the P.I.B. and prices and incomes policy. See, for example, Joan Mitchell, *The National Board for Prices and Incomes* (London: Secker & Warburg, 1972), A. Fels, *The British Prices and Incomes Board* (Cambridge: Cambridge University Press, 1972), W. Beckerman (ed.), *The Labour Government's Economic Record, 1964–70* (London: Duckworth, 1972), J. L. Fallick and R. F. Elliott, *Incomes Policies, Inflation and Relative Pay* (London: George Allen & Unwin, 1981), esp. Appendix, R. E. J. Chater, A. Dean and R. F. Elliott (eds.), *Incomes Policy* (Oxford: Clarendon Press, 1981), C. Balfour, *Incomes Policy and the Public Sector* (London: Routledge, 1972), F. T. Blackaby (ed.), *British Economic Policy 1960–74* (Cambridge: Cambridge University Press, 1978).

9 B.R.B. Minutes, 23 July 1964, 28 January 1965; Raymond–Beeching, 30 July 1964, B.R.B. 99–7–7 Pt. 1.

10 Raymond, memos. 14 April 1964, 19 March 1965, B.R.B. Minutes, 23 April 1964, joint meeting of B.R.B. and British Railways Management Committee, Minutes, 25 March 1965, B.R.B.

11 Fraser–Raymond, 23 June 1965, Raymond–Fraser, 8 July 1965, Raymond, Note on 'London Fares', 4 August 1965, B.R.B. 99–7–7 Pt. 2.

12 T.T., London Fares (British Railways) Order, 1966, No. 2, 18 July 1966.

13 Raymond–Castle, 18 November 1966, 27 February 1967, Castle–Raymond, 14 December 1966, 22 February 1967; 'Note of a Meeting between the Chairman B.R.B. and the Minister of Transport', 4 January 1967, B.R.B. 99–7–7 Pt. 2.

14 Shirley, memo. on 'London Fares', 18 July 1967, B.R.B. Minutes, 27 July 1967; Castle–Raymond, 22 June and 3 August 1967, B.R.B. 99–2–1 Pt. 4.

15 B.R.B. Minutes, 10 August 1967.

16 The L.T.B. decision had been given in March. In making its report on B.R.B., the P.I.B. made it clear that it saw no case for assimilation. See P.I.B., Report No. 72, Cmnd.3656, and report No. 56 on *Proposals by London Transport Board and British Railways Board for Fare Increases in London Area*, March 1968, P.P.1967–8, XXVII, Cmnd.3561.

17 B.R. Ordinary fares:

	Existing	Proposed	Tribunal ruling
1 mile	4d.	6d.	5d.
2 miles	8d.	1s. 0d.	9d.
4 miles	1s. 3d.	1s. 6d.	1s. 3d.
6 miles	1s. 9d.	2s. 0d.	1s. 9d.

Taken from P.I.B., Report No. 72, Cmnd. 3656, T.T., London Fares (British Railways) Order, 1968, No. 2, 16 August 1968, and see B.R.B. press release, 21 August 1968, B.R.B. P.R. & P. 99–7–1 Pt. 1.

18 These estimates are based on estimated annual yields of successive fares proposals. See, for example, B.R.B., 'Written Case for Application to Transport Tribunal', 30 May 1968, B.R.B. 99–7–7 Pt. 2.

19 Extract from Ministry note of meeting between Minister of Transport and Chairman B.R.B. at Brighton, 4 October 1966, B.R.B. 246–66–2; Raymond–

Castle, two letters, 21 November 1966, B.R.B. 99–2–1 Pt. 4; Commercial Conference Minutes, 18 April 1967, B.R.B. On government policy see *Prices and Incomes Standstill: Period of Severe Restraint*, November 1966, P.P.1966–7, LIX, Cmnd.3150, and *Prices and Incomes Policy after 30th June 1967*, March 1967, P.P.1966–7, LIX, Cmnd.3235.

20 Castle–Raymond, 9 March 1967, B.R.B. 99–2–1 Pt. 4.

21 Castle–Raymond, 21 March 1967, ibid., and Commercial Conference Minutes, 18 April 1967, B.R.B. The Board had proposed to increase the taper rates to the existing ordinary rate of 3.25d. a mile. Castle also made specific instructions in relation to juvenile concessionary season tickets: Castle–Raymond, 27 September 1967, B.R.B. 21–27–4.

22 Raymond–Castle, 15 August 1967, B.R.B. Finance 21–27–1 Pt. 1; P.I.B., Report No. 72, Cmnd.3656, pp. 1–2; Commercial Conference Special Meeting Minutes, 5 June 1968, B.R.B.; extract from note of a meeting of Chairmen of Nationalised Industries, 14 August 1967, B.R.B. 21–27–4. For further correspondence between Raymond and Castle, 22 May–27 September 1967, see B.R.B. 99–2–1 Pt. 4.

23 *S.C. Nat. Ind.: Min. Control*, 1967–8, M.O.E. 26 March 1968, Memo. of Guidance by Secretary of State, Department of Economic Affairs, 28 September 1967.

24 Raymond–Shirley and Johnson, 11 September 1967, B.R.B. 21–27–4.

25 James–Raymond, 13 November 1967, ibid.

26 P.I.B., Report No. 72, Cmnd.3656, p. 14.

27 Ibid. pp. 17–22; M. V. Posner, 'Policy towards Nationalized Industries', in Beckerman, *The Labour Government's Economic Record*, p. 255.

28 Commercial Conference Special Meeting Minutes, 5 June 1968, B.R.B.; James, B.R.B. Minutes, 13 June 1968, Johnson– Marsh, 6 May 1968, B.R.B. 21–17–4; General Managers' Committee Minutes, 21 February 1968, B.R.B.

29 Raymond, memo. to British Railways Management Committee on 'Passenger Fares Policy', 18 February 1964, British Railways Management Committee Minutes, 26 February 1964; Commercial Conference Minutes, 14 May 1965, B.R.B.

30 B.R.B. Minutes, 26 August 1965.

31 Cooper Bros., report to J.S.G. on 'British Railways – Passenger Marketing', 11 July 1967, B.R.B.; B.R.B., Memo. to National Board for Prices and Incomes, October 1967, and 'Proposals for Increases in Fares and Charges outside London – Headroom', 16 February 1968, B.R.B. 21–27–4.

32 Cf. the complaint that no specialist staff for commuter traffic or the London area had been appointed: J. H. Nunnelly, memo. 1 July 1965, Commercial Conference Minutes, 7 July 1965, B.R.B.

33 Cooper Bros., report to J.S.G., 11 July 1967, B.R.B.; James, 'What Went Wrong?', 6 September 1972, B.R.B. 27–1–14.

34 Marsh–Johnson, 20 June 1968, B.R.B. 21–27–5; Chairman's Conference Minutes, 10 June 1968; R.M.G. Minutes, 20 May 1970, B.R.B.

35 James–Raymond, 10 August and 28 October 1966, B.R.B. 246–66–2; Johnson–Marsh, 7 June 1968, B.R.B. 21–27–5.

36 Long, memo. on 'Passenger Income – 1970/1971: Pricing Action', 15 May 1970, R.M.G. Minutes, 20 May 1970, B.R.B.

37 Johnson–John Peyton, 7 July 1971, Richard Marsh–Peyton, 16 July 1971, note of Meeting of Chairmen of Nationalised Industries and the Chancellor

of the Exchequer, 14 July 1971, B.R.B. 362–40–25 Pt. 1; B.R. Corporate Finance Department, 'Effect on Results of Price Freeze', 6 September 1971, P. W. McGrath–Marsh, 21 September 1971, B.R.B. 362–40–27.

38 B.R.B., *R. & A. 1971*, I, p. 2. The D.O.E. also offered B.R.B. a higher grant for London and South East services: Marsh–Johnson, 4 August 1971, B.R.B. 362–40–25 pt. 1.

39 Bowick, memo. on 'Pricing Action Following Wages Settlement', 2 June 1972, B.R.B. Minutes, 8 June 1972; Finance Committee Minutes, 6 January 1971; R.M.G. Minutes, 20 June 1972, B.R.B.; Marsh–Peyton, 22 June 1972, B.R.B. 99–2–1 Pt. 6.

40 Finance Committee Minutes, 6 January 1971, B.R.B.

41 See *inter alia*, Fallick and Elliott, *Incomes Policies*, pp. 264–80, Chater, Dean and Elliott, *Incomes Policy*, pp. 9–28, and B. Towers, *British Incomes Policy* (Nottingham: Institute of Personnel Management, 1978).

42 B.R.B., *R. & A. 1973*, p. 3.

43 'Counter-Inflationary Measures. Note of a Meeting Held at 1 Victoria Street at 2.45 p.m. on Monday, 6 November 1972', Marsh, Papers on Pricing, 1970–5, B.R.B.

44 D. H. Jones (Executive Director (Freight)), memo. on 'Rail Pricing in 1973 and 1974', 1 August 1974, B.R.B. Minutes, 8 August 1974.

45 Ibid.; Peyton–Sir Arthur Cockfield, 7 June 1973, Marsh Papers, B.R.B.; B.R.B. Minutes, 14 June, 12 July and 9 August 1973, and B.R.B., *R. & A. 1974*, p. 3. The Price Commission insisted that the effect of industrial disputes on revenue should not be 'normalised' in the calculations and ruled that Social Grant be included in revenue. By rejecting 'normalisation' the Price Commission would not allow the effects of industrial disputes to be reversed to indicate a 'no dispute' situation, a ruling supported by the D.O.E.

46 Jones, memo. 1 August 1974, B.R.B.; R.M.G. Minutes, 15 January 1974, B.R.B.

47 Bosworth–Mulley, 22 July 1974, Mulley–Marsh, 5 August 1974, B.R.B. 99–2–59 pt. 1.

48 B.R.B. Minutes, 8 August 1974.

49 B.R.B., *R. & A. 1974*, p. 3.

50 Marsh–Mulley, 27 August 1974, B.R.B. 99–2–50 Pt. 1.

51 Cf. A. E. T. Griffiths (Executive Director (Passenger)), memo. for B.T.J.C.C. on 'Passenger Pricing', 6 February 1976, B.R.B. 99–2–1 Pt. 7.

52 *Reshaping*, I, pp. 40–1; B.R.B. Minutes, 8 October 1964; British Railways Productivity Council Minutes, 20 September 1963, B.R.B.

53 Commercial and Operating Committee Minutes, 4 April 1966; Williams, memo. on 'Oil Contracts; an Appraisal', 16 December 1963, British Railways Management Committee Minutes, 22 January 1964; R.M.G. Minutes, 27 January 1971, B.R.B.; S. C. Robbins (Executive Director (Freight)), memo. on 'Contracts for Petroleum Products in Bulk', November 1970, B.R.B. 95–6–2 Pt. 3.

54 Beeching–Marples, 24 December 1963, 14 February 1964, B.R.B. 81–1–1 Pt. 2; House, memo. on 'The Petroleum Industry', March 1966, Commercial and Operating Committee Minutes, 4 April 1966, B.R.B.

55 Williams, memo. on 'Oil Contracts: Rates and Costings', 16 December 1963, British Railways Management Committee Minutes, 22 January 1964; Shirley and Margetts, memo. on 'Oil Traffic Agreements', 26 July 1967, ibid. 23

August 1967; Commercial Conference Minutes, 12 March 1965, B.R.B. The traffic was required to make a 20 per cent contribution to indirect costs.

56 Movement Conference Minutes, 8 September 1967, British Railways Management Committee Minutes, 23 August 1967; Robbins, memo. November 1970, B.R.B. 95–6–2 Pt. 3.

57 Marsh, speech to Oil Industries Club, 19 November 1971, B.R.B. 95–6–2 Pt. 3. Cf. Robbins, memo. to General Managers' Committee on 'Oil Traffic Agreements – Profitability Exercise', 17 September 1968, B.R.B. Chief Executive's Files, X/41–3–2.

58 Cooper Bros., report to B.R.B. on 'Freight Marketing', 30 August 1968, Appendix B, B.R.B.

59 General Manager's Office, S.R., memo. on 'Coal Concentration Policy', 4 November 1965, B.R.B. 102–14–4 Pt. 1; Shirley, memo. on 'Progress Report on Coal Concentration', 20 October 1965, B.R.B. Minutes, 25 October 1965.

60 R. G. Smith–Robbins, 25 January 1968, B.R.B. 30–3–79; M. F. Dyer (Fuel Marketing Manager, L.M.R.)–R. L. E. Lawrence on 'Coal Class Traffic to Station Yards and Concentration Depots', 9 May 1969, and A. V. Barker–Robbins, 9 July 1969, X/41–1–8, B.R.B.; Geoffrey Freeman Allen, *British Railfreight Today and Tomorrow* (London: Ian Allan, 1984), pp. 107–9.

61 B.T.C. Minutes, 25 September 1958, B.R.B., and B.R.B. 102–16–21 Pt. 1.

62 Supplementary Memorandum of Agreement between the C.E.G.B. and the B.R.B., 1 December 1963, signed 7 January 1964, Raymond, memo. 2 January 1964, B.R.B. 102–15–21 Pt. 1.

63 Traffic Conference Minutes, 13 March 1964, B.R.B.; Arthur Dean (General Manager, N.E.R.)–Raymond, 16 March 1964; Long (Chief Commercial Officer), memo. on 'Meeting with National Coal Board', 4 November 1964; Beeching–Robens, 5 and 18 November 1964, Robens–Beeching, 13 November 1964, B.R.B. 107–15–21 Pt. 1.

64 Long *et al.*, memo. 27 March 1966, with Appendix A, draft heads of agreement, B.R.B. Minutes, 28 April 1966, B.R.B.; P. W. McGrath, memo. to Investment Committee, 19 March 1971, B.R.B. New Works 102–15–3 Pt. 3.

65 The 1963 Agreement with the C.E.G.B. provided for a fixed charge of 2s. 6d. (less 2d. when 32-ton wagons were used) plus 2.75d per ton-mile up to 30 miles, adjusted for inflation. Direct costs were estimated in 1966 at 1s. 2d. for 5, 10 and 20 miles: Long *et al.*, memo. 27 March 1966, B.R.B.

66 B.R.B. Minutes, 7 December 1967, 11 April and 10 June 1968; W. G. Thorpe–Johnson, 29 January 1969, enclosing 'BR and the Coal Industry. 1 – Why the merry-go-round has gone wrong', *Modern Railways*, February 1969, B.R.B. X/15–1–1; Robbins (Executive Director, (Freight)), 'Freight and Parcels Business Report 1971', March 1971, B.R.B. Minutes, 8 April 1971; P. E. Lazarus–J. E. H. Skerrett, 22 June 1970, B.R.B. New Works 172–345–2 Pt. 6.

67 *Reshaping*, I, pp. 142–6. About 12m. tons of wagon-load were earmarked for transfer to freightliners.

68 *Reshaping*, I, p. 147; Margetts, memo. on 'Liner Trains', 31 July 1963, B.R.B. Minutes, 8 August 1963; memo. on 'Liner Trains', November 1963, B.R.B. Minutes, 28 November 1963; Raymond–Castle, 23 September 1966, and B.R.B., Memo. to M.T. on 'National Freight Grid: Merchandise Services by Freightliner Trains', September 1966, B.R.B. 150–28–1 Pt. 4.

69 Unsigned memo. on 'Liner Trains', 30 October 1963, and H. R. Gomersall, memo. 16 October 1963, B.R.B. 150–28–1 Pt. 1. A return on gross outlay of 7 per cent was considered to be 'clearly inadequate'.
70 General Managers' Committee Minutes, 27 March 1968, B.R.B., and see also Robbins and J. Bonham-Carter, memo. on 'Quality of Freightliner Services', 9 February 1968, General Managers' Committee Minutes, 21 February 1968, and G. Zeitlin and J. A. Holehouse, memo. on 'Freightliner Services: Report on Quality of the Service', January 1968, B.R.B. 150–28–1 Pt. 5. On customer complaints see *Times*, 25 January 1968, and A. W. Hunter (British Paper and Board Makers' Association)–H. F. Heinemann (Board of Trade), 15 December 1967, in B.R.B. P.R. & P. 150–28–1 Pt. 7.
71 Margetts, memo. 30 November 1968, B.R.B. Minutes, 12 December 1968; Robbins (Chief Marketing Manager), memo. on 'Freightliner Profitability', 13 December 1968, B.R.B. 150–28–1 Pt. 5.
72 Raymond, *Sunday Times*, 7 January 1968; Robbins, 'Freight Business Report 1972', July 1972, B.R.B. See also K. M. Johnson and H. C. Garnett, *The Economics of Containerisation* (London: George Allen & Unwin, 1971).
73 Smith–Robbins, 25 January 1968, B.R.B. 30–3–79.
74 Gross revenue for full-load freight. Estimate of £117.6m. from Cooper Bros., report on 'Freight Marketing', August 1968, B.R.B. Total full-load business earned £170.6m., train-load £53.0m. In addition, freightliners earned £2.5m. Two-thirds of the 1967 coal traffic was carried in wagon-loads.
75 Raymond, memo. on 'What is Our Policy for Wagon Load Traffic?', 30 December 1963, Planning Committee Minutes, 14 January 1964, B.R.B.
76 Production-Engineering, report to J.S.G., February 1967; Cooper Bros., report on 'Freight Marketing', 30 August 1968, B.R.B.; Hammond–Ratter, 23 February 1967, Ratter–Hammond, 27 February 1967, and Hammond, memos. on 'P-E Report No. 4', 7 January and 2 March 1967, B.R.B. 21–1–28 Pts. 3 and 4. Production-Engineering had ceased to work for the J.S.G. after criticisms of its approach to the marketing remit.
77 McKenna–Thorpe on 'The Role of the Freight Marketing Department', 12 March 1968, and accompanying memo. on 'Common Sense and the Railway Freight Business', 23 February 1968, B.R.B. 30–3–79.
78 Planning Committee Minutes, 30 March 1966; Shirley, memo. on 'High Capacity Container Traffic', 21 July 1966, British Railways Management Committee Minutes, 21 September 1966, B.R.B.; B.R.B., Memo. to M.T. on 'National Freight Grid . . .', September 1966, B.R.B. 150–28–1 Pt. 4; Lazarus (M.T.)–Long, 24 February 1969, B.R.B. New Works 95–1–100 Pt. 2.
79 British Railways Management Committee Minutes, 23 June 1965, Commercial Committee Minutes, 19 October 1965, R. G. and K. V. Smith (Director of Costings, Commercial Research Manager), memo. on 'Wagon Load Traffic Test 1966', 9 December 1966, Commercial and Operating Committee Minutes, 10 January 1967, B.R.B.
80 Production-Engineering, report to J.S.G., February 1967, B.R.B.; Margetts, memo. to Shirley and James, 10 February 1967, B.R.B. 21–2–28 Pt. 4; B.R.B. Minutes, 11 June 1964.
81 Long, memo. on 'Quality of Service', 26 February 1965, Commercial Committee Minutes, 10 March 1965, B.R.B.
82 Cooper Bros, report on 'Freight Marketing', 30 August 1968, B.R.B. For internal criticisms of the plan see Operating Committee Minutes, 14 February

1967, Headquarters Executive Committee Minutes, 19 August 1968, B.R.B.
83 Wilson, memo. on 'Business Report – Railways', 29 May 1970, B.R.B. Minutes, 11 June 1970.
84 C. Sharp, 'The Allocation of Freight Traffic – A Survey', report to M.T., March 1970, pp. 32, 35–6, B.R.B.
85 B. T. Bayliss and S. L. Edwards, *Industrial Demand for Transport* (London: H.M.S.O., 1970), pp. 66–8.
86 B. M. Deakin and T. Seward, *Productivity in Transport. A Study of Employment, Capital, Output, Productivity and Technical Change* (Cambridge: Cambridge University Press, 1969), pp. 60–2.
87 Commercial Conference Minutes, 27 November 1964, B.R.B.
88 C. T. Rogers–Eric Merrill, 2 February 1965, B.R.B. P.R. & P. 95–5–5; Margetts, memo. 5 December 1963, British Railways Management Committee Minutes, 10 December 1963; Robbins, memo. to Commercial Committee on 'Executive Responsibility: General Post Office', 30 December 1965, Commercial Committee Minutes, 10 January 1966, B.R.B.
89 Margetts–Raymond, 19 July 1966, B.R.B. 21–27–2.
90 Raymond, memo. 16 October 1964, British Railways Management Committee Minutes, 25 November 1964, and see also Long and James, memo. on 'Traffic Costs and Freight Charges Policy', 16 October 1964, British Railways Management Committee Minutes, 21 October 1964, B.R.B.
91 James, memo. on 'Costs and Freight Traffic', 24 February 1966, British Railways Management Committee Minutes, 27 April 1966; Commercial Conference Minutes, 13 May 1966, B.R.B.; James–Raymond, 19 January 1967, B.R.B. 246–67–2.
92 Raymond–Castle, 15 August 1967, B.R.B. Finance 21–27–1 Pt. 1. He had told Fraser the same thing in November 1965.
93 R.M.G. Minutes, 20 May 1970, B.R.B.
94 Johnson, memo. on 'Budget Policy', 10 August 1967, B.R.B. 246–68–2.
95 B.R.B., Memo. on 'Freight Pricing Policy', 27 January 1977, *S.C. Nat. Ind.: Role of B.R.*, 1976–7.
96 Raymond–Fraser, 16 July 1965, Fraser–Raymond, 23 July 1965; 'Summary of Report on B.R.B. Financial Position', 20 September 1965, B.R.B. 240–1–5 Pt. 2. The final deficit in 1965 was £132m., £28m. over budget: Raymond–Fraser, 26 November 1965, enclosing B.R.B. report on 'Financial Position of the Board', November 1965, ibid.
97 B.R.B., report on 'Freight Plan 1968', October 1968, p. 11, B.R.B.
98 Castle–Raymond, 5 May 1967, and see also 25 May 1967, B.R.B. 240–1–5 Pt. 2. Raymond's response was a 13-page letter which emphasised that many factors, such as the general economic recession, were beyond the Board's control: Raymond–Castle, 22 May 1967, ibid.
99 Long, memo. 25 August 1966, Commercial and Operating Committee Minutes, 1 September 1966, B.R.B.
100 Dean, memo. to Planning Committee on 'The Future Framework of Rail Freight Services. Strategic Planning', 12 January 1967, and report on 'Forward Planning. The Future Framework of Rail Freight Services', 17 March 1967, B.R.B. 21–2–45.
101 P. Detmold (Central Planning Unit), 'The Integral Freight Plan', March 1967, B.R.B.
102 British Railways Management Committee Minutes, 24 May 1967, B.R.B.; J.

E. M. Roberts, memo. on 'Planning Organisation', 9 August 1967, B.R.B. PER 48–8–1 Pt. 1; Ratter, memo. on 'Planning of Rail Freight Services', 7 June 1967, B.R.B. New Works 95–1–200 Pt. 2; letter by S. J. Pears (Cooper Bros.) to J.S.G. on 'British Railways Board. Proposals for Management Structure', 2 June 1967, and Cooper Bros., report, 5 June 1967, B.R.B.

103 B.R.B. Minutes, 27 July 1967; Raymond–Long, 11 August 1967, B.R.B. 30–3–77.

104 K. V. Smith (Director of Planning), memo. on 'The Freight Situation', 15 February 1968, B.R.B. 95–1–100 Pt. 1.

105 Long, memo. 2 May 1968, B.R.B. Minutes, 22 February and 9 May 1968; Robbins–A. V. Barker on 'British Steel Corporation', 23 September 1968, B.R.B. X/41–2–1; Johnson–Thorpe, 20 February 1968, B.R.B. 95–1–100 Pt. 1.

106 Robbins, confidential report on 'Studies into the Possible Withdrawal of Freight Services from Selected Areas and Lines', May 1971; confidential memo. on 'Studies into the Possible Withdrawal of Freight Services – East Anglia Area' (Norwich, Ipswich, Whitemoor), August 1971, R.M.G. Minutes, 25 August 1971, B.R.B.

107 Robbins, memo. on 'The Development of a Selective Air-Braked Wagonload Service', 14 May 1973, Railway Management Group Minutes, 23 May 1973, B.R.B. The name 'Speedlink' was introduced in 1977.

108 Serpell, at meeting of B.R.B. and M.T. officials, 16 January 1969, and Lazarus–Long, 24 February 1969, B.R.B. 95–1–100 Pt. 1 and New Works 95–1–100.

109 On criticisms see Michael Bosworth–Johnson, 25 June 1969, B.R.B. 95–1–100 Pt. 3, and on American interest in B.R.B. planning see Long–Johnson, 24 February 1968, B.R.B. 23–1–40 Pt. 1.

110 B.R.B., report on 'Freight Plan 1968', October 1968, pp. 17–19, 34–7, 51–3, B.R.B.

111 Ibid. pp. 38–43.

112 Chairman's Conference Minutes, 21 October and 28 November 1968, B.R.B.; B.R.B. Minutes, 11 December 1968; Lazarus–Long, 24 February 1969, Bosworth–Johnson, 25 June 1969, Lazarus–Bosworth, 8 August 1969, B.R.B. New Works 95–1–100 Pts. 2–4.

113 Skerrett–Johnson, 15 January 1970, Skerrett–Sharp (D.O.E.), 30 July 1973, ibid. Pts. 5, 9.

114 R.M.G. Minutes, 27 October 1971; B.R.B., Second Corporate Plan, February 1972, B9, C3–4; B.R.B., Railway Policy Review, December 1972, Support Paper A on 'The Freight Business', B.R.B.

115 Operating Committee Minutes, 20 January 1965; General Managers' Committee Minutes, 24 April 1968 (note reservations of Ibbotson and Lawrence), and 26 February 1969; R.M.G. Minutes, 17 December 1969; Movement Conference Minutes, 15 January 1970, B.R.B.

116 B.R.B. Minutes, 27 May 1971; J. M. Moore–Bosworth, 2 August 1971, B.R.B. 95–1–200 Pt. 2; B.R.B., *R. & A. 1974*, p. 9; Bowick, evidence to *S.C. Nat. Ind.: Role of B.R.*, 1976–7, 19 October 1976, QQ. 367–9.

117 R.M.G. Minutes, 23 May 1973, 18 December 1974, B.R.B.; D. S. Binnie (Executive Director, Freight), memo. on 'Development of Airbraked Wagonload Services', December 1974, B.R.B. 95–1–30.

118 R.M.G. Minutes, 25 February 1970, 21 April 1971, B.R.B.

119 Robbins, 'Freight Business Report', 1972 and 1973, B.R.B. 95–1–108.
120 Bowick–Marsh, 18 June 1973, enclosing B.R.B. 'Pricing Policy and Profitability Assessment in Railways', June 1973, Marsh Papers, B.R.B.
121 Executive Directors' Conference Minutes, 15 March 1976, B.R.B.

12. Investment, labour relations and productivity

1 A. E. Robson, report, August 1968, B.R.B.
2 1963–73 data from C.S.O., *National Income and Expenditure 1963–1973* (1974), Table 58 (railway figures differ from those used in this study and exclude leasing 1971–3); Richard Pryke, *Public Enterprise in Practice. The British Experience of Nationalization over Two Decades* (London: MacGibbon and Kee, 1971), p. 289, and cf. his snapshot for 1977 in *The Nationalised Industries. Policies and Performance since 1968* (Oxford: Martin Robertson, 1981), p. 2.
3 B.R.B., *R. & A. 1972*, p. 1, *1973*, p. 3.
4 Cf. J. H. Nunneley (Chief Passenger Manager) and J. Bonham-Carter (Chief Operating Officer), report on 'Multiple Unit Stock – Future Requirements', March 1968, B.R.B., and Railway Policy Review, December 1972, Support Paper D on 'Investment', B.R.B.
5 A. Paterson (Chief Civil Engineer), memo. on 'British Railways. Civil Engineering Department. Ten-Year Plan', January 1969, B.R.B. New Works 195–10–2 Pt. 3; I. M. Campbell (Executive Director (Systems and Operations))–David Bowick (Chief Executive (Railways)) on 'Project: Installation of C.W.R., Comparison with Jointed Track', 11 March 1975, B.R.B. New Works PNW27/1.
6 C. P. Scott-Malden–H. R. Gomersall (Chief Officer (New Works)), 1 August 1967, B.R.B. Finance Planning File, 10–20–102. See also J. E. H. Skerrett (Chief Officer (New Works))–Campbell, 26 November 1973, B.R.B. Signalling and Telecomm. File, 206–1–1 Pt. 2.
7 Signalling and Telecomm. Department Statistics, 1955–73, B.R.B. Signalling and Telecomm. Engineering ref. 250–1–22; B.R.B. Railway Policy Review, December 1972, Support Paper D on 'Investment', p. D5, B.R.B. (signalbox data from B.R.B., *R. & A. 1973*, p. 8).
8 Cf. W. O. Reynolds (Executive Director, Systems and Operations)–regions, 17 December 1970, B.R.B. New Works 145–1–2 Pt. 6.
9 Ryde–Shanklin was also electrified in 1967. For details, see J. Johnson and R. A. Long, *British Railways Engineering 1948–80* (London: Mechanical Engineering Publications, 1981), pp. 227ff.
10 When the Euston station project was put up in March 1962 the overall rate of return on railway finance was estimated to be only 3.7–6.8 per cent depending on the scale of property development: London Midland Area Board Special Meeting Minutes, 8 March 1962, B.R.B. As costs rose, this proved to be optimistic. See Johnson, memo. 22 October 1965, B.R.B. Minutes, 2 November 1965. The final result was buried in the back-check on the electrification as a whole. See B.R.B. Minutes, 12 September 1968. On the failure of the L.M.R.'s office development scheme see ibid. 25 April 1963 and H. C. Johnson–Wansbrough-Jones, 19 April 1963, Beeching–Marples, 2 May 1963, Minutes of a Meeting of Railway Sites Ltd, L.M.R. and Chief Officer (New Works), 27 September 1963, B.R.B. New Works 336–3–50 Pt.

2. Several factors were at work here, besides the concern of local and central government about office-building in central London. For example, Railway Sites Ltd argued that Victoria offered more profitable opportunities than Euston and appear to have been rather lukewarm about the latter.

11 Sir James Dunnett–Beeching, 14 September 1961, B.R.B. 106–2–12; memo. to Works and Equipment Committee, 14 February 1962, Works and Equipment Committee Minutes, 20 February 1962, B.R.B. For Birmingham the return on the station facilities was put at 0.1 per cent, and on the commercial development at 15 per cent. Both projects encountered several problems before completion.

12 Cf. Oliver Marriott, *The Property Boom* (London: Hamish Hamilton, 1967), pp. 96–9. For Bristol Parkway the discounted rate of return was put at 62 per cent, with break-even year at 10 per cent 1974. Skerrett–G. Wilson, 18 March 1971, B.R.B. New Works 326–3–80. Estimated expenditure of £197,300 became £229,900.

13 Report, Proceedings, Evidence, Appendices, of *S.C. Nat. Ind.: Min. Control*, July 1968. See also F. T. Blackaby (ed.), *British Economic Policy 1960–74* (Cambridge: Cambridge University Press, 1978), pp. 486–98, 510–12.

14 Serpell–Wansbrough-Jones, 20 October 1960 and reply, 19 April 1961; 'Note of a Meeting Held in Mr. Serpell's Room . . . 21 February 1961'; Finance Department Paper on 'Investment Projects: Financial Information Required', 21 August 1962, and James–Shirley, 21 June 1963, B.R.B. New Works 23–4–4 Pt. 1.

15 Serpell–Ratter, 15 August 1962, enclosing 'Draft Letter to the British Transport Commission. Criteria for Capital Investment in Railways', Serpell–Wansbrough-Jones, 18 September 1963, enclosing 'Criteria for Capital Investment in Railways' (reproduced in Appendix 34, Annex A, *S.C. Nat. Ind.: Min. Control*); P. R. Sheaf (M.T.), note, 17 January 1964, B.R.B. New Works 23–4–4, Pts. 1 and 2; B.R.B. Minutes, 26 September 1963.

16 Notes of joint meeting of the Works and Equipment and Finance Committees on 9 February 1961, B.R.B. New Works 23–4–4 Pt. 1; Shirley–Beeching, 4 July 1963, and Wansbrough-Jones–Serpell, 18 October 1963, B.R.B. 23–4–9; Osborn, paper, 8 August 1961, Ratter, memo, 2 November 1961, B.T.C. Minutes, 13 July, 9 August and 12 October 1961 and 8 February 1962, B.R.B.

17 Treasury, 'Appraisal of Nationalised Industry Investment Projects – Suggested Points for Discussion', January 1965, and revised version sent with Padmore–Beeching, 15 April 1965, B.R.B. New Works 23–4–4 Pt. 2. See also A. J. Merrett and A. Sykes, *The Finance and Analysis of Capital Projects* (London: Longmans, 1963); N.E.D.O., *Investment Appraisal* (London: H.M.S.O., 2nd edn, 1967); Treasury paper on 'Appraisal', Annex A to Memo., February 1967, in *S.C. Nat. Ind.: Min. Control*, 1967–8, M.O.E., 16 March 1967, and Treasury Memo. on 'The Test Discount Rate', May 1968, in ibid. Appendix 7.

18 James, memo. to Regional Chief Accountants on 'Investment Criteria', 21 May 1965, B.R.B. New Works 23–4–6 Pt. 2; Finance Department, 'Investment Criteria', 29 September 1965, B.R.B. New Works 23–4–4 Pt. 2, reproduced in Annex C to Appendix 34, *S.C. Nat. Ind.: Min. Control*, 1968.

19 The paper (undated) is Annex B, ibid. See also M.T., Memo. on 'Rail Investment' for Treasury Working Party on Transport Investment, March 1966, B.R.B. New Works 23–4–4 Pt. 2, Gomersall, note on 'Relationship between the Ministry of Transport and the British Railways Board on Investment Matters', 7 March 1969, ibid. Pt. 3.

20 *Nationalised Industries. A Review of Economic and Financial Objectives*, November 1967, P.P. 1967–8, XXXIX, Cmnd. 3437, pp. 4–7.

21 Dunnett–Beeching, 18 September and 26 October 1962, Beeching–Dunnett, 4 October and 15 November 1962, B.R.B. 23–4–9; Foster–Gomersall, 23 September 1963, (Commercial Department (Economics Division), report, 2 February 1965, etc., in B.R.B. New Works 23–4–6 Pt. 2.

22 Report of *S.C. Nat. Ind.: Min. Control*, July 1968, pp. 98–9.

23 Lazarus–Arnold Kentridge, 28 January 1970, enclosing draft document on 'British Railways Board Investment', and Bosworth, memo. 4 February 1970, B.R.B. Minutes, 12 February 1970; Skerrett, memo. to Railway Investment Panel, 8 May 1972, B.R.B. New Works 23–4–6 Pt. 6; *Select Committee on Nationalised Industries – Capital Investment Procedures*, P.P. 1973–4, X, M.O.E., 14 February 1973, containing B.R.B. Memo. on 'Decisions on Major Capital Investments', 6 June 1972.

24 Cooper Bros., report on 'Investment Appraisal', 20 December 1967, B.R.B.

25 James–General Managers on 'Financial Appraisal of Investment Proposals', enclosing Financial Services Department document on 'Investment Appraisal', 8 October 1968, B.R.B. New Works 23–4–4 Pt. 2.

26 Skerrett, memo. 8 May 1972, with enclosures, including 'Investment Criteria', 26 April 1972, B.R.B. New Works 23–4–4 Pt. 6; report of *S.C. Nat. Ind.: Cap. Inv.*, December 1973, p. xxx.

27 *The Nationalised Industries*, March 1978, P.P.1977–8, XXXVII, Cmnd.7131, pp. 22–5, 33–7.

28 Griffiths (Executive Director, Passenger), memo. 21 September 1972, B.R.B. Finance 27–1–14.

29 Cf. B.R.B./M.T. joint meetings, e.g. 25 August 1964, 10 March 1965, B.R.B. New Works 23–4–3.

30 Evidence of Raymond, *S.C. Nat. Ind.: Min. Control*, 27 April 1967, QQ.597–8; evidence of Bosworth and Skerrett, *S.C. Nat. Ind.: Cap. Inv.*, 14 February 1973, QQ.562–5.

31 Gomersall–Scott-Malden, 13 May 1966; Raymond–Shirley, 5 August 1966, Raymond–Castle, 8 August 1966, Castle–Raymond, 10 August 1966; Memo. giving diary of events 13 July 1964–3 January 1967, in B.R.B. New Works 173–64–2. For published information, see *S.C. Nat. Ind.: Min. Control*, 1968, Appendices 27 and 34 (Annex K).

32 Scott-Malden–Bosworth, 19 March 1969, B.R.B. New Works 23–4–4 Pt. 3.

33 James–Shirley, 17 August 1966, enclosing note on 'New Build of Locomotive Hauled Passenger Coaching Stock', B.R.B. New Works 173–64–2; Scott-Malden–Gomersall, 8 August 1966, B.R.B. New Works 176–506–33.

34 Gomersall, note, 7 March 1969, B.R.B. New Works 23–4–4 Pt. 3.

35 *Par. Deb. (Commons)*, vol. 773 (Session 1968–9), Written Answer, 22 November 1968, Marsh–Parker, 355; Mulley, Written Answer to Ian Mikardo, *Parl. Deb. (Commons)*, vol. 794 (Session 1969–70), 19 January

1970, *80*. See also C. D. Foster, *Politics, Finance and the Role of Economists* (London: George Allen & Unwin, 1971), pp. 48–52.

36 Gomersall, aide-mémoire on 'Back-Checking of Investment Projects', February 1969, B.R.B. New Works 23–3–14 Pt. 3. Unfortunately, Pts. 1 and 2 of this file appear to have been destroyed.

37 A. S. Duncan (Audit Division), confidential report on 'The Derby Technical Centre Project', 14 February 1968, and N. R. Bellwood, memo. 26 February 1968, B.R.B. New Works 23–4–4 Pt. 2; Investment Committee Minutes, 19 October 1971, and K. M. Smith (Planning and Development Manager, B.T.H.)–R. H. Johnson (Project Officer, Way and Works) on 'St. Andrews: Backcheck', 8 October 1971, B.T.H., St Andrews Box, File 10, B.R.B.

38 B.R.B. Minutes, 13 February 1969; Minutes of a meeting on 'Back Checking of Investment Decisions' held at the Treasury, 25 February 1969, B.R.B. New Works 23–3–14 Pt. 3.

39 S. P. Kemp (M.T.)–Skerrett, 29 August 1969, and note of a meeting to discuss Track Rationalisation Grant Scheme, 14 January 1970, ibid.

40 P. W. McGrath (Controller of Corporate Finance), memo. 24 September 1970, Investment Committee Minutes, 29 September 1970, B.R.B.; McGrath, memo. 31 December 1970; Skerrett–A. G. Lyall (M.T.), 15 October 1970, B.R.B. New Works 23–3–14 Pt. 3; Skerrett, memo. to Railway Investment Panel, with enclosures, 3 November 1971, B.R.B. New Works 1–305.

41 B.R.B. New Works 23–3–36 Pt. 1 (starts November 1973); Department of Transport, *Railway Finances. Report of a Committee Chaired by Sir David Serpell* (London: H.M.S.O., 1983), pp. 41–6.

42 Beeching–Marples, 14 July 1964, B.R.B. New Works 23–4–3.

43 Scott-Malden, notes of a meeting held on 10 March 1965; Callaghan–Raymond, 5 August, Raymond–Callaghan, 12 August 1965; J. Drummond (Treasury)–Raymond, 18 August 1965, ibid.

44 Shirley, memo. 23 September 1966, B.R.B. Minutes, 21 October 1966, B.R.B.; *Parl. Deb. (Commons)*, vol. 735 (Session 1966–7), Written Answer, 9 November 1966, S. Swingler–D. Mitchell, *295*.

45 Chairman's Conference Minutes, 22 July 1968, B.R.B.; *Parl. Deb. (Commons)*, vol. 756 (Session 1967–8), Written Answer, 20 December 1967, J. Morris–J. C. G. Dance, *408*.

46 Tait and Skerrett, memo. to Investment Committee, 10 September 1969, Bosworth, memo. on 'Investment Projects', 30 September 1969, Bosworth–Lazarus, 13 November 1969, B.R.B. 23–4–2 Pts. 5 and 6.

47 In addition, the Ministry postponed the repayment of capital amounting to £180m. B.R.B., *R. & A. 1968*, I, p. 5, II, p. 94.

48 Cf. General Managers Committee Minutes, 21 February and 24 April 1968, H.Q. Executive Committee Minutes, 11 and 18 March 1968, B.R.B.

49 R.M.G. Minutes, 26 and 27 August 1969; Chairman's Conference Minutes, 1 April 1969, B.R.B.

50 Chairman's Conference Minutes, 23 March 1970, B.R.B. Minutes, 12 March 1970, and see correspondence between Lazarus and Bosworth, and Johnson and Mulley, December 1969–February 1970, B.R.B. 23–4–2 Pts. 6 and 7.

51 B.R.B. Minutes, 11 March, 12 August and 11 November 1971; Tait (Executive Director, Finance), memo. to R.M.G. on 'Leasing of Railway Assets', 19 April 1972, B.R.B. 23–4–100 Pt. 1; Finance Committee Minutes, 3 May

1972 and 1 May 1974, B.R.B.; Peyton–Marsh, 13 November, Marsh–Peyton, 20 November 1973, B.R.B. 23–4–100 Pt. 2.

52 Notes of a discussion at R.M.G., 22 September 1970, and cf. Moore (D.O.E.)–Bosworth, 28 April 1971, B.R.B. 23–4–2 Pt. 8; James, 'What Went Wrong', 6 September 1972, B.R.B. Finance 27–1–14.

53 Johnson–Marsh, 30 September 1969, B.R.B. New Works 182–6–22 Pt. 9.

54 This should not be taken to imply that projects always failed to achieve what was forecast. For example, a back-check on the Tinsley Marshalling Yard/diesel maintenance depot/freight concentration depot (Grimethorpe) in 1969 showed that the investment of £9.9m. had realised £1.322m. in net revenue improvement, compared with £1.43m. forecast (at 1968 prices). Skerrett, memo. 25 July 1969, B.R.B. New Works 343–16–54 Pt. 3.

55 Dunbar had been an L.N.E.R. traffic apprentice in 1924, and had moved up through the District Superintendent and Operating Superintendent posts. McLeod had been an L.N.E.R. traffic apprentice in 1928–9 and 1932, and had moved up via the posts of District Goods and Assistant Goods Manager. Information from B.R.B.

56 The A.S.L.E.F. Presidents were Albert Atkinson (1963–4), Les Kirk (1965–7), George Thomas (1968–71), Les Feltham (1972–3) and Bill Ronksley (1974–81). Information from A.S.L.E.F.

57 R.S.J.C., Verbatim Notes, 7 November 1963, B.R.B.; R.S.N.T., Decision No. 27, 14 February 1964.

58 Charles McLeod, *All Change. Railway Industrial Relations in the Sixties* (London: Gower Press, 1970), p. 120; R.S.N.C. Minutes, 13 December 1963, B.R.B.

59 R.S.N.C., Verbatim Notes, 6 November 1964; McLeod, R.S.N.T., Verbatim Notes, 4 and 7 December 1964, B.R.B.

60 R.S.N.T., Decision No. 35, December 1964, and No. 36, May 1965.

61 Fraser–Raymond, 24 June 1965, Raymond–Fraser, 30 June 1965, Raymond Papers, B.R.B.

62 'Note of Meeting with Chairman of B.R.B. . . .', 7 October 1965, ibid.

63 Cf. A.S.L.E.F., Report of Proceedings of Annual Assembly of Delegates, 7–17 June 1966 (presidential comments on E.C. report), and A.S.L.E.F. E.C. Minutes, 15 October 1965, A.S.L.E.F., and N.U.R. E.C. Special Meeting Minutes, 19 January 1966, N.U.R. Proc., 1966, I, N.U.R.

64 P. S. Bagwell, *The Railwaymen*, II, *The Beeching Era and After* (London: George Allen & Unwin, 1982), p. 168.

65 'Note of Meeting between the Chairman of B.R.B. and Mr. Aubrey Jones at N.B.P.I. on 25 November 1965', Raymond Papers, B.R.B.

66 B.R.B. Paper No. 27 on 'Summing Up'; 'Note of Meeting . . . 25 November 1965', Raymond Papers, B.R.B.

67 Dunbar, notes of informal discussions with the Investigating Committee, 1 November 1965, B.R.B. I.R. 82–2–34 Pt. 1.

68 Raymond–General Managers, 8 February 1966, B.R.B. 82–4–4 Pt. 1.

69 N.U.R., *National Union of Railwaymen and the PIB* (London: N.U.R., 1966), pp. 12–17, 22–8.

70 P.I.B., Report No. 8 on *Pay and Conditions of British Railways Staff (Conciliation, Salaried and Workshops Grades)*, January 1966, P.P.1965–6, VI, Cmnd.2873, pp. 8, 10–12, 15.

71 Ibid., pp. 18, 20–2. The P.I.B. also recommended that the Board's offer re.

improved holidays should stand, and that the pension scheme was inadequate and should be re-examined.

72 B.R.B. press release, 14 January 1966, Greene–Raymond, 20 January 1966, Raymond Papers, B.R.B.; N.U.R. E.C. Special Meeting Minutes, 19 January 1966, N.U.R. Proc., 1966, I, N.U.R.

73 'Record of Communication between Ministers, Chairman . . . and the Railway Trade Unions arising as a result of the Report No. 8 (Cmnd.2873) . . .'; J. C. Burgh, memo. on 'Decisions Reached at a Meeeting on the Railway Pay Dispute Held by the First Secretary . . . on 31 January 1966', p. 1, Raymond Papers, B.R.B.

74 N.U.R. Special Meeting Minutes, 10, 11 and 11–12 February 1966, N.U.R. Proc., 1966, I. N.U.R.; B. Castle, *The Castle Diaries 1964–70* (London: Weidenfeld & Nicolson, 1984), pp. 95–106; Bagwell, *The Railwaymen*, II, pp. 170–2.

75 *Report of a Court of Inquiry under Mr. A. J. Scamp into the Issues Arising in Negotiations between the British Railways Board, the Associated Society of Locomotive Engineers and Firemen and the National Union of Railwaymen*, September 1965, P.P.1964–5, XVII, Cmnd.2779, pp. 6–9; R.S.C., 'Productivity – Footplate Staff', containing 'Report of Management Working Party', 3 December 1964, B.R.B.

76 R.S.C., 'Productivity – Footplate Staff', 3 December 1964, B.R.B. Up-dated figures plus the figure of 2,300 appear in *Report of a Court of Inquiry under . . . Scamp*, Cmnd.2779, pp. 6–7.

77 It was hoped that 10,000 firemen would go, saving £9m. per annum. McLeod, memo. on 'Productivity – Trainmen', 5 January 1965, B.R.B. I.R. 81–19–4.

78 Griffiths and Kirk of A.S.L.E.F. met McLeod and Nicholson (Director of Industrial Relations) of B.R.B. on 18 December 1964; memo. on 'Footplate Staff – Application for Productivity Payment', 18 December 1964, ibid. See also R.S.N.C. Sub-Committee Minutes, 11 and 28 January, 18 March and 13 May 1965, B.R.B.

79 Memo. on 'Productivity – Footplate Staff', appendix to meeting, 13 May 1965, B.R.B. I.R. 81–19–4. Mileage payments of 6d. to drivers for 65–79 loaded train-miles run, rising by 6d. per 15 miles to 2s. 6d. for 125–39 miles (short) and 3s. 11d. ($\frac{1}{2}$-hour's pay) for 140–7 miles rising to 46s. 10d. for 223–30 miles (long) were increased substantially: 5s. for up to 65 miles, rising to 12s. 6d. for 105–24 miles (short), and 15s. 7d. (2 hours' pay) for 125–32 miles and 19s. 6d. for 140–7 miles rising by $\frac{1}{2}$-hour's pay per 8 miles to 62s. 6d. for 223–30 miles (long). Freezing of these bonuses from 1968 caused resentment in A.S.L.E.F.

80 Memo. on 'Productivity Payments: Trainmen', 15 June 1965; note for papers, 7 July 1965, B.R.B. I.R. 81–9–4. Unrest on Southern Region was exacerbated by R.S.N.T. Decision No. 38 of 11 June 1965, which gave the guards mileage payments which were marginally better than those for secondmen.

81 A nine-point set of conditions effectively rejected all of the proposals to relax the 1957 Agreement: *Locomotive Journal*, September 1965, *Financial Times*, 11 August 1965.

82 B.R.B. I.R. Department memo. on 'Productivity Payments: Footplate Staff', 4 August 1965, appendix F, and R.S.N.C. Sub-Committee Minutes, 6 Septem-

ber 1965, B.R.B. I.R. 81–19–4. The 1957 limitation on single-manning between midnight and 6 a.m. had already been relaxed re trains running to 1 a.m. or starting at 5 a.m. The unions offered to alter this to 2 a.m. and 4 a.m.

83 A.S.L.E.F. E.C. Minutes, 20 July 1965, and Report of Proceedings of Special Assembly of Delegates, 10–11 August 1965, and Report of Proceedings of Annual Assembly of Delegates, 7 June 1966, A.S.L.E.F. On Scamp, see *Financial Times*, 9 September 1965.

84 Raymond–Dunbar, 8 September 1965, B.R.B. I.R. 81–19–4.

85 *Report of a Court of Inquiry under . . . Scamp*, Cmnd.2779, pp. 3, 12–15, 19, 22–44.

86 B.R.B., Memo. of 'Agreement in Regard to the Manning of Diesel and Electric Locomotives and Multiple-Unit Trains', 28 October 1965. This is reproduced in *Report of a Court of Inquiry under Professor D. J. Robertson into a Dispute between the British Railways Board and the National Union of Railwaymen concerning Guards and Shunters*, October 1967, P.P.1966–7, XXXVIII, Cmnd.3426.

87 British Railways Management Committee Minutes, 26 July 1967, and B.R.B. I.R. Department, memo. on 'Review of Trainmen's Earnings, Productivity and Related Matters', October 1967, L. F. Neal Papers, R.S.C./I.R. Box 350, B.R.B.

88 Bowick, memo. to H.Q. Executive Committee, 14 November 1968, B.R.B. 75–50–25; Margetts–Raymond on 'Footplate Staff Made Surplus to Requirements', 17 February 1967, Dunbar Papers, R.S.C./I.R. Box. 281, B.R.B.

89 B.R.B. I.R. Department, 'Diary of Events', Neal Papers; British Railways Management Committee Minutes, 24 August 1966, B.R.B.; Dunbar–McLeod, 14 January 1967, Dunbar Papers; 'Memo. of Meeting between B.R.B. and A.S.L.E.F. and N.U.R', 6 January 1967; A. J. Scamp, 'Interpretation of Agreement of 28 October 1965 . . .', 12 January 1978, Neal Papers, R.S.C./I.R. Box 281, B.R.B.

90 Raymond–Margetts, Neal and Ibbotson, 30 March 1967, ibid. Raymond was particularly concerned about the misleading impression given by B.R.B. in its presentation of data.

91 B.R.B. Minutes, 13 April 1967, British Railways Management Committee Minutes, 23 August 1967, B.R.B.

92 *Report of a Court of Inquiry under . . . Robertson*, Cmnd.3426, pp. 22, 30–1; Management Brief on 'Productivity Payment for Guards' (n.d.), B.R.B. P.R. & P. 81–19–5, and British Railways Management Committee Minutes, 25 October 1967, B.R.B.

93 'Inquiry by Mr. A. J. Scamp into whether the recent productivity agreement between the B.R.B. and the N.U.R. is in conflict with the 1965 Single Manning Agreement', 30 November 1967, B.R.B. 81–19–5.

94 *Daily Sketch*, 1 December 1967; H. Wilson, *The Labour Government, 1964–70. A Personal Record* (Penguin edn., 1974), pp. 604–6.

95 Information from B.R.B. for 1984–5 (weekday turns excluding H.S.T.). 1971 data from G. R. Papworth (Development Officer (Production Planning)), report on 'Train Crew Productivity. An Analysis of the Extent and Causes of Double Manning of Locomotives and Multiple Units', August 1971, B.R.B.

96 Ibid.

97 Beeching–Greene, 21 February and 21 May 1964, B.R.B. I.R. 150–28–11; J.

W. Wickes–J. A. Dobson, 3 June 1970, enclosing 'B.R.B. Personnel Dept. Introduction of Freightliner Services. Summary of Developments with N.U.R. Regarding Open Terminals' (n.d.), B.R.B. I.R. 150–28–2 Pt. 8.

98 McLeod, *All Change*, p. 96.

99 Greene–Dunbar, 16 February 1965, B.R.B. I.R. 150–28–11; *Guardian*, 28 January 1965.

100 *Parl. Deb. (Commons)*, vol. 711 (Session 1964–5), 28 April 1965, Fraser, oral answer to Goodhew and Peter Mills, 421; 'Memo. of Meeting between Chairman of B.R.B. and Representatives of the N.U.R., A.S.L.E.F., and T.S.S.A. . . . 11 August 1965'; Greene–Raymond, 26 August and 22 September 1965, Raymond–Board, 25 August and 2 December 1965, B.R.B. I.R. 150–28–11.

101 R. W. Jackson (Liner Trains Manager), memo. on 'Freightliner Project', 22 August 1966, Robbins (Chief Marketing Manager), memo. on 'Freightliner – Stage I Development', 8 February 1967, B.R.B. I.R. 150–28–2 Pt. 7.

102 *Financial Times*, 2 September 1966; B.R.B., Memo. to M.T. on 'National Freight Grid Merchandise Services by Freightliner Trains', 5 October 1966, B.R.B. I.R. 150–28–2 Pt. 7.

103 Castle–Raymond, 1 November 1966, B.R.B. I.R. 150–28–7 Pt. 7; Castle, *Diaries*, p. 93.

104 *Times*, 21 July 1966.

105 'Notes of Meeting with Minister . . . 10/2/1967', B.R.B. 150–28–2 Pt. 7. For the role of the Road Haulage Association see *Railway Gazette*, 3 February 1967.

106 J. Scanlon (Glasgow), *Railway Review*, 24 February 1967, a reply to Castle in ibid., 17 February 1967.

107 B.R.B., press release, 19 October 1965, Robbins *et al.*, memo. to Works and Equipment Committee, 31 August 1966, B.R.B. 150–26–2; N.U.R. E.C. Minutes, 10 February 1967, N.U.R. Proc., 1967, I, N.U.R.; *The Economist*, 18 February 1967; *Financial Times*, 15 February 1967; Castle, *Diaries*, pp. 218–20; *Commercial Motor*, 17 February 1967.

108 Robbins *et al.*, memo. (n.d.), B.R.B. Minutes, 27 January 1966; N.U.R. E.C. Minutes, 17 and 28 February, 2 March 1967, N.U.R. Proc., 1967, I, NU.R.; *Railway Review*, 10 March 1967, Castle, *Diaries*, pp. 224–31. The suggestion here is that the Board approached hauliers with a view to forcing the open terminals issue if talks broke down. Cf. Raymond–Shirley, Margetts and Neal, 13 February 1967, B.R.B. I.R. 150–28–2 Pt. 7, and B.R.B. I.R. 150–26–9.

109 Memo. of Agreement between B.R.B. and the N.U.R., 7 June 1967, and Annexure to Memo. of Agreement, B.R.B. I.R. 150–28–2 Pt. 8.

110 Greene, *Railway Review*, 30 June 1967; Planning Committee Minutes, 20 January 1965, B.R.B. 98–93–4; N.U.R. E.C. Minutes, 13, 22, 23, 24, 29 and 30 June 1967; N.U.R. Agenda and Decisions of A.G.M. 1967 95 (a), N.U.R. Proc., 1967, I, N.U.R.

111 Ibbotson–McLeod, 13 June 1967, B.R.B. I.R. 150–28–2 Pt. 8.

112 'Notes of Meeting, March 10, 1966 at 10 Downing St.', B.R.B. 82–4–4 Pt. 1; B.R.B. I.R. Department, *Pay and Efficiency* (November 1967), p. 6. Workshop staff were not included in the inquiry.

113 B.R.B. I.R. Department, memo. on 'Railway Pay and Efficiency', enclosing 'Productivity and Efficiency – Progress Report' (June 1966), July 1966,

British Railways Management Committee Minutes, 27 July 1966, B.R.B.; Raymond–Gunter, Doc.I on 'Staff and Investment', 4 May 1967, Raymond Papers, B.R.B.

114 General Managers–Raymond, 9–11 February 1966, B.R.B. 82–4–4 Pt. 1, and I.R. Department memo. on 'Bonus and Productivity Payments – Railways Wages Staff', 6 May 1966, B.R.B. I.R. 82–4–4 Pt. 1.

115 General Managers' Conference Minutes, 21 March 1966, B.R.B.

116 General Managers' Committee, 'Interim Report on Pay Structure', June 1966, B.R.B. 82–4–4 Pt. 1.

117 B.R.B. I.R. Department, 'Report on Revision of Conciliation Grades Wages Structure', March 1966, and memo. on 'Railway Pay and Efficiency', July 1966. These, with the Bowick Committee's interim report, were discussed by the British Railways Management Committee: Minutes, 27 July 1966, B.R.B., and see B.R.B. 82–4–4 Pt. 1.

118 McLeod–Raymond, private note, 21 March 1966, Raymond Papers, B.R.B.; McLeod–General Managers, 21 March 1966, B.R.B. 82–4–4 Pt. 4.

119 A. Flanders, The Fawley Productivity Agreements (London: Faber and Faber, 1964); J. Torode, 'Len Neal and the NUR–ASLEF Feud', Personnel, I (March 1968), 23–6.

120 Raymond–Castle, 18 July 1966, B.R.B. 48–2–21; B.R.B. Minutes, 8 December 1966.

121 The official historian of N.U.R. comes to a similar conclusion: Bagwell, The Railwaymen, II, p. 173, and see also L. F. Neal, 'Productivity Breakthrough for British Railways', Railway Gazette, 20 September 1968.

122 A. S. Marre (Min. of Labour, Chairman of Sub-Group), report, 14 July 1967, Raymond Papers, B.R.B.

123 'Note of Meeting between Minister of Labour and L. F. Neal . . . 15th June 1967', ibid.; B.R.B. I.R. Department, Pay and Efficiency (November 1967). This was discussed by the Joint Group on 11 December.

124 B.R.B. I.R. Department, Pay and Efficiency. The Board's Offer (February 1968), pp. 1–23; 'Memo. of Meeting, 23 February 1968', and Johnson–Gunter, 30 January 1968, B.R.B. P.R. & P. 82–2–34 Pt. 2; B.R.B. Minutes, 14 March 1968. Castle called the scheme 'barely self-financing and therefore not really a productivity scheme at all': Diaries, p. 371.

125 R.S.N.T., Decision No. 41, 6 June 1968, pp. 7–10; B.R.B. Financial Services Department, note on 'N.U.R./A.S.L.E.F. Dispute. Estimated Effect', 10 July 1968, B.R.B. P.R. & P. 82–52–2 Pt. 7.

126 'Memo of Meeting Held at 222 Marylebone Road . . . 22nd June, 1968', R.S.C., Wage Negotiations, 1967–8, 'Proceedings Leading to R.S.N.T. . . . . 41, . . .', B.R.B.; Castle, Diaries, p. 477.

127 'Productivity Agreement between the N.U.R. and the British Railways Board, July 5, 1968 at Penzance (Conciliation Staff other than Footplate)', and ibid., '(Footplate Staff)', R.S.C., Wage Negotiations, 1967–8; B.R.B. Special Meeting Minutes, 3 July 1968, B.R.B.; Castle Diaries, p. 478.

128 Merrill–Johnson, 5 July 1968, B.R.B. P.R. & P. 82–52–2 Pt. 7.

129 Bowick–General Managers, etc., 9 July 1968, R.S.C., Wage Negotiations, 1967–8, B.R.B. Separate negotiations for clerical staff, supervisors and workshop staff produced agreements in July 1968 and April 1969, B.R.B., R. & A. 1968, I, p. 43; McLeod, All Change, pp. 162–5.

130 Cf. The Economist, 13 July 1968.

131 B.R.B. I.R. Department, *Pay and Efficiency. Agreement between the B.R.B. and National Union of Railwaymen* (August 1968); *Pay and Efficiency (Footplate Staff). Agreement between B.R.B., A.S.L.E.F. and the N.U.R.* (August 1968). See also L. F. Neal, 'Railway Pay and Efficiency Stage I. A Commentary for Railway Managers', 15 August 1968, B.R.B. P.R. & P. 82–2–34 Pt. 3.

132 B.R.B. Minutes, 8 August and 12 September 1968, B.R.B. H.Q. Executive Committee Minutes, 19 August and 16 September 1968, B.R.B.

133 Thorpe–General Managers, 7 October 1968, B.R.B. P.R. & P. 82–2–34 Pt. 3; Bowick, progress reports, 2 October and 2 November 1969, B.R.B. Minutes, 9 October and 11 November 1969; 'Pay and Efficiency: Monitoring of Results. Period up to 31/12/1968', B.R.B. I.R. 82–4–4; Bagwell, *The Railwaymen*, II, p. 191, and *Railway Gazette*, 20 September 1968.

134 B.R.B. H.Q. Executive Committee Minutes, 16 September 1968, General Managers' Committee Minutes, 23 April 1969, B.R.B.

135 Draft Memo. to Chairman's Conference on 'P and E: Stage II', B.R.B. P.R. & P. 82–2–34 Pt. 4; J. L. Fallick and R. F. Elliott, *Incomes Policies, Inflation and Relative Pay* (London: George Allen & Unwin, 1981), pp. 109, 112; Blackaby, *British Economic Policy*, pp. 375–8.

136 General Managers' Conference Minutes, 18 December 1968; General Managers' Committee Minutes, 23 July 1969; Bowick, memo. to E.C. (Railways) on '1970: Preliminary Forecast: Pay and Efficiency', 7 May 1969, B.R.B. P.R. & P. 82–2–34 Pt. 4; Bowick, memo. on 'Pay and Efficiency Stage II: An Outline', 3 July 1969, B.R.B. Minutes, 10 July 1969.

137 B.R.B., *Pay and Efficiency (Stage Two). Conciliation Staff Other than Footplate Staff* (August 1969), and *Pay and Efficiency (Footplate Staff)* (September 1969). The closed shop agreement came after many years of campaigning. See Bagwell, *The Railwaymen*, II, pp. 198–208.

138 Bowick, progress report, 2 November 1969, B.R.B. Minutes, 11 November 1969.

139 R.M.G. Minutes, 23–4 September 1969, B.R.B.

140 Neal–Johnson, 19 November 1969, B.R.B. P.R. & P. 82–2–34 Pt. 5.

141 'Meeting of R.S.J.C. . . . 13/3/1970', Wurr Papers, B.R.B.

142 R.M.G. Minutes, 25 March 1970, B.R.B.

143 J. Clemmett–Bowick, 14 January 1971, B.R.B. I.R. 82–4–300 Pt. 4; Bowick, report on 'Personnel', October 1970, B.R.B. Minutes, 11–12 November 1970; Bowick, memo. on 'Imbalance of Earnings: Consolidation', 1 October 1970, R.M.G. Minutes, 28 October 1970, B.R.B.

144 See Clemmett–Neal, 26 November 1970, and Clemmett–Bowick, 2 December 1970, and other correspondence in B.R.B. I.R. 82–4–300 Pt. 3.

145 Cf. *The Economist*, 26 February 1971, *Guardian*, 13 March 1971.

146 R.M.G. Minutes, 22–3 September 1970, B.R.B.

147 Memo. on 'Nationalised Chairmen's Lunch with Ministers . . . 15/9/1971' in I.R./R.S.C. Box 412, B.R.B.

148 Memo. on 'Railway Pay Talks 1972', 16 February 1972, R.S.C./I.R. Box 413; Chairman's Conference Minutes, 3 and 7 February 1972, B.R.B.; *Guardian*, 25 February 1972.

149 Farrimond annoyed the N.U.R. by asking them for their minimum requirements then attempting to bargain them down. As press interest in the talks intensified, he suggested that the two sides continue the negotiations aboard a

B.R.B. ferry, but Greene rejected the idea, saying he couldn't swim. Bagwell, *The Railwaymen*, II, pp. 246–7, *New Statesman*, 16 June 1972.
150 Statement by Jarratt, 16 April 1972, B.R.B. P.R. & P. 82–2–34 Pt. 7. Bagwell, *The Railwaymen*, II, ch. 7, gives a detailed account of the 1971–2 negotiations.
151 Bowick, note to Marsh, 5 May 1972, B.R.B. P.R. & P. 82–2–34 Pt. 7.
152 B.R.B., *R. & A. 1972*, p. 14.
153 *New Statesman*, 16 June 1972.
154 Richard Marsh, *On and Off the Rails. An Autobiography* (London: Weidenfeld & Nicolson, 1978), p. 176.
155 B.R.B., *R. & A. 1973*, p. 6.
156 B.R.B., 'Review of Pay Structure for Salaried and Conciliation-Grade Staff. The Board's Submission to the Railway Staff National Tribunal, April 1974', May 1974, B.R.B.; Buckton, statement to R.S.N.C., 28 September 1973, B.R.B.; Bagwell, *The Railwaymen*, II, pp. 215–19.
157 Cf. British Railways Management Committee Minutes, 23 September 1964, B.R.B.
158 Holroyd–Farrimond and Clemmett, 22 February 1972, in R.S.C./I.R. Box 413, B.R.B.
159 Based on real costs data in Appendix A, Table 4, deflated by output data in Appendix C, Table 1.
160 The calculation for 1960–70 is influenced by the loss of freightliner and sundries staff in 1969. However, the thesis of higher productivity growth in the 1960s is confirmed by growth rates for other periods, e.g. 1960–8: labour productivity 4.66 per cent per annum, 'total factor productivity' 2.12 per cent; 1962–8: labour 7.50 per cent, 'total factor productivity' 4.66 per cent. See Appendix C.
161 C. D. Jones, 'The Performance of British Railways 1962 to 1968', *Journal of Transport Economics and Policy*, IV (May 1970), 162–70; Pryke, *Nationalised Industries*, pp. 76, 81.
162 Derived from Appendix C, Table 2.
163 Data from B.R.B. Most of the information is published either in the Annual Report and Accounts, or in the Ministry of Transport/Department of the Environment volumes of transport statistics from the mid-1960s.

13. Conclusion

1 T. R. Gourvish, 'The Railways and the Development of Managerial Enterprise in Britain, 1850–1939', in K. Kobayashi and H. Morikawa (ed.), *Development of Managerial Enterprise. The International Conference on Business History 12* (Tokyo: University of Tokyo Press, 1986), p. 195.
2 T. R. Gourvish, *Railways in the British Economy, 1830–1914* (London: Macmillan, 1980), pp. 49–56.
3 Cf. for example, R. J. Irving, 'The Profitability and Performance of British Railways, 1870–1914, *Economic History Review*, 2nd ser., XXXI (1978), 46–65.
4 Wilson, communication with author, 28 March 1983.
5 Parker, Dimbleby Lecture, 1983, B.R.B.
6 Ibid.

7 Edith Penrose, *The Theory of the Growth of the Firm* (Oxford: Basil Blackwell, 1959; 2nd edn, 1980), A. D. Chandler, Jnr, *Strategy and Structure. Chapters in the History of Industrial Enterprise* (Cambridge, Mass.: M.I.T. Press, 1962), and see Leslie Hannah (ed.), *Management Strategy and Business Development* (London: Macmillan, 1976).

8 Macmillan–Leathers, 7 May 1952, MT62/142, P.R.O.

9 B. Castle, *The Castle Diaries 1964–70* (London: Weidenfeld & Nicolson, 1984), p. 335.

10 In a recent parody, an ex-Falklands veteran was encouraged to apply for the post of B.R.B. Chairman, since he had 'not travelled on a train since the Suez Petroleum Crisis of 1956': Steve Bell, 'If . . .', *Guardian*, 23 August 1983.

11 P.I.B., Report No. 107 on *Top Salaries in the Private Sector and Nationalised Industries*, March 1969, P.P.1968–9, XLIII, Cmnd.3970.

12 *Times*, 11 October 1977.

13 Review Body on Top Salaries, Report No. 10: *Second Report on Top Salaries*, June 1978, pp. 1–2, 31, P.P.1977–8, XLVIII, Cmnd.7253.

14 J. Hilliard, economist seconded to Review body, in Report No. 6: *First Report on Top Salaries*, December 1974, Appendix G, P.P.1974–5, XXXII, Cmnd.6846.

15 H. E. Osborn, memo. on 'Financial Outlook', 5 February 1958, B.T.C. Finance Committee Minutes, 12 February 1958; B.T.C. Minutes, 18 December 1958, 15 and 22 January 1959, B.R.B.

16 The direction in 1967 that nationalised industries should follow precise guidelines for investment – discount rates of 8 per cent, altered to 10 per cent in 1969 – and pricing – at marginal cost – conflicted with the retention of a specific rate of return objective, since the pricing and investment rules would themselves determine cash flow and hence the return. Cf. D. L. Bevan, 'The Nationalized Industries', in Derek Morris (ed.), *The Economic System in the United Kingdom* (Oxford: Oxford University Press, 1977), pp. 440–1.

17 For a general survey of the literature see D. Steel, 'Looking at the Nationalized Industries', *Royal Institute of Public Administration Newsletter*, III (Summer 1983), 10–11, and note especially L. Tivey, *Nationalisation in British Industry* (London: Jonathan Cape, 2nd edn, 1973), N.E.D.O., *A Study of the U.K. Nationalised Industries* (London: H.M.S.O., 1976), and K. Jones, 'Policy Towards the Nationalised Industries', in F. T. Blackaby (ed.), *British Economic Policy, 1960–74* (Cambridge: Cambridge University Press, 1978), p. 511.

18 Cf. Arthur Knight, *Private Enterprise and Public Intervention: The Courtaulds Experience* (London: George Allen & Unwin, 1974), pp. 67–8, 97–215, cit. by Bernard W. E. Alford, 'The Chandler Thesis – Some General Observations', in Hannah, *Management Strategy*, p. 64.

19 Sir Donald Fergusson, Permanent-Secretary, Ministry of Fuel and Power, note, 18 June 1952, MT62/138, P.R.O.

20 Cf. B.R.B., *R. & A.* 1984–5, p. 9.

21 Michael Burrage, 'Nationalization and the Professional Ideal', *Sociology*, VII (1973), 253–72. See also James A. Dunn, Jnr, 'Railroad Policies in Europe and the United States: The Impact of Ideology, Institutions, and Social Conditions', *Public Policy*, XXV (Spring 1977), 205–40.

22 Cf. Kenneth Cowling *et al.*, *Mergers and Economic Performance* (Cambridge: Cambridge University Press, 1980), p. 370.

23 Tait–James, 22 September 1972, B.R.B. Finance 27–1–4.
24 Sir Robert Reid, 'All Change for Railway Management – How British Rail is Facing the Challenge of Competition', address to the Institute of Administrative Management, 23 April 1985, B.R.B.
25 Ibid.
26 B.R.B. and Institute for Transport Studies, University of Leeds, *A Comparative Study of European Rail Performance* (London: 1979), pp. 46, 52–3.
27 John Davies, Secretary of State for Trade and Industry, *Parl. Deb. (Commons)*, vol. 805 (Session 1970–1), 4 November 1970, 1212, quoted in Blackaby, *British Economic Policy*, p. 55.
28 This followed the failure of the Rehabilitation Plan of 1979. See Japanese National Railways (J.N.R.), press release, 10 January 1985, and G. R. Burt, 'Report of a Visit to Japanese National Railways . . . April 1983', August 1983, B.R.B.
29 For a recent survey of the state of the art see Bernard de Fontgalland, *The World Railway System* (Cambridge: Cambridge University Press, 1984), pp. 113–37.

Select bibliography

There is a vast literature on both the nationalised industries in general and the railways in particular. What follows is very much a personal choice.

BOOKS, ARTICLES

Acworth, Sir William M., *The Elements of Railway Economics* (Oxford: Oxford University Press, 1924 edn.).

Aldcroft, Derek H., *British Railways in Transition: The Economic Problems of Britain's Railways since 1914* (London: Macmillan, 1968).
'Innovation on the Railways: The Lag in Diesel and Electric Traction', in *Studies in British Transport History 1870–1970* (Newton Abbot: David & Charles, 1974).

Alderman, Geoffrey, *The Railway Interest* (Leicester: Leicester University Press, 1973).

Allen, Cecil J., *The Locomotive Exchanges, 1870–1948* (London: Ian Allan, 1949).
New Light on the Locomotive Exchanges (London: Ian Allan, 1950).

Allen, Geoffrey Freeman, *British Rail After Beeching* (London: Ian Allan, 1966).
British Railfreight Today and Tomorrow (London: Ian Allan, 1984).
British Railways Today and Tomorrow (London: Ian Allan, 1959).
'Corporate Planning', *Modern Railways* (September 1968).

Arkle, E. W., 'The Branch Line Problem', *Journal of the Institute of Transport*, XXIV (March 1951).

Bagwell, Philip S., *The Railwaymen*, I, *The History of the National Union of Railwaymen* (London: George Allen & Unwin, 1963); II, *The Beeching Era and After* (London: George Allen & Unwin, 1982).
The Transport Revolution from 1770 (London: Batsford, 1974).

Balfour, Campbell, *Incomes Policy and the Public Sector* (London: Routledge, 1972).

Barker, Theodore, C., and Robbins, Michael, *A History of London Transport*, II, *The Twentieth Century to 1970* (London: George Allen & Unwin, 1974).

Barker, Theodore C. and Savage, Christopher I., *An Economic History of Transport in Britain* (London: Hutchinson, 1974).

Barry, E. Eldon, *Nationalisation in British Politics* (London: Cape, 1965).

Bayliss, Brian T., and Edwards, Samuel L., *Industrial Demand for Transport* (London: H.M.S.O., 1970).

Beckerman, Wilfrid (ed.), *The Labour Government's Economic Record, 1964–70* (London: Duckworth, 1972).

Beesley, Michael E., 'Financial Criteria for Investment in Railways', *Bulletin of the Oxford Institute of Statistics*, XXIV (February 1962).

Beesley, Michael E. and Walters, Alan A., 'Investment in British Railways', *Westminster Bank Review* (May 1955).

Bell, Robert, *History of the British Railways During the War, 1939–45* (London: Railway Gazette, 1946).

Bellerby, John R. (ed.), *Economic Reconstruction. A Study of Post-War Problems* (London: Macmillan, 1943).

Bevan, D. L., 'The Nationalized Industries', in Morris, Derek (ed.), *The Economic System in the United Kingdom* (Oxford: Oxford University Press, 1977).

Birkenhead, Lord (Smith, Frederick W. F.), *Walter Monckton* (London: Weidenfeld & Nicolson, 1969).

Blackaby, Frank (ed.), *British Economic Policy 1960–74* (Cambridge: Cambridge University Press, 1978).

Bonavia, Michael R., *The Birth of British Rail* (London: George Allen & Unwin, 1979).

British Rail. The First 25 Years (Newton Abbot: David & Charles, 1981).

British Railway Policy between the Wars (Manchester: Manchester University Press, 1981).

The Organisation of British Railways (London: Ian Allan, 1971).

Boyd-Carpenter, John, *Way of Life* (London: Sidgwick & Jackson, 1980).

B.R.B., *The Development of the Major Railway Trunk Routes* (London: B.R.B., 1965).

Measuring Cost and Profitability in British Rail (London: B.R.B., 1978).

An Opportunity for Change (London: B.R.B., 1976).

The Reshaping of British Railways (London: H.M.S.O., 1963).

A Study of the Relative True Costs of Rail and Road Freight Transport over Trunk Routes (London: B.R.B., 1964).

B.R.B. and Association of County Councils, *Review of Rural Railways* (London: 1984).

B.R.B. and Institute for Transport Studies, University of Leeds, *A Comparative Study of European Rail Performance* (London: 1979).

British Institute of Management, *Is Corporate Planning Necessary?* (London: B.I.M., 1968).

B.T.C., *Financial Situation and Prospects of British Transport* (London: B.T.C., 1956).

Modernisation and Re-equipment of British Railways (London: B.T.C., 1955).

The System of Electrification for British Railways (London: B.T.C., 1956).

Burrage, Michael, 'Nationalization and the Professional Ideal', *Sociology*, VII (1973).

Burtt, Philip, *Railway Rates, Principles and Problems* (London: Pitman & Sons, 1926).

Butler, David E., *The British General Election of 1955* (London: Macmillan, 1955).

Butler, Lord (Richard A.), *The Art of Memory: Friends in Perspective* (London: Hodder & Stoughton, 1982).

Button, K. J., 'Transport Policy in the United Kingdom: 1968–1974', *Three Banks Review*, CIII (September 1974).

Cairncross, Sir Alec, 'Incomes Policy: Retrospect and Prospect', *Three Banks Review*, C (December 1973).
(ed.), *The Managed Economy* (Oxford: Blackwell, 1970).
Years of Recovery. British Economic Policy 1945–51 (London: Methuen, 1985).
Castle, Barbara, *The Castle Diaries 1964–70* (London: Weidenfeld & Nicolson, 1984).
Chandler, Alfred D., Jr., *Strategy and Structure. Chapters in the History of Industrial Enterprise* (Cambridge, Mass.: M.I.T. Press, 1962).
Charlesworth, George, *A History of British Motorways* (London: Telford, 1984).
Chater, Robin E. J., Dean, Andrew, and Elliott, Robert F. (eds.), *Incomes Policy* (Oxford: Clarendon Press, 1981).
Chester, Sir Norman, *The Nationalisation of British Industry 1945–51* (London: H.M.S.O., 1975).
Clarke, Sir Richard, *Public Expenditure, Management and Control* (London: Macmillan, 1978).
Clegg, Hugh A., *The Changing System of Industrial Relations in Great Britain* (Oxford: Blackwell, 1979).
Coates, David, *The Labour Party and the Struggle for Socialism* (Cambridge: Cambridge University Press, 1975).
Coleman, Donald C., *Courtaulds. An Economic and Social History, III, Crisis and Change 1940–1965* (Oxford: Clarendon Press, 1980).
Cook, Pauline L., *Railway Workshops: The Problem of Contraction* (Cambridge: Cambridge University Press, 1964).
Cowling, Keith, *et al.*, *Mergers and Economic Performance* (Cambridge: Cambridge University Press, 1980).
Cox, Ernest S., *Locomotive Panorama*, (2 vols., London: Ian Allan, 1966).
Crossman, Richard H. S., *The Diaries of a Cabinet Minister* (3 vols., London: Hamish Hamilton and Jonathan Cape, 1975–7).
Cullingworth, John B., *Environmental Planning 1939–1969, I, Reconstruction and Land Use Planning 1939–47* (London, H.M.S.O., 1975).
Daniels, Gerald, and Dench, Les, *Passengers No More* (London: Ian Allan, 3rd edn, 1980).
Davenport, Nicholas E. H., *Memoirs of a City Radical* (London: Weidenfeld & Nicolson, 1974).
de Fontgelland, Bernard, *The World Railway System* (Cambridge: Cambridge University Press, 1984).
Deakin, Brian M. and Seward, Thelma, *Productivity in Transport. A Study of Employment, Capital, Output, Productivity and Technical Change* (Cambridge: Cambridge University Press, 1969).
Dear, D. Mansfield, 'Some Thoughts on the Comparative Costs of Road and Rail Transport', *Bulletin of the Oxford Institute of Statistics*, XXIV (February 1962).
Department of Transport, *Railway Finances. Report of a Committee Chaired by Sir David Serpell* (London: H.M.S.O., 1983).
Dodgson, John S., 'British Rail After Serpell', *Three Banks Review*, CXL (December 1983).
Donoughue, Bernard, and Jones, George W., *Herbert Morrison. Portrait of a Politician* (London: Weidenfeld & Nicolson, 1973).
Dow, J. C. R., *The Management of the British Economy 1945–60* (Cambridge: Cambridge University Press, 1965).

Dyos, H. J., and Aldcroft, Derek H., *British Transport. An Economic Survey from the Seventeenth Century to the Twentieth* (Leicester: Leicester University Press, 1969).

Eden, Sir Anthony (Lord Avon), *Full Circle* (London: Cassell, 1960).

Elliot, Sir John, *On and Off the Rails* (London: George Allen & Unwin, 1982).

Else, P. K., and Howe, M., 'Cost Benefit Analysis and the Withdrawal of Railway Services', *Journal of Transport Economics and Policy*, III (May 1969).

Emerson, A. H., 'Electrification of the London Midland Main Line from Euston', *Proceedings of the Institution of Mechanical Engineers*, CLXXXI (1966–7).

Fallick, J. L. and Elliott, Robert, F., *Incomes Policies, Inflation and Relative Pay* (London: George Allen & Unwin, 1981).

Feinstein, Charles H., *National Income, Expenditure and Output of the United Kingdom, 1855–1965* (Cambridge: Cambridge University Press, 1972).

Fels, Allan, *The British Prices and Incomes Board* (Cambridge: Cambridge University Press, 1972).

Fiennes, Gerard F., *I Tried to Run a Railway* (London: Ian Allan, 1967).

'Running a Region: WR and ER', *Modern Railways*, XXIII (October 1967).

Flanders, Allan, *The Fawley Productivity Agreements* (London: Faber and Faber, 1964).

Foot, Michael M., *Aneurin Bevan: A Biography, I, 1897–1945* (London: MacGibbon & Kee, 1962), II, *1945–60* (London: Davis-Poynter, 1973).

Foster, Christopher D., *Politics, Finance and the Role of Economists* (London: George Allen & Unwin, 1971).

'Some Notes on Railway Costs and Costing', *Bulletin of the Oxford Institute of Statistics*, XXIV (February 1962).

'Surplus Criteria for Investment', *Bulletin of the Oxford Institute of Statistics*, XXII (November 1960).

The Transport Problem (1st edn, London: Blackie, 1963; 2nd edn, London: Croom Helm, 1975).

Goodman, Geoffrey, *The Awkward Warrior. Frank Cousins, His Life and Times* (London: Davis-Poynter, 1979).

Gourvish, Terence R., *Mark Huish and the London and North Western Railway* (Leicester: Leicester University Press, 1972).

Railways in the British Economy 1830–1914 (London: Macmillan, 1980).

'The Railways and the Development of Managerial Enterprise in Britain, 1850–1939', in Kobayaski, Kesaji and Morikawa, Hidemasa (ed.), *Development of Managerial Enterprise. The International Conference on Business History 12* (Tokyo: University of Tokyo Press, 1986).

Grinyer, Peter H. and Wooller, Jeff, *Corporate Models Today: A New Tool for Financial Management* (London: Institute of Chartered Accountants in England & Wales, 1975).

Guillebaud, Claude W., *The Role of the Arbitrator in Industrial Wages Disputes* (Welwyn: Nisbet, 1970).

Gwilliam, Kenneth M., 'Institutions and Objectives in Transport Policy', *Journal of Transport Economics and Policy*, XIII (January 1979).

Transport and Public Policy (London: George Allen & Unwin, 1964).

Hannah, Leslie, *Engineers, Managers and Politicians. The First Fifteen Years of Nationalised Electricity Supply in Britain* (London: Macmillan, 1982).

(ed.), *Management Strategy and Business Development* (London: Macmillan, 1976).

Harris, John, and Williams, Glyn, *Corporate Management and Financial Planning. The British Rail Experience* (St Albans: Elek, 1980).

Harrison, A. A., 'Railway Freight Charges', *Journal of the Institute of Transport,* XXVII (July 1957).

Hartshorn, J. E., 'Doublethink about Transport Deficits', *The Banker,* CVI (December 1956).

Hillman, Jordan J., *The Parliamentary Structuring of British Road–Rail Freight Coordination* (Evanston, Illinois: Northwestern University Transportation Center, 1973).

Hillman, Mayer, and Whalley, Anne, *The Social Consequences of Rail Closures* (London: Policy Studies Institute, 1980).

Howe, M., 'The Transport Act, 1962, and the Consumers' Consultative Committees', *Public Administration,* XLII (Spring 1964).

Howe, M., and Else, P. K., 'Railway Closures: Recent Changes in Machinery and Policy', *Public Administration,* XLVI (Summer 1968).

Howe, M., and Mills, G., 'Consumer Representation and the Withdrawal of Railway Services', *Public Administration,* XXXVIII (Autumn 1960).

'The Withdrawal of Railway Services', *Economic Journal,* LXX (June 1960).

Hurcomb, Sir Cyril (Lord Hurcomb), 'The Obligation to Carry', *Journal of The Institute of Transport,* XXVII (January 1957).

Hurstfield, Joel, *The Control of Raw Materials* (London: H.M.S.O., 1953).

Johnson, Henry C., 'Main Line Electrification – A First Appraisal', *Journal of the Institute of Transport,* XXXII (January 1968).

Johnson, John, and Long, Robert A., *British Railways Engineering 1948–80* (London: Mechanical Engineering Publications, 1981).

Johnson, K. M., and Garnett, Harry C., *The Economics of Containerisation* (London: George Allen & Unwin, 1971).

Jones, C. D., 'The Performance of British Railways 1962 to 1968', *Journal of Transport Economics and Policy,* IV (May 1970).

Jones, K., 'Policy Towards the Nationalised Industries', in Blackaby, Frank T. (ed.), *British Economic Policy 1960–74* (Cambridge: Cambridge University Press, 1978).

Joy, Stewart, 'British Railways' Track Costs', *Journal of Industrial Economics,* XIII (November 1964).

'The "Standby" Concept on Railways', *Journal of Transport Economics and Policy,* I (September 1967).

The Train That Ran Away. A Business History of British Railways 1948–1968 (London: Ian Allan, 1973).

Kelf-Cohen, Reuben, *Nationalisation in Britain* (London: Macmillan, 1958).

Twenty Years of Nationalisation. The British Experience (London: Macmillan, 1969).

King, Cecil H., *The Cecil King Diary 1965–1970* (London: Jonathan Cape, 1972).

Knight, Arthur, *Private Enterprise and Public Intervention: The Courtaulds Experience* (London: George Allen & Unwin, 1974).

Leruez, Jacques, *Economic Planning & Politics in Britain* (London: Martin Robertson, 1975).

L.N.E.R., *The State and the Railways: An Alternative to Nationalisation* (London, L.N.E.R., 1946).

Lund, G. H. K., 'The Study of Work', *British Transport Review,* VII (December 1962).

McKenna, Frank, *The Railway Workers 1840–1970* (London: Faber and Faber, 1980).

McKillop, Norman, *The Lighted Flame. A History of the Associated Society of Locomotive Engineers and Firemen* (London: Thomas Nelson, 1950).

McLeod, Charles, *All Change. Railway Industrial Relations in the Sixties* (London: Gower Press, 1970).

Macmillan, Harold, *Pointing the Way 1959–1961* (London: Macmillan, 1972). *Riding the storm 1956–1959* (London: Macmillan, 1971).

Marriott, Oliver, *The Property Boom* (London: Hamish Hamilton, 1967).

Marsh, Sir Richard (Lord Marsh), *On and Off the Rails. An Autobiography* (London: Weidenfeld & Nicolson, 1978).

Merrett, Anthony J., and Sykes, Allen, *The Finance and Analysis of Capital Projects* (London: Longmans, 1963).

Mills, G., and Howe, M., 'On Planning Railway Investment', *Bulletin of the Oxford Institute of Statistics*, XXIV (February 1962).

Milne, Alistair M., and Laing, Austen, *The Obligation To Carry* (London: Institute of Transport, 1956).

Mitchell, Joan, *The National Board for Prices and Incomes* (London: Secker & Warburg, 1972).

Moran, Lord (Charles McMoran Wilson), *Winston Churchill: The Struggle for Survival, 1940–1965* (London: Constable, 1966).

M.T., *The Cambrian Coast Line* (London: H.M.S.O., 1969).

M.T. and B.R.B., *British Railways Network for Development* (London: H.M.S.O., 1967).

Munby, Denys L., 'Mrs. Castle's Transport Policy', *Journal of Transport Economics and Policy*, II (May 1968).
'Economic Problems of British Railways', *Bulletin of the Oxford Institute of Statistics*, XXIV (February 1962).
'The Productivity of British Railways', *Bulletin of the Oxford Institute of Statistics*, XXIV (February 1962).
'The Reshaping of British Railways', *Journal of Industrial Economics*, XI (July 1963).

Munby, Denys L., and Watson, A. H. (eds.), *Inland Transport Statistics: Great Britain 1900–1970*, I (Oxford: Oxford University Press, 1978).

Murphy, Brian, *ASLEF 1880–1980. A Hundred Years of the Locoman's Trade Union* (London: A.S.L.E.F., 1980).

N.E.D.O., *Investment Appraisal* (London: H.M.S.O., 2nd edn, 1967). *A Study of the U.K. Nationalised Industries* (London: H.M.S.O., 1976).

Newton, Charles H., *Railway Accounts* (London: Pitman & Sons, 1930).

N.U.R., *National Union of Railwaymen and the PIB* (London: N.U.R., 1966). *Planning Transport For You* (London: N.U.R., 1959).

Parker, Hugh, 'Managing the Managers. The Role of the Board', *The Director*, XX (May 1968).

Pearson, Arthur J., 'Developments and Prospects in British Transport', *Journal of the Institute of Transport*, XXV (May 1953).
Man of the Rail (London: George Allen & Unwin, 1967).
Railways and the Nation (London: George Allen & Unwin, 1964).

Plowden, Stephen, *Taming Traffic* (London: Deutsch, 1980).

Polyani, George, *Contrasts in Nationalised Transport since 1947* (London: Institute of Economic Affairs, 1968).

Pollins, Harold, *Britain's Railways* (Newton Abbot: David & Charles, 1971).

Posner, Michael V., 'Policy towards Nationalized Industries', in Beckerman, Wilfrid (ed.), *The Labour Government's Economic Record, 1964–70* (London: Duckworth, 1972).

'Pricing and Investment in Nationalised Industries', in Cairncross, Alec (ed.), *The Managed Economy* (Oxford: Blackwell, 1970).

Price, R. W. R., 'Public Expenditure', in Blackaby, F. T. (ed.), *British Economic Policy 1960–74* (Cambridge: Cambridge University Press, 1978).

Pryke, Richard W. S., *The Nationalised Industries. Policies and Performance since 1968* (Oxford: Martin Robertson, 1981).

Public Enterprise in Practice. The British Experience of Nationalization over Two Decades (London: MacGibbon and Kee, 1971).

Pryke, Richard, W. S., and Dodgson, John S., *The Rail Problem* (London: Martin Robertson, 1975).

Ray, G. F., and Saunders, C. T., 'Problems and Policies for Inland Transport', in Beckerman, Wilfrid, *et al.* (eds.), *The British Economy in 1975* (Cambridge: Cambridge University Press, 1965).

R.Co.A., *British Railways and the Future* (London: R.Co.A., 1946).

Reader, William J., *Imperial Chemical Industries. A History* (2 vols., London: Oxford University Press, 1970, 1975).

Redfern, Philip, 'Net Investment in Fixed Assets in the United Kingdom, 1938–53', *Journal of the Royal Statistical Society*, Series A, CXVIII (1955).

Reith, John C. W. (Lord Reith), *Into the Wind* (London: Hodder, 1949).

Richards, K.,'The Economics of the Cambrian Coast Line', *Journal of Transport Economics and Policy*, VI (September 1972).

Robens, Alfred (Lord Robens), *Ten Year Stint* (London: Cassell, 1972).

Robson, William A., *Nationalised Industry and Public Ownership* (London: George Allen & Unwin, 1960).

(ed.), *Problems of Nationalized Industries* (London: George Allen & Unwin, 1952).

Rogers, Hugh C. B., *The Last Steam Locomotive Engineer: R. A. Riddles, C.B.E.* (London: George Allen & Unwin, 1970).

Rogow, Arnold A., *The Labour Government and British Industry 1945–1951* (Oxford: Blackwell, 1955).

Sampson, Anthony, *Anatomy of Britain Today* (London: Hodder & Stoughton, 1965).

Savage, Christopher I., *Inland Transport* (London: H.M.S.O., 1957).

Shanks, Michael (ed.), *The Lessons of Public Enterprise* (London: Jonathan Cape, 1963).

Sissons, Michael, and French, Philip (eds.), *Age of Austerity* (London: Hodder, 1963).

Starkie, David, *The Motorway Age* (Oxford: Pergamon, 1982).

Steel, David, 'Looking at the Nationalized Industries', *Royal Institute of Public Administration Newsletter*, III (Summer 1983).

Stewart, J. C., 'The Marketing and Pricing of Railway Freight Transport', *Journal of the Institute of Transport*, XXXI (May 1966).

Stewart, Margaret, *Frank Cousins: A Study* (London: Hutchinson, 1968).

Stuart, Charles (ed.), *The Reith Diaries* (London: Collins, 1975).

Sugden, Robert, 'Cost Benefit Analysis and the Withdrawal of Railway Services', *Yorkshire Bulletin of Economic Research*, XXIV (May 1972).

Thomas, David St J., *The Rural Transport Problem* (London: Routledge, 1963).
Thomson, A. W. J. and Hunter, L. C., *The Nationalized Transport Industries* (London: Heinemann, 1973).
Tivey, Leonard J., *Nationalisation in British Industry* (London: Jonathan Cape, 2nd edn, 1973).
Torode, John, 'Len Neal and the NUR–ASLEF Feud', *Personnel*, I (March 1968).
Towers, Brian, *British Incomes Policy* (Nottingham: Institute of Personnel Management, 1978).
Tufnell, R. M., *The Diesel Impact on British Rail* (London: Mechanical Engineering Publications, 1979).
Turner, Graham, *Business in Britain* (London: Eyre & Spottiswoode, 1969).
Walker, Gilbert, J., 'Competition in Transport as an Instrument of Policy', *Economic Journal*, LXVI (September 1956).
Economic Planning by Programme and Control in Great Britain (London: Heinemann, 1957).
Road and Rail (London: George Allen & Unwin, 1942).
'The Transport Act, 1947', *Economic Journal*, LVIII (March 1948).
'Transport Policy Before and After 1953', *Oxford Economic Papers*, V (1953).
Wedderburn, Dorothy, *Redundancy and the Railwaymen* (Cambridge: Cambridge University Press, 1965).
Williams, B., 'Transport Act, 1947: Some Benefits and Dangers', *Journal of the Institute of Transport*, XXIV (May 1951).
Williams, Philip M., *Hugh Gaitskell: A Political Biography* (London: Jonathan Cape, 1979).
Wilson, Harold, 'The Financial Problem of British Transport' (typescript, London: 1951).
The Labour Government, 1964–70. A Personal Record (London: Weidenfeld & Nicolson, 1971).
Wilson, Reginald H. (Sir), 'The Accounting and Financial Structure of British Transport', *British Transport Review*, I (April 1950).
'Structure and Purpose in Transport Organisation', *Journal of the Institute of Transport*, XXVII (January 1957).
Technical Modernization and New Freight Charges on British Railways (London: B.T.C., 1958).
Worswick, G. D. N. and Ady, P. H. (eds.), *The British Economy 1945–1950* (Oxford: Clarendon Press, 1952).
The British Economy in the Nineteen-Fifties (Oxford: Clarendon Press, 1962).

Index

Lightning Source UK Ltd.
Milton Keynes UK
UKHW040727300622
405106UK00010B/22